HEILMAN

ENVIRONMENTAL LAW AND POLICY:

A COURSEBOOK ON

NATURE, LAW, AND SOCIETY

Zygmunt J.B. Plater
Boston College Law School

Robert H. Abrams
Wayne State University Law School

William Goldfarb
Cook College, Rutgers The State University of New Jersey

AMERICAN CASEBOOK SERIES®

WEST PUBLISHING COMPANY
ST. PAUL, MINNESOTA
1992

First Printing, 1992
Second Printing, 1992

Printed in the United States of America

Library of Congress Cataloging-in-Publication Data

Plater, Zygmunt J.B., 1943–
Environmental law and policy : a coursebook on nature, law, and society : cases, materials, and text / Zygmunt J.B. Plater, Robert H. Abrams, William Goldfarb.
p. cm. — (American casebook)
Includes index.
ISBN 0-314-00341-X
1. Environmental law—United States—Cases. 2. Environmental policy—United States. I. Abrams, Robert H., 1948– II. Goldfarb, William. III. Title. IV. Series: American casebook series.
KF3775.A7P55 1991
344.73'046—dc20
[347.30446] 91-41577
CIP

TEXT IS PRINTED ON 10% POST CONSUMER RECYCLED PAPER

PRINTED WITH SOY INK

3rd Reprint—1995

This book was printed on recycled paper using Trump Mediaeval type set on Macintosh personal computers. The entire book was produced ready for printing using electronic publishing methods, including the writing, editing, design, and layout.

Design and electronic production by Michael Kitchen, PIXELANTICS, An Electronic Design & Publication Studio, Newton, Massachusetts.

DEDICATION

To our families

and to all who act to protect this fragile planet.

Foreword

Joseph L. Sax

In introducing a 1986 symposium on environmental law I observed that the subject, born perhaps twenty years earlier, had changed dramatically in that short span. Despite the predictions of some observers that the environmental movement and environmental law would be passing fads, the tide was racing the other way. I wrote that, far from fading away, environmental law had become institutionalized, an accepted and significant enterprise both for government and for attorneys.[1]

Now, a half-dozen years later, it seems more like a flood, challenging our ability to assimilate its force and volume. There is so much environmental law that few academics still try to focus on the entire field.

A survey of environmental law teachers[2] that I conducted in 1989 revealed that many of us feel that our broader goals as teachers are no longer being met in the basic environmental law course. Massive legislative interventions in the pollution control field have seemed to call forth an inordinate focus on statutory detail while broader perspectives on the subject recede. Rich and exciting cognate areas like natural resources management, land use, and international issues are shunted to the side or ignored totally.

Environmental Law and Policy: Nature, Law, and Society can be seen as a first "second generation" environmental law book. Its major teaching premise is that environmental law will continue to grow and evolve. By employing a legal process orientation, the book responds to the desire to teach broadly without sacrificing attention to regulatory detail. By breaking down statutes into categories that reflect their underlying regulatory technique, this book also makes teaching statutory analysis a more fruitful endeavor. Students are taught about the different ways in which statutes address environmental problems, including the strengths and weaknesses of each generic statutory type. Beyond simplifying the task of teaching the statutory portions of the course, this approach insures that the student's knowledge does not become obsolete as statutes and regulations are amended and altered.

This book captures the diversity that is a hallmark of contemporary environmental law. The staples are, of course, present, including materials on air and water pollution control, toxic torts and other common law approaches, conflicts between private and public rights, and the procedures of the administrative state. Beyond

---

Professor Sax is the James H. House and Hiram H. Hurd Professor of Environmental Regulation, University of California, Berkeley School of Law.

1. Sax, Introduction to Environmental Law Symposium, 19 J. Law Reform 797 (1986).

2. Sax, Environmental Law in the Law Schools: What We Teach and How We Feel About It, 19 ELR 10251 (1989)(noted in Author's Preface *infra).*

that, the volume also addresses the "hot" topical areas of risk assessment, regulation of toxics, and hazardous materials. Still other important issues, like public trust law, economic incentives to environmental improvement, endangered species protection, alternative dispute resolution, and international law have their own chapters. The book seriously addresses the role citizens play in environmental decision making.

This is a challenging book designed in response to a challenging subject matter. I am confident that it will help make teaching environmental law as enjoyable and rewarding as it was in the early days.

Summary Table of Contents

Table of Contents

Chapter 2
LAW AND ECONOMICS, UNCERTAINTY AND RISK, IN ENVIRONMENTAL DECISION-MAKING

PART TWO: THE FOUNDATION OF ENVIRONMENTAL LAW: TRADITIONAL COMMON LAW THEORIES & FUNDAMENTAL ISSUES OF REMEDIES AND LIABILITIES

Chapter 3
ENVIRONMENTAL TORTS AND REMEDIES:
FITTING ENVIRONMENTAL CASES INTO COMMON LAW THEORIES

Chapter 8:
FUNDAMENTAL ENVIRONMENTAL RIGHTS: FEDERAL AND STATE CONSTITUTIONS, AND THE PUBLIC TRUST DOCTRINE

Chapter 9
PUBLIC POWERS AND PRIVATE PROPERTY RIGHTS: CONSTITUTIONAL AUTHORITY AND LIMITATIONS

PART FOUR: ENVIRONMENTAL STATUTES & THE ADMINISTRATIVE STATE, and A TAXONOMY OF ENVIRONMENTAL STATUTES

PART FIVE: TRENDS IN ENVIRONMENTAL LAW

REFERENCE

AUTHORS' PREFACE

"When we try to pick out anything by itself, we find it hitched to everything else in the universe," John Muir, founder of the Sierra Club, once said.[1] Indeed, "Everything is connected to everything else" is the First Law of ecology. This is depressing news for anyone trying to write a coursebook on environmental law. It means that it is impossible to capture in one book a field that ultimately takes on the entire planet as its subject matter.

So this is primarily a book about environmental law. Environmental law necessarily includes environmental science, environmental economics, and environmental policy as essential elements of its analysis. To keep the enterprise manageable, however, this book chooses to focus on law.

Even so, environmental law has become so complex and bulky that courses in the subject run the risk of bogging down, a danger that has encouraged us to use a different approach to organizing the field.

The logjam in current environmental law teaching was chronicled recently by Professor Joseph Sax, a pioneer in the teaching of environmental law. After polling more than a hundred colleagues,[2] he reported that "bewilderment and frustration were the most common themes....

"The subject seems to have overwhelmed us. Virtually every law teacher – however broad his or her overlook – wants to introduce students to the specific materials in the field, and to provide some experience and familiarity with it. Yet, every such attempt is an encounter with statutes of numbing complexity and detail. My respondents did not find their unease markedly alleviated when they shifted (as most had) from broad survey courses to those that focused primarily on one illustrative statute, usually the Clean Air Act.

"Complexity as such does not seem to be the problem. Lawyers enjoy puzzles. What discourages law teachers is rather a sense of being drawn into a system in which enormous energy must be expended on something that is ultimately vacuous. As I read the letters, I imagined spending years learning the minutiae of an extraordinarily difficult language, only to find, at the end, that it wasn't a language of communication at all, but just empty babble.... Jim Krier at the University of Michigan spoke for many when he said: 'Environmental law has come to be a bore...if the idea is to "teach" the "law" that we find in "the books." There is too much junk there, too many details.... Project this picture a bit and what you have for the future...is a bunch of lawyers who don't really know anything worth knowing.'

"A common adaptation to this state is to make the best of a bad thing. Environmental regulatory laws can be used to teach about the administrative

1. J. Muir, My First Summer in the Sierra 211 (1911).

2. Sax, Environmental Law in the Law Schools: What We Teach and How We Feel About It, 19 ELR 10251 (1989).

process, judicial review, or techniques of statutory analysis. Some among us, however, doubt that they are well suited even for that purpose. John Leshy of Arizona State observed: 'Frankly, I dislike teaching [the pollution side of environmental law].... It is mostly just administrative law in an environmental context.... I found it difficult to identify, much less organize a course around, some overarching themes in the regulatory patterns. They seem to me to be quite ad hoc...bureaucratic responses to pressing problems.'

"I sense that my colleagues would be more tolerant of the current laws if they were convinced that, for all the limitations of the regulatory genre, those statutes represented a best effort to cope with terribly difficult dilemmas – if they were persuaded that we were at least inching along in the right direction.

"But that is not the case.... The sense of discouragement that emerges [was] made explicit in comments...by David Getches of the University of Colorado. He observes that we have more and more 'environmental artillery': more lawyers working on problems that seem increasingly sophisticated, with ever greater economic stakes, and at the same time ever greater attenuation from the ultimate causes and concerns that gave rise to the field. 'Lawyers in great numbers are finding jobs doing environmental law,' he says. But 'law, lawyers, law schools, and law students seem to have so little to do with *environment* as seen by knowledgeable people.'"

How then does this coursebook handle the numbing complexity and detail of modern environmental law? Without getting too entangled in the intricacies of environmental science and policy analysis, the book invites and attempts to integrate into the law an awareness of what has gone wrong between humans and their natural habitat. Using a legal process structure, the book tries to probe every nook and cranny of the legal system, exploring ways in which environmental attorneys have attempted to use law imaginatively to remedy environmental problems.

Environmental law is a relatively young subject. Courses were first introduced, and only in a few law schools, around 1970. Initially most environmental law materials were drawn from other well-established legal sub-disciplines, such as land use, tort, criminal law, property, and constitutional law. The complex administrative subculture that now dominates pollution control was barely in its formative stages. The innovative burden of pioneering environmental lawyers was to adapt and harness an array of legal tools designed for other societal purposes as an effective means to promote environmental quality.

Since 1970, environmental law itself has matured. Interest has grown to the point that environmental law is a standard offering at more than one hundred-fifty law schools. Environmental consciousness, the number of students trained in environmental science, and the number of statutes directed at pollution and other forms of environmental degradation have all grown dramatically. The task facing environmental lawyers today is to handle the remarkable bulk of both statutory and nonstatutory environmental protection law.

This coursebook has a relatively long history. It began as a collection of teaching materials developed for an experimental course taught to graduate and undergraduate students at the University of Michigan in 1971. Since then "Nature, Law, and Society" has been taught in more than a dozen law schools and environmental studies programs. Strongly influenced by Professor Sax and his advocacy of citizen involvement in environmental decision-making, the materials aim to prepare environmentally interested and concerned students to be active participants in the processes that shape their environmental future. In addition to teaching students about the substance of the laws pertaining to the environment, the course pursues a broader goal of teaching about how the legal system functions in an area of vital public concerns.

Most other casebooks are organized on a medium-by-medium basis – divided into air, water, noise, land use, toxics, wildlife, nuclear, and so on – typically focusing on just one or two of these. That particular approach does not appear to make the subject more accessible to students, nor does it make the subject more "teachable." Quite the opposite. To split the course up along resource headings introduces weary, often redundant, sojourns through seemingly endless fields of legislative and regulatory overkill. It also forces students and teachers into an unrewarding pursuit of detail[3] that obscures rather than illuminates the ways in which the legal process can be employed to improve environmental decisionmaking.

In the face of the numbing mass and complexity of modern environmental law, this coursebook uses the structure of the legal system as its organizing principle, selecting the best examples of how the process works, including a sampling of classic environmental cases, without particular regard for the type of pollution or policy involved. The way the legal system works, not the intricacy of some media-specific physical science area, is our primary concern. The book's larger organization, therefore, tries to build around the major blocks of the legal system itself.

More than a score of years have passed since the first Earth Day and compilation of the original edition of this coursebook, a collection of materials that has changed many times over while retaining the same conceptual approach. This book aims to give students analytical skills and a solid doctrinal footing in the field, along with encouraging a taste for the pleasures of creative lawyering in meeting the challenges of our troubled ecological context. Ultimately we are guardedly optimistic that environmental problems can be solved, and that law will be a sensitive part of the solution.

NOTE ON EDITING CONVENTIONS USED IN THIS BOOK

In editing materials for this book we have tried to make the text as smooth as possible to the reader's eye, and to keep the amount of text as short as possible, while covering this dauntingly broad and expansive field. This has required quite a bit of editorial surgery on text and excerpted materials.

3. Taking the example of the federal Environmental Protection Agency, "today EPA employs over fourteen thousand people. Its major environmental statutes fill a 654 page book and the regulations encompass eleven volumes and 8608 pages of the Code of Federal Regulations. EPA's operating programs require about $2.7 billion, and the Superfund and Leaking Underground Storage Tank programs require an additional $1.6 billion." Reitze, Environmental Policy – It Is Time for a New Beginning, 14 Colum. J. Envtl. L. 111, 111–112 (1988).

Within excerpts, many internal citations (especially string citations) are simply excised, with no indication by ellipsis, or are dropped to footnotes. (In some cases in the text itself, when discussing general scientific or other nonlegal data, only limited citations are supplied.) Footnotes in excerpted materials, when they remain, do not have their original numbers. Where a footnote holds special importance to subsequent commentators, its original number is mentioned. Judicial opinions are often drastically cut and edited, indicated only by simple ellipsis, and in a few cases portions of the opinion are reordered to make the presentation flow more smoothly. As with most casebooks, if the reader wishes to delve into a particular case or text, the excerpts here should serve to get the inquiry started, but there is no substitute for going back to the original full text.

Various departures from literary convention and "Blue Book" style have been incorporated throughout the book to improve scansion (as in eliminating brackets on [i]nitial capitalization changes, or our simplified *infra* and *supra* references). Case opinion excerpts, however, usually retain the originating court's stylistic idiosyncrasies. Swarms of acronyms have invaded environmental law – EISs, NIMBY, LULUs, PSD, SARA, ToSCA, ad infinitum – so to help the reader cope, the back reference pages (which contain all reference sections except the Table of Contents), also include a Glossary of Abbreviations.

Gender-sensitivity was a virtually unknown editing concept until the 'Sixties. Accordingly many classic cases, and some modern texts as well, address all significant parties as male. In this book the pronouns "he" and "she" when used generically should be understood to refer inclusively to all persons regardless of gender (although in retrospect it seems most polluters appear here as male).

ACKNOWLEDGEMENTS

This book sometimes seems to have evolved with as much biodiversity of input as any marsh or rainforest. Dozens of people have helped shape and reshape it. For all who know the work of Professor Joseph Sax, now teaching at Berkeley, the mark of his thinking and advice on our efforts will be discernible throughout these pages. In its earliest form the book derives from materials prepared in 1971 by a committee of law students at the University of Michigan, including two of the present authors, for a course called Nature, Law, and Society offered to graduate and undergraduate students. Of that group, Peter W. Schroth served not only as a major editor but also as the administrator of the course, a thankless and demanding task; without his energetic work the whole project might well have died a-borning. The Nature, Law, and Society project was supported and advised by Joe Sax, and Professor William Stapp of the School of Natural Resources; they served graciously and well as mentors and midwives. Since then the materials have gone through repeated re-incarnations, in each case profiting from the experience, advice, and contributions of colleagues, research assistants, and students at the succession of schools at which we have taught them: Boston College Law School, Harvard Law School, Michigan Law School, Rutgers, the University of Tennessee College of Law, and Wayne State

Law School. We also appreciate greatly the suggestions and comments received from almost a dozen colleagues at other schools around the country who used interim versions of some or all of the book in their classes. This, in fact, was the way that Professor Goldfarb came to join the project.

For support and assistance at Wayne Law School, we warmly thank Dean John Reed. Among the students who contributed to the book, we want to thank especially Cecelia Littleton Bonner, Albert Bedecarré, Daniel Cronin, Patrick J. Dolan, Andrew Y. Lee, Carole LoConte, Kathleen Marie Quinn, Karen Hiyama Schodowski, Diane Smith, Nancy Swistock Snyder, Nicholas W. F. Targ, and the Boston College Law School Conservation Research Group.[4] The Boston College Law School Library reference staff repeatedly provided indispensable detective work and support; Mark Sullivan seems to have been the one who consistently got our most fiendish requests, and always calmly came through. As for the many authors and publishers who graciously granted us permission to reprint portions of their works, a complete listing follows immediately after the text.

For the huge counter-entropic task of managing mutating drafts, and bringing the book into physical existence, we thank Frances Piscatelli, Kathy King, Susan Noonan, Brenda Pepe, and Mary Curran at Boston College Law School. Without their labor, and the truly extraordinary support we received from Dean Daniel Coquillette, the coursebook would still be a smudgy stack of xeroxed class materials. In this computer age, helpful humans are still an indispensable necessity. We do, however, also owe a debt to the computers of the WESTLAW system and Mead Data-Central's LEXIS, and the people who built and provided us with those services, and also to the computer (and eyes and brains) of Michael Kitchen, for design and typesetting wizardry.

Ultimately, our greatest warm thanks and appreciation must be reserved for our families, who naïvely expressed pleasure when they heard of this project.

Z.J.B.P.
R.H.A.
W.G.

November, 1991

4. Tables of authorities were compiled under deadline pressures by the much-appreciated efforts of Conservation Research Group volunteers, including Craig Kelley, Kristin Cihak, John Ellis, and Catherine Smith.

Introduction

We travel together, passengers on a little space ship, dependent on its vulnerable resources of air and soil, all committed for our safety to its security and peace, preserved from annihilation only by the care, the work, and, I will say, the love we bestow on our fragile craft.

– Adlai Stevenson, at the United Nations, 1965

SPACESHIP EARTH

David Brower, one of the founding elders of the 20th century American environmental movement, who played the title role in Encounters with the Archdruid, John McPhee's book about environmentalism in America,[1] once spoke to a class of law students. Standing tall in front of the class, white-haired and raw-boned with piercing blue eyes, Brower stretched out his arm, with thumb and forefinger held about two inches apart, and said:

> Imagine if you will our entire planet reduced to this, the size of an egg.... If the planet Earth were reduced to the size of an egg, what do you think the proportionate volume of all its air, its atmosphere, would be? And what would be the total volume of the water that, along with air and sunlight, sustains life on this Earth?... According to the computations I've seen, the sum total of atmosphere veiled around this egg planet Earth would be equivalent to no more than the volume of a little pea wrapped around the globe. And the water? That would be no more than a matchhead, a tiny volume spread thin enough to fill the oceans, rivers and lakes of the world.[2]

Looking at the students, Brower asked,

> Thinking of those limits, can you any longer not believe that our planet is a tremendously vulnerable little system, totally dependent on this fragile tissue of air and water, a thin fabric of life support made up of all the air and water the Earth will ever have?[3]

Like the astronauts who reported dramatic and startling personal reactions to their first glimpse down upon planet Earth from their position in outer space, the images of Brower's egg and Stevenson's Spaceship Earth force us to recognize our interrelatedness with all other human and natural systems that make up the planet.

1. McPhee, Encounters with the Archdruid (1971).

2. In fact, the relative scale of the mass of atmosphere and water to the planet Earth is apparently even more dramatic. According to Dr. Heinrich Holland of Harvard's geology department, taking the relative *masses* of Earth's air and water (as opposed to spatial volume which is a misleading construct), the atmosphere constitutes less than one millionth of the planet's mass, and the water less than one thousandth.

3. Brower was speaking on a beach on Mission Point Peninsula, Grand Traverse Bay, Michigan, October 1977.

The Earth is indeed one small, limited, totally self-contained entity, a single natural system (albeit made up of many interconnected and interdependent systems) containing great richness, diversity, and vulnerability.

As the First Law of Ecology holds, everything is connected to everything else. Environmentalists tend to be conservative at least in this regard: out of utilitarian caution as well as ethical impulse they tend to value the dynamic natural equilibriums that have evolved over millennia, and they distrust the wholesale human intrusions on the balance that have occurred particularly since the arrival of the industrial age. Every act of technology or human behavior is likely to have direct and indirect results, some quite drastic, unpredictable, and long-term in their effects. Who but environmentalists would have foreseen that the choice of coalburning methods in the Midwest would hurt maple sugar producers in Vermont, and leach lead into the water supplies of eastern New England homes 700 miles away? Yet acid rain was a natural chemical reaction just waiting to be triggered. It is important, environmentalists say, to look wide and long before we leap.

Unfortunately, the long view, looking out for long-term negative consequences, does not seem instinctive to the human brain. Quite the contrary. If it can, the human species consistently tends to overlook long-term problems including ecological repercussions, focusing instead on the more upbeat realm of short-term payoffs. The supposition is that as problems start piling up one can ignore them, get around them, pass them off or away downstream and downwind, or one can move on to new frontiers. Brower's egg planet reminds us that there are no such frontiers left; everything goes somewhere and remains within the system in which we must continue to live.

Environmental law attempts to build foresight into the human decisional system, along with an awareness of costs and values that are typically invisible because, though real, they exist outside the formal market economy. Often environmental law works after the fact, attempting to force accountings for depredations that have already occurred, hoping to deter future repetitions. Environmental law has also developed elaborate doctrines attempting to anticipate and prevent environmental disruptions. The goal is to incorporate a process of fair, overall, comprehensive accounting of real costs, benefits, and alternatives into major public and private decisionmaking.

Over the past 20 years there has been a dramatic change in the stature of the field. It is no longer dismissable as the fad of a disgruntled minority; it is now the stuff of presidential campaigns. There are now more environmental lawyers in the United States than there are labor lawyers. Given these toeholds and the reality of environmental problems, the field inevitably will continue to grow ever more intricate, challenging, and important.

THE BOOK'S PERSPECTIVE

There are a few further necessary comments. Our bias, for example. If it isn't already, we wish to make it clear that we personally approach many, though not all, environmental cases from the perspective of environmental plaintiffs, the citizens and public interest groups who initiate these cases. Thus our approach will often be "how can this problem be corrected within the legal system?" presuming in most cases that a problem does exist. This approach seems realistic and useful as well as defensible, however, because the doctrines of environmental law have always been (and still are) developed primarily by the efforts of citizen environmentalists.

To understand environmental law one must understand environmental plaintiffs, especially the individuals and increasingly professionalized groups who make up the active environmental "movement." Environmental defendants do not offer any similarly broad countervailing theory of environmental defense.[4] So to get deeper into the swamps of environmental law, in practical terms one must follow the activists' trail. Whether readers ultimately view the field from the point of view of plaintiffs or defense, an understanding of the plaintiffs' perspective is indispensable to a recognition of what's going on.

STRUCTURE

The structure of this coursebook should be clear from the table of contents. It surveys environmental law issues throughout the vast range of American legal process (with brief glimpses beyond into international environmental law, a field which is just starting to grow, often on the American model.)

Most books on environmental law are organized by physical science categories: air pollution, water pollution, toxics, etc. This book contains material from each such area, but instead is organized like the legal system itself, building upon a base of common law and constitutional law, continuing on to statutory and administrative law. We find that this approach is a faster and more efficient way of getting students into the deeper and more important legal questions of environmental law. The text includes many classic cases. In large part the aim is not to teach hypertechnical details of current law, especially regulatory standards, like the current parts per million hydrocarbon standard for automobile tailpipe emissions. Environmental law changes daily. We aim rather to show the structure, and how it works. This book is used for the first, and often the only, course in environmental law, and we therefore feel obligated to leave students with a well-rounded legal overview. Because of time constraints, courses organized other ways often cover one type of pollution, including legal issues most important to that area, but leave students with only vague notions about application of the full range of legal concepts to other kinds of environmental problems.

4. Legal defenses typically amount to a series of attempts to avoid the issue – "the facts aren't sufficiently shown"; "the plaintiffs don't have the right to be heard in this court"; "the matter has continued for so long that the law is estopped from changing the status quo"; "enforcement of the law would violate our constitutional rights"; in short, "the law should not be applied."

Part I of the book begins with a brief review of ecological analysis, environmental politics, economics, and risk assessment.

Part II, based on this review and orientation, examines the traditional legal structures and remedies of the common law upon which environmental law doctrines have been based, including an analysis of how environmental plaintiffs have attempted to integrate environmental concerns into the system.

Part III turns to the relationship between private and public law, surveying an array of statutes arising in a toxics case, followed by materials on criminal, constitutional, and quasi-constitutional law as potential sources of enforceable environmental rights. The section includes issues of private due process rights, federal-state relations, and the public trust doctrine (which may be environmental law's single most dramatic contribution to the modern legal system).

Part IV studies the administrative state, after a brief introduction to administrative law in the environmental context, through a systematic study of "statutory taxonomies" illustrating the array of statutory and regulatory approaches that have been applied in the modern administrative state.

Part V offers a parting overview of current trends in the development of environmental law, including ADR (Alternative Dispute Resolution methods), the recent flowering of international environmental law, and a gaze toward the future.

GOING BEYOND THE BOOK

An environmental law course is broad in scope. The text and commentary in this book often incorporate an analysis of source material, cases, and issues extending far beyond the excerpted textual material. The excerpted material often serves to supplement the text, rather than vice versa as in most law course books. To provide more depth and familiarity with detail, students and professors have often added other components to the coursework. Some students take a concurrent nonlaw course, for example in field biology, toxicology, or environmental policy. Some take on projects or internships with active groups outside academe. Some classes have carried one chosen problem area through the course of the term, or kept track of an ongoing local controversy – a particular toxic disposal case, wildlife or park management issue, mining, dredging, or dam project. Others have assigned short individual research papers, class presentations, field visits, and so on, and each of these has been valuable in providing reinforcing feedback to the analyses and techniques of environmental law set out broadly in the book.

Some very fine loose-leaf services[5] provide information updates on a regular, often weekly, basis: The Environmental Law Reporter*†(cases and analyses by The Environmental Law Institute); The Environment Reporter*† (cases, statutes, and current developments by the Bureau of National Affairs); the BNA International Environmental Reporter*†; the BNA Chemical Regulation Reporter*†, the BNA

5. Sources available on the WESTLAW computer database system are indicated by an asterisk *; sources available on LEXIS are indicated by †.

Toxics Law Reporter*†, and the BNA Asbestos Abatement Reporter.† Student subscriptions to activist newsletters are also available and valuable: The Amicus Journal, Natural Resources Defense Council, 122 E.42d St., Suite 4500, NYC 10168; Earth Island Institute's E.I. Journal, 300 Broadway, San Francisco CA 94133; Environmental Defense Fund's monthly EDF Letter, 257 Park Ave. S, NYC 10010; Not Man Apart, Friends of the Earth, 530 7th St. SE, Washington DC 20003; the National Wildlife Federation's Weekly News Report, 1416 P. St. NW, Washington DC 20036; RESOLVE, published by Center for Environmental Dispute Resolution, World Wildlife Fund and The Conservation Foundation, 1250 24th St. NW, Washington, DC 20037; and the Sierra Club National Newsletter, 320 Pennsylvania Ave. SE, Washington DC 20003. The National Wildlife Federation's Conservation Directory is a useful catalogue of hundreds of environmental organizations; the Federation also has a Congressional Hotline recording for legislative updates at 202-797-6655. Many industry organizations also publish newsletters and are pleased to provide extensive materials in support of their positions.

A number of excellent law reviews specialize in environmental law, including (listed alphabetically) the Boston College Environmental Affairs Law Review*†, Colorado Journal of International Environmental Law, Columbia Journal of Environmental Law, Ecology Law Quarterly, Environmental Law*†, Harvard Environmental Law Review, Journal of Environmental Law and Litigation, Journal of Land Use and Environmental Law, Land and Water Law Review, Natural Resources Journal, Natural Resources and Environment (ABA), Public Land Law Review, Stanford Environmental Law Journal, Tulane Environmental Law Journal, UCLA Journal of Environmental Law and Policy, and Virginia Environmental Law Journal.

Background books on environmental analysis provide helpful orientation in this sprawling field. Worthwhile books include Eugene Odum's Fundamentals of Ecology, Rachel Carson's Silent Spring, Barry Commoner's The Closing Circle, and the fountainhead – Aldo Leopold's Sand County Almanac.

The best environmental law hornbook we know is Professor William Rodgers' Handbook on Environmental Law. Professor Rodgers and Professor Frank Grad have each published helpful multivolume treatises as well. West Publishing Company produces a very useful annual statutory compilation, Selected Environmental Law Statutes. Joseph Sax's Defending the Environment (1971) continues to be a vivid introduction to the use of law in solving the pervasive social, economic, and ecological problems we call "environmental."

And don't be daunted by the "numbing complexity and detail" of some sectors of environmental law. Since everything is connected to everything else, if one just picks up a trail and follows it, it will lead to all there is to know.

ENVIRONMENTAL LAW AND POLICY:

A COURSEBOOK ON

NATURE, LAW, AND SOCIETY

Part One

PERSPECTIVES ON ENVIRONMENTAL LAW

This noblest patrimony ever yet inherited by any people must be husbanded and preserved with care in such manner that future generations shall not reproach us for having squandered what was justly theirs.

– The Whig Almanac, 1843

Chapter 1

THE ENVIRONMENTAL PERSPECTIVE AND A SIMPLE CASE

Introduction

The ecological future of the planet is being shaped by its geophysical past; by continuing natural forces of sun, rain, wind, water, seismics, vulcanism, and diversifying biological evolution; and by humans, corporations, and government. These last three are very recent arrivals and relatively trivial in mass. They have proved, however, to have a remarkable capacity for causing planetary effects, for good and ill, and environmental law focuses upon them in doing its work.

The process of governing modern society and its natural habitat is a process of contending forces, in which environmental law is certainly not a monolith, although it is increasingly a central player.

To understand the perspectives of environmental law, one must operate on two levels. First it is necessary to understand the environmentalists' view of how decisions *should* be made: rational societal decisions based on a characteristic long-term overview accounting of facts and values. The physical world in which humans operate is comprised of a complex series of interdependent ecosystems supporting a rich variety of species and natural phenomena, where every action has its consequences on the ecological equilibrium. Parallel to this descriptive premise is a normative premise that the on-going maintenance and (where possible) enhancement of the viability of those ecosystems is desirable, even beyond the economic and human utility values that are associated with environmental quality.

Then one must understand the very different question of how human decisions are actually made – because governing decisions (using the term "governing" in the broadest sense to mean the way the society runs itself), do not automatically proceed on the basis of objective facts and logic, but rather are the results of all the various forces that are brought to bear, including human nature, politics, and the participants' tunnel vision, as well as law. Every environmental law case thus implies both a factual analysis and an analysis of the contending forces that shape issues within the economic and legal systems.

There is little that is revolutionary in the environmental perspective, but in a materialistic society it is not hard to see how actions viewed as desirable from the environmental perspective might be very differently viewed from other perspectives. Consider governmental regulations requiring the installation of expensive, mileage-reducing auto pollution control equipment: that choice may be undesirable to those who place a higher value on achieving other goals like improving their material standard of living. From the environmental perspective, reduction in pollution is generally a desirable outcome, although even radical environmentalists may be hesitant to impose large social costs in order to obtain trivial ecosystem benefits. From the perspective of those deeply concerned with improving the lot of the poor, marginal increases in air pollution may appear to have less adverse impact on the poor than their being denied the opportunity to purchase and use automobiles due to higher costs imposed by mandatory pollution controls. The environmental perspective does not exist in a vacuum. Tradeoffs between short-term material welfare and long-term ecological integrity do occur, although environmentalists often argue against false tradeoff decisions where rational alternatives are available. "You have to choose: either economic development, or environmental quality, you can't have both." – that cliché is the classic false tradeoff.

A. THE BREADTH AND SCOPE OF ENVIRONMENTAL PROBLEMS

Consider the amazing diversity of the field called environmental law. It includes:

- Chemical wastes buried in a suburban field.
- Seal puppies clubbed to death on floating ice packs in the Gulf of St. Lawrence.
- Uranium fuel rods shipped to nuclear power plants in India.
- Toxic gases spreading from chemical plants to poison surrounding low-income neighborhoods in Italy, India, and Kansas.
- The imminent extinction of an endangered snapdragon plant in Maine.
- A superhighway cutting through a park and low-income neighborhood in Memphis.
- Hairdressing salons in Yosemite National Park.
- Carcinogenic chemical fire-retardant in infant sleepwear.
- The cutting of shade trees along rural roads.
- A Tennessee river and its fertile valley eliminated by a federal recreational dam.
- A factory emitting smoke from its stacks and liquid wastes from its drain-pipes.
- A centuries-old church bulldozed for a parking lot.
- Non-returnable bottles lying along highways and in urban trash.
- Burning Rainforests, and desertification in the Third World.
- New Jersey's refusal to permit Philadelphia's garbage to be disposed of in New Jersey landfills.
- Rat bites and lead poisoning in an urban slum.
- Redwood trees turned into tomato stakes; our remnant ancient forests cut for subsidized export.
- Asbestos dust in local elementary schools.

- Chlorofluorocarbons thinning stratospheric ozone, causing increased ultraviolet radiation hazards on earth.
- A primitive tribe in Panama threatened by extension of the Pan-American Highway through their jungle territory.
- Global warming.

And hundreds more.

All of these widely diverse situations are labelled "environmental" issues, and activists called "environmentalists" have taken legal action on each of them (and hundreds of others) over the past few decades, with varying degrees of success. Each case involves a highly individualized set of scientific facts, economic and political issues, and social and natural consequences. Many of them have no obvious connection with others on the list, beyond their environmental label. The different areas have become so voluminously complex that an expert working on water pollution law, for example, typically has no time to do anything else. A person studying the science and law of endangered plants may have no special knowledge of any other environmental area, and no ties to individuals working on other kinds of environmental cases. Given this diversity, the term "environmental" may seem uselessly broad, describing nothing in particular. At worst, the environmental label can give each of these situations a quixotic implication that may serve to detract from serious public consideration of the merits, though this is changing.

There is, however, a special environmental perspective that provides a common ground for all environmental cases. The positions taken by environmentalists are typically based upon a broadened accounting of the considerations involved in decision-making.

Almost every environmental case starts in response to someone's decision to do something: new products or technologies; construction projects; the start, continuation or cessation of various programs that affect the physical world. The people who make these decisions are usually not environmentalists. Indeed, the environmental position often surfaces relatively late in the game, long after the planning stage and well into the implementation stage, when citizens finally see bulldozers rolling. A common complaint of the environmental camp is that these ongoing decisions are predicated on irrationally and unrealistically narrow grounds. The proposed actions, it is argued, unwisely ignore facts, costs, and impacts on social and natural values that have real importance to the well-being of the community. By virtue of their broad view of problems and sometimes skeptical view of benefits, environmentalists often end up sounding negative.

Take the example of the Memphis superhighway, studied in the *Overton Park* case.[1] Federal and state highway planners wanted to locate Interstate-40 along a route that would minimize the costs of land acquisition and the inconvenience of lawsuits. With that strategy in mind, the planned road ran straight through an urban park and the city's poorer communities. The local citizen environmentalists argued that this decision took no account of the natural and social value of parkland,

1. Citizens to Preserve Overton Park v. Volpe, 401 U.S. 402 (1971), in Chapter 11.

especially a park serving low-income communities that had no other open-space options. It was argued that the highway officials' cost considerations, based only upon the cost of condemning land and constructing the roadway, ignored the considerable social values inherent in a stable, cohesive, low-income urban neighborhood. Furthermore, if the full costs and values were taken into account, alternative routes existed that were both preferable and available. The citizens found some law – as it turned out, an environmental law having to do with the protection of parklands from rededication to highway use – that made part of their point and won the issue.

Environmentalists are often compelled to accomplish their ends by legal indirection, using doctrines originally intended for application in other situations. But there is a political hazard involved in using legal technicalities as leverage for larger issues. One conspicuous example is the "snail darter" endangered species case chronicled in Chapter 13. Another is the attempt to re-route the Trans-Alaska Pipeline. In the pipeline case, to avoid the perils of maritime transport, the environmentalists tried to push the oil industry toward a safer overland pipeline route through Canada. They used a statutory technicality, limiting the permissible width of governmental rights-of-way, that they found in the Mineral Lands Leasing Act of 1920. A successful antipipeline injunction was reversed by Congress in an action that swept away not only the technical stumbling block, but simultaneously exempted the pipeline from compliance with environmental laws as well. The design of the Alaska pipeline was substantially improved by the environmentalists' efforts, though the pipeline still ran to the tankers at Valdez, but their legal tactics promoted a stereotype of environmentalists as meddling outsiders. Calling for comprehensive rational analysis of actions does not guarantee popularity or respect, particularly if one comes back later to the wreck of the Exxon-Valdez and says, "I told you so."

The "established" players in government – not to mention the business establishment – have been slow to welcome environmentalists and environmental laws into the system. Environmentalists have generally been "outsiders" who win legislative battles only when they are able to mobilize public opinion outside the political capitals, and then they are forced to defend their victories against a process of political erosion. Since environmental statutes and regulations come rather late, and are often watered down, environmental attorneys early on became experts in using law developed in other fields to serve the purposes of environmental advocacy. It is a skill and orientation that continues to characterize environmental law.

B. THE ECOLOGICAL AND ETHICAL BASES OF ENVIRONMENTAL LAW

Environmental economics and politics play their role in environmental law, as we will see, but other important analytical filters are initially provided by ecology, the environmental sciences, and environmental ethics.

Section 1. ECOLOGY (MICRO AND MACRO)

Law draws many lessons and arguments from ecology and the other flourishing environmental sciences. Modern environmentalists have drawn inspiration and momentum from two giants in the field, Rachel Carson and Aldo Leopold. Here are two brief examples of their work:

Rachel Carson, Silent Spring

54-57, 61 (1962)

There are few studies more fascinating, and at the same time more neglected, than those of the teeming populations that exist in the dark realms of the soil. Perhaps the most essential organisms in the soil are the smallest – the invisible hosts of bacteria and threadlike fungi. Statistics of their abundance take us at once into astronomical figures. A teaspoonful of topsoil may contain billions of bacteria. In spite of their minute size, the total weight of this host of bacteria in the top foot of a single acre of fertile soil may be as much as a thousand pounds. Ray fungi, bacteria, [and] small green cells called algae, these make up the microscopic plant life of the soil [and are] the principal agents of decay, reducing plant and animal residues to their component minerals. The vast cyclic movements of chemical elements such as carbon and nitrogen through soil and air and living tissue could not proceed without these microplants. Without the nitrogen-fixing bacteria, for example, plants would starve for want of nitrogen, though surrounded by a sea of nitrogen-containing air. Other organisms form carbon dioxide, which, as carbonic acid, aids in dissolving rock. Still other soil microbes perform various oxidations and reductions by which minerals such as iron, manganese, and sulfur are transformed and made available to plants.

Also present in prodigious numbers are microscopic mites and primitive wingless insects called springtails. Despite their small size they play an important part in breaking down the residues of plants, aiding in the slow conversion of the litter of the forest floor to soil. The specialization of some of these minute creatures for their task is almost incredible. Several species of mites, for example, can begin life only within the fallen needles of a spruce tree. Sheltered here, they digest out the inner tissues of the needle. When the mites have completed their development only the outer layer of the cells remains. The truly staggering task of dealing with the tremendous amount of plant material in the annual leaf fall belongs to some of the small insects of the soil and the forest floor. They macerate and digest the leaves, and aid in mixing the decomposed matter with surface soil.

Besides all this horde of minute but ceaselessly toiling creatures there are of course many larger forms, for soil life runs the gamut from bacteria to mammals. Some are permanent residents of the dark subsurface layers; some hibernate or spend definite parts of their life cycles in underground chambers; some freely come and go between their burrows and the upper world. In general the effect of all this habitation of the soil is to aerate it and improve both its drainage and the penetration of water throughout the layers of plant growth.

Of all the larger inhabitants of the soil, probably none is more important than the earthworm. Over three quarters of a century ago, Charles Darwin...gave the world its first understanding of the fundamental role of earthworms as geologic agents for the transport of soil – a picture of surface rocks being gradually covered by fine soil brought up from below by the worms, in annual amounts running from many tons to the acre in most favorable areas.[2] At the same time, quantities of organic matter contained in leaves and grass (as much as 20 pounds to the square yard in six months) are drawn down into the burrows and incorporated in soil. Darwin's calculations showed that the toil of earthworms might add a layer of soil an inch to inch and a half thick in a ten-year period. And this is by no means all they do: their burrows aerate the soil, keep it well drained, and aid the penetration of plant roots.... The soil community, then, consists of a web of interwoven lives, each in some way related to the others – the living creatures depending on the soil, but the soil in turn a vital element of the earth only so long as this community within it flourishes.

The problem that concerns us here is one that has received little consideration: What happens to these incredibly numerous and vitally necessary inhabitants of soil when poisonous chemicals are carried down into their world, either introduced directly as soil "sterilants" or borne on the rain that has picked up a lethal contamination as it filters through the leaf canopy of forest and orchard cropland? Is it reasonable to suppose that we can apply a broad-spectrum insecticide to kill the burrowing larval stages of a crop-destroying insect, for example, without also killing the "good" insects whose function may be the essential one of breaking down matter? Or can we use a nonspecific fungicide without also killing the fungi that inhabit the roots of many trees in a beneficial association that aids the tree in extracting nutrients from the soil?...

Chemical control of insects seems to have proceeded on the assumption that the soil could and would sustain any amount of...poisons without striking back. The very nature of the world of the soil has been largely ignored.... A group of specialists who met to discuss the ecology of the soil...summed up the hazards of using such potent and little understood tools.... "A few false moves on the part of man may result in destruction of soil productivity, and the arthropods may well take over."

Aldo Leopold, A Sand County Almanac
214-220 (1948, 1968 ed.)

The image commonly employed in conservation education is "the balance of nature." For reasons too lengthy to detail here, this figure of speech fails to describe accurately what little we know about the land mechanism. A much truer image is the one employed in ecology: the biotic pyramid.... Plants absorb energy from the sun. This energy flows through a circuit called the biota, which may be represented by a pyramid consisting of layers. The bottom layer is the soil. A plant layer rests on the soil, an insect layer on the plants, a bird and rodent layer on the insects, and so on up through various animal groups to the apex layer, which consists of the larger carnivores....

In the beginning, the pyramid of life was low and squat; the food chains short and simple. Evolution has added layer after layer, link after link. Man is one of thousands of accretions to the height and complexity of the pyramid. Science has given us many doubts, but it has given us at least one certainty: the trend of evolution is to elaborate and diversify the biota. Land, then, is not merely soil; it is a fountain of energy flowing through soils, plants, and animals. Food chains are the living channels which conduct energy upward; death and decay return to the soil. The

2. C. Darwin, The Formation of Vegetable Mould, through the Action of Worms, with Observations on Their Habits (1897).

circuit is not closed; some energy is dissipated in decay, some is added by absorption from the air, some is stored in soils, peats, and long-lived forests; but it is a sustained circuit, like a slowly augmented revolving fund of life....

The velocity and character of the upward flow of energy depend on the complex structure of the plant and animal community, much as the upward flow of sap in a tree depends on its complex cellular organization. Without this complexity, normal circulation would presumably not occur. Structure means the characteristic numbers, as well as the characteristic kinds and functions, of the component species. This interdependence between the complex structure of the land and its smooth functioning as an energy unit is one of its basic attributes.

When a change occurs in one part of the circuit, many other parts must adjust themselves to it. Change does not necessarily obstruct or divert the flow of energy; evolution is a long series of self-induced changes, the net result of which has been to elaborate the flow mechanism and to lengthen the circuit. Evolutionary changes, however, are usually slow and local. Man's invention of tools has enabled him to make changes of unprecedented violence, rapidity, and scope.... The combined evidence of history and ecology seems to support one general deduction: the less violent the man-made changes, the greater the probability of successful readjustment in the pyramid.... This deduction runs counter to our current philosophy, which assumes that because a small increase in density enriched human life, that an indefinite increase will enrich it indefinitely. Ecology knows of no density relationship that holds for indefinitely wide limits. All gains from density are subject to a law of diminishing returns.

And, for broader ecological consequences:

T. Sancton, What on Earth Are We Doing?

Time, 2 January 1989, 24-30

One generation passeth away, and another generation cometh: but the earth abideth forever. – *Ecclesiastes*

No, not forever. At the outside limit, the earth will probably last another 4 billion to 5 billion years. By that time, scientists predict, the sun will have burned up so much of its own hydrogen fuel that it will expand and incinerate the surrounding planets, including the earth. A nuclear cataclysm, on the other hand, could destroy the earth tomorrow. Somewhere within those extremes lies the life expectancy of this wondrous, swirling globe. How long it endures and the quality of life it can support do not depend alone on the immutable laws of physics. For man has reached a point in his evolution where he has the power to affect, for better or worse, the present and future state of the planet.

Through most of the 2 million years or so of existence, man has thrived in earth's environment – perhaps too well. By 1800 there were 1 billion human beings bestriding the planet. That number had doubled by 1930 and doubled again by 1975. If current birthrates hold, the world's present population of 5.1 billion will double again in 40 more years. The frightening irony is that this exponential growth in the human population – the very sign of homo sapiens' success as an organism – could doom the earth as a human habitat.

The reason is not so much the sheer numbers, though 40,000 babies die of starvation each day in Third World countries, but the reckless way in which humanity has treated its planetary host. Like the evil genies that flew from Pandora's box, technological advances have provided the means of upsetting nature's equilibrium, that intricate set of biological, physical and chemical interactions that make up the web of life. Starting at the dawn of the Industrial Revolution, smokestacks have disgorged noxious gases into the atmosphere, factories have dumped toxic wastes into rivers and streams, automobiles have guzzled irreplaceable fossil fuels and fouled the air with their detritus in the name of progress, forests have been denuded, lakes poisoned with pesticides, underground aquifers pumped dry. For decades scientists have warned of the possible consequences of all this profligacy. No one paid much attention.

[In 1988, however,] the earth spoke like God warning Noah of the deluge. Its message was loud and clear, and suddenly people began to listen, to ponder what portents the message held. In the U.S., a three-month drought baked the soil from California to Georgia, reducing the country's grain harvest by 31 percent and killing thousands of head of livestock. A stubborn seven-week heat wave drove temperatures above 100° F. across much of the country, raising fears that the dreaded "greenhouse effect" – global warming as a result of the buildup of carbon dioxide and other gases in the atmosphere – might already be under way. Parched by the lack of rain, the Western forests of the U.S., including Yellowstone National Park, went up in flames, also igniting a bitter conservationist controversy. And on many of the country's beaches, garbage, raw sewage and medical wastes washed up to spoil the fun of bathers and confront them personally with the growing despoliation of the oceans.

Similar pollution closed beaches on the Mediterranean, the North Sea and the English Channel. Killer hurricanes ripped through the Caribbean and floods devastated Bangladesh, reminders of nature's raw power. In Soviet Armenia a monstrous earthquake killed some 55,000 people. That too was a natural disaster, but its high casualty count, owing largely to the construction of cheap high-rise apartment blocks over a well-known fault area, illustrated the carelessness that has become humanity's habit in dealing with nature.

There were other forebodings of environmental disaster. In the U.S. it was revealed that federal weapons-making plants had recklessly and secretly littered large areas with radioactive waste. The further depletion of the atmosphere's ozone layer, which helps block cancer-causing rays, testified to the continued overuse of atmosphere-destroying chlorofluorocarbons emanating from such sources as spray cans and air-conditioners. Perhaps most ominous of all, the destruction of the tropical forests, home to at least half of the earth's plant and animal species, continued at a rate equal to one football field a second.

Most of these evils had been going on for a long time, and some of the worst disasters apparently had nothing to do with human behavior. Yet this year's bout of freakish weather and environmental horror stories seemed to act as a powerful catalyst for worldwide public opinion. Everyone suddenly sensed that this gyrating globe, this precious repository of all the life that we know of, was in danger. No single individual, no event, no movement captured imaginations or dominated headlines more than the clump of rock and soil and water and air that is our common home....

What would happen if nothing were done about the earth's imperiled state? According to computer projections, the accumulation of CO_2 in the atmosphere could drive up the planet's average temperature 3° F. to 9° F. by the middle of the next century. That could cause the oceans to rise by several feet, flooding coastal areas and ruining huge tracts of farmland through salinization. Changing weather patterns could make huge areas infertile or uninhabitable, touching off refugee movements unprecedented in history.

Toxic waste and radioactive contamination could lead to shortages of safe drinking water, the sine qua non of human existence. And in a world that could house between 8 billion and 14 billion people by the mid-21st century, there is a strong likelihood of mass starvation. It is even possible to envision the world so wryly and chillingly prophesied by the typewriting cockroach in Donald Marquis' *archy and mehitabel*: "man is making deserts of the earth/ it won't be long now/ before man will have it used up/ so that nothing but ants/ and centipedes and scorpions/ can find a living on it."

There are those who believe the worst scenarios are alarmist and ill founded. Some scientists contest the global warming theory or predict that natural processes will counter its effects. Kenneth E. F. Watt, professor of environmental studies at the University of California at Davis, has gone so far as to call the greenhouse effect "the laugh of the century." S. Fred Singer, a geophysicist working for the U.S. Department of Transportation, predicts that any greenhouse warming will be balanced by an increase in heat-reflecting clouds. The skeptics could be right, but it is far too risky to do nothing while awaiting absolute proof of disaster.

Whatever the validity of this or that theory, the earth will not remain as it is now. From its beginnings as a chunk of molten rock and gas some 4.5 billion years ago, the planet has seen continents form, move together and drift apart like jigsaw-puzzle pieces. Successive ice ages have sent glaciers creeping down from the polar caps. Mountain ranges have jutted up from ocean beds, and landmasses have disappeared beneath the waves.

Previous shifts in the earth's climate or topology have been accompanied by waves of extinctions. The most spectacular example is the dying off of the great dinosaurs during the Cretaceous period (136 million to 65 million years ago). No one knows exactly what killed the dinosaurs, although a radical change in environmental conditions seems a likely answer. One popular theory is that a huge meteor crashed to earth and kicked up such vast clouds of dust that sunlight was obscured and plants destroyed. Result: the dinosaurs starved to death.

Whether or not that theory is correct, an event of no less magnitude is taking place at this very moment, but this time its agent is man. The wholesale burning and cutting of forests in Brazil and other countries, as one major example, are destroying irreplaceable species every day. Says Harvard biologist E.O. Wilson: "The extinctions ongoing worldwide promise to be a least as great as the mass extinction that occurred at the end of the age of dinosaurs."...

The invention of laborsaving machines, the discovery of anesthetics and vaccines, the development of efficient transportation and communication systems [are] some of the greatest achievements of modern times. But, increasingly, technology has come up against the law of unexpected consequences. Advances in health care have lengthened life-spans, lowered infant mortality rates and, thus, aggravated the population problem. The use of pesticides has increased crop yields but polluted water supplies. The invention of automobiles and jet planes has revolutionized travel but sullied the atmosphere....

Let there be no illusions. Taking effective action to halt the massive injury to the earth's environment will require a mobilization of political will, international cooperation and sacrifice unknown except in wartime. Yet humanity is in a war right now, and it is not too draconian to call it a war for survival. It is a war in which all nations must be allies. Both the causes and effects of the problems that threaten the earth are global, and they must be attacked globally....

COMMENTARY AND QUESTIONS

1. The depressing perspectives of global ecology, and the law. To Sancton, the global challenge facing the environment is only capable of redress through an altering of attitudes toward use and preservation of natural resources that would dramatically change lifestyles in virtually all parts of the world. What role, if any, does law play in that process? Laws can prohibit directly and indirectly some forms of environmental carnage, as with attempts to protect endangered species. The effectiveness of such attempts, however, remains an open question. Finding laws that seem capable of effecting larger behavioral changes, such as reducing global emissions of greenhouse gases produced by fossil fuel consumption and deforestation, remains more problematic. The law often adopts Abbie Hoffman's compromise advice to "think globally, act locally."

Arnold Reitze, in a penetrating article reviewing 20 years of environmental efforts,[3] dourly noted that virtually all global environmental degradation can be traced back to three major human phenomena – population, consumption, and pollution – all of which are out of control. Of these, the most devastating is population pressure. Relentless population growth undercuts the hopes of nationbuilders and those who try to apply industrial, social, economic, and legal technology to alleviate the ills of humankind and the planet. Dehumanizing poverty, hunger, homelessness, and lack of opportunity are increasing in both relative and absolute terms. The numbers and problems of the underclass grow rather than shrink. Society, instead of moving toward global cooperation, often seems to be degenerating into mutually antagonistic tribes. These human conditions can themselves be considered "environmental" problems. And they have the disastrous further consequence of reducing the terms of human decision-making to purely short-term coping and survival, so that long-term ecological rationality seems a wistful impossibility. Urban decay, children having children, desertification, desperate exploitation of resources – these may be products of the "population bomb" and it is far from clear what law can do about it. In fact, Reitze noted, governments find the problems of population and malconsumption so hard to handle that they tend to ignore them, and focus instead on pollution, which, although serious, is the least important of the major causes of environmental degradation.

This book, to some extent, incorporates that mistake. It is far easier to study legal remedies for controlling pollution than for controlling population and market consumption patterns. The coursebook looks beyond pollution, however, and the legal process approach can be flexibly extended as far as environmental analysis can

3. Environmental Policy – It is Time for a New Beginning, 14 Colum. J. Envtl. L. 111 (1989).

go. Law will be a participant in the mission to bring humankind and the planet into equilibrium, even if that sometimes appears to be a quixotic quest.

2. A need for integrated environmental management? Reality exists in the holistic, integrated overview, but knowledge and the capacity to manage discrete problems build from the bottom, from a narrow, incisive, specialized focus. A 1988 strategy report prepared by the U.S. Environmental Protection Agency[4] began with a fundamental declaration that EPA should take an overall "systems approach" that views the environment as an integrated whole, and should coordinate all protection strategies on that basis. The proposal has global implications, considered in the last chapter of this book. Perhaps ironically, however, the rest of the EPA report was organized on a medium-by-medium approach – air, water, toxics, noise, land use, and so on. Is it practically inevitable that bureaucrats, legislators, lawyers, litigants, and humans generally will focus on narrow slices of the environmental dilemma? In an increasingly specialized world, how do we keep our eyes open to the whole?

Section 2. ENVIRONMENTAL ETHICS

Aldo Leopold, A Sand County Almanac

129-130, 203, 224-225 (1948)

THINKING LIKE A MOUNTAIN

Only the mountain has lived long enough to listen objectively to the howl of a wolf.... My own conviction on this score dates from the day I saw a wolf die. We were eating lunch on a high rimrock, at the foot of which a turbulent river elbowed its way. We saw what we thought was a doe fording the torrent, her breast awash in white water. When she climbed the bank toward us and shook out her tail, we realized our error: it was a wolf. A half-dozen others, evidently grown pups, sprang from the willows and all joined in a welcoming mêlée of wagging tails and playful maulings. What was literally a pile of wolves writhed and tumbled in the center of an open flat at the foot of our rimrock.

In those days we had never heard of passing up a chance to kill a wolf. In a second we were pumping lead into the pack, but with more excitement than accuracy.... When our rifles were empty, the old wolf was down, and a pup was dragging a leg into impassable slide-rocks. We reached the old wolf in time to watch a fierce green fire dying in her eyes. I realized then, and have known ever since, that there was something new to me in those eyes – something known only to her and to the mountain. I was young then, and full of trigger-itch; I thought that because fewer wolves meant more deer, that no wolves would mean hunters' paradise. But after seeing the green fire die, I sensed that neither the wolf nor the mountain agreed with such a view....

4. L. Thomas, Environmental Progress and Challenges: EPA Update (1988).

THE LAND ETHIC...

There is as yet no ethic dealing with man's relation to land and to the animals and plants which grow upon it.... The extension of ethics to this...element in human environment is, if I read the evidence correctly, an evolutionary possibility and an ecological necessity.... The "key-log" which must be moved to release the evolutionary process for an ethic is simply this: quit thinking about decent land-use as solely an economic problem. Examine each question in terms of what is ethically and esthetically right, as well as what is economically expedient. A thing is right when it tends to preserve the integrity, stability, and beauty of the biotic community. It is wrong when it tends otherwise.

AN ENVIRONMENTAL ETHIC BEYOND UTILITARIANISM?

Leopold's lyrical ecology has inspired two generations of environmental scientists, and a vigorous ongoing ethical debate. Isn't the environment more than a commodity and medium for human designs? Shouldn't there be a recognized moral and ethical standard extending beyond pure human self-interest, recognizing the normative rights of the planet, of nature itself?

It is true, of course, that many environmentalists (like most chapters of this book) do indeed focus on utilitarian arguments for environmental quality: basic human self-interest, health and economics, should force society not to ignore ecological balances. Even Leopold himself is ambiguous. He continues the wolf-killing story by showing how wolves are important in controlling populations of deer and other foraging animals that otherwise will strip the forests bare and turn cattle ranges to dustbowls. When he later criticizes current land use policy because "it assumes, falsely, I think, that the economic parts of the biotic clock will function without the uneconomic parts," he is again making a utilitarian argument.

But the fire dying in the she-wolf's eyes, that is something else.

Could it be that humans are not indeed the measure of all things? Are we instead only one part of a larger ecological community, with responsibilities accompanying our undoubted powers and rights? Is there, in other words, a moral-legal basis for environmentalism beyond utilitarianism? This question increasingly reappears in environmental law cases. When a project is stopped because it threatens extinction for some endangered insect, or a court considers awards of natural resource damages for ecosystems destroyed by oil spills, the law must reach beyond the normal justifications founded upon net human benefit.[5]

Should we declare that the wolf herself has legal rights, rights that, although not absolute, must nevertheless be substantively weighed in the legal process? Impressive work has been devoted to animal rights and natural rights theories.[6] Nagging problems arise, however, in drawing lines. Is sentiency the litmus? If not, shouldn't

---

5. See Chapters 3, 8, and 13 on natural resource remedies and endangered species law.

6. See Roderick Nash's Rights of Nature: A History of Environmental Ethics (1989); H. Rolston, Environmental Ethics: Duties to and Values in the Natural World (1988); and R. Nozick, Anarchy, State and Utopia 35-42 (1975), and the literature that has followed it.

plants, rocks, and hills as well be able to claim these rights?[7] Unless the broader view prevails, the ethic ignores the rights of ecosystems. If natural rights can be defined, moreover, who defines them and determines when and how they are to be applied and weighed against human rights and the rights of other entities in the system?

Taking another approach, can it be argued that a God commands ecological sensitivity? Many have criticized the Bible's call for humans to conquer nature:

> Be the terror and dread of all the wild beasts and all the birds of heaven, of everything that crawls on the ground and all the fish of the sea; they are handed over to you.... Teem over the earth and be lord of it. Genesis 9:1-2,7.[8]

But other strands in Judaeo-Christian theology and other religious cultures cast humans in a less domineering role. Primitive humans were probably deists; the mountains and rivers had spirits, and humans spoke with the trees and animals they were about to kill for their use. In many Eastern and Native American[9] cultures, gods are intimately linked with nature; humans are merely a part of the web, the Tao. Human disruption of nature is deplored as having destroyed "the age of perfect virtue, when men lived in common with birds and beasts, as forming one family."[10] The Dalai Lama, speaking of his Buddhism, said "We have always considered ourselves as part of our environment."[11] The great Jewish philosopher Maimonides dramatically recanted his early Greek-inspired view of human primacy: "It should not be believed that all things exist for the sake of the existence of man. On the contrary, all the other beings, too, have been intended for their own sakes and not for the sake of something else."[12]

Christianity, whose God became a human, has been more resistant to any diminution of human-centeredness. The Protestant ethic, when it appeared, fit

7. See Christopher Stone, Should Trees Have Standing? (1972).

8. Calvin and many other Christian theologians have argued that God "created all things for man's sake." Institutes of Religion 182; bk.1, ch. 14, 22 (Battles edition 1961); see generally J.A. Passmore, Man's Responsibility for Nature (1974) (hereafter Passmore).

9. "Human beings are not superior to the rest of creation. If human beings were to drop out of the cycle of life, the earth would heal itself and go on. But if any of the other elements would drop out – air, water, animal or plant life – human beings and the earth itself would end." Audrey Shenandoan, Onandaga tribe, NY. This echoes the "Gaia" hypothesis that the planet Earth itself is a living, self-regulating organism; disruptions will modify the system, and life as we know it may disappear, though the planet will ultimately strike a new balance. J. Lovelock, The Ages of Gaia, (1988); A. Miller, Gaia Connections (1991). In this sense, the planet Earth may not be so "fragile." Cf. Dedication at page iii *supra*.

10. Chuang Tsu, 4th c. B.C., in Passmore at 7-8. "When humans interfere with the Tao, the sky becomes filthy, the equilibrium crumbles, creatures become extinct." Lao-tzu, Tao Te Ching (500 B.C.).

11. He continues, "Our scriptures speak of the container and the contained. The world is the container – our house – and we are the contained – the contents of the container.... As a boy studying Buddhism I was taught the importance of a caring attitude toward the environment. Our practice of nonviolence applies not just to human beings but to all sentient beings.... In Buddhist practice we get so used to this idea of nonviolence and the ending of all suffering that we become accustomed to not harming or destroying anything indiscriminately. Although we do not believe that trees or flowers have minds, we treat them also with respect. Thus we share a sense of universal responsibility for both mankind and nature." H.H. the 14th Dalai Lama, and G. Rowell, My Tibet 79-80 (1990).

12. See Passmore, at 12.

nicely with the Industrial Revolution's conquest of nature. Fundamentalist Christians' resistance to the notion that humans evolved as part of the natural world demonstrates a continuing need to see humans as separate and distinct from nature. But others can now read the Old Testament, particularly the Noah story, as affirming the sanctity and uniqueness of every living species, and setting humans the task of preserving the earth's natural heritage. Some new Christian scholarship urges an active ethic of human "stewardship" over all Creation.[13] These theological debates between human-centered and more interrelational metaphysics have been paralleled in the dialogues of nonreligious philosophy as well.[14]

Without a clearly divine or natural source of a moral ethic for the environment, the ethic, if it is to exist, must come from humans. Much of any human-based environmental ethic will of course continue to be based on utilitarianism: if we want our species' descendants to survive on the planet we must take the sensitive cautious long view. But beyond self-interest, further distinctions can extend the ethic. We may indeed currently be the dominant species on the earth, possessing earth-changing knowledge, technology, and physical powers, but along with these powers may come ethical responsibilities. Perhaps these are responsibilities to past generations and to the future, to steward and pass on the extraordinary legacy we have received. A classic legal algorithm holds that for every power there is a countervailing responsibility. The ability to destroy surely does not carry with it the moral right to do so, tempered only by the limitations of self-interest against self-inflicted wounds. That would be too juvenile, too male adolescent a norm for a species that has been maturing for three million years.

From the fact of human intellectual development come other bases for an environmental ethic. On one hand are the arguments that proceed from our superiorities, like the claim for an ecological *noblesse oblige*: because humans uniquely have been able, in some settings at least, to move beyond the bare demands of food, shelter, and survival to build an abstract culture, and to understand the effects of our actions upon the planet, our species has a high calling to protect the less powerful parts of the ecological community in which we live. Aesthetic principles, also a unique human development, likewise argue for an extended stewardship.

On the other hand are the arguments from humility. It has become a cliché to say that the more one knows, the more one realizes one does not know. The greater the expansion of our knowledge and technology, the vaster the realm of the unknown. When we look into the she-wolf's eyes with Leopold, some of what we feel may be anthropomorphic sympathy. But the fire dying there may also spark a recognition that we will never know the world she knows, and that should make us hesitant to make ourselves the measure of it all. Ultimately humans may be impelled to honor an environmental ethic protecting the planet's ecology for the

---

13. Fellows of the Calvin Center for Christian Scholarship, Earthkeeping: Christian Stewardship of Natural Resources (1980); P. Riesenberg, The Inalienability of Sovereignty in Medieval Political Thought (1956) explores medieval concepts of human (and royal) stewardship.

14. Goethe and Henry More were early outposts in the resistance to the human-centeredness of Bacon, Descartes, and even Kant. See generally Passmore, 16-23.

same reason that they are impelled to climb Mt. Everest: because it is there. The very existence – the "is-ness" – of the wolf and her rivers and mountains, separate from humans, makes the ethic fitting and proper for recognition.

When the question arises, as it continually does in legislatures, agencies, courts, and saloons, "Why protect such-and-such particular part of the environment?" environmentalists will undoubtedly continue to argue practically, "Because it may turn out to be important to us, or to hurt us if we lose it." But often, when the setting and the light are right, won't many also feel a further pull, leading beyond the stark counsels of human utility?

C. ENVIRONMENTAL ANALYSIS: ROAD SALT – A PARADIGM THAT HAS NOT YET FOUND A LEGAL FORUM

The following environmental controversy has as yet hardly touched the legal system. It nevertheless demonstrates how an environmental issue with economic and political dimensions confronts governmental and legal processes. Readers in the Frost Belt states are living in the midst of this exercise. For readers in Sun Belt states, it offers a bemusing and instructive opportunity to scrutinize a classic environmental dilemma from a safe distance.

Section 1. SOME FACTS ABOUT SALT

Like King Lear, one can learn much from salt. In 1976, the U.S. Environmental Protection Agency (EPA) prepared a major analysis of the effects of highway de-icing salt, based on 331 prior research projects and reports.[15] Dr. Charles Wurster, of the State University of New York's Marine Sciences Research Center, published this summary of the EPA report:

Wurster, Of Salt . . .

New York Times, 4 March 1978, 21.

The use of salt on roads for snow and ice removal has increased in the last 15 years. About nine million tons, more than 10 percent of all salt produced in the world, are applied annually to American highways in snowy states.

The benefits of salt for road de-icing – and its costs – are rarely questioned. A recent report of the EPA, which weighed the costs and benefits of the practice, includes surprises.

The costs of salting begin with $200 million for the salt and its application. Roadside vegetation destroyed by salt, particularly shade trees, was estimated by EPA to add another $150 million. Underground water mains, telephone cables and electric lines are corroded by salt seepage, adding another $10 million in damages. The Consolidated Edison Company, which owns the world's largest underground electrical system, estimated that road salt did $5 million in damages during the winter of 1973-74.

Salt finds its way into drinking-water supplies, especially ground-water aquifers, thereby becoming a health hazard. Recent research implicates salt intake as a causative factor in hypertension, heart disease and other circulatory problems, as

15. EPA Document 600/2-76-105 (May 1976).

well as various liver, kidney and metabolic disorders. It is estimated that at least 20 percent of Americans should restrict salt intake.

Individuals can control the salt that is added to foods, but salt in drinking water is harder to manage. About 27 percent of the drinking water supplies in Massachusetts are contaminated with road salt, and New Hampshire has a state-financed system for replacing contaminated wells. Long Island is especially vulnerable, since its sole drinking water is ground water recharged by precipitation, including highway runoff.

The EPA estimated that 25 percent of the population in the Snow Belt drinks water contaminated with road salt. The cost of providing pure water for these people was put at $150 million, but no objective cost was ascribed to health damage.

Salt damages bridges and other highway structures, best exemplified by the deterioration and collapse of New York City's West Side Highway. Corrosion by salt is believed to have been a major cause of the failure. The EPA estimated the national annual cost of damage to highway structures by salt at $500 million.

But the largest and most obvious cost of road salt is automobile corrosion, estimated by the EPA at $2 billion annually, or an average of about $34 per car per year in the Snow Belt. Heavy salting of highways hastens auto depreciation by about 20 percent. Telephone company vehicles last twice as long in the South as they do in New England.

Although they are usually assumed without question, the benefits of road salting have proven elusive to substantiate. At temperatures near or slightly below freezing, salt hastens melting and increases traction. But at lower temperatures, salt makes dry snow shiny and more slippery, and causes it to stick on windshields hampering vision. Salt also prolongs street wetness, reducing the friction.

Solid evidence of increased safety is lacking, because inadequate studies have been confounded by too many variables. The effects of salting are often inseparable from the effects of plowing and sanding. A Michigan study found fewer accidents during years when salt was used, but the number of storms and quantity of snowfall were ignored. Other studies showed no effects on accident rates.

Salt usually permits faster driving which would benefit emergency vehicles but is a mixed blessing for others. In snow, people tend to drive slowly and have "fender benders," but after salt applications they tend to drive faster and have more serious accidents.

The benefits of salt in preventing accidents, if any, are small. Not surprisingly, this conclusion is disputed by the salt industry, which claims great benefits from its use.

An interesting benefit-cost analysis results. Whereas benefits are uncertain but apparently small (except to the salt and automobile industries), costs total nearly $3 billion per year. Only a small amount of the cost is the salt itself, 93 percent consisting of indirect costs, borne especially by owners of motor vehicles.

Road salting should be re-examined. Reduced salting, combined with increased plowing, tire modifications, and driver education in snow driving might yield better results at lower costs.

The EPA report summarized by Dr. Wurster contains many other fascinating details:

- The state of Alaska gets along without using any road salt.
- The citizens of Michigan, leading the world in auto production, also lead in auto corrosion, losing $198,630,000 each year in salt-caused depreciation, which almost matches the total cost of salt application in the nation.
- Urban shade trees are vulnerable to salt, and have monetizable values[16] (a 15" diameter tree was valued at $1,767; if a tree starts showing leaf damage from salt it is beyond saving).
- So much salt has spilled into the Great Lakes that parts of the Lake Michigan depths now have a marine salt water ecology.
- Salt infiltrates through concrete and sets up a powerful pressure reaction with reinforcing steel, causing potholes and overpass damage.
- All things being equal, people favor the "bare pavement" look of salted roads because the visual impression is misleadingly clearer than that of a scraped and sanded roadway.
- Salt intake is a critical factor in many health afflictions including hypertension, cardiovascular diseases, renal and liver diseases and metabolic disorders, but no studies have focused on the widespread effects of highway salt on drinking water supplies.
- The report also notes that highway salt can be harmful to fish and wildlife, but doesn't pursue these costs. It makes extensive cost comparisons with a "scrape, sand, and selective salting" alternative model. (The net cost of the unlimited salting model was almost twice that of the restricted model.) The report doesn't review any totally no-salt strategies.

Section 2. EVALUATING THE BENEFITS, COSTS, AND ALTERNATIVES TO SALTING

Is salt an "environmental" problem? Although it involves potential damages to public health, vegetation, fish, and wildlife, these are precisely the areas that are least covered in the report. They are the concerns that lie at the end of an indirect chain of causation, and are the hardest to prove and least quantifiable in money terms. The mere presence of these interconnected human and natural effects, and the narrowed basis upon which the salt decision is made, put the issue squarely in the realm of environmental concern.

Salting is a classic example of how humans typically think in terms of "one-shot technology." You've got an ice problem? Bam, you zap it with salt, and the ice goes away. You've got bugs? You zap them with parathion and the bugs drop dead. Who wants to bother with thinking about where the salt or parathion go after the zap? Out of sight, out of mind. Environmentalists, however, remind us that everything goes somewhere and has residual consequences. We will live in a closed system with those residuals long after the ice and bugs are gone.

16. Throughout this book, the words "monetized" and "monetizable" are used in the informal sense of attributing market value, not in the technical sense of converting to legal obligation.

Dr. Wurster's article demonstrates the elements of a classic environmental policy analysis, equally applicable to a polluting factory or a federal dam-building project. First, the decision as it is actually made: the road commissions decide to put salt on roads because, for them, it is a logical benefit-cost-alternatives decision. They get bare roads for $200 million a year. But this ignores at least 93 percent of the true costs, as seen by environmentalists.

COSTS, ECONOMIC AND NATURAL

Environmentalists typically argue that the costs of a proposal are far greater than the limited costs considered by those who make the decision. Here are the conservative EPA estimates of the total yearly costs of road salting that can be monetized (stated in millions):[17]

Water Supplies	$ 150	
Vegetation	50	
Highway Structures	500	
Vehicles	2,000	
Utilities	10	
Salt Purchase & Application	200	**TOTAL: $2.91 billion**

This set of costs is, of course, not complete. Remarkably, the analyzed costs completely exclude health costs, beyond a factor based on substitute drinking water supply, and do not include any fish and wildlife or aesthetic values. They also ignore the costs which occur at the source of the salt, such as harms caused by mining, which typically include local water pollution from mine run-off and leachate.

As is usually the case in environmental matters, most of these costs are indirect and borne in small amounts by a large, dispersed class of adversely affected individuals. In many cases, however, the majority of costs are not so easily monetizable. In the case of seal pups slaughtered on the ice, what cost is attributable to human revulsion at the inhumanity of the massacre, not to mention to the seals themselves? Benefit-cost analysis is a rational process only to the degree that it incorporates full consideration of real costs and benefits, whether or not they are monetizable. This requires conceptual weighing as well as monetary weighing, a very tough assignment. One noted economist asserts that when faced with non-monetizeable costs, a properly conducted benefit-cost analysis will list such items to reveal that they are properly a part of the analysis even if not represented by a numerical figure of their worth:

> For any real world choice, there will always be some considerations that cannot easily be enumerated or valued, where the analysis becomes quite conjectural. Benefit-cost analysis does not, and should not, try to hide this uncertainty. The sensible way to deal with uncertainty about some aspects of a benefit or cost is to quantify what can be quantified, to array and rank non-quantifiable factors, and to proceed as far as possible.[18]

17. All salt figures are in the EPA Report's 1976 dollars.
18. E. Gramlich, A Guide to Benefit-Cost Analysis 5 (2d ed., 1990).

One of the difficulties in achieving practical acceptance of the environmental perspective and its comprehensive benefit-cost-alternatives analysis is that many public and private decision-makers are responsive only to data that reckons the costs *they* must bear in relation to the project. There is an understandable inclination to ignore costs that are either indirect, externalized or unmonetized. A federal pork barrel dam project tends to ignore the values of free-flowing rivers, disrupted communities, and loss of farmland. A polluting factory tends to ignore the far-flung health, property, ecological, and aesthetic damages caused by the hazardous liquids and fumes it emits. Environmentalists spurred by a normative preference for ecosystem protection (and those seeking an accurate benefit-cost analysis) will note that establishing a major new factory will not only cause costs associated with air and water pollution. They will also point out that the project requires the construction of roads and schools, police and fire protection, and the like. These are all costs that ought to be counted in the decision whether or not to go forward with a plant, but these are not often costs borne by the plant as part of its cost of construction or maintenance, and these costs may be overlooked by governmental regulators (even assuming that there is a governmental agency empowered to block the project because of an unfavorable benefit-cost analysis).

The point is, of course, that most of these kinds of costs are hidden from direct public view, and not chargeable to the persons who decide to impose them.[19] Returning to the salt problem, how many of the salt costs listed above, for example, will have to be paid by the road commissions that choose to use salt?

BENEFITS

The classic environmental response to a proposal's claimed benefits is to doubt them. The decision-makers in the official marketplace have decided to go ahead for their direct market reasons, but why is a supersonic transport plane needed? Will this new factory bring in as much local revenue as claimed? Does this area need another recreational reservoir? Are coats made of baby seal skins really necessary?

In the case of highway salt, this argument focuses on the lack of proof of benefits from the "bare pavement" model. What is the value of a road that appears to be clear, especially if it retains a film of icy slush? What is the value of faster-moving traffic, especially in light of the evidence that accidents on salted road systems are more likely to be fatal than the scrape-and-sand model's "fender-benders"? The environmentalist would admit the benefits of time saved and disruptions avoided by highway salting, but would argue that these benefits are illusory, or insubstantial, when offset by costs. In practice, on the other hand, the operative valuation of salt's benefits is based on intuitive judgments made by highway commissions that the "bare-pavement" result of salting is worth more than the yearly $200 million cost of buying and applying salt insofar as they are concerned. And in this as in other cases where valuation is difficult, one is tempted to leave the benefit calculus to administrative discretion and the marketplace.

---

19. See the discussion of decisionmakers' cost "externalization" in Chapter 2.

ALTERNATIVES

The analysis of a proposal's benefits and costs is meaningless unless it is linked to a comparison of alternatives. Environmentalists can accurately be regarded as narrow-minded negativists if they merely attack proposals, without reviewing alternative courses of action. One alternative in every case, of course, is the "no-action" alternative. When developers planned to build a dam that would flood part of the Grand Canyon for power and water supply, environmentalists were able to show that those benefits were not needed at that time and place, in light of the social costs. The better option was to do nothing.

Often the analysis of alternatives turns upon whether the action can better take place with a different design, location, timing, process, etc. A particular factory might be a better neighbor, for example, if it installed pollution-control mechanisms, used a higher temperature process, or located itself downwind. Beverage bottles would cause less litter and save energy and raw materials if they were returnable. In the Memphis highway case, the citizens argued for location and construction designs that were feasible and prudent alternatives to going through the middle of their park.

In the case of salt, the purpose of the proposed action – removal of snow from the highways so as to allow traffic to move – is clearly necessary. Only the most troglodytic environmentalist would argue that traffic should come to a halt when the snow falls. Rather, the analysis should turn to a comparison of realistic alternatives. Installation of infra-red electric melting devices in highway pavements might be effective and avoid all the indirect costs of salting, but the direct costs would be outrageous. Scraping and cindering, with or without selective location-specific salting, clearly are feasible alternatives, because that was the preferred method prior to the shift to salt in the 1960s. More recently, salt substitutes having many of the same snow melting characteristics, yet lacking the destructive characteristics of sodium chloride, have become viable alternatives. Calcium magnesium acetate (CMA), made by Chevron from recycled milk whey, avoids the destructive effects of salt and rebuilds salt-damaged soils by replacing stripped magnesium and calcium – but it costs \$300-600 as opposed to salt's \$20 – 70 per ton.

Even putting to one side the unmonetized costs in the public health arena that are not accounted for by EPA, it appears reasonable that the non-salt alternatives might realize savings of almost \$2 billion per year when compared with continued use of salt. This would be true even if the direct costs increased fivefold, from \$200 million to \$1 billion; the actual overall costs would still drop more than \$1.9 billion.

Assume that a careful study did conclusively prove that the United States was losing a net \$2 billion annually, unnecessarily, to road salt. In all probability, what would occur? Probably not much.

Section 3. THE HEART OF THE MATTER – CONTENDING FORCES, AND THE ROLE OF NONGOVERNMENTAL ORGANIZATIONS

Even though modern environmental law has carried environmental analysis into the heart of the governmental process, so far as can be determined the 1976 EPA salt study has not produced any changes in federal policy or practice. This might well be so even if it had conclusively established annual net losses of more than $2 billion. Why?

Look at the participants in the process. Salt manufacturers (in the U.S., primarily deep-mining companies) have expanded their production enormously over the past thirty years. Because of the growth of the road salt market, their payrolls and capital investments have increased. Because of their financial position, the salt producers and associated industries have a strong incentive and capacity to encourage the sale of salt. They have little or no financial accountability for the consequences of salt use; these costs are therefore irrelevant or "external" to their business decisions. Accordingly the salt industry organizes to increase production and promote the sale of road salt through advertising and trade publications that stress the low initial cost and high effectiveness of intensive salt use. To promote its position nationally, the industry formed the American Salt Institute, a lobbying and trade association located in the Washington D.C. area.

Which leads to government: At the operative level, of course, it is government agencies that actually spread salt on highways. Local and state highway commissions, however, are in the same narrowed decisional situation as the salt industry itself. They want the most removal punch for the money, and have virtually no accountability or concern for costs beyond their initial expenditures to get the job done. "The problem," says Chevron's Dan Walter, "is that the benefit of CMA does not go back to the governmental agency that pays for de-icers, typically state maintenance departments. If a bridge on an interstate highway must be replaced, the federal government will pay 80 percent of the cost. Therefore the highway department cannot justify paying over $600 per ton for CMA."[20] Accordingly they turn to intensive use of salt. The officials of the highway agencies also have their national associations, which have ties to the Highway Users Federation (the trade coalition that represents and lobbies for the many players in the highway industry) which in turn has ties to the Salt Institute. Nor does the Federal Highway Administration in the U.S. Department of Transportation demonstrate much incentive to challenge the salting procedures. It has traditionally been linked in interest to the corporate highway lobby.

In another corner of the legal system, however, the state and federal governments do have resource protection agencies that are designed to regulate and protect against the kinds of danger involved here. What will they do? The EPA did take action: it wrote the study. But it did nothing more. The environmental regulatory agencies, especially in recent years, have been constrained in their financial and political resources. It is extremely difficult for them internally and externally to

20. U.S. Water News, Salt-free Road De-icer Remains Stymied by Bureaucratic Red Tape, Jan. 1990 at 11.

oppose ongoing government decisions. With the negative effects of salting so diffused, indirect, and hard to quantify in cumulative form, it has been difficult to place the salt problem on the governmental agenda. Absent a political push, the environmental and health agencies have done nothing, with the exception of a few inquiries about local well water contamination.

What about the legislatures? It would of course be possible for a local or state legislative body or Congress to pass a law in response to the problem. (Some local communities have in fact adopted no-salt policies.) But merely pointing out a factual case to a legislative committee does not get the job done. Environmental groups learned early that legislatures and politicians generally respond to pressures, rather than out of some vague loyalty to the "public interest." Government is a process of contending forces. Several state legislators have unsuccessfully proposed salt-limitation bills. As soon as proposals surface in governmental agencies or legislatures, however, representatives of the industry (and perhaps the local highway commissions) can respond throughout the governmental process – in committee rooms, in offices and bureaus, in the corridors, and in the expense-account restaurants – emphasizing the direct cost savings in doing things consistent with their own market interests. Given the nature of the problem, and the immense resources of the market players, a rational overview analysis of the public interest is likely to be lost, no matter how compelling the facts.

Until the 1960s, there was generally no contest at all. The governmental process was essentially bi-polar, composed of market forces and regulatory government. Until the late 1800s, the private marketplace was the dominant "government" of the United States. (In some senses it still is, for, in a society that is basically structured by the private corporate market, the vast majority of daily actions and personal incentives are shaped by economic decisions.) In the trust-busting era, however, the laissez-faire theory of governance began to be supplemented by selective government regulation. Left to itself, the market ignores major external considerations that a society must deal with. Government intervention was necessary in order to impose certain non-market values upon the market, through laws on child labor, antitrust, worker safety, consumer fraud, and so on. The bi-polar system of government – agencies counter-balancing the market to protect the public interest – was never clearer than in the New Deal. But over time, government agencies tend to come ever closer to the corporate entities they regulate, as demonstrated by the highway commissions and highway-related industries. Given the dominant position of the market in everyday lives, this so-called "capture" phenomenon really doesn't come as a surprise, nor does the well-funded persuasive force of the marketplace in the legislatures. Many of the lions of the past – the ICC, SEC, FCC, CAB, FTC and others – became the lambs of the mid-century, and this taming-down of the watchdogs became especially notable in the Reagan era.

The comfortable bi-polar structure of government, however, has been wedged open in the last twenty years by the strident presence of non-market NGOs (non-governmental organizations). These so-called public-interest citizen groups, with environmentalists in the vanguard, have re-invigorated a process of active pluralistic democracy. This book repeatedly emphasizes the central role played by citizen activists in the creation and continuing development of modern environmental law. The legal system would have much dimmer prospects in its efforts at conserving the planet without the informed participation of citizen-environmentalists.

Who are the environmentalists? At one pole they include the ecoguerrillas of the EarthFirst! movement, and the "Greens" and "deep ecologists" dedicated to iconoclastic political action, then ranging rightward across a wide spectrum of groups and programs all the way to the silkstockinged salons of Brahmin conservationists. Environmentalism today includes citizens from a wide range of income levels and racial backgrounds.[21] At every point across the spectrum stand environmental lawyers and legal advocacy groups. Environmentalists are often volunteers, unfunded by the market or official government, attempting to bring their concerns into government processes that so often seem to ignore them. Ultimately environmentalists of all stripes are saying that the society cannot afford to make its decisions in a manner that leaves so many real values and consequences out of its calculus. Someone has to be in a place to say that the Emperor is not wearing clothes.

Section 4. THE STRATEGIES OF AN ENVIRONMENTAL LAW CASE

Back to the annual $2 billion in net salt damage: assuming again that they could prove the facts of destructive, unnecessary waste, how can environmentalists marshal sufficient force to interpose their arguments into the process?

MARKETPLACE REMEDIES

Theoretically, they can work within the private marketplace, either buying out the salt producers, mobilizing boycotts, or advertising salt's harms sufficiently to dry up the market. A moment's reflection on costs in the modern marketplace and the environmentalists' volunteer status will reveal the limits of this approach. And then there is ADR (Alternative Dispute Resolution), negotiation, mediation, and the like. Avoiding the battlefield mode of dispute resolution is a growing and desirable trend, and probably 90 percent of legal controversies are ultimately settled out of court. The problem is that, without the portent of legal battle, it is highly unlikely that the market players would willingly sit down to negotiate any compromises.

PUBLIC LAW REMEDIES: PETITIONING THE AGENCIES

The argument can be taken to the administrative agencies, through petitions and requests for administrative hearings. As previously noted, however, the highway commissions' dominating constraint of direct budgetary costs is likely to prevent serious rethinking of the policy, and the environmental protection agencies probably lack the political momentum to undertake such a crusade. Imagine the lot of the administrative official who did decide to take on the problem. After

21. The early predominance of white upper-middle-income activists has been changing due to outreach by national environmental organizations, and grassroots efforts of groups like Highlander Center, New Market, Tennessee; Citizens for a Better America, Halifax, Virginia; Native Americans for a Clean Environment, Tahlequah, Oklahoma; Tools for Change, San Francisco; and the national inner-city Natural Guard, based in Washington D.C.

presentation of petitions, public testimony, and a scattering of news stories, the citizens go home, leaving the official to face the constant presence and pressure of the salt producers and their cohorts who recognize a threat to their interests.

PETITIONING THE LEGISLATURE

Prospects are somewhat brighter on the legislative side. Particularly at the local level, petitions and testimony may represent sufficient potential votes to command attention. Even if a local government passes an ordinance notwithstanding the pressures of the market forces and its own highway commission, however, the environmental analysis still runs into strategic problems of scale. There are tens of thousands of local governments in the Frost Belt, each of which would have to be educated and pushed to take action, because the salt problem spreads so widely. Even if one town were to halt the practice, its citizens' cars and even water supplies would pick up the problem elsewhere. State or federal legislation is less likely, because the issue and its active constituency, relatively speaking, are minor in scale. To get legislative attention, the environmentalists would need an altruistic legislative crusader, a vivid crisis, or a blockbusting TV exposé.

THE MEDIA

The media have often and accurately been called a branch of government. Media attention on an issue can be extremely effective. It makes politicians respond for reasons that lie in the theatrical nature of the governing process as well as in the quest for votes. But media coverage is often just "info-tainment," hard to mobilize and keep focused. An effective media strategy is highly contingent upon citizens' ability to interest the media in the issue, to transmit sufficient detail to reporters (and note how complex most environmental analyses are, in comparison to straightforward market arguments, that "salt clears roads," etc.), to focus coverage on the relevant governmental target, and perhaps hardest, to keep the media on the story as long as required.

SUE THEM

Notice that all of the prior strategies focus upon rational persuasion. As such they are appealing, for one likes to think that human society has the capacity to respond to logic, analysis, and concerned debate. Realistically, however, many environmental cases must turn to the force of law to give practical effect to their arguments – the threat of legal action to force negotiated consideration of public environmental values, or the actuality of legal action when threats are not enough.

If a fundamental problem of our economic system is that decision-makers won't take account of many of the real costs they impose unless they themselves have to pay for them,[22] then environmental law fundamentally is the art of presenting the bill for environmental social costs, most often by litigation.

22. This is the basic "cost-externalization" syndrome studied in the next chapter. The managers of a factory, for example, will often try to pass on to others ("externalize") as much of the costs of their operations as they can, while holding onto, or "internalizing," maximum benefits, i.e. income, as analyzed further in Chapter 2.

The legal weaponry available to environmental activists in the United States is remarkably broad. Most of the available legal actions are based on actions in court. Although there are often useful opportunities to intervene directly in agency proceedings, most such interventions are backed up by the litigation option. In this country courts have their fingers in the widest array of pies.

Here are some of the available lawsuits, all of which have possible applications to the salt problem:

- *Tort actions*: Property owners can sue for injury to their homes, farms, cars; representatives of the public can sue against salt as a public nuisance. Salt could be the basis of several creative tort law suits, posing interesting procedural problems but offering the potential of money damages or injunctions, in individual or class actions. To date only a very few such cases have been reported.[23]
- *Constitutional claims*: Particular actions by government officials may run afoul of the federal or state constitution by violating due process rights, taking property without compensation, unlawfully restricting interstate commerce, etc. Salt might be the subject of an inverse condemnation claim.
- *Public trust theories*: This is a newly resurrected ancient remedy protecting the public's common resource base inherited from prior generations. Salt use may violate public trust duties of government to protect water quality, natural resources and other resources, and even highways.
- *Statutorily-based actions*: There are a host of statutes that could be the basis of citizen enforcement, some clearly not so intended by their originating legislators. Salt, for instance, might be classified as a point-source discharge of a pollutant under the Clean Water Act when it washes from highway drains into roadside watercourses.[24] Salt dust may give rise to sanctions under the Clean Air Act. No such suits have yet been tried, but the creativity of statutes is that they are applied and developed at the initiative of suing parties, and evolve over time.
- *Administrative law litigation*: Administrative law offers two major formats: the approach of pressuring regulatory agencies to take action against a problem (e.g., mandamus to obtain EPA enforcement of the Clean Water Act), and suit against those agencies that are the direct cause of problems (for example, a suit against state highway commissions for the "arbitrary and capricious" irrtionality of their decision to salt).
- *International law*: This field covers international treaties and conventions, and transboundary pollution cases. In the latter case, it is clearly possible that Canadian waters would be injured by cumulative salt infiltration into the Great Lakes drainage system, with possible arbitral and litigative remedies.

23. See Morash v. Commonwealth, 296 N.E.2d 461 (Mass. 1973); Mueller v. Brunn, 313 N.W.2d 790 (Wis. 1982).

24. This possibility might be affected by future implementation of the 1986 Clean Water Act amendments, which classified highway runoff as stormwater discharge with a postponed regulatory schedule. Future EPA stormwater regulations therefore may eventually address the salt issue, at least in urban areas.

The list goes on, each avenue raising a sequence of technical and procedural problems as well – standing to sue, class actions, estoppel, how to finance these suits, and so on. Some litigation approaches would be quite limited in their direct effects, and some quite far-reaching (depending on class actions or the effect of precedent for broadening their impact).

Ultimately it is necessary to remind ourselves that the genius of the Anglo-American system of law is that it is always in flux, though the process remains the same. Creative use of legal theories has shaped today's environmental law and will continue to do so. Perhaps some day environmental mediation and consensus negotiation will resolve the pressing questions of the day. For now, however, sweet reason and facts alone have insufficient force in the system. They require the support of credible legal leverages, mobilized to make their point in a vastly complex confrontational system. To give effect to values and analyses, one must know the full array of ways to play the game.

OVERVIEW

It is important to put the efforts of environmentalists in strategic perspective. If one accepts the premise that in most cases environmentalists are defending real public values that are being ignored, and doing so as volunteers, not for profit – and that on the other side market decisions are being made by persons who will have a direct, narrow profit or power stake in the proposed actions – then it seems that *a priori* the broader values should be dominant.

They are not. Environmentalists lose most battles, the complaints of business to the contrary notwithstanding. Try to name a dozen major government projects or programs that have been permanently stopped or ameliorated by environmentalists. Pollution continues in air, water, toxic wastes, noise, land abuse.... Anyone who has watched a state legislative hearing, an agency proceeding on regulation of an industry, or a court enforcement action against a large polluter, knows the heavy guns that the marketplace can bring to bear against "the do-gooders." The relative weakness of environmentalists in absolute terms would be justified if their concerns were trivial, or their input not sufficiently expert. (Often volunteer environmentalists *don't* do their homework well enough to compete with well-funded market opposition.) But the environmental accounting approach is not trivial, and environmentalists have necessarily become more expert in science, economics, politics, and law. Of the vast array of challengeable projects, only a tiny handful can be contested, so only the worst, in economic and ecological terms, can be challenged. Of these, most will survive environmental attacks anyway. It would not be so if the environmental side of the debate were funded in any rough parity with the marketplace, but that has never been the case.

Yet if the problems posed by greenhouse gases, for example, are more important than private and governmental market decision-makers consider them to be, it is critical that the environmental position be heard effectively. If acid rain in the Northeast is eroding the lead from urban pipes into water supplies, wiping out life in mountain lakes and fragile water-based vegetation systems, then it is critical that upwind state governments and industries do not make the narrow "free market" decisions on how much air pollution is "economically reasonable."

It should come as little surprise that "environmentalism" is a task as broad as government itself, highly frustrating, burdensome, never permanently successful or satisfying, altruistic, necessary.

Most environmentalists will tell you that they lose more cases than they win. For what it's worth, before the 1970s, environmentalists were almost never successful in being heard, and that has clearly changed. Perhaps the success of environmental efforts should be measured in the (unmeasurable) numbers of bad projects, programs or polluting plants that nowadays are not proposed, for fear of "those damned environmentalists."

And the salt goes on.

These must be the years when America pays its debts to the past by reclaiming the purity of its air, its water and our living environment. It is literally now or never.

— Richard Nixon, 1970

Chapter 2

LAW AND ECONOMICS, UNCERTAINTY AND RISK, IN ENVIRONMENTAL DECISION-MAKING

Economic concerns play a vital role in setting policy in an industrialized democracy like the United States. The well-being of the citizenry is, to a significant extent, linked to economic performance. Increasingly, prospective courses of action are evaluated by reference to their economic consequences. In this way, economics has a role to play in understanding modern environmental law controversies.

Environmental law is often portrayed as being in competition with economic development and increased productive activity. If environmental laws result in blocking construction of a huge dam and reservoir project, for example, certain forms of economic development associated with the project do not occur. Similarly, stringent air pollution control laws that result in cleaner air and improved public health do so by requiring "dirty" plants to cease operation, or imposing costs on manufacturers who must install pollution control devices. In some cases these added costs make products sufficiently more expensive so that consumers no longer buy as many units and production levels and jobs in the production sector must be scaled back. Even so, the hidden costs of dirty air to health and ecology may outweigh the costs imposed by pollution control. Informed judgments must be made about trade-offs between environmental quality and economic activity. The environmental perspective does not reflexively condemn economic activity; it insists only that decisions to pursue environmentally detrimental activities be made in a way that gives an adequate accounting of the full range of impacts. As President Barber Conable of the World Bank summarized it, "Good ecology is good economics."[1]

The enhanced role of economics in the decisional process has been accompanied by a growth in the use of tools of analysis developed in the study of economics as a social science. One of these, a branch of microeconomics called "welfare economics," is concerned with how forms of economic analysis can be used to guide policy determinations. Much of what follows is devoted to understanding ways in which analytical tools of welfare economics are brought to bear on issues in environmental law.

1. Conable, Address to the World Resources Institute, May 5, 1987.

A. ECONOMIC ANALYSIS OF LAW AND THE PURSUIT OF EFFICIENCY

In the latter half of the twentieth century, legal thinking and legal scholarship have been profoundly influenced by concepts borrowed from the discipline of economics:

> Partly, it is because economics is seen today as comprising much more than the narrow attempt to model general equilibrium or the decision-making of firms and households. To understand those topics, economists postulate a type of human agent who seeks rationally to maximize the satisfaction of his own wants in a context where others are engaged in a similar enterprise, against a finite stock of resources. That simple image of agent-as-maximizer proved remarkably fertile as economists were able to model interactions among very large numbers of people using the most modest assumptions, and to generate abstract results that were in fact quite powerful and interesting when applied to the messier reality of commerce, consumption and production in modern capitalist societies. Given that success, it was natural to try to extend these models of human choice and interaction into other fields and to apply them to other problems.[2]

Environmental degradation, on a very simple level, appears to be explained by the traditional tools and assumptions of economic analysis. Consider the expected actions of a rational maximizer who operates a factory that generates unwanted wastes as part of the production process. If the wastes are discharged into the atmosphere or some nearby water body, they pollute the quality of the airshed or watershed. In the absence of a legal rule either forbidding pollution or requiring a polluter to pay for harms caused to others by the pollution, a rational maximizing producer will make no expenditures for pollution control because to do so will increase costs and thereby reduce profits. Historically, experience confirms this thesis. In response to non-existent or lax pollution control laws, pollution of air and water as a low-cost means of disposing of unwanted waste products was a prevalent practice.

Economic analysis of pollution does not stop with merely identifying an incentive that leads an individual rational actor to engage in polluting activity. Economists also consider aggregate social welfare, which is generally treated as the sum of the welfare of all individuals. For this reason, economists look at the effects of pollution on others. In this simple example, those others are people downwind or downstream from the plant who are made worse off by the pollution. The harm to these individuals (and their activities) is a cost to them, and the sum of those costs is a cost of the polluting activity to society as a whole. Thus, economists, like environmentalists, are interested in the costs that pollution thrusts upon its victims.

At least implicitly at this point, economic analysis offers a tool for normative analysis of the polluting behavior.[3] Assuming that the goal of a society is to

2. Waldron, Criticizing Economic Analysis of Law, 99 Yale L.J. 1441 (1990).

3. The more explicit version of the normative claims of economists relates to the pursuit of efficiency.

maximize aggregate welfare, it is possible to determine if the production involved improves total social welfare in spite of the pollution it causes. To do this, one need only calculate the total dollar value of the social benefits (the sum of individual benefits associated with the production) and compare it to the total dollar value of the social costs (the sum of individual costs) associated with the production. This is a benefit-cost calculation similar to that associated with the environmental perspective.

The benefit side of that calculation is made simpler by the presence of a functioning market system. Economists measure the benefits of the activity on the basis of willingness to pay. Thus, under economic analysis, the total receipts earned through the sale of the product measure the benefits of its production. The cost side of the equation begins in the same way, that is, all of the firm's costs of production are toted up. The essentials of production, things such as materials and labor, are purchased in a market system. They too are easy to evaluate. The total social cost calculation is made more problematic by the absence of a market in which pollution effects are freely traded and the difficulty of placing a value on the harms suffered by the victims of pollution.

Assume for a moment (1) that a market for pollution effects exists, and (2) that the polluter has purchased from all interested parties the right to deposit pollution in the air or water. In that event, the cost side of the equation, like the benefit side of the equation, could be reckoned solely by tallying the benefits and costs to the producer. Recalling the terminology introduced in Chapter 1, all of the costs would be "internal" to the polluting firm's own benefit-cost accounting. Were that the case, and production was still profitable, even after paying the full costs, the firm would go ahead and produce the good. More vitally, the economic analysis of the activity would likewise be favorable because total social welfare would be increased.

There are several points to be noted at this juncture. First, this simple form of economic analysis of social welfare functions is premised on equating the benefits and costs of an activity with the dollar value of goods and "bads"[4] in the marketplace. Markets, as economists themselves understand, do not always exist or function well. Wherever markets are unavailable or imperfect, economic analysis must try to account for that fact in order to be valid. Second, the reliance on markets takes the pre-existing distribution of wealth as a given. However, not all individuals or organizations have the same amount of money available to them to compete in the purchase of goods and services. These imbalances can affect the vitality of presuming that the overall interests of society are best measured by market values. Third, just as the poor are to some extent disenfranchised by markets, the interests of the future are likewise underrepresented. The unborn generations who will inherit nuclear wastes generated in this century have no say in today's marketplace. Economic analysis addresses this issue by trying to evaluate

4. A "bad" here is intended to include the price one might need to pay someone to endure something unpleasant. In the pollution example, what is really at issue is the choice by affected parties to accept money, and the goods and services that money can buy, for the loss of health and amenity value.

future benefits and costs and to calculate their present value.[5] Finally, the reliance on markets is an entirely homocentric means of evaluating outcomes. Trees and fish do not buy and sell goods and bads. This observation is not an adequate grounds for abandoning economic analysis, but it too tempers unquestioning reliance on market outcomes.

Returning to the uses of the tools of economic analysis, rational choice theory aids those who seek to alter polluter behavior. Presumably, excessive air and water pollution will continue to recur until rational maximizers find it less profitable to pollute than to make other arrangements for disposal of unwanted by-products. Rational choice theory predicts that making pollution more expensive to the polluter than other environmentally less harmful methods of disposal will effect a reduction in pollution with a corresponding improvement in environmental quality. Law intersects with this simple economic analysis because the devices that change the calculus facing polluters are imposed by the legal system. Common law or statutory liability rules allow polluters to be sued for harm caused to others by the release of pollution. Alternatively, the law may, on threat of penalties that are a cost to polluters, prescribe installation of pollution control equipment, or mandate reductions in emissions. A different legal control mechanism is to enact a tax on effluents so that polluters must pay a specified charge for each unit of pollution discharged into the environment. Regardless of the legal means adopted, belief in rational choice theory undergirds the strategy: those making the law expect that regulated parties, in order to minimize costs, will reduce pollution.

Beyond providing rational choice theory as an analytic and explanatory tool, economic analysis attempts at times to be normative. That is, economic analysis has developed criteria to evaluate alternative courses of action as either better, or best. The umbrella term that is associated with these attempts to evaluate actions is "efficiency." In general, an allocation or use of resources is described as being "efficient" when the greatest total net benefits have been derived from their employment.[6] In more colloquial terms, the goal is to "make the most of what you've got."

Here again is a common ground shared between the environmental perspective and the pursuit of efficiency. Efforts at resource conservation, a mainstay of the environmental movement, are often attempts to make better use of resources. If, for example, changing over to water-saving plumbing fixtures and increasing the use of xerophytic landscaping allows a thirsty city like Los Angeles to serve its

---

5. As discussed more fully in subpart D of this chapter, this effort is not wholly successful.

6. Economists have developed a number of definitions of efficiency that are both technical and precise. These tests tend to be linked to rational choice theory because they often look to the position of individuals in regard to the maximization of their individual welfare. The most familiar and widely accepted efficiency criterion is the one developed by Vilfredo Pareto that bears his name. A trade or transfer of resources satisfies the Pareto criterion if, as a result, no one is harmed and some people are better off. Other efficiency criteria, associated with the work of Nicholas Kaldor and Tibor Scitovsky, test whether a change in policy is an improvement by inquiring if the people who gain from the change evaluate their gains at a higher dollar figure than the dollar figure that losers attach to their losses. Abram Bergson offers yet another approach by measuring the desirability of changes with reference to an explicit social welfare function. See E. Mansfield, Microeconomics: Theory and Applications 460, 482–83 (5th ed. 1985).

population's water needs with 20 percent less water, an array of unattractive adverse ecological consequences are avoided. Less water can be withdrawn from natural systems such as Mono Lake or the Sacramento and San Joachin River delta. This is efficient. The changes in lifestyle are neither expensive in terms of the investment required, nor do they significantly reduce the Angelenos' enjoyment of life. Water conservation, in this setting, allows a lesser amount of water to provide most of the same benefits as were obtained from a larger amount of water in the past, while incurring decreased total social and environmental costs.

There is a strain of legal scholarship associated with the "Chicago School" of economics, often labelled "economic analysis of law," that sees the promotion of economic efficiency as a major function of law:

> Rights are to be assigned in a way that promotes the efficient use of resources. In some cases this assignment will be the natural result of parties' dealings with one another: if a right is not already assigned to the person who can use it most productively, he should be in a position to purchase it from someone making a less productive use and still be in a position to derive advantage from the purchase. However, in cases where such dealings are impeded by transaction costs, it is the task of a court to determine how the rights would have been transferred apart from those costs and to assign them accordingly.[7]

Assuming, *arguendo*, that law ought to promote efficiency, the assessment of what is efficient in environmental cases is at times difficult to determine. Economic analysis of law appears to approach the choice of a rule of law in a way that is largely unrelated to the real questions of societal judgment that must underlie the issue. As an example of normative economic analysis of law, take the issue of air pollution and ask, "Ought there be a right of manufacturers freely to discharge pollutants into the air?" In selecting a legal rule for pollution rights, a proponent of economic analysis of law would first assess whether market mechanisms exist that result in efficient use of the affected resources (air, health, materials and labor needed to construct, install, and maintain pollution control devices, etc.). Legal intervention would be warranted only if market failure appeared likely. Here, market failure is likely because the harms of pollution are widely dispersed and fall on individuals and resource complexes that are not likely to be able to bargain with the polluter Transaction costs will impede the efficient allocation of the resource by market mechanisms alone.[8]

Should market mechanisms be unsuccessful in achieving accurate accommodation of competing interests, the second phase of economic analysis of pollution rights law tries to assess what outcome is efficient and adopt a legal rule leading to that outcome. Economic analysis of law as a basis for prescription of rules is a less useful analytical device at this stage, especially from an ecological perspective. Efficiency is not a criterion that is concerned with natural systems as much as it is

7. Waldron, note 2 *supra*, at 1442.

8. Cases in which meaningful bargaining can take place between polluter and pollution victim will usually reach an "efficient" outcome without regard to the legal rule adopted. This may seem counterintuitive, but the basis for this claim is explored in detail in subchapter B, *infra*. The choice of legal rule will affect welfare and the level of pollution that is found to be efficient usually will be influenced somewhat by the initial entitlement either to pollute or to enjoy clean air.

concerned with the material satisfaction of human desires. Even when the desires of ecologically sensitive individuals are taken into account, reliance on most measures of efficiency[9] invites efforts at quantification in dollar terms as a means of facilitating comparisons. These efforts at monetization are highly imprecise and are also skewed in a way that disfavors environmental interests because they tend to minimize the value of subjectively measured satisfactions. Furthermore, they too heavily discount future values, such as preserving a natural patrimony for future generations.

Apart from giving insufficient weight to ecological values in making interpersonal welfare comparisons, considering only efficiency in adopting rules of law is a barren approach. The inquiry neglects common notions of responsibility for one's acts that are captured in the "polluter pays" principle. Similarly, the inquiry has no concern for the undemocratic power that may be granted to the polluting entity to impose its choice about the use of resources on a large class of neighbors without their consent. In this way, normative economic analysis ignores traditional American democratic norms and ideals. Professor Waldron put it this way:

> [Economic analysis of law] raises but does not settle a number of important questions. Why is the promotion of efficiency to be taken as the aim of the legal process? Why not justice or the maximization of utility or some other value that requires us to go beyond efficiency (however that is understood)?[10]

It is possible to make too much of the potential antipathy between the environmental perspective and the reliance of economic analysis of law on efficiency as a norm for choosing rules of law. Environmental law as it exists today is a complex and variegated field. It is emphatically not an area of law that is dominated by one particular mode of analysis. For that reason, what remains most important about the interaction of environmental law and economics is the light that the tools of economic analysis can shed on problems of environmental law. The subsequent material in this chapter takes this cue and focuses on how economic science illuminates the character of environmental controversies, and at times contributes to their rational solution.

B. ENVIRONMENTAL LAW AS A RESPONSE TO THE PROBLEM OF A FINITE COMMONS

A large proportion of what fits under the title of environmental law has to do with governmental intervention to regulate the behavior of individuals and firms having untoward environmental consequences. Laws restricting emission of pollutants are, of course, the prime example. To many, the wisdom and necessity of engaging in that type of legal coercion of behavior is self-evident. In the eyes of the economist, the apparent nub of the problem (assuming that humans are for the most part rational actors who seek to improve their own welfare) is the occasional divergence between conduct that maximizes individual welfare, and conduct that

9. The major efficiency criteria are described in note 6, *supra*.

10. Waldron, note 2 *supra*, at 1442.

maximizes total social welfare. This section explores the economic approach to the matter and attempts to relate it to law and the assignment of property rights, including the right to control resource utilization decisions.

Section 1. THE CHARACTERISTICS OF A COMMONS

American law is predicated on a variety of unarticulated as well as explicit assumptions about the relationship of the government to the governed, and about the institutions comprising that relationship. An important institution in this regard is the ownership of private property. Under Lockean political theory, property law would not be necessary under Eden-like conditions of plenty, where there is no competition for resources, because all desired items would be abundant. With increasing population and limited goods at hand, however, a means for dividing up available goods has to be created. To Locke, the institution of exclusive property fit nicely with his sense of the order of God's universe, and it also responded to social needs under the changed state of nature.[11] Private property would induce people to act to improve their lot by assuring them of the fruits of their labors in gathering nature's bounty or in otherwise refining the products of nature to make human life more comfortable. Non-exclusive rights to property would fail to produce incentives for engaging in productive work. Like the tenets of modern economics, Locke's theory subscribes to rational choice theory: human actors are assumed to act in their own rational self interest. With regard to private property items, this means that owners will do whatever will maximize their advantage in regard to the property.

Unfortunately, much of the natural world is a commons, which puts it on a collision course with the dynamics of human behavior based on private property-related rational choices. Air, water, oceans, wildlife – these are parts of the planet's bounty that are open to use by all and not readily converted into private property. Other natural systems share characteristics of commons but are more easily reduced to ownership – forests, prairies, wetlands, hydrocarbons, and other resources – although something vital may ultimately be lost in the process. In explaining how humans make decisions with regard to private property, economics also explains why commons suffer. If we're lucky, economics can also help to prescribe legal solutions.

Garrett Hardin, The Tragedy of the Commons

162 Science 1243, 1243-1248 (December 13, 1968)

The tragedy of the commons develops this way. Picture a pasture open to all. It is to be expected that each herdsman will try to keep as many cattle as possible on the commons. Such an arrangement may work reasonably satisfactorily for centuries because tribal wars, poaching, and disease keep the numbers of both man and beast well below the carrying capacity of the land. Finally, however, comes the day of reckoning, that is, the day when the long-desired goal of social stability becomes a reality. At this point, the inherent logic of the commons remorselessly generates tragedy.

---

11. For a more thorough discussion of John Locke's view of private property, see Sanders, The Lockean Proviso, 10 Harv. J.L. & Pub. Pol'y 401 (1988).

As a rational being, each herdsman seeks to maximize his gain. Explicitly or implicitly, more or less consciously, he asks, "What is the utility to me of adding one more animal to my herd?" This utility has one negative and one positive component.

1) The positive component is a function of the increment of one animal. Since the herdsman receives all the proceeds from the sale of the additional animal, the positive utility is nearly +1.

2) The negative component is a function of the additional overgrazing created by one more animal. Since, however, the effects of overgrazing are shared by all the herdsmen, the negative utility for any particular decision-making herdsman is only a fraction of -1.

Adding together the component partial utilities, the rational herdsman concludes that the only sensible course for him to pursue is to add another animal to his herd. And another; and another.... But his is the conclusion reached by each and every rational herdsman sharing a commons. Therein is the tragedy. Each man is locked into a system that compels him to increase his herd without limit – in a world that is limited. Ruin is the destination toward which all men rush, each pursuing his own best interest in a society that believes in the freedom of the commons. Freedom in a commons brings ruin to all.

Some would say that this is a platitude. Would that it were! In a sense, it was learned thousands of years ago, but natural selection favors the forces of psychological denial. The individual benefits as an individual from his ability to deny the truth even though society as a whole, of which he is a part, suffers. Education can counteract the natural tendency to do the wrong thing, but the inexorable succession of generations requires that the basis for this knowledge be constantly refreshed....

In an approximate way, the logic of the commons has been understood for a long time, perhaps since the discovery of agriculture or the invention of private property in real estate. But it is understood mostly only in special cases which are not sufficiently generalized. Even at this late date, cattlemen leasing national land on the western ranges demonstrate no more than an ambivalent understanding, in constantly pressuring federal authorities to increase the head count to the point where overgrazing produces erosion and weed dominance. Likewise, the oceans of the world continue to suffer from the survival of the philosophy of the commons. Maritime nations still respond automatically to the shibboleth of the "freedom of the seas." Professing to believe in the "inexhaustible resources of the oceans," they bring species after species of fish and whales closer to extinction.

The National Parks present another instance of the working out of the tragedy of the commons. At present, they are open to all, without limit. The parks themselves are limited in extent – there is only one Yosemite Valley – whereas population seems to grow without limit. The values that visitors seek in the parks are steadily eroded. Plainly, we must soon cease to treat the parks as commons or they will be of no value to anyone.

What shall we do? We have several options. We might sell them off as private property. We might keep them as public property, but allocate the right to enter them. The allocation might be on the basis of wealth, by the use of an auction system. It might be on the basis of merit, as defined by some agreed-upon standards. It might be by lottery. Or it might be on a first-come, first-served basis, administered to long queues. These, I think, are all the reasonable possibilities. They are all objectionable. But we must choose – or acquiesce in the destruction of the commons that we call our National Parks.

POLLUTION

In a reverse way, the tragedy of the commons reappears in problems of pollution. Here it is not a question of taking something out of the commons, but of putting something in – sewage, or chemical, radioactive, and heat wastes into water; noxious and dangerous fumes into the air; and distracting and unpleasant advertising signs into the line of sight. The calculations of utility are much the same as before. The rational man finds that his share of the cost of the wastes he discharges into the commons is less than the cost of purifying his wastes before releasing them. Since this is true for everyone, we are locked into a system of "fouling our own nest," so long as we behave only as independent, rational, free-enterprisers.

The tragedy of the commons as a food basket is averted by private property, or something formally like it. But the air and waters surrounding us cannot readily be fenced, and so the tragedy of the commons as a cesspool must be prevented by different means, by coercive laws or taxing devices that make it cheaper for the polluter to treat his pollutants than to discharge them untreated. We have not progressed as far with the solution of this problem as we have with the first. Indeed, our particular concept of private property, which deters us from exhausting the positive resources of the earth, favors pollution. The owner of a factory on the bank of a stream – whose property extends to the middle of the stream – often has difficulty seeing why it is not his natural right to muddy the waters flowing past his door. The law, always behind the times, requires elaborate stitching and fitting to adapt it to this newly perceived aspect of the commons.

The pollution problem is a consequence of population. It did not much matter how a lonely American frontiersman disposed of his waste. "Flowing water purifies itself every 10 miles," my grandfather used to say, and the myth was near enough to the truth when he was a boy, for there were not too many people. But as population became denser, the natural chemical and biological recycling processes became overloaded, calling for a redefinition of property rights.

HOW TO LEGISLATE TEMPERANCE?

Analysis of the pollution problem as a function of population density uncovers a not generally recognized principle of morality, namely: the morality of an act is a function of the state of the system at the time it is performed....

That morality is system-sensitive escaped the attention of most codifiers of ethics in the past. "Thou shalt not..." is the form of traditional ethical directives which make no allowance for particular circumstances. The laws of our society follow a complex, crowded, changeable world. Our epicyclic solution is to augment statutory law with administrative law. Since it is practically impossible to spell out all the conditions under which it is safe to burn trash in the back yard or to run an automobile without smog-control, by law we delegate the details to bureaus. The result is administrative law, which is rightly feared for an ancient reason – Quis custodiet ipsos custodes? – "Who shall watch the watchers themselves?" John Adams said that we must have "a government of laws and not men." Bureau administrators, trying to evaluate the morality of acts in the total system, are singularly liable to corruption, producing a government by men, not laws.

Prohibition is easy to legislate (though not necessarily to enforce); but how do we legislate temperance? Experience indicates that it can be accomplished best through the mediation of administrative law. We limit possibilities unnecessarily if we suppose that the sentiment of Quis custodiet denies us the use of administrative law. We should rather retain the phrase as a perpetual reminder of fearful dangers we cannot avoid. The great challenge facing us now is to invent the corrective feedbacks that are needed to keep custodians honest. We must find ways to legitimate the needed authority of both the custodians and the corrective feedbacks.

PATHOGENIC EFFECTS OF CONSCIENCE

The long-term disadvantage of an appeal to conscience [as a means to mitigate the tragedy of the commons] should be enough to condemn it; but has serious short-term disadvantages as well. If we ask a man who is exploiting a commons to desist "in the name of conscience," what are we saying to him? What does he hear?... Sooner or later, consciously or subconsciously, he senses that he has received two communications, and that they are contradictory: (i)(the intended communication) "If you don't do as we ask, we will openly condemn you for not acting like a responsible citizen"; (ii)(the unintended communication) "If you do behave as we ask, we will secretly condemn you for a simpleton who can be shamed into standing aside while the rest of us exploit the commons."

Every man then is caught in what Bateson has called a "double bind." Bateson and his co-workers have made a plausible case for viewing the double bind as an important causative factor in the genesis of schizophrenia. The double bind may not always be so damaging, but it always endangers the mental health of anyone to whom it is applied. "A bad conscience," said Nietzsche, "is a kind of illness."

To conjure up a conscience in others is tempting to anyone who wishes to extend his control beyond the legal limits. Leaders at the highest level succumb to this temptation. Has any President during the past generation failed to call on labor unions to moderate voluntarily their demands for higher wages, or to steel companies to honor voluntary guidelines on prices? I can recall none. The rhetoric used on such occasions is designed to produce feelings of guilt in non-cooperators....

If the word responsibility is to be used at all, I suggest that it be in the sense Charles Frankel uses it. "Responsibility," says this philosopher, "is the product of definite social arrangements." Notice that Frankel calls for social arrangements – not propaganda.

MUTUAL COERCION MUTUALLY AGREED UPON

The social arrangements that produce responsibility are arrangements that create coercion, of some sort. Consider bank-robbing. The man who takes money from a bank acts as if the bank were a commons. How do we prevent such action? Certainly not by trying to control his behavior solely by a verbal appeal to his sense of responsibility. Rather than rely on propaganda we follow Frankel's lead and insist that a bank is not a commons; we seek the definite social arrangements that will keep it from becoming a commons. That this would infringe on the freedom of would-be robbers we neither deny nor regret....

To say that we mutually agree to coercion is not to say that we are required to enjoy it, or even to pretend we enjoy it. Who enjoys taxes? We all grumble about them. But we accept compulsory taxes because we recognize that voluntary taxes would favor the conscienceless. We institute and (grumblingly) support taxes and other coercive devices to escape the horror of the commons.

An alternative to the commons need not be perfectly just to be preferable. With real estate and other material goods, the alternative we have chosen is the institution of private property coupled with legal inheritance. Is this system perfectly just? As a genetically trained biologist I deny that it is. It seems to me that, if there are to be differences in individual inheritance, legal action should be perfectly correlated with biological inheritance – that those who are biologically more fit to be the custodians of property and power should legally inherit more. But genetic recombination continually makes a mockery of the doctrine of "like father, like son" implicit in our laws of legal inheritance. An idiot can inherit millions, and a trust fund can keep his estate intact. We must admit that our legal system of private property plus inheritance is unjust – but we put up with it because we are not convinced, at the moment, that anyone has invented a better system. The alternative of the commons is too horrifying to contemplate. Injustice is preferable to total ruin.

It is one of the peculiarities of the warfare between reform and the status quo that it is thoughtlessly governed by a double standard. Whenever a reform measure is proposed it is often defeated when its opponents triumphantly discover a flaw in it. As Kingsley Davis has pointed out, worshippers of the status quo sometimes imply that no reform is possible without unanimous agreement, an implication contrary to historical fact. As nearly as I can make out, automatic rejection of proposed reforms is based on one of two unconscious assumptions: (i) that the status quo is perfect; or (ii) that the choice we face is between reform and no action; if the proposed reform is imperfect, we presumably should take no action at all, while we wait for a perfect proposal.

But we can never do nothing. That which we have done for thousands of years is also action. It also produces evils. Once we are aware that the status quo is action, we can then compare its discoverable advantages and disadvantages with the predicted advantages and disadvantages of the proposed reform, discounting as best we can for our lack of experience. On the basis of such a comparison, we can make a rational decision which will not involve the unworkable assumption that only perfect systems are tolerable.

RECOGNITION OF NECESSITY

Perhaps the simplest summary of this analysis of man's population problems is this: the commons, if justifiable at all, is justifiable only under conditions of low-population density. As the human population has increased, the commons has had to be abandoned in one aspect after another.

First we abandoned the commons in food gathering, enclosing farm land and restricting pastures and hunting and fishing areas. These restrictions are still not complete throughout the world.

Somewhat later we saw that the commons as a place for waste disposal would also have to be abandoned. Restrictions on the disposal of domestic sewage are widely accepted in the Western world; we are still struggling to close the commons to pollution by automobiles, factories, insecticide sprayers, fertilizing operations, and atomic energy installations.

In a still more embryonic state is our recognition of the evils of the commons in matters of pleasure. There is almost no restriction on the propagation of sound waves in the public medium. The shopping public is assaulted with mindless music, without its consent. Our government is paying out billions of dollars to create a supersonic transport which will disturb 50,000 people for every one person who is whisked from coast to coast 3 hours faster. Advertisers muddy the airwaves of radio and television and pollute the view of travelers. We are a long way from outlawing the commons in matters of pleasure. Is this because our Puritan inheritance makes us view pleasure as something of a sin, and pain (that is, the pollution of advertising) as the sign of virtue?

Every new enclosure of the commons involves the infringement of somebody's personal liberty. Infringements made in the distant past are accepted because no contemporary complains of a loss. It is the newly proposed infringements that we vigorously oppose; cries of "rights" and "freedom" fill the air. But what does "freedom" mean? When men mutually agreed to pass laws against robbing, mankind became more free, not less so. Individuals locked into the logic of the commons are free only to bring on universal ruin; once they see the necessity of mutual coercion, they become free to pursue other goals. I believe it was Hegel who said, "Freedom is the recognition of necessity."

COMMENTARY AND QUESTIONS

1. The pessimism and optimism of the commons. Does Hardin seem too optimistic about the chances for averting the tragedy of the commons? Some who have considered the matter find Hardin's view (that necessity will make palatable the freedom from ruin that can be achieved by "mutual coercion, mutually agreed upon") to be grossly over-optimistic. See W. Ophuls, Ecology and the Politics of Scarcity 145–165 (1977). At the opposite pole are the "cornucopialists." Susan Cox, for example, argues that problems of the commons are not of the magnitude that Hardin fears. In her assessment, society has in fact adequately managed such problems through the ages, with the major lapses coming in times of cultural shifts. See Cox, No Tragedy of the Commons, 7 Envtl. Ethics 49 (1985).

2. Extrapolating to global scale. How far beyond the cow pasture does the commons concept apply? Does Hardin's analysis still apply when the scale is much grander? For example, a forest or lake would seem to present the same localized observable effects of individual decisions, but what about the commons of the continental air mass, or the oceans? The uses of these commons are so diverse and diffuse that it is difficult to demonstrate who is causing what effects. Even here, although individual actions hurting the common resource are often invisible, diffuse or unaccountable, those actions can be cumulatively critical. The difficulty of grand scale lies in discovering what initial coercions will avert the tragedy. On the global scale, Hardin's own analysis focuses on global population control. Environmental law, as you will see, addresses the problem of cumulative effects in a wide variety of ways.

3. Measuring sustainable yield. Another fundamental problem with the commons is defining the level of sustainability. It isn't easy to define the point where cows exceed the sustainable carrying capacity of the commons. It is far harder to define the acceptable level of imposition on a common resource like air or water ("assimilative capacity"). Is anything less than purity a negative burden on the commons? What constitutes tolerable depreciation, and what constitutes Hardin's downward spiral to disaster? See the discussion of environmental standard setting in Chapters 15–19.

4. The commons and positive outcomes. How do you decide what things should be maintained in common ownership rather than being reduced to a form of exclusive private property? Locke, Bentham, and Adam Smith all noted how private property ownership and the right to exclude others play a crucial role in motivating political and economic life. As Professor Carol Rose writes:

> The right to exclude others has often been cited as the most important characteristic of private property. This right, it is said, makes private property fruitful by enabling owners to capture the full value of their individual investments, thus encouraging everyone to put time and labor into the development of the resources. Moreover, exclusive control makes it possible for owners to identify other owners, and for all to exchange the fruits of their labors until these things arrive in the hands of those who value them most highly – to the great cumulative advantage of all.[12]

What kinds of things are better suited to public ownership and communal use? Rose cites public libraries and public highways as examples of successful commons. What of lakes and rivers? Forests? Antarctica? In most of the world, private land owners do not own resources beneath their land; the public retains the right to determine their use and development.

5. Law as mutual coercion. Assuming that much of the commons paradigm is relevant to analyzing environmental policy, note how Hardin sets up a critical role for the law but doesn't specify its operation. If nonmandatory policies or physical privatization are unlikely to work on a pollution commons (are they?), what kinds of legal intervention are likely to be effective and appropriate to avoiding the tragedy of the commons? Criminal sanctions, taxes, individual lawsuits, administrative bureaucracies? The choice is not easy. In practice, environmental law opts for a sort of pragmatic biodiversity – encouraging a wide range of control mechanisms.

Section 2. EXTERNALITIES AND AN ECONOMIC ANALYSIS OF THE COMMONS

Many of the disjunctions between social good and private good raised by the road salt hypothetical and Hardin's examples of the commons are described by economists in terms of "externalities." External costs are also a fundamental concept of environmental analysis, representing costs that are excluded from a decision-maker's own consideration – not internalized – because someone else will have to pay or absorb them. Humans by their nature do not generally respond to negatives (like the salt pollution effects encountered in Chapter 1) that they do not themselves

12. Rose, The Comedy of the Commons, 53 U. Chi. L. Rev. 711, 711–12 (1986).

experience. Corporations, in this sense, are even more human than humans: they are resolutely driven by self interest, responding to the equations of profit maximization with, understandably, no inherent charitable impulse to take on costs when not required to do so.

The process of identifying externalized costs, and then inserting them into some form of legal accounting so that they will be internalized within market and government decisions, constitutes one of the basic strategies of environmental law. In his book, Intermediate Microeconomics, Professor Hal Varian defined both negative and positive consumption and production externalities:

> We say that an economic situation involves a consumption externality if one consumer cares directly about another agent's production or consumption. For example, I have definite preferences about my neighbor playing loud music at 3 in the morning, or the person next to me in a restaurant smoking a cheap cigar, or the amount of pollution produced by local automobiles. These are all examples of negative consumption externalities. On the other hand, I may get pleasure from observing my neighbor's flower garden – this is an example of a positive consumption externality.
>
> Similarly, a production externality arises when the production possibilities of one firm are influenced by the choices of another firm or consumer.... A fishery cares about the amount of pollutants dumped into its fishing area, since this will negatively influence its catch.
>
> The crucial feature of externalities is that there are goods people care about that are not sold on markets. There is no market for loud music at 3 in the morning, or drifting smoke from cheap cigars, or a neighbor who keeps a beautiful flower garden. It is this lack of markets for externalities that causes problems....
>
> The market mechanism is capable of achieving Pareto efficient allocations when externalities are not present. If externalities are present, the market will not necessarily result in a Pareto efficient provision of resources. However, there are other social institutions such as the legal system, or government intervention, that can "mimic" the market mechanism to some degree and thereby achieve Pareto efficiency.[13]

The problem is that natural systems, and commons in particular, often appear to be free goods to private and corporate decision-makers. Wastes and pollution seem to disappear costlessly into the commons, out of sight, out of economic mind.

For environmental law purposes, the focus is primarily on negative externalities, whether consumptive or productive. Implicit in the economists' analysis is the behavioral fact that individual actors will be skillful in maximizing the amount of negatives they can treat as externalities and pass off, while minimizing the positives that escape unaccounted for from their enterprises. As in Hardin's commons, the challenge is to create markets that force an accounting for negatives, thus forcing decision-makers to pay their just bills or cease polluting.

13. H. Varian, Intermediate Microeconomics 542-43 (1987).

A CASE STUDY IN ECONOMIC BEHAVIOR AND POTENTIAL LEGAL RESPONSES

The following narrative presents a dramatic pollution case that illustrates the economic context of industrial behavior. As you read, note the different kinds of serious negative externalities – to occupational health conditions within the factories, to air, water and environmental quality outside the plants, and to ultimate consumers exposed to pesticides – and consider who within the corporate and legal systems should or could have taken account of them.

Goldfarb, Kepone: A Case Study

8 Environmental Law 645 (1978)

Hopewell (population approximately 24,000) is an industrial city located on the banks of the James River in southern Virginia. Calling itself "the Chemical Capital of the South," Hopewell has actively recruited large chemical manufacturers. Consequently, Firestone, Hercules, Continental Can, and Allied Chemical have located chemical plants in Hopewell.

Allied Chemical opened its Hopewell plant in 1928. This was the first industrial plant capable of utilizing atmospheric nitrogen for the production of ammonia and nitrogen fertilizer. Eventually, Allied's Hopewell plant became the Hopewell "complex," which in 1975 was Hopewell's largest employer with 4,000 workers.

The initial batch of 500 pounds of a pesticide named Kepone was produced by Allied in 1949. Two patents for the process were awarded to it in 1952. Allied did not consider Kepone to be a major pesticide. With less than $200,000 in annual sales over a 16 year period, Kepone production never exceeded 0.1 percent of America's total pesticide production. Kepone was intended primarily for export to Europe for use against the Colorado Potato Beetle, and to South America to control the Banana Root Borer.

Before moving to commercial production, Allied subjected Kepone to an extensive series of toxicity tests. Such tests were necessary in order to obtain registration under the federal pesticide laws.[14] The results of this research revealed Kepone to be highly toxic to all species tested: it caused cancer, liver damage, reproductive system failure, and inhibition of growth and muscular coordination in fish, mammals, and birds. Upon being presented with the test results, Allied voluntarily withdrew its petition to the Food and Drug Administration for the establishment of Kepone residue tolerances for agricultural products.

Kepone is a chlorinated hydrocarbon pesticide, a chemical relative of DDT, Aldrin/Dieldrin, and Mirex (all of which have been banned by the United States Environmental Protection Agency – EPA). As such, Kepone is a contact poison, capable of being absorbed through the skin or cuticle; it is lipophilic (fat soluble), but insoluble in water: it is persistent in the environment; and it will bioaccumulate in the fatty tissues of the body. The exact mechanism by which chlorinated hydrocarbons kill target pests is uncertain. What is known is that they are nerve poisons, interfering with the transmission of electrical impulses along nerve channels. The results of contact with Kepone are loss of control over muscular coordination, convulsions, DDT-like tremors and eventually death.

---

14. Eds.: The Federal Insecticide, Fungicide, and Rodenticide Act (FIFRA) (now codified at 7 U.S.C.A. §§135–136 (1976)) is the applicable statute. It is considered in Chapter 16.

Despite the unfavorable toxicity test results, Allied deemed Kepone ready for commercial production, and contracted with the Nease Chemical Company of State College, Pennsylvania, to produce it for them. The relationship between Allied and Nease lasted from 1958 through 1960. Allied entered into a similar arrangement with Hooker Chemical during the early 60's.

By 1966 even more negative test results had been associated with Kepone, but Allied nevertheless decided to manufacture Kepone on an increased basis in its own Semi-Works facility in Hopewell. In preparation for production, an area supervisor of the Semi-Works was asked to develop a production manual. This manual was to contain operating and safety instructions for the production process. The supervisor naturally consulted available toxicity research results, and his recommended precautions reflect the test findings. At Allied, Kepone spills and dust were closely controlled, and workers wore safety glasses, and rubber boots and gloves. Allied's Kepone operations were directed by William Moore until 1968, and thereafter by Virgil Hundtofte.

Prior to preparation of the production manual, there had been no recorded case of human exposure of Kepone to the level of acute poisoning. Allied apparently discounted such a possibility, regardless of the documented adverse effects of Kepone on animals. However, a witness for the United States at the trial testified that Allied should have suspected "that the same symptomology would be induced in man if exposed to Kepone."

In 1970, the Federal government resurrected the Refuse Act Permit Program, which required all industries discharging wastes into navigable waters to obtain permits from the U.S. Army Corps of Engineers.[15] The Allied complex at Hopewell had three pipes discharging directly into a stream called Gravelly Run, a tributary of the James River. One of these pipes originated at the Semi-Works where Kepone was manufactured. The Refuse Act Permit (RAP) application was discussed by Allied's plant managers and their assistants, who found themselves on the horns of a dilemma. Allied was discharging Kepone process wastes without treatment of any kind, and the installation of pollution control equipment would be expensive. Moreover, planning was being conducted for the construction of a regional sewage treatment plant which would treat the wastes of all industries in Hopewell, but the municipal treatment plant would not be completed before 1975. What should Allied do during the construction period?

Allied decided to list the Semi-Works discharge as a temporary phenomenon which would be discontinued within two years. In such cases a short form RAP application required only that the discharge be identified as a "temporary discharge." (Allied gratuitously added that it was unmetered and unsampled.) Thus, neither Kepone nor two plastics products (TAIC and THEIC) also manufactured at the Semi-Works were listed by Allied on its RAP application, even though Allied quite clearly did not intend to terminate production at Hopewell.

In 1972 the RAP expired, but a new permit program had been enacted – the National Pollutant Discharge Elimination System (NPDES) permit program under the Federal Water Pollution Control Act Amendments of 1972 (FWPCA). The NPDES permit program is administered by EPA instead of the Corps of Engineers.[16]

15. The Refuse Act is studied at the start of Chapter 7.

16. 33 U.S.C.A. §§1251-1376 (Supp. V 1973); §1342(a)(1)(Supp. V 1975). The federal Clean Water Act is studied in Chapter 19.

EPA requested data on the nature, volume, and strength of Allied's discharges, and again the dilemma manifested itself. One of Hundtofte's assistants prepared an option memorandum, outlining three strategies which Allied might follow: (1) to do nothing and hope for a lack of enforcement by EPA; (2) to divert the Semi-Works effluent to another outfall pipe for which a permit had been obtained; or (3) to slowly improve the Semi-Works effluent so as to "buy time" until completion of the municipal system. None of these last options was selected, and, as in 1970, Allied submitted data to the Federal government describing the Semi-Works discharges as unmetered, unsampled, temporary outfalls. As a result, between 1966 and 1974 Allied discharged untreated Kepone and plastics wastes into Gravelly Run without revealing the nature of its discharges to the Federal government.

In 1973 Allied underwent a corporate reorganization, during which control of the Semi-Works facility was transferred from the Agricultural Division to the Plastics Division. The transfer took place in expectation of the Agriculture Division's impending move to new facilities in Baton Rouge, Louisiana. Virgil Hundtofte, plant manager of Allied's Agricultural Division at Hopewell, and William Moore, Research Director, made plans to retire from the company rather than relocate. (Hundtofte had been with Allied in Hopewell since 1965, and Moore since 1948.)

One effect of the reorganization was a reorientation of production priorities among the products manufactured at the Semi-Works. Kepone production had decreased steadily, but THEIC, which had been manufactured in small quantities for eighteen years, suddenly found a lucrative market calling for a doubling of production. THEIC and Kepone shared certain production equipment, and with the surge in demand for THEIC a decision was made in 1973 to "toll" Kepone production. Tolling is a common arrangement in the chemical industry whereby another company performs processing work for a fee or "toll" and then returns the final product. The keynote of a tolling arrangement is that during the processing period legal title to the materials and product remains in the supplier, in this case Allied.

In January, 1973, when the decision to toll Kepone was divulged, William Moore saw his opportunity to remain in Virginia and continue in the Kepone manufacturing business. He immediately contacted Hundtofte, who had recently resigned from Allied and gone to work for a fuel oil distributor. Moore and Hundtofte agreed to form a corporation and bid for the Kepone tolling contract. On November 9, 1973, Life Science Products Company (LSP) was incorporated under the laws of the Commonwealth of Virginia. Moore and Hundtofte were the only shareholders, directors, and officers of LSP. Less than a month later, the tolling agreement between Allied and LSP was signed. Allied had solicited bids from Hooker Chemical, Nease Chemical, Velsicol and LSP, but LSP's bid was by far the lowest: 54 cents per pound for 500,000 pounds of Kepone. Nease Chemical (which, it may be recalled, manufactured Kepone for Allied from 1958 through 1960) declined to bid, but responded that if it chose to bid on the contract it would cost Nease 30 cents per pound for waste disposal alone. Hooker (Nease's successor) bid $3.00 per pound.

The details of the tolling agreement are important because the question of Allied's responsibility for LSP's illegal acts loomed large at the trial. The contract provided that Allied would supply – at its own expense – all of the raw materials for Kepone production, with the title to remain in Allied. Within certain broad limits, Allied would determine the monthly production rate of Kepone, which would be packed in Allied containers and transported in Allied trucks. Allied also agreed to

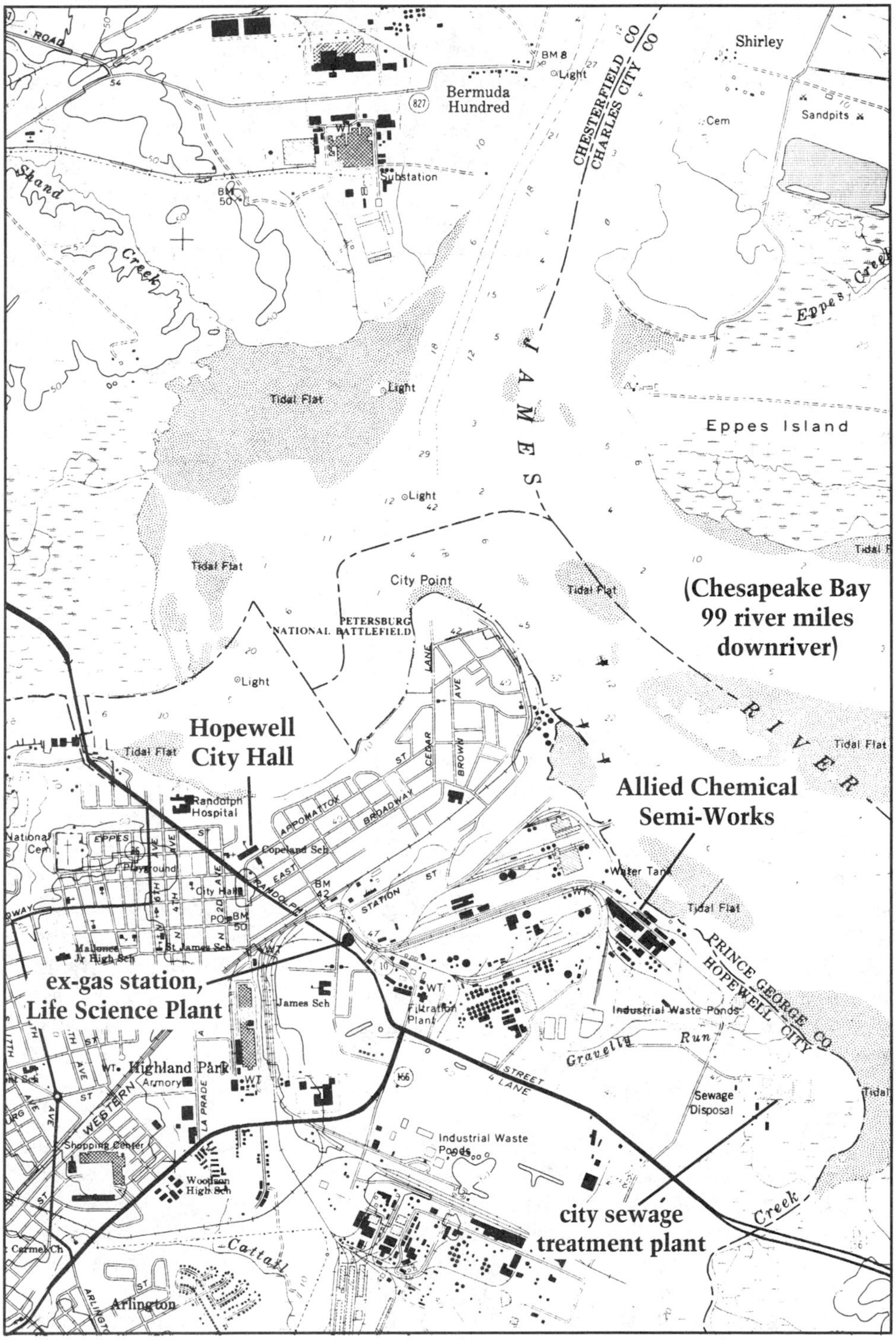

ADAPTED FROM USGS MAP NO. 37077-C3-TF-024 HOPEWELL QUADRANGLE

Schematic overview of the Allied Chemical Semi-Works and Life Science Products Co. in Hopewell, Virginia, site of the Kepone pesticide controversy.

pay LSP's taxes, other than corporate income taxes. LSP was to receive between 32 and 38 cents per pound for 650,000 pounds or more of Kepone. Through a capital surcharge arrangement, Allied was to pay for all of LSP's approved capital expenditures, whether for production or pollution control, except for land and building. If LSP was closed for pollution violations during the first year of the contract, Allied had the option to purchase LSP's assets for $25,000. And if the contract was terminated by either party for any reason, LSP agreed to refrain from producing Kepone for anyone else.

The relationship between Allied and LSP was only partially defined by the tolling agreement. Moore and Hundtofte promised Allied that they would not dispose of their shares in LSP without Allied's consent. Moreover, Allied assisted LSP in many ways – in obtaining loans and equipment from outside sources, in meeting temporary cash deficits, in augmenting fuel supplies during the oil embargo, and in attaining greater efficiency by the use of Allied facilities. Most importantly, LSP's effluent was sampled and analyzed by Allied personnel after Virginia ordered such testing. Before that (up to October 1974), LSP had tested its effluent only by a visual check – if the effluent was cloudy, the presence of suspended Kepone was indicated.

Allied officials regularly toured the LSP plant, and were informed by mail of the waste disposal problems which LSP faced almost from its inception. Whereas Allied had discharged the residues of its Kepone production process directly into tributaries of the James River, LSP decided to discharge into the Hopewell sewer system, despite the fact that the regional treatment plant was still under construction. By this means, LSP could avoid having to apply for an NPDES permit, which is not required of "indirect dischargers" (dischargers into municipal treatment systems).[17] Having made the decision to "plug in" to the Hopewell system, LSP contacted C.L. Jones, Director of Hopewell's Department of Public Works, for permission. At the time, Hopewell possessed a primary waste treatment plant – a series of filters and settling tanks without biological or chemical treatment other than disinfection and sludge digestion. Such a rudimentary system would not degrade Kepone, but would merely divide Kepone effluent between outfall pipe and sludge. Jones, who had been Plant Manager of Allied's Hopewell Semi-Works prior to Hundtofte, recommended to Hopewell's City Manager that LSP be permitted to discharge. Permission was granted in November of 1973, conditioned only upon the treatment plant not being interfered with by LSP's wastes. (In order to assure that no damage would be done to the sludge digester at the treatment plant, LSP was asked by Hopewell to meet a pretreatment standard of three parts per million of Kepone.) Thus, LSP became the only industry in Hopewell allowed to discharge into the municipal sewerage system.

LSP commenced operations in March, 1974, and almost immediately large quantities of Kepone began flowing into Hopewell's treatment plant. In October, a state inspector discovered that the sludge digester at the plant was inoperative, and his investigation revealed LSP to be the source of contamination. Prior to the plant breakdown, the State was apparently unaware that Kepone was being discharged into the Hopewell system because Hopewell's application for an NPDES permit for its treatment plant (filed October 10, 1973, about a month before plug-in permission was granted to LSP) made no mention of any industrial discharge into the municipal

17. 33 U.S.C.A. §1317(b)(Supp. V 1975) as amended by Clean Water Act of 1977. Pub. L. No. 95–217, 33 U.S.C.A. §1317(b)(West Supp. 1977); 49 C.F.R. §125.4(a)(1977).

system.[18] Moreover, additional information filed by Hopewell in July, 1974, did not include notice of LSP's discharges. When the State brought the situation to the attention of LSP and Hopewell officials, LSP's discharges were not prohibited even though the pretreatment standard was being violated. Instead, a study was commenced to determine a "safe" effluent limit for Kepone. Finally, in June of 1975, a more restrictive pretreatment standard was imposed on LSP (.5 parts per billion). EPA, which had been informed of the situation, agreed to this compromise even though it had earlier recommended a stricter effluent limitation. In order to meet this standard LSP had to further pretreat its wastes and hold its discharges in tanks until such time as discharge would not violate the pretreatment standard (i.e. even-out the flow). Allied had participated in the negotiations among LSP, Hopewell, Virginia, and EPA, and Allied opted to pay for the necessary pollution control equipment. Allied and LSP then began to discuss the capital costs of expanding Kepone production to 2,500,000 pounds per year in order to meet an increasing demand in the European market. (From the inception of LSP, Allied had constantly requested increased Kepone production.) However, even after the new equipment was installed, the pretreatment standard was violated in nineteen out of twenty-one samplings.

On July 7, 1975, as LSP was preparing for increased Kepone production, one of its employees visited Dr. Chou, a Hopewell internist, complaining of tremors, weight loss, quickened pulse rate, unusual eye movements, and a tender, enlarged liver. Such symptoms were not unusual among LSP employees, but were generally dismissed as "the shakes" – a necessary price to be paid for the $5.00 per hour wage they received. Although about twenty physicians had been consulted during the sixteen months of LSP's existence, only Dr. Chou suspected a connection between the ailments and the workplace environment. After questioning his patient and taking a blood sample, Dr. Chou forwarded the sample to the Center for Disease Control in Atlanta, where an analysis for Kepone could be performed. The tests disclosed that the blood sample contained 7.5 parts per million of Kepone, an astounding concentration to be found in human blood. Federal doctors then contacted the Virginia State Epidemiologist, Dr. Robert Jackson, who quickly arranged a meeting with Hundtofte and Moore.[19]

When Jackson toured the plant he was appalled: "Kepone was everywhere"; conditions were "incredible"; workers were "virtually swimming in the stuff." Workers wore no protective equipment, nor had warning signs been posted. Seven out of ten production workers present had "the shakes" so severely that they required immediate hospitalization. On July 25, 1975, LSP voluntarily closed out its operations under threat of a closure order by the Virginia Department of Health. Further investigation divulged seventy-five cases of acute Kepone poisoning among

18. The Virginia State Water Control Board was by this time administering the NPDES program pending formal delegation by EPA, 33 U.S.C.A. §1342(b)(Supp. V 1975) provides that the states may administer the NPDES program.

19. Meetings had previously been requested by the Virginia State Department of Labor and Industry, but LSP had been successful in postponing them. Even though a former LSP worker had filed a complaint with the United States Occupational Safety and Health Administration (a branch of the United States Department of Labor), that agency had also failed to inspect the LSP factory. Only one Federal official, an EPA pesticide inspector, visited LSP before 1973; but he was not authorized to enter the production area. Other media under EPA jurisdiction – air and water pollution – had been delegated to State and local officials. At various times representatives of the Virginia Air Pollution Control Board, Water Pollution Control Board, and State Health Department had all visited LSP, but they were not responsible for inspecting LSP's working conditions.

LSP workers and high levels of Kepone in the blood of some of their family members. Moreover, there was found to be massive contamination of air, soil, and especially water in the vicinity of the plant. As a result, the State of Virginia closed one hundred miles of the James River and its tributaries to fishing. (The river has since been reopened to fishing for those species which do not bioaccumulate Kepone.) EPA referred the case to the United States Attorney for the Northern District of Virginia, who in early 1976 convened a grand jury to hear testimony pending possible criminal indictment.... [The Kepone chronicle continues in Chapters 3 and 7.]

COMMENTARY AND QUESTIONS

1. A systems breakdown? The chronology of this case over the years after 1949 involved dozens of management decisions, many of them inevitably involving corporate attorneys. It seems unlikely that the corporate players were ignorant of the hazardous externalities in the workplace, in the surrounding environment, and to human consumers overseas. To what extent did the system oblige them to consider those externalized costs? Consider the Allied attorneys working sequentially on the patents, franchise agreements, export permits, occupational health regulations, disposal practices, RAP applications, and other critical actions. Could they have raised the hazards issue?

If attorneys and decision-makers within the corporation were unable or unwilling to raise the issues, who else was to account for them? The federal agencies? The local city government, and the Commonwealth of Virginia? No one acted until a foreign-born doctor blew the whistle. Why hadn't lawsuits been filed by somebody early on?

2. The Kepone cases. Only one civil judgment resulting from the Kepone affair was ever reported, the *Pruitt* case in Chapter 3, which involved pollution effects more than a hundred miles away in Chesapeake Bay. Dozens of plaintiffs filed legal claims against Allied, including workers and their families, nonemployees exposed in the neighborhood, and government bodies that faced massive remedial expenses. Why do you suppose no decided civil cases except *Pruitt* can be found on the public record? In most settlement agreements (reportedly running into millions of dollars in the Kepone cases), a standard provision is that no details of the settlement are to be released. The facts of settled cases may be important in helping other injured persons pursue legal remedies. This explains Allied's desire to suppress the information, but as a matter of social policy, shouldn't such information be shared freely?

3. Kepone as a problem of the commons. To what extent did the behavior of the individual and corporate Kepone producers reflect the cost-externalizing tendency? In ignoring the foreseeable costs to human health, water quality, fisheries resources, and the like, were Allied and LSP being irrational? Shortsighted? Evil? Most industries, at least before the mid-1970s, regarded pollution as a normal industrial by-product. Likewise important, in that era the prospect of legal accountability was quite unlikely.

4. Law. How can the law alter the economic setting in which this disaster evolved? Notice that the problems associated with the activities of Allied and LSP were regulated by numerous state and federal agencies throughout the relevant period. This suggests that then, as now, a law's enforceability and its institutional follow-through within the legal system are as vital as its substance.

C. DIFFERENT STRATEGIES FOR REFORMING THE ECONOMICS OF POLLUTION

Section 1. THE MARKET STRATEGY OF ECONOMISTS

Economists generally prefer to correct the injurious effects of externalities (the contributions externalities make to inefficiency) through the creation of functioning markets, in effect privatizing the commons economically. Professor Varian, for example, ascribes the absence of functioning markets, in part, to a failure of law to provide sufficiently well-defined and transferable legal rights. To demonstrate his point he posits two roommates, each having a certain amount of money and each having a different attitude toward smoke in the shared room. If the legal entitlement to clean air were certain and were considered to be a property right of the non-smoker, Varian describes how the two roommates would engage in a Pareto efficient trade whereby the non-smoker might trade some of the entitlement to smoke-free air for some of the smoker's money.[20] A trade will take place if the non-smoker values having additional money more than the surrender of some portion of the right to clean air and the smoker values the ability to smoke by the agreed amount more than the money that must be paid. The precise amount of smoke and clean air would be determined, not by a rulemaker who can only guess at how much the affected parties value their clean air and smoke, but by the parties themselves in a way that maximizes utility. If a trade is mutually satisfactory to both participants it is by definition Pareto efficient.

Professor Varian's materials on externalities not only probe the use of markets as a means of eliminating the inefficiencies associated with externalities; they also discuss how cost internalization techniques allow efficient levels of production to be calculated in the absence of functioning markets. The hypothetical used to explore internalization is one that posits a steel producer whose discharge of effluents adversely impacts a fishery. The production function of the steel firm, reflecting a lack of pollution control law, treats the current cost of discharging effluents as zero. Nevertheless, the steel firm has knowledge of how much expense would be incurred for installation of various levels of effluent control. The production function for the fishery is affected by pollution and reflects the effluent discharges of the steel company. As pollution increases, so does the cost of fishing (perhaps having to seek more distant grounds, perhaps having to discard some part of the catch as inedible, etc.). To measure the degree of effluent reduction that would be optimal, a simple expedient is employed: the two firms are treated as if they were

20. Likewise, in the opposite case of legal entitlement, the smoker would be better off by selling some of the unlimited right to smoke. In fact, any legal rule, as long as it is sufficiently precise in defining the property rights of the two roommates, will permit them to bargain for an efficient outcome. See H. Varian, Intermediate Microeconomics, 546–47 (1987).

merged. At that point, there is no longer any external cost at all. The efficient outcome can be calculated by maximizing the "merged" firm's welfare, for at that point the private costs of the merged firm account for social costs (harm to fishery) that had previously been ignored by the steelmaker in its decisional process.

COMMENTARY AND QUESTIONS

1. Externalities and moral fault. Economists do not view negative externalities as inherently bad. For them, the goal is not the elimination of externalities so much as it is elimination of the distortions that externalities impose on resource allocation. Is there, nevertheless, moral fault involved in the production of negative externalities? It is difficult to read about the Kepone case without feeling outraged by the conduct of Allied, LSP, and the individuals involved. Is the same moral condemnation of polluters for imposing external costs on their neighbors always valid? For example, is burning coal to generate the electricity that supports vital human activities immoral because it emits combustion by-products into the atmosphere? Is the perceived "fault" involved in the coal-burning example legal in origin, stemming from invasion of the legal right (also the initial economic endowment) of the plant's neighbors to be free from pollution?

2. Law as entitlement, and the welfare effects of market transfers. Efficient market exchanges, as contemplated in the smoker/non-smoker situation have an effect on wealth distribution. Those who must pay for change are less well-off, in absolute terms, than they would have been if the original distribution of entitlements had been more favorable to them. What role, if any, should welfare consequences play in shaping environmental law rules? What role, if any, should the relative cost bearing abilities of the parties have in selecting the rule of entitlements? For example, should the potential welfare distribution effects of efficiency-seeking influence the assignment of initial endowments, such as a right to pollute versus a right to be free of pollution, in a controversy pitting a large, well-capitalized industrial polluter against its neighbors?

3. The Coase theorem. A central theme of the economists' strategy stresses the need for law to create property rights that are capable of being traded via a market exchange. A famous article by Nobel laureate Ronald Coase demonstrates that through bargaining starting from a clear legal rule of entitlement, the same outcome will be reached irrespective of which of two different parties holds the legal entitlement. See The Problem of Social Cost, 3 J.L. & Econ. 1 (1960). Coase's demonstration relies on assumptions about the equal access of all participants to information, and the absence of transaction costs. Perhaps efficiency maximizing bargaining seems likely to occur in a simple model such as the smoker/non-smoker hypothetical, or in a dispute between a neighboring rancher and farmer over fencing (Coase's hypothetical). Is bargaining toward an efficient solution likely to be easy when a large number of parties are joint holders of a legal right, as would be the case if a generalized right to clean air were acknowledged? The difficulties of organizing a group of victims of pollution to bargain as one (a form of "transaction costs") would pose one problem. Additionally, members of the group might refuse to participate, in the belief that they will be able to reap the shared benefit without active participation. This is a version of the "free rider" problem. Would the bargaining go better if the initial legal right were assigned to the polluter?

4. Poorly-defined property rights as an impediment to efficient trading. Recalling the steel mill/fishery hypothetical, if either the merger of the two firms or a voluntary trade between them will lead to an optimal result, why doesn't that behavior take place? Looking at merger, it ought to be plain that it is in the interests of both firms to merge and internalize the externality because, as Varian points out, "if the joint profits of the two firms with coordination exceed the sum of the profits without coordination, then the current owners could each be bought out for an amount equal to the present value of the stream of profits for their firm, the two firms could be coordinated, and the buyer could retain the excess profits." Varian, Intermediate Microeconomics, at 557. In answer to why the coordinating merger doesn't take place, Varian asserts that in many cases it does. He then says that inefficiency-producing externalities do arise in cases of poorly defined property rights. In particular, he analyzes the Tragedy of the Commons using Hardin's cow grazing example as an archetype of poorly defined property rights.

5. Taxes as an alternative to markets. Besides merger, what other solutions to the steel mill/fishery externality can be employed? The microeconomics texts offer two. One is the creation of a market like that of the smoker/non-smoker hypothetical. The second is to place a tax (called a Pigouvian tax) on the production of pollution. The difficulty with the Pigouvian tax is in knowing how high to set the tax: too high and the steel firm's lost profit due to output restriction will exceed the fishery firm's increased profit due to improved environmental conditions; too low and the steel company's savings on pollution control will still be outweighed by the loss in fishery.

6. Economic analysis and automobile emissions. Are automobile emissions an externality? Is there a "tragedy of the commons" problem? Would a Pigouvian tax avert (or at least limit) the tragedy? Such a tax would provide an incentive to drive less, to use cleaner fuels and to develop engines that emit less pollutants. Could the same behavioral changes be mandated by legislative fiat rather than by a tax? Is it practicable to fashion a market for automobile emissions trading, or to merge all of the entities whose actions affect and are affected by the commons? The principal legal approach to automobile emissions is considered in Chapter 17. Efforts to adopt a market-oriented regulatory approach are studied in Chapter 20.

Section 2. ECONOMICS AND GOVERNMENTAL REGULATION OF POLLUTERS

A major portion of this book analyzes several various types of regulation that are applied to the governance of environmental problems. To use Hardin's terms, the book explores many forms that mutually agreed upon mutual coercion can take legally. It should come as no surprise that economists have studied the types of regulation that are applied, and concluded that some forms of regulation are preferable to others.

Adherents of economic analysis prefer those types of regulatory action that achieve the same improvement in environmental quality while imposing lower total social costs than other possible regulatory strategies. Put most simply, achieving the same result at a lower cost is more efficient. For example, assume that a given degree of effluent reductions is desired and the regulatory question is whether to require emission controls (devices that clean the effluent stream as it leaves the plant) or process changes (changes in production methods that reduce the amount of untreated effluent being produced).

To make the example more concrete, assume that the desired environmental improvement is reduction of SO_2 (sulfurdioxide) emissions from a factory that burns coal as a source of energy for its production processes: the plant currently emits 50 tons per year and the goal is to reduce emissions to only 20 tons per year. The plant may reduce its emissions by cleansing the effluent stream – it can install filters or an electrostatic precipitator, or other devices that remove the SO_2 from the waste stream prior to emission into the atmosphere. Alternatively, the plant could change the type of coal it burns to coal that is naturally low in sulfur and reduce its SO_2 emissions in that way. If both methods can achieve the 30 ton per year reduction, the choice between them ought to be the one that involves the lowest total social costs. Correlatively, the important point of this simple hypothetical for those given power to regulate, is that the means of regulation chosen must be one that leads to the selection of the lowest cost option.

How is the regulator to know which approach, emission controls or process changes, achieves the result at lowest cost? At this point, adherents of economic analysis offer the suggestion that the regulator need not make that calculation because the affected plant operator, acting out of self interest, will choose the least cost method of achieving the 30 ton per year reduction in emissions. Moreover, it is possible that in a world containing hundreds or thousands of SO_2 emitters all of whom are to be regulated, the least cost solution for achieving SO_2 reductions of any given magnitude may vary from plant to plant, so that some ought to install emissions controls and others ought to change production processes. The most efficient regulatory solution, therefore, is not to command and control the specific decisions of the polluters. Instead, it is more efficient to create a system of performance standards, setting the end result that must be achieved, relying on the market-based decisions of the individual firms to fill in the details of how to achieve compliance. After all, each firm knows far more about its own particular processes and abilities to change than does the governmental regulator. The cost of regulation itself is also reduced because the regulator need not invest time and effort in learning a great deal about the ins and outs of the production cycle of each regulated entity.

Once the hypothetical is expanded to include the polluting activities of many firms rather than a single firm, the argument of the adherents of economic analysis goes a step further than merely allowing each affected firm to choose between emission control and process changes. The overall least-cost pollution control effort might be obtained only if some firms (those for whom any form of pollution reduction is expensive) continue to pollute at present (or even expanded) levels, while other firms (those for whom pollution control is relatively inexpensive) cut their emissions by more than a proportionate amount. The job of the regulator in this setting is merely to fix the overall limits on allowable pollution, and then to create a market system that allows the regulated firms to trade allowances to pollute among themselves. The predicted result is that pollution will be reduced in the desired amount by the firms for which pollution avoidance is less expensive, and the allowable pollution will be emitted by those firms for which the cost of avoiding pollution is higher. In that way, the desired emission reductions will be achieved and the total amount of scarce resources devoted to pollution control will be minimized. More pointedly, the total social cost of the desired environmental improvement will be much less than if every firm is subjected to command and control regulations that make mandatory a particular form or degree of emission reductions or the implementation of certain process changes.

Plainly, the adherents of economic analysis are not alone in their preference for minimizing the cost of effective pollution control, for it would be wasteful to devote more of society's scarce resources than necessary to accomplish any given result, environmental or otherwise. The point at which the adherents of economic analysis and others part company has more to do with the degree of confidence that they place in market-based systems to actually achieve the desired outcomes in the real world. A more detailed analysis, using economic incentives as a part of the regulatory system, appears in Chapter 18.

COMMENTARY AND QUESTIONS

1. An economist's approach to equitable distribution of wealth. The discussion of the role of economics in environmental quality issues frequently focuses on efficiency. Efficiency, no matter how desirable in a rationalist world, is not the only value that a society should pursue. Economics recognizes a need to account for the distributive consequences of using market allocation as a principal engine of social organization. If market allocations result in unfair distribution of social benefits, that, too, just like malfunctioning markets, is a justification for governmental intervention in the market system to readjust the distribution of benefits. In assessing what constitutes fairness in this distributional context, economists have no special insights, nor do they suffer any disabilities – they are as sensitive and compassionate as individual conscience and world view may dictate.

When it comes to forms of intervention into the functioning of free markets in the name of equity, however, adherents of market allocations do have preferences. In general, they find it preferable to give cash stipends to individuals who have too small a share of the benefits pie, and then let those individuals maximize their own welfare by selecting and purchasing the precise mix of benefits they most desire given their improved financial position.

Consider in this light the question of environmental improvement of polluted inner city neighborhoods populated by citizens who are economically disadvantaged. Environmental improvement will increase their welfare, by improving living conditions and reducing some health risks caused by exposure to the existing pollution. Assume that society is willing to devote a fixed sum of money, $X, to improve the lot of this group of people. Which will generate greater benefits for the affected group, a government financed program of environmental improvement or a direct grant of funds to those same inhabitants?

2. Beyond the horizons of economic efficiency and equity. Mark Sagoff has argued that efficiency and equity should not be the principal driving forces of "social regulation," a broad category of governmental actions that includes regulation of environmental quality. Instead, in his notable book on environmental economics, he advocates including ethical, aesthetic, and cultural goals in the process:

> The positive thesis...is that social regulation expresses what we believe, what we are, what we stand for as a nation, not simply what we want to buy as individuals. Social regulation reflects public values we choose collectively, and these may conflict with wants and interests we pursue individually. M. Sagoff, The Economy of the Earth 16 (1989).

D. MEASURING PROJECT BENEFITS AND ENVIRONMENTAL COSTS

Section 1. THE CHALLENGE OF BENEFIT-COST ACCOUNTING

Without regard to whether the mode of analysis is that of economics or the environmental perspective, it is vitally important to be able to account for the benefits and costs of any given project or proposal, viewed, of course, in the context of available alternatives. In the world of private sector market-oriented decision-making, benefit-cost accounting is no more nor less than taking an accurate measure of a firm's internal welfare function. In the realm of public policy decision-making there is likewise a need to assess the potential benefits and costs of proposed courses of action.

Historically, benefit-cost analysis has long been associated with governmental public works construction projects. From the outset of the twentieth century onward, government-sponsored projects have theoretically been evaluated in this fashion, often facing a legal requirement that the ratio of benefits to costs must exceed 1 to 1 in order for the project to qualify for the expenditure of public funds. This tally sheet function, long applied to such environmentally disruptive activities as dam building, swamp draining, and similar public investments, very early recognized that the benefits and costs of a project would frequently include the project's impacts on natural systems and the human uses made of those natural systems.

The recognition of environmental values by benefit-cost accountants as part of their work does not insure that benefit-cost analysis will not be environmentally problematic. Paralleling the corporate tendency to externalize environmental costs is a bureaucratic tendency to overstate project benefits and understate project costs in an effort to allow the "pork barrel" to roll on. Despite an emerging set of cost accounting principles designed to address the natural resource effects of projects, environmental costs remain prominent among the classes of costs most readily subject to downward manipulation.

The thrust of benefit-cost analysis is to facilitate the ready comparison of alternative courses of action, especially when one of the options is to do nothing other than continue the status quo. As one expert in the field says, "Benefit-cost analysis is beguiling in its simplicity and seems to have very wide ramifications. In evaluating any choice, just add up the benefits, subtract the costs, and choose the alternative that maximizes the net benefits."[21] As we have seen from the start with Chapter 1's highway salting, when benefit-cost analysis is performed with thoroughness and careful consideration of environmental impacts and alternatives, it is a strong ally of the environmental perspective. When done in a superficial manner, however, relying primarily on easily-quantified market impacts, benefit-cost analysis easily becomes a means of obscuring environmental costs in order to cast proposed projects in an overly favorable light.

Benefit-cost analysis relies heavily on concepts and methodologies developed by economists. Whenever a benefit-cost analysis is performed, the choice that will come out looking the best by that test will be the choice that maximizes net social benefits. This is the language of economics and is very little removed from the idea of efficiency. Measuring the values to be toted up as benefits and costs is both a science and an art. The tools of measurement include such things as sophisticated supply and demand functions, discount rates, equilibrium models, distributional coefficients, and glorified intuition.

Environmental lawyers need not be economists in order to recognize the difference between a well done benefit-cost analysis and one that has the hallmarks of an *ex post facto* rationalization for an insular decision. Nevertheless, when a legal or policy debate has focused on the benefits and costs of a project, the expertise of an economist or public policy analyst is as indispensable as is the counsel of an expert toxicologist on matters of toxicology, or a hydrogeologist on matters of the movement of contaminants in groundwater. As in other areas, lawyers need not be experts, but must have a general understanding of the expert's processes of analysis, and familiarity with terms that are likely to be encountered.

Within the study of benefit-cost analysis, some analytical classifications have been developed for grouping types of projects and proposals. Of particular interest for environmental law is the analysis of "physical investment" cases, because a large number of environmental cases fall into that category. In lay terms, the generic physical investment case is one that produces some valuable resource such as oil, or flood control. In his text on benefit-cost analysis, Professor Gramlich observes that physical investment cases raise standard problems regarding valuation of resources, uncertainty, discounting, and dealing with the gains and losses of different groups, but these cases frequently have a unique character as well:

> Unlike many other benefit-cost issues, where it might sometimes seem that the stakes are rather small, environmental issues can often attain significant proportions [in physical investment cases]. When deciding to build a dam that will kill an endangered species or a power plant that will generate long-lived nuclear contaminants, public sector decision-makers are often being asked to make very fundamental choices. To a large degree, these choices

21. E. Gramlich, A Guide to Benefit-Cost Analysis 2 (2d ed. 1990).

> may not be the stuff of economics, that marginalist discipline. But as with questions of valuing human lives and assessing distributional changes, there are some techniques and styles of reasoning that can still help focus analysis on the fundamentals....[22]

The various devices that Gramlich describes as useful in the physical investment setting are numerous and their description tends toward complex, formula-ridden microeconomics. The environmental costs of physical investment projects that Gramlich characterizes as difficult to measure take several forms, two of which are particularly noteworthy. One is a sort of opportunity cost – for example, the lost benefits of having the Alaska National Wildlife Refuge serve effectively as a wildlife refuge in the event that proposals for oil exploration and drilling are approved.[23] The principal difficulty here is valuation: there is no obvious means for deciding how much a refuge is worth. The second difficulty of performing a benefit-cost analysis in the environmental context might best be described as evaluating residual costs. Here Gramlich gives the example of estimating the long-term cost of disposing of nuclear wastes. The process of discounting costs that will accrue in the future down to present value, and uncertainty about the range of costs that may be incurred, make assigning present values highly problematic.

The following materials delve briefly into the process of placing values on non-market resources and measuring environmental impacts that may occur in the future. A brief third section follows, sketching the emerging concepts of ecological economics.

Section 2. MEASURING RESOURCE VALUES

There are several ways in which natural resource effects can be made part of a benefit-cost analysis:

> Various methodologies have been proposed to calculate damages to natural resources. If the resource or service is traded in the marketplace, damages may be calculated based upon either the diminution of market price or an appraisal. If the resource is not traded in the marketplace, a variety of non-market techniques can be used. These include the travel cost method, which utilizes the costs of travel to a recreation site as a surrogate for the price of recreation services; the hedonic price method, which attempts indirectly to find the effect of the resource injury on, say, the price of land; the unit day value method, which uses a table of values to determine the value per day of various recreational activities; and the contingent valuation method, which is based upon a survey of people to determine their willingness to pay for (or to accept) environmental goods (or bads).[24]

Even simple examples serve to demonstrate that the array of methodologies just noted does not lead to a qualification of environmental costs without the need for

22. Id. at 134–35.

23. Exploration alone has some environmental costs that would adversely affect the refuge, but the greater disruption of production would destroy the essential characteristics of the area and eliminate its value as a refuge.

24. Cicchetti & Peck, Assessing Natural Resource Damages: The Case Against Contingent Value Survey Methods, 4 Natural Resources & the Environment 6 (Spring 1989).

using data sets that may be very difficult to obtain. In evaluating the loss of environmental resources there is, for example, no ready market to establish just how much 64,000 acres of wilderness in Montana, or six miles of high-quality trout stream in Pennsylvania, are worth. The benefit-cost analyst tries to find a more readily monetizable activity that bears a close relation to the value of wilderness or a recreational fishery. In both instances the cost that users of the resource spend is a possible "shadow price" that can be employed to calculate the value, in economic terms, of the present use of the resource. In the wilderness example, the users of the resource incur a travel cost; in the fishery example, users incur expenses for licenses, bait and tackle, and perhaps expenses for overnight lodging along with travel costs. To make a benefit evaluation, data must be collected about how many users there are, where they come from, what they spend on the activity and so forth. As a general rule, this data is not particularly reliable as it is not the sort of material that is routinely measured and recorded.

More fundamentally, from the environmental perspective, indeed, from almost any perspective, this method of using shadow prices is likely to omit values of great significance. In one case the cost may be destruction of critical habitat for a threatened or endangered species; in another case the cost may be the destruction of a breathtaking view. The shadow price methods focus only on quasi-commercial values, but that is only a start in assigning weight to those values. For that reason, it is important to note that a technique like the travel cost method of determining a shadow price produces only a *lower bound estimate* of the costs involved should the wilderness or fishery be destroyed, not a full estimate of the total costs.[25]

COMMENTARY AND QUESTIONS

1. The cost of losing a wildlife refuge. As to recurring proposals to open the Arctic National Wildlife Refuge and similar preservation areas to hydrocarbon development, is it clear that any of the several resource valuation methods will produce a reliable figure for environmental costs, or do all the possible methods provide a figure that is merely a lower bound estimate of the costs? The remoteness and impracticality of travel to such refuges raises the question of whether "use" oriented valuation methods are likely to produce a value that reflects the refuges' ecological importance. The travel cost per visit will be very high, but the number of visitors will be minuscule. One might even argue that refuge purposes are best served (and thus the value of refuges will be greater) if the number of human visits is lower, not higher. In terms reminiscent of the philosopher Berkeley, does a polar bear growling in the tundra make any noise if no one is there to hear it? Such concerns reflect what are sometimes referred to as "existence values." Wasn't this the kind of thing Sagoff had in mind in advocating laws (social regulation) motivated by values other than those that motivate us as consumers? These issues are explored further in the context of the Alaska oil spill in Chapter 3, at 163 *infra*.

2. Replacement value and mitigation cost. An alternative to quantifying environmental damage costs in their own right is to consider the cost of either replacing the

25. E. Gramlich, A Guide to Benefit-Cost Analysis 136–38 (2d ed. 1990).

damaged environmental resource or the cost of altering the proposed project in a way that will not harm resources. If a wetland is to be destroyed, replacement cost could be measured as the cost of purchasing similar property and dedicating it to use as a wetland. If a wetland was going to be dewatered by construction of a road that blocked the natural inflow of water, mitigation costs would be measured by the additional expenditure needed to assure the wetland of a continued water supply. Are these means of measuring environmental costs more accurate than the previously-discussed methods? Can replacement value and mitigation costs be used in benefit-cost analysis and later ignored when the project is constructed? Plainly, the answer is yes. Benefit-cost analysis is intended to evaluate a project's desirability. The considerations that go into actually building a project are governed by the applicable substantive governing law. This duality between informed judgement and physical action is reflected in some National Environmental Policy Act cases where agencies propose mitigation efforts to justify a project, and later decline to implement them. See Chapter 12.

3. Environmental benefits of reduced pollution. The benefits of environmental improvements are equally hard to evaluate. A reduction of air pollution in Los Angeles can be achieved through major alterations in transportation practices. How great are the potential benefits? Without question, the benefits include a reduction of pollution-induced death and illness. Is the value of those improvements adequately measured in terms of salary income earned by people who live longer and the reduction in health care costs for pollution-induced illness? The real benefits also include productivity gains from a workforce that has less eye irritation and suffers fewer headaches from breathing polluted air. Is it arbitrary to say, as did one recent benefit-cost analysis of the subject, that each avoided headache is worth a specific dollar amount? Is it even more arbitrary to ignore those benefits altogether?

4. Cost externalization in the bureaucratic sector. As noted in Section 1, government officials in the public works agencies feel internal agency incentives to inflate project benefits and understate project costs. Their "production" is measured in cubic yards of concrete poured, or miles of roadway built, or acres of waterway drained, dug, or dammed. Their "profit" is measured in terms of jobs gained for the agency and its contractors, renewed federal appropriations from the public purse, dollars passed through local public works constituencies, and political capital gained at federal, state, and local levels. Internal "costs" are measured in terms of political capital expended, hassles, and opportunity costs. Dollars, supplied by the taxpayers, are often only indirectly felt as determinative costs. With their project promotion orientation, most public works agencies would rather not consider or internalize broader assessments of project costs. The fact is that many public works projects cannot be justified by their real benefit-cost merits. The internal reckoning that drives many such projects is an agency's need to keep its agenda full and appropriations flowing: a rolling stone gathers momentum. The survival and perpetuation of the organization is a basic loyalty and a compelling managerial responsibility. Accurate accounting of costs and benefits does not necessarily serve the pork barrel agenda. Bureaucratic instinct is to maintain the flow of direct internal organizational benefits, not to serve some nebulous public good concept of net benefit-cost accounting. These pressures underlie the benefit-cost assessment process.

Section 3. INTERGENERATIONAL JUSTICE AND THE DISCOUNT RATE

Physical investment projects that disrupt the environment are typically long-lived. Their official benefits will be enjoyed, and at least some of their costs will be borne, a number of years into the future. Benefit-cost analysis, in order to be effective, must include a way to compare those future pluses and minuses with more immediate items, such as the costs incurred at the outset on mortar and concrete. In effect, there must be a common denominator in order for a meaningful comparison to take place, and that common denominator is to discount future benefits and costs down to present value.

The formal means by which analysts discount benefits and costs to present value may be unfamiliar, but the concept is an intuitively familiar one. The familiar adage that a bird in the hand is worth two in the bush suggests that the uncertainty of what will come to pass makes the present value of a benefit greater than its future value. An even more explicit recognition of the reduced value of future benefits is the charging of interest for the extension of credit, even where borrowers are certain to repay so that risk is not a part of the "cost" of credit. The bank will make a student loan today on condition that it be paid back the full amount lent plus something more at a specified time in the future. The "something more" covers not only the cost of initiating the loan and the risk of default,[26] it also reflects the fact that our society values present consumption more than future consumption. As another example, the fact that banks will pay 5 percent interest on a fully insured savings deposit for a year means that a dollar placed in the account will be worth $1.05 one year hence. This shows that the present value of the benefit of being paid $1.05 in one year is no more than $1.00. Another way to describe the reason for discounting is to say that devoting current assets to production of future benefits incurs an "opportunity cost," that is, a loss of the alternative present benefits that could have been obtained.

Economists and others acknowledge that future value is less than present value. There are highly competitive markets that offer a fairly reliable indication of just how much society as a whole discounts future values, and that indicator is called a discount rate – usually the prevailing interest rate for a sound, safe investment. Once a discount rate is adopted, a formula can be used to calculate future values, not just a year from now, but also any number of years into the future. The present value of a future benefit depends critically upon the discount rate chosen.[27] If a 1 percent rate is used, a $1 million benefit ten years hence has a present value of

26. Were the loan "guaranteed" by the national government, as many are, a lower, but still more than 0 percent, rate of interest would be charged, making it clear that the cost of credit reflects more than risk-taking alone.

27. The formula for discounted present value of a future benefit is $B_t/(1+r)^t$, where B is the dollar value of the future benefit to be obtained, t is the number of years in the future when the benefit will be obtained and r is the discount rate.

$905,287. If instead the rate is 10 percent, the present value of future benefits falls sharply to only $385,543; at 15 percent the present value is a mere $247,185.

Government pork barrel projects have been notorious over the years for selecting an unrealistically low discount rate. As the figures just set forth reveal, this tends to inflate the value of the stream of future benefits, thus making the good aspects of the project, things such as electric generation and flood control, look better. Simultaneously, the unrealistically low discount rate tends to inflate future costs, including the costs of adverse environmental effects. Although this might appear to be even-handed, it almost assuredly is not. Benefits are often unrealistically inflated. As to costs, the most easily quantified environmental harms accrue in the near term – items such as fish kills when a free flowing stream is first impounded. More important, long-term environmental costs tend to be underestimated due to the difficulty of their quantification.

The question of how a discount rate is selected remains important. The following excerpt provides a brief and somewhat technical glance at how economists approach the issue of choosing a discount rate for long-lived public projects.

J. Stiglitz, Discount Rates for Social Cost-Benefit Analysis
Economics of the Public Sector, 226–27 (1986).

In our discussion of private cost-benefit analysis, we noted that a dollar next year or the year after was not worth as much as a dollar today. Hence, income to be received in the future or expenses to be incurred in the future had to be discounted. In deciding whether to undertake a project, we look at its present discounted value. The discount factor private firms use is $1/(1 + r)$ where r is the rate of interest the firm has to pay. The question is, what discount rate should the government use? The discount rate used by the government is sometimes called the social discount rate. The central question of concern is the relationship between this and the interest rate faced by consumers, on the one hand, and producers, on the other.

For evaluating long-lived projects, such as dams, the choice of the discount rate is crucial: a project that looks very favorable using a 3 percent interest rate may look very unattractive at a 10 percent rate. If markets worked perfectly, the market interest rate would reflect the opportunity cost of the resources used and the relative evaluation of income at different dates. But there is a widespread belief that capital markets do not work well. Moreover, taxes may introduce large distortions. Thus it is not clear which of the various market rates of interest, if any, should be used: for instance, should it be the rate at which the government can borrow, or should it be the rate at which the typical taxpayer can borrow?

Although no consensus has been reached among economists at a practical level, there is some agreement about the principles. First, one needs to consider how a project will affect the economy, and to whom the benefits (and costs) accrue. Then one weighs the benefits and costs accruing to different individuals using a social welfare function. One might give less weight to increases in consumption to future generations than to increases in consumption to the current generation, because one believes that, as a result of technological progress, they will be better off on any account.

This assessment of how projects affect different generations is particularly important for long-lived projects, where the costs may be borne by one generation, and the benefits received by succeeding generations. The assessment of these projects entails a trade-off between individuals of different generations. What is at issue is the intergenerational distribution of income or welfare. We can talk about society's marginal rate of substitution of one generation's income for another, just as we can talk of an individual's marginal rate of substitution of consumption in one period for another. The question is, "What is the relationship between society's marginal rate of substitution and the market rate of interest?" The answer depends on how successful the government has been in adjusting the intergenerational distribution of income to reflect society's judgments concerning the appropriate intertemporal distribution.

In the absence of an active government policy, there is no reason that the intergenerational distribution of welfare generated by the market has any optimality properties; there is no reason to believe, in other words, that there will be any systematic relationship between the market rate of interest and the society's marginal rate of substitution between this generation's consumption and that of the next generation.[28] Using the market rate of interest may result in too high a discount rate, or too low a discount rate.

Disagreements arise among economists concerning the impact of the project being evaluated, the extent to which the government has used other policy instruments to bring about the appropriate intergenerational distribution of income, and consequently, how increments to income of different generations should be valued. For instance, some economists are particularly concerned about the extent to which public projects displace (or "crowd out") private projects. These economists tend to argue for using the rate at which firms can obtain financing.

COMMENTARY AND QUESTIONS

1. Discount rates used by private firms. Can you infer from the discussion of fixing the discount rate for public projects what the standard view is about the appropriate rate to be used in private projects? In general, because private investors make their decisions with reference to the value of alternative investments, they discount their stream of returns by the real interest rate.[29]

2. Improved conditions as a justification for discounting. Stiglitz describes, in addition to discounting, a second process by which intergenerational benefits and costs can be adjusted: the use of social welfare functions. He suggests that one might opt to give less weight to the benefits accruing to future generations because technology will make them "better off on any account." Is this technological optimism justified as an historical matter? Almost surely that answer is "Yes." Material standards of living have been rising for many generations, with much of the welfare gain being attributable to technological innovation. Is an inductive argument predicting more of the same in the future valid? Here there is room for

28. We sometimes refer to this marginal rate of substitution as the social rate of time preference.

29. The real interest rate is distinguished from the nominal interest rate which would reflect the additional premium that would account for predicted inflation. In present value calculations it is important to work in consistent terms. If real rates are used, both the benefit and cost streams must be measured in real terms; if nominal rates are used, again, both the benefit and cost streams must use nominal terms that are inflation-adjusted.

speculation on both sides of the question. That technological progress will continue to produce material improvements is as obvious as the revolutionary changes being made possible by microchips and electronic devices. The more nagging question is whether the potential degradation in environmental quality will outstrip the positive side of the ledger.

3. Moral hazard and future costs. The paradigmatic case that Stiglitz has in mind is a large current investment, such as a major dam that will provide flood control and hydroelectric generation for decades into the future, that places most of the cost on the present generation and awards most of the benefit to future generations. There is no moral hazard in opting to burden oneself (impose present costs) for the benefit of others (future generations). Is the same true of a project that provides current and short-term benefits while saddling future generations with major costs? One high visibility environmental law debate that illustrates this question is the promotion of nuclear electric generation that will burden future generations with potentially significant costs for long-term waste disposal and/or treatment. See Baltimore Gas & Electric Co. v. Natural Resources Defense Council, 462 U.S. 87 (1983); Pacific Gas & Electric Co. v. California State Energy Resources Comm., 461 U.S. 190 (1983), cases considered in Chapters 10 and 11.

4. Does discounting miss the point? Some observers resist the very idea of applying market discount approaches to issues of planetary ecological management. In a recent essay, Peter Brown argues that "there are some things that are not, and should not be, discounted. No one asks, 'What is the optimal rate of shredding for the U.S. Constitution?' On the contrary, we assume that we should preserve the historic document for posterity. This is precisely analogous to what many people think we should do with respect to these issues; but all this response demonstrates is that [market accounting] doesn't tell us what the discount rate with respect to these issues should be, or even whether there should be one." Moreover, "in any situation where there is a long-term asymmetry between costs and benefits, as is the case with global warming, discounting imperils the future by undervaluing it. Although the costs of averting the greenhouse effect are paid in the present, the benefits accrue in the distant future. The discounted value of harms that occur a century from now are insignificant when compared with the present costs of avoiding them. As D'Arge, Schulze, and Brookshire argue in Carbon Dioxide and Intergenerational Choice, 'a complete loss of the world's GNP a hundred years from now would be worth about one million dollars today if discounted by the present prime rate.'"[30]

5. Discounting for uncertainty. How should benefit-cost analysis evaluate events that are uncertain to occur? Is there a difference in evaluating the costs of a decision that will increase toxic exposure-induced cancer deaths by two persons per thousand and a decision that might not increase cancer deaths at all, or might increase them by four persons per thousand exposures? The problem of valuing loss

---

30. Brown, Greenhouse Economics: Think Before You Count, Report from the Institute for Philosophy & Public Policy 10, 11 (1991).

of human life is common to the two situations, but the number of lives at stake is uncertain in the second example. Studies demonstrate that there is "consumer preference" for certainty. Alternatively stated, there is consumer aversion to certain forms of risk-taking. To reflect this, benefit-cost analysis has developed methods for figuring in the disutility of uncertainty. The crux of the adjustment is to discount the value of uncertain benefits, and attach a premium to uncertain disfavored costs. The next subpart explores in greater depth the issues surrounding uncertainty and risk in environmental law settings.

Section 4. NEW ENVIRONMENTAL ECONOMICS

Running through the several examples of economic analysis of environmental concerns, beginning with pollution and ending with benefit-cost analysis and choosing discount rates, traditional economists betray a general lack of sensitivity to the environmental perspective. At each turn, it seems that the tools of classical economics are not attuned to measuring and accounting for long-term impacts on the environment. Some economists, however, have recently begun developing alternate modes of analysis that explicitly account for environmental quality. This "green" school of economics voices a new perspective on national and international economic policy:

Passell, Rebel Economists Add Ecological Cost To Price of Progress

New York Times, November 27, 1990, C1, col. 5.

Could biologists, ecologists and other natural scientists have more to say about the economics of the environment than economists themselves?

Researchers calling themselves ecological economists are challenging traditional economics on its own turf, accusing economists of mismeasuring development, underestimating the intangible costs of pollution and ignoring society's responsibilities to future generations.

While many economists dismiss the ideas of their fellow scientists and critics as both unoriginal and loosely reasoned, these notions are finding a respectful audience in bastions of the establishment, particularly those that deal with the third world. The rebels' ideas have special application for countries that depend heavily on their natural resources....

If the rebels succeed in the goal set by Robert Costanza, a biologist at the University of Maryland and a founder of the five year old International Society of Ecological Economists, they will persuade governments to give the "sustainability" of natural "life support systems" priority over conventionally measured economic growth. That could mean radical changes in policy, sharply reducing efforts to improve living standards through investments in land-intensive agriculture and resource extraction.

But succeed or fail, they will almost certainly force economists to face up to the issue that traditional analysis tends to undervalue environmental resources. And they may kindle public debate on some very uncomfortable questions, everything from the need for population control to the compensation owed by the present generation to those who will inherit radioactive reactor wastes in the year 3000....

CALCULATING DEPRECIATION

Robert Repetto and his colleagues at the World Resources Institute have been widely applauded for an attempt to correct a common distortion introduced by conventional economics practices: the failure to include natural resource depletion in national income accounts.

When economists measure a nation's net output, they subtract capital depreciation, the loss of machines, vehicles and buildings in the ongoing production process. But they rarely account for gains or losses of less tangible forms of capital, like human skills. Equally important, they neglect changes in reserves of natural resources, which are typically large (and negative) in poor countries.

The Repetto team used the example of Indonesia to show how important this omission can be in gauging national development. Losses from soil erosion, they calculated, reduce the net value of crop production by about 40 percent. And net losses of forest resources actually exceed timber harvests. Moreover, from 1980 to 1984 depletion of oil fields reduced the value of Indonesia's reserves base by about $10 billion annually, roughly 15 percent of national income.

In industrialized countries, where total output is much larger relative to natural resources depletion, similar extensions of conventional accounting methods have been used to calculate the impact of environmental degradation. Japan, Germany, and France all have ambitious projects under way. And the United Nations Statistical Office is working on a general framework for environment and natural resource accounting.

SEEKING A NEW FRAMEWORK

But ecological economists are not ready to permit researchers like Mr. Repetto, who accept the basic tenets of modern economic theory, to be the profession's toughest critics. What economics needs, they argue, is a whole new framework, one that fits economic production into ecological systems, rather than the other way around.

To Herman Daly at the World Bank, David Pearce at the University of London, and Paul Ehrlich at Stanford University, the key goal is the achievement of "sustainability" – adjusting economic activity so it does not damage the natural systems that underpin all functioning economies. Too many economists, they argue, simply assume that the biosphere can roll with any economic punch and bounce back for more.

But sustainability is proving hard to define and even harder to measure. One approach, now popular among ecological economists, is to calculate energy balances on the assumption that energy supplies represent the ultimate constraint on human activity. Mr. Costanza, for example, measures the amount of energy absorbed by swampland in order to compute the swamp's value.... Economists have been down this road before. Nicholas Georgescu-Roegen, an eccentric Rumanian economist...spent a career mulling the relationship between economics and the laws of thermodynamics. The amount of energy in the universe is constant, but the amount available for work in a closed (economic) system is limited and constantly in decline....

Mr. Daly, an economist by training who long ago defected to the enemy, approaches sustainability from another angle. He constructed an "index of sustainable economic welfare," adjusting conventionally measured output for environmental damage, resource depletion, the availability of leisure, even the degree of income equality. The index suggests that Americans' sustainable welfare peaked more than a decade ago, that "economic development" as contrasted with economic growth has stopped.

William Nordhaus, [an economist at Yale University] and the Nobel Prize-winning economist James Tobin put together a less ambitious "measurement of economic welfare" in the early 1970s in response to Marxists, whose claims to be creating more liveable societies were then taken seriously. The two economists found that the output omitted from regular income accounts – like the fruits of household labor – roughly offset the unmeasured costs, like pollution. Thus growth in economic welfare (in advanced industrialized economies, anyway) roughly tracked the growth in conventionally measured output.

At the heart of the sustainability question, Mr. Nordhaus argues, is the issue of endowing future generations with at least as much productive capacity as this generation inherited. Current levels of economic activity may deplete valuable resources and degrade ecological systems in irreversible ways, he acknowledges. But this generation will also pass on precious new technologies, cures for fatal diseases, incredibly efficient means for processing information, for example. Who is to judge whether our resource-stripping, environmentally stressful ways will more than offset this technological bounty?

TECHNOLOGICAL PESSIMISTS

Robert Hahn, an economist at the American Enterprise Institute, offers another way of parsing the question. Traditional economics implicitly assumes that as a practical matter no wasting asset, whether it be oil or the atmospheric ozone layer, is absolutely critical to economic growth or human welfare. Ecological economists, by contrast, are technological pessimists: if nations are not careful, they will make the planet uninhabitable.

No one really knows who is right. And to Mr. Hahn, the appropriate response to uncertainty is not agnosticism. It makes sense, he argues, to err on the side of caution where the penalty in output forgone is not high. The ecological economists thus score most tellingly, Mr. Hahn suggests, in their criticism of traditional economists' live-and-let-live approach to population issues.

Traditional economics, with its focus on the welfare of individuals, has generally been indifferent to the overall scale of economic activity. But for any given living standard, it is virtually certain that more people mean more damage to ecological systems, whose carrying capacities are poorly understood. Thus, it may matter critically whether the world's population stabilizes at, say, 10 billion rather than 20 billion.

It is not yet clear whether the ecologists will establish a beachhead in the economists' carefully constructed intellectual empire. What they have already demonstrated, though, is that environmental economics is too important to be left by default to economists....

COMMENTARY AND QUESTIONS

1. Measuring national product. The standard measure of national economic activity currently in use is gross national product (GNP). In measuring GNP, no account is taken of the costs imposed by pollution or by a nation's dwindling stock of natural resources. These omissions constitute a fundamental inconsistency, because the output measured to make up GNP does take account of the depletion of other capital resources, such as the depreciation of plant and equipment. Is there any plausible reason for these omissions? Would a concept of *net* national product be more conducive to making the environmental costs of economic activity more highly visible? "Conventional measures of output...cannot be used as accurate measures of true changes in economic welfare...." Seneca and Taussig, Environmental Economics 325–27 (1974). See also the German Federal Statistical Office's "Gross Ecological Product" project, cited in Hinrichsen, Economists' Shining Lie, 13 Amicus J. 3 (Spring 1991).

2. Population and more Tragedy of the Commons. Hardin's brief article excerpted earlier in this chapter is undoubtedly one of the most influential ever written. Do you hear strains of the tragedy of the commons in virtually every position expressed by the economists cited in the newspaper article? Even Robert Hahn, a champion of market solutions to environmental problems, sounds a Hardin-like caution on issues of population control. What is the relationship between sustainability and population? At a simplistic level, the argument is one of human welfare – if the earth's sustainable bounty is likened to a pie, everyone can have a larger piece if there are fewer with whom to share. The more intractable issues arise in trying to calculate or predict whether the additional stress that greater population puts on the earth's resources will exceed sustainability, either temporarily or irreversibly.

E. UNCERTAINTY, RISK, AND ENVIRONMENTAL LAW

Technological advances have played a vital role in improving living standards in modern industrialized societies, but the gains from technological innovation have associated costs, many of which are environmental costs. The internal combustion engine that revolutionized travel by making the automobile so convenient and useful has brought with it serious air pollution and huge demands for oil, whose production and distribution have often marred natural systems. Beyond ailments traceable to air pollution, automobile use can be said to cause adverse health effects for tens of thousands of people killed and injured in collisions each year. In deciding to embrace the automobile, societies implicitly accept the costs and risks that technology entails.

In the last quarter of this century, and looking ahead into the future, the possibilities for improving the human condition through technological advances remain abundant. Advances in science open possibilities of new cures for diseases, bioremediation of oil spills and other escapes of hazardous pollutants into the environment, new energy sources, and a seemingly endless list of other possibilities. In deciding whether to embrace these technologies, a rational decision-maker must weigh benefits and costs fully, using the various techniques previously laid out and keeping a careful eye out not to undervalue the ecological impacts of an activity.

As the areas of technological advance increasingly become areas at the edge of scientific knowledge and understanding, new difficulties beset the evaluation process. When the time comes to calculate the impacts of some of these new technologies, adequate information is unavailable because even the scientific community is uncertain of exactly what to expect. Even so, in almost all cases it is possible to sketch at least some broad categories of possible consequences and to have an idea of how likely it is that those consequences will come to pass. This is an assessment of the risk that inheres in employing a technology. Having assessed the risk, the problem still remains of determining whether to encounter it, and if so, on what terms. This involves selecting a means of risk management. The materials in this section explore the problems of uncertainty and risk regarding health and environmental effects, and the treatment uncertainty and risk receive in legal decision-making.

These materials are more than a mere adjunct to economic analysis and benefit-cost analysis in particular. While risk assessment under conditions of uncertainty is a subset of more general benefit and cost assessment, the fact of uncertainty infuses the process with a different character. The comparison is no longer a choice between known outcomes. The traditional interplay of individuals, legislators, agencies and courts and the traditional methods and processes of decision no longer seem well adapted to the task. Even the usual lines of rational argument about what outcomes are preferable, challenging specific elements of valuation or a proposal's distributive consequences, seem to overlook important issues. Risk management under conditions of uncertainty is distinctive and the number of cases raising health and environmental risk management issues is increasing.

To give a flavor of some of the problems that face legal decision-makers in risk management cases, these materials begin with a relatively simple case involving a court in the task of managing risks associated with hazardous waste disposal. Thereafter the materials take up risk assessment and risk management separately. The risk assessment section focuses on cancer risks and how they are demonstrated. The risk management section is more general in scope, defining what is at stake in risk management and considering in preliminary fashion questions of institutional competence of courts and agencies as risk managers.

Section 1. HARM THAT MAY NOT COME TO PASS: *WILSONVILLE* AS A CASE STUDY

The case that follows involves the NIMBY ("Not in my back yard!") phenomenon in which a local citizenry brings an attack on a hazardous waste disposal facility being operated in its midst. While there is some evidence that the plant is causing a degree of present interference with the community, emitting odors and causing small spills from vehicles bringing materials for disposal, the crux of the complaint is that the facility threatens to become a major problem in the future. The two principal scenarios that the plaintiffs build their case around are (1) leakage from the site with attendant contamination of groundwater supplies and (2) explosion and fire. The evidence at trial was sharply contradictory, with experts for plaintiffs and defendant taking radically divergent positions on the possibility and probability of the scenarios' occurrence and on the harms that would ensue if stored materials escaped from the disposal site.

The opinion of the Illinois Supreme Court was lengthy and recounted in detail many technical assessments made by the experts at trial. In editing the case, far more than usual of the evidentiary material and its evaluation by the court has been retained to give a sense of how the litigation was conducted, what scientific knowledge could be brought to bear on the problem, and how the court reacted to the risks to health and environment posed by the dumpsite and the plaintiffs' desire for its closure. The legal issue of greatest significance is that of deciding when a court should intervene in a dispute to enjoin conduct involving risk of future harm.

Village of Wilsonville v. SCA Services, Inc.
Supreme Court of Illinois, 1981
86 Ill. 2d 1, 426 N.E.2d 824.

CLARK, J. On April 18, 1977, the plaintiff village of Wilsonville (the village) filed a complaint seeking injunctive relief in the circuit court of Macoupin County. Plaintiffs Macoupin County and the Macoupin County Farm Bureau were granted leave to intervene.... The gravamen of the complaints was that the operation of the defendant's chemical-waste-disposal site presents a public nuisance and a hazard to the health of the citizens of the village, the county and the State. The Attorney General of Illinois filed a complaint on May 26, 1977, seeking an injunction pursuant to the Environmental Protection Act (Ill. Rev. Stat. 1975, ch. 111½).... Trial began on June 7, 1978, consumed 104 days, and resulted in judgment for the plaintiffs on August 28, 1978. The trial court's judgment order concluded that the site constitutes a nuisance and enjoined the defendant from operating its hazardous-chemical waste landfill in Wilsonville. It ordered the defendant to remove all toxic waste buried there, along with all contaminated soil found at the disposal site as a result of the operation of the landfill. Further, the court ordered the defendant to restore and reclaim the site. The defendant appealed....

The defendant has operated a chemical waste landfill since 1977. The site comprises approximately 130 acres, 90 of which are within the village limits of the plaintiff village. The remaining 40 acres are adjacent to the village. The defendant enters into agreements with generators of toxic chemical waste to haul the waste away from the generators' locations. The defendant then delivers it to the Wilsonville site, tests random samples of chemical waste, and then deposits the waste in trenches. There are seven trenches at the site. Each one is approximately 15 feet deep, 50 feet wide, and 250 to 350 feet long. Approximately 95 percent of the waste materials were buried in 55-gallon steel drums, and the remainder is contained in double-wall paper bags. After the materials are deposited in the trenches, uncompacted clay is placed between groups of containers and a minimum of one foot of clay is placed between the top drum and the top clay level of the trench.

The site is bordered on the east, west, and south by farmland and on the north by the village. The entire site, the village, and much of the surrounding area is located above the abandoned Superior Coal Mine No. 4, which operated from 1917 to 1954. The No. 6 seam of the mine was exploited in this area at a depth of 312 feet. The mining method used to extract coal was the room-and-panel method, whereby about 50 percent of the coal is left in pillars which provide some support for the earth above the mine. There was testimony at trial by Dr. Nolan Augenbaugh, chairman of the Department of Mining, Petroleum and Geological Engineering at the University of Missouri at Rolla, that pillar failure can occur in any mine where there is a readjustment of stress. Also on the defendant's site is a 30- to 40-feet-high pile of "gob," or mine spoil of coal, shale, and clay, which was accumulated over the time the mine was operated. Acid drainage from the mine has seeped into the ground and contaminated three surface drainage channels at the site. The defendant has attempted to remedy this situation by covering the surface of the "gob pile" with excess soil from the trenches.

There are 14 monitoring wells along the perimeter of the site. They are designed to detect liquids which seep through the soil and into the wells. They are not designed to contain liquids, however. In fact, monitoring wells Nos. 5 and 6 are 650 feet apart, which would allow many materials to pass between those two wells and not be discovered. The wells are sampled quarterly by a private laboratory, and test results are submitted to the Illinois Environmental Protection Agency (IEPA). Additional water samples are taken from three surface channels and are tested and reported in the same manner as samples taken from the wells. The surface drainage and the ground-water drainage from the site are to the south, away from the village and toward farmland.

The village has no sewage-treatment plant and no municipally owned sewage system. Most homes are served by septic tanks, and some homes and businesses are connected to private sewers. The water-distribution system is centralized, and water is purchased from Gillespie, Illinois. The system was built in 1952 after the village tried unsuccessfully to find sufficient water by drilling municipal wells in the area. There are still 73 water wells in the village, some of which are used to water gardens or wash cars. At least one well is used to water pets, and another is used for drinking water. South of defendant's site, approximately one-half mile from the gob pile, is the Vassi Spring, the owner of which intends to use it as his water supply when he builds his home. Further south are four more springs used to water livestock.

On February 11, 1976, the defendant applied to the IEPA for a permit to develop and operate the hazardous-waste landfill. A developmental permit was issued by the IEPA on May 19, 1976. After a preoperation inspection was conducted by the IEPA, an operational permit was issued to the defendant on September 28, 1976. Each delivery of waste material to the site must be accompanied by a supplemental permit issued by the IEPA. A supplemental permit specifies the chemical nature and quantity of the waste to be deposited at the sites. Between November 12, 1976, and June 7, 1977, the first day of trial, the defendant had obtained 185 such permits.

The materials deposited at the site include polychlorinated biphenyls (PCBs), a neurotoxic, possibly carcinogenic chemical which it has been illegal to produce in this country since 1979. Due to the extensive use of PCBs in electrical equipment such as transformers, capacitors, and heat-transfer systems, and in hydraulic systems, any PCBs that were produced legally now have to be disposed of when they are no longer in use. PCBs have been stored at the site in liquid, solid and semi-solid form. Additionally, there are a number of now-empty drums which had once contained PCBs, which are also buried at the site. Other materials buried at the site in large quantities are solid cyanide, a substance known as C5, 6, paint sludge, asbestos, pesticides, mercury, and arsenic. Considerable evidence was adduced to show that these and other substances deposited at the site are extremely toxic to human beings. Some of the adverse reactions which could result from exposure to these materials are pulmonary diseases, cancer, brain damage, and birth defects.

The general geologic profile of the site shows a surface layer of about 10 feet of loess (wind-blown silt and clay material), under which lies 40 to 65 feet of glacial till. In the till material there is a thin sand layer of a few inches to approximately two feet. Some ground water has been found in the sand layer. All trenches dug at the site have between 10 to 15 feet of glacial till below them. The glacial till is reported to be very dense and is not very permeable. Thus liquids do not travel through it quickly.

Permeability studies conducted before the site opened by John Mathes, a professional engineer hired by the defendant, indicate permeability results ranging from 7.4×10^{-8} centimeters per second to 1.2×10^{-8} centimeters per second (cm/sec.). (The larger the negative exponent is, the less permeable the soil. E.g., a finding of 10^{-8} cm/sec. indicates that the soil is less permeable than would a reading of 10^{-4} cm/sec.) Dr. James Williams, an engineering geologist with the Missouri Geology and Land Survey, also made permeability findings on behalf of the defendant from samples taken from the site after it opened. Dr. Williams' results ranged from 7×10^{-6}cm/sec. to 1×10^{-7} cm/sec. Dr. Williams testified on cross-examination that the general permeability of the site is considered to be greater than 1×10^{-8} cm./sec. and that he would not expect the average permeability of the soil to be as low as that used for samples. In the interim between the opening of the site and the time of trial, the IEPA adopted a suggested permeability standard of 1×10^{-8} cm/sec. for hazardous-waste landfills.

Subsidence of the earth underneath the site is another contention raised by the plaintiffs to support their thesis that the site is unsafe and is therefore an enjoinable nuisance. Dr. Nolan Augenbaugh testified extensively at trial. Dr. Augenbaugh took pictures of the area from an airplane as well as at ground level. During his testimony, he pointed out where subsidence occurred in the pictures he had taken. Dr. Augenbaugh stated that he had observed subsidence in a wheat field on the Wilbur Sawyer farm on June 17, 1977. Dr. Augenbaugh also testified that a subsidence basin lies to the northeast of the disposal site. The pictures also indicate, according to Dr. Augenbaugh, fractures in the ground. One picture depicts a fault, which, Dr. Augenbaugh explained, is a "fracture where there's been differential movement of the two blocks. One block has been moved more than the other block." Sawyer, the farmer, told Dr. Augenbaugh the cracks had begun to appear approximately two months before, which would have been spring 1977. Several of these subsidences and fractures are located approximately one-half mile from the western boundary of the lower part of the disposal site. Dr. Augenbaugh testified that, in his opinion, subsidence can and will occur at the disposal site. Further, that ruptures in the earth would occur which, like an open pipe, would act as conduits for artesian water to reach the trenches, thereby contaminating the water.

Dr. Augenbaugh was recalled to testify on rebuttal. He testified that on March 22, 1978, he returned to the Sawyer farm. With the use of a backhoe, Dr. Augenbaugh had a trench dug across the subsidence cracks which he had observed earlier. When the digging was completed, there was a trench nine feet long and approximately three feet wide, with a maximum depth of a little over eight feet. Photographs were taken and slides prepared of the operation at the site. As the trench was being dug, water began to seep into the trench at a depth of approximately 4 to 4½ feet. Dr. Augenbaugh testified that the water flowed from subsidence fractures which were below the surface of the ground. Dr. Augenbaugh then poured some green dye into a surface fracture which was located approximately 10 feet away from the trench. The green dye entered the trench through two openings within 25 minutes.

Thomas O. Glover, a mining engineer and liaison officer with the United States Bureau of Mining, Department of the Interior, also testified regarding subsidence. Glover defined subsidence as the settling of the ground, due to the diminution of the underground support structure, and either the pillars pushing into the fine clay bottom below the coal system, or the roof fracturing immediately above the coal seam and continuing to the surface. He stated that subsidence normally can be expected to appear, on the average, 40 years after a mine has closed down. Glover never visited the instant disposal site, but he had examined the information relative to Superior Mine No. 4 and he had witnessed subsidences many times in the field over the course of 27 years as a mining engineer. Glover offered the opinion that there is a possibility of subsidence wherever coal is mined and underground support is removed.

Several of the defendant's expert witnesses, James Douglas Andrews, the designer of the site and a consulting engineer for the defendant, John A. Mathes, an engineer, Steven Hunt, a geologist with the Illinois State Geological Survey (ISGS), and Paul B. DuMontelle, an engineering geologist with ISGS and coordinator of environmental geology for the Survey, testified in summary that there would be subsidence at the site, but that it would not be deep, would close in a short time, and could be repaired by means of engineering techniques.

Another of plaintiffs' witnesses, Dr. Arthur Zahalsky, offered the opinion that an "explosive interaction," resulting in chemical explosions, fires, or emissions of poisonous gases, will occur at the site. Dr. Zahalsky is a professor of biochemistry and head of the laboratory of biochemical parasitology at Southern Illinois University at Edwardsville. He testified in essence that if sufficient oxygen could reach the buried chemicals, and he believed it could, then an explosive interaction of unknown date of occurrence, magnitude, and duration is likely. Moreover, Dr. Zahalsky testified that it is unknown what interactions might occur when the waste materials combine after the deterioration of the steel containers and paper bags.

The defendant challenged Dr. Zahalsky's opinion during cross-examination and requested him to diagram the precise chemical formula which would result in an explosive interaction. Dr. Zahalsky testified that a precise formula could not be diagrammed. He stated that the defendant's trench logs indicate that several of the chemical wastes have flash points less than 80 degrees Fahrenheit. Zahalsky reviewed the trench logs and gave examples of chemicals, such as paranitroaniline, which is a strong oxidizing agent and may be explosive, and also paint sludge, which has a flash point of less than 80 degrees Fahrenheit, which could result in a chemical fire. Dr. Zahalsky offered one scenario in which acidic chlorinated degreasers would interact with waste phenolics, releasing the phenolics so that the flash point would be achieved, thereby setting off the paint sludges which, in turn, would set off paint wastes, which would achieve the temperature sufficient for the ignition and combustion of liquid PCBs. All of these materials are deposited together in trench No. 3.

Finally, considerable testimony was adduced, much of it conflicting, as to dust, odors, and spills of chemical waste which have occurred in the village. Various residents testified that dust emanating from the site blew toward their houses. Also, odors which caused burning eyes, running noses, headaches, nausea, and shortness of breath were mentioned in testimony. The odors themselves were said to resemble, among other things, fertilizer, insecticide, and burning rubber. There was further testimony that the dust and odors interfered with the witnesses' ability to use their yards for gardening or other recreational uses. The defendant presented witnesses who denied that the disposal site was the source of any odors, and that the odors resulted from the local practices of openly burning refuse and dumping sewage into a nearby creek.

There was testimony that trucks carrying the waste materials to the disposal site via Wilson Avenue, the main street of the village, sometimes spilled toxic liquids onto the street. The evidence is undisputed, both from the defendant's receiving reports and testimony from IEPA inspectors, that many drums arrived on the site leaking waste materials....

The defendant has raised several issues on appeal: (1) whether the finding of the circuit and appellate courts that the waste-disposal site is a prospective nuisance is contrary to the manifest weight of the evidence; (2) whether those courts applied the wrong legal standard in finding that the waste-disposal site constitutes a prospective nuisance; (3) whether the circuit and appellate courts erred in failing to balance the equities, either in finding a prospective nuisance or in fashioning relief; (4) whether the courts erred in failing to defer to, or to otherwise weight, the role of the IEPA, the United States Environmental Protection Agency (USEPA), and the Illinois State Geological Survey (ISGS); (5) whether the courts erred in finding that plaintiffs have no adequate remedy at law; (6) whether the courts erred in ordering a mandatory injunction; and, finally, (7) whether the courts' decisions constituted a taking of property without due process of law.

We conclude that the evidence in this case sufficiently establishes by a preponderance of the evidence that the chemical-waste-disposal site is a nuisance both presently and prospectively....

The defendant points out three areas where, it argues, the trial court made erroneous findings of fact. The defendant refers to: (1) Dr. Arthur Zahalsky's opinion testimony concerning an explosive interaction and Dr. Stephen Hall's testimony which concurred in that opinion; (2) evidence concerning soil permeability; and, (3) infiltration of water into the trenches, and of migration out of the defendant's trenches of chemical waste either through the "bathtub effect" or subsidence.

We have reviewed the extensive record compiled in this case. While it is true that the defendant vigorously challenged the evidence concerning an explosive interaction, permeability, and infiltration and migration due to subsidence, the defendant has not overcome the natural and logical conclusions which could be drawn from the evidence. Findings of fact made by the trial court will not be set aside unless they are contrary to the manifest weight of the evidence....

The defendant [to refute the conclusions of Drs. Zahalsky and Hall] particularly relies upon the opinion of Dr. Raymond D. Harbison, a professor of pharmacology at Vanderbilt University, a toxicologist and consultant to the USEPA on toxic-waste handling. Dr. Harbison offered the opinion that the instant site is the most advanced scientific landfill in this country, and that the inventory system and the "absolute confinement" of the materials to the site render the interaction of the chemicals an impossibility.

At bottom, Dr. Harbison's opinion is premised upon his belief that the materials at the site will be sufficiently confined so that they will not pose a threat to the health or lives of the residents of the village. Dr. Harbison's opinions were discounted by the trial court, however, due to the substantial evidence which shows that the soil is more permeable than originally thought; that there is migration of water out of the trenches; and that there is subsidence in the area. Moreover, Dr. Harbison's opinion must be further discounted due to his erroneous statement that the waste materials will be sufficiently confined since "there is no ground water to be contaminated anyway below the particular site." Dr. Harbison later amended that statement to say there was no "usable water supply below the site" in terms of volume. This statement is also erroneous and also ignores evidence that the ground water would flow from beneath the site, thereby transporting any contamination into Cahokia Creek and could eventually flow into the Mississippi River. Thus we will not overturn the trial court's findings on this issue. They are amply supported by the manifest weight of the evidence.

The defendant next contends that the appellate and circuit courts misinterpreted the permeability tests admitted into evidence. It is argued that permeability coefficients are but one factor in determining the permeability of soil. We agree, but the fact remains that the defendant placed a good deal of emphasis on the tests conducted by John Mathes and Dr. Williams, which show that the soil at the site is more permeable than the IEPA suggested standard of 1×10^{-8} cm/sec. These courts also relied upon the testimony of Dr. Williams, defendant's witness, that the soil was probably even more permeable than indicated in the tests. Based on this evidence the trial court was correct in finding that the permeable nature of the soil, as demonstrated by the coefficients, as one of several factors, poses a threat of migration of chemical waste away from the disposal site. That finding will not be disturbed.

The defendant also contends that the trial court's finding that subsidence warrants closing of the site is erroneous. The defendant argues that, assuming arguendo that subsidence would occur at the site, it could be counteracted by engineering techniques. This issue becomes complicated by the fact that the IEPA adopted a regulation providing that Class I disposal sites (i.e., chemical-waste-disposal sites), must be secure without engineering. The USEPA, however, has recently adopted regulations to require all landfill sites to establish containment-engineering systems to detect and prevent migration of chemicals. (45 Fed. Reg. 33,239-42 (May 1980).) Moreover, the General Assembly has, since the inception of this suit, passed a statute prohibiting the placement of a hazardous-waste-disposal site above a shaft or tunneled mine.... The instant disposal site is above an inactive tunneled mine lying partly within the corporate limits of the village of Wilsonville. Without an express statutory provision stating an act is to have retroactive effect, it can only be applied prospectively. Thus, the defendant cannot be thought to be in violation of the foregoing provision. The fact remains, however, that the instant site, which is intended to be permanent, is located above an inactive tunneled mine.

Moreover, Dr. Nolan Augenbaugh testified at great length, supported by many photographs, of the considerable subsidence which has already occurred near the site. In Dr. Augenbaugh's opinion, subsidence will occur at the site itself. The defendant's experts testified that any subsidence would be negligible and shallow and would not present a threat to health or life. Dr. Augenbaugh refuted this testimony. He stated that subsidence would permit chemical-waste materials to seep into the ground water. In addition, Dr. Augenbaugh testified that subsidence would create a "bathtub effect" by permitting water to get into the trenches, eventually rise to the surface, overflow, and contaminate the ground around the site. We think the circuit court was fully justified in giving more weight to Dr. Augenbaugh's well-documented opinion than to the opinions of defendant's experts. We will not disturb that finding....

[A long discussion about the nature of Illinois nuisance law follows. Nuisance law is studied in Chapter 3.]

Moreover, the trial court did engage in a balancing process, as is made clear by the following excerpt from the trial court's memorandum opinion:

> It is the opinion of the Court that the state of the law is such that nuisance cannot be justified on the ground of necessity, pecuniary interest, convenience or economic advantage.

The Court understands as does counsel that there is a need for disposal of industrial hazardous wastes. However, where disposal of wastes creates a nuisance said disposal site may be closed through legal action.

Whether or not a business is useful or necessary or whether or not it contributes to the welfare and/or prosperity of the community are elements to be considered in a serious manner but said elements are not determinative as to whether or not the operation is a nuisance.

The importance of an industry to the wealth and prosperity of an area does not as a matter of law give to it rights superior to the primary or natural rights of citizens who live nearby. However, such matters may be considered and have been in this case....

The defendant's next contention is that the courts below were in error when they failed to require a showing of a substantial risk of certain and extreme future harm before enjoining operation of the defendant's site. We deem it necessary to explain that a prospective nuisance is a fit candidate for injunctive relief. Prosser states: "Both public and private nuisances require some substantial interference with the interest involved. Since nuisance is a common subject of equity jurisdiction, the damage against which an injunction is asked is often merely threatened or potential; but even in such cases, there must be at least a threat of a substantial invasion of the plaintiff's interests." (Prosser, Torts §87, at 577 (4th ed. 1971).) The defendant does not dispute this proposition; it does, however, argue that the trial court did not follow the proper standard for determining when a prospective nuisance may be enjoined. The defendant argues that the proper standard to be used is that an injunction is proper only if there is a "dangerous probability" that the threatened or potential injury will occur. (See Restatement (Second) of Torts §933(1), at 561, comment b (1979).) The defendant further argues that the appellate court looked only at the potential consequences of not enjoining the operation of the site as a nuisance and not at the likelihood of whether harm would occur. The defendant assigns error on this basis.

We agree with the defendant's statement of the law, but not with its urged application to the facts of this case....

In this case there can be no doubt but that it is highly probable that the chemical-waste-disposal site will bring about a substantial injury. Without again reviewing the extensive evidence adduced at trial, we think it is sufficiently clear that it is highly probable that the instant site will constitute a public nuisance if, through either an explosive interaction, migration, subsidence, or the "bathtub effect," the highly toxic chemical wastes deposited at the site escape and contaminate the air, water, or ground around the site. That such an event will occur was positively attested to by several expert witnesses. A court does not have to wait for it to happen before it can enjoin such a result. Additionally, the fact is that the condition of a nuisance is already present at the site due to the location of the site and the manner in which it has been operated. Thus, it is only the damage which is prospective. Under these circumstances, if a court can prevent any damage from occurring, it should do so....

The next issue we consider is whether the trial court erroneously granted a permanent injunction.... Defendant cites Harrison v. Indiana Auto Shredders Co., 528 F.2d 1107 (7th Cir. 1975), for the proposition that the court must balance the relative harm and benefit to the plaintiff and defendant before a court may enjoin a nuisance. (528 F.2d 1107, 1109)....

In *Harrison*, an auto shredder operated its business in a residential neighborhood in Indianapolis.... The court concluded in *Harrison* that since the defendant was not in violation of any relevant zoning standards, and since the shredder did not pose an imminent hazard to the public health, the defendant should not be prevented from continuing to operate. The court then ordered that the defendant be permitted a reasonable time to "launder its objectionable features."

This case is readily distinguishable for the reason that the gist of this case is that the defendant is engaged in an extremely hazardous undertaking at an unsuitable location, which seriously and imminently poses a threat to the public health. We are acutely aware that the service provided by the defendant is a valuable and necessary one. We also know that it is preferable to have chemical-waste-disposal sites than to have illegal dumping in rivers, streams, and deserted areas. But a site such as defendant's, if it is to do the job it is intended to do, must be located in a secure place, where it will pose no threat to health or life, now, or in the future. This site was intended to be a permanent disposal site for the deposit of extremely hazardous chemical-waste materials. Yet this site is located above an abandoned tunneled mine where subsidence is occurring several years ahead of when it was anticipated. Also, the permeability-coefficient samples taken by defendant's experts, though not conclusive alone, indicate that the soil is more permeable at the site than expected. Moreover, the spillage, odors, and dust caused by the presence of the disposal site indicate why it was inadvisable to locate the site so near the plaintiff village.

Therefore, we conclude that in fashioning relief in this case the trial court did balance relative hardship to be caused to the plaintiffs and defendant, and did fashion reasonable relief when it ordered the exhumation of all material from the site and the reclamation of the surrounding area. The instant site is akin to Mr. Justice Sutherland's observation that "Nuisance may be merely a right thing in a wrong place – like a pig in the parlor instead of the barnyard." Village of Euclid v. Ambler Realty Co., 272 U.S. 365, 388 (1926).

We are also cognizant of amicus USEPA's suggestion in its brief and affidavits filed with the appellate court which urge that we remand to the circuit court so that alternatives to closure of the site and exhumation of the waste materials may be considered. The USEPA states: "Heavy equipment may damage drums, releasing wastes and possibly causing gaseous emissions, fires, and explosions. Repackaging and transporting damaged drums also risks releasing wastes. Workers performing the exhumation face dangers from contact with or inhalation of wastes; these risks cannot be completely eliminated with protective clothing and breathing apparatus. Nearby residents may also be endangered." It is ironic that the host of horribles mentioned by the USEPA in support of keeping the site open includes some of the same hazards which the plaintiffs have raised as reasons in favor of closing the site....

Accordingly, for all the reasons stated, the judgments of the circuit and appellate courts are affirmed and the cause is remanded to the circuit court to enable it to retain jurisdiction to supervise the enforcement of its order. Affirmed and remanded.

RYAN, J., concurring:

While I agree with both the result reached by the majority and the reasoning employed supporting the opinion, I wish to add a brief comment.... Any injunction is, by its very nature, the product of a court's balancing of competing interests, with a result equitably obtained. Prosser, in discussing the law of nuisance...states:

> If the possibility [of harm] is merely uncertain or contingent [the plaintiff] may be left to his remedy after the nuisance has occurred. Prosser, Torts §90, at 603 (4th ed. 1971).

Prosser thus recognizes that there are cases in which the possibility of inflicting harm is slight and where the plaintiff may be left to his remedy at law. However, I believe that there are situations where the harm that is potential is so devastating that equity should afford relief even though the possibility of the harmful result occurring is uncertain or contingent. The Restatement's position applicable to preventative injunctive relief in general is that "the more serious the impending harm, the less justification there is for taking the chances that are involved in pronouncing the harm too remote." Restatement (Second) of Torts §933, at 561, comment b (1979). If the harm that may result is severe, a lesser possibility of it occurring should be required to support injunctive relief. Conversely, if the potential harm is less severe, a greater possibility that it will happen should be required. Also, in the balancing of competing interests, a court may find a situation where the potential harm is such that a plaintiff will be left to his remedy at law if the possibility of it occurring is slight. This balancing test allows the court to consider a wider range of factors and avoids the anomalous result possible under a more restrictive alternative where a person engaged in an ultrahazardous activity with potentially catastrophic results would be allowed to continue until he has driven an entire community to the brink of certain disaster. A court of equity need not wait so long to provide relief.

Although the "dangerous probability" test has certainly been met in this case, I would be willing to enjoin the activity on a showing of probability of occurrence substantially less than that which the facts presented to this court reveal, due to the extremely hazardous nature of the chemicals being dumped and the potentially catastrophic results.

COMMENTARY AND QUESTIONS

1. Avoiding a hostile forum. What, if anything, could SCA Services have done differently in defending the lawsuit? If this is a NIMBY problem, submitting to trial in Macoupin County Circuit Court leaves the defendant vulnerable to local bias. If diversity of citizenship were present, defendant could have removed the case to federal court, if that would help.

2. Expert testimony and appropriate outcomes. There are several technical factual issues dividing the plaintiffs and the defendants. Why were the plaintiffs' experts believed rather than the defendants'? Whose witnesses were better prepared to testify regarding the actual possibilities of release of materials from the Wilsonville site? It should be a matter for concern that poor trial preparation by defendants and their experts may have resulted in exhumation of dangerous wastes for shipment and disposal at another site, an outcome that may involve far greater health and safety risks than leaving the wastes in place and improving containment measures at the current site. Whose job is it to protect the larger public interest in having this case reach the "right" outcome?

Virtually all lawsuits involve parties on different sides of the case who are genuine adversaries with regard to the matters under dispute. In cases like *Wilsonville*, where there are complex scientific disputes, are there "neutral" parties to whom the courts can look for unbiased enlightenment? What of the regulatory agencies? How well did the United States Environmental Protection Agency and the Illinois Environmental Protection Agency (IEPA) acquit themselves in this case? What best explains their lackluster performance?

3. The relevance of general standards and regulatory approval. Of what relevance are the non-case specific actions of the regulatory community, such as a subsequently promulgated USEPA guideline that explicitly preferred high temperature incineration of PCB-contaminated materials to land-based disposal? Is that regulation a better guide to determining safety than IEPA's issuance of 185 disposal permits for the Wilsonville site? To what extent is it appropriate for the site operator to rely on licensure as a guarantee of a right to continue to operate the facility? This matter is considered more fully in Chapter 22.

4. Equity and rationality in the disposal of wastes. Of what relevance, if any, is the fact that the wastes in question were not locally generated? Do the local Wilsonville citizens have a valid claim that they are being forced to bear the costs of the disposal for remote producers like a Monsanto facility in St. Louis, whose wastes had been moved to Wilsonville from a prior site in Dittmer, Missouri? Conversely, isn't it preferable to site wastes in Wilsonville (a rural area) rather than in St. Louis (a population center)?

5. The zero-infinity problem. There is very little debate about the fact that the odors and the small in-town spills justify a grant of relief to plaintiffs under a nuisance theory. The *Wilsonville* case is interesting for its treatment of potential future harms. In essence, the plaintiffs are asking the court to intervene on their behalf and force the closure of a lawful business that has yet to harm them in any significant way. Are there general principles that should guide a court when that is the relief being sought? In this regard, the concurring opinion addresses what is sometimes called the zero-infinity problem. Justice Ryan contends that the court is justified in enjoining present action that holds even a tiny chance of catastrophic consequences. Do you agree that a two-factor calculus is appropriate – the court should consider both the gravity of the threatened harm and the likelihood of its occurrence? Is there a point at which the remoteness in time or likelihood of occurrence of the harm precludes a court from enjoining the conduct? A number of the selections that follow speak to the general topic of risk management in similar settings.

6. The array and adequacy of available remedies. Even absent an injunction, the defendant remains liable for remedying the harms when and if they do occur. That threat of liability provides incentives for the defendant to guard against allowing the event to occur. Are those incentives adequate protection for the potential victims of the event? Should the decision to enjoin be affected by the efficacy of post-accident remediation? Groundwater decontamination is expensive but feasible, especially if an improved monitoring system would detect leaks as soon as the immediate containment was breached.

7. The consequences. What is the net effect of the *Wilsonville* case on the availability of hazardous waste disposal sites? Under what circumstances would a prudent investor invest in a company that proposed to build such sites? As the cost of operating such facilities escalates, the cost to their customers rises. Will the cost of disposing of hazardous wastes eventually get too high and stifle important activities that generate hazardous wastes? Will increased disposal costs lead to "voluntary" waste minimization programs? Recalling the definition of law as mutual coercion, mutually agreed upon, under what circumstances would it be appropriate to *require* a locality to accept the presence of a hazardous waste facility?

Section 2. RISK DEFINITION AND RISK MANAGEMENT

Law can be viewed as a set of official strategies for discouraging socially injurious activities and encouraging socially beneficial ones. In order to define legal mechanisms that achieve social goals, the consequences of particular activities must be predicted with accuracy. The inadequacy of current scientific knowledge (scientific uncertainty) frequently inhibits determining with sufficient certainty whether a particular event will occur, and, even if it will occur, what and how severe its effects will be.

The legal system responds to scientific uncertainty in a variety of ways that have as a common denominator the need to make a decision in real cases as they are posed. Obviously, courts and lawyers can have no more certain basis for the evaluation of complex scientific problems than do the very scientists whose work establishes that the knowledge needed for accurate prediction of outcomes is lacking. While it might be more comforting to postpone making any legal decision until science advances, there is a very real sense in which the failure of the law to act is itself an action. Take, as an example, the lack of a proven method for the safe long-term disposal of spent fuel rods from nuclear power plants. Assume that an electric utility proposes to build a nuclear power plant. If that private decision is in any way open to legal review – in a licensure proceeding before an administrative agency, or in a lawsuit – and if the "costs" of spent fuel disposal are relevant, the legal system has no way to avoid making a decision. If the project goes forward, it is a decision to run the uncertain risks; if the project is halted, it is a decision to avoid the risks.

Recognizing that judges and juries lack expertise in matters of scientific uncertainty, courts generally avoid delving into the available scientific evidence in cases of scientific uncertainty. Instead, the legal system employs procedural devices and erects presumptions that allow courts to reach a decision without pretending to know the unknown. Two legal devices are most evident in this regard, allocation of burdens of proof and doctrines of judicial deference to administrative agencies. The common law traditionally places the burden of proof on plaintiffs attempting to prevent future injury or obtain compensation for past injury. Uncertainty is thus the ally of the defendant. In cases involving judicial review of decisions taken by an administrative agency, deferential review by the courts places the burden of uncertainty on those contesting the agency decision.

Adopting presumptions and doctrines of deference in cases of scientific uncertainty is a defensible judicial expedient. What those devices fail to do, however, is to plumb the difficult policy choices that cases of scientific uncertainty present. It is both harrowing and dangerous to confront the uncertainties of some forms of genetic engineering. Conversely, the failure to take advantage of that technology may, if matters take a quite different turn, deprive humankind of improved medicines, hardier plant stocks that can prevent famine in harsh climates, oil-eating microbes that can help reclaim soiled environments and other advances that improve the human condition without unacceptable ecological costs.

The materials that follow in this section are intended to do what the expedients of presumption and deference do not do – try to offer a basis for arriving at policy judgments in cases of scientific uncertainty. The materials first develop a vocabulary for addressing the issue, speaking of safety and risk, as well as uncertainty. Next, the materials concentrate on exploring strategies for risk management, examining contrasting perspectives on the desirability of encountering certain types of risks that are commonly associated with environmental concerns. The final section explores in some depth the tools of risk assessment in a particular area of great scientific uncertainty, the causation of cancer by exposure to hazardous materials. This analysis centers on excerpts from *Reserve Mining*, a famous case concerned with the assessment of cancer risks.

a. RISK AND SAFETY

"Risk" is often defined as a measure of (1) the probability that a particular act will cause damage to human health and the environment, and (2) the severity of any damage that may occur. "Safety" is a judgment of the acceptability of risk. Although no activity is risk-free, an act is considered to be safe if its risks are judged to be acceptable.[31]

P. Sandman, Risk Communication: Facing Public Outrage
EPA Journal 21–22, November 1987.

If you make a list of environmental risks in order of how many people they kill each year, then list them again in order of how alarming they are to the general public, the two lists will be very different. The first list will also be very debatable, of course; we don't really know how many deaths are attributable to, say, geological radon or toxic wastes. But we do know enough to be nearly certain that radon kills more Americans each year than all our Superfund sites combined. Yet...millions who choose not to test their homes for radon are deeply worried about toxic wastes.

31. See generally W. Lowrance, Of Acceptable Risk (1976).

The conclusion is inescapable: the risks that kill you are not necessarily the risks that anger and frighten you....

The core problem is one of definition. To the experts, risk means expected annual mortality. But to the public (and even to the experts when they go home at night), risk means much more than that. Let's redefine terms. Call the death rate (what the experts mean by risk) "hazard." Call all the other factors, collectively, "outrage." Risk, then, is the sum of hazard and outrage. The public pays too little attention to hazard; the experts pay absolutely no attention to outrage. Not surprisingly, they rank risks differently.

Risk perception scholars have identified more than 20 "outrage factors." Here are a few of the main ones:

- *Voluntariness*: A voluntary risk is much more acceptable to people than a coerced risk, because it generates no outrage. Consider the difference between getting pushed down a mountain on slippery sticks and deciding to go skiing.
- *Control*: Almost everybody feels safer driving than riding shotgun. When prevention and mitigation are in the individual's hands, the risk (though not the hazard) is much lower than when they are in the hands of a government agency.
- *Fairness*: People who must endure greater risks than their neighbors, without access to greater benefits, are naturally outraged – especially if the rationale for so burdening them looks more like politics than science. Greater outrage, of course, means greater risk.
- *Process*: Does the agency come across as trustworthy or dishonest, concerned or arrogant? Does it tell the community what's going on before the real decisions are made? Does it listen and respond to community concerns?
- *Morality*: American society has decided over the last two decades that pollution isn't just harmful – it's evil. But talking about cost-risk tradeoffs sounds very callous when the risk is morally relevant. Imagine a police chief insisting that an occasional child-molester is an "acceptable risk."
- *Familiarity*: Exotic, high-tech facilities provoke more outrage than familiar risks (your home, your car, your jar of peanut butter).
- *Memorability*: A memorable incident – Love Canal, Bhopal, Times Beach – makes the risk easier to imagine, and thus (as we have defined the term) more risky. A potent symbol – the 55-gallon drum – can do the same thing.
- *Dread*: Some illnesses are more dreaded than others; compare AIDS and cancer with, say, emphysema. The long latency of most cancers and the undetectability of most carcinogens add to the dread.
- *Diffusion in time and space*: Hazard A kills 50 anonymous people a year across the country. Hazard B has one chance in 10 of wiping out its neighborhood of 5,000 people sometime in the next decade. Risk assessment tells us the two have the same expected annual mortality: 50. "Outrage assessment" tells us A is probably acceptable and B is certainly not.

These "outrage factors" are *not* distortions in the public's perception of risk. They explain why people worry more about Superfund sites than geological radon, more about industrial emissions of dimethylmeatloaf than aflatoxin peanut butter.

There is a peculiar paradox here. Many risk experts resist the pressure to consider outrage in making risk management decisions; they insist that "the data" alone, not the "irrational" public, should determine policy. But we have *two decades of data* indicating that voluntariness, control, fairness, and the rest are important components of our society's definition of risk. When a risk manager continues to ignore these factors – and continues to be surprised by the public's response of outrage – it is worth asking whose behavior is irrational.

COMMENTARY AND QUESTIONS

1. The law and outrage. Should legal institutions take outrage into account? Is a court better equipped to do so than a politically responsible actor, such as a legislator or an executive branch administrative official? At least one way to read the *Wilsonville* case is as a demonstration of the chasm between the professional hazard evaluators and the public risk bearers. The professional evaluators, the administrative agencies, found no problem. The risk bearers, the citizens of Wilsonville, found a remedy in the judicial system.

2. How EPA considers risk in environmental protection. Risk assessment is a burgeoning field in the realm of environmental regulation. For a summary of the methods of analysis used by the United States Environmental Protection Agency in performing risk assessment, see C. Coperland & M. Simpson, Considering Risk in Environmental Protection, 8 Congressional Research Service Review (No. 10) at 7-9 (1987). That article describes the risk quantification procedure that the federal government uses to evaluate health risks of hazardous substances. The two-fold inquiry first identifies the hazard, usually relying on epidemiologic studies, animal bioassays, short-term bioassays and chemical structure-activity studies. The second prong of the inquiry attempts to look at the exposure side of the problem, considering the magnitude (frequency and intensity) of the exposure to the substance that will be suffered by the populace and then trying to make an assessment of the likely response of exposed individuals to the exposure.

b. RISK MANAGEMENT BY THE LEGAL SYSTEM

P. Huber, Safety and the Second Best: The Hazards of Public Risk Management in the Courts

85 Colum. L. Rev. 277, 277–81, 301–07, 329–37 (1985).

The recent and devastating chemical plant tragedy in Bhopal, India, will do little to reassure skeptics about the advantages of technological innovation and development. Those who already view the chemical, nuclear, pharmaceutical, and other high-tech industries with profound suspicion and fear can now point to the 2200 dead of Bhopal as martyrs to unbridled technological tyranny. And Bhopal will henceforth serve as the shrine of Nemesis for those who would defend the value of high technology.

But Bhopal is only one painfully vivid example in a much larger, longstanding legal debate in this country. The debate reflects a deep division among legal commentators regarding the role of mass production and technological change in the improvement of social welfare. Long before Bhopal, the standard diagnosis in many judicial opinions and in much of our scholarly legal literature has been that our society produces too much "public" risk, through its excessive or unwise use of dangerous new technology and the tools of mass production. The standard prescription has been for lawyers to do something about it. This Article argues that the diagnosis is probably wrong and that the prescription should certainly be rejected.

The legal debate about risks is very much a debate about "public" risks. These are threats to human health or safety that are centrally or mass-produced, broadly distributed, and largely outside the individual risk bearer's direct understanding and control. Public risks usually derive from new or especially complex technology – they are the hazards of large-scale electric power plants, air transport in jumbo jets, mass-produced vaccines, chemical additives and contaminants in food, or recombinant-DNA technology. For many lawyers, "advancements" such as these arouse deep suspicion and concern. "Private risks," by contrast, are discretely produced, localized, personally controlled, or of natural origin. They are the risks of cottage industries, wood stoves, transportation by car, or exposure to natural toxins or pathogens. Typically, private risks arouse little anxiety among legal commentators.

The legal system's almost obsessive preoccupation with public risks is, in my view, entirely misguided. I wish to develop this argument soberly; there can be no technological arrogance in the shadow of Bhopal. But the facts and the regulatory arguments seem plain nonetheless. First, public risks are progressive – they improve the overall state of our risk environment – whenever the incremental risk created is smaller than the quantum of existing privately-created risk that is displaced. The point may seem obvious, but the fact that a large number of judges and legal commentators ignore it suggests otherwise.

Second, the judicial system is, for a variety of reasons, incapable of engaging in the aggregative calculus of risk created and risk averted that progressive public-risk management requires. While it is not my goal to replace an absolutist's aversion to public risk with an absolutist's embrace of it, I will argue that the judicial role sought (and achieved) by many commentators is imprudently biased against many progressive, risk-reducing (though still risky) technologies. This bias significantly hinders our progress towards a healthier, safer environment.

My arguments grow out of a single paradox of the risk economy: greater private safety is often to be found in the greater acceptance of public risk....

THE ATTACK ON THE WINDMILL

How much public risk is too much? And who shall decide how much is too much? Most of the legal debate revolves around these two questions. For many legal scholars and judges, the answer to the first question is almost self-evident: we currently bear more public risk than we should, because we have been too ready to accept the hazards of new or mass-production technology. Answers to the second question tend to be longer and more varied, but most have the same general thrust: lawyers and judges are well positioned to assess the problem and supply the additional deterrence that is so plainly needed. It is this pair of answers (both of which are, in my view, quite wrong) that this Part describes....

EXCESS PUBLIC RISK

Life is already unacceptably hazardous, and likely to grow more so as the result of excessively rapid and overwhelming technological change. This is the common starting point in much of the legal commentary. How is the point to be proved? First, by referring to the public's aversion to public risks. Second, by reciting the myriad public terrors already in our midst. Third, by developing the microeconomic and philosophical underpinnings of a case against means of production that entail public hazards.

Lawyers opposed to public risks are in good company. The public consensus, if there is one, seems to be that risk-taking, like abortion, religion, travel, or marriage, should be a private affair. Indeed, consumer hostility to public risk is matched only by consumer affection for private risk. Illustrations of this division of preferences abound. The aerial spraying of malathion in a California program to combat the Mediterranean fruit fly provokes passionate opposition, but consumers eagerly spray tens of thousands of gallons of the same pesticide in their own, private gardens. A proposal to vent small amounts of radioactive gas and water from the damaged nuclear reactor at Three Mile Island in the course of cleaning up that facility – a comparatively minuscule investment in public risk with clear risk-reducing benefits – causes panic. But a proposal to ban saccharin – a proposal to curtail, as these things go, a fairly substantial investment in comparatively "private" patterns of risk taking – precipitates what was described in the New York Times as panic buying of the sweetener. Mass aircraft accidents arouse great concern, and the mandatory use of seat belts in planes is accepted without a murmur. But in the much more hazardous private-risk environment of automobile travel, seat belt interlock systems or mandatory seat belt laws encounter vociferous consumer opposition. Mandatory vaccination programs are vigorously attacked in the courts, but individuals also come to court to insist on their right to be treated with medical quackery of every description, apricot pits providing a recent and much-publicized example.

Panic, protest, and organized resistance thus greet almost every venture that entails new public risk. Meanwhile, efforts to restrain private risk-taking are denounced as grave attacks on personal freedom. Some litigants have seriously maintained – and some courts have agreed – that the Constitution itself enshrines both the right to bear a private risk and the right not to be exposed to a public one. In short, shared risks, like shared goods, are thought to be almost un-American – a collectivist affront to individual autonomy and self-reliance.

The layperson's aversion to public risks is shared by much of the legal community. Lawyers, for the most part, are convinced that there is too much public risk out there, and they generally begin their indictment of public risks by citing some that they especially dislike. Professor Yellin, for example, uses as his paradigm case the hazards of generating nuclear power, but he also points to chemical pesticides, air and water pollution, occupational hazards, and "complex environmental decisions" of every description – the "ominous, not yet fully understood risks to public health [that] involve decisions that may seriously alter our physical environment." Professor Rosenberg's concern centers on similar targets: the risks accompanying "the production, distribution, marketing, consumption, and disposal of toxic agents." He lists as examples "asbestos, Agent Orange and Agent White, Three-Mile Island, dioxin, and a string of acronyms – DES, PCB, PBB and IUD," drugs, and aircraft disasters. Numerous other commentators have similar lists of concerns, and all supply citations to cases in which judges and juries have echoed these fears.

It is easy enough to clothe a visceral aversion to public risk in the robes of market efficiency or social justice. So easy, in fact, that the exercise has become quite reflexive and mechanical in much of the legal literature.

To the lawyer qua economist, risk is a cost – the cost of confining, disposing of, or simply coexisting with hazardous matter or energy. The cost can, of course, vary enormously, depending on how wisely a particular hazard is managed. It is nevertheless ascertainable. As with all other costs, the lawyer-economist will contend, the creator of a risk must shoulder it if markets are to operate "efficiently." A producer of risk who is not held strictly accountable for the unconsented-to consequences of that risk will generate risk in socially undesirable amounts. The result will be a market failure. Or so the story goes.

The lawyer qua philosopher may reach similar conclusions about public risks on somewhat different grounds. Our libertarian, individualistic, political ideal forbids one person from imposing unconsented-to burdens on another. Burdens that take the form of external threats to health or safety are especially objectionable intrusions on the risk bearer's private space and personal autonomy. Like the lawyer-economist, the lawyer-philosopher is therefore opposed to external risk. The mass producer of a dangerous good, or the operator of a hazardous power plant, acts antisocially. Her conduct is worse than economically inefficient – it is morally wrong. Or so the story goes.

Arguments along these lines are wheeled out, with pedestrian regularity, by those opposed to everything from nuclear power to synthetic sweeteners. Absent the risk bearer's individual, fully informed, and entirely free consent, any activity that creates public risk is, pro tanto, both a threat to market efficiency and an infringement on the just entitlements of the risk bearer. Public risks are an absolute bad. We want as few of them as possible.

THE JUDICIAL ROLE

Though there is somewhat less unanimity about precisely why it is that a nation with a large and powerful government, fifty autonomous state governments, and 650,000 lawyers, has apparently allowed public-risk technology to run so wild, the consensus is that the existing, agency-centered system of risk regulation inadequately deters the production of public risk. Help from the legal community is therefore in order. It may come before the accident, or after it, but in either event its thrust should be to discourage new dangerous technologies and the instrumentalities of mass-produced risks. Professor Yellin's and Professor Rosenberg's proposals typify the two larger schools of thought.

Professor Yellin urges the courts to improve preaccident decision-making. He advocates closer judicial scrutiny of "broad new regulatory departures." When an agency approves a novel technological venture that entails new public risk, the courts, suitably advised by "a committee of scientists, engineers, and lawyers to act as standing masters," should supply a "second" (read "final") opinion.

Professor Rosenberg, for his part, suggests a greater degree of judicial intervention after the public risk has been approved and is in place. The courts, again advised by "court-appointed experts, special masters, and blue-ribbon juries," should impose tort liability on public risk creators sooner, more often, and in larger amount. To this end, the cost of risk itself, rather than consummated injury, is to be made compensable – when, and only when, it is a "public" or "mass exposure" risk. Questions of legal causation are to be resolved under a relaxed "proportionality" rule, that will hold risk creators liable for the proportion of total injuries attributable to their activities, even when no single plaintiff can accurately claim that her injury was, more likely than not, caused by the defendant's conduct.

The Yellin and Rosenberg prescriptions are complementary in their intended effect on activities that create public risks. More before-the-accident review and stricter after-the-accident liability are mutually reinforcing responses to the same perceived problem – the excess creation of public risks. At first blush, it is hard to think of any reason not to applaud. Indeed, many do, by citation to or by development of Yellin's and Rosenberg's proposals.

[Major portions of the article are omitted here, including a segment in which Huber presents a case study of how vaccine development and use has been greatly over-deterred by the cost of paying damage awards to injured victims of the vaccine. Also omitted is a segment that argues against treating damage awards against public risk producers as desirable cost internalization. To internalize those costs, Huber argues, in the absence of imposing corresponding costs against natural risk producers, such as disease, leads to a distortion of risk consumption. He invokes the theory of second best in favor of non-internalization of public risks stating, "patchy, erratic risk internalization may impose greater costs on the safer substitutes within particular markets, and so may encourage a shift in consumption to the more hazardous." Huber claims that the morality of public risks also must be judged with reference to the private risks they retire, not merely on the basis of harms they may inflict. To prove that changes in lifestyle associated with public risk creating behaviors have made life safer in the aggregate, Huber invokes evidence of decreasing mortality and increases in life expectancy in the last several centuries. He then argues more narrowly that the degree of capitalization and expertise surrounding most public risk ventures are likely to make them more safe than the private risk counterparts that they displace.]

On close, objective examination one almost invariably discovers that public risk alternatives provide goods and services with less risk (per unit of good) than the private-supply substitutes. The reasons are not difficult to discover. Large, centralized, capital-intensive production facilities are easier to operate safely than their small, distributed, labor-intensive alternatives. The very characteristics of mass production and distribution that make public risks possible in the first place also make mass production inherently safer than the private-production alternative. The central- or mass-producers can and do deliver goods and services with much less attendant risk than distributed- or discrete-producers (including Nature) possibly could....

THE JUDICIAL ROLE IN MANAGING PUBLIC RISKS

The second large question in the public risk debate follows naturally from the first; who should decide how much public risk is enough? Since some measure of public risk is not only inevitable but desirable, some institution must be directed to define the measure and specify its ingredients....

Public control of public risks is therefore necessary, both to prevent the excess generation of public risk and to make possible the acceptance of as much public risk as is socially desirable. The government regulator, a single, central decision-maker, acts as the consumers' collective "broker" in a particular risk market. The regulator – whoever it may be – must perform at least two tasks. One, of course, is to reject unfavorable investments in public risk. The regulator has the resources to proceed against creators of unacceptable public risks. Here we have the more familiar regulator, government, saying "no," placing limits on the risks individuals may create.

But the regulator's second function is to acquiesce in risk creation. To represent his principal effectively, a broker in a risk market, like a broker in any other setting, must be able to buy as well as to sell. A centralized risk-regulatory system must not only reject bad public risk choices but also supply the public's consent to good ones. This is most clearly illustrated in comprehensively regulated industries such as those producing electric power, drugs, pesticides, and many other products of modern technology. In these areas, risk creators start with no freedom to do anything at all until they receive express regulatory permission. The nay-saying regulatory role then effectively disappears; the regulator's task is to serve as a retail deregulator, giving case-by-case consent to new ventures that entail public risks.

The administrative agencies are, of course, the more familiar regulators, wielding authority over public risks of every variety. But the courts are also vigorous regulators, and it is their role that most concerns me here. The courts are pivotal actors in the prospective approval of new technological ventures. They possess considerable authority to review agency approvals of new sources of risk, whether the risk involves a new vaccine, power plant, pesticide, or food additive. And in areas not subject to comprehensive administrative regulation the courts can use injunctions to act as first-tier gatekeepers of the risk environment. The courts are also heavily engaged in the retrospective regulation of public risks. Damage actions sounding in nuisance, negligence, strict liability, and absolute liability are powerful instruments of regulation. Indeed, the legal community invented the "emission fee" for dealing with hazards such as pollution long before the economists had much to say about it. Every risk creator and every risk bearer knows that the damage action, and most particularly an action seeking punitive damages, is potent medicine for regulating public risks.

[Huber's specific attacks on the judicial system as regulator are omitted.]

PRIVATE INJURY AND PUBLIC SAFETY: THE COURTS AND THE AGENCIES

My discussion in the previous Part brings me to two conclusions. First, governmental control of public risks is both necessary and useful. Many public risks should be excluded if they are not yet a part of our environment, or controlled if they already are. Government regulation, moreover, is also needed to fulfill the second half of the regulatory function – to supply our collective consent to public risks that are judged to be good risk investments. Second, the courts are institutionally predisposed to favor regressive public risk choices. The courts systematically prefer old risks to new ones and discretely produced or natural hazards to mass-produced substitutes, and have neither the inclination nor the expertise to distinguish sources of truly "excess" risk from their risky yet risk-reducing counterparts.

Who then should decide how much public risk we will accept and in what areas? The answer is painfully obvious to almost everyone outside the legal community: expert administrative agencies, not lawyers. To make life safer, faster, we need not more scientists in the legal process, but fewer lawyers in the scientific one. The legal system has no special competence to assess and compare public risks, and the legal process is not designed or equipped to conduct the broad-ranging, aggregative inquiries on which sensible public-risk choices are built. Expert administrative agencies, troubled and erratic though they may be, remain best able to regulate public risks in a manner calculated to advance the public health and welfare....

COMMENTARY AND QUESTIONS

1. Other voices in the debate. Particularly at the outset, Huber is responding to the work of commentators who have taken the other side of the debate, that is, others who have argued that public risk is being over-produced. Two articles in particular provoked Huber's attacks: Yellin, High Technology and the Courts: Nuclear Power and the Need for Institutional Reform, 94 Harv. L. Rev. 489 (1981) and Rosenberg,

The Causal Connection in Mass Exposure Cases: A Public Law Vision of the Tort System, 97 Harv. L. Rev. 851 (1984).

2. Accounting for the benefits of risk reduction. Polemics and specifics aside, as a matter of societal cost accounting, isn't one of Huber's central points – that the widely dispersed, small magnitude benefits of activities that pose public risks are often undervalued – quite similar to arguments made by environmentalists that many widely dispersed, small magnitude ecosystem costs are undervalued?

3. Giving credit for external benefits. Is it clear that the production of external benefits, such as the reduced private risk of disease in the wake of a mass vaccination program, justifies freeing public risk producers from damages for those harms palpably caused by them? Is a more just solution available by finding a way to internalize those benefits?

4. Nuclear power as a risk-reducing technology. Accept for a moment Huber's challenge to put aside preconceptions about the dangers of nuclear power. How might Huber champion nuclear power in preference to fossil fuel generation of electricity? Nuclear power reduces the risk of ecosystem harms due to the emission of sulfur oxides from coal-fired power plants, a major cause of acid rain. Likewise, nuclear energy use reduces the risk of massive ecological harms that would accompany the global warming threatened by the production of greenhouse gases. Are courts in a position to measure the trade-offs? Huber, in his mocking comparison of wood stoves to nuclear power plants, conveniently omits elaborate discussion about the back end of the nuclear fuel cycle, the extreme difficulties of nuclear waste disposal, but even putting all the factors on the table, is it certain that nuclear is a bad choice? Is the problem that Huber should address (but doesn't) the problem of risk assessment in high uncertainty situations? How do you think Huber would analyze a technology that provided many calculable benefits but also posed an ever-so-slight chance of destroying most of the world?

5. Rethinking institutional competence. The excerpt omits the bulk of Huber's institutional competence critique in which he finds fault with courts making decisions that seek to minimize the sum of private and public risk. After study of the materials in the next two chapters concerned with judicial resolution of environmental cases, and toxic tort issues in particular, try to construct an evaluation of the strengths and weaknesses of courts as makers of risk policy.

6. Attacking Huber's assessment of institutional competence. Huber's frequently sarcastic tone invites equally sarcastic responses. A more probing line of responding to Huber raises doubts about whether, as Huber claims, (1) courts over-deter investment in public risk and (2) reliance on administrative agencies is more likely to achieve acceptance of the optimal amount of public risk. The most direct effort at meeting Huber's arguments in that way is made by Professors C. Gillette and J. Krier in their article, Risk, Courts, and Agencies, 138 U. Pa. L. Rev. 1027 (1990). Gillette and Krier identify a method for deciding whether courts are too generous or too stingy to plaintiffs who challenge activities involving public risks. There are two lines of inquiry, one into process bias and one into access bias. They say:

> Process bias arises from the interplay of legal doctrine and adjudicative decision-makers. It concerns the ways in which judges and juries interpret and apply the law that defines the rights and liabilities of the parties before them. Access bias, on the other hand, arises from the interplay of legal doctrine, the structure of litigation, and the nature of public risk. It concerns the ways in which victims decide whether (given prevailing doctrine, among other things) litigation is worthwhile, and the ability of victims to initiate claims. Access is anterior to process; only when obstacles to access are overcome, so that claims are actually filed and prosecuted, can process bias come into play.

They then focus on the failings of professional risk assessment (i.e., hazard alone) to account for the multi-dimensional character of the layperson's perception of risk.

> Whatever its motivations, the experts' approach to risk is obviously not senseless. Yet neither is the public's approach. This is why we said in the introduction to this section that the problem comes down to one of competing rationalities. Admit this, and it unarguably follows that the choice of approach is an ethical and political one that technical experts have neither the knowledge nor the authority to dictate, because the issue transcends technocratic expertise. Were we to defer to agencies simply on the basis of their technical proficiency, the ethical-political question would be begged entirely. Agencies could be expected to resort to methods the use of which denies the very values at stake (it is, after all, the claim of methodological proficiency that grounds the argument for deference in the first place). And, to return to the idea with which we began this section, methodological proclivities would bias agency risk processing in the direction of too much public risk – as viewed from the public's perspective.

Gillette and Krier also conclude that access bias unduly restricts the number of public risk cases heard by the courts, and that access bias also skews the administrative process in favor of over-acceptance of public risks.

7. Body counting. Is "body counting" (limiting risk assessment to an objective assessment of hazard) as barren an enterprise as it is made out to be? It does provide one measure of the comparative impacts of alternative courses of action. Can that much be admitted without weakening the force of the argument that other factors ought to control social decisions? Is body counting a misleadingly certain measure in cases where there is great uncertainty about outcomes?

8. Managing risk strategically. Should risk management be proactive or reactive? Talbot Page distinguishes between situations of "environmental risk" and "classical pollution." Environmental risk situations are characterized by factors such as ignorance of mechanism, modest benefits when balanced against potentially catastrophic social costs, low probability of occurrence, latency, collective risk, and irreversibility. One frequently encounters the zero-infinity problem in cases of environmental risk. For Page, when dealing with environmental risk situations, decision-makers should "minimize false negatives" (i.e., minimize treating a dangerous situation as if it were benign). In other words, in the case of environmental risk, "When in doubt, regulate!" With classical pollutants, on the other hand, we can continue to minimize false positives (i.e., minimize treating a benign situation as if it were dangerous). Page believes that the common law and criminal law have traditionally minimized false positives. At another point in his article, Page recommends a balancing test for managing environmental risk, comparing "the cost of a false negative weighted by its probability with the cost of a false positive weighted by its probability, and choosing the alternative with the lower weighted cost." See Page, A Generic View of Toxic Chemicals and Similar Risks, 7 Ecol. L. Q. 207 (1978). Would Peter Huber agree with Page?

Section 3. THE SPECIAL CASE OF CANCER RISK AND CAUSATION

It should come as little surprise that regulation of cancer risks is an area of special concern in modern environmental law. There is a wealth of scientific evidence that correlates exposure to a wide variety of hazardous materials with cancer in humans and other species. Moreover, as many of the preceding materials have pointed out, the public is significantly risk averse to the sorts of cancer risks that are generated by exposure to hazardous materials that have been released into the environment as pollution or discarded waste.

The use of laws to regulate cancer-causing materials and to provide remedies to those who have been injured by its release requires an unusual effort to marry scientific evidence and legal doctrine. The crux of the problem lies in the limited scientific proof presently available linking exposure to a hazardous material with the subsequent onset of cancer. The precise etiology of diseases is often unknown and will vary depending on the carcinogen and the type of cancer involved. Presumably, sufficient exposure to a carcinogen precipitates a change in genetic or cellular structure. Over time, perhaps a very long time, the change is replicated and eventually alters the functional qualities of cells involved, causing them to multiply or attack other cells. The law has always functioned best with better-understood paths of causation, as when the smoke and particulate pollution from a neighboring factory cause immediate, observable physical and health damage to nearby neighbors.

Scientific inquiry into the linkage between exposure to suspected carcinogens and the subsequent onset of disease employs several quantitative techniques that estimate the magnitude of carcinogenic risks. In Leape, Quantitative Risk Assessment in the Regulation of Environmental Carcinogens, 4 Harv. Envtl. L. Rev. 86 (1980), the rudiments of how science approaches these problems is laid out in a straight forward fashion. Data on the carcinogenicity of a particular substance is usually developed in one of three ways – epidemiological studies, animal bioassay studies, or single cell tests. Data on exposure is even more difficult to develop because it involves generating a catalogue of sources of a particular carcinogen and a modelling of pathways by which that substance reaches humans. Only then can a guess about actual doses be made.

The uncertainty involved in estimating the potency of carcinogens and the degree of exposure to them is not the only lack of precision in assessing the risks of exposure to potential carcinogens. To translate those figures into a population-wide risk assessment is even more daunting. This latter step generally involves two sorts of extrapolation. First, the risk assessor must extrapolate from observed effects on subgroups of the population to the population as a whole. If a subgroup is, for some undisclosed reason, particularly susceptible or particularly resistant to contracting cancer, the extrapolation magnifies the degree of inaccuracy of the underlying data. Second, because most data is derived from high exposure settings, the risk assessor must attempt to predict the degree to which lower doses result in lowered cancer rates. Here the question of "threshold" doses becomes acute; that is, the risk assessor must decide if there is some level of exposure for which it will be assumed that there is literally a zero risk of contracting cancer. Given the relatively large numbers of persons who may be exposed to low-level doses, the threshold safe level question holds the potential to influence profoundly the risk assessment.

COMMENTARY AND QUESTIONS

1. The anthropocentric nature of risk assessment. Cancer risk assessment usually includes only human health effects. Should risk assessment also consider ecosystem effects? Are ecosystem effects more, less, or as important as human health effects? Assuming that an accounting for ecosystem effects is appropriate, do some environmental losses count more than others? Are, for example, unusual or endangered ecosystems more important than relatively common ones?

2. Outrage and cancer risk. Why does quantitative cancer risk assessment, as described in the text above, systematically ignore "outrage" factors? Presumably, their absence is not indicative of their insubstantiality; rather, it should be taken as a sign that outrage is more in the nature of a qualitative factor. How are quantitative and qualitative factors to be compared?

3. The fallacy of numeration. Is quantitative risk assessment viable, in light of the profound scientific uncertainties inherent in predicting carcinogenicity? Leape asserts that in many cases the uncertainties so confound the quantification process that it is even impossible to measure the extent of potential error reliably. Does expressing such crude estimates in numerical form create a "fallacy of numeration" by which risk assessments are given undue credibility because they seem to be so precise?

4. How safe is safe enough in dealing with cancer risks? Once risk is quantified insofar as is possible, the regulatory concern switches to the judgmental process of deciding what level of risk is little enough so that the risk should be encountered. Investigators have found that federal agencies are relatively consistent in defining "acceptable risk." More often than not, if a substance is expected to increase the number of cancer cases by more than four in 1000 over a lifetime of exposure, federal agencies decide to regulate that substance to reduce the risk below that level. If a substance is expected to increase the number of cases by less than one in a million, the chemical is rarely regulated. Between these extremes, federal decision-makers conduct cost-effectiveness analyses, which weight the cost of the regulation against the number of lives that regulation is likely to save. If the cost falls below $2 million per life saved, the substance is regulated. Travis, Richter, Crouch, Wilson, & Klema, Cancer Risk Management, 21 Envtl. Sci. Tech. 15 (1987).

What justifies the choice of these levels for regulatory action and forbearance? Is it moral to weigh human lives against dollars? Should the risks of a particular substance be counterbalanced by its benefits to society? Should zero risk levels be set for carcinogens with no known safe levels of threshold exposure? Given the uncertainties involved in quantifying acceptable risk, should an "ample margin of safety" be factored in to compensate for uncertainty? Should the relevant population consist of the general public? The most sensitive persons? The most exposed persons? See, Marchant and Danzeisen, Acceptable Risk For Hazardous Air Pollutants, 13 Harv. Envtl. L. Rev. 535 (1989).

In the view of Professor Harold Green, Congress is "the primary authority guiding the risk-management decisions of the courts and regulatory agencies," and Congress defines acceptable risk in "more a political than a scientific, or even a rational" way. "Although scientific analysis and quantification may have some input into legislative considerations of risk reduction strategies, the final statute will usually be influenced more heavily by subjective and political factors than by objective, scientific ones." The Role of Congress in Risk Management, 16 ELR 10220 (1983). Should Congress be more scientific, or is this inconsistent with the nature of the political process? Should Congress establish broad public policy and allow expert administrative agencies to set the actual numbers, or would this approach result in Congress abdicating its legislative responsibilities in favor of agencies?

5. Turning quantitative risk into legal causation. As has long been understood, moving from quantitative risk assessment data to a claim of causation that will satisfy judicial decision-makers, requires a step beyond that act of quantification. In discussing the linkage of cigarette smoking to cancer, for example, a 1964 report of the Surgeon General's Advisory Committee stated:

> Statistical methods cannot establish proof of a causal relationship in an association. The causal significance of an association is a matter of judgment which goes beyond any statement of statistical probability. To judge or evaluate the causal significance of the association between the attribute or agent and the disease, or effect upon health, a number of criteria must be utilized, no one of which is an all-sufficient basis for judgment. These criteria include: (a) the consistency of the association; (b) the strength of the association; (c) the specificity of the association; (d) the temporal relationship of the association; and (e) the coherence of the association.[32]

Proof of causation in cases seeking recoveries for damages caused by exposure to toxic carcinogens is explored further in Chapter 4. The following case illustrates, in a judicial setting, many of the issues involved in assessing and managing cancer risks.

---

32. See U.S. Surgeon General's Advisory Committee on Smoking and Health, Smoking and Health 20 (1964).

Reserve Mining v. United States Environmental Protection Agency[33]
United States Court of Appeals, Eighth Circuit, 1975.
514 F.2d 492.

BRIGHT, C.J. The United States, the States of Michigan, Wisconsin, and Minnesota, and several environmental groups seek an injunction ordering Reserve Mining Company to cease discharging wastes from its iron ore processing plant in Silver Bay, Minnesota, into the ambient air of Silver Bay and the waters of Lake Superior.... The district court granted the requested relief and ordered that the discharges immediately cease, thus effectively closing the plant....

In 1947, Reserve Mining Company (Reserve), then contemplating a venture in which it would mine low-grade iron ore ("taconite") present in Minnesota's Mesabi Iron Range and process the ore into iron-rich pellets at facilities bordering on Lake Superior, received a permit from the State of Minnesota to discharge the wastes (called "tailings") from its processing operations into the lake.

Reserve commenced the processing of taconite ore in Silver Bay, Minnesota, in 1955 and that operation continues today. Taconite mined near Babbitt, Minnesota, is shipped by rail some 47 miles to the Silver Bay "beneficiating" plant where it is concentrated into pellets containing some 65 percent iron ore. The process involves crushing the taconite into fine granules, separating out the metallic iron with huge magnets, and flushing the residual tailings into Lake Superior. The tailings enter the lake as a slurry of approximately 1.5 percent solids. The slurry acts as a heavy density current bearing the bulk of the suspended particles to the lake bottom. In this manner, approximately 67,000 tons of tailings are discharged daily.

The states and the United States commenced efforts to procure abatement of these discharges as early as mid-1969. These efforts, however, produced only an unsuccessful series of administrative conferences and unsuccessful state court proceedings....

Until June 8, 1973, the case was essentially a water pollution abatement case, but on that date the focus of the controversy shifted to the public health impact of the tailings discharge and Reserve's emissions into the ambient air. Arguing the health issue in the district court, plaintiffs maintained that the taconite ore mined by Reserve contained an asbestiform variety of the amphibole mineral

33. An entire legal process course could be taught out of the *Reserve Mining* case, which involved federal and state statutory and common law; federal, state, and private plaintiffs against corporate defendants and their labor and municipal supporters; carcinogenic pollutants and the esthetics of a pristine Great Lake; air and water pollution; convoluted industrial economics and much chemistry and technology; nine trips to the federal district court (one hearing lasting nine months), two to the state courts, four to the Eighth Circuit, one to the Supreme Court in an unsuccessful petition to revoke a stay; injunctions, stays, modified injunctions, mandamus orders (also stayed, and reinstated); an elaborate permit and standard-setting administrative system; counterclaims by industry for tort damages owing to "negligently issued permits"; a federal statute which, after 60 years of dormancy, suddenly imposed new prohibitions through a twist of statutory interpretation; plus an appellate order forcing the district judge to recuse himself for bias formed in the course of trial. Reserve Mining Co. v. Minnesota Pollution Control Agency, 434 F. Supp. 1191 (D. Minn. 1976); United States v. Reserve Mining Co., 417 F. Supp. 791 (D. Minn. 1976); 417 F. Supp. 789 (D. Minn.), aff'd, 543 F.2d 1210 (8th Cir. 1976); 412 F. Supp. 705 (D. Minn. 1976); 408 F. Supp. 1212 (D. Minn. 1976); 394 F. Supp. 233 (D. Minn. 1974), modified sub nom. Reserve Mining Co. v. EPA, 514 F.2d 492 (8th Cir. 1975), modified en banc sub nom. Reserve Mining Co. v. Lord, 529 F.2d 181 (8th Cir. 1976) (recusal order); 380 F. Supp. 11 (D. Minn.), stayed, 498 F.2d 1073 (8th Cir.), motion to vacate stay denied, 418 U.S. 911, motion to vacate or modify stay denied, 419 U.S. 802 (1974) (Douglas, J., dissenting). See also Reserve Mining Co. v. Herbst, 256 N.W.2d 808 (Minn. 1977); Reserve Mining Co. v. Minnesota Pollution Control Agency, 294 Minn. 300, 200 N.W.2d 142 (1972); see N.Y. Times, Apr. 25, 1982, at 31, col.1.

cummingtonite-grunerite, and that the processing of the ore resulted in the discharge into the air and water of mineral fibers substantially identical and in some instances identical to amosite asbestos. This contention raised an immediate health issue, since inhalation of asbestos at occupational levels of exposure is associated with an increased incidence of various forms of cancer.... In an effort to assess the health hazard, the parties presented extensive expert scientific and medical testimony, and the court itself appointed certain expert witnesses, who assumed the task of assisting the court in the evaluation of scientific testimony and supervising court-sponsored studies to measure the levels of asbestos fibers in the air near Silver Bay, in Lake Superior water, and in the tissues of deceased Duluth residents....

The trial court based its closure decision on two independent determinations. First...the court had concluded that the discharges "substantially endanger" the exposed populations. Second, the court had concluded that, although a method of abatement providing for an alternate means of disposal of wastes [land disposal] with some turn-around time represented a desirable middle course in this litigation, Reserve had demonstrated such intransigence on the issue of abating its water discharge as to render any such middle course impossible....

HEALTH ISSUES...THE DISCHARGE INTO AIR

Much of the scientific knowledge regarding asbestos disease pathology derives from epidemiological studies of asbestos workers occupationally exposed to and inhaling high levels of asbestos dust. Studies of workers naturally exposed to asbestos dust have shown "excess" cancer deaths and a significant incidence of asbestosis. [Asbestosis, a respiratory disease, is a diffuse scarring of the lung resulting from the inhalation of asbestos dust.] The principal excess cancers are cancer of the lung, the pleura (mesothelioma) and gastrointestinal tract ("GI" cancer)....

Several principles of asbestos-related disease pathology emerge from these occupational studies. One principal relates to the so-called 20-year rule, meaning that there is a latent period of cancer development of at least 20 years. Another basic principle is the importance of initial exposure, demonstrated by significant increases in the incidence of cancer even among asbestos manufacturing workers employed for less than three months (although the incidence of disease does increase upon longer exposure). Finally, these studies indicate that threshold values and dose response relationships, although probably operative with respect to asbestos-induced cancer, are not quantifiable on the basis of existing data.

Additionally, some studies implicate asbestos as a possible pathogenic agent in circumstances of exposure less severe than occupational levels....

At issue in the present case is the similarity of the circumstances of Reserve's discharge into the air to those circumstances known to result in asbestos-related disease. This inquiry may be divided into two stages: first, circumstances relating to the nature of the discharge and, second, circumstances relating to the level of the discharge (and resulting level of exposure).

The comparability of the nature of Reserve's discharge to the nature of the discharge in known disease situations raises two principal questions. The first is whether the discharged fibers are identical or substantially identical to fibers known to cause disease; the second is whether the length of the fibers discharged is a relevant factor in assessing pathogenic effects. The district court found that

Reserve's discharge includes known pathogenic fibers and that a lower risk to health could not be assigned to this discharge for reasons of fiber length....

The trial court heard extensive evidence as to the chemistry, crystallography, and morphology of the cummingtonite-grunerite present in the mined ore. This evidence demonstrated that, at the level of the individual fiber, a portion of Reserve's cummingtonite-grunerite cannot be meaningfully distinguished from amosite asbestos....

The second question, that of fiber length, reflects a current dispute among scientists as to whether "short" fibers (i.e., fibers less than five microns in length) have any pathogenic effect. Most of the fibers detected in Reserve's discharges may be termed "short." The evidence adduced at trial included conflicting scientific studies and diverse opinions on this question. Several Reserve witnesses testified concerning animal studies which seem to demonstrate that short fibers are non-tumorogenic. Plaintiffs offered opposing evidence based on contrary studies. Dr. Brown [a court-appointed expert] noted his general criticism of the studies on fiber size, stating that the researchers typically did not use electron microscopy to properly "size" the fibers, and thus it cannot be said that the animals are in fact being exposed to only short or only long fibers.

Presented with this conflicting and uncertain evidence from animal experimentation, and the fact that there are no human epidemiological studies bearing on the issue, the district court concluded that short fibers could not be assigned a lower relative risk than long fibers. [The standard set by the Secretary of Labor for permissible occupational exposure to asbestos is drawn in terms of fibers in excess of five microns in length. A dispute surfaced at trial over whether this standard should be read as endorsing the safety of fibers less than five microns. The district court ruled in the negative, and this conclusion was accepted by the appellate court.]....

The experts indicated that the counting of fibers represents a scientifically perilous undertaking, and that any particular count can only suggest the actual fiber concentration that may be present. Nevertheless, Dr. Taylor's [another court-appointed expert's] computation indicating some excess of asbestiform fibers in the air of Silver Bay over that of the control city of St. Paul appears statistically significant and cannot be disregarded. Thus...while the actual level of fibers in the air of Silver Bay is essentially unknown, it may be said that fibers are present at levels significantly higher than levels found in another Minnesota community removed from this air contamination.

Given the presence of excess fibers, we must now assess the effects of this exposure on the public. We note first...that the exposure here cannot be equated with the factory exposures which have been clearly linked to excess cancers and asbestosis. Our inquiry, however, does not end there. Asbestos-related disease...has been associated with exposure levels considerably less than normal occupational exposure. The studies indicating that mesothelioma is associated with the lower levels of exposure typical of residence near an asbestos mine or mill or in the household of an asbestos worker are of significance. Although these studies do not possess the methodological strengths of the occupational studies, they must be considered in the medical evaluation of Reserve's discharge into the air....

Plaintiff's hypothesis that Reserve's air emissions represent a significant threat to the public health touches numerous scientific disciplines, and an overall evaluation demands broad scientific understanding. We think it significant that Dr.

Brown, an impartial witness whose court-appointed task was to address the health issue in its entirety, joined with plaintiff's witnesses in viewing as reasonable the hypothesis that Reserve's discharges present a threat to public health. Although...Dr. Brown found the evidence insufficient to make a scientific probability statement as to whether adverse health consequences would in fact ensue, he expressed a public health concern over the continued long-term emission of fibers into the air. We quote his testimony...

> Based on the scientific evidence, I would be unable to predict...that cancer would be found in Silver Bay. Now, going beyond that, it seems to me...where it has been shown that a known human carcinogen...is in the air of any community, and if it could be lowered I would say, as a physician that, yes, it should be lowered. And if it could be taken out of the air completely, I would be even more happy....

THE DISCHARGE INTO WATER

All epidemiological studies which associate asbestos fibers with harm to health are based upon inhalation of these fibers by humans. Thus, although medical opinion agrees that fibers entering the respiratory tract can interact with body tissues and produce disease, it is unknown whether the same can be said of fibers entering the digestive tract. If asbestos fibers do not interact with digestive tissue, they are presumably eliminated as waste without harmful effect on the body.

The evidence bearing upon possible harm from ingestion of fibers falls into three areas: first, the court-sponsored tissue study, designed to measure whether asbestos fibers are present in the tissues of long-time Duluth residents; second, animal experiments designed to measure whether, as a biological phenomenon, fibers can penetrate the gastrointestinal mucosa and thus interact with body tissues; third, the increased incidence of gastrointestinal cancer among workers occupationally exposed to asbestos, and the hypothesis that this increase may be due to the ingestion of fibers initially inhaled. [A review of the generally inconclusive findings of these three inquiries is omitted.]

The second primary uncertainty with respect to ingestion involves the attempt to assess whether the level of exposure from drinking water is hazardous. Of course, this inquiry is handicapped by the great variation in fiber counts, and Dr. Brown's admonition that only a qualitative, and not a quantitative, statement can be made about the presence of fibers....

The record does show that the ingestion of asbestos fibers poses some risk to health, but to an undetermined degree. Given the circumstances, Dr. Brown testified that the possibility of a future excess incidence of cancer attributable to the discharge cannot be ignored:

> I would say that it is conceivable that gastrointestinal cancers can develop from the ingestion of asbestos, and what I don't know, Your Honor, is just how low that level of ingestion must be before the likelihood of GI cancer becomes so remote as to be, for all intents and purposes, ignored as a real live possibility....
>
> After some degree of exposure to the literature and to the testimony given in this trial I would say that the scientific evidence that I have seen is not complete in terms of allowing me to draw a conclusion one way or another concerning the problem of a public health hazard in the water in Lake Superior....

> As a medical person, sir, I think that I have to err, if err I do, on the side of what is best for the greatest number. And having concluded...the carcinogenicity of asbestos, I can come to no conclusion, sir, other than that the fibers should not be present in the drinking water of the people of the North Shore.

The preceding extensive discussion of the evidence demonstrates that the medical and scientific conclusions here in dispute clearly lie "on the frontiers of scientific knowledge."...

In assessing probabilities in this case, it cannot be said that the probability of harm is more likely than not. Moreover, the level of probability does not readily convert into a prediction of consequences. On this record, it cannot be forecast that the rates of cancer will increase from drinking Lake Superior water or breathing Silver Bay air. The best that can be said is that the existence of this asbestos contaminant in air and water gives rise to a reasonable medical concern for the public health. The public's exposure to asbestos fibers in air and water creates some health risk. Such a contaminant should be removed....

REMEDY

As we have demonstrated, Reserve's air and water discharges pose a danger to the public health and justify judicial action of a preventive nature.

In fashioning relief in a case such as this involving a possibility of future harm, a court should strike a balance between the benefits conferred and the hazards created by Reserve's facility. In its pleadings, Reserve directs attention to the [undenied] benefits arising from its operations...as follows:

> In reliance upon the State and Federal permits...[Reserve] constructed its plant at Silver Bay Minnesota. [Reserve] also developed the Villages of Babbitt and Silver Bay and their schools and other necessary facilities where many of [Reserve's] employees live with their families, as do the merchants, doctors, teachers, and so forth who serve them. [Reserve's] capital investment exceeds $350,000,000. As of June 30, 1970, [Reserve] had 3,367 employees. During the calendar year 1969, its total payroll was approximately $31,700,000; and it expended the sum of $27,400,000 for the purchase of supplies and paid state and local taxes amounting to $4,250,000. [Reserve's] annual production of 10,000,000 tons of taconite pellets represents approximately...15 percent of the production of the Great Lakes [ore] and about 12 percent of the total production of the United States. Between four and six people are supported by each job in the mining industry, including those directly involved in the mining industry and those employed in directly and indirectly related fields.

The district court justified its immediate closure of Reserve's facility by characterizing Reserve's discharges as "substantially" endangering the health of persons breathing air and drinking water containing the asbestos-like fibers contained in Reserve's discharge. The term "substantially" in no way measures the danger in terms of either probabilities or consequences. Yet such an assessment seems essential in fashioning a judicial remedy.

Concededly, the trial court considered many appropriate factors in arriving at a remedy, such as (a) the nature of the anticipated harm, (b) the burden on Reserve and its employees from the issuance of the injunction, (c) the financial ability of Reserve to convert to other methods of waste disposal, and (d) a margin of safety for the public.

An additional crucial element necessary for a proper assessment of the health hazard rests upon a proper analysis of the probabilities of harm....

With respect to the water, these probabilities must be deemed low for they do not rest on a history of past health harm attributable to ingestion but on a medical theory implicating the ingestion of asbestos fibers as a causative factor in increasing the rates of gastrointestinal cancer among asbestos workers. With respect to air, the assessment of the risk of harm rests on a higher degree of proof, a correlation between the inhalation of asbestos dust and subsequent illness. But here, too, the hazard cannot be measured in terms of predictability, but the assessment must be made without direct proof. But, the hazard in both air and water can be measured in only the most general terms as a concern for the public health resting upon a reasonable medical theory. Serious consequences could result if the hypothesis on which it is based should ultimately prove true.

A court is not powerless to act in these circumstances. But an immediate injunction cannot be justified in striking a balance between unpredictable health effects and the clearly predictable social and economic consequences that would follow the plant closing.

In addition to the health risk posed by Reserve's discharges, the district court premised its immediate termination of the discharges upon Reserve's persistent refusal to implement a reasonable alternative plan for on-land disposal of tailings.

During these appeal proceedings, Reserve had indicated its willingness to deposit its tailings on land and to properly filter its air emissions. At oral argument, Reserve advised us of a willingness to spend $243 million in plant alterations and construction to halt its pollution of air and water. Reserve's offer to continue operations and proceed to construction of land disposal facilities for its tailings [at Milepost 7], if permitted to do so by the State of Minnesota, when viewed in conjunction with the uncertain quality of the health risk created by Reserve's discharges, weighs heavily against a ruling which closes Reserve's plant immediately.

Indeed, the intervening union argues, with some persuasiveness, that ill-health effects resulting from the prolonged unemployment of the head of the family on a closing of the Reserve facility may be more certain than the harm from drinking Lake Superior water or breathing Silver Bay air.

Furthermore, Congress has generally geared its national environmental policy to allowing polluting industries a reasonable period of time to make adjustments in their efforts to conform to federal standards. In the absence of an imminent hazard to health or welfare, any other program for abatement of pollution would be inherently unreasonable and invite great economic and social disruption. Some pollution and ensuing environmental damage are, unfortunately, an inevitable concomitant of a heavily industrialized economy. In the absence of actual harm, a legal standard requiring immediate cessation of industrial operations will cause unnecessary economic loss, including unemployment, and, in a case such as this, jeopardize a continuing domestic source of critical metals without conferring adequate countervailing benefits.

We believe that...the district court abused its discretion by immediately closing this major industrial plant. In this case, the risk of harm to the public is potential, not imminent or certain, and Reserve says it earnestly seeks a practical way to abate the pollution. A remedy should be fashioned which will serve the ultimate public weal by ensuring clean air, clean water, and continued jobs in an industry vital to the nation's welfare....

Reserve shall be given a reasonable time to stop discharging its wastes into Lake Superior....

Pending final action by Minnesota on the present permit application, Reserve must promptly take all steps necessary to comply with Minnesota law applicable to its air emissions....

Furthermore, Reserve must use such available technology as will reduce the asbestos fiber count in the ambient air at Silver Bay below a medically significant level. According to the record in this case, controls may be deemed adequate which will reduce the fiber count to the level ordinarily found in the ambient air of a city such as St. Paul.

We wish to make it clear that we view the air emission as presenting a hazard of greater significance than the water discharge. Accordingly...Reserve must immediately proceed with the planning and implementation of such emission controls as may be reasonably and practically effectuated under the circumstances....

Additionally, the district court should take proper steps to ensure that filtered water remains available in affected communities to the same extent as is now provided by the Corps of Engineers, although not necessarily at the expense of the Corps....

COMMENTARY AND QUESTIONS

1. Court-initiated scientific inquiry. Both the district and appellate courts relied heavily on court-appointed witnesses and court-sponsored studies. What are the advantages and disadvantages of court-initiated investigations? Should we empanel special "science courts" to settle disputes involving pervasive scientific uncertainty? What about "environmental courts" to adjudicate environmental disputes?

2. The remedy selected and its implementation. Why was it necessary to compel Reserve to cease its discharges into Lake Superior and switch to land disposal when filtration plants for public drinking water could have been built (at Reserve's expense) at a fraction of the cost? Was land disposal necessarily a better alternative to discharging tailings into Lake Superior?

Did the appellate court deal satisfactorily with Reserve's "intransigence"? Should it have set a definite "reasonable time" for Reserve's compliance? Judge Lord, the district court judge in this case, later became so angry at Reserve's procrastination tactics that he excoriated Reserve from the bench and was removed from the case for bias by the appellate court. His successor, Judge Devitt, fined Reserve nearly a million dollars for violating its discharge permit, and an extra two hundred thousand dollars for withholding evidence. The Minnesota Department of Natural Resources rejected Reserve's application for a land discharge permit on health, safety, economic, and environmental reasons, recommending another site. After further negotiations over the permit to land discharge, Reserve did not begin the planned land disposal until 1980, five years after the appellate court decision. Bartlett, The Reserve Mining Controversy (1980). Ironically, Reserve shut down several years later, not because of burdensome pollution control requirements, but because of the general decline of the U.S. steel industry in the face of foreign competition.

3. Technology-based standards as a proactive norm. Did the appellate court act proactively or reactively? (Using Talbot Page's terms, did it minimize false positives or false negatives?) Was this a case of "environmental risk"? Did the court apply Page's balancing test for managing environmental risk? In light of the scientific uncertainties involved in establishing risks to public health, should all waste disposers be required to install the best available technology (economically achievable) even though no risk has yet been proven?

4. Deference to the regulators. Should the district and appellate courts have deferred to the original federal and state permits granted to Reserve's Silver Bay plant, and to the United States Department of Labor's occupational exposure standard for asbestos fibers of five microns in length minimum, as Huber might suggest? Most extended judicial discussions of risk management occur in the context of judicial review of administrative decisions made under the authority of federal statutes containing different approaches to risk management. In these cases, courts generally defer to agency decisions, especially those "on the frontiers of scientific knowledge." Compare Ethyl Corp v. EPA, 541 F.2d 1 (D.C. Cir. 1976(upholding EPA's phaseout of lead in gasoline) with Industrial Union Department, AFL-CIO v. American Petroleum Institute, 448 U.S. 607 (1980)(requiring further justification for OSHA's reduction of the permissible occupational exposure levels for benzene from 10 ppm to 1 ppm). See Latin, The Significance Of Toxic Health Risks: An Essay On Legal Decision-making Under Uncertainty, 10 Ecology. L.Q. 339 (1982). Courts also perform risk assessment when evaluating environmental impact documents for new technology under the National Environmental Policy Act. (See Chapter 12) For example, biotechnology may pose a zero-infinity dilemma. See Foundation On Economic Trends v. Heckler, 756 F.2d 143 (1985); Pimentel et al., Benefits and Risks of Genetic Engineering in Agriculture, 39 Bioscience 606 (1989).

5. *Reserve* and *Wilsonville* compared. Both *Reserve Mining* and *Wilsonville* involved the question of whether an injunction should be granted in a case where the occurrence of future harm is uncertain. Injunctions were issued in both situations, but the terms of the *Wilsonville* injunction were more drastic than those in *Reserve*. (The *Wilsonville* facility was shut down, but the *Reserve* plant was not.) Can you explain these different judicial responses to toxic substance risk? Would the *Reserve* court have agreed with Judge Ryan's concurring opinion in *Wilsonville*?

6. Relativity of risks. Individuals take on some risks voluntarily, like choosing to smoke cigarettes or driving cars. Some risks are taken on involuntarily, like breathing air and drinking water in Silver Bay, Minnesota that may contain very small amounts of asbestos fibers. Which activities are statistically more likely to lead to harm? Which does the legal system focus upon? If the answers to these questions are not the same, is that a problem or does the law primarily seek to protect the public against *unchosen* risks, against involuntary and unnecessary tradeoffs?

"Econs" basically believe that material wealth is the highest human value, and justice, fairness, dignity, and protecting the helpless all cost money and are therefore "economically inefficient." The money would be better spent on much more transcendent things, like pet rocks, hemorrhoid pads, and other items needed to satisfy AGGREGATE DEMAND.

Econs prove their theories by devising little mathematical formulas which assume whole truckloads of untrue things and then come to a particular conclusion. The conclusion is always – get this – "the market will take care of it itself." According to the Econs – I am not making this up, either – there is a GIANT INVISIBLE DISEMBODIED HAND that magically takes care of everything. Before you get too excited about this, remember that this is the same invisible hand that gave us the invisible GREAT DEPRESSION. Oh. That *invisible hand.*

When you point out that the assumptions in the formulas are simplistic (a euphemism for "false"), the Econs get really testy and tell you that you don't understand the discipline.[1]

— James Gordon, *How Not to Succeed in Law School*
100 Yale Law Journal 1679, 1699 (1991)

1. In his article Professor Gordon provides helpful analysis for understanding all the hidden realities of legal education. He contrasts, for instance, the "Econs" of the University of Chicago Law and Economics tribe with the "Crits" of the Critical Legal Studies movement: "While Crits believe that all law is aimed at SUPPORTING free market capitalism, the Econs believe that all law is an unwarranted INTERFERENCE with free market capitalism. Other than that, the two groups pretty much see eye to eye."

PART TWO

THE FOUNDATION OF ENVIRONMENTAL LAW:

TRADITIONAL COMMON LAW THEORIES & FUNDAMENTAL ISSUES OF REMEDIES AND LIABILITY

Although many of today's environmental controversies involve public law statutes and regulations, in functional terms the common law made by judges and private litigants over the course of the last 800 years continues to play a critical role in environmental law.

Each year many environmental cases involving localized pollution are filed under common law theories. These local cases undoubtedly make up the numerical majority of environmental cases generally. Even so, when an oil tanker disaster strikes the waters and shores of a coastal state, or a chemical factory's dump-site poisons land and groundwater, the major remedies litigated by injured parties are likewise based almost entirely on common law. After the wreck of the Exxon-Valdez, for example, the lawsuits filed by the State of Alaska and its citizens relied on tort and public trust theories to respond to that vast catastrophe. The common law is a fertile hunting ground for environmental lawyers trying to get a handle on some of the most modern ecological problems, and underscores the critical role played by private litigation in U.S. environmental law.

The common law also provides the conceptual underpinning for most statutes and regulations. Legislatures and agencies rely on the continued existence of common law to fill gaps in public law and to guide courts and agencies in their interpretation of statutes and rules. Statutes may come and go, but the common law generally rolls on.

Many fundamental issues raised in environmental law, moreover, will continue to be raised first in the common law realm. Questions of proof, uncertainty, balances of risk, fault, and other liability issues, foreseeability, standards of care, technological feasibility, causation, long-term residual injuries, remedies, practical deterrence, enforceability, and so on – all these are found first in the common law. Despite the existence of innumerable federal and state environmental statutes, and reams of administrative regulations, the common law of environmental protections remains vigorous and important.

Chapter 3

ENVIRONMENTAL TORTS AND REMEDIES: FITTING ENVIRONMENTAL CASES INTO COMMON LAW THEORIES

This chapter begins with the classic case of Oscar Boomer and the Atlantic Cement Company. Many law students have already encountered the case in a torts or property class. Some aspects of the *Boomer* legal analysis may therefore already be familiar. In this coursebook *Boomer* serves as a case study of private intentional nuisance torts, strategies, defenses, the wide range of available environmental remedies, and some new twists in environmental litigation. It can simultaneously be a vehicle for developing the ecological, economic, and political accounting that underlies every environmental case. The chapter proceeds from *Boomer* to a more general study of how tort law has been adapted to fit environmental cases, leading to Chapter 4 and the special lessons it draws from a parade of modern toxic chemical cases.

A. PRIVATE NUISANCE, INTENTIONAL TORT, AND THE CLASSIC *BOOMER* CASE

Section 1. SEEKING A REMEDY FOR A TYPICAL POLLUTION PROBLEM

The *Boomer* case was brought as a common law tort action, based on a complaint by the victims of air pollution against the factory whose emissions were causing an injury to plaintiffs' property. The case sounds in intentional private nuisance,[1] the doctrine which serves as the basis for suit in the majority of today's non-statutory environmental law cases.

Tort law in general, and nuisance in particular, offer an aggrieved plaintiff the possibility of monetary recoveries and a variety of injunctive remedies. With its roots in everyday tort law, nuisance is a familiar sort of claim to judges and lawyers alike. Just as in the typical negligence lawsuit for damages based on injuries suffered in an automobile accident, the plaintiff in a nuisance action must carry the burden of proving that she has suffered harm, that the defendant's conduct is the cause of that harm, and that defendant's conduct is of a type for which the law affords a remedy.

---

1. As later discussed in greater detail, there are two different nuisance theories, public and private, each of which can be litigated on the basis of intentional conduct, negligence, or strict liability. Both theories of nuisance draw upon the old maxim "sic utere tuo ut alienum non laedas," or "one should use her own property in such a manner as not to injure the interests of others." Private nuisance, the first to be discussed here, is concerned with individual private property rights in land. Public nuisance stems from the violation of a range of public interests in the maintenance of health, safety, and morals. The dramatic differences between them, and between intentional and negligent theories of culpability, will soon be apparent.

As you read through *Boomer*, picture the practicalities of litigating the case, and the environmental benefit-cost-alternatives analysis that might be applied to the controversy between Mr. Boomer and his industrial neighbor.

Boomer et al. v. Atlantic Cement Company

New York Court of Appeals, 1970
26 N.Y.2d 219, 257 N.E.2d 870, 309 N.Y.S.2d 312

BERGAN, J. Defendant operates a large cement plant near Albany. These are actions for injunction and damages by neighboring land owners alleging injury to property from dirt, smoke and vibration emanating from the plant. A nuisance has been found after trial, temporary damages have been allowed; but an injunction has been denied.

The public concern with air pollution arising from many sources in industry and in transportation is currently accorded ever wider recognition accompanied by a growing sense of responsibility in State and Federal Governments to control it. Cement plants are obvious sources of air pollution in the neighborhoods where they operate.

But there is now before the court private litigation in which individual property owners have sought specific relief from a single plant operation. The threshold question raised by the division of view on this appeal is whether the court should resolve the litigation between the parties now before it as equitably as seems possible; or whether, seeking promotion of the general public welfare, it should channel private litigation into broad public objectives.

A court performs its essential function when it decides the rights of parties before it. Its decision of private controversies may sometimes greatly affect public issues. Large questions of law are often resolved by the manner in which private litigation is decided. But this is normally an incident to the court's main function to settle controversy. It is a rare exercise of judicial power to use a decision in private litigation as a purposeful mechanism to achieve direct public objectives greatly beyond the rights and interests before the court.

Effective control of air pollution is a problem presently far from solution even with the full public and financial powers of government. In large measure adequate technical procedures are yet to be developed and some that appear possible may be economically impracticable.

It seems apparent that the amelioration of air pollution will depend on technical research in great depth; on a carefully balanced consideration of the economic impact of close regulation; and of the actual effect on public health. It is likely to require massive public expenditure and to demand more than any local community can accomplish and to depend on regional and interstate controls.

A court should not try to do this on its own as a by-product of private litigation and it seems manifest that the judicial establishment is neither equipped in the limited nature of any judgment it can pronounce nor prepared to lay down and implement an effective policy for the elimination of air pollution. This is an area beyond the circumference of one private lawsuit. It is a direct responsibility for government and should not thus be undertaken as an incident to solving a dispute between property owners and a single cement plant – one of many – in the Hudson River valley.

The cement making operations of defendant have been found by the court of Special Term to have damaged the nearby properties of plaintiffs in these two actions. That court, as it has been noted, accordingly found defendant maintained a nuisance and this has been affirmed at the Appellate Division. The trial judge had made a simple, direct finding that "the discharge of large quantities of dust upon each of the properties and excessive vibration from blasting deprived each party of the reasonable use of his property and thereby prevented his enjoyment of life and liberty therein." The judge continued, however: "I have given careful consideration to the plea of plaintiffs that an injunction should issue in this action. Although the Supreme Court has the power to grant and enforce an injunction, equity forbids its employment in this instance. The defendant's immense investment in the Hudson River Valley, its contribution to the Capital District's economy and its immediate help to the education of children in the Town of Coeymans through the payment of substantial sums in school and property taxes leads me to the conclusion that an injunction would produce great public...hardship." The total damage to plaintiffs' properties is, however, relatively small in comparison with the value of defendant's operation and with the consequences of the injunction which plaintiffs seek.

The ground for the denial of injunction, notwithstanding the finding both that there is a nuisance and that plaintiffs have been damaged substantially, is the large disparity in economic consequences of the nuisance and of the injunction. This theory cannot, however, be sustained without overruling a doctrine which has been consistently reaffirmed in several leading cases in this court and which has never been disavowed here, namely that where a nuisance has been found and where there has been any substantial damage shown by the party complaining an injunction will be granted.

The rule in New York has been that such a nuisance will be enjoined although marked disparity be shown in economic consequence between the effect of the injunction and the effect of the nuisance.

The problem of disparity in economic consequence was sharply in focus in Whalen v. Union Bag & Paper Co., 101 N.E. 805. A pulp mill entailing an investment of more than a million dollars polluted a stream in which plaintiff, who owned a farm, was "a lower riparian owner." The economic loss to plaintiff from this pollution was small. This court, reversing the Appellate Division, reinstated the injunction granted by the Special Term against the argument of the mill owner that in view of "the slight advantage to plaintiff and the great loss that will be inflicted on defendant" an injunction should not be granted. "Such a balancing of injuries cannot be justified by the circumstances of this case," Judge Werner noted. He continued: "Although the damage to the plaintiff may be slight as compared with the defendant's expense of abating the condition, that is not a good reason for refusing an injunction."

Thus the unconditional injunction granted at Special Term was reinstated. The rule laid down in that case, then, is that whenever the damage resulting from a nuisance is found not "unsubstantial," viz., $100 a year, injunction would follow. This states a rule that had been followed in this court with marked consistency.

There are cases where injunction has been denied. McCann v. Chasm Power Co., 105 N.E. 416 is one of them. There, however, the damage shown by plaintiffs was not only unsubstantial, it was non-existent. Plaintiffs owned a rocky bank of the stream in which defendant had raised the level of the water. This had no economic or other adverse consequence to plaintiffs, and thus injunctive relief was denied.

Similar is the basis for denial of injunction where no benefit to plaintiffs could be seen from the injunction sought. Thus if, within Whalen v. Union Bag & Paper Co., which authoritatively states the rule in New York, the damage to plaintiffs in these present cases from defendant's cement plant is "not unsubstantial," an injunction should follow.

Although the court at Special Term and the Appellate Division held that an injunction should be denied, it was found that plaintiffs had been damaged in various specific amounts up to the time of the trial and damages to the respective plaintiffs were awarded for those amounts. The effect of this was, injunction having been denied, plaintiffs could maintain successive actions at law for damages thereafter as further damage was incurred.

The court at Special Term also found the amount of permanent damage attributable to each plaintiff, for the guidance of the parties in the event both sides stipulated to the payment and acceptance of such permanent damage as a settlement of all the controversies among the parties. The total of permanent damages to all plaintiffs thus found was $185,000. This basis of adjustment has not resulted in any stipulation by the parties.

This result at Special Term and at the Appellate Division is a departure from a rule that has become settled; but to follow the rule literally in these cases would be to close down the plant at once. This court is fully agreed to avoid that immediately drastic remedy; the difference in view is how best to avoid it.[2]

One alternative is to grant the injunction but postpone its effect to a specified future date to give opportunity for technical advances to permit defendant to eliminate the nuisance; another is to grant the injunction conditioned on the payment of permanent damages to plaintiffs which would compensate them for the total economic loss to their property present and future caused by defendant's operations. For reasons which will be developed the court chooses the latter alternative.

If the injunction were to be granted unless within a short period – e.g., 18 months – the nuisance be abated by improved methods, there would be no assurance that any significant technical improvement would occur.

The parties could settle this private litigation at any time if defendant paid enough money and the imminent threat of closing the plant would build up the pressure on defendant. If there were no improved techniques found, there would inevitably be applications to the court at Special Term for extensions of time to perform on showing of good faith efforts to find such techniques.

Moreover, techniques to eliminate dust and other annoying by-products of cement making are unlikely to be developed by any research the defendant can undertake within any short period, but will depend on the total resources of the cement industry nationwide and throughout the world. The problem is universal wherever cement is made.

For obvious reasons the rate of the research is beyond control of defendant. If at the end of 18 months the whole industry has not found a technical solution a court would be hard put to close down this one cement plant if due regard be given to equitable principles.

On the other hand, to grant the injunction unless defendant pays plaintiffs such permanent damages as may be fixed by the court seems to do justice between the

---

2. Respondent's investment in the plant is in excess of $45,000,000. There are over 300 people employed there.

contending parties. All of the attributions of economic loss to the properties on which plaintiffs' complaints are based will have been redressed.

The nuisance complained of by these plaintiffs may have other public or private consequences, but these particular parties are the only ones who have sought remedies and the judgment proposed will fully redress them. The limitation of relief granted is a limitation only within the four corners of these actions and does not foreclose public health or other public agencies from seeking proper relief in a proper court.

It seems reasonable to think that the risk of being required to pay permanent damages to injured property owners by cement plant owners would itself be a reasonable effective spur to research for improved techniques to minimize nuisance.

The power of the court to condition on equitable grounds the continuance of an injunction on the payment of permanent damages seems undoubted.

The damage base here suggested is consistent with the general rule in those nuisance cases where damages are allowed. "Where a nuisance is of such a permanent and unabatable character that a single recovery can be had, including the whole damage past and future resulting therefrom, there can be but one recovery" (66 C.J.S. Nuisances §140, 947). It has been said that permanent damages are allowed where the loss recoverable would obviously be small as compared with the cost of removal of the nuisance (Kentucky-Ohio Gas Co. v. Bowling, 95 S.W.2d 1).

The present cases and the remedy here proposed are in a number of other respects rather similar to Northern Indiana Public Service Co. v. W. J. & M. S. Vesey, 200 N.E. 620 decided by the Supreme Court of Indiana. The gases, odors, ammonia, and smoke from the Northern Indiana company's gas plant damaged the nearby Vesey greenhouse operation. An injunction and damages were sought, but an injunction was denied and the relief granted was limited to permanent damages "present, past, and future."

Denial of injunction was grounded on a public interest in the operation of the gas plant and on the court's conclusion "that less injury would be occasioned by requiring the appellant (Public Service) to pay the appellee (Vesey) all damages suffered by it...than by enjoining the operation of the gas plant"; and that the maintenance and operation of the gas plant should not be enjoined.

The Indiana Supreme Court opinion continued: When the trial court refused injunctive relief to the appellee upon the ground of public interest in the continuance of the gas plant, it properly retained jurisdiction of the case and awarded full compensation to the appellee. This is upon the general equitable principle that equity will give full relief in one action and prevent a multiplicity of suits....

Thus it seems fair to both sides to grant permanent damages to plaintiffs which will terminate this private litigation. The theory of damage is the "servitude on land" of plaintiffs imposed by defendant's nuisance. (See United States v. Causby, 328 U.S. 256, 261, 262, 267, where the term "servitude" addressed to the land was used by Justice Douglas relating to the effect of airplane noise on property near an airport.)

The judgment, by allowance of permanent damages imposing a servitude on land, which is the basis of the actions, would preclude future recovery by plaintiffs or their grantees.

This should be placed beyond debate by a provision of the judgment that the payment by defendant and the acceptance by plaintiffs of permanent damages found by the court shall be in compensation for a servitude on the land.

Although the Trial Term has found permanent damages as a possible basis of settlement of the litigation, on remission the court should be entirely free to examine this subject. It may again find the permanent damage already found, or make new findings.

The orders should be reversed, without costs, and the cases remitted to Supreme Court, Albany County to grant an injunction which shall be vacated upon payment by defendant of such amounts of permanent damage to the respective plaintiffs as shall for this purpose be determined by the court.

JASEN, J., dissenting.

I agree with the majority that a reversal is required here, but I do not subscribe to the newly enunciated doctrine of assessment of permanent damages, in lieu of an injunction, where substantial property rights have been impaired by the creation of a nuisance.

It has long been the rule in this State, as the majority acknowledges, that a nuisance which results in substantial continuing damage to neighbors must be enjoined. (Whalen v. Union Bag & Paper Co., 101 N.E. 805; Campbell v. Seaman, 63 N.Y. 568; see, also, Kennedy v. Moog Servocontrols, 237 N.E.2d 356.) To now change the rule to permit the cement company to continue polluting the air indefinitely upon the payment of permanent damages is, in my opinion, compounding the magnitude of a very serious problem in our State and Nation today.

In recognition of this problem, the Legislature of this State has enacted the Air Pollution Control Act declaring that it is the State policy to require the use of all available and reasonable methods to prevent and control air pollution.

The harmful nature and widespread occurrence of air pollution have been extensively documented. Congressional hearings have revealed that air pollution causes substantial property damage, as well as being a contributing factor to a rising incidence of lung cancer, emphysema, bronchitis and asthma.

The specific problem faced here is known as particulate contamination because of the fine dust particles emanating from defendant's cement plant. The particular type of nuisance is not new, having appeared in many cases for at least the past 60 years. (See Hulbert v. California Portland Cement Co., 118 P. 928 (Cal. 1911).) It is interesting to note that cement production has recently been identified as a significant source of particulate contamination in the Hudson Valley. This type of pollution, wherein very small particles escape and stay in the atmosphere, has been denominated as the type of air pollution which produces the greatest hazard to human health. We have thus a nuisance which not only is damaging to the plaintiffs, but also is decidedly harmful to the general public.

I see grave dangers in overruling our long-established rule of granting an injunction where a nuisance results in substantial continuing damage. In permitting the injunction to become inoperative upon the payment of permanent damages, the majority is, in effect, licensing a continuing wrong. It is the same as saying to the cement company, you may continue to do harm to your neighbors so long as you pay a fee for it. Furthermore, once such permanent damages are assessed and paid, the incentive to alleviate the wrong would be eliminated, thereby continuing air pollution of an area without abatement.

It is true that some courts have sanctioned the remedy here proposed by the majority in a number of cases, but none of the authorities relied upon by the majority are analogous to the situation before us. In those cases, the courts, in denying an injunction and awarding money damages, grounded their decision on a showing that the use to which the property was intended to be put was primarily for the public benefit. Here, on the other hand, it is clearly established that the cement company is creating a continuing air pollution nuisance primarily for its own private interest with no public benefit.

This kind of inverse condemnation may not be invoked by a private person or corporation for private gain or advantage. Inverse condemnation should only be permitted when the public is primarily served in the taking or impairment of property. The promotion of the interests of the polluting cement company has, in my opinion, no public use or benefit.

Nor is it constitutionally permissible to impose a servitude on land, without consent of the owner, by payment of permanent damages where the continuing impairment of the land is for a private use. This is made clear by the State Constitution Art. I, §7(a) which provides that "private property shall not be taken for *public* use without just compensation" (emphasis added). It is, of course, significant that the section makes no mention of taking for a private use.

In sum, then, by constitutional mandate as well as by judicial pronouncement, the permanent impairment of private property for private purposes is not authorized in the absence of clearly demonstrated public benefit and use.

I would enjoin the defendant cement company from continuing the discharge of dust particles upon its neighbors' properties unless, within 18 months, the cement company abated this nuisance.[3]

It is not my intention to cause the removal of the cement plant from the Albany area, but to recognize the urgency of the problem stemming from this stationary source of air pollution, and to allow the company a specified period of time to develop a means to alleviate this nuisance.

I am aware that the trial court found that the most modern dust control devices available have been installed in defendant's plant, but, I submit, this does not mean that better and more effective dust control devices could not be developed within the time allowed to abate the pollution.

Moreover, I believe it is incumbent upon the defendant to develop such devices, since the cement company, at the time the plant commenced production (1962), was well aware of the plaintiffs' presence in the area, as well as the probable consequences of its contemplated operation. Yet, it still chose to build and operate the plant at this site.

In a day when there is a growing concern for clean air, highly developed industry should not expect acquiescence by the courts, but should, instead, plan its operations to eliminate contamination of our air and damage to its neighbors.

Accordingly, the orders of the Appellate Division, insofar as they denied the injunction, should be reversed, and the actions remitted to Supreme Court, Albany County to grant an injunction to take effect 18 months hence, unless the nuisance is abated by improved techniques prior to said date.

FULD, C.J., and BURKE and SCILEPPI, JJ., concur with BERGAN, J.

3. The issuance of an injunction to become effective in the future is not an entirely new concept. For instance, in Schwarzenbach v. Oneonta Light & Power Co., 100 N.E. 1134, an injunction against the maintenance of a dam spilling water on plaintiff's property was issued to become effective one year hence.

COMMENTARY AND QUESTIONS

1. *Boomer* as an environmental case. Do you think that Oscar Boomer regarded himself as an environmentalist? Mr. Boomer clearly wanted to stop the cement dust falling on him and get compensation. He may well have thought of environmentalists as a bunch of birdwatchers and tree huggers. Note that although there were undoubtedly a number of ecological consequences to natural resources in the area polluted by cement dust, the case is totally silent about these, focusing instead upon injury to plaintiffs' personal and real property. Injury to human health and property remains the primary focus of much environmental litigation. Human quality of life is an important part of environmental concern. The law, however, is slowly growing conscious of the tangible importance of ecological natural resource harms as well.

2. *Boomer* and the cement company's "cost externalization." Besides its interesting holdings on permanent damages and balancing, many aspects of the *Boomer* case reflect classic environmental perceptions. The case involved a typical industrial setting, with the cement company doing its own internal benefit-cost analysis that made discharge of waste dust into the commons the rational disposal option. Absent successful legal action, the company would have had to account for almost none of the pollution's cost, even if the total of actual costs to natural systems, human health, and property in the affected area extending downwind many miles were actually greater than the cost of installing better control equipment (or might even have exceeded total net benefits to the company).

The problem is that natural and human environmental costs are typically spread so far and wide, or are so hard to take account of and quantify in monetary terms, that the overall accounting is rarely done.

3. The "cost internalizing" effect of the *Boomer* lawsuit. To the extent that common law litigation like *Boomer* forces a factory to provide relief to plaintiffs, to that same extent the company is forced to internalize some of the negative effects of its pollution as a cost of doing business, to be passed on to its consumers. How much gets internalized here? The *Boomer* decision resulted in internalizing some of the private property damage suffered by the Boomers and their neighbors. What *Boomer* does not even attempt to do is to trace more carefully *all* of the negative consumption externalities caused by the pollution. Why not? Does the difficulty lie in cost accounting? Recall from the discussions in Chapter 2 how difficult it would be to provide an accurate measure of the harms to affected natural resources (forests, wildlife, etc.) or the low-level adverse human health effects of particulate pollution. Does the difficulty stem from the lack of an advocate for the environment? Oscar Boomer may or may not care deeply about the environment, but it is probably not in his self-interest to spend vast amounts of effort and energy trying to marshal evidence on damages to the commons beyond his own private property. Even if such evidence could be assembled and litigated, it might not be worthwhile, or efficient, to do so.

Class actions offer a vehicle for expanded internalization and dramatically increase defendants' incentives to clean up. *Boomer* was not filed as a class action case, although it could have been. Would that have achieved more rational results? See Wright, The Cost-Internalization Case for Class Actions, 21 Stan. L. Rev. 383 (1969), and page 173 *infra*, on environmental use of class actions.

Do we have the time or luxury, on the other hand, to consider all the diverse external costs of each industrial operation? The cacophony of voices raised by a host of far-off pollution victims in such efforts might mean that nothing gets done. Some pollution is necessary to progress, say the Chicago School pragmatists. It has to occur somewhere. The market's accounting dictates that it occur here, in a rural area where only a few relatively low income people will be affected. There is no complaint about health effects in *Boomer*, so the effects of cement dust pollution may be relatively slight. The benefits of cement are clearly substantial. Does the rough accounting reached in *Boomer* thus suffice? Does society have the luxury of performing an endless analysis of the benefits and costs of every enterprise like the Atlantic Cement Company, or should such scrutiny be reserved for cases of more dramatic environmental impact?

4. Tactics, politics, and the urge to litigate. If the cement dust pollution was so obvious in this case, why didn't Boomer and his lawyer go straight to the state air pollution agency? Albany, the state capital, was close by, and the official state pollution control agency possessed statutory authority, extensive regulations, public funding appropriated for enforcement, and expertise. What practical advantages in getting relief persuade pollution victims to take on the burdens of litigating in common law courts, rather than trusting to the official public law system?

The United States is an unusually litigious society. For that reason, it may seem natural that when the Boomers felt themselves aggrieved by the action of their cement plant neighbor, they resorted to a lawsuit in an effort to obtain redress. Speculating about the reasons for that choice by the Boomers reveals a great deal about the attraction of the common law as a system for environmental governance in American society.

The avenues of potential redress for the Boomers other than a lawsuit were not particularly promising because of the Boomers' lack of access and influence in decisional processes. In the private corporate decision, of course, the Boomers' interests were not likely to be of great concern. But the public law, both state and local, might have been expected to be different.

The construction of a major facility like a cement plant is usually the subject of local governmental land use regulations, most often zoning. If the project was consistent with existing local zoning classifications, there was no opportunity for Boomer to oppose the project in the zoning board forum; if, however, the use was one not initially allowed by the zoning, the project proponents would have had to seek a zoning change in order to construct the plant. Even if the project were consistent with existing zoning, some communities require permits for either the siting or the construction of large facilities.

Are the various local regulatory systems likely to provide people like the Boomers a sympathetic local forum in which to oppose the plant before it is built? The $45 million in equities weigh heavily in the balance. Today, as communities prostrate themselves in efforts to attract the economic benefits that come with major industrial facilities, the pressures to grant needed permits are substantial. Except for immediate neighbors of the plant who may suffer, like the Boomers, most of the community will find its immediate self-interest aligned with having the plant built.

What about the state pollution control system? As studied later, beginning in Chapter 6, the regulatory statutes are highly complex and primarily concerned with the general business of pollution control, not with providing discrete local remedies for relatively small individual claims. The statutes are primarily tools for governmental regulation of polluters, and opportunities for individual citizens to play a significant role in that process are few. The regulators are seldom eager to expand their dialogue with regulated parties into a multi-dimensional process in which citizens seek results that are often at odds with the agency's own view of proper outcome. This is not to say that seeking the aid of public authorities charged with control of pollution is always unavailing, but merely that it is a process over which the private citizen has little control.

Compare the official public law processes to an ordinary common law tort suit. Plaintiffs can hire a lawyer, probably on a contingent fee basis, who seeks relief at the local courthouse where the opportunity to win damages and injunctions provides a strong self-interest incentive to prosecute the case, a flexible scope of remedies, and broad, familiar theories for the judge to apply, without any need for entering the quagmire of administrative proceedings where the outcome can be so heavily influenced by politics and regional economics. Plaintiffs can exercise a measure of control over the litigation, selecting the lawyer, perhaps helping to develop the evidence, and the litigation process can to some extent equalize the parties to the controversy. And unlike the agency regulatory process, of course, the common law can provide damage recoveries for the plaintiff's injuries. There is, moreover, a growing literature in the civil procedure area addressing the psychological benefits of the litigation process. In addition to its various participatory characteristics, litigation usually leads to a definitive end, sometimes providing a personal sense of vindication, and always at least providing closure, itself an important benefit.

5. Environmental tort remedies. Tort actions illustrate other advantages of common law remedies in environmental cases. Tort law typically looks to community standards of appropriateness; it provides jury trials, so that the actual decision-makers on whether community standards have been met are local citizens themselves. As a means of seeking redress, tort cases demystify the technicalities of environmental cases, reverting to shared community understandings about what is right and what is wrong.

When plaintiffs successfully establish defendant's liability under an environmental tort cause of action, one remedy is automatic: the award of compensatory damages for tort injuries suffered. The well-established checklist of compensatory damage categories includes recoveries for health and property damage, lost profits and earnings, pain and suffering, and the like. Environmental cases occasionally add new remedy theories, noted later. The *Boomer* case concerned only property damages, but added the relatively novel permanent damage approach in lieu of an injunction.

After a court awards compensatory damages, typically for past rather than permanent injuries, courts then move to the further question of whether an injunction will be issued. Mirroring *Boomer*, the grant of an injunction in virtually all modern courts is never automatic, but depends upon a balancing of the equities. Accepting that principle, does an environmental perspective on the *Boomer* case reveal any problems with the court's balance? Would you mention the cement dust's more general public effects? Following Judge Jasen's lead, would you have proposed alternative forms of injunction? These and other issues are developed below in this chapter's subpart D on remedies.

Section 2. THE PRIMA FACIE ENVIRONMENTAL PRIVATE NUISANCE CASE

THE ELEMENTS OF THE CAUSE OF ACTION

Nuisance can roughly be described as use of property by one party so as to (a) interfere substantially with the reasonable use, enjoyment or value of another's property, (b) injure life or health, (c) offend the senses or violate principles of decency, or (d) obstruct free passage or use of highways, navigable streams, public parks and beaches, and other public rights.

Nuisance is divided into two distinctive branches: Private nuisance is based on interference with individual plaintiffs' private property rights in land, ((a) and (b) above), while public nuisance stems from violations of "public rights" of varying descriptions (primarily (c) and (d)). Public nuisance, although it can provide extremely useful and creative remedies for environmental problems, poses some special practical difficulties for private plaintiffs, noted later in this chapter. Until recently, almost all environmental nuisance actions have been brought in private nuisance.

The elements of a prima facie case of private nuisance, when it is brought as an "intentional" tort action like *Boomer*, merely require plaintiffs to prove that:

(1) they have suffered substantial unreasonable interference with property use,
(2) the interference was caused by defendant's use of its land, and
(3) that the defendant acted "intentionally."

What kind of evidence would be necessary to establish these elements in a case like *Boomer*? An effective plaintiffs' attorney might want to learn something about the effect of alkaline cement dust on paint, metal, gardens, and peoples' health; dust sampling techniques; the industry's prior knowledge of cement dust problems; citizen complaints; and so on.

After the plaintiff presents credible evidence on these three elements, the burden then shifts to the corporate defendant to raise its defenses, many of which pose interesting environmental issues. At the first line of defense – when defendant attempts to deny the truth of plaintiff's various factual allegations – denials of causation often enmesh environmental litigation in scientific quandaries. Then, even if the alleged facts of a prima facie case are proved, an array of affirmative defenses apply, noted in this chapter's subpart B *infra.*

If the plaintiff successfully avoids the defenses and proves the tort's elements at trial, liability is established and compensatory damages, at least, will be awarded. In *Boomer* the damages sought for past injuries were straightforward property claims, but modern cases present a parade of other damage claims – for physical illnesses, aesthetics, risk, fear of cancer, as well as for punitive damages. *Boomer* also raises further remedy issues of permanent damages and the wide powers of equitable relief. All these are noted later.

INTENTION AND NEGLIGENCE

Both public and private nuisance are usually brought as "intentional" rather than negligence-based tort actions. Environmental law gives new importance to this distinction. In most tort causes of action, plaintiffs can choose to base their case on one or more of the three basic theories of tort culpability. As one court set out the range of choices:

> An action to redress a private nuisance can be maintained upon allegations that the defendant's conduct is (1) intentional...(2) negligent or reckless, or (3) actionable under the rules governing [strict] liability for abnormally dangerous conditions or activities. State of New York v. Schenectady Chemicals, Inc., 459 N.Y.S.2d 971, 976 (1983).

How do you determine which basis for private nuisance Oscar Boomer's lawyer chose? In the cement dust setting he probably could not have based his action on strict liability, but could have used either or both of the other theories, intentional tort and negligence. As in most nuisance cases, the *Boomer* litigation never states which private nuisance theory is being applied.

Although intentional torts are not given much attention in the standard law school curriculum, environmental law early on discovered the dramatic advantages of intentional tort theories.

The *Boomer* case, viewed analytically, was brought as an intentional tort, not under a negligence theory, because it based liability on findings of plaintiffs' injuries without further findings on the defendant's unreasonableness that would be required in order to establish negligence. In intentional tort cases plaintiffs must show that the defendant acted knowing that such injuries were substantially certain to occur. This "civil intent" is quite different from criminal intent, amounting merely to substantial foreseeability. Plaintiffs are aided in proving intent by a legal presumption that an actor intends the natural consequences of an act. Once the plaintiff has shown that the defendant knew or should have known that the pollution was substantially certain to cause negative effects to persons like the plaintiff, the inquiry shifts to the seriousness of plaintiff's injury – was plaintiff suffering an unreasonable burden? – and proof that it was actually the defendant that caused the harm. Liability based on intent is quite direct and decisive.

Compare intentional private nuisance to the elements of nuisance liability under a negligence theory. In negligence cases, plaintiffs must show that injury was caused by the defendant's breach of a duty of care owed to them; defendant's conduct must be shown to be unreasonable in all the circumstances. If, instead of merely showing an unreasonable burden on themselves and defendant's civil intent, plaintiffs like Boomer had to prove that defendant's conduct itself was "unreasonable" in order to make a prima facie case, they would quickly run into serious problems establishing liability, with a host of additional negligence requirements and defenses. What exactly was the defendant's duty of care, was it breached, did the breach directly cause the plaintiffs' injuries, did the plaintiff miss an opportunity to prevent or mitigate? The defendant might also avoid negligence liability by showing that it is only doing what all other such factories are doing, that further pollution controls would be too expensive, that plaintiffs were contributorily negligent, or even that its production is socially more important than plaintiffs' injuries.

Notice what a difference this makes in plaintiffs' attempts to obtain a pollution accounting. If the court applies a negligence theory, the plaintiffs must show that the defendant corporation acted unreasonably in all the balance of circumstances, which is no easy task; if they don't succeed they will recover nothing. If, on the other hand, the case is pleaded and proved under intentional tort, "fault" is not an issue, and the question of whether the defendant was unreasonable, and the balance of defendant's economic importance and utility, are wholly irrelevant, at least to the question of liability. The focus is upon the unreasonableness of burdens suffered by plaintiffs, which is a very different question from whether defendant acted unreasonably.

If plaintiffs are shown to be suffering an unreasonable burden in intentional tort, liability follows and defendant's payment of damages for neighborhood pollution becomes a straightforward cost of doing business. Modern environmental intentional torts therefore serve as matter-of-fact cost internalizers, and the concept of fault is increasingly irrelevant, either bypassed or diluted by the concept of civil intent.

Over the years many courts have confused the issues of what constitutes liability in nuisance with choice of remedy. Thus there have been some nuisance cases in which courts denied relief, finding defendants' conduct reasonable under the circumstances, as when major industrial facilities inflicted substantial damage on nearby houses. In doing so those courts replicated the over-simplification of an old English dictum, "Le utility del chose excusera le noisomeness del stink."[4]

Negligence is far more familiar than intentional tort to most attorneys and judges. Many appear not to know there is a difference, which may explain why courts sometimes apply negligence concepts in intentional tort cases. Environmen-

4. Roughly, "The usefulness of the thing will excuse the pollution." The Legal French appears to be a version of Ranketts case: "Si home fait Candells deins un vill, per que il caufe un noyfom fent al Inhabitants, uncore ceo neft alcun Nusans, car le needfulnefs de eux difpenfera ove le noifomnefs del fmell." P. 3 Ja.B.R. Rolle's Abridgement, Nusans, 139 (1684).

tal lawyers filing nuisance actions often bear the burden of clarifying the difference in the course of litigation. It is worth the effort. But if a court allows the decision on tort liability itself (not just the decision whether to enjoin the defendant) to depend on the comparative importance of the parties' activities, it creates an all or nothing contest. Such negligence-type balances inevitably favor industry and by definition completely ignore the negative burdens suffered by the losers. An early American pollution case, Madison v. Ducktown Sulfur, Copper & Iron Co., 83 S.W. 658 (Tenn. 1904), clearly rejected this mistaken version of intentional tort. Faced with farmers whose lands were being destroyed by the belching acid emissions of a primitive but important copper smelting factory, the *Ducktown* court held that a comparison of public importance and reasonableness was not relevant to establishing nuisance liability; rather, the comparative "balancing of equities" goes to the subsequent question of whether an injunction will be issued in addition to payment of compensatory damages. This is precisely the approach followed by the *Boomer* court. These remedy issues are discussed at length later in this chapter.

POLLUTION AS AN INTERFERENCE WITH PLAINTIFFS' PROPERTY RIGHTS

To prevent the intentional private nuisance action from becoming too disruptive, the law requires plaintiffs to prove that the interference with their rights is substantial and unreasonable; mere annoyance is not nuisance. By using the word "unreasonable," however, the possibility of confusion arises because that term is universally applied in the negligence equation. Courts in intentional nuisance cases may mistakenly import a question of the "unreasonableness of defendant's conduct" into their determinations of liability, instead of simply addressing the question of whether plaintiffs have suffered an unreasonable burden.

Where does mere annoyance end and substantial interference with the use and enjoyment of land begin? This is a typical legal problem of line drawing, where there are easy cases at the extremes: from the continuous emission of noxious solvent fumes from a paint factory, which would quite clearly be a nuisance, to a neighbor's occasional cooking of brussel sprouts, the smell of which is merely unpleasant and not legally a nuisance. These examples suggest, first, that the question is one of fact, not of law, and second, that the standard is an objective community standard rather than the subjective standard of the affected individual. Should that be so?

Environmental litigators must often look for the cheapest available probative evidence to make their cases. In *Boomer*, for example, corroded gutters, soiled wash from the clothesline, or cement dust-coated vegetables might be effective exhibits for proving the unreasonable burden on plaintiffs, because they graphically demonstrate that defendant's conduct materially interfered with plaintiffs' ordinary activities. What other physical evidence of pollution damage is likely to be persuasive? Can testimonial evidence of inconvenience, such as the need to dust windowsills, be equally effective? An aggrieved householder may be a vivid witness, able to express anger at defendant's unwarranted intrusions. Or would it be preferable to present third-party testimony, such as that of a real estate agent who observed the grit and dust and could correlate those phenomena with estimates of reduced market value of the parcel, or a doctor or occupational safety specialist who could testify about the health threat of airborne particulates while also describing the conditions at the plaintiff's house? Does the utility of such evidence vary depending on whether the case is being tried to a jury rather than to a judge sitting alone? (As in other common law torts, of course, in nuisance cases where damages are sought either party has the right to demand a jury.)

THE QUALITATIVE CONDUCT OF THE POLLUTER

What did the Atlantic Cement Company do that was "wrong"? The trial judge found that the cement plant had "installed at great expense the most efficient devices available to prevent the discharge of dust and polluted air into the atmosphere." Must the plaintiff prove "fault," as in a negligence case, showing that defendant's conduct was careless or unreasonable in some way? If that were so, then the case would be actionable in negligence, and the doctrine of intentional nuisance would be redundant.

In proving an intentional tort, must the plaintiffs show that the defendant's conduct was undertaken with malice aforethought, or was intended to harm the plaintiff? Not at all. Those are questions typically raised by the criminal law, under which the mental state of the actor is of great concern. In general, however, the tort of private nuisance imposes only the modest requirement that the defendant know with substantial certainty that such an injury was likely to occur to someone. In *Boomer*, the cement company had ignored the neighbors' repeated complaints and petitions, which virtually proves the civil intent element. In most pollution cases, the obvious likelihood that pollutants will travel into neighboring areas answers most quibbles on this point.

CAUSATION

In the *Boomer* case there was little dispute that the damages alleged by plaintiffs were caused by the Atlantic Cement Company, a new major industrial facility located in an area previously devoted to rural uses. In many environmental cases, however, proof of defendant's causation of plaintiffs' harm is extremely difficult. In a heavily industrialized area, for example, how do plaintiffs prove which of several factories is (are) the culprit(s) and to what degree? Prevailing wind charts and chemical or microscopic analysis of the invasive material may point to one installation rather than another, but the job of proof can be technically demanding. In appropriate cases, plaintiffs may try to establish joint and several liability between several polluters joined as defendants, all of whom may have contributed to the nuisance. If plaintiffs prevail, the burden shifts to the several defendants to apportion the loss among themselves. Joint and several liability will be studied with the toxics cases in the next chapter. The toxics cases also raise further tough causation problems, as, for example, when plaintiffs try to prove the etiology of long-latent diseases deriving from past chemical exposures. If Mr. Boomer had contracted chronic bronchial asthma, how easy would it be to recover health damages from Atlantic? See Chapter 4.

B. DEFENSES IN ENVIRONMENTAL TORT SUITS

There are two principal ways to defend a torts case: the defendant can deny and refute a critical element of the plaintiffs' prima facie case, or else can try to raise and prove an affirmative defense. As to affirmative defenses, a laundry list of the most common ones can be found in Fed. R. Civ. P. Rule 8(c). A quick review of that list shows only a few – discharge in bankruptcy, estoppel, laches, and res judicata – that might have a bearing on a typical nuisance lawsuit.

Apart from the standard affirmative defenses, environmental lawsuits confront a number of more specialized defenses. In a recent New York chemical dump case involving the "Loeffel" site, the court reviewed an array of defenses:

State of New York v. Schenectady Chemical Co.

N.Y. Supreme Court, Rensselaer County, 1983
117 Misc.2d 960, 459 N.Y.S.2d 971.

[The court first heard the defendant manufacturer's arguments that the elements of a common-law cause of action did not exist, and that cleanup costs were not recoverable. Finding that these arguments lacked merit, the court turned to an illustrative laundry list composed mostly of affirmative defenses:]

The defendant has raised many additional objections.... It is argued that the action is untimely. The limitation applicable to a nuisance cause of action is the three-year period provided in N.Y. Civ. Prac. L. & R. 214. The rule with respect to an ongoing nuisance, as here alleged, is that the action continually accrues anew upon each day of the wrong although the recovery of money damages is limited to the three-year period immediately prior to suit. Defendant's contention that the limitation period should accrue upon the last day of dumping lacks merit since the law has long been settled that, "the right to maintain an action for...nuisance continues as long as the nuisance exists...."

The argument that [the governmental plaintiff] lacks standing to maintain the action because the waters are private rather than public cannot withstand scrutiny. The amended complaint alleges that the waste has migrated from the Loeffel site into neighboring surface and ground water, including two streams. By statute "waters" is defined to include "all other bodies of surface or underground water... public or private (except those private waters which do not combine or effect a junction with natural surface or underground waters)...."

[As to an attempted constitutional prescriptive rights defense, the state high court has] rejected [the] claim that protecting water from pollution somehow violated a due process property right, stating that the argument was "untenable since such rights do not attach to water itself and in any event are required to yield to public health and public safety."

Defendant's next contention is that the complaint must be dismissed since the requested relief is speculative and to some degree not authorized or appropriate. A complaint will not be dismissed due to a prayer for inappropriate relief so long as some right to recover is demonstrated.

The court will dismiss the demand for attorney's fees since that relief is not available in the absence of a statute or contract authorizing same.[5]

5. [Eds. This is not necessarily true. Equity can award fees. See Chapter 11, Part D §1(c).]

The objection that the complaint is improperly set forth as eight separate and distinct causes of action instead of one is not a basis for relief. While better pled as a single nuisance cause of action, the method employed here does not constitute improper splitting since all claims are contained in a single action.

As to the request for dismissal for failure to join necessary parties, i.e., other alleged tortfeasors guilty of dumping at the site, the rule is that those contributing to a nuisance are liable jointly and severally and "it is fundamental that a plaintiff...is free to choose his defendant." If defendant feels that others may have contributed to plaintiff's damage it should commence the appropriate third-party practice.

The argument that plaintiff has released [co-defendants] General Electric Company and Bendix and thus defendant is released, must fail. First of all the...purported releases have not been furnished, lending credence to plaintiff's assertion that they do not yet exist. More importantly, plaintiff has averred that the language of the proposed releases will specifically reserve its rights against defendant; thus, [defendant] will not be discharged.

The defenses of res judicata and collateral estoppel due to the order and judgment of March 4, 1968 in Ingraham v. Loeffels Oil Removal & Serv. Co. are not available since this action involves different parties upon different causes of action, and defendant's responsibility, if any, was never addressed in the prior action.

Likewise, dismissal is not warranted under N.Y. Civ. Prac. L. & R. 3211 due to "another action pending between the same parties for the same cause of action," since the pending case of Thornton v. General Electric does not involve the identical parties and causes of action.

The defense that the statutory scheme of the Environmental Conservation Law is exclusive and bars common law actions is directly contradicted by §17-1101 of that law....

Likewise, the complaint cannot be dismissed upon defendant's "state of the art" defenses.... The fact that a manufacturer may have complied with the latest industry standards is no defense to an action to abate a nuisance since, as stated earlier with respect to public nuisances and inherently dangerous activities, fault is not an issue, the inquiry being limited to whether the condition created, not the conduct creating it, is causing damage to the public.

The final argument for dismissal worthy of discussion is the contention that by hiring a private contractor licensed to dispose of chemical wastes the defendant has met its legal duty and cannot be held liable for the contractor's wrongdoing. Defendant [however, can] be found liable for Loeffel's acts if: (1) it was negligent in retaining an incompetent contractor; (2) it failed, with knowledge thereof, to remedy or prevent an unlawful act; (3) the work itself was illegal; (4) the work itself was inherently dangerous; or (5) the work involved the creation of a nuisance....

[The opinion on the merits in *Schenectady Chemical* appears at 122 *infra*.]

COMMENTARY AND QUESTIONS

1. Evaluating *Schenectady Chemical's* defenses. Consider each of the foregoing defensive arguments made by the chemical company. Which of them deserve legitimate attention when such environmental cases go to trial? Although the company's lawyers raised a welter of attempted defenses, there are more:

2. The permit defense. One common line of defense in environmental cases, the "permit defense," is a form of pre-emption argument based on defendant's assertion that the polluting activity is being conducted under the terms of a valid government permit. (A number of pollution permit systems are explored *infra*, Chapters 15 and following.) This defense is consistently rejected in intentional nuisance cases, unless the statute creating the permit system has expressly repealed the availability of common law remedies in the field. Because environmental activists are keenly aware of this issue, virtually all pollution statutes have specifically rejected industry lobbyists' attempts to pre-empt common law by making statutory permit enforcement the exclusive pollution remedy. Where a case is argued as a negligence-based nuisance, on the other hand, courts have been readier to take notice of permit compliance as one element of defining defendant's duty of reasonable care and its breach. In policy terms, why shouldn't permit compliance always be a good defense?

3. Primary jurisdiction. The "primary jurisdiction" defense is less dramatic but equally disliked by environmental plaintiffs. Under this defense, the defendant urges the judge to suspend the common law suit, in order to await enforcement by the government agency with jurisdiction over the matter. The argument is not that common law remedies do not co-exist with the public law remedy, but rather that courts should initially defer to the expertise, official appropriateness, and uniformity function represented by the statutory regulators. Environmental plaintiffs bemoan such remands to the agencies. Why? The fact that polluters want to be sent to the official agencies gives some indication of which forum is more likely to provide effective remedies against them (as well as giving an ironic twist to familiar corporate arguments denouncing the bureaucratic state). Plaintiffs try to resist the primary jurisdiction defense by arguing that the reasons for deference to agencies don't apply in their case, that only a court can offer them damage remedies, that unlike the public law system the common law is designed to deal with localized controversies, and so on.[6] Primary jurisdiction is not a well-understood nor widely litigated defense. It invites interesting environmental arguments on both sides of the question.

4. Industry practice and custom. Can a defendant prevail by proving that her conduct was "normal and customary industry practice," reasonable and accepted within that industry? This can be a useful defense in negligence actions, although in some cases courts find that the industry practice is negligent. But the *Ducktown* precedent, confronting this defense, shows why there is a strategic difference between intentional and negligent tort: Proof that defendant is doing things as well as others in her industry does not rebut the fact that, even using those methods, the pollution is substantially certain to occur. As with contributory negligence and other negligence-oriented defenses, the intentional tort finesses the defense. In the *Boomer* case, as in the *Schenectady Chemical* excerpt above, the defense made was even stronger, alleging that the defendant's plant was "state-of-the-art." If indeed the defendant can prove that there is no cleaner pollution control technology available, a consequent finding of the reasonableness of defendant's conduct is

6. See Comment, Primary Jurisdiction in Environmental Cases, 48 Indiana L.J. 676 (1973).

likely to defeat a negligence liability claim. Why shouldn't that be a good defense against intentional tort claims?

5. Statutes of limitation and other time bars. Can statutes of limitations provide a good defense for operators of longstanding nuisances? What if a state has a three-year general torts statute of limitation, and an offending plant commenced operations five years before the suit is brought? Not all state courts have treated the question alike, but the majority position seems to be like *Schenectady Chemical's*, that if the pollution is a "continuing nuisance," each day is a separate injury, so that a lawsuit can recapture all losses within the period of the statute of limitations. When, however, a nuisance is of a "permanent" nature (loosely defined as a nuisance plainly intended from the first to continue to operate for many years in exactly the same way, like a major electric generation facility), the defendant may use the tort statute of limitations to bar untimely suits. In such cases, the statute begins to run from the time at which the cause of action first accrues to the plaintiff. See Goldstein v. Potomac Electric Power Co., 404 A.2d 1064 (Md. 1979). Do you see that the two different scenarios are not always clearly distinguishable?[7]

Even where a lawsuit is brought within the statute of limitations, a defendant may claim to have acquired a prescriptive private right to pollute, noted in Chapter 5 at page 238 *infra*; the prescriptive period is usually in the ten-to-twenty year range. Other estoppel arguments are also available against injunction suits under the equitable defense of laches. As in *Schenectady*, however, public rights usually override such private defenses. As to when limitations start to run, see page 221 *infra*.

6. Coming to the nuisance. A few states still recognize a special defense (a form of estoppel defense) called "coming to the nuisance." As the name suggests, the thrust of the claim is that the defendant had become established in the area before the plaintiff arrived, so the injury to plaintiff was, in effect, self-inflicted. Would a coming to the nuisance defense have prevailed in *Boomer*? As indicated by its lack of widespread recognition, the defense of coming to the nuisance is flawed analytically. Although the defendant may have begun operations that did no palpable harm to neighboring landowners at the time, with the advent of the injury to plaintiff the question is who enjoys the better right – plaintiff to the quiet enjoyment of her land, or defendant to continue the operation of its factory in the same fashion? To say, as a defendant does in raising this defense, that plaintiff could have avoided the conflict by settling elsewhere, begs the question whether defendant had any legal right to insist that plaintiff do so. In the last analysis, defendant is seeking to use another's land as its disposal site without ever having purchased that privilege from its neighbor. Most modern courts do not seem fully to understand the defense's internal flaws. Instead they most frequently point to the existence of tight housing markets, or zoning ordinances, to affirm the primacy of residential uses. The defense accordingly may still be applied in some rural areas.

7. For more on toxic tort statute of limitations issues, see pages 221–222 *infra*.

7. The best defense is a good offense? One interesting environmental defense tactic is the filing of "SLAPPs" – strategic lawsuits against public participation. When public-interest citizen activists bring actions to enforce the common law or statutory law against polluters, developers, public utilities, and ranchers or other entrepreneurs using federal lands, in at least one hundred recent cases defendants have sued or countersued for damages averaging $7,400,000.[8] To get around the First Amendment's petition protection, defense lawyers argue in tort: plaintiffs' allegations amount to libel, slander, defamation, interference with business advantage, and abuse of judicial process.

On their merits, SLAPP suits are overwhelmingly thrown out of court if plaintiffs persevere in resisting them. The fear and burden on volunteer activists of defending against these intimidation suits, however, in practice has resulted in the collapse of many citizen initiatives. Well-heeled defendants can justify spending time and money on SLAPP suits as tax-deductible business expenses, knowing that the citizen plaintiffs are likely to be greatly hindered, or halted, in their efforts regardless of the SLAPP suit's minimal merits. Given the disparate status of the players and the courts' current lack of rigor against attorneys bringing such suits, environmental plaintiffs' ability to obtain sanctions (as allowed under Federal Rule of Civil Procedure II) against SLAPP attorneys remains largely theoretical.

8. The strategies of environmental defendants. Environmental defenses are predominantly directed toward blocking plaintiffs' claims from going to trial. Where plaintiffs can prove the factual elements of an intentional tort claim, there is no general substantive theory of environmental defense available to polluters for avoiding payment of environmental damages as a cost of doing business. As you go through environmental case law, keep an eye on the various defense strategies that are mobilized. Understandably, they are often attempts to duck the merits, or to switch them into forums that are more politically and economically sensitive to defendants' interests.

C. A COMPENDIUM OF TORT CAUSES OF ACTION AND SPECIAL ISSUES THEY RAISE

A variety of common law theories beyond private nuisance can provide a basis for environmental lawsuits, each with particular requirements and utility. In each case a plaintiff must fit the defendant's conduct into a theory on which liability can be based, and must prove damage and causation. In general, damage and causation elements are the same for all torts; the principal difference among the torts lies in the definition of the other elements of each theory.

---

8. SLAPPS have also issued in response to the filing of petitions and testimony by activists in legislative and executive proceedings. See generally Canan & Pring, Studying Strategic Lawsuits Against Public Participation, 22 Law & Soc'y Rev. 385 (1988:2); Pring, Intimidation Suits Against Citizens: A Risk for Public Policy Advocates, 7 Nat. L.J. 16 (1985); Comment, Counterclaim and Countersuit Harassment of Private Environmental Plaintiffs, 74 Mich. L. Rev. 106 (1975).

Modern tort law to some extent still reflects the old English common law courts' formulaic writ system. Under that arcane and rigid system, a plaintiff would have to select a single writ, such as trespass on the case (the writ that has grown into the typical modern day negligence cause of action), and then prove facts that precisely "fit the writ."

In the adaptation of tort law to environmental cases, the importance of the old writ system is greatly reduced by modern civil procedure's lenient fact pleading, eliminating the traps of hypertechnical writ allegations, and the procedure of pleading in the alternative. Today, an environmental plaintiff can allege the facts of pollution, and in a single lawsuit claim that defendant is maintaining a private nuisance and a public nuisance, committing a trespass, and causing personal injuries, and allege separate claims for recovery in each tort (except trespass) based on negligence, intentional conduct, and strict liability. The old writ system has produced differences that give the torts different tactical and strategic advantages, and sometimes continues to have confusing effects like mixing negligence and intention theories.

In analyzing each of the tort theories here, consider the different demands they place upon plaintiffs and defendants, and the different advantages they offer for capturing and bringing environmental values into the legal balance.

Section 1. PUBLIC NUISANCE

Public nuisance, quite unlike private nuisance, is descended from criminal offenses against the public peace. Over time public nuisance became a civil action as well, providing remedies for violations of public rights. Traditionally it has applied to cases like the blocking of public rights of way, or offenses against public sensitivities and decency, like boisterous saloons and bawdy houses or, in modern times, pornography shops. In typical public nuisance actions, public prosecutors bring lawsuits seeking injunctions to force cessation of nuisances (often preferring the tort approach even where statutory remedies apply). Public nuisance is usually litigated as an intentional tort. In some circumstances public nuisance actions can be brought by private plaintiffs, and public nuisances can simultaneously be private nuisances. In analyzing the following cases, consider the tactical advantages public nuisance offers prosecutors and private plaintiffs.

State of New York v. Schenectady Chemical Co.

N.Y. Supreme Court, Rensselaer County, 1983
117 Misc.2d 960, 459 N.Y.S.2d 971.

[The portion of the opinion dealing with defenses appears at 117 *supra*.]

The court must decide if the State, either by statute or common law, can maintain an action to compel a chemical company to pay the costs of cleaning up a dump site so as to prevent pollution of surface and ground water when the dumping took place between 15 to 30 years ago at a site owned by an independent contractor hired by the chemical company to dispose of the waste material....

The amended complaint contains the following factual assertions. The action is brought by the State in its role as guardian of the environment against Schenectady

Chemicals, Inc. with respect to a chemical dump site located on Mead Road, Rensselaer County, New York (hereinafter referred to as the "Loeffel site"). Since 1906 Schenectady Chemicals has manufactured paints, alkyl phenols and other chemical products, a byproduct of which is waste, including but not limited to phenol, benzene, toluene, xylene, formaldehyde, vinyl chloride, chlorobenzene, 1,2 dichlorobenzene, 1,4 dichlorobenzene, trichloroethylene, chloroform, ethyl benzene, nethylene chloride, 1,1 dichloroethane, 1,2 dichloroethane, trans-1,2 dichloroethylene, lead, copper, chromium, selenium, and arsenic. These chemical wastes are dangerous to human, animal and plant life, and the defendant was so aware. During the 1950s until the mid-1960s the defendant disposed of its chemical wastes by way of contract with Dewey Loeffel, or one of Mr. Loeffel's corporations. Mr. Loeffel made pick-ups at the defendant's manufacturing plants and disposed of the material by dumping directly into lagoons at the Loeffel site, and in some instances by burying the wastes. It is alleged that with knowledge of the danger of environmental contamination if its wastes were not properly disposed, and knowing of Loeffel's methods, Schenectady Chemicals: (1) hired an incompetent independent contractor to dispose of the wastes; and (2) failed to fully advise Loeffel of the dangerous nature of the waste material and recommend proper disposal methods.

It is alleged that the Loeffel site is approximately 13 acres of low-lying swamp land located in a residential-agricultural area in Rensselaer County with surface soil consisting mainly of gravel and sand. The ground water beneath the site is part of an aquifer which serves as the sole source of water for thousands of area residents and domestic animals. The site drains into two surface streams, one a tributary of the Valatie Kill, and the other a tributary of Nassau Lake. During the period in question approximately 46,300 tons of chemical wastes were deposited at the Loeffel site, of which 17.8 percent, or 8,250 tons, came from defendant. The other material was generated by General Electric Company and Bendix Corporation and has been so inextricably mixed with defendant's as to become indistinguishable....

The complaint alleges that over the years the chemical wastes have migrated into the surrounding air, surface and ground water contaminating at least one area drinking well and so polluting, or threatening to pollute, the area surface and ground water as to constitute an unreasonable threat to the public well-being and a continuing public nuisance. As a result, the Department of Environmental Conservation (DEC) developed a plan to prevent further migration of chemical wastes from the site, and General Electric and Bendix have agreed to pay 82.2 percent of the costs thereof. Defendant's refusal to pay its portion of the clean-up costs gives rise to this suit.

The fourth through eighth causes of action rely upon a nuisance theory. The "term nuisance, which in itself means no more than harm, injury, inconvenience, or annoyance...arises from a series of historical accidents covering the invasion of different kinds of interests and referring to various kinds of conduct on the part of defendants." Copart Inds. v. Consolidated Edison Co., 362 N.E.2d 968. Nuisances are classified as either private or public. In *Copart,* the Court of Appeals described a public nuisance as:

> A public, or as sometimes termed a common, nuisance is an offense against the State and is subject to abatement or prosecution on application of the proper governmental agency. It consists of conduct or omissions which offend, interfere with or cause damage to the public in the exercise of rights common to all in a manner such as to offend public morals, interfere with use

by the public of a public place or endanger or injure the property, health, safety or comfort of a considerable number of persons. 362 N.E.2d at 968....

[The court permitted the public nuisance to be litigated based on both intentional and strict liability theories.] While ordinarily nuisance is an action pursued against the owner of land for some wrongful activity conducted thereon, "everyone who creates a nuisance or participates in the creation or maintenance of a nuisance are liable jointly and severally for the wrong and injury done thereby" 17 Carmody-Wait 2d, N.Y.Prac., §107:59, 334. Even a non-landowner can be liable for taking part in the creation of a nuisance upon the property of another. Thus, in Hine v. Air-Don Co., 250 N.Y.S. 75, the Third Department held that it was for the jury to decide if the defendant had taken part in the creation of a nuisance so as to render it liable to the injured plaintiff through the act of leaving the unassembled parts of a furnace in a pile upon a public sidewalk. In Caso v. District Council, 350 N.Y.S.2d 173, the defendant, a union of employees working for municipal sewage treatment plants, engaged in an illegal strike resulting in one billion gallons of raw sewage being emitted into the East River. The plaintiffs, officials of Nassau County and affected towns on Long Island, sued on behalf of their governmental units seeking compensatory and punitive damages for injury done to their water and beaches. The union moved to dismiss the complaint, alleging that no such cause of action existed.... The Second Department stated, "A common law cause of action in nuisance would appear to be the appropriate remedy in the instant case." 350 N.Y.S.2d 177.

The common law is not static. Society has repeatedly been confronted with new inventions and products that, through foreseen and unforeseen events, have imposed dangers upon society (explosives are an example). The courts have reacted by expanding the common law to meet the challenge, in some instances imposing absolute liability upon the party who, either through manufacture or use, has sought to profit from marketing a new invention or product. The modern chemical industry, and the problems engendered through the disposal of its byproducts, is, to a large extent, a creature of the twentieth century. Since the Second World War hundreds of previously unknown chemicals have been created. The wastes produced have been dumped, sometimes openly and sometimes surreptitiously, at thousands of sites across the country. Belatedly it has been discovered that the waste products are polluting the air and water and pose a consequent threat to all life forms. Someone must pay to correct the problem, and the determination of who is essentially a political question to be decided in the legislative arena. As Judge Bergan noted in Boomer v. Atlantic Cement Co., resolution of the issues raised in society's attempt to ameliorate pollution are to a large extent beyond the ken of the judicial branch. Nonetheless, courts must resolve the issues raised by litigants and, in that vein, this court holds that the fourth through seventh causes of action of the amended complaint state viable causes of action sounding in nuisance.

[In subsequent proceedings, the case was settled out of court, with no admission of liability. There was, however, a consent judgment whereby the defendant paid $498,500 in damages. Additionally, the defendant was not excused from paying for future damages if pollution migrated off the site. Eds.]

COMMENTARY AND QUESTIONS

1. Why public nuisance? Why did the government prosecutors in this case use common law instead of the elaborate federal and state statutory provisions that were available for decontamination of toxic sites? Does public nuisance provide greater efficiency in establishing liability and obtaining effective remedies? This case may also illustrate how liberal the concept of "intentional" tort can be. How did the court determine civil intent? What did the defendant know was substantially certain to happen? In a public nuisance action brought by the appropriate public official, is the remedial calculus regarding grant of an injunction, including a balancing of the equities, the same as in *Boomer*? The public plaintiff is clothed with a presumptive authority to speak for the common good. Does that mean that the interests represented by the public official presumptively outweigh the costs to a private nuisance-maker when equities are balanced, or does it merely mean that (unlike in *Boomer*) the public values are allowed onto the scale?

2. Vicarious liability. Did Schenectady Chemical create the nuisance in this case or did Loeffel? Here Loeffel and his various companies are independent contractors. One who hires an independent contractor will usually not be vicariously liable for the contractor's acts.[9] Do you think Loeffel's creation of a nuisance should be imputed to Schenectady in any event? Is your answer based on the law of independent contractors or on a sense that the court is not about to let a large chemical concern hide behind a small (probably bankrupt) disposal firm?

3. Aquifers attract toxics. Note the horrendous siting of this toxic dump, in a low-lying wetland with sub-strata of gravel and sand, precisely the kind of geology that carries groundwater and acts as an aquifer recharge area. Perversely, many dumpers over the years have chosen marshes and gravel quarries as the most convenient dumping spots – out of sight, out of mind. Once within an aquifer, a toxic plume spreads widely, and decontamination of the subsoil is grossly expensive and time-consuming if not impossible.

The following public nuisance case is best known for its strange remedy, but the environmental implications of its cause of action are likewise notable:

Spur Industries, Inc. v. Del Webb Development Co.
Supreme Court of Arizona, 1972
108 Ariz. 178, 494 P.2d 700

CAMERON, J. The area in question is located in Maricopa County, Arizona, some 14 to 15 miles west of the urban area of Phoenix, on the Phoenix-Wickenburg Highway, also known as Grand Avenue. About two miles south of Grand Avenue is Olive Avenue which runs east and west. 111th Avenue runs north and south as does the Agua Fria River immediately to the west.

Farming started in this area about 1911. In 1929, with the completion of the Carl Pleasant Dam, gravity flow water became available to the property. By 1950, the only urban areas in the vicinity were the agriculturally related communities of Peoria, El Mirage, and Surprise located along Grand Avenue. Along 111th Avenue approximately one mile south of Grand Avenue and 1½ miles north of Olive

9. Employers will typically be liable for the acts of an independent contractor only where they colluded in wrongful acts, or where strict liability can be proved. Some environmental attorneys have gotten around this bar by suing employers for their "negligent choice of independent contractor."

Avenue, the community of Youngtown was commenced in 1954. Youngtown is a retirement community appealing primarily to senior citizens.

In 1956, Spur's predecessors in interest, H. Marion Welborn and the Northside Hay Mill and Trading Company, developed feedlots about ½ mile south of Olive Avenue. The area is well suited for cattle feeding and in 1959, there were 25 cattle feeding pens or dairy operations within a 7 mile radius of the location.... In April and May of 1959, the Northside Hay Mill was feeding between 6,000 and 7,000 head of cattle and Welborn approximately 1,500 head on a combined area of 35 acres.

In May of 1959, Del Webb began to plan the development of an urban area to be known as Sun City. For this purpose, the Marinette and Santa Fe Ranches, some 20,000 acres of farmland, were purchased for $15,000,000 or $750.00 per acre. This price was considerably less than the price of land located near the urban area of Phoenix, and along with the success of Youngtown was a factor influencing the decision to purchase the property in question.

By September 1959, Del Webb had started construction of a golf course south of Grand Avenue and Spur's predecessors had started to level ground for more feedlot area. In 1960, Spur purchased the property... and began a rebuilding and expansion program extending both to the north and south of the original facilities. By 1962 Spur's expansion program was completed and had expanded from approximately 35 acres to 114 acres.

Accompanied by an extensive advertising campaign, homes were first offered by Del Webb in January 1960 and the first unit to be completed was south of Grand Avenue and approximately 2½ miles north of Spur. By May 2, 1960, there were 450 to 500 houses completed or under construction. At this time, Del Webb did not consider odors from the Spur feed pens a problem. [In 1963 Webb's staff knew of the potential conflict, but decided to continue its southward development.] By December 1967, Del Webb's property had extended south to Olive Avenue and Spur was within 500 feet of Olive Avenue to the north.... Del Webb continued to develop in a southerly direction until sales resistance became so great that the parcels were difficult if not impossible to sell.... Del Webb filed its original complaint alleging that in excess of 1,300 lots in the southwest portion were unfit for development for sale as residential lots because of the operation of the Spur feedlot.

Del Webb's suit complained that the Spur feeding operation was a public nuisance because of the flies and the odor which were drifting or being blown by the prevailing south to north wind over the southern portion of Sun City. At the time of the suit, Spur was feeding between 20,000 and 30,000 head of cattle, and the facts amply support the finding of the trial court that the pens had become a nuisance to the people who resided in the southern part of Del Webb's development. The testimony indicated that cattle in a commercial feedlot will produce 35 to 40 pounds of wet manure per day, per head, or over a million pounds of wet manure per day for 30,000 head of cattle, and that despite the admittedly good feedlot management and good housekeeping practices by Spur, the resulting odor and flies produced an annoying if not unhealthy situation as far as the senior citizens of southern Sun City were concerned. There is no doubt that some of the citizens of Sun City were unable to enjoy the outdoor living which Del Webb had advertised and that Del Webb was faced with sales resistance from prospective purchasers as well as strong and persistent complaints from the people who had purchased homes in that area....

It is noted, however, that neither the citizens of Sun City nor Youngtown are represented in this lawsuit and the suit is solely between Del Webb Development Company and Spur Industries.... It is clear that as to the citizens of Sun City, the operation of Spur's feedlot was both a public and a private nuisance. They could have successfully maintained an action to abate the nuisance. Del Webb, having shown a special injury in the loss of sales, has a standing to bring suit to enjoin the nuisance. The judgment of the trial court permanently enjoining the operation of the feedlot is affirmed.

A suit to enjoin a nuisance sounds in equity and the courts have long recognized a special responsibility to the public when acting as a court of equity: Courts of equity may, and frequently do, go much further both to give and withhold relief in furtherance of the public interest than they are accustomed to go when only private interests are involved. Accordingly, the granting or withholding of relief may properly be dependent upon considerations of public interest.... 27 Am. Jur. 2d, Equity, §104, 626.

In addition to protecting the public interest, however, courts of equity are concerned with protecting the operator of a lawful, albeit noxious, business from the result of a knowing and willful encroachment by others near his business.

In the so-called "coming to the nuisance" cases, the courts have held that the residential landowner may not have relief if he knowingly came into a neighborhood reserved for industrial or agricultural endeavors and has been damaged thereby:

> Plaintiffs chose to live in an area uncontrolled by zoning laws or restrictive covenants and remote from urban development. In such an area plaintiffs cannot complain that legitimate agricultural pursuits are being carried on in the vicinity, nor can plaintiffs, having chosen to build in an agricultural area, complain that the agricultural pursuits carried on in the area depreciate the value of their homes....[citations omitted]

Were Webb the only party injured, we would feel justified in holding that the doctrine of "coming to the nuisance" would have been a bar to the relief asked by Webb, and, on the other hand, had Spur located the feedlot near the outskirts of a city and had the city grown toward the feedlot, Spur would have to suffer the cost of abating the nuisance as to those people locating within the growth pattern of the expanding city....

There was no indication in the instant case at the time Spur and its predecessors located in western Maricopa County that a new city would spring up, full blown, alongside the feeding operations and that the developer of that city would ask the court to order Spur to move because of the new city. Spur is required to move not because of any wrongdoing on the part of Spur, but because of a proper and legitimate regard of the courts for the rights and interests of the public.

Del Webb, on the other hand, is entitled to the relief prayed for (a permanent injunction), not because Webb is blameless, but because of the damage to the people who have been encouraged to purchase homes in Sun City. It does not equitably or legally follow, however, that Webb, being entitled to the injunction, is then free of any liability to Spur if Webb has in fact been the cause of the damage Spur has sustained. It does not seem harsh to require a developer, who has taken advantage of the lesser land values in a rural area as well as the availability of large tracts of land on which to build and develop a new town or city in the area, to indemnify those who are forced to leave as a result.

Having brought people to the nuisance to the foreseeable detriment of Spur, Webb must indemnify Spur for a reasonable amount of the cost of moving or shutting down. It should be noted that this relief to Spur is limited to a case wherein a developer has, with foreseeability, brought into a previously agricultural or industrial area the population which makes necessary the granting of an injunction against a lawful business and for which the business has no adequate relief.

It is therefore the decision of this court that the matter be remanded to the trial court for a hearing upon the damages sustained by the defendant Spur as a reasonable and direct result of the granting of the permanent injunction. Since the result of the appeal may appear novel and both sides have obtained a measure of relief, it is ordered that each side will bear its own costs.

COMMENTARY AND QUESTIONS

1. The twist in *Spur*. On remand, Webb settled, reportedly paying Spur more than $1 million in moving costs. In a subsequent case, the Arizona court also allowed Spur to sue for indemnity, so that Webb would have to reimburse the feedlot for tort damages Spur might have to pay to individual homeowners. Spur v. Superior Court, 505 P.2d 1377 (Ariz. 1973). The unusual feature of the *Spur* case is not its public nuisance theory, but its remedy, conditioning the injunction on plaintiff's payment of moving costs. Is this a case about comparative fault? The court seems to consider that it was the developer's fault that caused the conflict. Is Spur's nuisance therefore based on some kind of no-fault liability? What if the only suit for injunction and damages had been brought by homeowners, not Webb? What if Webb lacked funds to pay Spur? Doesn't this get the court into judicial land use decisions, as noted below?

On a larger scale, it is useful to note that agricultural pollution cases generally can only be litigated under common law theories, because the farm lobbies' political strength has successfully inserted blanket exemptions for agriculture into all significant federal and state pollution statutes. But farmers clearly need protection against tort suits filed by hypersensitive newcomers in rural areas. Since *Spur*, common law courts have not evolved a satisfactory balancing process for protecting rural farming from nuisance suits, but more than 40 states have enacted "right-to-farm" tort exemption statutes for rural areas.

2. The tactical advantages of public nuisance. What advantages did Webb get from suing in public nuisance? Part of his strategy was to get around the coming-to-the-nuisance defense. Did Webb also get a broader basis for nuisance claims than he would have under private nuisance, even class action private nuisance? The court unhesitatingly balanced the overall public interest against Spur. Note, moreover, that there was no proof of personal injury or property damage in *Spur*. The court said that "the odor and flies produced an annoying if *not unhealthy* situation," and seemed to focus on the aesthetics and quality of life of the community of Sun City. Would Oscar Boomer have gained from filing his case in public nuisance? Aesthetic nuisance litigation, applied to billboards, junkyards, and the like, is typically based on public nuisance.

3. A widening role for environmental public nuisance? Public nuisance has traditionally been applied against actions which injure life or health; offend the senses; violate principles of decency; obstruct free passage or use of highways, navigable streams, public parks, and beaches; and otherwise disrupt public rights.

USDA PHOTOS

Inset map from Spur *decision, 494 P.2d 702, and two views of feedlot operations like those involved in* Spur. *Rather than grazing, the cattle have feed and water brought to them. Densities sometimes reach 400+ per acre, with predictable liquid and solid waste and animal health consequences. Note the manure runoff in lower photograph; in some feedlots the wastes do not drain off but accumulate where the cattle stand.*

These definitions obviously possess great potential to expand with contemporary sensibilities to incorporate a wide range of environmental values. How far into novel environmental settings can public nuisance be extended? The aesthetic enjoyment of low-tech visitors to a Walden Pond, a desert park, or a wilderness river can be disturbed by just a few individuals with boom-boxes or all-terrain vehicles. Are these public nuisances? Is smoking in public becoming litigatable as public nuisance? Destruction of historic monuments? Could public nuisance injunctions, if the facts had been known, have blocked the importation of alien species like gypsy moths, poisonous walking catfish, carp, and starlings into the U.S.? Can public nuisance be used where consequences are potentially disastrous but probabilities are uncertain, as with recombinant DNA genetic engineering experimentation outside the laboratory? For an ancient doctrine, the flexibility and scope of public nuisance give it remarkable evolutionary potential.

4. Public nuisance/private plaintiffs. Public nuisance, deriving from criminal law, is in the first instance supposed to be litigated by public prosecutors, but local and state governments often are not enthusiastic about litigation and are sometimes themselves the defendants in public nuisance actions. Private plaintiffs have thus played a major role in the expansion of public nuisance. Private standing, however, has traditionally posed a procedural barrier: in order to sue in public nuisance, private plaintiffs have to show "special injury" different in kind, and not just in degree, from the public as a whole. In *Spur*, for example, Webb's "sales resistance" is special injury. A homeowner in the neighborhood might or might not be granted special injury standing. A disgusted county resident with no health or property damage traditionally would have no hope of suing in public nuisance. Isn't it somewhat paradoxical that in order to represent public values in public nuisance, which offers wide attractions to environmental plaintiffs, they must prove that they are substantially different from the public? Recent amendments to the Restatement 2d of Torts §421c attempt to extend standing in public nuisance, for injunctive relief only, to any person "having standing to sue as a representative of the general public, as a citizen in a citizen suit, or class representative in a class action." Many courts have continued to follow the old special injury rule, although a number of states hold that any bodily injury is *per se* special.

5. Judicial zoning under public nuisance? Given the Arizona court's holding in *Spur*, would it have issued an injunction against Webb's southward development if Spur had timely brought such an action in 1962? The court clearly considered the natural and appropriate use for the area to be agricultural rather than urban. In a number of fascinating cases, courts have issued injunctions against, for instance, funeral parlors and gas stations in unzoned residential areas, judicially recognizing their primarily residential character. Powell v. Taylor, 263 S.W.2d 906 (Ark. 1954)(funeral parlor); State v. Feezell, 400 S.W.2d 716 (Tenn. 1966)(crematorium). In Harrison v. Indiana Auto Shredders, 528 F.2d 1102 (7th Cir. 1975), however, the court permitted a noisy, smelly, gas-and-dust emitting automobile shredding and recycling operation to locate in a low-income neighborhood, merely awarding damages, evidently classifying the neighborhood as less deserving of equitable protection. In Bove v. Donner-Hanna Coke Corp., 258 N.Y.S. 229, 233 (1932), the court denied even damages to a woman whose home was polluted by installation of a smelly coke oven, saying that "it is true that...when the plaintiff built her house, the land on which these coke ovens now stand was a hickory grove. But...this region was never fitted for a residential district; for years it has been peculiarly adapted for factory sites." Recognizing the environmental potential for incorporating evolving public sensibilities into public nuisance, do you nevertheless feel uncomfortable with the role that judges can play in dictating appropriate uses for particular parcels of land?

Section 2. TRESPASS

Borland v. Sanders Lead Company, Inc.

Supreme Court of Alabama, 1979
369 So. 2d 523

JONES, J. This appeal involves the right of a property owner, in an action for trespass, to recover damages for pollution of his property.... J.H. Borland, Sr., and Sarah M. Borland, Appellants, own approximately 159 acres of land, located just south of Troy, Alabama, on Henderson Road. On this property, Appellants raise cattle, grow several different crops, and have a large pecan orchard.

In 1968, the Appellee, Sanders Lead Company, started an operation for the recovery of lead from used automobile batteries. This operation is conducted on property just east of the Borlands' property across Henderson Road. The Appellee's smelter was placed on the west edge of their property, that part nearest to the Appellants' property. The smelter is used to reduce the plates from used automobile batteries. It is alleged by Appellants that the smelting process results in the emission of lead particulates and sulfoxide gases.

It is undisputed that Appellee installed a filter system, commonly known as a "bag house," to intercept these lead particulates which otherwise would be emitted into the atmosphere. The "bag house" is a building containing fiber bags. The smoke emitting from the furnace is passed through two cooling systems before passing through the "bag house" so that the fiber bags will not catch fire. If properly installed and used, an efficient "bag house" will recover over 99 percent of the lead emitted. On two occasions, the cooling system at Appellee's smeltering plant has failed to function properly, resulting in the "bag house's" catching fire on both occasions. There is a dispute as to the efficiency of Appellee's "bag house" throughout its operation. Appellants allege that, because of the problems with the "bag house," their property has been damaged by a dangerous accumulation of lead particulates and sulfoxide deposits on their property....

It is apparent from a further reading of the final decree that the trial Court was under the mistaken impression that compliance with the Alabama Air Pollution Control Act shielded the Defendant from liability for damages caused by pollutants emitting from its smelter. This is not the law in this State.... Furthermore, the trial Court incorrectly applied the law of this State in concluding that, because there was evidence showing that the Plaintiffs' farm had increased in value as industrial property, due to its proximity to the lead plant, Plaintiffs could not recover of the Defendant. Such a rule, in effect, would permit private condemnation, which, unquestionably, is impermissible...[and] overlooks the fact that the appreciation factor is totally unrelated to the wrongful acts complained of....

Alabama law clearly provides an appropriate remedy for Plaintiffs who have been directly injured by the deleterious effects of pollutants created by another party's acts. In Rushing v. Hooper-McDonald, Inc., 300 So.2d 94 (Ala. 1974), this Court held, in a case of first impression, that a trespass need not be inflicted directly on another's realty, but may be committed by discharging foreign polluting matter at a point beyond the boundary of such realty. *Rushing* specifically held that a trespass is committed by one who knowingly discharges asphalt in such a manner that it will in due course invade a neighbor's realty and cause harm.

In *Rushing*, this Court cited with approval Restatement, 2d, Torts, §158, and particularly emphasized a portion of the Comments under this section, which recites:

> In order that there may be a trespass under the rule stated in this Section, it is not necessary that the foreign matter should be thrown directly and immediately upon the other's land. It is enough that an act is done with knowledge that it will to a substantial certainty result in entry of foreign matters.

Rushing further cited with approval the case of Martin v. Reynolds Metals Co., 342 P.2d 790 (Or. 1959). In *Martin*, a case remarkably similar to the present case, the Plaintiffs sought recovery from the Defendant aluminum company, for trespass. The Plaintiffs in *Martin* alleged that the operation by Defendants of an aluminum reduction plant caused certain fluoride compounds in the form of gases and particulates, invisible to the naked eye, to become airborne and settle on Plaintiffs' property, rendering it unfit for raising livestock. Plaintiffs in the present case allege that the operation of Defendant's lead reduction plant causes an emission of lead particulates, and SO_2, invisible to the naked eye, which emissions have settled on their property, making it unsuitable for raising cattle or growing crops.

The Defendants in *Martin* contended that there had not been a sufficient invasion of Plaintiffs' property to constitute trespass, but, at most, Defendant's acts constituted a nuisance. This would have allowed the Defendants to set up Oregon's two-year statute of limitations applicable to non-possessory injuries to land rather than Oregon's six-year statute for trespass to land.

The *Martin* Court pointed out that trespass and nuisance are separate torts for the protection of different interests invaded – trespass protecting the possessor's interest in exclusive possession of property and nuisance protecting the interest in use and enjoyment. The Court noted, and we agree, that the same conduct on the part of defendant may, and often does, result in the actionable invasion of both interests....

The modern action for trespass to land stemmed inexorably from the common law action for trespass which lay when the injury was both direct and substantial. Nuisance, on the other hand, would lie when injuries were indirect and less substantial. A fictitious "dimensional" test arose, which obviated the necessity of determining whether the intrusion was "direct" and "substantial." If the intruding agent could be seen by the naked eye, the intrusion was considered a trespass. If the agent could not be seen, it was considered indirect and less substantial, hence, a nuisance.... The *Martin* Court rejected the dimensional test and substituted in its place a force and energy test, stating:

> The view recognizing a trespassory invasion where there is no "thing" which can be seen with the naked eye undoubtedly runs counter to the definition of trespass expressed in some quarters. It is quite possible that in an earlier day when science had not yet peered into the molecular and atomic world of small particles, the courts could not fit an invasion through unseen physical instrumentalities into the requirement that a trespass can result only from a direct invasion. But in this atomic age even the uneducated know the great and awful force contained in the atom and what it can do to a man's property if it is released. In fact, the now famous equation $E=mc^2$ has taught us that mass and energy are equivalents and that our concept of 'things' must be reframed. If these observations on science in relation to the law of trespass should appear theoretical and unreal in the abstract, they become very practical and real to the possessor of land when the unseen force cracks the foundation of his house. The force is just as real if it is chemical in nature.... Viewed in this way we may define trespass as an intrusion which invades the

possessor's protected interest in exclusive possession, whether that intrusion is by visible or invisible pieces of matter or by energy which can be measured only by the mathematical language of the physicist. We are of the opinion, therefore, that the intrusion of the fluoride particulates in the present case constituted a trespass.

It might appear, at first blush, from our holding today that every property owner in this State would have a cause of action against any neighboring industry which emitted particulate matter into the atmosphere, or even a passing motorist, whose exhaust emissions come to rest upon another's property. But we hasten to point out that there is a point where the entry is so lacking in substance that the law will refuse to recognize it, applying the maxim de minimis non curat lex – the law does not concern itself with trifles. In the present case, however, we are not faced with a trifling complaint. The Plaintiffs in this case have suffered, if the evidence is believed, a real and substantial invasion of a protected interest.

Although we view this decision as an application, and not an extension, of our present law of trespass, we feel that a brief restatement and summary of the principles involved in this area would be appropriate. Whether an invasion of a property interest is a trespass or a nuisance does not depend upon whether the intruding agent is "tangible" or "intangible." Instead, an analysis must be made to determine the interest interfered with. If the intrusion interferes with the right to exclusive possession of property, the law of trespass applies. If the intrusion is to the interest in use and enjoyment of property, the law of nuisance applies. As previously observed, however, the remedies of trespass and nuisance are not necessarily mutually exclusive.

While the direct/indirect analysis of the nature of the intrusion is not a valid method of determining trespass vis-a-vis nuisance, this analysis must be made in order to determine the elements necessary to prove trespass. If the intrusion is direct, then, under our present law, actual damages need not be shown; nominal damages may be awarded and this will support punitive damages....

Under the modern theory of trespass, the law presently allows an action to be maintained in trespass for invasions that, at one time, were considered indirect and, hence, only a nuisance. In order to recover in trespass for this type of invasion (i.e., the asphalt piled in such a way as to run onto plaintiff's property, or the pollution emitting from a defendant's smoke stack, such as in the present case), a plaintiff must show (1) an invasion affecting an interest in the exclusive possession of his property; (2) an intentional doing of the act which results in the invasion; (3) reasonable foreseeability that the act done could result in an invasion of plaintiff's possessory interest; and (4) substantial damages to the res [i.e., unlike direct trespasses which need not show substantial damages]....

If, as a result of the defendant's operation, the polluting substance is deposited upon the plaintiff's property, thus interfering with his exclusive possessory interest by causing substantial damage to the res, then the plaintiff may seek his remedy in trespass, though his alternative remedy in nuisance may co-exist.... Reversed and remanded.

COMMENTARY AND QUESTIONS

1. Trespass and tactics. As the *Borland* and *Martin* courts both noted, pollution may be simultaneously both a trespass and a nuisance, and be litigated as either or both. Why do plaintiffs sue in trespass instead of nuisance? Trespass carries a number of internal restrictions, including those noted by the court and the fact that in most states it cannot be based on mere negligence liability. The statute of limitations for trespass, however, often extends back further in time than nuisance, as it did in *Martin*; damages are available for all consequential injuries throughout the actual chain of causation, not only those foreseeable; and trespass actions seem to encourage the grant of injunctions by emphasizing the fact of an unconsented invasion, penetration, or incursion onto private property. Even judges quite unattuned to environmental issues have acknowledged that "a man's home is his castle," and issued injunctions.

2. How far can trespass go? After *Borland*, Alabama apparently requires actual and substantial injury for an "indirect" trespass like a pollution case. Most other states, however, do not. If courts apply $E=mc^2$ to determine whether there has been "physical invasion" of plaintiff's property, is there any limit to how far the trespass action may apply? Noise? Light photons? Low-frequency electromagnetic radiation from high voltage transmission facilities? An ugly view? Has the distinction between trespass and nuisance become purely semantic; does it any longer make sense?

3. Defenses in *Borland*. Note the defendant's attempt to use the "permit defense." The court's reasoning reflects a distinction between the remedial purposes of the common law and the regulatory purposes of the pollution control statutes – the former is concerned with redress for local injuries, the latter is concerned with minimum public health and welfare standards. Defendant also raised as a partial defense to the assessment of damages the argument that it had caused no loss to the plaintiff because the land had appreciated in value due to its value as commercial property which derived from its proximity to defendant's lead plant. The appellate court rejected the defense. If change in property value is not the measure of damage, what is? Is it possible to base the measure of damages on the change in value of the land as used for purposes desired by the plaintiff?

Section 3. NEGLIGENT NUISANCE, AND NEGLIGENCE

Negligence has seldom been the sole theory of recovery in successful environmental cases. The apparent reason for the relatively rare use of the negligence cause of action is that in cases involving injury to property, like most of those studied thus far, the intentional nuisance or trespass theories (or strict liability, considered in the following section) are easier to prove than negligence. The principal domain of the negligence cause of action is the traditional lawsuit by an injured victim to recover for bodily injuries caused by the defendant's negligence. Personal injury cases do arise in the environmental setting, and are occasionally litigated on negligence theories, see Greyhound v. Blakely, 262 F.2d 401 (9th Cir. 1958), but more typically are litigated under strict liability.

The following case illustrates some of the reasons why there are not many modern negligent nuisance actions.

Dillon v. Acme Oil Company

New York Supreme Court, General Term, 1888
49 Hun 565, 18 N.Y. St. Rep. 477, 2 N.Y.S. 289

HAIGHT, J. The evidence tends to show that the plaintiff's wells were contaminated with oil and rendered unfit for use. The evidence also tends to show that there has been occasional leakage and spilling of oil and the refuse thereof upon the ground at the refinery where the crude is manufactured into refined oil; that the earth had become saturated with it around the refinery.... The plaintiff's premises...are twenty rods away. There is a public street and a railroad, with several tracks, intervening between the plaintiff's and defendant's premises. Taking into consideration the character of the surface soil, it hardly seems possible or probable that the oil upon the ground, at the defendant's refinery, would soak or percolate through the ground collaterally upon the surface so great a distance as to contaminate the plaintiff's wells from the surface. It appeared, upon the trial, that some feet under the surface there was a stratum of gravel, and the more rational and probable theory, to our minds, is that the oil at the refinery had percolated through the earth downward until some subterranean water vein was reached, probably in the stratum of gravel, from which it was conveyed into the wells. And this theory appears to have been the one upon which the case was tried. The court found, as a fact, that the works of the defendant were constructed and operated as well as such works could be, having reference to the location and nature of the business. The question is, therefore, presented as to whether there could be a recovery for contaminating a subterranean water stream or vein when the defendant is pursuing a legitimate business with works constructed and operated as well as they could be. It is said to be a legal maxim, that every man must so use his own property as not to injure that of another, but this maxim is not to be construed so as to deprive a party from using that which he owns for legitimate purposes, provided, in so doing, he exercise proper care and skill to prevent unnecessary injury to others....

It is only in exceptional cases that the channels of subterranean streams are known and their courses defined; it is only in such exceptional cases that the owner can know beforehand that his works will affect his neighbor's wells or supply of water, and we are, therefore, of the opinion that in the absence of negligence and of knowledge as to the existence of such subterranean water-courses, when the business is legitimate and conducted with care and skill, there can be no liability if such subterranean courses become contaminated....

COMMENTARY AND QUESTIONS

1. Negligence defenses. The *Dillon* court based its holding in part on lack of foreseeability, an element that would equally have undercut intentional tort liability. (Was it indeed not foreseeable that oil spilled on the ground would contaminate the groundwater?) But the weight accorded defendant's "legitimate business conducted with care and skill," and its implicit balance of utilities, provided a virtually unbeatable defense under the negligent nuisance theory.

In a case where a coal processing operation's burning refuse piles released clouds of hydrogen sulfide gas that stunk up an entire neighborhood and caused housepaint to turn black, the Pennsylvania Supreme Court also used negligence theories to deny liability. The Court noted that the defendants "used every known means to prevent damage or injury to adjoining properties," but, unfortunately, "there is no known method by which such fires can be extinguished." Quoting two lower court opinions in similar cases, the Court continued:

> The plaintiffs are subject to annoyance [but] it is probable that upon reflection they will...still conclude that, after all, one's bread is more important than landscape or clear skies. Without smoke, Pittsburgh would have remained a very pretty *village*....
>
> The general rule that one must use his own land so as not to injure that of another – otherwise he is liable in damages – is subject to the exception that every man has the right to the natural use and enjoyment of his own property, and if while lawfully in such use and enjoyment, without negligence or malice on his part, an unavoidable loss occurs to his neighbor, it is *damnum absque injuria*, for the rightful use of one's own land may cause damage to another, without any legal wrong. Waschak v. Moffat, 109 A.2d 310, 316-17 (Pa. 1954)(emphasis in original).

Given the defensive effects of such negligence principles, it is unsurprising that most experienced plaintiffs attorneys in pollution cases avoid reliance on negligence theories, and try to clarify for trial judges the significant differences between negligent and intentional torts.

2. The uses of negligence. A few environmental suits not based on personal injuries are decided on negligence theories. See Rotella v. McGovern, 288 A.2d 258 (R.I. 1972)(negligent sewer maintenance produced sewage flood in basement). One of the advantages of negligence to plaintiffs, beyond its familiarity to bench and bar, is the extensive array of damage theories developed in negligence case law, including pain and suffering, offering opportunities for "running up" damage awards. Another is that tort claims acts waiving sovereign immunity may only cover negligence. Under some insurance policies, moreover, defendants will only be covered for accidental discharges, not for "intentional" pollution, so a negligence judgment is more likely to be paid. See e.g., Technicon Electronic Corp. v. American Home Assurance Co., 542 N.E.2d 1048 (N.Y. 1989). Where violations of environmental laws and regulations are proved, plaintiffs' job of proving defendants' negligence may be greatly facilitated. As a tactical matter, even in intentional tort cases it may be to plaintiffs' advantage to present evidence of what the defendant could have done more carefully.

3. The deterrence value of negligence actions. Does the threat of negligence verdicts deter would-be polluters? There is no necessary relationship between the amount awarded to plaintiff and either the costs of avoiding the pollution or the culpability of defendant's conduct. Given the reputation of some negligence litigators, the possibility of large negligence damage awards would surely catch defendants' attention. Most cases, however, continue to proceed on non-negligence theories.

Section 4. STRICT LIABILITY

The Restatement 2d of Torts, §519 provides that:

(1) One who carries on an abnormally dangerous activity is subject to liability for harm to the person, land or chattels of another resulting from the activity, although he has exercised the utmost care to prevent such harm.

(2) Such strict liability is limited to the kind of harm, the risk of which makes the activity abnormally dangerous.

§520 lists the factors to be used when determining what constitutes an abnormally dangerous activity:

In determining whether an activity is abnormally dangerous, the following factors are to be considered:

(a) Whether the activity involves a high degree of risk of some harm to the person, land, or chattels of others;
(b) Whether the gravity of the harm which may result from it is likely to be great;
(c) Whether the risk cannot be eliminated by the exercise of reasonable care;
(d) Whether the activity is not a matter of common usage;
(e) Whether the activity is inappropriate to the place where it is carried on; and
(f) The value of the activity to the community.

Branch v. Western Petroleum, Inc.

Supreme Court of Utah, 1982
657 P.2d 267

STEWART, J. The Branches, the plaintiff property owners, sued for damages for the pollution of their culinary water wells caused by percolation of defendant Western Petroleum Inc.'s formation waters into the subterranean water system that feeds the wells....

In December 1975, Western purchased forty acres of land in a rural area north of Roosevelt, Utah, which had previously been used as a gravel pit. Western used the property solely for the disposal of formation water, a waste water produced by oil wells while drilling for oil. Formation water contains oil, gas and high concentrations of salt and chemicals, making it unfit for culinary or agricultural uses. The formation water was transported by truck from various oil-producing sites and emptied into the disposal pit with the intent that the toxic water would dissipate through evaporation into the air and percolation into the ground. Alternative sites for disposing of the water were available to Western, but at a greater expense.

In 1976, the Branches purchased a parcel of property immediately adjacent to, and at an elevation of approximately 200 to 300 feet lower than, Western's property. The twenty-one acre parcel had on it a "diligence" well, which had been in existence since 1929, some outbuildings, and a home. After acquiring the property, the Branches made some $60,000 worth of improvements to the home and premises. Prior owners of the property used the water from the well for a grade A dairy and later a grade B dairy. Both dairy operations required that the water be approved for fitness and purity by appropriate state agencies. The Branches, as had all prior owners since 1929, used water from the diligence well for culinary purposes. The water from the diligence well was described as being sweet to the taste and of a high quality until December of 1976.

Two months after purchasing the property, the Branches noticed that the well water began to take on a peculiar taste and had the distinctive smell of petroleum products. Soap added to the water would no longer form suds. They observed that polluted water from Western's disposal pit was running onto the surface of the Branches' property and, on one occasion, reached their basement, causing damage to food stored there. After testing the diligence well water and finding it unfit for human consumption, and after their rabbits and one hundred chickens had died, apparently from the polluted water, the Branches began trucking water to their property from outside sources. In November, 1977, the Branches dug an additional well south of their home. Water from the new well was tested and found safe for culinary purposes. But after a few months, the new well also ceased producing potable water, and on advice of the State Health Department, the Branches ceased using the new well for culinary purposes and hauled water to their property almost until the time of trial.

The Branches requested Western to cease dumping formation water in the disposal pit, but Western refused unless the Branches would post a bond to cover the costs....

At trial the major issue was whether and how Western's formation waters caused the pollution of the Branches' wells. Western's expert, Mr. Ferris, a private geologist with approximately two years professional experience in the Rocky Mountain area, and the Branches' expert, Mr. Montgomery, a state geologist who had spent nine years working for the Utah Division of Water Resources, agreed that the subsurface waters consist of shallow groundwater and a deeper aquifer known as the Duchesne Formation. The Duchesne Formation produces the culinary water which is tapped by the Branches' wells. The two experts also agreed that formation water in the disposal pit was percolating into the subsurface waters, but they disagreed on whether thc polluted waters had merely entered the shallow groundwaters or had percolated down into the Duchesne Formation....

The jury obviously considered Montgomery the more convincing of the two experts. It found, in response to special interrogatories, that "defendant's use of the evaporation pit for the dumping of formation water [was] a cause of the pollution of the water in plaintiffs' [wells]," and that Western caused 66 percent of the pollution in Branches' original well and 52 percent of the pollution in the new well. The rest of the pollution was found to be caused by other unspecified "parties or conditions."...

The major substantive dispute is whether the trial court erred in entering judgment against Western on the basis of strict liability for pollution of the Branches' wells. Western argues that other states have based liability for pollution of subterranean waters on either negligence, [intentional] nuisance, or trespass, and that since the Branches failed to allege nuisance or trespass, "the only accepted theory upon which this case could be based is negligence." Therefore, according to Western, the trial court erred in entering judgment on the basis of strict liability. Western further submits that since the court did not instruct the jury on proximate cause and comparative negligence, the judgment cannot stand. The Branches, on the other hand, take the position that Western created an abnormally dangerous condition by collecting contaminated water on its land for the purpose of having it seep or percolate into the groundwater and that, therefore, the law of strict liability controls....

In England under the common law, percolating water was considered part of the freehold and subject to private ownership. In American law it is generally recognized that a landowner has no absolute right to pollute percolating waters. In this state, a landowner has no such absolute right because percolating waters belong to the people of the state. For that reason, and because percolating waters are migratory and the rights of the landowners to those waters are correlative, such waters are subject to the maxim that one may not use his land so as to pollute percolating waters to the injury of another.

As Utah is one of the most arid states in the union, the protection of the purity of the water is of critical importance, and the Legislature has enacted laws for the protection of both surface and subterranean waters....

The landmark case of Rylands v. Fletcher, 3 H. & C. 774, 159 Eng. Rep. 737 (1865), rev'd in Fletcher v. Rylands, L.R. 1 Ex. 265 (1866), aff'd in Rylands v. Fletcher, L.R. 3 H.L. 330 (1868), held that one who uses his land in an unnatural way and thereby creates a dangerous condition or engages in an abnormal activity may be strictly liable for injuries resulting from that condition or activity. Whether a condition or activity is considered abnormal is defined in terms of whether the condition or activity is unduly dangerous or inappropriate to the place where it is maintained. That doctrine was the genesis of §519 of the Restatement of Torts (1939), which, however, limited strict liability to "ultrahazardous activities."

Although Rylands v. Fletcher was initially rejected by a number of states, its influence has been substantial in the United States. According to the latest edition of Dean Prosser's treatise on torts, only seven American jurisdictions have rejected the rule of that case, while some thirty jurisdictions have essentially approved the rule. Indeed, the strict liability rule of the Restatement of Torts was broadened in §519 of the Restatement 2d of Torts by making it applicable to "abnormally dangerous activities."

There are two separate, although somewhat related, grounds for holding Western strictly liable for the pollution of the Branches' wells. First, the facts of the case support application of the rule of strict liability because the ponding of the toxic formation water in an area adjacent to the Branches' wells constituted an abnormally dangerous and inappropriate use of the land in light of its proximity to the Branches' property and was unduly dangerous to the Branches' use of their well water. Several cases on comparable facts have applied strict liability due to the abnormal danger of polluting activity. For example, Mowrer v. Ashland Oil & Refining Co., 518 F.2d 659 (7th Cir. 1975), applied strict liability to the leakage of crude oil and salt water into a fresh water well; Yommer v. McKenzie, 257 A.2d 138 (Md. 1969), applied the same rule to the seepage of gasoline from an underground tank into an adjoining landowner's well; Cities Service Co. v. Florida, 312 So. 2d 799 (Fla. 1975), applied strict liability to the escape of phosphate slime into a creek and river. See also Bumbarger v. Walker, 164 A.2d 144 (Pa. 1960)(strict liability for well pollution caused by defendant's mine blasting). See generally Clark-Aiken Co. v. Cromwell-Wright Co., 323 N.E.2d 876 (Mass. 1975)(strict liability applied to escape of impounded water); Indiana Harbor Belt Railroad Co. v. American Cyanamid Co., 517 F. Supp. 314 (N.D. Ill. 1981)(strict liability applied to spillage of toxic chemical that resulted in property damage and pollution of water supply); W. Prosser, Torts §78 at 512-13 and cases there cited. See also Atlas Chemical Industries, Inc. v. Anderson, 514 S.W.2d 309 (Tex. Civ. App. 6 Dist., 1974), aff'd 524 S.W.2d 681 (1975), where the Texas court, distinguishing a case relied upon by Western, Turner v. Big Lake Oil Co., 96 S.W.2d 221 (Tex. 1936), held the defendant strictly liable for polluting surface streams with industrial wastes. The strict liability rule of Rylands

v. Fletcher was held to apply to pollution cases "in which the defendant has set the substance in motion for escape, such as the discharge of the harmful effluent or the emission of a harmful gas or substance."[10]

In concluding that strict liability should govern in that case, the court in *Atlas Chemical* reasoned that the common law rules of tort liability in pollution cases "should be in conformity with the public policy of this state as declared by the Legislature in the Texas Water Code." Id. at 315. The court also found support for the rule of strict liability in the policy consideration that an industry should not be able to use its property in such a way as to inflict injury on the property of its neighbors because to do so would result in effect in appropriating the neighbor's property to one's own use. An industrial polluter can and should assume the costs of pollution as a cost of doing business rather than charge the loss to a wholly innocent party. The court in *Atlas Chemical* stated:

> We know of no acceptable rule of jurisprudence which permits those engaged in important and desirable enterprises to injure with impunity those who are engaged in enterprises of lesser economic significance. The costs of injuries resulting from pollution must be internalized by industry as a cost of production and borne by consumers or shareholders, or both, and not by the injured individual.

We think these reasons adequately support application of the rule of strict liability in this case.

In sum, the trial court properly ruled that Western was strictly liable for the damage which it caused the Branches. Since liability was properly based on strict liability, the failure of the trial court to give instructions on comparative negligence and proximate cause was not error. Contributory negligence is neither a defense to a nuisance action, nor to an action based on strict liability. The issue of actual causation was decided in favor of the Branches, and there was no issue of proximate causation to be decided....

---

10. *Atlas Chemical, supra,* at 314. Even if Western did not know that the formation water would enter the aquifer and cause damage to plaintiffs' wells, it could have determined the likelihood of that consequence. As Professor Davis has stated:

> A polluter should not be absolved from liability just because he may not be able to anticipate the movement of the polluted groundwater he created. This defense should not be recognized for several reasons. First, the hydrology of groundwater movement is much better understood now than it was when many of the early groundwater pollution cases were decided. Even though precise mapping of groundwater movement in any particular location is still expensive, it is within the reach of any major waste producer which proposes to inject wastes underground. Disposal wells need porous formations for successful waste injection and the appropriate hydrologic tests would insure a successful injection well. Therefore, persons deliberately disposing of wastes underground ought to be required to act in accordance with the information gained by such testing regarding the movement of the injected wastes and their probable effects on neighboring groundwater uses. If they do not make such tests, they should be charged with the information they would have gained had they made them. Second, it is generally known now that liquids placed on the ground will seep into the soil and may enter the body of groundwter percolating beneath the surface. Persons causing groundwater pollution, in ways other than by deliberate underground disposal, should be charged with such knowledge and should not be insulated from liability for groundwater pollution by claiming that they know nothing more about groundwater movement than was known in 1843 when Acton v. Blundell was decided. Although a particular polluter might still legitimately claim he could not predict particular injurious consequences of his activity, he can no longer claim legitimately that the polluting material vanished from the earth once it seeped beneath the surface. He knows it will go somewhere. Such a defense to nuisance liability is not recognized in surface watercourse and air pollution cases. Groundwater pollution cases should not recognize it either.

Davis, Groundwater Pollution: Case Law Theories for Relief, 39 Mo. L. Rev. 117, 145-46 (1974). See also Wood v. Picillo, 443 A.2d 1244, 1249 (R.I. 1982). [This is note 6 in the original.]

COMMENTARY AND QUESTIONS

1. Why strict liability? Analytically, the *Branch* case is a private nuisance action, based on strict liability grounds rather than negligence or intent. What advantages does strict liability offer plaintiffs? Beyond shortcutting various foreseeability elements and defenses in toxic dumping cases like *Schenectady Chemical,* strict liability also automatically extends liability to chemical generators despite their use of independent contractors as intermediaries.

2. "Abnormally dangerous." In *Branch,* what is found to be ultrahazardous or abnormally dangerous under the terms of Restatement §519-520? Is oil an abnormally dangerous material? Or is storage of oil-drilling wastewater an abnormally dangerous activity? On the facts of *Branch,* the closest analogy to *Rylands* is disposing of formation waters by placing them in an impoundment near a property line or recharge area for local wells. Is that enough?

3. Foreseeability. Did Western know that the formation water would reach the wells? It appears that they did not foresee such an occurrence, and even after the fact disputed its occurrence through the testimony of their expert witness. To what degree is foreseeability relevant? In its footnote 6, the court relies on Professor Davis' argument to reject the importance of defendant's foreknowledge of events. What is Davis' argument? It first simply charges highly-capitalized waste disposers with foreseeing whatever testing would have revealed; it second simply recognizes that liquids tend to percolate down into aquifers, and it charges defendants with that knowledge, something that the law refused to do in an earlier era when less was known about hydrogeology. So stated, would there be sufficient evidence of foreseeability in *Branch* to reflect intent? In many settings these cases could just as well be litigated under intentional public or private nuisance.

4. Strict liability for what harms? The court points out the nonchalance of Western in its attitude toward the Branch's rights and its lack of inquiry into the pollution laws of Utah. Why is this relevant in a strict liability case? The answer lies with a claim for punitive damages, discussed in the following section on remedies.

In Langan v. Valicopters, 567 P.2d 218 (Wash. 1977), an aerial crop-dusting service had allowed its pesticide sprays to drift onto an organic farm. No crops were killed. The plaintiffs' injury claim was based purely on their crops' loss of "organic" certification caused by the spray. The court went step by step through Restatement §§519 and 520 and applied strict liability. Looking at §519(2), would you? If pesticide spraying is indeed an abnormally dangerous activity, what kinds of ecological harms can be recouped, by whom? Was Allied Chemical's making and dumping of Kepone an abnormally dangerous activity? If so, is damage to the environment the kind of hazard that made it dangerous, or is strict liability limited to personal injuries?

5. Environmental applications of other tort theories. Beyond the preceding commonly encountered torts, environmental cases filed by creative plaintiffs can be based on theories of "battery" (where pollution is characterized as unconsented intentional physical contact with plaintiffs' bodies), Martin v. National Steel, 607 F. Supp. 1430 (S.D. Ill. 1985); "waste" to land (where degradation of rented land, life estates, or a defeasible fee injures the reversion), U.S. v. Denver RGR Co., 190 F. 825 (D. Colo. 1911); water-based violations of "reasonable use" (impacting riparian property rights), Thompson v. Enz, 154 N.W.2d 473 (Mich. 1967), and other flexible applications of existing doctrine, each presenting different litigation requirements and potential benefits. Environmental plaintiffs are continually exploring and rethinking old tort options in order to develop new litigation approaches and tactics.

D. REMEDIES IN ENVIRONMENTAL LITIGATION

Many novel issues arise in the context of environmental law remedies. The following sections explore equitable remedies, damages, restoration remedies, and natural resources remedies. Criminal penalties are considered in Chapter 7, and administrative sanctions in Part IV's chapters on the administrative state.

Section 1. EQUITY AND INJUNCTIONS

Plater, Statutory Violations and Equitable Discretion
70 California Law Review 524, 545-546, 533-544 (1982)

The exercise of equitable jurisdiction, particularly the availability of injunctions, has increased over the years. The anachronistic requirement of a property interest in order to invoke equity has been scrapped of necessity, and other impediments have been removed. Despite regular protestations to the contrary, the status of the injunction has become a common, widely used judicial remedy precisely because of its ability to fine-tune the requirements of private conduct in a complex, modern society. Its development parallels the expansion of cases [in environmental law and] in civil rights and other constitutional areas, where damage remedies are insufficient or miss the point....

When equity's application in traditional common law cases is subjected to careful analysis, some basic clarifications emerge. Analytically, it can be argued that the umbrella terms "balancing the equities" and "equitable discretion" obscure what are really three separate areas of balancing, three different functions fulfilled by three different types of equitable relativism. The three areas are:

1. *Threshold balancing*, based in both law and equity, tests whether plaintiffs can maintain their actions. This stage includes questions of laches, clean hands, other estoppels, the lack of an adequate remedy at law, proof of irreparable harm, and similar issues.
2. *Determination of contending conducts* ascertains which conduct will be permitted to continue and which will be subordinated. It often involves the question of abatement, a separate issue from the question of liability for past injuries to protected interests.
3. *Discretion in fashioning remedies* involves a process of tailoring remedies to implement the second stage determination of contending conducts.

Consider, for example, the relatively simple field of private nuisance torts where equity has traditionally played an active role. The classic *Ducktown Sulphur* case demonstrates all three of equity's distinctly different roles. In that turn-of-the-century case, 83 S.W. 658 (Tenn. 1904), the court had to deal with an early example of an environmental tradeoff. The smelting industry was getting underway in the foothills of southeastern Tennessee and northern Georgia. It was likely to provide sizable revenues for the entrepreneurs of Atlanta and Chattanooga, jobs for local residents, and copper and other materials for the nation's industrial economy. The copper ore was mined in nearby hills, then smelted in large open-air piles layered with firewood and coal. This firing process, however, produced acidic "sulphurectic" air emissions that eventually turned nearly a hundred square miles of hills into a remarkably stark, denuded desert, its topsoil slowly washing away down sterile, chemical-laden streams. The plaintiffs were farmers whose fields and orchards began to die as the smelting got underway.

The Tennessee high court held that the smelting was a continuing private nuisance, but after long and careful deliberation allowed the defendant industries to continue operations despite their drastic impact upon the plaintiffs' land and livelihood. The court required only that the mills compensate the plaintiffs for their losses. In common parlance, it awarded legal compensatory damages but denied any injunctive remedy, based on a balancing of equities. The *Ducktown* court certainly balanced the equities. Analytically, however, it did so not once but thrice:

Threshold Balancing. The first type of balancing addresses threshold questions which plaintiffs must survive if a cause of action is to be heard. Some issues appear in the guise of affirmative legal defenses: laches and coming to the nuisance, for example, are legal defenses grounded in principles of equitable estoppel. Other issues – clean hands, additional estoppel principles, proof of irreparable harm, and the inadequacy of legal remedies – are more specifically equitable, brought to bear only where the plaintiff seeks equitable remedies. Each of these threshold issues involves comparisons and balances that are part of the longstanding discretionary processes of equity. The *Ducktown* court made several such determinations, excluding some plaintiffs on laches grounds as to certain defendants, confirming their rights to sue as to others, and noting injuries to land that analytically made equitable remedies potentially available on grounds of irreparability.

The Determination of Contending Conducts. After plaintiffs survive equity's threshold gauntlet, nonstatutory litigation moves to the application of rules of conduct. The major discretionary function of the equity court at this second stage is the determination of whether the defendant's conduct will be permitted to continue. To reach this abatement determination, however, courts must first consider issues of liability....

The initial question is whether defendants are liable at all, whether their conduct is "illegal" under the common law.... Plaintiffs in private nuisance cases and in other common law areas seek equitable remedies – particularly injunctions – as well as damages. In such cases, once tort liability is found, the court turns to the different question of whether defendant's conduct will be abated....

The *Ducktown* abatement question focused on the desirability and consequences of the competing forms of conduct, considering relative hardship between the parties, the balance of comparative social utility between the two competing conducts, and the public interest (which usually amounts to the same thing). The court declared:

> A judgment for damages in this class of cases is a matter of absolute right, where injury is shown. A decree for an injunction is a matter of sound legal

> discretion, to be granted or withheld as that discretion shall dictate, after a full and careful considerations of every element appertaining to the injury.

Citing a series of equity cases in which the utility of defendant's enterprises weighed against injunctions, the court's "careful consideration" began with a question that virtually answered itself:

> Shall the complainants be granted, by way of damages, the full measure of relief to which their injuries entitle them or shall we go further, and grant their request to blot out two great mining and manufacturing enterprises, destroy half of the taxable values of a country, and drive more than 10,000 people from their homes?...

The tort debts owed by one party to the other might be decided by uniformly applicable substantive tort principles, but questions of the life and death of farms and smelting plants – of who must stop and who may go on – were left to the flexible hands and heart of equity. In short, courts have used equity to define and exercise a separate judicial role, grounded upon a rational discretion and working beyond the rigid rules of the law.

Tailoring the Remedies.... At this point in a lawsuit, law and equity have determined all the substantive issues, and only the equitable function of implementation remains. If the court had decided in the second stage balance that defendant's conduct may continue, the award of legal damages for past injuries ends the question of remedy. In that situation no equitable remedy is necessary unless required to enforce payment of damages.

When the court determines that defendant's conduct may not continue, on the other hand, a full array of equitable options exists. If defendants agree to abate their activity voluntarily, the court has the option of not issuing any formal equitable remedy at all. This point...is taken for granted in the common law setting: an injunction need not issue if the court finds that the abatement decision will be implemented without it, but will usually issue where there is any doubt on the matter. Between these two extremes lies the declaratory judgment, a remedy slightly more formal and more assertive than the no-injunction option but similarly unenforceable through contempt proceedings. Yet in the case of good faith defendants, a declaratory judgment or less may be all that is necessary to implement the court's abatement decision.

The strength and flexibility of injunctions, however, makes them attractive as the remedy of choice in many cases. Equity courts shape injunctions in multifarious forms: injunctions to halt an enterprise completely, to shut down a particular component activity, to scale down overall activity by a certain percentage, to halt a specific offensive effect, to abate after a lapse of a specific term if certain performance standards are not achieved – these are but a few. Injunctions also serve different tactical ends. They can be wielded to drag a rambunctiously recalcitrant defendant into compliance, to tighten the reins on slipshod defendants whose compliance efforts may be sloppy, or merely to add a final reassuring level of certainty to a good faith defendant's compliance. In short, "the plastic remedies of the chancery are moulded to the needs of justice."

COMMENTARY AND QUESTIONS

1. A range of equitable remedies. The last paragraph offers a reminder that injunctions can be far more subtly crafted than mere cease-and-desist prohibitions. When Oscar Boomer went to his lawyer's office, he undoubtedly wanted to stop that cursed cement dust, and the remedy he instinctively favored for the factory was to shut it down. When most attorneys consider remedies beyond damages they are equally unsubtle; the only injunction they conceive of is an order halting the defendants in their tracks. Environmental attorneys can increase the force and effect of their litigation efforts, however, by considering a range of appropriate, innovative equitable remedies and proposing them to the court. Consider each of the following equity options available as remedies in settings ranging from localized pollution like *Boomer* to massive episodes like coastal oil spills:

- decrees encouraging technological innovation, like Judge Jasen's proposed order in *Boomer*, postponing shutdowns for a set term, to be effective thereafter unless clean technology can be applied;
- decrees ordering, say, a 30 percent cutback in production until cleaner technology is achieved;
- decrees restricting defendant's activity during times when weather conditions are particularly likely to cause pollution damage;
- decrees requiring ongoing corporate monitoring of offsite pollution;
- decrees requiring defendants actively to clean up their externalized pollution;
- decrees ordering installation of particular specified control technology;
- decrees ordering restitution of profits gained from avoidance of pollution controls;
- decrees requiring periodic reporting to the court;
- decrees ordering "restoration" of trees, soil, personal property, and natural resources;
- appointment of equitable trial masters under Fed. R. Civ. P. 53 for managing complex factual and procedural issues prior to judgment;
- appointment of post-decree monitors to oversee defendants' compliance with court orders, backed by subpoena powers and reporting to the courts;
- environmental receiverships, so that where defendant firms can't or won't comply with environmental requirements, courts will take over and run them through appointed equitable receiverships;

and other creative applications of this remarkable judicial power.

Injunctions decree whatever a court chooses to prescribe, and their prescriptive capabilities are given extra credibility by the criminal contempt-of-court penalties they carry with them.

When an injunction commands a halt to a polluting activity, it acts like a decisive statutory prohibition. Is that cost internalization? The more subtle equitable orders noted above can clearly improve the internalization process. In the Oregon aluminum factory cases cited in *Borland*, the courts prescribed precisely which pollution control devices defendants had to install, setting strict schedules. What about cleanup or restoration orders? There is no doctrinal reason why equity cannot take sensitive account of the natural resource consequences of wrongful acts, and remedy them in accord with modern public policy. Defendants' realization that they may have to pay restitution of profits, or to clean or replace soil, trees, or other property, drastically changes the economic calculus of industrial waste disposal, and raises ecological consciousness. See Verdiccio, Environmental Restoration Orders,12 Envtl. Aff. L. Rev. 171 (1985).

2. The balance of equities. The *Boomer* case is perhaps most famous for its rejection of the traditional New York common law rule that an injunction would routinely issue to shut down a continuing nuisance, in favor of the more flexible balancing the equities doctrine. Was the court undercutting environmental protection and sound policy when it reversed the automatic rule? What do you suppose the tendency of trial courts had been in prior nuisance cases when they realized that any finding of nuisance liability would automatically trigger a shutdown of industrial operations?

A fundamental canon of equity law is that an equitable decree must do equity. That means it must be sensitive to public as well as private consequences of proposed restrictions. Under the *Ducktown* principle, it was surely fitting and relevant that the *Boomer* court considered public interests weighing in favor of continued plant operation. But what items were allowed into the balance of equities in *Boomer*? Do they appear to include all relevant information for a full-scale balancing? The court weighed items of both public and private concern affirmatively in favor of the defendant, against the proposed injunction. What did it weigh in favor of the injunction for plaintiffs? A more evenhanded approach might have allowed plaintiffs to present evidence of the cement plant's adverse impacts on the community at large. Why does the majority explicitly remove public health issues from its consideration? In light of the public interest element in equitable balancing, which he himself applied in favor of the defendant, doesn't Justice Bergan's refusal to intrude "broad public objectives" into a simple suit between "individual property owners and a single cement plant" ring hollow? How would you have argued the point?

Would the equities of the case have been different if the Boomers, well before construction of the cement plant, had repeatedly told Atlantic Cement Company that they feared the dust would escape and injure them, only to receive assurances that there would be no problem? See Smith v. Staso Milling Co., 18 F.2d 736 (2d Cir. 1927)(opinion by Learned Hand granting an injunction in such circumstances, under Vermont nuisance law.)

Note that when courts balance the equities to determine what kind of order to issue, they are not restricted to facts and values incorporated in the elements of the cause of action, nor even to the evidence adduced on the trial record. This means that in appropriate cases the equitable balancing can include consideration of a broad range of public environmental concerns that could not be directly litigated, including a community's quality of life, ecological consequences to natural resources, and declared public policies of local, state, and federal governments.

3. Constraints on equitable remedies. In addition to equity's particular threshold and balancing requirements noted in the equitable discretion article excerpt, equity law presents other constraints to environmental litigants. One of the most interesting is the defense of "prospective" or "anticipatory nuisance" seen in Chapter 2's *Wilsonville* case. The traditional rule was that in order to get an injunction against proposed actions, one had to prove the probability of serious injury or that it was a "nuisance per se"; otherwise the law would "wait and see." But in environmental litigation plaintiffs are often attempting to stop activities that have no legal track record. In Wallace v. Andersonville Docks, 489 S.W.2d 532 (Tenn. 1972), for example, a court refused on those grounds to halt a cross-country motorcycle race through a state reserve. Or a case may pose a "zero-infinity" problem – release of a particular chemical or gene-altered organism may have only a small possibility of negative effects, but if they occur they may be catastrophic. As a result the common law abdicated all such issues to the tender mercies of public authorities. There are signs, as in Judge Ryan's concurrence in *Wilsonville*, that the situation is changing. See Sharp, Rehabilitating the Anticipatory Nuisance Doctrine, 15 Envtl. Aff. L. Rev. 627 (1988).

4. Other equitable actions. The present focus on equitable remedies should not obscure the fact that although equity is usually employed to supply remedies for common law or statutory causes of action, there are some causes of action which are themselves based on the traditional equity jurisdiction. Substantive equitable claims thus may have environmental importance in cases involving fraud, bankruptcy, and trust law (the latter plays a major role in Chapter 8). Does equity embody a creative free-floating cause of action? In other words, can a judge issue an injunction whenever she is convinced that a wrong is occurring? Conventional wisdom holds rather that plaintiffs must show injury to a legal right.

5. Restoration remedies. Modern environmental cases have also brought new and expanded currency to the old remedy of restoration. One of the traditional aims of legal damages and equitable orders has always been to return innocent plaintiffs to the position they would have occupied but for the wrongdoing. As a measure of damages for harms to land, the Restatement 2d of Torts §929(a) prescribes "the difference between the value of the land before the harm and the value after the harm, *or* at [plaintiff's] election in an appropriate case, the cost of restoration that has been or may be reasonably incurred." [emphasis added.] The restoration concept has great environmental utility, but raises some knotty problems. Note the potency of the restoration remedy in *Schenectady Chemical*, page 123 *supra*, and *Wilsonville*, page 68 *supra*, where plaintiffs forced defendants to remove polluted soils and restore the land. In these cases, was restoration ordered for its putative safety advantages, or to restore the status quo ante?

Restoration is a powerful deterrent to dumpers: one may initially save hundreds of dollars by disposing of toxins carelessly, but the cost of gathering and removing them can be geometrically more expensive, running into hundreds of thousands or millions of dollars. If you might be caught, it is far cheaper to treat and dispose of chemicals properly at the outset, when you have them in one place, than to recapture them after they have dispersed and percolated through a mile or more of underground gravel aquifer. Restoration provides a compelling deterrent in other settings, too. If a defendant wrongfully chops down trccs, for instance, the ill-gotten profits may quickly be dwarfed by the costs of restoration, especially if the court's order requires replanting equivalent mature trees.

Equitable restoration orders also tend to rehabilitate natural values that would be excluded from the usual monetary interests balanced in legal actions. Consider the effect of an order requiring Allied to cleanse the polluted sediments of the James River and Chesapeake Bay, or Atlantic Cement to reclaim its cement dust. See the discussion of natural resources restoration remedies at page 163 *infra*.

These images, however, suggest some problems inherent in restoration. Restoration may be impossible, or so grossly expensive that it makes no sense. How does a court decide when to order restoration? In a Louisiana case a court noted that the polluted property "is swamp, subject to overflowing by the Mississippi River...used seasonally for grazing...hunting and fishing.... Its value was set at $375 per acre, or slightly over $200,000 for the 550 acres affected.... The restoration of the property, according to plaintiff's witness, would take about seven years, involve the use of 100 trucks running continuously during that time and would cost $170 million...." Ewell v. Petro Processors, 364 So. 2d 604, 608 (La. App. 1978). The court understandably denied the restoration, instead merely awarding the difference in market value, a remedy that left all the toxins in the ground and groundwater. The judge must have suspected that plaintiffs might use a restoration injunction to extort a hefty cash payoff from the defendants, or, if restoration damages were granted, might not actually spend them on restoration. Some case law makes likelihood of actual restoration a consideration in the decision. Puerto Rico v. S.S. Zoe Colocotroni, 628 F.2d 652, 676 (1st Cir. 1980). Should courts presume that market value ($375 per acre in *Ewell*) sets an appropriate maximum remedy?

But there are countervailing examples. Take the case of a defendant who maliciously destroys a private arboretum, clearcutting five acres of exotic imported trees and vegetation. Such a defendant might argue that she has actually *improved* the plaintiff's position in terms of development-based market value; a similar claim was made in *Borland*. On what appropriate basis can damages be awarded, if not to return plaintiffs somehow to their status quo ante? See Restatement of Torts 2d §929.

Section 2. DAMAGES

a. COMPENSATORY DAMAGE REMEDIES – PAST DAMAGES

The typical tort plaintiff seeks an award of compensatory damages for past injuries, whether or not an injunction is also being sought. Unlike injunctive relief, compensatory damages follow automatically upon a finding of defendant's liability. Compensatory damages can include sums awarded for all forms of property damage, injuries to the plaintiff's health, loss of consortium, etc. In *Boomer*, there was little dispute about the amount of damages awarded for past harms. Damages included injury to stored automobiles and other personal property, and, as to real property, the "loss of rental value or loss of usable value," averaging $60 per plaintiff per month. Imputed rental value attempts to gauge the burden imposed by pollution upon the lives of the plaintiffs, assuming that the amount of rent that people would be willing to pay adequately captures the sum total of life-quality values involved. Does it?

Compare the elements of damage allowed in *Boomer* to those found in the typical personal injury lawsuit. In the latter, the plaintiff's recovery is generally made up of two broad categories: (1) compensation for monetary losses such as lost wages, medical expenses, and automobile repair costs; and (2) compensation for intangibles, especially pain and suffering, but also anxiety and emotional trauma. The *Boomer* damages were limited to the first category. Is there any reason to ignore intangible elements of damage? What if Oscar and June Boomer had long been planning on this farm as their idyllic retreat from the sights and sounds of urban America? "Hedonic damages" offer an interesting new remedy theory. Traditional recoveries compensate for injuries and pain sustained, and look to the future only in terms of lost profits or earnings. Hedonics compensate for losses of future quality of life, a broader concept that has obvious applicability in environmental law. See Sherrod v. Berry, 629 F. Supp 155 (N.D. Ill. 1985), affirmed 827 F.2d 195 (7th Cir. 1987), reversed on rehearing 856 F.2d 802 (7th Cir. 1988).[11]

Note, however, that most damage awards make provision only for injuries to human plaintiffs. Possibilities for getting natural resource damages are noted in Section 3 *infra*.

b. PERMANENT DAMAGES

Here is part of the *Boomer* trial court's original opinion denying an injunction and suggesting permanent damages:

Boomer v. Atlantic Cement Company

New York Supreme Court, 1967
287 N.Y.S.2d 112

HERZBERG, J. The ownership of property will be protected unless there are other considerations which forbid, as inequitable, the remedy of the prohibitive or mandatory injunction [but if] the protection of a legal right would do a plaintiff but comparatively little good and would produce great public or private hardship, equity will withhold its discreet and beneficent hand and remit the plaintiff to his legal rights and remedies.... After reviewing the evidence in this action, I find that an injunction would produce great public hardship.... I find that the reasonable market value of each property as of September 1, 1962 (the date of the commencement of operations by Atlantic), the reasonable market value as of June 1, 1967 (the time of trial), and the permanent loss to each plaintiff, are as follows:

11. Though the Seventh Circuit vacated and remanded the lower court's opinion, it did so on other grounds. The Seventh Circuit's prior approval of the hedonic damages, described as testimony that was "invaluable to the jury," 827 F.2d at 206, was not expressly overturned; subsequently, other courts have awarded hedonic damages. See also McClurg, It's a Wonderful Life: The Case for Hedonic Damages in Wrongful Death Cases, 66 Notre Dame L. Rev. 57 (1990).

	REASONABLE MARKET VALUE		PERMANENT DAMAGES
	9/1/62	6/1/67	
Oscar H. Boomer and June C. Boomer	25,000	12,500	12,500
Theodore J. Richard and Miriam W. Richard			
Real Property	30,000	12,000	18,000
Business	40,000	16,000	24,000
Avie Kinley, Martha Kinley and Mary Kinley	140,000	70,000	70,000
Kenneth Livengood and Delores Livengood	18,000	7,000	11,000
Floyd W. Millious and Barbara A. Millious	20,000	8,000	12,000
Joseph L. Ventura and Carrie Ventura	25,000	12,500	12,500
James W. McCall	22,000	11,000	11,000
Charles J. Meilak and Angelina Meilak	26,000	12,000	14,000
		Total	**$185,000**

COMMENTARY AND QUESTIONS

1. The measure of permanent damages. Permanent damages are supposed to account for all the named plaintiffs' private property rights lost to cement dust. In theory, these damages ought to be equal in value to the relief that would have been obtained from the denied injunction. Are they? Market values do capture the current best estimate of what the land's future profitable economic uses will be, discounted back into present dollars, in terms of what a willing buyer would pay a willing seller. According to Herzberg's formula, however, what would be the permanent damages if in the years between 1962 and 1967 Boomer's property value, as polluted, had appreciated, along with general land values, back to $24,999?

Even if the accounting is accurately done (subtracting *present* value as polluted from *present* value as it would be without pollution) the net result of the refusal of an injunction and award of permanent damages is to force Boomer unwillingly to sell Atlantic Cement Company an easement to pollute at its market value. Can the court assess an extra amount to account for his unwillingness to sell? On remand, the trial court found the actual loss of market value to be $140,000, and then added a further $35,000, while admitting that it really couldn't define why: "If analogy is found in Newton's experiment with prisms showing that white light is composed of all the colors of the spectrum, each lending its own characteristics to a degree when passed through a prism, all the approaches to valuation entering into the informed mind and sensitive conscience of the court lend to an appropriate degree in the resulting decision." 340 N.Y.S.2d 97, 2d at 108 (1972). See also Hiley, Involuntary Sale Damages In Permanent Nuisance Cases: A Bigger Bang From *Boomer*, 14 Envtl. Aff. L. Rev. 61, 86-91 (1986). How is the court to choose between a forced sale of rights and the possibility that plaintiffs will use defendant's large sunk capital investment to "extort" a grossly exaggerated price for surrender of their rights?

2. Do permanent damages create private expropriation? Dissenting Judge Jasen in *Boomer* and some commentators have argued that permanent damages are unconstitutional because they amount to private exercise of the condemnation power, "which, unquestionably, is impermissible," said the *Borland* court. But is it? Defendants in cases like *Boomer* are using common law rather than the police power. There are other precedents for private forced purchases – to get access easements to landlocked parcels, to transport water over neighboring lands, or to build milldams – each justified by theories of public necessity. The right to deposit pollution on neighbors, however, is quite a different kind of claimed "necessity." Are such forced sales justified by theories of efficient use of scarce resources?

3. The decision to award permanent damages. Traditionally courts did not award permanent damages, instead permitting the plaintiff to return to court over time to prove a new case. What institutional factors relating to the court system workload and judicial competence militate for and against the old approach? As a litigant in a case like *Boomer*, how valuable to you is the sense of closure that accompanies the award of permanent damages?

4. The future of permanent damages. Despite much discussion in the literature, the *Boomer* decision's permanent damage remedy has not often been applied by subsequent courts. Is it a remedy that deserves more attention, assuming that standards for measuring the damages can be defined, or is there something organically wrong in a remedy that displaces permanent injunctions and is based on discounted future values? Do permanent damages imply that pollution is acceptable as long as polluters pay?

c. PUNITIVE DAMAGES

Punitive damages are extraordinary in a variety of ways. Law in general is conservative about intervening in the private ordering of affairs. Even when an injury that befalls one member of society can be said to have been caused by another member of society, the first impulse of the legal system is to erect relatively high barriers before the power of the state, acting through its courts, will redistribute the loss away from the victim. These barriers are, of course, the various elements of tort, contract, or other causes of action that the plaintiff must be able to prove by a preponderance of the evidence. In tort, the non-strict liability branches all involve culpable conduct. Even strict liability torts involve conduct that has been singled out for special loss-shifting treatment because (in most cases and especially in toxic tort cases) the defendants knowingly engaged in conduct involving great dangers. And even when these barriers are scaled, all that is awarded is compensation designed to make plaintiff whole, restoring the status quo before the defendant's act injured the plaintiff. Permanent damages and past compensatory damages are both pegged to determinations of actual damages suffered.

Punitive damages are based on the egregious wrongfulness of the defendant's conduct. When available, they add a new dimension to damage remedies, serving functions quite different from compensation – retributive punishment and deterrence. Thus in some cases plaintiffs may get $5,000 in compensatory damages, and $100,000 or more in punitives. Punitive damages find justification in the fact that, as the name implies, they are intended to *punish* fault, or reckless disregard for others, even in cases where fault is not an element of the tort. The forty or so states permitting awards of punitive damages typically prescribe them for cases where the defendant's conduct was found to be "willful," "wanton," "malicious," or "reckless." Because it is the wrongful character of defendant's conduct that is the issue, there need be no proportionality between the amount of punitive damages and the actual harm inflicted.

Punitive damages may also serve other purposes, including camouflaged compensation. To some environmental attorneys punitive awards are readily justifiable, not only to force defendants to confront the seriousness of environmental concerns, but more practically as a means of capturing and internalizing some of the unrecovered intangible costs, like ecological injuries to natural resources and property damages to persons downwind for whom injuries were real but insufficient to justify litigation. In the latter cases, punitives are forms of extended compensation for externalities. Further, punitive awards serve as a bounty incentive for private citizen enforcement of environmental standards, acknowledging that public officials are often unable to do so. Injured plaintiffs may also be especially deserving, having suffered disproportionately. To some observers, punitives raise serious concerns because of their absence of standards for quantification, their potential for duplication in multiple lawsuits, and their lack of direct nexus to the externalities imposed by the defendants.

Branch v. Western Petroleum, Inc.
Supreme Court of Utah, 1982
657 P.2d 267, 277-78

[After discussing strict liability in its opinion excerpted at page 137 *supra*, the court went on to discuss punitive damages for the oil company's failure to protect groundwater:]

Western's final contention on its appeal challenges the award of punitive damages. It argues that punitive damages are appropriate only when willful and malicious conduct is shown and that the court erred in including the phrase "reckless indifference and disregard" in its instruction on punitive damages. However, punitive damages may be awarded when one acts with reckless indifference and disregard of the law and his fellow citizens:

> This presumed malice or malice in law does not consist of personal hate or ill will of one person towards another but rather refers to that state of mind which is reckless of law and of the legal rights of the citizen in a person's conduct toward that citizen.... In such cases malice in law will be implied from unjustifiable conduct which causes the injury complained of or from a wrongful act intentionally done without cause or excuse. Terry v. Zions Cooperative, 605 P.2d 314, 327 (Utah, 1979).

The evidence in this case meets that standard. Western discharged the waste water into the disposal pit intending that it seep into and percolate through the soil. Thus, the pollution of the percolating waters was willful and carried out in disregard of the rights of the Branches. Moreover, Western compounded the Branches' problems by its trespass on their land, the spraying of waste water over their land and the failure to comply with state law. In addition, Western continued its dumping activities even after notice of the pollution of the diligence well. The punitive damage award was adequately supported by evidence of reckless indifference toward, and disregard of, the Branches' rights.

Furthermore, there is no merit to Western's contention that the award of punitive damages was excessive and influenced by passion or prejudice rather than reason. The jury was properly instructed that the purpose of exemplary damages is to deter defendant and others from engaging in similar conduct....

Fischer v. Johns-Manville Corp.

Supreme Court of New Jersey, 1986
103 N.J. 643, 512 A.2d 466.

[Plaintiff in this case was awarded punitive damages for lung injuries caused by exposure to asbestos more than forty years earlier. The defendant challenged the award on a number of grounds. Only a small excerpt of the court's discussion is reprinted.]

CLIFFORD, J. The remoteness [in time] of the tortious conduct spawns arguments that it would be inequitable to impose punitive damages in litigation that does not take place until years after the offending event. One such argument posits that changing social values render punishable conduct that would never have been punished at the time it occurred. Professor David Owen cautions against overlooking the prevailing moral and business standards of the time involved. Problems in Assessing Punitive Damages Against Manufacturers of Defective Products, 49 U. Chi. L. Rev. 1, 13-14 (1982). In an earlier article Professor Owen grouped "manufacturer misconduct" into five categories: (1) fraudulent-type, affirmative conduct designed to mislead the public, (2) knowing violations of safety standards, (3) inadequate testing and quality-control, manufacturing procedures, (4) failure to warn of known dangers, and (5) post-marketing failures to remedy known dangers. Punitive Damages in Products Liability Litigation, 74 Mich. L. Rev. at 1329-61 (1976).

We do not perceive that any "changing social values" are implicated in this case, which we view as falling within Professor Owen's categories one and four. Punitive damages were available in this state well before James Fischer was exposed to asbestos. Allen v. Craig, 13 N.J.L. 294 (1833). We cannot imagine that the conduct proven in this case would have been viewed as any less egregious in the 1940s, when the exposure commenced, than it is today. In this connection we share the Appellate Division's reaction to defendant's "knowingly and deliberately...subjecting (James Fischer) as an asbestos worker to serious health hazards with utter and reckless disregard of his safety and well-being." 472 A.2d 577.

It is indeed appalling to us that Johns-Manville had so much information on the hazards to asbestos workers as early as the mid-1930s and that it not only failed to use that information to protect these workers but, more egregiously, that it also attempted to withhold this information from the public. It is also clear that even though Johns-Manville may have taken some remedial steps decades ago to protect its own employees, it apparently did nothing to warn and protect those who, like plaintiff, were employed by Johns-Manville customers engaged in the manufacture and fabrication of asbestos products.

Another concern created by the time gap between exposure and litigation is that the corporate personnel who made the decisions at the time of the exposure are no longer with the defendant company, possibly no longer alive. From this fact it is argued that punitive damages are inappropriate because they will not punish the true wrongdoers. But as many courts have observed, this contention ignores the nature of a corporation as a separate legal entity. Although the responsible management personnel may escape punishment, the corporation itself will not. "It is agency at the time of the tortious act, not at the time of litigation, that determines the corporation's liability." Moran v. Johns-Manville Sales Corp., 691 F.2d 811, 817 (6th Cir. 1982). We are reminded that a primary goal of punitive damages is general deterrence – that is, the deterrence of others from engaging in similar conduct. That purpose is, of course, well served regardless of changes in personnel within the offending corporation.

A related argument, which similarly ignores the legal nature of corporations, is that punitive damages unfairly punish innocent shareholders. This argument has been rejected repeatedly. It is the corporation, not the individual shareholders, that is recognized as an ongoing legal entity engaged in manufacturing and distributing products. True, payment of punitive damages claims will deplete corporate assets, which will possibly produce a reduction in net worth and thereby result in a reduction in the value of individual shares. But the same is true of compensatory damages. Both are possible legal consequences of the commission of harmful acts in the course of doing business. To the same extent that damages claims may affect shareholders adversely, so do profitable sales of harmful products redound to their benefit (at least temporarily). These are the risks and rewards that await investors. Also, we would not consider it harmful were shareholders to be encouraged by decisions such as this to give close scrutiny to corporate practices in making investment decisions.

Another characteristic of asbestos litigation is found in the startling numbers that reflect the massive amount of litigation generated by exposure to asbestos. Although we are mindful of the fact that the case before us involves one worker, whose exposure to asbestos caused legally compensable injury to him and his wife – it is not a class action, not a "mass" case – nevertheless we would be remiss were we to ignore the society-wide nature of the asbestos problem. Recognizing the mass-tort nature of asbestos litigation, we address the concerns that that characteristic of the litigation brings to a decision to allow punitive damages.

Studies show that between eleven million and thirteen million workers have been exposed to asbestos. More than 30,000 lawsuits have been filed already for damages caused by that exposure, with no indication that there are no more victims who will seek redress. Of the multitude of lawsuits that are faced by asbestos defendants as a group, Johns-Manville alone has been named in more than 11,000 cases. New claims are stayed because Johns-Manville is attempting reorganization under federal bankruptcy law. In re Johns-Manville Corp., 26 B.R. 420 (Bkrtcy. S.D.N.Y.1983).

Defendant argues that the amount of compensatory damages assessed and to be assessed is so great that it will effectively serve the functions of punitive damages – that is, defendants are more than sufficiently punished and deterred. We are not at all satisfied, however, that compensatory damages effectively serve the same functions as punitive damages, even when they amount to staggering sums. Compensatory damages are often foreseeable as to amount, within certain limits difficult to reduce to a formula but nonetheless familiar to the liability insurance industry. Anticipation of these damages will allow potential defendants, aware of dangers of a product, to factor those anticipated damages into a cost-benefit analysis and to decide whether to market a particular product. The risk and amount of such damages can, and in some cases will, be reflected in the cost of a product, in which event the product will be marketed in its dangerous condition.

Without punitive damages a manufacturer who is aware of a dangerous feature of its product but nevertheless knowingly chooses to market it in that condition, willfully concealing from the public information regarding the dangers of the product, would be far better off than an innocent manufacturer who markets a product later discovered to be dangerous – this, because both will be subjected to the same compensatory damages, but the innocent manufacturer, unable to anticipate those damages, will not have incorporated the cost of those damages into the cost of the product. All else being equal, the law should not place the innocent manufacturer in a worse position than that of a knowing wrongdoer. Punitive damages tend to meet this need.[12]

Defendant argues further that the cumulative effect of punitive damages in mass-tort litigation is "potentially catastrophic." The Johns-Manville bankruptcy is offered as proof of this effect. We fail to see the distinction, in the case of Johns-Manville, between the effect of compensatory damages and that of punitive damages....

Heretofore the typical setting for punitive damage claims has been the two-party lawsuit in which, more often than not, a punitive damages award was supported by a showing of some element of malice or intentional wrongdoing, directed by a defendant to the specific plaintiff. Even if the actual object of the malicious conduct was unknown to defendant, the conduct nevertheless was directed at a single person or a very limited group of potential plaintiffs.

Punishable conduct in a products liability action, on the other hand, will often affect countless potential plaintiffs whose identities are unknown to defendant at the time of the culpable conduct. We agree with the Illinois court that the mere fact that a defendant, "through outrageous misconduct...manage(s) to seriously injure a large number of persons" should not relieve it of liability for punitive damages. Froud v. Celotex Corp., 437 N.E.2d 910, 913 (1982), rev'd on other grounds, 456 N.E.2d 131 (Ill. 1983).

Of greater concern to us is the possibility that asbestos defendants' assets may become so depleted by early awards that the defendants will no longer be in existence and able to pay compensatory damages to later plaintiffs. Again, it is difficult if not impossible to ascertain the additional impact of punitive damages as compared to the impact of mass compensatory damages alone.

Many of the policy arguments against punitive damages in mass tort litigation cases can be traced to Roginsky v. Richardson-Merrell, Inc., 378 F.2d 832 (2d Cir. 1967). The Roginsky court denied punitive damages to a plaintiff who suffered cataracts caused by MER/29, an anti-cholesterol drug. Although the denial of punitive damages rested on a determination that the evidence was insufficient to send the matter to the jury, the court expressed several concerns over allowing punitive damages for injuries to multiple plaintiffs. The fear that punitive damages would lead to "overkill" turned out to be unfounded in the MER/29 litigation.

12. In addition, it is questionable how much punishment is effected by compensatory damages alone, which are generally covered by liability insurance. We consider our observation in that regard to be valid despite a restricted insurance market and increasing insurance costs.

Approximately 1500 claims were made, of which only eleven were tried to a jury verdict. Punitive damages were awarded in only three of those cases, one of which was reversed on appeal. While we do not discount entirely the possibility of punitive damage "overkill" in asbestos litigation, we do recognize that the vast majority of cases settle without trial.

Accepting the possibility of punitive damage "overkill," we turn to means of addressing that problem. Because the problem is nationwide, several possible remedial steps can be effective only on a nationwide basis, and hence are beyond our reach. One such solution is the setting of a cap on total punitive damages against each defendant. Such a cap would be ineffective unless applied uniformly. To adopt such a cap in New Jersey would be to deprive our citizens of punitive damages without the concomitant benefit of assuring the availability of compensatory damages for later plaintiffs. This we decline to do....

At the state court level we are powerless to implement solutions to the nationwide problems created by asbestos exposure and litigation arising from that exposure. That does not mean, however, that we cannot institute some controls over runaway punitive damages. When a defendant manufacturer engages in conduct warranting the imposition of punitive damages, the harm caused may run to countless plaintiffs. Each individual plaintiff can fairly charge that the manufacturer's conduct was egregious as to him and that punitive damages should be assessed in his lawsuit.... Nonetheless, there should be some limits placed on the total punishment exacted from a culpable defendant. We conclude that a reasonable imposition of those limits would permit a defendant to introduce evidence of other punitive damage awards already assessed against and paid by it, as well as evidence of its own financial status and the effect a punitive award would have....

We realize that defendants may be reluctant to alert juries to the fact that other courts or juries have assessed punitive damages for conduct similar to that being considered by the jury in a given case. Although the evidence may convince a jury that a defendant has been sufficiently punished, the same evidence could nudge a jury closer to a determination that punishment is warranted. That is a risk of jury trial. The willingness to accept that risk is a matter of strategy for defendant and its counsel, no different from other strategy choices facing trial lawyers every day.

When evidence of other punitive awards is introduced, trial courts should instruct juries to consider whether the defendant has been sufficiently punished, keeping in mind that punitive damages are meant to punish and deter defendants for the benefit of society, not to compensate individual plaintiffs.

A further protection may be afforded defendants by the judicious exercise of remittitur. Should a trial court determine that an award is "manifestly outrageous" or "grossly excessive," it may reduce that award or order a new trial on punitive damages. In evaluating the excessiveness of challenged punitive damage awards, trial courts are expressly authorized to consider prior punitive damage awards....

COMMENTARY AND QUESTIONS

1. Do all intentional torts deserve punitive damages? Could Oscar Boomer have gotten punitive damages against Atlantic Cement? Boomer proved that the cement dust pollution was an intentional tort; so wasn't it "willful," justifying punitives? In McElwain v. Georgia Pacific Corp., a pulp mill air pollution case, the court majority allowed punitive damages in a case very much like *Boomer*:

> The intentional disregard of the interest of another is the equivalent of legal malice, and justifies punitive damages for trespass. Where there is proof of an intentional, unjustifiable infliction of harm with deliberate disregard of the social consequences, the question of award of punitive damages is for the jury.
>
> It is abundantly clear from the record that defendant knew when it decided to construct its [paper] mill in Toledo, that there was danger, if not a probability, that the mill would cause damage to adjoining property.... The jury could have found that during the period involved in this action the defendant had not done everything reasonably possible to eliminate or minimize the damage to adjoining properties by its mill. 421 P.2d 957, 958 (Or. 1966).

The dissenting justice in *McElwain* strongly disagreed, arguing that actual malice was a necessary and desirable requirement for award of punitive damages. Which is right? These and related questions resurface in the toxic tort cases.

2. The availability and measure of punitives. Analyzing *Branch, McElwain,* and *Fischer,* is the availability of punitive damages restricted to situations where defendants' conduct is extreme and anti-social?

What is the proper measure of punitive damages? What checks are imposed? In a jury case, the process by which punitive damages are awarded most often begins with plaintiffs' closing argument urging the jury, in accordance with the judge's charge, to award punitives because the defendant's conduct has been shown to "merit" such an award. Thereafter, a jury instruction will be given to the effect that the prevailing plaintiffs are also entitled to punitive damages if the standard for disregard or indifference to the rights of others is met. Rather less is said in the jury charge about how those awards are to be calculated. Are juries free to vent their spleen?

3. Proving punitives. What kind of proof is likely to incite a jury to award punitives? In a book on the asbestos litigation, Paul Brodeur chronicled the industry's 40 year-long "conspiracy of silence" in failing to warn workers or consumers about the fatal dangers of asbestos exposure that it had known about at least since the 1940s. Brodeur quotes a company memo written by Dr. Kenneth W. Smith, Johns-Manville's medical director, after a 1949 study showed that of 708 asbestos workers like Fischer, only four did not have asbestosis:

> It must be remembered that although these men have the X-ray evidence of asbestosis, they are working today and definitely are not disabled.... They have not been told of this diagnosis for it is felt that as long as the man feels well, is happy at home and at work, and his physical condition remains good, nothing should be said. When he becomes disabled and sick, then the diagnosis should be made and the claim submitted by the Company. The fibrosis of this disease is irreversible and permanent so that eventually compensation will be paid to each of these men. But as long as the man is not disabled it is felt that he should not be told of his condition so that he can live

> and work in peace and the Company can benefit by his many years of experience. Should the man be told of his condition today there is a very definite possibility that he would become mentally and physically ill, simply through the knowledge that he has asbestosis.

Another memo from a later year revealed a conversation about a 52-year old man:

> "Advanced pneumoconiosis," Dr. Smith declared after looking at the patient's medical file.
>
> "Should we change him?" inquired Sheckler [a safety and health supervisor for the company, who wanted to know if a transfer to a non-dusty area was in order].
>
> "Won't make any difference," Smith replied.
>
> "If he hits sixty-five, I will be surprised," Dr. DuBow [a plant physician] said.
>
> On the basis of such advice, Sheckler decided to take no action other than to watch the patient carefully and retire him on disability, if, as he put it, it became "necessary." And as to a woman testing positive for advanced asbestosis, "If she is called in, she will get hysterical, and I am sure you'll have a claim on your hands," so nothing was done. See P. Brodeur, Outrageous Misconduct: The Asbestos Industry on Trial 102–03, 145–46 (1985).

And so contaminated workers were not informed, nor were new employees entering the plant's work force in succeeding years told of the fatal hazard. Analyze why these items of evidence might have an effect on punitive damages (and why, as in the Kepone case, the system couldn't rely upon the medical profession for warnings and correction).

4. Punitive problems in mass cases. The *Fischer* case, involving a single plaintiff, raises many of the problems that have impelled some state legislatures to yield to industry lobbyists and prohibit punitive damages altogether, or to restrict their availability to special cases of malice, or to cap maximum awards. Are you satisfied with the *Fischer* court's rejoinders to these arguments? The facts of environmental cases often arouse anger and outrage in juries. If a defendant has limited funds, or if juries in sequential cases award duplicative punitive damages for a single mass exposure, there is at least the possibility of unfairness to defendants and other potential plaintiffs. In the 180 Exxon-Valdez cases, proposals were made for mandatory certification of one all-inclusive punitive damage claim. Should there be a national clearinghouse coordinating punitive damage claims filed against mass tortfeasors? Or is the risk of an avalanche of punitive-minded juries just part of the game?

5. Constitutional checks on the award of punitive damages? The United States Supreme Court has decided two cases considering what constitutional limitations might apply to the award of punitive damages. In Browning-Ferris Industries of Vermont v. Kelco Disposal, 492 U.S. 257 (1989), the Court held that the Eighth Amendment's excessive fines clause does not apply to awards of punitive damages in cases between private parties. In Pacific Mut. Life Ins. Co. v. Haslip, 111 S.Ct.

1032 (1991), the Court acknowledged that awards of punitive damages could in some cases violate due process. The jury verdict of $800,000 in *Haslip*, more than four times the compensatory damages in the case, was upheld because the Alabama courts had applied seven test criteria in reviewing the punitives award: (1) the reasonable relationship between the amount awarded and the harm caused or threatened by defendant's action; (2) the reprehensibility, duration, frequency, and consciousness of defendant's conduct; (3) the profitability of the action; (4) the defendant's financial position; (5) the costs of litigation; (6) whether criminal sanctions had been imposed (which would mitigate the punitives award); and (7) whether defendant had had to pay other civil awards.

6. Remittitur. As the *Fischer* and *Haslip* cases noted, appellate (and even trial court) judges can and do at times order a rollback of punitive damage verdicts that they consider excessive, but there are virtually no generally agreed-upon common law judicial standards for remittitur. The Alabama courts' tests in *Haslip* are just a start. How would they tend to apply in environmental cases? Can uncompensated ecological damages be considered? See Garcia, Remittitur in Environmental Cases, 16 Envtl. Aff. L. Rev. 119 (1988).

d. REMOTENESS; INDIRECT ECONOMIC DAMAGES

The element of causation in tort has two distinct facets, termed cause-in-fact and proximate cause. Cause-in-fact refers to the everyday notion of cause and effect, like the row of dominoes linking the act that precipitates the fall of the first to the fall of the last. The usual linguistic test of cause-in-fact is "but for" – the plaintiff must show that but for the act of defendant, the plaintiff's injury would not have occurred. As will be seen in later cases where all that can be proved is that defendant increased the probability of the harm that befell plaintiffs, strict adherence to but-for causation would unfairly doom these cases to failure.

Proximate causation is concerned with the problem of remoteness. At times, but-for causation extends to great distances, perhaps linking defendant's conduct to losses that are beyond the scope of responsibility that defendant should bear. If a highway oil spill negligently caused by defendant's tanker truck causes a traffic jam that delays the delivery van that was carrying a needed part to fix the machine that was to make the widget that the plaintiff had contracted to supply to a customer who had to have it by today, and the cash from the sale was needed to pay the bill to ward off repossession of... etc., somewhere along the line it may be appropriate to limit the availability of remedies for the far-off consequences of wrongful acts, especially where injuries are purely economic. Where do you draw that line?

The following is the only civil case arising from the Kepone debacle[13] ever to go to judgment. It raises questions about how far down the chain of causation liability can be extended. It is important to note that the plaintiffs in this case are not alleging physical injuries to themselves or their property. This is a case of long distance *economic* harms. (Allied quickly settled any and all local physical injury claims.)

---

13. See Chapter 2, at page 42 *supra*.

Pruitt v. Allied Chemical Corp.

United States District Court, Eastern District of Virginia, 1981
523 F. Supp. 975

MERHIGE, D.J. Plaintiffs bring the instant action against Allied Chemical Corporation ("Allied") for Allied's alleged pollution of the James River and Chesapeake Bay with the chemical agent commonly known as Kepone....

Plaintiffs allegedly engage in a variety of different businesses and professions related to the harvesting and sale of marine life from the Chesapeake Bay. All claim to have suffered economic harm from defendant's alleged discharges of Kepone into the James River and thence into the Bay. Plaintiffs assert their right to compensation under each of the dozen counts to their complaint [including claims in negligence and strict liability]....

It is commonly stated that the general rule both in admiralty and at common law has been that a plaintiff cannot recover for indirect economic harm. The logical basis for this rule is obscure. Although Courts have frequently stated that economic losses are "not foreseeable" or "too remote," these explanations alone are rarely apposite. As one well-respected commentator has noted, "the loss to plaintiff in each case...would be readily recoverable if the test of duty – or remoteness – usually associated with the law of negligence were applied...."[14]

Given the conflicting case law from other jurisdictions, together with the fact that there exists no Virginia law on indirect, economic damages, the Court has considered more theoretical sources in order to find a principled basis for its decision. There now exists a considerable amount of literature on the economic rationale for tort law. In general, scholars in the field rely on Judge Learned Hand's classic statement of negligence to argue that a principal purpose of tort law is to maximize social utility: where the costs of accidents exceed the costs of preventing them, the law will impose liability.

The difficulty in the present case is how to measure the cost of Kepone pollution. In the instant action, those costs were borne most directly by the wildlife of the Chesapeake Bay. The fact that no one individual claims property rights to the Bay's wildlife could arguably preclude liability. The Court doubts, however, whether such a result would be just. Nor would a denial of liability serve social utility: many citizens, both directly and indirectly, derive benefit from the Bay and its marine life. Destruction of the Bay's wildlife should not be a costless activity.

In fact, even defendant in the present action admits that commercial fishermen are entitled to compensation for any loss of profits they may prove to have been caused by defendant's negligence. The entitlement given these fishermen presumably arises from what might be called a constructive property interest in the Bay's harvestable species. These professional watermen are entitled to recover despite any direct physical damage to their own property. Presumably, sports fishermen share the same entitlement to legal redress for damage to the Bay's ecology. The Court perceives no valid distinction between recognition of commercial damages suffered by those who fish for profit and personal harm suffered by those who fish for sport.

---

14. James, Limitations of Liability for Economic Loss Caused by Negligence: A Pragmatic Appraisal, 25 Vand. L. Rev. 43 (1972). Prof. James has gone on to state that "the prevailing distinction between indirect economic loss and physical damage is probably a crude and unreliable one that may need reexamination if a limitation on liability for pragmatic reasons is to be retained." Id. at 50-51.

The claims now considered by the Court, however, are not those of direct users of the Bay, commercial or personal. Instead, defendant has challenged the right of those who buy and sell to direct users of the Bay, to maintain a suit. Defendant would have the Court draw a sharp and impregnable distinction between parties who exploited the Bay directly, and those who relied on it indirectly....

None of the plaintiffs here – including commercial fishermen – has suffered any direct damage to his private property. All have allegedly suffered economic loss as a result of harm to the Bay's ecology. Apart from these similarities, the different categories of plaintiffs depend on the Bay in varying degrees of immediacy. The commercial fishermen here fit within a category established in Union Oil Co. v. Oppen, 501 F.2d 558 (9th Cir. 1974)(the Santa Barbara oil spill case): they "lawfully and directly make use of a resource of the sea." The use that marina and charterboat owners make of the water, though hardly less legal, is slightly less direct. (And indeed, businesses in similar situations have been held entitled to recover in other courts.) Still less direct, but far from nonexistent, is the link between the Bay and the seafood dealers, restaurants, and tackle shops that seek relief (as do the employees of these establishments).

One meaningful distinction to be made among the various categories of plaintiffs here arises from a desire to avoid double-counting in calculating damages. Any seafood harvested by the commercial fishermen here would have been bought and sold several times before finally being purchased for consumption. Considerations both of equity and social utility suggest that just as defendant should not be able to escape liability for destruction of publicly owned marine life entirely, it should not be caused to pay repeatedly for the same damage.

The Court notes, however, that allowance for recovery of plaintiffs' lost profits here would not in all cases result in double-counting of damages. Plaintiffs in categories B, C, D, E, and F[15] allegedly lost profits when deprived of supplies of seafood. Those profits represented a return on the investment of each of the plaintiffs in material and labor in their businesses, and thus the independent loss to each would not amount to double-counting. Conversely, defendants could not be expected to pay, as a maximum, more than the replacement value of a plaintiff's actual investment, even if the stream of profits lost when extrapolated into the future, would yield greater damages.

Tracing the stream of profits flowing from the Bay's seafood, however, involves the Court in other complexities. The employees of the enterprises named in categories B through F, for example, had no physical investment in their employers' businesses. Yet if plaintiff's allegations are proven, these employees undoubtedly lost wages and faced a less favorable job market than they would have, but for defendant's acts, and they have thus been harmed by defendant. What is more, the number of parties with a potential cause of action against defendant is hardly exhausted in plaintiffs' complaint. In theory, parties who bought and sold to and from the plaintiffs named here also suffered losses in business, as did their employees. In short, the set of potential plaintiffs seems almost infinite.

Perhaps because of the large set of potential plaintiffs, even the commentators most critical of the general rule on indirect damages have acknowledged that some limitation to liability, even when damages are foreseeable, is advisable. Rather than allowing plaintiffs to risk a failure of proof as damages become increasingly remote and diffuse, courts have, in many cases, raised an absolute bar to recovery.

15. Respectively, seafood wholesalers, retailers, processors, distributors and restaurateurs.

The Court thus finds itself with a perceived need to limit liability, without any articulated reason for excluding any particular set of plaintiffs. Other courts have had to make similar decisions.[16] The Court concludes that plaintiffs who purchased and marketed seafood from commercial fishermen suffered damages that are not legally cognizable, because insufficiently direct. This does not mean that the Court finds that defendant's alleged acts were not the cause of plaintiffs' losses, or that plaintiffs' losses were in any sense unforeseeable. In fact, in part because the damages alleged by plaintiffs here were so foreseeable, the Court holds that those plaintiffs in categories G, H and I[17] have suffered legally cognizable damages. The Court does so for several reasons. The United States Court of Appeals for the Fourth Circuit has held, in admiralty, that a defendant should "pay...once, but no more" for damages inflicted. While commercial fishing interests are protected by allowing the fishermen themselves to recover, it is unlikely that sportsfishing interests would be equally protected. Because the damages each sportsman suffered are likely to be both small and difficult to establish, it is unlikely that a significant proportion of such fishermen will seek legal redress. Only if some set of surrogate plaintiffs is entitled to press its own claims which flow from the damage to the Bay's sportfishing industry will the proper balance of social forces be preserved. Accordingly, the Court holds that to the extent plaintiffs in categories G, H and I suffered losses in sales of goods and services to sports fishermen as a result of defendant's tortious behavior, they have stated a legally cognizable claim.

Defendant hardly has reason to complain of the equity of the Court's holding. First, it benefited above from the Court's exclusion of the claims of innocent businessmen in categories B through F who are probable victims of their alleged acts. Here, the Court applies different restrictions on liability for reasons of equity and efficiency previously addressed. Second, the "directness" of the harm, at least to plaintiffs in categories G and I,[18] is high here. Both operate on the water or at its edge. Finally, the Court is influenced by similar decisions as to liability in cases such as Maddox v. International Paper Co., 105 F. Supp. 89 (W.D. La. 1951) and Masonite Corp. v. Steede, 23 So. 2d 756 (Miss. 1945). The Court's conclusion results from consideration of all these factors, and an attempt to tailor justice to the facts of the instant case....

COMMENTARY AND QUESTIONS

1. The rationale for barring indirect damages. Is there any compelling reason for the traditional tort law rule that forbade recovery of indirect economic losses in the absence of physical injury? Could the reason be institutional, seeking to limit the number of cases in which courts were called upon to make necessarily speculative determinations about the course of future events? Could the reason instead represent an inductive overgeneralization, that in a substantial majority of cases

---

16. See e.g., Judge Kaufmann's opinion in Petition of Kinsman Transit Co., 388 F.2d 821, 824-25 (2d Cir. 1968), where the court noted that "in the final analysis the circumlocution whether posed in terms of 'foreseeability,' 'duty,' 'proximate cause,' 'remoteness,' etc. seems unavoidable," and then turned to Judge Andrews well-known statement in Palsgraf v. Long Island R.R. Co., 162 N.E. 99, 104 (N.Y. 1928): "It is all a question of expediency...of fair judgment, always keeping in mind the fact that we endeavor to make a rule in each case that will be practical and in keeping with the general understanding of mankind."

17. Boat (G), tackle and bait shop (H), and marina owners (I) respectively.

18. Generally boat and marina owners.

lacking physical damage there is likewise no credible economic damage? The bar against indirect recoveries has been widely applied in maritime tort cases under the rule of *Robins Drydock*, 275 U.S. 303 (1927), and has attracted criticism as a major barrier to oil spill plaintiffs in cases like the Exxon-Valdez spill, although statutory exceptions sometimes apply. See Mulhern, Marine Pollution: A Tort Recovery Standard for Pure Economic Losses, 18 Envtl. Aff. L. Rev. 85 (1990).

2. Of double-counting and foreseeable losses. What is the double-counting danger that is raised by defendants? The judge is correct in saying that the sum of the lost profits of the several categories of victims, by definition a net figure, is inherently free of double counting problems. Is it correct to limit the award to "replacement value of a plaintiff's actual investment"? What if a plaintiff bought a going fishing business at an unreasonably low price. Is there any reason to allow defendant to deprive that victim of the anticipated net income the wise investment would have generated?

The judge draws the line at the water's edge. Is that fair to inland plaintiffs who are foreseeable victims of massive contamination of the Bay? How does a recovery by the commercial fishermen in any way protect the interests of the owners and employees of a cannery that can no longer process fish from the Bay? And are you satisfied with the allowance of sport fishery industry recoveries as a proxy for natural resource damage?

Surveying the range of legal actions so far noted in the Kepone case, how complete an accounting did Allied Chemical face from private litigation?

Section 3. NATURAL RESOURCES REMEDIES

Because the vast majority of environmental litigation is directed at recouping losses to humans and their property, one tends to lose sight of ecological reality: that human injuries are not necessarily the major consequences of disruptions of the natural equilibrium. When a wrongdoer destroys or injures natural resources, the law can do an adequate enough job establishing fault or equivalent basis for liability. The riddle, as noted in Chapter 2 at 63, is how to define and apply remedies for injuries beyond damages to humans. Over the past decade, environmental law has, in a variety of ways, committed itself to answering that question. The Clean Water and Superfund Acts both require the federal government to "identify the best available procedures to determine [natural resources] damages, including both direct and indirect injury, destruction or loss."[19] But the valuation process, and the directions in which natural resource remedies are moving, remain uncertain. The Exxon-Valdez oil spill provides a classic example.

Shortly after midnight on March 24, 1989, the single-hulled supertanker Exxon-Valdez sliced into the submerged granite of Bligh Reef in Alaska's Prince William

19. CWA, 33 U.S.C.A. §1321(f)(4)(5), CERCLA, 42 U.S.C.A. §9651(C)(2).

Sound. Pushed by northeasterly winds, the eleven million gallons of crude oil that spewed from the wreck spread out over 1,000 miles of coastal waters.[20]

The ecosystem hit by the Exxon-Valdez spill was extraordinarily rich. Affected species included herring, black cod, cutthroat trout, dolly varden, shark, halibut, rock fish, shell fish, fin fish, several species of salmon, sea otters, fur seals, steller's sea lions, harbor porpoises, dall porpoises, killer whales, hump-back whales, minke whales, fin whales, blue whales, gray whales, deer, fox, coyotes, black bears, brown bears, bald eagles, several species of gulls, hundreds of thousands of sea birds, such as kittiwakes, puffins, hawks, guillemots, murres, murreletes, loons, grebes, diving ducks, dungeness crabs, pot shrimp, trawl shrimp...and these were just the upper layers of the ecological pyramid. The waters and wildlife of thé Gulf of Alaska were among the most fertile coastal communities on earth, built upon a confluence of ocean currents rich in micro-organisms, zooplankton and phytoplankton.

In the aftermath of the Exxon-Valdez oil spill, more than one hundred and eighty civil suits were filed, almost all by people claiming injury to their economic interests. Some of those economic claims are relatively uninteresting – claims for direct property losses and diminution of market value. Others raise the tough questions debated in this section, about how far economic recoveries can extend along a chain of "indirect" causation, from commercial fishers, to processors, distributors, ship owners, outfitters, and restauranteurs, none of whom sustained actual physical damage.

The State of Alaska's lawsuit likewise included many predictable economic claims – loss of tourism and recreation; reimbursement for out-of-pocket cleanup efforts by towns, native American tribes, and the State; emotional distress and disruption of citizens' lives; and so on – but the State also asked the trial court to award damages and injunctions that would capture a broader swath of values, based on natural resources losses. As you read the following brief excerpts from the State's 40-page complaint, note the problems faced in defining and separating human and ecological remedies:

"If seven maids with seven mops
Swept it for half a year, do you suppose," the Walrus said,
"That they could get it clear?"
"I doubt it," said the Carpenter,
And shed a bitter tear.

— Lewis Carroll, Through the Looking Glass, 1871

20. As to fault, the wreck was an accident waiting to happen, attributable to cost-cutting and complacency within the oil industry, abetted by lassitude within the U.S. Coast Guard and state and federal regulatory agencies. See State of Alaska Oil Spill Commission, Spill: The Wreck of the Exxon-Valdez: Lessons for the Safe Transportation of Oil (1990).

IN THE SUPERIOR COURT FOR THE STATE OF ALASKA
THIRD JUDICIAL DISTRICT

THE STATE OF ALASKA, on its own behalf, and as public trustee and as *parens patriae* for the citizens of the State, Plaintiff,	Case No. 3AN8906852CIV
vs.	
EXXON CORPORATION, a New Jersey corporation; EXXON PIPELINE COMPANY, a Delaware corporation; EXXON SHIPPING COMPANY, a Delaware corporation; ALYESKA PIPELINE SERVICE COMPANY, a Delaware corporation; et al. Defendants.	COMPLAINTS FOR COMPENSATORY AND PUNITIVE DAMAGES, CIVIL PENALTIES AND INJUNCTIVE RELIEF

DEFINITIONS

...20. "Environmental damages" includes, but is not limited to, one or more types of damages to use and enjoyment values derived from State lands, waters, and resources:

(1) Use values, including consumptive and nonconsumptive uses;

(2) Nonuse values, including existence, intrinsic, option, bequest, temporal, and quasi-option values;

(3) Values derived from the existence of management options and the expertise and data to exercise and support same;

(4) Values associated with the necessity or desirability of restoration, replacement, assessment or monitoring;

(5) Other ecosystem existing values....

DAMAGES TO PLAINTIFF

61. As a result of the oil spill from the EXXON-VALDEZ, over a thousand square miles of State lands, waters, and resources have suffered severe environmental damage. A growing number of coastal and inland sounds and bays, beaches, tidelands, tidal pools, wetlands, estuaries, and other sensitive elements of the ecosystems have been devastated; thousands of mammals, fowl, and fish have been killed or injured; anadromous streams, near shore environments and other fish and wildlife critical habitats have been contaminated; aesthetics and scenic quality have been destroyed or impaired, together with attendant opportunities for recreational experiences; air quality has deteriorated through the escape of evaporating pollutants; commercial fisheries have been sharply curtailed, with adverse biological and economic consequences; the greater ecosystem in the spill area has been deprived of its pristine condition with attendant damage to the condition of, and interrelationship among, living creatures comprising the system; and the manage-

ment opportunities available through the knowledge and data base generated from prior experience with the ecosystem have been compromised....

RELIEF SOUGHT

WHEREFORE, plaintiff prays that this Court:

...Award all compensatory and punitive damages authorized under the common law, including, but not limited to, environmental and economic damages. Award all compensatory and punitive damages authorized under the general maritime law.

Order that the defendants be permanently enjoined to remove all spilled oil and to restore the surface and subsurface lands, wildlife, waters, fisheries, shellfish and associated marine resources, air and other State lands, waters and resources affected directly or indirectly by the spill;

Order immediate and continuing environmental monitoring and assessment of the conditions of the air, waters and subsurface and surface lands, fisheries, shellfish and the associated marine resources and other natural resources... [and]

...Award such other and further relief as this Court deems just and proper.

DATED this 15th day of August, 1989.

Douglas B. Baily
Attorney General

COMMENTARY AND QUESTIONS

1. Non-marketplace human-based remedies. Natural resources remedies are intended to go beyond the mere commodity-pricing approach of the marketplace. As the appellate court wrote when Ohio challenged the Clean Water Act and Superfund natural resource regulations,

> it is the incompleteness of market processes that give rise to the need for [non-market valuation].... While it is not irrational to look to market price as *one* factor in determining the use value of a resource, it is unreasonable to view market price as the exclusive factor, or even the predominant one. From the bald eagle to the blue whale and snail darter, natural resources have values that are not fully captured by the market system.... Option and existence values may represent 'passive' use, they nonetheless reflect utility derived by humans from a resource, and thus *prima facie* ought to be included in a damage assessment.[21]

Note how the court returns to humans. Likewise, although the Alaska complaint begins its narration of damages with environmental losses, even within the definition of "environmental damages" many if not all of the contentions are for human-based economic recovery.[22]

---

21. Ohio v. U.S. Department of Interior, 880 F.2d 432, 464 (D.C. Cir. 1989)(emphasis in original).

22. Beyond the realm of natural resources, the Alaska complaint also raises environmental questions regarding remedies for the dramatic disruptions to the Alaska Native communities along the coast, where the prior-existing complex and stable subsistence culture may never recover from the onslaughts of oil and oilspill cleanup salaries. The complaint also seeks remedies for non-economic human losses in psychological stresses suffered by many non-Native Alaskans whose lives were severely impacted by the spill.

The term "use value," for instance, seeks to capture values for things that don't actually trade in the marketplace, but uses an attributed market value. "Consumptive value" attributes a value to lost resource uses of sportsmen and tourists who would have taken wildlife in hunting or fishing pursuits. "Non-consumptive" uses include the ecosystem's value to photographers, bird watchers, and the like. Some "non-use" values are based on attributed human value: what it means to people just to know the resource is there, even if they never actively use it; it is "option value" if they may use it. "Bequest value" reflects the resource as a legacy passed by the present generation to its children. "Temporal" and "quasi-option" values assess unknown future values foreclosed. There is a wide range of economic methods for estimating or "shadow pricing" some of these values, including travel cost (the amount that people are willing to spend to travel to such places); "hedonic" value, using market activity preferences; implied speculative rent values; and contingent valuation methods (CVM) based on public opinion surveys about willingness to pay (as in a hypothetical tax).[23]

Fundamentally, each of these approaches creates a hypothetical human market for resources, an approach which requires that the component fish, wildlife, bugs, and micro-organisms of an ecosystem be made sufficiently recognizable and attractive to a human audience to deserve monetary recognition.

2. Natural resources' own intrinsic value? None of the preceding remedies pretends to assess the value of the resources in and of themselves. It seems presumptuous, however, to argue that humans are the sole measure of what has been lost in an ecological catastrophe (although only humans, of course, are in a position to raise the intrinsic ethical claims). If courts can look beyond human-based values, as both law and ethics may currently be inviting them to do, serious questions arise. Can you talk intelligently about the lost wildlife's value to itself? First, it's dead; second, it's wildlife, not human. The flora and fauna and their ecosystem leave no probate estates for wrongful death recoveries. Who can sue, for what purpose, and for what measure of relief?

Who can sue? Given our legal system, it would be vastly easier to sue for the loss of resources if they were citizens, or someone owned them. In the absence of either, the state of Alaska can file its claims for remedies based on its "parens patriae" and public trustee roles, and environmentalists can sue as public trust beneficiaries (see Chapter 8), but the nature and extent of standing to recover for intrinsic natural resources losses are not self-evident.

What is the purpose of seeking natural resources damages? The dead wildlife cannot be brought back to life. In ordinary tort law the purpose of damages is a delicate mix of restoring plaintiffs to their prior position and taxing wrongdoers for their wrongdoing. "Destruction of the Bay's wildlife should not be a costless activity," said the judge in the *Pruitt* Kepone case earlier in this chapter. To this extent the

23. See Cross, Natural Resource Damage Valuation, 42 Vand. L. Rev. 269 (1989), and see text and notes at page 56 *supra*. [Chapter 2, D(2)]

punitive damages sought in the Alaska complaint may be an attempt to capture unquantifiable intrinsic losses, and deter future wrongful actions.

But what is the measure of loss? The wildlife and their ecological pyramid had an "existence value" that is gone. The fact that they used to be there, and no longer are, reflects the disruption of an evolved ecological community that didn't just happen to be there, but had adapted and developed over thousands and millions of years. What is the value of the components of that system, especially the vast numbers of small rather prosaic protozoans, sea slugs, and the like?[24]

The fundamental problem of damage valuation for the *per se* loss of wildlife is that the intrinsic worth of natural resources does not conveniently fit the terms of economic accountability.

3. Ecological restoration remedies. The shortcomings in human-based valuations, and the perplexities of awarding intrinsic value natural resources damages, propel the law increasingly toward performance-based relief – restoration or mitigation remedies.

Restoration, as an in-kind ecological remedy, represents two different rationales: first, the aim to put things back as they were before defendants' wrongdoing occurred, a satisfying and understandable objective; second, to provide a performance standard as a proxy for the otherwise difficult task of valuing what has been lost. The court cuts through the riddles of natural resources valuation by ordering that the wrong be undone. If a piece of forest was wrongfully clear-cut, how fitting to order soil restoration and replanting of mature trees, shrubs, and undergrowth. As with human-based restoration remedies, page 147 *supra*, natural resources remediation is a way to capture widespread values within judicial relief and raise potent deterrent examples for prospective wrongdoers. Restoration presents serious questions, however, not least the definition of what restoration means.

What does Alaska's complaint mean when it demands restoration? As requested, it is clearly impossible. It is technically and economically infeasible to recapture more than about 20 percent of any major oil spill. Most is now lodged deep within ocean bottom sediments, travelling in solution through ocean currents, or located within the tissues of coastal and marine wildlife, the strata of coastal beaches, etc. What would the cost of a partial restoration undertaking be, if it could be done? And might not the removal of oil, through solvents or organic methods, cause more destruction than the oil itself?

In fact, a natural restoration process begins as soon as an oil spill catastrophe occurs. Volatiles evaporate into the air and are diffused; hydrocarbons begin a very slow

24. In some cases, courts have tried to value the wildlife itself in terms of what it would bring at a meat market or pet store. In a case where millions of baby striped bass were sucked into the cooling intakes of a power plant, the court awarded the per pound price of striped bass in the fish market; zoos may have set a special market value by buying animals like sea otters, sometimes for tens of thousands of dollars; sea slugs have a value as delicacies in Japanese restaurants. Does this sound like an appropriate approach for estimating the intrinsic value of ecological losses?

process of breaking down and becoming ever-more diluted components of the ecosystem. With the action of wind, waves, sun, and time, within 50 years the Gulf of Alaska is likely to be very similar to its condition prior to the oil spill (although several species may be gone). If that is the case, then what is meant by a legally-mandated restoration? Various ecosystem components can indeed be added immediately by human actions: hatcheries can be created to propagate fish, birds, even mayflies and plankton, and those efforts, although they risk a sort of suburban homogenizing of the naturally diverse gene pool, nevertheless can serve a useful function. But if one begins with the curve of natural restoration, apparently the primary rationale of legal restoration remedies is to accelerate, artificially, the rate of natural recovery, a somewhat ambiguous undertaking even if it is feasible.

Restoration can arguably be vastly more expensive than it is worthwhile, which guarantees that it will attract strong resistance. The Clean Water and Superfund Acts both provide for "the restoration or replacement of natural resources damaged or destroyed as a result of discharge of oil or a hazardous substance.... Sums recovered shall be used to restore, rehabilitate, or acquire the equivalent of such natural resources[25] by the appropriate agencies. As issued by Secretary James Watt, however, the required regulations on natural resources remedies provided that the measure of damages should be "the *lesser* of restoration or replacement costs, or diminution of use values." The *Ohio* court struck down the regulations, declaring that "the Department of Interior erred by establishing a strong presumption in favor of market price,"[26] and emphasized the preferability of restoration.

But cost must play some part in the balance. An army of biologists can be deployed, sopping up oil with sponges, and propagating myriad tiny organisms and higher lifeforms to rebuild shattered food chains; sands and mud can be imported; floating filtration plants can be installed. The costs would be astronomical, however, and the results uncertain. In a case arising from a Puerto Rican oil spill, the First Circuit had to balance the feasibility and cost of restoration against a statutory restoration mandate. Puerto Rico had asked for removal and replacement of oil-soaked bottom sediments, and replanting of thousands of poisoned mangroves, at a cost of $7 million, or alternatively an award of "replacement value" based on a biologist's estimate that 92 million creatures had been destroyed, and a guesstimate that they averaged a replacement value or cost of $.06 each, totaling $5,526,583.20. The court decided that "the appropriate primary standard for determining damages in a case such as this, is the cost reasonably to be incurred by the sovereign or its designated agency to restore or rehabilitate the environment in the affected area to its pre-existing condition, or as close thereto as is feasible *without grossly disproportionate expenditures*...with attention to such factors as technical feasibility, harmful side effects, compatibility with or duplication of such regeneration as is naturally to be expected, and the extent to which efforts beyond a certain point would become either redundant or disproportionately expensive." The court rejected the government's $7 million remedy as "impractical, inordinately expensive, and

25. 33 U.S.C.A. §1321(f)(4)(5), echoed in Superfund, 42 U.S.C.A. §9651(C)(2).

26. Ohio v. U.S. Department of Interior, 880 F.2d 432, 464 (D.C. Cir. 1989) (emphasis added).

unjustifiably dangerous to the healthy mangroves and marine animals still present in the area to be restored," and the second, replacement value theory on the ground that the government was not actually proposing to replace the 92 million creatures into the contaminated bay "which, being contaminated with oil, would hardly support them...."[27] Was this a judgment based on a finding that the cost was "grossly disproportionate," or that actual restoration was infeasible in the circumstances? If restoration is feasible, how does one weigh the cost of natural resources restoration?

4. Must restoration awards be used to restore? If Alaska recovers $500 million in damages based on the cost of feasible restoration, can the Governor then take the money and use it to build roads through the wilderness, which, he says, are a more worthwhile project? Under the law of the case or the public trust doctrine to be examined in Chapter 8, it would seem that restoration awards are impressed with a trust for that general purpose, but it is not clearly so.

5. Mitigation and substituted resources. As to mitigation, a lawsuit filed by environmentalists in the Alaska oil spill case, following up on suggestions in the Clean Water Act, requested the establishment of a fund or foundation for "the acquisition of equivalent [and additional] natural resources" as an alternative remedy where restoration was ecologically or economically infeasible.[28] Is such mitigation-by-acquisition a satisfactory natural resources remedy? In effect it merely secures (as a park or reserve) existing resources that otherwise might face destruction by economic development. Does it add or replace anything beyond what existed in the aftermath of an ecological catastrophe?

6. Prospects. Restoration and mitigation remedies obviously offer important options to courts and agencies faced with damaged ecosystems. Ultimately, they and other natural resources remedies are not a neatly quantifiable concept, as they would be if they merely paralleled marketplace assessments. Natural resources remedies have been written into statutes and are evolving as part of the common law, so the issues raised here, with their ambiguities and opportunities, will continue. Should their development be left to judicial hands, or should such complex modern questions be turned over to the administrative agency process?

By conducting ourselves ethically toward all creatures, we enter into a spiritual relationship with the universe.

– Albert Schweitzer

27. Puerto Rico v. S.S. Zoe Colocotroni, 628 F.2d 652, 676, 677 (1st Cir. 1980) (emphasis added).

28. National Wildlife Fed. et al. v. Exxon Corp., Alyeska Pipeline Service Co. et al., Super. Ct., 3d Dist. Alaska, 3 AN-89-2533 civ (1989).

Chapter 4

TOXIC TORTS: BEYOND THE TRADITIONAL COMMON LAW SETTING

Toxic torts are a rapidly growing area of legal practice. Toxic exposures occur in various ways. Workers may use toxics on the job; ordinary citizens may be exposed to substances released into the environment. Some exposures are deliberate, as in the use of prescription drugs. As scientific knowledge of health hazards associated with exposure to toxic substances grows, the search for effective remedies for toxic injuries keeps pace, bringing more cases into the legal system.

The materials that follow survey a number of toxic tort problems. First come the difficulties posed by the multiplicity of parties in mass toxic torts. When a case has large numbers of plaintiffs it can pose practical problems of case management, and doctrinal problems of extending liability throughout long chains of causation. When a case involves multiple polluters it raises questions of particularizing and apportioning defendants' liability. Then there is the often dicey area of proof of causation in fact, with long periods between exposures and harms, and a chronic uncertainty that puts juries at the frontiers of medical knowledge. Finally come a host of new theories of recovery for toxic exposures. The special circumstances of toxics cases set them apart from traditional tort law, although they continue to be interrelated. Some toxic tort issues, such as remoteness of harms, imposition of joint and several liability, and assessment of punitive damages, are also relevant to conventional cases. Many conventional issues, like the choice of liability theories from intentional nuisance and trespass, negligence and strict liability, are essential to the toxic tort case as well.

A. MULTIPLE PLAINTIFFS AND THE MANAGEABILITY OF MASS TOXIC TORT LITIGATION

Section 1. PROBLEMS OF MULTIPLICITY: LITIGATABILITY

The common law put down its roots in an age where its rigid formal procedures could be applied in lawsuits that might be described as simple binary litigation: one plaintiff, one defendant. The litigation was also bi-polar, having two clearly defined sides on the pivotal issue. Outcomes were likewise all-or-nothing; the plaintiff would either recover fully, or not at all. Traditionally, the rigid formalities of English law required the parties to select a single form of action (such as trespass), and thereafter reduce their dispute to a single contested issue (such as whether the emissions of the defendant were the cause-in-fact of the plaintiff's injury). Through intricate and bewildering pleading devices, all other issues were removed from the lawsuit. The rigidity was not a problem in most cases because in a simpler era most tort victims were injured in discrete events, involving clear direct injury to only a few people at a time. Toxic torts, however, are often mass torts of staggering complexity, often with multiple defendants and involving large classes of victims. Examples include asbestos exposure as in the *Fischer* case in Chapter 3, where literally millions of people may have suffered serious harm; pesticide and herbicide spraying as in the Agent Orange cases;[1] and principal cases in this section where plaintiffs included all persons living downwind of fallout from nuclear testing in Nevada (Allen v. United States) and all persons who drank water from contaminated public wells (Anderson v. W. R. Grace & Co. and Ayers v. Jackson Township). With their multiplicity of claims, those cases present serious questions about proof of remote causation for long-latent disease, about the transaction costs of extended litigation, about defendants' ability to pay, and about the fairness of compensating victims far removed from defendant's action.

In the environmental law context, the impact of changes in procedure has been absolutely essential to the emergence of meaningful common law remedies for injuries caused by both conventional and toxic tort. The complexity of many environmental cases as to matters of fact, issues of causation, measurement of damage, etc., would have been virtually impossible to litigate in a meaningful fashion without a procedural system that allowed for the concurrent pleading and proof of many theories and issues. Additionally, the advent of procedural devices allowing joinder of claims and joinder of parties has allowed a would-be plaintiff in a case involving great legal difficulty and expense to pool resources with other plaintiffs facing the same problem.[2]

When a toxic substance has entered the environment and when large numbers of potential plaintiffs have been exposed to it, sometimes on a nationwide scale, serious logistical problems confront the legal system. Many of the issues of liability, defenses, and proof will be exactly the same in hundreds and thousands of cases; to litigate them separately or even state by state would be wastefully redundant. Other issues may, however, be highly particular to individual plaintiffs. Litigation costs to plaintiffs and defendants alike become astronomical, and themselves become part of the tactical setting.

Compare an air pollution nuisance case of the *Boomer* variety. In that case as litigated, only a small number of individuals sued, each claiming fairly significant amounts of harm. They were all aided in their efforts to force the cement company to pay for their damage by the fact that their individual cost of seeking a remedy was reduced by the sharing of litigation expenses with their co-plaintiffs. As litigated, however, the *Boomer* case probably did not go as far in this direction as possible. There were numerous individuals owning land at a slightly greater remove from the cement plant who suffered lesser degrees of intrusion with their quiet enjoyment of their property. While the law of nuisance at some point says insubstantial loss of quiet enjoyment is not a violation of legal rights because the degree of interference

1. See P. Schuck, Agent Orange on Trial: Mass Toxic Disasters in the Courts (1988).

2. In the American legal system, usually, absent special equitable considerations or legislation, each party must pay its own attorneys and expert witness fees. See Chapter 11 at Part D, §1(c) *infra*.

is not unreasonable, it remains quite likely that many people suffering some unreasonable injuries did not sue because the amount of their individual recovery would not justify the expense and hassle of pursuing the litigation. These people may sue later,[3] but they may not. Institutionally for the court system, efficiency would be better served if there is only one lawsuit on behalf of *all* of the victims of the pollution rather than in multiple lawsuits. In joined or class actions, the court's workload is reduced because the basic underlying facts have to be resolved only once. Economic efficiency is also served because composite lawsuits internalize a greater portion of the costs of the pollution. See Wright, The Cost-Internalization Case for Class Actions, 21 Stan. L. Rev. 383 (1969).

Toxic torts, the subject of this chapter, are frequently ideal candidates for joined litigation because they are often mass torts: large numbers of individuals injured through the same pattern of events. One generic pattern involves a toxic release (or a series of releases) that exposes a community to hazardous materials. To some degree, that was the backdrop of both the *Kepone* and the *Reserve Mining* cases introduced in Chapter 2. Two cases considered in this chapter, Anderson v. W.R. Grace & Co. and Ayers v. Jackson Township, also fit that pattern. In these cases, the impetus to group litigation lies both in the commonality of the questions presented for legal resolution and in the economies of scale obtained by pooling resources for litigation.

Section 2. CLASS ACTIONS

Modern procedure offers the class action device as an opportunity for bringing all pollution or toxic tort victims into a single lawsuit. In class actions, a large class of persons who are similarly situated in regard to the dispute being litigated are represented in litigation by a single member of the class or by a small group drawn from the class. The procedural rules governing class actions go to considerable lengths to insure full and fair representation of the members of the class. Rule 23 of the Federal Rules of Civil Procedure is the most prominent of the class action rules, operative in all federal court litigation, and serving as a model for the procedural rules of many of the states.

Most environmental class actions are litigated under the following two provisions of Rule 23:

(b)(2) the party opposing the class has acted or refused to act on grounds generally applicable to the class, thereby making appropriate final injunctive relief or corresponding declaratory relief with respect to the class as a whole; or

(b)(3) the court finds that the questions of law or fact common to the members of the class predominate over any questions affecting only individual members, and that a class action is superior to other available methods for the fair and efficient adjudication of the controversy.

3. Subsequent plaintiffs in some cases will benefit by the *Boomer* court's findings. This will depend on their ability to invoke the doctrine of collateral estoppel without mutuality of estoppel. Such parties are "free riders" on Boomer's efforts, but their recovery extends the sum of costs internalized by legal action.

The court exercises considerable control over cases that are maintained as a class action. The court decides whether the class action device is appropriate and must consider factors such as the ability of the class representative fully and fairly to represent the class, the interest of individual class member plaintiffs in controlling the prosecution of their own claims, the desirability of concentrating the litigation in a single court and, perhaps most importantly for mass toxic tort cases, "the difficulties likely to be encountered in the management of a class action."

Imagine, for example, the difficulty of a trial that seeks to present all of the health related claims arising from the widespread use of asbestos as insulating material in this country.[4] Who are the plaintiffs? Looking narrowly, the group still includes millions of construction workers, some who have contracted forms of cancer, others who have not, but who are now at far greater risk of developing cancer in the future. Who are the defendants? This second group, again looking narrowly, includes the hundreds (perhaps thousands) of companies that produced and distributed asbestos. Some of these companies were long aware of the harmful nature of contact with the product and concealed that fact, others may have been unaware. And what are the damages? And who is responsible for what share of the damages? And which particular defendant's product caused which particular plaintiff's injury when so much of the material was of a generic type that might be impossible to identify many years after the exposure to the asbestos.

The inescapable conclusion, considering that manageability is an element in class action suitability, may be that no one class action can possibly take on so massive a problem, and that class action treatment may be inappropriate generally. Attempts to set up an alternative system with a special fund and arbitrational tribunal for asbestos claims (the "Wellington Agreement") have not succeeded either. While the asbestos problem is close to unique in its scale, it is not unique in displaying horrific manageability problems.

As you will see in the materials in this chapter, environmental lawyers have become inventive and adaptive in using various procedural devices to overcome the manageability problems incident to the multiparty nature of many toxic tort cases. Where class actions are likely to be unmanageable, for example, the plaintiffs have in some cases opted to select "flagship" plaintiffs. These plaintiffs are similar to those who would have been selected as class representatives – their claims are among the most typical. If they win, the understanding, made clear to the defendant, is that other claims will follow. At times, courts will require these later lawsuits to relitigate the disputed issues from scratch; other courts will allow later cases to make collateral use of determinations that were squarely faced in the earlier lawsuit.[5]

---

4. See, e.g., Jenkins v. Raymark Industries, 782 F.2d 468 (5th Cir. 1986). In *Jenkins*, the Court of Appeals approved trial court certification of a district-wide class action (the judicial district covered a part of Texas) to determine certain issues of liability against thirteen defendant asbestos manufacturers. The class, at the time of certification, included over 1,000 plaintiffs and continued to grow as asbestos–related disease manifested itself in additional exposed victims. Of course, if trial of an asbestos case like *Jenkins* appears daunting, consider the alternative of having that same trial 1,000+ times over! The total number of American workers exposed to asbestos was estimated by the *Jenkins* court to be "at least 21 million."

5. The use of the results in prior litigation to foreclose relitigation of claims or issues – res judicata – is subdivided into two branches, one that prevents the relitigation of entire claims (merger and

COMMENTARY AND QUESTIONS

1. Multiparty litigation as a cure for access bias. Recall the concept of access bias raised by Professors Gillette and Krier in Chapter 2. In their view, deserving cases challenging defendants who create public risks are often deterred from even entering the judicial system by barriers to entry. Class actions and flagship lawsuits are among the tools that reduce access bias against those who seek to internalize costs that are externalized by public risk creators. Leaving a more particularized answer for courses in complex litigation, do class actions and other forms of representative litigation seem likely to overcome the problem of access bias in the toxic tort setting?

2. The multiplier effect of multiparty litigation. To a defendant, what is the impact of procedural devices that result in the joinder of multiple similar claims into a single lawsuit? One obvious result is that the amount at risk in the event of an award of damages may increase manyfold. In the toxic tort area, where the injuries are often serious, this may turn many cases into a "you bet your company" scenario. Is there anything unfair in this? In general, plaintiffs can be expected to meet any such claims by defendants by pointing out that it is the defendants whose actions touched the lives of so many people. Can an individual plaintiff with a marginal case, by turning to a multiparty device, "extort" a handsome settlement of the case? Here it seems more plausible that defendants can make credible claims of unfairness, but even in this context the cost of responding to (or settling) marginal claims is a cost faced by virtually all enterprises, not just toxic tort defendants.

3. The benefits of using multiparty devices. There are ways in which the resort to multiparty litigation can make outcomes more just. Initially, to the extent that multiparty litigation reduces the need for repetitive litigation, the cost savings to the parties on both sides make the process preferable. There are at least two other settings in which having all of the claims joined in a single lawsuit holds a potential for making outcomes more just. On the plaintiffs' side, consider what happens when total liability exceeds a defendant's assets. If the litigation occurs in a piecemeal fashion, the early winners will collect their full damages, and later winners may find the defendant bankrupt and unable to pay any part of their claims. If the litigation all takes place in a single lawsuit, the proceeds can be divided up in a common fund that is proportioned to the individual entitlements of every deserving party. On the defendants' side, consider punitive damages. Assume that the conduct involved is such that punitive damages are awarded. If the litigation is piecemeal, punitive damages may be imposed numerous times, by numerous juries, each failing to take full account of what other punitive damages have been imposed. If only a single lawsuit is involved, a one-time-for-all award would more accurately measure the

---

bar) and another that prevents the relitigation of previously decided issues (collateral estoppel). In the successful flagship plaintiff toxic tort setting, later plaintiffs who were not parties of record in the first lawsuit would seek issue-preclusion against defendant on issues such as causation, or liability for the toxic release. The term that describes this use of the results of prior litigation is "offensive use of collateral estoppel without mutuality of estoppel." The leading federal case on the subject is Parklane Hosiery Co. v. Shore, 439 U.S. 322 (1979).

extent of punishment that should be imposed on the defendant. As Judge Clifford noted later in the *Fischer* asbestos case:

> Perhaps the most likely solution to the problem of cumulative punitive damages lies in the use of a class action for those damages.... Several courts have recognized the usefulness of class certification in mass tort cases. In re "Agent Orange" Product Liability Litigation, 100 F.R.D. 718, 735 (E.D.N.Y.)(class certified for affirmative defenses and causation issues, mandatory certification on punitive damages); [In re Asbestos Litigation, 628 F. Supp. 774 (D.N.J. 1986).]... A federal district court in Pennsylvania certified a nationwide class of plaintiff school authorities in asbestos property damage cases. In re Asbestos School Litigation, 104 F.R.D. 422 (1984), rev'd, 789 F.2d 996 (3d Cir. 1986)[6].... Defendants as well as plaintiffs can seek class certification. See *Dalkon Shield*, 693 F.2d 847, 849 n. 2 (9th Cir. 1982). In addition, the asbestos industry itself is free to – and has begun to – develop alternatives and supplements to federal class action. [The judge mentions the now-collapsed Wellington Agreement.] 512 A.2d at 480.

B. MULTIPLE TORTFEASORS AND JOINT AND SEVERAL LIABILITY

The traditional analysis of causation in tort is more difficult when more than one defendant is involved in the case. First, the but-for problem rears its head again. When the acts of several parties converge to effect a result that injures plaintiff, tort law must find a way to allocate the loss. Traditionally, the plaintiff had to show which of several actors was responsible for the damage and to what extent, or all recovery would be denied. If there were six independent upwind industrial polluters all using coal for their boiler fuel, the plaintiff would be hard pressed to segregate the emissions of any of them as responsible for the injuries. Gradually the doctrine of joint and several liability has developed to allow liability in such circumstances. As to payment, assuming that defendants are found to be joint tortfeasors, the common law allowed the plaintiff to collect the full judgment from any one of the jointly liable defendants, but it forbade that defendant from shifting a portion of the loss to co-tortfeasors. Modern tort law has also recoiled at that unfairness, but the problem of loss apportionment in hazardous waste toxic tort cases remains a major area of litigation.[7]

Velsicol Chemical Corporation v. Rowe

Supreme Court of Tennessee, 1976
543 S.W.2d 337

[The original plaintiffs, residents and homeowners in the Alton Park area of Chattanooga, sued Velsicol Chemical for damages allegedly caused them by pollutants emitted from its chemical manufacturing plant. The complaint alleged that Velsicol's emissions contaminated the air and water, creating a nuisance and a trespass in depositing quantities of chemicals and other pollutants upon plaintiffs'

6. The class was ultimately decertified because of insufficient factual findings.

7. For the most part, the question of intra-defendant allocation of loss will be studied in conjunction with the statutory materials relating to the management of hazardous waste sites and their clean-ups. See Chapters 6 and 21, *infra* .

properties. Because plaintiffs alleged that Velsicol had intentionally disregarded past injunctions, they also asked for punitive damages. Velsicol, however, argued that there were five other chemical polluters in the Alton Park area who could have caused or contributed to plaintiffs' injuries. This raised the question, first, whether plaintiffs could choose to proceed only against Velsicol, and second, if they prevailed, whether Velsicol could then turn and sue the five for contribution in paying damages.]

BROCK, J. ... It has been suggested that joint torts be divided into four basic categories, viz., (1) the actors knowingly join in the performance of the tortious act or acts; (2) the actors fail to perform a common duty owed to the plaintiff; (3) there is a special relationship between the parties (e.g., master and servant or joint entrepreneurs); and (4) although there is no concert of action, nevertheless, the independent acts of several actors concur to produce indivisible harmful consequences. 1 Harper & James, Law of Torts, §10.1. While acknowledging that the last category, which may be termed independent, concurring torts, may not fall within the traditional definition of "joint torts," the authors note an increasing tendency in judicial decisions and among legal commentators to impose joint and several liability for such wrongs and thus to establish such torts as "joint" in their practical or legal effect.

The primary concern in dealing with independent, concurring torts is the proper extent of the liability of such wrongdoers, i.e., when should tortfeasors who do not act in concert, but whose acts combine to produce injury to the plaintiff, be held individually liable for the entire damage? It has been suggested that the proper approach should be to look to the combined effect of the several acts:

> If the acts result in separate and distinct injuries, then each wrongdoer is liable only for the damage caused by his acts. However, if the combined result is a single and indivisible injury, the liability should be entire. Thus the distinction to be made is between injuries which are divisible and those which are indivisible. Jackson, Joint Torts & Several Liability, 17 Tex. L. Rev. 399, 406 (1939).

The requirement of "indivisibility" can mean either that the harm is not even theoretically divisible, as death or total destruction of a building, or that the harm, while theoretically divisible, is single in a practical sense in that the plaintiff is not able to apportion it among the wrongdoers with reasonable certainty, as where a stream is polluted as the result of refuse from several factories.

In Landers v. East Texas Salt Water Disposal Co., 248 S.W.2d 731 (Tex. 1952), the plaintiff sued the defendant salt water disposal company and an oil company jointly and severally for the damage resulting when they independently deposited salt water in his lake. The court, apparently assuming that neither defendant acting alone would have caused the entire damage, extended the liability of such wrongdoers by holding them, in effect, to be jointly and severally liable, with the reservation that any one defendant could reduce his liability by showing the amount of damage caused by his acts only, or the amount that was caused by other defendants. The Texas court said:

> Where the tortious acts of two or more wrongdoers join to produce an indivisible injury, that is, an injury which cannot be apportioned with reasonable certainty to the individual wrongdoers, all of the wrongdoers will be held jointly and severally liable for the entire damages and the injured

> party may proceed to judgment against any one separately or against all in one suit. 248 S.W.2d at 734.

More recently, in Michie v. Great Lakes Steel, 495 F.2d 213 (6th Cir. 1974), residents of LaSalle, Ontario, brought a nuisance action in federal court, claiming that air pollutants from defendants' manufacturing plants across the Detroit River caused diminution of the value of their property, impairment of their health, and interference with the use and enjoyment of their land. Each plaintiff claimed at least $11,000 joint damage against these defendants, charging that the defendants were jointly and severally liable.

Relying upon Michigan automobile cases involving successive collisions, the Court reasoned that in any claim for relief there was a manifest unfairness in "putting on the injured party the impossible burden of proving the specific shares of harm done by each [defendant]," quoting *Landers*. The Court concluded that the Michigan Supreme Court would extend the principle of the automobile collision cases to the *Michie* facts and held that joint and several liability is applicable in nuisance actions. It is our conclusion that the rule stated and applied in the *Landers* and *Michie* cases is...consonant with modern legal thought and pragmatic concepts of justice....

After filing an answer generally denying the plaintiffs' allegations, Velsicol filed a third-party complaint against five third-party defendants, alleging that each of them operated a plant in the Alton Park area, that during the period alleged in the original complaint each of them emitted pollutants of the air and water, and that by reason of these facts the third-party defendants are liable to Velsicol for "whatever amount of recovery is made by said plaintiffs."...

The common law rule was that there could be no contribution between those who were regarded as "joint tortfeasors," when one had discharged the claim of the injured plaintiff.... Prosser, §50 and n. 38. The rule was originally adopted by the English courts in Merryweather v. Nixon, 101 Eng. Rep. (K.B. 1799). Apparently, the basis of the rule was the unwillingness of the court to allow anyone to found a cause of action upon his own deliberate wrong, an aspect of the "unclean hands" doctrine. When, in the United States, the codes of civil procedure permitted joinder of defendants who were merely negligent, such defendants came to be called "joint tortfeasors," and the reason for the rule against contribution was lost to sight. The great majority of American jurisdictions applied the rule of no-contribution to all situations, even those in which independent, but concurrent, acts of negligence had contributed to a single resulting injury. A small minority of states – including Tennessee – eventually came to a contrary conclusion, allowing contribution among joint tortfeasors without the aid of legislation. Davis v. Broad St. Garage, 232 S.W.2d 355 (1950); Huggins v. Graves, 210 F. Supp. 98 (E.D. Tenn. 1962).... In *Huggins*, the federal district judge concluded that:

> [t]he right of contribution exists under Tennessee law as between joint tortfeasors in a negligence action in the absence of willful or wanton negligence upon the part of the party seeking contribution. Moreover, this result accords with reason and, as stated by the Tennessee Supreme Court in the *Davis* case, "justice, right, and equity demand this conclusion." 210 F. Supp. at 103.

Any remaining uncertainty regarding the extent of the right of contribution among joint tortfeasors in Tennessee was dispelled by the 1968 enactment of the Tennessee Uniform Contribution Among Tortfeasors Act. TCA 23-3104, 3105 (1975). Excluding intentional tortfeasors, the Tennessee Uniform Act provides that the right to contribution arises upon the satisfaction of two general conditions. First, there must be "two (2) or more persons...jointly or severally liable in tort for the same injury to person or property...." Secondly, one of those jointly or severally liable must have paid more than his pro rata share of the common liability.

Obviously, the meaning of the phrase "jointly or severally liable" is of primary importance in determining the right of contribution under our law. An early Tennessee case, Swain v. Tennessee Copper Co., 78 S.W. 93 (1903), stated that the test of joint liability is "whether each of the parties is liable for the entire injury done." It would appear that the Court was begging the question:

> If they [the defendants] are joint tortfeasors, each one is responsible for the damage resulting from the acts of all the wrongdoers, and they may all be sued severally or jointly; but, if they are not joint tortfeasors, each is liable only for the injury contributed by him, and can only be sued in a separate action therefor. 78 S.W. at 94.

The factual situation presented in the *Swain* case was markedly similar to that in the instant case. The plaintiff-landowners brought suit against two neighboring copper smelting plants, alleging that the noxious fumes emitted from their respective hearths became "indistinguishably mingled," creating "a great nuisance." The Court, however, refused to acknowledge that the harm done to the plaintiffs' land was indivisible. Rather, the Court said:

> Proof of the extent and capacity of the several plants causing the damages complained of, the tonnage of ores treated by each of them, the time each has been in operation, their comparative proximity or distance from the plaintiff's lands, the usual condition of the air currents in that locality, and many other facts and circumstances, will show with substantial certainty the extent of the injury inflicted by each of the defendants.... Id. at 99.

Apparently, the Court was not troubled by the fact that it would be extremely difficult, if not impossible, for the plaintiff to apportion his damages among the defendants. The rationale of the *Swain* decision is shown:

> If it were otherwise...one defendant, however little he might have contributed to the injury, would be liable for all the damages caused by the wrongful acts of all the other defendants, and he would have no remedy against the latter, because no contribution could be enforced by the tortfeasors. Id. at 97, quoting Miller v. Highland Ditch Co., 25 P. 550 (Cal.1891).

Such was the state of our law regarding contribution among tortfeasors at the time *Swain* was decided. Since that time, however, as above indicated, we have developed not only a common law right of contribution among tortfeasors but the legislature has passed a uniform act specifically granting such a right. Thus, the no-contribution rationale of the *Swain* case has collapsed, so that we look elsewhere for the import of the phrase "jointly or severally liable."

In Waller v. Skelton, 212 S.W.2d 690 (1948), it was no defense for a defendant, who drove over the crest of a hill on the wrong side of the road in the face of congested oncoming traffic and collided with the oncoming car in which plaintiff was riding, that a motorist who was driving behind plaintiff's car negligently collided with plaintiff's car, contributing to the plaintiff's injuries. Since the following motorist's negligence was concurrent with the defendant's negligence, the Court reasoned, each would be jointly and severally liable for all of plaintiff's injury. Relying upon various legal authorities, the Court said:

> A defendant's negligent act, in order to be the proximate or legal cause of plaintiff's injuries, need not have been the whole cause or the only factor in bringing them about. It was enough if such act was a substantial factor in causing them. 212 S.W.2d at 696.

While not relying on the "single, indivisible injury" theory, the Court did decide that where successive impacts with different negligently operated vehicles contributed to or combined to cause the aggregate harm suffered, the plaintiff is entitled to a joint and several recovery against both tortfeasors....

We depart from *Swain*...and adopt the rule of *Landers* and *Michie* for determining joint and several liability when an indivisible injury has been caused by the concurrent, but independent, wrongful acts or omissions of two or more wrongdoers, whether the case be one of negligence or nuisance. We hold that the third-party complaint may stand as a claim for contribution by one tortfeasor from other alleged joint tortfeasors....

COMMENTARY AND QUESTIONS

1. Problems of joint liability. In *Rowe*, and the *Landers* and *Michie* cases it discusses, is it clear that the plaintiffs have suffered a single harm from the air or water pollution? The plaintiffs have suffered a single type of harm in each of the three instances, but no single defendant is the cause-in-fact of the entire extent of the harm suffered. What justifies "extending" the liability of each potential defendant? Is the extension effectively offset by the availability of an action for contribution?

In each of those cases, the court presumes that the injuries were probably caused by multiple defendants, each of whom contributed a part. What if it had been a "single bullet" injury, however? Take the example of a landfill with a thousand toxic barrels in it, all unmarked, and just one unidentifiable barrel escapes in a flood to poison a city's drinking water. Even if one knows all seven companies that dumped there, it is clear that only one unidentifiable defendant caused the poisoning. Unless one company dumped more than 50 percent of the barrels, each defendant can say that it is statistically unlikely that it caused the pollution (therefore arguing that it is unreasonable or unconstitutional to assess liability), yet together it is clear that one of them did it. This is a Summers v. Tice problem, 199 P.2d 1 (Cal. 1948), similar to the DES market-share liability cases (e.g., Sindell v. Abbot Laboratories, 607 P.2d 924 (Cal. 1980), where recovery, however, was limited to each defendant's *pro rata* share.) Can it be answered by the concert of action principles with which the *Rowe* excerpt begins? The answer that seems to be evolving in toxic tort law is a blend of strict liability, concert of action, and enterprise liability, permitting courts to shift the impossible burden of proving which defendant caused the harm from innocent plaintiffs to the class of defendants, all of whom may have been careless or risky in dumping toxic barrels, but all but one of whom is innocent in such a case.

A further extension is the "Blue Bus" theory: if plaintiff was injured by a fast-moving hit and run bus on a dark and lonely road one night, can you use the fact that 70 percent of the buses on that route belong to the Blue Bus Company to assess full (or 70 percent) liability against that defendant? Nesson, Agent Orange Meets the Blue Bus: Factfinding at the Frontier of Knowledge, 66 B.U.L. Rev. (1986).

2. Contribution and indemnity. Traditionally, contribution and indemnity were independent causes of action that became available only after a tortfeasor had paid more than its appropriate share of a judgment for the plaintiff. With the rise of more liberal joinder rules, in particular FRCP 14 and its state court counterparts, defendants who are sued alone may join potential contributors and indemnitors in the original action. This encourages efficiency by joining more of the issues in a single lawsuit, but it does not alter the plaintiff's option to enforce the ensuing judgment *in toto* against a single defendant. When is that option important?

Under the common law, the Uniform Contribution Among Tortfeasors Act (UCATA), and Uniform Comparative Fault Act (UCFA), contribution is usually *pro rata* unless there is some other provable basis on which to apportion the injury. The emergence and growth of comparative negligence in recent years has led to apportionment in accordance with the respective percentages of negligence. In cases founded on intentional nuisance, trespass and strict liability, comparative fault would seem to be irrelevant, but there too some courts nevertheless divide responsibility according to the Acts' comparative fault principles. Dole v. Dow Chemical, 282 N.E.2d 288 (N.Y. 1972). See Phillips, Contribution and Indemnity in Products Liability, 42 Tenn. L. Rev. 85 (1974). What avenues might a polluter in *Rowe* consider in trying to pay less than a *pro rata* amount?

3. Predecessor landowners' liability. Can the prior owner of a contaminated parcel of land be held liable for common law damages when the toxics are subsequently discovered? Some forms of predecessor liability are straightforwardly available – within the constraints of statutes of limitation, prior owners who polluted the land will be liable to injured neighbors who sue in tort; federal and state cleanup statutes generally extend regulatory liability to prior owners (see Chapters 6 and 21). But other areas can be more problematic.

What about suits by private individuals who purchase contaminated land? The traditional property doctrine is *caveat emptor*, buyer beware. Unlike the case of contracts for the sale of goods, sellers of land are held to no implied warranty that the land will be fit for use. While awaiting the development of such an implied warranty, can landowners sue predecessor owners (particularly those who can be shown to have known about the toxics, not to mention those who actually dumped them) under nuisance theories? In Philadelphia Electric Co. v. Hercules, 762 F.2d 303 (3d Cir. 1985), the court held that private nuisance was unavailable, because that tort was designed for suits between owners of different parcels of land. It dismissed the public nuisance claims on standing grounds. If plaintiffs can show special injury, might public nuisance claims work? Does a claim of abnormally dangerous activity improve the situation by adding strict liability to the equation? See T&E Industries v. Safety Light Corp., 587 A.2d 1249 (N.J. 1991) (court allows strict liability in favor of landowner against predecessor in title).

The question of liability against and between predecessor and successor corporations is more fully developed, with liability typically cutting through changes in corporate form. See Civins, Environmental Law Concerns in Real Estate Transactions, 43 Sw. L. J. 819 (1990).

C. CAUSATION: BEYOND MEDICAL CERTAINTY – LATENCY, LOW-LEVEL, AND MULTIPLE EXPOSURES

Conventional tort law is adapted to injuries that are identifiably and immediately caused by a traumatic impact, such as an automobile accident. Toxic torts seldom exhibit that pattern. Illness develops slowly over time and the etiology of the typical diseases caused by toxic torts – cancers, and mutagenic changes – cannot be readily proved to be a direct result of the toxic exposure for which the defendant is responsible. In this setting, the proof of causation is made even more tenuous by the fact that in addition to defendant's action, other potential causes for which defendant is not responsible are simultaneously at work, like exposure to cigarette smoke. With regard to a cancer that develops many years after a toxic exposure, the usual evidence will address the degree to which the exposure increased the risk of contracting the disease. Given medical uncertainty and the vagaries of statistical proof, toxics cases often compel the courts either to go to the frontiers of science and beyond, or leave plaintiffs with no relief, alternatives that many judges find dismaying, although not Judge Jenkins in the following radiation exposure case.

Section 1. PROOF OF CAUSATION: FACTUAL CONNECTIONS, STATISTICAL PROOF?

The following case dealing with mass exposures to radioactive materials presents an unusually detailed discussion of legal proof of causation in circumstances where science can offer no certainty. The excerpted analysis may be tough going, but that is part of the point. The judge undoubtedly was convinced that it would be inappropriate and unfair to dismiss the case in light of the proven facts, but because causation was scientifically unclear, his liability analysis had to be extraordinarily complex. Going through the *Allen* excerpts, most readers are expected to get only a sense of the problem, not a command of it. And you have reason to thank as well as curse your editors: the original opinion is 191 pages long.

Allen v. United States

United States District Court for the District of Utah, 1984
588 F. Supp 247

JENKINS, J. This case is concerned with atoms, with government, with people, with legal relationships, and with social values.... It is concerned with the duty, if any, that the United States government had to tell its people, particularly those in proximity to the experiment site, what it knew or should have known about the dangers to them from the government's experiments with nuclear fission....

The complaint in this action alleges that each plaintiff, or his predecessor, has suffered injury or death as a proximate result of exposure to radioactive fallout [from bomb tests held between 1951 and 1963] that drifted away from the Nevada Test Site and settled upon communities and isolated populations in southern Utah, northern Arizona and southeastern Nevada. Each of the plaintiffs or their decedents resided in that area. Each claims serious loss due to radiation-caused cancer or leukemia. Each asserts that the injury suffered resulted from the negligence of the United States in conducting open-air nuclear testing, in monitoring testing results, in failing to inform persons at hazard of attendant dangers from such testing and in failing to inform such persons how to avoid or minimize or mitigate such dangers....

The following is the testimony of Frank Butrico, an off-site monitor assigned to St. George. When HARRY [the atomic bomb tested] was detonated at 5:05 a.m. on May 19, 1953, Butrico was not made aware of the fallout until it registered on his own instruments – off the scale, indicating exposure rates of greater than 350 millirems per hour. Upon seeing the abnormal readings [at 8:50 a.m.], Butrico called William Johnson, a safety official at NTS;

Q: What did Mr. Johnson tell you to do at the time of that first telephone conversation?

A: Check the instruments and be sure that at a different point some distance away...to take another reading. I reported back that the instrument was still off scale....

At about 9:45 a.m., Butrico called Johnson back for instructions:

Q: And did Mr. Johnson have a concrete plan for you to carry out at that point?

A: No, other than...that we were going to wash cars and we were going to try to get people indoors. To do this via some communication mechanism such as radio or television...at about noon it was time to take some kind of a break, and communications were opened up with the command post...and I had indicated that I was going back to the motel to wash up because I, very foolishly, probably, was traveling around St. George without any head cover and I was getting some pretty high readings in my hair.

Q: Did you take any readings on your own body?

A: Yes, indoors. So it was obvious that it was off me and not around me.

Q: Do you remember what those readings were?

A: Approximately what they were outside just for brief moments, but then they dropped considerably. And I'd indicated I was going to go ahead and shower as much as I could and get some shampoo and get some of that stuff out of my hair....

Q: Did [Mr. Johnson] tell you to decontaminate yourself?

A: Well, we were just having this kind of a conversation that I was pretty hot, and that I was going to do this, and this was a good idea....

Q: Did Mr. Johnson tell you that you should tell other people in St. George to decontaminate themselves?

A: No, that subject was not brought up....

Q: [The people of St. George] who were out of doors between 8:50, and 10:15 when the radio message came would have gotten the same exposures you did?

A: Yes....

Q: And they were never advised to shower and discard their clothes as you were?

A: That was never brought up, nor was it suggested....

THE QUESTION OF CAUSATION

Before any findings as to duty or negligent breach of duty may be applied to determine the question of liability, each plaintiff must show that he has suffered injury as a result of the defendant's conduct, at least in part.

The plaintiff's starting point on the road to a tort recovery is to be able to pick the defendant out of the crowd; that is, to demonstrate factually that there is a reason why this particular person is the defendant. This is usually called the causation or factual causation issue. I find "factual connection" to be a more accurate term. Factual connection in the manner in which the term is used herein, carries no connotation of fault or of liability. It is the means of selecting a particular defendant on whom to focus the process of the legal system. It is the statement of what happened between plaintiff and defendant. Whether the factual connection between plaintiff's injury and defendant will lead to liability depends upon plaintiff successfully establishing the remainder of the issues that are relevant to the determination of liability. Thode, Tort Analysis: Duty-Risk v. Proximate Cause and the Rational Allocation of Functions Between Judge and Jury, 1977 Utah L. Rev. 1, 2 (1977).

The reason for this requirement was stated long ago by Professor Beale:

> Starting with a human act, we must next find a causal relation between the act and the harmful result for in our law – and, it is believed, in any civilized law – liability cannot be imputed to a man unless it is in some degree a result of his act. Beale, The Proximate Consequences of an Act, 33 Harv. L. Rev. 633, 637 (1920).

In most cases, the factual connection between defendant's conduct and plaintiff's injury is not genuinely in dispute. Often, the cause-and-effect relationship is obvious: A's vehicle strikes B, injuring him; a bottle of A's product explodes, injuring B; water impounded on A's property flows onto B's land, causing immediate damage. In this case, the factual connection singling out the defendant as the source of the plaintiffs' injuries and deaths is very much in genuine dispute. Determination of the cause-in-fact, or factual connection, issue is complicated by the nature of the injuries suffered (various forms of cancer and leukemia), the nature of the causation mechanism alleged (ionizing radiation from nuclear fallout, as opposed to ionizing radiation from other sources, or other carcinogenic mechanisms), the extraordinary time factors and other variables involved in tracing any causal relationship between the two.

At this point, there appears to be no question whether or not ionizing radiation causes cancer and leukemia. It does. Once more, however, it seems important to clarify what is meant by "cause" in relation to radiation and cancer:

When we refer to radiation as a cause, we do not mean that it causes every case of cancer or leukemia. Indeed, the evidence we have indicating radiation in the causation of cancer and leukemia shows that not all cases of cancer are caused by radiation. Second, when we refer to radiation as a cause of cancer, we do not mean that every individual exposed to a certain amount of radiation will develop cancer. We simply mean that a population exposed to a certain dose of radiation will show a greater incidence of cancer than that same population would have shown in the absence of the added radiation. J. Gofman, M.D., Radiation and Human Health, 54-55 (1981).

The question of cause-in-fact is additionally complicated by the long delay, known often as the *latency period*, between the exposure to radiation and the observed cancer or leukemia. Assuming that cancer originates in a single cell, or a few cells, in a particular organ or tissue, it may take years before those cells multiply into the millions or billions that comprise a detectable tumor. As Dr. John Gofman explains, cancer is characterized by "the unregulated, uncontrolled proliferation of the descendants of a single changed cell. It is not that cancer cells divide more rapidly than normal cells; rather it is that they keep on dividing when there is no need for them."

The problem of the latency period is one factor distinguishing radiation/cancer causation questions from the cause-in-fact relationships found in most tort cases.... The great length of time involved (*e.g.*, A irradiates B, who develops a tumor 22 years later) allows the possible involvement of "intervening causes," sources of injury wholly apart from the defendant's activities, which obscure the factual connection between the plaintiff's injury and the defendant's purportedly wrongful conduct. The mere passage of time is sufficient to raise doubts about "cause" in the minds of a legal system accustomed to far more immediate chains of events.

The non-specific nature of the alleged injury further obscures the causal relationship between the defendant's conduct and the biological effects which are identified as consequences. Wounds and injuries from firearms, knives, heavy machinery, or other dangerous implements, for example, have particular qualities which are readily traced to source. Acute poisoning by specific toxic chemicals may be identified by specific symptoms or effects coinciding with the detected presence of the substance itself. Even acute radiation syndrome resulting from short-term exposure to 25 or more rads is fairly easily traced to source by blood counts and more externalized symptoms now identified to such exposure.

When the injury alleged, the biological consequence, is some form of cancer or leukemia, such specific clues as to cause, or source, are usually lacking:

> Once established, a radiation-induced cancer cannot be distinguished from a cancer of the same organ arising from the unknown causes we so commonly lump together as "spontaneous...." Gofman at 59.

Ionizing radiation – or other carcinogens – seem to add to the number of cancers already occurring in people, rather than producing new, distinct varieties of cancer. The intrinsic nature of the alleged injury itself thus restricts the ability of the plaintiffs to demonstrate through evidence a direct cause-in-fact relationship between radiation from any source and their own cancers or leukemias. At least within the scope of our present knowledge, the injury is not specifically traceable to the asserted cause on an injury-by-injury basis.

This does not, however, end the inquiry. That the court cannot now peer into the damaged cells of a plaintiff to determine that the cancer or leukemia was radiation-induced does *not* mean (1) that the damage was not in fact caused by radiation; (2) that the radiation damage involved did not result from the defendant's conduct; or (3) that a satisfactory factual connection can never be established between plaintiff's injury and defendant's conduct for purposes of determining liability. Experience and the evidence in the record indicate that indeed it can.

If plaintiff cannot establish a cause-in-fact connection between his injury and defendant's conduct that will support liability...plaintiff should attempt to establish the most exclusive factual connection that he can between his injury and the defendant. This will normally involve some kind of a relationship between plaintiff and defendant.... Thode at 5.

The more exclusive the factual connections that may be established by evidence, the stronger the rational basis for focusing the tools of legal analysis upon a specific defendant's conduct.

For example, the fact that both plaintiff and defendant are members of the human race is one of the less exclusive connections possible and does nothing to explain why this defendant is before the court. That the defendant was in the area when plaintiff was injured establishes a more exclusive connection. Id. at 6.

That the defendant was engaged in risk-creating conduct of a particular type, and plaintiff's injuries are consistent with the kind of harm that is predicted and observed when such risks are created, makes the factual connection seem even more exclusive – exclusive of other defendants, other connections, other "causes."

Whether any of these factual connections will lead to liability is, as Professor Thode reminds us, "an issue involving *the scope of the legal system's protection afforded to plaintiff* and is not an issue of factual causation." Id. at 6 (emphasis added).

Several relevant cases may be analyzed cogently in terms of factual connections rather than direct proof, tracing cause-in-fact....

A number of cases involving destruction of property by two or more fires or sources of fire, or similar problems may be cited wherein a factual connection establishing a rational relationship between plaintiff's injury and a defendant's conduct has been relied upon to reach questions of liability, even though a specific cause-in-fact relationship is not clearly identified. [Discussion of Summers v. Tice and similar cases omitted.] There are several cases in which the factual connection to plaintiff's injury is the defendant's failure to warn plaintiff or otherwise safeguard the plaintiff from risk or hazard. E.g., Haft v. Lone Palm Hotel, 478 P.2d 465 (Cal. 1970) (father and son drowned in motel swimming pool; motel neither provided lifeguard nor warning that none was present); Reynolds v. Texas & Pac. Ry. Co., 37 La. Ann. 694 (1885) (plaintiff emerging from brightly lit train station onto unlit stairway at night, falls and is injured; negligence of railroad in not lighting stairway "multiplied" chance of accident); Kirincich v. Standard Dredging Co., 112 F.2d 163, 164-65 (3d Cir. 1940) (failure of crew to throw life preserver to drowning seaman); Berry v. Farmers Exchange, 286 P. 46 (Wash. 1930) (failure of building owners to provide fire escape not sufficient factual connection). See also Malone, Ruminations on Cause-in-Fact, 9 Stan. L. Rev. 60, 77-81 (1956).

Sometimes the connection seems too improbable to the court to establish any basis for liability. See e.g., Kramer Service, Inc. v. Wilkins, 186 So. 625 (Miss. 1939) ("no probability" that plaintiff's skin cancer was caused by cut resulting from falling glass). In other cases, it does not appear improbable at all. See e.g., Daly v. Bergstedt, 126 N.W.2d 242 (Minn. 1964) (evidence of factual connection between injury from fall in defendant's store and subsequent tumor at site of bruise held sufficient to support verdict for plaintiff).

In some of the cases in which plaintiff has been injured, but has no means of identifying the specific cause-in-fact of the injury, the burden of proof has been placed upon the *defendant* to establish the factual details of the incident and show that defendant's conduct did not contribute to the victim's injury. Summers v. Tice is probably the best known example....

In other cases, where plaintiff has produced evidence of factual connection sufficient to permit the drawing of a rational inference of causation – of some contribution by defendant's conduct to plaintiff's injury – it has been left to the defendant to prove otherwise. In Basko v. Sterling Drug Co., 416 F.2d at 429, the

Second Circuit relied upon §432(2) of the Restatement 2d of Torts in holding that such an inference of causation may support a finding of liability. That section states:

> If two forces are actively operating, one because of the actor's negligence, the other not because of any misconduct on his part, and each of itself is sufficient to bring about harm to another, the actor's negligence may be found to be a substantial factor in bringing it about.

If defendant's negligent conduct is found to be a "substantial factor," it may in Restatement parlance be judged to be the "legal cause" of plaintiff's injury, i.e., defendant could be held liable based upon determination of the *legal* issues relating to liability (scope of duty, negligence, etc.). "The reason for imposing liability in such a situation," the court explains, is that the "defendant has committed a wrong and this has been *a* cause of the injury; further, such negligent conduct will be more effectively deterred by imposing liability than by giving the wrongdoer a windfall in cases where an all-sufficient innocent cause happens to concur with his wrong in producing the harm." 2 Harper and James, at 1123. Similarly, Judge Learned Hand stated that "the single tortfeasor cannot be allowed to escape through the meshes of a logical net. He is a wrongdoer; let him unravel the casuistries resulting from his wrong." Navigazione Libera T.S.A. v. Newtown Creek Towing Co., 98 F.2d 694, 697 (2d Cir. 1938).

Implicitly the *Basko* opinion shifts the burden to defendant to produce evidence refuting causation if he is to escape liability once plaintiff has established a "substantial" factual connection between defendant's conduct and her own injuries, the principle expressed in Restatement §432 comment b (1965). Thus a defendant may be held liable for negligent conduct with factual connections to plaintiff's injuries even where other concurrent forces of human, "natural" or unknown origin have similar connections....

The case of Haft v. Lone Palm Hotel highlights an additional reason for assigning to the tortfeasor the burden of extricating himself from a tangle of causal forces. Thc defendant hotel's failure to maintain a lifeguard at its swimming pool did not merely aggravate the risks which took effect in the drowning of plaintiff's decedents; it also deprived the parties and the court of a potentially important witness on the subject of cause-in-fact, the lifeguard himself....

Likewise, the Government's negligent failure to adequately monitor and record the actual external and internal radiation exposures of off-site residents on a person-specific basis has yielded many glaring deficiencies in the evidentiary record as it relates directly to the question of causation. The current multi-million dollar effort to reconstruct the radiation dosages received by plaintiffs or their decedents is constantly hampered by the failure of the off-site radiation safety personnel to gather whole categories of exposure data at the time that the exposures actually took place. Furthermore, had Government personnel provided adequate warnings of risk and information as to precautions minimizing the amount of exposure, a materially different picture as to appropriate inferences about factual connection and cause-in-fact might now be presented. Accurate monitoring of persons largely was not undertaken; adequate warnings and information were almost entirely omitted from the operational radiation safety activities. A strong additional reason for shifting the burden of proof on the cause-in-fact question is thus readily apparent from the record.

This is not to say that this court presumes a causal relationship from the Government's negligence. To the contrary, as Dean Leon Green explains, "it will be noticed in these cases that the factual details of the immediate environment out of which the case arose must be shown with considerable particularity. Causal relation will not be presumed from the fact of injury or from a showing defendant has violated his duty." Yet so long as the evidence will support an inference that defendant's conduct *contributed* to the victim's injury, even though other inferences can be drawn that it did not, or that his injury was due to other causes, "it is for the finder of fact" – this court – "to draw the most appropriate inference using the court's own best judgment, experience and common sense in light of all the circumstances." Green, The Causal Relation Issue in Negligence Law, 60 Mich. L. Rev. 543, 560 (1962). This is true even in cases when it may be extremely difficult to establish a factual connection, where "the parties may have to rely almost wholly on scientific proof, i.e., the opinions of experts, and they may differ widely in their opinions." Id. at 561.

A useful analogy may perhaps be drawn from some of the currently proposed schemes for compensating long-term injuries to health allegedly caused by exposure to toxic chemicals and chemical wastes. The causation problems facing many toxic waste plaintiffs are strikingly similar to those facing plaintiffs alleging nuclear fall-out injuries in this and other cases. Consider, for example, the problem of the "indeterminate plaintiff":

> We may know, for example, that a *group* of people has a specific type of cancer and that some of them contracted that cancer from exposure to the defendant's waste, but we do not know which *individuals* of that group were affected by the waste. The character of toxic waste injuries causes this uncertainty. We know what causes a broken leg or a black eye and can decide liability based on whether or not those causes were controlled by the defendant, but we do not know the mechanics of causation of cancers and nervous disorders. We are still at the elementary stage of knowing simply that they *can* be caused entirely or in part by exposures to certain substances; we cannot tie the exposures more precisely to the injuries. Note, The Inapplicability of Traditional Tort Analysis to Environmental Risks: The Example of Toxic Waste Pollution Victim Compensation, 35 Stan. L. Rev. 575, 582 (1983) (emphasis in original); Delgado, Beyond *Sindell*: Relaxation of Cause-in-Fact Rules for Indeterminate Plaintiffs, 70 Calif. L. Rev. 881, 881-83 (1982).

As the Note explains, "a toxic tort plaintiff typically can show only a 'causal linkage' between the toxic substance to which he was exposed and his type of disease or affliction." Like exposure to ionizing radiation, "most toxic tort injuries are of indeterminate causation. The etiology of the disease is unclear and the disease may occur in the absence of the suspect toxic contaminant." Id. at 583 & n. 31. The concept of "causal linkage," coined by Professor Calabresi, refers to an empirically based belief that the act or activity in question will, if repeated in the future, increase the likelihood that the injury under consideration will also occur, see Calabresi, Concerning Cause and the Law of Torts: An Essay for Harry Kalven, Jr., 43 U. Chi. L. Rev. 69, 72 (1975)....

Each of the prior cases analyzed has dealt to some extent with the problem of indeterminate causation. In each case, the court has applied common-law principles to fashion a remedial process that fairly compensates plaintiff's injuries while relieving the defendant of the burden of those harms which defendant can reasonably prove were *not* in fact a consequence of his risk-creating, negligent conduct. A remedial framework can certainly be fashioned to meet the circumstances and requirements of the parties and issues now before this court in this action. To that end, this court now holds as follows: Where a defendant who negligently creates a radiological hazard which puts an identifiable population group at increased risk, and a member of that group at risk develops a biological condition which is consistent with having been caused by the hazard to which he has been negligently subjected, such consistency having been demonstrated by substantial, appropriate, persuasive and connecting factors, a fact finder *may* reasonably conclude that the hazard caused the condition absent persuasive proof to the contrary offered by the defendant.

In this case, such factors shall include, among others: (1) the probability that plaintiff was exposed to ionizing radiation due to nuclear fallout from atmospheric testing at the Nevada Test Site at rates in excess of natural background radiation; (2) that plaintiff's injury is of a type consistent with those known to be caused by exposure to radiation; and (3) that plaintiff resided in geographical proximity to the Nevada Test Site for some time between 1951 and 1962. Other factual connections may include but are not limited to such things as time and extent of exposure to fallout, radiation sensitivity factors such as age or special sensitivities of the afflicted organ or tissue, retroactive internal or external dose estimation by current researchers, a latency period consistent with a radiation etiology, or an observed statistical incidence of the alleged injury greater than the expected incidence in the same population.

The Restatement (2d) of Torts offers some guidance for determining whether defendant's conduct amounts to a "substantial factor":

> §433. The following considerations are in themselves or in combination with one another important in determining whether the actor's conduct is a substantial factor in bringing about harm to another:
>
> (a) the number of other factors which contribute in producing the harm and the extent of the effect which they have in producing it;
> (b) whether the actor's conduct has created a force or series of forces which are in continuous and active operation up to the time of the harm, or has created a situation harmless unless acted upon by other forces for which the actor is not responsible; and
> (c) lapse of time.

One consideration is easily resolved; exposure to ionizing radiation from nuclear fallout cannot fairly be described as "a situation harmless unless acted upon by other forces." See also id. §§440-452. Others are more difficult:

> Experience has shown that where a great length of time has elapsed between the author's negligence and harm to another, a great number of contributing factors may have operated, many of which may be difficult or impossible of actual proof.... However where it is evident that the influence of the actor's negligence is still a substantial factor, mere lapse of time, no matter how long, is not sufficient to prevent it from being the legal cause of the other's harm. Id., comment f.

Implicit in the finding of "substantial factor" based upon relevant considerations is the exercise of sound judgment in light of the evidence. As both the court of appeals and the Restatement remind us, "the plaintiff need not prove his case beyond a reasonable doubt. In fact, 'He is not required to eliminate entirely all possibility that the defendant's conduct is not a cause....'"

THE PROBLEM OF MATHEMATICAL PROOF

In a case where a plaintiff tries to establish a factual connection between a particular "cause" and a delayed, non-specific effect such as cancer or leukemia, the strongest evidence of the relationship is likely to be statistical in form. Where the injuries are causally indistinguishable, and where experts cannot determine whether an individual injury arises from culpable human cause or non-culpable natural causes, evidence that there is an increased incidence of the injury in a population following exposure to defendant's risk-creating conduct may justify an inference of "causal linkage" between defendant's conduct and plaintiff's injuries.... The search for increased incidence of injury among groups receiving more or less radiation exposure is the classic approach to researching induction of cancer and leukemia by ionizing radiation. See e.g., J. Gofman, Radiation and Human Health (1981), PX-1046, and the studies discussed therein; Hiroshima and Nagasaki, *supra* at 187-332; the UNSCEAR Report (1977), PX-706/DX-605; the BEIR-III Report (1980), DX-1025. Where there is an increase of observed cases of a particular cancer or leukemia over the number statistically "expected" to normally appear, the question arises whether it may be rationally inferred that the increase is causally connected to specific human activity. The scientific papers and reports will often speak of whether a deviation from the expected numbers of cases is "statistically significant," supporting a hypothesis of causation, or whether the perceived increase is attributable to random variation in the studied population, i.e., to chance. The mathematical tests of significance commonly used in research tend to be stringent; for an increase to be considered "statistically significant," the probability that it can be attributed to random chance usually must be five percent or less (p=0.05). In other words, if the level of significance chosen by the researcher is p=0.05, then an observed correlation is "significant" if there is 1 chance in 20 – or less – that the increase resulted from chance. H. Young, Statistical Treatment of Experimental Data 131-32 (pap. ed. 1962). In scientific practice, levels of significance of 0.01 or 0.001 are used providing an even more stringent test of a chosen hypothetical relationship. R. Burlington & D. May, Handbook of Probability and Statistics with Tables 228 (2d ed. 1970). Where p=0.01 or 0.001, the probability that the observed correlation resulted from random chance is 1 in 100, or 1 in 1,000, respectively. Whether a statistical increase or relationship is "significant" depends first upon what arbitrary level of significance a researcher has selected in analyzing the data. A researcher selecting an arbitrary level of p=0.05 has determined that where the probability is 1 in 20 that something resulted from random chance (and conversely, that the probability is 19 out of 20 that it did *not* result from chance), the relationship will be deemed "significant"; where, for instance, the probability is 1 in 19 that events happened by chance (p=0.0526), the relationship will be deemed statistically "insignificant" – even though the probability is 94.73 percent or 18 chances out of 19 that the observed relationship is not a random event. Though deemed "insignificant" by the researcher, the certainty that the observed increase is related to its hypothetical cause rather than mere chance is still far more likely than not. Perhaps an accurate method of reporting would be to indicate at what level of certainty the statistical relationship is "significant." See J. Gofman, Radiation and Human Health 811-12 (1981), PX-1046. This would permit more immediate evaluation of the degree of certainty or randomness that is involved. The cold statement that a given relationship is not "statistically significant" cannot be read to mean "there is no probability of a relationship." Whether a correlation between a cause and a group of effects is more likely than not – particularly in a legal sense – is a different question from that answered by tests of statistical significance, which often distinguish narrow differences in degree of probability.

[The court criticizes at length the statisticians' requirement of 95 percent probability for significance....] The inherent limitations in the concept of statistical significance are particularly important to the evaluation of statistical studies of relatively small populations, or groups of subjects....

Where the normal incidence of a particular cancer in a specific age group in a large population is 50 cases per 100,000 persons, the probable incidence in a population of 1,000 would be 0.5 cases. It's absurd to talk of one-half a case of cancer. There will likely be one case, or none at all. But what would *two* cases signify? Or three? Random chance operating in a small group, or doubling or tripling of cancer incidence by a suspected carcinogenic agent? The methods of the statistician approach such data with deliberate caution. That data from small populations must be handled with care does not mean that it cannot provide substantial evidence in aid of our effort to describe and understand events. Mathematical or statistical evidence, when properly combined with other varieties of evidence in the same case can "supply a useful link in the process of proof." Tribe, Trial by Mathematics: Precision and Ritual in the Legal Process, 84 Harv. L. Rev. 1329, 1350 (1971). If relied upon as a guide rather than as an answer, the statistical evidence offered in this case provides material assistance in evaluating the factual connection between nuclear fallout and plaintiffs' injuries.

The value of the available statistical data concerning radiation and cancer in off-site communities is not confined by arbitrary tests of "statistical significance." Nor is the court constrained by simplistic models of causal probability impressed upon the judicial "preponderance of the evidence" standard.

It is suggested, for example, that in the following scenario plaintiff's proof would fail to satisfy the standard:

> Before the defendant's arrival, the region experienced a stable ("background") rate of 100 cases of the injury per year. After the defendant's arrival, the number of cases increases to 190 and remains constant. Expert testimony establishes that the increased incidence of the injury can only be attributed to the conduct of the defendant.... Delgado, Beyond *Sindell*... 70 Calif. L. Rev. 881, 885 (1982).

In such a case, it is argued, "no victim can make it appear more probable than not that his or her injury stemmed from defendant's conduct." Id. at 887. "[S]uch evidence says little about the cause of the plaintiff's particular injury: Unless that statistical increase is greater than 100 percent, his injury probably was *not* caused by the exposure, and he will recover nothing." Note, Inapplicability of Traditional Tort Analysis, *supra*, 35 Stan. L. Rev. at 584.

First, such argument assumes the absence of other factual connections tying the increased risk to plaintiff's particular injury. Yet even standing alone, the statistical evidence in the hypothetical cases plainly establishes the defendant's probable contribution of approximately 90 additional injuries to the community – a substantial factual connection. Whether causal inferences should be drawn which will carry the case to the additional issues of risks, scope of duty and culpable breach of duty, e.g., negligence, is a question of judgment resting in part upon policy. The court must determine those risks for which the defendant should be held responsible. Malone, Ruminations on Cause-in-Fact, 9 Stan. L. Rev. 60 (1956). Whether the defendant is ultimately held responsible for an injury which may likely have occurred anyway is inherently a question of policy, not of factual connection or causation. The mechanical application of a "greater-than-100 percent-increase" test in this context represents merely the refabrication of the "but-for" test of causation in mathematical form: but – for defendant's 50 plus percent share of the statistically identified injuries, plaintiff would probably not have been hurt.

In cases where, as here, defendant's duty extends to protection of plaintiff from even the *possibility* of harm, or where, as here, defendant's wrongful conduct arguably has denied to plaintiff a potential *opportunity* to avoid serious or lethal injury, analysis using "but-for" tests in any form falls far short of the mark.

Two centuries of experience in tort law teach us that "[a] victim's hurt as the result, at least in part, of a defendant's conduct may be highly improbable and yet admittedly true, while on the other hand it may be highly probable and yet the result of other cause factors." Green, 60 Mich. L. Rev. at 557. Like statistical significance, mathematical probability aids in resolving the complex questions of causation raised by this lawsuit, but is not itself the answer to those questions....

[Liability was found against the government. The judgment was reversed on appeal on sovereign immunity grounds, 816 F.2d 1417 (10th Cir. 1987).]

COMMENTARY AND QUESTIONS

1. Innovative civil procedure. *Allen* was not litigated as a class action despite having more than 1,100 plaintiffs. Instead it was treated as a consolidation of separate actions from which "typical" or "flagship" plaintiffs were selected for trial with a conscious intent to avoid duplication of effort by the use of res judicata doctrines, in particular permitting plaintiffs to make offensive use of collateral estoppel without mutuality of estoppel. See Parklane Hosiery v. Shore, 439 U.S. 322 (1979). The trial was a major undertaking involving the testimony of 98 witnesses, the receipt of 1,692 documentary exhibits (over 54,000 pages) producing a 7,000-page transcript.

2. Causation connection. Is the "factual connection" in a toxic tort case on a par with *Summer's* simultaneous firing of shotgun pellets by the two hunters, resulting in plaintiff's immediate injury? Are you persuaded by Professor Thode's assertion that the showing of factual connections between defendant's conduct and plaintiff's injury raises legal questions about the scope of liability (usually thought of as proximate cause) rather than legal questions about factual causation? Is the use of "substantial factor" analysis too generous to plaintiffs?

3. Causation: law vs. science. Lack of knowledge of the etiology of toxic exposure-induced diseases precludes proof of the precise role of defendant's conduct in causing plaintiff's loss. As a result, most proof about that relationship is group proof, based on plaintiff's status as part of a group whose post-exposure health is other than what was expected in the absence of the exposure. For that reason, toxic tort cases rely heavily on mathematical and statistical evidence. Judge Jenkins' opinion does a good job of explaining concepts such as statistical significance and demonstrating that levels of significance usually required in scientific research greatly exceed the demands of the legal system. Likewise, in omitted segments of the opinion, he explains the concepts of dose-response relationships and dosimetry (588 F. Supp at 419–28).

4. Causation: statistical tests. Is the *Allen* opinion equally persuasive when it turns to exploring the probativeness of mathematical and statistical evidence? Consider here the argument that defendant ought not be liable unless it is more likely than not that defendant caused plaintiff's injury – a test that will be failed if there is less than a 100 percent increase in incidence of the disease in the relevant population. Is the judge correct that this is another incarnation of the ritualistic insistence on but-for causation, rather than accepting the substantial factor analysis that has become prevalent in ordinary tort settings and toxic tort settings alike? In thinking about this question, it may be helpful to focus on the cases in which Delgado and Judge Jenkins would grant summary judgment or a directed verdict to either plaintiff or defendant.

5. Sovereign immunity in *Allen*. The *Allen* case was ultimately reversed on appeal on sovereign immunity grounds, but its holdings on causation have been widely quoted despite the reversal. How did the plaintiffs think they would avoid sovereign immunity in *Allen*? It is fairly clear that if the radiation exposure had been caused by a private corporation, as in the Karen Silkwood plutonium case, Silkwood v. Kerr-McGee, 464 U.S. 238 (1984), see Chapter 6, there would typically be no such bar. What if private tortfeasors are government contractors? See Boyle v. United Technologies, 792 F.2d 413, 414 (1986)(extending immunity to some government contractors).

Chevron Chemical Company v. Ferebee

United States Court of Appeals for the District of Columbia, 1984

736 F.2d 1529

[Richard Ferebee was a worker at the federal government's Beltsville Agricultural Research Center. He was exposed to the insecticide Paraquat, made by Chevron, on a number of occasions over a three year period, and once even collapsed after having walked behind a tractor spraying the pesticide. Ferebee developed severe lung fibrosis. In a wrongful death action brought by his family after his death, the jury awarded extensive damages against the pesticide manufacturer.]

MIKVA, C.J. This is an appeal by Chevron Chemical Company from a judgment rendered against it after a jury trial in a suit brought by the minor children and the estate of Richard Ferebee....

Even before 1977, Mr. Ferebee was not a picture of perfect health. He was overweight, suffered from high blood pressure, and had a life-long sinus problem. Nonetheless, in late 1977, according to Mr. Ferebee's testimony, he began to notice a marked change in his physical condition, most notably increasing shortness of breath. Over the next several years, Mr. Ferebee's condition progressively deteriorated. In November of 1979 he checked into Capitol Hill Hospital, where Dr. Muhammad Yusuf, a pulmonary specialist, diagnosed Ferebee's disease as pulmonary fibrosis. Dr. Yusuf referred Mr. Ferebee to the National Institutes of Health, where he was treated during 1981 and 1982 by Dr. Ronald G. Crystal, Chief of the Pulmonary Branch of the Heart, Lung, and Blood Institute. After several consultations and tests, both Drs. Yusuf and Crystal concluded that Ferebee's pulmonary fibrosis was caused by paraquat poisoning. Mr. Ferebee's lung condition continued to degenerate, and on March 18, 1982, he died.

In the legal action prosecuted by Ferebee's estate and minor children, appellees presented both of Mr. Ferebee's treating physicians as expert witnesses. Both Dr. Yusuf and Dr. Crystal testified that, in their opinion, paraquat had caused Mr. Ferebee's pulmonary fibrosis. To support this view, they relied not only upon their own observation of Mr. Ferebee and the medical tests performed on him, but also upon medical studies which, they asserted, suggested that dermal absorption of paraquat can lead to chronic lung abnormalities of the sort characterized as pulmonary fibrosis. Appellees then argued to the jury that Chevron had not adequately labelled paraquat to warn against the possibility that chronic skin exposure could lead to lung disease and death and that this failure was a proximate cause of Mr. Ferebee's illness and death.

Under [Maryland] law as interpreted by the trial judge, appellees had the burden of proving, by a preponderance of the evidence, the following elements:

(1) That paraquat proximately caused Mr. Ferebee's illness and death;
(2) That paraquat is inherently dangerous;
(3) That Chevron knew, or should have known, at the time it sold the paraquat used by Mr. Ferebee, that the chemical was inherently dangerous;
(4) That the resulting duty to provide an adequate warning of the danger was not met; and
(5) That the inadequacy of the warning proximately caused Mr. Ferebee's illness and death.

Chevron does not dispute that this is a correct statement of the elements necessary to recover under Maryland strict liability principles in a failure-to-warn suit. Nonetheless, Chevron seeks to overturn the jury's verdict on the theory that, with the exception of the second element, the jury could not reasonably have inferred from the conflicting testimony the existence of any of these elements. A review of the conflicting testimony with respect to each of these elements makes it clear that Chevron cannot sustain the heavy burden it must carry to overturn a jury's verdict. We also reject Chevron's legal claim that other federal law preempts this tort action.

An appellate court's function in reviewing the denial of a judgment notwithstanding the verdict is very limited.... The appellate court does not assess witness credibility nor weigh the evidence, but rather seeks to verify only that fair-minded jurors could reach the verdict rendered.... Judges, both trial and appellate, have no special competence to resolve the complex and refractory causal issues raised by the attempt to link low-level [long-term] exposure to toxic chemicals with human disease. On questions such as these, which stand at the frontier of current medical and epidemiological inquiry, if experts are willing to testify that such a link exists, it is for the jury to decide whether to credit the testimony....

CAUSATION

Chevron first argues that the jury was obligated to reject appellee's theory that long-term exposure to paraquat caused Ferebee's illness and death. Chevron acknowledges that paraquat is known to be toxic, but argues that it is only acutely toxic – that is, that any injuries resulting from exposure to paraquat occur within a very short time of exposure, such as days or weeks, and that when exposure ceases, so too does the injury. In this case, Ferebee did not experience any of the symptoms of pulmonary fibrosis until late 1978, at which point it had been ten months since he last sprayed paraquat, and his chronic inflammatory lung disease continued to worsen long after his final use of paraquat in August of 1979. Plaintiffs' theory of recovery was thus that paraquat, when absorbed through the skin, can attack the lungs in such a way as to cause chronic and self-perpetuating inflammation. Chevron argues that there has never been any evidence nor any suggestion that paraquat can cause chronic injury of this sort and that, in any event, Ferebee could not have been exposed to enough paraquat to injure him in this fashion.

The short answer to Chevron's argument is that two expert witnesses refuted it and that the jury was entitled to believe those experts. Both Drs. Crystal and Yusuf, who are eminent specialists in pulmonary medicine and who were Ferebee's treating physicians, testified that paraquat poisoning was the cause of Ferebee's illness and death. Both admitted that cases like Ferebee's were rare, but Dr. Crystal identified three other cases he felt were similar to that of Mr. Ferebee. Chevron argues that these cases can be distinguished from Mr. Ferebee's, but it is not our role to decide the merits of Chevron's attempted distinctions; Dr. Crystal thought the cases were similar, and the jury was entitled to believe him. Chevron of course introduced its own experts who were of the view that Ferebee's illness was not caused by paraquat, but the testimony of those witnesses, who did not treat Mr. Ferebee or examine him, can hardly be deemed so substantial that the jury had no choice but to accept it. The experts on both sides relied on essentially the same diagnostic methodology; they differed solely on the conclusions they drew from the test results and other information. The case was thus a classic battle of the experts, a battle in which the jury must decide the victor....

Finally, Chevron argues that its expert, Dr. Fisher, proved that it was physically impossible for Ferebee to have been exposed to enough paraquat to cause him any injury. Dr. Fisher's testimony, however, went only to the amount of paraquat necessary to cause the short-term illnesses that have long been recognized to follow from paraquat exposure. Accepting Dr. Fisher's testimony as true, as plaintiffs did not at trial, it still would not necessarily follow that the same amount is needed to trigger a chronic disease like that which Ferebee allegedly contacted. The jury could therefore have concluded that Ferebee had been exposed to sufficient amounts of paraquat to cause the chronic disease from which he suffered – even if that exposure was not substantial enough to produce acute symptoms. The dose-response relationship at low levels of exposure for admittedly toxic chemicals like paraquat is one of the most sharply contested questions currently being debated in the medical community, see generally Leape, Quantitative Risk Assessment in Regulation of Environmental Carcinogens, 4 Harv. Envtl. L. Rev. 86, 100-103 (1980); surely it would be rash for a court to declare as a matter of law that, below a certain threshold level of exposure, dermal absorption of paraquat has no detrimental effect. We therefore conclude that there was sufficient evidence of causation to justify submission of that issue to the jury...and allow the jury's verdict to stand.

COMMENTARY AND QUESTIONS

1. Causation: the jury as medical factfinders. Chevron attacked causation in two ways, challenging the course of Ferebee's illness as inconsistent with lung illness caused by paraquat and claiming that the dose/response pattern consistent with Ferebee's illness required far higher levels of exposure than Ferebee encountered. The jury, at least implicitly, rejected those attacks. Is it appropriate that juries, skilled in neither law nor science, be given so vital a role in determining such a technical issue? What other possibilities exist?

2. Duty to warn. A basic theory of the *Ferebee* case here was a failure to warn adequately of the dangers of paraquat. Warnings were on the package, but they did not refer to dermal absorption and lung disease. The warnings, which included the language "CAN KILL IF SWALLOWED, HARMFUL TO THE EYES AND SKIN" certainly indicated that paraquat isn't an appropriate skin lotion, but the warning did not specifically mention adverse consequences of dermal contact other than skin irritation. This failure in the warning to disclose consequences of exposure known to Chevron was deemed sufficient to support the jury finding. Does a failure-to-warn theory lessen the burdens of proving causation?

3. Other causes? Mr. Ferebee worked at the Agricultural Research Center for more than 13 years, during which time he was exposed to a number of different insecticides, pesticides, and herbicides. Why was this case litigated only against Chevron? It may well be that substantial exposure to paraquat could be proven, and only paraquat had any scientific linkage to lung fibrosis. How would you feel about the case if you knew that Mr. Ferebee had been a three-pack-a-day chain smoker?

4. The limits of *Allen* and *Ferebee*. *Allen* and *Ferebee* do not by any means represent established majority holdings in the field of causation, although the "substantial factor" analysis has been increasingly adopted by state tort law, and juries are increasingly permitted to operate at the forefront of science.

5. The importance of expert testimony. Cases such as *Allen* and *Ferebee* pose the distinction between legal and scientific proof. The dilemma confronting courts arises bccausc cascs involving claims of toxic exposure-caused injury must frequently be decided before the scientific community has accumulated sufficient data to establish scientific causation. If courts adopt a scientific standard of causation, then plaintiffs will invariably lose where the cases involve matters "at the frontier of current medical and epidemiological inquiry." If, on the other hand, courts impose no limits on plaintiffs' ability to place a particular theory of causation before the trier of fact (almost always a lay jury in toxic tort cases), then quackery, coincidence, or the sympathy of jurors with injured parties could lead to findings of causation where the preponderance of credible evidence fvors the defendant.

Courts have responded to this dilemma by developing rules governing the admissibility of evidence. In matters of a scientific or technical nature, for example, virtually all courts require that testimony be given only by experts having appropriate qualifications. Although this requirement provides a safeguard of sorts, plaintiffs' and defendants' bars both have developed cadres of qualified expert witnesses skilled in presenting their respective opposing views on toxic injury causation. A growing number of courts are demanding more than mere expertise, and are increasingly sophisticated about the difference between legal and scientific proof.

6. Rubanick v. Witco Chemical: a methodologically-based admissibility test. In Rubanick v. Witco Chemical Corp., 593 A.2d 733 (N.J. 1991), the survivors of two men who had worked at a chemical plant where they had been exposed to polychlorinated biphenyls (PCBs), a toxic substance, claimed that their decedents' fatal colon cancer was caused by that exposure. Plaintiff Rubanick's sole witness, Dr. Earl Balis, was a biochemist who, although he had never examined Rubanick, was unquestionably one of the world's leading colon cancer researchers. This was the first time that Dr. Balis had testified as an expert witness. (He told the court that he hoped it would be his last.) Dr. Balis testified that exposure to PCBs caused plaintiff Rubanick's colon cancer based on the following factors: (1) the extremely low incidence of cancer in males under 30 (Rubanick was 29 years old when he died); (2) Rubanick's personal history, e.g., his diet, the fact that he was a nonsmoker, and that he did not come from a "cancer family" (whose members are at high risk of cancer due to genetic predisposition to the disease); (3) the fact that five out of 105 employees at Witco had developed some kind of cancer during the relevant period; (4) Rubanick's frequent exposure to large quantities of PCBs; (5) "a very large body of evidence" showing that PCBs cause cancer in experimental animals; and (6) 13 articles on the effects of exposure to PCBs in animals and human beings that, according to Dr. Balis, supported his opinion that PCBs are human carcinogens. The trial court asked Balis whether his theory that PCBs cause cancer in human beings finds support in the scientific community. Answering that most of the scientific community "pays [no] attention to PCBs whatsoever," Balis noted that 13 of the 39 papers he had reviewed on the subject supported his opinion.

Applying the conventional rule , the trial court excluded Dr. Balis' testimony from jury consideration because his conclusions weren't "accepted by at least a substantial minority of the applicable scientific community." 542 A.2d 975 (N.J.Super. 1988). The court of appeals reversed, holding that toxic tort cases – where scientific certainty is impossible and most theories of causation were still novel and controversial – required a different standard. 576 A.2d 4 (1990).

Upholding the admissibility of Dr. Balis' testimony, the state Supreme Court considered whether, in order to be admissible, the conclusions of an expert witness's testimony must have received general acceptance within the scientific community. 593 A.2d 733 (N.J. 1991):

> The scientific method...fails to address or accomodate the needs and goals of the tort system.... "The differences between the judicial and scientific-technological processes are profound and pervasive. Failure to recognize that difference has led to judicial expressions of frustration and an unfortunate tendency to rest judicial decisions on current, and often transient, 'truths' and 'facts' of science and technology. The purpose and function of science is to learn physical facts.... The purpose and function of law is to resolve disputes and to facilitate a structure for the organization of a just society – in a word, to provide justice."[8]
>
> Several courts have taken a more flexible approach to the admission of causation theories in toxic-tort litigation. Those courts have looked not to

8. Quoting an article by Judge Markey: Needed: A Judicial Welcome for Technology – Star Wars or Stare Decisis?, 79 F.R.D. 209, 210 (1979).

> whether the theories have been generally accepted by the scientific community, but rather to whether the scientific knowledge is sufficiently founded or based on a sound methodology, leaving the decision to credit the theory to the finder of fact. [The court discusses *Ferebee* as an example of this trend.]
>
> Accordingly, we hold that in toxic-tort litigation, a scientific theory of causation that has not yet reached general acceptance [by at least a substantial minority of scientists] may be found to be sufficiently reliable if it is based on a sound, adequately-founded scientific methodology involving data and information of the type reasonably relied on by experts in the scientific field. The evidence of such scientific knowledge must be proferred by an expert who is sufficiently qualified by education, knowledge, training, and experience in the specific field of science. The expert must possess a demonstrated professional capability to assess the scientific significance of the underlying data and information, to apply the scientific methodology, and to explain the bases for the opinion reached.
>
> We appreciate that the process for determining the admissibility of such scientific evidence will be complicated and the ultimate decision difficult. In determining if the scientific methodology is sound and well-founded, courts should consider whether others in the field use similar methodologies.... It is not essential that there be general agreement with the opinions drawn from the methodology used. There must merely be some expert consensus that the methodology and underlying data are generally followed by experts in the field....
>
> We do not believe that in determining the soundness of the methodology the trial court should directly and independently determine as a matter of law that a controversial and complex scientific methodology is sound. The critical determination is whether comparable experts accept the soundness of the methodology, including the reasonableness of relying on this type of underlying data and information.... Thus, the inquiry is not the reliability of the expert's ultimate opinion.... The proper inquiry is whether comparable experts in the field would actually rely on that information....[9]

Does such a methodology-based standard raise other problems? Will hearings on admissibility, for example, degenerate into an infinite regression of experts testifying to the soundness of other experts' evaluations of methodologies? Will the "battle of the experts" be replaced by the "battle of the credentials"?

---

9. 593 A.2d at 741–749. As to expert witnesses' credentials, the court said:

> The qualifications of the expert proferring relatively new scientific knowledge must be factored into the determination of the soundness of the methodology used....
>
> The necessary inquiry into the expert's qualifications implicates an additional concern relating to "the hired gun phenomenon".... The answer to the problem...should consist of greater judicial vigilance in scrutinizing the status of the expert and in directing the factfinder to those factors that bear relevantly on the expert's credibility.... 593 A.2d at 749–750.

Section 2. THE LOGISTICS OF LITIGATING TOXIC CONTAMINATION

THE WOBURN, MASSACHUSETTS, CONTAMINATED WELLWATER CASE

The following account of Anderson et al. v. W.R. Grace Co. and Beatrice Foods, the Woburn toxics case,[10] written by the plaintiffs' attorney, is intended to convey a sense of the tasks facing plaintiffs trying to prove causation:

Jan Schlichtmann, Eight Families Sue W.R. Grace and Beatrice Foods for Poisoning City Wells with Solvents, Causing Leukemia, Disease, and Death

(1988)

The Woburn case began with a mother's horror that her child had leukemia. Anne Anderson had moved to Woburn, Massachusetts, a small city 13 miles north of Boston, with her husband and daughter in 1965. Over the next few years she gave birth to two more children. Although all of the children seemed to have more than their fair share of colds, sore throats, and infections, James, the youngest, seemed to get sick more than the others and recovered slower. In the winter of 1971, when Jimmy did not get over the latest round of flu, the family doctor referred Ms. Anderson to a specialist at Massachusetts General Hospital in Boston. The specialist told Anne that Jimmy had cancer in his bone marrow. Treatment would be long and painful.

Anne Anderson's distress soon gave way to the realization that she was not the only mother in Woburn with a child suffering from leukemia. There were other Woburn mothers who sat quietly in the waiting room at Massachusetts General while their children received chemotherapy – women and children from her neighborhood, whose homes were a block or two from her own.... In May, 1979, two of the city wells were found to be contaminated with toxic industrial solvents, including trichloroethylene (TCE) and tetrachloroethylene, suspected carcinogens.... The Center for Disease Control (CDC) and the Massachusetts Department of Public Health confirmed that the children in Woburn were coming down with leukemia at a rate significantly higher than would be expected. Within a six block radius of the Anderson home there were seven other children with leukemia. Many other cases were also documented throughout the East Woburn community. But the health agencies couldn't say if the contaminated well water had anything to do with the leukemia in the neighborhood. The EPA and the state environmental agency confirmed that the aquifer feeding the two contaminated city wells was heavily polluted with industrial solvents but could not say from whose property the contamination was coming or when the wells had become contaminated.

With the help of a local minister, Ms. Anderson organized members of the community into a vocal and active citizens' environmental group, For A Cleaner

---

10. Anderson v. W.R. Grace, U.S.D.C. Mass. C.A. No. 82-1672-S (May, 1982); Anderson v. W.R. Grace, 628 F. Supp. 1219 (D.C. Mass. 1986) (Summary judgment rulings); Anderson v. Cryovac, Inc., 805 F.2d 1 (1st Cir. 1986) (Gag order reversed); Anderson v. Beatrice Foods Co., 127 F.R.D. 1 (D. Mass. 1989); Anderson v. Beatrice Foods Co., 862 F.2d 910 (1st Cir. 1988); cert. denied, Anderson v. Beatrice Foods Co., 900 F.2d 388 (1st Cir. 1990). The narrative that follows is a heavily edited version of a paper based on The Woburn Case: Stricken Families Take On a Chemical Giant and Win, ATLA Rep. (Sept. 1987). The case is the subject of a book, P. Brown and E. Mikkelson, No Safe Place (1990). (Full disclosure notice: one of this casebook's authors worked with plaintiffs on the case.)

Environment (FACE), to monitor and prod the governmental agencies. Jimmy's death in January, 1981, strengthened her resolve. She and seven other families hired a tort lawyer.

A review of the work done by the governmental agencies up through 1981 made it clear that evidence for the case would in large measure have to be obtained by the plaintiffs themselves. In March, 1982, the EPA issued its report regarding the contamination of the aquifer. It drew no conclusions concerning the sources of the well contamination. The CDC and State Department of Health were still unsure of the next step to take.

The EPA field data available as of March, 1982, was reviewed by Robert Harris, a professor of chemical engineering, who concluded that the likely sources of the well contamination were the properties of the W.R. Grace Company, twenty-four hundred feet northeast, and a tannery owned by Beatrice Foods, six hundred feet west of the contaminated wells. In May, 1982, suit was filed against Grace and Beatrice on behalf of the eight families. In seven of the families a child had contracted leukemia. Five of those children had died from the disease. In one family an adult suffered from the disease.

The filing of suit received intense public and media attention. The defendants, especially Grace, responded by publicly denouncing the suit as baseless. They denied that their plant in Woburn used the chemicals, or that it could have contributed to the contamination.

In response to the plaintiffs' interrogatories as to chemical use and disposal, Grace moved to dismiss.... Grace contended that plaintiffs' attorneys had no good faith basis to assert that Grace used the chemicals found in the wells, that it disposed of them so as to contaminate the aquifer, or that the chemicals could cause leukemia. The proceedings over Grace's unsuccessful Rule 11[11] motion to dismiss consumed the entire first year of litigation.

Thereafter, in February, 1983, Grace was forced to answer plaintiffs' interrogatories. In its answers, Grace admitted that it had used the same type of chemicals found in the wells, and had disposed of "small quantities" of the chemicals on the ground to the rear of the plant building, as well as burying several drums in a pit. The grudging revelations by Grace of its chemical use and disposal practices sharply contrasted with information Grace had previously provided the EPA during that agency's investigation the year before. The EPA subsequently ordered Grace, Beatrice, and another company, Unifirst, to conduct on-site investigations of their properties to determine if their properties were contributing to the pollution of the aquifer. EPA lethargy over the next two years, however, prompted plaintiffs to conduct their own on-site investigations.

In January, 1984, a year after Grace was ordered to investigate its property and after its consultant's report documented contamination at the site, Grace moved for summary judgment on the basis that plaintiffs could not prove that the contaminated water caused the children's leukemia. In support of its motion, Grace submitted the affidavits of two hematologists, Drs. Maloney and Jandl, who asserted that there was no scientific basis for an opinion that the chemicals found in the contaminated wells could cause leukemia.

---

11. Since its original promulgation, FRCP Rule 11 has provided for the striking of pleadings and the imposition of disciplinary sanctions on the attorney, the client, or both to check abuses in pleadings and litigation.

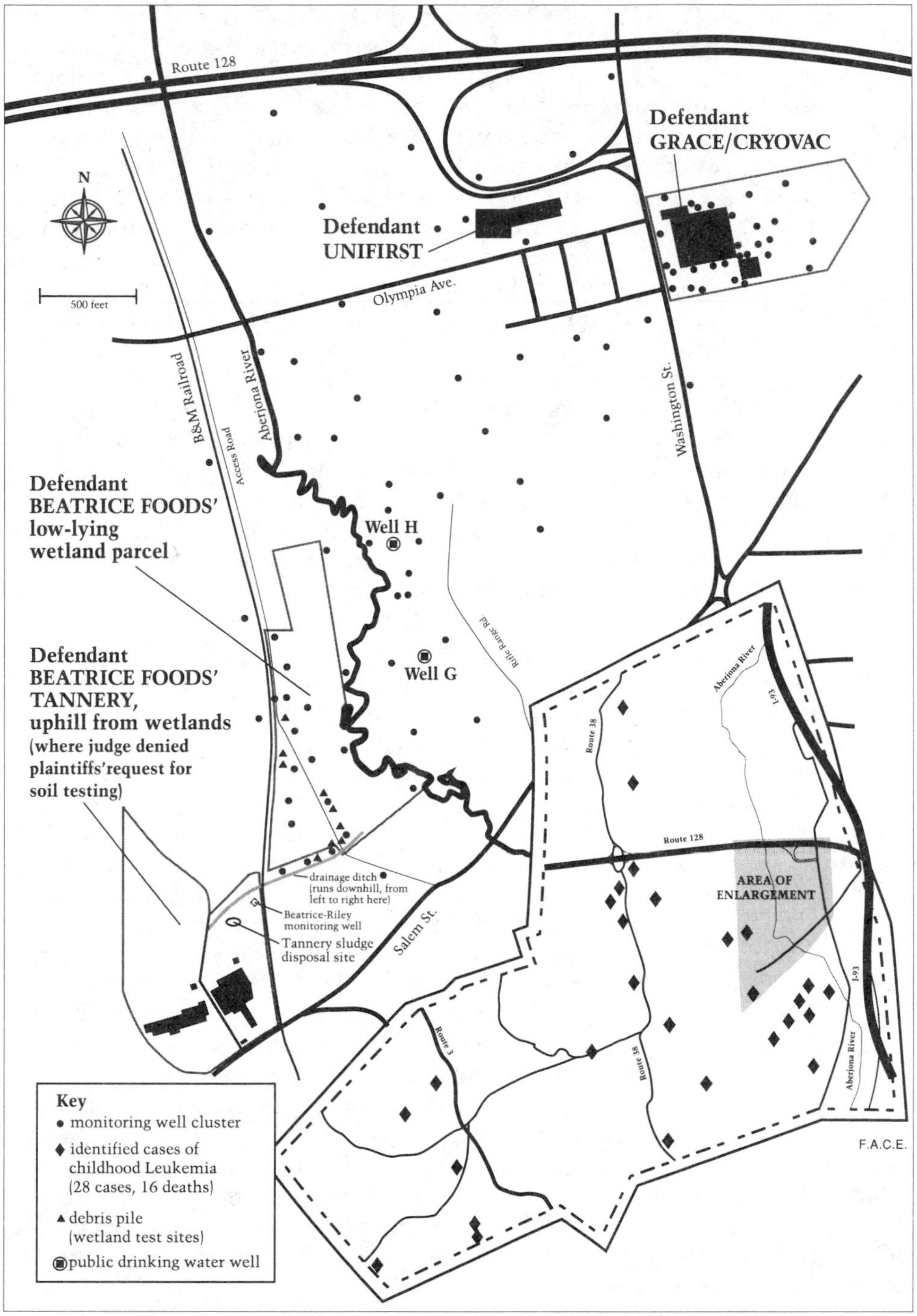

LARGE MAP: *adapted from exhibit at trial, Anderson, et al. v. W.R. Grace Co., Beatrice Foods, Unifirst Co., et al., showing location of Public Wells G and H, the three main defendants, the Beatrice wetland parcel that was a major source of contamination, and the Aberjona River, a creek wending through the middle of the area.* ***INSET OVERVIEW MAP:*** *shows the area served by wells G and H, and the 28 identified childhood leukemia cases (16 fatal) that occurred there between the time the wells opened and the time of the trial.*

In the fall of 1983, plaintiffs had retained Dr. Allen S. Levin, an immunopathologist, who had a great deal of clinical experience treating people exposed to toxic substances. Dr. Levin was very knowledgeable regarding the effects of toxic exposure on the body's immune system. The plaintiffs' medical records, which had been systematically collected, were reviewed by Dr. Levin. In addition, he ordered blood tests of the surviving family members which were conducted at the Massachusetts General Hospital immuno-pathology lab. The review of the families' medical records revealed a pattern of infection, skin disorders, gastrointestinal problems, genito-urinary problems, and cardiac problems as well as cancer. The blood tests which looked at the absolute numbers and ratios of "T-cells," which are the specialized cells of the immune system, demonstrated striking abnormalities in many of the family members. Also, Harvard scientists examining health survey data from Woburn had concluded that there was an association between certain childhood disorders including leukemia and availability of water from the contaminated wells. This marked the first time that such an association had been shown.

In his affidavit opposing summary judgment, Dr. Levin outlined the scientific methodology he followed in concluding that exposure to the contaminated water caused leukemia in the families. In so doing, he illustrated how a clinician makes use of epidemiological data, like the Harvard health study, not to prove causation in an individual case, but in conjunction with clinical data, history, examination and tests, to assist in forming opinions as to the likely etiology of a patient's disease.

Levin began by discussing the scientific knowledge regarding the capacity of the solvents found in the water to harm the building blocks of the body's cells, DNA and its constituents, making them potentially cancerous. He outlined how solvent exposure can damage the immune system, the role of which is to remove these cancerous elements. By both creating opportunities for cancer and weakening the body's ability to remove it, he explained how solvent exposure can increase a host's susceptibility to cancer. Further, Dr. Levin pointed to scientific studies of animals and human populations showing a statistical relation between solvent exposure and cancer. After establishing the toxic nature of the chemicals, and the mechanism of harm, Dr. Levin turned his attention to the Woburn population exposed to the solvent-contaminated water. The government health studies done in Woburn showed that the community was suffering from an increased incidence of childhood leukemia. The Harvard health study demonstrated that this increased incidence of leukemia and other childhood disorders was associated with exposure to the contaminated water. Their relationship indicated that exposure to the contaminated well water had affected the population's ability to fight disease and cancer. Finally, Dr. Levin discussed the medical histories and test results of individual family members. The histories were consistent with people suffering from chemical exposure, and the blood tests demonstrated that this group of people had been resisting a carcinogen on a chronic basis. For these reasons he concluded that in all probability the exposure to the solvents in the water "substantially contributed" to the family members succumbing to leukemia.

Plaintiffs argued that to overcome Grace's motion for summary judgment it was their burden merely to show that there was factual dispute on the issue of causation. The court's role was not to determine which expert's opinion was more persuasive, but rather whether reasonable experts could disagree about whether the exposure to the contaminated water caused the plaintiffs' leukemias. If the court was satisfied that the expert's conclusion regarding the etiology of plaintiffs' disease was based on sound scientific methodology and principles, then the expert's conclusion, even if considered controversial, was sufficient to sustain plaintiffs' burden. The court in a brief opinion determined that the issue of medical causation as to leukemia was "hotly contested" and denied the defendant's motion for summary judgment in an unpublished opinion, July, 1984.

Over the next year and a half plaintiffs' medical condition was extensively examined. In an effort to establish a basis for proving a connection between exposure to the water and leukemia, the impact of toxic exposure on the health of the surviving plaintiffs was brought into sharper focus. The theory of cancer causation based on the toxic effects of the solvents on the body's immune system led to the examination of other organ systems which were known to be affected by solvents, namely the nerves and heart. Complete health histories, examinations, and tests were performed by experts in immunology and internal medicine to establish the overall health and condition of the plaintiffs, and to rule out other causes for their health problems. The plaintiffs were also extensively examined by experts in neurology, neuropsychology, and cardiology. The detailed testing in these specialties provided objective evidence that the surviving plaintiffs had indeed suffered significant damage to these organ systems. In addition, psychiatric examination revealed the interplay between the impact of the exposure on the body and the knowledge of it on the mind.

Because a domestic population had never before been examined and tested so extensively to determine the effects of exposure to solvents contaminating a drinking water supply, the unique findings of the clinicians studying the Woburn population was further supplemented and supported by work of scientists in toxicology, genetics, and epidemiology. The scientific effort included the establishment for the first time of control groups and scientific benchmarks for study of populations exposed to contaminated drinking water....

COMMENTARY AND QUESTIONS

1. Lawyers as epidemiologists. The Woburn case study continues in the next section. In the narrative up to this point, however, note the extensive preparations made by the plaintiffs to try to prove causation. To what extent are plaintiffs preparing to go beyond the judicial tests of *Allen* and *Ferebee* to prove an individualized causative nexus to the plaintiffs whose blood they tested?

As a practical note, the Woburn case produced new scientific research on epidemiology with its T-cell surveys. Who financed those extraordinarily expensive trial preparations? Unifirst, one of the original defendants, settled with the plaintiffs for $1 million. A trial lawyers' group provided a further stipend, and plaintiffs' attorney sought personal loans to finance the case. During the course of the trial, plaintiffs' attorney had his automobile and condo foreclosed upon by the lenders.

2. Negative circumstantial evidence? In several recent cases, plaintiffs' attorneys have tried to avoid the near-impossibility of proving the epidemiological causative linkage between defendant's toxin and plaintiff's particular disease by negative inference. In a recent Colorado suit concerning hydrazine exposure, an epidemiologist testified that after analyzing the range of possible causes, he had concluded that "there is no other more plausible cause of these cases of cancer than [plaintiffs'] exposures to water contaminated with...carcinogens." This opinion was echoed by other experts. The judge, although she specifically stated a willingness to consider circumstantial evidence, ultimately dismissed the action for insufficient proof of actual hydrazine exposure. Renaud v. Martin Marietta Corp., 749 F. Supp 1545 (D.C. Colo. 1990). The logic of attempting to prove causation by a process of eliminating other less likely possible causes remains potentially useful. See Rubanick v. Witco Chem. Co., 593 A.2d 733 (N.J., 1991), noted at page 197 *supra.* (The jury could consider a variety of circumstantial indications of causation of the cancer death of the young, otherwise healthy factory worker).

D. NEW REMEDIES IN TOXICS CASES

Toxic tort cases present special problems in the scope of liability for damages, including unique claims based on increased risk of contracting an exposure-induced disease for example, seeking present compensation for future damages that may or may not come to pass. The cases in this section, Anderson v. W.R. Grace and Ayers v. Jackson Township, also review claims for fear and emotional distress in the toxic tort setting.[12]

These are hotly contested issues. The stakes are high. Toxic exposures often create mass torts; damages are multiplied by the number of victims. The types of damage in dispute are significant items such as increased medical expenses and damages caused by catastrophic diseases. Many of the losses are either uninsured or uninsurable and become major unexpected costs for the defendants. The intensity with which the cases are litigated, coupled with the fact that plaintiffs have been pressing for novel extensions of tort liability, has led to some unusual friction between lawyers representing plaintiffs and those representing defendants. One recent defense-oriented article began with the following introduction:

> The sphere of injuries for which plaintiffs may seek compensation in toxic tort cases is, it seems, bounded only by the ingenuity of counsel and by the human capacity to feel wronged.... To meet these more exotic toxic injury claims, the defense counsel in toxic tort cases must counter ingenious allegations with equally ingenious defenses.[13]

Section 1. COMPENSABLE ITEMS: CANCERPHOBIA, RISK, AND QUALITY OF LIFE

Anderson v. W.R. Grace & Co., Beatrice Foods Co., et al.
United States District Court for the District of Massachusetts, 1986
628 F. Supp. 1219

MEMORANDUM AND ORDER ON DEFENDANTS' JOINT MOTION FOR PARTIAL SUMMARY JUDGMENT

SKINNER, D.J. This case arises out of the defendants' alleged contamination of the

12. Also present in the cases are issues dealing with statutes of limitations and governmental immunity that will receive attention only in the note materials.

13. Pagliaro & Lynch, No Pain, No Gain: Current Trends In Determining Compensable Injury In Toxic Tort Cases, 4 BNA Toxics L. Rep. 271 (1989).

groundwater in certain areas of Woburn, Massachusetts, with chemicals, including trichloroethylene and tetrachloroethylene. Plaintiffs allege that two of Woburn's water wells, Wells G and H, drew upon the contaminated water until the wells were closed in 1979 and that exposure to this contaminated water caused them to suffer severe injuries.

Of the 33 plaintiffs in this action, five are the administrators of minors who died of leukemia allegedly caused by exposure to the chemicals. They bring suit for wrongful death and conscious pain and suffering. Sixteen of the 28 living plaintiffs are members of the decedents' immediate families. These plaintiffs seek to recover for the emotional distress caused by witnessing the decedents' deaths. Three of the living plaintiffs also contracted leukemia and currently are either in remission or treatment for the disease. The 25 non-leukemic plaintiffs allege that exposure to the contaminated water caused a variety of illnesses and damaged their bodily systems. All of the living plaintiffs seek to recover for their illnesses and other damage, increased risk of developing future illness, and emotional distress....

W.R. Grace & Co. and Beatrice Foods Co. (collectively "defendants"), have jointly moved for partial summary judgment on several of plaintiffs' claims. They contend that: ...the emotional distress claims of the plaintiffs who have not contracted leukemia may not stand because the emotional distress was not caused by any physical injury; and the plaintiffs' claims for increased risk of developing serious illness in the future are not recognized under Massachusetts law....

[Claims for physical injuries had already survived a summary judgment motion in 1984.]

CLAIMS FOR EMOTIONAL DISTRESS

Defendants move for summary judgment on plaintiffs' claims of emotional distress on the grounds that the non-leukemic plaintiffs' distress was not caused by any physical injury. They also move for summary judgment on the emotional distress claims of plaintiffs who witnessed a family member die of leukemia, arguing that Massachusetts law does not recognize such a claim....

(1) PHYSICAL INJURY

In seeking summary judgment on the non-leukemic plaintiffs' claims for emotional distress, defendants rely on Payton v. Abbott Labs, 437 N.E.2d 171 (Mass. 1982). In *Payton*, the Supreme Judicial Court answered a certified question as follows:

> [I]n order for...plaintiffs to recover for negligently inflicted emotional distress, [they] must allege and prove [they] suffered physical harm as a result of the conduct which caused the emotional distress. We answer, further, that a plaintiff's physical harm must either cause or be caused by the emotional distress alleged, and that the physical harm must be manifested by objective symptomatology and substantiated by expert medical testimony. (437 N.E.2d at 181.)

Defendants attack plaintiffs' claims of emotional distress at three points: they argue that plaintiffs did not suffer physical harm as a result of defendants' allegedly negligent conduct; that, if the plaintiffs did suffer any harm, it was not "manifested by objective symptomatology"; and that any manifest physical harm did not cause the claimed emotional distress....

Each plaintiff states that exposure to contaminants in the water drawn from Wells G and H "affected my body's ability to fight disease, [and] caused harm to my body's organ systems, including my respiratory, immunological, blood, central nervous, gastro-intestinal, urinary-renal systems...." This alleged harm is sufficient to maintain plaintiffs' claims for emotional distress under *Payton*. As used in that opinion, the term "physical harm" denotes "harm to the bodies of the plaintiffs." 437 N.E.2d at 175 n.4. In requiring physical harm rather than mere "injury" as an element of proof in a claim for emotional distress, the court required that a plaintiff show some actual physical damage as a predicate to suit.

Defendants argue that plaintiffs' alleged harm is "subcellular" and therefore not the type of harm required to support a claim for emotional distress under *Payton*. I disagree. The Supreme Judicial Court requires that plaintiffs' physical harm be "manifested by objective symptomatology and substantiated by expert medical testimony." 437 N.E.2d at 181. In setting forth this requirement, the court did not distinguish between gross and subcellular harm. Instead, the court drew a line between harm which can be proven to exist through expert medical testimony based on objective evidence and harm which is merely speculative or based solely on a plaintiff's unsupported assertions. Upon review of the pleadings and the affidavits of plaintiffs' expert, I cannot say as a matter of law that this standard will not be met at trial.

The alleged damages to plaintiffs' bodily systems is manifested by the many ailments which plaintiffs claim to have suffered as a result of exposure to the contaminated water. Dr. Levin apparently will testify to the existence of changes in plaintiffs' bodies caused by exposure to the contaminated water. He will base his testimony on objective evidence of these changes, including the maladies listed.... Dr. Levin explicitly states that the changes in plaintiffs' systems have "produced illnesses related to these systems." Although the affidavit does not specifically identify the illnesses suffered by each plaintiff as a result of the changes, nor state that plaintiffs suffered more ailments than the average person would have over the same time span, it is sufficient evidence of harm to support the existence of a factual dispute and bar summary judgment.

Under *Payton*, of course, injury is not sufficient. The harm allegedly caused by defendants' conduct must either have caused or been caused by the emotional distress.... However, certain elements of plaintiffs' emotional distress stem from the physical harm to their immune systems allegedly caused by defendants' conduct and [these] are compensable. Plaintiffs have stated that the illnesses contributed to by exposure to the contaminated water have caused them anxiety and pain. The excerpts from plaintiffs' depositions appended to defendants' motion indicate that plaintiffs are also worried over the increased susceptibility to disease which results from the alleged harm to their immune systems and exposure to carcinogens. As these elements of emotional distress arise out of plaintiffs' injuries, plaintiffs may seek to recover for them.

Defendants contend that plaintiffs' physical harm did not "cause" plaintiffs' distress over their increased susceptibility to disease. They argue that the fear arose out of discussions between plaintiffs and their expert witness, Dr. Levin, in which the expert informed plaintiffs of their suppressed immune systems. Assuming, as I must for purposes of the motion, that Dr. Levin is telling the truth, this argument is frivolous.

Plaintiffs can recover "only for that degree of emotional distress which a reasonable person normally would have experienced under [the] circumstances."

437 N.E.2d at 181. The Supreme Judicial Court has explicitly stated that the reasonableness of a claim for emotional distress is to be determined by the trier of fact. Accordingly, defendants' motion for summary judgment on the non-leukemic plaintiffs' claims for emotional distress is DENIED.

(2) WITNESSING DEATH OF A FAMILY MEMBER

The second issue raised by defendants' motions is whether Massachusetts recognizes a claim for emotional distress for witnessing a family member die of a disease allegedly caused by defendants' conduct. This differs from the question considered in the preceding section because the concern now is whether the plaintiffs can recover for distress caused by witnessing the injuries of others, not by their own condition. The plaintiffs do not claim any physical harm resulted from this emotional distress.

The plaintiffs proceed on alternative theories: (1) that they were in the "zone of danger," Restatement 2d of Torts §313(2), and (2) that they themselves were the victims of an "impact" from the same tortious conduct that caused the death of the children.... The Supreme Judicial Court has [held that] damages may be recovered for emotional distress over injury to a child or spouse when the plaintiff suffers contemporaneous physical injury from the same tortious conduct that caused the injury to the close relative. Cimino v. Milford Keg, Inc., 431 N.E.2d 920, 927 (Mass. 1982)....

Plaintiffs would be entitled to go forward on the basis of *Cimino*, if it were not for three further prudential limitations on recovery of a bystander for emotional distress resulting from injuries to another. These are the requirements of physical proximity to the accident, temporal proximity to the negligent act, and familial proximity to the victim. The plaintiffs in this case were present during the illness and death of the children, and at least 16 of them...are immediate family members of the decedents, but they do not meet the [temporal proximity] test....

For emotional distress to be compensable under Massachusetts law...the distress must result from immediate apprehension of the defendant's negligence or its consequences. In each of the cases in which recovery for the emotional distress of a bystander has been allowed, there has been a dramatic traumatic shock causing immediate emotional distress. Such is not the case here. There is no indication in the Massachusetts cases that liability would be extended to a family member's emotional distress which built over time during the prolonged illness of a child.

Imposition of liability in that case, while logically indistinguishable from the trauma situation, would violate the Massachusetts court's demonstrated prudential inclination to keep the scope of liability within manageable bounds....

CLAIMS FOR INCREASED RISK OF FUTURE ILLNESS.

Plaintiffs seek to recover damages for the increased risk of serious illness they claim resulted from consumption of and exposure to contaminated water.... In Massachusetts,

> [a] plaintiff is entitled to compensation for all damages that reasonably are to be expected to follow, but not to those that possibly may follow, the injury which he has suffered. He is not restricted to compensation for suffering and expense which by a fair preponderance of the evidence he has proved will inevitably follow. He is entitled to compensation for suffering and expense which by a fair preponderance of the evidence he has satisfied the jury reasonably are to be expected to follow, so far as human knowledge can foretell. Pullen v. Boston Elevated Ry. Co., 94 N.E. 469, 471 (Mass. 1911).

In addition, when there is a "reasonable probability" that future expenses will be required to remedy the consequences of a defendant's negligence, the jury may consider the expense in awarding damages. Menard v. Collins, 9 N.E.2d 387 (Mass. 1937). Plaintiffs argue that these cases indicate that Massachusetts accepts the general rule of tort law that "[o]ne injured by the tort of another is entitled to recover damages for all harm, past, present and prospective, legally caused by the tort." Restatement 2d of Torts §910. I agree, subject to two caveats. First, as is indicated by *Pullen* and *Menard*, when an injured person seeks to recover for harms that may result in the future, recovery depends on establishing a "reasonable probability" that the harm will occur. See Restatement 2d of Torts §912. Second, recovery for future harm in an action assumes that a cause of action for that harm has accrued at the time recovery is sought. See Restatement 2d of Torts §910....

Defendants argue that the cause of action for any future serious illness, including leukemia and other cancers, has not yet accrued because the injury has not yet occurred.[14] This is the rationale of the discovery rule applied to latent disease cases in Massachusetts under which the injury is equated with the manifestation of the disease. The question thus becomes whether, upon the manifestation of one or more diseases, a cause of action accrues for all prospective diseases so that a plaintiff may seek to recover for physically distinct and separate diseases which may develop in the future.

The answer to this question depends on the connection between the illnesses plaintiffs have suffered and fear they will suffer in the future. Unfortunately, the nature of plaintiffs' claim for increased risk of future illness is unclear on two counts. Nothing in the present record indicates the magnitude of the increased risk, or the diseases which plaintiffs may suffer....

A further reason for denying plaintiffs' damages for the increased risk of future harm in this action is the inevitable inequity which would result if recovery were allowed. To award damages based on a mere mathematical probability would significantly undercompensate those who actually develop cancer and would be a windfall to those who do not. [citations omitted] In addition, if plaintiffs could show that they were more likely than not to suffer cancer or other future illness, full recovery would be allowed for all plaintiffs, even though only some number more than half would actually develop the illness. In such a case, the defendant would overcompensate the injured class.

Accordingly, action on plaintiffs' claims for the increased risk of serious future illness, including cancer, must be delayed....

COMMENTARY AND QUESTIONS

1. Physical harm/emotional distress. What is the relevance of physical harm in a claim for emotional distress? Is it possible that an individual could be greatly distressed without suffering any injury whatever? The usual rationale for a physical harm requirement is the desire to prevent fictitious claims. It may be underinclusive in those genuine cases where a victim suffers emotionally without physical damage, and it may be overinclusive in allowing claims of emotional distress by unprincipled plaintiffs who suffer no distress at all.

14. The weight of authority would deny plaintiffs a cause of action solely for increased risk because no "injury" has occurred.

In *Anderson*, satisfaction of the physical harm requirement by subcellular T-cell effects seems to be a needless formality.[15] Are the physical damage requirement and the required causal link between physical injury and emotional distress intended to substitute for a policy debate about whether the defendant's conduct should, as a matter of law and policy, result in liability for this type of injury? Recall that one of the functions of the proximate cause inquiry is to limit the extent of liability that could be imposed using but-for causation carried to extreme lengths. Pruitt v. Allied Chemical Co., *supra*, page 160, however, shows that proximate cause analyses may also resort to arbitrary rules to guide their application.

Even if you are hostile to attempts to limit emotional distress claims for those personally victimized by contamination, is the argument for prudential limitations stronger in the case of those who suffer by witnessing the suffering of others? These claims are no less real to their victims, nor are they any less credible, in the context of watching an immediate family member die an agonizing and unnecessary death, than are first party claims for infliction of emotional distress. Is it simply too expensive to compensate these non-economic losses and still maintain affordable prices for goods that produce hazardous materials as by-products of their manufacture?

2. Novel civil procedure: "polyfurcation." The holdings on emotional distress in *Anderson* never went to trial, because the judge in February, 1986, split the case into four multiple sequential phases. Under FRCP 42(b), a judge may phase a trial in the interests of efficiency, so basic questions, like liability, are raised and litigated first in a separate trial; then consequential issues, like remedies, are litigated as necessary. The Woburn judge, however, split the liability issue itself three ways. He set Phase 1 to determine whether defendants' contaminants ever reached the public wells, Phase 2 on causation of leukemia, Phase 3 on other injuries to other family members, and Phase 4 on punitive damages. Only the first phase ever went to trial, and it was limited to the question of liability for groundwater flow. Plaintiffs' attorneys generally oppose such multiple phasing because it "cuts the heart out" of the continuity of the story they are trying to present to the jury. The Woburn jury nevertheless came in with a verdict against defendant Grace in Phase 1, and Grace quickly settled for $8 million dollars in damages. Does that outcome reinforce the rationale for phasing, or support the plaintiffs' fear of dilution? See Bedecarré, Polyfurcation of Liability Issues in Environmental Tort Cases, 17 Envtl. Aff. L. Rev. 123 (1989).

3. Special jury questions. The Woburn plaintiffs' case encountered another tactical disadvantage when the judge required the jury in the Phase 1 trial, instead of simply bringing in a simple verdict on whether the defendants' contamination reached the wells or not, to specify the particular time at which each of four chemicals reached the wells. The questions were so complex that even the jury verdict against Grace

---

15. The defendants and the court could entertain no real doubt about the plaintiffs' sufferings. The defendants may think that the plaintiffs are suffering needlessly, i.e., that nothing will come of the exposures, but it is hard to believe that they discredit the claims of fear and anxiety.

was internally inconsistent, and jury members confessed their extreme confusion about the highly technical subquestions they were required to answer. See Pacelle, Contaminated Verdict, The American Lawyer 75 (Dec. 1986); cf. Brodin, Accuracy, Efficiency, and Accountability in the Litigation Process: The Case for the Fact Verdict, 59 U. Cin. L. Rev. 15 (1990). (Confronted with the inconsistencies in the Woburn jury's answers, the judge overturned the verdict and ordered a new trial. Grace's decision, after weighing its options, to settle for $8 million, came the same day despite the overturned verdict.)

4. The "highly extraordinary" defense. Under Restatement 2d Torts §435(1), foreseeability is not a requirement for liability in strict liability cases. Section 435(2), however, provides that liability can be excused where "looking back from the harm to the actor's negligent conduct, it appears to the court highly extraordinary that it should have brought about the harm." This grant of discretion to the trial judge was designed to nullify liability where there are statistically amazing chains of causation, as in the classic *Palsgraf* case, 162 N.E. 99 (N.Y. 1928). In the Woburn case the judge applied §435(2) to excuse the Beatrice tannery from any liability prior to the time it was told by an engineer that the groundwater under its property flowed laterally 800 feet, under a small stream, to the public wells. How does this square with Professor Davis' analysis in footnote 6 in *Branch*, page 140 *supra*, which implies that groundwater pollution is foreseeable, and certainly not extraordinary? The judge also inexplicably did not allow plaintiffs to test for contamination at the tannery site and its disposal lagoons, restricting testing to a downhill wetland parcel. The jury then decided that with the restricted evidence it could not make the required specialized findings for chemical exposure in Beatrices' narrowed window of liability. The leukemia victims' case against Beatrice went up and down through the federal courts over the next two years, on issues of rulings at trial and revelations that, during discovery, defendants' attorneys had concealed several incriminating requested test reports showing contamination at the tannery sites. A final petition for certiorari was denied. 111 S. Ct. 233 (1990). The federal government was more successful than the leukemia plaintiffs. The EPA ultimately negotiated a $69 million dollar settlement of the defendants' civil, criminal, and cleanup liability for the toxic contamination.

5. The logistics of toxic torts cases. Does the account of the Woburn case give some indication of the enormous burdens imposed on plaintiffs trying to use the common law to redress their injuries in complex circumstances? As with all litigation, students must be reminded that a case does not develop and prove itself at trial; each step of the litigation involves guesses and gambles, rationing of time and resources, choices made and viable options foregone. The actions of judges, not to mention attorneys and juries, are not necessarily predictable. Facts and procedural rulings can be slippery. Because of the burdens and complexities of the process, opportunities for appeal may offer no effective redress for mistakes. What ultimately emerges is a potpourri of happenstance that may or may not accord with one's sense of justice.

Ayers v. Township of Jackson

Supreme Court of New Jersey, 1987
106 N.J. 557, 525 A.2d 287

STEIN, J. The litigation involves claims for damages sustained because plaintiffs' well water was contaminated by toxic pollutants leaching into the Cohansey Aquifer from a landfill established and operated by Jackson Township. After an extensive trial, the jury found that the township had created a "nuisance" and a "dangerous condition" by virtue of its operation of the landfill, that its conduct was "palpably unreasonable" – a prerequisite to recovery under N.J.S.A. 59:4-2 [The sovereign immunity tort claims waiver] – and that it was the proximate cause of the contamination of plaintiffs' water supply. The jury verdict resulted in an aggregate judgment of $15,854,392.78, to be divided among the plaintiffs in varying amounts. The jury returned individual awards for each of the plaintiffs that varied in accordance with such factors as proximity to the landfill, duration and extent of the exposure to contaminants, and the age of the claimant.

The verdict provided compensation for three distinct claims of injury: $2,056,480 was awarded for emotional distress caused by the knowledge that they had ingested water contaminated by toxic chemicals for up to six years; $5,396,940 was awarded for the deterioration of their quality of life during the twenty months when they were deprived of running water; and $8,204,500 was awarded to cover the future cost of annual medical surveillance that plaintiffs' expert testified would be necessary because of plaintiffs' increased susceptibility to cancer and other diseases. The balance of the verdict, approximately $96,500, represented miscellaneous expenses not involved in this appeal....

The evidence at trial provided ample support for the jury's conclusion that the township had operated the Legler landfill in a palpably unreasonable manner, a finding that the township did not contest before the Appellate Division....

At trial plaintiffs offered expert testimony to prove that the chemical contamination of their wells was caused by the township's improper operation of the landfill. The testimony established that, in varying concentrations, the following chemical substances had infiltrated various wells used by plaintiffs as a water source: acetone; benzene; chlorobenzene; chloroform; dichlorofluoromethane; ethylbenzene; methylene chloride; methyl isobutyl ketone; 1,1,2,2-tetrachloroethane; tetrahydrofuran; 1,1,1-trichloroethane; and trichloroethylene. A groundwater expert described the probable movement and concentration of the chemicals as they migrated from the landfill toward plaintiffs' wells. A toxicologist summarized the known hazardous characteristics of the chemical substances. He testified that of the twelve identified chemicals, four were known carcinogens. Other potential toxic effects identified by the toxicologist included liver and kidney damage, mutations and alterations in genetic material, damage to blood and reproductive systems, neurological damage, and skin irritations. The toxicologist also testified about differences in the extent of the chemical exposure experienced by various plaintiffs. An expert in the diagnosis and treatment of diseases caused by exposure to toxic substances testified that the plaintiffs required annual medical examinations to afford the earliest possible diagnosis of chemically induced illnesses. Her opinion was that a program of regular medical surveillance for plaintiffs would improve prospects for cure, treatment, prolongation of life, and minimization of pain and disability.

A substantial number – more than 150 – of the plaintiffs gave testimony with respect to damages, describing in detail the impairment of their quality of life during the period that they were without running water, and the emotional distress they suffered. With regard to the emotional distress claims, the plaintiffs' testimony detailed their emotional reactions to the chemical contamination of their wells and the deprivation of their water supply, as well as their fears for the health of their family members. Expert psychological testimony was offered to document plaintiffs' claims that they had sustained compensable psychological damage as a result of the contamination of their wells.

QUALITY OF LIFE

In November, 1978, the residents of the Legler area of Jackson Township were advised by the local Board of Health not to drink their well water, and to limit washing and bathing to avoid prolonged exposure to the water. Initially, the township provided water to the affected residents in water tanks that were transported by tank trucks to various locations in the neighborhood. Plaintiffs brought their own containers, filled them with water from the tanks, and transported the water to their homes. This water-supply system was soon discontinued and replaced by a home-delivery system. Residents in need of water tied a white cloth on their mailbox and received a 40 gallon barrel containing a plastic liner filled with water. The filled barrels weighed in excess of 100 pounds and were dropped off, as needed, on the properties of the Legler-area residents. The family-members frequently were required to move the barrels to a protected area, either inside a garage or inside the residence. Residents who stored the barrels in garages testified that the water froze in cold weather. Other residents rolled or dragged their barrels into their homes.... One witness, who suffered from arthritis, testified to hauling her water for drinking, cooking and bathing up nine steps because, as she said, [t]here was no way that I could get the water upstairs except by hauling pot after pot out of the containers...which was a considerable amount of hauling everyday just to use for drinking and bathing the children and cooking. As the Appellate Division noted, the lack of running water was an understandable source of tension and friction among members of the plaintiffs' households, who for nearly two years were compelled to obtain water in this primitive manner.

The trial court charged the jury that plaintiffs' claim for "quality of life" damages encompassed "inconveniences, aggravation, and unnecessary expenditure of time and effort related to the use of the water hauled to their homes, as well as to other disruption in their lives, including disharmony in the family unit." The aggregate jury verdict on this claim was $5,396,940. This represented an average award of slightly over $16,000 for each plaintiff; thus, a family unit consisting of four plaintiffs received an average award of approximately $64,000.

In the Appellate Division and before this Court, defendant argues that this segment of the verdict is barred by the New Jersey Tort Claims Act, which provides: "No damages shall be awarded against a public entity or public employee for pain and suffering...." The Appellate Division rejected the township's contention, concluding that there was a clear distinction between the subjectively measured damages for pain and suffering, which are not compensable by the Tort Claims Act, and these which objectively affect quality of life by causing an interference with the use of one's land through inconvenience and the disruption of daily activities.

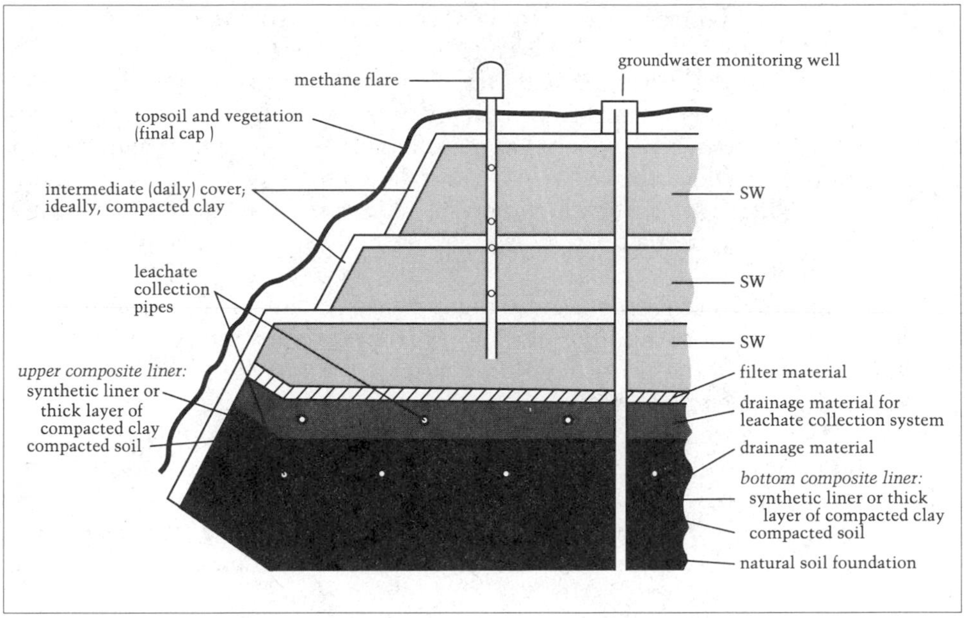

ADAPTED FROM OFFICE OF TECHNOLOGY ASSESSMENT DIAGRAM

Schematic cutaway diagram of the corner of a state-of-the-art solid waste landfill, showing protective liner layers, water-repelling capping, and internal drainage and monitoring system. As in the Ayers v. Twp. of Jackson case, solid waste landfill operations in practice are often much less fastidious about design and maintenance; moreover, as one state official said, the basic rule of liners is that they'll all eventually leak.

We agree with the Appellate Division's conclusion.... As the Appellate Division acknowledged, plaintiffs' claim for quality of life damages is derived from the law of nuisance.

EMOTIONAL DISTRESS

The jury verdict awarded plaintiffs damages for emotional distress in the aggregate amount of $2,056,480. The individual verdicts ranged from $40 to $14,000.

Many of the plaintiffs testified about their emotional reactions to the knowledge that their well-water was contaminated. Most of the plaintiffs' testimony on the issue of emotional distress was relatively brief and general. Typically, their testimony did not indicate that the emotional distress resulted in physical symptoms or required medical treatment.... Nevertheless, the consistent thrust of the testimony offered by numerous witnesses was that they suffered anxiety, stress, fear, and depression, and that these feelings were directly and causally related to the knowledge that they and members of their family had ingested and been exposed to contaminated water for a substantial time period.

Plaintiffs also presented testimony from an experienced clinical psychologist, Dr. Margaret Gibbs...[who] testified that the sample of 88 plaintiffs she tested manifested abnormally high levels of stress, depression, health concerns, and psychological problems. She expressed the opinion that the psychological conditions observed by her were causally related to the contamination of plaintiffs' water supply....

The township challenged the jury verdict awarding damages for emotional distress on two grounds. The township contended that plaintiffs had not proved that the emotional distress experienced by them was manifested by any discernible physical symptoms or injuries, arguing that proof of related physical symptoms was a prerequisite to recovery.... Plaintiffs maintain...that their emotional distress claims are compensable because we have abandoned the requirement of physical impact as a condition to recovery for emotional distress. We acknowledge that our cases no longer require proof of causally-related physical impact to sustain a recovery for emotional distress....

In addition, the township contended that the jury verdict for emotional distress constituted damages for "pain and suffering resulting from any injury," recovery for which is expressly barred by the Tort Claims Act, N.J.S.A. 59:9-2(d).... We have no doubt, based on our review of the record, that many of the plaintiffs understandably experienced substantial emotional distress as a result of the contamination of their water supply. However, the legislature has expressly determined that the pain and suffering occasioned by their emotional distress is not compensable by damages from Jackson Township. The New Jersey Tort Claims Act bars the recovery of such damages. Accordingly, we [reverse] the jury verdict awarding damages for emotional distress.

CLAIMS FOR ENHANCED RISK, AND MEDICAL SURVEILLANCE

No claims were asserted by plaintiffs seeking recovery for specific illnesses caused by their exposure to chemicals. Rather, they claim damages for the enhanced risk of future illness attributable to such exposure. They also seek to recover the expenses of annual medical examinations to monitor their physical health and detect symptoms of disease at the earliest possible opportunity....

The trial court granted defendant's motion for summary judgment dismissing the enhanced risk claim. It held that plaintiffs' proofs, with the benefit of all favorable inferences, would not establish a "reasonable probability" that plaintiffs would sustain future injury as a result of chemical contamination of their water supply. With regard to the claims for medical surveillance expenses...the jury verdict included damages of $8,204,500 for medical surveillance. The Appellate Division reversed, concluding that the claims for medical surveillance expenses, like the claims for "enhanced risk," were too speculative to warrant recognition under the Tort Claims Act.... As a result of the trial court's and Appellate Division's rulings, plaintiffs are left to await actual manifestation of physical injury attributable to their exposure to toxic chemicals before they can institute and sustain a damage claim for personal injuries against the defendant.... In the interim, under the Appellate Division ruling, any plaintiff who obtains regular or periodic medical surveillance for the express purpose of detecting adverse physical conditions attributable to exposure to toxic chemicals must personally bear the expense of that evaluation to the extent its cost is not covered by plaintiffs' own health insurance.

In our view, these decisions fall short of effectuating the policies of the Tort Claims Act where claims are asserted against a public entity for wrongful exposure to toxic chemicals. Although we concur with the Appellate Division's refusal to recognize plaintiffs' damage claim based on enhanced risk, we disagree with its conclusion that an award for medical surveillance damages cannot be supported by this record.

Our evaluation of the enhanced risk and medical surveillance claims requires that we focus on a critical issue in the management of toxic tort litigation: at what stage in the evolution of a toxic injury should tort law intercede by requiring the responsible party to pay damages?

At the outset, we must recognize that the issues presented by this case and others like it will be recurring. We note the difficulty that both law and science experience in attempting to deal with the emerging complexities of industrialized society and the consequent implications for human health. One facet of that problem is represented here, in the form of years of inadequate and improper waste disposal practices. However dimly or callously the consequences of those waste management practices may have been perceived, those consequences are now upon us. According to the Senate Committee on Environment and Public Works, more than ninety percent of all hazardous chemical wastes produced in the United States have been disposed of improperly. S. Rep. No. 848, 96th Cong., 2d Sess. 3 (1980) (citing EPA estimates).

In addition to the staggering problem of removing – or at least containing – the hazardous remnants of past practices, there remains the moral and legal problem of compensating the human victims of past misuse of chemical products.... In the absence of statutory or administrative mechanisms for processing injury claims resulting from environmental contamination, courts have struggled to accommodate common-law tort doctrines to the peculiar characteristics of toxic-tort litigation.

Although state statutes of limitations are invariably identified as procedural obstacles to mass exposure litigation, the extent of the problem posed by such statutes varies widely among jurisdictions. Ginsberg & Weiss, 9 Hofstra L. Rev. at 921 & n.259; Developments – Toxic Waste, 99 Harv. L. Rev. 1606-07. Because of the long latency period typical of illnesses caused by chemical pollutants, victims often discover their injury and the existence of a cause of action long after the expiration of the personal-injury statute of limitations, where the limitations period is calculated from the date of the exposure. Most jurisdictions have remedied this problem by adopting a version of the "discovery rule" that tolls the statute until the injury is discovered. Few states follow New Jersey's discovery rule that tolls the statute until the victim discovers both the injury and the facts suggesting that a third party may be responsible. However, we note that CERCLA now pre-empts state statutes of limitation where they provide that the limitations period for personal-injury or property-damage suits prompted by exposure to hazardous substances starts on a date earlier than the "federally required commencement date." That term is defined as "the date plaintiff knew (or reasonably should have known) that the personal injury or property damages...were caused or contributed to by the hazardous substance...concerned." (Superfund Amendments and Authorization Act of 1986, 42 U.S.C.A. §9658.)

The single controversy rule "requires that a party include in the action all related claims against an adversary and its failure to do so precludes the maintenance of a second action." Aetna Ins. Co. v. Gilchrist, 85 N.J. at 556-57. The doctrine may bar recovery where, as here, suit is instituted to recover damages to compensate for the immediate consequences of toxic pollution, but the initiation of additional litigation depends upon when, if ever, physical injuries threatened by the pollution are manifested. It is appropriate that all of the parties in interest understand that neither the single controversy doctrine nor the statute of limitations will preclude a timely-filed cause of action for damages prompted by the future "discovery" of a disease or injury related to the tortious conduct at issue in this litigation. The bar of the statute of limitations is avoided...under New Jersey's discovery rule. Moreover, the single controversy rule...cannot sensibly be applied to a toxic-tort claim filed when disease is manifested years after the exposure, merely because the same plaintiff sued previously to recover for property damage or other injuries. In such a case, the rule is literally inapplicable since, as noted, the second cause of action does not accrue until the disease is manifested; hence, it could not have been joined with the earlier claims.

[The court then ruled that "neither the statute of limitations nor the single controversy rule should bar timely causes of action in toxic-tort cases instituted after discovery of a disease or injury related to tortious conduct, although there has been prior litigation between the parties of different claims based on the same tortious conduct." The court then turned its attention to the difficulties facing toxic tort plaintiffs in proving negligence, the usual basis for recovery, and the great difficulty posed by the causation issue. The discussion paralleled the analysis in Allen v. United States, but on a rather more general plane, and then continued on to the enhanced risk and medical surveillance claims.]

Among the recent toxic tort cases rejecting liability for damages based on enhanced risk is Anderson v. W.R. Grace & Co.... The majority of courts that have considered the enhanced risk issue have agreed with the disposition of the district court in *Anderson*.... Other courts have acknowledged the propriety of the enhanced risk cause of action, but have emphasized the requirement that proof of future injury be reasonably certain.... Additionally, several courts have permitted recovery for increased risk of disease, but only where the plaintiff exhibited some present manifestation of disease.

We observe that the overwhelming weight of the scholarship on this issue favors a right of recovery for tortious conduct that causes a significantly enhanced risk of injury. For the most part, the commentators concede the inadequacy of common-law remedies for toxic-tort victims. Instead, they recommend statutory or administrative mechanisms that would permit compensation to be awarded on the basis of exposure and significant risk of disease, without the necessity of proving the existence of present injury.

Our disposition of this difficult and important issue requires that we choose between two alternatives, each having a potential for imposing unfair and undesirable consequences on the affected interests. A holding that recognizes a cause of action for unquantified enhanced risk claims exposes the tort system, and the public it serves, to the task of litigating vast numbers of claims for compensation based on threats of injuries that may never occur. It imposes on judges and juries the burden of assessing damages for the risk of potential disease, without clear guidelines to determine what level of compensation may be appropriate. It would undoubtedly increase already escalating insurance rates. It is clear that the recognition of an "enhanced risk" cause of action, particularly when the risk is unquantified, would generate substantial litigation that would be difficult to manage and resolve.

Our dissenting colleague, arguing in favor of recognizing a cause of action based on an unquantified claim of enhanced risk, points out that "courts have not allowed the difficulty of quantifying injury to prevent them from offering compensation for assault, trespass, emotional distress, invasion of privacy or damage to reputation." Although lawsuits grounded in one or more of these causes of action may involve claims for damages that are difficult to quantify, such damages are awarded on the basis of events that have occurred and can be proved at the time of trial. In contrast, the compensability of the enhanced risk claim depends upon the likelihood of an event that has not yet occurred and may never occur – the contracting of one or more diseases the risk of which has been enhanced by defendant's conduct. It is the highly contingent and speculative quality of an unquantified claim based on enhanced risk that renders it novel and difficult to manage and resolve....

On the other hand, denial of the enhanced-risk cause of action may mean that some of these plaintiffs will be unable to obtain compensation for their injury. Those who contract diseases in the future because of their exposure to chemicals in their well water may be unable to prove a causal relationship between such exposure and their disease...because of the difficulty of proving that injuries manifested in the future were not the product of intervening events or causes.... We are conscious of the admonition that in construing the Act courts should "exercise restraint in the acceptance of novel causes of action against public entities." Comment, N.J.S.A. 59:2-1. In our view, the speculative nature of an unquantified enhanced risk claim, the difficulties inherent in adjudicating such claims, and the policies underlying the Tort Claims Act argue persuasively against the recognition of this cause of action...for the unquantified enhanced risk of disease.

The claim for medical surveillance expenses stands on a different footing from the claim based on enhanced risk. It seeks to recover the cost of periodic medical examinations intended to monitor plaintiffs' health and facilitate early diagnosis and treatment of disease caused by plaintiffs' exposure to toxic chemicals. At trial, competent medical testimony was offered to prove that a program of regular medical testing and evaluation was reasonably necessary and consistent with contemporary scientific principles applied by physicians experienced in the diagnosis and treatment of chemically-induced injuries.

The Appellate Division's rejection of the medical surveillance claim is rooted in the premise that even if medical experts testify convincingly that medical surveillance is necessary, the claim for compensation for these costs must fail, as a matter of law, if the risk of injury is not quantified, or, if quantified, is not reasonably probable. This analysis assumes that the reasonableness of medical intervention, and, therefore, its compensability, depends solely on the sufficiency of proof that the occurrence of the disease is probable. We think this formulation unduly impedes the ability of courts to recognize that medical science may necessarily and properly intervene [with a course of surveillance monitoring] where there is a significant but unquantified risk of serious disease....

An application of tort law that allows post-injury, pre-symptom recovery in toxic tort litigation for reasonable medical surveillance costs is manifestly consistent with the public interest in early detection and treatment of disease. Recognition of pre-symptom claims for medical surveillance serves other important public interests. The difficulty of proving causation, where the disease is manifested years after exposure, has caused many commentators to suggest that tort law has no capacity to deter polluters, because the costs of proper disposal are often viewed by polluters as exceeding the risk of tort liability. However, permitting recovery for reasonable pre-symptom, medical-surveillance expenses subjects polluters to significant liability when proof of the causal connection between the tortious conduct and the plaintiffs' exposure to chemicals is likely to be most readily available. The availability of a substantial remedy before the consequences of the plaintiffs' exposure are manifest may also have the beneficial effect of preventing or mitigating serious future illnesses and thus reduce the overall costs to the responsible parties.

Other considerations compel recognition of a pre-symptom medical surveillance claim. It is inequitable for an individual, wrongfully exposed to dangerous toxic chemicals but unable to prove that disease is likely, to have to pay his own expenses when medical intervention is clearly reasonable and necessary....

Our conclusion regarding the compensability of medical surveillance expenses is not dissimilar to the result in the *Reserve Mining* case (514 F.2d 492 (1975))…. The likelihood of disease is but one element in determining the reasonableness of medical intervention for the plaintiffs in this case. Other critical factors are the significance and extent of their exposure to chemicals, the toxicity of the chemicals, the seriousness of the diseases for which individuals are at risk, and the value of early diagnosis…. Accordingly, we hold that the cost of medical surveillance is a compensable item of damages where the proofs demonstrate, through reliable expert testimony predicated upon the significance and extent of exposure to chemicals, the toxicity of the chemicals, the seriousness of the diseases for which individuals are at risk, the relative increase in the chance of onset of disease in those exposed, and the value of early diagnosis, that such surveillance to monitor the effect of exposure to toxic chemicals is reasonable and necessary…notwithstanding the fact that the extent of plaintiffs' impaired health is unquantified….

The medical surveillance issue was tried as if it were a conventional claim for compensatory damages susceptible to a jury verdict in a lump sum…. The indeterminate nature of damage claims in toxic-tort litigation [however] suggests that the use of court-supervised funds to pay medical-surveillance claims as they accrue, rather than lump-sum verdicts, may provide a more efficient mechanism for compensating plaintiffs [and]…is a highly appropriate exercise of the Court's equitable powers. Such a mechanism offers significant advantages over a lump-sum verdict. [In] Tort Claims Act cases, it provides a method for offsetting a defendant's liability by payments from collateral sources. Although the parties in this case sharply dispute the availability of insurance coverage for surveillance-type costs, a fund could provide a convenient method for establishing credits in the event insurance benefits were available for some, if not all, of the plaintiffs…. However, we decline to upset the jury verdict awarding medical-surveillance damages in this case. Such a result would be unfair to these plaintiffs, since the medical-surveillance issue was tried conventionally. We also recognize that the fund mechanism that we now endorse in toxic-tort cases is novel and represents a sharp break with our prevailing practice. In such circumstances, we have previously recognized the wisdom of limiting the application of a new rule of law…. Accordingly, the judgment of the Appellate Division setting aside the jury verdict for medical surveillance damages is reversed and the jury verdict is reinstated….

HANDLER, J., concurring in part and dissenting in part.

The Court does not dispute the fact of toxic contamination, nor does it contest the characterization of a significantly enhanced risk of disease as a tortiously inflicted injury. The majority also admits that "[d]ismissal of the enhanced risk claims may effectively preclude any recovery for injuries caused by exposure to chemicals in plaintiffs' wells." The Court exaggerates the difficulties in recognizing this cause of action and minimizes the imperative to provide fair compensation for seriously injurious wrongs.

The majority concludes that plaintiffs' injury cannot be redressed. Its reasons for treating their claims differently from other injury claims are an unsupported fear of "vast numbers of claims" and a belief that no "clear guidelines [exist] to determine what level of compensation may be appropriate…." It nowhere explains why a risk that generates the "reasonable probability" of future injury can be compensated while one that "significantly enhances" the likelihood of future injury cannot…. If it is just and fair, and it is, to compensate a victim in one case for an unquantified enhanced risk of future disease, it cannot be right to deny recovery in a second case also involving a claim of unquantified enhanced risk.... The courts have not allowed the difficulty of quantifying injury to prevent them from offering compensation for assault, trespass, emotional distress, invasion of privacy, or damage to reputation. The claim in this case involves a tortious invasion, as much an invasion as the trespass of gas and microscopic deposits on someone else's property.... The plaintiffs' claim of an unquantified enhanced risk should not be characterized as "depend[ing] upon the likelihood of an event that has not yet occurred and may never occur." The injury involved is an actual event: exposure to toxic chemicals. Among the consequences of this unconsented-to invasion are genetic damage and a tangible risk of a major disease, a peril that is real even though it cannot be precisely measured or weighed. The peril, moreover, is unquestionably greater than that experienced by persons not similarly exposed to toxic chemicals.... Like claims based on the doctrines of trespass, assault, invasion of privacy, or defamation, the damages suffered are not solely actual consequential damages, but also the disvalue of being subjected to an intrinsically harmful event. The risk of dreadful disease resulting from toxic exposure and contamination is...frightening and palpable....

COMMENTARY AND QUESTIONS

1. Damages for subjective human intangibles. What items of damage are included in the "quality of life" recovery? Is there any recognition of the stigma of living in a contaminated community? Is there any argument that separates toxic tort cases from ordinary tort cases when it comes to compensation for subjective intangibles? The mass exposure aspect of toxic tort cases implies that defendant's financial exposure may be great. Under what circumstances will that justify modification of the ordinary substantive rules?

2. The medical surveillance remedy. The surveillance monitoring fund remedy invented by the attorneys in *Ayers* has been picked up in several other states as a response to the problems of long-term toxic torts' latency. Would the *Anderson* court have allowed medical surveillance, although it foreclosed recovery for risk?

3. Cancerphobia. There is a growing number of cases which have, in various degrees, accepted the concept of recovery for "cancerphobia," post-exposure anxiety that is an understandable reaction to exposure to carcinogenic chemicals. Some courts have allowed recovery for fear of cancer risk even though they have denied recovery for the risk itself. See Sterling v. Velsicol, 855 F.2d 1188 (6th Cir. 1988). The reluctance of courts to open a floodgate of cases based on fear with no attendant physical injury has led to a high standard in some states. In New Jersey, for instance, the *Ironbound* cases held that the neighbors of an Agent Orange production facility who had been contaminated by that defoliant could not recover for cancerphobia because their distress was not sufficiently "severe and substantial." Ironbound Health Rights Advisory Commission v. Diamond Shamrock Chemicals Co., 578 A.2d 1248 (N.J. Super. 1990); see also Gale and Goyer, Recovery for Cancerphobia and Increased Rick of Cancer, 15 Cumb. L. Rev. 734 (1985).

Part of the courts' hesitancy in the cancerphobia cases, and in other mass tort environmental cases, is that the theories of common law liability prove too much.

The reasonable fears of chemical contamination are so serious and so widespread that a defendant who pollutes a community might readily face a billion dollars in jury verdicts, and the American economy cannot stand the imposition of such tort liability. When courts raise the threshold barriers to tort recovery in mass toxic tort cases, are they making a social policy judgment that for reasons of social utility the damages for non-physical injuries must remain where they lie?

4. Toxic torts, latency compensation. Pre-illness claims are inherently enigmatic. On one hand, compensation can mulct defendants of damages even in cases where illness never occurs. This results in a form of systematic over-compensation. On the other hand, to refuse compensation is to ignore the goal of complete compensation because defendant's conduct has made plaintiffs less well-off. If proof of that is needed, consider whether an individual would voluntarily choose to drink contaminated water for several years. See R. Posner, Economic Analysis of Law 149 (2d ed., 1977). Likewise, consider what a prudent insurer of health risks would do if it discovered that an applicant for insurance had suffered a major toxic exposure, as had the plaintiffs in *Ayers*. Are there persuasive rebuttals to these assertions of over- and under-compensation? Is there a further argument that compensation for enhanced risk systematically undercompensates those victims who actually contract the feared disease?

To what extent is it necessary to know whether subsequent lawsuits (when diseases actually appear) will be barred by the statute of limitations or by doctrines of res judicata? As a policy matter, the majority in *Ayers* tries to indicate in dicta that New Jersey courts should be receptive to later suits. The court couples that assurance with its perception that courts are facing only the beginning of a flood of toxic tort litigation, to justify its conservative wait-and-see, wait-and-sue approach to enhanced risk. Would Judge Jenkins in *Allen* have been likely to take the same approach?

5. Sovereign immunity. Most sovereigns in history have not encouraged their citizens (or anyone else, for that matter) to sue them in the sovereign's own courts. The idea of sovereign immunity has long been a powerful part of the American law. In the nineteenth and twentieth centuries, however, numerous attacks on the unfairness and irrationality of immunity were mounted and eventually took their toll. In an era where government is acknowledged to have many similarities to other corporate entities, why, for example, should a pedestrian negligently run down by a government-owned vehicle find her suit barred by governmental immunity when no such bar would encumber a suit against a private company? Why should Jackson Township be any less responsible for harms caused by its dump operations than a private landfill operator?

Over time the courts, and to a lesser extent legislatures, responded to arguments favoring a partial abolition of governmental immunity. On the common law front, a popular innovation is to distinguish between cases in which the governmental defendant is performing a governmental function, and those in which it is engaging in a mere proprietary function.[16] For example, setting the standard for airborne lead pollution would be governmental in character, and immune; running a hot dog stand at the public beach would be proprietary in character and subject to suit. In between lies a lot of room for closer questions. Another popular judicial device for limiting immunity is to grant official immunity for acts that are clothed with discretion (again, standard-setting is a good example) but to hold officials liable for negligence or intentional torts in the performance of mere ministerial functions.[17] Some legislatures have taken similar initiatives, while a larger number have codified what the courts have done, sometimes modifying the scope of the judicial abrogation of immunity, other times not.

In recent years, with the advent of widely publicized tort recoveries and a manifold increase in governmental liability insurance costs, a reaction to the liberalized abrogation of immunity has taken place. This is the backdrop to the statute construed in *Ayers* that re-establishes the concept of governmental immunity in New Jersey and then abrogates that immunity under statutorily-defined circumstances. Even in those cases where New Jersey abrogates its governmental immunity, the statute expressly denies damages for pain and suffering and kindred intangible items of damage.

6. A Note on statutes of limitation. Toxic tort cases raise a number of difficult statute of limitations problems. As an initial matter, the discovery by plaintiffs that they are victims of a tort is seldom concurrent with the defendant's tortious conduct. Even in *Ferebee* (the paraquat spraying case) the plaintiff's decedent was unaware of the harm caused to him by the exposures until sometime significantly after the initial exposure occurred. Likewise in *Ayers* and *Anderson* the groundwater contamination and plaintiffs' subsequent ingestion of it began well in advance of plaintiffs' learning that contamination had occurred, and perhaps years in advance of plaintiffs suffering any physical injury from having ingested the water.

The courts have adopted two devices for dealing with statutes of limitations problems. The first doctrine relates to defining when a cause of action accrues. A lawsuit cannot be brought by a plaintiff to vindicate a cause of action before the cause of action has accrued to the plaintiff. To do otherwise defies logic, asking plaintiff to act on a legal right not yet in existence. The doctrine is intended to protect the courts themselves from the burden of adjudicating unripe controversies. In fairness to plaintiffs refused access to courts by the accrual rule, it is universally held that statutes of limitations only begin to run from the time a cause of action has accrued to the plaintiff. Most courts have held that accrual occurs only when all of the elements necessary for successful prosecution of the claim have occurred, and a central element of any tort claim is the injury to the plaintiff.

---

16. "Proprietary" implies there is no functional difference from a privately-owned profitmaking enterprise; "governmental" implies a function carried on in satisfaction of a public duty.

17. "Ministerial" implies that the public employee is simply implementing explicit governmental duties; "discretionary" acts are based on a broader, less constrained grant of delegated authority to act.

The second major development in limitation of actions law that operates to protect plaintiffs in toxic tort cases is the so-called "discovery rule." It too helps to define when a cause of action accrues. In that portion of the *Anderson* opinion addressing the effect of the statute of limitations on wrongful death claims being pressed on behalf of area children who had died of leukemia after drinking water from the polluted wells, the court stated the general discovery rule:

> The discovery rule is a method of defining when a cause of action accrues. The principle behind the rule is that "a plaintiff should be put on notice before his or her claim is barred by the passage of time." The notice required by the rule includes knowledge of both the injury and its cause–that plaintiff "has been harmed as a result of defendant's conduct." 628 F. Supp. at 1224 (citations omitted).[18]

It should be clear that the discovery rule addresses the problem of long latency periods intervening between tortious exposure and the onset of disease. If the statute of limitations has not yet begun to run until the disease is manifest, then plaintiffs will have ample opportunity to bring suit after the onset of the disease. There may be some proof difficulties in reconstructing the events surrounding exposure, but it is at least reasonable to consider these the lesser of evils. The principal alternatives to the discovery rule are requiring defendants to compensate all exposure victims as if they have developed the disease, or abandoning the discovery rule, and thereby limiting plaintiffs to damages that became manifest within a short time of exposure.

Ayers recognizes the existence of an additional potential discovery rule problem, the operation of the rules of res judicata (in particular merger and bar) that the New Jersey court labels "the single controversy rule." In most instances, in order to avoid duplicative and inefficient litigation of a case, all claims must be joined in a single suit. To the extent that claims have been omitted and not placed in issue, the single controversy rule deems them extinguished and "merged" into the original judgment. In cases like *Ayers* the pitfall of the single controversy rule is that later-initiated claims for matured illness will be allowed by the discovery rule, only to be barred by merger. The New Jersey approach to this problem is to recognize that the policies of the discovery rule would be set at naught if merger and bar were applied. The court points out that merger and bar only apply to cases that could have been brought at the time of the first suit, and here, technically speaking, the cause of action for bodily injury would not yet have come into existence.

7. A note on "tort reform." Over the years there have been recurring calls for tort reform from plaintiffs as well as defendants, the latter often based on perceptions

---

18. This particular form of the discovery rule, requiring that the plaintiff must have discovered both the fact of injury and who caused it before the statute starts running, is not a majority rule although it appears to be gaining. More states toll the statue of limitations in these toxic tort cases only until discovery of the injury. See Development in the Law – Toxic Waste Litigation. 99 Harv. L. Rev. 1458, 1906-07 (1986). Some state legislatures are enacting statutes of limitations that expressly disallow the operation of the discovery rule. These states appear to be motivated by concern for the burdens placed on present-day operators of businesses by large judgments for "ancient torts" committed by officers and employees who have no present relation to the defendant entity.

of the growing size of tort recoveries, others on the basis that the common law tort system is ill-suited to coping with the problems of mass tort and toxics cases, and so on. One example of such a call for tort reform is the report produced by the Grad Commission, in which areas such as negligence, trespass, nuisance, and strict liability were examined in their relation to environmental tort claims and remedies.[19]

In recent years, environmental tort cases have regularly provided the nation's largest recoveries. In 1989, for instance, the Wall Street Journal was not pleased to report that the 1989 record was $76 million for each of two workers exposed to asbestos. Coyne and McCoubrey v. Celotex, (settled)(Wall St. J. 9 Feb. 1990, B1.) The plaintiffs' bar responds that the average recovery in tort cases has not increased disproportionately, and that the insurance industry, in decrying the need to raise premiums, focuses on tort payments to the exclusion of its own internal investment policies. That debate is likely to be noisy and continuing.

On the specific question of mass toxic torts, however, there is a sufficient body of scholarship arguing that the nature of epidemiology, the size of exposed plaintiff classes, the emotional and economic repercussions of litigation, and the problems of latency all combine to recommend statutory and administrative overrides of the tort law. See Trauberman, Statutory Reform of "Toxic Torts," 7 Harv. Envtl. L. Rev. 177, 188-202 (1983). The size and complexity of proposed public law remedies for mass torts, however, and their alleged vulnerability to political pressure from industry defendants, combine to raise substantial doubts within the environmental bar.

The short of it appears to be that tort law is a known commodity that carries its own internal incentives to prosecution of claims. Public law management cannot easily replicate the tort law's claims-processing mechanism. For the time being, matters are likely to continue as they are at present, with common law the active and tangible foundation for most toxic tort law, with occasional intervention from the public law system.

---

19. F. Grad, et al., Injuries and Damages From Hazardous Wastes – Analysis and Improvement of Legal Remedies: A Report to Congress in Compliance With Section 301(e) of the Comprehensive Environmental Response, Compensation, and Liability Act of 1980 (P.L. 96-510) by the Superfund Section 301(e) Study Group, S. Rep. No. 12, 97th Cong., 2d Sess. (1982).

Chapter 5

ENVIRONMENTAL REMEDIES DRAWN FROM OTHER FIELDS OF LAW: CORPORATE LAW, CONTRACTS, AND PROPERTY

This chapter is short. Its purpose is to illustrate that environmental law is where you find it. In most modern legal practice, given the innate conservatism of the profession, practitioners typically apply tried and true remedies to controversies they encounter. Environmental practice, however, has always been slightly maverick. It attempts to raise values and issues of fact that have long been ignored and unacknowledged by established economic and political institutions, and it often has to raise them in novel ways.

The dramatic evolution of environmental tort law demonstrates the ability of the legal system to find flexible solutions for modern problems when old doctrines are creatively applied and litigated. This chapter surveys a variety of other sectors of the legal system to see how they also may sometimes be creatively applied to implement modern environmental concerns in the absence of specific environmental legislation on point. The areas noted are corporate law, property law, and contract law, but the methods used by the imaginative environmental lawyer can potentially stretch to all areas of modern legal practice. This chapter, then, offers examples and invitations to expand legal analysis beyond the calcified ruts of familiar practice.

A. A CORPORATE LAW RETROSPECTIVE – THE PACIFIC LUMBER CONTROVERSY

Anderberg, Wall Street Sleaze: How the Hostile Takeover of Pacific Lumber Led to the Clear-Cutting of Coastal Redwoods

10 Amicus Journal No. 2, 8 (1988).

Debate has been vigorous over the effects of so-called junk-bond financing on American corporations and the United States economy in general, and whether it forces a healthy reassessment by managers and investors of a company's business or rather simply benefits the deal makers who undertake highly debt-leveraged corporate acquisitions.

But, many people on both sides of the debate agree, one junk bond-financed acquisition in northern California may result in a horror story in which mighty coastal redwoods are clear-cut in order to amortize junk debt incurred in the hostile takeover of a once venerated timber company.

Prior to 1985, the family-run Pacific Lumber Company was widely respected as the most environmentally sensitive timber company in the industry. While other lumber companies often overharvested their inventory of redwoods and firs and depleted their long-term yield (scarring the landscape and wreaking havoc on the local economy), Pacific Lumber selectively cut old-growth redwoods under a sustained-yield policy that allowed new lumber to grow faster than old lumber was cut. For over forty years the company refused to clear-cut any of its forest holdings. The company was even known to have worked closely with the Save the Redwoods League, agreeing to preserve critical acreage until it could be incorporated into the national park system.... Even after the company went public in 1975 (with its stock trading on the New York Stock Exchange), the company was still considered by environmentalists and employees alike as a "bulwark of responsibility."

Pacific Lumber was also unique in one other respect. While its 189,000-acre holdings do not even make it the largest timber company in its area, Pacific Lumber owns by far the largest majority of the virgin old-growth redwoods (*Sequoia sempervirens*, or Coast redwoods) that are not already incorporated into federal, state, or regional park systems. A tall relic of a vast forest system that prior to the Ice Age covered millions of acres, virgin old-growth redwoods today occupy some 110,000 acres. The trees, some more than twenty centuries old, grow in magnificent and serene groves. About 70 percent of this acreage is protected as parkland, and the lion-sized share that is not (some 16,000 to 17,000 acres) is owned by Pacific Lumber and was thought to be relatively safe.

A certain Charles E. Hurwitz changed all this one early September morning in 1985. While denominating himself as a Texas farm boy, Hurwitz is, in fact, a corporate raider, who through his investment vehicle Maxxam Group, Inc. of New York (the former Simplicity Pattern Company) has built a large fortune by making heavily debt-financed acquisitions of companies whose assets (as measured by the price of their stock on an established stock exchange) are undervalued and thus can be purchased at a relative bargain.

The very factors that made Pacific Lumber so venerated among environmentalists and others may have made it a sitting duck for Hurwitz. Pacific Lumber in effect had stockpiled its inventory of redwoods, allowing trees to grow for decades before selectively cutting them in a manner designed to maintain consistent harvests. A corporate raider could obtain control of such vast timber reserves, radically increase harvests to increase cash flow and short-term profits, and subsequently sell the company. Augmenting the situation was Pacific Lumber's conservative management ("under-managed," according to Hurwitz) which resulted in the company's having a fairly low stock price (perhaps even significantly lower than the net asset value of its timber), flat earnings, and no significant debt load.

Beginning on that fateful September morning in 1985, Hurwitz moved to obtain control of Pacific Lumber, initially through a hostile tender offer (an offer to purchase on the open market approximately 22 million shares of Pacific Lumber that were traded on the New York Stock Exchange). By January, 1986, Hurwitz's MAXXAM Group had completed its acquisition of the outstanding stock of Pacific Lumber, but at a cost: some $868 million, approximately $680.5 million of which was debt-financed by three issues of high-interest, low-grade investment (risky) "junk bonds," debt instruments that [were] the forte of Wall Street investment banking house Drexel Burnham Lambert. They are backed solely by the assets of Pacific Lumber, not by MAXXAM. Perhaps more telling, the purchasers of the junk bonds (primarily large institutional investors) can look for repayment of interest and principal on such bonds *only* from the sale or other use of Pacific Lumber's assets.

After obtaining control of Pacific Lumber, and as is common in a highly debt-leveraged acquisition, Hurwitz first sold the company's non-timber assets (the corporate headquarters for $30 million and an unrelated cutting and welding operation for about $250 million). Hurwitz then turned his attention to the remaining large asset of Pacific Lumber: its inventory of coastal redwoods. In 1986, Hurwitz stepped up harvests from 137 million to 248 million board feet per year (including clear-cutting of selected tracts of up to 500 acres and the harvesting of virgin redwoods), conceding in testimony before the California legislature that the increase in harvest was primarily to pay off the massive debt load incurred in acquiring Pacific Lumber. Many have noted that the interest payments on the junk debt used to acquire Pacific Lumber [amount to] $83 million a year, more than Pacific Lumber's preacquisition cash flow.

Many environmentalists, residents, and even company loggers worry that not only is Pacific Lumber destroying a national treasure, but that the trees are being harvested at a rate that will ultimately jeopardize the sustained yield of the forests and the economy of the local region. Said one Pacific Lumber worker: "They're just leveling everything.... They're destroying the future, leaving nothing for the next generation." And Woody Murphy, a great-grandson of the Murphy that built Pacific Lumber into a venerated logging company, said, "And when they're through, it'll be a moonscape."

Pacific Lumber executives claim that if they reduce timber cutting after twenty years of intense harvesting to preacquisition harvest levels, Pacific Lumber's lands will still have a substantial inventory of redwoods and Douglas fir left for the future....

Meanwhile, Hurwitz claims he was victimized in the Pacific Lumber takeover by Drexel Burnham Lambert investment banker Dennis B. Levine, who allegedly leaked insider information concerning the prospective acquisition to arbitrageur (and convicted felon) Ivan Boesky, who used such information to quietly purchase large blocks of Pacific Lumber stock (thereby driving up its market price) shortly before Hurwitz's acquisition was announced. The Justice Department, Securities and Exchange Commission, and New York Stock Exchange are investigating the charges.

Ironically, Hurwitz may fail for economic reasons in his bid to use the coastal redwoods to pay off his junk bonds. John E. Mack, Jr., an analyst with Warberg, Rowe, and Pittman, Akroyd, Inc., states that Hurwitz may end up "flooding the market" with redwood, lowering prices, and destroying the company's ability to liquidate its inventory at a profit.

At the very least, Pacific Lumber is a vignette of what Representative John D. Dingell (D. Michigan) calls "the takeover and dismemberment of a good corporate citizen"; a hostile corporate acquisition that turned the most respected timber company in America into the least respected, while radically increasing the debt-load and jeopardizing the economic health of a soundly run company. "This case has enormous implications," warns Representative Ron Wyden (D. Oregon), a member of the House Banking, Finance and Urban Affairs Subcommittee that is investigating the Pacific Lumber acquisition. "I'm not convinced it's responsible for management to cut trees to pay debts to people who live thousands of miles away...."

Even more troubling is the question of whether other industries involved in the extraction of our nation's natural resources and whose operations have a critical effect on the overall quality of our environment could suffer the fate of the Pacific Lumber Company and the *Sequoia sempervirens*. Are we in danger of becoming a country in which our natural resources will be dismembered in transactions that benefit nobody but the deal makers?

Boundary line and clearcut area of a Maxxam Corporation (Pacific Lumber Co.) redwood clearcutting operation, located above All Species Creek, southeast of Eureka, California. The trees in the distance are old-growth redwoods 3 to 6 feet in diameter, averaging more than 200 feet tall, as were the trees in the clearcut area.

COMMENTARY AND QUESTIONS

1. Corporate law and social responsibility. Corporations are the fundamental building blocks of the American economy, and since economic decisions are so often the causes of long-term negative environmental effects, corporate law is an obvious candidate for environmental attorneys' attention. Corporate attorneys have learned to their dismay about dozens of statutory areas where they now must be sensitive to environmental concerns – in modern air, water, and chemical pollution regulations, in SEC reporting, lender liability, real estate transactions, tax treatment of pollution control, and so on. But getting legislatures to pass effective new statutes restricting corporate conduct is immensely difficult.

This section is not aimed at the depredations of junk bond raiders. Although leveraged buyouts still continue, junk bond financing is increasingly out of fashion. Rather, the *Pacific Lumber* case raises the larger question: Does corporate law contain any inherent principles of corporate responsibility that, in the absence of legislation, can be mobilized to induce corporations to take account of environmental harms?

It is difficult to intrude long-term public and intangible values into the corporate arena, unless they can be made to serve the interests of the corporation and its shareholders. In the recent past, the primary approach for insinuating environmental concerns into corporate practice has been through non-legal means, as environmentalists try through demonstrations, media, shareholder ballot questions, and boycotts to convince corporate officers and shareholders to make environmentally sensitive corporate policy. These efforts have been laudable but typically quite unsuccessful, as public interest environmental initiatives drown in a flood of institutional proxies, short-term profit maximization, and management indifference. A corporation is not in business to accomplish the public's good. Long-term problems, intangible costs, and any costs that can be externalized are not the concern of the corporate entity. Corporate managers, in fact, might be held liable if they expended corporate assets for purposes which cannot be justified in terms of protecting and enhancing the value of the corporation. It is this singlemindedness that has helped to build the world's greatest national economy and underlies the problem of corporate social responsibility.[1]

2. Valdez Principles. More recently, especially under clouds of media coverage generated by dramatic chemical contaminations, oil spills, and other corporate disasters, many corporations, especially those vulnerable to public identification of names and trademarks, have taken hesitant steps toward internalizing some

---

1. The difference between the long-term and short-term corporate perspectives illustrates other problems in American corporate law. In Japan, for instance, corporate executives are evaluated based on their contribution to the corporation's long-term growth and strength. In American practice, however, executives are typically evaluated based upon net earnings performance per quarter. Money reinvested in the corporation – in research and development, energy conservation, or environmental planning – is regarded as a cost and weighed against earnings. If internal corporate reward systems are based on short-term gratification they tend to undermine long-term needs for productivity and competitiveness, not to mention environmental rationality.

environmental sensitivity. In the wake of the Exxon-Valdez oil spill, for instance, a group of environmental organizations, the Coalition for Environmentally Responsible Economics (CERES), has had some success in persuading corporations to accept the "Valdez Principles," a statement of long-term corporate commitment to environmental values. The Valdez Principles urge companies to abide by the following code:

1. *Protection of the biosphere.* We will minimize and strive to eliminate the release of any pollutants that may cause environmental damage to the air, water, or earth or its inhabitants. We will safeguard habitats and rivers, lakes, wetlands, coastal zones and oceans, and will minimize contributing to the greenhouse effect, depletion of the ozone layer, acid rain, or smog.

2. *Sustainable use of natural resources.* We will make sustainable use of renewable resources such as water, soils and forests. We will conserve non-renewable natural resources through efficient use and careful planning. We will protect wildlife habitat, open spaces and wilderness while preserving biodiversity.

3. *Reduction and disposal of waste.* We will minimize the creation of waste, especially hazardous waste, and wherever possible recycle materials. We will dispose of all waste through safe and responsible methods.

4. *Wise use of energy.* We will make every effort to use environmentally safe and sustainable energy sources to meet our needs. We will invest in improved energy efficiency and conservation in our operations. We will maximize the energy efficiency of products we produce or sell.

5. *Risk reduction.* We will minimize the environmental, health and safety risks to our employees and the communities in which we operate by employing safe technologies and operating procedures and by being constantly prepared for emergencies.

6. *Marketing of safe products and services.* We will sell products or services that minimize adverse environmental impacts and that are safe as consumers commonly use them. We will inform consumers of the environmental impacts of our products and services.

7. *Damage compensation.* We will take responsibility for any harm we cause to the environment by making every effort to fully restore the environment and to compensate those persons who are adversely effected.

8. *Disclosure.* We will disclose to our employees and to the public incidents relating to our operations that cause environmental harm or pose safety or health hazards. We will disclose potential environmental, health, or safety hazards posed by our operations, and we will not take any action against employees who report any condition that creates a danger to the environment or poses health and safety hazards.

9. *Environmental directors and managers.* At least one member of the Board of Directors will be a person qualified to represent environmental interests. We will commit management resources to implement these Principles, including the funding of the office of Vice-President for Environmental Affairs or an equivalent executive position, reporting directly to the CEO, to monitor and report upon our implementation efforts.

10. *Assessment and annual audit.* We will conduct and make public an annual self-evaluation of our progress in implementing these Principles and in complying with all applicable laws and regulations throughout our worldwide operations. We will work towards the timely creation of independent environmental audit procedures which we will complete annually and make available to the public.

If adopted and implemented by all major corporations, the Valdez Principles could go far toward changing the current linkage between economic productivity and long-term ecological degradation. But is it realistic to think that corporate conscience and consumer awareness will attract sufficient adherence to the Principles to give them practical effect? Charles Hurwitz was reported to have defined his corporate Golden Rule as "He who has the gold, rules."[2]

3. Exploring corporate law remedies. The classic problem presented by the Pacific Lumber story is that there was no obvious feature of corporate law that could resist the logic of the raider who takes aim at a "sitting duck," a debt-free company with long-term environmentally-sensitive management policies, and replaces it with a drastic cut-and-run corporate regime. The standard answer is that as long as shareholders receive a fair price for their shares, corporate law has no complaints. Hurwitz purchased Pacific Lumber's shares at forty dollars, when previously they had been selling, albeit under-valued, for around thirty.

But are there doctrines of corporate law that could have been mobilized to attempt to rectify the Pacific Lumber problem in court actions seeking damages or injunctions? (Statutory efforts had failed in the state legislature.) The Murphy family originally tried unsuccessfully to halt the takeover with a shareholders' derivative suit arguing that the board had failed to exercise due care. But other approaches may deserve exploration.

Here is a brainstorming checklist for analyzing how corporate law might have been employed to take account of the Pacific Lumber problem:

TIMING: Note that there are two different settings for legal action – preventive action before a takeover, and retrospective action afterward. The preventive action is tactically preferable.

REMEDIES TO BE SOUGHT: *Injunctions* – to block a takeover in advance, or, afterward, to reconvey back to the old corporation, refinance, slow down the

2. Los Angeles Times, 10 April 1987. See also Comment, The Valdez Principles: Is What's Good for America Good for General Motors?, 8 Yale L. & Pol'y Rev. 180 (1990).

cutting, replace various corporate directors and officers, etc.; and *Damages*, after the fact, to recapture windfalls, losses of asset values, potential bankruptcy losses, etc.

PLAYERS: *Defendants* – the raiders, investment bankers, directors and officers charged with wrongful conduct; and *Plaintiffs* – minority shareholders, possibly labor representatives, anti-takeover directors and officers.[3]

WRONGFUL ACTS ALLEGED

- *Injury to the environment*: But in corporate lawsuits, judges are not interested in such claims.
- *Injury to the region*: Likewise useless.
- *Injury to the employee work force*: This claim has some slight chance of being heard under a few states' corporate law, as in New York.
- *Violation of duty of due care*: An umbrella minimum standard applying to management practices before and after a takeover. But courts tend to defer to corporate decisions under the "business judgment" rule unless more specific violations are claimed. (Injury *to the corporation itself* is the major premise to be developed in this and subsequent inquiries.)
- *Failure to supervise*: Where directors fail to take account of relevant issues and facts like the rate of cutting, they permit inaccurate asset inventories, etc.
- *Self-dealing*: This gets around the business judgment rule, if officers and director shareholders stand to gain more than others if the takeover goes through.
- *Breach of duty of loyalty*: Where a raider becomes chief executive officer of the captured company and presides over its cut-rate dismemberment, or where management officers go along with a takeover to save their own jobs, especially if the price is alleged to be too low.
- *Duty of intrinsic fairness*: This largely replicates the preceding standard.
- *Fair price*: If the management knows that the takeover price paid per share is an undervaluation, not a fair price, it breaches its duties by acquiescing.
- *Loss of value of going concern*: Although some economic doctrines argue otherwise, the strip-and-sell tactic of junk-bond raiders may result in firesale prices and fail to capture the value of the assembled company as a going concern.
- *Waste of assets*: If an accelerated cutting regime floods the market and depresses prices, the raider's exploitation policy results in a diminished return on corporate assets, the trees.
- *Violation of long-term profit maximization*: This is a key novel claim. Most corporate law decisions ignore the long-term values that environmentalists want to stress, in favor of short-term, quarter-to-quarter profit maximization,

3. Many of the following possible remedies are far easier to apply where the old management opposes the takeover bid, as in internal corporate maneuvers like "poison pills," and "asset lockups" selling prime assets via long-term contracts to a white knight or the employee pension plan.

reflected in maximum current share value. But it can be argued that the long-term values of the company are greater, even discounted into the future, than the short-term raider's price, if the sustained managed harvest over time will maximize the company's market position, given foreseeable market price premiums for prime resources in the future. This is especially so with a timber company where the tree resource assets will grow each year that they aren't cut down. To the extent this is so, current market prices will be undervalued.

- *Loss of corporate personality*: This picks up from the preceding: if a corporation has established a "corporate personality" or "corporate culture" emphasizing long-term profit maximization (and especially if, like Pacific Lumber before and after takeover, it represented that policy to investors) a new theory allows a court to take account of the long-term. The Time-Warner-Paramount litigation, 571 A.2d 1140 (Del. 1989), accepted the directors' right (but not duty) "to follow a course designed to achieve long-term value even at the cost of immediate value maximization." If this is a right of directors, in appropriate cases it may become a duty.
- *Loss of investment quality*: Similar to the preceding, where a stable old blue chip company is turned into a junk-bond volatile issue.
- *Risking bankruptcy*: Where a company is bought out, but is maintained as a separate entity and stripped of assets, bankruptcy may well follow.
- *Rule 10(b)(5) of the Securities and Exchange Act*: This can effect liability for failure to disclose environmental violations to investors if shareholders might suffer under those violations.
- *Other securities law violations*: By studying a takeover's history, it may be possible to show that the raider's stock purchases were done improperly, as by hiding initial purchases in violation of federal disclosure laws, etc.
- *Other violations of duty of care*: There are other potential claims: increasing the likelihood of harmful police power regulation, risking eminent domain condemnation, loss of corporate reputation and good will, dislocating a skilled labor pool with attendant costs, and so on.

Ultimately, it is not clear which of these attempts, if any, would be likely to achieve some corporate law accounting of the Pacific Lumber cut-and-run problem. Given the ecological and economic dangers of corporate behavior, however, the corporate law theatre is worth the effort, as imaginative environmental attorneys attempt to save corporate America and the national economy from tunnel vision.

B. PROPERTY AND CONTRACT LAW IN ENVIRONMENTAL LITIGATION

Strip-mining is a highly emotional modern controversy of the "energy v. environment" variety, and also a classic environmental problem in terms of overview benefit-cost accounting. The market's production method – bulldozing, dynamiting, and shovelling off all soil, vegetation and substrate lying over the coal – tends to externalize and thus ignore the serious costs it imposes on neighboring communities and the environment, unless an adequate statute is passed and enforced, or unless plaintiffs can find a relevant cause of action. In the following section, one of the oldest questions of property and contract law – what exactly was conveyed by the document? – shapes lawsuits that trigger the full array of modern economic and scientific issues raised by strip-mining and its attendant land and water pollution.

Section 1. STRIP MINING AND THE BROAD FORM DEED

Buchanan v. Watson
Kentucky Court of Appeals, 1956
290 S.W.2d 40

In this declaratory judgment action, two questions are presented: May the owner of minerals underlying a tract of land remove coal therefrom by a strip mining process which results in the destruction of the surface by another? If so, is the owner of the coal liable for damages to the surface owner for such surface rights as may be destroyed? The Chancellor decided both questions in the affirmative. He held that the coal could be strip mined but damages must be paid for the destruction of the surface owner's interest in the surface and the timber thereon. Both parties appeal.

The meaning and effect of a mineral deed dated May 19, 1903, from Miles Cole and wife to John C.C. Mayo, covering 129.47 acres of land in Magoffin County, are involved. Appellant has the exclusive right to mine the coal under this land by virtue of a lease from Elkhorn Coal Corporation, successor in title to Mayo. Appellees purchased 20 acres of the surface of this boundary by deed dated June 19, 1943, for a recited consideration of $75. About 1.5 acres of coal lie around the top of a mountain and within the 20-acre tract.

The Cole deed, severing the minerals, granted and conveyed "property, rights and privileges, in, of, to, on, under, concerning and appurtenant.... All the coal, minerals and mineral products...such of the standing timber as may be, or by the Grantee, his heirs or representatives, its successors, or assigns, be deemed necessary for mining purposes...use and operate the same and surface thereof...in any and every manner that may be deemed necessary or convenient for mining, and therefrom removing...and in the use of said land and surface thereof by the Grantee, his heirs or representatives, successors and assigns, shall be free from, and is, and are, hereby released from liability or claim of damage to the said Grantor, their representatives, heirs and assigns.... There is reserved to the Grantor all the timber upon the said land, except that necessary for mining, and the purpose hereinbefore mentioned, and the free use of land for agricultural purposes, so far as such use is consistent with the property, rights and privileges hereby bargained, sold, granted or conveyed, and the right to mine and use coal for Grantor's own personal household and domestic purposes."

Thus, the deed created two separate and distinct estates in the land under which, insofar as the 20 acres are concerned, appellant and appellees now claim.

The Chancellor found that the only feasible and economical way to mine the coal in question was by the strip and auger method of mining. He further found that such operation would result in the destruction of the timber and the surface above and adjacent to the coal.

Appellant contends that since all of the coal was conveyed it may be mined by any method, and the appellees' surface rights are subordinate to the rights of the appellant. Appellees contend that it was not contemplated that a mining process would be used which would destroy the surface and timber of a substantial area and the surface rights may not be violated in such manner.

This question has been considered in other states with conflicting conclusions. [citations omitted]. In the foregoing cases, an attempt was made to determine what the parties intended with respect to the method of removal of the coal. In the present case, the Chancellor found from a reading of the deed that the parties thereto had not contemplated the strip and auger method of mining nor did they contemplate that any portion of the surface of the land would be destroyed or rendered valueless for agricultural purposes or growing timber. The deed by express language did not exclude or include this method of mining, although the proof shows that such mining methods were known and had been used prior to the date of the deed. It seems clear that the parties intended the conveyance of the coal. To deny the right to remove it by the only feasible method is to defeat the principal purpose of the deed....

Having decided that appellant is entitled to "strip mine" the coal, when is he liable to the surface owner for damage for destruction of the surface or the growing timber thereon?

Two fundamental rules for construction of deeds are set forth in McIntire v. Marian Coal Co., 227 S.W. 298, 299. They are: "that a deed which grants land and certain specific rights and privileges, there being no ambiguity in the instrument, will be construed according to its terms, and enforced strictly according to its terms. But, where there is ambiguity or uncertainty in the deed, it will be construed most strongly against the grantor and in favor of the grantee," and "that the instrument shall be construed most strongly against the grantors and in favor of the grantee both upon the grant of the property and the rights and privileges specified...."

The deed in this case conveyed virtually all rights necessary to carry out the mining of the coal, including a waiver of damages. The reservations of timber and agricultural use in favor of the grantor were to be exercised only insofar as such uses were consistent with the rights conveyed to the grantee. It was obvious that the estate reserved to the grantor was to be subservient to the dominant estate of the grantee. The paramount purpose of the conveyance was to enable the grantee, or his successor in title, to remove the coal from under the surface of this land. The value of the land lay under the surface, not on it.

The rights of the respective owner of the surface and of the minerals underneath in similar deeds have been determined and declared. The owner of the mineral has the paramount right to the use of the surface in the prosecution of its business for any purpose of necessity or convenience, unless this power is exercised oppressively, arbitrarily, wantonly, or maliciously, in which event the surface owner may recover for damages so occasioned....

The rule has become so firmly established that it is a rule of property law governing the rights under many mineral deeds covering much acreage in Eastern Kentucky. To disturb this rule now would create great confusion and much hardship in a segment of an industry that can ill-afford such a blow. It is especially desirable that the law of property rights should remain stable after it has been settled. The doctrine of stare decisis requires that we do not depart from the established rule.

ZBP

A stripmine in the Cumberland Mountains near the Kentucky-Tennessee border. Note the results of the primitive blast and scrape method, and its consequences in erosion, mudslides, and disruption of natural water flows. Photograph is taken from the unstable edge of an excavated seam higher up on the mountain. When trees start to lean, it means that the surface of the mountain is beginning to "creep" or slide. Mines on the mountains in the distance extract coal from the same horizontal seams.

Martin v. Kentucky Oak Mining Co.
Kentucky Court of Appeals, 1968
429 S.W.2d 395

[The majority of the court followed *Buchanan, supra.*]

HILL, J., dissenting.

I dissent from the majority opinion.... Strip mining was neither heard of nor dreamed of in 1905 in Knott County, the locality of the coal land in question. There was no railroad in Knott County until long thereafter. Neither was there a navigable stream in that County. About the only coal mined in those days was from the out-croppings in creek beds, where a small quantity was obtained by the use of a new-found tool – the coal pick....

I concede that prior to the decision in Buchanan v. Watson, there was a long line of cases by this court holding that the grantees under similar "broad form" deeds had a right to use the surface for any purpose "deemed necessary or convenient" by the grantee. However, all those cases prior to *Buchanan* involved deep-mining methods, which was the method of mining contemplated by the parties in 1905. But *Buchanan* really got out in left field when it ignored and disregarded all the rights of the surface owner. This court on many occasions recognized that the surface owner had at least some semblance of right when it held that the owner of the coal must leave pillars of coal to support the surface.... This court decided in Wiser Oil Co. v. Conley, 346 S.W.2d 718 (1970), that "even though...the water-flooding process was known prior to...the date of execution of the lease, and was employed to some extent...we concluded that it was the intention of the parties that oil should be produced by drilling in the customary manner that prevailed when the lease was executed." *Wiser* and *Buchanan* are as inconsistent as sin and salvation.

I am shocked and appalled that the court of last resort in the beautiful state of Kentucky would ignore the logic and reasoning of the great majority of other states and lend its approval and encouragement to the diabolical devastation and destruction of a large part of the surface of this fair state without compensation to the owners thereof.

COMMENTARY AND QUESTIONS

1. Stripmining and stripmine regulation. In the Appalachians, coal veins typically lie horizontally in multiple layers beneath the hills. Can you visualize the effects of *Buchanan*'s "strip and auger" method? Soil and rock were being bulldozed off each successive layer of coal, pushing debris over the side of the hill. When the walls of rock over the coal became too high, the stripminers bored multiple huge parallel auger holes into the heart of the mountain, draining its groundwater and destabilizing the remaining rock. The air and water pollution consequences of stripmining can be severe, coupled with disruption of land and downhill watercourses.

Both state and federal governments have passed stripmining controls. At the state level, many regulatory systems have been dominated by the industry. At the federal level, regulation under the Surface Mining Control and Reclamation Act (SMCRA)[4] has had a similarly checkered history, being almost completely diluted during the

4. The attorney for appellants in *Martin* was the late Harry Caudill, who wrote Night Comes to the Cumberlands (1963) and three other anguishing chronicles of Appalachia and stripmining.

Reagan years under Interior Secretary James Watt. To many non-Kentucky environmental lawyers, at least, common law remedies often appear to be more fruitful than public law.[5]

2. The court's deed interpretation. When the *Buchanan* court applies the canon of interpretation against the grantor of a deed, does it justifiably ignore the fact that most broadform deeds were prepared by grantees, and that many grantors signed with an "X"? To what extent can you make arguments beyond the question of exactly what the intention of the parties to the broadform deed had been? Is there an argument that the subdivision of a parcel of land into two separate estates, surface and subsurface, necessarily implies that a party who owns just one estate cannot destroy the existence of the other? What do you make of the fact that many original subsurface deeds were purchased for $3.00 an acre, which was often more than the full assessed value of a full fee simple?

Section 2. PRIVATE AGREEMENTS AND WARRANTIES

The stripmining cases demonstrate an area of environmental law that is not based on theories of fault, but rather on the legal consequences of private parties' express and implied agreements. In some situations it may be practically or politically far more feasible to use such bases for assigning legal rights and duties than to turn to tort and its analogs. Theories based on private agreement draw legal rights and duties from individual consensual choice, in a doctrinal area accustomed to adapting to changing circumstances. Private contract and property law offer an extended range of mechanisms and remedies that can be useful in implementing environmental objectives.

Privately-created land use restrictions are a prime case in point. A deed much like the following was prepared for a beautiful 1000 acre parcel of beach, dunes, wetlands, tidal rivers, and a coastal headland in Maine, owned by a family that was coming under increasing tax pressure to subdivide and develop the property.

Indenture

(1) KNOW ALL MEN BY THESE PRESENTS that X, Y, and Z of Little Neck in the County of Bath, State of Maine, parties of the first part, in consideration of one dollar and other good and valuable consideration paid by Ocean College, Kennebunkport, Maine, party of the second part, receipt of which is hereby acknowledged,

(2) DO HEREBY give, grant, bargain, sell, and convey unto the said party of the second part a certain parcel of land comprising one thousand twenty two acres, more or less, situated at Little Neck, Maine, and bounded as follows: Beginning at iron peg at top of bluff on east side of Cranberry Creek, North one hundred rods, [etc.]...

(3) ALONG WITH the covenants, conditions, easements, and other liabilities and interests thereto attached or created by this document, including the provisions of

5. In 1974 the Kentucky legislature actually passed a statute requiring stripmining consent by all who owned any interest in land, but the high court quickly declared it an unconstitutional taking. DNR v. No. 8 Limited, 528 S.W.2d 684 (Ky. 1975).

a conveyance executed this day between parties of the first part and The Nature Conservancy, Inc., a New York Corporation.

(4) TO HAVE AND TO HOLD the granted premises, with all privileges, liabilities, and appurtenances, to the said Ocean College, its heirs and assigns, to their own use and behoof forever, IN FEE SIMPLE, BUT IF the land is ever used for purposes other than conservation management, academic research, or college-based public service, the Maine Coast Heritage Trust shall have the right to take possession in fee simple absolute.

(5) [Here follow extensive ecologically crafted restrictive covenants – agreements that natural dune formations will never be altered, that a warden will be employed full-time to supervise the preserve, that no non-native flora or fauna will be brought onto the property, and the like – and restricted easements of access....]

[A conveyance executed the same day conveyed the development rights via an open space easement to The Nature Conservancy, Inc., a preservationist charity.]

COMMENTARY AND QUESTIONS

1. The conservation restrictions' multiple intents. What was the economic intent of this conveyance and attached instruments? To what extent will it achieve environmental goals? The family retained several private inholdings within the granted parcel, with easements to continue to use the whole for recreation. The combination of ecological altruism and tax planning can be a potent incentive for preservation. Does the restriction on public access that goes along with this deed detract from its usefulness, or protect it?

2. The broad reach of private land controls. Private land controls can incorporate whatever terms and values the private parties want, far beyond the range of governmental regulations. Until 1948 they could even apply racial land restrictions. Today private land controls can dictate the color of buildings, the kinds of trees to be planted, the total non-development of some developable areas, and so on. In addition, private land controls are likely to remain attached to the deeded lands forever. Is there a rational basis upon which to distinguish desirable private land use planning from capricious restraints on future use of scarce resource?

3. Prescriptive easements. In many states you can acquire an "easement by prescription" by using land without permission for a statutory term (often 5 to 10 years). This resembles "squatters' rights" in adverse possession of land. A "right to dump" can be an easement, so some polluters have claimed an "easement to pollute" particular streams into which they have discharged waste over the years, thus claiming immunity from private nuisance suits. In the absence of a statute, how could private plaintiffs overcome the polluters' "rights"? It may be useful to note that the "right to dump" prescriptive easements are strictly defined in terms of the quantity and quality of discharges that were established over the term. Is it also relevant that squatters' rights are generally not recognized where they are in competition with *public* rights? See Anneberg v. Kurtz, 28 S.E.2d 769, 773 (Ga. 1944).

4. Equitable restrictions. On Shady Mountain in Tennessee, a land developer from Chattanooga had sold ten lots to families who moved in and, pursuant to covenants in their deeds, built single-family homes. Thereafter she stopped sales for a while, and later leased lots #11-18 to a coal strip-mining company which had just moved onto the land and was ready to bulldoze and blast. The government control agencies, as usual, had no interest in restricting the strip-mining. Some activist law students stopped the strip-mine operation for the families by a property law action based on a negative reciprocal covenant (sometimes confusingly called an "equitable servitude"). When a seller subdivides lots and begins to sell them with a similar or uniform set of restrictions, there is an enforceable implied equitable promise that *all* lots will similarly be held to the earlier restrictions.

5. Toxic breach of implied warranty of title. What happens if a buyer discovers toxic contaminants on the land between the day the contract to purchase was made and the date set for the transfer of title? The law creates an implied warranty that sellers will provide good marketable title at the closing. Will the mere presence of toxics on the land create a "cloud on the title" allowing purchasers to rescind contracts based upon violation of the warranty? The consequences of such a rule would be drastic. Because it would threaten marketability of any affected parcel, it would practically compel environmental assessment audits of all major land purchases. It is not yet clear how pollution per se affects the implied warranty of marketable title (unless the government has slapped a lien on the title). Should buyers be able to rescind in such cases? Note that, having notice, they probably could not claim the "innocent landowner" exception from Superfund liability. (In practice, most residential cases contracts are made contingent on buyers obtaining financing, so all the buyer has to do in such cases is tell the bank about the chemicals and her financing will be withdrawn, triggering the contract release clause.)

6. Breach of warranty – products liability. The Uniform Commercial Code's §2314, the implied warranty of merchantability warranting that products are fit for ordinary use, also has a potential use in environmental cases. Using warranty theories, as distinct from strict tort liability defective products cases, plaintiffs have sought remedies for formaldehyde insulation pollution inside mobile homes, for radiation effects from products using radium, for the deleterious effects of cigarettes, and for other environmental situations, with varying results. Brummett v. Skyline Corp., No. C-81-0103-L(B), slip opinion (W.D. Ky. June 3, 1985) (formaldehyde); Allen v. U.S. Radium Corp., No. L-013851-84, slip opinion (N.J. Super. 1984) (radium radiation); Cipollone v. Liggett Group, Inc., 893 F.2d 541 (3d Cir. 1990), cert. granted 111 St. Ct. 1386 (1991) (cigarettes, action based on claim of express warranty); Wingo v. Celotex Corp., et al., 834 F.2d 375 (4th Cir. 1987) (asbestos). In other cases, express warranty claims are possible where manufacturers have incorrectly alleged that products are safe or environmentally benign. Contract-based warranty actions, with their opportunity for consequential damages under UCC §2714, may in some cases offer advantages over tort theories that are worth exploring.

7. Environmental breach of federal contract. Most government-supply contracts made by corporations – and these run into the billions of dollars each year – contain a standard clause agreeing that suppliers will comply with all relevant statutes and regulations, including environmental protection laws. When a supplier is discovered in violation of such laws, there are potential remedies for breach of contract and misrepresentation. These remedies gain special impetus from the fact that citizens are granted standing under the Federal False Claims Act, 31 U.S.C.A. §3729, to bring such actions even if the official parties aren't interested in doing so; treble damages are available, with a 25% bounty thereof payable to the individual plaintiffs. Does this bear further investigation?

8. Other horizons for environmental law. There are undoubtedly dozens of other situations in which environmental issues can be raised using statutory or nonstatutory legal doctrines drawn from areas of modern practice that have rarely or never before been so applied – from labor law, tax, equity, antitrust, public utilities, consumer protection, banking, admiralty, and so on, as well as corporate law, property, and contract. In Chapter 8, for example, the use of trust law – applied by analogy through the environmental public trust doctrine – provides the basis for one of the most significant developments in modern environmental law.

The point is, environmental law is where you find it.

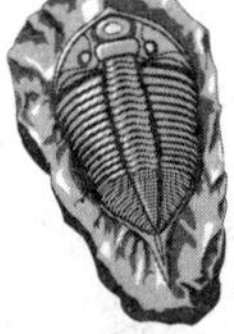

They were careless people...they smashed up things and creatures and then retreated back into their money or their vast carelessness...and let other people clean up the mess they had made....

— F. Scott Fitzgerald
The Great Gatsby (1925)

PART THREE

FROM COMMON LAW TO PUBLIC LAW: THE STRUCTURE AND POWER OF GOVERNMENT

The range, potency, and policy ramifications of environmental tort cases explored in Part Two provide a testimonial to the creative power of the American common law system. This Part Three, however, explores the expanding realm of governmental regulation that has arisen to supplement and occasionally replace the common law.

Common law is able to adapt and provide effective remedies for many victims who suffer injuries caused in ways that were almost unimaginable at the time the underlying legal doctrines were given their basic content. Conversely, however, the common law alone, even when supplemented by imaginative use of other bodies of law, is often not capable of handling larger problems of environmental degradation. Common law remedies may be too limited in character: they neither provide redress for widespread public harms, nor do they provide a mechanism that allows for insightful anticipatory intervention that would avert the harmful consequences of environmentally unsound practices. Stated differently, tort judgments for damages, and even injunctions, are generally private remedies for past wrongs. The remedies are limited to those whose interests are represented in court, and many would-be plaintiffs are deterred from making that effort by the difficulty and expense of legal action. In that way tort law remedies fail to compensate and assist all victims of pollution and other environmental harms, and the law governing environmental tort cases is reactive rather than protective.

Unlike governmental regulation, the usual posture of tort law cases, despite exceptions like *Wilsonville* at page 68 *supra*, is to act after environmental harm has occurred. Tort judgments indirectly may function proactively and on a general level, but only insofar as they deter others from engaging in the kind of conduct that gave rise to liability, or can support specific injunctions against further pollution. Finally, tort remedies seldom consider and address the full range of adverse ecosystem impacts. Most natural resource impacts are not the subject of recoveries, and the cumulative nature of the effects of many lesser polluting facilities are rarely aggregated and considered. Perhaps most important, many courts still view injunctions halting or altering polluting behavior as exceptions rather than the rule.

The limitations of tort law in addressing the widespread public harms caused by pollution and other environmentally degrading activity provide a backdrop for introducing the role of "public law" in securing broader environmental protection. Public environmental law is active; it features the government working affirmatively to protect and improve environmental quality. The materials introduced here operate in general at a broader level than that of resolving specific disputes. Statutes of general application, administrative regulations, criminal law, constitutions, and natural law theories of rights all fall in the realm of public law.

The chapters of this Part Three also look at structural relations between the national and state governments in matters of environmental regulation, and consider the special protections that the Constitution gives to private property. Part Four of this coursebook will provide more intensive studies of statutes, agency regulations, and the administrative process.

Chapter 6

THE INTERPLAY OF COMMON LAW AND STATUTES

This chapter introduces statutory efforts to address environmental problems. Here statutes are studied as public law mechanisms that are built on common law foundations and become part of a larger legal process.

The chapter opens by highlighting the breadth and variety of environmental statutes. This is done in subpart A by a brief survey of the numerous environmental statutes that might have been applied to the events surrounding the release of Kepone into the James River, studied earlier at pages 42 and 160. The principal goal here is to acquaint you with the broad range of public law statutes.

The next portion of the chapter, subpart B, explores the difference in origin and scope between statutes and the common law and the similarities of statutes and common law when it comes to deciding specific cases and making successive applications of law to a series of cases. Small portions of the two major federal laws most directly regulating hazardous wastes are used as examples.[1] The substantive interpretation of these statutes, and of most statutes, is strongly influenced by the common law. The interpretation given to these two statutes begins with the application of general principles – the so-called canons of construction – and thereafter proceeds on an incremental basis as additional cases are presented for decision.

The remaining subpart of the chapter examines complementary topics that help define the relationship between statutes and other remedies for environmental harms. These are (1) the extent to which the enactment of public law regulatory statutes creates and supports additional private remedies for environmental harms, (2) the extent to which the common law is limited by statutes promulgated in the same field, and (3) an examination of the short happy life of federal public law in the pollution field, which was largely eliminated by the Supreme Court based upon the passage of protective statutes. These are important questions. Who should make environmental law, legislatures, judges, or both? As a matter of democratic theory, the generally preferred institution for lawmaking is the popularly elected legislature. In the environmental field, despite the potential reach of legislative supremacy, legislatures have usually not been eager to displace the working of the common law. Most legislation has sought to supplement or clarify pre-existing common law norms. But that is not always the case.

---

1. These are the Resource Recovery and Conservation Act (RCRA), 42 U.S.C.A. §§6901-6992k and the Comprehensive Environmental Response, Compensation and Liability Act (CERCLA)(also known as "Superfund"), 42 U.S.C.A. §§9601–9675.

In reading this chapter, there are a few areas of comparison between common law and statutes that you should keep in mind. First and most obviously, statutes are products of the political and legislative process, and therefore have a greater claim of legitimacy in the policymaking area than does common law framed by courts adjudicating specific cases. Second, the "public interest" element is often not an overt feature of common law cases. In effect, the focus in common law cases is on doing justice in individual cases rather than protecting the larger public interest. That, you will remember, was the express position of the *Boomer* majority. Courts deciding cases under statutory provisions may be far more willing to interject public interest elements into their decisions. Third, there will inevitably be instances in which the legislative branch enacts laws that fail to answer all the difficult questions that arise in a regulated area, and courts will often be forced to resolve those issues when appropriate cases are presented for decision. Similarly, even the most artfully drafted statute will usually leave some minor uncertainties requiring resolution through the process of statutory interpretation.

A. A STATUTORY MOSAIC AND A THIRD LOOK AT THE KEPONE CASE

The chemical poisoning of the James River by Kepone discharges was considered at length in Chapter 2 as an example of antisocial, but economically rational, behavior that relied on externalizing the cost of controlling the release of hazardous chemical wastes. Pruitt v. Allied Chemical in Chapter 3 returned to the Kepone debacle in considering common law compensation for remote victims of a tort. The failure of the market system to protect the commons, and the failure of the common law fully to remediate injuries to persons dependent on the commons, both demonstrate that effective environmental protection requires a far greater arsenal of legal control mechanisms than the common law alone.

Governmental regulation at the national, state, and local levels typically complements the legal system's common law remedies. The most significant development in modern environmental law in the second half of the twentieth century has been the growth in environmental statutes that take on the anticipatory, proactive regulatory function that the common law does not. The Kepone case is a good vehicle for introducing the broad array of regulatory statutes that might have been applied to the activities of Allied and LSP. The Kepone incident occurred despite a large number of available public law statutes and regulations, making it an unfortunate, but not uncommon, case of regulatory failure. It is helpful, nevertheless, to review the disparate and varied tangle of environmental laws potentially applicable to environmentally harmful activity.

The list of statutes that follows is not meant to be exhaustive and the descriptions of their operative provisions are quite general. They do, however, show the range of activities subject to environmental regulation. There is, from a lawyer's perspective, a special value to going through this list. Put yourself in the role of an attorney whose clients have learned of the Kepone releases and want them controlled. If a simple phone call or letter of complaint to the regulatory authorities does not seem likely to obtain the desired results, one must lay out all the possible lines of legal argument and evaluate their potential for achieving desired results. The common law theories studied previously in Chapter 3 must be on that list. They should be joined there by a long list of potential statutory and regulatory avenues for controlling offending behavior. While the emphasis here is on federal statutes, it is important to note that state and local laws normally require even more permits than the federal government. Many federal statutes have direct state equivalents, and some issues are regulated only by state and local police power systems. The scope of the following survey is intended to emphasize that every legal analysis of an environmental problem should begin by thinking broadly and imaginatively.

1. THE OCCUPATIONAL SAFETY AND HEALTH ACT[2] (OSHA)

Administered by the Occupational Health and Safety Administration, OSHA addresses environmental conditions within the work place. The agency sets general industry standards, and a wide range of specific health and safety standards, focusing on working conditions. In the Allied/Kepone setting, OSHA standards would involve safety of physical structures, ladders, gangways, mixing vats, and so forth, but also more relevantly a variety of exposure standards related to the handling of toxic materials and harmful physical agents including hazardous wastes. Air quality within the plant is subject to OSHA standards set in general terms or with reference to the particular materials being used. OSHA also requires certain chemicals to be labeled with warnings, so that workers have notice of the hazardous materials they are handling. OSHA is enforced through inspection by federal agents who make random inspections or who respond to clandestine complaints by workers. The agency has drawn criticism from both sides – from labor representatives who feel that it's a paper tiger with soft or unenforced standards, and employers who treat it as a meddling and less-than-completely-competent regulatory agency. In a number of situations OSHA's standards, however weak, have been held to have a preemptive effect upon more stringent state standards. In the Allied/Kepone setting, however, that had never been a problem given the rather low level of Virginia's state safety enforcement. OSHA's enforcement efforts often seem to fall short. Many cases involving environmental injuries to workers note that OSHA had failed to detect flagrant toxic problems in its inspections, or had totally failed to make inspections in the first place.

2. THE CLEAN AIR ACT (CAA)[3]

In the process of producing chemicals, Allied Chemical, like most modern factories, produces a variety of air pollution emissions that are regulated under the provisions of the federal Clean Air Act. At the time of the Kepone controversy, emissions that would have been regulated by the CAA would probably have been limited to the usual smoke and fumes produced in industrial boilers and power generation facilities. Normal emissions from power generation, including sulphur

2. 29 U.S.C.A. §651 et seq. (1970).

3. 42 U.S.C.A. §7401 et seq. (1970).

oxides, hydrocarbons, nitrogen oxides, and the like, are subject to a joint federal-state control mechanism under §§108, 109, and 110. The federal government requires each state government to draw up and enforce a "state implementation plan" (SIP), which assigns permitted levels of emissions for all air pollution sources in the state, calculated so as to reduce the overall ambient level of those pollutants in the locality down to the basic federal "primary standard" for each pollutant. In negotiation with the federal Environmental Protection Agency (EPA), the state of Virginia had set out a series of models and permit requirements for all industrial facilities in the state, including Allied, at levels that the state calculated would be sufficient to achieve the federally required ambient air quality levels.

Apart from its general regulation of conventional air pollutants, the CAA also requires EPA to regulate hazardous air pollutants. The levels of airborne pollutants in the Kepone production area were so high that they might be expected to be subject to regulation under §112 of the CAA which called for national emission standards for hazardous air pollutants (NESHAPs). Unfortunately, that was not the case. First, the focus of the CAA was on emissions to the external ambient air, not conditions within a plant. Although on some days it was reported that external venting of Kepone dust hindered visibility on the neighboring street, most attention focused on air quality within the workplace. Second and more fundamentally, §112, despite its promise, was not fully implemented by EPA, so that only a few hazardous substances had been regulated with particularity, and those regulated would not have included the airborne carcinogens involved at LSP.

3. THE REFUSE ACT/RIVERS AND HARBORS APPROPRIATIONS ACT OF 1899[4]

The Rivers and Harbors Appropriations Act of 1899 gave the United States Army Corps of Engineers a wide ranging jurisdiction over various alterations of navigable waters. Initially, these sections were used mainly to control piers and wharves and dredge and fill operations. Thus, if Allied Chemical wished to dike the banks of Gravelly Run, the small stream behind the Semi-Works, or dredge new channels for water discharge, it might require a special Corps of Engineers permit. Far more important, a subsection of the Rivers and Harbors Act known as the "Refuse Act" (33 U.S.C.A. §407), however, prohibited the discharge of "refuse matter of any kind or description whatsoever" into navigable waters, or other waters of the United States that fed into navigable waters, without a permit from the U.S. Army Corps of Engineers. Eventually, this authority was construed to include a power to prohibit or permit pollution discharges into the navigable waters of the United States. The criminal sanctions of the Refuse Act made it potentially the nation's strongest federal environmental statute, at least through the first 60 years of the 20th century. During most of this time, however, the statute was virtually unenforced against water pollution because it was justifiably thought that Congress had intended it to apply only to structural obstacles to navigation. In the late 1960s, however, the Refuse Act was rediscovered by environmentalists and it was put into active use as an enforcement tool.

4. Pub.L. 97–322, now codified, as amended, at 33 U.S.C.A. §§401 et seq.

Allied Chemical had never requested a Refuse Act permit for its discharges into Gravelly Run. It was thus vulnerable in the early 1970s to criminal prosecution and the threat of major criminal fines or imprisonment of its corporate officers. That its company's lawyers took the statute seriously is evidenced by the fact that LSP went to great lengths to connect into the Hopewell municipal treatment plant, almost certainly in an effort to take advantage of the Refuse Act's exemption for liquid pollutants flowing into navigable waters from streets and sewers.

4. THE CLEAN WATER ACT (CWA)

In 1972, as noted in the Goldfarb narrative, Allied Chemical had to respond to a newly strengthened piece of federal water pollution control legislation, the 1972 Federal Water Pollution Control Act Amendments (FWPCA).[5] That statute put teeth into the federal government's water pollution regulatory statutes, which previously had been hortatory but non-mandatory. FWPCA, which in 1977 was retitled the Clean Water Act (CWA), was a composite affair, combining new amendments with the provisions of other federal statutes, including the Refuse Act and the Water Quality Improvement Act of 1970.

The goal of the CWA is "to restore and maintain the chemical, physical, and biological integrity of the nation's waters." It also, like the CAA, is a federal-state partnership. Under the terms of the statute, states are invited to take on the powers and responsibilities of the federal statute including administration of the National Pollutant Discharge Elimination System (NPDES). Many states, however, decided that they did not want to take on those powers and duties; Virginia, prior to 1975, had not become an NPDES-certified state system. This left two completely different water control systems applicable to factories in such states – the NPDES federal permit system administered by the regional office of the federal EPA and the pre-existing state regulatory system.

Under §301 of the CWA, the EPA publishes effluent standard regulations for many industrial classes and categories, requiring them to employ the best available technology (BAT) determined to be achievable for treating each industrial effluent. These pollution standards are to be applied to every "point source" in the nation. NPDES permits are thus required for most pipes, ditches, channels, tunnels, conduits, fissures, or other discernable, discrete conveyances of liquid waste. Allied had the legal responsibility to report each drainpipe or outfall in its operation, along with its contents, and to hold its pollutant levels to the standards set by the EPA. This typically was difficult and expensive. Allied apparently never moved to report its Kepone water pollution under FWPCA. Thus, despite a statute of obvious applicability to the Kepone case, the situation managed to evade regulation until long after the catastrophic harm was done.

Section 307 of the CWA, as it stood during much of the relevant period, authorized EPA to issue special standards in the case of particular toxic pollutants. Toxic pollution standards under §307 were to be set "at that level which the EPA administrator determines provides an ample margin of safety" without reference to

5. 33 U.S.C.A. §1251 et seq.

technical or economic feasibility, a high standard indeed. In some cases variances were available, if a company established that it was meeting "best available technology" standards with no harm to water quality. Although EPA had the authority to shut down factories that failed to comply with these standards, and Congress had declared a strong national goal of "fishable, swimmable waters by 1985," the CWA, especially in regard to toxic pollutants, was not enforced in such a draconian manner. Needless to say, LSP and Allied were not controlled in regard to their Kepone discharges.

5. THE FEDERAL INSECTICIDE, FUNGICIDE, AND RODENTICIDE ACT (FIFRA)[6]

FIFRA requires any person distributing, selling, offering, or receiving any pesticide to register the poison with the EPA. The federal government is required to grant registration for a pesticide once it determines that (1) the pesticide is effective as claimed, (2) the labelling and other data supplied by the manufacturer conform to federal standards, and (3) the poison will perform its functions without "unreasonable risks to humans and the environment, taking into account the economic, social, and environmental costs and benefits of the pesticide's intended use" and that the pesticide will not cause "unreasonable risk" when applied in accordance with the directions for its use. Some registrations can be granted that restrict a pesticide's use to professional applicators, where the application of the material in question is particularly dangerous. All registrations must also be followed, under FIFRA, by establishing official "tolerance levels" that set the maximum permissible exposure for each chemical. Registrations, once granted with practicable tolerance levels, are akin to perpetual licenses to market the product. Registrations can be cancelled or suspended, but in those cases the statute, until very recently, required that the government compensate the manufacturer for all existing supplies of materials that could no longer be marketed.

FIFRA, of course, applied to many of Allied's operations and to the production of Kepone in particular. For many years, FIFRA was administered by the United States Department of Agriculture. During that era, the scrutiny given to registration petitions was much weaker. Kepone was registered in 1957; it was cancelled in 1977. (Because Allied never succeeded in getting the federal government to establish tolerance levels for Kepone, however, the pesticide was only sold overseas and never used legally in the United States.) Had Allied or LSP been in violation of FIFRA due to manufacturing, marketing, and distributing its Kepone without valid registration for it, a number of remedies would have been available under FIFRA. These would have included possible confiscation of the product and the materials to be used for its continued manufacture. Once illegal conduct was discovered, those remedies would effectively force the cessation of pollution by effectively banning production. More importantly, if Kepone had been refused FIFRA registration, its

6. 7 U.S.C.A. §§136–136y. FIFRA has undergone numerous amendments since its initial passage in 1947. For a time, beginning in 1972, it was subsumed within an umbrella statute entitled the Federal Environmental Pesticide Control Act (FEPCA), but by later amendment FIFRA was restored as the statute's name.

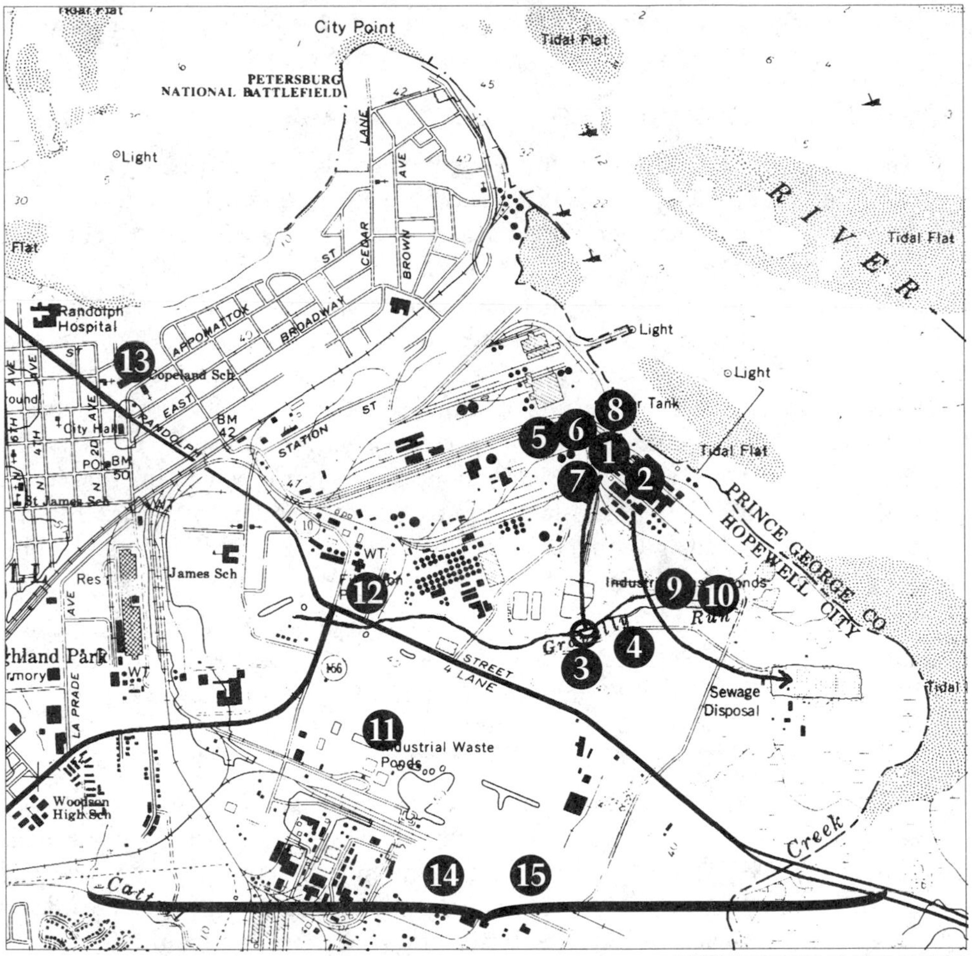

BASED ON USGS MAP NO. 37077-C3-TF-O24

A SCHEMATIC STATUTORY MOSAIC

A hypothetical montage of state and federal environmental programs that might apply in a chemical production setting like the Allied Chemical Kepone case (see pages 42–48 supra*)(an equivalent array would apply to the Life Sciences plant's production).*

1. State and federal workplace statutes, OSHA
2. State and federal air statutes, CAA
3. Federal Refuse Act
4. Federal water statutes, CWA
5. Federal pesticide product registration statute, FIFRA
6. Federal toxics substances act, ToSCA
7. State and federal hazardous materials transport controls
8. Federal Hazardous Substances Act
9. State and federal solid waste disposal statutes, SWDA
10. Federal solid waste statute, RCRA
11. State and federal cleanup statutes, CERCLA (Superfund)
12. State and federal drinking water controls, SDWA
13. State and federal notification statutes, EPCRA
14. State and federal comprehensive envt'l review statutes, NEPA
15. Other applicable local, state, and federal regulatory programs

sale would have been virtually impossible, so its production in more than experimental quantities would not have occurred in the first place.

6. THE TOXIC SUBSTANCES CONTROL ACT (ToSCA)[7]

ToSCA is directed to the chemical manufacturing industry. It has several features. First and foremost it is designed to insure testing by manufacturers to identify hazards to human health and the environment associated with chemical substances before they are permitted to be manufactured and sold. (For this reason ToSCA can be categorized as a "market access" regulatory system.) Testing and disclosure of test results to the government are required whenever EPA publishes a test rule requirement. The statute operates somewhat like a permit system in that EPA can act upon adverse test results to forbid or limit the uses made of a chemical substance. In this way, failure of EPA to act to restrict use of a substance acts like a grant of a permit, and a ban on use functions like a permit denial. In other major sections ToSCA attempts to regulate responses to PCB and asbestos hazards and establishes national goals for indoor radon abatement, while offering states technical and other assistance.

ToSCA would not have applied to Kepone production at LSP. First, §2602(2)(B)(ii) excludes substances regulated under FIFRA. Second, ToSCA only became effective in 1976, after production of Kepone at LSP had ceased.

7. THE HAZARDOUS MATERIALS TRANSPORTATION ACT

The Hazardous Materials Transportation Act,[8] provides for extensive regulation of hazardous substances in transit by the United States Department of Transportation. There are requirements for spill control and prevention, and for central reporting in the event of spills of toxic or hazardous substances. The statute invites state regulation consistent with the terms of the Act. States may impose higher restrictions, so long as they do not unreasonably burden interstate commerce. Virginia had not accepted that invitation, so transport of pesticides and other economic poisons produced by Allied's Hopewell Semi-Works and LSP were essentially under federal control. The federal regulation in place at the relevant time involved labelling and vehicle equipment requirements that would have had no impact on Allied and LSP.

8. THE FEDERAL HAZARDOUS SUBSTANCE ACT

Under the Federal Hazardous Substance Act[9], a broad concurrent jurisdiction over toxins, hazardous substances, corrosives, irritants, and other similar chemical substances is granted to the Consumer Product Safety Commission (CPSC). The CPSC issues regulations for the introduction of such products into interstate commerce; heavy penalties including both fines and imprisonment are theoretically available for breach of the statute or regulations. Corporate defendants may be

7. 15 U.S.C.A. §§2601–2671.
8. 49 U.S.C.A. §§1801–1812.
9. 15 U.S.C.A. §1261 (1960).

liable for introducing hazardous substances into commerce regardless of their knowledge or motivations. Kepone, however, is not a consumer product within the definition of this law, so none of the Act's provisions would apply to Allied or LSP.

9. THE SOLID WASTE DISPOSAL ACT OF 1965 (SWDA)[10] AND THE RESOURCE RECOVERY ACT OF 1970 (RRA)[11]

These federal statutes were the first steps in a series of federal initiatives that have been taken in the management of solid waste. From 1965 to 1970 under the SWDA, the law recognized the existence of a major environmental problem that the legislation itself deemed "a rising tide of scrap, discarded, and waste materials." Initially, however, the operative provisions of the law were limited to research and grant programs that studied the problem rather than regulated it. The RRA amended the SWDA, changing the emphasis from studying disposal practices to a focus on recovery of materials and energy from the solid waste stream.

After the 1970 amendments, the SWDA remained a research and grant program that sought to develop and demonstrate technologies for successful recovery and reuse of solid waste. Even that limited mission was further undercut by very modest funding.[12] The RRA's reporting requirements and bureaucratic study responsibilities, however, proved to be somewhat useful. They led to the generation and collection of data that triggered serious concern about the problems of solid waste management, and greatly hastened passage of the Resource Conservation and Recovery Act (RCRA) amendments to the SWDA in 1976.

The original SWDA and RRA would have had no impact on the disposal of Kepone wastes by Allied and LSP. RCRA, however, as discussed below, would have had a significant impact on events in Hopewell.

10. THE RESOURCE CONSERVATION AND RECOVERY ACT OF 1976 (RCRA)[13]

The RCRA amendments to the SWDA so transformed the SWDA that most contemporary discussions of federal solid waste legislation refer to the governing law simply as RCRA. Landmark legislation when it was passed in 1976, RCRA has become even more prominent after substantial strengthening amendments in 1984. Subsequently it has been further expanded to include coverage of leaking underground storage tanks and medical wastes. RCRA did what the original SWDA and RRA did not do – it regulated the waste cycle, and it did so with an exceptional degree of rigor and detail.[14]

RCRA's broad reach is reflected in its definition of solid waste. Among other items, solid waste includes "solid, liquid, semisolid, or contained gaseous material

10. Pub.L. 89–272, 79 Stat. 992.

11. Pub.L. 91–512, 84 Stat. 1227.

12. See W. Rodgers, Handbook on Environmental Law 632 (1977).

13. 42 U.S.C.A. §§6901–6991K.

14. Chapter 22 looks at many regulatory aspects of RCRA in some detail. Subpart B of this chapter considers RCRA's provisions that can be used to obtain a clean up of released wastes that pose an imminent danger to public health or to the environment.

resulting from industrial, commercial, mining, and agricultural operations...."[15] RCRA viewed the solid waste problem as part of an organic process with an established life cycle beginning with generation of the waste and ending with its treatment, storage, or disposal. Particularly in regard to what it defines as hazardous waste, RCRA attempts to regulate all aspects of that life cycle, an approach that quickly was dubbed, somewhat imprecisely, "cradle to grave" regulation. In addition to a tracking system that follows the transportation and disposal of hazardous waste from the time of its generation, RCRA authorizes the EPA to engage in corrective actions that can prevent or remedy problems associated with the release of hazardous wastes into the environment. RCRA and the administrative regulations that have been promulgated under its requirements provide voluminous standards for the treatment, storage, and disposal of hazardous waste.

Had RCRA been in force at the time that Allied and LSP were engaged in Kepone manufacture, it would certainly have had an impact. Absent a valid NPDES permit that included the discharge of Kepone wastes, the disposal of Kepone-laden wastewater would have been governed by RCRA. Beyond that, LSP simply dumped some of its wastes in a pile behind the plant. These actions would likewise have violated RCRA.

By way of remedies for RCRA violation, EPA is authorized to seek civil and criminal penalties of substantial magnitude. More importantly from a public health and environmental standpoint, EPA is also empowered under 42 U.S.C.A. §6973 (RCRA §7003) to sue for or to issue an administrative order for a corrective action that would alleviate any "imminent and substantial endangerment to health or the environment...." As RCRA has been interpreted, both Allied and LSP would be liable under its provisions, and that means that the resources of Allied as well as those of LSP would have been available to pay the costs associated with taking corrective action.

11. THE COMPREHENSIVE ENVIRONMENTAL RESPONSE, COMPENSATION AND LIABILITY ACT (CERCLA, OR "SUPERFUND")[16]

The far better-known companion statute to RCRA in the toxics disposal remedial field is the "Superfund" law, formally titled the Comprehensive Environmental Response, Compensation and Liability Act of 1980 (CERCLA). In CERCLA, and especially after its amendment and reauthorization in 1986,[17] Congress established a mechanism to insure that funding would be available to pay for cleanups at the most serious sites of contamination.

The need for the "fund" part of a Superfund law may not be immediately obvious. After all, if state common law is inadequate to fix liability on the industries that generate, transport, and dispose of hazardous wastes, a federal law imposing

15. 42 U.S.C.A. §6903(27). There are also some significant exceptions to the definition of solid waste. The most significant exceptions are sewage, discharges permitted under the Clean Water Act, irrigation return flows and certain nuclear materials.

16. 42 U.S.C.A. §§9601 to 9675.

17. Superfund Amendments and Reauthorization Act of 1986, (SARA) Pub.L. 99-499, 100 Stat. 1613.

liability on a somewhat broader range of potentially responsible parties would seem to be all that is needed. Under such a law, those responsible for hazardous releases could be ordered to undertake a cleanup and to compensate others damaged by their releases. This latter damage calculation would include any cleanup expenses incurred by third parties or government.

The major reasons for the fund component of Superfund are that the responsible parties cannot always be identified – as in the notorious practice of "midnight dumping"– and that responsible parties may be unable to pay the amount of the cleanup costs. The reason that the fund must be "super" is a function of cost. Purging a hazardous waste site of contaminants can be a multi-million dollar undertaking.

The principal statutory mechanisms of CERCLA were succinctly described at the time of its enactment:

> Essentially, CERCLA authorizes governmental responses to actual and threatened releases of a wide range of harmful substances. Parties causing releases of such substances may then be held liable without regard to fault for certain damages resulting from the release, which primarily include government incurred costs for cleanup, removal and resources restoration. To ensure that such injuries are redressed, the law establishes a $1.6 billion [$8.5 billion, after SARA in 1986] Hazardous Substances Response Fund, financed jointly by industry and the federal government over five years. When polluters are unknown, or are unable or unwilling to provide recompense, a claim for specified damages may be filed against the fund. Payment of claims by the fund then subrogates the fund to the rights of the claimant.[18]

Focusing on specific remedial provisions, CERCLA's provisions retrace the imminent hazard provisions of RCRA described above[19] and add provisions that relate to recoupment and allocation of cleanup costs already incurred in response to hazardous waste releases.[20]

CERCLA, like RCRA, would have had obvious applicability to the actions of Allied and LSP, both of whom would be liable parties under CERCLA.[21] On the remedial side, CERCLA adds the possibility of a governmentally funded cleanup with recoupment of the costs from responsible parties. CERCLA, and the National Contingency Plan (NCP) it requires, also set standards that govern the cleanup process to insure that the removal and remedial actions taken are adequate to protect both health and environment. There are also liability provisions that call for the assessment and payment of natural resource damages for environmental harms caused by the release of hazardous materials.

---

18. Comment, Superfund at Square One: Promising Statutory Framework Requires Forceful EPA Implementation, 11 ELR 10101 (1981).

19. See CERCLA, §106, codified at 42 U.S.C.A. §9606.

20. See CERCLA, §107, codified at 42 U.S.C.A. §9607. The text of this provision appears beginning at page 261. The 1986 Amendments to §107, while adding some material, do not to make major changes in the scope and coverage of §107. Its impact with regard to the liability of "innocent purchasers" of realty that is discovered to be contaminated is significantly affected by the amendments to §9601(35) wherein the obligations of purchasers to use due diligence to discover the presence of contaminants are spelled out.

21. CERCLA is a strict liability law; the precise basis for the liability of Allied and LSP under CERCLA §§106 & 107 will be studied further in subpart B of this chapter and Chapter 21.

12. THE SAFE DRINKING WATER ACT (SDWA)[22]

The best-known elements of this law are its requirements fixing water quality levels for drinking water suppliers. These quality standards are set by the federal government to insure an adequate margin of safety for public health. The statute also prohibits the use of lead pipes, solder, or flux in drinking water delivery systems.

A second major component of this law is the protection of underground drinking water supply sources. While the development of direct regulatory programs is left to the states, the EPA must set guidelines which form a baseline to be met by the states in their programs. A key element in this program is the identification of public drinking water supply aquifers and their protection. The protections offered include restrictions on certain activities near well fields. Also among the primary concerns in this part of the law is control of the injection of wastes, the practice of pumping waste liquids into abandoned wells and drill holes as a method of disposal. Disposal by injection is a longstanding practice in both the hydrocarbon production industry (oil and gas) and the chemical industry, and was seldom comprehensively regulated in the past. Like many other federal laws under which the states are given major duties, the SDWA provides for federal research programs as well as technical and financial assistance to the states. It probably would not have had an impact on the Kepone case.

13. THE EMERGENCY PLANNING AND COMMUNITY RIGHT-TO-KNOW ACT (EPCRTKA, OR EPCRA)[23]

One basic thrust of this law requires the states to establish state-wide and local emergency response planning committees charged with developing emergency plans. Among their important features, plans are to identify facilities in the community that contain substantial amounts of hazardous materials and provide for emergency actions that should be taken in the event of a release of those substances, including giving notice to the affected public. An additional thrust of the Act is mandatory public reporting of the nature and characteristics of certain hazardous materials. By this means, public officials should be better prepared to respond in the event of releases.

Consider the impact that EPCRA would have had on the Allied and LSP situation. Any of the unpermitted releases of Kepone would have been covered by EPCRA, and the failure of Allied or LSP to report them to local officials would have been a violation of the law. If Allied had reported, the obvious implications for Hopewell would probably have triggered local responses. In a sense, speculation on the impact of EPCRA on the Kepone case shows just how far the regulatory climate has changed since the 1970s. EPCRA is a statute two generations removed from the law as it was at the time of the Kepone releases in question. It presupposes a post-RCRA universe in which hazardous materials are comprehensively tracked, and builds additional public interest protective regulation upon that.

---

22. 42 U.S.C.A §§300f–300j-26.

23. 42 U.S.C.A. §§11001–11050; the Act can also properly be called SARA's Title III.

14. THE NATIONAL ENVIRONMENTAL POLICY ACT (NEPA)[24]

Perhaps the most significant single federal environmental statute in the past two decades has been the National Environmental Policy Act. Effective January 1, 1970, NEPA does not stipulate any pollution control measures, nor in fact does it establish any direct regulation of any private industry. Nevertheless, as noted in Chapter 12 *infra*, NEPA has provided the environmental movement with a strategic statutory foundation in court because of the pervasive connections between government and business, and NEPA's quite accidental litigable requirement that all federal agencies must prepare an environmental impact statement (EIS). Under NEPA's §102(2c), agencies must write EISs when they are about to undertake any "major federal action significantly affecting the human environment."

For purposes of this statutory overview, it should be noted that environmental citizen watchdog groups could have demanded an EIS from various federal agencies issuing permits to Allied, where the permits related to actions that allegedly could cause significant environmental affects. A Corps of Engineers permit to alter the banks of Gravelly Run, for instance, would be likely to require an environmental impact statement. Many federal permits in the various statutory toxic regulation systems are also potentially subject to NEPA. In some cases permits to be issued by the EPA for environmental protection are exempt from NEPA. The potential for citizens to require agencies to issue EISs in a number of different statutory settings presented in this regulatory mosaic, however, means that NEPA is often likely to be available as a litigation tool.

15. OTHER FEDERAL STATUTES

There are, in addition, a wide variety of other federal statutes that directly or indirectly might be involved in the Allied Chemical Semi-Works' environmental regulatory history. If the plant were officially classified as lying within the coastal zone of Virginia, for instance, it would be subject to a variety of federal and state consistency reviews under the federal Coastal Zone Management Act,[25] to assure that it was not contradictory to the purposes of safe management and conservation of the coastal zone. The Noise Control Act, as amended by the Quiet Communities Act,[26] establishes federal standards for various noise sources, and specifically invites further stricter state control of noise sources. The federal Freedom of Information Act (FOIA)[27] provides a basis for public disclosure of information that Allied supplies to a federal regulatory agency; under FOIA, documents are to be disclosed upon request to any person, subject only to narrowly defined exemptions for material that is clearly confidential. Even the Federal Aeronautics Act may apply to Allied; that statute requires the FAA to be notified and approve of plans for construction of smokestacks, and to certify proper lighting thereon for the protection of aircraft at night. Other federal statutes undoubtedly will be applicable in various cases.

24. 42 U.S.C.A. §§4331–4335, 4341–4347 (1969).

25. 33 U.S.C.A. §§1251–1376 (1970).

26. 42 U.S.C.A. 4901–4918 (1972); Pub.L. 95–609 (1978)

27. 5 U.S.C.A. §552 (1966).

16. A BROAD RANGE OF STATE STATUTES

If the foregoing catalogue of federal statutes seems extensive, it should be remembered that there are, and were, far more non-federal regulations potentially applicable to the Allied Chemical Semi-Works, given the police power jurisdictions of state and local governments. Virginia has a number of state statutes closely paralleling the functions of federal statutes. In other areas, the state government regulates concerns not covered at all by federal regulation. The state statutes in the Kepone case were evidently not being stringently enforced. It is, nevertheless, a fundamental requirement for attorneys representing clients like Allied, or citizen environmental groups attempting to watchdog a polluter's actions, to understand the full array of state regulatory provisions potentially applicable to a plant.

The following list gives an indication of the kinds of permits that might be required in setting up a plant like the Allied Semi-Works under the provisions of state and local statutory law. In many cases citizens can intervene with environmental challenges in permit issuance processes.

AGENCY:	REGULATORY REQUIREMENT:
State air, water, natural resources commissions	[A dozen or so permits directly analogous to the federal permits noted above]
plus	
State Department of Labor	Permit for boiler installation
State Department of Labor	Permit for any elevators involved in a plant
State Department of Natural Resources	Permit for dredging and filling as required on site
State Water Resources Commission	Permit for alteration of channels or floodplains, or any drains
State Department of Natural Resources	Permit for construction in zone close to major bodies of water
State Department of Health	Approval of sanitary sewer system
State Police	Approval for above-ground storage of flammable liquids
County Road Commission	Permit for altering or temporary closing of highways for construction
County Health Commission	Permit for alteration of any drains
County Health Commission	Approval of sewer system
Local Township	Building, electrical, and plumbing permits
Local Township	Permits for water use and sewerage
State Air Pollution Commission	Permit for boilers and diesel generators
State Department of Aeronautics	Permit for construction of high smokestacks
State Water Resource Commission	Permit for use of water during plant construction, operation, and sewage treatment (in addition to state water pollution control, or NPDES permit)
State Department of Natural Resources	Soil erosion and sedimentation permit
State Department of Natural Resources	Inland streams alteration permit
State Public Utilities Commission	Permit for construction of high voltage electric transmission lines
State Public Utilities Commission	Permission for connection to high voltage electric transmission lines
State Department of Highways	Permit for alteration of highway access
State Public Utilities Commission	Railroad spur construction, alteration, and connection to existing railroad spurs
State Public Utilities Commission	Permits for building grade crossings across railroad tracks
State Public Utilities Commission	Construction permit for operation of electrical substation
County, and Local Municipality	Zoning permits

COMMENTARY AND QUESTIONS

1. Public law/private law: different roles. Do the topics addressed by the various public law statutes just described lend themselves to "private law" resolution? What distinguishes the two categories? Is it the proactive side of the statutes, whereby they attempt to prevent harms from occurring? Is it standard-setting, deciding how much of chemical X constitutes a threat of harm to health? Is it broad policy-making, deciding that aquifers reasonably well-suited to use for drinking water ought to remain inviolate for that purpose, or deciding that people of a community have a right to know what chemicals are present on the premises of various facilities in that area?

2. The continuing role of common law. Do these statutes comprehensively cover all issues and areas involved in environmental controversies? The common law continues in force except insofar as it is expressly or necessarily overridden by statute. This means that it continues as a freestanding separate corpus of law applicable to environmental cases alongside state and federal statutes. The common law serves as the broad foundation upon which the various statutory accretions produced by legislatures and agencies are superimposed.

So what relevant legal coverage does the common law provide in the environmental setting that statutes fail to treat? Contrast how the Kepone case would be handled by public law and common law. In general, what functions does the statutory law not play in these cases? In similar regard note that although more than a dozen state and federal statutes apply to oil production and transport, yet in the wake of the Exxon-Valdez oil spill disaster, the State of Alaska's litigation against the oil companies was non-statutory, based upon common law theories. Why? The public law's lack of compensation remedies is part, but not all, of the answer.

Thinking structurally about the differences between private and public law helps to explain the complementary roles of the two systems. Private litigation seeks to particularize the event at hand. It is controlled by the litigants, who are antagonists in disputes that pit them one against the other, contesting the impacts of particular environmentally harmful events on their private interests. That the common law should provide individualized remedies in appropriate cases of this type is a concept almost as old as the common law itself. The common law provides the rules of decision, and the legal system provides the impartial forum for decision. Public law is more concerned with the larger social implications of behavior–protecting public health generally, setting aggregative rules about the sharing of the commons, managing the ongoing business of human and economic activity in the state.

3. Regulatory failure and the Kepone disaster. Despite the litany of statutes that were in place at the time that Allied Chemical and LSP's actions so badly polluted the James River, the pollution took place anyway. One means of explaining the failure of the statutes and regulations is to note that even public law is not self-enforcing in most settings. After reviewing the various statutes and taking into account the tort suits that might have been brought, it seems likely that most lawyers asked to mount a legal challenge to the activities of Allied and LSP could have found successful grounds on which to do so. What was lacking were clients willing to confront the activities in question, or zealous regulatory officials unwilling to accommodate Allied and LSP.

Could that same regulatory failure take place today? The answer in a post-RCRA world, at least when a major company is involved, is that so many inspections and oversights occur that it would be almost impossible to hide the laxity of control as in the Kepone case. Even with a smaller firm like LSP, it seems hard to imagine that their practices today could long escape detection.

In part, the current likelihood of improved governmental enforcement reflects changes in regulatory inspection procedures. One of the administrative changes produced by pollution cases like the Kepone incident was that federal inspectors were given a broader responsibility to consider violations of laws other than the specific one for which they were inspecting. Thus, for example, an OSHA inspector would now be expected to report to EPA about likely violations of air toxics control standards, water pollution, or RCRA violations stemming from apparently improper handling of hazardous materials. Although this cross-reporting does not break down the medium-by-medium approach entirely, it is a step toward integrated environmental reporting and inspection procedures.

A second reason for the increased likelihood today that Kepone discharges would be detected and acted upon by regulatory authorities at a far earlier stage is the change in public perceptions about hazardous materials. Looking back at the Kepone story, there seems to have been a conspiracy of silence that went far beyond individuals like Hundtofte and Moore. The local sewage treatment plant officials did not act vigorously, state and federal inspectors did not see things they should have, plant and community doctors either suppressed or did not recognize symptoms of chemical poisoning, workers did not file anonymous complaints or take advantage of whistleblower protections that appear in virtually all modern regulatory statutes, and so on. Today, with the NIMBY phenomenon and statutes like EPCRA, the public attitude toward these hazards is dramatically different. Community norms have changed, new and more effective laws have been passed, and laws and regulations that were quiescent in the 1960s and 1970s are now enforced with greater rigor, especially in regard to hazardous materials. Citizen enforcement provisions, moreover, are now built into most major pollution statutes, encouraging standing for enforcement.

B. THE ROLE OF JUDGES IN GIVING MEANING TO STATUTES: THE EXAMPLE OF RCRA AND CERCLA

In the foregoing array of statutes, each legislative enactment requires interpretation and elaboration before its practical application. Typically that process initially takes place in an administrative agency because under most of the statutes an administrative agency is assigned regulatory tasks that require it to act to make the statute fully effective. Also typically, however, those agency interpretations and applications of statutes are soon thereafter second-guessed in a court of law. The administrative and judicial review processes usually draw upon both statutory and common law concepts, and create a continually developing "common law of statutes."

The common law of statutes includes several distinct ideas. Among the most traditional of these ideas is that judges, in trying to ascertain the meaning and effect of statutes, rely on the accumulated body of experience interpreting statutes that has been built up through decisions of previous cases interpreting statutes. The teachings of these cases are sometimes referred to as the canons of statutory construction. As some of the materials that follow will indicate, most of these canons are familiar-sounding bromides: "a later-enacted statute controls over an earlier-enacted statute," "a more specific provision controls over a more general provision," "statutes in derogation of the common law are to be narrowly construed," etc. The canons of construction, though useful, are vague enough and numerous enough that they are often contradictory and do not always provide a great deal of guidance to a court. Indeed, the canons often seem to be used as after-the-fact justifications for interpretations grounded upon some other line of analysis or belief.

A second traditional sense in which statutory interpretation has a common law character is the willingness of courts to consider similar precedents. Especially in modern times, statutes governing different subjects often adopt provisions that are similar (or identical) to provisions found in sister statutes. In the environmental field, for example, the so-called "saving to suitors" provision that permits other prior remedies to remain in force is common to several statutes.[28] Just as with the common law of judge-made rules, interpretations of particular statutory language take on precedential value, influencing subsequent cases involving identical or similar statutory enactments.

A third sense in which statutory interpretation in the American legal system has a common law quality was alluded to at the very outset of this section – there is universal acceptance of the proposition that the full meaning of a statute is developed through a dynamic process that includes judicial interpretation.[29] This does not substitute judicial supremacy for legislative supremacy; judges remain bound to honor legislative intent. Rather, it reflects the fact that legislation cannot and does not address all possible situations that may be within the ambit of a regulatory enactment.

Within this third form of common law influence on statutory interpretation and application, there are occasional instances in which the legislative branch has deliberately carved out a prominent role for courts. In the environmental field, one

28. See, e.g., Clean Water Act §505(e), 33 U.S.C.A. §1365(e); Clean Air Act §304(e), 42. U.S.C.A. §7604(e).

29. The acceptance of the active role of the judiciary in giving meaning to statutory enactments is one of the most distinctive features of American jurisprudence. It can be contrasted, for example, to the civil law systems that are common in Western Europe in which the legislation is controlling and the courts have no latitude whatever to deviate from the law as written in the codes.

example of this phenomenon is the Michigan Environmental Protection Act (MEPA) considered more fully in Chapter 8, *infra*. MEPA relies on the statutory creation of a cause of action that allows citizens to initiate claims for the protection against pollution, impairment, or destruction of the state's natural resources. The courts, in the truest common law fashion, are told to define the precise contours of the statutory cause of action. A second example of this phenomenon, and one that is the central focus of this section, involves RCRA and CERCLA, two federal statutes governing the cleanup of hazardous waste contamination. Here, as will be seen, Congress expended considerable effort filling in the details of the remedial sides of these two statutes, but also left many areas in need of judicial interpretation and clarification.

RCRA and CERCLA are probably the two most actively litigated statutes in current environmental law. Together, supplemented by state common law tort theories studied in Chapters 3 and 4, they form the legal basis for determining who will bear the costs associated with the release of hazardous materials on land and into groundwater.[30]

Section 1. THE BASICS OF STATUTORY LIABILITY FOR CLEANUP OF HAZARDOUS MATERIALS

The key statutory language of RCRA and CERCLA that imposes liability for cleanups appears in §7003 of RCRA and §§106 and 107 of CERCLA. The text of the RCRA provision is set forth in the *NEPACCO* case that appears later in this section at page 266. The relevant portions of §§106-107 are as follows:

42 U.S.C.A. §9606. Abatement actions

(a) Maintenance, jurisdiction, etc.

In addition to any other action taken by a State or local government, when the President determines that there may be an imminent and substantial endangerment to the public health or welfare or the environment because of an actual or threatened release of a hazardous substance from a facility, he may require the Attorney General of the United States to secure such relief as may be necessary to abate such danger or threat, and the district court of the United States in the district in which the threat occurs shall have jurisdiction to grant such relief as the public interest and the equities of the case may require. The President may also, after notice to the affected State, take other action under this section including, but not limited to, issuing such orders as may be necessary to protect public health and welfare and the environment....

(b) Fines; reimbursement

(1) Any person who, without sufficient cause, willfully violates, or fails or refuses to comply with, any order of the President under subsec-

30. The release of hazardous materials into the navigable waters (i.e., surface waters) of the United States is governed by the Clean Water Act, 33 U.S.C.A. §§1251 to 1387. Portions of that Act are studied in Chapter 19 *infra*.

tion (a) of this section may...be fined not more than $25,000 for each day in which such violation occurs or such failure to comply continues....

42 U.S.C.A. §9607. Liability

(a) Covered persons; scope; recoverable costs and damages; interest rate; "comparable maturity" date

Notwithstanding any other provision or rule of law, and subject only to the defenses set forth in subsection (b) of this section –

(1) the owner and operator of a vessel or a facility,

(2) any person who at the time of disposal of any hazardous substance owned or operated any facility at which such hazardous substances were disposed of,

(3) any person who by contract, agreement, or otherwise arranged for disposal or treatment, or arranged with a transporter for transport for disposal or treatment, of hazardous substances owned or possessed by such person, by any other party or entity, at any facility or incineration vessel owned or operated by another party or entity and containing such hazardous substances, and

(4) any person who accepts or accepted any hazardous substances for transport to disposal or treatment facilities, incineration vessels or sites selected by such person, from which there is a release, or a threatened release which causes the incurrence of response costs, of a hazardous substance, shall be liable for –

(A) all costs of removal or remedial action incurred by the United States Government or a State or an Indian tribe not inconsistent with the national contingency plan;

(B) any other necessary costs of response incurred by any other person consistent with the national contingency plan;

(C) damages for injury to, destruction of, or loss of natural resources, including the reasonable costs of assessing such injury, destruction, or loss resulting from such a release; and

(D) the costs of any health assessment or health effects study carried out under section 9604(i) of this title....

(b) Defenses

There shall be no liability under subsection (a) of this section for a person otherwise liable who can establish by a preponderance of the evidence that the release or threat of release of a hazardous substance and the damages resulting therefrom were caused solely by –

(1) an act of God;

(2) an act of war;

(3) an act or omission of a third party other than an employee or agent of the defendant, or than one whose act or omission occurs in

connection with a contractual relationship, existing directly or indirectly, with the defendant (except where the sole contractual arrangement arises from a published tariff and acceptance for carriage by a common carrier by rail), if the defendant establishes by a preponderance of the evidence that (a) he exercised due care with respect to the hazardous substance concerned, taking into consideration the characteristics of such hazardous substance, in light of all relevant facts and circumstances, and (b) he took precautions against foreseeable acts or omissions of any such third party and the consequences that could foreseeably result from such acts or omissions; or

(4) any combination of the foregoing paragraphs....

(f) Actions involving natural resources; maintenance, scope, etc.

(1) Natural resources liability

In the case of an injury to, destruction of, or loss of natural resources under subparagraph (C) of subsection (a) of this section liability shall be to the United States Government and to any State for natural resources within the State or belonging to, managed by, controlled by, or appertaining to such State and to any Indian tribe for natural resources belonging to, managed by, controlled by, or appertaining to such tribe....

A review of RCRA and CERCLA, particularly their definition sections, demonstrates that the universe of conduct that might fall within these laws is quite broad. Moreover, those same laws do not clearly describe the standards of liability that determine what conduct is actionable and what is not. This void has been filled by the courts. The following excerpt provides a roadmap to some of the major rulings that have emerged in defining the operation of CERCLA.

Rich, Personal Liability for Hazardous Waste Cleanup: An Examination of CERCLA §107

13 Boston College Environmental Affairs Law Review 643, 653-58 (1986)

Section 107 of CERCLA[31] designates certain parties who may be liable for the cleanup costs of a hazardous waste site. Section 107 imposes liability for cleanup costs and damage to natural resources[32] on: (1) past and present owners and operators of hazardous waste facilities; (2) persons who arrange for disposal of hazardous substances to facilities (usually generators); and (3) persons who transport hazardous substances to facilities from which there is a release or a threatened release of toxic chemicals that results in response costs. These responsible parties are liable for three types of costs incurred as a result of a release or a threatened release of hazardous waste: (1) governmental response costs (costs incurred by the federal government to clean up hazardous waste sites); (2) private response costs (costs

31. Ed. note: CERCLA §107 is codified as 42 U.S.C.A. §9607.

32. "Natural resources" under CERCLA means "fish, wildlife, biota, air, water, groundwater, drinking water supplies, and other such resources belonging to, managed by, held in trust by, appertaining to, or otherwise controlled by the United States...any state or local government, or any foreign government." 42 U.S.C.A. §9601(16)(1982).

incurred by other parties consistent with the National Contingency Plan), and (3) damages to natural resources.

Section 107 provides limited defenses. Parties otherwise liable under §107 may escape liability if they can establish that the release or threat of release of hazardous substances and resulting damages were caused by an act of God, an act of war, or an act or omission of a third party other than an employee or agent of the defendants, or one whose act or omission occurs in connection with a contractual relationship with the defendants. The third party exception applies only if defendants both exercised due carc with respect to the hazardous substance, and took necessary precautions against acts or omissions by the third party.

STRICT LIABILITY

In spite of the comprehensive nature of its hazardous waste cleanup provisions, CERCLA's standards of liability are vague. Congress removed references to strict liability and joint and several liability before the bill's final passage, leaving these matters for judicial interpretation.

The standard of liability under CERCLA is strict liability. Although it does not specifically mention strict liability, §101, CERCLA's definitional section, states that liability under CERCLA "shall be construed to be the standard of liability which obtains under §311 of the Federal Water Pollution Control Act." Although §311 of the Federal Water Pollution Control Act (FWPCA) does not explicitly mention strict liability, courts have inferred such liability from the language of that Act, which subjects certain parties to liability unless they can successfully assert one of the limited defenses specified. Congress' reference to FWPCA §311 in CERCLA is logical, because the same defenses to liability found in FWPCA §311 also appear in §107 of CERCLA. Courts construing CERCLA have therefore held parties strictly liable for statutory violations.

JOINT AND SEVERAL LIABILITY

Congress also deleted references to joint and several liability from the final version of CERCLA. The original Senate proposal specifically imposed joint and several liability, but this language was deleted from the final version of the bill as part of the "hastily drawn compromise which resulted in the enactment of CERCLA." Federal courts construing liability under CERCLA, however, uniformly have held that CERCLA permits, but does not mandate, joint and several liability. It is therefore within the discretion of the court to impose joint and several liability. Furthermore, some courts have held that joint and several liability should be imposed under CERCLA, unless the defendants can establish that a reasonable basis exists for apportioning the harm against them.[33]

CERCLA's standard of strict liability, coupled with the possibility of joint and several liability, places a heavy burden on defendants. CERCLA does, however, place some constraints on the amount of liability that courts may impose under §107. Section 107 liability is premised upon a governmental response pursuant to §104 and the National Contingency Plan, or a response by another party in accordance with the National Contingency Plan. Both §104 and the National Contingency Plan impose practical limitations on the extent and cost of hazardous waste cleanup operations....

33. U.S. v. Northeastern Pharm. & Chem. Co. (NEPACCO), 579 F. Supp. 823, 844 (W.D. Miss. 1984).

The National Contingency Plan establishes procedures and standards for responding to releases of hazardous substances, pollutants, and contaminants. These procedures include methods for discovering and investigating hazardous substance disposal facilities, for determining the appropriate extent of removal of the substances, for assuring that remedial actions are cost-effective, and for determining priorities among releases or threatened releases. The statute and the National Contingency Plan thus limit the extent of liability under CERCLA §107.

PERSONAL LIABILITY UNDER CERCLA §107

As discussed earlier, CERCLA imposes liability on: (1) past and present owners and operators of hazardous waste facilities; (2) persons who arrange for the transport of hazardous waste; and (3) persons who transport hazardous waste. These parties include individuals as well as corporations. The federal government has sought to hold both corporations and their corporate officers and employees responsible for the costs of hazardous waste cleanup under CERCLA. Although individual defendants have argued that their actions were the actions of the corporation, thereby shielding them from liability under the doctrine of limited liability, this argument has not succeeded. The few district courts to consider this issue uniformly have held that the corporate form does not shield individuals from personal liability where such individuals have exercised personal control over, or have actually been involved in, the disposal of hazardous waste.

COMMENTARY AND QUESTIONS

1. Reading statutes. CERCLA §§106 & 107 and RCRA §7003 are the first environmental law statutory texts in this coursebook. As you read these and other statutes, it is helpful to approach them with at least two things in mind. Most fundamentally, you must understand what it is that they are attempting to do and how they go about doing it. Looking (in a somewhat over-simplified way) at these statutes, for example, RCRA §7003 and CERCLA §106 intend to create means by which the federal government can get dangerous releases of hazardous materials cleaned up. They establish two avenues (court suits and administrative orders) which EPA follows in obtaining cleanups. The second task while reading new statutory material is "issue-spotting" the statute. Try to identify the points of a statute's operation that are both important and open to interpretation, for these are likely to be the issues that courts will be asked to address when the statute is applied. Consider CERCLA §107. Just by reading its terms it seems clear that subsection (a)(1-4), the provisions that define what categories of persons are liable, are going to be intensely litigated. The coverage issue is obviously important – if particular defendants are not within one of the categories, they are not liable for §107 cleanup costs. This can be a multi-million dollar issue in the case of extensive or hard-to-clean releases. The coverage terms like "owner" and "operator," and the liability term "shall be liable" – if not more fully defined elsewhere[34] – will need to be clarified. Reading statutes in this way

---

34. The terms owner and operator are defined in §101(20), 42 U.S.C.A. §9601(20). The application of the definitional section has itself been the subject of litigation. As explained in the excerpted material, the liability term was not fully defined and was settled by the courts.

anticipates many of the most active questions and controversies that are likely to surround the statutes' application.

2. Common law devices and interpreting CERCLA. Although the Rich excerpt mentions no canons of construction contributing to the interpretation given to CERCLA §107, examples of the two other kinds of common law development of statutes were prominent in §107's judicial interpretation. The "shall be liable" language and reference to §311 of the Federal Water Pollution Control Act (which became the Clean Water Act, CWA), led courts to look to cases interpreting the CWA as precedents for the interpretation of §107. The judicial treatment given to the issue of joint and several liability exemplifies the traditional lawmaking role of courts in filling in matters that statutes fail to address.

3. Summarizing CERCLA. Summarizing CERCLA is a pastime that has engaged countless scribes writing in academic and practitioner-oriented law journals. There are many fine summaries available tracing the evolving precedents that have played so central a role in defining CERCLA's impact. A useful and well-organized example is McSlarrow, Jones, and Murdock, A Decade of Superfund Litigation: CERCLA Case Law From 1981-1991, 21 ELR 10367 (1991).

4. A common law substitute for Superfund? What do CERCLA's §§106 and 107 accomplish that the common law could not?[35] Looking first at §106, by addressing both "actual or threatened" releases, §106 makes prospective relief routinely available. Under the common law, it is only the extraordinary case like *Wilsonville* that prevents a harm before it happens. Section 106 offers an extra-judicial remedy: EPA can go to court, but it can also issue its own administrative orders against polluters, a far more efficient and streamlined process. Moreover, EPA's administrative orders are, in a pragmatic sense, non-debatable. They are not subject to judicial review until after compliance, or by way of defense in an action seeking penalties for non-compliance (triple the amount of EPA's cleanup cost), or in defense of a proceeding seeking enforcement of the EPA §106 order.[36] The common law can do somewhat more of the things that §107 provides for. It is quite possible that a common law court would be willing to hold defendants who release hazardous materials into the environment strictly, jointly and severally liable even in the absence of a statute allowing it. Perhaps the common law might also adopt a relaxed standard of proof of causation similar to that of CERCLA in cases involving concurrent actions of multiple tortfeasors. (In the CERCLA cases, however, the furtherance of legislative policy is a key element underlying judicial willingness to relax traditional tort law standards of proof.) Going further, §107 does things that it would be very difficult for common law to do. The damage assessment of

---

35. CERCLA as a whole does many things that are far beyond the realm of common law possibility. Most obviously, its creation of a national fund from which cleanup expenses can be paid is one thing that the common law cannot readily do. Similarly, the creation of a National Priorities List that identifies and ranks sites as to the need for cleanup action is unthinkable without the intervention of a public law mandate. There are many other facets of CERCLA, and other environmental statutes and regulations, that touch on issues the common law cannot practically address.

36. See 42 U.S.C.A. §112(h).

§107(a)(4)(A) is not a traditional damage measure – it assesses the actual costs of environmental remediation, not the amount of a plaintiffs' loss. Compare, for example, the award of damages paid in *Boomer*. By providing damages for natural resources, §107(a)(4)(C) also moves a step beyond traditional tort law, and §107(a)(4)(D) makes clear that health studies are an item of recoverable damage, hardly a regular feature of damage awards under the common law.

5. Personal liability. The focus of the Rich excerpt is personal individual liability for §107 recoveries. The common cases in which this issue arises are those in which a hazardous waste generator, transporter, or disposer is a corporation, and a §107 action seeks to hold individual corporate officers or employees liable (for fiscal or punitive reasons). Their classic defense is to argue limited liability for corporate acts, the protective doctrine that provides such an important incentive to corporate entrepreneurialism. But courts increasingly have allowed application of individual personal liability for corporate officers under CERCLA and other statutes.

Analytically the cases usually fall into three categories:

The first category, occurring most often in small, closely held corporations, involves piercing the corporate veil when corporate structure stands as an impediment to reaching the assets of individuals who have directly profited from the corporation's activities, even though they may not have been personally involved in day-to-day operations. These cases require the sorts of rigorous showings that are required in non-CERCLA veil-piercing cases.

The second class of cases is where officers are held liable for their own wrongful personal actions, for instance where they themselves personally dumped toxics or directly ordered the illegal act.

The third class of individual liability is where individuals are held liable because of their status as managerial officers, responsible for directing the corporate activity in which violations occurred. Several of these liability theories are explored further in the criminal law materials at page 321 *infra*, and in the following case arising under CERCLA and RCRA:

United States v. Northeastern Pharmaceutical & Chemical Co. [*NEPACCO*]
United States Court of Appeals for the Eighth Circuit
810 F.2d 726 (1986)[37]

McMILLIAN, J. Northeastern Pharmaceutical & Chemical Co. (NEPACCO), Edwin Michaels, and John W. Lee appeal from a final judgment entered in the District Court for the Western District of Missouri finding them and Ronald Mills jointly and severally liable for response costs incurred by the government after December 11, 1980, and all future response costs relative to the cleanup of the Denney farm site that are not inconsistent with the national contingency plan (NCP) pursuant to

37. Cert. denied, 484 U.S. 848 (1988).

§§104 and 107 of the Comprehensive Environmental Response, Compensation, and Liability Act of 1980 (CERCLA), 42 U.S.C.A. §§9604, 9607....

The following statement of facts is taken in large part from the district court's excellent memorandum opinion, 579 F. Supp. 823 (W.D. Mo. 1984). NEPACCO was incorporated in 1966.... Although NEPACCO's corporate charter was forfeited in 1976 for failure to maintain an agent for service of process, NEPACCO did not file a certificate of voluntary dissolution with the secretary of state of Delaware. In 1974 its corporate assets were liquidated, and the proceeds were used to pay corporate debts and then distributed to the shareholders. Michaels [had] formed NEPACCO, was a major shareholder, and was its president. Lee was NEPACCO's vice-president, the supervisor of its manufacturing plant located in Verona, Missouri, and also a shareholder. Mills was employed as shift supervisor at NEPACCO's Verona plant.

From April 1970 to January 1972, NEPACCO manufactured the disinfectant hexachlorophene at its Verona plant. NEPACCO leased the plant from Syntex Agribusiness, Inc. (Syntex).... Michaels and Lee knew that NEPACCO's manufacturing process produced various hazardous and toxic byproducts, including 2,4,5-trichlorophenol (TCP), 2,3,7,8-tetrachlorodibenzo-p-dioxin (TCDD or dioxin), and toluene. The waste byproducts were pumped into a holding tank which was periodically emptied by waste haulers. Occasionally, however, excess waste byproducts were sealed in 55-gallon drums and then stored at the plant.

In July 1971 Mills approached NEPACCO plant manager Bill Ray with a proposal to dispose of the waste-filled 55-gallon drums on a farm owned by James Denney located about seven miles south of Verona. Ray visited the Denney farm and discussed the proposal with Lee; Lee approved the use of Mills' services and the Denney farm as a disposal site. In mid-July 1971 Mills and Gerald Lechner dumped approximately 85 of the 55-gallon drums into a large trench on the Denney farm (Denney farm site) that had been excavated by Leon Vaughn. Vaughn then filled in the trench. Only NEPACCO drums were disposed of at the Denney farm site.

In October 1979 the Environmental Protection Agency (EPA) received an anonymous tip that hazardous wastes had been disposed of at the Denney farm. Subsequent EPA investigation confirmed that hazardous wastes had in fact been disposed of at the Denney farm and that the site was not geologically suitable for the disposal of hazardous wastes. Between January and April 1980 the EPA prepared a plan for the cleanup of the Denney farm site and constructed an access road and a security fence. During April 1980 the EPA conducted an on-site investigation, exposed and sampled 13 of the 55-gallon drums, which were found to be badly deteriorated, and took water and soil samples. The samples were found to contain "alarmingly" high concentrations of dioxin, TCP and toluene.

In July 1980 the EPA installed a temporary cap over the trench to prevent the run-off of surface water and to minimize contamination of the surrounding soil and groundwater.... The 55-gallon drums are now stored in a specially constructed concrete bunker on the Denney farm. The drums as stored do not present an imminent and substantial endangerment to health or the environment; however, no plan for permanent disposal has been developed, and the site will continue to require testing and monitoring in the future.

In August 1980 the government filed its initial complaint against NEPACCO, the generator of the hazardous substances; Michaels and Lee, the corporate officers responsible for arranging for the disposal of the hazardous substances; Mills, the transporter of the hazardous substances; and Syntex, the owner and lessor of the Verona plant, seeking injunctive relief and reimbursement of response costs pursuant to RCRA §7003. In August 1982 the government filed an amended complaint adding counts for relief pursuant to CERCLA [which] was enacted after the filing of the initial complaint....

CERCLA RETROACTIVITY: APPLICATION OF CERCLA TO PRE-1980 ACTS

Appellants first argue the district court erred in applying CERCLA retroactively, that is, to impose liability for acts committed before its effective date, December 11, 1980. CERCLA §302(a) provides that "[u]nless otherwise provided, all provisions of this chapter shall be effective on December 11, 1980." Appellants argue that CERCLA should not apply to pre-enactment conduct that was neither negligent nor unlawful when committed. Appellants argue that all the conduct at issue occurred in the early 1970s, well before CERCLA became effective. Appellants also argue that there is no language supporting retroactive application in CERCLA's liability section, or in the legislative history. Appellants further argue that because CERCLA imposes a new kind of liability, retroactive application of CERCLA violates due process and the taking clause. We disagree.

The district court correctly found Congress intended CERCLA to apply retroactively. We acknowledge there is a presumption against the retroactive application of statutes. We hold, however, that CERCLA §302(a) is "merely a standard 'effective date' provision that indicates the date when an action can first be brought and when the time begins to run for issuing regulations and doing other future acts mandated by the statute."

Although CERCLA does not expressly provide for retroactivity, it is manifestly clear that Congress intended CERCLA to have retroactive effect. The language used in the key liability provision, CERCLA §107 refers to actions and conditions in the past tense: "any person who at the time of disposal of any hazardous substances owned or operated," CERCLA §107(a)(2), "any person who...arranged with a transporter for transport for disposal," CERCLA §107(a)(3), and "any person who...accepted any hazardous substances for transport to...sites selected by such person," CERCLA §107(a)(4).[38]

Further, the statutory scheme itself is overwhelmingly remedial and retroactive. CERCLA authorizes the EPA to force responsible parties to clean up inactive or abandoned hazardous substance sites, CERCLA §106, and authorizes federal, state and local governments and private parties to clean up such sites and then seek recovery of their response costs from responsible parties, CERCLA §§104, 107. In order to be effective, CERCLA must reach past conduct. CERCLA's backward-looking focus is confirmed by the legislative history. See generally H.R.Rep. No. 1016, 96th Cong., 2d Sess., reprinted in 1980 U.S. Code Cong. & Ad. News 6119 (CERCLA House Report). Congress intended CERCLA "to initiate and establish a comprehensive response and financing mechanism to abate and control the vast problems associated with abandoned and inactive hazardous waste disposal sites."

The district court also correctly found that retroactive application of CERCLA does not violate due process. Appellants argue CERCLA creates a new form of liability that is designed to deter and punish those who, according to current standards, improperly disposed of hazardous substances in the past. We disagree.

38. The court in United States v. South Carolina Recycling & Disposal, Inc., 20 ERC (BNA) 1753, 1760 (D.S.C. 1984), noted that CERCLA does not apply "retroactively" because it does not impose liability for past conduct; rather, CERCLA imposes liability upon those parties responsible for causing certain conditions, that is, the release or threatened release of hazardous substances, that are the present *or future* results of their *past* actions.

It is by now well established that legislative Acts adjusting the burdens and benefits of economic life come to the Court with a presumption of constitutionality, and that the burden is on one complaining of a due process violation to establish that the legislature has acted in an arbitrary and irrational way. [L]egislation readjusting rights and burdens is not unlawful solely because it upsets otherwise settled expectations. This is true even though the effect of the legislation is to impose a new duty or liability based on past acts. Usery v. Turner Elkhorn Mining Co., 428 U.S. 1, 15 (1976).

Due process is satisfied "simply by showing that the retroactive application of the legislation is itself justified by a rational legislative purpose." Pension Benefit Guaranty Corp. v. R.A. Gray & Co., 467 U.S. 717, 730 (1984). "Provided that the retroactive application of a statute is supported by a legitimate legislative purpose furthered by rational means, judgments about the wisdom of such legislation remain within the exclusive province of the legislative and executive branches...." Id. at 729.

Appellants failed to show that Congress acted in an arbitrary and irrational manner. Cleaning up inactive and abandoned hazardous waste disposal sites is a legitimate legislative purpose, and Congress acted in a rational manner in imposing liability for the cost of cleaning up such sites upon those parties who created and profited from the sites and upon the chemical industry as a whole. We hold retroactive application of CERCLA to impose liability upon responsible parties for acts committed before the effective date of the statute does not violate due process.

[The opinion went on to demonstrate at some length that pre-1980 cleanup expenditures, as well as pre-1980 acts of dumping, were covered by CERCLA.]

RCRA: STANDARD AND SCOPE OF §7003 LIABILITY

...We have considered the 1984 amendments and the accompanying legislative history and, for the reasons discussed below, we believe the 1984 amendments support the government's arguments about RCRA's standard and scope of liability and retroactivity.

The critical issue is the meaning of the phrase "contributing to." Before its amendment in 1984, RCRA §7003(a), 42 U.S.C. §6973(a), imposed liability upon any person "contributing to" "the handling, storage, treatment, transportation or disposal of any solid or hazardous waste" that "may present an imminent and substantial endangerment to health or the environment." The district court did not find either the statutory language or the statutory framework helpful in determining whether past non-negligent off-site generators and transporters were liable under RCRA §7003(a)(prior to the 1984 amendments). The district court then considered the legislative history of the 1980 amendments because "[t]he legislative history of the [RCRA] as originally enacted contains no specific discussion of the reach of §7003 and no mention of the reasons for its insertion...."

Then, in November 1984, Congress passed and President Reagan signed the 1984 amendments which were described as "clarifying" amendments and specifically addressed the standard and scope of liability of §7003(a). As amended in 1984, RCRA §7003(a), 42 U.S.C.A. §6973(a)(West Supp. 1986)(new language italicized; deleted language in brackets), now provides in pertinent part:

> Notwithstanding any other provision of this chapter, upon receipt of evidence that the *past or present* handling, storage, treatment, transportation or disposal of any solid waste or hazardous waste may present an

> imminent and substantial endangerment to health or the environment, the Administrator may bring suit on behalf of the United States in the appropriate district court [to immediately restrain any person] *against any person (including any past or present generator, past or present transporter, or past or present owner or operator of a treatment, storage, or disposal facility) who has contributed or who is* contributing to such handling, storage, treatment, transportation or disposal [to stop] *to restrain such person from* such handling, storage, treatment, transportation, or disposal [or to take such other action as may be necessary], *to order such person to take such other action as may be necessary, or both.*

As amended, RCRA §7003(a) specifically applies to past generators and transporters. Congress' intent with respect to the standard of liability under RCRA §7003(a) as amended by the 1984 amendments, is clearly set forth in the accompanying House Conference Report. The House Conference Report also expressly disapproved of the *Wade* and *Waste Industries* cases, which were relied upon by the NEPACCO [trial] court, as well as the *NEPACCO* [trial court] decision itself. The House Conference Report stated:

> Section 7003 focuses on the abatement of conditions threatening health and the environment and not particularly human activity. Therefore, it has *always reached those persons who have contributed in the past or are presently contributing to the endangerment, including but not limited to generators, regardless of fault or negligence.* The amendment, by adding the words "have contributed" is merely intended to clarify the existing authority. Thus, for example, *non-negligent generators whose wastes are no longer being deposited or dumped at a particular site may be ordered to abate the hazard to health or the environment posed by the leaking of the wastes they once generated and which have been deposited on the site.* The amendment reflects the long-standing view that generators and other persons involved in the handling, storage, treatment, transportation or disposal of hazardous wastes must share in the responsibility for the abatement of the hazards arising from their activities. The section was intended and is intended to abate conditions resulting from past activities. Hence, the district court decisions in United States v. Wade, 546 F. Supp. 785 (E.D. Pa. 1982), United States v. Waste Industries, Inc. 556 F. Supp. 1301 (E.D. N.C. 1983), and United States v. Northeastern Pharmaceutical & Chemical Co., 579 F. Supp. 823 (W.D. Mo. 1984), which restricted the application of section 7003, are inconsistent with the authority conferred by the section as initially enacted and with these clarifying amendments. H.R.Conf. Rep. No. 1133, 98th Cong., 2d Sess. 119 (1984)(emphasis added).

Thus, following the 1984 amendments, past off-site generators and transporters are within the scope of RCRA §7003(a). We reverse that part of the district court judgment holding that RCRA does not apply to past non-negligent off-site generators and transporters.

SCOPE OF LIABILITY

The district court found NEPACCO liable as the "owner or operator" of a "facility" (the NEPACCO plant) under CERCLA §107(a)(1) and as a "person" who arranged for the transportation and disposal of hazardous substances under CERCLA §107(a)(3). The district court found Lee liable as a "person" who arranged for the disposal of hazardous substances under CERCLA §107(a)(3) and as an "owner or operator" of the NEPACCO plant under CERCLA §107(a)(1) by "piercing the corporate veil." Id. at 848-49. The district court also found Michaels liable as an "owner or operator" of the NEPACCO plant under CERCLA §107(a)(1).

Appellants concede NEPACCO is liable under CERCLA §107(a)(3) for arranging for the transportation and disposal of hazardous substances at the Denney farm site. Because NEPACCO's assets have already been liquidated and distributed to its shareholders, however, it is unlikely that the government will be able to recover anything from NEPACCO.

Appellants argue (1) they cannot be held liable as "owners or operators" of a "facility" because "facility" refers to the place where hazardous substances are located and they did not own or operate the Denney farm site, (2) Lee cannot be held individually liable for arranging for the transportation and disposal of hazardous substances because he did not "own or possess" the hazardous substances and because he made those arrangements as a corporate officer or employee acting on behalf of NEPACCO, and (3) the district court erred in finding Lee and Michaels individually liable by "piercing the corporate veil." Appellants have not claimed that any of CERCLA's limited affirmative defenses apply to them.

The government argues Lee can be held individually liable without "piercing the corporate veil," under CERCLA §107(a)(3), and that Lee and Michaels can be held individually liable as "contributors" under RCRA §7003(a). For the reasons discussed below, we agree with the government's liability arguments.

LIABILITY UNDER CERCLA §107(A)(1)

First, appellants argue the district court erred in finding them liable under CERCLA §107(a)(1) as the "owners and operators" of a "facility" where hazardous substances are located. Appellants argue that, regardless of their relationship to the NEPACCO plant, they neither owned nor operated the Denney farm site, and that it is the Denney farm site, not the NEPACCO plant, that is a "facility" for purposes of "owner and operator" liability under CERCLA §107(a)(1). We agree.

CERCLA defines the term "facility" in part as "any site or area where a hazardous substance has been deposited, stored, disposed of, or placed, or otherwise come to be located." CERCLA §101(9)(B); see New York v. Shore Realty Corp., 759 F.2d 1032, 1043 n.15 (2d Cir. 1985). The term "facility" should be construed very broadly to include "virtually any place at which hazardous wastes have been dumped, or otherwise disposed of." United States v. Ward, 618 F. Supp. at 895. In the present case, however, the place where the hazardous substances were disposed of and where the government has concentrated its cleanup efforts is the Denney farm site, not the NEPACCO plant. The Denney farm site is the "facility." Because NEPACCO, Lee and Michaels did not own or operate the Denney farm site, they cannot be held liable as the "owners or operators" of a "facility" where hazardous substances are located under CERCLA §107(a)(1).

INDIVIDUAL LIABILITY UNDER CERCLA §107(A)(3)

CERCLA §107(a)(3) imposes strict liability upon "any person" who arranged for the disposal or transportation for disposal of hazardous substances. As defined by statute, the term "person" includes both individuals and corporations and does not exclude corporate officers or employees. Congress could have limited the statutory definition of "person" but chose not to do so. Compare CERCLA §101(20)(A)(limiting definition of "owner or operator"). Moreover, construction of CERCLA to impose liability upon only the corporation and not the individual corporate officers and employees who are responsible for making corporate decisions about the handling and disposal of hazardous substances would open an enormous, and clearly unintended, loophole in the statutory scheme.

First, Lee argues he cannot be held individually liable for having arranged for the transportation and disposal of hazardous substances under CERCLA §107(a)(3) because he did not personally own or possess the hazardous substances. Lee argues NEPACCO owned or possessed the hazardous substances.

The government argues Lee "possessed" the hazardous substances within the meaning of CERCLA §107(a)(3) because, as NEPACCO's plant supervisor, Lee had actual "control" over the NEPACCO plant's hazardous substances. We agree. It is the authority to control the handling and disposal of hazardous substances that is critical under the statutory scheme. The district court found that Lee, as plant supervisor, actually knew about, had immediate supervision over, and was directly responsible for arranging for the transportation and disposal of the NEPACCO plant's hazardous substances at the Denney farm site. We believe requiring proof of personal ownership or actual physical possession of hazardous substances as a precondition for liability under CERCLA §107(a)(3) would be inconsistent with the broad remedial purposes of CERCLA.

Next, Lee argues that because he arranged for the transportation and disposal of the hazardous substances as a corporate officer or employee acting on behalf of NEPACCO, he cannot be held individually liable for NEPACCO's violations. Lee also argues the district court erred in disregarding the corporate entity by "piercing the corporate veil" because there was no evidence that NEPACCO was inadequately capitalized, the corporate formalities were not observed, individual and corporate interests were not separate, personal and corporate funds were commingled or corporate property was diverted, or the corporate form was used unjustly or fraudulently.

The government argues Lee can be held individually liable, without "piercing the corporate veil," because Lee personally arranged for the disposal of hazardous substances in violation of CERCLA §107(a)(3). We agree. As discussed below, Lee can be held individually liable because he personally participated in conduct that violated CERCLA; this personal liability is distinct from the derivative liability that results from "piercing the corporate veil." "The effect of piercing a corporate veil is to hold the owner [of the corporation] liable. The rationale for piercing the corporate veil is that the corporation is something less than a bona fide independent entity." Donsco, Inc. v. Casper Corp., 587 F.2d 602, 606 (3d Cir. 1978). Here, Lee is liable because he personally participated in the wrongful conduct and not because he is one of the owners of what may have been a less than bona fide corporation. For this reason, we need not decide whether the district court erred in piercing the corporate veil under these circumstances.

We now turn to Lee's basic argument. Lee argues that he cannot be held individually liable for NEPACCO's wrongful conduct because he acted solely as a corporate officer or employee on behalf of NEPACCO. The liability imposed upon Lee, however, was not derivative but personal. Liability was not premised solely upon Lee's status as a corporate officer or employee. Rather, Lee is individually liable under CERCLA §107(a)(3) because he personally arranged for the transportation and disposal of hazardous substances on behalf of NEPACCO and thus actually participated in NEPACCO's CERCLA violations.

> A corporate officer is individually liable for the torts he [or she] personally commits [on behalf of the corporation] and cannot shield himself [or herself] behind a corporation when he [or she] is an actual participant in the tort. The fact that an officer is acting for a corporation also may make the corporation vicariously or secondarily liable under the doctrine of respondeat superior; it does not however relieve the individual of his [or her] responsibility. Donsco, Inc. v. Casper Corp., 587 F.2d at 606. Thus, Lee's personal involvement in NEPACCO's CERCLA violations made him individually liable.

INDIVIDUAL LIABILITY UNDER RCRA §7003(A)

The district court did not reach the question of individual liability under RCRA because it concluded that RCRA did not impose liability upon past non-negligent off-site generators like NEPACCO.... RCRA is applicable to past non-negligent off-site generators. The government argues Lee and Michaels are individually liable as "contributors" under RCRA §7003(a). We agree.

RCRA §7003(a) imposes strict liability upon "any person" who is contributing or who has contributed to the disposal of hazardous substances that may present an imminent and substantial endangerment to health or the environment. As defined by statute, the term "person" includes both individuals and corporations and does not exclude corporate officers and employees. As with the CERCLA definition of "person," Congress could have limited the RCRA definition of "person" but did not do so. [Again] compare CERCLA §101(20)(A)(limiting definition of "owner and operator"). More importantly, imposing liability upon only the corporation, but not those corporate officers and employees who actually make corporate decisions, would be inconsistent with Congress' intent to impose liability upon the persons who are involved in the handling and disposal of hazardous substances.

Our analysis of the scope of individual liability under the RCRA is similar to our analysis of the scope of individual liability under CERCLA. NEPACCO violated RCRA §7003(a) by "contributing to" the disposal of hazardous substances at the Denney farm site that presented an imminent and substantial endangerment to health and the environment. Thus, Lee and Michaels can be held individually liable if they were personally involved in or directly responsible for corporate acts in violation of RCRA.

We hold Lee and Michaels are individually liable as "contributors" under RCRA §7003(a). Lee actually participated in the conduct that violated RCRA; he personally arranged for the transportation and disposal of hazardous substances that presented an imminent and substantial endangerment to health and the environment. Unlike Lee, Michaels was not personally involved in the actual decision to transport and dispose of the hazardous substances. As NEPACCO's corporate president and as a major NEPACCO shareholder, however, Michaels was the individual in charge of and directly responsible for all of NEPACCO's operations, including those at the Verona plant, and he had the ultimate authority to control the disposal of NEPACCO's hazardous substances. Cf. New York v. Shore Realty Corp., 759 F.2d at 1052–53 (shareholder-manager held liable under CERCLA).

In summary, we hold Lee individually liable for arranging for the transportation and disposal of hazardous substances in violation of CERCLA §107(a)(3), and Lee and Michaels individually liable for contributing to an imminent and substantial endangerment to health and the environment in violation of RCRA §7003(a)....

BURDEN OF PROOF OF RESPONSE COSTS

The district court found appellants had the burden of proving the government's response costs were inconsistent with the NCP, and that response costs that are not inconsistent with the NCP are conclusively presumed to be reasonable and therefore recoverable. Appellants argue the district court erred in requiring them to prove the response costs were inconsistent with the NCP, not cost-effective or unnecessary. Appellants further argue the district court erred in assuming that all costs that are consistent with the NCP are conclusively presumed to be reasonable. Appellants note that the information and facts necessary to establish consistency with the NCP are matters within the possession of the government.

We believe the district court's analysis is correct. CERCLA §107(a)(4)(A) states that the government may recover from responsible parties "all costs of removal or remedial action...not inconsistent with the [NCP]." The statutory language itself establishes an exception for costs that are inconsistent with the NCP, but appellants, as the parties claiming the benefit of the exception, have the burden of proving that certain costs are inconsistent with the NCP and, therefore, not recoverable....

Because determining the appropriate removal and remedial action involves specialized knowledge and expertise, the choice of a particular cleanup method is a matter within the discretion of the EPA. The applicable standard of review is whether the agency's choice is arbitrary and capricious. As explained in United States v. Ward –

> If [appellants] wish the court to review the consistency of [the government's] actions with the NCP, then they are essentially alleging that the EPA did not carry out its statutory duties. The statute provides liability except for costs "not inconsistent" with the NCP. This language requires deference by this court to the judgment of agency professionals. [Appellants], therefore, may not seek to have the court substitute its own judgment for that of the EPA. [Appellants] may only show that the EPA's decision about the method of cleanup was "inconsistent" with the NCP in that the EPA was arbitrary and capricious in the discharge of their duties under the NCP. 618 F. Supp. at 900.

Here, appellants failed to show that the government's response costs were inconsistent with the NCP. Appellants also failed to show that the EPA acted arbitrarily and capriciously in choosing the particular method it used to clean up the Denney farm site....

GIBSON, J., concurring in part and dissenting in part.

I concur with the court's opinion except for [those] parts holding that RCRA §7003(a) imposes liability on past off-site nonnegligent generators and transporters and determining that the government could recover its response costs from Lee and Michaels under §7003(a). I respectfully dissent from the court's opinion as to those points.

The majority's analysis of liability under the RCRA focuses exclusively on the legislative history of the 1984 amendments to the RCRA. The majority particularly rely on House Conference Report No. 1133, which singles out the district court's opinion and states that it is "inconsistent with the authority conferred by [§7003] as initially enacted and with these clarifying amendments." H.R.Conf.Rep. No. 1133, 98th Cong., 2d Sess. 119 (1984), reprinted in 1984 U.S. Code Cong. & Ad. News 5649, 5690. The Conference Report also states that §7003 "has always" reached nonnegligent generators and transporters. Id. From these statements, the majority conclude that "the 98th Congress made clear that the intention of the 94th

Congress in enacting the RCRA in 1976 had been to impose liability upon past nonnegligent off-site generators and transporters of hazardous waste." Thus, the majority hold that the RCRA as it read prior to the 1984 amendments imposed strict liability upon past generators and transporters and that the district court erred in holding that proof of fault or negligence was necessary for the government to recover its response costs under the RCRA.

I think that the 1984 House Conference Report is nothing more than a blatant effort by members of a later Congress to graft their personal views of the scope of liability under the RCRA onto the original Act. It is bootstrapping, and the majority fail to recognize it as such. The Conference Report characterizes the 1984 amendments as "clarifying" the RCRA. The "clarifying" amendments to §7003, however, did not alter the crucial phrase "contributing to," the construction of which the majority acknowledge as "the critical issue," other than to cast it in both the present and the past tense: "has contributed to or... is contributing." 42 U.S.C.A. §6973(a). Nor do the amendments supply a definition for this phrase. The amendments to section 7003(a) are directed toward changing the scope of the section to reach past as well as present and future generators and transporters of hazardous waste. I believe this to be a substantive change, rather than a clarification. In any event, because the amendments did not relate to the "contributing to" language, the statements in the House Conference report regarding the standard of liability under §7003(a) – negligence versus strict liability – are wholly gratuitous.

COMMENTARY AND QUESTIONS

1. Private plaintiffs and cleanup legislation. *NEPACCO*, like many other cases brought under RCRA and CERCLA, features the United States as plaintiff. Private plaintiffs may also sue to enforce those statutes. For example, a subsection of the citizen suit provision of RCRA, 42 U.S.C. §6972(a)(1), authorizes private suits to enforce violation of any of RCRA's regulatory mechanisms, or the imminent hazard provision. Still, even with the presence of a citizen suit provision allowing its enforcement, RCRA has been held to create no private cause of action for damages.[39] See Walls v. Waste Resource Corp., 761 F.2d 311 (6th Cir. 1985). CERCLA does allow private recovery of response costs, a matter that is considered more fully later in this section.

2. Retroactivity. Prior to the amendment of RCRA and CERCLA, the retroactivity problem was quite perplexing to the courts, and at least a few found (on constitutional as well as statutory interpretation grounds) that the statutes were not to be applied to past non-negligent off-site generators. Is it clear that prior to CERCLA's passage, toxic dumping was "legal"? What would other arguments for non-retroactivity have been? See United States v. Wade *(Wade I)*, 546 F. Supp. 786 (E.D. Pa. 1982).

3. The strategy of avoiding §107 recoveries. In *Wade I*, the government sought an injunctive order requiring the defendant generators to clean up the site under CERCLA §106. As will be studied more fully in Chapter 21, CERCLA provides for

39. For a discussion of when a private cause of action may be implied from a regulatory enactment, see *infra* at 301.

creation of a Superfund from which the government may draw to pay for the cleanup of hazardous waste contamination. The government, when it uses the fund to pay for cleanups, may then sue responsible parties to recoup sums spent and thereby replenish the fund. Given the existence of Superfund cleanup funding and recoupment provisions under §107, and state law damage remedies, is it clear to you why EPA might seek such an order? Few if any of the parties ordered to clean a site are in a position to do the work themselves. Viewed in this light the order to clean a site looks like an order to pay a contractor to clean the site, which looks like a damage remedy. When first authorized Superfund had only $1.6 billion available under §107 and the pace of efforts that would have replenished the fund was slow. By obtaining relief under the imminent hazard prongs of RCRA §7003 and CERCLA §106, EPA could bypass the potential cash flow problem facing Superfund cleanups. By 1986 EPA's position was validated by the fact that CERCLA reimbursement was very problematic: a study conducted by EPA's Inspector General revealed that only 1.1 percent of $1.3 billion expended on Superfund cleanups up to 1986 had been recovered and put back into the fund.

4. The relevance of the views of a subsequent Congress. Who gets the better of the debate between the majority and the dissent about the relevance of 1984 legislative history to the interpretation of 1980 language? What should not be obscured is that the 1984 Congress is free to adopt prospectively whatever rule it wants; this is simply an exercise of its constitutional power to legislate granted by Article I. Whatever the state of prior legislation, a later Congress is not required to continue it unchanged. In contrast, what is involved here is the meaning of a provision that the 1980 Congress had enacted as law. Aren't questions of statutory interpretation to be decided by courts, not subsequent legislatures? What is the relevance of the views of members of a later Congress as evidence of what members of the 1980 Congress actually intended? Are they legislative history?

5. Arranging for disposal under CERCLA §107(a)(3). The most far-reaching development in the *NEPACCO* case is probably its ruling that holds Michaels personally liable under RCRA §7003 as a person who "contributed" to the disposal of hazardous waste, even though Michaels was not involved in the day-to-day operations of the plant in Verona, Missouri. The key phrases in the court's holding on this point cast a broad net – Michaels was "the individual in charge and directly responsible...and he had ultimate authority to control the disposal of NEPACCO's hazardous substances." Doesn't that description fit almost all chief operating officers of corporations? Looking at CERCLA §107(a)(3), can the "arranging for disposal" language of that liability section be read as broadly? One court has proposed a liability standard based on ability to prevent improper disposal:[40]

> This standard is different, but more stringent on the whole than traditional corporate liability, yet it requires more than mere status as a corporate officer or director.... The test – whether the individual in a close corporation could

40. See also the further discussion of executive liability in Chapter 7 at 343 *infra*.

have prevented or significantly abated the release of hazardous substances – allows the fact-finder to impose liability on a case-by-case basis.... Michigan v. ARCO Industries Corp., 723 F. Supp. 1214, 1219 (W.D. Mich. 1989).

As discussed in the next section of this chapter, setting appropriate limits to the scope of liability in "ability to control" situations has become an even hotter issue in other contexts. The *ARCO Industries* standard applies to close corporations, i.e. corporations owned and controlled by just a few shareholders. Is there any reason why the same standard would not be equally well-suited to determining liability of corporate offers in large publicly-held corporations?

6. Selling hazardous materials as a form of disposal. Given the breadth of RCRA and CERCLA liability, is it possible that the sale of products that contain hazardous materials such as creosote (a wood preservative that is itself a hazardous substance) can be considered "arranging for disposal" of those materials under §107(a)(3) of CERCLA? Congress did not define the term "arranged" in the statute and courts have had to supply a definition. In general, the courts have been quick to reject liability, protecting the sellers of products containing hazardous substances from liability. See, e.g., Edward Hines Lumber Co. v. Vulcan Materials Co., 685 F. Supp. 651 (N.D. Ill. 1988), aff'd on other grounds, 861 F.2d 155 (7th Cir. 1988). See also Gaba, Interpreting Section 107 (a)(3) of CERCLA: When Has A Person "Arranged For Disposal"?, 44 Sw. L. J. 1313 (1991).

Section 2. THE CLASSES OF PARTIES WHO MAY BE HELD LIABLE UNDER CERCLA

CERCLA holds liable all persons or entities classified as owners or operators of treatment, storage, or disposal ("TSD") facilities, and generators[41] and transporters of hazardous waste. These terms are, in part, easily understood, especially in the case of generators and transporters. Owners and operators is a more specialized term and is defined as follows by §101(20) of CERCLA:

> (A) The term "owner or operator" means (i) in the case of a vessel, any person owning, operating, or chartering by demise, such vessel, (ii) in the case of an onshore facility or an offshore facility, any person owning or operating such facility, and (iii) in the case of any facility, title or control of which was conveyed due to bankruptcy, foreclosure, tax delinquency, abandonment, or similar means to a unit of State or local government, any person who owned, operated or otherwise controlled activities at such facility immediately beforehand. Such term does not include a person, who, without participating in the management of a vessel or facility, holds indicia of ownership primarily to protect his security interest in the vessel or facility....

41. Generator liability is traceable to the previously reproduced provision in §107(a)(3) holding liable persons who arranged for disposal of hazardous materials that later are the subject of a removal or remedial action.

(D) The term "owner or operator" does not include a unit of State or local government which acquired ownership or control involuntarily through bankruptcy, tax delinquency, abandonment, or other circumstances in which the government involuntarily acquires title by virtue of its function as sovereign. The exclusion provided under this paragraph shall not apply to any State or local government which has caused or contributed to the release or threatened release of a hazardous substance from the facility, and such a State or local government shall be subject to the provisions of this chapter in the same manner and to the same extent, both procedurally and substantively, as any nongovernmental entity, including liability under section 9607 of this title.

The courts have played an important role in delineating the contours of hazardous waste liability through case law interpreting the statutory terms. In the *NEPACCO* case, for instance, portions of the opinion recounted examples of the "common law" of past, non-negligent off-site generator liability under RCRA §7003.

The owner and operator provisions of CERCLA, despite the presence of explicit statutory definition, have proved troublesome. Three major areas of litigation have emerged. The first line of cases concerns the potential liability of lenders who make loans to operators of TSD facilities or to generators. Frequently, when the borrower encounters financial difficulty, the lender will try to salvage its loan by becoming involved in the operation of the debtor's business. Not surprisingly, the presence of a solvent entity (the lender) participating in the affairs of a financially troubled TSD facility or generator makes an inviting target for a CERCLA plaintiff.

In one of the first cases attempting to extend liability in this fashion, United States v. Maryland Bank and Trust, 632 F. Supp. 573 (D. Md. 1986), the United States pressed a §107 claim against a bank that formerly held a mortgage on a Superfund site and later purchased the site at a foreclosure sale. The court found that the government had stated an actionable claim. The case first held that current owners, even those who were not "operators" of a site, were liable under CERCLA. This position is widely held, see, e.g., New York v. Shore Realty, 759 F.2d 1032 (2d Cir. 1985). More unusual, however, the *Maryland Bank* court, on the government's motion for summary judgment, addressed the §107(b)(3) affirmative defense raised by the bank. That statutory defense is available to those who can demonstrate that the release of hazardous materials was caused solely by a third party. The court found that there remained genuine issues of material fact regarding the government's allegations that the bank's pattern of loans and its on-going business relationship with the waste site operator vitiated the defense. Nevertheless, the court made plain its view that, if proven, the facts alleged by the government would deprive the bank of the defense.

Later leading cases, particularly United States v. Fleet Factors Corp., 901 F.2d 1550 (11th Cir. 1990), cert. denied, 111 S. Ct. 752 (1991), have affirmed and significantly expanded this line of liability. The *Fleet Factors* opinion states:

> Under the standard we adopt today, a secured creditor may incur section 9607(a)(2) liability, without being an operator, by participating in the

> financial management of a facility to a degree indicating a capacity to influence the corporation's treatment of hazardous wastes. 901 F.2d at 1557.

More recently, however, in In re Bergsoe Metal Corp. 910 F.2d 688 (9th Cir. 1990), the Ninth Circuit declined to embrace the *Fleet Factors* standard, stating "It is clear from the statute that, whatever the precise parameters of 'participation,' there must be *some* actual management of the facility before a secured creditor will fall outside of the exception [of §101(20)(A)]."

The second line of cases focuses less on expanding the class of operators and more on expanding the class of owners. For the most part, these cases involve pinning down who really owns the facility. Here the issues are ones of corporate structure, such as the relationship of a parent corporation to a subsidiary, or corporate succession, such as deciding whether a successor corporation is responsible for the liabilities of the entity it took over.[42]

Finally, there is a great deal of legal uncertainty surrounding the statutory effort to exonerate innocent purchasers of contaminated parcels from liability. As noted in the previous discussion of the *Maryland Bank* case, current owners of contaminated property are liable under §107 unless they can establish the affirmative defense that the contamination was solely due to the act of a third person with whom they had no contractual dealings. This defense protects property owners against unauthorized "midnight dumping" but it does not protect them against the misdeeds of predecessors in their chain of title, with whom they will often be in a contractual relationship. Congress, aware of this problem, tried to address it by amendments now codified in §101(35), which appears in Question 7 below.

COMMENTARY AND QUESTIONS

1. The Superfund Amendments and Reauthorization Act of 1986 (SARA). In 1986 Congress revisited a number of areas of CERCLA in a far-reaching set of amendments that also reauthorized the continuing operation of the Superfund system. Pub. No. 99-499. SARA, as the 1986 legislation is known, spoke to a number of liability issues, usually in ways that confirmed broad judicial interpretations of the liability provisions. As in §101(35) noted in Question 7, Congress clarified a variety of questions about the scope of the statute. SARA did not cut back on the scope of CERCLA liability. To the contrary, the generally pro-liability posture of SARA led some experts in the field to suggest that its acronym ought to be changed to RACHEL because the Reauthorization Act Confirms How Everyone's Liable. See, e.g., United States v. Kramer, 757 F. Supp. 397 (D.N.J. 1991); Glass, Superfund and SARA: Are There Any Defenses Left?, 12 Harv. Envtl L. Rev. 385 (1988). In the same vein, one commentator has written, "With only slight exaggeration, one government lawyer has described a [CERCLA] trial as requiring only that the Justice Department lawyer stand up and recite: 'May it please the Court, I represent the government and therefore I win.'" Marzulla, Superfund 1991: How Insurance Firms Can Help Clean Up the Nation's Hazardous Waste, 4 TXLR 685 (1989).

---

42. These issues are not limited to the ownership of TSD facilities, they can also arise in the context of deciding who is a generator or transporter.

2. *Fleet Factors* as a Pyrrhic victory for EPA. The breadth of the test applied by the 11th Circuit for lender liability in the *Fleet Factors* case has proved to be problematic for EPA. The decision raised a storm of protest from the lending industry, not just private lenders but also federal agencies like the Federal Deposit Insurance Corporation and Resolution Trust Company. One industry fear was that the typical efforts of secured lenders to prevent default on loans and/or the loss of collateral would frequently render them liable under CERCLA despite their status as secured creditors under §101(20)(A). The second fear was that foreclosers would also be liable because they might not be considered innocent purchasers under §101(35)(A)(ii). If the federal banking establishment and lenders generally are up in arms about *Fleet Factors*, what is likely to result?

Should Congress rewrite the pertinent parts of the statute? See Note, Will CERCLA Be Unbroken? Repairing the Damage After *Fleet Factors*, 59 Fordham L. Rev. 135, 164-168 (1990). Should EPA issue an administrative rule interpreting the relevant provisions to narrow the scope of liability? EPA has taken initial steps down this path. See EPA, Draft Proposal Defining Lender Liability Issues Under the Secured Creditor Exemption of CERCLA (Sept. 14, 1990).[43] Should the matter be left to the courts to resolve the conflicts between the tests for liability set forth in *Fleet Factors* and *In re Bergsoe*?

3. Trustee liability. Real property or businesses are at times held in trust by a trustee for the benefit of the trust's beneficiaries. In the event that the property is the site of a release of hazardous materials, or the business generates hazardous materials that are disposed of at a site at which there is a release, CERCLA liability is unaffected by the fact that the property is a trust. That is, as to trust assets the trustee will be susceptible to CERCLA liability like any other potentially responsible party (PRP). The more probing question is under what circumstances the trustee (whether an individual, a bank trust department, or a corporation) can be made to pay for CERCLA liability out of the trustee's own assets. Is there any meaningful sense in which a trustee actively operating a business is not an owner or operator, or a generator? Should the trustee's personal assets be added to those of the trust as assets available for the cleanup of CERCLA sites? Thus far there is surprisingly little case law on this point. In United States v. Burns, the motion of the defendant trustee for partial summary judgment on the issue of his personal liability was denied. This is perhaps unsurprising, for as one commentator puts it:

> Generally, a trustee is personally liable for torts "committed in the course of the administration of the trust to the same extent that he would be liable if he held the property free of trust." Restatement (2d) of Trusts §264 (1959). When the trustee is found liable, however, he will have a right of indemnification against trust assets if the liability was incurred "in the proper administration of the estate or trust...and if the fiduciary was not personally at fault." Of

43. The draft was widely leaked and was published at 5 TXLR 650 (Oct. 17, 1990). A revised draft has also been leaked, but its text has yet to be published. In a later Toxics Law Reporter article describing the revision, it was characterized as having made allowances for the ordinary practices of secured creditors and foreclosing lenders. See 5 TXLR 1170 (Feb. 20, 1991).

> course, the underlying logic of the common law standard stumbles somewhat in the hazardous waste context, because a liable (but blameless) trustee might find his right of indemnification worthless where the trust constitutes a net liability. Note, The Potentially Responsible Trustee: Probable Target For CERCLA Liability, 77 Va. L. Rev. 113, 116 n.21 (1991).

How should banks and other deep-pocket trustees adjust their trust practices?

4. "The time has come," the walrus said, "to talk of many things...of 'subsids,' parents, shareholders, of cabbages and kings." The courts consistently have construed CERCLA's scope of liability broadly in a variety of contexts that involve scrutinizing a corporation's form. At times this has gone beyond the traditional common law doctrine that allows for piercing the corporate veil when corporate form is being used as a sham to defraud creditors. To go beyond traditional rules of corporate law in imposing liability on owners of corporations is a very delicate matter because one of the principal assurances of corporate form is that only corporate assets are put at risk by corporate activities; personal assets of a corporation's owners are not supposed to be put at risk. As a matter of policy, adherence to this general principle is quite important. Limited liability invites the formation of new companies that may or may not survive, and is thus vital to economic innovation and dynamism. Shareholder immunity from liability is likewise a vital element in capital formation. Without it shareholders would be inhibited from purchasing stock as a form of investment in corporations. Despite all of these dangers, CERCLA liability has been extended beyond the normal limits of corporate law in a number of disparate settings:

> *Corporate parent-subsidiary relationships:* It is not unusual for a corporate parent to create a number of subsidiary corporations that engage in different activities. In fact, the use of subsidiaries may be a legitimate attempt to protect the parent against claims for excess liabilities of a subsidiary that is going to enter a risk-laden field, such as hazardous materials operations in a post-CERCLA world. When the subsidiary is a mere sham, the common law has long disregarded the corporate form, usually looking to a series of factors to determine if the subsidiary was a bona fide separate entity. The factors include whether the subsidiary was adequately capitalized, the extent to which the parent retained direct control of the subsidiary's action, the presence of interlocking directorates and common corporate officers, etc. Many of the CERCLA cases, however, have included concepts of ability to control as a vital issue. In the parent-subsidiary context the parent, by virtue of its ownership of the subsidiary, always has a long-term power to control the subsidiary's actions. Thus far the cases have not been quick to disregard the corporate form, although a split in the circuits has developed. The leading case that vindicates the usual principles of corporate law is Joslyn Manufacturing Co. v. T. L. James & Co., 696 F. Supp. 222 (W.D. La. 1988), aff'd, 893 F.2d 80 (5th Cir. 1990), cert. denied, 111 S. Ct. 1017, (1991). The leading case imposing liability on a corporate parent based on a showing that would not qualify for traditional common law veil-piercing is United States v. Kayser-Roth Corp., 724 F. Supp. 15, aff'd, 910 F.2d 24 (1st Cir. 1990), cert. denied, 111 S. Ct. 957 (1991).

Corporate shareholders of dissolved corporations: Corporations at times wind up their affairs and go out of existence through a state law dissolution process. Dissolution provides a period of time after a petition for dissolution is filed in which claims against the corporation may be brought and satisfied from corporate assets that would otherwise be distributed to the corporation's shareholders. Usually, in order to have a measure of finality in these matters, claims that are not filed during the designated period are thereafter barred. The issue in the CERCLA context is whether a post-dissolution suit can be brought against shareholders to whom corporate assets were distributed. Again, in the absence of fraud, the usual rule of corporation law is that such suits are barred. The leading federal case on point is Onan Corp. v. Industrial Steel Container Co., 909 F.2d 511 (8th Cir. 1990), cert. denied, 111 S. Ct. 431 (1990); but see United States v. Sharon Steel, 681 F. Supp. 1492, 1495–98 (D. Utah 1987)(construing CERCLA as pre-emptive of state dissolution law).

As a matter of policy, it is not fundamentally important that corporate assets distributed upon dissolution should be transferred to shareholders free of claims related to corporate wrongdoing. Stated differently, the policy favoring repose and finality that is behind the usual operation of dissolution proceedings is not as vital to the functioning of the corporate system as are the interests in protecting the limited liability aspects of corporate form. Indeed, there is a sense in which failure to seek recovery of the distributed corporate assets allows the shareholders to retain ill-gotten gains, especially if the corporation was actively engaged in environmental misdeeds during its existence. At least one recent case described in the BNA Toxics Law Reporter shows some possible movement toward liability in such cases. In that case a state trial court, on both CERCLA and state law theories, held the shareholders of a dissolved corporation liable to a party that had cleaned up hazardous contamination released by the dissolved corporation. See U-Haul Co. of Inland Northwest v. Yakima Rex Spray Co., No. 90-2-00155-4 (Wash. Super. Ct. Yakima City. Aug. 24, 1990) discussed at 5 TXLR 534.

Successor corporations: Often one corporation will purchase the productive assets of another, either via merger, through the purchase of stock, or through the purchase of the assets themselves. Corporate law has developed general principles that establish when successor corporations will be held to have purchased the liabilities of their predecessors. EPA has issued a guidance document that sets forth its general approach to issues of corporate succession:

In establishing successor liability under CERCLA, the Agency should initially utilize the "continuity of business operation" approach of federal law. However, to provide additional support or an alternative basis for successor corporation liability, the Agency should be prepared to apply the traditional exemptions to the general rule of non-liability in asset acquisitions. EPA Memorandum of Courtney Price, Liability of Corporate Shareholders and Successor Corporations For Abandoned Sites Under [CERCLA] at 15-16 (June 13, 1984).

At least one commentator has argued that this position marks a substantial expansion of successor liability because the continuation of the business entity test ignores the nuances of asset transfer that are often a key to determining successor liability under traditional state corporation law. See Wallace, Liability of Corporations and Corporate Officers, Directors, and Shareholders Under Superfund: Should Corporate and Agency Law Concepts Apply?, 14 J. Corp. L. 839, 879-884 (1989). The business continuation standard, instead, has its roots in the modern products liability revolution that has so greatly expanded liability in that realm.

In general, the courts have been receptive to imposing successor liability in CERCLA cases, even in some situations where the common law would not. See, e.g., Smith Land & Improvement Corp. v. Celotex Corp., 851 F.2d 86 (3d Cir. 1988), cert. denied, 488 U.S. 1029 (1990); Louisiana-Pacific Corp. v. Asarco, Inc., 909 F.2d 1260 (9th Cir. 1990).

5. How the courts make CERCLA liability policy. After the preceding three notes' long forays into the nuts and bolts of CERCLA liability, the prominent role of courts in framing the contours of CERCLA as part of a case-by-case development should be apparent. What is less clear is whether the courts are interpreting statutes or making law. In any event, the courts are not merely engaged in a rote process of statutory interpretation that deduces the intent of Congress through a series of simple logical steps. The process of judicial interpretation frequently calls upon courts to weigh and balance competing policy concerns, giving the process of statutory interpretation much of the same dynamism as the common law. The Sixth Circuit, in a successor liability case, reflected on the role of courts in these terms:

> The Supreme Court has stated that "the authority to construe a statute is fundamentally different from the authority to fashion a new rule or to provide a new remedy which Congress has decided not to adopt." Northwest Airlines, Inc. v. Transport Workers Union of America, 451 U.S. 77, 97 (1981). As Justice Stevens wrote in *Northwest Airlines*, "Broadly worded constitutional and statutory provisions necessarily have been given concrete meaning and application by a process of case-by-case judicial decisions in the common-law tradition." Id. at 95.
>
> Of course, the line separating statutory interpretation and judicial lawmaking is not always clear and sharp. If a statute is found to be abundantly clear and well defined, a judicial decision that expands or contracts its reach or adds or deletes remedies fashions federal common law. On the other hand, if the court detects only gaps in definitions or descriptions, it may fill these interstices of the statute by exercising its authority to interpret or construe the statute. As the Supreme Court has stated, these two exercises of judicial authority are fundamentally different, and they are subject to different standards. The authority to construe a statute lies at the very heart of judicial power and is not subject to rigorous scrutiny. The rule is otherwise with respect to outright judicial lawmaking, however. Before a federal court may fashion a body of federal common law, it must find either (1) that Congress painted with a broad brush and left it to the courts to "flesh out" the statute

> by fashioning a body of substantive federal law, or (2) that a federal rule of decision is necessary to protect uniquely federal interests. Anspec Company, Inc. v. Johnson Controls, Inc., 922 F.2d 1240, 1245 (6th Cir. 1991).

Which sort of exercise are the courts engaged in when they address issues such as successor liability? The court in *Anspec* held that CERCLA issues are matters of statutory construction and that CERCLA, properly construed, intended to impose liability on successor corporations. The making of federal common law will be considered later in this chapter.

6. Would you buy this land? Assume that you are a commercial investor and are aware of a contaminated parcel that is otherwise well suited for investment. Should you purchase the property? As is made plain by CERCLA §101(35) set forth in the next question, as a purchaser of the property with knowledge of its contamination you would be liable for cleanup costs as a responsible party under CERCLA. If the sum of the purchase price plus the cost of cleanup is sufficiently low that the parcel freed of contamination is worth more than that sum, the purchase should be consummated. In the case of badly contaminated parcels, however, the cleanup costs alone often dwarf the "clean" market value of the parcel. Those are problem cases for society because one important goal of CERCLA is (or ought to be) the return of contaminated sites to productive use. What can be done in those cases? For a series of suggestions, see Motiuk & Monaghan, Incentives and Protections for Prospective Purchasers and Operators of Contaminated Property, 5 TXLR 1536 (1991).

Would the presence of a state law strict liability cause of action against former owners whose acts contaminated the parcel alter the calculation of the desirability of its purchase? The availability of such a claim would increase the attractiveness of the parcel. New Jersey has taken a step in this direction. See T & E Industries, Inc. v. Safety Light Corp., 587 A.2d 1249 (N.J. 1991).

7. The "act of a third party" defense. CERCLA §107(b)(3) permits a defense when the hazardous release or threatened release is caused solely by the act of a third party with whom the defendant has little or no relation. Section 107 was set forth at the outset of the CERCLA materials in this chapter. Section 101(35) in relevant part reads as follows:

> (A) The term "contractual relationship," for the purpose of §9607(b)(3) of this title includes, but is not limited to, land contracts, deeds or other instruments transferring title or possession, unless the real property on which the facility concerned is located was acquired by the defendant after the disposal or placement of the hazardous substance on, in, or at the facility, and one or more of the circumstances described in clause (i), (ii), or (iii) is also established by the defendant by a preponderance of the evidence:
>
> (i) At the time the defendant acquired the facility the defendant did not know and had no reason to know that any hazardous

substance which is the subject of the release or threatened release was disposed of on, in, or at the facility.

(ii) The defendant is a government entity which acquired the facility by escheat, or through any other involuntary transfer or acquisition, or through the exercise of eminent domain authority by purchase or condemnation.

(iii) The defendant acquired the facility by inheritance or bequest. In addition to establishing the foregoing, the defendant must establish that he has satisfied the requirements of §9607(b)(3)(a) and (b) of this title.

(B) To establish that the defendant had no reason to know, as provided in clause (i) of subparagraph (A) of this paragraph, the defendant must have undertaken, at the time of acquisition, all appropriate inquiry into the previous ownership and uses of the property consistent with good commercial or customary practice in an effort to minimize liability. For purposes of the preceding sentence the court shall take into account any specialized knowledge or experience on the part of the defendant, the relationship of the purchase price to the value of the property if uncontaminated, commonly known or reasonably ascertainable information about the property, the obviousness of the presence or likely presence of contamination at the property, and the ability to detect such contamination by appropriate inspection....

Consider whether that defense is available in the following hypothetical situation: RHA is considering buying a piece of commercial property that shows no obvious signs of contamination. Under what circumstances, if any, will RHA be free from §107(a)(1) owners liability if in the future it is discovered that previously disposed of hazardous substances are buried under the surface and are releasing toxic contaminants into the groundwater?

Section 3. THE GOVERNMENT'S RELAXED BURDEN OF PROOF OF CAUSATION IN CERCLA CASES

You will recall from the earlier material on toxic tort litigation the difficulty that plaintiffs encounter in proving that the defendant's activities are the cause in fact of plaintiff's injuries. Even in a strict liability regime, that same difficulty could scuttle much of CERCLA's effectiveness if the government in every case had to trace each facet of cleanup costs to the actions of a particular defendant. This is especially true in older sites or midnight dumping sites where the records of what wastes were deposited by whom are sketchy or non-existent. The courts confronted this problem within the first years following CERCLA's enactment.

United States v. Wade *(Wade II)*

United States District Court, Eastern District of Pennsylvania
577 F. Supp. 1326 (1983)

[The Wade litigation involved a large disposal site in Chester, Pennsylvania. The site was an extraordinarily high visibility one, having been the scene of a major fire in 1978 which damaged many of the several thousand tank cars and drums stored on the property. After testing discovered the presence of more than fifty hazardous substances at the site, many of which were leaking into the groundwater and from there into the Delaware River, legal action was instituted.

The Wade site was among the first sites for which the United States EPA sought remedies under RCRA and CERCLA. The litigation began in 1979 with the filing of a RCRA §7003 complaint. Shortly after the enactment of CERCLA in 1980, an amended complaint added counts under CERCLA §§106 and 107. The United States sought both injunctive relief as to the cleanup of the site and monetary relief for the response costs incurred by the government and others who had already undertaken steps to begin to seal the site and remove additional wastes still stored there. The parties sued by the United States included the site's owner (Wade), several off-site generators and some of the transporters who had deposited materials at the site. Earlier litigation had focused on the scope and retroactivity of the major statutes; the excerpted portion of this decision addresses only the issue of proof of causation.]

NEWCOMER, J. This is a civil action brought by the United States against several parties allegedly responsible for the creation of a hazardous waste dump in Chester, Pennsylvania. The government seeks injunctive relief against Melvin R. Wade, the owner of the dump site, ABM Disposal Service, the company which transported the hazardous substances to the site, and Ellis Barnhouse and Franklin P. Tyson, the owners of ABM during the time period at issue ("non-generator defendants"). The government also seeks reimbursement of the costs incurred and to be incurred in cleaning up the site from the non-generator defendants as well as from Apollo Metals, Inc., Congoleum Corporation, Gould, Inc., and Sandvik, Inc. ("generator defendants").

The claims for injunctive relief are brought pursuant to §7003 of the Resource Conservation and Recovery Act of 1976 ("RCRA"), 42 U.S.C.A. §6973, and §106 of CERCLA, 42 U.S.C.A. §9606. The claims for monetary relief are based on §107(a) of CERCLA, 42 U.S.C.A. §9607(a), as well as a common law theory of restitution. Presently before the Court are the government's motions for partial summary judgment on the issue of joint and several liability under §107(a) against each of the defendants....

The generator defendants' motions for summary judgment on the CERCLA claims generally advance two arguments. First, they argue that the government has not and cannot establish the requisite causal relationship between their wastes and the costs incurred by the government in cleaning up the site....

THE CAUSATION ARGUMENT

...Even assuming the government proves that a given defendant's waste was in fact disposed of at the Wade site, the generator defendants argue it must also prove that a particular defendant's actual waste is presently at the site and has been the subject of a removal or remedial measure before that defendant can be held liable. In the alternative, the generator defendants argue that at a minimum the government must link its costs incurred to waste of the sort created by a generator before that generator may be held liable....

Part of the generator defendants' argument revolves around the use of the word "such" in referring to the "hazardous substances" [in CERCLA §107(a)(3)] contained at the dump site or "facility." It could be read to require that the facility contain a particular defendant's waste. On the other hand it could be read merely to require that hazardous substances like those found in a defendant's waste must be present at the site. The legislative history provides no enlightenment on this point. I believe that the less stringent requirement was the one intended by Congress.

The government's experts have admitted that scientific technique has not advanced to a point that the identity of the generator of a specific quantity of waste can be stated with certainty. All that can be said is that a site contains the same kind of hazardous substances as are found in a generator's waste. Thus, to require a plaintiff under CERCLA to "fingerprint" wastes is to eviscerate the statute. Given two possible constructions of a statute, one which renders it useless should be rejected. Generators are adequately protected by requiring a plaintiff to prove that a defendant's waste was disposed of at a site and that the substances that make the defendant's waste hazardous are also present at the site....[44]

I turn now to the generator defendants' contention that the government must link its costs incurred to wastes of the sort created by them.

A reading of the literal language of the statute suggests that the generator defendants read too much into this portion of its causation requirement. Stripping away the excess language, the statute appears to impose liability on a generator who has (1) disposed of its hazardous substances (2) at a facility which now contains hazardous substances of the sort disposed of by the generator (3) if there is a release of that or some other type of hazardous substance (4) which causes the incurrence of response costs. Thus, the release which results in the incurrence of response costs and liability need only be of *"a"* hazardous substance [the language of CERCLA §107(a)(4)] and not necessarily one contained in the defendant's waste. The only required nexus between the defendant and the site is that the defendant have dumped his waste there and that the hazardous substances found in the defendant's waste are also found at the site. I base my disagreement with defendants' reading in part on the Act's use of "such" to modify "hazardous substance" in paragraph three and the switch to "a" in paragraph four....

Deletion of the causation language contained in the House-passed bill and the Senate draft is not dispositive of the causation issue. Nevertheless, the substitution of the present language for the prior causation requirement evidences a legislative intent which is in accordance with my reading of the Act.

COMMENTARY AND QUESTION

1. Comparison to toxic tort cases. How does the relaxation of the government's burdens in proving causation in CERCLA cases compare with handling of burden of proof issues in traditional and toxic tort cases that were studied in Chapters 3 and 4?

Section 4. JOINT AND SEVERAL LIABILITY IN CERCLA CASES

United States v. Monsanto Company

United States Court of Appeals for the Fourth Circuit, 1988
858 F.2d 160

[In this case the federal and state governments sued to recover response costs following releases and threatened releases of hazardous material at a waste storage

44. I also reject the arguments that the government must establish that the generator selected the site at which the wastes were dumped and that transfer of ownership of the waste to ABM at the time of pick-up for disposal absolves the generator of liability. Neither argument finds any support in the language of the statute.

facility. The district court found defendants jointly and severally liable as owners, operators, and generators of hazardous waste, and defendants appealed. Additional facts are supplied in the opinion.]

SITE-OWNERS' LIABILITY

In light of the strict liability imposed by §107(a), we cannot agree with the site-owners contention that they are not within the class of owners Congress intended to hold liable. The traditional elements of tort culpability on which the site-owners rely simply are absent from the statute. The plain language of §107(a)(2) extends liability to owners of waste facilities regardless of their degree of participation in the subsequent disposal of hazardous waste.

Under §107(a)(2), any person who owned a facility at a time when hazardous substances were deposited there may be held liable for all costs of removal or remedial action if a release or threatened release of a hazardous substance occurs. The site-owners do not dispute their ownership of the Bluff Road facility, or the fact that releases occurred there during their period of ownership. Under these circumstances, all the prerequisites to §107(a) liability have been satisfied.[45] See New York v. Shore Realty, 759 F.2d 1032, 1043-44 (2d Cir. 1985)(site-owner held liable under CERCLA §107(a)(1) even though he did not contribute to the presence or cause the release of hazardous substances at the facility)....

GENERATOR DEFENDANTS' LIABILITY

The generator defendants first contend that the district court misinterpreted §107(a)(3) because it failed to read into the statute a requirement that the governments prove a nexus between the waste they sent to the site and the resulting environmental harm. They maintain that the statutory phrase "containing such hazardous substances" requires proof that the specific substances they generated and sent to the site were present at the facility at the time of release. The district court held, however, that the statute was satisfied by proof that hazardous substances "like" those contained in the generator defendants' waste were found at the site. United States v. South Carolina Recycling and Disposal, Inc., 653 F. Supp. 984, 991-92 (D.S.C. 1986)(SCRDI). We agree with the district court's interpretation.

---

45. The site-owners' relative degree of fault would, of course, be relevant in any subsequent action for contribution brought pursuant to 42 U.S.C.A. §9613(f)(West Supp. 1987). Congress, in the Superfund Amendments and Reauthorization Act of 1986, Pub.L. 99-499, §113 (1986)(hereafter SARA), established a right of contribution in favor of defendants sued under CERCLA §107(a). Section 113(f)(1) provides:

> Any person may seek contribution from any other person who is liable or potentially liable under §9607(a) of this title, during or following any civil action under §9606 of this title or under §9607(a) of this title. Such claims shall be brought in accordance with this section and the Federal Rules of Civil Procedure, and shall be governed by Federal law. In resolving contribution claims, the court may allocate response costs among liable parties using such equitable factors as the court determines are appropriate. Nothing in this subsection shall diminish the right of any person to bring an action for contribution in the absence of a civil action under §9606 or §9607 of this title.

The legislative history of this amendment suggests that in arriving at an equitable allocation of costs, a court may consider, among other things, the degree of involvement by parties in the generation, transportation, treatment, storage, or disposal of hazardous substances. H.R.Rep. No. 253(III), 99th Cong., 1st Sess. 19 (1985), reprinted in 1986 U.S. Code Cong. & Admin. News 2835, 3038, 3042.

Reduced of surplus language, §107(a)(3) and (4) impose liability on off-site waste generators who:

> arranged for disposal...of hazardous substances...at any facility...*containing such hazardous substances*...from which there is a release...of a hazardous substance. (emphasis supplied).

In our view, the plain meaning of the adjective "such" in the phrase "containing such hazardous substances" is "[a]like, similar, of the like kind." Black's Law Dictionary 1284 (5th ed. 1979). As used in the statute, the phrase "such hazardous substances" denotes hazardous substances alike, similar, or of a like kind to those that were present in a generator defendant's waste or that could have been produced by the mixture of the defendant's waste with other waste present at the site. It does not mean that the plaintiff must trace the ownership of each generic chemical compound found at a site. Absent proof that a generator defendant's specific waste remained at a facility at the time of release, a showing of chemical similarity between hazardous substances is sufficient.

The overall structure of CERCLA's liability provisions also militates against the generator defendants' "proof of ownership" argument. In *Shore Realty*, the Second Circuit held with respect to site-owners that requiring proof of ownership at any time later than the time of disposal would go far toward rendering the §107(b) defenses superfluous. We agree with the court's reading of the statute and conclude that its reasoning applies equally to the generator defendants' contentions. As the statute provides –"(n)otwithstanding any other provision or rule of law"– liability under §107(a) is "subject *only* to the defenses set forth" in §107(b)(emphasis added). Each of the three defenses established in §107(b) "carves out from liability an exception based on causation." *Shore Realty*, 759 F.2d at 1044. Congress has, therefore, allocated the burden of disproving causation to the defendant who profited from the generation and inexpensive disposal of hazardous waste. We decline to interpret the statute in a way that would neutralize the force of Congress' intent.

Finally, the purpose underlying CERCLA's liability provisions counsels against the generator defendants' argument. Throughout the statute's legislative history, there appears the recurring theme of facilitating prompt action to remedy the environmental blight of unscrupulous waste disposal. In deleting causation language from §107(a), we assume as have many other courts that Congress knew of the synergistic and migratory capacities of leaking chemical waste, and the technological infeasibility of tracing improperly disposed waste to its source. In view of this, we will not frustrate the statute's salutary goals by engrafting a "proof of ownership" requirement, which in practice, would be as onerous as the language Congress saw fit to delete. See United States v. Wade, 577 F. Supp. 1326, 1332 (E.D. Pa.1983)("To require a plaintiff under CERCLA to 'fingerprint' wastes is to eviscerate the statute.")...

The appellants next challenge the district court's imposition of joint and several liability for the governments' response costs.[46] The court concluded that joint and several liability was appropriate because the environmental harm at Bluff Road was "indivisible" and the appellants had "failed to meet their burden of proving otherwise."

---

46. The site-owners limit their joint and several liability argument to the contention that it is inequitable under the circumstances of this case, i.e., their limited degree of participation in waste disposal activities at Bluff Road. As we have stated, however, such equitable factors are relevant in subsequent actions for contribution. They are not pertinent to the question of joint and several liability, which focuses principally on the divisibility among responsible parties of the harm to the environment.

While CERCLA does not mandate the imposition of joint and several liability, it permits it in cases of indivisible harm. In each case, the court must consider traditional and evolving principles of federal common law, which Congress has left to the courts to supply interstitially.

Under common law rules, when two or more persons act independently to cause a single harm for which there is a reasonable basis of apportionment according to the contribution of each, each is held liable only for the portion of harm that he causes. When such persons cause a single and indivisible harm, however, they are held liable jointly and severally for the entire harm. We think these principles, as reflected in the Restatement (Second) of Torts, represent the correct and uniform federal rules applicable to CERCLA cases.

Section 433A of the Restatement (Second) of Torts (1965) provides:

> (1) Damages for harm are to be apportioned among two or more causes where
>
> (a) there are distinct harms, or
>
> (b) there is a reasonable basis for determining the contribution of each cause to a single harm.
>
> (2) Damages for any other harm cannot be apportioned among two or more causes.

Placing their argument into the Restatement framework, the generator defendants concede that the environmental damage at Bluff Road constituted a "single harm," but contend that there was a reasonable basis for apportioning the harm. They observe that each of the off-site generators with whom SCRDI contracted sent a potentially identifiable volume of waste to the Bluff Road site, and they maintain that liability should have been apportioned according to the volume they deposited as compared to the total volume disposed of there by all parties. In light of the conditions at Bluff Road, we cannot accept this method as a basis for apportionment.

The generator defendants bore the burden of establishing a reasonable basis for apportioning liability among responsible parties. United States v. Chem-Dyne Corp., 572 F. Supp. 802, 810 (S.D. Ohio 1983); Restatement (Second) of Torts §433B (1965).[47] To meet this burden, the generator defendants had to establish that the environmental harm at Bluff Road was divisible among responsible parties. They presented no evidence, however, showing a relationship between waste volume, the release of hazardous substances, and the harm at the site.[48] Further, in light of the commingling of hazardous substances, the district court could not have reasonably apportioned liability without some evidence disclosing the individual and interac-

---

47. Section 433(b)(2) of the Restatement (Second) of Torts (1965) provides:

> Where the tortious conduct of two or more actors has combined to bring about harm to the plaintiff, and one or more actors seeks to limit his liability on the ground that the harm is capable of apportionment among them, the burden of proof as to the apportionment is upon each such actor.

48. At minimum, such evidence was crucial to demonstrate that a volumetric apportionment scheme was reasonable. The governments presented considerable evidence identifying numerous hazardous substances found at Bluff Road. An EPA investigator reported, for example, that in the first cleanup phase RAD Services encountered substances "in every hazard class, including explosives such as crystallized dynamite and nitroglycerine. Numerous examples were found of oxidizers, flammable and nonflammable liquids, poisons, corrosives, containerized gases, and even a small amount of radioactive material." Under these circumstances, volumetric apportionment based on the overall quantity of waste, as opposed to the quantity and quality of hazardous substances contained in the waste would have made little sense.

tive qualities of the substances deposited there. Common sense counsels that a million gallons of certain substances could be mixed together without significant consequences, whereas a few pints of others improperly mixed could result in disastrous consequences.[49] Under other circumstances proportionate volumes of hazardous substances may well be probative of contributory harm.[50] In this case, however, volume could not establish the effective contribution of each waste generator to the harm at the Bluff Road site.

Although we find no error in the trial court's imposition of joint and several liability, we share the appellants' concern that they not be ultimately responsible for reimbursing more than their just portion of the governments' response costs.[51] In its refusal to apportion liability, the district court likewise recognized the validity of their demand that they not be required to shoulder a disproportionate amount of the costs. It ruled, however, that making the governments whole for response costs was the primary consideration and that cost allocation was a matter "more appropriately considered in an action for contribution between responsible parties after plaintiff has been made whole." *SCRDI*, 653 F. Supp. at 995 & n. 8. Had we sat in place of the district court, we would have ruled as it did on the apportionment issue, but may well have retained the action to dispose of the contribution questions. That procedural course, however, was committed to the trial court's discretion and we find no abuse of it. As we have stated, the defendants still have the right to sue responsible parties for contribution, and in that action they may assert both legal and equitable theories of cost allocation.[52]

WIDENER,C. J., concurred in part, dissented in part, and filed an opinion.

COMMENTARY AND QUESTIONS

1. The choice of joint and several liability. Do you see how, strategically, joint and several liability is the concept (imported from common law) that makes CERCLA so potent? Courts uniformly interpret CERCLA as manifesting an intent on the part of Congress to allow joint and several liability among potentially responsible parties

49. We agree with the district court that evidence disclosing the relative toxicity, migratory potential, and synergistic capacity of the hazardous substances at the site would be relevant to establishing divisibility of harm.

50. Volumetric contributions provide a reasonable basis for apportioning liability only if it can be reasonably assumed, or it has been demonstrated, that independent factors had no substantial effect on the harm to the environment. Cf. Restatement (Second) of Torts §433A comment d, illustrations 4, 5 (1965).

51. The final judgment holds the defendants liable for slightly less than half of the total costs incurred in the cleanup, while it appears that the generator defendants collectively produced approximately 22 percent of the waste that SCRDI handled. Other evidence indicates that agencies of the federal government produced more waste than did generator defendant Monsanto, and suggests that the amounts contributed by the settling parties do not bear a strictly proportionate relationship to the total costs of cleaning the facility. We note, however, that a substantial portion of the final judgment is attributable to litigation costs. We also observe that the EPA has contributed upwards of $50,000 to the Bluff Road cleanup, and that any further claims against the EPA and other responsible government instrumentalities may be resolved in a contribution action pursuant to CERCLA §113(f).

52. Contrary to the generator defendants' request, it would be premature for us to interpret the effect of settlement on the rights of nonsettling parties in contribution actions under CERCLA §113(f)(2). We observe, however, that the possibility this subsection precludes contribution actions against settling parties signals legislative policy to encourage settlement in CERCLA cleanup actions. At the same time, we recognize that the language of CERCLA's new contribution provisions reveals Congress' concern that the relative culpability of each responsible party be considered in determining the proportionate share of costs each must bear.

(PRPs). The consequence of imposing joint and several liability is potentially to shift the entire burden of cleanup onto any identifiable PRP. Similarly, the *Monsanto* opinion also relflects the standard view in holding that courts should decide case-by-case whether harm is sufficiently severable to apportion liability.

Is the determination to invoke joint and several liability justified by the same sort of appeal to necessity that led to the relaxation of the causation requirement in CERCLA cases? It has some of the same feel about it insofar as the approach of the Restatement of Torts 2d links the imposition of joint and several liability to issues of proving causation of harm. There is, however, a greater effort to rationalize the imposition of joint and several liability as a logical outgrowth of the remedial character of CERCLA. The *Monsanto* court seems to be saying that Congress wanted a ready source of funds to be applied to cleanups – a goal that is facilitated by being able to tap the assets of any one of the responsible parties for the entire cost of a cleanup. That, of course, is exactly what the imposition of joint and several liability allows.

2. The unfairness of joint and several liability. Isn't it patently unfair to make a deep pocket responsible party, such as Monsanto, pay for an entire cleanup when it is demonstrable that they are but one of several causes of the problem? The *Wade* cases justify the initial imposition of potentially unfair allocations in reliance on the later ability of the unfairly burdened party to reallocate some part of the loss by obtaining contribution from fellow joint tortfeasors. Although this topic will be considered at length in Chapter 21, *infra*, can you predict why it may prove difficult for parties who pay more than their fair share in a government cleanup action to recover an appropriate amount via contribution?

3. Divisibility of harm or of costs? In cases like *Monsanto*, the indivisibility of the environmental harm is the predicate for application of joint and several liability. In United States v. Kramer, 757 F. Supp. 397 (D.N.J. 1991), the generator defendants at a landfill site argued as a defense that the bulk of the anticipated $60 million cleanup cost was attributable to the quantitatively large volume of municipal solid waste and sludge deposited at the site. More narrowly, the non-municipal generator defendants sought to limit their liability to an amount that could be calculated arithmetically as the difference between the cleanup cost with, and without, their waste being present at the site. Why might this approach prove less costly to the non-municipal defendants?

Given the limited ability of municipalities to raise large sums of money, an apportionment that left the lion's share of the liability with the municipalities could pose a collectability problem for EPA. To date EPA has frequently limited its efforts to recover a "fair" share from municipalities at sites where other potentially responsible parties (PRPs) can be identified and pursued. As an example, at the Kramer site EPA did not name the municipalities as defendants in its original complaint, but they remained vulnerable to contribution claims from the named defendants.

SECTION 5. PRIVATE LITIGATION UNDER CERCLA §107

You will recall that under §107(a)(2)(B) even non-governmental entities are accorded a remedy to recover for costs that are consistent with the National Contingency Plan (NCP).[53] In this way CERCLA expressly authorizes private litigants to seek recoveries from PRPs. This cause of action is complementary to causes of action that may exist under the common law, for the allowable scope of recovery relates exclusively to costs that are incurred in the cleanup of a contaminated site. Items such as recovery for personal injuries, or loss of amenity value, remain the province of traditional actions in tort.

The typical scenarios of private §107 actions involve current owners of contaminated property as plaintiffs suing either former occupiers of the property, parties whose wastes were disposed of there, or parties whose wastes have migrated there.[54] In some cases, the current owner will already have been ordered to clean the site by the government; in other cases, the cleanup effort may have preceded governmental involvement. For some time there was ambiguity about whether costs could be incurred consistent with the NCP in advance of a governmentally-initiated investigation or cleanup order. That matter has been resolved by the courts in favor of broad recovery. See, e.g., Wickland Oil Terminals v. Asarco, Inc., 792 F.2d 887 (9th Cir. 1986).

The private cause of action under §107 has four basic elements: the plaintiff must prove that (1) the site in question is a "facility," (2) the defendant is a liable party under CERCLA §107(a), (3) a release or threatened release of a hazardous substance has occurred at the facility, and (4) the plaintiff has incurred response costs consistent with the NCP in responding to the release or threatened release. Given the broad readings given to CERCLA liability issues, the consistency (with the NCP) requirement has often been the most ardently litigated issue in private §107 suits.[55]

General Electric Co. v. Litton Industrial Automation Systems, Inc, 920 F.2d 1415 (1990), cert. denied, 111 S. Ct. 1390 (1991), appears to be emerging as the leading case on consistency with the NCP. In that case, Litton merged with a former owner and occupant of land now owned by GE. From 1959 to 1962, during the occupancy of the company taken over by Litton, improper disposal of cyanide based electroplating wastes, sludges, and other pollutants had occurred on the parcel. In the early 1980s, GE and the Missouri Department of Natural Resources (MDNR) investigated the site and decided that no cleanup was necessary. In 1984, GE sold the site to a commercial real estate developer. Shortly thereafter, the MDNR changed its position on the need for a cleanup, at which point GE was threatened with CERCLA lawsuits by both its vendee and MDNR. Negotiations followed in which GE agreed

---

53. The NCP is discussed more fully in Chapter 21, *infra*. For present purposes the NCP can be understood as a set of guidelines framed by the United States that delineate the proper procedures and actions that are to be taken in cleaning up a Superfund site.

54. Adversely affected adjacent landowners are also allowed to sue. See, e.g., Standard Equipment, Inc. v. The Boeing Co., No. C84-1129 (W.D. Wash. 1986).

55. See Steinway, Private Cost Recovery Actions Under CERCLA: The Impact of the Consistency Requirements, 4 TXLR 1364 (1990).

to clean up the site and did so to the satisfaction of MDNR.

Thereafter GE sued Litton under §107. Litton's most vigorous defense was that the cleanup was not consistent with the NCP. The District Court ruled in favor of GE, awarding $940,000 as reimbursement for response costs and an additional $419,000 in attorney fees. See General Electric Co. v. Litton Business Systems, 715 F. Supp. 949 (W.D. Mo. 1989). In reviewing the critical finding that the costs incurred were consistent with the NCP despite having omitted some detailed requirements mentioned in the NCP, the court wrote:

> We are satisfied that the thorough evaluation that was performed here is consistent with the NCP, specifically with 40 CFR §300.65(b)(2). The site evaluation does not have to comply strictly with the letter of the NCP, but only must be consistent with its requirements. It is not necessary that every factor mentioned by the NCP be dealt with explicitly; thus, for instance, a failure to consider explicitly the weather conditions factor is not fatal to an evaluation's consistency with the NCP. 920 F.2d at 1420.[56]

COMMENTARY AND QUESTIONS

1. The purpose of the consistency requirement. Why must cleanups be consistent with the NCP to allow recovery in a §107 action? Why isn't the key issue whether the response action was effective? One answer was suggested by counsel for Litton in the oral argument in the Eighth Circuit when he indicated that defendants in private cost recovery suits need protection from parties that voluntarily perform "a Rolls-Royce cleanup when a Volkswagen one would do." See 5 TXLR 651 (1990). On the other end of the scale, NCP-consistent cleanups are a means of guaranteeing that the effort is effective. Particularly under the new NCP (discussed in Chapter 21), satisfying its requirements would help to insure an effective cleanup.

2. Standing in the shoes of the government. In a private §107 action, should the plaintiff enjoy all of the same advantages (joint and several strict liability with a relaxed standard of causation) as the government does when it sues PRPs? In general, the cases seem to point in that direction. In Dedham Water Co. v. Cumberland Farms Dairy, Inc. 889 F.2d 1146 (1st Cir. 1989), for example, the appeals court reversed a ruling that had required the plaintiff to prove which of two possible sources had caused the contamination of its well that had given rise to CERCLA response costs. The court drew heavily on the liberal liability provisions of CERCLA to find that "a literal reading of the statute imposes liability if releases or threatened releases from defendant's facility cause the plaintiff to incur response costs; it does *not* say that liability is imposed only if the defendant causes actual contamination of the plaintiff's property." (Emphasis by the court.) Does it seem odd to hold a party like Cumberland Farms liable when the facts as found by the trial court (and not overturned on appeal) were that two other nearby operations "were 'probable' causes" of the contamination of plaintiff's wells? Isn't this like the *Wade II* relaxed standard of causation that, in effect, treats all parties whose acts are potential causes of the pollution as being actual causes of the problem?

---

56. But see Channel Master Satellite Systems Inc. v. JFD Electronics Corp., 748 F. Supp. 373 (E.D.N.C. 1990)(favoring strict compliance with NCP).

3. Private CERCLA lawsuits seeking contribution. Are all CERCLA §107 private actions in reality claims for contribution? The answer is clearly no because the plaintiff in a §107 suit will at times be a party who is not a PRP, such as an innocent neighbor like Dedham Water Company. Often, however, the plaintiff will be a PRP who has paid a disproportionate share and seeks to use a §107 action to vindicate the statutory right of contribution created by §113(f)(1). When the suit sounds in contribution, the issue of loss allocation includes assigning a share to the plaintiff. In that context the rote application of strict joint and several liability of defendants for the entire loss is no longer appropriate. The problem of loss allocation in such cases is also considered in Chapter 21.

4. A reminder about state law remedies. Even if it borders on redundancy, it is important to keep in mind the continuing availability of state statutory and common law remedies for environmental harms caused by hazardous materials. Despite the broad federal efforts to govern hazardous groundwater contamination reflected in both RCRA and CERCLA, Congress was well aware that they were entering a field having a strong tradition of state regulatory and remedial primacy. Both RCRA and CERCLA contain provisions extending authority to states to enact additional more stringent measures.[57] Beyond that, §114(a) of CERCLA provides:

> Nothing in this chapter shall be construed or interpreted as pre-empting any State from imposing any additional liability or requirements with respect to the release of hazardous substances within such State.[58]

Section 6. INSURANCE AND INSOLVENCY: LOOKING BEYOND CERCLA

Matters of insurance and insolvency are of concern in the larger structure of RCRA and CERCLA. Both insurance and insolvency touch upon the fiscal condition of the actors who play on the hazardous waste stage. RCRA and CERCLA, however, did not fully address the legal issues of insurance and insolvency that would arise. While these issues are many and varied, this section will note only a few of the issues of highest visibility and importance.

Conventional liability insurance is, in essence, a form of indemnity contract under which the insurer agrees to make whole the insured (up to policy limits) in the event that the insured is adjudged liable to a third party for the risks covered by the policy. Typically, most businesses will carry a comprehensive general liability (CGL) insurance policy to meet liabilities that arise in connection with operation of

---

57. RCRA §3009, codified at 42 U.S.C.A. §6929; CERCLA §114(a), codified at 42 U.S.C.A. §9614(a).

58. Despite this expressly non-pre-emptive character, there are narrow areas of state legislative authority that are pre-empted by CERCLA and RCRA. These cases arise when states enact their own mini-Superfund laws and fund them via a tax like that used to fund CERCLA. See Exxon Corp. v. Hunt, 475 U.S. 355 (1986). There have also been cases pre-empting local regulation of RCRA-regulated waste handling facilities. See ENSCO Inc. v. Dumas, 807 F.2d 743 (8th Cir. 1986)(pre-empting local waste handling regulations that bar methods encouraged by RCRA).

The pre-emption of common law by statutes is generally disfavored; the canon of statutory construction cautions that statutes in derogation of common law are to be narrowly construed. Nevertheless, in an era of vast regulatory intervention into the control of pollution and waste disposal, there is some movement toward finding that comprehensive statutory enactments do oust the common law. These matters are considered in greater detail later in this chapter.

the business and its premises.

For the study of the hazardous waste field, the important question under these CGL policies is whether liability for releases of hazardous wastes is covered by the policies in question. As a legal matter, this is no more than an issue of contract interpretation, but, as both a practical matter and as a public policy matter, the answer is quite significant. Practically, huge sums of money are at risk, for cleanups have proven remarkably expensive, often costing many millions of dollars to perform at a single site. As a matter of policy, the shifting of the loss to insurance companies tends to spread the loss more broadly and makes additional assets available to meet cleanup costs. To engage in that loss spreading, however, may allow the parties who actually engaged in the inappropriate disposal to avoid bearing the real cost of their behavior.

Keep in mind that much of the contamination caused by the escape of hazardous materials took place through inappropriate waste handing practices that occurred many years ago, before the dangers of such practices were widely understood. The CGL policies from that era did not expressly address the issue of whether the harms and losses caused by those releases were covered by the policy. What was clear in most policies was that the costs of ordinary "pollution," such as the day-in and day-out emission of particulates from a smokestack, were not considered to be covered by CGL policies. On the other hand, sudden mishaps, such as explosions, even if they involved the waste stream, were covered by the policies. To accomplish this, most CGL policies included language that is referred to as the "pollution exclusion." A typical version of the exclusion states, "This policy excludes...bodily injury or property damage arising out of the discharge, dispersal, release or escape of...toxic chemicals, liquids or gasses...but this exclusion does not apply if such discharge, dispersal, release or escape is sudden and accidental." See, e.g., Allstate Insurance Co. v. Klock Oil Co., 426 N.Y.S.2d 603, 604 (1980).

The results in cases that have considered whether the pollution exclusion bars coverage for typical CERCLA-type liabilities are many and varied. The issue, being one of contract interpretation, is governed by state law, and therefore each state is free to decide the question for itself. Over time, a significant number of states have faced the interpretive question and a split of authority has developed. The list of decisions on the issue grows and changes with sufficient frequency that it is difficult to keep abreast of it.

Insolvency issues have led the development of CERCLA into another area of law, that of bankruptcy. A fundamental tension exists between the remedial goals and aspirations of CERCLA and the objectives of bankruptcy law. One goal of bankruptcy law is to distribute the bankrupt's assets fairly among all of the creditors. A second objective is to provide the bankrupt with a fresh start, freed of the previous debts. In contrast, a central concern animating CERCLA is assuring the availability of sufficient resources for the cleanup of hazardous release sites. Accordingly, CERCLA has a strong interest in making all the bankrupt's assets, both present and future, available to remediate the hazards that the PRP bankrupt has helped to create. This CERCLA-based interest collides with bankruptcy law when bankruptcy law seeks to protect co-creditors through a fair division of the available assets.

Specifically, bankruptcy law gives preference to secured creditors over unsecured creditors such as the government would be in regard to a CERCLA recovery. As a second matter, under normal bankruptcy law the debtor can expect to be absolved from personal post-bankruptcy obligations relating to CERCLA liabilities.

Congress did nothing to broker the competition between these two statutory children, CERCLA and the bankruptcy act. That task, like so many others associated with CERCLA, has fallen to the courts. A few important issues have emerged, two of which have already been addressed by the United States Supreme Court. To probe the entire range of CERCLA-bankruptcy issues would lead too far astray into the workings of the bankruptcy law, but a summary of those two decisions provides a preliminary view of the interaction of the two statutes.

The United States Supreme Court first approached the intersection of toxic contamination liability and bankruptcy law in Kovacs v. Ohio, 469 U.S. 274 (1985). In *Kovacs,* the State of Ohio had obtained an injunction ordering Kovacs, the chief executive officer of Chem-Dyne Corp., and others to clean up a dumpsite that the company had operated. Kovacs and the others failed to fulfill their obligations under the injunction and Ohio then had the dumpsite as well as Chem-Dyne's and Kovacs' other assets legally entrusted to a receiver. Kovacs then filed for personal bankruptcy.

Ohio, seeking to insure that Kovacs' post-bankruptcy earnings would be available to help pay for the costs of the still incomplete cleanup, sought a declaration that Kovacs' obligation under the injunction was not a "debt" or a "claim" dischargeable in bankruptcy. Stated differently, Ohio sought a declaration that Kovacs would still have to pay for the cleanup even in the event his petition for a discharge in bankruptcy was granted. The specific legal argument put forth was that the equitable cleanup duty imposed on Kovacs by the Ohio injunction fell outside of the definition of claims subject to discharge appearing in §101(4)(B) of the Bankruptcy Code.

The United States Supreme Court ruled in favor of Kovacs. Adopting the reasoning of the lower courts, Justice White's majority opinion quoted the bankruptcy court which had said "There is no suggestion by plaintiff [Ohio] that defendant [Kovacs] can render performance under the affirmative obligation other than by the payment of money." It therefore found the obligation indistinguishable from a typical claim for money that is discharged in bankruptcy. The Court in dicta emphasized what it did not decide and offered some hint of what it might do in other settings. The Court observed (among other things) that (1) Kovacs' potential criminal liability was unaffected by the discharge, that (2) a fine or monetary penalty imposed prior to bankruptcy was non-dischargeable under §523(a)(7) of the bankruptcy code, that (3) the existing injunction was enforceable insofar as it restrained Kovacs from doing certain acts unrelated to the payment of money, and that (4) anyone lawfully in possession of the property, including the bankruptcy trustee or a vendee of the trustee, would be subject to compliance with state environmental laws.

The last of these dicta is of special significance. In all cases where the cleanup of a site is going to be expensive in relation to the value of a site, it does not take too much imagination to conclude that a trustee in bankruptcy of a contaminated hazardous waste site will try to unload the property to a vendee. By the same token, no prudent vendee is going to purchase from the trustee a site clouded by the nearly certain imposition of a costly cleanup. Bankruptcy law authorizes a trustee to abandon property that is burdensome to the bankrupt's estate. The abandonment power was the key issue in the second Supreme Court decision in this field.

In Midlantic National Bank v. New Jersey Department of Environmental Protection, 474 U.S. (1986), the court considered whether §554(a) of the Bankruptcy Code, 11 U.S.C.A. §554(a),[59] authorizes a trustee in bankruptcy to abandon property in contravention of state laws or regulations that are reasonably designed to protect the public's health or safety.

The facts in *Midlantic* are complicated, involving a bankrupt waste disposal facility operator, Quanta Resources, that operated two separate sites, one in New York and one in New Jersey. At the New York site, the trustee in bankruptcy concluded that the real property, contaminated by as much as 70,000 gallons of PCB-contaminated oil, was a burden to the estate of the bankrupt and abandoned the property. The City and the State of New York objected in the bankruptcy court, contending that abandonment would threaten the public's health and safety, and would violate state and federal environmental law. The State and City stressed public policy considerations reflected in applicable local laws, and the requirement of 28 U.S.C.A. §959(b), that a trustee "manage and operate" the property of the estate "according to the requirements of the valid laws of the State in which such property is situated." The bankruptcy court allowed the abandonment. Shortly thereafter a similar scenario followed as to the New Jersey site, again culminating in abandonment. The United States District Court affirmed the abandonment, but the Third Circuit Court of Appeals reversed, at which point certiorari was granted.

In the United States Supreme Court, the key element in the decision was the interplay between statutes and common law in giving content to the bankruptcy act. As Justice Powell's majority opinion observed:

> Before the 1978 revisions of the Bankruptcy Code, the trustee's abandonment power had been limited by a judicially developed doctrine intended to protect legitimate state or federal interests. This was made clear by the few relevant cases.... Thus, when Congress enacted §554, there were well-recognized restrictions on a trustee's abandonment power. In codifying the judicially developed rule of abandonment, Congress also presumably included the established corollary that a trustee could not exercise his abandonment power in violation of certain state and federal laws. The normal rule of statutory construction is that if Congress intends for legislation to change the interpretation of a judicially created concept, it makes that intent specific.

He went on to give weight to the special emphasis of Congress on toxic pollution issues as an additional ground supporting a refusal to allow abandonment:

---

59. Section 554(a) reads:

> After notice and a hearing, the trustee may abandon any property of the estate that is burdensome to the estate or that is of inconsequential value and benefit to the estate.

> Although the reasons elaborated above suffice for us to conclude that Congress did not intend for the abandonment power to abrogate certain state and local laws, we find additional support for restricting that power in repeated congressional emphasis on its "goal of protecting the environment against toxic pollution." Chemical Manufacturers Assn., Inc. v. Natural Resources Defense Council, Inc., 470 U.S. 116, 143, (1985).[60]

COMMENTARY AND QUESTIONS

1. Legislative cognizance of the common law. In the very brief excerpt from Justice Powell's majority opinion, notice the reliance on the canon of statutory construction that the legislature is presumed to be aware of the common law, and a legislative intent to alter or repeal common law must be specific. Why is that a guiding principle of American jurisprudence? One begins by recognizing the different level of generality at which the two branches, legislature and judiciary, operate. Legislation, if it is to avoid interminable detail and internal inconsistency, must tend to be more general and of broader scope. Fine-tuning of general concepts to keep multiple legislative policies work intact often requires judicial case-by-case analysis. Once an accommodation of competing policies has been reached by the courts, it is less disruptive if subsequent legislation is presumed to continue that accommodation. Taking the example used by Justice Powell, the earlier version of the Bankruptcy Act included unqualified provisions favoring the bankrupt and trustee in ways similar to the abandonment power of §554. The judiciary had fashioned exceptions to those provisions based on the policy of promoting compliance with federal and state laws. Applying the above-mentioned canon of statutory construction, subsequent legislative silence concerning the judicially-created exceptions continued those common law exceptions.

2. *Midlantic* as paradigm. How often will abandonment of the dumpsite be attempted by trustees in bankruptcy? The usual scenario will involve large cleanup liabilities incurred by a thinly capitalized dumpsite operator. Particularly in urban settings, the site itself is probably the operator's major asset, due to the high value of industrial real estate. With that asset suddenly devalued due to the contamination and the cleanup obligation, bankruptcies and attempted abandonments are likely.

3. To the victor go the spoils, but what are the spoils? What is won in *Midlantic*? The fact that a trustee cannot abandon the burdensome dumpsite renders the trustee a target for compliance with environmental laws as suggested by the *Kovacs* dictum. But how much is that worth? Plainly the answer will in part depend on the financial strength of the bankrupt debtor apart from the environmental liability.

Still, to say that the state can avoid abandonment is not self-evidently a great victory for the state – consider where the state would have been had abandonment been

60. Justice Rehnquist, joined by three other dissenters, opposed the majority's view that state law should be allowed to bar abandonment.

allowed. The state still would have been able to submit a claim in the bankruptcy proceeding for the amounts it stands to recover under CERCLA and any other state laws. These amounts will include cleanup costs and damage costs. The catch, from the state's point of view, is that those claims are unsecured and will be joined with the claims of all other unsecured creditors. These claims will be paid on a pro rata basis to the extent that the bankrupt's remaining assets permit after secured creditors and others having priority have been wholly satisfied. The prospects for complete recoveries are poor.

Despite the dim prospects for ordinary unsecured creditors' recoveries, the greatest advantage of forcing trustees to remain in possession lies in the fact that current expenses of maintaining property are paid by the trustee during the pendency of the bankruptcy proceedings before the claims of creditors are paid. Thus, items such as installing fencing, providing guards, etc., would be paid currently, 100 cents on the dollar, by the trustee using whatever assets the bankrupt has left, rather than becoming part of the state's claim against the bankrupt estate which would be compromised in the bankruptcy proceeding. More significantly, as was pointed out by the four dissenters in *Midlantic*, the trustee's obligation to maintain the property might easily be held to include undertaking a state law-ordered cleanup. Were that the case, then the avoidance of abandonment is the equivalent of obtaining a preference, a right to be paid by the estate before the claims of other creditors are considered. This view seems to be that taken by the appellate court in the New Jersey portion of the *Midlantic* case. See In re Quanta Resources Corp., 739 F.2d 912 and 739 F.2d 927 (3d Cir. 1984).

Cases in the wake of *Midlantic* appear to be granting the government the preferred position its seeks. See In re Mowbray Engineering Co., 67 Bkr. Rptr. 34 (Bkr. M.D. Ala. 1986). In that case response costs were ruled to be "administrative expenses" entitled to first priority payment under Chapter 11 of the bankruptcy code. The trustee was, however, permitted to abandon the site to the government, but remained liable for the response costs as "administrative expenses." After abandonment, if the government sells the property, any proceeds in excess of its uncompensated response costs must be turned over to the trustee for benefit of other creditors.

4. The losers in *Midlantic*. Who is hurt by the *Midlantic* rule, on the assumption that it gives governmental response costs a priority in payment? The simple answer is unsecured creditors, and note that neighbors suffering contamination damages are usually members of the unsecured creditor class. Consider a situation where a groundwater contamination problem has apparently caused cancer in identified individuals. Assuming that the defendant causing the injuries faces bankruptcy, due in part to the high cost of decontaminating the site, is it appropriate that the expense of cleanup be exacted before any individuals are compensated?

C. THE EFFECT OF ENVIRONMENTAL STATUTES ON THE COMMON LAW

Having explored at some length the impact of the common law on statutes, this subpart turns the lens the other way and examines how the presence of statutes influences common law adjudication of environmental cases. In the American legal system ordinary statutes have the ability to alter or replace common law. The nature of this power might seem to be a one-way ratchet that continually reduces the reach of the common law, but that is not the case. Most often, statutes leave the common law undisturbed. Beyond that, statutes can either expand or contract the availability of common law remedies.

Statutes can expand the availability of common law relief in two principal ways – by making existing causes of action more fruitful, or by authorizing courts to create new common law causes of action. For example, statutes substituting the moderated defense of comparative negligence for the blanket defense of contributory negligence have led to an increase in the availability of tort recoveries for plaintiffs in negligence cases. The passage of regulatory legislation can erect standards of conduct for the regulated party, the breach of which can be used by appropriate plaintiffs to prove negligence. More profoundly, the enactment of a regulatory scheme by statute can by implication give rise to the creation of a whole new non-statutory private cause of action for violation of the statute.

Statutes that reduce the reach of common law also operate on those same two levels, either by altering the rules of existing common law causes of action, or by entirely eliminating causes of action. Legislation can limit the amount of tort recoveries or add new defenses, like allowing the "state-of-the-art" defense for protecting manufacturers in product liability suits. (Initiatives of this character are frequently labelled "tort reform" by their proponents.) Whole areas of recovery may be eliminated, as was done at the turn of the twentieth century through the substitution of workers compensation systems for tort remedies in the field of workplace injuries. The creation of a statutory remedy and the ouster of common law remedies, however, do not always go hand in hand as part of an explicit legislative quid-pro-quo. At times, statutes may curtail the common law without providing any new remedial options in return. This happens when continuation of common law recoveries is inconsistent with the statutory regime, and, under the principle of legislative supremacy, the common law must give way. The general presumption, on the other hand, is that common law provisions are not ousted and remain co-existing with statutory law.

IMPLIED PRIVATE CAUSES OF ACTION

Regulatory statutes are primarily intended to fix a standard of conduct for the regulated party and provide for enforcement of the regulations by an administrative agency according to the express terms of the statute. Occasionally, the legislation will also identify and expressly create private rights to sue and recover in favor of parties injured by conduct that amounts to a violation of the statutory standards. In addition, in a very narrow set of circumstances, courts will imply from a regulatory statute a private cause of action even where the legislation itself did not address the matter. The United States Supreme Court has developed a four factor test to determine if it would be permissible for a court to imply a private cause of action. It stated:

> In determining whether a private remedy is implicit in a statute not expressly providing one, several factors are relevant. First, is the plaintiff "one of the class for whose especial benefit the statute was enacted," [emphasis by J. Brennan], that is, does the statute create a federal right in favor of the plaintiff? Second, is there any indication of legislative intent, explicit or implicit, either to create such a remedy or to deny one? Third, is it consistent with the underlying purposes of the legislative scheme to imply such a remedy for the plaintiff? And finally, is the cause of action one traditionally relegated to state law, in an area basically the concern of the States, so that it would be inappropriate to infer a cause of action based solely on federal law?[61]

In the years since Cort v. Ash, the Supreme Court has been hesitant in using this power to expand the realm of remedies created by federal statutes beyond those remedies expressly authorized by the Congress. In the environmental area no implied private causes of action have been recognized. In California v. Sierra Club, 451 U.S. 287 (1981), the Court roundly rejected a call for an implied private cause of action under §10 of the Rivers and Harbors Act that prohibited obstruction of navigable waterways.

COMMENTARY AND QUESTIONS

1. Implying remedies under RCRA and CERCLA. In thinking about environmental cases and the relationship of regulatory and remedial statutes such as RCRA and CERCLA to pre-existing common law remedies, are private causes of action likely to be implied? Is there, in broad gauge legislation like RCRA and CERCLA, an identifiable "especial" class of beneficiaries? What would be the indications of legislative intent to create such a remedy? Does the fact that CERCLA creates causes of action in favor of private parties indicate that no additional causes of action may be implied from CERCLA itself or from related statutes like RCRA, ToSCA, etc.?

2. Violation as proof of negligence. Even if a private cause of action cannot be implied, is violation of a federal regulatory statute or its implementing regulations relevant in proving negligence in, for example, the handling of hazardous materials? Tort law addresses this topic quite extensively, placing several threshold requirements on statutory violations before they can be used to help prove negligence:

> Once the statute is determined to be applicable – which is to say, once it is interpreted as designed to protect the class of persons in which the plaintiff is included, against the risk of the type of harm which has in fact occurred as a result of its violation – and once its breach has been established, probably a majority of courts hold that the issue of negligence is thereupon conclusively determined, in the absence of sufficient excuse, and that the court must so direct the jury. This usually is expressed by saying that the

61. Cort v. Ash, 422 U.S. 66, 78 (1975).

> unexcused violation is negligence "per se," or in itself.... A large number of courts have held that a violation is only evidence of negligence, or prima facie evidence thereof, which may be accepted or rejected according to all of the evidence. Prosser and Keeton on the Law of Torts 229-30 (5th ed. 1984).

3. Dim prospects for implying private environmental remedies. In this modern era of elaborate congressional consideration of legislation prior to enactment, under what conditions, if any, can congressional intent to create a remedy be implied where Congress itself provided none? The *Cannon* case, 441 U.S. 677 (1979), is the most prominent example of the Court finding an implied remedy in favor of a plaintiff. That case involved a private cause of action for an act of alleged discrimination by a member of the class to be protected against discrimination by the relevant federal statute. Do any of the federal environmental laws in the hazardous substances area offer narrowly-targeted benefits?

4. Public law citizen suits: private attorneys-general and the private enforcement of statutory violations. Consider the difference between lawsuits where citizens seek implied remedies for harms sustained to themselves as a result of violations of environmental statutes, and the very different case of citizen suits to enforce statutes' regulatory aspects. The latter category, where citizens try to take on public law tasks that are being neglected by the official agencies of government, raises illuminating questions about "establishment" politics and the role of citizens in the modern state. Plainly, in the second context, the citizens are seeking to provide a public benefit by assisting in the enforcement of legislated statutory norms, acting in a sense as private attorneys-general. In that context, the remedy being sought by citizen suits is precisely what Congress originally sought to provide in enacting the statute.

The prospect of citizen involvement in shaping the administrative enforcement agenda understandably arouses bureaucratic opposition, even in cases where agencies are not cozy with the industries they regulate. Objections to citizen enforcement of environmental laws are raised on the ground that it may interfere with the regulatory prerogatives of enforcement agencies. This may involve forcing regulators to intervene before their case is fully prepared, or citizen enforcement may seek punishment for violations that regulators wish to leave unprosecuted for good policy reasons. Historically there are many examples of federal environmental cases refusing citizen enforcement, usually describing their reasoning as based on the law of standing to sue. See, e.g., People for Environmental Progress v. Leisz, 373 F. Supp. 589 (C.D. Cal. 1984)(refusing private enforcement of a FIFRA violation). What might increase the courts' receptivity to citizen enforcement actions?

In the realm of contemporary federal environmental laws, the battle appears to have been won by the advocates of an active pluralistic role for citizen litigation. The difficult questions about the propriety of unwanted citizen involvement in enforcement have largely been legislated out of existence by Congress. Almost all major federal environmental laws now have citizen suit provisions that expressly authorize statutory enforcement by private citizens, usually after appropriate advance notice to relevant federal agencies. See, e.g., 33 U.S.C.A. §1365 (Clean Water Act §505); 42 U.S.C.A. §7604 (Clean Air Act §304). The modern citizen standing provisions reflect the reality that environmental protection – under both public and common law – has largely been forged by citizen efforts rather than governmental leadership. Although counterpressures are of course also discernible in the corporate and political sectors, and in the judiciary, the United States, more than any other industrial democracy, today acknowledges the legitimate role of citizens and nongovernmental public interest organizations in its administrative program.

OUSTER OR CO-EXISTENCE? ENVIRONMENTAL STATUTES AND STATE COMMON LAW

A frequent phenomenon in modern environmental law is the argument by statutorily-regulated defendants that their common law liabilities have been completely superseded by the existence of public law legislation. (Such implied ouster of common law by regulatory statutes is sometimes referred to as "pre-emption.")[62] The extent to which statutes reduce the operative sphere of state common law depends on legislative intent. In the relatively few instances in which legislation expressly ousts common law, the intent to supersede is patent and the role of the courts is ministerial. All they are required to do is give effect to the legislated change. When legislation is silent as to its effect on common law, the court is equally bound to give effect to the relevant legislation, but to do so the court must divine the legislature's intent on the issue of ouster of common law.

Courts have long experience in all fields of law in trying to assess the impact of statutory changes on the common law. Although the law of a few states is different, most courts begin their inquiry into the effect of a statute on common law with the traditional canon that statutes in derogation of common law must be narrowly construed.[63] This is a basic proposition of statutory construction. One treatise on the subject states –

> Where there is any doubt about their meaning or intent [statutes] are given the effect which makes the least rather than the most change in the common law. The rule of strict construction of statutes in derogation of the common law reflects the insight that changes in the existing order of things are generally effected on a piecemeal rather than a wholesale basis. Thus it appears that, for the purpose of the rule, "common law" should be understood to carry its broadest meaning of the existing body of law, rather than

---

62. As a descriptive matter, use of the term "pre-emption" is acceptable and appears in many judicial opinions addressing this subject. As a technical matter, the term "pre-emption" was initially introduced into modern American jurisprudence as part of the phrase "federal pre-emption" and referred to the exclusion by Congress of state regulatory authority from subject areas that Congress had addressed and intended to be regulated solely by the national government. Analytically, there is sufficient distinction between federal pre-emption and the ouster of common law by statutes that in this book we generally reserve the term pre-emption for the federal pre-emption setting and use the term ouster for cases in which continued operation of the common law is inconsistent with legislation, either state or federal, governing the same events.

63. See Jennings v. Hodges, 129 N.W.2d 59, 65 (S.D. 1964)("The rule followed in most jurisdictions is that [a] statute...in derogation of the common law must be strictly construed...That is not the rule in this state.").

the narrower definition of an ancient body of Anglo-American judge-made principles.[64]

There are numerous opportunities for the question of ouster of common law to arise in the environmental area. The spate of pollution control legislation enacted in the latter portion of the twentieth century has raised the question of its effect on the common law of nuisance and trespass as remedies for the harms done to neighbors downwind and downstream. The rule favoring the continuation of the common law in cases where there is not express ouster has held sway.[65]

In most of these cases, the judicial opinions are very clear in applying the rule of statutory construction favoring non-ouster of common law as an aid in determining legislative intent. A typical example is Renken v. Harvey Aluminum, 226 F. Supp. 169 (D. Ore. 1963). In that fluoride pollution trespass case, the court was faced with the claim by an aluminum producer that Oregon's state statutes regulating air pollution had ousted all common law remedies not expressly saved by the relevant legislation. The court said:

> Defendant's contention that the Oregon Air Pollution Law pre-empts this field is without foundation. Specifically recognized by ORS 449.820 is the right by an individual to prosecute a suit to abate a private or public nuisance. The record in this case is sufficiently broad to be viewed as a suit to abate a nuisance, as well as a suit to enjoin a continuing trespass. For that matter, a continuing trespass could well be a nuisance. [Other Oregon] cases recognize that the deposit of smoke screenings and particulates on the lands of another amounts to a nuisance. The rule of construction "expressio unius est exclusio alterius,"[66] for which defendant contends, is not a rule of law, but is a mere guide in determining intent and such a rule must be harmonized with all other rules of construction. It is a rule which should be applied with caution and merely as an auxiliary rule to determine the legislative intention....
>
> Surely, the Oregon Legislature employed the word ["nuisance" in a broad] sense when enacting ORS 449.820. Furthermore, all statutes which encroach on personal or property rights of an individual are to be construed strictly, and in the absence of express words or necessary implication, it will be presumed that such statute is not intended to interfere with or prejudice a private right or title.
>
> We must assume that the Oregon Legislature was familiar with this rule of construction and that it never intended, by this legislation, to deprive individuals, such as plaintiffs, of their common law right to enjoin a flagrant

---

64. Sutherland's Statutory Construction, §61.01 (1986 ed.).

65. See Biddix v. Hendredon Furniture Industries, Inc., 331 S.E.2d 717, 720 (N.C. App. 1985)("statutes in abrogation of the common law are strictly construed," holding that a nuisance action survives enactment of the state water pollution control laws and the federal Clean Water Act); cf. In re Glacier Bay, 746 F. Supp. 1379, 1384 (D. Alaska 1990)("Statutes which invade the general maritime law are read with a presumption favoring the retention of long-established and familiar principles except when a statutory purpose to the contrary is evident," finding such a purpose that *expanded* beyond the common law norms the damages recoverable for an oil spill).

66. Eds: Idiomatic translation: "the expression of one thing excludes all others." In this context the argument was that the express legislative saving of common law nuisance actions excluded the saving of trespass and other common law remedies.67. 226 F. Supp. at 175-76.

violation of those rights nor to pursue their right to enjoin a continuing trespass in a proper Court.[67]

The crux of the argument favoring the implied ouster of common law by statutes is that the legislature intended the legislation it passed, not common law, to provide the yardstick by which the legality of conduct is measured. Conduct that meets the legislative standard, so the argument goes, should not give rise to liability at common law. As a corollary matter the argument can be extended to say that even when the regulated party violates the statute itself, the remedies for failure to live up to the statutory command are only those prescribed by the statute itself. Adding common law remedies would allegedly distort the balance struck by the legislation.

Despite the norms of statutory construction referred to above, defendants' arguments favoring ouster of common law, though self-serving, are not always fatuous. When a regulatory program is comprehensive and the need for uniform regulation is substantial, the argument for implied legislative intent to oust common law is at its strongest. The following case was litigated on a claim that a federal statute foreclosed state common law remedies.

SILKWOOD v. KERR-McGEE CORPORATION

United States Supreme Court, 1984
464 U.S. 238, 104 S. Ct. 615, 78 L. Ed. 2d 443

WHITE, J. Last term, this Court examined the relationship between federal and state authority in the nuclear energy field and concluded that states are precluded from regulating the safety aspects of nuclear energy. Pacific Gas & Electric Co. v. State Energy Resources Conservation & Development Comm'n, 461 U.S. 190 (1983). This case requires us to determine whether a state-authorized award of punitive damages arising out of the escape of plutonium from a federally-licensed nuclear facility is pre-empted either because it falls within that forbidden field or because it conflicts with some other aspect of the Atomic Energy Act.

Karen Silkwood was a laboratory analyst for Kerr-McGee at its Cimmaron plant near Crescent, Oklahoma. The plant fabricated plutonium fuel pins for use as reactor fuel in nuclear power plants. Accordingly, the plant was subject to licensing and regulation by the Nuclear Regulatory Commission (NRC) pursuant to the Atomic Energy Act, 42 U.S.C.A. §§2011-2284 (1976 ed. and Supp. V).

During a three-day period of November 1974, Silkwood was contaminated by plutonium from the Cimmaron plant....

Bill Silkwood, Karen's father, brought the present diversity action in his capacity as administrator of her estate. The action was based on common law tort principles under Oklahoma law and was designed to recover for the contamination injuries to Karen's person and property....

During the course of the trial, evidence was presented which tended to show that Kerr-McGee did not always comply with NRC regulations. One Kerr-McGee witness conceded that the amount of plutonium which was unaccounted for during the period in question exceeded permissible limits.[68] An NRC official testified that

67. 226 F. Supp. at 175–76.

68. After allowing for hold-up (plutonium which remains in the equipment after a very thorough cleanout), the inventory difference (opening less closing) for the 1972–1976 period was 4.4 kilograms. This represented 0.522 percent of the 842 kilograms received by Kerr-McGee during that period. The NRC permits an inventory difference of .5 percent.

he did not feel that Kerr-McGee was conforming its conduct to the "as low as reasonably achievable" standard.[69] There was also some evidence that the level of plutonium in Silkwood's apartment may have exceeded that permitted in an unrestricted area such as a residence.

However, there was also evidence that Kerr-McGee complied with most federal regulations. The NRC official testified that there were no serious personnel exposures at the plant and that Kerr-McGee did not exceed the regulatory requirements with respect to exposure levels that would result in significant health hazards. In addition, Kerr-McGee introduced the Commission's report on the investigation of the Silkwood incident in which the Commission determined that Kerr-McGee's only violation of regulations throughout the incident was its failure to maintain a record of the dates of two urine samples submitted by Silkwood.

The trial court determined that Kerr-McGee had not shown that the contamination occurred during the course of Silkwood's employment. Accordingly, the court precluded the jury from deciding whether the personal injury claim was covered by Oklahoma's Workers' Compensation Act.... Instead, the court submitted the claims to the jury on alternative theories of strict liability and negligence.[70]

The court also instructed the jury with respect to punitive damages.... The jury returned a verdict in favor of Silkwood, finding actual damages of $505,000 ($500,000 for personal injuries and $5,000 for property damage) and punitive damages of $10,000,000. The trial court entered judgment against Kerr-McGee in that amount....

In *Pacific Gas & Electric*, an examination of the statutory scheme and legislative history of the Atomic Energy Act convinced us that "Congress...intended that the federal government regulate the radiological safety aspects involved...in the construction and operation of a nuclear plant." 461 U.S. at 205. Thus, we concluded that "the federal government has occupied the entire field of nuclear safety concerns, except the limited powers expressly ceded to the states." Id. at 212.

Kerr-McGee argues that our ruling in *Pacific Gas & Electric* is dispositive of the issue in this case. Noting that "regulation can be as effectively asserted through an award of damages as through some form of preventive relief," Kerr-McGee submits that because the state-authorized award of punitive damages in this case punishes and deters conduct related to radiation hazards, it falls within the prohibited field. However, a review of the same legislative history which prompted our holding in *Pacific Gas & Electric*, coupled with an examination of Congress' actions with respect to other portions of the Atomic Energy Act, convinces us that the preempted field does not extend as far as Kerr-McGee would have it....

Congress' decision to prohibit the states from regulating the safety aspects of nuclear development was premised on its belief that the Commission was more qualified to determine what type of safety standards should be enacted in this complex area. As Congress was informed by the AEC, the 1959 legislation provided

69. Federal regulations require that "persons engaged in activities under licenses issued by the Nuclear Regulatory Commission...make every reasonable effort to maintain radiation exposures, and releases of radioactive materials in effluents to unrestricted areas, as low as is reasonably achievable." 10 CFR 20.1(c)(1983). In 1974, the regulation required reasonable efforts to maintain exposures and releases "as far below the limits specified [in other portions of the regulations] as practicable." The difference in the terminology is not significant. 40 Fed.Reg. 33029 (1975).

70. In an effort to avoid a new trial in the event that the Court of Appeals disagreed with its ruling on the applicability of strict liability principles, the court instructed the jury to answer a special interrogatory as to whether Kerr-McGee negligently allowed the plutonium to escape from its plant. The jury answered in the affirmative.

for continued federal control over the more hazardous materials because "the technical safety considerations are of such complexity that it is not likely that any State would be prepared to deal with them during the foreseeable future." H.R. Rep. No. 1125, 86th Cong., 1st Sess. 3 (1959). If there were nothing more, this concern over the states' inability to formulate effective standards and the foreclosure of the states from conditioning the operation of nuclear plants on compliance with state-imposed safety standards arguably would disallow resort to state-law remedies by those suffering injuries from radiation in a nuclear plant. There is, however, ample evidence that Congress had no intention of forbidding the states from providing such remedies.

Indeed, there is no indication that Congress even seriously considered precluding the use of such remedies either when it enacted the Atomic Energy Act in 1954 and or when it amended it in 1959. This silence takes on added significance in light of Congress' failure to provide any federal remedy for persons injured by such conduct. It is difficult to believe that Congress would, without comment, remove all means of judicial recourse for those injured by illegal conduct.

More importantly, the only congressional discussion concerning the relationship between the Atomic Energy Act and state tort remedies indicates that Congress assumed that such remedies would be available. After the 1954 law was enacted, private companies contemplating entry into the nuclear industry expressed concern over potentially bankrupting state-law suits arising out of a nuclear incident. As a result, in 1957 Congress passed the Price-Anderson Act, an amendment to the Atomic Energy Act. Pub.L. 85-256 (1957). That Act established an indemnification scheme under which operators of licensed nuclear facilities could be required to obtain up to $60 million in private financial protection against such suits. The government would then provide indemnification for the next $500 million of liability, and the resulting $560 million would be the limit of liability for any one nuclear incident.

Although the Price-Anderson Act does not apply to the present situation, the discussion preceding its enactment and subsequent amendment indicates that Congress assumed that persons injured by nuclear accidents were free to utilize existing state tort law remedies. The Joint Committee Report on the original version of the Price-Anderson Act explained the relationship between the Act and existing state tort law as follows:

> Since the rights of third parties who are injured are established by State law, there is no interference with the State law until there is a likelihood that the damages exceed the amount of financial responsibility required together with the amount of the indemnity. At that point the Federal interference is limited to the prohibition of making payments through the state courts and to prorating the proceeds available. S.Rep. No. 296, 85th Cong., 1st Sess. 9 (1957)....

Kerr-McGee focuses on the differences between compensatory and punitive damages awards and asserts that, at most, Congress intended to allow the former. This argument, however, is misdirected because our inquiry is not whether Congress expressly allowed punitive damages awards. Punitive damages have long been a part of traditional state tort law. As we noted above, Congress assumed that traditional principles of state tort law would apply with full force unless they were expressly supplanted. Thus, it is Kerr-McGee's burden to show that Congress intended to preclude such awards. Yet, the company is unable to point to anything in the legislative history or in the regulations that indicates that punitive damages were not to be allowed. To the contrary, the regulations issued implementing the insurance provisions of the Price-Anderson Act themselves contemplate that punitive damages might be awarded under state law....

We do not suggest that there could never be an instance in which the federal law would pre-empt the recovery of damages based on state law. But insofar as damages for radiation injuries are concerned, pre-emption should not be judged on the basis that the federal government has so completely occupied the field of safety that state remedies are foreclosed but on whether there is an irreconcilable conflict between the federal and state standards or whether the imposition of a state standard in a damages action would frustrate the objectives of the federal law. We perceive no such conflict or frustration in the circumstances of this case.

The United States, as amicus curiae, contends that the award of punitive damages in this case is pre-empted because it conflicts with the federal remedial scheme, noting that the NRC is authorized to impose civil penalties on licensees when federal standards have been violated. 42 U.S.C.A. §2282 (1976 ed. and Supp. V). However, the award of punitive damages in the present case does not conflict with that scheme. Paying both federal fines and state-imposed punitive damages for the same incident would not appear to be physically impossible. Nor does exposure to punitive damages frustrate any purpose of the federal remedial scheme.

Kerr-McGee contends that the award is pre-empted because it frustrates Congress' express desire "to encourage widespread participation in the development and utilization of atomic energy for peaceful purposes." 42 U.S.C.A. §2013(d). In *Pacific Gas & Electric*, we observed that "there is little doubt that a primary purpose of the Atomic Energy Act was, and continues to be, the promotion of nuclear power." 461 U.S. at 221. However, we also observed that "the promotion of nuclear power is not to be accomplished 'at all costs.'" Id. at 222. Indeed, the provision cited by Kerr-McGee goes on to state that atomic energy should be developed and utilized only to the extent it is consistent "with the health and safety of the public." 42 U.S.C.A. §2013(d). Congress therefore disclaimed any interest in promoting the development and utilization of atomic energy by means that fail to provide adequate remedies for those who are injured by exposure to hazardous nuclear materials. Thus, the award of punitive damages in this case does not hinder the accomplishment of the purpose stated in §2013(d)....

COMMENTARY & QUESTIONS

1. The lines of dissent in *Silkwood*. *Silkwood* was a 5–4 decision that sparked two separate dissents. Both dissents relied heavily on *Pacific Gas & Electric*, the case decided the previous year that figured so prominently in the majority opinion. Excerpts from that case appear in Chapter 10, at page 483, *infra*. Justice Powell, joined by all of the other dissenters, attacked the majority for allowing state common law to punish safety violations that the NRC, Congress' choice as the sole regulator of nuclear safety, had not felt merited punishment:

> The Court's decision, in effect, authorizes lay juries and judges in each of the states to make regulatory judgments as to whether a federally licensed nuclear facility is being operated safely. Such judgments then become the predicate to imposing heavy punitive damages. This authority is approved in this case even though the Nuclear Regulatory Commission (NRC) – the agency

> authorized by Congress to assure the safety of nuclear facilities – found no relevant violation of its stringent safety requirements worthy of punishment. The decision today also comes less than a year after we explicitly held that federal law has "pre-empted" all "state safety regulations" except certain limited powers "expressly ceded to the states." *Pacific Gas & Electric*, 461 U.S. at 212 (1983). There is no express authorization in federal law of the authority the Court today finds in a state's common law of torts.[71]

Justice Blackmun, writing separately, distinguished the partial ouster of common law punitive damages from the ouster of common law compensatory damages. He saw the issue in the case as being "whether the jury can impose a fine on a nuclear operator in addition to whatever compensatory award is given." He wrote:

> It is to be noted, of course, that the same pre-emption analysis produces the opposite conclusion when applied to an award of compensatory damages. It is true that the prospect of compensating victims of nuclear accidents will affect a licensee's safety calculus. Compensatory damages therefore have an indirect impact on daily operations of a nuclear facility. But so did the state statute upheld in *Pacific Gas*. The crucial distinction between compensatory and punitive damages is that the purpose of punitive damages is to regulate safety, whereas the purpose of compensatory damages is to compensate victims. Because the Federal Government does not regulate the compensation of victims, and because it is inconceivable that Congress intended to leave victims with no remedy at all,[72] the pre-emption analysis established by *Pacific Gas* comfortably accommodates – indeed it compels – the conclusion that compensatory damages are not pre-empted whereas punitive damages are.

2. Common law damage remedies as surrogate performance standards. Regulatory statutes often establish standards of performance that must be achieved. The variety of such standards is described in some detail in Chapter 15 and following chapters. Taking a cue from Justice Powell's dissent in *Silkwood*, a defendant operator of a radiopharmaceutical plant argued that to allow common law relief for injuries caused by the escape of radioactive material was tantamount to setting a standard for radioactive emission that was inconsistent with the regulatory standard. Bennett v. Mallinckrodt, Inc., 698 S.W.2d 854 (Mo. App.), cert. denied, 476 U.S. 1176 (1985). The argument was considered and rejected:

> Permitting plaintiffs' petition to state a claim for relief under Missouri law, Mallinckrodt argues, would create an irreconcilable conflict between Missouri and federal standards. Mallinckrodt contends that subjecting it to state

---

71. 464 U.S. at 274. (Opinion of Powell, J., dissenting).

72. In *Pacific Gas*, the Court relied on the fact that there was no federal regulation of the economic considerations of nuclear power as clear evidence that Congress intended to leave such concerns to consideration of the States:

> The Nuclear Regulatory Commission...does not purport to exercise its authority based on economic considerations.... It is almost inconceivable that Congress would have left a regulatory vacuum; the only reasonable inference is that Congress intended the States to make these judgments. 461 U.S. at 207-208.

The absence of federal regulation governing the compensation of victims of nuclear accidents is strong evidence that Congress intended the matter to be left to the States.

> tort liability effectively establishes a "zero-release standard." More specifically, Mallinckrodt argues, that if a permissible release is to be determined by a jury "after the fact on an ad hoc basis," a federal licensee, like Mallinckrodt, "could assure avoidance of liability only by a zero release of emissions." This state imposed standard, Mallinckrodt reasons, irreconcilably conflicts with federal standards.
>
> Mallinckrodt's logic is questionable.... As other manufacturers, producers and operators functioning in a regulated field, Mallinckrodt is not guaranteed absolute insulation from the consequences of its acts through compliance with federal regulation. Thus, the issue here is not whether Mallinckrodt will be assured of freedom from liability. Rather, the issue is whether there is an irreconcilable conflict between our state standards and federal standards; an issue which, in turn, is answered by whether it is impossible for Mallinckrodt to comply with both federal standards and those standards implicitly reflected in plaintiffs' petition. *Silkwood*, 104 S. Ct. at 626....
>
> Mallinckrodt has not shown our state standards to be more stringent than federal standards, nor has it shown our state standards to be theoretically or practically impossible to meet, if our state standards are in fact more stringent. Moreover, even if Mallinckrodt cannot reduce its radiation emissions below the federal standards, Missouri can decide that, as between Mallinckrodt and plaintiffs, Mallinckrodt ought to bear the costs of compensating those injuries that could have been prevented with a theoretical emission rate lower than the rate approved by the NRC. On the present record, payment of damages and compliance with federal standards are clearly possible. Mallinckrodt can continue to meet federal standards, and, if found wanting by state standards, simply pay the piper....
>
> In short, common law liability does not impose requirements on Mallinckrodt; rather, it allows Mallinckrodt to choose between risking liability by not changing its behavior or attempting to negate the risk by lowering its emission rates.[73]

3. The permit defense revisited. The *Mallinckrodt* case in the previous note has a great deal in common with the permit defense introduced in Chapter 3. See page 134, *supra*. That defense consists of a regulated defendant claiming that so long as the defendant is in compliance with a permit it obtained from a regulatory agency, the permit operates as a defense to tort claims. Is there any difference between the claim of ouster of common law by the enactment of regulatory regimes and the permit defense? Don't both arguments amount to a claim by the defendant that the statute provides the sole measure of what conduct on its part is actionable? After reading the *Silkwood* and *Mallinckrodt* cases, it is plain that courts are loathe to attribute such an intent to the legislature, even in cases where the same legislation has been interpreted to have intended that the conduct of the defendant be subject to only one regulatory authority.

4. Ouster of common law injunctive remedies. Imagine that the *Silkwood* plaintiffs, employing a prevention-of-nuisance theory like that of the *Wilsonville* case at page

73. 698 S.W.2d at 859-60.

68 *supra*, had sought an injunction requiring Kerr-McGee to institute specified radiation-handling processes to reduce the escape of plutonium from the workplace in the future. Why is it so clear that the common law injunction remedy would be unavailable, while the imposition of punitive damages for failing to control the escape of plutonium was not ousted? See Brown v. Kerr-McGee Chemical Corp., 767 F.2d 1234 (1985), cert. denied, 475 U.S. 1006 (1986).

5. More canons of statutory construction. In a famous article that sought to demonstrate that the canons of construction were more like semantic clichés than rules of construction, Karl Llewellyn wrote:

> When it comes to presenting a proposed construction in court, there is an accepted conventional vocabulary. As in case-law, the accepted convention still, unhappily, requires discussion as if only one single correct meaning could exist. Hence there are two opposing canons on almost every point.[74]

In two lists that he labelled "Thrust" and "Parry" Llewellyn then set out the opposing canons. For the thrust that "statutes in derogation of the common law will not be extended by construction" he parried with, "such acts will be liberally construed if their nature is remedial." In the environmental litigation context, and especially from the environmental perspective, are those two canons inconsistent, or do they tend to favor environmental plaintiffs in both instances? There is no need to belabor the point this "Thrust" canon aids in providing environmental remedies by preserving common law actions like nuisance. But the "Parry" canon seems to also have the effect of expanding the range of remedial options by finding that remedial statutes ought to be read broadly.

In re Glacier Bay, 746 F. Supp. 1379 (D. Alaska 1990), is an excellent example of the "Parry" serving the needs of environmental plaintiffs. In that case plaintiff fishermen brought an action under the Trans-Alaska Pipeline Authorization Act (TAPAA), 43 U.S.C.A. §§1651-1655 to recover for economic losses caused by an oil spill. In particular, §1653(c)(1) establishes strict liability for damages from oil spills up to $100 million. The *defendants* argued that the statute's damage remedy should be construed to alter the common law as little as possible. On that basis they contended that the statute allowed recovery only for the same types of damages as those allowed by the common law of maritime torts. Under the well-settled maritime tort rule of Robins Dry Dock & Repair Co. v. Flint, 275 U.S. 303 (1927), when only pecuniary loss without physical injury is suffered, a plaintiff may not recover for the loss of the financial benefits of a contract or prospective trade.

At this point, the "Parry" came into play to favor the environmental plaintiffs. The court observed that "the purpose of §1653(c) is to provide adequate compensation for damage caused by spills of TAPS oil" and that the statutory language allowing damages included the phrase "notwithstanding the provisions of any other law." Reading that phrase in conjunction with the statutory language that included "all

---

74. Llewellyn, Remarks on the Theory of Appellate Decision and the Rules or Canons About How Statutes Are To Be Construed, 3 Vand. L. Rev. 395, 401 (1950).

damages" sustained by "any person," the court stated that "while that language does not address the *Robins Dry Dock* rule by name, it does address the subject matter of the rule, i.e. recoverable damages." The *Glacier Bay* court, after making additional findings favoring the broadening of remedies, construed §1653(c) to abrogate the *Robins Dry Dock* common law limitation on damages.

THE SHORT-LIVED REIGN OF THE FEDERAL COMMON LAW OF INTERSTATE WATER POLLUTION NUISANCE

Imagine a case in which a polluter in one state emits effluents that travel downwind or downstream into a neighboring state, or a case in which the water pollution affects a water body that forms the boundary between two states. It seems appropriate that an injured party in the non-source state ought to be able to resort to a common law nuisance action seeking abatement, damages, or both. The question, however, might arise: under which state's common law should the case be tried, the source's, or the victim's? An appealing answer is to select neither – and instead, in the interests of national uniformity regarding matters of interstate concern, develop a federal common law of interstate pollution nuisance.

In the modern American federal system, however, creating a federal common law is not a solution that is routinely undertaken. In part, this is the residual baggage of the famous case of Erie Railroad v. Tompkins, 304 U.S. 64 (1938), which disavowed the power of the federal courts to create a "general federal common law," and largely limited the power to make common law to the state courts. Over the years since Erie a few areas of federal judicial common law have retained their vitality, most notably admiralty and the resolution of controversies among sister states. In the post-*Erie* world there was also some growth of federal common law in areas where the federal government had an overriding interest in promoting national uniformity – labor relations being the most notable example.[75]

Interstate pollution nuisance cases, to the extent they were similar to other state versus state natural resource controversies, fit well as candidates for the generation of a federal common law solution. In an early case, Justice Holmes had argued eloquently for a federal measure of legal relief in favor of the adversely affected sovereign:

> The caution with which demands of this sort, on the part of a state, for relief from injuries analogous to torts, must be examined, is dwelt upon in Missouri v. Illinois, 200 U.S. 496, 520, 521. But it is plain that some such demands must be recognized, if the grounds alleged are proved. When the States by their union made the forcible abatement of outside nuisances impossible to each, they did not thereby agree to submit to whatever might be done. They did not renounce the possibility of making reasonable demands on the ground of their still remaining quasi-sovereign interests; and the alternative to force is a suit in this court. (Missouri v. Illinois, 180 U.S. 208, 241.) Georgia v. Tennessee Copper Co., 206 U.S. 230, 237 (1907).

75. The areas mentioned are areas in which the desirability of a single national law is strong. In modern times, admiralty may no longer fit in that category. In the early years of nationhood, to have a single law of admiralty was vital because admiralty greatly affected the relationships between the emerging nation and its overseas trading partners.

It was only a short further step to translate the availability of such relief into a justification for creating of a federal common law of interstate pollution nuisance. A leading decision considering the question stated:

> Federal common law and not the varying common law of the individual States is, we think, entitled and necessary to be recognized as a basis for dealing in uniform standard with the environmental rights of a State against improper impairment by sources outside its domain. The more would this seem to be imperative in the present era of growing concern on the part of a State about its ecological conditions and impairments of them. In the outside sources of such impairment, more conflicting disputes, increasing assertions and proliferating contentions would seem to be inevitable. Until the field has been made the subject of comprehensive legislation or authorized administrative standards, only a federal common law basis can provide an adequate means for dealing with such claims as alleged federal rights. And the logic and practicality of regarding such claims as being entitled to be asserted within the federal-question jurisdiction of §1331(a) would seem to be self-evident. Texas v. Pankey, 441 F.2d 236, 241-242 (10th Cir. 1971).

The *Pankey* decision proved prophetic. In Illinois v. City of Milwaukee (*Milwaukee I*), 406 U.S. 91 (1972), the Supreme Court announced that federal common law was available to adjudicate an interstate water pollution claim raised by the State of Illinois against interstate pollution caused by discharges of sewage from Wisconsin sources. The opinion recited and strong federal interest in the nation's waters and cited *Pankey* and its arguments with favor. Importantly, the Court raised the question of the relationship of federal common law to federal statutory governance of the issue. At the time, there were several federal statutes offering some limited governance of water pollution, but none addressed interstate pollution as an independent matter. Justice Douglas' majority opinion found little difficulty in saying there had been no ouster of the common law by statutory efforts in the same field. Perhaps acknowledging the environmental awakening of Congress, he said, "It may happen that new federal laws and new federal regulations may in time pre-empt the field of federal common law of nuisance. But until that comes to pass, federal courts will be empowered to appraise the equities of suits alleging creation of a public nuisance by water pollution."

The Douglas dictum, too, would prove prophetic. In 1972, only months after the decision in *Milwaukee I*, Congress enacted the Federal Water Pollution Control Act Amendments of 1972[76] These amendments totally overhauled federal water pollution control law, creating a comprehensive scheme of regulations that addressed (among many other items) control and permitting of sewage treatment plants. The new federal law also provided mechanisms by which downstream states, such as Illinois in the *Milwaukee* controversy, could seek to have their their concerns made a part of the upstream source state's permitting process. Meanwhile, the result in *Milwaukee* I had led to the initiation of a new lawsuit by Illinois that worked its way through the federal court system eventually reaching the United States Supreme

76. Pub. L. 92-500 (1972)

Court. The stage was now set for consideration of whether the major strengthening of federal water pollution control law had ousted the federal common law of interstate water pollution nuisance.

In Illinois v. City of Milwaukee (*Milwaukee II)*, 451 U.S. 304 (1981), the United States Supreme Court, in an opinion authored by Justice Rehnquist, held that the 1972 amendments had ousted federal common law. Illinois had argued that the ouster of federal common law by statute should be disfavored, just as is the case regarding the ouster of state common law. Noting that the historic deference owed by all federal law to state law was not present in this setting, Justice Rehnquist began from the assumption, "that it is for Congress, not the federal courts, to articulate the appropriate standards to be applied as a matter of federal law." In contrast to the vague regulatory regime in place at the time *Milwaukee I* was decided, the new law had spoken with sufficient precision to the problems raised by Illinois to render the continuation of federal common law inappropriate. The sewage treatment plants in question were subject to EPA-approved pollution controls as part of a carefully crafted congressional scheme of regulation. The issues involved were of a highly technical engineering nature that augured in favor of remitting them to the expertise of an administrative agency rather than forcing generalist judges to resolve them. Moreover, Illinois was not without an avenue for vindicating its concerns under the federal statute. Notice must be given to affected states of permit applications having interstate impacts, and affected states are allowed to participate in the process, with EPA being given the power to disapprove of a permit if, in EPA's view, the affected state's interests are inadequately protected by the permit-granting agency of the source state.

In subsequent cases seeking the application of federal common law to environmental disputes, *Milwaukee II* has had the effect of creating a strong, almost irrebuttable, presumption that there will be no room for the operation of federal common law so long as the federal statute in question is "comprehensive." The prototypical application of this position is found in Middlesex County Sewage Authority v. National Sea Clammers Association, 453 U.S. 1 (1981). In *Sea Clammers,* seafood harvesters brought a federal common law action protesting marine dumping by defendants. The plaintiffs also alleged violations of both the Clean Water Act (the law at issue in *Milwaukee II*) and the Marine Protection, Research, and Sanctuaries Act, another major federal statute addressed to the protection of marine environments, and sought remedies for those violations via implied private causes of action. Both claims were given short shift by the Court. The key element in the ruling was that the complex and "comprehensive" nature of the federal laws governing law and precluded a tenable implication that Congress intended additional extra-statutory federal remedies. Here the holding seems somewhat ironic. Despite their comprehensiveness, both of the statutes under consideration failed to provide an express remedy for their alleged violation in these circumstances. Nevertheless, precisely because of their comprehensiveness, neither implied private causes of action nor federal common law is available to redress the statutory violations alleged by the Sea Clammers.

COMMENTARY & QUESTIONS

1. State common law and federal common law: different likelihoods of ouster. When studying these materials on the ouster of common law by statutes, it is quite important to distinguish between ouster of federal common law by federal statutes and ouster of state common law by state or federal statutes. As a matter of political theory and constitutional fact, the states began the constitutional process as complete, full-purpose sovereigns, possessed of all of the powers of independent nations. They created a national government and even granted it supremacy, but only as to a limited range of subjects. The states retained all else and for that reason can be described as the "residual sovereigns" in our federal system.

What do these constitutional truisms mean when focusing on the issue of common law power and its ouster? First, they help to explain the historic decision in Erie Railroad v. Tompkins, *supra*, and the narrow ambit it accorded for federal common law. *Erie* made the point that the common law power of the federal judiciary was not the broad general common law power of state court judges. The areas of federal lawmaking competence are limited by the Constitution. The subject matter of the *Erie* case, a local tort action for injuries to a pedestrian struck by a train, was not a proper subject for the fashioning of a federal rule of decision, whether by congressional legislation or by the judiciary. The mere fact that a federal court was authorized to hear a case involving that subject matter did not mean that the court was authorized to create a federal common law.

More important to environmental law, the constitutionally different postures of the two sovereigns makes it likely that the roles of their respective judges in making common law and in having that common law ousted by legislation is different. Just as the national government is a limited government, the federal common lawmaking power of the federal courts is a limited power – it arises only in cases that touch upon subjects over which the national government has been granted power. Moreover, as will be described more fully in Chapter 10, even those areas where the federal government is granted power, the concurrent power of the states to continue to regulate is usually preserved.[77] This means that even in the absence of federal legislation and in advance of the fashioning of federal common law, a court deciding a case that was concerned with a subject of federal power, might nonetheless be able to decide the case by looking at state law, either statutory or common law. This availability of "residual" state law reduces the need for federal courts to generate a uniquely federal common law.

This notion that state law may govern in preference to the creation of federal common law in an area of federal legislative competence is perhaps a difficult one. Although it is not articulated with great clarity in the excerpt, there was no federal statutory remedy for the interstate pollution at issue in *Milwaukee I* at the time of its decision in early 1972. Had Justice Douglas not decided in favor of recognizing

77. The cases in which state power is pre-empted by the exercise of federal authority, or impermissible because of its adverse impact on interstate commerce, are studied in detail in Chapter 10.

federal common law of interstate water pollution nuisance, the case would have been litigated on state law theories, either statutory or common law.

A second example may help clarify this point. Before the enactment of CERCLA in 1980, there could be no doubt that Congress, under its power to legislate in areas affecting interstate commerce, was empowered to pass statutes governing the cleanup of hazardous waste releases. If, however, a pre-1980 lawsuit had been initiated in federal court seeking a remedy for the problem based on federal common law, it is almost certain that the court would have found that it was not authorized to create a federal common law to decide the case. The facts so prominent in justifying the resort to federal common law in Texas v. Pankey and *Milwaukee I* – (1) interstate impact of the action and (2) claims made by a sovereign state based on activities outside of its borders are absent in this hypothetical. If the case is one where the federal court has jurisdiction despite the absence of a claim based on federal law,[78] the case must be decided using state law. State statutory remedies might be available, but in their absence, or if those statutory remedies are not exclusive, state common law would also be applicable.

There is one final point to be made in regard to ouster of common law. Although federal common law is considered to be ousted by subsequent legislation that "comprehensively" addresses the field, that is not the case for state common law. Federal common law is exceptional in nature, it is generated only within a narrow range of circumstances, and it is more easily found to be displaced by legislation. State common law is residual law, it is presumptively available unless something is clearly intended to displace it.

2. Drawing conclusions from congressional silence. It is the basic premise of the *Milwaukee II* decision compelling? It is no doubt plausible that Congress may have intended that regulated polluters need look only to the federal regulatory scheme (as implemented by a complying state like Wisconsin) as the exclusive measure of their federal obligations to abate pollution. But the question remains whether Congress, whose legislation was silent on the issue, did intend to exclude the previously recognized federal common law of interstate water pollution nuisance from continuing as a supplement to the new statutory effort. What are the strongest points for and against the majority opinion?

3. The statute's language expressly preserving remedies. In *Milwaukee II* Justice Blackmun reaches a different conclusion regarding the intent of Congress. The arguments are numerous, but §505 (e) is certainly the focal point. It provides:

> Nothing in this section shall restrict any right which *any person* (or class of persons) may have under *any statute or common law* to seek enforcement of any effluent standard or limitation *or to seek any other relief* (including relief against the Administrator or a State agency). 33 U.S.C.A. §1365 (e)(emphasis added in Justice Blackmun's dissent).

78. The principal example of such a case would be where the plaintiff and defendant are citizens of different states. See 28 U.S.C.A. §1332(a)(1).

Blackmun asserted that the provision meant what it said in preserving pre-existing rights under "any" common law. The majority had addressed this argument by stressing the introductory phrase – "Nothing *in this section*" – as opposed to having said – "Nothing *in this statute*." Section 505 is the standard citizen suit provision that allows citizens to sue for violations of the Act. Rehnquist reads §505(e) to mean that the section's express authorization of citizen suits does not oust other pre-existing remedies, but that the statute as a whole could have the effect of ousting the remedies of federal common law.

4. The allure of unitary regulation. The creation of a mandatory federal regulatory system, even one with cooperative state participation in administration, creates the possibility that sources of pollution can look forward to being governed by a single unitary system of regulation. What are the advantages of such a system from the polluter's point of view? Does the continued existence of federal common law remedies compromise the certainty that would be created by unitary regulation? Does the continued existence of state common law remedies have a different effect? The *Milwaukee II* Supreme Court majority opinion concedes that Congress did not intend to oust state common law. Specifically looking at §510 of the statute which preserved the authority of states to enact more stringent limitations on the discharge of pollutants than those mandated by the federal statute, the majority observed:

> Section 510 provides that nothing in the Act shall preclude States from adopting and enforcing limitations on the discharge of pollutants more stringent than those adopted under the Act. It is one thing, however, to say that States may adopt more stringent limitations through state administrative processes, or even that States may establish such limitations through state nuisance law, and apply them to in-state dischargers. It is quite another to say that the States may call upon federal courts to employ federal common law to establish more stringent standards applicable to out-of-state dischargers. Any standards established under federal common law are federal standards, and so the authority of States to impose more stringent standards under §510 would not seem relevant. 451 U.S. at 328.

5. Common law remedies open to "downstream" states. The result in *Milwaukee II*, in effect, was to remit Illinois to a lawsuit based on state common law. Illinois took that course, and sought to have the suit adjudicated under its own nuisance law rather than Wisconsin's common law of nuisance. Illinois was again rebuffed. See Illinois v. Milwaukee (*Milwaukee III*), 731 F.2d 403 (1984), cert. denied, 469 U.S. 1196 (1985). Two years later, International Paper Co. v. Ouellette, 479 U.S. 481 (1987), a case very similar to *Milwaukee III*, reached the Supreme Court. There the Court held that in an interstate water pollution nuisance suit brought against a New York polluter by its Vermont victims, the nuisance law of the source state (New York) must be the law applied. In part, Justice Powell's majority opinion stated:

> After examining the CWA as a whole, its purposes and its history, we are convinced that if affected States were allowed to impose separate discharge standards on a single point source, the inevitable result would be a serious

> interference with the achievement of the "full purposes and objectives of Congress."...
>
> An interpretation of the saving clause [§505(e)] that preserved actions brought under an affected State's law would disrupt this balance of interests. If a New York source were liable for violations of Vermont law, that law could effectively override both the permit requirements and the policy choices made by the source State. The affected State's nuisance laws would subject the point source to the threat of legal and equitable penalties if the permit standards were less stringent than those imposed by the affected State. Such penalties would compel the source to adopt different control standards and a different compliance schedule from those approved by the EPA, even though the affected State had not engaged in the same weighing of the costs and benefits. This case illustrates the problems with such a rule. If the Vermont court ruled that respondents were entitled to the full amount of damages and injunctive relief sought in the complaint, at a minimum IPC would have to change its methods of doing business and controlling pollution to avoid the threat of ongoing liability. In suits such as this, an affected-state court also could require the source to cease operations by ordering immediate abatement. Critically, these liabilities would attach even though the source had complied fully with its state and federal permit obligations. The inevitable result of such suits would be that Vermont and other States could do indirectly what they could not do directly – regulate the conduct of out-of-state sources.[79]

6. Statutory remedies open to downstream states. How important to the majority opinion is it that downstream states do have some administrative avenues for making their concerns known under the 1972 amendments? Are the avenues left open to downstream states very promising? The right of the downstream state to participate in the permitting decision is salutary, but the forum may be far from a sympathetic one. Using the *Milwaukee* litigation as an example, the cost of eliminating separate and combined sewer overflows to the extent required in the nuisance litigation was orders of magnitude greater than the cost of compliance with the Wisconsin permit and court order. That higher cost, if passed on to Milwaukee area taxpayers, was estimated to be several thousands of dollars per year per household. Wouldn't a Wisconsin commission be reluctant to impose those costs for benefits that will be enjoyed primarily by the residents of Chicago, Illinois?

The more substantial protection available to downstream states in cases where remedies would impose extraordinary costs on an upstream state seems to be their ability to appeal to EPA to veto the permit. A case pending in the Supreme Court as this book went to press involves that process and adds an important twist for the law of interstate water pollution. See Oklahoma v. EPA, 908 F.2d 595 (10th Cir. 1990), cert. granted, 111 S. Ct. 2849 (1991). In that case, Fayetteville, Arkansas was issued a NPDES permit by EPA[80] to discharge into a stream that later flowed into Oklahoma. Oklahoma pursued its option to participate in the permit process. It argued (and EPA

79. 479 U.S. at 495.

80. Arkansas had not yet qualified to be delegated the permitting function under the CWA.

agreed) that any permit issued to Fayetteville must be sufficiently stringent to assure that no relevant water quality standards, including those of the downstream state, will be violated by the discharge.[81] The basis for the argument begins with the language of CWA §301(b)(1)(C). That section, entitled "Effluent limitations" provides in part that in addition to meeting technology-based standards –

> there *shall be achieved*...any more stringent limitation, including those *necessary to meet* water quality standards...established pursuant to any State law or regulations...or *required to implement* any applicable water quality standard established pursuant to this chapter. (Emphasis by the court at 908 F.2d 606.)

EPA had previously approved Oklahoma's water quality standards (WQS) for the waters in question and, therefore, found those standards to be ones that must be considered in the permit process. Arkansas objected to this interpretation of the CWA on the ground that it introduced the precise kind of multi-state regulation and chaos that *Ouellette* and *Milwaukee III* had ruled against. In this line of argument, Arkansas relied heavily on very broad dicta that appeared in *Ouellette*.[82] The court rejected the consequences of Arkansas' approach:

> The full ramifications of Arkansas' formulation of the Clean Water Act issue are exposed once it is realized that an upstream state has the ability (if not the legal right) largely to control the quality of certain waters of a downstream state. It can accomplish this simply by setting and enforcing its own water quality standards and releasing water of that quality to the downstream state. If the upstream state's water quality standards are lower than those considered desirable by the downstream state, so will be the actual quality of the interstate waters in the downstream state. In other words, the lowest common denominator will prevail. The ultimate question posed to this court is whose water quality standards take precedence under the Clean Water Act – the upstream state's, the downstream state's, the federal government's, or nobody's. We conclude that no state "imposes" its standards on another state, but rather that the Clean Water Act mandates compliance with federal law, including federally approved water quality standards of affected states. 908 F.2d 602.

Is the decision in Oklahoma v. EPA seriously at odds with achieving a system of unitary regulation of pollution control? Didn't Oklahoma do precisely what the opinion in *Milwaukee II* seemed to call for a downstream state to do – take advantage of the opportunities provided by the Clean Water Act itself?

---

81. EPA found that the permit it granted to Fayetteville did not risk a violation of Oklahoma's water quality standards. Oklahoma challenged that finding.

82. As two examples, the majority in *Ouellette* had stated:

> We hold that when a court considers a state-law claim concerning interstate water pollution that is subject to the CWA, the court must apply the law of the State in which the point source is located. 479 U.S. at 487.
>
> ...We conclude that the CWA precludes a court from applying the law of an affected State against an out-of-state source. 479 U.S. at 494.

Chapter 7

THE FORCE OF THE CRIMINAL LAW IN ENVIRONMENTAL CASES

Criminal law in our legal system wields a potentially heavy hand in comparison to civil law: convicted defendants face actual personal time in jail as well as punitive fines that may be quite large and cannot be charged to insurance or deducted from income taxes as business expenses. Criminal law seeks to punish bad actors in order to accomplish several different public policy objectives not so directly involved in civil law: revenge and retribution for bad actions, rehabilitation (although this is often merely theoretical), incapacitation (the prevention of repeat offenses by holding perpetrators in prison), specific deterrence by making the defendant apprehensive about future conduct, and general deterrence by showing other potential culprits that crime does not pay.

It would seem inevitable that criminal law would be enlisted in legal efforts to protect the environment, at least once the 1960s and 1970s had brought a broad environmental consciousness to government and the general public. "Throw the bums in jail" is at least as natural as "Sue the bastards" as a gut reaction to many pollution controversies. Yet only in the last few years have environmental prosecutions ceased being rare occurrences, and they still remain a miniscule proportion of the environmental litigation total.

The rarity of criminal prosecutions for environmental violations has not been based upon a lack of criminal law on the books. Most of the major environmental statutes passed in the last 20 years, and the extensive regulatory structures built upon them, do contain criminal penalty provisions along with the more familiar civil penalties. Many other state and federal penal laws with potential application to environmental cases, particularly those in the area of public health, lie virtually unused. Nevertheless, criminal law prosecutions of environmental offenses can play a special role in the legal system's response to problems of pollution and environmental quality. Whether that role is ultimately effective, or well-advised, is the subject of some debate.

The following is an illuminating example of how such criminal laws lingering on the statute books can have dramatic application in the environmental setting.

A. THE 1899 REFUSE ACT, REDISCOVERED IN THE 1960S

In the 1960s, when environmental activists following the lead of Rep. Henry Reuss of Wisconsin discovered the 1899 Refuse Act (passed in 1899 as a part of the Federal Rivers and Harbors Appropriation Act of that year[1]), they read its terms with pleased anticipation:

§407 Deposit of Refuse in Navigable Waters Generally

It shall not be lawful to throw, discharge, or deposit or cause, suffer, or procure to be thrown, discharged, or deposited either from or out of any ship, barge, or other floating craft of any kind, or from the shore, wharf, manufacturing establishment, or mill of any kind, any refuse matter of any kind or description whatever other than that flowing from streets and sewers and passing therefrom in a liquid state, into any navigable water of the United States, or into any tributary of any navigable water from which the same shall float or be washed into such navigable water: and it shall not be lawful to deposit, or cause, suffer, or procure to be deposited material of any kind in any place on the bank of any navigable water, where the same shall be liable to be washed into such navigable water, either by ordinary or high tides, or by storms or floods, or otherwise, whereby navigation shall or may be impeded or obstructed: *Provided*, That nothing herein contained shall extend to, apply to, or prohibit the operations in connection with the improvement of navigable waters or construction of public works, considered necessary and proper by the United States officers supervising such improvement or public work: *And provided further*, That the Secretary of the Army, whenever in the judgment of the Chief of Engineers anchorage and navigation will not be injured thereby, may permit the deposit of any material above mentioned in navigable waters, within limits to be defined and under conditions to be prescribed by him, provided application is made to him prior to depositing such material; and whenever any permit is so granted the conditions thereof shall be strictly complied with, and any violation thereof shall be unlawful....

§411. Penalty for Wrongful Deposit of Refuse: Use of or Injury to Harbor Improvements, and Obstruction of Navigable Waters Generally

Every person and every corporation that shall violate or that shall knowingly aid, abet, authorize, or instigate a violation of the provisions of...this title shall be guilty of a misdemeanor, and on conviction thereof shall be punished by a fine not exceeding $2,500 nor less than $500, or by imprisonment (in the case of a natural person) for not less than thirty days nor more than one year, or by both such fine and imprisonment, in the discretion of the court, one-half of said fine to be paid to the person or persons giving information which shall lead to conviction.

COMMENTARY AND QUESTIONS

1. The Refuse Act in the 1960s. Upon the discovery of the Refuse Act, a number of prosecutions were begun across the country, as United States District Attorneys

1. Pub. L. 97-322, codified at 33 U.C.S.A. §§401 et seq.

responded to the 1960s explosion of environmental consciousness in the media and the electorate. The opportunity for prosecution under the Refuse Act was an unexpected boon to the environmental movement. Most people had presumed that there were no existing environmental laws with teeth in them, and that legal action would therefore have to await legislative action. Instead, prosecutors were able to go immediately against a wide range of defendants, from small dumpers to major corporations, obtaining convictions quickly and decisively, and levying substantial fines. The American Chamber of Commerce and the National Association of Manufacturers were horrified by this legal development, and began to urge repeal of the Refuse Act. The Act may therefore take some of the credit for industry's willingness to go along with a new federal water pollution control act in 1972. For a time, the Refuse Act was undoubtedly the nation's most direct and effective environmental statute.

2. Ease of prosecution. If you were an environmentally-minded U.S. Attorney in the 1960s, and the Refuse Act was brought to your attention along with bottles and samples of muck from a particular water pollution outfall pipe, why would you find your case against the suspect dumper so easy to prove? Note first of all the geographical scope of the statute. To what geographical areas does it *not* apply? To what polluting materials does it apply? Is it clear that it applies to liquid pollutants? All liquid pollutants? And what are the elements of the criminal offense? Because the Refuse Act had not been generally recognized as a pollution statute, and because most polluters considered the federal government to be apathetic about pollution, virtually no dischargers had obtained a permit from the U.S. Army Corps of Engineers. Not much more had to be proved. The Supreme Court helped by holding, in U.S. v. Republic Steel, 362 U.S. 482, 491 (1960), that the Act meant what it said in plain words: pollution was "refuse," and where there were doubts, the Act should be read "charitably in light of the purpose to be served." Whose purpose, and when? What about the question of criminal "mens rea" or intent? Section 411 contains the requirement that defendants who aid and abet must be acting "knowingly." Does that apply to all prohibited acts as a requirement for prosecution? The syntax of the "knowing" phrase seems to apply only to aiding and abetting, not to direct violations of §407. Does it violate the process to convict a person who didn't know she was doing wrong? What does "knowing" mean? Does it mean that a person was not acting unconsciously? Does it mean that a defendant must know that she does not have a permit and that federal law requires one? These questions are considered later in this chapter.

3. The decision to prosecute. At first, in the initial fervor of the nation's environmental awakening, U.S. Attorneys began energetically to prosecute many of the cases that were brought to their attention by citizen groups, newspapers, and federal and state investigators. Over the next few years, however, the adverse reaction of defendants began to have a chilling effect on prosecutions. In 1970 the Nixon administration published the following mandatory Department of Justice guideline:

> U.S. DEPARTMENT OF JUSTICE, GUIDELINES FOR LITIGATION UNDER THE REFUSE ACT:
>
> 11. The Policy of the Department of Justice with respect to the enforcement of the Refuse Act for purposes other than the protection of the navigable capacity of national waters, is not to attempt to use it as a pollution abatement statute in competition with the federal water pollution act [Eds: the federal act at this time was a completely ineffective enforcement statute that had never successfully been used against a polluter] or with state pollution abatement procedures, but rather to use it to supplement that Act by bringing appropriate actions either to punish the occasional or recalcitrant polluter, or to abate continuing sources of pollution which for some reason or other have not been subjected to a proceeding conducted by the Federal Water Quality Administration or by a State, or where in the opinion of the Federal Water Quality Administration the polluter has failed to comply with obligations under such a procedure. To this end, the instructions...below encourage United States Attorneys to use the Refuse Act to punish or prevent significant discharges which are either accidental or infrequent, but which are not of a continuing nature resulting from the ordinary operations of a manufacturing plant....Therefore in order that we might coordinate our litigation with the programs of the Federal Water Quality Administration, civil and criminal actions against manufacturing plants which continuously discharge refuse into the navigable waters of the United States are not among the types of actions which the United States Attorneys may initiate on their own authority.

What was the effect of this directive? What tactical difference did it make in the nation's use of the Refuse Act as a major water pollution statute? Who would be affected by the Refuse Act after this directive went into effect?

4. Citizen prosecution – qui tam? If federal (and potentially state) prosecutors decline to prosecute a particular action, for whatever prosecutorial discretion reason, the violation is unlikely to be criminally prosecuted. In some circumstances citizens attempted to obtain prosecution of particularly egregious polluters by seeking to file qui tam actions themselves against polluters. The qui tam action is a traditional remedy by which a citizen can bring a law suit "in the name of the King," particularly where the citizen has a direct personal stake in the prosecution. The potential reward offered in §411 of the Refuse Act appears to be sufficient to establish a standing basis for citizen prosecutors. As it happened, the courts were generally inhospitable to citizen qui tam actions under the Refuse Act, so that initiation of prosecution depended upon political, social, and media pressures applied to prosecutorial authorities. Most qui tam suits were dismissed. See U.S. ex rel. Mattson v. Northwest Paper Company, 327 F. Supp. 87 (Minn. 1971), although some courts allowed such cases to be brought, see, e.g., Alameda Conservation Association v. California, 437 F.2d 1087 (9th Cir. 1971), cert. denied, 402 U.S. 908 (1971).

5. Statutory interpretation. What is "refuse"? If it includes pollution (which is indeed a leap of sorts), what about the argument that it does not include oil spills, because oil is a valuable commodity that is not being disposed of as waste, but rather was lost by accident? See U.S. v. Standard Oil Company, 384 U.S. 224 (1966). As the courts developed the doctrines of the Refuse Act, ultimately even temperature changes came to be regarded as "refuse" and thereby violations of the statute. Does it make any difference to you whether environmental damage has been caused maliciously, intentionally, negligently, or merely by unforeseeable accident? In each case the Refuse Act would still permit prosecution, representing as it does a statute for which, apparently, willfulness is not a required element for conviction.

The Refuse Act holds lessons beyond criminal law. What does it teach you about the life history of statutory enactments? When the Refuse Act was passed in 1898, what do you suppose was the subject of the debates in Congress? What was the intended "evil" that the statute was designed to prevent? Whom did Congress expect would be prosecuted? If you had been listening to the legislative debates in 1898, what societal interests would have been amongst the primary intended beneficiaries of the Refuse Act? Industrial corporations were the primary targets of Refuse Act prosecutions in the 1960s. Is there any question in your mind what would have happened if someone had told the Congress in 1898 that the statute would be applied against manufacturers producing liquid pollution wastes?

A criminal statute is a potent piece of legislatively-created law. It is, however, both a crude blunt instrument and a relatively unguided missile. The words that it embodies continue to be law while surrounding circumstances may change. The legislators who write a statute do not thereafter act as judges determining how it should be applied; the separation of powers sees to that. If the words of the statute are perfectly clear, its application follows, even seventy years after the statute was written. If the citizen activists who pushed prosecutions of the Refuse Act knew that the legislature that had passed the law intended that it have no application to circumstances like pollution, were they being unethical in seeking prosecutions under the Act?

6. Permits. Even if prosecutions under the Refuse Act were not certain to follow, many polluters in the 1960s understandably wanted to avoid the possibility of being prosecuted, and started seeking permits from the Corps of Engineers to cover their effluent outfall pipes. Under the terms of the statute, is it clear that the Corps of Engineers' Chief of Engineers can issue permits allowing pollution to continue? Must a permit's issuance or denial be based solely on questions of anchorage and navigation, or can the Corps include amongst its considerations other national policies, especially after January 1, 1970, when the National Environmental Policy Act of 1969 (see Chapter 12) became law? NEPA declared it the duty of all federal government agencies to seek to further environmental quality. See Zabel v. Tabb, 430 F.2d 199 (5th Cir. 1970). *Must* the Corps of Engineers base its permit issuance on considerations of public health and environmental quality?

7. Implied civil remedies? Injunctions? Why did the 1898 Congress make it a criminal offense rather than providing for civil penalties, damages, and injunctions? Can a court that finds a polluter in violation of the criminal offense tack on civil remedies as well, by "implying civil remedies" from the penal statute? Some 1960s Refuse Act cases did so. U.S. v. Jellico Industries, 3 ERC 1519 (M.D. Tenn. 1971). The

Supreme Court's Cort v. Ash doctrine, 422 U.S. 66 (1975), noted in Chapter 6 at page 302 *supra*, severely limited such civil remedy add-ons.

8. Juries. Remember that in virtually all environmental prosecutions, the defendants will have the right to a jury. How is that likely to affect the course and outcome of criminal proceedings? Is it any surprise that most of the reported appellate cases (i.e. where there is an appeal because defendants lost at trial and were convicted) are cases tried to a judge without a jury? In all probability, why didn't they request juries in those cases?

Prophesying jury reactions and jury verdicts has become a major feature of the defense attorney's art. Besides the individual proclivities of each juror, there are situational differences that can have great bearing. How dramatic is the environmental consequence of the indicted offense? How readily can the jury see itself in the role of the defendant rather than the victims? What deference attaches to corporate white collar defendants? Is jury nullification – always a possibility in the Anglo-American jury system – a reasonable tactic, or is the jury's hyper-vindictiveness rather to be feared?

9. The effectiveness of the Refuse Act. The effectiveness of the Refuse Act, if one means by that its effectiveness in getting the attention of American polluters, was extraordinary. Why does criminal law have this effect? In reality, not many executives can expect to go to jail, and their corporations certainly can be expected to pay any individual fines that corporate officers are assessed in criminal prosecutions. There remains, however, a small chance of going to jail. Furthermore, whether deserved or not, conviction of a criminal offense, even a misdemeanor, attaches some special stigma to corporate officials, unlike civil penalties that are just a nominal cost of doing business when you run too close to the line. Even though the chance of being convicted may be small, the uncertain possibility is something that no executive lives with easily.

Some of the provisions of the Refuse Act were amended by the Federal Water Pollution Control Act Amendments of 1972, now the Clean Water Act, a statute that established a direct, enforceable federal water pollution control system, albeit with less decisive teeth than the Refuse Act. See Chapter 19. Except for the permit program, however, the provisions of the Refuse Act set out here are largely still in force. Ten to fifteen major Refuse Act prosecutions are initiated each year by the Department of Justice, mostly under §407. According to one federal prosecutor, the old statute has major advantages over comparable provisions of the modern Clean Water Act. Under the latter statute, for example, one who spills pollutants into the water has a legal obligation to report the spill to federal authorities, but gains immunity from prosecution for virtually all matters covered by such information. The Refuse Act includes no such immunity. The Refuse Act continues to serve as an indication of the perils and potential of environmental criminal statutes.

10. Questioning the effectiveness of criminal prosecutions. What particular effectiveness does a criminal statute add to the system of pollution laws? In a sense, environmental criminal statutes are crude blunt instruments. If prosecutions are actually brought, they certainly do pack a punch. But do they constitute overkill? Especially where pollution prosecutions were limited to "accidental" spills by the Nixon guidelines, is it clear that the Refuse Act's criminal penalties were appropriate? Criminal fines bear no necessary relationship to the amount of harm caused by pollution, and they are not paid into a pollution control fund. Jail sentences used to vary widely from judge to judge, although now the federal sentencing guidelines have reduced the variations between sentences for similar offenses. See page 335 *infra*.

Even in the most dramatic cases, criminal prosecutions pose logistical and political problems. The Exxon-Valdez oil spill of March 24, 1989, for example, was the worst oil spill in the history of the United States, with environmental consequences that will to some extent be irreparable and in any event will require decades for Prince William Sound to return to a natural equilibrium roughly similar to that preceding the accident. Social and economic dislocations have likewise been drastic. It now appears probable that the Alaskan spill was not caused only or even primarily by the known alcoholism of the tanker's captain. At least in part there also appears to have been a consistent course of corporate conduct shortcutting safety procedures, cutting back on necessary shipboard personnel to save on payrolls, and perhaps even using financial incentives to encourage ships to run at higher speeds regardless of weather and water conditions. If these and other assertions were proved true and causative, the corporation and its officers would face criminal charges under the Refuse Act §407 and other federal statutes, as well as state laws. What purpose would be served by such prosecutions in light of the civil costs and loss of good will that the corporation has already sustained? What special problems would be encountered? What does it say about environmental criminal prosecutions that both the federal and Alaska state governments strenuously avoided criminal trials against Exxon, Alyeska, and their executives?

Nevertheless, many environmentalists continue to urge criminal prosecutions. Often criminal proceedings proceed parallel to civil proceedings brought by citizen plaintiffs. In such circumstances, courts in a civil tort litigation often defer to the ongoing criminal litigation, waiting for its conclusion before proceeding with civil suit. Does this make sense? Environmental citizen plaintiffs, of course, are pleased when prior criminal litigation produces a conviction of the defendant they are suing for damages and injunctions in parallel civil proceedings. In many cases, issues determined against polluters in criminal proceedings need not be relitigated in subsequent civil cases. Are there corresponding negative consequences of environmental criminal prosecutions?

B. THE RECENT WILLINGNESS TO PROSECUTE ENVIRONMENTAL CRIMES

People of the State of Illinois v. Film Recovery Systems, Inc.; Metallic Marketing Systems; Charles Kirschbaum; Daniel Rodriguez; Steven O'Neil

Circuit Court, Cook County, Illinois, 4th Division

No. 83-11091 (involuntary manslaughter); No. 84-5064 (murder), June 14, 1985

ORAL VERDICT FROM THE BENCH

BANKS, J. This court is being reconvened this afternoon in order for me to render a decision in the case against Film Recovery Systems, Inc., Metallic Marketing Systems, Inc., Steven O'Neil, Charles Kirschbaum, and Daniel Rodriguez.

The record should be clear the defendants are charged with the following offenses: Steven O'Neil, Charles Kirschbaum, and Daniel Rodriguez are charged by way of indictment No. 84 C–5064 with murder as defined in Chapter 38 Section 9-1-a-2, that being "A person who kills an individual without lawful justification commits murder if, in performing the acts which cause the death, such person knows that such acts create a strong probability of death or great bodily harm to the individual or another." Also, the defendants Film Recovery Systems, and Metallic Marketing Systems, Inc. are charged by way of indictment No. 83 C–11091 with involuntary manslaughter and fourteen counts of reckless conduct. Also, Steven O'Neil, Daniel Rodriguez, and Charles Kirschbaum are charged in the same indictment with fourteen counts of reckless conduct.

Before I render a decision in this case, I would like to set forth some of the reasons for my decision. I would like to make it known and make it perfectly clear that the reasons I state are not the total basis for my decision in this case. My decision in this case is based on total review of all evidence presented in this case by both the State and Defense. The evidence reviewed and taken into consideration in making my finding was the oral testimony given by the defendants, plus a review of all exhibits which were presented; also, weighing the credibility of all the witnesses who appeared before this Court. That which I will allude to now, I believe, is essential in reaching the decision that I have reached. During my deliberations and evaluations of all the evidence, let it be known that I never forgot the most important concept in criminal law, that being the defendants are presumed innocent and that it is the burden of the State that they must prove guilt beyond a reasonable doubt.

I hereby make the following findings: No. 1: Stefan Golab died of acute cyanide toxicity. I arrived at that conclusion in the following way: many witnesses testified to the conditions of the air in the plant; not only workers, but independent witnesses as well, such as insurance inspectors, OSHA inspectors, Environmental Protection Agency inspectors, police officers and other service representatives. The testimony of the police investigators is the most important because although we do not know the actual amount of hydrogen cyanide gas in the air on February 10, 1983, the date of the death of Stefan Golab, the police officers testified as to the air quality on the date in question. They were the investigating officers after the incident had occurred, and their symptoms were classical symptoms, which, according to the Material Safety Data Sheet, would occur if exposed to hydrogen cyanide gas at high levels. These symptoms were nausea, burning throat, burning eyes, difficulty breathing, plus others.

No. 2: I believe also the Medical Examiner, because in the Medical Examiner and toxicologist reports, the victim had a blood cyanide level of 3.45 micrograms per millilitre, which is a lethal dose and can be fatal. The manufacturer states that sodium cyanide, which has a brand name or trade name of Cyanogran, which is manufactured by the DuPont Company, when mixed with a weak alkali, with water in this case, which is a weak alkali, has a pH of approximately seven, will create hydrogen cyanide gas.

I find that the conditions under which the workers in the plant performed their duties was totally unsafe. There was an insufficient amount of safety equipment present on the premises. There were no safety instructions given to the workers.

The workers were not properly warned of the hazards and dangers of working with cyanide. The warning signs were totally inadequate. The warning signs were written in Spanish and English. The warning signs stated the words "poison" or "veneno," meaning poison in Spanish. The problem with that is that there were more than Spanish and American workers working in this plant. Aside from the Spanish and American workers, there was Stefan Golab, plus other Polish workers. The evidence has shown that Stefan Golab did not speak English, could not read or write English, so a sign in Spanish had no benefit to that man at all.

The Cyanogran label, which is on all the drums that were delivered to Film Recovery, which is Exhibit 13, if I recall correctly, which is the brand name for sodium cyanide, states that there are three ways in which cyanide can be fatal; one being inhalation of the gas hydrogen cyanide, one being ingestion of sodium cyanide, and third, the absorption into the skin of the sodium cyanide or the liquid that was produced by the sodium cyanide in water. This was not told to the workers, and most of the workers, including Stefan Golab, could not read the label because they could not read English; therefore, he had no knowledge of the potential danger from inhalation or absorption into their bodies.

I also find the defendants were totally knowledgeable in the dangers which are associated with the use of cyanide. This I ascertained through the testimony of the witnesses, including the defendants. The defendants knew that the workers were becoming nauseated and vomiting. The workers complained to all three of the defendants. Steven O'Neil testified on May 28, 1985, as stated in the transcript on page 5-4, and I quote, "I was aware of all of the hazardous nature of cyanide." He knew hydrogen cyanide gas was present. He knew hydrogen cyanide gas, if inhaled, could be fatal. Charles Kirschbaum saw workers vomiting. He was given a Material Safety Data Sheet. He read the label, and he knew what it said. He said that he did not wear the same equipment the workers did because he did not do the same work as the workers, even though he testified to the contrary. Daniel Rodriguez knew the workers got sick at the plant. He testified to that. He could read the label, and he read it many times.

I also find that Steven O'Neil, who was the President of Film Recovery Systems, President of Metallic Marketing Systems, Metallic Marketing Systems owning fifty percent of Film Recovery Systems, was in control and exercised control over both Film Recovery Systems and Metallic Marketing Systems before and after the death of Stefan Golab, which was on February 10, 1983.

Using all the facts stated above and all other evidence pertinent to this case, I find that the conditions present in the work place which caused sickness and injury to workers was reckless conduct. I also find that the death of Stefan Golab was not accidental but in fact murder. I also find that the defendants created the conditions present in the plant by their acts of omission and commission.

I also find that the defendants were either officers or high managerial personnel of both Film Recovery Systems and Metallic Marketing Systems, Inc. I also find that to state that a corporation cannot be convicted of a crime because it has no mind and it cannot therefore have a mental state in order to infer knowledge on a corporation is totally erroneous. It is my belief that the mind and mental state of a corporation is the mind and mental state of the directors, officers, and high managerial personnel because they act on behalf of the corporation for both the benefit of the corporation and for themselves; and if the corporation's officers, directors, and high managerial personnel act within the scope of their corporate responsibilities and employment for their benefit and for the benefit of the profits of the corporation, the corporation must be held liable for what occurred in the work place.

Therefore, it is the decision of this Court that the defendants Steven O'Neil, Charles Kirschbaum and Daniel Rodriguez are guilty of murder both as individuals and also as officers and high managerial personnel of Film Recovery Systems and Metallic Marketing Systems, Inc.

> I also find that they are guilty of murder and reckless conduct, all fourteen counts, shall be entered upon the record and judgment thereon on the findings shall be entered.

I also find that because of the negligence and reckless behavior of both Film Recovery Systems, Inc. and Metallic Marketing Systems as corporate entities in allowing their officers and high managerial personnel to operate the corporation in such a manner as to cause death to one worker and injuries to other workers, that the defendant corporations Film Recovery Systems and Metallic Marketing Systems, the corporations are guilty of involuntary manslaughter and fourteen counts of reckless conduct.

I hereby find that Film Recovery Systems and Metallic Marketing Systems are guilty as charged, and enter judgment on all the findings, as to the fourteen counts of reckless conduct and involuntary manslaughter.

Finally, and this is the most important part and most difficult part for a Judge, I believe because the cloak of innocence has been removed from the accused and because the charge of murder, which the defendants have been found guilty of, does not carry probation and carries a minimum of twenty years in the penitentiary, it is my duty to revoke all bail and the defendants shall be remanded to the custody of the Sheriff's Office, awaiting sentencing, and it is the order of this Court that the bonds be revoked.

At this time, gentlemen, I am going to set a date for sentencing....

Steven Ferrey, Hard Time: Criminal Prosecution for Polluters
10.4 Amicus Journal 11 (Fall 1988)

On the surface, it was a model company. It recycled valuable minerals from waste materials, and had a stellar record on hiring minorities. But beyond the facade lurked a darker, more ominous, and deadly story.

Film Recovery Systems Inc., a company near Chicago, extracted trace amounts of silver from hospitals' discarded X-ray film by using sodium cyanide. In its heyday, the company employed eighty workers and earned about $18 million annually.

But in its unventilated workroom, employees hunched over 140 bubbling, foaming cauldrons of sodium cyanide. They were issued no protective gear and were not instructed in safety measures. While manually stirring these vats, sodium cyanide slopped over the sides, soaking the workers' clothing and skin. The air was choked with the fumes of hydrogen cyanide gas.

Film Recovery employed illegal Mexican and Polish immigrant laborers almost exclusively in its silver-recovery process. Employees later revealed that legal workers were not offered jobs. Few workers spoke English; even fewer could read. The common antidote for cyanide poisoning, amyl nitrite, was not available at the facility. Even the skull-and-crossbones warning labels on the drums of the cyanide were covered over or obscured by management. One day in February 1983, Stefan Golab, a Polish immigrant, stumbled into the lunchroom, fell to the floor with nausea, and died from acute cyanide poisoning. He was fifty-nine years old.

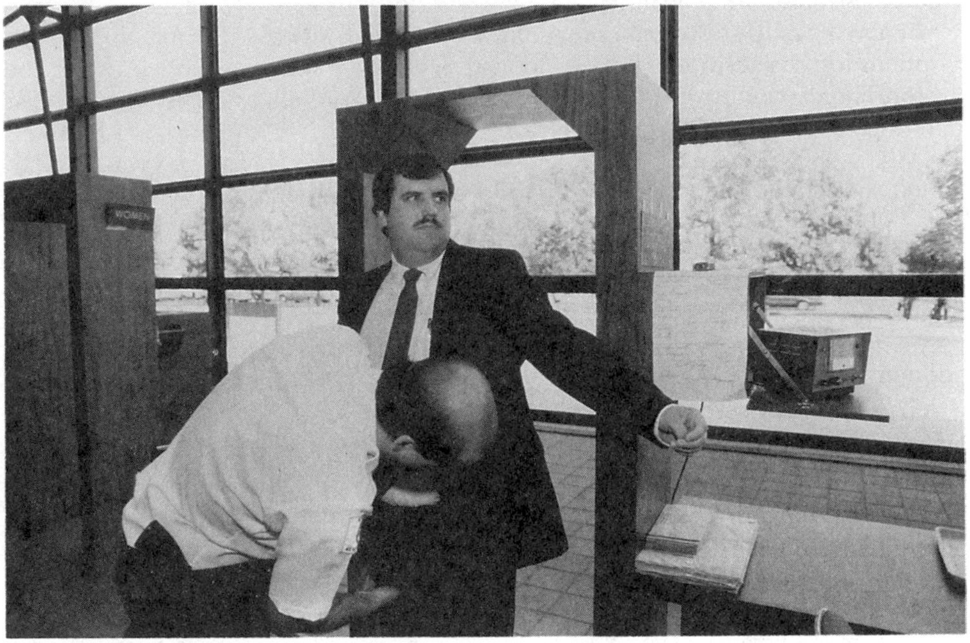

SCOTT SANDERS/DAILY HERALD, ARLINGTON HEIGHTS, ILLINOIS

Former president of Film Recovery Systems Inc., Steven O'Neil, being searched before being sentenced to twenty-five years in prison for the job-related death of an employee at his Elk Grove Village plant. Prosecutors said O'Neil and two other executives were "motivated by greed and greed alone."

"It was the most outrageous situation I have ever seen, coldly calculated to risk the public's and workers' health," remembers Jay Magnuson, deputy chief of the Public Interest Bureau, Cook County (Illinois) State's Attorney's Office. Magnuson went to the mat. He prosecuted Film Recovery President Steven O'Neil, the plant manager, and the foreman, for murder. "Callously, they knowingly maintained an unsafe plant environment that was likely to cause death to workers," Magnuson remarks. "I never had a second thought that they should be convicted for murder."...

The tragedy of Stephan Golab's death is compounded by the fact that the government agency responsible for regulating Film Recovery had given the firm a clean bill of health only months before. In the fall of 1982, inspectors from the federal Occupational Safety and Health Administration (OSHA) visited the plant, but they never got past the front office, where they saw nothing out of the ordinary in the company's paperwork. They did not walk the additional twenty-five feet beyond the office doors to observe Golab and others hunched over gurgling vats of cyanide.

After Golab's death, OSHA inspectors descended on the plant, fining management the seemingly arbitrary and insignificant amount of $4,855. Film Recovery refused to pay, so OSHA reduced it by half, though to this day it has not collected.

These on-site activities were just the tip of the criminal iceberg. Investigators later discovered almost 15 million pounds of cyanide waste from Film Recovery that had been dumped illegally in rented truck trailers parked in other parts of

Illinois. The EPA used $4.5 million of taxpayer's funds to clean up this toxic debris. Decontamination of the facility cost the building's landlord $250,000.

Five years ago, jail sentences for polluters were unheard of. At worst, the penalty for violating environmental or workplace safety laws was a modest fine. On the remote chance of getting caught, the fines could be rationalized as just another cost of doing business.

But times are changing. Federal and state laws covering hazardous waste, clean air, clean water, and workplace safety impose stiff civil and criminal penalties of up to $25,000 per violation. Like expanding reflections in a carnival mirror, one transgression magnifies into multiple dimensions. A single polluting action can violate several laws simultaneously, and each day of violation is counted by the courts as if it were a new violation. A single act of pollution becomes a serious and compounded felony. "Corporate America will readily take notice of environmental statutes when they start going to jail for their violations," says Glenn Sechen, assistant prosecutor for Cook County. "It simply ceases to be a cost of doing business when it becomes their own necks."

The impact of environmental prosecution has been refocused on individuals. The protective wall between corporate actions and corporate executives is eroding. In Los Angeles County alone, where the district attorney's office now investigates every workplace accident as a possible criminal violation, 125 criminal environmental prosecutions by the city attorney's office resulted in convictions in all but one instance. Twenty-seven corporate executives and employees currently are serving jail terms for their offenses, and forty-five more cases are in various stages of prosecution.

The U.S. Department of Justice has brought criminal indictments against 328 individuals and 117 corporations for environmental pollution. The courts have imposed 203 years of jail time and collected $12 million in fines. Sixty-four years of those sentences already have been served. Of those sentenced, about one-third were corporate presidents, 12 percent were vice-presidents, an additional 5 percent were corporate officers, and 20 percent were managers or foremen. Less than 25 percent of those sentenced to jail were the workers who actually released the pollution.

How high in the corporate hierarchy prosecutions reach is a function of employee cooperation in providing evidence against co-workers. An emerging lesson is that the middle of a large corporate ladder can be a perilous place to perch in a company that ignores environmental requirements. At the lower end of the corporation, the "Nuremberg defense" can be an effective escape. Prosecutors are reticent to indict lower-level personnel who claim that they unknowingly were "just following orders" when breaking an environmental law.

Correspondingly, in large corporations, the top-level management may not have direct knowledge of polluting activities. The buck often stops on the desk of middle-level managers, identified by employees as the ones giving the orders to engage in polluting activities. Ironically, a large corporation, with a diffuse management structure and unclear lines of responsibility, may shield executives from potential criminal liability.

In a survey of environmental prosecutions on the East Coast, the most prevalent source of information resulting in prosecutions came from citizen complaints rather than government inspections. The typical company cited was small, employing less than fifty persons. An examination of dispositions in criminal environmental prosecutions reveals that about a quarter are dismissed before a verdict, about half result in guilty pleas by defendants, and of the remaining cases that proceed through a trial, three quarters result in convictions while about a quarter result in acquittals.

Despite successful prosecutorial records in several states, most local prosecutors do not actively pursue criminal environmental polluters. The barriers can be daunting. "Judges understand a smoking gun and a bag of heroin as criminal. They do not understand environmental pollution," laments Lieutenant Gary Long of the Illinois State Police environmental unit.

Some prosecutors argue privately that criminal court judges, experienced in dealing with common criminals, are uncomfortable with prosecution of executives in Gucci loafers. The very large penalties in environmental statutes ($25,000 per violation per day) also are outside normal venue of criminal court jurists. For many local judges, deciding the proper criminal sanction for a corporate executive "is like walking in new snow," according to John Lynch, assistant district attorney in Los Angeles.

Problems of proof can be substantial. Documenting the facts and dates of actual polluting activities can prove elusive without help from informants. Allegations against criminal defendants must be proved beyond reasonable doubt. Not all convictions result in jail sentences, and not all jail sentences actually are served. Liberal use of suspended sentences, immediate probation, sentences served on weekends only, and other "innovative" programs mitigate the service of "hard" time. A typical jail sentence is about sixty to ninety days.

Environmental criminals often qualify for treatment that Lynch describes as "commit a crime, go to your room." With jails overcrowded, convicted executives typically fit the profile for release programs: they have ties to the community, references from prominent persons, and are not violent or likely to flee. Consequently, some serve time by wearing an identification bracelet and confining their activities to their homes.

Despite practical problems, criminal prosecution has assumed center stage in environmental enforcement. For an executive, the prospect of incarceration with violent felons focuses the attention like few other sanctions. In return for no jail time, defendants often are willing to plead guilty to violations carrying very large fines.

The battle against knowing polluters is far from won. Where a sociologist might predict that aggressive criminal prosecution would deter wrongdoing, the laws of economics exert a countervailing force.... To dispose of a barrel of hazardous waste legally today, the cost may be as high as $400. The economics of waste disposal tempts many to ignore the laws governing proper waste handling and disposal, and the chances of being caught still are small.

And defendants' costs usually are paid by the corporation, not by the accused executive. These legal costs are tax-deductible business expenses. Corporations often also pay the fines on behalf of their executives. But until the corporation also can serve time, criminal prosecution of individual corporate executives will remain the most potent weapon in the expanding arsenal of environmental enforcement.

COMMENTARY AND QUESTIONS

1. *Film Recovery* and pre-emption. What is your assessment of the regulatory reliability of the federal Occupational Safety and Health Administration (OSHA) in the *Film Recovery* case? It would seem that OSHA had ample opportunity to find and correct the extreme dangers of the workplace but for some reason had not been militant. Even after the fact, the minimal fine levied by OSHA was protested, and reduced. Despite an agency's general fecklessness, however, defendants are sometimes successful in persuading courts that the existence of federal statutory remedies precludes and pre-empts application of general state criminal statutes. See People v. Chicago Magnet Wire, 510 N.E.2d 1173 (Ill. App. 1987) (reversed in 1989 by the Illinois Supreme Court).

2. The consequences of *Film Recovery*. *Film Recovery* was probably the decade's most important environmental prosecution because of the dramatic way it was covered by the press (the first time in living memory that a corporate executive had been prosecuted for murder in connection with environmental pollution). As of 1991, however, none of the defendants in *Film Recovery* had yet seen the inside of a jail, or paid a cent in fines. Steven O'Neil was sentenced to twenty-five years in jail, but in late 1991 his appeal was still moving through the appellate courts. Another defendant, David MacKay, fled to the state of Utah which for some reason has refused to extradite him back to Illinois. The appeals of the others were delayed for an extended period of time by a state court of appeals decision holding the homicide statute pre-empted by the OSHA statute. See *Chicago Magnet Wire, supra.*

Film Recovery was a homicide prosecution. The vast majority of potential environmental prosecutions are probably of a lesser order of magnitude. In this media-sensitive age, however, *Film Recovery's* homicide convictions have encouraged prosecution of other kinds of crimes as well. The result of that one case has had the effect of galvanizing environmental prosecutions throughout the country. In Los Angeles, District Attorney Ira Reiner made a name for his department by setting up an environmental crime specialty division with 10 attorneys, 8 investigators, and the full resources of the department behind it, prosecuting a wide range of offenses. According to David Guthman, a prosecutor in the L.A. District Attorney's office, public recognition of the DA's willingness to prosecute environmental crimes has led to the development of a new specialty amongst those who practice L.A. law. Those who specialize in environmental defense work are currently billing at $400 an hour with no market resistance from their frightened clientele. "Clients will say, 'If I'm being sued for dumping toxic wastes, I don't care what it costs to pay the lawyer. I just need to get out of this problem,'" said Lawrence Bright, vice president of Hildebrandt Inc., a consulting firm for lawyers and the corporations that use them. Top Lawyers Get $400 an Hour as Fees, L.A. Times, 18 Sept. 1989, 1.

3. Federal prosecutions. Environmental prosecutions have been heating up at the federal level as well. During the 1970s, under Jimmy Carter, an avowed conservationist, only 25 federal environmental prosecutions were commenced. Between 1982 and 1989 there were more than 450 indictments, more than 325 pleas or convictions, almost 100 of them against corporations, with assessed fines of over $13 million (although 20 percent or more of these appear to have been suspended) and jail terms of more than 200 years (mostly against noncorporate individual offenders), with nearly 65 years of jail time actually being served. How did this happen in a Reagan era?

4. Environmental application of federal sentencing guidelines. The United States Sentencing Commission, originally set up by the Reagan Administration as part of its "law and order" policies, ended up establishing remarkably stringent punishments for environmental crimes. Under its uniform sentencing guidelines, as authorized by the Sentencing Reform Act of 1984, 28 U.S.C.A. Title 58, the illegal discharge of pollutants, without a permit or in violation of the terms of a permit, requires a sentence of 20-27 months in jail without parole. The toxic chemical and pesticide provisions further illustrate the process: Simple misuse is "level 8" conduct; if it involves repetitive discharges, the level moves up to 14; if there was active danger to the public, it moves to level 23; if any evacuation had to be ordered, it rises to level 27; if there was illegal transportation of the toxics, it goes to level 31. Then the conduct level is multiplied by a nature-of-the-offense factor: "no prior criminal record" results in a 60-70 month final sentence; if there have been prior convictions the multiplier can go to a factor of four or more, resulting in a sentence of 120 months! What practical courtroom consequences are likely to follow from this battery of strict sentencing prescriptions?

For a fascinating glimpse into how the sentencing guidelines can be applied in environmental cases, see U.S. v. Rutana, 932 F.2d 1155, cert. denied 1991, LEXIS 5818 (6th Cir. 1991)(district courts leniency to a corporate executive was misplaced; case remanded for stricter sentencing).

C. PROBLEMS IN CORPORATE PROSECUTIONS FOR ENVIRONMENTAL CRIMES

By the nature of the American economic system, much of the pollution dumped into the air and waters of the U.S. comes from corporate polluters, especially the most toxic of such waste streams. Successful prosecution of criminal environmental violations always faces an array of difficulties not encountered in civil lawsuits, notably in Fifth Amendment and other limitations on discovery, and the special burden of proof required to prove defendants guilty "beyond a reasonable doubt," not just liable by a simple preponderance of the evidence. These difficulties are particularly pronounced in the case of prosecutions of corporations and corporate executives.

Section 1. THE FIFTH AMENDMENT AND THE CORPORATION

A corporation can claim Fifth Amendment protections against regulatory takings and violations of procedural due process. Can a corporation take the Fifth, refusing to produce documents that may tend to incriminate it, as a natural person can? The Supreme Court's answer apparently is "No." See Hale v. Henkel, 201 U.S. 43 (1906); U.S. v. Morton Salt, 338 U.S. 632 (1950); Bellis v. U.S., 417 U.S. 85 (1974). In some cases the corporation cannot even claim attorney-client privilege. People v. Keuffel & Esser Co., 181 Cal. App. 3d 785, 227 Cal. Reptr. 13 (1986)(zinc pollution). Not only can't the company claim Fifth Amendment privilege, but it also must deliver up documents in its possession even if they directly incriminate the individuals who make up the corporation. In such circumstances, by virtue of their corporate positions, corporate officers effectively lose the protections of the Fifth Amendment.

Section 2. DIFFICULTIES IN PROVING COLLECTIVE ACTIVITY CRIMES

Goldfarb, Kepone: A Case Study

8 Environmental Law 645 (1978)

[The narrative history of the Allied Chemical Kepone case was set out earlier in Chapter 2 at page 42 *supra*. The present excerpt picks up with the criminal indictments filed in the case....]

INDICTMENTS AND PLEAS

On May 7, 1976, the Federal grand jury in Richmond, Virginia, handed up two indictments charging Allied, LSP, the City of Hopewell, and six individuals with a total of 1,097 counts (separate offenses) relating to the Kepone incident at Hopewell. Then on July 28th, the grand jury was reconvened to hear further evidence, and the result was a third indictment issued on August 2, 1976.

Indictment #1 charged Allied with 941 counts: 940 alleged violations of the Refuse Act and FWPCA for discharging Kepone, TAIC, and THEIC from Allied's Semi-Works without permits; and one count for an alleged conspiracy to violate control laws among Allied and five of its employees. Each of the individual defendants was also charged with conspiracy to defraud the United States by providing false information regarding the Semi-Works effluent.

Indictment #2 charged Allied, LSP, Hundtofte, Moore, and the City of Hopewell with 153 counts apiece relating to the allegedly unlawful discharge of Kepone by LSP into the Hopewell sewer system. In addition, Hopewell was charged with three counts of failure to report the presence of Kepone in its municipal treatment works.

The belated Indictment #3 contained only one count, charging Allied, LSP, Hundtofte, and Moore with conspiracy relating to LSP's discharge of Kepone.

None of the indictments related to conditions within the LSP plant, because the Federal Occupational Safety and Health Act does not provide for criminal sanctions in cases such as this.

The corporate and individual defendants were confronted by the prospect of heavy fines and jail terms if found guilty and accorded maximum sentences. Allied faced a maximum fine of more than $17 million; LSP and its co-owners $3.8 million each; the City of Hopewell 3.9 million; and the alleged co-conspirators $10,000 on each conspiracy count. The more serious potential penalty, however, was imprisonment. The counts for discharging without a permit – 940 counts in Indictment #1 and 153 in Indictment #2 – carried a maximum jail term of one year on each count. The possible penalty on the conspiracy counts was up to five years on each count.

On May 21, 1976, each of the defendants was arraigned and each pleaded not guilty on all counts. The Kepone defendants elected to forego a jury trial, probably because they were reluctant to entrust their fates to the lay representatives of an outraged public.

Indictment #1 charged Allied with being directly liable for 940 counts of discharging wastes from its own Semi-Works plant without a permit, and with vicarious liability for LSP's discharge. Indictment #2 charged LSP, Hundtofte, and Moore with direct responsibility for the discharges of Kepone by LSP into the Hopewell sewer system. Moreover, Hopewell was indicted for violation of its own permit and failure to report the presence of Kepone in its treatment works.

As for vicarious liability, Indictment #2 charged Allied and Hopewell with responsibility for LSP's discharges. The conspiracy counts can be found in Indictments #1 and #3.

The direct liability aspects of this case are relatively unimportant from a legal standpoint, and will be treated in summary fashion. Allied was clearly in violation of the Refuse Act, which makes discharging without a permit a criminal act regardless of the presence or absence of criminal intent. The FWPCA and CWA do, however, require proof of "willful or negligent" conduct for the imposition of criminal penalties. But the FWPCA goes beyond the Refuse Act by explicitly extending liability to a "responsible corporate officer" for the illegal acts of his corporation. LSP as discharger and Hundtofte and Moore as its only officers obviously contravened the FWPCA by discharging pollutants which interfered with the Hopewell treatment plant (a violation of federal regulations)[2] and continuously violating pretreatment standards – all with the knowledge of Hundtofte and Moore. The City of Hopewell was clearly in violation of its own NPDES permit by discharging an unpermitted and unreported substance (Kepone) with knowledge of its presence in the system.

Given the clear-cut direct criminal liability in this case, it is not surprising that the defendants after having made some unsuccessful preliminary motions, chose to change their pleas from "not guilty" to nolo contendere on the direct liability counts.

There are two main reasons for entering a nolo plea. First, carrying less of a stigma than "guilty," it may be part of a plea bargaining process in which a prosecutor agrees that in return for avoiding the delay and expense of a trial he will accept a nolo plea and request the judge to impose a sentence which is lighter than the maximum. Second, the conviction of a defendant after a nolo plea cannot be used as evidence in another legal proceeding arising out of the same set of facts – for example, in a civil action for damages. Had the defendant pleaded or been found guilty, on the other hand, such a conviction would be a prima facie case by the plaintiff in a related civil case.

The City of Hopewell was the first defendant to request that its plea be changed from "not guilty" to nolo. The prosecutor had been especially diligent in his plea bargaining with Hopewell because of the problems inherent in imposing criminal liability and sanctions on municipalities. The position of a municipality as a criminal defendant is an anomalous one; it is a direct representative of the public; it is not a profit-making enterprise, but a public service organization; and the law imposes no clear criminal liability upon municipal officials for municipal conduct other than for criminal acts arising from their own venality (e.g., bribery, extortion, election fraud, etc.). As for sanctions, how can a municipality be imprisoned? And how meaningful is it to threaten woefully overburdened and often impoverished municipalities with heavy fines? Given the exigencies of modern urban life, juries will not convict municipalities and judges will be lenient in sentencing them. Water pollution control law adds other variations to this theme. Municipalities must rely on large Federal grants in order to construct the sophisticated systems required to cleanse urban residential and industrial wastes. What if a municipality is in violation of its NDES permit because of an inability to procure Federal construction

2. See 40 C.F.R. §128.131(1977). This section of the CWA regulations prohibits the introduction of waste into a publicly owned treatment plant which interferes with the operation of or the performance of the plant.

grant funds? Or, as in the case of Hopewell, because of a delay in the completion of a regional treatment plant? Furthermore, the FWPCA makes "responsible corporate officers" criminally responsible for corporate criminal acts; however, there is no comparable provision for "responsible municipal officials." Thus, the problem of enforcing pollution control laws (either civilly or criminally) against municipalities such as Hopewell is one of the most compelling perplexities in environmental law.

On June 25, 1976, Hopewell requested that the court allow it to change its plea to nolo for ten counts of Indictment #2. The United States then moved to dismiss the remaining 146 counts against Hopewell. The bargain was accepted by the court, and Hopewell was convicted of violating the FWPCA by discharging Kepone from its treatment plant without a permit, and, more importantly as will appear, aiding and abetting LSP's illegal discharges of Kepone and other pollutants.

Virgil Hundtofte was next to plea bargain. He was permitted to plead nolo on 79 of the 153 counts of Indictment #2 (the remaining 74 counts were dismissed), and to plead "guilty" to a reduced charge of conspiring to furnish false information to the Federal government. Hundtofte also pleaded nolo to the single conspiracy count of Indictment #3. Apparently, Hundtofte also consented to appear as a witness for the United States against Allied. William Moore and LSP plea bargained in a manner similar to Hundtofte.

Finally, Allied unexpectedly requested permission to plead nolo on 940 counts of Indictment #1. The prosecutor objected vehemently to Allied's request, but Judge Merhige accepted the nolo plea "in the interest of justice." By pleading nolo, Allied was anticipating that civil actions would be filed against it based on the Kepone discharges. (Indeed, damage suits aggregating more than $200 million were brought against Allied and others.) Thus, Judge Merhige, in accepting Allied's nolo plea, afforded Allied a profound tactical advantage in subsequent civil suits.

As a result of plea bargaining, all relevant defendants had pleaded nolo to all outstanding counts charging direct violations of pollution control laws. In addition, all of the relevant major defendants except Allied had pleaded either guilty or nolo to the conspiracy counts of Indictments #1 and #3. Thus, the only significant issues remaining for the trial were the 153 counts of Indictment #2 charging Allied with responsibility for LSP's discharges into the Hopewell sewer system (Hopewell had already been convicted on ten counts of Indictment #2), and the conspiracy counts against Allied. However, the ease with which the United States obtained convictions on the counts involving direct violations of law stands in stark contrast to its inability to establish any vicarious liability or conspiracy regarding Allied.

TRIAL AND SENTENCING

The court quickly disposed of the count against Allied charging conspiracy to provide false information to the United States. By pretrial motion, Allied sought a ruling dismissing the count on the ground that, as a matter of law, a corporation cannot be in conspiracy with its own employees who are acting within the scope of their authority. Since, argued Allied, it was the duty of the plant management at Hopewell to prepare permit applications and submit them to Federal agencies, there could be no conspiracy regarding these applications because a conspiracy must include at least two persons, and corporate employees are not separate and distinct persons when acting within their authority. In other words, Allied was arguing that it could not be in conspiracy with itself. The court agreed, and dismissed the count as to Allied.

Although the 153 counts of Indictment #2 and the single conspiracy count of Indictment #3 represented less than ten percent of the total number of counts in the three indictments, they were undoubtedly the most controversial and significant from the standpoint of law and public policy since they held Allied responsible for the criminal acts of LSP. The United States was anxious to establish a precedent that tolling, or its equivalents in other industries, should not be utilized to circumvent pollution control laws. In the words of the prosecutor, "we're trying to establish that these large chemical companies which seek to farm out these contracts will remain liable...for any violations of law that may occur...."[3]

The legal presumption is that corporations separate in law are separate in fact, even if they are parent and wholly-owned subsidiary. Therefore, the burden of proof is on the plaintiff (in a civil action) or the government (in a criminal action) to establish that although ostensibly separate and distinct, two corporations are so involved and entwined in each other's operations that they are really one and the same enterprise. (In a criminal case it must be proven beyond a reasonable doubt that one of the corporations is mere form without substance.) Only then can a judgment against one be enforced against both of them. This is called "piercing the corporate veil."

It is another axiom of corporate law that a corporation is responsible for damages and fines only to the extent of its own assets, as distinguished from those of its shareholders. Consequently, corporations are tempted to spin off risky activities to thinly capitalized subsidiaries or other "friendly" companies. This trend is especially pronounced where the severed operation involves environmental pollution, because despite assertions to the contrary virtually all pollution control and safety programs are more lenient with regard to "economically weak" firms. A struggling corporation is more likely to obtain enforcement delays or exceptions to pollution control laws on the ground that the costs of full or immediate compliance would compel a shutdown.[4]

In attempting to hold Allied criminally liable for LSP's discharges, the United States relied upon four legal theories: (1) that LSP was an *instrumentality* of Allied; (2) that LSP was an *agent* of Allied; (3) that Allied was an *accomplice* of LSP; and (4) that Allied and LSP were engaged in a *conspiracy* to violate pollution control laws.

Under the instrumentality theory, the United States was called upon to prove "actual domination" of LSP by Allied. Somewhat less was necessary to establish an agency relationship: a continuous right of control by Allied (rather than actual domination), along with a consent by LSP to produce Kepone primarily for the benefit of Allied, and at least a tacit acceptance by Allied, if not an explicit condonation, of LSP's unlawful acts. Imposing accomplice liability depended upon proving that Allied "aided and abetted" LSP's illegal discharges. Accomplice liability moves from the realm of control to that of association and assistance, preserving the autonomy of accomplice and perpetrator. It is a kind of vicarious liability that does not require the corporate veil to be pierced. Finally, a conspiracy

3. Arnold Reitze characterizes tolling as "corporate buccaneering," comparing it to the practice of English sovereigns in the sixteenth century of encouraging private individuals to become pirates by outfitting them and covertly granting them immunity from English law, and then sharing in the spoils while denying responsibility for the privateers' depredations. But whatever its analogues, tolling is an inevitable result of the status accorded to corporations by the American legal system.

4. The courts have generally been reluctant to grant injunctions against corporations who are attempting to comply with pollution control standards where such injunctions would force the corporation out of business. See, e.g., Boomer v. Atlantic Cement Co., in Chapter 3.

is a formal or informal agreement to commit another crime. Under a conspiracy theory, Allied and LSP would also be treated as distinct entities.

At the trial, witnesses for the United States, including Hundtofte and Moore, emphasized Allied's close knowledge of Kepone production and toxicity; the relationship of Allied to Hundtofte and Moore; the onesideness of the tolling agreement; Allied's provision of services to LSP – including sampling its effluent on a regular basis, and tours of the LSP plant by Allied's employees and consultants; and Allied's constant urging of LSP to greater Kepone production. A key date was July 7, 1975, when Allied officials allegedly met with Hundtofte and Moore and were specifically informed that LSP could not meet the new .5 parts per billion pretreatment standard and still increase production. According to the testimony, Allied was then told that new capital was necessary if production was to be increased, and Allied agreed to furnish these funds. But, urged the prosecutor, even after July 7th (and before the new equipment was procured), Allied was supplying raw materials and insisting upon production increases, while continuing to sample LSP's effluent.

The defense relied on letters from LSP to Allied, allegedly written over a period of years, reassuring Allied that LSP was not discharging in violation of the law. Allied's reasonable reliance on these letters, it was urged, refuted the "instrumentality" and "agency" theories and also precluded the requisite criminal intent to aid and abet LSP's illegal discharges and to agree upon an illegal course of conduct (conspire). Counsel for Allied also highlighted Allied's willingness to pay for LSP's pollution control equipment, claiming that Allied could not have intended to break the law when it was spending money to ensure LSP's compliance.

Without a formal opinion in the case, the court exonerated Allied on all counts involving vicarious liability. While Judge Merhige's remarks during and after the trial were cryptic, he did indicate that he was not convinced beyond a reasonable doubt of Allied's having possessed the necessary intent upon which to base a conviction.

Whatever one's own evaluation of the evidence, it is difficult to see how in a similar case a conviction could be obtained unless the defendant made explicit and unambiguous incriminating statements. Given the presumptions of innocence and against vicarious liability, the burdens placed upon the prosecution are overwhelming. Even counts based on accomplice and conspiracy theories, which do not require that the corporate veil be pierced, encounter the massive obstacles of proving intent to aid and abet, and to agree on illegal acts. (Moreover, conspiracy has not yet overcome the stigma attached to it by the abuse of conspiracy indictments during the 1960s).

The court's decision on the vicarious liability counts received little attention from the press. But it would appear that there is now a strong incentive for corporations to enter into tolling agreements in order to evade the costs of pollution control.

Much greater publicity was accorded to the imposition of the maximum fine on Allied for its own discharges. For its conviction on the 940 counts of Indictment #1 (to which it pleaded "nolo"), Allied was fined $13.2 million. However, Judge Merhige made it clear that he would reconsider the amount of the fine if Allied "voluntarily" took action to alleviate the damage caused by its discharges. Accordingly, Allied sought a reduction in sentence based on its having set aside $8 million to fund the Virginia Environmental Endowment, a nonprofit corporation which would perform research and implement programs to mitigate the environmental effects of Kepone. Judge Merhige then adjusted the fine to $5 million. Taking into consideration all of Allied's "voluntary" expenditures, the fine actually paid was $13,356,202.[5]

Before discussing the effects of the fine on Allied, let us return to the other defendants. Hundtofte and Moore were fined $25,000 each. LSP received a fine of close to $4 million, a meaningless gesture in light of LSP's lack of assets. Finally, the city of Hopewell was fined $10,000. Referring to the Hopewell fine, Judge Merhige stated that "heavy fines would serve no purpose. The penalties would come from municipal tax revenues. It amounts to a transfer of money from one pocket of the taxpayer to another."

Did the Kepone sentences actually do justice? Did they achieve the retribution and deterrence (both of the defendants and prospective violators) for which the criminal law strives?

A $13.3 million fine is not unduly burdensome to a corporation which does $3 billion in annual sales. But what about the intangible effects of the sentence? Was Allied's "corporate image" tarnished, as its attorneys claimed prior to sentencing? This argument would deserve greater credence if Allied's operations were more closely related to the general public; but in fact Allied sells almost all of its chemicals to other corporations, which are presumably unimpressed by "corporate image." Moreover, the price of Allied's shares since the sentencing reflects no discernible loss of investor confidence. On the other hand, insofar as corporate executives are concerned about prestige and status in addition to money, the publicity given to the case undoubtedly acted as a deterrent, both within Allied and throughout corporate society.

Would it have better served the purposes of the criminal law to have imposed jail terms on some of Allied's executives, and perhaps Hundtofte and Moore? The American public does not look favorably upon the imprisonment of corporate officers for corporate crimes. This explains why jail terms were never a viable alternative in the Kepone case. (Judge Merhige commented that "nobody is going to jail in this case.") Moreover, the imprisonment of corporate officers frequently does more harm than good, fostering a "demonology myth" that a few greedy industrialists are responsible for the pollution problem, whereas pollution is a pervasive result of our economic system's "externalization" of certain costs of production. The light fines imposed upon Hundtofte and Moore typify the generous treatment which cooperating corporate officials can expect to receive at the hands of the law.

But is not the function of the criminal law in pollution cases really a symbolic one? To stigmatize an offender so as to achieve deterrence? And to effectuate a catharsis of public outrage? And is it not the function of the *civil law* to achieve financial deterrence by affording compensation to injured plaintiffs?

Allied is civilly liable to the United States for the costs of cleaning up the James River. But dredging the river might be dangerous because of the possible resuspension of Kepone which has sunk to the bottom. Allied has also been named as a defendant in civil actions brought by local residents and LSP employees demanding more than $200 million in damages. However, Allied is insured for these claims, and the only financial effect which the civil actions will have on Allied is the speculative prospect of increased insurance premiums (which Allied will undoubtedly pass on to its customers in the form of higher, albeit not uncompetitive, prices). Ultimately,

5. Allied may be able to treat this sum as a business expenditure under §162 of the Internal Revenue Code, or as a charitable deduction under §170 on its income tax returns.

the general public will pay for Allied's Kepone pollution through increased prices for all consumer goods containing chemicals.

There are those who feel that the only way to punish a corporation is to punish its shareholders, who at least theoretically control the corporation. Shareholders suffer as a result of decreased sales, not increased costs which can be passed through to consumers. Current law allows EPA to blacklist (deprive of Federal contracts) certain polluting facilities. But these provisions do not apply to entire companies, as distinguished from individual facilities, and they only apply to facilities which deal directly with the United States. Allied as a whole does very little business directly with the United States government, and its Hopewell facility does almost none.

After the Kepone dust has cleared, it will remain questionable whether the entire course of legal proceedings in the Kepone cases has been only "symbolic assurance"– a show of justice without the real thing.

COMMENTARY AND QUESTIONS

1. The judge, and the absence of a jury. Where was the jury in this criminal prosecution? Obviously Allied and its indicted executives chose to waive their constitutional right to a jury. Was this a good move? Note the effect of Judge Merhige's rulings on pleadings, on required elements of collective action crimes, and on sentencing, as well as his comments at the early stages of trial ("Nobody is going to jail..."). What effect did these have on the litigative parties? If there had been a jury, would there have been a different judicial posture?

2. The perils of plea bargaining. The negotiations between the U.S. Attorney's office and Hundtofte, Moore, and the City of Hopewell illustrate the potential benefits of plea bargaining to both prosecutor and defendants. Note, however, that bargains struck between the parties do not bind the judge. A tough judge could have refused to dismiss the original counts or to allow the lesser pleas, or could have ignored the prosecutors' recommendations for lighter sentences. Judges can go softer on defendants than the terms of a bargain, as well. Judge Merhige felt free to ignore the U.S. Attorney's opposition to Allied's nolo plea, even though it undermined the prosecutors' basis for the prior plea bargains. Can defendants or prosecutors whose plea bargains have not been followed by the trial judge get relief from an appellate court? Not likely. In environmental cases, where criminal liability is a relatively novel phenomenon for judges, the reliability of plea bargaining for both sides may be relatively unpredictable.

3. Allied's vicarious liability. It is not clear why Judge Merhige dismissed all the vicarious liability counts against Allied. Does it appear that Allied was a stranger to the sloppy operations at Life Science's plant? Did Allied not have the requisite knowledge of what was going on? Should "tolling" agreements legally insulate corporate principals from the pollution of their "independent" subcontractors? If the United States had appealed dismissal of the counts holding Allied vicariously liable for LSP's pollution, which argument on the Kepone facts – "instrumentality," "agency," "accomplice," or "conspiracy" – would have appeared strongest?

4. The Kepone reckoning, criminal and civil. The *Allied* criminal case took more than two years of prosecutorial efforts by governmental attorneys. In light of the other civil remedies available, was it worth the effort? Note the *Pruitt* damages action at page 160 *supra*, and the fact that Allied was forced to settle dozens of lawsuits brought by workers and directly injured neighbors with total payments amounting to more than $15 million.

Section 3. EXECUTIVE LIABILITY FOR ACTS OR OMISSIONS BY SUBORDINATES

United States v. Park

United States Supreme Court, 1975
421 U.S. 658, 95 S. Ct. 1903, 44 L.Ed.2d 489

BURGER, C.J. Acme Markets, Inc., is a national retail food chain with approximately 36,000 employees, 874 retail outlets, 12 general warehouses, and four special warehouses. Its headquarters, including the office of the president, respondent Park, who is chief executive officer of the corporation, are located in Philadelphia, Pa. In a five-count information filed in the United States District Court for the District of Maryland, the Government charged Acme and respondent with violations of the Federal Food, Drug and Cosmetic Act. Each count of the information alleged that the defendants had received food that had been shipped in interstate commerce and that, while the food was being held for sale in Acme's Baltimore warehouse following shipment in interstate commerce, they caused it to be held in a building accessible to rodents and to be exposed to contamination by rodents. These acts were alleged to have resulted in the food's being adulterated within the meaning of 21 U.S.C. §§342(a)(3) and (4), in violation of 21 U.S.C. §331(k).

Acme pleaded guilty to each count of the information. Respondent pleaded not guilty. The evidence at trial demonstrated that in April 1970 the Food and Drug Administration (FDA) advised respondent by letter of insanitary conditions in Acme's Philadelphia warehouse. In 1971 the FDA found that similar conditions existed in the firm's Baltimore warehouse. An FDA consumer safety officer testified concerning evidence of rodent infestation and other insanitary conditions discovered during a 12-day inspection of the Baltimore warehouse in November and December 1971. He also related that a second inspection of the warehouse had been conducted in March 1972. On that occasion the inspectors found that there had been improvement in the sanitary conditions, but that "there was still evidence of rodent activity in the building and in the warehouse and we found some rodent-contaminated lots of food items."

...The Government's final witness, Acme's vice president for legal affairs and assistant secretary, identified respondent as the president and chief executive officer of the company and read a bylaw prescribing the duties of the chief executive officer. He testified that respondent functioned by delegating "normal operating duties," including sanitation, but that he retained "certain things, which are the big, broad, principles of the operation of the company," and had "the responsibility of seeing that they all work together."

At the close of the Government's case in chief, respondent moved for a judgment of acquittal on the ground that "the evidence in chief has shown that Mr. Park is not personally concerned in this Food and Drug violation." The trial judge denied the motion, stating that United States v. Dotterweich, 320 U.S. 277 (1943), was controlling.

Respondent was the only defense witness. He testified that, although all of Acme's employees were in a sense under his general direction, the company had an "organizational structure for responsibilities for certain functions" according to which different phases of its operation were "assigned to individuals who, in turn, have staff and departments under them." He identified those individuals responsible for sanitation, and related that upon receipt of the January 1972 FDA letter, he had conferred with the vice president for legal affairs, who informed him that the Baltimore division vice president "was investigating the situation immediately and would be taking corrective action and would be preparing a summary of the corrective action to reply to the letter." Respondent stated that he did not "believe there was anything [he] could have done more constructively than what [he] found was being done."

On cross-examination, respondent conceded that providing sanitary conditions for food offered for sale to the public was something that he was "responsible for in the entire operation of the company," and he stated that it was one of many phases of the company that he assigned to "dependable subordinates." Respondent was asked about and, over the objections of his counsel, admitted receiving, the April 1970 letter addressed to him from the FDA regarding insanitary conditions at Acme's Philadelphia warehouse.... Finally, in response to questions concerning the Philadelphia and Baltimore incidents, respondent admitted that the Baltimore problem indicated the system for handling sanitation "wasn't working perfectly" and that as Acme's chief executive officer he was responsible for "any result which occurs in our company."

...The jury found respondent guilty on all counts of the information, and he was subsequently sentenced to pay a fine of $50 on each count.

The Court of Appeals reversed the conviction and remanded for a new trial. The court viewed the Government as arguing "that the conviction may be predicated solely upon a showing that...[respondent] was the President of the offending corporation" and it stated that as "a general proposition, some act of commission or omission is an essential element of every crime."... It reasoned that, although our decision in United States v. Dotterweich, 320 U.S. at 281, had construed the statutory provisions under which respondent was tried to dispense with the traditional element of "awareness of some wrongdoing," the Court had not construed them as dispensing with the element of "wrongful action." The Court of Appeals concluded that...proof of this element was required by due process.... We reverse.

In *Dotterweich* [on similar facts to *Park* concerning contaminated drugs] a jury...convicted Dotterweich, the corporation's president and general manager. The Court of Appeals reversed the conviction on the ground that only the drug dealer, whether corporation or individual, was subject to the criminal provisions of the Act, and that where the dealer was a corporation, an individual connected therewith might be held personally only if he was operating the corporation "as his 'alter ego.'"...

In reversing the judgment of the Court of Appeals and reinstating Dotterweich's conviction, this Court looked to the purposes of the Act and noted that they "touch phases of the lives and health of people which, in the circumstances of modern industrialism, are largely beyond self-protection." 320 U.S. at 280. It observed that the Act is of "a now familiar type" which "dispenses with the conventional requirement for criminal conduct – awareness of some wrongdoing. In the interest of the larger good it puts the burden of acting at hazard upon a person otherwise innocent but standing in responsible relation to a public danger." Id. at 280-281.

Central to the Court's conclusion that individuals other than proprietors are subject to the criminal provisions of the Act was the reality that "the only way in which a corporation can act is through the individuals who act on its behalf." Id., at 281. The Court also noted that corporate officers had been subject to criminal liability under the Federal Food and Drug Act of 1966, and it observed that a contrary result under the 1938 legislation would be incompatible with the expressed intent of Congress to "enlarge and stiffen the penal net" and to discourage a view of the Act's criminal penalties as a "'license fee for the conduct of an illegitimate business.'" 320 U.S. at 282-283.

At the same time, however, the Court was aware of the concern which was the motivating factor in the Court of Appeals' decision, that literal enforcement "might operate too harshly by sweeping within its condemnation any person however remotely entangled in the proscribed shipment." A limiting principle, in the form of "settled doctrines of criminal law" defining those who "are responsible for the commission of a misdemeanor," was available. In this context, the Court concluded, those doctrines dictated that the offense was committed "by all who...have...a responsible share in the furtherance of the transaction which the statute outlaws." Id. at 284.

The Court recognized that, because the Act dispenses with the need to prove "consciousness of wrongdoing," it may result in hardship even as applied to those who share "responsibility in the business process resulting in" a violation. It regarded as "too treacherous" an attempt "to define or even to indicate by way of illustration the class of employees which stands in such a responsible relation." The question of responsibility, the Court said, depends "on the evidence produced at the trial and its submission – assuming the evidence warrants it – to the jury under appropriate guidance." The Court added: "In such matters the good sense of prosecutors, the wise guidance of trial judges, and the ultimate judgment of juries must be trusted." Id., at 284-285.

The rule that corporate employees who have "a responsible share in the furtherance of the transaction which the statute outlaws" are subject to the criminal provisions of the Act was not formulated in a vacuum. Cf. Morissette v. United States, 342 U.S. 246, 258 (1952). Cases under Federal Food and Drug Act of 1906 reflected the view both that knowledge or intent were not required to be proved in prosecutions under its criminal provisions, and that responsible corporate agents could be subjected to the liability thereby imposed. see e.g. United States v. Mayfield, 177 F. 765 (N.D. Ala. 1910). Moreover, the principle had been recognized that a corporate agent, through whose act, default, or omission the corporation committed a crime, was himself guilty individually of that crime. The principle had been applied whether or not the crime required "consciousness of wrongdoing," and it had been applied not only to those corporate agents who themselves committed the criminal act, but also to those who by virtue of their managerial positions or other similar relation to the actor could be deemed responsible for its commission.

In the latter class of cases, the liability of managerial officers did not depend on their knowledge of, or personal participation in, the act made criminal by the statute. Rather, where the statute under which they were prosecuted dispensed with "consciousness of wrongdoing," an omission or failure to act was deemed a sufficient basis for a responsible corporate agent's liability. It was enough in such cases that, by virtue of the relationship he bore to the corporation, the agent had the power to prevent the act complained of [citations omitted].

The rationale of the interpretation given the Act in *Dotterweich*, as holding criminally accountable the persons whose failure to exercise the authority and supervisory responsibility reposed in them by the business organization resulted in the violation complained of, has been confirmed in our subsequent cases. Thus, the Court has reaffirmed the proposition that "the public interest in the purity of its food is so great as to warrant the imposition of the highest standard of care on distributors." Smith v. California, 361 U.S. 147, 152 (1959). In order to make "distributors of food the strictest censors of their merchandise," the Act punishes "neglect where the law requires care, or inaction where it imposes a duty." Morissette v. United States, *supra* at 255. "The accused, if he does not will the violation, usually is in a position to prevent it with no more care than society might reasonably expect and no more exertion than it might reasonably exact from one who assumed his responsibilities." Id. at 256.

The theory upon which responsible corporate agents are held criminally accountable for "causing" violations of the Act permits a claim that a defendant was "powerless" to prevent or correct the violation to "be raised defensively at a trial on the merits." United States v. Wiesenfeld Warehouse Co., 376 U.S. 86, 91 (1964). If such a claim is made, the defendant has the burden of coming forward with evidence, but this does not alter the Government's ultimate burden of proving beyond a reasonable doubt the defendant's guilt, including his power, in light of the duty imposed by the Act, to prevent or correct the prohibited condition. Congress has seen fit to enforce the accountability of responsible corporate agents dealing with products which may affect the health of consumers by penal sanctions case in rigorous terms, and the obligation of the courts is to give the effect so long as they do not violate the Constitution.

We cannot agree with the Court of Appeals that it was incumbent upon the District Court to instruct the jury that the Government had the burden of establishing "wrongful action" in the sense in which the Court of Appeals used that phrase. The concept of a "responsible relationship" to, or a "responsible share" in, a violation of the Act indeed imports some measure of blameworthiness; but it is equally clear that the Government establishes a prima facie case when it introduces evidence sufficient to warrant a finding by the trier of the facts that the defendant had, by reason of his position in the corporation, responsibility and authority either to prevent in the first instance, or promptly to correct, the violation complained of, and that he failed to do so.

COMMENTARY AND QUESTIONS

1. Fighting over principles? Note that this case went up to the Supreme Court of the United States on appeal of a sentence of $50 for each of five counts. Why did Mr. Park bother? The corporation itself was also prosecuted, but did not attempt to fight the charges.

2. Who gets targeted? Could the government, if it had wished, have prosecuted the actual workers whose acts or omissions had caused the contamination? Many statutes can be so applied, but governmental prosecutors often understandably choose to prosecute higher up the corporate chain of command if they can. The U.S. Department of Justice's environmental crimes division has a policy of prosecuting in each case the highest-ranking corporate officer who had any responsibility for overseeing environmental compliance. See Starr, Countering Environmental Crimes, 13 Envtl. Aff. L. Rev. 379 (1986).

3. Defensive organizational responses. Aware of new liabilities as well as the growing public concern for the environment, many corporations are altering their internal structures to ensure environmental compliance. One common change is creation of a centralized office charged with company-wide oversight. A particular mandate is to try to ensure that pollution standards are not compromised for the sake of production, particularly given the pressures to cut corners common in times of recession. Giving the Environment Teeth, N.Y. Times, 3 Mar. 1991, Section 3, 29.

4. Executive liability, civil as well as criminal. *Park* demonstrates judicial willingness to extend federal criminal liability far up the corporate executive ladder. Although this chapter focuses on criminal liability, it is appropriate to note the similarities to executive civil liability issues raised in the NEPACCO case, page 266 *supra*.

As with civil liability, corporate officers can be held criminally liable for their individual acts where they themselves dumped toxics or directly ordered employees to do so (this is obvious, but is rarely easy to prove). They also can be held liable, both civilly and criminally, for actions that take place within areas of their corporate responsibility and authority.[6] In some cases, where a corporate officer is in active daily managerial control of the area of corporate activity that caused a statutory violation, liability may reflect an inference that the executive in fact personally ordered, encouraged, or winked at the acts – where these facts cannot be directly proved.[7] In other cases liability appears to be based on a more indirect nexus – the officer's status and general authority over corporate matters. In *Dotterweich*, Justice Frankfurter held that, at least with regard to public health crimes, it is permissible to place the burden on corporate individuals who are in a position to prevent the harm from occurring "rather than to throw the hazard on the innocent public who are wholly helpless." 320 U.S. at 285. In a Vermont case, the court based liability on a finding that "each individual defendant here was either personally involved in corporate acts of Staco, *or was in a position* as a corporate officer or majority stockholder *to have ultimate control.*" Vermont v. Staco Inc., 27 ERC 1084 (DC Vt. 1988)(emphasis added). See generally Seymour, Civil and Criminal Liability of Corporate Officers under Federal Environmental Laws, 20 Env. Rptr. 337 (1989). Seymour notes that "even though...actual operating functions had been delegated to subordinate employees who exercised responsibility over the everyday operations of the company, the court...in *Park*...indicated that with the power to delegate comes a corresponding obligation on the part of high-level corporate officers to control the behavior of subordinates...." Failure to discover and correct violations, as well as failure to provide adequate supervision, can be the basis of criminal as well as civil liability. 20 Env. Rptr. at 342. How far up the ladder does such responsibility go? Is the CEO of a Big Three automaker personally liable for an acid spill in one of the company's plating plants in Seattle? The latter, indirect theory of executive

6. The first theory of officer liability noted in the prior chapter – the concept of piercing the corporate veil – is not relevant in the criminal setting, where individual responsibility rather than availability of assets is the issue. See page 266 *supra*.

7. This may explain the liability found against certain officers in the cases of U.S. v. Carolawn Co., 21 ERC 2124 (D.C. S.C. 1984); U.S. v. Pollution Abatement Services, Inc. of Oswego, 763 F.2d 133 (2d Cir. 1985); and In re BED, EPA No. TSCA-IV-860001, 12/8/88.

responsibility, which comes closest to executive strict liability, raises special problems in the criminal setting. What if the defendant has no specific knowledge of the illegal acts? The degree to which penal sanctions can then be applied is considered in the following section of this chapter: some statutes are written without a requirement of proof of knowledge, but constitutional questions arise whether knowledge is nevertheless required. Civil liability is freer of such constraints. Into which liability theory does *Park* fall, or defendant Michaels' circumstances in *NEPACCO* at page 266 *supra*?

The same defenses that may be available to executives in criminal actions – inability to prevent the violation, or ignorance of the violation – are sometimes available in the civil context as well. In any case, criminal sanctions, because of their stigma and potential severity, are generally more credible as deterrents than civil penalties.

5. Corporate ignorance as a defense. In *Park* the defendant admitted knowing fairly specifically that there was a violation of federal law that was not being corrected. What if, as in most cases, executives say they did not know that the criminal violation was occurring? How far does the criminal responsibility set out in *Park* and *Dotterweich* extend beyond the facts of those two cases? Could prosecutors – who are continually amazed by how little, according to litigation affidavits, corporate executives know about what really goes on in their factories – base executive criminal liability on a theory of "willful ignorance"? Some executives surely instruct their employees that they "don't want to know" how certain things get done, "just get it done."

On January 1, 1991, the "California Corporate Criminal Liability Act" went into effect, making it a crime whenever a corporation or manager has "actual knowledge" of a serious concealed danger associated with a product or business practice, and knowingly fails within 15 days (or immediately if there is imminent risk of great bodily harm or death) to notify the state occupational safety and health agency and affected employees. The statute provides that knowledge need not be actual awareness, but may simply be possession of facts that would lead a reasonable person to believe that a danger exists. Questions about how much knowledge or intent must be proved in criminal prosecutions continue in the following materials.

D. KNOWLEDGE AND INTENT

Where statutes do require knowledge, how much must be proved to show a "knowing" violation? In a number of environmental statutes, like §411 of the Refuse Act, criminal sanctions are provided for without any requirement for proving that the defendant acted "knowingly" with criminal intent or "scienter."

United States v. White Fuel Corporation
United States Court of Appeals for the First Circuit, 1974
498 F.2d 619

CAMPBELL, J. White Fuel Corporation was convicted after a jury-waived trial of violating §13 of the Rivers and Harbors Act of 1899, 33 U.S.C. §407 [the Refuse Act].

White Fuel operates a tank farm abutting a small cove off the Reserved Channel, part of Boston harbor. Both the cove and the channel are navigable waters of the United States. On May 3, 1972, the Coast Guard found oil in the waters of the cove. White Fuel, which in January 1972 had been alerted by state authorities to possible oil spillage problems, immediately undertook to clean up the oil and to trace its source. Although at first an oil-water separator and later a leaky pipe were suspected, experts called in by White Fuel finally determined that the oil was seeping from an immense accumulation (approximately half a million gallons) which had gathered under White Fuel's property. White Fuel concedes, and the court found, that it owned the oil, which continued to seep into the cove throughout the summer of 1972 even though White Fuel worked diligently to drain or divert the accumulation. By September it was successful and seepage had ceased....

The district court found that the seepage was a violation of the Refuse Act and imposed a $1,000 fine. The court denied White Fuel's motion for judgment of acquittal and, ruling that intent or scienter is irrelevant to guilt, also denied White Fuel's offer to present evidence that it had not known of the underground deposit, had not appreciated its hazards, and had acted diligently when the deposit became known. The court held that White Fuel's only defense would be to show that third parties caused the oil seepage – that "this oil escaped from a source other than that under the control of the defendant." White Fuel contends that the government was required to prove scienter or at least negligence as part of its case, and that the court erred by precluding the proffered defense.

In the seventy-five years since enactment, no court to our knowledge has held that there must be proof of scienter; to the contrary, the Refuse Act has commonly been termed a strict liability statute. The offense falls within the category of public welfare offenses which:

> are not in the nature of positive aggressions or invasions, with which the common law so often dealt, but are in the nature of neglect where the law requires care, or inaction where it imposes a duty.... The accused, if he does not will the violation, usually is in a position to prevent it with no more care than society might reasonably expect and no more exertion than it might reasonably exact from one who assumed his responsibilities. Morissette v. U.S., 342 U.S. 246, 255-256 (1952)....

In the present circumstances we see no unfairness in predicating liability on actual non-compliance.... Whatever occasional harshness this could entail is offset by the moderateness of the permitted fine, the fact that the statute's command – to keep refuse out of the public waters – scarcely imposes an impossible burden, and the benefit to society of having an easily defined, enforceable standard which inspires performance rather than excuses.... As a corporate defendant like White Fuels cannot be imprisoned, we need not consider to what extent absolute liability would carry over to cases where incarceration is a real possibility.

COMMENTARY AND QUESTIONS

1. Statutes imposing no-fault criminal liability. Courts regularly confront penal statutory provisions that appear to impose liability without fault, and defendants regularly challenge such interpretations.

In United States v. Hoflin, 880 F.2d 1033 (9th Cir. 1989), a city's Director of Public Works was convicted under RCRA §6928(d)(2)(A) of ordering his workers to take fourteen barrels filled with waste highway paint to the grounds of the sewage treatment plant, dig a hole, and dump the drums in. Some of the drums were rusted and leaking, and at least one burst open in the process. The hole was not deep enough, so the employees crushed the drums with a front-end loader to make them fit, and they were then covered with sand. Hoflin appealed on the grounds that the jury should have been required to find that he *knew* the city did not have a permit to dispose of the barrels. RCRA §6928(d)(2)(A) provides–

> (d) CRIMINAL PENALTIES. Any person who...
>
> (2) knowingly treats, stores or disposes of any hazardous waste identified or listed under this subchapter either–
>
> (A) without having obtained a permit under §6925 of this title...; or
>
> (B) in knowing violation of any material condition or requirement of such permit; ...
>
> shall, upon conviction, be subject to [fines, imprisonment, or both].

The Ninth Circuit interpreted this provision to require only proof that Hoflin knew the paint wastes were hazardous, not to require proof that he knew there wasn't any permit. The Third Circuit, in U.S. v. Johnson & Towers, Inc., 741 F.2d 662 (3d Cir. 1984) decided the other way – at least as regards prosecution of subordinate employees; the "knowingly" requirement is implied from Subsection (d)(2) into 2(A). Which court has the better of the statutory interpretation? Do you see also that in cases like *Hoflin* ignorance of the law is no defense? The court did not require proof that Hoflin knew the hazardous dumping was illegal. It used the argument made in *White Fuels*, that for regulatory "public welfare" statutes involving grave issues of public health, there is no need to prove mens rea unless statutory terms require it. Does the public welfare offense argument presume that when something is so noxious, everyone must know it is likely to be illegal? Many other environmental statutes besides RCRA would seem to fit this category.

If courts decide that proof of defendants' knowledge is required, what practical consequences for criminal prosecution are likely to follow?

2. Innocent mind, culpable deeds? The White Fuel Company does not fit easily into the role of environmental bandit or scofflaw. What purpose is there in hitting the company with criminal penalties? As a fallback position (supplementing its argument that prosccution required criminal intent), White Fuel argued that at least some form of negligence would have to be found in order to apply criminal sanctions, and that in its actions it had been careful, an exemplary corporate citizen. Does this claim stand on stronger ground? The court held, however, that there was no such generalized due care defense available: "Merely to attempt to formulate, let alone apply, such negligence standards, would be to risk crippling the Refuse Act as an enforcement tool." To what extent does your conception of criminal punishment incorporate notions of *fault*? To what extent is fault a feature of accountability in environmental law and environmental analysis generally?

3. Void for vagueness. Note also that polluters can defend on the basis that they didn't have sufficient knowledge of their activity's illegality because the terms of the criminal statute or regulation were too unclear to put them on notice. This "void for vagueness" challenge is a serious due process argument, but it has been held in some pollution conviction cases that "in the field of regulatory statutes governing business activities, where the acts limited are in a narrow category, greater leeway is allowed than in statutes applicable to the general public." People v. Martin, 259 Cal. Rptr. 770, 773 (1989) (a dumper of toxics disputed the specificity of "hazardous wastes"); U.S. v. Protex, 874 F.2d 740 (10th Cir. 1989) (chemical company convicted of "knowing endangerment" of workers who suffered solvent poisoning, under 42 U.S.C.A. §6928(e), of RCRA.)

4. Doesn't constitutional due process require criminal intent or fault? The White Fuel Company, which acted neither intentionally nor negligently in spilling its oil, was a corporation and faced only a small fine. What if the defendant is a person facing larger fines or jail? Are strict liability crimes subject to no due process mens rea requirements? A tentative answer is offered in the following case.

United States v. Wulff

United States Court of Appeals for the Sixth Circuit, 1985
758 F.2d 1121

On September 15, 1983, a federal grand jury returned a one-count indictment charging the defendant with selling migratory bird parts in violation of 16 U.S.C. §§703 and 707(b)(2). Section 707(b)(2) provides as follows:

> (b)Whoever, in violation of §§703 to 711 of this title, shall – (2) sell, offer for sale, barter or offer to barter, any migratory bird shall be guilty of a felony and shall be fined not more than $2,000 or imprisoned not more than two years, or both...

[Non-commercial actions, on the other hand, are merely misdemeanors. The statute does not mention "knowing" or "willful" action; thus on its face it is a strict liability criminal offense, not requiring any showing of knowledge in order to gain convictions. Eds.]

The indictment was based on a sale made by the defendant to a special agent of the United States Fish and Wildlife Service of a necklace made of red-tailed hawk and great-horned owl talons. Both birds are protected species under the Migratory Bird Treaty Act....

[The district court dismissed the felony indictment, distinguishing the following language from Morissette v. U.S., 342 U.S. 246 (1952), a Supreme Court decision that was also cited in the *White Fuels* case:]

> Many of these strict liability offenses are not in the nature of positive aggressions or invasions, with which the common law so often dealt, but are in the nature of neglect where the law requires care, or inaction where it imposes a duty. Many violations of such regulations result in no direct or immediate injury to person or property but merely create the danger or probability of it which the law seeks to minimize. While such offenses do not threaten the security of the state in the manner of treason, they may be regarded as offenses against its authority, for their occurrence impairs the efficiency of controls deemed essential to the social order as presently

> constituted. In this respect, whatever the intent of the violator, the injury is the same, and the consequences are injurious or not according to fortuity. Hence, legislation applicable to such offenses, as a matter of policy, does not specify intent as a necessary element. The accused, if he does not will the violation, usually is in a position to prevent it with no more care than society might reasonably expect and no more exertion than it might reasonably exact from one who assumed his responsibilities. *Also, penalties commonly are relatively small, and conviction does no grave damage to an offender's reputation.* Under such considerations, courts have turned to construing statutes and regulations which make no mention of intent as dispensing with it and holding that the guilty act alone makes out the crime. This has not, however, been without expressions of misgiving. 342 U.S. at 255-56 (emphasis supplied).

The district court next turned to the case of Holdridge v. United States, 282 F.2d 302 (8th Cir. 1960):

> Where a federal criminal statute omits mention of intent and where it seems to involve what is basically a matter of policy, where the standard imposed is, under the circumstances, reasonable and adherence thereto properly expected of a person, where the penalty is relatively small, where conviction does not gravely besmirch, where the statutory crime is not taken over from the common law, and where congressional purpose is supporting, the statute can be construed as one not requiring criminal intent. The elimination of this element is then not violative of the due process clause....

Applying these legal precedents to the facts before it, the district court noted that the felony statutory penalty involved in this case included a maximum sentence of two years' imprisonment or a fine of $2,000.00, or both. The district court felt that these were not "relatively small penalties." The district court further noted that a convicted felon loses his right to vote, his right to sit on a jury and his right to possess a gun, among other civil rights, for the rest of his life. The district court was of the opinion that a felony conviction irreparably damages one's reputation. Based on these findings, the district court held that the MBTA felony penalty provisions did not meet the criteria of *Holdridge, supra*, and, accordingly, concluded that §707(b)(2) is violative of due process of law....

Dilemmas similar to the one presented in this case have been resolved in the past by reading a requirement of scienter into an otherwise silent statute. See, e.g., *Morissette, supra*, 342 U.S. at 263.... In our opinion, we cannot read a requirement of scienter into §707(b)(2).... An element of scienter can be read into an otherwise silent statute only where the crime is one borrowed from the common law.... The question before us today is not whether Congress made a rational choice in legislating a felony conviction for the commercialization of protected birds. Rather, we must decide whether the absence of a requirement that the government prove some degree of scienter violates the defendant's right to due process.

We believe the proper guidance for the resolution of this issue can be found in Judge, now Justice, Blackmun's opinion in *Holdridge, supra*. Extrapolating from *Holdridge*, the proper test would appear to be as follows: The elimination of the element of criminal intent does not violate the due process clause where (1) the penalty is relatively small, and (2) where conviction does not gravely besmirch. As the district court held, §707(b)(2) does not meet these criteria. The felony penalty carries a maximum sentence of two years' imprisonment or $2,000.00 fine, or both.

"This is not, in this Court's mind, a relatively small penalty." United States v. St. Pierre, 578 F. Supp. 1424, 1429 (D.S.D. 1983)(concluding that imposition of felony penalty under §707(b) would violate due process, and therefore directing that if defendant were convicted, the court would sentence under the misdemeanor provision). In addition, as the district judge noted, a felony conviction irreparably damages one's reputation, and in Michigan a convicted felon loses, among other civil rights, his right to sit on a jury and his right to possess a gun....

We are of the opinion that in order for one to be convicted of a felony under the MBTA, a crime unknown to the common law which carries a substantial penalty, Congress must require the prosecution to prove the defendant acted with some degree of scienter. Otherwise, a person acting with a completely innocent state of mind could be subjected to a severe penalty and grave damage to his reputation. This, in our opinion, the Constitution does not allow.

COMMENTARY AND QUESTIONS

1. A lone *Wulff*? Other appellate courts have differed from the Sixth Circuit's constitutional scienter requirements presented in *Wulff*. In U.S. v. Engler, 806 F.2d 425 (3d Cir. 1986) on almost precisely the same facts as *Wulff*, the Third Circuit upheld a strict liability MBTA conviction for the innocent sale of a protected falcon in interstate commerce. The Supreme Court, *Engler* noted, has indicated that due process may set some limits on criminal strict liability, but has never set out any guidelines. The Court has said that "public policy may require that in prohibition or punishment of particular acts, it may be provided that he who shall do them shall do them at his peril and will not be heard to plead in defense good faith or ignorance.... Legislation may, in particular instances be harsh, but...this court cannot set aside legislation because it is harsh." Shevlin-Carpenter v. Minn., 218 U.S. 57, 70 (1910).

Reading *Wulff* against *Morisette*, the *Engler* court ridiculed *Wulff*'s "besmirchment" line-drawing between felonies and misdemeanors, and went on to add a practical element to the due process balance: "Where the offenses prohibited and made punishable are capable of inflicting widespread injury, and where the requirement of proof of the offender's guilty knowledge and wrongful intent would render enforcement of the prohibition difficult if not impossible (i.e., would in effect tend to nullify the statute), the legislative intent to dispense with mens rea as an element of the offense has justifiable basis." (A practical argument leading in the other direction is that, insofar as a statute is designed to *deter* proscribed acts, proof of knowing, or at least careless, acts seems logically necessary.)

The *Engler* court hinted, moreover, that scienter could often be implied from the public welfare context: "Due process is not violated by the imposition of strict liability as part of a regulatory measure in the interest of public safety, which may well be premised on the theory that one would hardly be surprised to learn that the prohibited conduct is not an innocent act.... Strict liability for omissions which are not '*per se* blameworthy' may violate due process because such derelictions are 'unlike the commission of acts, or the failure to act under circumstances that should alert the doer to the consequences of his deed.' The capture and sale of species protected by the MBTA is not 'conduct that is wholly passive,' but more closely resembles conduct 'that one would hardly be surprised to learn...is not innocent.'"[8]

Does the sale of endangered wildlife violate the public welfare or constitute an act that is obviously not innocent? The court said that "the prohibition of such sales furthers "a national interest of very nearly the first magnitude." Do you agree? The *Engler* tests add practical public policy enforcement elements to *Wulff*'s considerations of defendants' personal burdens. Does the utilitarian impact of criminal enforcement outweigh the fairness issues raised by strict liability environmental prosecutions?

2. A scienter requirement balance? In *White Fuels, Wulff,* and *Engler*, the courts considered the crimes to be "public welfare offenses," so that proof of criminal intent was not necessarily required by the Constitution. Are some public welfare offenses more dramatic than others, so "less" scienter is required, or in such cases does more "besmirchment" of individual reputation occur, thus requiring proof of "more" scienter? Should distinctions be drawn between protections of endangered birds and protections of human health against toxic pollution?

3. Strict liability and sentencing options. In these strict liability crime cases would you feel differently about convictions that lead only to fines, and convictions that lead to incarceration? Fines and imprisonment are the standard criminal sanctions available to environmental prosecutors. Besides criminal injunctions, it might also deserve mention that *probation* is an available remedy in prosecutions against corporations as well as individuals. Probation can, of course, be used to blunt the force of other remedies, when used by sentencing judges to suspend fines and jail sentences so long as probation conditions are not violated. If, on the other hand, judges apply it as a *supplement* rather than as a substitute for fines and imprisonment, probation allows a court to maintain a watchful eye and tough control over defendants who otherwise might cut corners in future environmental compliance. A court can set out very specific terms for probation, with particular action requirements and performance standards (not to mention community service penance obligations) monitored by a probation officer to whom the defendant corporation must report regularly "like a common criminal." If the terms of probation are violated, the corporate defendants know that further specified penalties will be directly forthcoming. See Gruner, To Let the Punishment Fit the Organization: Sanctioning Corporate Offenders through Corporate Probation, 16 Am. J. Crim. L. 1 (1988).

4. An overview critique of criminalization for environmental injuries. In his book The Limits of the Criminal Sanction (1968), Professor Herbert Packer surveyed modern justifications for criminal punishment. He sharply criticized criminal penalties based on evolving concepts of "morality"[9] as ambiguous and problematic.

8. 806 F.2d at 435, citing due process distinctions set out in U.S. v. Freed, 401 U.S. at 608, and *Dotterweich*.

9. He was particularly concerned with criminalization of "victimless crimes" like gambling, addiction, prostitution, homosexuality, etc.

His criticism, as it implicitly applies to environmental cases, questions the propriety of making corporate activities "immoral" that have been accepted business practice for years. Penal sanctions should be justified on utilitarian grounds.

> What can we discern about the utilitarian modes of prevention – deterrence, intimidation, incapacitation, and rehabilitation?... [A] utilitarian case for defining conduct as criminal can best be made in situations where both deterrence and incapacitation are effective....
>
> There is a vast area of criminal proscription that...deals with legitimate economic activity..."white-collar crime"..."regulatory offenses" ...the vast and disorganized set of proscriptions...used for the job of regulating the mode in which business enterprise by individuals and corporations is carried on....Our inquiry is into the general utility of ancillary reliance on the criminal sanction in the economic sphere.... What, generally speaking, are the purposes for which we invoke the criminal sanction to deal with economic offenses? There is really only one. These proscriptions are uniquely *deterrent* in their thrust. Through them we seek to maintain a high standard of conformity among those who might be tempted to further their own economic advantage by violating the law. These are, generally speaking, sanctions addressed to the law-abiding... Intimidation...incapacitation [and] rehabilitative effect [are not the reasons for] the imposition of criminal punishment on those pillars of the community who happen to get convicted of economic offenses....
>
> There is much to be said in favor of a probable high deterrent efficacy for criminal punishment in the field of economic activity. People who value their standing in the community are likely to be especially sensitive to the stigma associated with a criminal conviction, as well as to the antecedent unpleasantnesses of the criminal process. Furthermore, the kind of conduct that runs afoul of economic regulation is neither happenstance nor impulsive: people who...knowingly sell adulterated foods have ample opportunity to calculate their courses of action, to weigh the risks against the advantages, and to take into account the possibility that their conduct will expose them to being branded as criminal. The other side of this coin is that it takes a substantial enforcement effort, and the resources required to bring the threat up to its minimal level of credibility might be better expended in noncriminal modes of regulation.... Furthermore, there is the totally unexplored issue of what it takes to give the criminal sanction its bite when "respectable" offenders are involved. Is the fact of conviction enough? (Conversely, is the fact of accusation enough? If so, and especially if the conviction rate is not high, there may be a substantial question of fairness raised.)... How important is publicity?...
>
> There is a complex and subtle relationship between vigorous enforcement of a criminal prohibition and public acceptance of the propriety of employing criminal sanctions.... The criminal law does not ordinarily permit one person to be held criminally liable for the acts of another unless it can be shown that he aided in their commission or, at the very least, recklessly tolerated their commission.... There are two possible lines of solution. One is to relax the

> requirements for the imposition of vicarious liability. On the whole this has not been done with respect to serious offenses because of an understandable reluctance to expose a man to criminal punishment without convincing proof of personal guilt. The other course is to impose criminal liability on the corporation itself. This the law has regularly done, and we are now accustomed to seeing corporate entities convicted of committing crimes....
>
> Of course, the only punishment that can be imposed on a corporation is a fine, apart from the stigma of conviction itself. How real that stigma is may be doubted.... John Doe has friends and neighbors; a corporation has none.... A substantial proportion of America's 500 largest industrial concerns have been convicted of one or more economic regulatory offenses, but it has never been shown to make any difference to their economic position.
>
> Given the difficulty of attributing guilt to individuals for corporate crime and the rather ineffective sanctions available against the corporation itself, one may well ask whether the present degree of reliance on the criminal sanction in the field of economic regulation may not be misplaced....[10]

Whatever the specific validity of Packer's conclusions, his analysis reminds us of the special nature of criminal punishment – its costs, consequences, and variable degrees of efficacy. How do you weigh the fitness of criminalization in the various areas of environmental behavior, in terms of accomplishing the traditional objectives of penal law noted at the beginning of this chapter – societal revenge and retribution, general deterrence, incapacitation, specific deterrence, rehabilitation?

5. Economics. How about the overview economic analysis that underlies so much of modern environmental law? Environmentalists use legal remedies to make producers take full account of the environmental costs and values, tangible and intangible, imposed by their activities. When environmental prosecutions successfully skewer a polluting defendant, does that necessarily skew the economics of rational accounting, or can it make a nice fit with the rest of the common law and administrative civil remedies in modern environmental legal process?

6. Ecoguerrillas and the criminal law? And for a completely different angle on enviro-criminal law, how should the legal system treat activists like EarthFirst! when they spike trees to frustrate legal redwood logging, or sabotage highway layouts and electric transmission lines? Is the "necessity defense" available to override the letter of the law? See California v. McMillan, San Luis Obispo Mun. Ct. 87-D00518 (1987)(necessity defense applied to a nuclear protest case), and E. Abbey, The Monkeywrench Gang (1975).

10. Packer, The Limits of the Criminal Sanction, 249–250, 258–59, 356–58, 363.

Chapter 8

FUNDAMENTAL ENVIRONMENTAL RIGHTS: FEDERAL AND STATE CONSTITUTIONS, AND THE PUBLIC TRUST DOCTRINE

A. A FEDERAL CONSTITUTIONAL RIGHT TO ENVIRONMENTAL QUALITY?

Perhaps as a legacy of the mid-20th century, when the courts of the United States played such a crucial role in the assertion of individual and pluralistic democratic rights, many early environmental activists looked to constitutional law for support. We Americans like to find vindication for any and all cherished principles within the text of the federal Constitution, particularly within the Bill of Rights. In 1969, during debates on the National Environmental Policy Act, several legislators asserted that a constitutional right to environmental quality already existed, but that claim was not widely accepted.[1] Some environmental litigators have hoped to stretch the Ninth Amendment (as the Court did in Griswold v. Connecticut, 381 U.S. 479, 486 (1965) and its progeny, defining the unwritten constitutional right of privacy) to define a constitutionally-based right to a clean, unspoiled environment. Others have tried to float the argument that whenever a governmental entity gives a permit to a polluting industry, that is "state action," transforming the polluters' actions so that they are open to claims of due process takings or equal protection violations.

Beyond the difficulties involved in defining just exactly where such claims of right might come from and what exactly they would mean, the courts have appeared hesitant to adopt the constitutional assertions because of the way they would vastly complicate environmental litigation. Perhaps environmental cases are daunting enough without raising the ante to the level of a constitutional battle.

Tanner et al. v. Armco Steel et al.
United States District Court, Southern District of Texas, 1972
340 F. Supp. 532

NOEL, J. Plaintiffs, residents of Harris County, Texas, bring this action to recover for injuries allegedly sustained as a result of the exposure of their persons and their residence to air pollutants emitted by defendants' petroleum refineries and plants located along the Houston Ship Channel. It is asserted that plaintiff George W.

1. See Congr. Rec., Dec. 20, 1969, 40, 417.

Tanner, as a proximate result of these emissions, has suffered pulmonary damage with consequent medical expenses and loss of income to himself and his family. By way of remedy, it appears from the rather prolix complaint that plaintiffs pray "to recover their damages from the Defendants, jointly and severally, for their personal injuries, past and future medical expenses, pain and suffering, loss of services, mental anguish, loss of support, damages to the homestead and lands of the Tanners, general damages, puntative (sic) damages and all other damages allowed by law, in the combined amount of FIVE MILLION DOLLARS."

As this action between private parties would appear to sound in tort, and as diversity of citizenship has not been pleaded, the threshold question of federal jurisdiction immediately arises. Arguing that such jurisdiction is lacking and that a claim upon which relief can be granted has not been stated, sixteen defendants have filed motions to dismiss....

In their jurisdictional statement, citing a potpourri of federal constitutional and statutory provisions, plaintiffs purport to construct a claim upon the following foundations: (1) the Constitution of the United States "in its entirety"; (2) the Due Process Clause of the Fifth Amendment; (3) the Ninth Amendment; (4) the Fourteenth Amendment in conjunction with the Civil Rights Act of 1871; 42 U.S.C.A. §1983, and its jurisdictional statute, 28 U.S.C.A. §1343; (5) the National Environmental Policy Act of 1969, 42 U.S.C.A. §§4321 et seq.; (6) and, finally, the general federal question jurisdictional statute, 28 U.S.C.A. §1331 (a). All of the foregoing shall now be considered seriatim.

The allusion in the complaint to the Federal Constitution "in its entirety" is not a plain statement of the ground upon which the Court's jurisdiction depends, and is therefore insufficient pleading under Rule 8(a)(1), Fed.R.Civ.P.

Plaintiffs next assert that their claim arises under the Due Process Clause of the Fifth Amendment to the Federal Constitution, and is therefore cognizable in this Court. The contention is without merit. It is well settled that the Fifth Amendment operates only as a restraint upon the National Government and upon the States through the Fourteenth Amendment, but is not directed against the actions of private individuals such as defendants. It is not alleged in the instant complaint that the Federal Government is involved in the activity complained of. In their responsive brief, plaintiffs do assert that federal funds are given to the State of Texas and City of Houston for the purpose of antipollution efforts. The relevance of this is not immediately apparent; however, taken as true, it clearly does not amount to federal complicity or participation in the alleged transgressions of the defendant private corporations, and it just as clearly will not support a Fifth Amendment claim.

Plaintiffs next seek solace in the Ninth Amendment, and concede on brief that this is a pioneering enterprise:

> This case is believed to be unique in that counsel for the Tanners is not aware of any other cases that have sought damages for personal injuries caused by air pollution in the United States District Courts based upon the premise that the right to a healthy and clean environment is at the very foundation of this nation and guaranteed by the laws and Constitution of the United States. Plaintiffs maintain that their right not to be personally injured by the actions of the Defendants and their right to non-interference with their privacy and the air that they breathe are protected by the Ninth Amendment....

Since its promulgation, the Ninth Amendment has lain largely quiescent, its most ambitious sortie being in the form of a concurrence in Griswold v. Connecticut, 381 U.S. 479, 486 (1965) (concurring opinion of Mr. Justice Goldberg). The parties have cited and the Court has found no reported case in which the Ninth Amendment has been construed to embrace the rights here asserted. Such a construction would be ahistorical and would represent essentially a policy decision. In effect, plaintiffs invite this Court to enact a law. Since our system reserves to the legislative branch the task of legislating, this Court must decline the invitation. The Ninth Amendment, through its "penumbra" or otherwise, embodies no legally assertable right to a healthful environment. Environmental Defense Fund, Inc. v. Corp of Engineers, 325 F. Supp. 728, 739 (E.D.Ark. 1971).

Plaintiffs also contend that this action is entertainable by reason of the Fourteenth Amendment in conjunction with the Civil Rights Act of 1871, 42 U.S.C.A. §1983, and its jurisdictional counterpart, 28 U.S.C.A. §1343. The Supreme Court of the United States, in Adickes v. S.H. Kress & Co., 398 U.S. 144, 150 (1970), has recently defined plaintiffs' task:

> The terms of §1983 make plain two elements that are necessary for recovery. First, the plaintiff must prove that the defendant has deprived him of a right secured by the "Constitution and laws" of the United States. Second, the plaintiff must show that the defendant deprived him of this constitutional right "under color of any statute, ordinance, regulation, custom, or usage, of any State or Territory." This second element requires that the plaintiff show that the defendant acted "under color of law."

Therefore, it is clear that a sufficiently stated claim under §1983 must embrace two elements properly alleged: (1) a constitutional deprivation, and (2) state action. On brief, all parties have devoted considerable attention to state action, the second requisite.

This Court is persuaded that plaintiffs have not alleged the quantum of state or municipal regulatory involvement necessary to clothe defendants with the mantle of the State for the purposes of §1983. However, it is unnecessary to dwell upon the point at length. For, assuming arguendo that state action were present, the fact remains that the first requisite of a §1983 suit – constitutional deprivation – has not been satisfied.

Taking as true all factual allegations in the complaint, plaintiffs have failed to allege a violation by defendants of any judicially cognizable federal constitutional right which would entitle them to the relief sought. Once again, the parties have cited and the Court has found no reported case which persuasively suggests that the Fourteenth Amendment is susceptible of the interpretation urged. Although there has been something of a boom recently in what Judge Seals of this court has described as "grandiose claims of the right of the general populace to enjoy a decent environment", Bass Anglers Sportsman's Society of America v. United States Plywood-Champion Papers, Inc., 324 F. Supp. 302, 303 (S.D.Tex.1971), such claims "have been more successful in theory than in operation." Rheingold, A Primer on Environmental Litigation, 38 Brooklyn L.Rev. 113, 126 (1971). In view of the dearth of supportive authority, this Court must decline "to embrace the exhilarating opportunity of anticipating a doctrine which may be in the womb of time, but whose birth is distant." Spector Motor Service v. Walsh, 139 F.2d 809, 823 (2d Cir. 1943) (L. Hand, J., dissenting); cf. Environmental Defense Fund, Inc. v. Corps of Engineers, 325 F. Supp. at 739.

First, there is not a scintilla of persuasive content in the words, origin, or historical setting of the Fourteenth Amendment to support the assertion that environmental rights were to be accorded its protection. To perceive such content in the Amendment would be to turn somersaults with history. For, as the Congressional sponsor of a proposed federal environmental amendment recently observed:

> We are frank to say that such a provision to the Constitution would have been meaningless to those attending the Constitutional Convention in Philadelphia almost 200 years ago. Indeed, this amendment would have been altogether unpersuasive twenty years ago, although the handwriting was then visible on the wall, if one cared to look for it. Remarks of Representative Richard L. Ottinger of New York, Cong. Rec. 17116 (1968), quoted at Platt, Toward Constitutional Recognition of the Environment, 56 A.B.A.J. 1061 (1970).

Second, it is apparent that nowhere in the Fourteenth Amendment – or its "incorporated" amendment – can be found the decisional standards to guide a court in determining whether the plaintiffs' hypothetical environmental rights have been infringed, and, if so, what remedies are to be fashioned. Such a task would be difficult enough with the guidance of a statute, but to undertake it in the complete absence of statutory standards would be simply to ignore the limitations of judicial decision-making.

Third, from an institutional viewpoint, the judicial process, through constitutional litigation, is peculiarly ill-suited to solving problems of environmental control. Because such problems frequently call for the delicate balancing of competing social interests, as well as the application of specialized expertise, it would appear that their resolution is best consigned initially to the legislative and administrative processes. Furthermore, the inevitable trade-off between economic and ecological values presents a subject matter which is inherently political, and which is far too serious to relegate to the ad hoc process of "government by lawsuit" in the midst of a statutory vacuum.

Finally, to the extent that an environmental controversy such as this is presently justiciable, it is within the province of the law of torts, to wit: nuisance. There would seem little good reason in law or policy to conjure with the Fourteenth Amendment and §1983 for the purpose of producing the wholesale transformation of state tort suits into federal cases. In any event, if such a result is deemed desirable in order to cope with pollution on a nationwide scale, then it should be accomplished by Congress through legislation, and not by the courts through jurisdictional alchemy....

For the foregoing reasons, this Court holds that no legally enforceable right to a healthful environment, giving rise to an action for damages, is guaranteed by the Fourteenth Amendment or any other provision of the Federal Constitution. As the United States Supreme Court recently observed in rejecting a similarly imaginative constitutional claim, "the Constitution does not provide judicial remedies for every social and economic ill." Lindsey v. Normet, 405 U.S. 56 (1972). It follows, of course, that a claim under §1983 has not been stated and subject matter jurisdiction under 28 U.S.C.A. §1343 has not been invoked....

National Wildlife Federation, Environmental Quality Amendment to the U.S. Constitution (Tentative Proposed Draft, 1991)

["The National Wildlife Federation believes that the right to breathe clean air, drink pure water and live in a healthy environment is as inalienable as the right to free speech and freedom of worship. But fundamental rights mean nothing without fundamental laws to protect them. That is why the Federation is proposing an amendment to the United States Constitution that will ensure a quality environment for current and future generations of Americans. The proposed amendment would embody the following principle:][2]

> Each person has the right to clean air, pure water, productive soils and to the conservation of the natural, scenic, historic, recreational, aesthetic and economic values of America's natural resources. There shall be no entitlement, public or private, competent to impair these rights. It is the responsibility of the United States and of the several States as public trustees to safeguard them for the present and for the benefit of posterity.

Krier, The Environment, the Constitution, and the Coupling Fallacy
32 Michigan Law Quadrangle Notes 35 (1988)

Shortly after the environmental movement first got underway, almost 20 years ago now, there appeared a little parade of articles urging a constitutional right to a clean environment. While a few of the articles campaigned for an amendment to this effect, most of them reasoned that an amendment to this effect was unnecessary. They argued that the right in question is already in the Constitution, however inconspicuously – in the Ninth Amendment, say, or in the concept of ordered liberty protected by the Due Process Clause, or in the so-called penumbra of the Bill of Rights. They asked the courts simply to acknowledge this reading, but the courts did not. The United States Supreme Court has not subscribed to any of the theories advanced by the articles, and neither have the lower federal courts nor the state courts, with a couple of inconsequential exceptions.

Why should something so fundamental as the environment go unrecognized in something so fundamental as the Constitution? True, there is no explicit statement of an environmental right in the constitutional text, but it hardly follows that such a right could not be read in, and in a principled way... So why no constitutional right to environmental quality? Two reasons are usually given, but I think they boil down to one. "The asserted right lacks any foundations in the constitutional text or in history." Call this the *doctrinal* reason against the right.... Critics of a constitutional environmental right also insist that such a right would reach well beyond the range of judicial competence, in both the immediate sense of technical capacity and the more remote sense of political legitimacy. This is the *functional* reason against the right.... If the constitutional right were recognized, courts would be ultimately responsible for large resource allocation decisions, and this could mean that they would have to use economic and other methods of technical analysis when there is no reason to suppose that they know how; and they would have to determine the distributional impacts of various environmental policy alternatives, a determination that is itself a difficult technical matter, and then trade these impacts off against allocational efficiency without the assistance of any accepted guide for making such

2. The Federation cautions that "the exact amendment language is subject to further constitutional and legal analysis." Five other draft amendments have been suggested. The debate is coordinated by the Comprehensive Environmental Amendment Project, 4353 E-119, Thorton, CO 80233.

tradeoffs; and they would have to confront the polycentric and dynamic characteristics of environmental policy and figure the impact of alternatives on research and development in the field of pollution control technology, not to mention...the impacts of one environmental policy – dealing with air quality, say – on other environmental media, such as water and land; and they would have to puzzle over questions having to do with values and preferences and intergenerational justice; and there is little if any principled basis for any of this, so how would the courts manage? And even if they managed, they would still be left with the embarrassing problem of figuring out how to implement the constitutionally required programs. Courts lack the competence, technical and political, for all of these tasks....

The functional considerations...point to the conclusion that environmental matters are "more appropriately left to the judgment of the legislature" and to "majoritarian determination."

In other words, to politics...

Even my former colleague Joseph Sax, perhaps the foremost advocate of an active judicial role in matters of environmental law, concluded in his book *Defending the Environment* that there should not be a constitutional right, because a court "should not be authorized to function as an environmental czar against the clear wishes of the public and its elected representatives."

But look at what Sax (and everybody else, apparently) has done: The idea of a *constitutional* right has been coupled with the idea of *judicial* management of the right. So far as I can tell, the entire debate on this issue – which seems to have ended with the appearance of Professor Stewart's article a decade ago[3] – has gone forth on the singular notion that the Constitution and the courts are necessarily coupled together. But that notion, however typical, is hardly necessary, even as a matter of doctrine. Political question doctrine, for instance. Whatever disputes there might be about its marginal meanings, the central core of political question doctrine is conventional enough that I can simply quote an encyclopedia on the subject. An entry labeled "Political Question" in the *Encyclopedia of the American Constitution* says that the Supreme Court recognized as early as the turn of the last century "that decisions on some governmental questions [and here the author, Philippa Strum, could have added the words *arising from constitutional provisions*] lie entirely within the discretion of the 'political' branches of the national government – the President and Congress – and thus outside the proper scope of judicial review." In other words, decision on political questions are not justiciable. That is what Ms. Strum says at the beginning of her essay. This is what she says at the end:

> The [political question] device...enables the judiciary to maintain its independence by withdrawing from no-win situations.... The Supreme Court, declaring the presence of a political question, tacitly admits that it cannot find and therefore cannot ratify a social consensus.... The political question doctrine, which permits the Court to restrain itself from precipitating impossible situations that might tear the social fabric, gives the electorate and its representatives time to work out their own rules....

The Court has used the doctrine when it would otherwise have to define obscure terms (such as "republican form of government") the content of which can be resolved only by picking one political philosophy over another, or when it would

3. [Stewart, The Development of Administrative and Quasi-Constitutional Law in Judicial Review of Environmental Decision-making: Lessons from the Clean Air Act, 62 Iowa L.R. 713, 750-758 (1977).]

have to develop principles beyond its capabilities, or when it would have to announce unenforceable judgments. All of this sounds strangely familiar. To my mind, political question doctrine provides a ready answer to the functional case against constitutional status for environmental quality, because it lets us uncouple the Constitution and the courts. That the judiciary is incompetent to define and manage certain kinds of constitutional conceptions is simply not a conclusive, and maybe not even a very interesting, objection to the conceptions themselves. The argument to the contrary is faulty. It commits what can neatly be called the coupling fallacy.

Is mine just a debater's point? What good is...a constitutional provision without the courts directly behind it? There are a number of answers that come immediately to mind: Recognition of the environment as an item with nonjusticiable constitutional status might, without contradicting the purposes of political question doctrine, allow courts to insist that the legislative and executive branches consider environmental values in an open and reasoned way in the policy process, no matter what those branches ultimately conclude. Similarly, recognition might give courts room to construe ambiguous legislation in favor of environmental values when the competing values at stake in the legislation's meaning are not of constitutional dimension; or room to manipulate the burden of proof in cases involving the environment; and so on....

The Constitution itself, as a whole, is a symbol held in immeasurable esteem by millions of people who have never even read it. It follows that to be an item in the Constitution, explicitly or not, is to take on a meaning larger than meanings that can be captured in, or reduced to, mere operations. A republican form of government stands for something quite without the courts and even if Congress itself cannot articulate, other than by decisions in the name of the form, just what that something is.

If I were a conscientious legislator or executive who had taken my oath to heart, the fact that environmental quality had constitutional status would make the environment mean something more to me than otherwise, even if I could not articulate the meaning in the absence of reaching decisions on particular issues. It would make the environment mean more to me even if, but more likely especially because, questions of environmental quality were regarded as nonjusticiable, so that I and my colleagues had the last word on the questions. My sense of the significance of having the environment in the Constitution might be remote, but the consequences of the environment being there in the document could be immediate, as when some formerly loyal group of my constituents asked me to make a close call against environmental interests and I could point out to them that, under the circumstances, I felt *constitutionally* bound to do otherwise....

If, as seems to be the case, the legislature (along with the executive) is the relatively competent branch in the case of environmental matters, then it is difficult for me to understand why it could not conscientiously interpret the Constitution – purely and explicitly for its own purposes, and purely in light of its own instrumental competence – in such a way as to recognize the enduring importance of environmental quality. The doctrinal arguments that might seem to stand in the way may in fact be to the side, because they are arguments based on a reading of the Constitution for purely judicial purposes. But our purposes are not judicial at all.

Congress would not be expanding its legislative authority by interpreting the Constitution in a manner that recognizes environmental quality, because the Commerce Clause already gives Congress broad power to legislate in the area.

Moreover, the interpretation I have in mind need not be considered to create congressional obligations or limitations – not, at least, justiciable ones. The interpretation would be simply hortatory. (The environmental amendments to state constitutions have been regarded by state courts in this way.) For these reasons, I have shied away from couching my own argument in terms of a constitutional right to environmental quality; I have spoken, rather, of constitutional status.

I don't know whether it would be easy to convince Congress to exercise its interpretive prerogative...in favor of environmental values. I am confident that the chances that Congress could be so moved are better than the chances of obtaining an amendment or of convincing the Court to take sympathetic action....

COMMENTARY AND QUESTIONS

1. An unenforceable constitutional right to environmental quality? How does the federal constitutional right advocated by Professor Krier differ from those argued for in *Tanner*? Would there really be any consequent improvement to the environment if such a right existed but was not judicially enforceable? What kind of faith in the political process does Krier's position require? Doesn't it presume a great deal about legislators' ability to deal with issues on the principled merits, and the ability of the electoral process to correlate voter behavior with subtle issues of abstract principle? There is a danger that such an unenforceable right would be merely another misleading act of "symbolic assurance," as when Congress in an election year authorizes billions for pollution control, but later refuses to appropriate the funds. Empty symbolic assurances in an age of sound-bite politics can pose a demoralizing threat to the political process.

If an aspirational constitutional right for environmental quality were established, legions of environmental plaintiffs' attorneys would inevitably try to use it in litigation. How likely is it that Krier's prudential restriction against judicial enforcement would hold? If such a right were established, *should* the restriction hold?

2. Why talk of *rights*? In the federal sphere and elsewhere it may be useful to ask why environmentalists (and other citizen activists generally) find the process of trying to define various "rights" so compelling. Some legal thinkers have begun reconsidering the emphasis on rights, exploring the need to define complementary civic responsibilities in order to balance the social contract. Mary Ann Glendon, Rights Talk: The Impoverishment of Political Discourse (1991). This perspective is not a naïve call for law and order and citizens' respect for authority. Professor Glendon notes that corporations and public agencies also require lessons in civic responsibility, and implies recognition of the fact that citizens – some employing rights arguments – have often played an active role in trying to make civic governance work.

In some settings, a focus on rights may not be particularly useful. Professor Cass Sunstein, a supporter of many regulatory programs introduced through citizen clamor in the 1960s and 1970s, noted in a review of Professor Glendon's book that:

> efforts to think about social and economic problems in terms of rights can obscure those problems. A claimed right to clean air or water, or safe products or workplaces, makes little sense in light of the need for close assessment, in particular cases, of the advantages of greater environmental protection, or more safety, as compared with the (sometimes) accompanying disadvantages of higher prices, lower wages, less employment, and more poverty. To the extent that the regulatory programs of the 1970s were billed as vindications of "rights," they severely impaired political deliberation about their content....
>
> Often, rights emerge precisely because of the refusal of private and public institutions to recognize and carry out their duties. When the environment is degraded, or when the vulnerable are simply left to fend for themselves, it should be unsurprising to find vigorous claims for "rights." The claims for a right to clean air and water, to food, to a decent place to live, to a safe workplace, or to "free reproductive choice" – all these must be understood in their context, as responses to failures of social responsibility. Sunstein, Rightalk, 205 The New Republic No. 10, 33, 34-36 (Sept. 2, 1991).[4]

Faced with corporate, bureaucratic, and legislative inertia, in other words, citizens may be impelled to wave the crude blunt instrument of rights talk to capture the political and legal processes' practical attention.

B. THE PUBLIC TRUST DOCTRINE

"By the law of nature, these things are common to mankind: the air, running water, the sea, and consequently the shores of the sea...."

— Institutes of Justinian, 2.1.1, (529 A.D.)

"...So neither can the king intrude upon the common property, thus understood, and appropriate it to himself or to the fiscal purposes of the nation. [T]he enjoyment of it is a natural right which cannot be infringed or taken away, unless by arbitrary power, and that, in theory at least, [can]not exist in a free government...."

— Arnold v. Mundy, 6 N.J.L. 1, 87-88 (1821)

Section 1. THE MODERN REDISCOVERY OF THE PUBLIC TRUST DOCTRINE

Joseph L. Sax, Defending The Environment: A Strategy for Citizen Action
163–165 (1970)

Long ago there developed in the law of the Roman Empire a legal theory known as the "doctrine of the public trust." It was founded upon the very sensible idea that certain common properties, such as rivers, the seashore, and the air, were held by government in trusteeship for the free and unimpeded use of the general public. Our

4. Professor Sunstein is the author of After the Rights Revolution: Reconceiving the Regulatory State (1990).

contemporary concerns about "the environment" bear a very close conceptual relationship to this venerable legal doctrine.

Under the Roman law, perpetual use of common properties "was dedicated to the public." As one scholar, R.W. Lee, noted: "In general the shore was not owned by individuals. One test suggests that it was the property of the Roman people. More often it is regarded as owned by no one, the public having undefined rights of use and enjoyment."[5] Similarly in England, according to R.S. Hall, the law developed that "the ownership of the shore, as between the public and the King, has been settled in favor of the King: but...this ownership is, and had been immemorially, liable to certain general rights of egress and regress, for fishing, trading, and other uses claimed and used by his subjects."

American law adopted the general idea of trusteeship but rarely applied it to any but a few sorts of public properties such as shorelands and parks. The content and purpose of the doctrine never received a careful explication, though occasionally a comment can be found in the cases to the effect that it is "inconceivable" that any person would claim a private-property interest in the navigable waters of the United States, assertable against the free and general use of the public at large. And from time to time provisions can be found, as in the Northwest Ordinance of 1787, which stated that "the navigable waters leading into the Mississippi...shall be common highways and forever free...to the citizens of the United States..."

The scattered evidence, taken together, suggests that the idea of a public trusteeship rests upon three related principles. First, that certain interests – like the air and the sea – have such importance to the citizenry as a whole that is would be unwise to make them the subject of private ownership. Second, that they partake so much of the bounty of nature, rather than of individual enterprise, that they should be made freely available to the entire citizenry without regard to economic status. And, finally, that it is a principle purpose of government to promote the interests of the general public rather than to redistribute public goods from broad public uses to restricted private benefit....

Sax, The Public Trust Doctrine in Natural Resource Law: Effective Judicial Intervention

68 Michigan Law Rev. 471, 489-502 (1970)

The most celebrated public trust case in the American law is the decision of the United States Supreme Court in Illinois Central Railroad Company v. Illinois[6]. In 1869 the Illinois legislature made an extensive grant of submerged lands, in fee simple, to the Illinois Central Railroad. That grant included all the land underlying Lake Michigan for one mile out from the shoreline and extending one mile in length along the central business district of Chicago – more than one thousand acres of incalculable value, comprising virtually the whole commercial waterfront of the

---

5. [The Latin concepts are *res comunes* and *res nullius*. The former referred to such things which, while not susceptible to exclusive ownership, can be enjoyed and used by everyone (such as water, air, and light); the latter referred to things which belonged to no one, "either because they were unappropriated by anyone, such as unoccupied lands or wild animals, or things similar to *res sacrae* or *res religiosae* 'to which a religious character prevents any human right of property attaching.'" Coquillette, Mosses from an Old Manse: Another Look at Some Historic Property Cases about the Environment, 64 Cornell L. Rev. 761, 803 n. 196 (1979); Black's Law Dictionary 1304-1305, 1306 (6th ed. 1990). For more on Justinian's Institutes, see Jolowicz, Historical Introduction to the Study of Roman Law, 502-503 (2d ed. 1954).]

6. 146 U.S. 387 (1892).

city. By 1873 the legislature had repented of its excessive generosity, and it repealed the 1869 grant; it then brought an action to have the original grant declared invalid.

The Supreme Court upheld the state's claim and wrote one of the very few opinions in which an express conveyance of trust lands has been held to be beyond the power of a state legislature.... But the Court did not actually prohibit the disposition of trust lands to private parties; its holding was much more limited. What a state may not do, the Court said, is to divest itself of authority to govern the whole of an area in which it has responsibility to exercise its police power; to grant almost the entire waterfront of a major city to a private company is, in effect, to abdicate legislative authority over navigation.

But the mere granting of property to a private owner does not ipso facto prevent the exercise of the police power, for states routinely exercise a great deal of regulatory authority over privately owned land. The Court's decision makes sense only because the Court determined that the states have special regulatory obligations over shorelands, obligations which are inconsistent with large-scale private ownership. The Court stated that the title under which Illinois held the navigable waters of Lake Michigan is

> different in character from that which the state holds in lands intended for sale.... It is a title held in trust for the people of the state that they may enjoy the navigation of the waters, carry on commerce over them, and have liberty of fishing therein freed from the obstruction or interference of private parties.

With this language, the Court articulated a principle that has become the central substantive thought in public trust litigation. When a state holds a resource which is available for the free use of the general public, a court will look with considerable skepticism upon *any* governmental conduct which is calculated *either* to reallocate the resource to more restricted uses *or* to subject public uses to the self-interest of private parties.

The Court in *Illinois Central* did not specify its reasons for adopting the position which it took, but the attitude implicit in the decision is fairly obvious.... While there may be good reason to use governmental resources to benefit some group smaller than the whole citizenry, there is usually some relatively obvious reason for the subsidy, such as a need to assist the farmer or the urban poor. In addition, there is ordinarily some plainly rational basis for the reallocative structure of any such programs – whether it be taxing the more affluent to support the poor or using the tax base of a large community to sustain programs in a smaller unit of government. Although courts are disinclined to examine these issues through a rigorous economic analysis, it seems fair to say that the foregoing observations are consistent with a general view of the function of government. Accordingly, the court's suspicions are naturally aroused when they are faced with a program which seems quite at odds with such a view of government.

In *Illinois Central*, for example, everything seems to have been backwards. There appears to have been no good reason for taxing the general public in order to support a substantial private enterprise in obtaining control of the waterfront. There was no reason to believe that private ownership would have provided incentives for needed developments, as might have been the case with land grants in remote areas of the country; and if the resource was to be maintained for traditional uses, it was unlikely that private management would have produced more efficient or attractive services to the public. Indeed, the public benefits that could have been achieved by private ownership are not easy to identify.

Although the facts of *Illinois Central* were highly unusual – and the grant in that case was particularly egregious – the case remains an important precedent. The model for judicial skepticism it built poses a set of relevant standards for current, less dramatic instances of dubious governmental conduct. For instance, a court should look skeptically at programs which infringe broad public uses in favor of narrower ones. Similarly there should be a special burden of justification on government when such results are brought into question. But *Illinois Central* also raises more far-reaching issues. For example, what are the implications for the workings of the democratic process when such programs, although ultimately found to be unjustifiable, are nonetheless promulgated through democratic institutions? Furthermore, what does the existence of those seeming imperfections in the democratic process imply about the role of the courts, which, *Illinois Central* notwithstanding, are generally reluctant to hold invalid the acts of co-equal branches of government?

THE CONTEMPORARY DOCTRINE OF THE PUBLIC TRUST: AN INSTRUMENT FOR DEMOCRATIZATION: THE MASSACHUSETTS APPROACH

The *Illinois Central* problem has had its most significant modern exegesis in Massachusetts. In that state, the Supreme Judicial Court has shown a clear recognition of the potential for abuse which exists whenever power over lands is given to a body which is not directly responsive to the electorate. To counteract the influence which private interest groups may have with administrative agencies and to encourage policy decisions to be made openly at the legislative level, the Massachusetts court has developed a rule that a change in the use of public lands is impermissible without a clear showing of legislative approval.

In Gould v. Greylock Reservation Commission,[7] the Supreme Judicial Court of Massachusetts took the major step in developing the doctrine applicable to changes in the use of lands dedicated to the public interest. Because *Gould* is such an important case in the development of the public trust doctrine, and because the implications of the case are so far-reaching, it is important to have a clear understanding of both the facts of the case and the court's decision.

Mount Greylock, about which the controversy centered, is the highest summit of an isolated range which is surrounded by lands of considerably lower elevation. In 1888 a group of citizens, interested in preserving the mountain as an unspoiled natural forest, promoted the creation of an association for the purpose of laying out a public park on it. The state ultimately acquired about 9,000 acres, and the legislature enacted a statute creating the Greylock Reservation Commission and giving it certain of the powers of a park commission. By 1953 the reservation contained a camp ground, a few ski trails, a small lodge, a memorial tower, some TV and radio facilities, and a parking area and garage. In that year, the legislature enacted a statute creating an Authority to construct and operate on Mount Greylock an aerial tramway and certain other facilities, and it authorized the original commission to lease to the Authority "any portion of the Mount Greylock Reservation."

For some time the Authority was unable to obtain the financing necessary to go forward with its desire to build a ski development, but eventually it made an arrangement for the underwriting of revenue bonds. Under that arrangement the

---

7. 350 Mass. 410, 215 N.E. 2d 114 (1966).

underwriters, organized as a joint venture corporation called American Resort Services, were to lease 4,000 acres of the reservation from the Commission. On that land, the management corporation was to build and manage an elaborate ski development, for which it was to receive forty percent of the net operations revenue of the enterprise. The underwriters required these complex and extensive arrangements so that the enterprise would be attractive for potential purchasers of bonds.

After the arrangements had been made, but before the project went forward, five citizens of the county in which the reservation is located brought an action against both the Greylock Reservation Commission and the Tramway Authority. The plaintiffs brought the suit as beneficiaries of the public trust under which the reservation was said to be held, and they asked that the court declare invalid both the lease of the 4,000 acres of reservation land and the agreement between the Authority and the management corporation. They asked the court to examine the statutes authorizing the project, and to interpret them narrowly to prevent both the extensive development contemplated and the transfer of supervisory powers into the hands of a profit-making corporation. The case seemed an exceedingly difficult one for the plaintiffs, both because the statutes creating the Authority were phrased in extremely general terms, and because legislative grants of power to administrative agencies are usually read quite broadly. Certainly, in light of the statute, it could not be said that the legislature desired Mount Greylock to be preserved in its natural state, nor could the legislature be said to have prohibited leasing agreements with a management agency. Nonetheless, the court held both the lease and the management agreement invalid on the ground that they were in excess of the statutory grant of authority.

Gould cannot be considered merely a conventional exercise in legislative interpretation. It is, rather, a judicial response to a situation in which public powers were being used to achieve a most peculiar purpose.[8] Thus, the critical passage in the decision is that in which the court stated:

> The profit sharing feature and some aspects of the project itself strongly suggest a commercial enterprise. In addition to the absence of any clear or express statutory authorization of as broad a delegation of responsibility by the Authority as is given by the management agreement, we find no express grant to the Authority of power to permit use of public lands and of the Authority's borrowed funds for what seems, in part at least, a commercial venture for private profit.

In coming to this recognition, the court took note of the unusual developments which led to the project. What had begun as authorization to a public agency to construct a tramway had developed into a proposal for an elaborate ski area. Since ski resorts are popular and profitable private enterprises, it seems slightly odd in itself that a state would undertake such a development. Furthermore, the public authority had gradually turned over most of its supervisory powers to a private consortium and had been compelled by economic circumstances to agree to a bargain which heavily favored the private investment house.

It hardly seems surprising, then, that the court questioned why a state should

8. For a confirmation that the "feel" of a case is critical to its decision, the *Gould* case should be compared with People ex rel. Kurcharski v. McGovern, 245 N.E. 2d 472 (Ill. 1969). In the latter case, the court upheld recreational developments in a forest preserve, despite a limited statute of authorization, apparently because the public action seemed reasonable and it was the posture of the objector which gave rise to suspicion.

subordinate a public park, serving a useful purpose as relatively undeveloped land, to the demands of private investors for building such a commercial facility. The court, faced with such a situation, could hardly have been expected to have treated the case as if it involved nothing but formal legal issues concerning the state's authority to change the use of a certain tract of land.

Yet the court was unwilling to invalidate an act of the legislature on the sole ground that it involved a modification of the use of public trust land. Instead, the court devised a legal rule which imposed a presumption that the state does not ordinarily intend to divert trust properties in such a manner as to lessen public uses. Such a rule would not require a court to perform the odious and judicially dangerous act of telling a legislature that it is not acting in the public interest, but rather would utilize the court's interpretive powers in accordance with an assumption that the legislature is acting to maintain broad public uses. Under the Massachusetts courts' rule, that assumption is to guide interpretations, and is to be altered only if the legislature clearly indicates that it has a different view of the public interest than that which the court would attribute to it.

Although such a rule may seem to be an elaborate example of judicial indirection, it is in fact directly responsive to the central problem of public trust controversies. There must be some means by which a court can keep a check on legislative grants of public lands while ensuring that historical uses may be modified to accommodate contemporary public needs and that the power to make such modifications resides in a branch of government which is responsive to public demands....

While it will seldom be true that a particular governmental act can be termed corrupt, it will often be the case that the whole of the public interest has not been adequately considered by the legislative or administrative officials whose conduct has been brought into question. In those cases, which are at the center of concern with the public trust, there is a strong, if not demonstrable, implication that the acts in question represent a response to limited and self-interested proponents of public action. It is not difficult to perceive the reason for the legislative and administrative actions which give rise to such cases, for public officials are frequently subjected to intensive representations on behalf of interests seeking official concessions to support proposed enterprises. The concessions desired by those interests are often of limited visibility to the general public so that public sentiment is not aroused; but the importance of the grants to those who seek them may lead to extraordinarily vigorous and persistent efforts. It is in these situations that public trust lands are likely to be put in jeopardy and that legislative watchfulness is likely to be at the lowest levels. To send such a case back for express legislative authority is to create through the courts an openness and visibility which is the publics principle protection against overreaching, but which is often absent in the routine political process. Thus, the courts should intervene to provide the most appropriate climate for democratic policy making.

Gould v. Greylock Reservation Commission is an important case for two reasons. First, it provides a useful illustration that it is possible for rather dubious projects to clear all the legislative and administrative hurdles which have been set up to protect the public interest. Second, and more significantly, the technique which the court used to confront the basic issues suggests a fruitful mode for carrying on such litigation. Moreover, *Gould* is not unique; it is one of a line of exceedingly important cases in which the Massachusetts court has produced a remarkable body of modern public trust interpretation by using the technique which it developed in that case.

THE DEVELOPMENT OF THE MASSACHUSETTS RESPONSE TO THE PROBLEM OF LOW VISIBILITY POLICY DECISIONS

Gould, like *Illinois Central,* was concerned with the most overt sort of imposition on the public interest; commercial interests had obtained advantages which infringed directly on public uses and promoted private profits. But the Massachusetts court has also confronted a mere pervasive, if more subtle, problem – that concerning projects which clearly have *some* public justification. Such cases arise when, for example, a highway department seeks to take a piece of parkland or to fill a wetland. It is clear that the appropriate agencies hear and attend to the voices which call for getting the job of road building done as quickly and cheaply as possible. But there are also individuals who put a high premium on the maintenance of parks, wetlands, and open space. Are their voices adequately heard and their claims adequately taken into account in the decisional process?

There is no single answer to that question. Sometimes, to be sure, the objectors in a community are alert and highly organized and make their views known very clearly. In other situations, a project will go forward quietly and will approach the point of irreversibility before those who would question it can initiate their questioning. Such situations are hardly consonant with a democratic view of government and are undesirable even when they are the result of mere inadvertence on the part of public agencies. But it often appears that there is a conscious effort to minimize public awareness and participation[9]. Situations of that sort arise almost daily in the thousands of resource development and conservation matters that come before state and federal agencies. Often the picture is not a pretty one. Yet many courts respond to objections simply by asserting that protection of the public interest has been vested in some public agency,[10] and that it is not appropriate for citizens or the courts to involve themselves with second-guessing the official vindicators of the public interest.

---

9. Cases of this nature are numerous. One was brought to light...after the massive oil leakage off the Santa Barbara coast. In that instance, the governmental agency charged with protecting the public interest decided against holding public hearings prior to granting approval for a project because the agency "preferred not to stir the natives up any more than possible [sic]" Interoffice Memo from Eugene W. Standley, Staff Engineer, U.S. Dept. of the Interior, Feb. 15, 1968. When questions were raised, the agency publicly responded by saying, "we feel maximum provision has been made for the local environment and that further delay in the lease sale would not be consistent with the national interest." N.Y. Times, March 25, 1969, at 30, col. 6 (quoting from a letter from the Undersecretary of the Interior to the chairman of the board of supervisors of Santa Barbara County). But the agency privately indicated that "The 'heat' has not died down but we can keep trying to alleviate the fears of the people," *id.* at col 3, and noted that pressures were being applied by the oil company whose equipment worth "millions of dollars" was being held "in anticipation."

There are a variety of other ways in which agencies minimize public participation in their deliberations. For example, the duty to hold a public hearing may technically be satisfied by holding a hearing which is "announced" to the public by posting a notice on an obscure bulletin board in a post office. Nashville I-40 Steering Comm. v. Ellington, 387 F.2d 179, 183 (6th Cir. 1967), cert. denied, 390 U.S. 921 (1968). Alternatively, a statutory hearing requirement may simply be ignored, and the argument later made that despite the omission no citizen has legal standing to challenge the agency's action. See D.C. Fed'n. of Civic Ass'ns., Inc. v. Airis, 391 F. 2d 478 (D.C. Cir. 1968).

10. E.g., Harrison-Halsted Community Group v. Housing & Home Fin. Agency, 310 F.2d 99, 105 (7th Cir. 1962), cert. denied, 373 U.S. 914 (1963): "The legislature, through its lawfully created agencies, rather than 'interested' citizens, is the guardian of the public needs to be served by social legislation."

As a result of *Gould* and the cases which followed it, the situation is considerably better in Massachusetts. That state's Supreme Judicial Court has penetrated one of the very difficult problems of American government – inequality of access to, and influence over, administrative agencies. It has struck directly at low-visibility decision-making, which is the most pervasive manifestation of the problem. By a simple but ingenious flick of the doctrinal wrist, the court has forced agencies to bear the burden of obtaining specific, overt approval of efforts to invade the public trust.

The court has accomplished that result by extending the application of a well-established rule designed to mitigate traditional conflicts between public agencies arising when one agency seeks to condemn land held by another. Under that established rule, one agency cannot take land vested in another agency without explicit authorizing legislation; otherwise the two agencies might successively try to take and retake property ad infinitum. Clearly, that principle evolved as a judicial means of avoiding conflict between agencies. The Massachusetts court has turned it into an affirmative tool for private citizens to use against governmental agencies which are assertedly acting contrary to the public interest. Thus, the legal doctrine did not formally change, but an extremely important modification was made in its application. It now operates to overrule the doctrine that citizens must acquiesce in discretionary administrative actions which are not plainly in contravention of law. The administrative agencies now have the burden of establishing an affirmative case before the legislature in the full light of public attention.

Having set the stage in cases involving conflict between public agencies, the Massachusetts court took the important step of intervention on behalf of private citizens in *Gould*. The next year, that court further emphasized its views in Sacco v. Department of Public Works[11]. In that case, residents of the town of Arlington sought to enjoin the Department of Public Works from filling a great pond as part of its plan to relocate part of a state highway. The department thought it had all the legislative authority it needed, for it was operating under two particularly broad statutes. The court not only found the statutory power inadequate, but actually used it against the Department. As to the first statute, the court noted that it has previously decided that it did not regard "general reference to unspecified "public land" as a conferring...of a blanket power to take...any land of the Commonwealth which the Authority chooses." The court's response to the second statute was even more vehement and clearly reveals the court's feeling about these cases. With scarcely disguised irritation, the court said:

> ...the improvement of public lands contemplated by this section does not include the widening of a State highway. It seems rather that the improvement of public lands which the legislature provided for...is to preserve such lands so that they may be enjoyed by the people for recreational purposes.

The court then noted the legislature had recently passed a law directing the department to "provide for the protection of water resources, fish and wildlife and recreational values", and stated that it did not believe that the new law "represented an abrupt change in legislative policy", but rather "an abiding legislative concern for the preservation of our great ponds" – a concern which the court obviously did not think the Department of Public Works shared.[12]

11. 227 N.E.2d 478 (Mass. 1967).

12. 227 N.E.2d at 480. The ultimate result of such litigation is usually a honing down of developers' demands or a modification of their methods. Thus, in *Sacco*, counsel for the plaintiffs reported

Despite the strong and explicit language of the court, the Department of Public Works continued to march to its own tune. A year later it was back in court, this time in Robbins v. Department of Public Works,[13] a case involving the acquisition of some wetlands for its highway program. The suit was instituted by private citizens to protect Fowl Meadows, a "wetlands of considerable natural beauty...often used for nature study and recreation." The meadows were owned and administered by the Metropolitan District Commission, a state parklands agency, which had agreed with the Department of Public Works to transfer the meadows to it for highway use. The case is of particular significance because the agency whose specific function it was to protect parklands for the public was named as a co-defendant with the highway agency. Moreover, the applicable statute required that the transfer receive the approval of both the Governor and the state council, and such approval had been given. The court's willingness to entertain a citizens' suit against all these guardians of the citizenry is a measure of the Massachusetts court's skepticism about administrative discretion in dealings with public resources.

The statute at issue in *Robbins* was considerably more explicit than that which was at issue in *Sacco*; the *Robbins* court itself noted that "admittedly there are significant differences.... For example, [the statute in *Robbins*] is not an eminent domain statute; it concerns only 'land of the commonwealth'; it requires that the transfer have the approval of the Governor and Council; and it restricts the new use to the 'laying out or relocation of any highway'."

Even with these differences, the court held, the statute failed to "state with the requisite degrees of explicitness a legislative intention to effect the diversion of use which the DPW seeks to accomplish." The court then set out the standard which must be met if there is to be adequate evidence of legislative intent. That standard is patently designed to thrust such matters before the public, by requiring that the legislature specify the reallocative policy being undertaken; a court could not be more explicit in its effort to make the legislative and administrative processes more responsive to the will of the general public and less susceptible to the tendency to make decisions which, as a result of inequalities of access, do not fully reflect the general will:

> We think it is essential to the expression of plain and explicit authority to divert parklands, Great Ponds, reservations and kindred areas to new and inconsistent public uses that the Legislature identify the land and that there appear in the legislation not only a statement of the new use but a statement or recital showing in some way legislative awareness of the existing public

---

that, "after the decision the legislature enacted a bill granting the DPW authority to take 4.7 acres of Spy Pond for the highway. The Department had wanted a much broader bill, but it was hoist [sic] by its own petard in that it had insisted throughout the litigation that all it needed was 4.7 acres." Letter from Robert J. Muldoon to the author, July 21, 1969. In Robbins v. Department of Pub. Works, 244 N.W. 2d 577 (Mass. 1969), counsel for the objectors wrote the following as to the outcome of litigation:

> [A]fter a Herculean effort, the House of Representatives in Massachusetts voted 130-92 to authorize a feasibility study of a westerly route, such as we have been working for. However, our local Public Works Department brought out its troops in the form of at least six men who spent most of the week in the State House and, after reconsideration, obtained a bill for an opposite route by the narrow score of 109-105. The Senate concurred after removing some amendments...but, in the meantime, the Governor has stated in public and written us that he will not permit the transfer of the requisite parkland. Letter from Stuart Debard to the author, Sept. 5, 1969.

13. 244 N.E.2d 577 (Mass. 1968).

use. In short, the legislation should express not merely the public will for the new use but its willingness to surrender or forgo the existing use.

Finding the statute in question clearly inadequate under this test, the court ordered the issuance of a writ of mandamus commanding that the land not be transferred to the Department of Public Works until legislation authorizing such transfer was duly enacted.

Thus, in cases which followed *Gould*, the Massachusetts court has clearly demonstrated both an awareness of the problems which are central to public trust litigation and a willingness to ensure that those problems are not ignored by decision-making bodies. The court has not attempted to make policy decisions concerning the proper use of public trust lands, but has instead developed a means for ensuring that those who do make the decisions do so in a publicly visible manner. The court has served notice to all concerned that it will view with skepticism any dispositions of trust lands and will not allow them unless it is perfectly clear that the dispositions have been fully considered by the legislature.

COMMENTARY AND QUESTIONS

1. The history of the public trust doctrine in the United States. The article from which you have just read excerpts can claim the majority of credit for the active presence of the public trust doctrine in American environmental law. (It has been so often cited as the seminal work in the field that Professor Sax was recently introduced at a conference on western public interest law as "Seminal Sax" and received a standing ovation on the point.) But the public trust doctrine did exist earlier in the case law of the United States, waiting to be re-discovered (somewhat like the Refuse Act of 1899). In 1810, in the Pennsylvania case of Carson v. Glazer, 2 Binn. 475, the Pennsylvania court asserted the public trust doctrine to affirm that no one could own the rights to fish in a Pennsylvania river, as against the public. That case is notable, moreover, not only for the fact that it used the term "trust" in the very modern sense that Sax uses it, but also that the court quite matter of factly extended the traditional trust from navigable waters and ocean waters to inland waterways with no suggestion of navigability. The New Jersey Supreme Court followed in Arnold v. Mundy, 6 N.J.L. 1 (1821), asserting that no one could own shellfishing beds as against the public. Subsequent cases prior to *Illinois Central* had established the same principle. Martin v. Waddell, 41 U.S. 367 (1842). Accordingly, there does not seem to be much dispute about the existence of the public trust doctrine within the body of American law. The questions that have arisen about the public trust doctrine do not deny that fact; rather, they debate the terms upon which the trust exists and applies.

2. The public trust as trust law. The public trust doctrine is an equitable doctrine which shares its elements with the far more commonly litigated doctrine of private trusts. In both cases, what are the elements of a trust situation? First there must be the "thing" about which the trust is concerned, the "corpus" or "res", a defined bundle of assets that are owned and managed under the trust framework. Then there is the trustee, a person or entity legally charged with responsibilities and rights. Trustees in Anglo-American law actually "own" the resources in terms of legal title. They accordingly have the right to manage, sell, lease, develop, etc., the assets, but only insofar as a careful fiduciary would and could so as to protect the existence of the assets and achieve the purposes of the trust. When trustees own a parcel of land in an urban area, as in the case of a number of private or charitable trusts, they may go to an equity court and request permission to sell, lease, or develop the trust property so as to maximize the economic benefits that typically constitute the trust terms in private trusts. The "terms" of a trust, however, differ from trust to trust and are critically important. When a trust has been set up by the "trustor" or "settlor" of the trust (the prior owner who created it), the trustees must follow the precise dictates and terms of the trust stipulations. If a trust is mandated to maximize the financial security of family members, then the management of the assets will be judged by the careful economic standards necessary to achieve that end. If the trust is set up to care for a park or an educational institution, then the primary trust standard is to maintain the character of the trust property.

While the legal title of a trust rests with the trustee, the real "equitable" or "beneficial" title to the property, enforceable in court, is held by the "beneficiaries." In most trusts the court's enforcement and oversight comes at the request of beneficiaries, any one of whom has standing to call for an accounting from the trustees, in court.

These then are the generic elements of a trust. Can you roughly identify how each of them is to be defined in the case of the public trust doctrine? In a public trust, who is the trustee, who are the beneficiaries, what is the corpus, what are the terms? (The identity of the settlor probably depends upon your theological inclinations).

3. What is the public trust and where is it going? There is little controversy about the existence of the public trust historically in the United States. But what, exactly, is it? Is it a common law doctrine? If so, how is it that it can overturn a *statutory* enactment? Is it a federal or state doctrine? Note that in *Illinois Central* the doctrine was used by a federal court to overcome the action of a sovereign state. Does the doctrine apply to the federal government as well? In several cases, courts have asserted that the federal government is equally accountable and restricted under the terms of the public trust doctrine. See In Re Steuart Transp. Co., 495 F. Supp. 38, 40 (E.D. Va. 1980); U.S. v. 1.8 Acres, 523 F. Supp. 120, 124 (D. Mass. 1981). The federal government is a creature of the states by delegation through the act of union and the federal Constitution. If the federal government is therefore exercising delegated sovereign powers, it would appear straightforward that it cannot have greater rights and fewer limitations than the entities that created it. Is the public trust then a principle of federal common law? A number of courts and commentators have indicated that neither the federal government nor the state governments can act to abolish the public trust doctrine. See Marks v. Whitney, 491 P. 2d 374, 380-81 (Cal. 1971). As trustees, the state sovereignties and federal government are bound by the terms of the trust. Is it then a principle of federal constitutional law? If so, where does it lie?

Where is the public trust going? If it is clear that governments – state and perhaps federal – are the trustees, then what is the scope of the assets held in trust? Is it just tidal waters or navigation and fishing in tidal waters? The doctrine has already spread far beyond that locale, as we will see. It clearly applies on dry land as well, but the ultimate scope of the doctrine is not clearly delineated, at least not yet.[14]

What are the terms of the trust? Does it require an absolute freeze on the present use of all public trust resources? If the beneficiaries are future citizens as well as present (and past) citizens, then it appears that a simple majority vote of a present-day legislature may not be enough to permit irrevocable diversion or alienation of trust resources. Professor Sax discusses the Massachusetts cases as merely requiring a specific legislative authorization for sale or alteration of the trust assets. Isn't that ultimately just a procedural requirement? As in *Illinois Central,* doesn't the trust really mean that a court reviewing the trustee's actions may hold, even where statutory authorization is specific, that the statute violates *substantive* trust standards, and so overturn the legislative action? Note that trust doctrines are not absolute – after the *Illinois Central* case, the U.S. Supreme Court and state supreme courts have sometimes found that a conscientious balancing of public trust interests permitted alteration of trust assets. See Milwaukee v. State, 214 N.W. 820 (Wis. 1927), and State v. Public Service Comm'n, 81 N.W.2d 71 (Wis. 1957), where the issue was the proposed filling of a small percentage of Lake Wingra in the town of Madison, Wisconsin, for the purposes of making a park area more enjoyable and accessible. The court held, after a careful balancing of public trust considerations, that this action would not violate the trust.

And what are the standards of the trust? The following modern Illinois case experiments with the process of defining such standards.

Section 2. APPLYING THE MODERN PUBLIC TRUST DOCTRINE

Paepke v. Building Commission

Supreme Court of Illinois, 1970
46 Ill. 2d 330, 263 N.E.2d 11

BURT, J. Plaintiffs, who are citizens, residents, taxpayers and property owners of the city of Chicago, appeal from an order of the circuit court of Cook County dismissing their complaint by which they sought to prevent defendants, Public Building Commission of Chicago, the City of Chicago, the Board of Education of Chicago, and the Chicago Park District from implementing plans to construct school and recreational facilities in Washington and Douglas parks. This court has jurisdiction on direct appeal because of the constitutional questions involved....

The Public Building Commission of Chicago, at the request of the Board of Education of the City of Chicago, has undertaken a program involving the construction, alteration, repair, renovation, and rehabilitation of public schools in the city, together with park, recreational, playground, and other related public facilities which will be leased by the Building Commission to the Board of

14. See Rieser, Ecological Preservation as a Sovereign Right, 15 Harv. Env. L.Rev. 393 (1991); Coastal States Org., Putting the Public Trust to Work (symposium proceedings, 1990)(including a 29-state survey); Symposium, 19 Envtl. Law 425 et eqs. (1990).

Education, the Chicago Park District, and other governmental agencies. The commission has selected, located, and designated sites within the territorial limits of the city of Chicago as sites to be acquired for the erection and construction of elementary, middle, and high schools to serve about 30,000 pupils, together with park, recreation, and playground facilities. Each of the sites has been recommended by the Department of Development and Planning of the City of Chicago in accord with the comprehensive plan for the City of Chicago and in cooperation with the Board of Education of the City of Chicago and also the Chicago Park District in connection with the sites in which the Chicago Park District is involved. Some of these sites have already been approved by the city council of the city of Chicago.

A site has been designated in Washington Park for the erection of a school-park facility. The Chicago Park District proposes to convey to the Public Building Commission of Chicago for such purposes a total of 3.839 acres located in the northwest portion of the park about 250 feet from the northern boundary. On 2.586 acres of this site the building commission proposes to construct a middle school for approximately 1500 students to be leased to the Board of Education of the City of Chicago. The remaining 1.253 acres would be utilized in the construction of a gymnasium and recreational facilities which will be leased to the Chicago Park District. Construction had started on this site at the time suit was filed but had not proceeded to a point where original use of the land would no longer be possible. Of the sites thus far selected by the Public Building Commission of Chicago and approved by the city council of the city of Chicago only the 2.6 acres in Washington Park involves property in a park which is to be used for school construction.

It is plaintiffs' theory that the parks in question are so dedicated that they are held in public trust for use only as park or recreational grounds and that those of them who are property owners adjacent to or in the vicinity of a park dedicated by the acts of 1869 have a private property right to the continuation of the park use of which even the legislature cannot deprive them. They further contend that all plaintiffs who are citizens and residents of any area of the city have a public property right to enforce the public trust existing by reason of the dedication of the parks as aforesaid and to require that no change of park use be permitted because the legislature has not explicitly and openly so provided by statute....

Such dedication having been made by the sovereign, the agencies created by it hold the properties in trust for the uses and purposes specified and for the benefit of the public. See Illinois Central Railroad Co. v. Illinois, 146 U.S. 387 (1892); Sax, The Public Trust Doctrine in Natural Resource Law: Effective Judicial Intervention, 68 Mich. L. Rev. 471-566. [extensive quotations from Professor Sax's article omitted.]

With this much background we approach the first question presented in this appeal: Have plaintiffs who are property owners adjacent to or in the vicinity of the parks dedicated by the acts of 1869 a private property right to continuation of the park use of which even the legislature cannot deprive them? This question must be answered in the negative. The mere dedication by the sovereign of lands to public park uses does not give property owners adjoining or in the vicinity of the park the right to have the use continue unchanged even though, when the park was established, abutting or adjoining owners were assessed for special benefits conferred. Reicheldarfer v. Quinn, 287 U.S. 315. In the cited cases, Rock Creek Park in the District of Columbia had been created by act of Congress providing that the lands "were perpetually dedicated and set apart as a public park or pleasure ground for the benefit and enjoyment of the people of the United States." A later act of

Congress authorized the Commissioners of the District of Columbia to construct a fire engine house in the park. The Supreme Court held that the plaintiffs derived no rights against the government and had no interest protected by the constitution against diminution by the government, however unreasonable its action might be....

As to the interests of plaintiffs and their standing to bring the action, the trial judge found that they had no rights sufficient to enable them to maintain the action "except as taxpayers." If the public trust doctrine is to have any meaning or vitality at all, however, the members of the public, at least taxpayers who are the beneficiaries of that trust, must have the right and standing to enforce it. To tell them that they must wait upon governmental action is often an effectual denial of the right for all time. The conclusion we have reached is in accord with decisions in other jurisdictions, see, e.g., [*Robbins* and *Gould*, the Massachusetts cases], wherein plaintiffs' rights as residents in a trust of public lands were enforced without question.

As to the second part of the question, whether there has been a sufficient manifestation of legislative intent to permit the diversion and reallocation contemplated by the plan proposed by defendants, it should be remembered that in People ex rel. Stamos v. Public Building Comm'n, 40 Ill.2d 164, this court had before it the very plan and program here involved which was examined in detail in the light of the many constitutional objections raised. We found that the applicable statutes authorized the program of schools and recreational facilities in parks which is now sought to be implemented in Washington Park and possibly in Douglas Park by the defendants here.

Plaintiffs argue nevertheless that before defendants can be allowed to carry out their plan the legislature must clearly and specifically state with reference to the park or parks in question explicit authority to divert to new public uses and that there must appear in that legislation not only a statement of the new use but a statement or recital showing in some way an awareness on the part of the legislature of the existing public use. Their position is based mainly upon the line of Massachusetts cases.... It is our conclusion, as we found in the *Stamos* case, that present statutes, including the Public Building Commission Act, authorize a plan such as that evolved for a Washington Park presently, and we further find that the intention expressed in that legislation is sufficiently broad, comprehensive and definite to allow the diversion in use involved here.

In passing we think it appropriate to refer to the approach developed by the courts of our sister State, Wisconsin, in dealing with diversion problems. In at least two cases, City of Madison v. State, 83 N.W.2d 674, and State v. Public Service Comm'n, 81 N.W.2d 71, the Supreme Court of Wisconsin approved proposed diversions in the use of public trust lands under conditions which demonstrated (1) that public bodies would control use of the area in question, (2) that the area would be devoted to public purposes and open to the public, (3) the diminution of the area of original use would be small compared with the entire area, (4) that none of the public uses of the original area would be destroyed or greatly impaired and (5) that the disappointment of those wanting to use the area of new use for former purposes was negligible when compared to the greater convenience to be afforded those members of the public using the new facility. We believe that the present plans for Washington Park meet all of these tests. While not controlling under the issues as presented in this case, we believe that standards such as those might serve as a useful guide for future administrative action....

In conclusion, let it be said that this court is fully aware of the fact that the issues presented in this case illustrate the classic struggle between those members of the public who would preserve our parks and open lands in their pristine purity and those charged with administrative responsibilities who, under the pressures of the changing needs of an increasingly complex society, find it necessary, in good faith and for the public good, to encroach to some extent upon lands heretofore considered inviolate to change. The resolution of this conflict in any given case is for the legislature and not the courts. The courts can serve only as an instrument of determining legislative intent as evidenced by existing legislation measured against constitutional limitations. In this process the courts must deal with legislation as enacted and not with speculative consideration of legislative wisdom. As previously indicated in this opinion, existing legislation does not warrant the restrictive interpretation plaintiffs would place upon it.

The judgment of the circuit court of Cook County dismissing plaintiffs complaint is affirmed.

COMMENTARY AND QUESTIONS

1. Three different settings for the trust. The *Paepke* setting is an example of governmental "diversion" of trust property, the second category of public trust situations referred to by Professor Sax. The first type of trust case is the "alienation" situation like *Illinois Central*, where government attempts to transfer public trust assets to a private party. The possibility of continued governmental oversight notwithstanding, such actions are especially likely to reduce public use. In the second category of cases, represented implicitly by some of the Massachusetts cases, the government is attempting to divert ownership and use of a public trust asset from one governmental agency to another. In the diversion cases, typically, one governmental agency holding public trust resource lands for protection purposes proposes to transfer them to another agency that has a primary mission and inclination to exploit and develop public property.[15] A third category, which might be called the "resource-defense" or "derogation" cases, can be discerned in cases where government or private developers threaten to pollute or destroy trust assets, most often seen in the water pollution setting.[16]

2. The scope of the trust. Note here in the *Paepke* case how matter-of-factly the court accepts the assumption that the public trust doctrine, developed in the oceans of the Roman Empire, applies to a public parkland. In fact there has been little serious argument in the public trust cases over the past two decades about whether the public trust doctrine can appropriately be applied to dedicated parklands. The fundamental idea of a park, it appears, is a long-term special management relationship between land, people, and government. (This may help to explain why

15. Lying in a grey area between the alienation and diversion categories are cases like Vermont v. Central Vt. Ry., 571 A.2d 1128 (1989), where the state supreme court held that a public utility railroad company's grant of lands on the shores of Lake Champlain would be restricted to public trust uses, where the company, which held title, wanted to undertake resort and commercial development of the lands.

16. See e.g. Tennessee Code Annotated §§70.324 et seq.; beyond water resources, see the redwood cases, invoking the trust to protect redwoods against erosion and destruction. 396 F. Supp. 90 (N.D. Cal. 1974), 398 F. Supp. 284 (N.D.Cal. 1975).

Professor Sax's public trust scholarship moved quite naturally into an extensive study of the meaning of parks and wilderness in the 20th Century. See Sax, Mountains without Handrails (1981).) What is a "park"? The United States invented the idea of national parks, but there is a continuing debate about what they mean. If the public trust doctrine applies to "parks," does it apply to state or federal forests? Is the concept of "dedication," in some terms, implied or express, the distinguishing factor?

3. The *Paepke* court's balancing process: a substantive, not merely a procedural standard? Professor Sax's discussion of the Massachusetts cases in his 1970 article might lead a development-minded legislature to believe that all it had to do to override the trust was to pass exceedingly specific authorization for a proposed project. The *Paepke* case implies that governments have substantive trusteeship duties, not just procedural requirements. Is the *Paepke* court's holding based on the Wisconsin (substantive) or the Massachusetts (procedural) trust analysis? Would Sax approve of the *Paepke* court's application of his theories?

Under the Wisconsin tests, proposed alterations of trust resources will apparently be tested by scrutiny of the actual balance struck between trust obligations and values on one hand and economic or other legislative development motives on the other. The public trust's long-term legacy value is presumed to be primary; departures from the trust apparently bear the substantive burden of persuasion. Although courts review the acts of other branches of government deferentially, equity precedents for trust accountings from public officials, as in charitable trusts, argue for less deference. When the government is acting as a trustee, it comes before the equity court as a fiduciary subject to special scrutiny.[17]

The standards applied by the *Paepke* court, and the process by which it applied them, have the ring of good common sense. The court recognizes that parklands are important public trust resources, and takes seriously, it seems, its role of determining whether or not the diversion ordered by the governmental process will be permitted to chop a piece out of Washington Park. What do you think of the Wisconsin standards and the way the *Paepke* court applied them to the case? Take the five tests one by one and ask yourself whether they sufficiently capture the protective ideas of the public trust. Is there anything missing that could be added as a litigable standard in *Paepke*?

With reference to this last question, ask yourself why the city of Chicago was diverting this section of parkland to its school department's use. Is this the only place in this area of Chicago where the school board can build a new school and facilities? Or is it rather an economic trade-off? Presumably, since they have the

17. See People ex rel. Scott v. Chicago Park District, 360 N.E.2d 773 (Ill. 1977). The Illinois legislature wanted to convey 194.6 acres of submerged lands under Lake Michigan to United States Steel – remarkably like the circumstances of *Illinois Central*. Despite a legislative assertion in the bill that the conveyance would result in "the conversion of otherwise useless and unproductive submerged land into an important commercial development to the benefit of the people of the State of Illinois," the court wasn't biting. "The self-serving recitation of a public purpose within a legislative enactment is not conclusive of the existence of such purpose." 360 N.E.2d at 781.

power of eminent domain, the school board and city authorities could take 3.8 acres anywhere in this part of the city. The only problem is cost, because it would surely cost a great deal more to take private property than to grab public property for free. But that motive – saving cash – will in every case result in diversion or destruction of public trust resources. In the *Overton Park* case, analyzed later on in these materials, the Supreme Court of the United States interpreted a statutory formulation by which the Congress, faced with the same dilemma of automatic trade-offs, declared that no parkland shall be taken for a federal-aid highway unless there is "no feasible and prudent alternative." Professor Sax would clearly not object to that standard.

For another formulation of the balance, see Payne v. Kassab, 312 A.2d 86, 94-94 (Pa. App. 1973). The *Payne* court, citing no precedent, asserted that a change in use of public trust parkland must meet three standards: (1) compliance with applicable statutes and regulations; (2) a reasonable effort to minimize environmental "incursions" resulting from the change in use; and (3) benefits must outweigh any resulting harms. The third test is clearly the key to determining whether there will be a meaningful trust balance or a mere conclusory bureaucratic writeoff: Will harms be weighed in terms of long-term intangible trust values, or market dollars? Will benefits be accounted realistically, or in the promoters' hyperbolic terms? Will alternatives be scrupulously weighed against the proposal? Only where the range of considerations is that complete are the sensitive principles of the trust honored.

4. A diversity of values: tradeoffs? If the city of Chicago was merely trying to save a few dollars and could just as well have condemned private land near the park for its school, that surely should be weighed against the city's proposal. But should the court also consider whether particular proposed alternative locations would disrupt stable, low-income, minority neighborhoods?

Or what if protection of the public trust resource imposes heavy water conservation burdens and expenses on millions of citizens, rich and poor, in a major American city?

National Audubon Society v. Superior Court of Alpine County (*Mono Lake*)
Supreme Court of California, 1983
33 Cal.3d 419, 189 Cal.Reptr. 346, 658 P.2d 709

[The City of Los Angeles, located in its dry coastal enclave on the southern California coast, has 3 million inhabitants, and continues to grow by 5+ percent each year. To assure that water supplies critical to its survival and growth would remain available, city officials thought that they had locked up sufficient appropriated/contract water rights in the Sierra Nevada Mountains[18] to last well into the 21st century. Then, using the public trust doctrine, plaintiff environmentalists filed a lawsuit against Los Angeles' water diversions. The case eventually came to the California Supreme Court on a federal trial judge's request for clarification of the state's public trust doctrine:]

18. The bitter battles over those water rights formed part of the political backdrop for Roman Polanski's movie "Chinatown."

BROUSSARD, J. ...Mono Lake, the second largest lake in California, sits at the base of the Sierra Nevada escarpment near the eastern entrance to Yosemite National Park. The lake is saline; it contains no fish but supports a large population of brine shrimp which feed vast numbers of nesting and migratory birds. Islands in the lake protect a large breeding colony of California gulls, and the lake itself serves as a haven on the migration route for thousands of Northern Phalarope, Wilson's Phalarope, and Eared Grebe. Towers and spires of tufa on the north and south shores are matters of geological interest and a tourist attraction.

Although Mono Lake receives some water from rain and snow on the lake surface, historically most of its supply came from snowmelt in the Sierra Nevada. Five freshwater streams – Mill, Lee Vining, Walker, Parker and Rush Creeks – arise near the crest of the range and carry the annual runoff to the west shore of the lake. In 1940, however, the Division of Water Resources granted the Department of Water and Power of the City of Los Angeles (hereafter DWP) a permit to appropriate virtually the entire flow of four of the five streams flowing into the lake. DWP promptly constructed facilities to divert about half the flow of these streams into DWP's Owens Valley aqueduct. In 1970 DWP completed a second diversion tunnel, and since that time has taken virtually the entire flow of these streams.

As a result of these diversions, the level of the lake has dropped; the surface area has diminished by one-third; one of the two principal islands in the lake has become a peninsula, exposing the gull rookery there to coyotes and other predators and causing the gulls to abandon the former island. The ultimate effect of continued diversions is a matter of intense dispute, but there seems little doubt that both the scenic beauty and the ecological values of Mono Lake are imperiled....

The case brings together for the first time two systems of legal thought; the appropriative water rights system which since the days of the gold rush has dominated California water law, and the public trust doctrine which, after evolving as a shield for the protection of tidelands, now extends its protective scope to navigable lakes. Ever since we first recognized that the public trust protects environmental and recreational values (Marks v. Whitney, 491 P.2d 374 (1971)), the two systems of legal thought have been on a collision course. Johnson, Public Trust Protection for Stream Flows and Lake Levels, 14 U.C. Davis L.Rev. 233 (1980)). They meet in a unique and dramatic setting which highlights the clash of values. Mono Lake is a scenic and ecological treasure of national significance, imperiled by continued diversions of water; yet, the need of Los Angeles for water is apparent, its reliance on rights granted by the board evident, the cost of curtailing diversions substantial.

Attempting to integrate the teachings and values of both the public trust and the appropriative water rights system, we have arrived at certain conclusions which we briefly summarize here. In our opinion, the core of the public trust doctrine is the state's authority as sovereign to exercise a continuous supervision and control over the navigable waters of the state and the lands underlying those waters. This authority applies to the waters tributary to Mono Lake and bars DWP or any other party from claiming a vested right to divert waters once it becomes clear that such diversions harm the interests protected by the public trust. The corollary rule which evolved in tideland and lakeshore cases barring conveyance of rights free of the trust except to serve trust purposes cannot, however, apply without modification to flowing waters. The prosperity and habitability of much of this state requires the diversion of great quantities of water from its streams for purposes unconnected to any navigation, commerce, fishing recreation, or ecological use relating to the source stream. The state must have the power to grant nonvested usufructuary rights to appropriate water even if diversions harm public trust uses. Approval of such diversion without considering public trust values, however, may result in needless destruction of those values. Accordingly, we believe that before state courts and agencies approve water diversions they should consider the effect of such diversions upon interests protected by the public trust, and attempt, so far as feasible, to avoid or minimize any harm to those interests....

DWP expects that its future diversions of about 100,000 acre-feet per year will lower the lake's surface level another 43 feet and reduce its surface area by about 22 square miles over the next 80 to 100 years, at which point the lake will gradually approach environmental equilibrium (the point at which inflow from precipitation, groundwater and nondiverted tributaries equals outflow by evaporation and other means). At this point, according to DWP, the lake will stabilize at a level 6,330 feet above the sea's, with a surface area of approximately 38 square miles. Thus, by DWP's own estimates, unabated diversions will ultimately produce a lake that is about 56 percent smaller on the surface and 42 percent shallower than its natural size.

Plaintiffs consider these projections unrealistically optimistic. They allege that, 50 years hence, the lake will be at least 50 feet shallower than it now is, and hold less than 20 percent of its natural volume. Further, plaintiffs fear that "the lake will not stabilize at this level", but "may continue to reduce in size until it is dried up." Moreover, unlike DWP, plaintiffs believe that the lake's gradual recession indirectly causes a host of adverse environmental impacts. Many of these alleged impacts are related to an increase in the lake's salinity, caused by the decrease in its water volume.

As noted above, Mono Lake has no outlets. The lake loses water only by evaporation and seepage. Natural salts do not evaporate with water, but are left behind. Prior to commencement of the DWP diversions, this naturally rising salinity was balanced by a constant and substantial supply of fresh water from the tributaries. Now, however, DWP diverts most of the fresh water inflow. The resultant imbalance between inflow and outflow not only diminishes the lake's size, but also drastically increases its salinity....

Plaintiffs predict that the lake's steadily increasing salinity, if unchecked, will wreck havoc throughout the local food chain. They contend that the lake's algae, and the brine shrimp and brine flies that feed on it, cannot survive the projected salinity increase. To support this assertion, plaintiffs point to a 50 percent reduction in the shrimp hatch for the spring of 1980 and a startling 95 percent reduction for the spring of 1981. These reductions affirm experimental evidence indicating that brine shrimp populations diminish as the salinity of the water surrounding them increases. (See Task Force Report at 20-21) DWP admits these substantial reductions, but blames them on factors other than salinity.

DWP's diversions also present several threats to the millions of local and migratory birds using the lake. First, since many species of birds feed on the lake's brine shrimp, any reduction in shrimp population allegedly caused by rising salinity endangers a major avian food source. The Task Force Report considered it "unlikely that any of Mono Lake's major bird species...will persist at the lake if populations of invertebrates disappear." (Task Force Report at p. 20) Second, the increasing salinity makes it more difficult for the birds to maintain osmotic equilibrium with their environment.

The California gull is especially endangered, both by the increase in salinity and by loss of nesting sites. Ninety-five percent of this state's gull population and 25 percent of the total species population nests at the lake. (Task Force Report at 21). Most of the gulls nest on islands in the lake. As the lake recedes, land between the shore and some of the islands has been exposed, offering such predators as the coyote easy access to the gull nests and chicks. In 1979, coyotes reached Negrit Island, once the most popular nesting site, and the number of gull nests at the lake declined sharply. In 1981, 95 percent of the hatched chicks did not survive to maturity. Plaintiffs blame this decline and alarming mortality rate on the predator access created by the land bridges; DWP suggest numerous other causes, such as increased ambient temperatures and human activities, and claims that the joining of some islands with the mainlands is offset by the emergence of new islands due to the lake's recession.

Plaintiff allege that DWP's diversions adversely affect the human species and its activities as well. First, as the lake recedes, it has exposed more than 18,000 acres of lake bed composed of very fine silt which, once dry, easily becomes airborne in winds. This silt contains a high concentration of alkali and other minerals that irritate the mucous membranes and respiratory systems of humans and other animals. (See Task Force Report at 22). While the precise extent of this threat to the public health has yet to be determined, such threat as exists can be expected to increase with the exposure of additional lake bed. DWP, however, claims that its diversions neither affect the air quality in Mono Basin nor present a hazard to human health.

Furthermore, the lake's recession obviously diminishes its value as an economic, recreational, and scenic resource. Of course, there will be less lake to use and enjoy. The declining shrimp hatch depresses a local shrimping industry. The rings of dry lake bed are difficult to traverse on foot, and thus impair human access to the lake, and reduce the lake's substantial scenic value. Mono Lake has long been treasured as a unique scenic, recreational and scientific resource (see, e.g., City of Los Angeles v. Aitken, *supra*, 10 Cal.App. 2d 460, 462-463; Task Force Report at pp. 22-24), but continued diversions threaten to turn it into a desert wasteland like the dry bed of Owens Lake.

[This appeal comes as an inquiry from the federal court on an] important issue of California law: "What is the interrelationship of the public trust doctrine and the California water rights system, in the context of the right of the Los Angeles Department of Water and Power ('Department') to divert water from Mono Lake pursuant to permits and licenses issued under the California water rights system? In other words, is the public trust doctrine in this context subsumed in the California water rights system, or does it function independently of that system? Stated differently, can the plaintiffs challenge the Department's permits and licenses by arguing that those permits and licenses are limited by the public trust doctrine, or must the plaintiffs challenge the permits and licenses by arguing that the water diversions and uses authorized thereunder are not 'reasonable or beneficial' as required under the California water rights system?..."

[The State Superior] court entered summary judgment against plaintiffs. Its notice of intended ruling stated that "[t]he California water rights system is a comprehensive and exclusive system for determining the legality of the diversions of the City of Los Angeles in the Mono Basin.... The Public Trust Doctrine does not function independently of that system. This Court concludes that as regards the

© JIM STROUP/MONO LAKE COMMITTEE

© JIM STROUP/MONO LAKE COMMITTEE

Views of Mono Lake; top photograph shows the setting and tufa spires rising from the lake bed. Bottom photograph shows land bridge to Negit Island created by falling water levels in 1979 – because of feeder stream diversions to Los Angeles – allowing predators to destroy the island's nesting population of 38,000 California gulls, three-fourths of the gull's total population in the state.

right of the City of Los Angeles to divert waters in the Mono Basin that the Public Trust Doctrine is subsumed in the water rights system of the state ...."

We...set the case for argument....

THE PUBLIC TRUST DOCTRINE IN CALIFORNIA

"By the law of nature these things are common to mankind – the air, running water, the sea and consequently the shores of the sea." (Institutes of Justinian 2.1.1.) From this origin in Roman law, the English common law evolved the concept of the public trust, under which the sovereign owns "all of its navigable waterways and the lands lying beneath them 'as trustee of a public trust for the benefit of the people.'" (Colberg, Inc. v. State of California ex rel. Dept. Pub. Wks. (1967) 67 Cal. 2d 408, 416 [62 Cal. Reptr.. 401, 432 P.2d 3].) The State of California acquired title as trustee to such lands and waterways upon its admission to the union (City of Berkeley v. Superior Court (1980) 26 Cal. 3d 515, 521 [162 Cal. Reptr.. 327, 606 P.2d 362] and cases there cited); from the earliest days (see Eldridge v. Cowell (1854) 4 Cal. 80, 87) its judicial decisions have recognized and enforced the trust obligation.

Three aspects of the public trust doctrine require consideration in this opinion: the purpose of the trust; the scope of the trust, particularly as it applies to the nonnavigable tributaries of a navigable lake; and the powers and duties of the state as trustee of the public trust. We discuss these questions in the order listed.

THE PURPOSE OF THE PUBLIC TRUST

The objective of the public trust has evolved in tandem with the changing public perception of the values and uses of waterways. As we observed in Marks v. Whitney, *supra*, 6 Cal.3d 251, "[p]ublic trust easements [were] traditionally defined in terms of navigation, commerce and fisheries. They have been held to include the right to fish, hunt, bathe, swim, to use for boating and general recreation purposes the navigable waters of the state, and to use the bottom of the navigable waters for anchoring, standing, or other purposes. We went on, however, to hold that the traditional triad of uses–navigation, commerce and fishing–did not limit the public interest in the trust res. In language of special importance to the present setting, we stated that "[t]he public uses to which tidelands are subject are sufficiently flexible to encompass changing public needs. In administering the trust the state is not burdened with an outmoded classification favoring one mode of utilization over another. There is a growing public recognition that one of the most important public uses of the tidelands–a use encompassed within the tidelands trust–is the preservation of those lands in their natural state, so that they may serve as ecological units for scientific study, as open space, and as environments which provide food and habitat for birds and marine life, and which favorably affect the scenery and climate of the area."

Mono Lake is a navigable waterway. It supports a small local industry which harvests brine shrimp for sale as fish food, which endeavor probably qualifies the lake as a "fishery" under the traditional public trust cases. The principal values plaintiffs seek to protect, however, are recreational and ecological – the scenic views of the lake and its shore, the purity of the air, and the use of the lake for nesting and feeding by birds. Under Marks v. Whitney, *supra*, 6 Cal.3d 251, it is clear that protection of these values is among the purposes of the public trust.

THE SCOPE OF THE PUBLIC TRUST

Mono Lake is, as we have said, a navigable waterway. The beds, shores and waters of the lake are without question protected by the public trust. The streams diverted by DWP, however, are not themselves navigable. Accordingly, we must address in this case a question not discussed in any recent public trust case – whether the public trust limits conduct affecting nonnavigable tributaries to navigable waterways....

[T]he principles recognized by [our early public trust dambuilding and streambed gold mining] decisions apply fully to a case in which diversions from a nonnavigable tributary impair the public trust in a downstream river or lake. "If the public trust doctrine applies to constrain fills which destroy navigation and other public trust uses in navigable waters, it should equally apply to constrain the extraction of water that destroys navigation and other public interests. Both actions result in the same damage to the public interest." Johnson, Public Trust Protection of Stream Flows and Lake Levels, 14 U.C.Davis L.Rev. 233, 257-258 (1980)....

We conclude that the public trust doctrine, as recognized and developed in California decisions, protects navigable waters from harm caused by diversion of nonnavigable tributaries.

DUTIES AND POWERS OF THE STATE AS TRUSTEE

In the following review of the authority and obligations of the state as administrator of the public trust, the dominant theme is the state's sovereign power and duty to exercise continued supervision over the trust. One consequence, of importance to this and many other cases, is that parties acquiring rights in trust property generally hold those rights subject to the trust, and can assert no vested right to use those rights in a manner harmful to the trust.

As we noted recently in City of Berkeley v. Superior Court, *supra*, 26 Cal. 3d 515, the decision of the United States Supreme Court in Illinois Central Railroad Company v. Illinois, 146 U.S. 387, "remains the primary authority even today, almost nine decades after it was decided." The legislature, it held, did not have the power to convey the entire city waterfront free of trust, thus barring all future legislatures from protecting the public interest. The opinion declares that: "A grant of all the lands under the navigable waters of a State has never been adjudged to be within the legislative power; and any attempted grant of the kind would be held, if not absolutely void on its face, as subject to revocation. The State can no more abdicate its trust over property in which the whole people are interested, like navigable waters and soils under them...than it can abdicate its police powers in the administration of government and the preservation of the peace. In the administration of government the use of such powers may for a limited period be delegated to a municipality or other body, but there always remains with the State the right tor evoke those powers and exercise them in a more direct manner, and one more conformable to its wishes. So with trusts connected with public property, or property of a special character, like lands under navigable waterways, they cannot be placed entirely beyond the direction and control of the State." 146 U.S. at 453–454.

In summary, the foregoing cases amply demonstrate the continuing power of the state as administrator of the public trust, a power which extends to the revocation of previously granted right or to the enforcement of the trust against lands long thought free of the trust (see *City of Berkeley, supra*). Except for those rare instances in which a grantee may acquire a right to use former trust property free of trust restrictions, the grantee holds subject to the trust, and while he may assert a vested right to the servient estate (the right of use subject to the trust) and to any improvements he erects, he can claim no vested right to bar recognition of the trust or state action to carry out its purposes.

Since the public trust doctrine does not prevent the state from choosing between trust uses, the Attorney General of California, seeking to maximize state power under the trust, argues for a broad concept of trust uses. In his view, "trust uses" encompass all public uses, so that in practical effect the doctrine would impose no restrictions on the state's ability to allocate trust property." We know of no authority which supports this view of the public trust, except perhaps the dissenting opinion in Illinois Central Railroad Co. v. Illinois. Most decisions and commentators assume that "trust uses" relate to uses and activities in the vicinity of the lake, stream, or tidal reach at issue.... The tideland cases make this point clear: after *City of Berkeley*, no one could contend that the state could grant tidelands free of the trust merely because the grant served some public purpose, such as increasing tax revenues, or because the grantee might put the property to a commercial use....

Thus, the public trust is more than an affirmation of state power to use public property for public purposes. It is an affirmation of the duty of the state to protect the people's common heritage of streams, lakes, marshlands and tidelands, surrendering that right of protection only in rare cases when the abandonment of that right is consistent with the purposes of the trust....

THE RELATIONSHIP BETWEEN THE PUBLIC TRUST DOCTRINE AND THE CALIFORNIA WATER RIGHTS SYSTEM

As we have seen, the public trust doctrine and the appropriative water rights system administered by the Water Board developed independently of each other. Each developed comprehensive rules and principles which, if applied to the full extent of their scope, would occupy the field of allocation of stream waters to the exclusion of any competing system of legal thought. Plaintiffs, for example, argue that the public trust is antecedent to and thus limits all appropriative water rights, an argument which implies that most appropriative water rights in California were acquired and are presently being used unlawfully. Defendant DWP, on the other hand, argues that the public trust doctrine as to stream waters has been "subsumed" into the appropriative water rights system and, absorbed by that body of law, quietly disappeared: according to DWP, the recipient of a board license enjoys a vested right in perpetuity to take water without concern for the consequences to the trust.

We are unable to accept either position. In our opinion, both the public trust doctrine and the water rights system embody important precepts which make the law more responsive to the diverse needs and interests involved in the planning and allocation of water resources. To embrace one system of thought and reject the other would lead to an unbalanced structure, one which would either decry as a breach of trust appropriations essential to the economic development of this state, or deny any duty to protect or even consider the values promoted by the public trust. Therefore, seeking an accommodation which will make use of the pertinent principles of both the public trust doctrine and the appropriative water rights system, and drawing upon the history of the public trust and the water rights system, the body of judicial precedent, and the views of expert commentators, we reach the following conclusions:

a. The state as sovereign retains continuing supervisory control over its navigable waters and the lands beneath those waters. This principle, fundamental to the concept of the public trust, applies to rights in flowing waters as well as to rights in tidelands and lakeshores; it prevents any party from acquiring a vested right to appropriate water in a manner harmful to the interests protected by the public trust.

b. As a matter of current and historical necessity, the legislature, acting directly or through an authorized agency such as the Water Board, has the power to grant usufructuary licenses that will permit an appropriator to take water from flowing streams and use that water in a distant part of the state, even though this taking does not promote, and may unavoidably harm, the trust uses at the source stream. The population and economy of this state depend upon the appropriation of vast quantities of water for uses unrelated to in-stream trust values. California's constitution, its statutes, decisions, and commentators all emphasize the need to make efficient use of California's limited water resources: all recognize, at least implicitly, that efficient use requires diverting water from in-stream uses. Now that the economy and population centers of this state have developed in reliance upon appropriated water, it would be disingenuous to hold that such appropriations are and have always been improper to the extent that they harm public trust uses, and can be justified only upon theories of reliance or estoppel.

c. The state has an affirmative duty to take the public trust into account in the planning and allocation of water resources, and to protect public trust uses whenever feasible. Just as the history of this state shows that appropriation may be necessary for efficient use of water despite unavoidable harm to public trust values, it demonstrates that an appropriative water rights system administered without consideration of the public trust may cause unnecessary and unjustified harm to trust interests. (See Johnson, 14 U.C. Davis L. Rev. 233, 256-257; Robie, Some Reflections on Environmental Considerations in Water Rights Administration, 2 Ecology L.Q. 695, 710-711 (1972); Comment, 33 Hastings L.J. 653, 654.) As a matter of practical necessity the state may have to approve appropriations despite foreseeable harm to public trust uses. In so doing, however, the state must bear in mind its duty as trustee to consider the effect of the taking on the public trust (see United Plainsmen v. N.D. State Water Cons. Comm'n, 247 N.W. 2d 457, 462-463 (N.D. 1976), and to preserve, so far as consistent with the public interest, the uses protected by the trust.

Once the state has approved an appropriation, the public trust imposes a duty of continuing supervision over the taking and use of the appropriated water. In exercising its sovereign power to allocate water resources in the public interest, the state is not confined by past allocation decisions which may be incorrect in light of current knowledge or inconsistent with current needs.

The state accordingly has the power to reconsider allocation decisions even though those decisions were made after due consideration of their effect on the public trust. The case for reconsidering a particular decision, however, is even stronger when that decision failed to weigh and consider public trust uses. In the case before us, the salient fact is that no responsible body has ever determined the impact of diverting the entire flow of the Mono Lake tributaries into the Los Angeles Aqueduct. This is not a case in which the Legislature, the Water Board, or any judicial body has determined that the needs of Los Angeles outweigh the needs of the Mono Basin, that the benefit gained is worth the price. Neither has any responsible body determined whether some lesser taking would better balance the diverse interest. Instead, DWP acquired rights to the entire flow in 1940 from a water board which believed it lacked both the power and the duty to protect the Mono Lake environment, and continues to exercise those rights in apparent disregard for the resulting damage to the scenery, ecology, and human uses of Mono Lake.

It is clear that some responsible body ought to reconsider the allocation of the waters of the Mono Basin. No vested rights bar such reconsideration. We recognize the substantial concerns voiced by Los Angeles – the city's need for water, its reliance upon the 1940 board decision, the cost both in terms of money and environmental impact of obtaining water elsewhere. Such concerns must enter into any allocation decision. We hold only that they do not preclude a reconsideration and reallocation which also takes into account the impact of water diversion on the Mono Lake environment....

This has been a long and involved answer to the...questions posed by the federal district court. In summarizing our opinion, we will essay a shorter version of our response.

The federal court inquired first of the interrelationship between the public trust doctrine and the California water rights system, asking whether the "public trust doctrine in this context [is] subsumed in the California water rights system, or...function[s] independently of that system?" Our answer is "neither." The public trust doctrine and the appropriative water rights system are parts of an integrated system of water law. The public trust doctrine serves the function in that integrated system of preserving the continuing sovereign power of the state to protect public trust uses, a power which precludes anyone from acquiring a vested right to harm the public trust, and imposes a continuing duty on the state to take such uses into account in allocating water resources.

Restating its question, the federal court asked: "[C]an the plaintiffs challenge the Department's permits and licenses by arguing that those permits and licenses are limited by the public trust doctrine, or must the plaintiffs [argue] that the water diversions and uses authorized thereunder are not 'reasonable or beneficial' as required under the California water rights system?" We reply theat plaintiffs can rely on the public trust doctrine in seeking reconsideration of the allocation of the waters of the Mono Basin....

This opinion is but one step in the eventual resolution of the Mono Lake controversy. We do not dictate any particular allocation of water. Our objective is to resolve a legal conundrum in which two competing systems of thought – the public trust doctrine and the appropriative water rights system – existed independently of each other, espousing principles which seemingly suggested opposite results. We hope by integrating these two doctrines to clear away the legal barriers which have so far prevented either the Water Board or the courts from taking a new and objective look at the water resources of the mono Basin. The human and environmental uses of Mono Lake – uses protected by the public trust doctrine – deserve to be taken into account. Such uses should not be destroyed because the state mistakenly thought itself powerless to protect them.

COMMENTARY AND QUESTIONS

1. **Scope of the public trust doctrine.** Just what is the public trust resource that is being protected in *Mono Lake*? It clearly has not much to do with navigability. Is it the lake itself that is the public trust asset? If so, is it the lake in its original form, as it is today, or at some intermediate point? Is it the economic use of the water based on harvesting brine shrimp? Is it the brine shrimp themselves? The California gulls?

Mono Lake may stand for the proposition that the public trust doctrine is capable of reaching out and encompassing the ecological values of an entire functioning ecosystem. Does this mean all ecosystems, or just those ecosystems fortunate enough to inhabit a photogenic environment?

And note something else striking about *Mono Lake*. The decision apparently applies to *private* rights. True, the government of Los Angeles owns the water rights to the various streams flowing into Mono Lake, but it owns them by appropriating the water in the same way that those rights would be obtained and held by a private citizen. Does the public trust lie latent within private property rights? Marks v. Whitney, cited in the main opinion, held precisely that there was an inherent public right in privately-owned submerged lands, so that the private property owner was completely restricted unless the government gave permission to fill in the submerged lands and make them economically useful. What if you owned the oldest burr oak tree in Illinois, or the house in which Benjamin Franklin was born, or the land on which the state's oldest church was located, and in each case you wanted to bulldoze the property to make a profitable parking lot? Might the public trust doctrine apply with full force and litigibility to your case as well? What standards would apply?

2. **The terms of the trust balance.** Note that in this case, the state's Attorney-General argued against the applicability of the public trust doctrine. Why? Ultimately the court defined a public trust role for the state government that held it to a new and higher standard of decision-making. The state could no longer merely be a mechanism of majoritarian politics; it apparently now had enforceable long-term fiduciary obligations to an indefinite constituency including generations unborn.

After the decision in *Mono Lake*, what are the standards by which the public trust balance will be struck, to determine how much of Los Angeles' private water rights and how much of Mono Lake's public trust assets will be legally protected? There is a serious apples and oranges problem. How can two such disparate public interests be balanced? It is notable, however, that the courts have declared that the public trust doctrine cannot be abrogated, which apparently asserts that the trust obligations, whatever they are, must be substantively fulfilled. After *Mono Lake*, if you were an attorney for the Los Angeles Water Board, or on the other hand for the environmental coalition, how would you go about preparing for subsequent proceedings in state court to determine what actually would happen to Mono Lake? To what extent in that balance does the lack of prior notice of the trust's existence to owners of the water rights matter to you? Are public trust rights necessarily superior to private property rights, if indeed they conflict? If the trust balance results in a restriction of private water rights, do the losers have a right to compensation? See Chapter 9.

3. A reprise on *Mono Lake*. What further developments in California public trust law followed the decision in *Mono Lake*? The destiny of Mono Lake remains in doubt. The first few years following the California Supreme Court decision were unusually wet and the level of Mono Lake actually rose.[19] Then there was an extended drought. The Court had sent the case back to the Water Board to determine whether and to what extent Los Angeles should cut back its diversions from the Mono Lake tributaries in order to protect public trust values. Even if that task had been undertaken with maximum dispatch, it would have taken years before any final order actually changing the flows into Mono Lake would have been forthcoming. In fact, seven years after the decision, the Water Board has still not completed its investigations and its environmental report. In 1989, officials for the city of Los Angeles and the Mono Lake Committee reached an agreement whereby Los Angeles would abide by a court-set lake level and would give up some of its water rights, in exchange for assistance from the state in finding alternate sources of water. But controversy has continually recurred. An entirely new suit to protect the lake was successfully brought under two obscure provisions of the Fish and Game Code requiring releases from dams sufficient to re-establish and maintain fish populations below the dams.

There have also been developments in the principal case. While awaiting the Water Board studies, the trial court issued a preliminary injunction requiring that the lake be maintained at 6,377 feet above sea level, some two feet above its current level but still more than forty feet below the level it attained prior to L.A.'s diversion project. That case has now been expanded to encompass issues other than the balance between public trust and municipal supply needs (the plaintiffs have been concerned that their doctrinal public trust victory might be 'balanced away'). One such issue is violation of air quality requirements resulting from blowing dust created by exposure of shoreland flats as the lake level declined. Another is a claim to lake level maintenance on behalf of the U.S. government. The interest of the federal government has come to the fore because in 1984 Congress established a Mono Basin National Forest Scenic Area in order to protect the geological, ecological, and cultural resources of Mono Basin. The Scenic Area statute provides, however, that "nothing in [this law] shall be construed to...affect the present (or prospective) water rights of any person...including the City of Los Angeles." 16 U.S.C.A. §543c(h). For its part, despite a 1989 negotiated agreement and three trial court rehearings on minimum lake levels, the city continues to oppose the restrictions on withdrawal.

On yet another front, the State of California enacted a statute that makes as much as $60 million available to mitigate the cost to Los Angeles of finding a substitute for the reductions it will eventually bear at Mono Lake. The law anticipates innovations such as conservation, waste water reclamation, conjunctive use, and

19. This update is adapted from Sax, Abrams, and Thompson, Legal Control of Water Resources 588–596 (2d ed. 1991).

groundwater recharge. The idea of the law presumably is that state-wide sharing of the costs of finding alternatives will smooth the way to an actual solution of the controversy, and keep the legal dispute from continuing indefinitely. To date the prospect of money has not generated a quick or clear solution.

How will Los Angeles ultimately deal with its loss at Mono Lake? No one knows, and no one yet knows the extent of the potential loss. In an ordinary year the 10,000 acre-foot per year diversion represents about 15 percent of the city's total water supply. What are the current alternatives facing Los Angeles and other South Coast cities? The adaptation that would produce the least reverberations elsewhere would be reduction of demand through conservation. Alternatively, Los Angeles might purchase the water from other rights owners, most likely agricultural users. The possibility remains, however, that Los Angeles may use its Mono Lake losses to press for new water projects, in which case environmental concerns will simply have been shifted to a new arena.

The opinion in *Mono Lake* has spawned a number of interesting cases exploring the intersection of water rights and the public trust and further defining the balance between water needs and public trust interests that the *Mono Lake* court left for future determination. One case supported the state water board's requirement of upstream releases of water to protect the fish and wildlife of the Sacramento-San Joaquin River Delta against salt water intrusion.[20] A second significant case applied *Mono Lake* to an initial appropriation of water, permitting a requested diversion but imposing strict downstream flow maintenance requirements in order to protect public trust values below the point of diversion, primarily chinook salmon.[21]

The latter court's view of *Mono Lake* was that it –

> encourages and requires the trier of fact to balance and accommodate all legitimate competing interests in a body of water...rather than the "unbalanced structure" that would result from a flat preference for either instream or consumptive values.... Water quality [for municipal use] cannot be excluded from the analysis simply because it does not fit plaintiffs' and intervenors' conception of a public trust value. Neither, however, can the importance of the public trust be diluted by treating it as merely another beneficial use...co-equal with irrigation, power production, and municipal water supply.... Public trust doctrine occupies an exalted position in any judicial or administrative determination of water resource allocation....

The balance, in other words, still remains very unclear. In the arid West, waterfights tend to be longrunning battles.

20. [The "Delta" case, U.S. v. State Water Resources Control Board, 182 Cal. App. 3d 82, 227 Cal. Rptr. 161 (1986).]

21. [The "East Bay MUD" case, E.D.F. v. East Bay Munic. Util. Dist. (No. 425955, Superior Court, Alameda Co., California, Jan. 2, 1990).]

Section 3. HOW FAR DOES THE PUBLIC TRUST DOCTRINE GO?

The public trust doctrine asserts that certain special public rights and duties lie latent within various natural resources, whether publicly or privately owned, with consequences that can be dramatic. Once the public trust genie has been released from the bottle, moreover, it arguably can cast its shadow over situations previously unknown.

The following case unfolded in 1969, a short distance west of Colorado Springs, Colorado, where an accident of geology 10 million years ago had created a remarkably rich 6,000 acre area of fossil beds. The Florissant Fossil Beds, layer upon layer of paper-thin shales filled with biological artifacts, was a unique and nationally-famous archaeological site, featured in many junior high school textbooks. Congress, in desultory fashion, had been discussing whether to purchase the beds in order to create a national monument. Meanwhile, a group of private developers contracted to purchase the 6,000 acre tract. They had determined that in marketplace terms the area's best commercial use lay in subdivision construction, and the bulldozers were poised, ready to roll, to carve roads, driveways, and split-level foundations into the fragile fossil beds....

Defenders of Florissant v. Park Land Development Co. et. al.

(unreported) V. Yannacone, Environmental Law, 47-60 (1970)

IN THE UNITED STATES DISTRICT COURT FOR THE DISTRICT OF COLORADO

DEFENDERS of FLORISSANT, Inc., individually and on behalf of all those entitled to the full benefit use and enjoyment of the national natural resource that is the proposed *Florissant Fossil Beds National Monument*, and all those similarly situated,
Plaintiff,

vs.

PARK LAND COMPANY, CENTRAL ENTERPRISES, Inc.,
CLAUDE R. BLUE, *et al.*,
Defendants.

NOTICE OF MOTION

PLEASE TAKE NOTICE that the Plaintiffs will move this Court at the United States District Court House, Denver, Colorado, on the 8th day of July, 1969, at half past nine o'clock in the forenoon of that day, or as soon thereafter as counsel can be heard, for an order:

RESTRAINING the Defendants from any actions which may cause serious permanent or irreparable damage to the national natural resource that is the area included within the proposed Florissant Fossil Beds National Monument; or in the alternative,

DIRECTING the immediate hearing on the merits of the Plaintiff's application for a temporary injunction,

TOGETHER with such other and further relief as to the Court shall seem just and proper under the circumstances.

Respectfully submitted,
Victor J. Yannacone, Jr., Attorney for Plaintiff

VERIFIED COMPLAINT

The Plaintiffs, complaining of the Defendants by their attorney, Victor J. Yannacone, Jr., set forth and allege:

1. **Jurisdiction:** Jurisdiction of this Court is invoked under Title 28, Unites States Code, section 1331(a), "The district courts shall have original jurisdiction of all civil actions wherein the matter in controversy exceeds the sum or value of $10,000, exclusive of interest and costs, and arises under the Constitution, laws, or treaties of the United States."...

2. **Jurisdiction:** Jurisdiction of this Court is invoked under Title 28, United States Code, section 1343(3): "To redress the deprivation, under color of any State law, statute, ordinance, regulation, custom or usage, of any right, privilege or immunity secured by the Constitution of the United States or by any Act of Congress providing for equal rights of citizens or of all persons within jurisdiction of the United States."...

3. **Jurisdiction:** This is also a proceeding for Declaratory Judgment under Title 28, United States Code, sections 2201, and 2202, declaring the rights and legal relations of the parties to the matter in controversy, specifically:

(a) That the proposed Florissant Fossil Beds National Monument is a national natural resource.

(b) The right of all the people of the United States in and to the full benefit, use and enjoyment of the unique values of the proposed Florissant Fossil Beds National Monument, without diminution or degradation resulting from any of the activities of the Defendants or their Successors in interest, sought to be restrained herein.

(c) That the degradation of the unique National Natural Resources of the proposed Florissant Fossil Beds National Monument by the Defendants or their Successors in interest violates the rights of the Plaintiffs, guaranteed under the Ninth Amendment of the Constitution of the United States and protected by the due process and equal protection clauses of the Fifth and Fourteenth Amendments of the Constitution of the United States.

4. **Class Action:** The Plaintiff is a non-profit, public-benefit corporation duly organized and existing under Colorado law. DEFENDERS OF FLORISSANT, INC. is made up of scientists and other citizens dedicated to the preservation of this natural treasure....

5. **The Proposed Florissant Fossil Beds National Monument:** The proposed national monument comprises an area of 6,000 acres on the east slope of the Rocky Mountains. Located in a region of high recreation use and relatively close to a fast growing metropolitan complex, heavy visitation is expected.

The primary resources are the unique Oligocene lake beds with their plant and insect fossil-bearing layers and related geological features. These resources, combined with a scenic setting and secondary recreational and biological resources, constitute a relatively compact natural unit.

The ancient lake beds of Florissant preserve more species of terrestrial fossils than any other known site in the world. The insect fossils are of primary significance. They represent the evolution and modernization of insects better than any other known site in America. In addition, the fossil plants, emphasized dramatically by the petrified tree stumps and the great variety of leaf fossils, add greatly to the primary values. Fossils of spiders, other invertebrates, fish, and birds also have been found at Florissant.

The beds have been a famous collecting ground by numerous scientists for nearly a century and continue to be of great value for paleontological research.

The present-day vegetation is one of pine-covered hills and grassy meadows. In good years the wildflower display in June and July may be spectacular and is an acknowledged tourist attraction....

Geological History: Subsequent to the birth of the Rocky Mountains, 60 million years, ago, a period of erosion ensued. By Oligocene time, 40 million years ago, the mountains in the Florissant region had been reduced generally to a broad, gently rolling hill land–a piedmont of low relief and moderate elevation.

Volcanic eruptions covered the region with pyroclastics to a depth of 40 to 60 feet or more, and the drainage of the area was blocked, thus forming the Florissant Lake. The rolling slopes and the lakeshore were mantled by many types of deciduous trees and immense Sequoia groves.

Explosive eruptions and mud flows eventually filled the lake. The mud flows engulfed and buried the lakeshore trees which were gradually petrified. Insects, leaves, and other forms of life were carried to the lake bottom and preserved between alternating layers of volcanic ash. The source of the volcanic material appears to have been the Guffey volcano, 15 miles southwest of Florissant....

A number of the tree stumps, including large Sequoias, are exposed at the two commercially operated petrified forest areas. Some of these have been exposed by excavating around them. Many other stumps could be exposed by removing a very shallow over-burden. Some of the exposed stumps have fallen apart as a result of exposure; some are wired together by steel cables.

In addition to the insect, leaf, and wood fossils, the beds contain numerous microfossils. These occur in light-colored diatomited and sapropel laminae which alternate with one another, and in some places with light-colored pumice and graded tuff laminae. Ranking below the fossil insects and leaves in numbers of specimens found here are thin-shelled mollusks, and fresh water fishes. Several bird feathers and a few bird carcasses have been found.

Significance of Geological Resources: These deposits represent a small chapter of the geological history of the earth, but one very closely related to the present. What happened here in Oligocene times–the environment conditions that existed, the life forms that prevailed, the whole story–is written into the Florissant deposits. Scientists have revealed parts of this story; more remains to be told.

The rare quality of the Florissant site lies in the delicacy with which thousands of fragile insects, tree foliage, and other forms of life–completely absent, or extremely rare in most paleontological sites–have been preserved. There is no known locality in the world where so many terrestrial species of one time have been preserved. A total of 144 plant entities or species have been found there. Thirty of these are of uncertain affinity, but the remaining 114 are identifiable with modern species. Approximately 60,000 specimens of insect fossils have been collected here, the site having a world-ranking second only to the Baltic amber sites in Europe. Almost all the fossil butterflies of the new world have come from this site. Even the presence of fresh water diatoms in the Florissant beds is their earliest known occurrence.

The Florissant site has been visited by scientists for nearly a century, and almost all have expressed admiration for the quantity and remarkable perfection of the fossils discovered here. Textbooks of paleontology, historical geology, and entomology cite Florissant as an outstanding locality for fossil insects. Fossil leaves from here are noteworthy and have been described in paleontological and botanical literature. Probably no formation of such limited extent has ever been the subject of as large a body of literature as the Florissant lake beds (226 papers)....

In years of average or better rainfall, the wildflower display in June and July is truly spectacular; every open area is carpeted with paintedcup, many penstemon and crazyweed species, composites, mariposas, harebells, and other varieties. Under the aspens and in wet meadows may be found columbines, pedicularis, iris, shooting-stars, and many others. In August and early September, various sunflowers, groundsels, and fireweed take the place of the earlier flowers, and if there is a late summer rain, frequently this display is as spectacular as the earlier one.

There are many species of large and small mammals, including deer, antelope, elk, mountain lions, bobcats, coyotes, beaver, cottontail and jack rabbits, porcupines, one or more bat species, badgers, goldenmantled ground squirrels, chipmunks, Albert squirrels, whitetailed prairie dog, various mice species, and probably well over 100 bird species. In addition, there are numerous insect and butterfly species....

6. **The Defendant:** That upon information and belief, the defendants, individually and collectively, as their interests may appear, are the owners in fee of lands included within the proposed Florissant Fossil Beds National Monument.

Upon information and belief the defendants individually and collectively as their interests may appear are subject to the exercise of eminent domain by the United States of America upon final action by the Congress of the United States which, upon information and belief, should occur during the current session of the Congress.

7. **Defendants' Actions:** That upon information and belief, unless restrained by order of this Court, the Defendants, individually, or their Successors in Interest, will develop the area to be included within the proposed Florissant Fossil Beds National Monument, in such a way as to cause serious, permanent and irreparable damage to the unique national natural resource that is the Florissant Fossil Beds.

That the development of the region of the Florissant Fossil Beds in any way which involves road building, excavation, or covering the fossil beds with permanent dwelling units or building structures, will cause serious permanent and irreparable damage to the unique paleontological resource that is the Florissant Fossil Beds.

That there are uses of the area compatible with the private ownership thereof, and the preservation of the unique national natural resources, that are the proposed Florissant Fossil Beds....

That upon information and belief the operation of conventional building construction methods will cause serious permanent and irreparable damage to the unique national paleontological resource represented by the Florissant Fossil Beds.

That the development of the area encompassed within the proposed Florissant Fossil Beds National Monument by Defendants is not compatible with the maintenance of the unique national natural resources, that is the Florissant Fossil Beds.

Upon information and belief, the defendant Park Land Company, Claude R. Blue, Kenneth C. Woffard, J. R. Fontan, and M. L. Barnes, Jointly or severally intend to commence construction operations immediately which will cause serious permanent and irreparable damage to the National Natural Resource which is the Florissant Fossil Beds....

8. **Equitable Jurisdiction:** That this action is properly brought in equity before this court on the following grounds:

(a) The subject matter of the dispute is equitable in nature. This action is brought for the purpose of restraining the Defendants individually, and their Successors in Interest, from damaging or degrading the unique national natural resource that is, the Florissant Fossil Beds, within the area proposed for inclusion in the Florissant Fossil Beds National Monument. The injury which may be inflicted by the Defendants individually or their successors in Interest, if they are permitted to develop the area without regard for the unique national natural resources represented thereby, will be irreparable, in that it cannot be adequately compensated in damages. The declaratory judgment demanded by the Plaintiffs, together with the equitable relief related thereto are equitable remedies in the substance of character of the rights sought to be enforced or historically, in the province of the Court of Chancery.

(b) There is no adequate remedy at law. The law does not afford any remedy for the contemplated wrong to the American people resulting from the degradation of the unique national natural resources represented by the Florissant Fossil Beds from the development thereof by the Defendants and/or their Successors in Interest, in a way inconsistent with the protection of the paleontological, paleobotanical and palynological resources represented thereby. There is no plain adequate and complete remedy at law as practicable and efficient as the equitable relief sought herein. Nor would the damages sustained by the people of the United States as a result of the improper development of the area by the Defendants or their Successors in Interest, be capable of measurement and determination in any action at law.

9. **Trust:** That the Defendants individually and their Successors in Interest, hold the unique national natural resource of the Florissant Fossil Beds, with respect to its paleontological, paleobotanical and palynological values in trust for the full benefit, use and enjoyment of all the people of this generation, and those generations yet unborn.

That the maintenance of this trust is compatible with the proper efficient development of the resource represented by the area encompassed within the proposed Florissant Fossil Beds National Monument area.

That the administrative agencies of the Federal and State governments are incapable of preventing the irreparable damage which will result from the improper development of the region by the Defendants or their Successors in Interest without regard for the protection of the unique paleontological, paleobotanical and palynological values represented by the Florissant Fossil Beds.

That the maintenance of the trust is consistent with private ownership of the property and does not constitute any taking of the Defendant's property.

WHEREFORE, the plaintiffs individually and on behalf of all those entitled to the full benefit, use and enjoyment of the national resource that are the proposed Florissant Fossil Beds National Moment, respectfully pray:

That this Court take jurisdiction of the matter, and that a three judge court be convened to hear and determine this cause as provided by Title 28 U.S. Code, §2281, et seq. and upon such hearing:

(a) Grant judgment declaring the right of the Plaintiff and all others to the full benefit, use and enjoyment of the national natural resources that are the proposed Florissant Fossil Beds National Monument, without any degradation resulting from the improper development thereof by the Defendants and/or their Successors in Interest.

(b) That the Court issue such orders as will protect the unique paleontological, paleobotanical and palynological values encompassed within the Florissant Fossil Beds, pending the final hearing of determination of this action.

(c) That the Court issue such orders as will protect the unique paleontological and palynological values encompassed within the Florissant Fossil Beds.

(d) Together with all such other and further relief as to the Court may seem just, proper, and necessary under the circumstances to protect the unique national natural resources that are in the Florissant Fossil Beds.

Attorney for Plaintiff

[AFFIDAVIT]

STATE OF COLORADO, CITY AND COUNTY OF DENVER

Estella B. Leopold, being duly sworn deposes and says:

1. That she is a Paleontologist presently employed by the United States Geological Survey, and is personally familiar as a research scientist with the area to be included within the proposed Florissant Fossil Beds National Monument, and in particular the land and area presently being threatened by the activities of the Defendants with respect to excavation and road building.... [Dr. Leopold's affidavit then described and analyzed most of the material set out in the Complaint.]

The District Court dismissed the action for failure to state a claim upon which relief could be granted. The plaintiffs quickly appealed to the Tenth Circuit for temporary injunctive relief.

UNITED STATES COURT OF APPEALS FOR THE TENTH CIRCUIT

DEFENDERS OF FLORISSANT, INC., Individually and on behalf of all those entitled to the full benefit, use and enjoyment of the national natural resource that is the proposed FLORISSANT FOSSIL BEDS NATIONAL MONUMENT, and all those similarly situated,

Plaintiffs,

vs.

PARK LAND COMPANY; CENTRAL ENTERPRISES, INC., CLAUDE R. BLUE, KENNETH C. WOFFARD; J. R. FONTAN, M. L. BARNES; W. NATE SNARE, A. W. GREGG, R. MITSCHELE, MARILDA NELSON; DELBERT and EMMA WELLS; E. D. KELLY, JOHN BAKER, and their successors in interest, if any, as their interest may appear,

Defendants.

ORDER

Upon reading and filing the application of the plaintiffs herein for a temporary restraining order, together with the transcript of the hearing on the application of plaintiffs for similar relief before the United States District Court, District of Colorado on July 9, 1969, together with the oral application of counsel for the plaintiffs before this Court on this date, including a complete recital of all the efforts by counsel for the plaintiffs to secure the appearance of the defendants, Claude R. Blue and J. R. Thornton, individually and as partners of the Park Land Company, the principal defendant herein, including recital of the substance of the conference held among the parties in the United States District Courthouse Courtroom C on July 10, 1969, in which counsel for the plaintiff indicated he would secure further immediate temporary relief from the Circuit Court of Appeals having jurisdiction of this Circuit and the United States Supreme Court, and the representations by counsel for the defendants, Robert Johnson of Colorado Springs, that he would not enter a formal appearance under any circumstances in this action at this time, together with telegraphic notice at 10:00 A.M. and 12:00 P.M. on July 10, 1969, to Attorney Johnson, Claude R. Blue and J. R. Thornton, at the address in Colorado Springs furnished to plaintiff's counsel at the conference of July 9, 1969 and to which no reply had been received.

AND IT APPEARING TO THE COURT from the representations of counsel and the information contained in the verified complaint and exhibits annexed thereto, the affidavits submitted therewith of Dr. Estella Leopold, Paleontologist for the United

States Geological Survey, that the Florissant Fossil Beds represent a unique national natural resource, and that the excavation with road building or other construction equipment of these fossil beds will result in serious, permanent, irreparable damage and render the action for preliminary injunction pending for trial in the United States District Court on July 29, 1969, moot, and it appearing from the uncontradicted statements contained in the transcript of the hearing of July 9, 1969, conducted in the presence of defendants and their counsel and the similar representations of plaintiff's counsel before this Court, and that there will be no damage to the defendants by order of this Court restraining construction activities at the area of the Florissant Fossil Beds,

IT IS ORDERED that the defendants, jointly or severally, individually or collectively, or by their agents, servants or employees, their contract vendees or their successors in interest, be and are hereby restrained from disturbing the soil, or sub-soil or geologic formations at the Florissant Fossil Beds by any physical or mechanical means including, but not limited to excavation, grading, roadbuilding activity or other construction practice until a hearing on the merits of the plaintiff's application for preliminary injunction to be heard in the United States District Court, District of Colorado, on July 29, 1969, at 9:30 A.M.

IT IS FURTHER ORDERED that service of this order shall be made by the United States Marshal on any workman engaged in construction activities at the Florissant Fossil Beds forthwith and that personal service shall also be made on each of the defendants subject to the jurisdiction of the Court.

It is ordered that the effectiveness of the temporary restraining order issued by this court this date is conditioned upon the filing by the plaintiff with the Clerk of the United States District Court for the District of Colorado a cash bond in the amount of $500.00 for the payment of such costs and damages as may be incurred or suffered by any party who is found to have been wrongfully restrained during the period of the temporary restraining order.

ALFRED P. MURRAH, Chief Judge
JEAN S. BREITENSTEIN, Judge
JOHN J. HICKEY, Judge
United States Court of Appeals
Dated: July 10, 1969

[At the hearing for a preliminary injunction, the district court again dismissed the case. On appeal to the Tenth Circuit again, the appellate judges ordered that the above injunction be continued indefinitely, until further order of the Court of Appeals. The federal government authorized eminent domain purchase by a bill signed on August 14, 1969, P.L. 91-60, and the injunction remained in effect during the time that the federal government was acquiring the lands in question. The fossil beds are now a national monument.]

COMMENTARY AND QUESTIONS

1. The basis of the injunction? The injunction issued in the Florissant fossil beds case (which, it should be noted, is hardly a typical run of the mill environmental case) froze the use of the private land pending possible governmental purchase. What was the basis of the injunction? The court never issued an opinion, so the precise rationale is not clear. An injunction, in modern legal practice, is not itself a cause of action. It requires a foundation tort or other cause of action in order to be issued. In the course of oral argument in the trial court, the attorney for the fossil beds was asked by the judge what his cause of action was, and he replied that he did not have a clear cause of action. He was dismissed. The Tenth Circuit Court of Appeals panel later asked the same question, and attorney Yannacone replied, more or less, "Your Honors, if I told you that the U.S. Constitution somehow lay buried there in the fossil beds, would you let the bulldozers roll?" When the court said "Of course not, we'd issue an injunction," the attorney said, "Whatever you'd use there, I'm using here." Was it, in fact, the public trust?

The complaint uses the phrase "trust" in substantially the same manner as the public trust doctrine might be applied. Is that the basis of the case? Note that the "trustee," according to the plaintiffs' allegation, is not the government. The complaint asserted that the public trust resource was held in trust by the private owner, certainly a most disgruntled potential trustee.

2. The balancing process in *Florissant*. In the *Florissant* case, the environmentalists were attempting to hold up bulldozing of the fossil bed area until such time as the federal Congress would pony up the money to pay for purchasing it from the owners. Bills were proceeding in both the House and the Senate to that end, but the private developer, with an instinct, perhaps, for playing the role of environmental defendant to the dastardly hilt, reportedly announced that it was going to bulldoze some of the fragile areas immediately. The defendant corporation's only concession to the existence of the fossil beds was to offer to sell them to the environmental coalition for a price double what it had itself paid for the property the week before. If the environmentalists would not pay the 100 percent mark-up, the defendants clearly wished to proceed quickly, because eminent domain proceedings for governmental purchase, as we will see in the next chapter, would only pay them fair market value, which was presumptively the amount that they themselves had just paid for the land. In *Florissant*, the trust balance might have been very different if plaintiffs had sought to freeze the fossil beds permanently from development, without the imminent likelihood of governmental purchase that in fact settled the case. The trust balance may in that case have been a process of weighing the strategic time values of maintaining the status quo, as well as public and private rights.

Does it shock you that these privately-owned fossil beds were protected by the court with an injunctive order, freezing them from development, for aesthetic public reasons with no compensation required by the injunction? Chapter 9 considers constitutional takings issues at length.

3. Exploring the scope of the trust. Consider the following comment on researching the scope of the public trust –

> An initial obstacle in a state's active adoption of public trust theories, understandably, is the task of establishing the existence of the doctrine in the state's common law heritage. Courts may react hesitantly when faced with potent and unfamiliar legal doctrines introduced into litigation....

> The holdings of Supreme Court decisions clearly establish the existence and applicability of the doctrine in all of the states of the Union, while leaving the detailed articulation of the doctrine, in great part, to subsequent state adjudication.
>
> Often public trust law lies latent in a state's case law. Experience in Tennessee, which is not a leading state in environmental protection, may be indicative: In 1970 the public trust was an unfamiliar principle in Tennessee practice. The drafters of the 1972 water pollution act inserted the public trust concept into that statute (as to water quality only) but the effect of the trust language was not clear. When environmental law classes focused upon the public trust doctrine, however, they came up with a wealth of public trust law starting in the earliest days of statehood. More than 50 cases were found dealing with the trust (often in direct and express terms) in state parklands, lakes and watercourses, wildlife, roads and streets, railroad rights of way, subterranean water, and school lands.
>
> When the state's regional prison program subsequently proposed a diversion of state forest lands, cutting approximately 50 acres out of the center of a wild public preserve, the student researchers and local attorneys were able to marshal sufficient federal and state case law to convince the court that the trust existed, that citizens had standing as beneficiaries to enforce the trust, and that trust standards had to be complied with prior to any diversion of the resource.[22] Plater, The Non-Statutory Public Trust: Affirmative New Environmental Powers for Attorneys-General, Nat'l Assoc. of Attorneys-General Envntl. Control J., April 1976, 13–14.

The development of public trust law in California has been greatly influenced by the case of Marks v. Whitney, 491 P. 2d 374 (Cal. 1971). In *Marks*, the court applied the trust between two private parties to determine whether the owner of submerged lands could fill them in spite of detriment to private shoreowners as well as fish and ducks. In analyzing the trust, the *Marks* court wrote –

> Public trust easements are traditionally defined in terms of navigation, commerce, and fisheries. They have been held to include the right to fish, hunt, bathe, swim, to use for boating and general recreational purposes the navigable waters of the state, and to use the bottom of the navigable waters for anchoring, standing or other purposes....
>
> The public uses to which tidelands are subject are sufficiently flexible to encompass changing public needs. In administering the trust the state is not burdened with an outmoded classification favoring one mode of utilization over another. There is a growing public recognition that one of the most important public uses of the tidelands – a use encompassed within the tidelands trust – is the preservation of those lands in their natural state, so that they may serve as ecological units for scientific study, as open space, and

22. Marion County v. Luttrell, No. A-3586 (Chancery Ct., Davidson Co., Tenn., June 28, 1974). The case was finally resolved extrajudicially, without a statement by higher courts, through local citizens' political pressuring and dynamite threats against development of the forest resource. Citizen standing was also upheld on trust beneficiary principles in State *ex rel.* SOCM v. Fowinkle, No. A-2914-A (Chancery Ct., Davidson Co., Tenn., Nov. 2, 1973).

as environments which provide food and habitat for birds and marine life, and which favorably affect the scenery and climate of the area. It is not necessary to here define precisely all the public uses which encumber tidelands.... 491 P.2d at 380.[23]

4. The public trust doctrine: is it amphibious?[24] As the preceding excerpt from Marks v. Whitney demonstrates, the public trust in water resources has grown far beyond the traditional trust terms of Roman law. To what extent does it apply beyond water-based resources? Parklands are obviously included today, though unknown to Justinian. Why? What is it about parklands that makes them public trust resources? Is it an inherent premise of open, shared public use? During litigation over the state of Michigan's duty to keep oil wells out of a state forest preserve (West Mich. Env. Action Council v. NRC, The Pigeon River Case, cited at 422, *infra*), the assistant attorney general, arguing for the oil companies, asked, "Is all publicly-owned land now invested with the public trust, even dumps and highway yards?" It's a good question. If they are not, where is the line to be drawn?

Above the water line, the trust doctrine has been applied, at various times, to parks (*Paepke*, etc.); wildlife and archaeological artifacts (In re Steuart Transp. Co., 495 F.Supp 38 [E.D. Va. 1980] and Wade v. Kramer, 459 N.E. 2d 1025 [Ill. 1984]); beach access over uplands (Matthews v. Bay Head Imprvm't Assoc., 471 A.2d 355 [N.J. 1984]);[25] stream access, including the right to portage around barriers by traversing adjacent private land (Mont. Coalition for Stream Access v. Hildreth, 684 P.2d 1088 [Mont. 1984]); critical upland areas surrounding a redwood forest (Sierra Club v. Dept. of Interior, 396 F. Supp. 90, 398 F. Supp. 284 [N.D. Cal. 1974]); trees threatened by resort developments (Irish v. Green, 4 ERC 1402 [Mich. Cir. Ct. 1972]); trees damaged by oil spills (S.S. Zoe Colocotroni, 628 F. 2d 652 (1st Cir. 1980)[although these were water-based mangrove trees]); perhaps fossil beds, as we have seen; and more.

Take this not-so-hypothetical: after purchasing a painting by the renowned post-Impressionist Paul Cezanne for $900,000, two entrepreneurs in New York City announce that they have decided to cut it up into one-inch squares because their marketing analysis indicates they can sell off the tiny "authentic Cezannes" for more than $1.5 million. Could a public trust be argued here, or public nuisance? Who has standing to sue? What remedy – an injunction pending imminent public

---

23. "The public trust doctrine, like all common law principles, should not be considered fixed or static, but should be molded and extended to meet changing conditions and needs of the public it was created to benefit." Neptune City v. Avon-by-the-Sea, 294 A.2d 47, 54 (N.J. 1972).

24. See Scott Reed's article of the same name, 1 J. Envtl. Law & Litig. 107 (1986).

25. An active case law has developed around the question of public access to beaches, generally asserting the public's rights to use all beaches, sometimes including even the right to go over private land to reach the public beach area. See Matthews v. Bay Head Imprvm't Assoc., 471 A.2d 355 (N.J. 1984); Note, Public Trust Doctrine–Beach Access... 15 Seton Hall L.Rev. 344 (1985); D. Brower, Access to the Nation's Beaches: Legal and Planning Perspectives (1978). Massachusetts and Maine are anomalies, due to the courts' interpretation of a 1647 colonial ordinance issued under authority granted by the King purporting to convey private property grants down to the low water mark, subject only to a public easement for "fyshynge, fowleing, and navigation," but not for beach use. Opinion of the Justices, 313 N.E.2d 561 (Mass. 1974). There is some question whether the King himself possessed such authority.

purchase, as in *Florissant*? Would the same kind of theory be applicable to the protection of ancient petroglyphs – prehistoric human rock paintings – from willful destruction?

Once started on this road, the trust's complications abound, but the doctrine's recognition of intangible public values undeniably captures a piece of reality, the legal significance of a society's common cultural heritage.

5. The third category of public trust situations. Reviewing the list of different settings in which the trust doctrine has been applied identifies a third category beyond Professor Sax's alienation and diversion cases. Whenever the trust is used to support antipollution efforts (see Tennessee Water Pollution Contol Act, T.C.A. §§70.324 et seq., and State v. Amerada Hess, 350 F. Supp. 1060 [Md. 1972]), to prevent destruction of trust resources by public or private actors (see the redwood cases in the preceding note), or to recover damages for the destruction of trust assets (see In re Steuart Transp. Co., in the preceding note, or the state of Alaska's oilspill litigation), it is analytically focused on defense of the quality of the resource against derogation rather than protecting the character of ownership. Emperor Justinian, remember, began his list of public trust resources with *air*, for which issues of ownership are irrelevant, but issues of quality essential. In practice, however, the application of the trust analysis in this third, resource-defense, or "derogation" category parallels the alienation and diversion cases. The issue in each setting is to determine to what extent the qualities of the trust resources are to be preserved and stewarded against short-term exploitation.

6. Governmental use of the trust. Governments have often used the trust doctrine, most often to affirm the existence of their governmental powers to regulate, as in wildlife cases, where the state acts as trustee. In an oilspill case, for example, countering defendant's argument that neither the federal nor the state government plaintiffs "owned" the birds and ducks destroyed by oil, both governments successfully argued the public trust doctrine to win standing for recovery of damages. In re Steuart Transp. Co., in note 5, *supra*. The trust can aid in defending against regulatory takings challenges as well. When governments cite the trust in affirming their authority over a matter, however, might they concurrently also expand their active liabilities, opening themselves to trust suits by disgruntled environmentalist "beneficiaries"? This scenario may help explain the California attorney-general's enmity in *Mono Lake*, and why public trust law has generally been developed, like so many other areas of environmental law, through citizen rather than governmental efforts.

Section 4. THE PUBLIC TRUST AND PRIVATE PROPERTY RIGHTS

The public trust doctrine has major implications for private property rights, which explains much of the opposition encountered in the doctrine's continued development. When a gravel company is suddenly told that it may not quarry its lands because they are public trust wetlands, as in Potomac Sand and Gravel Co. v. Maryland, 293 A.2d 241 (Md. 1972), the trust doctrine can create unexpected economic losses, anger, and political backlash. Private property rights are far more sacrosanct, and public rights far less developed, in the United States than in any other modern nation – which helps explain some of the American economy's past dynamism as well as some of its environmental dilemmas.

Comprehensive consideration of conflicts between public rights and private property rights comprises the bulk of Chapter 9. For the moment, however, note how Professor Sax, as father (or at least midwife) of the modern public trust doctrine, framed this potent issue in evolutionary terms:

Sax, The Limits of Private Rights in Public Waters
19 Environmental Law 473, 476-478 (1989)

To understand the nature of the public [trust] claim on water, it is useful to look back to a time when the use of water to promote industrialization was considered a primary, if not exclusive, public goal.... [W]hen the public interest was seen as primarily developmental, people were permitted to use water in the service of development. They were not, however, being vested with a private property right that could be asserted against that interest when public goals changed. They obtained a right because they were making a use that was at the time compatible with the public interest. Their water right extended only as far as that compatibility.

This observation can be illustrated by reference to a famous (or perhaps infamous) old case, Sanderson v. Pennsylvania Coal Co.,[26] decided by the Supreme Court of Pennsylvania just over a hundred years ago. This was a property rights case about pollution. A coal company was mining and dumping its wastes in the river, and a downstream landowner objected, claiming that the traditional laws of riparian rights gave her a right to have the river flow down to her unchanged in quality and quantity. She also invoked the long-standing doctrine that each person must use his property so as not to damage the property of others. The coal company's discharges were plainly transgressing both these doctrines.

The coal company urged that "the law should be adjusted to the exigencies of the great industrial interests of the Commonwealth and that the production of an indispensable mineral...should not be crippled and endangered by adopting a rule that would make colliers answerable in damages for corrupting a stream."[27] Though the court at first refused to define the property rights in water to meet the demands of an industrial economy, it finally agreed with the coal company that the law should be "adjusted." On the fate of the plaintiff's property rights, the court had this to say:

> [W]e are of opinion that mere private personal inconvenience...must yield to the necessities of a great public industry, which...subserves a great public interest. To encourage the development of the great natural resources of a country, trifling inconveniences to particular persons must sometimes give way to the necessities of a great community.[28]

Thus the court recognized that property rights satisfactory in a preindustrial era must cede to the demands of the public interest of the time. When the public interest was developmental, traditional property rights in water – long-standing property

26. 86 Pa. 401, 6 A. 453 (1886).
27. 86 Pa. at 408.
28. Penn. Coal Co. v. Sanderson, 6 A. 453, 459 (1886).

rights to natural flow – yielded, just as they had before and have since in many other instances.[29] [T]hen, as now, the fundamental rule remains that beneficial use is the basis, measure, and limit of property rights in water. When uses cease to be seen as beneficial, however long standing, they are repudiated in favor of modern conceptions of beneficiality....

Sax, Liberating the Public Trust Doctrine from its Historical Shackles
14 University of California-Davis Law Review 185, 186-194 (1980)

It is unreasonable to view the public trust as simply a problem of alienation of publicly owned property into private hands, since many – if not most – of the depredations of public resources are brought about by public authorities who have received the permission of the state to proceed with their schemes. On the other hand, it is inconceivable that the trust doctrine should be viewed as a rigid prohibition, preventing all dispositions of trust property or utterly freezing as of a given moment the uses to which those properties have traditionally been put. It can hardly be the basis for any sensible legal doctrine that change itself is illegitimate.

At its heart, the public trust doctrine is not just a set of rules about tidelands, a restraint on alienation by the government or an historical inquiry into the circumstances of long-forgotten grants. And neither Roman Law nor the English experience with lands underlying tidal waters is the place to search for the core of the trust idea.[30]

---

29. See generally Horwitz, The Transformation in the Conception of Property In American Law 1780-1860, 40 U. Chi. L. Rev. 248 (1973). The strongest statement about limits appear in Justice Stewart's concurring opinion in Hughes v. Washington, 389 U.S. 290, 296-97 (1967) ("[A] State cannot be permitted to defeat the constitutional prohibition against taking property...by the simple device of asserting retroactively that the property it has taken never existed at all. Whether the decision here worked an unpredictable change in state law...presents a federal question."). See also Cherry v. Steiner, 716 F. 2d 687, 692 (9th Cir. 1983)("[A] state cannot validly effect a taking of property by the simple expedient of holding that the property right never existed"), cert. denied, 466 U.S. 931 (1984).

Beyond this, proposed constitutional limits on redefinition of property present a much knottier problem than may at first appear. It is not sufficient to suggest that only prospective changes are permissible. Otherwise property rules would be insulated from reconsideration, a result that the Supreme Court is unwilling to apply to its own decisions. For example, not long ago the Supreme Court itself suddenly changed the property rule that governs ownership of formerly submerged land when a river changes its course. Compare Bonnelli Cattle Co. v. Arizona, 414 U.S. 313 (1973) with Oregon ex rel. State Land Bd. v. Corvallis Sand & Gravel Co., 429 U.S. 363 (1977) (overruling the rule adopted in *Bonnelli*). The Supreme Court has repeatedly rejected the argument that a court decision changing state property law can, by itself, constitute a taking. E.g., Brinkerhoff-Faris Co. v. Hill, 281 U.S. 673 (1930); Tidal Oil Co. v. Flanagan, 263 U.S. 444 (1924); see also Brief of the States of Alaska, California, Montana, Nevada, North Dakota, Oregon, Utah, Washington, and Wyoming as Amici Curiae in Support of the Petition for a Writ of Certiorari at 8-12, Ariyoshi v. Robinson, 477 U.S. 902 (1986).

30. Roman law most likely reflects an effort at rational classification. The Romans began by classifying as conventional private property those things which were amenable to ordinary purchase, sale or inheritance. Then the Romans classified everything that could not be so categorized, i.e., temples, which were said to belong to the gods, public buildings, which belong to the State, and a number of other things, called *res communis* or *res nullius* – like the seashore and wildlife – which could not be said to belong to anyone.

In all probability, categories like *res communis* were a response to what the Romans conceived to be the physical nature of certain properties – things that were abundant and not amenable to private possession, and therefore not the subject of purchase, sale, exclusion or possession. While some of these things can be physically and economically privatized, in fact they were not privately owned in Roman times, and probably were not subject to demands for private ownership. The Romans did, however, grant certain persons some exclusive rights to fishery in the sea. They also removed small farmers from their lands and instituted larger-scale, slave-operated farms which were owned by rich persons.

The essence of property law is respect for reasonable expectations. The idea of justice at the root of private property protection calls for identification of those expectations which the legal system ought to recognize. We all appreciate the importance of expectations as an idea of justice, but our concern for expectations has traditionally been confined to private owners. We have tied the legal concern with expectations to private proprietorship and to formal title; and while we recognize that mere title is not enough to sustain every claim of expectation that is made under it, it is hard to imagine legally enforceable expectations unconnected to formal title. At the same time we know that, insofar as expectations underlie strong and deeply held legal-ethical ideals, they are not limited to title ownership.

In "The New Property," Professor Charles Reich introduced the notion that many things lacking traditional status as formal property – things like television or liquor licenses – in fact generate expectations quite like those that attach to traditional forms of property. Even interests that don't at all resemble ordinary property give rise to important values and expectations that cry for recognition, and sometimes get it. Much of the recent controversy over the federal highway program, and over urban renewal, was engendered by the prospect of the destruction of established communities. Similar problems are arising today with the inundation of established western communities by energy development projects. The root values that inhere in the maintenance of an established community have much in common with the established expectations that underlie the recognition of private property rights.

To put the idea of expectations in a broader context, one might say that stability, and the protection of stable relationships, is one of the most basic and persistent concerns of the legal system. Stability in ownership is what we protect with property rights; stability within a community is a major part of the business of the criminal law. Of course, stability does not mean the absence of change, nor does it mean political or legal reaction. It does mean a commitment to evolutionary rather than revolutionary change, for the rate of change and the capacity it provides for transition are precisely what separate continuity and adaptation from crisis and collapse.

Precisely the same point might be made from a biological perspective. The focus of environmental problems is not, as is sometimes suggested, the mere fact of change, which it is said environmental zealots cannot accommodate, but rather a rate of change so destabilizing as to provoke crises – social, biological, and (as we see in the context of energy prices) economic. The disappearance of various species from the earth in the natural, evolutionary process is totally different from the disappearance of species over a short time. The key difference is not the fact of change, but the rate of change. The essence of the problem raised by public trust litigation is the imposition of destabilizing forces that prevent effective adaptation.

The central idea of the public trust is preventing the destabilizing disappointment of expectations held in common but without formal recognition such as title.[31] The function of the public trust as a legal doctrine is to protect such public expectations against destabilizing changes, just as we protect conventional private

31. Land-use regulation, whether effectuated by private covenant or by public zoning, reflects a recognition of values common to the community. The regulations most often is a joint effort to protect values diffused among all property owners within the regulated area.

property from such changes.[32] So conceived, the trust doctrine would serve not only to embrace a much wider range of things than private ownership, but would also make clear that the legal system is pursuing a substantive goal identical to that for the management of natural resources. Concepts like renewability and sustained yield, so familiar to us in fisheries and forest management, are designed precisely to prevent the sort of sudden decline in stocks that is destabilizing and crisis-provoking. The legal system incorporates parallel concerns in protecting expectations, and it remains only to assure the legal principle's application more comprehensively.

I can put some flesh on these bare bones by referring to the historical experience that most clearly reveals the proper sources for the legal public trust doctrine today: the tradition of the commons in medieval Europe. A statement of regional French law in the 11th century declared that "the public highways and byways, running water and springs, meadows, pastures, forests, heaths and rocks...are not to be held by lords,... nor are they to be maintained...in any other way than that their people may always be able to use them." The wild places abundant in early settlements were commonly resorted to by members of nearby communities to cut wood and catch fish, to hunt and graze animals, to obtain peat and rushes from marshes, and brush and broom from the heaths. It was only natural that these places should be commonly available, since their common use was necessary for the maintenance of the feudal economy....

But as resources became scarce, objections by the lords to common rights were heard and were often the source of agrarian revolts. The peasants responded to these incursions with indignation: "Let the knights then feel our strength," one writer said. "[W]e can go to the woods as we will...to do there what we please in the clearings, waters, and trees." The [conflicting] claims did not ordinarily deny the legal or ethical possibility of private ownership. Rather, they asserted long-standing customary use and treated that assertion as a fact to be determined....[33]

Privatization and class separation were not the only pressures felt by the commons. The commons were also very valuable resources. In times of economic stringency, they became a battleground for sustenance between lords and peasants, a fertile source of controversy because their legal status was so often buried in a shadowy history of competing claims of title and custom.

32. I am persuaded that the absence of perceived destabilizing change is the underlying rationale for the...decision in Penn. Cent. Transp. Co. v. New York City, 438 U.S. 104 (1978), and Agins v. Tiburon, 100 S. Ct. 2138 (1980). By the time those proposals were initiated, sensible land owners knew, or should have known, that historical protection and open-space preservation were important public values and that they were increasingly being protected to the detriment of landowners. While it is impossible to specify exactly when owners will be charged with such knowledge, there comes a point at which expectations are being sharply disappointed. That is, at some point the imposition of such restraints is no longer seen as sharply destabilizing for the land-development industry. One might say the same about the long line of wetland-protection cases. As such laws become more and more commonplace, wetlands owners will not be able to claim an expectational right to develop as they did in the past.

33. In an English case of the 13th century, for example, men of the Archbishop of Canterbury of Mainstone complained that the Lord of Rochester stopped their ships going down the river and demanded a toll from them. It was argued that "they ought to give no toll...and ought to sail freely...and thus it was accustomed in the time of Archbishop Hubert Walter [in the past]." In response, it was said by Rochester, who sought to collect the toll, "that always from of old it has been used that, whether they were the ships of the archbishop [of Canterbury] or anyone else's, they were always accustomed and ought...to give tolls." Issue was thus joined, and the case was put to a jury for decision. Curia Regis Rolls, 15, No. 1079 (1234-1235).

This history of the commons does not demonstrate any absolute restraint upon the alienation of things comprising nature's bounty, for such things were frequently alienated away from community use. At the same time, despite alienation and formal ownership, mere title was not always sufficient to settle the controversies. One might have been able to trace a grant back a long time, but if common uses incompatible with the grant had developed, those uses had to be reckoned with. The more necessary the uses, the stronger the claims of justice that attached to the custom. By the same token, even long-standing uses could be attacked – sometimes for good and sometimes for base reasons – by appeal to claims of ownership right.

What brought disputes over the commons to crisis was neither title nor custom, taken alone, but the sharp disappointment of expectations, continuance of which was perceived as a necessity. A stable equilibrium was being disrupted by the rigorous application of laws and claims of title unjustified by any social or economic necessity.

The medieval customary law had the striking advantage of putting developed expectations, rather than formalities such as title ownership, at the center of attention. While such established uses were not determinative, the significance of the established uses to the sustenance of the community as a stable entity was, in one way or another, factored into the ultimate result....

To put these considerations into modern guise, consider the...case of City of Berkeley v. Superior Court of Alameda County.[34] Although the grantee's chain of title extended back more than 100 years, there was no claim of private use during that period. Thus the potential destabilizing effect of disappointing the grantee's expectations should carry less weight than traditional analysis would give it. At the same time, there was a long-standing public or common use. The court took actual use into account in fashioning a remedy, to be sure, but there is no established doctrinal basis for recognizing these values. The same notions may be influential in the Mono Lake controversy, where it is the recent destabilizing action of Los Angeles which is really critical, rather than the formalities of arrangements made decades ago.

I do not mean to suggest that the medieval doctrine of custom should be revived in the late 20th century under the name of the public trust. I do believe, however, that the public trust doctrine should be employed to help us reach the real issues – expectations and destabilization – whether the expectations are those of private property ownership, of a diffuse public benefit from ecosystem protection or of a community's water supply. The historical lesson of customary law is that the fact of expectations rather than some formality is central. Of course, title is not irrelevant where ownership is actually a surrogate for reliance and expectation and where non-recognition of title would in fact be destabilizing. Conversely, where title and expectations are not congruent, title should carry less weight. We do sometimes overtly recognize this point, as in the California cases of 1970 dealing with implied dedication of land permitting access to the sea.

Our task is to identify the trustee's obligation with an eye toward insulating those expectations that support social, economic and ecological systems from avoidable destabilization and disruption. Less acute intrusions should be selected where feasible. In dealing with projects proposed for bottomlands, for example, the trustee should ask whether they need to be water-based. Where the alternatives

---

34. [606 P.2d 362 (Cal. 1980), where property rights in submerged lands were held to be subordinated to the trust.]

include a solution which will sustain yields and support long-established human uses or biological communities, that approach should be required. Where traditional expectations must give way to new techniques or new needs, the transition should be as evolutionary – rather than revolutionary – as the new needs permit.

In our legal system there is always a question of separation of powers underlying substantive questions. In considering the rights of private property owners and their rightful expectations, we endow the courts with the final word. Since expectations so diffusely held are not explicitly recognized in the Constitution, courts have been less willing to take ultimate responsibility for public trust claims. Some courts have nonetheless found the trust responsibility to be a constitutional mandate to legislatures, based on the requirement that legislative acts be for public purposes. For these courts, a failure to recognize, or at least to consider and deal with, expectations could represent a failure to act for a public purpose.

But however appealing such interpretations may be sharp confrontations between courts and legislatures should be avoided wherever possible. The courts can do much to provoke a search for less disruptive alternatives below the constitutional level. They can assure that decisions made by mere administrative bodies are not allowed to impair trust interests in the absence of explicit, fully considered legislative judgments. Under the rubric of the legislative remand, courts can also press a legislature to fortify its decisions with a full consideration of less disruptive solutions. Finally, the courts can reduce the pressures that claims of private ownership put on public trust resources by looking to the history of common rights. The courts should recognize that mere unutilized title, however ancient, does not generate the sort of expectations central to the justness of property claims, and that long-standing public uses have an important place in the analysis.

With such an approach fully in operation, we could integrate legal doctrine and fundamental principles of intelligent resource management, instead of treating basic social decisions as if they were merely the province of a title examiner. We could draw sustenance from history, rather than viewing it as a sterile, manipulative game.

COMMENTARY AND QUESTIONS

1. Public trust skeptics. As noted earlier, because of its potential restrictions on public and private action, not everyone is enthusiastic about the public trust doctrine. See, for instance, Huffman, A Fish Out of Water: The Public Trust in a Constitutional Democracy, 19 Envtl. Law 527 (1989); Comment, The Public Trust Totem in Public Land Law: Ineffective - and Undesirable - Judicial Intervention, 10 Ecol. L.Q. 455 (1982); and Lazarus, Questioning the Public Trust Doctrine, 71 Iowa L. Rev. 631 (1986). Each of these expressed serious concerns about how public trust concepts would undermine normal market expectations about private property rights.

The trust's antagonists have not yet found a countervailing momentum to the evolution of public trust case law. At some level, no matter how uncertain its ultimate trajectory, the doctrine appears to fulfill some old and newly re-discovered needs.

2. A society's underlying expectations. When he says that "[t]he central idea of the public trust is preventing the destabilizing disappointment of expectations held in common...," Professor Sax is focusing on *public* expectations. When discussing the constitutional balance between public and private property rights, however, most commentators think primarily of private landowners' market expectations for what they can do with their property. Thus the holding in a 1988 Supreme Court public trust case turned in part on whether a state's assertion that it owned certain tidal wetlands upset "settled private expectations." Philips Petroleum Co. v. Mississippi, 484 U.S. 469 (1988)(deciding that it didn't, in an opinion emphasizing the traditional role of the states in defining their public trust; see also Shively v. Bowlby, 152 U.S. 1, 26 [1894]).

As environmental consciousness grows, public conceptions of public rights inevitably expand, and public and private property expectations follow suit. The United States has been learning to accept the end of the myth of the frontier, of unlimited resources, of the ability to walk away from mistakes to fresh terrain. The public trust doctrine reflects societal realities long accepted in other modern nation states, which have had to deal with problems of limited resources and high population densities. Does the public trust represent a tendency toward bringing American private property rights closer to those in other industrial nations' legal systems, where property owners generally have "privileges" to develop, rather than relatively unfettered "rights"? Does this prospect worry you? See Chapter 9.

3. What *is* the public trust? At this point, never mind where it is going. Are we in any better position to figure out what exactly the public trust doctrine *is*? Is it constitutional? Is it federal common law? Is it a Rawlsian, Lockian, "pre-political" natural right? Is it Professor Krier's constitutional right? Is it intergenerational democracy, mediating resource legacies over the years? Is it enforceable? Is it merely an administrative law "hard look" doctrine applied to natural resources? Is it like Burke's tree: we honor it for its years of growth, but also because we don't understand exactly from whence it comes?

C. STATE CONSTITUTIONS AND STATE ENVIRONMENTAL RIGHTS

Section 1. STATE CONSTITUTIONAL PROVISIONS

Constitution of the Commonwealth of Massachusetts, Article 49

The people shall have the right to clean air and water, freedom from excessive and unnecessary noise, and the natural, scenic, historic, and esthetic qualities of their environment; and the protection of the people in their right to the conservation, development and utilization of the agricultural, mineral, forest, water, air and other natural resources is hereby declared to be a public purpose.

The general court [legislature] shall have the power to enact legislation necessary or expedient to protect such rights.

In the furtherance of the foregoing powers, the general court shall have the power to provide for the taking, upon payment of just compensation therefor, or for the acquisition by purchase or otherwise, of lands and easements or such other interests therein as may be deemed necessary to accomplish these purposes.

Lands and easements taken or acquired for such purposes shall not be used for other purposes or otherwise disposed of except by laws enacted by the two thirds vote, taken by yeas and nays, of each branch of the general court.

Michigan Constitution, Article IV

§52. The conservation and development of the natural resources of the state are hereby declared to be of paramount public concern in the interest of the health, safety and general welfare of the people. The legislature shall provide for the protection of the air, water and other natural resources of the state from pollution, impairment and destruction.

Illinois Constitution, Article XI

§1. Public Policy – Legislative Responsibility

The public policy of the State and the duty of each person is to provide and maintain a healthful environment for the benefit of this and future generations. The General Assembly shall provide by law for the implementation and enforcement of this public policy.

§2. Rights of Individuals

Each person has the right to a healthful environment. Each person may enforce this right against any party, governmental or private, through appropriate legal proceedings subject to reasonable limitation and regulation as the General Assembly may provide by law.

New York Constitution, Article XIV

§4. The policy of the state shall be to conserve and protect its natural resources and scenic beauty and encourage the development and improvement of its agricultural lands for the production of food and other agricultural products. The legislature, in implementing this policy, shall include adequate provision for the abatement of air and water pollution and of excessive and unnecessary noise, the protection of agricultural lands, wetlands and shorelines, and the development and regulation of water resources. The legislature shall further provide for the acquisition of lands and waters, including improvements thereon and any interest therein outside the forest preserve counties, and the dedication of properties so acquired or now owned, which because of their natural beauty, wilderness character, or geographical, ecology or historical significance shall be preserved and administered for the use and enjoyment of the people. Properties so dedicated shall constitute the state nature and historical preserve and they shall not be taken or otherwise disposed of except by law enacted by two successive regular sessions of the legislature.

§5. A violation of any of the provisions of this article may be restrained at the suit of the people, or, with the consent of the supreme court in appellate division, on notice to the attorney-general at the suit of any citizen.

Constitution of the Commonwealth of Pennsylvania (1971) Article 1, §27

(Article 1, §27 is debated in the next case *infra.*)

The people have a right to clean air, pure water, and to the preservation of the natural, scenic, historic and esthetic values of the environment. Pennsylvania's public natural resources are the common property of all the people, including generations yet to come. As trustee of these resources, the Commonwealth shall conserve and maintain them for the benefit of all the people.

COMMENTARY AND QUESTIONS

1. Constitutional variations on a theme. There is significant diversity among these different state approaches to the declaration of constitutional rights. Which are clear, which unspecific? Which appear to be enforceable, and by whom? Which appear to be mere political posturing? Note how some of them resonate with the public trust doctrine. To what degree are they different from the public trust doctrine? For more on state constitutional provisions, see Howard, State Constitutions and the Environment, 58 Va.L.Rev. 193 (1972).

2. Judicial enforcement of state constitutional provisions. As Professor Krier has noted, just because you have a constitutional right doesn't necessarily mean that you can do anything with it in a court of law. The following case considers the problem of whether or not state constitutional provisions are self-executing.

Commonwealth v. National Gettysburg Tower, Inc.

Supreme Court of Pennsylvania, 1973
454 Pa. 193, 311 A.2d 588

[In this case the Commonwealth of Pennsylvania, acting through and by its Attorney General, sought to enjoin the defendant from erecting a steel tower more than 300 feet tall that would loom over a portion of the Gettysburg battlefield. The basis for the state's suit was the state constitution's environmental amendment, §27 of Article I the Pennsylvania Constitution, *supra.*]

...The chancellor, after making detailed findings concerning the location and characteristics of the tower and the neighborhood of the park, concluded that the Commonwealth had failed to show by clear and convincing proof that the natural, scenic, historic or aesthetic values of the Gettysburg environment would be injured by the erection of the tower. In order to reach the ultimate issue, the chancellor first found to be without merit the defense interposed by appellees that Article 1, §27 of the Pennsylvania Constitution – upon which the Commonwealth relied for the authority of the Attorney General to bring this suit – was not self-executing and, therefore, legislative authority was required before the suit could be brought....

By familiar principles, the appellees, as the owners of the site, may use their property as they please, provided they do not interfere with their neighbors' reasonable enjoyment of their properties and subject to reasonable regulations for the public good imposed under the police power of the State, of which there are none here....

Similarly, there is no statute of the Pennsylvania Legislature, which would authorize the Governor and the Attorney General to initiate actions like the law suit in the instant case. Rather, authority for the Commonwealth's suit is allegedly based entirely upon Article 1, §27 of the State Constitution, ratified by the voters of Pennsylvania on May 18, 1971.... [see constitutional text, *supra*.]

It is the Commonwealth's position that this amendment is self-executing; that the people have been given a right "to the preservation of the natural, scenic, historic and esthetic values of the environment", and "that no further legislation is necessary to vest these rights in the people."

The general principles of law involved in determining whether a particular provision of a constitution is self-executing were discussed at length in O'Neill v. White[35]:

> A Constitution is primarily a declaration of principles of the fundamental law. Its provisions are usually only commands to the legislature to enact laws to carry out the purposes of the framers of the Constitution, or mere restrictions upon the power of the legislature to pass laws, yet it is entirely within the power of those who establish and adopt the Constitution to make any of its provisions self-executing....
>
> Cooley's Constitutional Limitations (8th ed.), Vol. 1 p. 165 says: "But although none of the provisions of a constitution are to be looked upon as immaterial or merely advisory, there are some which, from the nature of the case, are as incapable of compulsory enforcement as are directory provisions in general. The reason is that, while the purpose may be to establish rights or to impose duties, they do not in and of themselves constitute a sufficient rule by means of which such right may be protected or such duty enforced. In such cases, before the constitutional provision can be made effectual, supplemental legislation must be had; and the provision may be in its nature mandatory to the legislature to enact the needful legislation, though back of it there lies no authority to enforce the command. Sometimes the constitution in terms requires the legislature to enact laws on a particular subject; and here it is obvious that the requirement has only a moral force: the legislature ought to obey it; but the right intended to be given is only assured when the legislation is voluntarily enacted."
>
> In Davis v. Burke, 179 U.S. 399, 403, the United States Supreme Court said: "Where a constitutional provision is complete in itself it needs no further legislation to put it in force. When it lays down certain general principles, as to enact laws upon a certain subject...or for uniform laws upon the subject of taxation, it may need more specific legislation to make it operative. In other words, it is self-executing only so far as it is susceptible of execution." 22 A.2d at 26-27.

The Commonwealth makes two arguments in support of its contention that §27 of Article 1 is self-executing. We find neither of them persuasive.

First, the Commonwealth emphasizes that the provision in question is part of Article 1 and that no provision of Article 1 has ever been judicially declared to be nonself-executing. The Commonwealth places particular emphasis on the wording of §25 of Article 1. See Erdman v. Mitchell, 56 A. 327 (Pa. 1903). Section 25 of Article 1 reads as follows:

> To guard against transgressions of the high powers which we have delegated, we declare that everything in this article is excepted out of the general powers of government and shall forever remain inviolate.

35. [22 A.2d 25 (Pa. 1941).]

However, it should be noted that Article 1 is entitled "Declaration of Rights" and all of the first twenty-six sections of Article 1 which state those specific rights, must be read as limiting the powers of government to interfere with the rights provided therein.

Section 25 of Article 1 should be read as summarizing the philosophy of the first twenty-four sections of Article 1, particularly when it declares that "...everything in this article is *excepted out of the general powers of government* and shall remain forever inviolate." (emphasis supplied.)

Unlike the first twenty-six sections of Article 1, §27, the one which concerns us in the instant case, does not merely contain a limitation on the powers of government. True, the first sentence of §27, which states:

> "The people have a right to clean air, pure water, and to the preservation of the natural, scenic, historic and esthetic values of the environment,"

can be read as limiting the right of government to interfere with the people's right to "clean air, pure water, and to the preservation of the natural, scenic, historic and aesthetic values of the environment." As such, the first part of §27, if read alone, could be read to be self-executing.

NATIONAL TOWER
Gettysburg, Pa.
GETTYSBURG
"Where history comes alive"
on top of the National Tower
Provisions for handicapped, deaf and blind
Foreign translations available of Sound Program

A brochure showing the tower

But the remaining provisions of §27, rather than limiting the powers of government, expand those powers. These provisions declare that the Commonwealth is the "trustee" of Pennsylvania's "public natural resources" and they give the Commonwealth the power to act "to conserve and maintain them for the benefit of all people." Insofar as the Commonwealth always had a recognized police power to regulate the use of land, and thus could establish standards for clean air and clean water consistent with the requirements of public health, §27 is merely a general reaffirmation of past law. It must be recognized, however, that up until now, aesthetic or historical considerations by themselves have not been considered sufficient to constitute a basis for the Commonwealth's exercise of its police power. See Kerr's Appeal, 294 Pa. 246, at 250.

Now for the first time, at least insofar as the state constitution is concerned, the Commonwealth has been given power to act in areas of purely aesthetic or historic concern.

The Commonwealth has cited no example of a situation where a constitutional provision which expanded the powers of government to act against individuals was held to be self-executing... It should be noted that §27 does not give the powers of a trustee of public natural resources to the *Governor* or to the *Attorney General* but to the *Commonwealth*.

If we were to sustain the Commonwealth's position that the amendment was self-executing, a property owner would not know and would have no way, short of expensive litigation, of finding out what he could do with his property. The fact that the owner contemplated a use similar to others that had not been enjoined would be no guarantee that the Commonwealth would not seek to enjoin his use. Since no executive department has been given authority to determine when to [sue] to protect the environment, there would be no way of obtaining, with respect to a particular use contemplated, an indication of what action the Commonwealth might take before the owner expended what could be significant sums of money for the purchase or the development of the property.

We do not believe that the framers of the environmental protection amendment could have intended such an unjust result...

To summarize, we believe that the provisions of §27 of Article 1 of the Constitution merely state the general principle of law that the Commonwealth is trustee of Pennsylvania's public natural resources with power to protect the "natural, scenic, historic and esthetic values" of its environment. If the amendment was self-executing, action taken under it would pose serious problems of constitutionality, under both the equal protection clause and the due process clause of the Fourteenth Amendment. Accordingly, before the environmental protection amendment can be made effective, supplemental legislation will be required to define the values which the amendment seeks to protect and to establish procedures by which the use of private property can be fairly regulated to protect those values....

ROBERTS, J. (concurring).

I agree that the order of the Commonwealth Court should be affirmed; however my reasons for affirmance are entirely different from those expressed in the opinion by Mr. Justice O'Brien (joined by Mr. Justice Pomeroy).

I believe that the Commonwealth, even prior to the recent adoption of Article I, Section 27 possessed the inherent sovereign power to protect and preserve for its citizens the natural and historic resources now enumerated in Section 27. The express language of the constitutional amendment merely recites the "inherent and independent rights" of mankind relative to the environment which are "recognized and unalterably established" by Article I, Section 1 of the Pennsylvania Constitution.

Prior to the adoption of Article I, Section 27, it was clear that as sovereign "the state has an interest independent of and behind the titles of its citizens, in all the earth and air within its domain...." Georgia v. Tennessee Copper Co., 206 U.S. 230, 237 (1907). The proposition has long been firmly established that

> [i]t is a fair and reasonable demand on the part of a sovereign that the air over its territory should not be polluted...that the forests on its mountains, be they better or worse, and whatever domestic destruction they have suffered, should not be further destroyed or threatened...that the crops and orchards on its hills should not be endangered.... Id. at 238.

Parklands and historical sites, as "natural resources",[36] are subject to the same considerations.

Moreover, "it must surely be conceded that, if the health and comfort of the inhabitants of a state are threatened, the state is the proper party to represent and defend them...." Missouri v. Illinois, 180 U.S. 208, 241 (1901). Since natural and historic resources are the common property of the citizens of a state, see McCready v. Virginia, 94 U.S. 391 (1876), the Commonwealth can – and always could – proceed as parens patriae acting on behalf of the citizens and in the interests of the community,[37] or as trustee of the state's public resources.[38]

However, in my view, the Commonwealth, on this record, has failed to establish its entitlement to the equitable relief it seeks, either on common-law or constitutional (prior or subsequent to Section 27) theories.... Moreover, I entertain serious reservations as to the propriety of granting the requested relief in this case in the absence of appropriate and articulated substantive and procedural standards.

MANDERINO, J., joins in this opinion. NIX, J., concurs in the result.

JONES, J., dissenting:

This Court has been given the opportunity to affirm the mandate of the public empowering the Commonwealth to prevent environmental abuses; instead, the Court has chosen to emasculate a constitutional amendment by declaring it not to be self-executing. I am compelled to dissent....

If the amendment was intended only to espouse a policy undisposed to enforcement without supplementing legislation, it would surely have taken a different form. But the amendment is not addressed to the General Assembly. It does not require the legislative creation of remedial measures. Instead, the amendment creates a public trust. The "natural, scenic, historic and aesthetic values of the environment" are the trust *res*, the Commonwealth, through its executive branch, is the trustee; the *people of this Commonwealth* are the trust beneficiaries. The amendment thus installs the common law public trust doctrine *as a constitutional right to environmental protection* susceptible to enforcement by an action in equity.

Each of the equivalent [environmental protection] amendments [in Massachusetts, Illinois, New York and Virginia] purports to establish a policy of environmental protection, but either omits the mode of enforcement or explicitly delegates the responsibility for implementation to the legislative branch. The Pennsylvania amendment defines enumerated rights within the scope of existing remedies. It imposes a fiduciary duty upon the Commonwealth to protect the people's "rights to clean air, pure water and to the preservation of the natural, scenic, historical and aesthetic values of the environment." The the language of the amendment is subject to judicial interpretation does not mean that the enactment must remain *an ineffectual constitutional platitude* until such time as the legislature acts.

---

36. See Snyder v. Bd. Park Comm'rs, 181 N.E. 483, 484 (Ohio 1932): "[W]e...are of the opinion that, to the extent to which a given area possesses elements or features which supply a human need and contribute to the health, welfare, and benefit of a community, and are essential for the well being of such a community and the proper enjoyment of its property devoted to park and recreational purposes, the same constitute natural resources."

37. See Georgia v. Pennsylvania R.R. Co., 324 U.S. 439 (1945); Sparhawk v. Union Passenger Ry. Co., 54 Pa. 401 (1867).

38. R.R. Co. v. Illinois, 146 U.S. 387 (1892); Sax, The Public Trust Doctrine in Natural Resource Law: Effective Judicial Intervention, 68 Mich.L.Rev. 471 (1970); cf. Abel v. Girard Trust Co., 73 A.2d 682, 685 (Pa. 1950); Restatement (2d) of Trusts §391 (1959); Broughton, The Proposed Pennsylvania Declaration of Environmental Rights, 41 Pa.B.Ass'n Q. 421, 422-23 (1970).

Because I believe Article 1, Section 27 is self-executing, I believe that our inquiry should have focused upon the ultimate issue of fact: does the proposed tower violate the rights of the people of the Commonwealth as secured by this amendment?...

The facts indicate that the proposed tower is a metal structure rising 310 feet above the ground. It is shaped like an hourglass; about 90 feet in diameter at the bottom, 30 feet in the middle and 70 feet at the top. The top level will include an observation deck, elevator housings, facilities for warning approaching aircraft and an illuminated American flag. The proposed site of the tower is an area around which the third day of the battle of Gettysburg was fought. It is located immediately south of the Gettysburg National Cemetery.

The Commonwealth presented compelling evidence that the proposed observation tower at Gettysburg would desecrate the natural, scenic, aesthetic and historic values of the Gettysburg environment. The director of the National Park Service, George Hartzog, appeared as a witness for the Commonwealth....

> I described it as a monstrosity. I advised Mr. Ottensteing that between all of the mistakes which I felt the federal government had made here, and all of the mistakes I felt the commercial interests had made here, nevertheless Gettysburg remained a very sacred symbol to the more than 200,000,000 people across the United States, and that an intrusion of this immensity would, in our judgment, be an absolute monstrosity in this kind of environment and I was very much opposed to it."

Mr. Hartzog offered eloquent testimony on the question of the tower's impact upon the Gettysburg environment....

> Q. Would it, in your opinion, be possible to measure the damage that would occur to this historic site if that tower were erected?
>
> A. Well, I don't think that you can measure these things in a normal system of values that we articulate in terms of dollars and cents. You measure them more in terms of matters of integrity and understanding and inspiration and involvement. And from this standpoint, I think a monstrous intrusion such as this tower is, into the historical, pastoral scene of the battlefield park and Eisenhower National Site and the National Cemetery and the place where Lincoln spoke, is just destructive of the integrity of its historical value.
>
> Q. And you are saying you can't put a price tag on those values?
>
> A. No, you can't. There is one Yorktown and there is one Gettysburg....

I would enjoin the construction of this tower by the authority of Article 1, Section 27 of the Pennsylvania Constitution. I dissent!!

EAGEN, J., joins in this opinion.

COMMENTARY AND QUESTIONS

1. A split decision on constitutional enforcement? As you count the votes on the different merits of this case, how many justices of the state supreme court were of the opinion that the tower did not amount to a violation of law? Clearly the tower won. How many of them, on the other hand, actually held that the constitutional provision was not self-executing? It appears that only the first two justices were convinced that §27 needed further legislative action. This reading of the court is supported by the fact that, like a number of other state high courts, the Pennsylvania Supreme Court has subsequently held that §27 of the state constitution is self-executing. Payne v. Kassab, 312 A.2d 86, 94 (Pa. Commw. 1973), aff'd, 361 A.2d 263 (1976).

2. The state constitution and the public trust. Note how the constitutional provision here was intertwined with the public trust doctrine, especially in Justice Robert's concurrence. How many of the justices appeared to accept that public trust principles were at least theoretically applicable to the private lands surrounding the battlefield? Did §27 add anything to pre-existing trust law?

3. Commercialization, and a parade of horribles. In hindsight, could you have litigated this case differently so as to have achieved a different result? One way might have been to remind the state supreme court that its decision could well spawn a rash of other towers surrounding the Gettysburg battlefield. If the image of the arrival of a thicket of towers and other tourist attractions (shooting galleries, water slides, cemetery-view ferris wheel rides?) would move the court, could it not draw the line here, enjoining the first tower?

One of the classic problems of public parklands is the way they attract the crassest commercialization to their boundaries – Estes Park at the gateway to the Rockies; West Yellowstone, Montana; and Pigeon Forge at the gateway to the Smokies National Park, with its Dinosaurland, Waterslides, Spaceship rides, Ripley's Believe-It-Or-Not, the Tourist Gardens of Christ, and the only hula dance-porpoise show in the Appalachians. Can the public trust doctrine extend to the surroundings of parklands, to protect park resources from the depredations of the tourist marketplace carnival? How about public nuisance? How about legislation? See (as usual) Sax, Helpless Giants: The National Parks and the Regulation of Private Lands, 74 Mich. L. Rev. 239-45 (1976). See also Chapter 14.

Section 2. STATE STATUTORY ENVIRONMENTAL RIGHTS: THE MICHIGAN ENVIRONMENTAL PROTECTION ACT (MEPA)

The Michigan Environmental Protection Act (MEPA)[39] is a rather unusual approach to environmental regulation. Principally the work of Professor Joseph Sax, MEPA is grounded on the belief that insular decisionmaking having adverse environmental impacts ought to be subject to judicial review and correction. Judicial relief to limit or forbid actions or planned actions can be obtained by showing that the action has (or will) "pollute, impair or destroy" natural resources or the public trust as it relates to those resources. Thereafter the burden switches to the defendant to rebut the claim of resource harm or to prove by way of an affirmative defense that there is no prudent and feasible alternative to the action that is consistent "with the promotion of the public health, safety and welfare in light of the state's paramount concern for the protection of its natural resources from pollution, impairment or destruction."

MEPA embodies an approach that encourages overall environmental assessment. It requires courts to consider wideranging environmental effects and alterna-

39. M.C.L.A. §§691.1201–.1207 (1970).

tives that may ordinarily be downplayed as a matter of regulatory convenience, cost externalization, or simply unintended oversight. Courts are authorized to issue declaratory or injunctive relief and may review administrative standards, directing that different standards be adopted if needed to protect the environment as MEPA requires. Damage remedies are not provided by MEPA; this omission was a deliberate compromise made to obtain passage of the statute.

Important statutory terms, such as "pollute, impair or destroy," and the term "natural resources" are not defined by the legislature. This requires the courts of Michigan to interpret the statute's broad language. In one of the first MEPA cases to reach the Michigan Supreme Court, Ray v. Mason Country Drain Commissioner, 224 N.W.2d 883 (Mich. 1975), that court found that MEPA charges the courts to create the equivalent of an environmental common law. In response to the defendant's claim that the statute was so broad as to be an unpermitted delegation of legislative authority to the courts, the opinion conceded that the legislature "paints the standard for environmental quality with a rather broad stroke of the brush, [but] the language used is neither elusive nor vague. 'Pollution,' 'impairment,' and 'destruction' are taken directly from the constitutional provision which sets forth this state's commitment to preserve the quality of our environment." 224 N.W.2d at 888, n.10.

Beyond the authorization to create a common law of environmental quality, another of MEPA's revolutionary features is the provision in §2 that states:

> **§2 (2).** In granting relief...where there is involved a standard for pollution or for an anti-pollution device or procedure, fixed by rule or otherwise, by an instrumentality or agency of the state or a political subdivision thereof, the court may:
>
> a. Determine the validity, applicability and reasonableness of the standard.
>
> b. When a court finds a standard to be deficient, direct the adoption of a standard approved and specified by the court.

Here MEPA expressly rejects the administrative law norm that courts should defer to agency expertise in standard-setting matters.[40] Although this power has seldom been exercised by the courts in MEPA cases, in one early case the judge literally rewrote the discharge permit of a small sewage treatment plant in order to reduce the noxious effects of its discharges on a downstream chain of lakes. See Lakeland Property Owners v. Township of Northfield, 3 ERC 1893, 2 ELR 20331 (Livingston Cty. Cir. Ct. 1972).

Perhaps the most difficult question that has arisen in MEPA cases is determining whether there is some minimum threshold of environmental harm that must be crossed before conduct is actionable under the statute.[41] Consider, for example, a case in which a road commission proposes to cut down a few trees at a forest's edge to widen a highway right-of-way to improve safety. How should this case be analyzed under MEPA? At some literal level, the tree cutting obviously involves the

---

40. Discussion of that deferential norm and its rationale is developed more fully in Chapter 11 Part B.

41. See Abrams, Thresholds of Harm in Environmental Litigation: The Michigan Environmental Protection Act as a Model of a Minimal Requirement, 7 Harv. Envtl L. Rev. 107, 114 (1983).

destruction of natural resources and, therefore, appears to establish a prima facie case. The situation can be analyzed two ways.

Under one view, the mundane nature of the act and its lack of significance in maintenance of the larger forest resource make it seem unlikely that the legislature intended such a barebones showing to constitute a prima facie case (that then forces the road commission to establish the affirmative defense of a lack of alternatives). One of the maxims of equity is that "the law does not concern itself with trifles."[42] Moreover, the prima facie case would be irrebuttable because the road commission would be unable to deny that it would be cutting the trees. Beyond that the affirmative defense is hard to establish if, for example, guard rails would provide similar safety benefits. In the end, the de minimis theory argues that the legislature could not have intended such small environmental impacts to "force" courts to require agencies or other defendants to alter their planned courses of action. Accordingly the "proper" interpretation of MEPA must either include an unstated minimum threshold of harm as an element of the claim, or define stautory terms like "natural resource" as having a more generalized meaning so that the "natural resource" is the entire forest and not the trees.

The other view is that the legislature was sufficiently worried about the cumulative effect of many small-scale decisions that the decision by a road commission to cut a few trees for highway improvement is precisely the insular decisionmaking that ought to be open to review.[43] Perhaps a guard rail is a feasible and prudent alternative that places lesser burdens on the natural resource base than tree cutting does. The potential burdens of incessant and trivial litigation have to be controlled by the wisdom of judges hearing cases. Rather than restricting the reach of MEPA, those judges must instead insure that small impact cases are not blown out of proportion.

In general, the courts have tended toward the threshold of harm approach. The tree cutting hypothetical bears a general resemblance to a decided case, City of Portage v. Kalamazoo County Road Commission, 355 N.W.2d 913 (Mich. App. 1984), that has become the leading small impact case. The key passage in that opinion states:

> The crucial issue is whether the threatened impact on the environment rises to a level which would justify judicial intervention. The Supreme Court has recognized that virtually all human activities can be found to adversely impact natural resources in some way or other. West Michigan Environmental Action Council v. Natural Resources Comm'n, 275 N.W.2d 538 (1979). It has been left to the courts to give precise meaning to the statute and to determine whether the proposed action can be found to rise to the level of impairment or destruction of natural resources so as to constitute an environmental risk and justify judicial intervention. Ray v. Mason County Drain Comm'r, 224 N.W.2d 883 (1975). A court is not empowered to enjoin any conduct which does not rise to the level of an environmental risk proscribed by the MEPA. As stated in Oscoda Chapter of PBB Action

42. De minimis non curat lex.

43. Note the parallel with the development of the public trust doctrine in Massachusetts which likewise aims to raising the level of visibility of decisions that adversely affect trust resources.

Committee, Inc. v. Dep't of Natural Resources, 268 N.W.2d 240 (1978)[dealing with disposal of toxin-contaminated cows]:

"That act does not confer plenary power on the courts to do whatever they may think preferable in environmental cases. Absent a finding that the conduct of the defendant has or is likely to pollute, impair or destroy, the court may not order another alternative even though it finds it more desirable." The standard, "has, or is likely to pollute, impair or destroy," is a limitation as well as a grant of power.

In determining whether the impact of a proposed action on wildlife is so significant as to constitute an environmental risk and require judicial intervention, the court should evaluate the environmental situation prior to the proposed action and compare it with the probable condition of the particular environment afterwards. The factors the court should consider include: (1) whether the natural resource involved is rare, unique, endangered, or has historical significance, (2) whether the resource is easily replaceable (for example, by replanting trees or restocking fish), (3) whether the proposed action will have any significant consequential effect on other natural resources (for example, whether wildlife will be lost if its habitat is impaired or destroyed), and (4) whether the direct or consequential impact on animals or vegetation will affect a critical number, considering the nature and location of the wildlife affected. The magnitude of the harm likely to result from the proposed action will depend on the characteristics of the resources involved. Esthetic considerations alone are not determinative of significant environmental impact. 355 N.W.2d at 915–16.

COMMENTARY & QUESTIONS

1. Standing to sue and targets of suit under MEPA. One of the deliberate choices made by MEPA was to open up the process of environmental decisionmaking and allow citizen participation. To that end the statute explicitly grants near-universal standing to bring suits by its provision that along with state officials and governmental entities, "any person, partnership, corporation, association, organization or other legal entity may maintain an action" for declaratory or equitable relief under MEPA. MEPA §2(1). In like fashion, the list of MEPA defendants includes not only governmental entities, but also private individuals, corporations, etc. The single notable omission from the list of potential defendants is the federal government.

2. MEPA as model legislation. Within a few years following its enactment, MEPA served as a model for similar statutes in six additional states,[44] but thereafter the concept seems to have languished. The failure of MEPA to be more widely copied is attributable, in part, to the enormous expansion in other environmental legislation that took place in the early 1970s. Some of the felt need for MEPA, the indifferent performance of environmental control agencies, seemed to have been addressed by the major federal statutes in the air and water quality fields that brought all of the states on board in the effort to control the most obvious sources of pollution.

44. Minn. Stat. Ann. §§116B.01-116B.13 (Supp. 1973); Mass. Ann. Laws, ch. 214, §10A (Supp. 1972); Conn. Gen. Stat. An. §§22a-20 (Supp. 1973); S. Dak. Comp. Laws. Ann. §§21-10A-1 to 21-10A-15 (Supp. 1973); Fla. Stat. Ann. §403.412; Ind. Ann. Stat. §§13-6-1-1 to 13-6-1-6 (1973).

3. The underutilization of MEPA. Despite its broad applicability and universal standing provisions, a longitudinal study of MEPA conducted by Professor Sax and a number of other researchers shows surprisingly small numbers of MEPA cases, with no more than a few dozen cases filed per year.[45] Those same studies reveal that the most frequent MEPA plaintiffs are governmental environmental enforcement agencies who use MEPA's injunctive remedies to supplement their other powers. Why are private suits uncommon? The evidence obtained from interviews with attorneys who have filed MEPA cases points toward the burdensome expenses of obtaining the expert testimony (often $10,000 to $15,000 even in relatively simple cases) needed to make out the credible prima facie showings. This also tends to explain the relative popularity of MEPA with pollution control agencies that have their own in-house expertise. Similarly, the absence of a damage remedy means that there is no potential fund of money available to help defray the cost of plaintiff's attorney's fees, making those fees a further disincentive to MEPA's use.[46]

4. A standard for threshold resource damages. The *Portage* two-part inquiry, with its accompanying four factors, has become the standard approach to the threshold of harm inquiry in natural resource cases in Michigan.

Have the courts altered the inquiry in a way inconsistent with the statutory language? Where did the term "environmental risk" that appears in both the language of the *Oscoda PBB* case and in *Portage* come from? The two cases are rather different in nature. The former was a challenge to the burial in clay-lined pits of the carcasses of PBB-contaminated cattle. The plaintiffs sought an injunction against the burial on the ground that the PBB could escape the pits and contaminate local groundwater aquifers. The decision in the case rested on a finding that plaintiffs had been unable to prove even a threat of such a release. Thus the risk language appearing in Justice Levin's plurality opinion is appropriate, assuming it is confined to using the word "risk" in relation to whether plaintiff has made a strong enough showing that the claimed resource impacts will occur at all. Is the concept of "risk" even relevant in discussing natural resource destruction, like that in *Portage* which is virtually certain to occur? See the discussion of risks in Chapter 2.

5. Assessing the Michigan experiment. The Michigan statute was hailed as a breakthrough in citizen reform of the environmental protection process, cursed as a disruptive attack on the state's economic integrity, and belittled as a minor procedural change in standing law. What lessons emerge from the Michigan experience to inform the statutory and common law development of environmental law in other states?

---

45. See generally Sax & Connor, Michigan's Environmental Protection Act of 1970: A Progress Report, 70 Mich. L. Rev. 1003 (1972); Sax & DiMento, Environmental Citizen Suits: Three Years' Experience Under the Michigan Environmental Protection Act, 4 Ecol. L.Q. 1 (1974); Haynes, Michigan's Environmental Protection Act in its Sixth Year: Substantive Environmental Law from Citizen Suits, 53 J. Urb. L. 589 (1976); Slone, The Michigan Environmental Protection Act: Bringing Citizen-Initiated Environmental Suits into the 1980s, 12 Ecol. L.Q. 271 (1985).

46. Plaintiffs, however, may be able to get expert witness and attorneys fees under equitable private attorney-general theories. See Chapter 11.

Chapter 9

PUBLIC POWERS AND PRIVATE PROPERTY RIGHTS: CONSTITUTIONAL AUTHORITY AND LIMITATIONS

Introduction

Government's role in environmental law is ambivalent. It is sometimes an environmental protector, and sometimes a destructive promoter. On one hand the power of the state can be a strong ally of environmentalists, since in most cases government actions are backed by substantial public resources and are presumed valid until proven to be unauthorized, arbitrary and capricious, or otherwise invalid. If, for example, a statute or regulation had established readily enforceable limits for cement dust pollution, Oscar Boomer might have had an easier time against the Atlantic Cement Company. On the other hand, environmentalists who question governmental development programs, like marsh-draining and highway construction, find them correspondingly difficult to oppose. Environmental legislation is a comparatively recent phenomenon at all levels of government, while official policies that subsidize development – land development, dam-building, agrichemical technology, highway proliferation at the expense of mass transit, timber cutting and log exports, etc. – have been around for a long time and are institutionalized in existing laws and agencies.

Accordingly, environmental law often becomes a struggle for the hearts and minds of government – of legislators, executive officers, and agency bureaucrats, federal, state and local.

Local, state, and federal governments each possess, as a basic attribute of sovereignty, the coercive "police power" – the power of government to force anyone within its jurisdiction to do or not to do things that the government believes would affect the health, safety, or general welfare of its citizens.[1] Thus government can prohibit you from dumping pollutants or filling a wetland, force you to sell your land for a public park or parking lot, or regulate your use of wilderness areas and wildlife. The police power includes, in other words, both physical and regulatory actions by government.

1. The police power resides in all state governments by definition, from which it has been broadly extended to local governments for various health, safety, and welfare purposes. The federal government does not possess a general police power, but the federal government exercises such a similar range of powers through its commerce, national defense, property, and other delegated authorities that its exercises of these powers are also at times referred to as "police power" actions.

Physical appropriations by government, eminent domain condemnations, are difficult to defend against. Government regulation can similarly be very forceful in its effect on private property. The toxics and pollution statutes already noted, and the array of statutes and rules studied later in this coursebook, are typically backed up by the prospect of fines, imprisonment, civil liabilities, or direct enforcement by police or other public officials. In the environmental field, mandatory government regulations are voluminous in number, and are often indispensable in achieving some overall management of resource problems, drawing lines and limits that private parties could never afford to litigate under the common law. Imagine the problem of defining in a tort suit how much chloride one plant can dump into a stream in a suburban neighborhood, then multiply by every stream in every locality, and hundreds of different pollutants, and it becomes obvious why some statewide and nationwide mandatory standard-setting is necessary.

Mandatory governmental requirements, by their very nature, lay heavy burdens upon regulated individuals and corporations, and are often bitterly resented, so defensive counterattacks against government actions inevitably occur.

Legal attacks upon environmental regulations are frequently based upon claims that they are unconstitutional in their effect upon private property. In this chapter the constitutional provisions involved in the combat between public and private rights are mostly drawn from the language of the Fifth Amendment to the U.S. Constitution (as incorporated in the Fourteenth Amendment for state actions and substantially replicated in corresponding provisions in most state constitutions):

> No person shall be...deprived of life, liberty, or property, without due process of law; nor shall private property be taken for public use, without just compensation.

Analytically, this language embodies two different constitutional rights applicable to private property: a right against deprivation without due process (substantive as well as procedural), and a protection against uncompensated "takings." Structurally, these rights are virtually identical. Whether the challenged physical action or regulations are state or federal, they are subjected to the same categories of constitutional attack in approximately the same manner.

Plater and Norine, Through the Looking Glass of Eminent Domain: Exploring the "Arbitrary and Capricious" Test and Substantive Rationality Review of Governmental Decisions,

16 Boston College Environmental Affairs Law Review 661, 707–12 (1989)

THE FOUR BASIC INQUIRIES IN SUBSTANTIVE JUDICIAL REVIEW

Dividing the areas of substantive judicial scrutiny [of governmental actions] into four separate diagnostic inquiries can clarify many issues of judicial review. These four substantive inquiries are discernible throughout the case law, and appear to encompass all nonstatutory substantive questions typically raised in judicial review of governmental action. Zoning cases, which offer frequent and familiar (if homely) examples of constitutional challenges, provide an area of litigation that helps illustrate issues in all four substantive categories.

1. AUTHORITY

A challenger to a zoning decision can assert the government's lack of general or specific authority to act. Such a challenge presents an *ultra vires* question, which clearly is constitutional. Ultra vires challenges involve substantive inquiry because they dispositively review the foundation of the right by which the government constrains private interests in the possession, use, and enjoyment of an individual parcel of property.

In the zoning setting, a plaintiff may attack a municipality by alleging that it has no power to pass a particular zone regulation for lack of sufficient delegated power under the state enabling statute, by alleging pre-emption of local or state authority, or the like. The same inquiry, of course, can be found in other kinds of cases throughout the range of federal and state regulatory actions arising under the police power and correlative powers ceded to the federal government. This inquiry is analytically a threshold question, not a focus on the particular merits of the governmental act challenged.

2. PROPER PUBLIC PURPOSE

The second category of challenges addresses proper public purpose. Zoning laws, for example, were originally attacked as not fitting within the "general welfare" component of the police power's classic triad of basic regulatory purposes: health, safety, and welfare. Once Euclid v. Ambler, 272 U.S. 365 (1926) established that the harmony of planned development constituted a proper, generalized public-welfare purpose, the attacks shifted to attempts to define further, particularized, improper purposes.

Such narrower "poison purpose" allegations have included, with varying degrees of success, claims that regulations were "purely aesthetic," were for "purely private purposes," were motivated by a desire to drive down land prices for future condemnation, were racially exclusionary or otherwise invidiously intended to discriminate, or, like some motorcycle helmet prohibitions, impermissibly protected individuals against their own rugged wills. Analogous attacks are regularly posed in other regulatory settings as well. This inquiry as to proper public purpose, too, is a form of threshold question, testing the propriety of the governmental objective rather than the nature of the actual decision itself.

3. MERITS REVIEW: MEANS RATIONALLY RELATED TO ENDS

The third category of challenges involves attacking a governmental action on its merits for lack of *rational relationship of means to ends....* Where the purposes of challenged governmental actions are perfectly proper, the design of an ordinance or the factual reasoning supporting a decision may nevertheless be insufficiently, illogically or erroneously related to achieving the purposes. Thus zoning acts have been struck down, as applied to specific parcels, when the lines drawn are found to bear no rational nexus to purposes, or when the pattern of regulation has insufficient supporting data or planning. The floodplain safety zone, for example, cannot rationally be applied to hilltop land; a residential zone cannot be applied to land that could never be used for residences.

Analytically, moreover, this third means-end inquiry may also incorporate "least drastic means" and equal protection review. Thus, when a zone discriminates against poor people or mobile homes, its distinctions and classifications can be challenged as not rationally related to the purposes of zoning. Beyond zoning, this third inquiry can be widely discerned in judicial declarations that governmental determinations and classifications must "have reasonable relation to a proper legislative purpose, and [be] neither arbitrary nor discriminatory [to satisfy] the requirements of due process," and must "rationally advance...a reasonable and identifiable governmental objective."

4. PRIVATE BURDEN

The fourth inquiry, the degree of burden imposed on the individual, is often the emotional heart of substantive review. Its most common manifestation is the allegation of "confiscatory" takings burdens in regulatory cases, asking a question basic to justice and democracy: how far can the collective power of the majority erode the property of the individual for the sake of public well-being? The usual answer in regulatory takings cases is what one of the authors has previously dubbed the "residuum" takings tests.[2] According to these tests, property owners must be left with a beneficial (or "profitable" or "reasonable") remaining use of their regulated property. These various versions of the diminution test require a fair amount of implicit balancing of potential public harms against private property losses, but, if such balancing is done, offer a workable and philosophically defensible test for application far beyond the field of land-use regulation. Of course, when physical appropriation of property is involved under eminent domain, the fourth inquiry is less a balancing than a straightforward measure of governmental payment at fair market value rates to compensate the burdened individual for property rights taken.

5. PROCEDURAL PROBLEMS

For the sake of comprehensiveness, it should be noted that courts also apply at least two different kinds of procedural scrutiny beyond strict statutory requirements. One type of scrutiny is the set of requirements owed to individuals in the form of procedural due process. This flourishing sector of constitutional litigation raises questions of notice, opportunity to contest issues at a hearing, the clarity of legal standards to be applied, and the opportunity to obtain review of the application of a law to a particular case.

The second type is that class of procedural requirements owed to the courts themselves. In order for federal courts to fulfill their Article III functions (and state courts their correlative duties), the processes of government must be such that they will produce a meaningful, reviewable record. Such a record must illuminate the basis of official actions and show whether the governmental actors have at least considered the relevant factors in reaching their determinations.

COMMENTARY AND QUESTION

1. An analytical approach to public-private property issues. The diagnostic categories noted in the excerpt are not carved in stone, but offer a useful analytical organization that can be applied to the often complex and confusing controversies surrounding exercises of public power upon private property, as noted in the following materials of this chapter.

2. Plater, The Takings Issue in a Natural Setting: Floodlines and the Police Power, 52 Texas L. Rev. 201 (1974).

Do you see why governmental regulations that violate Inquiries Number 1, 2, or 3 usually would be declared void on their face, while violations of the fourth are usually voided "as applied" to that particular land?

A. EMINENT DOMAIN CONDEMNATIONS

Eminent domain is one important subcomponent of the police power. Governments occasionally use the eminent domain power in the service of environmental goals, for instance to condemn land for parks. More frequently, however, the condemnation power is used in operations that do not take sufficient account of environmental values – cutting highways through wilderness, building publicly owned office towers in low-income neighborhoods, siting regional trash dumps or power plants, creating development parks in bucolic areas to attract industry, or (through delegation of power to private companies), condemning rights-of-way for power lines, pipelines, ditches, and drains, or taking private lands so that mining companies can operate strip mines. In each case, environmentalists would like to raise some legal questions.

Section 1. THE DOMAIN OF DEFERENCE

The power of the public to appropriate private property via condemnation is a universal attribute of sovereign governments, clearly necessary to the functioning of a modern state.[3] As a result, governmental eminent domain decisions in the United States have generally received a most respectful reception in courts, both state and federal. Given that the government concedes that it will pay just compensation for a taking, many courts in effect declare that they have no further questions.[4] The governmental agency's assertions of condemning authority, proper public purpose, and rational choice of means are, in practice, "well-nigh unassailable."[5]

The usual eminent-domain case is cut and dried. The condemning entity files a complaint in court against a parcel of land; the "remedy" sought is a court order transferring title. For the condemnation to succeed, the court need only be convinced:

1) That the condemning entity, which is normally either a unit of government or a public utility, has the power of eminent domain

3. Kohl v. United States, 91 U.S. 367, 371–372 (1875); the following text has been adapted from Plater and Norine, Through the Looking Glass of Eminent Domain: Exploring the "Arbitrary and Capricious" Test and Substantive Rationality Review of Governmental Decisions," 16 Envtl Aff. L. Rev. 661, 662-663 (1989)(hereafter "Looking Glass").

4. The general invulnerability of eminent domain appears to exist irrespective of which level of condemning authority is involved – federal, state, local, or public utility corporation. Analytically, as well, there are no meaningful differences between these condemnors. Each must have a proper grant of authority and must satisfy the other three categories of police power tests. Judicial review of the rationality of the condemnor's site-selection choice is typically very deferential. In most cases, condemnees cannot require a specific showing why a particular site was not chosen. The Colorado Supreme Court, however, has suggested that public utility condemnations may deserve more scrutiny than governmental takings. Arizona-Colorado Land & Cattle Co. v. District Court, 511 P.2d 23, 24–25 (Colo. 1975).

5. Berman v. Parker, 348 U.S. 26, 35 (1954).

under the applicable statutes, and follows the necessary procedures for its exercise;

2) that the condemnation is for a stated proper public purpose;
3) that the condemnation decision is not "arbitrary and capricious," (or, in some states, whether the condemnation is "necessary," usually an inquiry at the level of "Are highways necessary?" rather than "Is this particular land essential if a highway is to be built?"); and
4) that appropriate just compensation will be paid.

The location, amount of land to be taken, and ecological effects of condemnations are normally not open to question. In the vast majority of cases, then, the opponents of condemnation can only stand and fight on the issue of damages, which is to say the amount of compensation. They can only try to make the taking more expensive. This is often impossible for environmentalists, who do not own the subject property, and it is not very satisfying anyway, since money may be small comfort for the loss of a marsh or forest.

Section 2. CHALLENGING AN EMINENT DOMAIN CONDEMNATION

The wonder is that eminent domain condemnation, a governmental power that is so drastic and has such wide-ranging consequences, has been subjected to so little active judicial scrutiny. There are a variety of legal avenues, however, that potentially may be used to open up governmental eminent domain decisions to substantive judicial review, giving challengers the opportunity to nullify condemnations on the merits.

The primary target of such substantive challenges is the question of rationality or arbitrariness. If a court allows propertyowners a serious hearing on their claim of irrationality, and weighs that defense according to the standard tests of arbitrariness applied in other administrative law settings, substantive challenges can be successful.

One approach is available where propertyowners can claim that their land serves quasi-public environmental purposes. When one government tries to condemn another governmental entity's property, courts determine the winner under the "paramount public use" balance. Several courts have extended this defense to private lands.[6]

More broadly, some state courts matter-of-factly allow defenses alleging that a particular taking is "unnecessary."[7] Viewed analytically, however, there seem to be compelling arguments for a lessening of deference in federal and state courts generally.

Two hypothetical cases[8] help to set out the legal basis for serious substantive review of condemnation decisions.

---

6. Texas Eastern Transm. Co. v. Wildlife Preserves, 225 A.2d 130 (N.J. 1966); Merrill v. City of Manchester, 499 A.2d 216 (N.H. 1985)(the court weighed the "recreational, scenic and ecological importance" of the private land dedicated to open space preservation, against a proposed town industrial park taking); Oxford County Agricultural Society v. School District, 211 A.2d 893 (Me. 1965), and Middlebury College v. Central Power Corporation 143 A. 384 (Vt. 1928).

7. See Plater and Norine, Looking Glass, 16 Envtl. Aff. L. Rev. 661, 689–693.

8. The text is adapted from Plater and Norine, Looking Glass, at 671–677.

A MEANS-ENDS FACTUAL IMPLAUSIBILITY CASE

Assume that a federal agency with a clear grant of authority to condemn for statutory purposes, and an express statutory mandate to "promote regional economic development and water recreation," decides to build a public works project centered upon a dam and reservoir that will flood 8000 acres of river-valley lands. In rational-basis terms, there can be no realistic legal challenge to the forced sale of these 8000 acres and perhaps another 2000 acres necessary for use and operation of the reservoir. Taking those 10,000 acres is a direct and rational means for achieving the purposes of creating a reservoir. Assume that the agency, however, seeks to condemn a further *forty square miles* of adjacent land beyond the projected reservoir pool and service area, with the avowed objective of "shoreland industrial development," promoting the location of new water-based private industry in the area and new towns to serve the industrial parks.

This hypothetical is, in fact, the case of the Tennessee Valley Authority's Columbia Dam on the Duck River, as well as that of the Tellico Dam imbroglio.[9] In these circumstances, the 300 families whose forty square miles of farm land are being condemned for future non-reservoir shoreland development would typically voice a barrage of complaints: that this is a "land-grab," a taking of private land to be turned over to other private interests, a taking of "excess" land, a "socialistic" governmental land speculation, and so on. Defense attorneys in eminent domain cases have turned all of these kinds of verbal complaints into defensive legal arguments, all focused on alleged improper public purposes, and all dead losers.

Assume, however, one more fact: that the agency has previously used exactly the same rationale to condemn and hold a total of more than 200 square miles of non-reservoir dryland parcels in four other neighboring public works dam projects over the past twenty-five years, and that virtually no such industrial development has occurred therein. The condemnation defendants realistically cannot argue that industrial development is not a proper public policy or public purpose, but they do now have available a further argument: that they should be able to go forward with an offer of proof that condemnation of their lands is not rationally related to the accomplishment of the agency's expressed public purpose. That is, whereas a court initially could well have deferred to the agency's "experience and expertise" or "experimentation" as bases for allowing the first shorelands development projects, now that the factual record clearly shows the implausibility of ever achieving those purposes, private property owners must be allowed at least a practical chance to challenge the rational basis of such condemnations in court.

The private property owners would then attempt to produce a substantial quantum of evidence based on actual practical experience, demonstrating that the condemnation of their parcels did not actually serve the purpose of shoreland industrial development....

In brief, the private property owners' defense is that, based on the factual record,

9. By acquiring more than sixty square miles for the Tellico project, only 16,000 acres of which would be flooded even during the summer, TVA projected that it could resell up to 35 square miles of condemned farmlands to a hypothetical industrial city to be called "Timberlake," theoretically to be built by the Boeing Corporation with congressional subsidies.

no governmental official could reasonably believe that the governmental choice of means – condemnation of these lands – would achieve the avowed governmental ends of industrial development for the valley. Such a case is not a question of "excess condemnation"; rather, it is a case straightforwardly questioning the rational basis of the condemnation's basic shoreland development premise itself.

The fundamental problem of modern eminent domain law, however, is that, at least in practical terms, under the deferential standard of review applied in condemnation takings the defendants in most federal courts today would not be able to take even this first step. The agency's discretion and the rationality of its decisions to condemn, short of lunacy, are supported in court by a practically irrefutable presumption of validity. Many state courts, though not all, follow the federal courts' extremely deferential example.

A RATIONAL ALTERNATIVES CASE

The second paradigm requires the reviewing court to apply the rationality rule in a contextual setting, reviewing how an agency has chosen between several competing alternatives that admittedly would each achieve the public purpose. Poletown Neighborhood Council v. City of Detroit illustrates this paradigm.[10]

Assume that a federal redevelopment agency, working through the auspices of a city government, decides to encourage the construction of a new job-creating, manufacturing plant within city limits. It decides to condemn and raze an urban neighborhood of fifty square blocks – containing 1,100 homes, 144 businesses, 16 churches including two cathedrals, two schools, and a hospital – causing a substantial amount of personal and commercial distress, in order to turn over the 500-acre parcel to a major automobile manufacturer for construction of a Cadillac assembly plant.

The property owners might, as usual, attack the taking as based on an improper public purpose – a "private use," for example – and, as usual, would lose. They might argue further that condemnation payments will never provide sufficient funds for replacement of their homes and businesses at relocated sites, but, in the absence of special statutory provisions, this argument also fails because just compensation is assessed according to the market value of what is taken with no guarantee of relocation or replacement costs.

Assume further, however, that at the time the officials decided to condemn and raze the neighborhood there were at least four other empty industrial sites of 500 acres each available within city limits with equivalent access to rail, highways, and utilities. The landowners may now make a further argument: that, given the drastic burden imposed upon them, and the available alternative sites that cannot be

10. See 304 N.W.2d 455 (Mich. 1981)(per curiam); see also Crosby v. Young, 512 F. Supp. 1363, 1374 (E.D. Mich. 1981). For a factual chronicle of Poletown, see Poletown, 304 N.W.2d at 464–71 (Ryan, J., dissenting). See Jeanie Wylie, Poletown: Community Betrayed, Univ. of Illinois Press (1989); Bukowczyk, The Decline and Fall of a Detroit Neighborhood: Poletown vs. GM and the City of Detroit, 41 Wash. & Lee L. Rev. 49 (1984); Poletown Lives, (documentary film), Information Factory, 3512 Courville St., Detroit MI 48224. General Motors, despite the desperate efforts of property owners and Ralph Nader, successfully induced a federally-funded redevelopment condemnation project to give the corporation land in Poletown, a stable, mixed-race, low income neighborhood of Detroit, to build a Cadillac plant.

DAVID C. TURNLEY, DETROIT FREE PRESS

Detroit's Poletown area, before and after. General Motors and the city used eminent domain powers to eliminate everything standing on the 465 acres of this integrated low-income residential-commercial neighborhood – the homes of 4,200 people, 144 local businesses, 16 churches, two schools, and a hospital – in order to build a Cadillac assembly plant, despite the existence of alternative undeveloped industrial park sites in the area.

rationally distinguished from their neighborhood's site (except that they are *less* expensive to develop given the cost of condemnation to the city), no official could rationally have chosen to condemn their homes and businesses rather than go to one of the other four open sites.[11]

Such an argument is *not* a means-end argument that the condemnation of Parcel A will not in fact or logic serve the avowed public purpose of industrial development, but rather that, viewed in the factual context of drastic costs and available alternative sites B, C, D, and E, no rational official could have picked A. This version of rationality review is analytically more complex and difficult, dealing not with a basic factual implausibility but with a judicial cost-benefit-alternatives review. In effect, it involves judicial acknowledgment of a "less-drastic-means" inquiry in review of some governmental condemnation actions. Deference to governmental decisions is an even greater consideration here, but the fundamental question remains: if to serve the legitimate, expressed public purpose of industrial development a site must be chosen, but in light of the disproportionate private and public burdens no rational official could have thought that Parcel A was preferable for that legitimate purpose, does not a defendant have the right to ask a court to scrutinize the substance of the condemnation decision and rescind it if it fails the test?

These two paradigms present instances in which private property owners would want at least the opportunity to go forward with the burden of proving that a governmental decision is not rational, in terms showing that a rational official could not so have decided. In both these cases, however, the "arbitrary and capricious" standard would be honored in the breach. Federal courts currently do not take on a particularized rational basis scrutiny of governmental condemnation decisions, but instead defer in general terms to the exercise of official discretion, leaving condemnation defendants with no practical substantive review of takings decisions.

The paradigms are admittedly rather extreme examples of eminent domain condemnation, but such cases permit clearer insights into condemnation review. Lest they be thought hyperbolic, moreover, it should be remembered that both have actually occurred and may well occur again.

11. "The Poletown environmental impact statement identified nine potential sites for the Cadillac factory, but, from the beginning, General Motors' site criteria were so particular to the Poletown site that only it would fit. The company demanded 'an area of between 450 and 500 acres; a rectangular shape (3/4 mile by 1 mile); access to a long-haul railroad line; and access to the freeway system.'" 304 N.W.2d at 460 (Fitzgerald, J., dissenting).

Never clarified in the legal battle was the fact that others of the nine potential sites were basically "green field" sites fitting all but the rectangular criterion. In addition, they were also empty of houses, churches, and small businesses and thus available without the massive disruption of Poletown; but they all were rejected at GM's insistence, basically because they were not rectangular. Was shape a critical or a superficial requirement? When Detroit's planning office staffers inquired informally of GM, they were told that the corporation was insisting on a rectangle so that it could use the same blueprint layout of parking lots and assembly units as at an existing GM plant in Oklahoma. But could not the design of parking lots be shifted to fit the shape of the existing Detroit industrial sites? They could, the GM staff said, or a parking structure could be built instead of open lots to accommodate the plant worker's needs at the less disruptive sites. But GM adamantly refused to consider shifting the parking lot layout or building a parking structure. The latter could cause congestion, and either would require a modification of the Oklahoma blueprints, which the company simply declined to do. 'Once we had decided what we wanted, we would not retrench,' said one GM employee." Plater & Norine, Through the Looking Glass of Eminent Domain: Exploring the "Arbitrary and Capricious" Test and Substantive Rationality Review of Governmental Decisions, 16 Envtl. Aff. L. Rev. at 675, n. 37.

COMMENTARY AND QUESTIONS

1. The legal basis for more active review. The excerpted article goes on at interminable length with an analysis of the two cases, examining substantive rationality review of condemnation decisions based upon substantive due process and the potential application of state and federal administrative procedure acts long overlooked by condemnation attorneys.

The Supreme Court implicitly accepted a substantive due process test for eminent domain decisions in upholding Hawaii's land reform act: in order to meet constitutional requirements it must be shown that "the Legislature *rationally could have believed* that the [Act] would promote its objective." Hawaii v. Midkiff, 467 U.S. 229, 242 (1984)(O'Connor, J., emphasis in original).

Under administrative procedure acts, courts are directed to review and rescind government agency actions found to be "arbitrary and capricious."[12] Administrative law interprets that test far more rigorously than eminent domain case law does. The door is thus open for administrative law challenges of agency condemnations, and, by natural extension, of public utility condemnations.

In the Poletown case, the arguments actually made in court for the neighborhood were almost entirely based on challenges to the constitutionality of the public purpose in giving land to a private corporation, and predictably came to nought. See case cited in footnote 10 *supra*.

2. Uncorking judicial review of condemnation. Is this an area of practice that is about to awaken, after a century of torpor, under the pressures of environmental challenges to governmental condemnation decisions? Once judicial scrutiny is let loose in an area previously characterized by deference, do you realize how difficult it might be later to get the genie back into the bottle? In practical terms, how much would governments be burdened by the necessity of defending their condemnation decisions?

3. The politics of eminent domain. The political backdrop to environmentalists' efforts to open up judicial review of condemnation is interesting. On one hand, eminent domain is a longstanding rhetorical bugbear of "conservatives." On the other, those who get hit by government condemnations are rarely the wealthy and powerful, as in highway and porkbarrel water projects. Often, in fact, as in the *Poletown* case, private corporate interests stand foursquare with government in opposition to private property owners. Indeed, as in that case, the business bloc may have initiated and controlled the government's exercise of eminent domain from the start. In *Poletown*, who were the conservatives and who the liberals? Does anyone still know, in the environmental era, what those labels mean?

---

12. See 5 U.S.C.A. §706(a)(2), and Plater & Norine, "Looking Glass," Envtl. Aff. L. Rev. at 704-706; and see administrative law materials in Chapter 11.

B. INVERSE CONDEMNATION: A CONSTITUTIONAL TORT?

At first glance, inverse condemnation scarcely resembles eminent domain. The facts in the following material resemble tort cases, not constitutional law. Governmental actions here result in noise, vibrations, smells, and general disruptions to the neighboring environs.

Why then make these into constitutional cases? The simple answer is that it may not be easy to sue the government in certain tort settings because of sovereign immunity. If the federal, state, or local government performing a governmental function has not consented to be sued, the immunity doctrine is a complete defense to the tort action.[13] The right to challenge government action on constitutional grounds remains available, however, because the Constitution ranks higher in the hierarchy of laws than statutes and common law.

Why call it "inverse" condemnation? In an ordinary condemnation case, the government decides it wants someone's property, and sues to get it. As part of its suit, the government declares its willingness to pay the value of the property as set by the court. But what if, instead of suing to get the property, the government has in effect simply taken it physically? In that case, the victim of the taking may sue the government for compensation, and since the government becomes the defendant instead of the plaintiff, the proceeding is called inverse condemnation or "reverse condemnation." The plaintiff is effectively saying, "The government has in reality condemned my property by physically taking it without admitting it, so I want to sue them in court, to make them sue and pay me eminent domain compensation."

Of course, it may be that the reason the government didn't offer compensation was that it didn't think what it was doing was condemnation. As in the following cases, the government may have done something, like running an airport, which it didn't consider to affect private property at all.

In the usual eminent domain case, the only issue is the amount of compensation. In inverse condemnation cases, however, there are usually two major issues: whether there was a taking at all, and if so, what relief is due to the plaintiff.

Thornburg v. Port of Portland

Supreme Court of Oregon, 1962
233 Ore. 178, 376 P.2d 100

GOODWIN, J. The issues in their broadest sense concern rights of landowners adjacent to airports and the rights of the public in the airspace near the ground. Specifically, we must decide whether a noise-nuisance can amount to a taking.

The Port of Portland owns and operates the Portland International Airport. It has the power of eminent domain. It has used this power to surround itself with a substantial curtilage, but its formal acquisition stopped short of the land of the plaintiffs. For the purposes of this case, the parties have assumed that the Port is

13. The availability and extent of governmental liability, short of constitutional claims, depends on the vagaries of statutory and common law exceptions to immunity.

immune from ordinary tort liability. Further, it is conceded that injunctive relief would not be in the public interest. Aircraft are not ordinarily operated by the Port itself, but by third parties which use its facilities. Air navigation and other related operations are, for all practical purposes, regulated by a federal agency. The Port merely holds the airport open to the flying public.

The plaintiffs own and reside in a dwelling house located about 6,000 feet beyond the end of one runway and directly under the glide path of aircraft using it. Their land lies about 1,500 feet beyond the end of a second runway, but about 1,000 feet to one side of the glide path of aircraft using that runway.

The plaintiffs contend that flights from both runways have resulted in a taking of their property. Their principal complaint is that the noise from jet aircraft makes their land unusable. The jets use a runway the center line of which, if extended, would pass about 1,000 feet to one side of the plaintiffs' land. Some planes pass directly over the plaintiffs' land, but these are not, for the most part, the civilian and military jets which cause the most noise.

The plaintiffs' case proceeded on two theories: (1) Systematic flights directly over their land cause a substantial interference with their use and enjoyment of that land. This interference constitutes a nuisance. Such a nuisance, if persisted in by a private party, could ripen into a prescription. Such a continuing nuisance, when maintained by government, amounts to the taking of an easement, or, more precisely, presents a jury question whether there is a taking. (2) Systematic flights which pass close to their land, even though not directly overhead, likewise constitute the taking of an easement, for the same reasons, and upon the same authority.

The Port of Portland contends that its activities do not constitute the taking of easements in the plaintiffs' land. The Port argues: (1) The plaintiffs have no right to exclude or protest flights directly over their land, if such flights are so high as to be in the public domain, i.e., within navigable airspace as defined by federal law.[14] (2) The plaintiffs have no right to protest flights which do not cross the airspace above their land, since these could commit no trespass in any event. Accordingly, the Port contends, there is no interference with any legally protected interest of the plaintiffs and thus no taking of any property for which the plaintiffs are entitled to compensation. In short, the Port's theory is that the plaintiffs must endure the noise of the nearby airport with the same forbearance that is required of those who live near highways and railroads. The Port's arguments, supported as they are by substantial authority, prevailed in the lower court, even though they were not entirely responsive to the plaintiffs' case. (The plaintiffs founded their case upon a nuisance theory; the defendant answered that there was no trespass.)

The trial court proceeded as if the rights of the plaintiffs were limited by the imaginary lines that would describe a cube of airspace exactly 500 feet high and bounded on four sides by perpendicular extensions of the surface boundaries of their land. The trial court thus in effect adapted the law of trespass to the issues presented in this case, and held that unless there was a continuing trespass within the

14. The Air Commerce Act of 1926, as amended by the Civil Aeronautics Act of 1938, provided that the Civil Aeronautics Authority could prescribe air traffic rules. See 49 U.S.C.A. §551(a)(7)(1952). One of these rules fixed 500 feet as the minimum safe altitude over persons, vehicles, and structures. 14 CFR 60.107 (1947 Supp). There can be no doubt that Congress has, during all material times, denominated the airspace 500 feet above any person, vessel, vehicle or structure in other than congested areas as navigable airspace which is subject to a public right of transit. The authority of Congress to pass such legislation is bottomed on the commerce power, and the validity of the legislation is not in question.

described cube of space there could be no recovery. The trial court accordingly adopted the view that even if there was a nuisance, a nuisance could not give rise to a taking....

Since United States v. Causby, 328 U.S. 256 (1946), and particularly since Griggs v. Allegheny County, 369 U.S. 84 (1962), we know that easements can be taken by repeated low-level flights over private land. Such easements have been found in actions against the federal government (Causby) and in actions against municipal corporations (Griggs). When such easements are said to have been taken, compensation must be paid to the owners of the lands thus burdened. This much appears to be settled.

It is not so well settled, however, that the easements discussed in the *Causby* and *Griggs* cases are easements to impose upon lands near an airport a servitude of noise. Courts operating upon the theory that repeated trespasses form the basis of the easement have not found it necessary to decide whether a repeated nuisance, which may or may not have been an accompaniment of a trespass, could equally give rise to a servitude upon neighboring land. It must be remembered that in both the *Causby* and *Griggs* cases the flights were virtually at tree-top level. Accordingly, both decisions could perhaps be supported on trespass theories exclusively. Following the *Causby* case, several federal district courts held that while repeated flights at low levels directly over private land may amount to a taking for which compensation must be paid, repeated flights nearby but not directly overhead must be endured as mere "damages" which, for various reasons, may not be compensable....

After the case at bar had been argued and submitted, the United States Court of Appeals for the Tenth Circuit, which had previously held in Batten v. United States, 292 F.2d 144 (10th Cir. 1961), that a complaint sounding substantially in nuisance stated a cause of action under circumstances very like those now before us, held...that there must be a trespass before there can be a taking. Batten v. United States, 306 F.2d 580 (10th Cir. 1962). As pointed out in a dissent by Murrah, Chief Judge, the interference proven was substantial enough to impose a servitude upon the lands of the plaintiffs, and under the *Causby* and *Griggs* cases equally could have constituted a taking. 306 F.2d at 585.... We believe the dissenting view in the *Batten* case presents the better-reasoned analysis of the legal principles involved, and that if the majority view in the *Batten* case can be defended it must be defended frankly upon the ground that considerations of public policy justify the result: i.e., that private rights must yield to public convenience in this class of cases....

While not every wrong committed by government will amount to a taking of private property, there are some wrongs which do constitute a taking. Many of these wrongs involve trespassory activities. The inquiry must not beg the question, however, whether a nuisance can also amount to a taking. Whether a nuisance has, in fact, produced the results alleged by the plaintiff in this case is another matter; first we must decide whether a nuisance can ever constitute a taking. If there is a taking, then what is taken must be paid for....

If the government substantially deprives the owner of the use of his land, such deprivation is a taking for which the government must pay. If, on the other hand, the government merely commits some tort which does not deprive the owner of the use of his land, then there is no taking.

Therefore, unless there is some reason of public policy which bars compensation in cases of governmental nuisance as a matter of law, there is a question, in each case, as a matter of fact, whether or not the governmental activity complained of has resulted in so substantial an interference with use and enjoyment of one's land as to amount to a taking of private property for public use. This factual question, again barring some rule which says we may not ask it, is equally relevant whether the taking is trespassory or by a nuisance. A nuisance can be such an invasion of the rights of a possessor as to amount to a taking, in theory at least, any time a possessor is in fact ousted from the enjoyment of his land....

The plaintiffs concede that single-instance torts, as torts, are not compensable. Inverse condemnation, however, provides the remedy where an injunction would not be in the public interest, and where the continued interference amounts to a taking for which the constitution demands a remedy. In summary, a taking occurs whenever government acts in such a way as substantially to deprive an owner of the useful possession of that which he owns, either by repeated trespasses or by repeated non-trespassory invasions called "nuisance." If reparations are to be denied, they should be denied for reasons of policy which are themselves strong enough to counterbalance the constitutional demand that reparations be paid. None has been pointed out to us in this case.

If we accept, as we must upon established principles of the law of servitudes, the validity of the propositions that a noise can be a nuisance; that a nuisance can give rise to an easement; and that a noise coming straight down from above one's land can ripen into a taking if it is persistent enough and aggravated enough, then logically the same kind and degree of interference with the use and enjoyment of one's land can also be a taking even though the noise vector may come from some direction other than the perpendicular.

If a landowner has a right to be free from unreasonable interference caused by noise, as we hold that he has, then when does the noise burden become so unreasonable that the government must pay for the privilege of being permitted to continue to make the noise? Logically, the answer has to be given by the trier of fact.... The balancing of private rights and public necessity is not a novel problem.

Whether expressed in so many words or not, the principle found in the *Causby* [and] *Griggs*...cases is that when the government conducts an activity upon its own land which, after balancing the question of reasonableness, is sufficiently disturbing to the use and enjoyment of neighboring lands to amount to a taking thereof, then the public, and not the subservient landowner, should bear the cost of such public benefit.... The real question was not one of perpendicular extension of surface boundaries into the airspace, but a question of reasonableness based upon nuisance theories. In effect, the inquiry should have been whether the government had undertaken a course of conduct on its own land which, in simple fairness to its neighbors, required it to obtain more land so that the substantial burdens of the activity would fall upon public land, rather than upon that of involuntary contributors who happen to lie in the path of progress....

Logically, it makes no difference to a plaintiff disturbed in the use of his property whether the disturbing flights pass 501 feet or 499 feet above his land. If he is in fact ousted from the legitimate enjoyment of his land, it is to him an academic matter that the planes which have ousted him did not fly below 500 feet. The rule adopted by the majority of the state and federal courts is, then, an arbitrary one. The barring of actions when the flights are above 500 feet is also difficult to reconcile with the theory that recovery should be based upon nuisance concepts rather than upon the trespass theory which we have rejected. Whether a plaintiff is entitled to recover should depend upon the fact of a taking, and not upon an arbitrary rule. The ultimate question is whether there was a sufficient interference with the landowner's use and enjoyment to be a taking.... Congress may very properly declare certain airspace to be in the public domain for navigational purposes, but it does not necessarily follow that rights of navigation may be exercised unreasonably. The power to invade the rights of servient landowners no doubt reposes in the federal government, but there is a point beyond which such power may not be exercised without compensation. United States v. Causby. The same limitation applies to lesser governmental agencies....

PERRY, J., dissenting....

It should be noted that to reach a reversal of the judgment of the trial court, the majority rely upon the law of nuisance. The majority seem to admit that this has never been the law of this state, but argue that it should be. So far as I have been able to ascertain, no jurisdiction whose constitution reads as does ours has ever sustained such a proposition.... Where a flight directly over the land, by reason of noise and vibration, can be said in fact to cause serious interference in the owner's use and enjoyment of the property, it is a trespass, which is a constitutional taking, and requires full compensation.

In the matter before us, however, after searching the record, I am unable to find any evidence that would support a judgment of a taking, based on interference with the plaintiffs' use and enjoyment of the land by airplane flights above the 500-foot level....

That the definition of a constitutional taking has consistently been grounded in the appropriation of an interest in the realty itself has been a rule of law of long standing under the Constitution of the United States is shown by the case of Portsmouth Harbor Land & Hotel Co. v. United States, 260 U.S. 327 (1922). In this case damages were sought in inverse condemnation because of the establishment of a fort in which there were gun emplacements and shells were fired over and across the plaintiff's land. Mr. Justice Holmes, speaking for the court, said: "This is a claim in respect of land which, *or an interest in which*, is alleged to have been taken by the United States Government...." (italics mine)....

A nuisance, although a tort, does not contemplate a physical invasion of the property of another, but the use of a person's own property in such a way as to interfere with another's free enjoyment of his property.... Practically all human activities engaged in carrying out a commercial enterprise may interfere with someone's enjoyment of his property. It is the right of an owner of land to use his land in any lawful manner, and it is only when the manner of use creates a grave interference with another's enjoyment of his property that the law will seek to redress this type of wrong. This is a natural requirement of organized society. There must be some give and take to promote the well-being of all. The underlying basis in nuisance law is the common-sense thought that in organized society there must be an adjustment between reasonable use and personal discomfort. No such consideration is involved in the law of trespass.

Trespass of property which, as has been pointed out, effects a taking in a constitutional sense, comprehends a physical invasion of the property either by the person or by causing a physical object to enter upon or over the property of another.... Therefore, it is the taking of an owner's possessory interest in land as compared with interfering with an owner's use and enjoyment of his land that distinguishes a trespass which is a "taking" from a nuisance, which is not....

Since a nuisance interferes with the enjoyment of the right to possess land, different rules of law apply to the balancing of the interests of owners. An owner's use of his own land will not create liability unless his use causes substantial interference with another's enjoyment of his property. Also, the utility of the use that creates the nuisance must be weighed against the "gravity of the harm" (sic).

Such considerations are foreign to the law of trespass. A trespass imports damage and permits recovery, though no actual damage is caused. This rule of law is so well established, citation of authority is unnecessary. There can be no balancing of interests.

Where a permanent trespass is committed by government, the constitution will not permit a balancing of the value of the taking for the benefit of the public against the interests of an owner. The owner must be fully compensated for his loss....

A nuisance takes none of the title in the property. The full legal title rests in the owner. If the nuisance is abated in any manner, the damage suffered has ended and the land is again restored to its full value to the owner. On the other hand, if there is a taking, the property right of ownership or some interest therein has been transferred from the owner to the sovereign, and does not again revert to the original owner even though the use to which the property has been put by the sovereign ceases....

COMMENTARY AND QUESTIONS

1. Nuisance as a "servitude." The majority and dissent agree that a plane's physical trespass will constitute the taking of a servitude (more properly labelled an "easement"). They split over the rather technical point of whether a nuisance can do likewise. The distinction echoes a principle of eminent domain compensation allowing extensive recovery for "consequential" damages if government has condemned any piece of your real property, however tiny, but none if no land is taken. Both opinions ignore a fairly well-established line of cases holding that nuisances can create prescriptive easements to pollute (see Chapter 5). Both recognize that nuisance law involves more balancing than trespass law, although neither is very clear about intentional nuisance doctrine. To what extent should airport inverse condemnation cases balance the noise and vibrations suffered by plaintiffs against the public's need for an airport? Or should any substantial burden on neighbors be compensated as a cost of doing business? Should it make any difference that government, rather than a private entity, operates the harmful airport?

2. Extending physical inverse condemnation theories. There has been some limited extension of the inverse condemnation remedy beyond airport cases. Compensation has been ordered for loss of access (where a public road was converted to a limited-access highway), and loss of light and air (where a bridge or overpass was built alongside a house), even though no part of the plaintiffs' land or airspace was physically invaded. Land owners along major highways suffer very real problems with dust, noise, vibrations, flashing lights, and severe losses in property value. Are these compensable now? If so, the costs could bankrupt public highway programs.

Inverse condemnation claims can also arise in the wild. Can't it be argued that the government takes an easement in my property without compensation when it forbids me from fencing out the antelope that want to eat my grass (giving the antelope an easement of access over my land), or when I am forbidden to shoot the endangered grey wolf that still thinks my property is her territory and eats one of my cows every week, or when the Forest Service adopts a "let-burn" policy for national forests so that my private trees and vacation cabin are destroyed by fire? See U.S. v. Lawrence, 848 F.2d 1502 (10th Cir. 1988)(antelope); Christy v. Hodel, 857 F.2d 1324 (9th Cir. 1988)(grizzlies); Wiener, Uncle Sam and Forest Fires, 15 Envtl. L. 623 (1985); Keiter and Holscher, Wolf Recovery under the Endangered Species Act: a Study in Contemporary Federalism, 11 Public Land L. Rev. 19 (1990).

Pushing the doctrine even further, consider the fact that many Americans are starting to worry about clusters of leukemia and other ailments that have been correlated in some cases with the presence of high-tension electrical transmission facilities. If clients are worried about high electro-magnetic fields (EMF) on their property caused by utility transmission lines, but cannot prove tort liability, can an attorney file an inverse condemnation claim for a "taking" by the public utility company (which has the power of eminent domain) of an "electromagnetic easement" of right of way over their property? See Brodeur, Annals of Radiation: Calamity on Meadow Street, July 9, 1990 New Yorker Magazine at 50. Or likewise against the federal government for low frequency radio transmissions? Wisconsin v. Weinberger, 745 F.2d 412 (7th Cir. 1984). Or even to use a physical taking argument to circumvent sovereign immunity in tort cases like Nevin v. U.S., 696 F.2d 1229 (9th Cir. 1987), where members of the public were injured by clandestine governmental testing of bacillary and chemical agents in urban public areas? (As to the latter, public notice is now required by law. 52 U.S.C.A. §1520.)

C. CHALLENGES TO REGULATIONS AS UNCONSTITUTIONAL "TAKINGS"

Section 1. REGULATORY TAKINGS AND WETLANDS

Determining how far the collective power of the majority can intrude upon individual rights has always been one of the classic problems of democracy. When government regulates private property under the police power, moreover, tensions tend to get particularly hot because it does not generally pay for the privilege. Few Americans actively welcome the state's directive opinions about how they should use their land, especially when restrictions get in the way of private profits. In modern America, where rugged frontier individualism lives on in private property doctrines that built the world's greatest economy, environmental regulations may be particularly resented because they are relatively new to the scene, dealing with public "rights" and objectives that the market economy had never heard of before Silent Spring.

"Regulatory takings" attacks on environmental statutes and regulations are likely to occur wherever private property rights are impacted, which is to say they arise throughout the field. When a state prohibits building in wetlands, when the federal government prohibits billboards on interstate highways, when a local town council prohibits junkyards, or when a government entity proposes to restrict any of a host of other concerns – automobile pollution, trade in endangered species ivory, use of off-road vehicles on public lands, destruction of historic buildings, biogenetic experimentation and drug development, agricultural pesticides and herbicides, destruction of wildlife and its habitat, air and water pollution, stripmining, throwaway bottles, and so on – in each case the "invalid takings" argument will be heard loudly in the legislative and administrative process. These complaints about government high-handedness are sometimes coupled with a dire warning from the lobbyists that if the restriction is passed, those who vote for it as well as the agency regulators may find themselves personally liable for damages for violating the regulatees' civil rights.

Often the mere threat of a lawsuit raising a takings challenge is enough to dissuade legislators and city councils from passing environmental measures, even where the proposed regulation clearly would comply with judicial takings tests. Often, however, the legal tests of validity and invalidity are indeed not clear. As Professor Sax has written, "the 'crazy-quilt pattern' of Supreme Court doctrine has effectively been acknowledged by the Court itself, which has developed the habit of introducing its uniformly unsatisfactory opinions in this area with the understatement that 'no rigid rules' or 'set formula' are available to determine where [valid] regulation ends and [invalid] taking begins."[15]

When a restriction is actually challenged in court, the argument typically begins with the allegation of economic loss. (The first three areas of police power tests – authority, proper public purpose, and the restriction's reasonable relationship of means to ends – are relevant but usually are in effect conceded.) The attack alleges that even though the restriction does not take physical possession of all or part of the private property (which in virtually all cases would clearly require eminent domain compensation), it so restricts property rights that it amounts to a taking under the due process clause and the eminent domain clause of the Fifth Amendment and their state corollaries. The test is the same under either clause, and usually turns in some manner on the amount of property loss, viewed in a vacuum. If a court finds a restriction excessive, or confiscatory, the government can accept an equitable remedy nullifying the law as applied to the subject property, or agree to pay damages for the invalid taking (which explains why these verdicts are often confusingly referred to as "inverse condemnation" or "eminent domain").[16]

Paradoxically, although courts go to extraordinary lengths to defer to and uphold government police power condemnation actions, as seen above in Subpart B of this chapter, the judicial approach to regulatory acts is discernibly more critical. Given a loss of property values – an inevitability in most police power settings – many courts in effect shift the burden to government, ignoring the usual presumption of validity for governmental acts. Takings jurisprudence can be decisively consequential in all areas of government, but nowhere more pressingly and vividly than in the

15. Sax, Takings and the Police Power, 74 Yale L.J. 36, 37 (1964).

16. The *remedies* sought in regulatory challenges can be the same as in inverse condemnation and eminent domain cases: damages for the taking, or injunctions to block the government action. But the substantive elements of the claims are very different in the regulatory and the physical taking settings. See comment 7 at page 464 *infra*.

field of environmental protection. Always on the cutting edge, environmental law cases provide a major focus of takings controversy.

Although an inquiry into regulatory takings could be based in any of dozens of environmental fields, wetlands protection regulations are chosen here as the vehicle for raising some of the tough questions presented – questions of property law, private rights, public rights, democracy, fairness, and justice.

President's Council on Environmental Quality, Our Nation's Wetlands
1-2, 19-28, 50 (1978)[17]

The early settlers on this continent found a land of extraordinary physical beauty and fertility. Sparkling wild rivers coursed through mature forests, the woods teemed with game, and fish thrived in estuaries and the pure waters of mountain lakes....

Today we know that the gifts of clean water, fertile land, and bountiful energy supplies are not inexhaustible.... There has grown an increasing awareness of the need for making conscious, informed choices about further modification of the natural environment. Inland and coastal wetlands – only yesterday considered useless – are now seen as valuable endangered natural resources. Estimates of irreversibly altered or destroyed wetlands in the 48 continental states have already reached 40 to 50 percent.... Of California's original 3.5 million wetland acres, in 1954 only 450,000 remained. In 1959 it was estimated that 45 percent of Connecticut's coastal marshes had been lost since a 1914 survey. At current rates of destruction, it was predicted that only 14 percent might remain by the year 2000. Surveys disclosed that the Rainwater Basin of south-central Nebraska had lost over 80 percent of its marshes by the 1960s. Southeastern Wisconsin had lost 61 percent by 1968. An estimated one-half the wetlands in the prairie pothole region of the United States had been drained by 1950. It is estimated that 35,000 acres of prime prairie wetlands are now being sacrificed each year. A survey conducted by the Fish and Wildlife Service in 1974 revealed that over 40 percent of the potholes existing in 1964 in western Minnesota had been destroyed in that 10-year period....

Many former marshes and swamps are [today] vacation homes and marinas. Other wetlands are used as dumping grounds.... With greater affluence and increased population, the pressures for development of wetlands – for agricultural production, for highways, for residential and commercial building sites, for ports, for marinas, for parking lots, for industries and power plants which require large quantities of cooling water – seem destined to increase....

Evaluating all these uses is not easy. Clearly it is blatantly wasteful to turn a productive wetland into a dump. But it is harder to assign relative values to leaving a wetland in its natural state or using it for luxurious waterfront dwellings. Still more difficult is balancing the values between natural wetland and highly productive cultivated farmland. The results of past practices, recent scientific discoveries, and our changing priorities must all weigh in decisions on how much to conserve of the remainder of our wetland heritage – for the benefit of society as a whole and for the use and enjoyment of future generations.

17. Perhaps because wetlands protection was identified as an area of marked controversy between developers and conservationists, this report – produced during the Carter years – was quickly recalled and sequestered in 1981 by the incoming administration.

We do know that wetlands are vital fish and wildlife habitats. Two-thirds of the commercially important fish and shellfish harvested along the Atlantic and in the Gulf of Mexico depend on coastal estuaries and their wetlands for food sources, for spawning grounds, for nurseries for the young, or for all these critical purposes; for the Pacific coast, the figure is almost one-half. Wetlands provide essential resting, wintering, and nesting grounds for many species of migratory waterfowl, other waterbirds, and many songbirds. They are among the most productive ecosystems in the world. They are important in maintenance of ground water supplies and water purification. Marshes and swamps along coasts, rivers, and lakes protect shorelines and banks from erosion. Wetlands also have the capacity to store flood waters temporarily and in some instances to reduce the volume and severity of floods.

The less tangible values of wetlands may be classified as recreational, educational, scientific, and aesthetic. It is curious that the sight of tall marsh grasses dipping and bending with the wind and currents have been so little admired until recent years by any except a few naturalists and artists. The poets have offered us images with which we can readily express our wonder at the magnitude of the oceans and the mountains, but apparently they have been defeated by the fact that so few words rhyme with "swamp." Many of us who readily grasp the importance of preserving forests, sand dunes, and lakes for their aesthetic values alone remain blind to the less obvious charms of a healthy marsh bordered by deep yellow marsh marigolds or a swamp in which ospreys nest high in the cypresses....

WETLAND FUNCTIONS

An ecosystem is a unit of plants, animals, and their physical and chemical environment in which no one part exists independently of the others. The tidal wetlands and the estuary – where a stream's freshwater mixes with the saltwater of the sea – form a distinctive ecosystem in which plants and animals exist with each other and with the nonliving environment in a complex system of interdependencies.

THE FOOD WEB...

The source of the energy needed by all plants and animals to sustain life is the sun, but only plants have the capacity to transform the sun's energy into food through photosynthesis. This energy, in the form of plant material, carbohydrates, fats, and proteins, then becomes available to the entire animal world, including people.... Energy continues to flow as creatures feed on each other. As detritus is carried through the marsh, it is consumed by microorganisms, by fiddler crabs, by the larvae of marsh insects, and by mussels, clams, and other creatures which are then ingested by even larger animals. The energy from the sun which was harnessed by marsh vegetation reaches people as we consume the oysters and fish which feed in the estuary – or their predators which live in the coastal waters.

The estuary offers a veritable smorgasbord for the fish which visit seasonally and for those which enter with the tides. Their prey includes the mud-dwelling insects, worms, mollusks, and crustaceans and the young of other species which use the estuary as a nursery because of the abundance of food and the shelter of shallow water and grasses. As fish and shellfish which feed in the estuary swim into deeper waters, larger predatory fish await them. Birds also find a variety of food in and near the marshes. Hawks sweep the area in search of smaller birds and mice. The clapper rail hunts small fish, fiddler crabs, insects, and snails in the vegetation along the edges of the marsh.

Inland marshes also teem with life. Red-winged blackbirds nest in cattails and shrubs and fly out, displaying their gaudy epaulets, to feed on grain, snails, beetles, and grubs. Foraging herons stretch their long necks to snatch fish, frogs, or small crustaceans swimming about in the shallow waters, and kingfishers watch at the water's edge. Raccoons, which like people will feast on either plant or animal matter, prowl the marsh at dusk. Newly hatched ducklings take to the water where they conceal themselves from predators among the bordering plants.

WETLAND PRODUCTIVITY...

The estuary and tidal marshes are extraordinary natural systems in which tidal energy circulates nutrients, animals feed on plants and on each other, and excess nutrients are washed out to feed the organisms which live offshore. The crop is automatically cultivated and stored within the system, requiring neither human investment nor labor....

A primary measure of wetland productivity is fish yield. Of the 10 fish and shellfish most valuable commercially – shrimp, salmon, tuna, oysters, menhaden, crabs, lobsters, flounders, clams, and haddock – only tuna, lobsters, and haddock are not estuarine dependent. The highest-ranking commercial species in terms of quantity is menhaden, a wetland-dependent fish valued not for human consumption but for its oil, which is used in tanning leather, in paint and varnish, insect spray, and soap, and in fertilizer, animal feed, and fish food. The average annual harvest of menhaden for the 5 years 1969-73 was 1.9 billion pounds.

Figures on wetland-dependent fish yields have been the subject of numerous studies. The Georgia Game and Fish Commission estimated the per acre yield of freshwater wetland fish at 75 pounds. In Connecticut's marshy Niantic River, the annual scallop harvest is 15,000 bushels, amounting to 300 pounds per acre per year, which exceeds the beef yield on excellent grazing grounds. Wetland productivity also includes waterfowl....

POLLUTION CONTROL

There is general recognition of the fact that wetlands are vital to fish and wildlife. A subject of livelier debate and growing intensity is how wetlands function as pollution filtration systems and as natural flood control mechanisms. The implications of current scientific findings for these subjects are of great interest to ecologists, planners, and engineers.

The role of wetlands in reducing the pollution levels in water has recently become one of the most compelling arguments for their preservation. Because wetland ecosystems hold nutrients, they simultaneously act as a pollution filtration system. Water arriving from such "point" sources as waste water treatment plants and from such "nonpoint" sources as runoff from agricultural fields and city streets carries a high level of pollutants, particularly excess levels of nitrogen and phosphorous. As the water circulates through a wetland, the plants take up and use these pollutants as nutrients.

A study by the Georgia Water Quality Control Board of Mountain Creek, a tributary of the Alcovy River, showed that water heavily polluted with human sewage and chicken offal was designated clean after passing through 2.75 miles of swamp forest. A study of the Tinicum Marsh, located a few miles from the Philadelphia airport, measured pollutants in the broad tidal creek which transects the marshes and again when the water returned to the creek after draining for 2–5

SOUTH FLORIDA WATER MANAGEMENT DISTRICT

An extensive wetland area, all privately-owned lands, lying ready for draining and development. Limited to their natural state, the wetlands have low market value. If drained, they may increase from ten to a hundred times in value.

This wetland overview happens to be the Kissimmee River wetlands of south-central Florida shortly before they were channelized and drained at government expense in 1961 by the Army Corps of Engineers.

The drainage project, which had been strongly opposed by environmentalists, created immensely valuable private lands. It also turned out to create a nightmare. The natural meandering streams and wetlands had served as a giant natural filter absorbing and cleaning the water of fertilizer runoffs, other nutrients, and pollution. Without the natural system, Lake Okechobee, a major water source for South Florida, immediately began to choke up with pollution, organic detritus, and eutrophication effects.

Now the Corps and Florida officials are attempting to return much of the river system to its original state, hoping to save public water supplies. To restore the river, however, will require $343.6 million (the 1961 channelizing cost less than $30 million), much of the current cost (see page 473 infra*) is for governmental compensation payable to private landowners for loss of dryland market values initially created by the public drainage project.*

hours. Chemical and bacteriological samplings indicated that the marshes significantly improved water quality by increasing the oxygen content and by reducing the nutrient load....

Interest currently centers on the role that river marshes play through their filtration function in protecting lakes from accelerated aging. In the natural and normally slow aging process, lakes accumulate nutrients and sediments and become so shallow that plants grow and emerge through the surface. When a lake accumulates excess quantities of nutrients through natural or manmade causes, the aging process is accelerated, as evidenced by increased turbidity and the growth of algae. Oxygen levels in the water drop and fish die....

FLOOD PROTECTION

One of the most innovative practical applications of current findings about wetland functions is the Charles River plan. Although some people still believe that engineers automatically insist on altering natural systems so that they can get on with their construction, the Corps of Engineers is responsible for devising the simplest yet the most innovative of plans for natural flood control in the Massachusetts Charles River watershed.

Within the Charles River watershed there are 20,000 acres of undeveloped wetland amounting to 10 percent of the entire drainage area. At times of high water, these wetlands absorb the water and release it slowly after the floodwaters recede.

"The logic of the scheme is compelling," said the Corps final report in 1972:

> Nature has already provided the least-cost solution to future flooding in the form of extensive wetlands which moderate extreme highs and lows in stream flow. Rather than attempt to improve on this natural protection mechanism, it is both prudent and economical to leave the hydrologic regime established over the millennia undisturbed. In the opinion of the study team, construction of any of the most likely alternatives, a 55,000 acre-foot reservoir, or extensive walls and dikes, can add nothing....

THE VALUE OF WETLANDS

In its study of the Charles River Basin, the Corps of Engineers tagged the annual flood control benefits of the Natural Valley Storage Plan at $1,203,000 – "The difference between annual flood losses based on present land use and conditions" of the 8,500 acres of wetlands and "those associated with projected 1990 loss of 30 percent of valley storage."

It is difficult to quantify the value of wetlands, and attempts to do so generate considerable disagreement, but because alternative approaches to engineering problems are often judged today by cost-benefit comparisons, such financial estimates are now common. Today a number of ecologists are attempting to apply accounting procedures to wetlands, making financial evaluations of the services which wetlands perform in their natural state and urging that the figures be seriously considered in decisions on uses of water resources.

Most quantifiers have concerned themselves solely with wetlands functions. Placing a dollar value on purely aesthetic delight may seem impossible to many scientists who feel on surer ground pricing wetlands in relation to damage projections or to the known commercial values of estuarine-dependent shellfish, for example....

State of Maine v. Johnson
Supreme Court of Maine, 1970
265 A.2d 711

MARDEN, J. On appeal from an injunction granted under the provisions of 12 M.R.S.A. §§4701-4709, the Wetlands Act, which places restrictions upon the alteration and use of wetlands, as therein defined, without permission from the municipal officers concerned and the State Wetlands Control Board. The Act is a conservation measure under the police power of the State to protect the ecology of areas bordering coastal waters.[18]

The appellants own a tract of land about 220 feet wide and 700 feet long extending across salt water marshes between Atlantic Avenue on the east and the Webhannet River on the west in the Town of Wells. Westerly of the lots fronting on Atlantic Avenue the strip has been subdivided into lots for sale. The easterly 260 feet approximately of the strip has been filled and bears seasonal dwellings. Westerly of this 260 foot development is marsh-land flooded at high tide and drained, upon receding tide, into the River by a network of what our Maine historical novelist Kenneth E. Roberts called "eel runs," but referred to in the record as creeks. Similar marsh-land, undeveloped, lies to the north and south of appellants' strip and westerly of the River, all of which makes up a substantial acreage (the extent not given in testimony, but of which we take judicial notice) of marshland known as the Wells Marshes. Appellants' land, by raising the grade above high water by the addition of fill, is adaptable to development for building purposes.

Following the effective date of the Act, an application to the municipal officers, with notice to the Wetlands Control Board, for permission to fill a portion of this land was denied by Board.... [Subsequently,] fill was deposited on the land in question, as the result of which the State sought an injunction....

---

18. Pertinent portions of the wetlands act are quoted:

§4701. No person, agency or municipality shall remove, fill, dredge or drain sanitary sewage into, or otherwise alter any coastal waters, as defined herein...without filing written notice of his intention to do so, including such plans as may be necessary to describe the proposed activity, with the municipal officers in the municipality affected and with the Wetlands Control Board.... The municipal officers shall hold a public hearing on the proposal.... For purposes of this chapter, coastal wetland is defined as any swamp, marsh, bog, beach, flat or other contiguous lowland above extreme low water which is subject to tidal action or normal storm flowage at any time excepting periods of maximum storm activity.

§4702. **Permits** Permits to undertake the proposed alteration shall be issued by the municipal officers within 7 days of such hearing providing the Wetlands Control Board approves. Such permit may be conditioned upon the applicant amending his proposal to take whatever measures are deemed necessary by either the municipality or the Wetlands Control Board to protect the public interest. Approval may be withheld by either the municipal officers or the board when in the opinion of either body the proposal would threaten the public safety, health or welfare, would adversely affect the value or enjoyment of the property of abutting owners, or would be damaging to the conservation of public or private water supplies or of wildlife or freshwater, estuarine or marine fisheries.

§4704. **Appeal** Appeal may be taken to the Superior Court within 30 days after the denial of a permit or the issuance of a conditional permit for the purpose of determining whether the action appealed from so restricts the use of the property as to deprive the owner of the reasonable use thereof, and is therefore an unreasonable exercise of police power, or which constitutes the equivalent of a taking without compensation. The court upon such a finding may set aside the action appealed from.

§4705. **Wetlands Control Board** The Wetlands Control Board shall be composed of the Commissioners of Sea and Shore Fisheries and of Inland Fisheries and Game, the Chairman of the Water and Air Environmental Improvement Commission, the Chairman of the State Highway Commission, the Forest Commissioner and the Commissioner of Health and Welfare or their delegates.

§4709. **Violations** Violators are subject to fine and/or injunctive process.

The record establishes that the land which the appellants propose to build up by fill and build upon for sale, or to be offered for sale to be built upon, are coastal wetlands within the definition of the Act and that the refusal by the Board to permit the deposit of such fill prevents the development as proposed. The single Justice found that the property is a portion of a salt marsh area, a valuable natural resource of the State, that the highest and best use for the land, so filled, is for housing, and that unfilled it has no commercial value.

The issue is...whether the [wetlands restrictions] so limit the use to plaintiffs of this land that such deprivation of use amounts to a taking of their property without constitutional due process and just compensation.[19]

Due process of law has a dual aspect, procedural and substantive. Procedurally, "notice and opportunity for hearing are of the essence."... The Act meets all requirements of procedural due process.

Substantively, [due process] is "the constitutional guaranty that no person shall be deprived of...property for arbitrary reasons, such a deprivation being constitutionally supportable only if the conduct from which the deprivation flows is proscribed by reasonable legislation (that is, legislation the enactment of which is within the scope of legislative authority) reasonably applied (that is, for a purpose consonant with the purpose of the legislation itself)." 16 Am. Jur. 2d, Constitutional Law §550.

It is this substantive due process which is challenged in the Act.... The constitutional aspect of the current problem is to be determined by consideration of the extent to which appellants are deprived of their usual incidents of ownership – for the conduct of the public authorities with relation to appellant's land is not a "taking" in the traditional sense. Our State has applied a strict construction of the constitutional provisions as to land.

We find no constitutional definition of the word "deprive," since the constitutionally protected right of property is not unlimited. It is subject to reasonable restraints and regulations in the public interest by means of the legitimate exercise of police power. The exercise of this police power may properly regulate the use of property and if the owner suffers injury "it is either damnum absque injuria, or, in the theory of law, he is compensated for it by sharing in the general benefits which the regulations are intended...to secure." The determination of unconstitutional deprivation is difficult and judicial decisions are diverse. Broadly speaking, deprivation of property contrary to constitutional guaranty occurs "if it deprives an owner of one of its essential attributes, destroys its value, restricts or interrupts its common, necessary, or profitable use, hampers the owner in the application of it to the purposes of trade, or imposes conditions upon the right to hold or use it and thereby seriously impairs its value."

Conditions so burdensome may be imposed that they are equivalent to an outright taking, although the title to the property and some vestiges of its uses remain in the owner.... A guiding principle appears in the frequently cited case of Pennsylvania Coal Company v. Mahon, 260 U.S. 393, 413 (1922), where Mr. Justice Holmes declared:

> Government hardly could go on if to some extent values incident to property could not be diminished without paying for every such change in the general

19. Maine Constitution Article I §6. "He shall not be...deprived of his...property...but by the law of the land."

"Section 21. Private property shall not be taken for public uses without just compensation...."

> law. As long recognized some values are enjoyed under an implied limitation and must yield to the police power. But obviously the implied limitation must have its limits or the contract and due process clauses are gone. One fact for consideration in determining such limits is the extent of the diminution. When it reaches a certain magnitude, in most if not in all cases there must be an exercise of eminent domain and compensation to sustain the act. So the question depends upon the particular facts.... We are in danger of forgetting that a strong public desire to improve the public condition is not enough to warrant achieving the desire by a shorter cut than the constitutional way of paying for the change. As we already have said this is a question of degree – and therefore cannot be disposed of by general propositions.

Confrontation between public interests and private interests is common in the application of zoning laws, with which the Wetlands Act may be analogized, and the great majority of which, upon their facts, are held to be reasonable exercise of the police power. There are, however, zoning restrictions which have been recognized as equivalent to a taking of the property restricted....

The same result has been reached as to zoning laws which identify their purposes as ones of conservation, flood control, and swampland preservation, and the rationale expressed in [cases] involving the "dredge and fill" act....

Between the public interest in braking and eventually stopping the insidious despoliation of our natural resources which have for so long been taken for granted, on the one hand, and the protection of appellants' property rights on the other, the issue is cast.

Here the single Justice has found that the area of which appellants' land is a part "is a valuable natural resource of the State of Maine and plays an important role in the conservation and development of aquatic and marine life, game birds and waterfowl," which bespeaks the public interest involved and the protection of which is sought by §4702 of the Act. With relation to appellants' interest the single Justice found that appellants' land absent the addition of fill "has no commercial value whatever." These findings are supported by the evidence and are conclusive.

As distinguished from conventional zoning for town protection, the area of Wetlands representing a "valuable natural resource of the State," of which appellants' holdings are but a minute part, is of state-wide concern. The benefits from its preservation extend beyond town limits and are state-wide. The cost of its preservation should be publicly borne. To leave appellants with commercially valueless land in upholding the restriction presently imposed, is to charge them with more than their just share of the cost of this state-wide conservation program, granting fully its commendable purpose.... Their compensation by sharing in the benefits which this restriction is intended to secure is so disproportionate to their deprivation of reasonable use that such exercise of the State's police power is unreasonable.

The application of the Wetlands restriction in the terms of the denial of appellants' proposal to fill, and enjoining them from so doing deprives them of the reasonable use of their property and...is both an unreasonable exercise of police power and equivalent to a taking....

Holding, as we do, that the prohibition against the filling of appellants' land, upon the facts peculiar to the case, is an unreasonable exercise of police power, it does not follow that the restriction as to draining sanitary sewage into coastal wetlands is subject to the same infirmity. Additional considerations of health and pollution which are "separable from and independent of" the "fill" restriction may well support validity of the acts in those areas of concern....

Sibson v. State
Supreme Court of New Hampshire, 1976
336 A.2d 239

[The facts of the case, and the text of the wetlands regulation, are virtually identical to those in the *Johnson* case. The Sibsons purchased a six-acre tract of saltmarsh for $18,500, legally filled a two-acre portion prior to the passage of the Act, and in 1972 sold the filled land with a house they had built on it for $75,000, placing a value of $50,000 on the house and $25,000 on the land. In 1973, the New Hampshire Wetlands Act went into effect, and, under its terms, the judicial referee found that "the unfilled portion of the marsh is of practically no pecuniary value to the plaintiffs."]

GRIFFITH, J. ...The plaintiffs do not seriously contest that the denial of the permit to fill was a proper exercise of the police power [i.e. under the authority, proper purpose, and rationality tests], but argue that this denial rendered their saltmarsh economically useless and therefore constitutes a taking. They rely upon a theory first promulgated by Justice Holmes in Pennsylvania Coal Co. v. Mahon, that "compensation is due a landholder when a regulation destroys all or substantially all of the value of the property affected or denies to the owners all of its beneficial use."

The referee found that the plaintiffs had recovered their total investment and made some profit. Since they had been able to fill two acres and build a house on their original six-acre tract, the dismissal of their appeal could be sustained on the basis that their land was not rendered useless, but that they had only been deprived of a speculative profit.

We prefer to decide the case on the present application to fill the four acres still retained by the plaintiffs. It is only when the state action appropriates property for the public use at the expense of the property owner that compensation is due. [In a case like this the regulation] is not an appropriation of the property to a public use, but the restraint of an injurious private use by the owner, and is therefore not within the principles of property taken under the right of eminent domain.

[In other cases, however, we have sometimes applied a different standard, holding that] there is no public taking unless the prohibition deprives the owner of the only use of his land.

Somewhat more analogous to the present cases are cases where individuals are required to cease heretofore lawful activities now determined harmful to the public. These cases generally involve state action thought to be required to protect the health, welfare and morals of the public or required by an emergency. The validity of the state action is determined by balancing the "importance of the public benefit which is sought to be promoted against the seriousness of the restriction of a private right sought to be imposed."

We hold that the denial of the permit to fill the saltmarsh of the plaintiffs was a valid exercise of the police power proscribing future activities that would be harmful to the public and that, therefore, there was not taking under the eminent domain clause.

GRIMES, J. concurring in the result in part and dissenting in part:

I am in complete sympathy with those who wish to preserve the marshes. However, I continue to agree with Judge Smith when over one hundred years ago he said that great public benefit "may afford an excellent reason for taking the plaintiff's land in a constitutional manner but not for taking it without compensation."

Because I fear this decision destroys private ownership in all undeveloped property in this State, I can concur in the result only as to that part of the marsh which lies below the mean high water mark of the Atlantic Ocean. I can concur to this extent because the State has an interest in the public waters which would be reduced by the fill....

As to the marsh above mean high water, the effect of the State's action is to compel the plaintiff to devote his land to a public purpose without compensation by denying him the right to put it to any other reasonably profitable use.

This constitutes a taking. Maine v. Johnson.... The effect of the principle adopted in today's decision is to undermine a great constitutional safeguard.

COMMENTARY AND QUESTION

1. Different approaches to wetlands takings. The majority of wetlands cases to date probably resemble *Johnson* rather than *Sibson*. Judges in wetlands cases are not oblivious to wetlands' ecological values. Even in *Johnson*, for example, the Maine court clearly paid attention to the arguments for protecting wetlands, but it did so only as a basis for establishing that the act served a proper public purpose. Having done so, doesn't the opinion then focus exclusively on the private loss, without further consideration of the environmental context? *Sibson* could also be explained by its limited view of private loss. Wetland regulations indeed have a dramatic impact on market values, but shouldn't the constitutional balance on takings burdens have some place in it for weighted consideration of ecological harms which motivated the legislative regulation in the first place? Courts have found it easy to recognize the costs "externalized" onto private property by regulation, but find less obvious the need for an accounting of harms externalized onto the public by private action. Not knowing how to do so, most courts remain focused exclusively on diminution of value, the market loss figure. Does the *Sibson* court's effort, which we will re-examine, offer a coherent alternative?

Section 2. DIMINUTION, THE DOMINANT TAKINGS TEST, AND "REASONABLE REMAINING USE"

The following case is the classic takings decision referred to in *Johnson*, *Sibson*, and virtually every other takings case since 1922. *Pennsylvania Coal* is the first case in which restricted property owners successfully persuaded the U.S. Supreme Court to expand the constitutional prohibition on uncompensated physical takings to nonphysical regulatory actions, focusing on the regulation's diminution effect on property values. The *Pennsylvania Coal* opinion, like its author, is suitably both eminent and enigmatic:

Pennsylvania Coal Co. v. Mahon
Supreme Court of the United States, 1922
260 U.S. 393, 43 S. Ct. 158

HOLMES, J. This is a bill in equity brought by the defendants in error to prevent the Pennsylvania Coal Company from mining under their property in such way as to remove the supports and cause a subsidence of the surface and of their house. The bill sets out a deed executed by the Coal Company in 1878, under which the plaintiffs claim. The deed conveys the surface but in express terms reserves the right to remove all the coal under the same and the grantee takes the premises with the risk and waives all claim for damages that may arise from mining out the coal. But the plaintiffs say that whatever may have been the Coal Company's rights, they were taken away by an Act of Pennsylvania, approved May 27, 1921 (P. L. 1198), commonly known there as the Kohler Act.... The statute forbids the mining of anthracite coal in such a way as to cause the subsidence of, among other things, any structure used as a human habitation [i.e., it forbade coal companies nearing the end of mining in underground coal seams from quarrying away parts of the supportive "pillars" of coal that had been kept in place to hold up the ceilings of the working mine if there were homes, public buildings, roads, lakes, or streams above].... As applied to this case the statute is admitted to destroy previously existing rights of property and contract. The question is whether the police power can be stretched so far.

Government hardly could go on if to some extent values incident to property could not be diminished without paying for every such change in the general law. As long recognized some values are enjoyed under an implied limitation and must yield to the police power. But obviously the implied limitation must have its limits or the contract and due process clauses are gone. One fact for consideration in determining such limits is the extent of the diminution. When it reaches a certain magnitude, in most if not in all cases there must be an exercise of eminent domain and compensation to sustain the act. So the question depends upon the particular facts. The greatest weight is given to the judgment of the legislature but it always is open to interested parties to contend that the legislature has gone beyond its constitutional power....

[In this case] the extent of the taking is great. It purports to abolish what is recognized in Pennsylvania as an estate in land – a very valuable estate – and what is declared by the Court below to be a contract hitherto binding the plaintiffs....

It is our opinion that the act cannot be sustained as an exercise of the police power, so far as it affects the mining of coal under streets or cities in places where the right to mine such coal has been reserved. As said in a Pennsylvania case, "For practical purposes, the right to coal consists in the right to mine it." Commonwealth v. Clearview Coal Co., 100 A. 820, 820 (Pa. 1917). What makes the right to mine coal valuable is that it can be exercised with profit. To make it commercially impracticable to mine certain coal has very nearly the same effect for constitutional purposes as appropriating or destroying it. This we think that we are warranted in assuming that the statute does.

The protection of private property in the Fifth Amendment presupposes that it is wanted for public use, but provides that it shall not be taken for such use without compensation. A similar assumption is made in the decisions upon the Fourteenth Amendment. When this seemingly absolute protection is found to be qualified by the police power, the natural tendency of human nature is to extend the qualifica-

HORGAN/LACKAWANNA HISTORICAL SOCIETY

Photographs from Scranton Pennsylvania showing mine subsidence cave-ins caused by removal of coal pillars beneath the city. The photo above, taken shortly before 1920, was presented to the legislature as part of the city's case for passage of the 1921 Kohler Act, which was declared unconstitutional in Pennsylvania Coal. *The bottom left photograph was taken in the first decade of the century. The residents of the home, Mr. and Mrs. Buckley, escaped safely by ladder up to the surface from their attic window.*

tion more and more until at last private property disappears. But that cannot be accomplished in this way under the Constitution of the United States.

The general rule at least is that while property may be regulated to a certain extent, if regulation goes too far it will be recognized as a taking. It may be doubted how far exceptional cases, like the blowing up of a house to stop a conflagration, go – and if they go beyond the general rule, whether they do not stand as much upon tradition as upon principle. In general it is not plain that a man's misfortunes or necessities will justify his shifting the damages to his neighbor's shoulders. We are in danger of forgetting that a strong public desire to improve the public condition is not enough to warrant achieving the desire by a shorter cut than the constitutional way of paying for the change. As we already have said this is a question of degree – and therefore cannot be disposed of by general propositions. But we regard this as going beyond any of the cases decided by this Court. We assume, of course, that the statute was passed upon the conviction that an exigency existed that would warrant it, and we assume that an exigency exists that would warrant the exercise of eminent domain. But the question at bottom is upon whom the loss of the changes desired should fall. So far as private persons or communities have seen fit to take the risk of acquiring only surface rights, we cannot see that the fact that their risk has become a danger warrants the giving to them greater rights than they bought. Decree reversed.

BRANDEIS, J., dissenting....

Coal in place is land, and the right of the owner to use his land is not absolute. He may not so use it as to create a public nuisance, and uses once harmless may, owing to changed conditions, seriously threaten the public welfare. Whenever they do, the Legislature has power to prohibit such uses without paying compensation; and the power to prohibit extends alike to the manner, the character and the purpose of the use.

Are we justified in declaring that the Legislature of Pennsylvania has, in restricting the right to mine anthracite, exercised this power so arbitrarily as to violate the Fourteenth Amendment? Every restriction upon the use of property imposed in the exercise of the police power deprives the owner of some right theretofore enjoyed, and is, in that sense, an abridgment by the state of rights in property without making compensation. But restriction imposed to protect the public health, safety or morals from dangers threatened is not a taking. The restriction here in question is merely the prohibition of a noxious use.... The state does not appropriate it or make any use of it. The state merely prevents the owner from making a use which interferes with paramount rights of the public.... The restriction upon the use of this property cannot, of course, be lawfully imposed, unless its purpose is to protect the public. But the purpose of a restriction does not cease to be public because incidentally some private persons may thereby receive gratuitously valuable special benefits.... Furthermore, a restriction, though imposed for a public purpose, will not be lawful unless the restriction is an appropriate means to the public end. But to keep coal in place is surely an appropriate means of preventing subsidence of the surface; and ordinarily it is the only available means. Restriction upon use does not become inappropriate as a means, merely because it deprives the owner of the only use to which the property can then be profitably put. The liquor and the oleomargarine cases settled that. Mugler v. Kansas, 123 U.S. 623, 668-669 (1887); Powell v. Pennsylvania, 127 U.S. 678, 682 (1888); Hadacheck v. Los Angeles, 239 U.S. 394 (1915). Nor is a restriction imposed through exercise of the police power inappropriate as a means, merely because the same end might be effected through exercise of the power of eminent domain, or otherwise at public expense. Every restriction upon the height of buildings might be secured through acquiring by eminent domain the right of each owner to build above the limiting height; but it is settled that the state need not resort to that power.

If by mining anthracite coal the owner would necessarily unloose poisonous gases, I suppose no one would doubt the power of the state to prevent the mining, without buying his coal fields. And why may not the state, likewise, without paying compensation, prohibit one from digging so deep or excavating so near the surface, as to expose the community to like dangers? In the latter case, as in the former, carrying on the business would be a public nuisance.

It is said that one fact for consideration in determining whether the limits of the police power have been exceeded is the extent of the resulting diminution in value, and that here the restriction destroys existing rights of property and contract. But values are relative. If we are to consider the value of the coal kept in place by the restriction, we should compare it with the value of all other parts of the land. That is, with the value not of the coal alone, but with the value of the whole property. The rights of an owner as against the public are not increased by dividing the interests in his property into surface and subsoil. The sum of the rights in the parts cannot be greater than the rights in the whole. The estate of an owner in land is grandiloquently described as extending ab orco usque ad coelum. But I suppose no one would contend that by selling his interest above 100 feet from the surface he could prevent the state from limiting, by the police power, the height of structures in a city. And why should a sale of underground rights bar the state's power? For aught that appears the value of the coal kept in place by the restriction may be negligible as compared with the value of the whole property, or even as compared with that part of it which is represented by the coal remaining in place and which may be extracted despite the statute.

Section 3. *PENNSYLVANIA COAL* TODAY: A RESIDUUM TEST

It was inevitable, perhaps, that such a difficult problem of democracy – defining the line between valid majoritarian regulatory demands and invalid confiscation of individual property rights when government regulation goes too far – would cause the courts such protracted difficulties.

Given the many different ways and degrees in which modern government can directly or incidentally burden private property, there can be no bright line objective test for delineating the frontier of regulations going "too far." Justice Holmes set out the dilemma in *Pennsylvania Coal.* Modern regulatory government is an irreversible necessity, Holmes realized, so all property owners must implicitly accept the possibility of substantial governmental restrictions under the states' police powers or their federal correlatives. But the mere fact that the public's interests are being rationally served by a regulation does not mean that individuals must accept any and all burdens. The Constitution must be interpreted to provide some reasonable protections to individuals' property rights so that private citizens do not end up providing a broad range of involuntary subsidies to the commonwealth. Without meaningful constitutional protection of private property, American units of government could not be trusted not to try to support themselves through a broad range of coerced regulatory subsidies unequally drawn from various regulated individuals and corporations. In *Pennsylvania Coal,* Holmes said the state must face scrutiny under the due process, contract, and eminent domain clauses. This logic was not new; it was discernible in several previous Supreme Court cases. What was new was that in *Pennsylvania Coal*, for the first time in the nation's history, Holmes' opinion actually struck down a regulation on the strength of a takings argument. In taking on that power and using it, it created the perplexing problem of developing a formula for defining just when invalid regulatory takings occur.[18]

The takings analysis advanced by Holmes in *Pennsylvania Coal* was characteristically perceptive, common-sensical, and flawed. It was quickly seized upon by succeeding generations of grateful courts, especially those tending toward a pro-corporate antiregulatory stance, as a beacon providing a verbal formulation for guidance in handling the daunting takings issue when it arose in judicial reviews of police power actions. Holmes, although he himself expressly said that he was presenting a limited, partial analysis, implying that other elements were relevant, in fact focused upon only one part of the dilemma, the degree of private loss: "One fact for consideration in determining such limits is the extent of the diminution." Because he discussed no other factor, many courts following his lead have tended to do the same. Whether they uphold or strike down challenged regulations, most courts tend to avoid defining any direct conception of how public and private rights are to be balanced against one another. Typically, as Holmes did in *Pennsylvania Coal*, public rights elements are discussed separately in a set of threshold inquiries based upon due process: Is there proper authority, a proper public purpose, a rational rather than an arbitrary or capricious regulatory scheme? Each of these typically is checked-off affirmatively. Then the effects upon private property rights are likewise analyzed separately, the degree of private economic diminution typically being viewed in a constitutional vacuum. Buttressed by Holmes' framing of the question, these diminution effects are viewed within the four corners of the particular piece of property, rather absolutely, without any relativity or proportionality to the surrounding constitutional context of public harms avoided. Brandeis in dissent tried to argue the relevance of context, but Holmes successfully evaded Brandeis's thoughtful hypotheticals.

Since *Pennsylvania Coal*, the courts' various verbal formulations typically verge on the tautological. At one extreme, a few courts defer so much to governmental acts that they virtually ignore particular regulatory effects upon private property rights in takings challenges, satisfying themselves that full due process has been accorded if only the public power requisites of authority, proper purpose, and rationality have been established.[19] At the opposite pole, many courts seem to focus

---

18. The Founding Fathers quite clearly did not intend that regulations could be takings (see Bosselman, Callies, and Banta, The Taking Issue (1973)) – a fact of constitutional history that gives pause to some who are otherwise strict-constructionists.

19. These courts say that where authority, proper purpose, and rationality are established, regulations do not amount to a taking or violation of due process if they cause incidental private property loss. See e.g. U.S. v. Central Eureka Mining Co., 357 U.S. 155, 165-169 (1958); Consolidated Rock Products v. Los Angeles, 370 P.2d 342, 346-347, 351-352 (Cal. 1962). By focusing on the first three tests, these courts disregard any question of the proportionality or fairness of the effect on individual private property. As to whether the private loss is "incidental," in point of fact property burdens are almost *always* incidental (if incidental means "not directly intended"), since imposing them is rarely the motivating public purpose.

only upon private diminution, in dramatic terms of "confiscation," "government land grabs," "socialism," and the like, that make proof of any substantial private loss a prelude to invalidation of the police power regulation. Either way, the tests operate in a vacuum. Even where courts discuss both public and private elements to some extent, as Holmes did in *Pennsylvania Coal*, they don't weigh them directly against one another because no judicial test for doing so has been established.

The situation is so amorphous that the U.S. Supreme Court for a long time ducked takings cases as much as it could, perhaps reflecting the Court's recognition that lack of an intelligible standard invites mere judicial gut reactions. Coinciding with the ascendancy of Mr. Justice Rehnquist, the Court has begun to show a heightened interest in taking on takings cases, often with the result of restricting police power regulation of economic interests.

Most courts today test takings under some version of what one of the authors has previously dubbed the "residuum" tests. These forms of the diminution test consider constitutional validity not so much in terms of how much has been lost to the property owner, as in terms of whether the remaining property value is constitutionally adequate. By far the most prevalent residuum test today (and the most prevalent test overall) is the "reasonable remaining use" test drawn from municipal zoning case law, widely followed by state and federal courts as a general test. When the Supreme Court had to determine whether New York City's historical preservation ordinance could block the owner of Grand Central station from raising a skyscraper over the old landmark, it used residuum reasoning. Pennsylvania Central Transportation Co. v. New York City, 438 U.S. 104 (1978). As articulated in the *Penn Central* court's final footnote[20] and a host of subsequent cases, police power regulations are valid if they leave property owners with some "economically viable" use. If not, they are putatively invalid. The courts may not know how to weigh public versus private rights one-on-one, but they usually do assert that a reasonable residual use is the minimal test of validity.

The "reasonable residuum" test developed in particular response to the problems posed by land use zoning. Following the lead of the model Standard State Zoning Enabling Act drafted in 1919, zoning presented the nation's first widespread takings question, intimately regulating land uses and in many cases depressing land values in thousands of cities and towns. Zoning was a novel form of the police power, making public planning part of the development process, serving purposes of "harmony" and "compatibility of uses" that went far beyond common law tort law. Euclid v. Ambler, the classic first zoning case in the Supreme Court,[21] established the validity of zoning but ducked the takings question. Whatever zoning was, the Court, for a variety of mixed political reasons, declared it basically OK if it followed the rules.

---

20. The Court's footnote 27 concluded that "if appellants can demonstrate at some point in the future that circumstances have changed such that the Terminal ceases to be...economically viable," appellants may obtain relief. The text of the majority opinion's final paragraph referred to a remaining "reasonable beneficial use." 438 U.S. at 138.

21. 272 U.S. 365 (1926).

Given the vagueness of zoning's specific objectives, it was especially hard to imagine how to weigh the constitutionality of its depressive effects on private property values. If my prohibited junkyard, gas station, or grocery store in the middle of a residential area could have earned me the equivalent of twice the sale price of a home each year, why was or wasn't that too much of a sacrifice on my part to make for the public's sake?

The reasonable residuum test provided the state courts, which have long dominated zoning law, with a rough and ready fallback minimum standard. Because the public "harms" that zoning addressed could not readily be quantified, like many environmental values, courts following *Euclid*'s lead had to figure out how zoning could ever be nonconfiscatory in the face of private loss, as the Supreme Court had indicated. If it was difficult to define how much private loss was too much, it was at least a practicable line to say that if too little was left over after zoning to provide an economically viable use, then zoning had probably gone too far as applied. Since 1926, the reasonable residuum test has served as an accepted takings norm for zoning cases. Moreover, since zoning cases have provided the vast majority of takings challenges, it is no surprise that the takings standard used in zoning cases came to be applied in other areas.

COMMENTARY AND QUESTIONS

1. Wetlands cases on a diminution baseline. Most wetlands takings cases, like most takings cases generally, focus on whether there is a reasonable remaining profitable use left to the regulated landowner. For the moment, presuming that many courts will continue to review regulations in this manner, note the games that can be played in the wetlands setting in determining how to measure whether there is a reasonable remaining use. If you do a schematic diagram of the *Johnson* case, it rapidly becomes clear that Dr. Johnson made a tidy profit from the earlier sale of dry land portions of his property that were previously sold for cottages. The court in *Johnson* asked the question whether there was a reasonable remaining profitable use *only of the regulated portion of the property*, not looking at the entire parcel. Note how the *Sibson* court looked at the regulations' effect on the private profit from the parcel as a whole, not merely the regulated portion. Not coincidentally, a focus on the regulated portion alone in wetland cases (and many other environmental settings) typically reveals that the regulation has eliminated virtually all economic value, while focus on the property owner's parcel as a whole often reveals a substantial profit that has been made or may be made in the future, rendering the regulation valid.

This question of what to consider as the baseline for judicial review of takings is an important fundamental point. If courts looked just at the regulated portion of property, many environmental regulations would be stuck down. Requiring catalytic converters on automobile engines would by this logic be held unconstitutional if automobile companies could not make a profit on that particular element of their automobiles; if a historical building cannot be profitably displayed to fee-paying visitors, historic preservation regulations would be void, even though the surrounding parcel of land supported profitable agricultural or other economic uses.

2. The judges' baseline game. The baseline question of what portion of property to view for the determination of diminution loss appeared in *Pennsylvania Coal* in Holmes' focus on the restricted pillar of coal, and Brandeis' argument that diminution should be viewed in the context of the entire coal field. Precisely the same arguments were repeated in the Supreme Court's 1987 opinion in Keystone Bituminous Coal Association v. Pennsylvania, 480 U.S. 470 (1987). Remarkably, *Keystone Bituminous* also involved a Pennsylvania statute requiring coal companies to keep underground pillars to support the surface. This time, for the majority, Justice Stevens successfully argued that the takings test should be based on the entire coal field owned by the coal company petitioners, not just on the coal pillars that the companies were required to leave untouched. After arguing (quite unconvincingly) that he was not overruling *Pennsylvania Coal,* Stevens wrote:

> Petitioners...claimed that they have been required to leave a bit less than 27 million tons of coal in place to support [protected surface] areas. The total coal in [their] thirteen mines amounts to over 1.46 billion tons. Thus [the Act] requires them to leave less than 2 percent of their coal in place.... Petitioners have never claimed that their mining operations, or even any specific mines, have been unprofitable since the Subsidence Act was passed. Instead Petitioners have sought to narrowly define certain segments of their property and assert that when so defined, the Subsidence Act denies economically viable use. They advance two alternative ways of carving their property in order to reach this conclusion. First, they focus on the specific tons of coal that they must leave in the ground under the Subsidence Act, and argue that the Commonwealth has effectively appropriated this coal since it has no other useful purpose if not mined. Second, they contend that the Commonwealth has taken a separate legal interest in property – the "support estate." Because our test for regulatory taking requires us to compare the value that has been taken from the property with the value that remains in the property, one of the critical questions is determining how to define the unit of property "whose value is to furnish the denominator of the fraction." Michelman, Property, Utility, and Fairness: Comments on the Ethical Foundations of Just Compensation Law, 80 Harv. L. Rev. 1165, 1192 (1967). In *Penn Central* the Court explained: "takings jurisprudence does not divide a single parcel into discrete segments and attempt to determine whether rights in a particular segment have been entirely abrogated. In deciding whether a particular governmental action has effected a taking, this Court focuses rather both on the character of the action and on the nature of the interference with rights *in the parcel as a whole....*"
>
> The 27 million tons of coal do not constitute a separate segment of property for takings law purposes. Many zoning ordinances place limits on the property owner's right to make profitable use of some segments of his property. A [setback] requirement that a building occupy no more than a specified percentage of the lot on which it is located could be characterized as a taking of the vacant area as readily as the requirement that coal pillars be left in place....
>
> The Court of Appeals...concluded that as a practical matter the support estate is always owned by either the owner of the surface or the owner of the

> minerals.... Its value is merely a part of the entire bundle of rights possessed by the owner of either the coal or the surface.

In vigorous dissent, Justice Rehnquist argued:

> In this case, enforcement of the Subsidence Act and its regulations will require Petitioners to leave approximately 27 million tons of coal in place. There is no question that this coal is an identifiable and separable property interest.... From the relevant perspective – that of the property owners – this interest has been destroyed every bit as much as if the government had proceeded to mine the coal for its own use.... In these circumstances I think it unnecessary to consider whether Petitioners may operate individual mines or their overall mining operations profitably, for they have been denied all use of 27 million tons of coal....
>
> Under Pennsylvania law, the support estate, the surface estate, and the mineral estate, are "three distinct estates in land which can be held in fee simple separate and distinct from each other...." Operation of this [Act] extinguishes the Petitioners' interests in their support estates, making worthless what they purchased as a separate right under Pennsylvania law. Like the restriction on mining particular coal, this complete interference with a property right extinguishes its value, and must be accompanied by just compensation.

Who got the better of this crucial definitional debate? Rehnquist argued further that there should be no difference between physical takings tests, like those applied in the airplane inverse condemnation cases, and regulatory takings, misleadingly citing *Causby*, the classic physical takings case for the proposition that "governmental action short of physical invasion may constitute a taking because such regulatory action might result in 'as complete [a loss] as if the government had entered upon the surface of the land and taken exclusive possession of it.'" 480 U.S. at 516, citing U.S. v. Causby, 328 U.S. 256, 261 (1946). In the airport cases, obviously, the taking of an easement, even though it amounted to a small fraction of the property value, would immediately require compensation as a governmental appropriation. Is there a distinction between physical and regulatory takings? If there isn't, whichever regulated interests regulated by government can be put into private easement form by attorneys would immediately require compensation, wouldn't they? Does that argument prove too much?

3. A challenger's baseline game. What if a property owner sells all the profitably developable portions of her property, and then goes to court claiming that the regulated leftover has no economic use? Presumably the court can take account of past profits as part of the balance. Does the timing of the regulation make any difference? What if a property owner consciously buys a heavily-regulated and completely undevelopable piece of land at a bargain price, and then goes to court claiming unconstitutional hardship? Some courts have held that property owners are estopped from attacking regulations that they knew about at the time of purchase; the majority of states, however, allow a person to buy land cheap, and then to argue that the regulation that had held down the purchase price was unconstitutional because it prevented profitable use. These states hold that one can never waive one's constitutional rights. The doctrine of "self-imposed hardship," however, developed in zoning law when challengers have consciously created sub-standard lots, argues that such diminution does not amount to a constitutional taking.

4. Defining "reasonable remaining use." If the courts are going to look only at whether there is a reasonable remaining use on whatever property baseline is defined, how does one determine what is a reasonable use? Compared to what? Presumably most land could be used to raise geraniums for sale, producing at least some small income. Is that enough? If the phrase means that the property owner must make a profit on the land, how much profit – 1 percent, 6 percent, 12 percent? And net profit based on what? If the landowner received the land free from her aunt, is that any different from just having purchased it for a million dollars? The standard answer in zoning cases seems to be that the land must be able to produce a reasonable profitable return, based on its market value in comparison to similarly situated parcels. Thus the market value of private property (which ignores externalized harms in much the same way as the industrial marketplace does) becomes the foundation of the typical constitutional takings equation.

5. A takings role for the public trust doctrine? Rex Lee, the ex-U.S. Solicitor General hired by the coal companies to attack Pennsylvania's Subsidence Act in *Keystone Bituminous*, decided on appeal not to challenge the portions of the mining regulations under the Act which forbade removal of pillars beneath streams and public waterbodies. Why? Did he recognize that there were pre-existing public trust rights, at least as to surface waters, so that no matter what property rights the private companies had bought, they had no right to drop lakes and streams into the depths of their coal mines?

Analytically, the public trust doctrine often offers a strategic and available argument to governments attempting to sustain environmental regulations against takings challenges, if they can identify pre-existing public trust rights incorporating the ecological status quo that would be destroyed by the prohibited private activity. Several state supreme courts have asserted that principle. Orion v. Washington, 747 P.2d 1062 (Wash. 1987); Potomac Sand & Gravel v. Governor of Maryland, 293 A.2d 241 (Md. 1972), cert. denied, 409 U.S. 1040 (1972). In Just v. Marinette County, 201 N.W. 2d 761 (Wisc. 1972), the Wisconsin Supreme Court upheld a wetland regulation, first, rather frivolously, on the theory that diminution should only be figured on the natural undeveloped value of the land as it had existed for 200 years, ignoring actual market values. More coherently, the court held that the wetlands were vested with a public trust that countered the private property diminution loss. Can you detect a hint of that argument within Judge Grimes' partial concurrence in *Sibson*?

Public trust rights are ever more widely recognized. Could Maine have argued that coastal wetlands are impressed with a public trust, even within private ownership, so that Dr. Johnson had no absolute right to develop? If rivers and wetlands are subject to the public trust, how about ancient virgin forests on private corporate lands in the Northwest, or protected wildlife eating and destroying private property in the settings noted at the end of the inverse condemnation section, comment 2 at page 441 *supra*?

If public trust rights exist within private property, then regulations merely give effect to a pre-existing potential limitation within the private title, and no regulatory taking can result therefrom. You cannot be deprived of what you never really had – an unfettered right to develop.

6. "Reciprocity of advantage." Picking up on a comment by Justice Holmes in *Pennsylvania Coal*, Justice Rehnquist also advanced the argument in *Keystone Bituminous* that since the early regulatory cases established that restrictions on property were constitutional if they provided a "reciprocity of advantage" to the regulated land-owner who shared in the restrictions' public benefits, the obverse was also true: if a property owner did not receive an equal advantagc from a regulation, then that established the restrictions' invalidity. No other justices have yet followed him down the reciprocity of advantage path, requiring that police power regulations be struck down if they don't provide benefits equal to regulatees' costs. What would happen if that test were adopted?

7. The "inverse condemnation" remedy transplanted to regulatory takings. We have seen in Subpart B of this chapter how a cause of action in inverse condemnation allowed plaintiffs to win a constitutional compensation claim against physical actions by government. The cases in this part of the chapter reflect the further possibility that compensation can be awarded – and be called "inverse condemnation" – when regulatory governmental actions, rather than physical acts, are determined to violate property rights. If courts find a regulation unconstitutional and require the government to pay compensation if it wants to continue to regulate,[22] analytically that is an inverse condemnation remedy.

Note, however, that there still is a major difference between the regulatory and the physical settings. In both cases, inverse condemnation can describe the cash *remedy* if it is awarded. The elements of the constitutional *causes of action* that lead to that remedy are very different, however. *Any* physical taking of land by the public (or of an easement to use land physically) requires compensation, regardless of how small the appropriation. See page 441 *supra*. In the regulatory context, Holmes and all subsequent courts have accepted the fact that *some* property loss is constitutionally permissible. The question in the regulatory cases is, "How much impact is too much?" If the same test of validity were applied in both settings, almost all regulations would be void. The regulated interest in virtually every case – the right to build in a wetland, the right to dump pollution into a river – could be characterized as governmental "taking" of an "easement," to wit the right to develop, or the right to pollute. See page 472 *infra*. This proves too much, so courts and scholars take more subtle approaches to regulatory takings analyses.

22. It is clear that governments have the choice whether to pay compensation and continue to apply the regulation that has been found to go too far, or to accept its nullification as to the challenger's property and thereby avoiding the need to pay (although temporary interim damages may be assessed). First English Evangelical Lutheran Church v. Los Angeles, 482 U.S. 304 (1987); see also page 472 *infra*.

Section 4. THE BOTTOM LINE: REGULATORY VALIDITY WHERE THERE IS NO REMAINING ECONOMIC USE

The "reasonable residuum" test does indeed generally provide a logical minimum standard of validity in zoning cases, but it may become less fitting when it is inverted into a universal test of invalidity, especially in circumstances, unlike most zoning settings, where public harms are discrete and obvious.[23] The problem of such promiscuous application of the reasonable remaining use test is that it of necessity focuses only upon a regulation's effect on private property. In the zoning context, the only tangible losses are to private market values: The public considerations involved in zoning a particular parcel are extremely intangible, so the rough justice of the reasonable remaining use test makes some sense as a practicable standard in the zoning setting. The test becomes quite illogical, however, where public harms are tangible.

As noted earlier, on its terms the "reasonable remaining use" formulation tests regulations in a complete vacuum, paying no heed to what kind or degree of public interest is involved, nor to the particular actions or settings of private property owners. Accordingly, quite strange results follow from the avowed terms of the test if courts do not employ an array of fudge factors and adjustments.

Imagine, for example, a hypothetical cyanide-manufacturer faced with a governmental ban on discharging cyanide into rivers. If the factory owners could show that their particular product cannot be produced without generating large amounts of cyanide waste water, which cannot economically be reused and must be discharged into surface waters, and that their custom-designed machinery and other plant assets can only be used for making that product, they would seemingly have made out an impregnable case of regulatory invalidity! The total value of the plant has been destroyed by the regulation. In fact, the plant's value is now a negative figure, because the customized machinery and factory assets will have to be removed before the land can be put to other economic uses. There is no remaining economically viable beneficial use, so the factory owners would be assured the constitutional right to dump their cyanide into the river, or be compensated fully for not doing so.

Can this be? To require government to pay for preventing harmful private actions, where protective regulations foreclose all profitable uses, would seem to let the Chicago school of economics run riot, diminishing the role of government as sovereign protector of the public, and recasting it in the role of a merchandising broker paying for public safety like any other desired commodity. The extent of private diminution caused by governmental regulation is certainly relevant in determining a regulation's validity, but viewed alone in a vacuum should never be completely determinative. The bottom line is that some regulations must necessarily be constitutional, as in the cyanide hypothetical, *even if they destroy all private property value*. Justice Brandeis was trying to raise this compelling point in *Pennsylvania Coal*: "If, by mining anthracite coal, the owner would necessarily

---

23. Portions of this text are adapted from Plater, The Takings Issue in a Natural Setting: Floodlines and the Police Power, 52 Texas L. Rev. 201, 244-252 (1974).

unloose poisonous gasses, I suppose no one would doubt the power of the state to prevent the mining without buying his coal fields." 260 U.S. at 418.

EXPLORING THE "NUISANCE EXCEPTION"

The possibility that complete property wipeouts may be constitutionally valid has not been totally ignored. Even Justice Rehnquist has noted the possibility.[24] Confronted with the cyanide factory example, he would undoubtedly explain the obvious constitutionality of the pollution regulation as falling within the "noxious use,"[25] or "nuisance exception...a narrow exception allowing the government to prevent a misuse or illegal use." *Keystone*, 480 U.S. at 512. See also Curtis v. Benson, 222 U.S. 78, 86 (1911). Because dumping cyanide can be readily labelled a public nuisance, that designation automatically removes it from any claim of private property rights. But as Justice Rehnquist applies the nuisance test, it is extremely narrow and tautological, a jurisprudence of labels that is useful only in obvious cases. By acknowledging a nuisance exception as a simple all-or-nothing ground for regulatory validity, judges who use it fail to inquire into *why* a nuisance is not being constitutionally protected in such cases. Isn't it because judges intuitively balance harms, and when they say that a regulation isn't an invalid taking because it restricts a "nuisance," they are implicitly holding that public harms imposed by the private action outweigh private rights? If this is so, the logic of that constitutional balance should extend beyond the nuisance label, which would allow the kinds of harms underlying environmental regulation in cases not formally recognized as "nuisances." Accepting the logic of Justice Rehnquist's nuisance exception would then go far toward clarifying the elements of takings jurisprudence.

Restricting the concept to a non-analytical labelling exercise, on the other hand, causes real problems. What gets labelled a nuisance, for instance? Only actions traditionally recognized as nuisances per se? That would seem unnecessarily restrictive a definition. On the other hand, the nuisance exception clearly doesn't mean that any act that is prohibited by a regulation is illegal and thus is not constitutionally protected. That would be a tautology on the permissive extreme, making it far too easy for government, because by definition virtually all environmental regulations declare restricted private property activities illegal.

The better course is for courts to enter into an open analysis and application of the basic logic of Justice Rehnquist's acknowledged takings exception for nuisances: private property uses can be constitutionally restricted and in some cases totally suppressed when they impose sufficiently serious burdens and costs upon their neighbors and the public, even if they have not been previously recognized as nuisances per se.

---

24. Penn Central, 438 U.S. at 145.

25. Noxious use cases replicate the circular reasoning semantics of the automatic nuisance exception. A classic example of the noxious use analysis is Mugler v. Kansas, 123 U.S. 623 (1887)(shutting down a brewery by regulation was no taking because alcohol was deemed a noxious use), or Miller v. Schoene, 276 U.S. 272 (1928)(statute requiring cedar trees to be destroyed was valid because they posed a disease threat to apple trees). These cases are analytically very interesting, but not because of their conclusory language dismissing the private property as noxious.

Take the example of an earthquake zone or mudslide ordinance in a region prone to seismic activity. If residences or other structures are forbidden on steep slopes within a hundred meters of earthquake faults, for example, the resulting diminution losses may drop market value from $100,000 an acre to less than $500. But the building of homes and other structures on slopes is not a nuisance recognized in the annals of the common law. Court review, however, would quite reasonably take account of the fact that, without the regulation, foreseeable losses to life and property, public services, and disaster relief might well be astronomical. Put in this context, a court should not hesitate to bring the precise public harms that prompted the legislature to pass the regulation in the first place into the active constitutional balance. Viewed in this context, a reasonable court assessing the validity of the earthquake zone would appropriately hold the regulation valid. Why? Because at the very least, property owners do not have the right to impose greater costs upon the public than they themselves would suffer from the restriction of their market activity. The same would seem to hold true in avalanche zones, or (far more commonly) in floodplain areas where regulations exclude residential structures from areas likely to be flooded.

Yet, the limited logic of the diminution test has become so dogmatic in many American courts that they strike down floodplain restrictions even where a developer plans to put 300 housing units in the path of an imminently foreseeable flood. Dooley v. Fairfield, 226 A.2d 509 (Conn. 1967). In a 1987 Supreme Court case, First English Evangelical Lutheran Church v. Los Angeles, 482 U.S. 304, decided on other grounds, Justice Rehnquist posited that a floodplain ordinance was an unconstitutional confiscation because it eliminated existing economic uses of a riverside campground area that the property owner had been using as a camp for handicapped children. This amounted to the argument that a property owner had a constitutional right to house 200 children in the path of impending floods, or be compensated fully for the prohibition of that use. On remand, the California appeals court refused to accept that conclusion, and the Supreme Court denied certiorari. 258 Cal. Rptr. 893 (1989), cert. denied, 110 S. Ct. 866 (1990).

The reasonable conclusion would seem to be that the constitutional balance of alleged environmental takings must be relative, not a simplistic all-or-nothing definition of whether or not something is a "nuisance" recognized by the courts. Otherwise the market value of private property losses will completely dominate the question. As in the floodplain setting, market values often ignore the potential for catastrophic impacts on the public and future inhabitants of regulated areas. Market values, after all, are set in such circumstances by the dumbest class of buyers – whoever will offer the highest price for a piece of residential riverfront land. To elevate that short-sighted market to a constitutional determinant is not a compelling exercise of constitutional logic.

A discriminating balancing process requires some proportionality between the degrees of public need and private loss. While minor threats to the public cannot justify devastating private losses, large personal losses may be supportable when great public interests are imperiled.

The essential proposition that distills from the confusion of the takings tests is that courts must explicitly recognize both the individual losses that government action causes and the costs that private uses impose upon the public. This approach forces courts to consider complex physical and ecological resource relationships and to distinguish between the different effects of property use. Using this process, the courts are in a far better position to undertake the balancing task that remains at the heart of judicial review. Reconstituted in this way, the balancing approach does two things: it offers one firm minimum constitutional conclusion and produces a two-stage takings inquiry that provides a more rational and workable rule.

The first stage of this "diminution-balancing" approach consists of implementing the assertion that regulations are always constitutionally valid when the costs that an unrestricted property use imposes upon the public would be greater than private diminution losses. No private loss, in other words, can be constitutionally excessive if it is less than the costs it would impose on others. So a plaintiff's prima facie case against a regulation would have the burden of showing not only economic loss but also that the private loss exceeds the public harms the regulation was reasonably designed to prevent.

As to the second stage of the takings balance, the zoning cases make clear that the plaintiff still must further show that no reasonable economic use remains, viewed over the plaintiff's entire contiguous parcel, not just the regulated segment thereof. If a court upholds an environmental regulation in such a fallback reasonable-residuum inquiry, presumptively the plaintiff would have fared no better under the old less explicit takings tests.

COMMENTARY AND QUESTIONS

1. Can wetland regulations prevail under a reformed takings test? The diminution-balancing test advocated in the preceding text would require a two-stage review, first to determine whether private losses exceed public harms, and second whether there is any reasonable remaining use. Won't wetland regulations fail both these tests, unless fortuitously the property owner's parcel contains buildable high ground outside of the wetlands area? The problem is, as to the second stage, that a wetlands parcel that is completely restricted typically has no appreciable commercial use. That leaves wetlands restrictions dependent upon the assertion of the first stage test, that building on wetlands will potentially cause more harm than the private losses sustained. But are courts willing to count wetland losses as "harms" in the same league as floodplain property and safety hazards, earthquake and mudslide hazards, avalanche hazards, or the other hypotheticals discussed earlier? The loss of a 5-acre parcel of wetlands, as noted in the *Johnson* case, is the loss of "a valuable natural resource [that] plays an important role in the conservation and development of aquatic and marine life, gamebirds and waterfowl." Coastal wetlands are the spawning areas for millions of dollars worth of commercial fish caught in the open ocean, and wetlands serve as natural sponges, buffering and holding high water conditions. Reading *Sibson*, note how the court took judicial notice of widespread ecological public harms from wetland destruction, in sustaining the validity of the ordinance. Does *Sibson* lead the way to a more articulated public rights balancing of private rights in the wetlands setting? But aren't the effects of wetlands losses rather abstract and remote, especially because they are based on cumulative losses of thousands of acres of wetlands?

In a Florida wetland mining case, Florida Rock Industries v. United States, 8 Cl. Ct. 160 (1985), the U.S. Army Corps of Engineers had denied a permit for phosphate rock mining that eventually would have destroyed two and a half square miles of wetlands in western Dade County, an area that already was losing extensive wetlands to other earlier permitted phosphate mining operations. Speaking for the court, Judge Kozinski took notice of the public harms argument made by the Corps as defendant, that property losses were allegedly permissible "because the proposed use of the property would cause pollution."... "Defendant argues that there is no right to use one's property so as to harm others, and government may therefore prohibit such uses without paying compensation." The judge then examined the extent of pollution effects from wetland mining, both to the subsurface groundwater, surface water, and nearby water courses, ultimately concluding that "plaintiff's proposed rock mine would not have resulted in pollution of the water supply." But what about the other negatives caused by destruction of wetlands? The *Florida Rock* opinion mentioned that the project would eliminate "valuable habitat and food chain resources," destroy wildlife, and replace "a place of great natural beauty, teeming with an astonishing variety of life forms" with "unsightly and barren...rock pits." It held, however, that the harm caused by the loss of the wetland was not entitled to judicial consideration because it was merely a question of "the public's continued enjoyment of the environmental and aesthetic values." "Courts do not view the public's interest in environmental and aesthetic values as a servitude upon all private property, but as a public benefit that is widely shared and therefore must be paid for by all," citing Maine v. Johnson. Injuries to human life and property would be considered, in other words, but not the more abstruse ecological values addressed by wetlands regulations.[26]

Would the argument of the public trust doctrine have changed Judge Kozinski's balance? If the water-based ecological resources of the wetlands were identified as public property rights under the public trust, would that have induced the judge to consider the effects of rock mining as a cognizable public harm?

2. Can a court consider ecological cumulation? Part of the perplex of *Florida Rock* is that, like so many other takings cases, it considers only those harms directly arising on the regulated property. But what of the reality that environmental losses

26. Judge Kozinski also applied a "reasonable-residuum," second-stage test. Instead of looking for "remaining market value," however, he said that land had to retain a "remaining [present] market use" in order for a restriction to survive. Even if the land still had market value, it could not be considered because speculative values could not be considered in order to avoid a taking. On appeal, the latter definition of market value was modified to recognize that present values based on future uses could be used. 791 F.2d 893 (11th Cir. 1986). On remand, however, the Claims Court determined that there was no reasonable remaining market value, and ordered compensation. 21 Cl. Ct. 161 (1990). Judge Kozinski's original comprehensive consideration of public harms was apparently accepted throughout the subsequent proceedings.

are cumulative? In the Maine and New Hampshire coastal wetlands cases, for instance, it might have been possible to show that if regulations were struck down, unless compensated (a fiscal impossibility), the cumulative loss of spawning resources would eliminate 20 percent of commercial fish stocks supporting a $400 million fisheries industry. Would that catch a judge's eye and be legitimately factored into the constitutional balance? If a harms-based takings test is applied case by case, without regard to cumulation, it would result in the piecemeal cumulative destruction of a widespread wetland resource. If harms are cumulated, on the other hand, it might be virtually impossible for any private property owner to overturn wetlands regulations. If a court cumulates public harms, should it also cumulate all private market value losses in order to balance constitutional factors? These and other constitutional and ecological conundrums are presented with particular vividness by the wetlands situation, although *Florida Rock* and *Sibson* are the rare exceptions in taking on the question of the overall balance of public versus private rights in takings cases.

3. Other takings tests. Among a wide variety of competing alternative takings test proposals, here are some more:

Professor Dunham proposed a shift away from consideration of private economic loss, instead basing a takings test on public purpose: if the public purpose is to prevent a harm, then the regulation is valid; if the public purpose is to obtain a free benefit without paying for it, then the regulation is a taking. In clear cases at either end of the spectrum, this test is obviously sensible. Do you see, however, how the definition of public purpose in the middle grey area is either subjective, or a tautological self-fulfilling prophecy? Dunham, A Legal & Economic Basis for City Planning, 58 Colum. L. Rev. 650 (1958); and Dunham, Flood Control Via the Police Power, 107 U. Pa. L. Rev. 1098 (1959).

Professor Sax argues that reviewing courts should look for "spillovers." Property owners have no right to impose spillover effects on surrounding parcels, and if they do the legislature can choose which activity to prohibit, without having to pay compensation. The problem here is that Professor Sax takes no account of spillovers' different magnitudes, qualities, or fairness expectations. He classes even visual effects as spillovers, so if house construction on my property would block public view of a beautiful landscape, the house could be prohibited without compensation. Sax, Takings: Private Property & Public Rights, 81 Yale L.J. 149, 155-72 (1971).

Another test, echoed occasionally in the Supreme Court but never the basis of a holding, is that courts should base takings holdings on "the extent to which the regulation has interfered with distinct investment-backed expectations." (See cases cited in Connolly v. Pension Benefit, 475 U.S. 211, 224-225 (1986).) This test appears to derive from a law review article by Professor Michelman, who urged, not as a constitutional taking test but as a social policy decision, that legislatures should compensate when the effects of their restrictions would upset the fairness and investment expectations of the marketplace. Michelman, Property, Utility, &

Fairness: Comments on the Ethical Foundations of "Just Compensation" Law, 80 Harv. L. Rev. 1165 (1967). Consider this test in the context of Brandeis' poison gas example in *Pennsylvania Coal*: if a landowner discovers, to her dismay, that her land contains poison gas deposits, so that it cannot safely be developed, her expectations clearly are frustrated; but is that constitutional injury, or merely bad luck? The legislature may well decide to reimburse her as charity, but must it?

As a different form of test, Judge Lehman once proposed a rubric that has struck a responsive chord with dozens of courts since then. A regulation will be unconstitutional, he wrote in Arverne Bay Construction Co. v. Thatcher, 15 N.E.2d 587 (N.Y. 1938), if it removes all valuable incidents from the property owner "except the duty to continue paying property taxes on the land." This quip is probably wrong: if property is regulated so as to have sharply reduced market value, landowners have a constitutional right to roll tax assessments back down to market value *as restricted*, eliminating most of the burden of property taxes thereon.

For better or worse, the diminution tests – in various forms and with various accomodations to the necessities of balancing public and private harms – are likely to dominate takings jurisprudence for the foreseeable future.

4. Rethinking rights. At the beginning of this chapter we noted that extremely rigorous defense of private property rights was a special characteristic of American democracy, and one of the commonly-credited reasons (along with the nation's extraordinary natural wealth available for exploitation) for the American economy's world dominance. In other nations more densely populated and less richly endowed, property rights resemble privileges and are tempered by public rights. In many countries, for instance, landowners have only qualified rights to mineral resources beneath the surface, and are forced to share the authority to permit mining, and royalties, with their governments. In most modern nations it would be unthinkable for property owners to assert a right to destroy permanently the utility and value of their land, but environmental defendants in this country have recurringly made that fundamental claim, as in the coal stripmining controversies.[27]

The awakening debate about civic responsibilities as counterweights to rights[28] invites further questions about the absolutist nature of the private property assertions so regularly heard contesting regulatory actions by federal, state, and local governments:

> [When rights in general] have a strident and absolutist character, they impoverish political and judicial discourse. They do not admit of compro-

27. The stripminers' claim would concede that activities can be restrained if substantial adverse effects extend beyond the boundaries of the private property, but may argue that, compared with their economic stakes, no more than de minimis spillovers occur. "And anyway," one miner told one of the authors, "these coal regions are economically just national sacrifice areas." In Germany, by way of contrast, the idea that land can be written off forever on a draconian economic balance would offend even the mining companies. See Plater, Coal Law from the Old World, 64 Ky. L.J. 473, 500–501 (1976).

28. See references to Professors Glendon and Sunstein's work, in Chapter 8 at page 364 *supra*.

> mise. They do not allow room for competing considerations. They impair and even foreclose deliberation. Rooted in 19th century ideas of absolute [private] sovereignty over property, they are ill-adapted to a long discussion of tradeoffs and competing needs. They are, moreover, overly individualistic [and focused on the short-term].... They miss the "dimension of sociality" and posit selfish, isolated individuals asserting what is theirs rather than participating in communal life. Sunstein, Rightalk, 205 The New Republic No. 10, 33 (Sept. 2, 1991).[29]

Although the rights-and-responsibilities theorists have sometimes been considered reactionaries, the more sophisticated civic debate they call for cannot be typecast. In the regulatory takings field, for instance, it could do much to temper the average court's preclusive focus on private effects to the exclusion of careful consideration of the public harms that motivate regulation.[30] Coupled with notions of the public trust – and modern acknowledgment of the loss of the mythical American frontier with its boundless resources and ability to absorb mistakes – might it mean that old conceptions of isolated private sovereign rights in land are changing?

Section 5. OTHER TAKINGS ISSUES: REMEDIES, EXACTIONS, AND INNOCENT LANDOWNER WIPEOUTS

a. TAKINGS REMEDIES

If a regulation is finally determined to be an invalid taking, two remedies are available: (1) an equitable injunction or declaration that the regulation is void as applied to that particular parcel, or (2) payment by the government for the taking under the rubric of "inverse condemnation" as it applies to regulatory takings. *First English*, 482 U.S. 304 (1987), made it clear that governments always have the choice. Do you see what the political effect would be if, as previously sought by industry, the Court had permitted plaintiffs to dictate the choice of remedy by suing only under a damage claim?

Governments will only rarely choose to buy off a regulated property owner if regulation has been found to be a taking. If it does so choose, it is not clear how compensation should be measured. Take a zoning example, with regard to a parcel that would have a full fee simple market value of $100,000 if unregulated. Assume that a court is willing to make especially precise findings of fact, and determines that market value after zoning is $20,000 and that is too little, hence unconstitutional, but that a remaining value of $60,000 would have been constitutional. How much would government have to pay, if it is not taking possession but only maintaining the regulation? $80,000? $40,000?

---

29. (Professor Sunstein is describing Professor Glendon's analysis. Mary Ann Glendon, Rights Talk: The Impoverishment of Political Discourse (1991).)

This dimension of sociality is fine, says the landowner, but why do *I* have to bear the brunt of your highminded civic protections?

30. After surveying the cases, Professor Sax observed that in most cases there apparently is "a hierarchy [of constitutional values] in which the right to profit stands first, with [only] a grudging exception for exigent public need." Sax, Takings, Private Property, and Public Rights, 81 Yale L.J. 149, at n. 7 (1971).

Even tougher is the question of valuing temporary takings, where the state decides to give up and suspend the regulation's application to the parcel, but the landowner, using another element of *First English*'s holding, demands compensation for the "temporary" taking between the time the regulation was applied and the time that it is suspended. What should the measure of such temporary damages be? If it is the difference in market value, that will often have *increased* between the time of the initial regulation and the time the regulation is released. Some courts have argued that "rent" must be paid by government, or even "lost profits." These latter figures can become huge, thereby chilling the exercise of the police power from the start, which may be the point in the first place. What local government wants to undertake an environmental regulation when affected property owners can argue that it confiscates their property, and force payment of millions in lost profits if a court agrees with them? See Almota Farmer's Elevator & Warehouse Company v. U.S., 409 U.S. 470 (1973)(rental value was used as the measure of damages in a physical appropriation case).

b. AMORTIZATION AND OFFSET ALTERNATIVES?

One way government can attempt to secure their regulations against takings challenges is by providing a period of delay before enforcement, to allow the property-owner to "amortize" and recoup her investment before it is shut down. If state or local governments wish to ban billboards, for example, they may provide a four-year amortization period. The billboard industry, one of the strongest lobbies in the nation, is sure to challenge the ban as a regulatory taking. How is amortization, which has been upheld in a wide variety of other property land use regulations, likely to fare against billboards? See Mayor and Council of New Castle v. Rollins Outdoor Advertising, Inc., 459 A.2d 541 (Del. 1983)(three years insufficient); Village of Skokie v. Walton, 456 N.E.2d 293 (Ill. App. 1983)(seven years OK). Is it relevant that a billboard company has long since written off the billboard in depreciation credits on its tax books for the Internal Revenue Service? Nat'l Advertising Co. v. County of Monterey, 464 P.2d 33 (Cal. 1970)(tax depreciation can be considered); Art Neon v. Denver, 488 F.2d 118 (10th Cir. 1973)(amortization need not await depreciation); Modjeska Sign Studios, Inc. v. Berle, 373 N.E.2d 255 (N.Y. 1977)(ditto).

Another possibility is a takings compensation offset. If, for example, the state and federal governments created thousands of acres of private agricultural land out of Florida swamps by channelizing the Kissimmee River at public expense, must they now, 30 years later, pay full dry-land market value when they decide that groundwater levels must be raised, returning some of the lands to wetlands (because the loss of marshes turned out to cause massive pollution effects in downstream water supplies and Lake Okeechobee)? Can a state condemning a billboard agree to pay its fair market value *minus an offset amount attributable to public expenditures*, i.e., excluding all value attributable to the highway? See U.S. v. Cors, 337 U.S. 325 (1949)(government expropriating a vessel need not pay higher values attributable to demand caused by government program). U.S. v. Miller, 317 U.S. 369 (1943). Successful offset arguments, however, are rare.

c. EXACTIONS AND THE *NOLLAN* CASE

Physical appropriations by the public, as opposed to mere regulatory prohibitions, are virtually always a taking. See Loretto v. Teleprompter, 458 U.S. 419 (1982). In many so-called 'exaction' cases, however, government regulations have been upheld when they required regulated landowners to provide free property for public parks, or public schools, or roadways, and the like, for public ownership and use, in return for getting development permits, as in subdivision regulation and urban "linkage" programs. In Nollan v. California Coastal Commission, 483 U.S. 825 (1987), the Supreme Court held that such exactions are valid where a landowner seeks permission from government to do something the government could prohibit outright if it wished (e.g., higher-density development of a coastline parcel of land). The government may require the landowner to give public easements over the private property as a condition of permit approval. In *Nollan*, however, the exaction was unconstitutional because the exacted physical easement was a public right of lateral passage along the high water mark, and there was no sufficient nexus between the purpose of the permit (regulation of coastal density) and the required exaction. If a government required landowners, for instance, to provide free open public right-of-way access from a highway across the private property to the beach, that would be constitutionally valid, because the need for public access was related to the ongoing increases in the density of side-by-side residential development along the coast.

Exactions, now confirmed by the Supreme Court in *Nollan* so long as a proper nexus is established, are likely to serve in many other environmental settings, although the degree to which the test requires directness of nexus and proportionality of burdens has not yet been established.

d. DUE PROCESS AND THE INNOCENT LANDOWNER

Here is a final, tough takings problem presented by environmental regulation: assume that your client has purchased a 3-acre piece of land for $20,000 in order to build a greenhouse. She begins digging foundations but suddenly hits fifty leaking unmarked barrels filled with toxic wastes. She notifies the appropriate government agencies, which congratulate her on her forthrightness, and then tell her that the bill for cleanup, for which she is responsible under state and federal statutes, will be $600,000! She turns to you and says, "This has got to be unconstitutional." That hypothetical situation was possible under the federal Superfund statute prior to SARA's 1986 "innocent landowner" exceptions, and is still possible under some state Superfund statutes and in other statutory settings.

Is there a viable constitutional argument against the validity of such heavy monetary burdens imposed by regulation, perhaps focusing on the innocent landowner's lack of fault, intent, or "nexus" to the causation of toxic leakage? The landowner is not, in any conventional sense, the cause of the problem. Would the legal challenges focus upon individual confiscatory effects, the fourth category of police power tests, or upon the third, "rational relationship," test?

Most property owners would reasonably expect that when they buy land, they are taking some chances; *caveat emptor*, buyer beware. But the most one thinks is being risked is the amount of the purchase price of the land. Environmental cases have demonstrated that potential liability may be a hundred times the purchase price of the land. This is a setting in which "fairness expectations" are clearly upset. Does that mean the regulations are unconstitutional?

In an acid mine pollution case, Commonwealth v. Barnes & Tucker Company, 371 A.2d 461 (Pa. 1977), the court noted that the mining company had proved that virtually all of the acid mine water draining from its mine came from the past wrongful activities of neighboring coal mines now abandoned. The court nevertheless held the defendant liable to pay for the entire cleanup, perhaps under some sort of theory of "enterprise liability," an approach that has been followed by other courts. But what about innocent nonindustry landowners, especially if they have not been negligent in failing to discover the toxic materials prior to buying the land?

The innocent landowner is constitutionally a tough problem. Clearly, the innocent owner's land still may be leaching poisonous materials into public groundwater. The landowner would seem to have some responsibility. To extend it, however, to the massive financial burden of cleaning up all toxic wastes on-site raises a difficult fairness problem that, given the heritage of the American bench and bar, is likely to become a serious and challenging constitutional point.

Chapter 10

ENVIRONMENTAL ISSUES IN THE DIVISION OF AUTHORITY BETWEEN FEDERAL AND STATE GOVERNMENTS

Major environmental law issues regularly arise from the tension that exists between the federal government and the states. The tension emanates from three elementary propositions of American constitutional law:

- The spheres of operation of the national government are limited rather than general;
- Within the enumerated areas of its competence the power of the national government is superior to the power of the states; and, correlatively,
- The states surrendered their power to exercise authority in any way that is inconsistent with the constitution or federal law.

These three constitutional truisms, although necessary to understanding modern federal-state relations, are of differing contemporary significance. Limitations on the range of permissible federal authority today have been rendered virtually irrelevant for the purposes of environmental law by the broad construction given to federal authority under the commerce power. Thus, in the environmental area, it is generally accurate to assume that the federal government, if it wishes to act, may do so.[1] This chapter explores the surprisingly sophisticated analysis required to understand how the latter two principles (federal supremacy and state limitation) can operate to disable state environmental regulation in some settings.

1. Federal authority occasionally faces half-hearted quibbles. In the field of wildlife law, for example, it is not clear by what power the federal government prohibits the killing of an endangered species population that exists only within the borders of a state. 16 U.S.C.A. §1531 et seq. In such cases, unless a treaty is relevant, the commerce power seems to be stretched to the limit, but the courts have not been seriously troubled by the challenge. See Bean, The Evolution of National Wildlife Law 21 (2d ed. 1983). The only other area commonly raising doubts about the reach of federal authority is direct federal enactment of land use controls, a function that is generally viewed as local in nature and intimately associated with traditional state prerogatives. Faced with vehement state and local opposition, the federal government has made little effort at direct land use control on lands not in federal ownership. (Lands owned by the federal government are subject to federal regulation as authorized by the property clause which allows Congress to "make all needful Rules and Regulations" for federal lands. U.S. Const., Art. IV, §3, cl. 2.)

A. PRE-EMPTION OF STATE AUTHORITY BY FEDERAL STATUTES AND IMPLEMENTING REGULATIONS

Section 1. THE POTENTIAL FORCE OF THE SUPREMACY CLAUSE AND THE DOCTRINE OF PRE-EMPTION OF STATE AUTHORITY

By now you have encountered environmental regulations imposed by each of the three levels of government – federal, state, and local. Some areas of environmental concern are subjected to concurrent regulatory efforts by authorities at more than one level. Inevitably cases arise in which compliance with the commands of both governments is either difficult or impossible, or in which the commands of different sovereigns are working at cross purposes to one another. Even more commonly, the commands of one government are more exacting than that of another. What is a polluter legally required to do when one government's law allows her to do one thing, while the law of another government commands her to do something different? In an early environmental pre-emptive case, for instance, diesel oil-fired boilers approved under federal regulations were subjected to tougher smoke pollution standards applied by the City of Detroit where the ships docked in Detroit for loading and unloading.[2] Mining companies with valid federal permits to mine federal land can suddenly be confronted with state restrictions that severely limit or forestall their mining.[3] And so on.

Real predicaments can arise from different governments' shared authority. Differences between concurrent regulations pose an important challenge for the legal system, which must find principles for coordinating the different provisions and resolving conflicts. In the American legal system these principles begin with constitutional analysis.

The supremacy clause of Article VI of the United States Constitution provides:

> This Constitution, and the Laws of the United States which shall be made in Pursuance thereof; and all Treaties made, or which shall be made, under the authority of the United States, shall be the supreme Law of the Land; and the Judges in every State shall be bound thereby, any Thing in the Constitution or Laws of any State to the Contrary notwithstanding.

Despite the grant of supremacy in the enumerated areas of national authority, the concept of American federalism has operated to preserve as much power to the states as possible. The spirit of that federalism is captured in the words of the Tenth Amendment:

> The powers not delegated to the United States by the Constitution, nor prohibited by it to the States, are reserved to the States respectively, or to the people.

---

2. Huron Portland Cement Co. v. Detroit, 362 U.S. 440 (1962)(noted at 498 *infra*; the city won).

3. This hypothetical resembles the situation in California Coastal Commission v. Granite Rock Company, 480 U.S. 572 (1987), that appears at page 499 *infra*.

The potentially antagonistic concepts of federal supremacy and the desire to maintain state authority, can be, and are, reconciled by creating a presumption in favor of the validity of concurrent regulation by both the federal and state governments.[4] Despite the supremacy of federal authority, if possible in each case it is presumed to be exercised in a way that does not disable the states' authority. In regulating the production, distribution, labelling and application of pesticides, for example, the federal government acts under its enumerated powers and the states and local governments act using their non-displaced powers.[5]

Should it wish to do so, Congress can act to forbid the states from regulating a subject of national concern, but that intention to pre-empt state authority needs to be manifest either in the legislation itself, or by implication from the scope and range of congressional action. Additionally, in cases of conflict between state law and federal law, even where Congress has not manifested an intent to pre-empt the entire field, the simple command of the supremacy clause is that where a state enactment is incompatible with federal law, the state regulatory effort must fall. The Supreme Court in Wisconsin Public Intervenor v. Mortier, 111 S.Ct. 2476 (1991), summarized the general framework of pre-emption analysis as follows:

> Under the Supremacy Clause, U.S. Const., Art. VI, cl. 2, state laws that "interfere with, or are contrary to the laws of congress, made in pursuance of the constitution" are invalid. Gibbons v. Ogden, 9 Wheat. 1, 211 (1824)(Marshall, C.J.). The ways in which federal law may pre-empt state law are well established and in the first instance turn on congressional intent. Congress' intent to supplant state authority in a particular field may be express in the terms of the statute. Absent explicit pre-emptive language, Congress' intent to supersede state law in a given area may nonetheless be implicit if a scheme of federal regulation is "so pervasive as to make reasonable the inference that Congress left no room for the States to supplement it," if "the Act of Congress...touch[es] a field in which the federal interest is so dominant that the federal system will be assumed to preclude enforcement of state laws on the same subject," or if the goals "sought to be obtained" and the "obligations imposed" reveal a purpose to preclude state authority. Rice v. Santa Fe Elevator Corp., 331 U.S. 218, 230 (1947). See Pacific Gas & Electric Co. v. State Energy Resources Conservation and Development Commission, 461 U.S. 190, 203-204 (1983). When considering pre-emption, "we start with the assumption that the historic police powers of the States were not to be superseded by the Federal Act unless that was the clear and manifest purpose of Congress." *Rice, supra*, 331 U.S. at 230.

---

4. Regulations issued by local governments via delegation of police power from state government are included here under the category of state regulation. It should also be noted that the same pre-emption arguments presented here between federal and state levels of government can also be made between state and local levels. Local returnable bottle ordinances, for instance, have been attacked by the throwaway bottle industry as allegedly pre-empted by the existence of state agency regulations in the consumer beverage field.

5. In the environmental field this will usually mean that the federal government acts pursuant to its very broadly construed power to regulate interstate commerce, and the states and local governments act pursuant to their traditional police power to regulate matters affecting health, safety, and welfare.

> Even when Congress has not chosen to occupy a particular field, pre-emption may occur to the extent that state and federal law actually conflict. Such a conflict arises when "compliance with both federal and state regulations is a physical impossibility," Florida Lime & Avocado Growers, Inc. v. Paul, 373 U.S. 132, 142-143 (1963), or when a state law "stands as an obstacle to the accomplishment and execution of the full purposes and objectives of Congress." Hines v. Davidowitz, 312 U.S. 52 (1941).
>
> It is, finally, axiomatic that "for the purposes of the Supremacy Clause, the constitutionality of local ordinances is analyzed in the same way as that of statewide laws." Hillsborough v. Automated Medical Laboratories, Inc., 471 U.S. 707, 713 (1985).

COMMENTARY AND QUESTIONS

1. The *Mortier* case in brief. *Mortier* involved a chemical applicator's pre-emption challenge to a local ordinance regulating pesticide spraying. The relevant federal statute, the Federal Insecticide, Fungicide, and Rodenticide Act (FIFRA), 7 U.S.C.A. §136 et seq., grants "states" the power to regulate pesticide applications more stringently than did FIFRA. It was argued that Congress, by granting "states" the power to regulate more stringently, impliedly precluded local governments from doing the same. Starting with the strong presumption against pre-emption in the quoted passage, the Supreme Court rejected the challenge. First, the Court found no express language in FIFRA that supersedes local authority. It interpreted the word "state" in the section permitting additional regulation as a generic term that allowed states the discretion to delegate that power to political subdivisions. The Court similarly found no implied intent to oust local governments. Finally, the Court ruled that the regulation in this case created no actual conflict with FIFRA (i.e., compliance with both was physically possible), and the concept of local regulation generally was consistent with FIFRA's goals.

Notice that in *Mortier*, as in most pre-emption cases, the federal pre-emption argument is not being raised by the federal government but by a regulated industry that does not want to comply with stricter state or local environmental standards.

2. Four categories of pre-emption cases. There are four discernably different categories of pre-emption delineated by the Court's language in *Mortier* and its previous cases.

The first is express pre-emption. This occurs when Congress, in the text of its legislation, directly declares that the federal regulatory scheme is to be exclusive of additional regulation. The second category of pre-emption is congressionally-*implied* pre-emption, where the statutory context or legislative history can support a court's holding that, by implication, Congress intended, as with express pre-emption, that the federal regulatory provisions be exclusive of additional regulation. The third form of pre-emption involves cases in which dual compliance with both federal and state regulation is practically impossible. These can be called physical-contradiction cases. An example would be a federal government requirement that freight trains pull 100 freight cars at a time (for energy efficiency, perhaps), where state or local regulations prohibited trains of more than 50.[6] Finally, the fourth form of pre-emption argument arises when a state law allegedly interferes with the accomplishment of the policy objectives of a federal law. This might be called policy-contradiction pre-emption. This type of argument is raised most dramatically in cases where states want to restrict nuclear plants for safety reasons, and confront federal laws intended in part to *promote* nuclear industry.[7] It might seem to border on misnomer to apply the "pre-emption" label to these physical contradiction and policy contradiction cases because they involve only the straightforward application of the supremacy clause. Their denomination as pre-emption cases arises mainly from the common analysis that goes into determining that there is a conflict between the challenged state law and the federal regulatory regime.

These four analytical categories explain the setting of virtually all regulatory pre-emption cases. Arguments claiming express pre-emption by Congress are relatively rare, primarily because Congress rarely expressly pre-empts anything. Physical contradiction claims by defendants occur regularly. Implied pre-emption arguments and policy-contradiction arguments, which are also often heard, resemble one another but are analytically distinct: implied pre-emption (our second category) is based on a court's interpretation of Congress's words and legislative intent – finding that Congress actually desired its statute to pre-empt state or local efforts. In policy-contradiction cases, on the other hand, Congress may not have intended pre-emption, but the court may find that effectuation of Congress's purposes requires pre-emption. In any event, successful pre-emption arguments, in any of the four categories, are relatively infrequent. Because the payoff to defendants can be dramatic, however – elimination of a whole level of liability on a matter – defense attorneys often raise pre-emption claims. For the environmental defense bar, moreover, pre-emption often seems to offer an opportunity for a complicated argument when no other defense appears to be available.

3. The scope of pre-emption. In all four categories of pre-emption arguments, there is a further need to define the scope of what is purportedly pre-empted. Pre-emption can be held to override specific provisions, or it can preclude shared authority from an entire field of regulation. The latter wide-ranging pre-emption – often called "field-occupancy" or "field pre-emption" – would exclude state and local regulations from a sphere reserved to federal authority even if the federal government had not promulgated any regulations in the particular area covered by state and local enactments. The scope of pre-emption in the field occupancy cases tends to be broad

---

6. The state or local requirement might be based on grade-crossing traffic reasons. A similar case where a federal regulation mandated a standard directly contradicted by the state standard, so that one could not physically comply with both, is Southern Pacific Co. v. Arizona, 325 U.S. 761 (766), which, however, was decided based on dormant commerce clause issues studied in subpart B *infra*.

7. In these cases, there is no physical contradiction: by complying with the state's tougher emission standard, one automatically complies with the federal, but the federal nuclear promotion policy is diluted. Even the nuclear policy-contradiction argument has not always prevailed, as seen later in this section. In determining whether Congress's *policy* has been contradicted, judges get to exercise far more personal subjectivity than in cases of straightforward physical contradiction. See *Pacific Gas and Electric*, 461 U.S. 190 (1983). Cf. Northern States Power Co. v. Minnesota, 447 F.2d 1143 (8th. Cir. 1971), aff'd 405 U.S. 1035 (1972).

– whole areas of regulation are put beyond the ambit of state control, nuclear safety regulations is the classic example. This preclusion occurs when the federal policy interest concerns overarching national interests or issues requiring national uniformity of regulation.[8]

The application of field pre-emption in environmental cases has, in general, been extremely rare. Two different factors seem to play a key role. First, Congress has frequently expressed its desire to tolerate non-uniformity in environmental standard-setting as long as federal minima are satisfied, thus limiting congressionally expressed or implied pre-emption. Second, environmental regulation has traditionally been an area of state regulatory competence, so the courts as well as the Congress are reluctant to find broad pre-emption. Futher, do you see why pre-emption arguments in the physical contradiction cases would almost always be particularized rather than field-pre-empted?

4. The role of Congress and the courts in finding pre-emption. Who makes the pre-emption decision, Congress or the courts? While the practical answer may be that the courts decide pre-emption cases, the legal process answer is that pre-emption must derive from Congress' authority and intent as effectuated by the statutes. The objective for courts in pre-emption cases, as in most cases of statutory interpretation, is to do the bidding of Congress, as long as Congress is acting within its proper sphere of authority. Different cases, however, present courts with different degrees of opportunity for applying their own judgments about what Congress intended.

5. The presumption against pre-emption. Where does the presumption against pre-emption originate? The presumption cannot have been created by Congress: Congress has never spoken in the abstract about the relation of its legislation to the residual power of states to regulate. The presumption must come from either the Constitution or the courts. Although the presumption may be a plausible means for accommodating federal supremacy with due regard for the role of the states, even the most ardent states' rights advocate would not claim that the Tenth Amendment *compels* the courts to erect such a presumption. It is more plausible to argue that the presumption is erected by the courts, guided by their sense of American political theory. Here matters of history surrounding the framing of the Constitution, the Federalist Papers, and similar materials that document the vitality of the states as sovereigns, even after the forming of the nation, all come to bear.

Is the presumption against federal pre-emption of state authority uniformly strong in all cases, or does it vary with the subject matter of the cases involved? A number of United States Supreme Court cases suggest that the presumption is of variable

---

8. Hines v. Davidowitz, 312 U.S. 52 (1947) is the source of the language that is now routinely used to describe field pre-emption based on policy contradiction. In *Hines* a Pennsylvania alien registration law was pre-empted because it was held to conflict with the need for national uniformity in the field of immigration and naturalization. The burden of compliance with the state registration law was quite modest and did not make it any harder to comply with parallel federal programs; nevertheless, the desirability of single uniform national standards swayed the Court. The result of *Hines* was the practical ouster of the states from all efforts to regulate aliens, for if a mere registration law conflicted with federal policy, almost any law would.

force. Anti-pre-emption presumption is strongest in cases where the state is regulating in an area of traditional state concern. See e.g., Hillsborough v. Automated Medical Laboratories, Inc., 471 U.S. 707, 712 (1985). Most environmental concerns, including land use regulation and pollution control as part of public health regulation, lie at the core of traditional state and local authority.

6. The non-pre-emption presumption as executive policy. During the Reagan Administration, federalism concerns were a matter of ideological and political importance. On October 26, 1987, Executive Order 12,612 announced a position on "Federalism." Invoking in §2(e) the words of Thomas Jefferson that the States are "the most competent administrations for our domestic concerns and the surest bulwarks against antirepublican tendencies," the Executive order went on to announce that "in the absence of clear constitutional or statutory authority, the presumption of sovereignty should rest with the individual States." §2(i). The order also includes the following position on pre-emption:

> §4 Special Requirements for Pre-emption.
>
> (a) To the extent permitted by law, Executive departments and agencies shall construe, in regulations and otherwise, a Federal statute to pre-empt State law only when the statute contains an express pre-emption provision or there is some other firm and palpable evidence compelling the conclusion that Congress intended pre-emption of State law, or when the exercise of State authority directly conflicts with the exercise of Federal authority under the Federal statute.

What legal force does this Executive Order have in cases raising issues of federal pre-emption? As a pure legal matter, it can be argued that the order has virtually no effect. The key issue in each case is congressional intent, and the policy views of the executive branch are simply irrelevant. More pragmatically, however, the views of the executive branch are quite important, especially in cases where the claim of pre-emption is based on doing violence to the interests of a federal program. In *Mortier*, for example, the federal Department of Justice participated in the litigation arguing *against* federal pre-emption. The executive branch thereby added not only its prestige to the arguments supporting local regulation of pesticides; it also added the tacit support of the Environmental Protection Agency, as the administering agency, that its regulatory program would not be impaired by allowing local regulation.

Section 2. CONGRESSIONAL PRECLUSION OF STATE LAW THROUGH OCCUPANCY OF THE FIELD

As pointed out in the preceding section, federal pre-emption of state authority usually involves either a form of contradiction between the federal law and the attempted concurrent state regulation or Congressional occupation of an entire field. The cases raising claims of field occupancy pre-emption, at least in the environmental area, virtually all arise in the field of regulation of nuclear materials and nuclear power plants. This is an area where Congress has long been viewed as having intended to pre-empt the fields of radiation safety and power plant construction and operations from state regulation. See Northern States Power Co. v. Minnesota, 447 F.2d 1143 (8th Cir. 1971), aff'd 405 U.S. 1035 (1972). In other areas of environmental law, viable claims of field occupancy probably have been headed off by the strong presumption against pre-emption in traditional areas of state regulation. Even in regard to the nuclear industry, the following case demonstrates that even though some field occupancy pre-emption is allowed in regard to nuclear energy production, the states can retain considerable latitude to act.

Pacific Gas and Electric v. California Energy Resources Conservation & Development Commission

United States Supreme Court, 1983

461 U.S. 190, 103 S.Ct. 1713, 75 L.Ed. 752

WHITE, J. The turning of swords into plowshares has symbolized the transformation of atomic power into a source of energy in American society. To facilitate this development the Federal Government relaxed its monopoly over fissionable materials and nuclear technology, and in its place, erected a complex scheme to promote the civilian development of nuclear energy, while seeking to safeguard the public and the environment from the unpredictable risks of a new technology. Early on, it was decided that the States would continue their traditional role in the regulation of electricity production. The interrelationship of federal and state authority in the nuclear energy field has not been simple; the federal regulatory structure has been frequently amended to optimize the partnership.

This case emerges from the intersection of the Federal Government's efforts to ensure that nuclear power is safe with the exercise of the historic state authority over the generation and sale of electricity. At issue is whether provisions in the 1976 amendments to California's Warren-Alquist Act, Cal. Pub. Res. Code Ann. §25524,[9] which condition the construction of nuclear plants on findings by the State Energy Resources Conservation and Development Commission that adequate storage

---

9. Eds.: In relevant part the statute provides:

California Civil Code §25524.2.

Disposal of high-level nuclear waste; conditions for plant certification and land use; findings; resolution of disaffirmance; vested rights

> No nuclear fission thermal powerplant, including any to which the provisions of this chapter do not otherwise apply, but excepting those exempted herein, shall be permitted land use in the state, or where applicable, be certified by the [State Energy Resources Conservation and Development] commission until both conditions (a) and (b) have been met:
>
> (a) The commission finds that there has been developed and that the United States through its authorized agency has approved and there exists a demonstrated technology or means for the disposal of high-level nuclear waste.
>
> (b) The commission has reported its findings and the reasons therefor pursuant to paragraph (a) to the Legislature. Such reports of findings shall be assigned to appropriate policy committees for review. The commission may proceed to certify nuclear fission thermal powerplants 100 legislative days after reporting its findings unless within those 100 legislative days either house of the Legislature adopts by a majority vote of its members a resolution disaffirming the findings of the commission made pursuant to paragraph (a)....
>
> (c) As used in this section, "technology or means for the disposal of high-level nuclear waste" means a method for the permanent and terminal disposition of high-level nuclear waste. It shall not necessarily require that facilities for the application of such technology and/or means be available at the time the commission makes its findings. Such disposition shall not necessarily preclude the possibility of an approved process for retrieval of such waste.

facilities and means of disposal are available for nuclear waste, are pre-empted by the Atomic Energy Act of 1954, 42 U.S.C. §2011 *et seq.*

A nuclear reactor must be periodically refueled and the "spent fuel" removed. This spent fuel is intensely radioactive and must be carefully stored. The general practice is to store the fuel in a water-filled pool at the reactor site. For many years, it was assumed that this fuel would be reprocessed; accordingly, the storage pools were designed as short-term holding facilities with limited storage capacities. As expectations for reprocessing remained unfulfilled, the spent fuel accumulated in the storage pools, creating the risk that nuclear reactors would have to be shut down. This could occur if there were insufficient room in the pool to store spent fuel and also if there were not enough space to hold the entire fuel core when certain inspections or emergencies required unloading of the reactor. In recent years, the problem has taken on special urgency. Some 8,000 metric tons of spent nuclear fuel have already accumulated, and it is projected that by the year 2000 there will be some 72,000 metric tons of spent fuel. Government studies indicate that a number of reactors could be forced to shut down in the near future due to the inability to store spent fuel.

There is a second dimension to the problem. Even with water-pools adequate to store safely all the spent fuel produced during the working lifetime of the reactor, permanent disposal is needed because the wastes will remain radioactive for thousands of years. A number of long-term nuclear waste management strategies have been extensively examined. These range from sinking the wastes in stable deep seabeds, to placing the wastes beneath ice sheets in Greenland and Antarctica, to ejecting the wastes into space by rocket. The greatest attention has been focused on disposing of the wastes in subsurface geologic repositories such as salt deposits. Problems of how and where to store nuclear wastes has engendered considerable scientific, political, and public debate. There are both safety and economic aspects to the nuclear waste issue: first, if not properly stored, nuclear wastes might leak and endanger both the environment and human health; second, the lack of a long-term disposal option increases the risk that the insufficiency of interim storage space for spent fuel will lead to reactor shutdowns, rendering nuclear energy an unpredictable and uneconomical adventure....

The Act requires that a utility seeking to build in California any electric power generating plant, including a nuclear powerplant must apply for certification to the State Energy Resources Conservation and Development Commission....

Section 25524.2 deals with the long-term solution to nuclear wastes. This section imposes a moratorium on the certification of new nuclear plants until the Energy Commission "finds that there has been developed and that the United States through its authorized agency has approved and there exists a demonstrated technology or means for the disposal of high-level nuclear waste ...." §§25524.2(a), (c). Such a finding must be reported to the state legislature, which may nullify it.

In 1978, petitioners Pacific Gas & Electric Co. and Southern California Edison Co. filed this action in the United States District Court, requesting a declaration that numerous provisions of the Warren-Alquist Act, including the two sections challenged here, are invalid under the Supremacy Clause because they are pre-empted by the Atomic Energy Act. The District Court held...that the two provisions are void because they are pre-empted by and in conflict with the Atomic Energy Act. 489 F. Supp. 699 (E.D. Cal. 1980). The Court of Appeals for the Ninth Circuit...held that the nuclear moratorium provisions of §25524.2 were not pre-empted because §§271 and 274(k) of the Atomic Energy Act, 42 U.S.C.A. §§2018 and 2021(k), constitute a congressional authorization for States to regulate nuclear powerplants "for purposes other than protection against radiation hazards." The court held that §25524.2 was not designed to provide protection against radiation hazards, but was adopted because "uncertainties in the nuclear fuel cycle make nuclear power an uneconomical and uncertain source of energy." 659 F.2d 903, at 925 (1981). Nor was the provision invalid as a barrier to fulfillment of the federal goal of encouraging the development of atomic energy. The granting of state authority in §§271 and 274(k), combined with recent federal enactments, demonstrated that Congress did not intend that nuclear power be developed "at all costs," but only that it proceed consistent with other priorities and subject to controls traditionally exercised by the States and expressly preserved by the federal statute....

It is well established that within constitutional limits, Congress may pre-empt state authority by so stating in express terms. Absent explicit pre-emptive language, Congress' intent to supersede state law altogether may be found from a " 'scheme of federal regulation ... so pervasive as to make reasonable the inference that Congress left no room for the States to supplement it,' because the 'Act of Congress may touch a field in which the federal interest is so dominant that the federal system will be assumed to preclude enforcement of state laws on the same subject,' or because 'the object sought to be obtained by the federal law and the character of obligations imposed by it may reveal the same purpose.' " Even where Congress has not entirely displaced state regulation in a specific area, state law is pre-empted to the extent that it actually conflicts with federal law. Such a conflict arises when "compliance with both federal and state regulations is a physical impossibility," or where state law "stands as an obstacle to the accomplishment and execution of the full purposes and objectives of Congress."

Petitioners, the United States, and supporting *amici*, present three major lines of argument as to why §25524.2 is pre-empted. First, they submit that the statute – because it regulates construction of nuclear plants and because it is allegedly predicated on safety concerns – ignores the division between federal and state authority created by the Atomic Energy Act, and falls within the field that the Federal Government has preserved for its own exclusive control. Second, the statute, and the judgments that underlie it, conflict with decisions concerning the nuclear waste disposal issue made by Congress and the Nuclear Regulatory Commission. Third, the California statute frustrates the federal goal of developing nuclear technology as a source of energy. We consider each of these contentions in turn.

Even a brief perusal of the Atomic Energy Act reveals that, despite its comprehensiveness, it does not at any point expressly require the States to construct or authorize nuclear powerplants or prohibit the States from deciding, as an absolute or conditional matter, not to permit the construction of any further reactors. Instead, petitioners argue that the Act is intended to preserve the Federal Government as the sole regulator of all matters nuclear, and that §25524.2 falls within the scope of this impliedly pre-empted field. But as we view the issue, Congress, in passing the 1954 Act and in subsequently amending it, intended that the federal government should regulate the radiological safety aspects involved in the construction and operation of a nuclear plant, but that the States retain their traditional responsibility in the field of regulating electrical utilities for determining questions of need, reliability, cost, and other related state concerns. Need for new power facilities, their economic feasibility, and rates and services, are areas that have been characteristically governed by the States....

So we start with the assumption that the historic police powers of the States were not to be superseded by the Federal Act "unless that was the clear and manifest purpose of Congress...."

[F]rom the passage of the Atomic Energy Act in 1954, through several revisions, and to the present day, Congress has preserved the dual regulation of nuclear-powered electricity generation: the Federal Government maintains complete control of the safety and "nuclear" aspects of energy generation; the States exercise their traditional authority over the need for additional generating capacity, the type of generating facilities to be licensed, land use, ratemaking, and the like.

The above is not particularly controversial. But deciding how §25524.2 is to be construed and classified is a more difficult proposition. At the outset, we emphasize that the statute does not seek to regulate the construction or operation of a nuclear powerplant. It would clearly be impermissible for California to attempt to do so, for such regulation, even if enacted out of non-safety concerns, would nevertheless directly conflict with the NRC's exclusive authority over plant construction and operation. Respondents appear to concede as much. Respondents do broadly argue, however, that although safety regulation of nuclear plants by States is forbidden, a State may completely prohibit new construction until its safety concerns are satisfied by the Federal Government. We reject this line of reasoning. State safety regulation is not pre-empted only when it conflicts with federal law. Rather, the Federal Government has occupied the entire field of nuclear safety concerns, except the limited powers expressly ceded to the States. When the Federal Government completely occupies a given field or an identifiable portion of it, as it has done here, the test of pre-emption is whether "the matter on which the State asserts the right to act is in any way regulated by the Federal Act." Rice v. Santa Fe Elevator Corp., 331 U.S. at 236. A state moratorium on nuclear construction grounded in safety concerns falls squarely within the prohibited field. Moreover, a state judgment that nuclear power is not safe enough to be further developed would conflict directly with the countervailing judgment of the NRC that nuclear construction may proceed notwithstanding extant uncertainties as to waste disposal. A state prohibition on nuclear construction for safety reasons would also be in the teeth of the Atomic Energy Act's objective to insure that nuclear technology be safe enough for widespread development and use – and would be pre-empted for that reason.

That being the case, it is necessary to determine whether there is a non-safety rationale for §25524.2. California has maintained, and the Court of Appeals agreed, that §25524.2 was aimed at economic problems, not radiation hazards....

Without a permanent means of disposal, the nuclear waste problem could become critical, leading to unpredictably high costs to contain the problem, or worse, shutdowns in reactors. "Waste disposal *safety*," the Reassessment Reports notes, "is not directly addressed by the bills, which ask only that a method [of waste disposal] be chosen and accepted by the federal government."

The Court of Appeals adopted this reading of §25524.2. Relying on the Reassessment Report, the court concluded:

> [S]ection 25524.2 is directed towards purposes other than protection against radiation hazards. While Proposition 15 would have required California to judge the safety of a proposed method of waste disposal, section 25524.2 leaves that judgment to the federal government. California is concerned not with the adequacy of the method, but rather with its existence. 659 F.2d at 925.

Our general practice is to place considerable confidence in the interpretations of state law reached by the federal courts of appeals.

Although these specific indicia of California's intent in enacting §25524.2 are subject to varying interpretation, there are two further reasons why we should not become embroiled in attempting to ascertain California's true motive. First, inquiry into legislative motive is often an unsatisfactory venture. What motivates one legislator to vote for a statute is not necessarily what motivates scores of others to enact it. Second, it would be particularly pointless for us to engage in such inquiry here when it is clear that the States have been allowed to retain authority over the need for electrical generating facilities easily sufficient to permit a State so inclined to halt the construction of new nuclear plants by refusing on economic grounds to issue certificates of public convenience in individual proceedings. In these circumstances, it should be up to Congress to determine whether a State has misused the authority left in its hands.

Therefore, we accept California's avowed economic purpose as the rationale for enacting §25524.2. Accordingly, the statute lies outside the occupied field of nuclear safety regulation.

Petitioners' second major argument concerns federal regulation aimed at the nuclear waste disposal problem itself. It is contended that §25524.2 conflicts with federal regulation of nuclear waste disposal, with the NRC's decision that it is permissible to continue to license reactors, notwithstanding uncertainty surrounding the waste disposal problem, and with Congress' recent passage of legislation directed at that problem....

California [has not, however] sought through §25524.2 to impose its own standards on nuclear waste disposal. The statute accepts that it is federal responsibility to develop and license such technology. As there is no attempt on California's part to enter this field, one which is occupied by the Federal Government, we do not find §25524.2 pre-empted any more by the NRC's obligations in the waste disposal field than by its licensing power over the plants themselves....

Finally, it is strongly contended that §25524.2 frustrates the Atomic Energy Act's purpose to develop the commercial use of nuclear power. It is well established that state law is pre-empted if it "stands as an obstacle to the accomplishment and execution of the full purposes and objectives of Congress."

There is little doubt that a primary purpose of the Atomic Energy Act was, and continues to be, the promotion of nuclear power. The Act itself states that it is a program "to encourage widespread participation in the development and utilization of atomic energy for peaceful purposes to the maximum extent consistent with the common defense and security and with the health and safety of the public." 42 U.S.C. §2013(d). The House and Senate Reports confirmed that it was a "major policy goal of the United States" that the involvement of private industry would "speed the further development of the peaceful uses of atomic energy...."

The Court of Appeals' suggestion that legislation since 1974 has indicated a "change in congressional outlook" is unconvincing. The court observed that Congress reorganized the Atomic Energy Commission in 1974 by dividing the promotional and safety responsibilities of the AEC, giving the former to the Energy Research and Development Administration (ERDA) and the latter to the NRC. Energy Reorganization Act of 1974, 88 Stat. 1233, 42 U.S.C. §5801 et seq. The evident desire of Congress to prevent safety from being compromised by promotional concerns does not translate into an abandonment of the objective of promoting nuclear power. The legislation was carefully drafted, in fact, to avoid any anti-nuclear sentiment....

The Court of Appeals is right, however, that the promotion of nuclear power is not to be accomplished "at all costs." The elaborate licensing and safety provisions and the continued preservation of state regulation in traditional areas belie that. Moreover, Congress has allowed the States to determine – as a matter of economics – whether a nuclear plant vis-à-vis a fossil fuel plant should be built. The decision of California to exercise that authority does not, in itself, constitute a basis for pre-emption. Therefore, while the argument of petitioners and the United States has considerable force, the legal reality remains that Congress has left sufficient authority in the States to allow the development of nuclear power to be slowed or even stopped for economic reasons. Given this statutory scheme, it is for Congress to rethink the division of regulatory authority in light of its possible exercise by the States to undercut a federal objective. The courts should not assume the role which our system assigns to Congress.

The judgment of the Court of Appeals is affirmed.

COMMENTARY AND QUESTIONS

1. The concurring, even less pre-emptive view in *Pacific Gas.* Justice Blackmun, joined by Justice Stevens, wrote separately, taking issue with the portion of the majority opinion arguing that a state could not prohibit nuclear power totally if it were motivated by safety. The first ground of disagreement was that the majority had overstated the scope of the field expressly occupied by Congress: it was not the broad field of nuclear safety concerns that Congress had addressed; it was only the narrower field "of how a nuclear power plant should be constructed and operated to protect against radiation hazards." The concurrence also viewed the promotion of nuclear power as only intending to make that option an available energy source, not a mandatory one. This difference in view would deflect a challenge based on policy contradiction pre-emption when a state imposed extremely rigorous standards, or declined to have nuclear power for whatever reason.

2. Congressional intent to pre-empt nuclear state safety standards. Congress pretty clearly intended to pre-empt nuclear radiation safety issues from state and local control. Whatever one's views about the nuclear establishment and the national decision to add nuclear power to America's energy policy, a strong case can be made for uniformity in setting nuclear radiation standards. The technical details of plant design and licensing are dictated by both applicable safety standards and available nuclear technology. If states set radiological emission standards different from federal standards, plants in different locations would be forced to employ different design and radiation control techniques. This variation would require expensive, unique designs for each such plant, making the cost of nuclear generation all the more expensive. Still, despite the logic in support of uniform standards, state governments feel that health, safety, and welfare are quintessentially state concerns. Many would like to require safer, lower levels of radiation emissions into their receiving air and water, based on state-of-the-art scientific research. Several states tried to do so, but were quashed. See *Northern States Power*, 447 F.2d 1143 (8th Cir. 1971), aff'd 405 U.S. 1035 (1972).

3. The "different purpose" test of pre-emption. The California legislation is but one of many examples that opposition to nuclear power plants has continued unabated since the advent of commercial reactors. The California legislation, in effect, placed a moratorium on nuclear development in the state. Do you suppose that fiscal responsibility was truly the driving purpose behind the state legislation and the popular referendum that preceded it?

Justice White declared that "the test of pre-emption is whether 'the matter on which the State asserts the right to act is in any way regulated by the Federal Act.'" He decided that it was not, mainly on the basis that California had a different purported purpose than safety when it regulated. Granting that the Supreme Court should not readily ignore a state's declarations about what its true legislative purpose was, nevertheless isn't the question also whether state regulation functionally determines matters that the federal government is supposed to decide, like questions of nuclear plant construction and design? What would Justice White do in the event that the NRC approves a technology for spent fuel reprocessing and the California Energy Commission or the Legislature still refuses to certify a nuclear power plant? Does it matter how expensive the reprocessing method is?

4. Beyond purpose: conflicting policies. Perhaps *Pacific Gas* and other pre-emption cases can be better understood as judicial recognition that many areas of modern life involve a wide array of important governmental policies – economic, social, environmental, health, and safety – and that none of these policies, even nuclear promotion, is so predominant as to override all other legitimate governmental concerns. At one level the resolution of this problem is semantic. The Court notes that if a field is "pervasively regulated" by the federal government, then the state can't enter it at all. The pervaded field might have been defined as anything affecting in any way the design and operation of nuclear plants, which would have precluded California's regulation. But the definition of pervasively regulated fields tends to be narrower, as with nuclear plant safety in *Pacific Gas*. If the courts decide that not everything remotely touching "nuclear design or safety" is pre-empted, then the way is open to permit a variety of governmental policies, state as well as federal, to be applied. (This is another example of how the policy contradiction argument leaves room for judicial subjectivity.) One may thus read *Pacific Gas* as an avenue toward democratic pluralism.

5. Federal pre-emption of tort remedies. In Silkwood v. Kerr-McGee, 464 U.S. 238 (1984), at page 306 *supra*, a sizeable award of state common law damages, both compensatory and punitive, were upheld against a claim of federal pre-emption of nuclear safety issues. After *Silkwood*, how likely is it that federal pre-emption of any state common law tort recoveries for injuries caused by a federally regulated activity will be found in the absence of express congressional language to that effect?

In English v. General Electric Company, __ U.S. __, 110 S.Ct. 2270 (1990), the Court revisited the subject of pre-emption of tort remedies in another case involving a nuclear materials processor as defendant. In that case the plaintiff reported workplace safety violations and eventually was fired by her employer. She sought a statutory remedy under a whistleblower's provision of the federal Energy Reorganization Act of 1974, but was denied relief on procedural grounds. She subsequently filed a state common law tort suit for intentional infliction of emotional distress and was met with the claim of federal pre-emption. A unanimous Supreme Court rejected the pre-emption argument. The Court stated:

> Although the decision in *Silkwood* was based in substantial part on legislative history suggesting that Congress did not intend to include in the pre-empted field state tort remedies for radiation-based injuries, we think it would be odd, if not irrational, to conclude that Congress intended to include tort actions stemming from retaliation against whistleblowers in the pre-empted field but intended not to include tort actions stemming from radiation damage suffered as a result of actual safety violations. 110 S.Ct. at 2279.

The court also rejected the narrower argument that the enactment of a federal whistleblower remedy precluded the availability of additional state law-based remedies that served a similar purpose.

6. Other environmental pre-emptions. Pre-emption issues have arisen in a variety of other environmental controversies, where regulated interests have attempted to use federal law to trump state or local regulations (or state law to trump local regulations). The cases include efforts to prevent local town governments from passing ordinances requiring stricter standards of herbicide and pesticide applicators, as in *Mortier*, to industry efforts to prevent states from requiring broader public availability of information on toxics in the workplace than federal OSHA standards provide. See e.g., CSX Transp. v. Public Util. Comm. of Ohio, 901 F.2d 497 (6th Cir. 1990)(federal rail safety act pre-empted most of the state hazardous material transport law); Assoc. Industries of Mass. v. Dep't of Labor, 898 F.2d 274 (1st Cir. 1990)(state asbestos abatement statute generally not pre-empted by OSHA); Ohio Manuf. Assoc. v. City of Akron, 801 F.2d 824 (6th Cir. 1984)(local "right to know" ordinance pre-empted by federal statute).

Section 3. CONTRADICTION-BASED FEDERAL PRE-EMPTION AND THE TOLERANCE OF CONCURRENT STATE REGULATION

As noted earlier, most environmental law cases involving claims of pre-emption of state authority by federal action are cases where state action is claimed to conflict with federal action. Some of these cases claim that there is an irreconcilable contradiction between the two sets of regulations, and that dual compliance is physically impossible. Other cases merely assert that the state law stands as an obstacle to the accomplishment of the federal regulatory scheme.

The impetus for states to seek to add their own environmental regulation, supplementing federal regulation, is easily understood. The federal government's environmental regulations are, for the most part, national in scope and take no account of local variation. Congress has often acknowledged the likelihood that states might want to enact more stringent regulation, and in a number of major federal laws have inserted express provisions inviting more stringent state regulation. That allows states that find their own special circumstances inadequately considered by national standards to address them with additional regulation. Even in the absence of congressional invitations to act, states may still find it necessary to do so. In the wake of the Exxon-Valdez oil spill, for example, Alaska and other coastal states began worrying that the federal government was not sufficiently protecting their state interests from potential disasters of oil and other hazardous waste transportation, particularly at sea. To some state observers, the Coast Guard often appeared to be operating as an adjunct of the marine transport industry, where many of its senior officers continue their careers after retiring from federal service. The following Supreme Court case exemplifies the kinds of pre-emption litigation that can ensue when states enter areas that are the subject of numerous federal statutory and regulatory efforts.

Ray v. Atlantic Richfield Co.

United States Supreme Court, 1978

435 U.S. 151, 98 S. Ct. 988, 55 L.Ed. 179

[This case involved a challenge to the constitutionality of the Washington Tanker Law,[10] which regulated the design, size, and movement of oil tankers in Puget Sound. Three operative provisions were challenged as having been pre-empted by federal regulation:

(1) a requirement that both "enrolled" (domestic coastal) oil tankers, and "registered" (foreign trade) tankers, of more than 50,000 deadweight tons (DWT), carry a Washington-licensed pilot while navigating the Sound (§88.16.180);

(2) a requirement that enrolled and registered oil tankers of from 40,000 to 125,000 DWT satisfy certain design or safety standards including "double bottoms" under all oil and liquid cargo compartments, or else use tug escorts while operating in the Sound (§88.16.190 (2)); and

(3) a ban on the operation of any supertankers in the Sound i.e. any tanker exceeding 125,000 DWT (§88.16.190 (1)).]

WHITE, J. Pursuant to the Ports and Waterways Safety Act of 1972 (PWSA),[11] navigation in Puget Sound, a body of inland water lying along the northwest coast of the State of Washington, is controlled in major respects by federal law. The PWSA also subjects to federal rule the design and operating characteristics of oil tankers.

This case arose when the Tanker Law was adopted with the aim of regulating in particular respects the design, size, and movement of oil tankers in Puget Sound. In response to the constitutional challenge to the law brought by the appellees herein, the District Court[12] held that under the Supremacy Clause, Art. VI, cl. 2, of the Constitution, which declares that the federal law "shall be the supreme Law of the Land," the Tanker Law could not co-exist with the PWSA and was totally invalid....

10. Ch. 125, 1975 Wash. Laws, 1st Extr. Sess., Wash. Rev. Code §88.16.170 et seq. (Supp. 1975) .

11. 86 Stat. 424, 33 U.S.C. §1221 et seq. (1970 ed., Supp. V), and 46 U.S.C. §391a (1970 ed., Supp. V).

12. Ed. note: When this case arose, challenges to state statutes based on invalidity as a matter of federal constitutional law were required to be heard by a United States District Court comprised of three judges.; appeals from that three-judge court went directly to the Supreme Court.

The Court's prior cases indicate that when a State's exercise of its police power is challenged under the Supremacy Clause, "we start with the assumption that the historic police powers of the States were not to be superseded by the Federal Act unless that was the clear and manifest purpose of Congress." Rice v. Santa Fe Elevator Corp., 331 U.S. 218, 230 (1947); Jones v. Rath Packing Co., 430 U.S. 519, 525 (1977). [The opinion recited at some length the litany of cases describing various categories of federal pre-emption – explicit and implicit, conflict-based, and field occupancy.]

With these principles in mind, we turn to an examination of each of the three operative provisions of the Tanker Law. We address first Wash. Rev. Code §88.16.180 (Supp. 1975), which requires both enrolled and registered oil tankers of at least 50,000 DWT to take on a pilot licensed by the State of Washington while navigating Puget Sound. The District Court held that insofar as the law required a tanker "enrolled in the coastwise trade" to have a local pilot on board, it was in direct conflict with 46 U.S.C. §§215, 364. We agree.

Section 364 provides that "every coastwise seagoing steam vessel subject to the navigation laws of the United States...not sailing under register, shall, when under way...be under the control and direction of pilots licensed by the Coast Guard." Section 215 adds that "[n]o State or municipal government shall impose upon pilots of steam vessels any obligation to procure a State or other license in addition to that issued by the United States...." It goes on to explain that the statute shall not be construed to "affect any regulation established by the laws of any State, requiring vessels entering or leaving a port in any such State, *other than coastwise steam vessels*, to take a pilot duly licensed or authorized by the laws of such State...." (emphasis added.) The Court has long held that these two statutes read together give the Federal Government exclusive authority to regulate pilots on enrolled vessels and that they preclude a State from imposing its own pilotage requirements upon them. Thus, to the extent that the Tanker Law requires enrolled tankers to take on state-licensed pilots, the District Court correctly concluded, as the State now concedes, that it was in conflict with federal law and was therefore invalid.

While the opinion of the court below indicated that the pilot provision of the Tanker Law was void only to the extent that it applied to tankers enrolled in the coastwise trade, the judgment itself declared the statute null and void in its entirety. No part of the statute was excepted from the scope of the injunctive relief. The judgment was overly broad, for just as it is clear that States may not regulate the pilots of enrolled vessels, it is equally clear that they are free to impose pilotage requirements on registered vessels entering and leaving their ports. Not only does 46 U.S.C.A. §215 so provide, as was noted above, but so also does §101(5) of the PWSA, 33 U.S.C.A. §1221(5)(1970 ed., Supp. V), which authorizes the Secretary of Transportation to "require pilots on self-propelled vessels engaged in the foreign trades in areas and under circumstances where a pilot is not otherwise required by State law to be on board until the State having jurisdiction of an area involved establishes a requirement for a pilot in that area or under the circumstances involved...." Accordingly, as appellees now agree, the State was free to require registered tankers in excess of 50,000 DWT to take on a state-licensed pilot upon entering Puget Sound.

We next deal with §88.16.190(2) of the Tanker Law, which requires enrolled and registered oil tankers of from 40,000 to 125,000 DWT to possess all of the following "standard safety features":

> "(a) Shaft horsepower in the ratio of one horsepower to each two and one-half deadweight tons; and

(b) Twin screws; and
(c) Double bottoms, underneath all oil and liquid cargo compartments; and
(d) Two radars in working order and operating, one of which must be collision avoidance radar; and
(e) Such other navigational position location systems as may be prescribed from time to time by the board of pilotage commissioners...."

This section contains a proviso, however, stating that if the "tanker is in ballast or is under escort of a tug or tugs with an aggregate shaft horsepower equivalent to five percent of the deadweight tons of that tanker..." the design requirements are not applicable. The District Court held invalid this alternative design/tug requirement of the Tanker Law. We agree insofar as we hold that the foregoing design requirements standing alone, are invalid in the light of the PWSA and its regulatory implementation.

[The Court briefly describes the Secretary's statutory authority to issue regulations regarding safety, marine environmental protection, and inspections....]

This statutory pattern shows that Congress, insofar as design characteristics are concerned, has entrusted to the Secretary the duty of determining which oil tankers are sufficiently safe to be allowed to proceed in the navigable waters of the United States. This indicates to us that Congress intended uniform national standards for design and construction of tankers that would foreclose the imposition of different or more stringent state requirements. In particular, as we see it, Congress did not anticipate that a vessel found to be in compliance with the Secretary's design and construction regulations and holding a Secretary's permit, or its equivalent, to carry the relevant cargo would nevertheless be barred by state law from operating in the navigable waters of the United States on the ground that its design characteristics constitute an undue hazard.

We do not question in the slightest the prior cases holding that enrolled and registered vessels must conform to "reasonable, nondiscriminatory conservation and environmental protection measures..." imposed by a State. Similarly, the mere fact that a vessel has been inspected and found to comply with the Secretary's vessel safety regulations does not prevent a State or city from enforcing local laws having other purposes, such as a local smoke abatement law. But in none of the relevant cases sustaining the application of state laws to federally licensed or inspected vessels did the federal licensing or inspection procedure implement a substantive rule of federal law addressed to the object also sought to be achieved by the challenged state regulation. Huron Portland Cement Co. v. Detroit [362 U.S. 440(1960)], for example, made it plain that there was "no overlap between the scope of the federal ship inspection laws and that of the municipal ordinance..." there involved. 362 U.S. at 446. The purpose of the "federal inspection statutes [was] to insure the seagoing safety of vessels...to affor[d] protection from the perils of maritime navigation," while "[b]y contrast, the sole aim of the Detroit ordinance [was] the elimination of air pollution to protect the health and enhance the cleanliness of the local community." Id. at 445....

Here, we have the very situation that Huron Portland Cement Co. v. Detroit... put aside. Title II aims at insuring vessel safety and protecting the marine environment; and the Secretary must issue all design and construction regulations that he deems necessary for these ends, after considering the specified statutory standards. The federal scheme thus aims precisely at the same ends as does §88.16.190 (2) of the Tanker Law. Furthermore, under the PWSA, after considering the statutory standards and issuing all design requirements that in his judgment are necessary, the Secretary inspects and certifies each vessel as sufficiently safe to protect the marine environment and issues a permit or its equivalent to carry tank-vessel cargoes. Refusing to accept the federal judgment, however, the State now seeks to exclude from Puget Sound vessels certified by the Secretary as having acceptable design characteristics, unless they satisfy the different and higher design requirements imposed by state law. The Supremacy Clause dictates that the federal judgment that a vessel is safe to navigate United States waters prevail over the contrary state judgment.

Enforcement of the state requirements would at least frustrate what seems to us to be the evident congressional intention to establish a uniform federal regime controlling the design of oil tankers. The original Tank Vessel Act, amended by Title II, sought to effect a "reasonable and uniform set of rules and regulations concerning ship construction...," H.R. Rep. No. 2962, 74th Cong., 2d Sess., 2 (1936); and far from evincing a different purpose, the Title II amendments strongly indicate that insofar as tanker design is concerned, Congress anticipated the enforcement of federal standards that would pre-empt state efforts to mandate different or higher design requirements.... [A long passage stressing the congressional desire for uniformity of regulation of vessels engaged international trade is omitted.]

Of course, that a tanker is certified under federal law as a safe vessel insofar as its design and construction characteristics are concerned does not mean that it is free to ignore otherwise valid state or federal rules or regulations that do not constitute design or construction specifications. Registered vessels, for example, as we have already indicated, must observe Washington's pilotage requirement.

In our view, both enrolled and registered vessels must also comply with the provision of the Tanker Law that requires tug escorts for tankers over 40,000 DWT that do not satisfy the design provisions specified in §88.16.190 (2). This conclusion requires analysis of Title I of the PWSA, 33 U.S.C.A. §§1221–1227 (1970 ed., Supp. V).

In order to prevent damage to vessels, structures, and shore areas, as well as environmental harm to navigable waters and the resources therein that might result from vessel or structure damage, Title I authorizes the Secretary to establish and operate "vessel traffic services and systems" for ports subject to congested traffic, as well as to require ships to comply with the systems and to have the equipment necessary to do so. §§1221(1) and (2). The Secretary may "control vessel traffic" under various hazardous conditions by specifying the times for vessel movement, by establishing size and speed limitations and vessel operating conditions, and by restricting vessel operation to those vessels having the particular operating characteristics which he considers necessary for safe operation under the circumstances. §1221(3). In addition, the Secretary may require vessels engaged in foreign trade to carry pilots until the State having jurisdiction establishes a pilot requirement, §1221(5); he may establish minimum safety equipment requirements for shore structures, §1221(7); and he may establish waterfront safety zones or other measures for limited, controlled, or conditional access when necessary for the protection of vessels, structures, waters, or shore areas, §1221(8).

In carrying out his responsibilities under the Act, the Secretary may issue rules and regulations. §1224. In doing so, he is directed to consider a wide variety of interests that might affect the exercise of his authority, such as possible environmental impact, the scope and degree of the hazards involved, and "vessel traffic characteristics including minimum interference with the flow of commercial traffic, traffic volume, the sizes and types of vessels, the usual nature of local

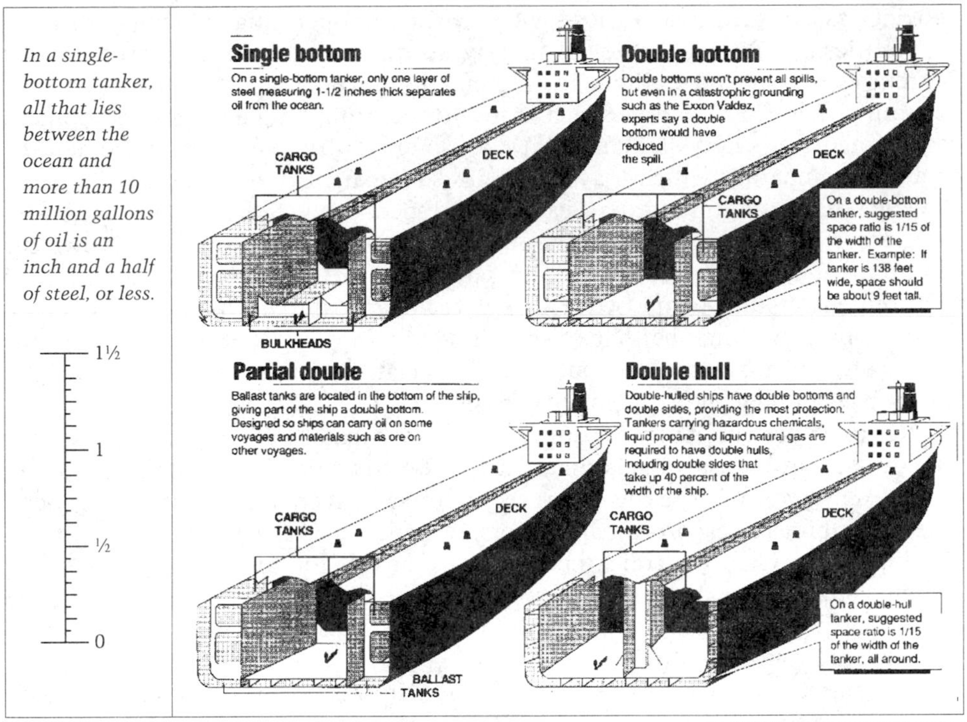

ELLIOTT BAY DESIGN GROUP SEATTLE

A diagrammatic comparison of tanker hull requirements. The state of Washington's double bottom requirement was one of the statutory provisions challenged in the Ray *case.*

cargoes, and similar factors." §1222(e). §1222(b) provides that nothing in Title I is to "prevent a State or political subdivision thereof from prescribing for structures only higher safety equipment requirements or safety standards than those which may be prescribed pursuant to this chapter."

Exercising this authority, the Secretary, through his delegate, the Coast Guard, has issued Navigation Safety Regulations, 33 CFR Part 164 (adopted at 42 Fed. Reg. 5956 (1977)). Of particular importance to this case, he has promulgated the Puget Sound Vessel Traffic System containing general rules, communication rules, vessel movement reporting requirements, a traffic separation scheme, special rules for ship movement in Rosario Strait, descriptions and geographic coordinates of the separation zones and traffic lanes, and a specification for precautionary areas and reporting points. There is also delegated to Coast Guard district commanders and captains of ports the authority to exercise the Secretary's powers under §1221(3) to direct the anchoring, mooring, and movements of vessels; temporarily to establish traffic routing schemes; and to specify vessel size and speed limitations and operating conditions. 33 CFR §160.35 (1976). Traffic in Rosario Strait is subject to a local Coast Guard rule prohibiting "the passage of more than one 70,000 DWT vessel through Rosario Strait in either direction at any given time." During the periods of bad weather, the size limitation is reduced to approximately 40,000 DWT.

A tug-escort provision is not a design requirement, such as is promulgated under Title II. It is more akin to an operating rule arising from the peculiarities of local waters that call for special precautionary measures, and, as such, is a safety measure clearly within the reach of the Secretary's authority under §§1221(3)(iii) and (iv) to establish "vessel size and speed limitations and vessel operating conditions" and to restrict vessel operation to those with "particular operating characteristics and capabilities...." Title I, however, merely authorizes and does not require the Secretary to issue regulations to implement the provisions of the Title; and assuming that §1222(b) prevents a State from issuing "higher safety equipment requirements or safety standards," it does so only with respect to those requirements or standards "which may be prescribed pursuant to this chapter."

The relevant inquiry under Title I with respect to the State's power to impose a tug-escort rule is thus whether the Secretary has either promulgated his own tug requirement for Puget Sound tanker navigation or has decided that no such requirement should be imposed at all. It does not appear to us that he has yet taken either course.... It may be that rules will be forthcoming that will pre-empt the State's present tug-escort rule, but until that occurs, the State's requirement need not give way under the Supremacy Clause.

Nor for constitutional purposes does it make substantial difference that under the Tanker Law those vessels that satisfy the State's design requirements are in effect exempted from the tug-escort requirement. Given the validity of a general rule prescribing tug escorts for all tankers, Washington is also privileged, insofar as the Supremacy Clause is concerned, to waive the rule for tankers having specified design characteristics.[13] For this reason, we conclude that the District Court erred in holding that the alternative tug requirement of §88.16.190(2) was invalid because of its conflict with the PWSA.

We cannot arrive at the same conclusion with respect to the remaining provision of the Tanker Law at issue here. §88.16.190(1) excludes from Puget Sound under any circumstances any tanker in excess of 125,000 DWT. In our view, this provision is invalid in light of Title I and the Secretary's actions taken thereunder.

[The Court found that the Secretary has the authority to establish "vessel size and speed limitations," and had acted at least enough to forbid the state's action.] Against this background, we think the pre-emptive impact of §1222(b) is an understandable expression of congressional intent. Furthermore, even without §1222(b), we would be reluctant to sustain the Tanker Law's absolute ban on tankers larger than 125,000 DWT. The Court has previously recognized that "where failure of...federal officials affirmatively to exercise their full authority takes on the character of a ruling that no such regulation is appropriate or approved pursuant to the policy of the statute," States are not permitted to use their police power to enact such a regulation. Bethlehem Steel Co. v. New York State Labor Relations Board, 330 U.S. 767, 774 (1947). We think that in this case the Secretary's failure to

13. We do not agree with appellees' assertion that the tug-escort provision, which is an alternative to the design requirements of the Tanker Law, will exert pressure on tanker owners to comply with the design standards and hence is an indirect method of achieving what they submit is beyond state power under Title II. The cost of tug escorts for all of appellee ARCO's tankers in Puget Sound is estimated at $277,500 per year. While not a negligible amount, it is only a fraction of the estimated cost of outfitting a single tanker with the safety features required by §88.16.190 (2). The Office of Technology Assessment of Congress has estimated that constructing a new tanker with a double bottom and twin screws, just two of the required features, would add roughly $8.8 million to the cost of a 150,000 DWT tanker. Thus, contrary to the appellees' contention, it is very doubtful that the provision will pressure tanker operators into complying with the design standards specified in §88.16.190 (2). While the tug provision may be viewed as a penalty for noncompliance with the State's design requirements, it does not "stan[d] as an obstacle to the accomplishment and execution of the full purposes and objectives of Congress." Hines v. Davidowitz, 312 U.S. 52, 67 (1941). The overall effect of §88.16.190 (2) is to require tankers of over 40,000 DWT to have a tug escort while they navigate Puget Sound, a result in no way inconsistent with the PWSA as it is currently being implemented.

promulgate a ban on the operations of oil tankers in excess of 125,000 DWT in Puget Sound takes on such a character. As noted above, a clear policy of the statute is that the Secretary shall carefully consider "the wide variety of interests which may be affected by the exercise of his authority," §1222(e), and that he shall restrict the application of vessel size limitations to those areas where they are particularly necessary. In the case of Puget Sound, the Secretary has exercised his authority in accordance with the statutory directives and has promulgated a vessel-traffic-control system which contains only a narrow limitation on the operation of supertankers. This being the case, we conclude that Washington is precluded from enforcing the size limitation contained in the Tanker Law....

MR. JUSTICE MARSHALL, with whom MR. JUSTICE BRENNAN and MR. JUSTICE REHNQUIST join, concurring in part and dissenting in part. [Opinion omitted.]

MR. JUSTICE STEVENS, with whom MR. JUSTICE POWELL joins, concurring in part and dissenting in part. [Opinion omitted.]

COMMENTARY AND QUESTIONS

1. Applying *Ray*. What regulations can coastal states, in the name of environmental protection, apply to marine transport of oil and hazardous materials after *Ray*? They are pre-empted in the design area and cannot insist on double hulls or similar requirements, but they remain free to impose tug escort requirements and pilotage requirements for vessels engaged in foreign trade. Can states use these permissible requirements in ways that would seriously limit the operations of the regulated vessels? Could the state require a whole flotilla of tug boats for each large vessel, for example, making the expense of entering Puget Sound prohibitive for large vessels? Perhaps a tug flotilla requirement would be too transparently an attempt to ban supertankers or impose design requirements on mid-size tankers, both of which are held to be pre-empted from state action. What if the additional state regulation was less transparently an effort to enter the pre-empted area? Even that may be pre-empted. The thrust of the footnote that mentions the expense of the actual tug escort provision implies that states cannot impose excessively burdensome requirements, even when legitimately pursuing goals that remain open for state regulation, because to do so would interfere with the accomplishment of federal objectives.

2. Design pre-emption and the need for uniformity. If the federal government issues a design standard and the state issues a design standard that is not identical to the federal one, there appears to be a patent conflict. But what if the state requirement is "merely" additional rather than different? Should the finding of conflict then turn on the degree of burden of adding the extra equipment? Even additional requirements that can easily be met are argued to be pre-empted on the theory that the adoption by the federal government of its design standard involves an implied rejection of any need for those additional requirements. A second argument is that ships call at many ports and might be subjected to multiple additional requirements and ought to be able to rely on maintaining conformity with a single body of regulation. (This also echoes the dormant Commerce Clause argument studied in the next subpart of this chapter.) How persuasive are these arguments? Their greatest weakness is that they proceed from implication alone – the pre-emption was not made explicit by Congress when it passed the law, nor by the federal agency involved when it promulgated regulations pursuant to the authority delegated to it by Congress. The key issue, therefore, is once again one of Congress's intent. Recall in this regard Executive Order 12,612, *supra* at page 482, establishing an administrative presumption against pre-emptive intent for all federal actions that do not expressly or inherently require pre-emption.

3. The Detroit smoke abatement ordinance case. In *Ray* the Court treads very gingerly around the case of Huron Portland Cement Co. v. Detroit, 362 U.S. 440 (1960). That case upheld a local Detroit smoke abatement ordinance that was applied to ships that docked at Detroit. The cement company owned and operated ships whose boilers had to remain fired while in port in order to operate the deck equipment for loading and unloading. The particular boilers in question had operational characteristics that caused them to violate Detroit's Smoke Abatement Code. Those same boilers were regulated by federal law; they were inspected by the Coast Guard and found to meet all applicable federal requirements. In regard to the relevant legislation the Court stated:

> ...46 U.S.C.A. §392(c) make[s] clear that inspection of boilers and related equipment is for the purpose of seeing to it that the equipment "may be safely employed in the service proposed."... By contrast, the sole aim of the Detroit ordinance is the elimination of air pollution to protect the health and enhance the cleanliness of the local community. 362 U.S. at 445.

This is another example of the "different purposes" test for establishing non-pre-emption. Does it prove too much? In *Huron Portland Cement*, for example, it was conceded that "structural alterations" of the vessels would be required in order for them to comply with the Detroit ordinance (i.e., the boilers could not easily be retrofitted to meet the Detroit standards and might have to be replaced). Why is that not offensive to the federal regime in *Huron Portland Cement*, whereas the design changes that Washington sought in *Ray* were pre-empted?

Section 4. PRE-EMPTING STATE INTERFERENCE WITH FEDERAL RESOURCE PROGRAMS?

Beginning in the latter half of the 19th century with the federal mining acts and the creation of the National Forest system on the federal public lands, Congress established numerous federal resource (as contrasted with regulatory) management programs designed to promote a variety of declared national interests. When states try to regulate the environmental impacts of federal programs and their licensees, thorny pre-emption issues arise.

Generically these cases most often raise the fourth type of pre-emption problem – claims that the state law interferes with the accomplishment of federal objectives. In broad terms the argument goes like this: the federal agency, by licensing the private activity as part of its resource management program, has affirmatively authorized the activity; state laws that bar or burden the activity therefore conflict with federal law. The counter-argument rests on the view that federal licenses or permits are not intended to divest states of their traditional police power authority, including environmental quality regulation. Cases like *Huron Portland Cement* and the general judicial reluctance to find pre-emption, in the absence of additional facts, tend to support the validity of concurrent state regulation.

Frequently, however, cases are complicated by the fact that many federal licensing programs also include their own environmental standards and reviews. If a federal agency imposes environmentally protective conditions on its licensees, the pre-emption argument is strengthened. At that point the additional state environmental review may be redundant and, more tellingly, inconsistent with federal determination of the proper balance between environmental quality and other national programmatic objectives. In this situation, concurrent state regulation arguably constitutes an interference with the federal program.

The Supreme Court decided two such cases in 1987 and 1990, one involving minimum streamflow requirements imposed on a federally-licensed hydropower facility and the other involving federally-permitted mining on National Forest lands. California v. Federal Energy Regulatory Commission, __ U.S. __, 110 S.Ct. 2024 (1990)(*Rock Creek*) exemplified that scenario. In that case a proposed hydroelectric facility on Rock Creek, a tributary of the American River in California, threatened to reduce stream flows in a way that would adversely affect fisheries. FERC, as part of its licensing process and pursuant to congressional directives,[14] reviewed information on these issues and granted the applicant a license that prescribed specified minimum stream flows. Since FERC's minimum flow standard allowed stream flows to decline to less than a third of the state's proposed minimum requirements, environmentalists would assess the situation as reflecting FERC's traditional industry viewpoint and low level of concern for environmental protection. The Supreme Court held that FERC's minimal standards governed;[15] California could not impose its own more environmentally protective stream flow requirements.[16]

California Coastal Commission v. Granite Rock Co., 480 U.S. 572 (1987), presented a much more subtle pre-emption problem. Granite Rock had obtained a

14. The Electric Consumers Protection Act of 1986, Pub. L. 99-495, codified as part of the Federal Power Act at 16 U.S.C.A. §797(e) and §803(a), requires FERC to consider fish and wildlife effects in making its licensure determinations, although in practice the statutory standards are neither substantively nor procedurally rigorous.

15. The Court applied the arguments of its 1946 decision in First Iowa Hydro-Electric Cooperative v. FPC, 328 U.S. 152, interpreting §27 of the FPA, which provides:

Nothing contained in this chapter shall be construed as affecting or intending to affect or in any way to interfere with the laws of the respective States relating to the control, appropriation, use, or distribution of water used in irrigation or for municipal or other uses, or any vested right acquired therein. 16 U.S.C.A. §821.

Faced with the seemingly clear intent of Congress to preserve state water regulatory powers, the *First Iowa* decision narrowed the clause's meaning, holding that its preservation of state jurisdiction is "confined to rights of the same nature as those relating to the use of water in irrigation or for municipal purposes." 328 U.S. at 175-176.

16. EJG/EM (E.D. Cal. July 9, 1991) the pre-emptive effect of *Rock Creek* was extended to divest the California State Water Resource Control Board (SWRCB) of the authority to require the FERC licensee to submit information on issues other than the availability of water. The SWRCB had required Nugget to provide more thorough analyses of the instream impacts of its project than those provided to FERC, at which point Nugget withdrew its application for a SWRCB permit and went to federal court seeking a pre-emption-based order to save it from having to "jump through a never-ending series of hoops...[that] relate to matters already reviewed by FERC," adding that "the delay and cost impose a tremendous hardship on plaintiff [Nugget]." The court pre-empted the SWRCB efforts.

permit from the U.S. Forest Service to mine for pharmaceutical grade white limestone in a portion of the Los Padres National Forest near Big Sur. Due to the land's proximity to the Pacific Coast, the area was also within the jurisdiction of the California Coastal Commission (CCC), a state agency having extensive land use planning and environment protection powers. Despite the existence of the federal permit, CCC directed Granite Rock to apply to it for an additional permit, a request that was met with a lawsuit claiming that the CCC's authority had been pre-empted.

The Ninth Circuit Court of Appeals decided in favor of Granite Rock's pre-emption argument, because the Forest Service, through its permit regulations, applied state environmental standards as the basis for its own permitting decisions.[17] Accordingly, the Ninth Circuit held, there was no remaining function for the state agency to perform. The Supreme Court reversed, requiring Granite Rock to submit to the state permit proceeding. One key to the ruling lay in the language of the Forest Service regulations, several of which called for federal licensees to comply with applicable state environmental quality standards; one regulation specifically mentioned state permits' usefulness for proving such compliance with state regulations. See 36 CFR §§228.5 (b), 228.8 (a-c, h).

The licensee's second major contention in the Supreme Court was that the CCC's actions were a thinly-veiled effort to reverse the Forest Service's choices under its land use planning mandate, contained in the National Forest Management Act of 1976, 16 U.S.C.A. §§1600-1614. CCC was trying to prohibit mining in an area that the Forest Service had determined was appropriate for mining. The majority found this challenge speculative; CCC had not acted to impose any conditions or requirements on Granite Rock prior to the filing of the lawsuit.

Justice O'Connor's majority opinion also drew a rather fine semantic distinction between land use planning and environmental protection:

> The California Coastal Commission alleges that it will use its permit requirement to impose reasonable environmental regulation.... Federal land use statutes and regulations, while arguably expressing an intent to pre-empt state land use planning, distinguish environmental regulation from land use planning.

COMMENTARY AND QUESTIONS

1. The case for finding pre-emption. *Granite Rock* presents a strong case for displacement of state authority because the parallel state authority that is to be exercised affects lands in federal ownership that are part of the National Forest system and that are being managed under an articulated "multiple use" mandate that establishes federal policies regarding the administration of National Forest tracts. To whatever extent the California Coastal Commission (CCC) might thwart a federally approved project, there is both an intrusion upon federal government planning and de facto imposition of state land use controls on federal land. These points motivated a dissent by Justice Powell (joined by Justice Stevens) and a dissent by Justice Scalia (joined by Justice White). Even so, a majority of the Court was

17. 768 F.2d 1077, 1083 (1985).

willing to support concurrent regulatory control as long as there was no concrete conflict of regulations. What can the CCC now impose by way of conditions that would not be in conflict with the Forest Service plan? Would erosion and dust emission control requirements that forced Granite Rock to keep excavated overburden covered during mining operations – or a strict post-mining reclamation requirement – be allowed? Does it matter how much compliance with such requirements would cost? What if, for example, the increased cost made the proposed mining project more expensive than other feasible alternative sites?

2. Local expertise and pluralism. What makes concurrent levels of regulatory authority so attractive? Concurrency is almost surely less efficient, adding costs for dual filings, studies, and processing, constantly posing opportunities for delay. Does concurrency sustain the traditional view of the states as primary regulators of environmental matters? In an era of massive federal statutory intervention in the environmental field, it seems hard to resist the conclusion that Congress and the federal bureaucratic army have become the primary regulatory system. Is local expertise at issue here? Is there any indication that the CCC is better apprised of the environmental consequences of the proposed action than the federal District Ranger? A different justification for concurrency lies in the desire to respect the sovereignty of the states. Making concurrency the norm arguably does not undercut federal authority; it simply places the burden on the federal government to announce its intentions to exercise unilateral control. It would appear that the environmental perspective is benefitted by concurrency. The theory is that two forums are better than one. The public environmental perspective may receive a more hospitable reception in one place rather than the other and a potentially destructive project must survive the rigors of both tests.

3. State regulation of the federal public lands. As an historical matter in the public lands area, it is only recently that the property clause of the United States Constitution has been recognized as supporting active federal management authority over federal lands. Nineteenth century cases frequently regarded that clause merely as an authority to own on the same basis as any other landholder, i.e., subject to state regulation. For an excellent discussion of this topic and many others relating to the federal public lands, see Cowart & Fairfax, Public Lands Federalism: Judicial Theory and Administrative Reality, 15 Ecol. L. Q. 375, 439-476 (1988). Cowart and Fairfax criticize the majority opinion in *Granite Rock*:

> The majority opinion fails to clarify either general pre-emption doctrine or its application to the public lands. Instead, the decision turns on a presumed fine-grained distinction between land use planning and environmental regulation. That distinction is unclear, unsupported by the public lands statutes and not at all helpful to state and federal legislators and administrators seeking to manage complex intermixed resources. [Id. at 463.]

Are these criticisms well taken? The distinction is indeed a fine one, but *Pacific Gas, Huron Portland Cement*, and *Ray* similarly draw distinctions based on the purposes of statutes. It is unfortunate that no clear guide was announced, but is it really within the power of the Court rather than Congress to unravel the complexities of concurrency?

4. Is pre-emption analysis better applied on a local or a national level? Consider the following criticism of the *Granite Rock* approach:

> The Court focused on the pre-emptive effect of the governing federal statutes and nationwide regulations. Some vehicle was needed, it rightly assumed, to avoid giving the states a veto over federal land uses. But the Court could better have addressed the issue by instead considering the pre-emption of state law at the lowest level – the pre-emption that occurs when a federal agency at the local level lawfully acts in a way that causes conflict with a state or local law. So long as federal action pre-empts at that level, pre-emption at a higher level is unneeded and, in this setting at least, undesirable. From an institutional perspective, pre-emption at the lowest level can best foster cooperative land planning on the scene. For a variety of reasons, pre-emption should occur only when a federal agency concludes, in a site-specific determination made in the course of statutory land-planning processes, that a particular federal use should override contrary state and local rules. Freyfogle, Granite Rock: Institutional Competence and the State Role in Federal Land Planning, 59 U. Colo. L. Rev. 475, 477 (1988).

5. State regulation of federal facilities? To what extent can states and local governments apply their environmental regulations to federal facilities in their territory? The question has recurred over the years, as Army posts allow toxics to leach into groundwater, federal hospitals violate air pollution standards, federal authorities authorize the construction of mammoth power transmission towers or radio transmission towers in historic zones, and so on. The simplest answer seems to be that the federal action trumps state and local regulations unless the basic federal statute accepts state jurisdiction, or unless the federal government has voluntarily agreed to accommodate state and local restraints. See Chapter 19.

6. Requirements for federal-state coordination? Given the numerous opportunities for overlapping federal-state jurisdictions over projects, activities, and regulatory programs, there are obvious advantages to coordinating their actions. The federal government has often subscribed to the rhetoric of federal-state coordination and has implemented a succession of formal procedural requirements aimed toward that end. For many years Circular A-95, issued by the federal Office of Management and Budget (OMB) in 1968, directed federal agencies to provide opportunities for advance consultation with state agencies whenever a federal proposal might affect state interests. If a state was about to be chosen as the site of a federal bombing range, waste dump, or penitentiary, the Governor's office was supposed to get early warning of it through A-95 procedures. Executive Order 12,372, "Intergovernmental Review of Federal Programs" (July 14, 1982), issued early in the Reagan presidency, supplanted A-95 and sought to establish a more responsive process. Supplementing the Intergovernmental Cooperation Act of 1968, 42 U.S.C.A. §4231(a), E.O. 12,372 called for federal agencies to "provide opportunities for consultation by elected officials of those State and local governments that would provide the non-Federal funds for, or that would be directly affected by, proposed Federal financial assistance or direct Federal development." Section 2(a) of the order encouraged states to develop a process for formulating a position to be communicated to the relevant federal agency and directed that federal agency to "utilize the State process to determine official views of State and local elected officials."

Executive Order 12,372 seems not to have lived up to its potential. It has done little to improve avenues of federal consultation with states and appears to be largely ignored by federal agencies. There have been no comprehensive studies by OMB or the congressional General Accounting Office of its impact, but the informally expressed opinion of one expert in intergovernmental relations was that the order has resulted in "a debilitation of the [prior] consultative process." The few cases that raise E.O. 12,372 arguments seem to provide a basis for using the order to insist on consultation. In Azzolina v. United States Postal Service, 602 F. Supp. 859, 863 (D.N.J. 1985),for example, a case involving siting of a post office, the court affirmed that "federal agencies are to provide opportunities for consultation and communication and to make efforts to accommodate state and local concerns." The court went on to note that federal agencies also have an obligation to develop a reviewable record in cases where they choose to act in disharmony with local planning objectives. The commentators are divided on the effect of the executive order. Compare Bell & Johnson, State Water Laws & Federal Water Uses: The History of Conflict, The Prospects for Accommodation, 21 Envtl. L. 1, 68-70 (1991) (the order is ineffectual), with Mandelker, Controlling Non-Point Source Water Pollution: Can It Be Done?, 65 Chicago-Kent L. Rev. 479, 490-91 (1989)(noting greater federal responsiveness to state planning concerns).

B. THE "DORMANT COMMERCE CLAUSE" – INVALIDATING STATE LAWS THAT EXCESSIVELY BURDEN INTERSTATE COMMERCE

As pointed out in the introductory segment of this chapter, the states voluntarily surrendered a portion of their sovereignty in order to form an effective nation. One area of substantial constitutional concern was the need for the states to integrate their economies in order to obtain the benefits of relatively free movement of goods among them and in foreign commerce. The national government was thus granted jurisdiction over interstate and international commerce.

Although the commerce clause is written as a grant of legislative authority to Congress, it has long been interpreted as at least partially self-executing. Even in advance of congressional action on a matter, courts have been willing to invalidate state laws that unduly burden or restrict the interstate movement of goods in commerce on the ground that they are inconsistent with the surrender of the commerce power to the national government. The fact that the courts may activate and use the commerce clause in cases where Congress has let its regulatory authority under the clause lie dormant gives rise to the label "dormant commerce clause" for this branch of constitutional analysis.

Action by the judiciary in dormant commerce clause cases in no degree reduces the plenary authority of Congress and the principle of legislative supremacy. Congress can always act to permit state action that courts have invalidated on this basis, or Congress can act to forbid state regulation of interstate commerce that courts have found to be constitutionally permissible. Dormant commerce clause issues frequently arise in the environmental protection context.

Section 1. THE BASICS OF DORMANT COMMERCE CLAUSE ADJUDICATION

City of Philadelphia v. New Jersey

United States Supreme Court, 1978
437 U.S. 617, 98 S. Ct. 2531, 57 L. Ed. 2d 475

STEWART, J. A New Jersey law prohibits the importation of most "solid or liquid waste which originated or was collected outside the territorial limits of the State..." In this case we are required to decide whether this statutory prohibition violates the Commerce Clause of the United States Constitution.

The statutory provision in question is Chapter 363 of 1973 N.J. Laws, which took effect in early 1974. In pertinent part it provides:

> No person shall bring into this State any solid or liquid waste which originated or was collected outside the territorial limits of the State, except garbage to be fed to swine in the State of New Jersey, until the commissioner [of the State Department of Environmental Protection] shall determine that such action can be permitted without endangering the public health, safety and welfare and has promulgated regulations permitting and regulating the treatment and disposal of such waste in this State. N.J. Stat. Ann. §13:1I-10.

As authorized by Ch. 363, the Commissioner promulgated regulations permitting four categories of waste to enter the State. Apart from these narrow exceptions, however, New Jersey closed its borders to all waste from other States.

Immediately affected by these developments were the operators of private landfills in New Jersey, and several cities in other States that had agreements with these operators for waste disposal....

Although the Constitution gives Congress the power to regulate commerce among the States, many subjects of potential federal regulation under that power inevitably escape congressional attention "because of their local character and their number and diversity." South Carolina State Highway Dept. v. Barnwell Bros., Inc., 303 U.S. 177, 185. In the absence of federal legislation, these subjects are open to control by the States so long as they act within the restraints imposed by the Commerce Clause itself. The bounds of these restraints appear nowhere in the words of the Commerce Clause, but have emerged gradually in the decisions of this Court giving effect to its basic purpose. That broad purpose was well expressed by Mr. Justice Jackson in his opinion for the Court in H.P. Hood & Sons, Inc. v. Du Mond, 336 U.S. 525, 537-538:

> This principle that our economic unit is the Nation, which alone has the gamut of powers necessary to control of the economy, including the vital power of erecting customs barriers against foreign competition, has as its corollary that the states are not separable economic units. As the Court said in Baldwin v. Seelig, 294 U.S. 511, 527, "what is ultimate is the principle that

> one state in its dealings with another may not place itself in a position of economic isolation."

The opinions of the Court through the years have reflected an alertness to the evils of "economic isolation" and protectionism, while at the same time recognizing that incidental burdens on interstate commerce may be unavoidable when a State legislates to safeguard the health and safety of its people. Thus, where simple economic protectionism is effected by state legislation, a virtually *per se* rule of invalidity has been erected. The clearest example of such legislation is a law that overtly blocks the flow of interstate commerce at a State's borders. But where other legislative objectives are credibly advanced and there is no patent discrimination against interstate trade, the Court has adopted a much more flexible approach, the general contours of which were outlined in Pike v. Bruce Church, Inc., 397 U.S. 137, 142:

> Where the statute regulates evenhandedly to effectuate a legitimate local public interest, and its effects on interstate commerce are only incidental, it will be upheld unless the burden imposed on such commerce is clearly excessive in relation to the putative local benefits.... If a legitimate local purpose is found, then the question becomes one of degree. And the extent of the burden that will be tolerated will of course depend on the nature of the local interest involved, and on whether it could be promoted as well with a lesser impact on interstate activities....

The crucial inquiry, therefore, must be directed to determining whether Ch. 363 is basically a protectionist measure, or whether it can fairly be viewed as a law directed to legitimate local concerns, with effects upon interstate commerce that are only incidental.

The purpose of Ch. 363 is set out in the statute itself as follows:

> The Legislature finds and determines that...the volume of solid and liquid waste continues to rapidly increase, that the treatment and disposal of these wastes continues to pose an even greater threat to the quality of the environment of New Jersey, that the available and appropriate land fill sites within the State are being diminished, that the environment continues to be threatened by the treatment and disposal of waste which originated or was collected outside the State, and that the public health, safety and welfare require that the treatment and disposal within this State of all wastes generated outside of the State be prohibited.

The New Jersey Supreme Court accepted this statement of the state legislature's purpose. The state court additionally found that New Jersey's existing landfill sites will be exhausted within a few years; that to go on using these sites or to develop new ones will take a heavy environmental toll, both from pollution and from loss of scarce open lands; that new techniques to divert waste from landfills to other methods of disposal and resource recovery processes are under development, but that these changes will require time; and finally, that "the extension of the lifespan of existing landfills, resulting from the exclusion of out-of-state waste, may be of crucial importance in preventing further virgin wetlands or other undeveloped lands from being devoted to landfill purposes." 348 A.2d at 509-512. Based on these findings, the court concluded that Ch. 363 was designed to protect, not the State's economy, but its environment, and that its substantial benefits outweigh its "slight" burden on interstate commerce. 348 A.2d at 515-519.

The appellants strenuously contend that Ch. 363, "while outwardly cloaked 'in the currently fashionable garb of environmental protection,'...is actually no more than a legislative effort to suppress competition and stabilize the cost of solid waste disposal for New Jersey residents...."

The appellees, on the other hand, deny that Ch. 363 was motivated by financial concerns or economic protectionism....

This dispute about ultimate legislative purpose need not be resolved, because its resolution would not be relevant to the constitutional issue to be decided in this case. Contrary to the evident assumption of the state court and the parties, the evil of protectionism can reside in legislative means as well as legislative ends. Thus, it does not matter whether the ultimate aim of Ch. 363 is to reduce the waste disposal costs of New Jersey residents or to save remaining open lands from pollution, for we assume New Jersey has every right to protect its residents' pocketbooks as well as their environment. And it may be assumed as well that New Jersey may pursue those ends by slowing the flow of all waste into the State's remaining landfills, even though interstate commerce may incidentally be affected. But whatever New Jersey's ultimate purpose, it may not be accomplished by discriminating against articles of commerce coming from outside the State unless there is some reason, apart from their origin, to treat them differently. Both on its face and in its plain effect, Ch. 363 violates this principle of nondiscrimination.

The Court has consistently found parochial legislation of this kind to be constitutionally invalid, whether the ultimate aim of the legislation was to assure a steady supply of milk by erecting barriers to allegedly ruinous outside competition, or to create jobs by keeping industry within the State, or to preserve the State's financial resources from depletion by fencing out indigent immigrants. In each of these cases, a presumably legitimate goal was sought to be achieved by the illegitimate means of isolating the State from the national economy.

Also relevant here are the Court's decisions holding that a State may not accord its own inhabitants a preferred right of access over consumers in other States to natural resources located within its borders. These cases stand for the basic principle that a "State is without power to prevent privately owned articles of trade from being shipped and sold in interstate commerce on the ground that they are required to satisfy local demands or because they are needed by the people of the State." Foster-Fountain Packing Co. v. Haydel, 278 U.S. 1, 10.

The New Jersey law at issue in this case falls squarely within the area that the Commerce Clause puts off limits to state regulation. On its face, it imposes on out-of-state commercial interests the full burden of conserving the State's remaining landfill space. It is true that in our previous cases the scarce natural resource was itself the article of commerce, whereas here the scarce resource and the article of commerce are distinct. But that difference is without consequence. In both instances, the State has overtly moved to slow or freeze the flow of commerce for protectionist reasons. It does not matter that the State has shut the article of commerce inside the State in one case and outside the State in the other. What is crucial is the attempt by one State to isolate itself from a problem common to many by erecting a barrier against the movement of interstate trade....

Today, cities in Pennsylvania and New York find it expedient or necessary to send their waste into New Jersey for disposal, and New Jersey claims the right to close its borders to such traffic. Tomorrow, cities in New Jersey may find it expedient or necessary to send their waste into Pennsylvania or New York for disposal, and those States might then claim the right to close their borders. The

Commerce Clause will protect New Jersey in the future, just as it protects her neighbors now, from efforts by one State to isolate itself in the stream of interstate commerce from a problem shared by all. The judgment is reversed.

COMMENTARY AND QUESTIONS

1. The similarities between dormant commerce clause and takings analyses. In Chapter 9, at page 426 *supra*, the analysis of private property-based takings challenges to environmental regulations employed four separate inquiries: (1) proper authority, (2) proper (and not poison) public purpose, (3) a sufficiently close means-ends rationality, and (4) avoidance of excessive burdens. Dormant commerce clause analysis follows that same analytical breakdown remarkably closely. As with takings, the first item, proper authority, is necessary but not usually controversial, and is seldom the inquiry that scuttles challenged state or local regulations.[18] The takings law inquiry into proper and poison purposes is plainly picked up in dormant commerce clause cases, as in *Philadelphia*, in judicial review of protectionism – the dichotomy between discriminatory legislation and even-handed legislation. The inquiries into means-end rationality and balancing of burdens also appear in dormant commerce clause cases. (See the Chicago phosphate ban case at page 512 *infra*.) In cases identified as discriminatory and protectionist, a far stricter means-ends fit and an absence of alternatives is required. In cases falling on the proper purpose side of the line, only basic rationality need be shown. Finally, as to the fourth inquiry, the avoidance of excessive burdens on the individual in the takings context finds a direct analogue in the avoidance of excessive burdens on interstate commerce in the dormant commerce clause cases.[19] If the burden on interstate commerce is disproportionate in comparison to the law's benefits, the law will be invalidated.

2. Discriminatory legislative purpose. The threshold inquiry in most dormant commerce clause cases is whether the challenged state law attempts to discriminate against interstate commerce. At least as a matter of the common language appearing in many of the cases, there is "a virtually per se rule of invalidity" for discriminatory legislation. As seen in Maine v. Taylor, 477 U.S. 131 (1986) at page 508 *infra*, however, even discriminatory legislation, upon a proper showing, can be sustained against a dormant commerce clause attack.

3. Even-handed legislation, the *Pike* test, and burden weighing. Regulation that is not deemed discriminatory against interstate commerce is subjected to the test set

---

18. The treatment of the environmental altruism issue in *Proctor & Gamble* at page 512 *infra*, may reflect a concern on the authority issue, however. Another way the authority question is raised, of course, is where a defendant argues that the state or local power is eliminated by pre-emption.

19. The analogy helps explain the shortcomings in commerce cases' use of the concept of "incidental burdens" as a test of validity. The *Philadelphia* court, citing Pike v. Bruce Church, states that "where the statute regulates evenhandedly to effectuate a legitimate local public interest, *and its effects on interstate commerce are only incidental*, it will be upheld unless the burden imposed on such commerce is clearly excessive in relation to the putative local benefits...." As in the takings setting, the term "incidental" would seem to mean "unintended." See page 505 *supra*. Thus in the commerce setting it is either redundant, duplicating the inquiry into improper protectionist purpose, or shortchanges a more detailed balance of the regulation's benefits and negative effects on commerce. (Note that the *Pike* quotation specifically requires that further balance.)

forth in the quotation from Pike v. Bruce Church, Inc. that appeared in the *Philadelphia* case. The purpose of the legislation must be legitimate (in furtherance of local public interest), and the burden on interstate commerce must be only "incidental." Even then, the burden on interstate commerce must be weighed against local benefits in a fairly complex calculus that seeks to account for the importance of the local benefit and the extent of the burden on interstate commerce. This line of analysis is more fully considered in conjunction with Procter & Gamble Corp. v. Chicago, at page 512 *infra.*

4. The potential breadth of the Philadelphia v. New Jersey ruling. Would it be fair to characterize the holding in *Philadelphia* as being that states may not, consistent with the dormant commerce clause, hoard their natural resources, including landfill sites? Is it also fair to characterize *Philadelphia* as holding that states cannot bar interstate movement, even of articles that are undesirable like refuse and other forms of waste? The Court confronted this latter problem because it felt the need to distinguish the *Philadelphia* situation from what it viewed as valid state quarantine laws. The Court found the two situations different because quarantine laws "did not discriminate against interstate commerce as such, but simply prevented traffic in noxious articles, whatever their origin." 437 U.S. at 617. Quarantine laws are discussed more fully at page 529 *infra.*

Maine v. Taylor

United States Supreme Court, 1986

477 U.S. 131, 106 S. Ct. 2440, 91 L. Ed. 2d 110

BLACKMUN, J. Once again, a little fish has caused a commotion. See Hughes v. Oklahoma, 441 U.S. 322 (1979); TVA v. Hill, 437 U.S. 153 (1978); Cappaert v. United States, 426 U.S. 128 (1976). The fish in this case is the golden shiner, a species of minnow commonly used as live bait in sport fishing.

Appellee Robert J. Taylor operates a bait business in Maine. Despite a Maine statute prohibiting the importation of live baitfish,[20] he arranged to have 158,000 live golden shiners delivered to him from outside the State. The shipment was intercepted, and a federal grand jury in the District of Maine indicted Taylor for violating and conspiring to violate the Lacey Act Amendments of 1981, 16 U.S.C. §§3371-3378. Section 3(a)(2)(A) of those Amendments makes it a federal crime "to import, export, transport, sell, receive, acquire, or purchase in interstate or foreign commerce ... any fish or wildlife taken, possessed, transported, or sold in violation of any law or regulation of any State or in violation of any foreign law."

Taylor moved to dismiss the indictment on the ground that Maine's import ban unconstitutionally burdens interstate commerce and therefore may not form the basis for a federal prosecution under the Lacey Act....

The Commerce Clause of the Constitution grants Congress the power "to regulate Commerce with foreign Nations, and among the several States, and with the Indian Tribes." Art. I, §8, cl. 3. "Although the Clause thus speaks in terms of powers bestowed upon Congress, the Court long has recognized that it also limits the power of the States to erect barriers against interstate trade." Lewis v. BT

20. "A person is guilty of importing live bait if he imports into this State any live fish, including smelts, which are commonly used for bait fishing in inland waters." Me. Rev. Stat. Ann., Tit. 12, §7613 (1981).

Investment Managers, Inc., 447 U.S. 27, 35 (1980). Maine's statute restricts interstate trade in the most direct manner possible, blocking all inward shipments of live baitfish at the State's border. Still, as both the District Court and the Court of Appeals recognized, this fact alone does not render the law unconstitutional. The limitation imposed by the Commerce Clause on state regulatory power "is by no means absolute," and "the States retain authority under their general police powers to regulate matters of 'legitimate local concern,' even though interstate commerce may be affected." Id. at 36.

In determining whether a State has overstepped its role in regulating interstate commerce, this Court has distinguished between state statutes that burden interstate transactions only incidentally, and those that affirmatively discriminate against such transactions. While statutes in the first group violate the Commerce Clause only if the burdens they impose on interstate trade are "clearly excessive in relation to the putative local benefits," Pike v. Bruce Church, Inc., 397 U.S. 137, 142 (1970), statutes in the second group are subject to more demanding scrutiny. The Court explained in Hughes v. Oklahoma, 441 U.S. 322, 336 (1979), that once a state law is shown to discriminate against interstate commerce "either on its face or in practical effect," the burden falls on the State to demonstrate both that the statute "serves a legitimate local purpose," and that this purpose could not be served as well by available nondiscriminatory means. See also, e.g., Sporhase v. Nebraska ex rel. Douglas, 458 U.S. 941, 957 (1982).

The District Court and the Court of Appeals both reasoned correctly that, since Maine's import ban discriminates on its face against interstate trade, it should be subject to the strict requirements of Hughes v. Oklahoma...

The evidentiary hearing on which the District Court based its conclusions was one before a magistrate. Three scientific experts testified for the prosecution and one for the defense. The prosecution experts testified that live baitfish imported into the State posed two significant threats to Maine's unique and fragile fisheries. First, Maine's population of wild fish – including its own indigenous golden shiners – would be placed at risk by three types of parasites prevalent in out-of-state baitfish, but not common to wild fish in Maine. Second, non-native species inadvertently included in shipments of live baitfish could disturb Maine's aquatic ecology to an unpredictable extent by competing with native fish for food or habitat, by preying on native species, or by disrupting the environment in more subtle ways.

The prosecution experts further testified that there was no satisfactory way to inspect shipments of live baitfish for parasites or commingled species.[21] According to their testimony, the small size of baitfish and the large quantities in which they are shipped made inspection for commingled species "a physical impossibility." Parasite inspection posed a separate set of difficulties because the examination procedure required destruction of the fish. Although statistical sampling and inspection techniques had been developed for salmonids (i.e., salmon and trout), so that a shipment could be certified parasite-free based on a standardized examination of only some of the fish, no scientifically accepted procedures of this sort were available for baitfish.[22]

21. The expert who examined appellee's shipment testified that, although his inspection of the shipment revealed only two of the three parasites he described as prevalent in baitfish outside Maine, "I certainly could not put my signature on a certificate to say that [none of the third parasite] was present in that lot."

22. According to the prosecution testimony, the design of sampling and inspection techniques must take into account the particular parasites of concern, and baitfish parasites differ from

Appellee's expert denied that any scientific justification supported Maine's total ban on the importation of baitfish. He testified that none of the three parasites discussed by the prosecution witnesses posed any significant threat to fish in the wild and that sampling techniques had not been developed for baitfish precisely because there was no need for them. He further testified that professional baitfish farmers raise their fish in ponds that have been freshly drained to ensure that no other species is inadvertently collected.

Weighing all the testimony, the magistrate concluded that both prongs of the *Hughes* test were satisfied, and accordingly that appellee's motion to dismiss the indictment should be denied....

The Commerce Clause significantly limits the ability of States and localities to regulate or otherwise burden the flow of interstate commerce, but it does not elevate free trade above all other values. As long as a State does not needlessly obstruct interstate trade or attempt to "place itself in a position of economic isolation," Baldwin v. G.A.F. Seelig, Inc., 294 U.S. 511, 527 (1935), it retains broad regulatory authority to protect the health and safety of its citizens and the integrity of its natural resources. The evidence in this case amply supports the District Court's findings that Maine's ban on the importation of live baitfish serves legitimate local purposes that could not adequately be served by available nondiscriminatory alternatives. This is not a case of arbitrary discrimination against interstate commerce; the record suggests that Maine has legitimate reasons, "apart from their origin, to treat [out-of-state baitfish] differently," Philadelphia v. New Jersey, 437 U.S. at 627. The judgment of the Court of Appeals setting aside appellee's conviction is therefore reversed.

STEVENS, J., dissenting.

There is something fishy about this case. Maine is the only State in the Union that blatantly discriminates against out-of-state baitfish by flatly prohibiting their importation. Although golden shiners are already present and thriving in Maine (and, perhaps not coincidentally, the subject of a flourishing domestic industry), Maine excludes golden shiners grown and harvested (and, perhaps not coincidentally sold) in other States. This kind of stark discrimination against out-of-state articles of commerce requires rigorous justification by the discriminating State. "When discrimination against commerce of the type we have found is demonstrated, the burden falls on the State to justify it both in terms of the local benefits flowing from the statute and the unavailability of nondiscriminatory alternatives adequate to preserve the local interests at stake." Hunt v. Washington Apple Advertising Comm'n, 432 U.S. 333, 353 (1977).

Like the District Court, the Court concludes that uncertainty about possible ecological effects from the possible presence of parasites and non-native species in shipments of out-of-state shiners suffices to carry the State's burden of proving a legitimate public purpose. The Court similarly concludes that the State has no obligation to develop feasible inspection procedures that would make a total ban unnecessary. It seems clear, however, that the presumption should run the other way. Since the State engages in obvious discrimination against out-of-state commerce, it should be put to its proof. Ambiguity about dangers and alternatives should actually defeat, rather than sustain, the discriminatory measure.

---

salmonid parasites. Appellee's expert agreed. There was also testimony that the physical layout of baitfarms makes inspection at the source of shipment particularly difficult, and that border inspections are not feasible because the fish would die in the time it takes to complete the tests.

This is not to derogate the State's interest in ecological purity. But the invocation of environmental protection or public health has never been thought to confer some kind of special dispensation from the general principle of nondiscrimination in interstate commerce....

COMMENTARY AND QUESTIONS

1. The demise of the "virtually *per se* rule of invalidity" for discriminatory legislation. Maine's ban on the importation of baitfish in *Taylor* is a case of the most blatantly discriminatory legislation: a total ban on the interstate movement of a product that would compete with locally produced goods in the local market. As the dissent argued, the traditional approach would mean that Maine would carry a very substantial burden of justification, one that seldom can be met. Did you find the evidence in favor of Maine's position persuasive?

Did the majority in *Taylor* actually apply the older rule? In the key passage, the doctrine seems to have shifted to a far less demanding test. Citing Hughes v. Oklahoma, the majority finds that the state merely needs "to demonstrate both that the statute `serves a legitimate local purpose,' and that this purpose could not be served as well by available nondiscriminatory means." In *Hughes*, an effort to limit out-of-state competition for the taking of minnows in Oklahoma waters was held to violate the dormant commerce clause. Should language taken from a case that fails even a relaxed standard of justification be seen as an indication that the old doctrine is no longer the law and that the Court intended to alter the previously settled rule of virtual *per se* invalidity? As a matter of good policy, which standard for testing the validity of discriminatory legislation is preferable, the test in *Taylor*, or in the older cases?

2. Fact finding and appellate review in dormant commerce clause cases. How important is it that the magistrate's fact findings favored Maine in *Taylor*? Appellate courts will only reject fact finding by lower courts when those findings are "clearly erroneous." That may explain the willingness of the majority to accept without skepticism the finding that Maine had no alternatives other than the baitfish ban available to it. The dissent is likewise willing to accept the facts as found, but it finds that those facts were insufficient to overcome the strong presumption against discriminatory legislation.

3. Of mixed purposes. What if, in addition to the legitimate purpose of protecting the Maine environment against baitfish parasites and exotic species, Maine also had its own economic self-interest in mind when it banned the importation of baitfish – does the presence of an illegitimate purpose contaminate the legitimate purpose for dormant commerce clause analysis? That question was raised but not decided in *Taylor* when a snippet of legislative testimony against repeal of the baitfish ban revealed a Maine natural resource official saying:

> We can't help asking why we should spend our money in Arkansas when it's far better spent at home? It is very clear that much more can be done here in Maine to provide our sportsmen with safe, home-grown bait. There is also

> the possibility that such an industry could develop a lucrative export market in neighboring states.

The Court avoided the issue by agreeing with the magistrate that those three sentences do not convert the baitfish ban into a piece of protectionist legislation.

Minnesota v. Clover Leaf Creamery Co., 449 U.S. 456 (1981), was another case in which the attack on State legislation contended that it was prompted by mixed environmental and protectionist motives. The Minnesota statute restricting certain types of milk containers arguably favored pulpwood manufacturers (a major Minnesota industry) and disfavored plastics manufacturers (a non-Minnesota industry). The Court found that the statute was not discriminatory, and proceeded to measure the burdens on interstate commerce under the *Pike* test,[23] eventually concluding that "even granting that the out-of-state plastics industry is burdened...we find that this burden is not 'clearly excessive' in light of the substantial state interest in promoting conservation of energy and other natural resources and easing solid waste disposal problems...." Is it likely that in most mixed motive cases, the courts will treat the statutes as even-handed, and invalidate them only if burdens on interstate commerce are too great? See e.g., Government Suppliers Consolidating Services, Inc. v. Bayh, 753 F. Supp. 739 (1990). Shouldn't the courts in these cases be trying to sustain the legislation in the absence of strong reasons for invalidation? When a legitimate purpose is present, there is little warrant for striking the statute down in the absence of demonstrable ill-effects on interstate commerce.

Section 2. ANALYZING BURDENS ON INTERSTATE COMMERCE

Even if *Taylor* ultimately has not transformed the judicial approach in dormant commerce clause discriminatory legislation cases into an approach far more like that applied in cases of even-handed legislation, it should be clear that all challenges to state statutes on dormant commerce clause grounds are going to raise the issue of weighing, in some fashion, the burden imposed on interstate commerce.

The case that follows involves a ban on phosphate detergents that was challenged by commercial entities in the phosphate detergent industry on dormant commerce clause grounds. The court goes to great pains to evaluate arguments based on interstate burdens and local benefits, thereby offering an insight into what is involved when courts enter those arenas.

Procter & Gamble Corp. v. Chicago

United States Circuit Court for the Seventh Circuit, 1975
509 F.2d 69, cert. denied, 421 U.S. 978

SWYGERT, C.J. This appeal presents the question of whether an ordinance of the City of Chicago that bans the use of detergents containing phosphates is unconstitutional on the ground that it results in an impermissible interference with interstate commerce. This district court decided that the ordinance is unconstitutional. We disagree.

---

23. The *Pike* test is explored more fully at page 519 *infra*.

The ordinance was adopted by the City Council after its Committee on Environmental Control had held public meetings for three days. The measure provided that the sale of detergents containing any phosphorous after June 30, 1972 constituted a criminal offense. Most detergents sold in this country contain phosphates which are compounds containing the element phosphorous.

The present action was brought seeking declaratory and injunctive relief. Plaintiff-appellee Procter and Gamble Company is a manufacturer of phosphate detergents. Plaintiff-appellee FMC Corporation processes and manufacturers sodium tripolyphosphate and other phosphate products for use in detergents....

A substantial amount of evidence, including exhaustive expert scientific and technical testimony by many witnesses, was presented both in court and by depositions....

The plaintiffs unquestionably showed that the ordinance has had an adverse effect upon their businesses which admittedly are national in scope. Procter and Gamble was unable to sell any detergents in the Chicago area for five months after June 30, 1972 and lost $4,700,000 in sales as a result. FMC lost $500,000 worth of sales of phosphates as a result of the ordinance. Further, whereas before the ordinance Procter's Chicago plant was able to supply over 96 percent of the requirement for the six-state "Chicago Plant Area," after the ordinance became effective the plant could supply only 51 percent, which necessitated shipments to this area from other Procter plants in Louisiana, Missouri, and Kansas. The result was the establishment of a different and, from the company's viewpoint, a less efficient interstate system of distribution of its products.

Evidence was also introduced concerning the warehousing practices of the retail grocery chains serving Chicago and the surrounding area. These chains, which include chains of independents, warehouse their products on an area-wide basis as opposed to a city-wide basis. Goods are purchased from the manufacturer and stored in warehouses for eventual distribution to the individual retail stores. In the Chicago area, the same warehouses also service stores in northern Illinois, northern Indiana, southern Wisconsin, and Michigan. At the warehouses, each product is stored in its own particular area called a slot. There was testimony that these warehouses will not "double slot" a product and thus refused to carry both phosphate and non-phosphate versions of the same product. The explanation is that there is not sufficient space in the warehouses and there would be the possibility of a violation of the ordinance if phosphate formulas were accidently shipped to Chicago stores. Of the seventeen major Chicago area customers of Procter and Gamble, fifteen chose to carry only non-phosphate detergents. The result has been that consumers in areas of Illinois and the other adjacent states where the sale of phosphate detergents is legal can purchase only non-phosphate formulas of the major detergents from stores which are part of these fifteen chains. Thus, the Chicago ordinance affected Procter and Gamble's ability to sell its phosphate detergents in other states.

The bulk of the evidence dealt with the nature and effect of phosphates and particularly their effect on the water moving in the Illinois Waterway. Phosphates are not a problem in and of themselves. They are not harmful to most humans and are even added to water by some communities for the purpose of softening. The aspect of phosphates that causes concern is their nutritive contribution to the eutrophication of rivers and lakes. Eutrophication is a process of aging, whereby a body of water becomes over-nourished in nutrient elements such that there occurs an extensive growth of green plants or nuisance algae. Nuisance algae can result in an unpleasant odor and a bad taste in drinking water. It is the elimination and prevention of these algae that is desirable.

Some controversy exists, however, concerning the relationship of phosphorous and eutrophication. An abundance of phosphorous does not always result in increased eutrophication. It is a more complex process and its exact nature is somewhat in dispute. Other nutrients including nitrogen and carbon are needed for eutrophication. So far as the nutrient aspect of eutrophication is concerned the important inquiry centers on the idea of the "limiting nutrient" or "limiting factor." The "limiting nutrient" is that nutrient that is in the shortest supply relative to the need for it for plant growth. It is the factor which limits any further aquatic growth. The district court found that phosphorous can be a "limiting factor" for nuisance algae only at .02 milligrams per liter or less. There is some evidence, however, that phosphorous is the nutrient that is most easily controlled.

The ordinance's most direct effect is on the Illinois Waterway because the City's sewage effluent flows into it. This Waterway, which includes the Illinois River, is a water source for some communities, but not for Chicago. The Waterway has a very high percentage of phosphorous. The district court determined that before the passage of the ordinance the amount of phosphorous present in this Waterway was at least twenty-five times as much as is necessary to sustain nuisance algae. Still, there is a question of whether there is any nuisance algae problem in the Illinois River. Although the City introduced photographs showing the presence of such algae, the district court concluded "that there was no significant amount of nuisance algae in the Illinois River." Explanations offered for this lack of growth included the excessive turbidity of the river which prevents needed sunlight, periodic flushing, and possibly some undefined trace elements which inhibit such growth. Also, the district court found that the elimination of Chicago phosphates alone would not result in reaching the "limiting factor" level, though a 66 percent reduction did result in at least part of the Waterway after the ordinance had been effect.

Finally, there is the evidence concerning Lake Michigan which is the source of Chicago's water supply. The danger of nuisance algae is more pronounced with regard to Lake Michigan because it does not have the flushing quality of a river. Moreover, the phosphorous concentration is at about the "limiting factor" of .02 milligrams per liter. But unlike some of the other communities along the lake, Chicago's sewage does not normally flow into the lake; only during excessively heavy rainstorms is one of two rivers reversed so that sewage flows into Lake Michigan. The district court determined that such reversals occurred only four times within a ten year period, though there was also testimony that the frequency of such reversals is increasing. As to the amount of phosphates entering the lake during a year in which a back-flow resulted, the conclusion of the district court was that detergents contributed only 250 tons or about three percent of the total entering the lake each year.

Based on this evidence the trial court determined that the phosphate ban was unconstitutional. It decided that the ordinance resulted in increased costs of manufacture and distribution and burdened interstate commerce. Once the plaintiffs had proven this much the court held that the City was then required to justify the ordinance by showing some need to protect the public health, safety, or welfare. Though it found that the "ordinance was enacted in good faith and for laudatory objectives," the justifications offered for the ordinance were not sufficient to outweigh its interference with interstate commerce. The court held that the City did have the power to protect the water quality for persons living downstream, but the ordinance by itself would not have any beneficial effect on the Illinois Waterway. The actual effect on Lake Michigan was apparently considered too minimal to support the legislation; the theory that the City could enact the ordinance in order to influence other communities to stop discharging phosphates into Lake Michigan was rejected. Though the court conceded that such an ordinance might be sustained in some other jurisdiction where the water supply situation is different, it concluded that Chicago could only enact the ordinance on a standby basis to become effective only when other controls have brought the phosphorous content of the Illinois Waterway down to the "limiting level."

It is difficult to discern the precise test that should be used to determine when a state or local legislative enactment's effect on an area of interstate commerce that has not been pre-empted by Congressional legislation is violative of the Commerce Clause of the Constitution. It is clear that we must first decide whether there is such an effect and what it is, for if we find no effect our inquiry need not progress. However, if some effect is found then we must proceed to consider whether the legislative body "has acted within its province, and whether the means of regulation chosen are reasonably adapted to the end sought." The more difficult question is whether our analysis should encompass an additional step if the legislation is found to be a reasonable means of achieving a legitimate end. The predominant test utilized by the Supreme Court appears to require that the burden imposed on interstate commerce be balanced against the local benefit in order to determine the ultimate question of constitutionality. See Bibb v. Navajo Freight Lines, Inc., 359 U.S. 520 (1959), and Southern Pacific Co. v. Arizona, 325 U.S. 761 (1945). The Court's most recent formulation is contained in Pike v. Bruce Church, Inc., 397 U.S. 137, 142 (1970):

> Where the statute regulates evenhandedly to effectuate a legitimate local public interest, and its effects on interstate commerce are only incidental, it will be upheld unless the burden imposed on such commerce is clearly excessive in relation to the putative local benefits.

There is some support, though, for the proposition that once it is determined that the legislation is a reasonable means of achieving a nondiscriminatory, legitimate goal it should be deemed constitutional and any further weighing process need not occur. [Arguably] this "third stage" balancing process is undesirable because it can lead to the usurpation of the legislative role....

The question that we are faced with is how much weight, if any, should be accorded the legislative body's determination that the means are reasonably related to achieving the end. In the present case we think that it is at this point that the *Pike* balancing stage occurs. The district court addressed this issue as if it was an ordinary factual dispute over a technical matter that should be decided without the benefit of a presumption. It is our view, however, that if the burden on interstate commerce is slight, and the area of legislation is one that is properly of local concern, the means chosen to accomplish this end should be deemed reasonably effective unless the party attacking the legislation demonstrates the contrary by clear and convincing proof. If it is determined that this presumption should be applied, no further balancing need be undertaken. The end has already been deemed legitimate and the burden on interstate commerce slight. If the legislation is a reasonable means to the end it is constitutional.

Having in mind the framework of our analysis, we begin by considering what, if any, burden was imposed on interstate commerce by this ordinance. The first major argument raised by the plaintiffs, and apparently accepted by the district court, is that the ordinance burdened interstate commerce by impairing the normal operation of companies having interstate sales and requiring these companies to create new, and less direct, shipping routes. This argument is based on the fact that Procter and Gamble's plant in the Chicago area could not adequately supply its six-state area with detergents because the plant had to manufacture two lines of detergent products and thus reduce its capacity. The result was that products had to be shipped to some of these states from plants which happened to be at different, and often further, locations. The principal cases relied on to support this theory involve interstate carriers whose ability to efficiently transport other's goods through particular states was permanently impaired. With our case, we are not confronted with a situation in which legislation has reduced the effectiveness of a means of transportation itself. In this context the ordinance is not a burden on interstate commerce, but is merely a "burden" on a company which happens to have interstate distribution facilities. The effect of the ordinance is that the particular interstate systems of distribution used by Procter and Gamble and other detergent companies before the passage of the ordinance can no longer be used. This is because of the freely chosen geographical locations of their various plants, not because of the requirements of this ordinance. There is no impairment of the ultimate ability to transport in interstate commerce in the most efficient and economical manner possible. While this factor might necessitate a change in certain production facilities, it does not rise to the level of an unconstitutional burden on interstate commerce.

Plaintiffs also argue that the ordinance is a burden on interstate commerce because there is a "potential for conflicting legislation." Other jurisdictions, including some within the Chicago marketing area have enacted phosphate detergent legislation, and it is urged that such local legislation might conflict with each other so as to inhibit the uniformity necessary for the national manufacture and distribution of detergents. It is claimed that Milwaukee has an ordinance that not only restricts phosphates, but also prohibits highly alkaline detergents which have been used as substitutes for phosphate detergents. But there is no evidence in the record to prove that any phosphate substitutes used by the appellees in Chicago violate Milwaukee's ordinance. The Supreme Court has indicated that in a case involving environmental legislation it is actual conflict, not potential conflict, that is relevant. Moreover, once again the plaintiffs have drawn the main support for their argument from the cases involving interstate carriers. The importance of uniformity is not as great in the present type of case in terms of interstate commerce. As Judge Stevens of this circuit has stated:

> We think it certainly is true where you have a carrier who necessarily goes from state to state carrying the goods of third parties there is a higher interest in uniformity throughout the nation, but with respect to a commercial enterprise such as a manufacturer of detergents there is not the same national interest in uniformity throughout the country....

No burden has been shown based on this theory.

Another argument presented by plaintiffs is that the ordinance burdens interstate commerce because it amounts to an embargo on a safe, useful and unique product of commerce without any corresponding local benefit. We find no merit to this argument. In essence, it is not a Commerce Clause argument but one based on substantive due process, an issue not before us. The only Commerce Clause cases cited for this proposition involve situations in which a state has attempted to achieve a local purpose by discriminating against out-of-state producers or manufacturers. There is no discrimination in this case. The ordinance does not require that detergents be manufactured in Chicago or Illinois and does not benefit manufacturers who are located there.

There is one theory of plaintiffs, however, in which we find some merit. This ordinance does have an extraterritorial effect because of the four-state warehouse marketing system employed by the major wholesale purchasers of detergents. Since a substantial number of the retail grocery stores within a 150 mile radius of Chicago are supplied from seventeen grocery warehouses in or near Chicago, the refusal of these warehouses to "double slot" detergents means that many people outside Chicago cannot buy phosphate detergents even though they wish to use them. Potential purchasers in other states are prevented from obtaining a detergent formula that manufacturers may legally sell in those states. Though the ordinance may not directly dictate such a result, one effect is that the free flow in commerce of a particular product is disrupted. Such a disruption must be deemed a burden on interstate commerce.

Still, there is the question of how substantial is this burden. It is important to realize that this burden is one that was not intended by the City Council, even though that factor is not determinative. The effect is an incidental one due to the nature of the grocery warehouse system over which the City Council has no control.

Moreover, all the potential purchasers of phosphate detergents in this area outside Chicago are not affected by the ordinance. Other jurisdictions in the Chicago marketing zone also have limitations on phosphate detergents. Purchasers in these areas are restricted by their own local legislation. And in the areas without such legislation phosphate detergents assumedly will be available at those stores which are not part of these chains. Two of the seventeen chains chose to carry phosphate formula detergents, so such products will also be available at those stores. While there might be people who cannot buy phosphate detergents in their own towns, the foregoing factors tend to lessen the burden. Indeed, there is the possibility that manufacturers might be able to "drop-ship" directly from the plant to stores in some areas. Although this might not be the customary or most economical procedure, Procter and Gamble distributes its products in this manner for about one percent of its total business.

We are troubled by the contention that these large warehouses absolutely refuse to stock two formulas of the same detergent. Procter and Gamble and the other two large detergent manufacturers are huge companies that could exert at least some "leverage" on those warehouses.... We are not totally persuaded by the grocery chains' explanation of why only one type of detergent can be stocked. The major reason presented is lack of space. But it would seem that the total number of boxes of detergents sold would be about the same whether two formulations or only one are offered....

Nor can we unquestionably accept the contention that carrying both types of detergents would result in a great risk of accidental shipments to and sale of phosphate detergents by stores within Chicago in violation of the ordinance. If this were the only concern we are sure that some procedure could be arranged to minimize this possibility. For instance, the cartons that contain boxes of phosphate could be made a different color so they would be easily distinguishable. Certainly under such a procedure the employees of the individual stores could recognize a mistake and not sell the illegal detergent.

We recognize that the Chicago ordinance combined with the grocery warehousing practice can result in interfering with the full distribution of phosphate detergents to areas outside of Chicago. But many of these consumers would probably have access to such products either at other stores or at chain stores that might receive drop-shipments. Our analysis has indicated that if there was sufficient demand it might even be possible that all the large warehouses would carry phosphate detergents. Overall, we conclude that the ordinance's effect on full access to certain products by consumers in parts of other states can only be classified as a slight burden on interstate commerce.

Having determined that the ordinance does impose some burden on interstate commerce, we are required to consider whether the interest sought to be served by the legislation is a legitimate local concern. As with most cases of this type, the goal of this legislation can be stated in its ultimate terms – protection of health and welfare. For purposes of our analysis, we believe that it would be more useful to express the objective simply as the prevention and elimination of nuisance algae. This is an environmental objective toward which local legislation may properly be aimed. In broad terms, this legislation is part of the overall attack on the problem of water pollution. Though there is federal intervention in this general area, this does not prevent local attempts to deal with one of our most immediate and difficult problems....

Indeed, Congress appears to have specifically encouraged such local legislation. The Federal Water Pollution Control Amendments of 1972 provide:

> Except as expressly provided in this chapter, nothing in this chapter shall (1) preclude or deny the right of any State or political subdivision thereof or interstate agency to adopt or enforce (A) any standard or limitation respecting discharges of pollutants, or (B) any requirements respecting control or abatement of pollution.

Moreover, as noted earlier, there are no discriminatory aspects associated with this purpose that might invalidate it. The objective is legitimately local and nondiscriminatory which means that it may properly be the end toward which local legislation is addressed.

Finally, we see no problem in the fact that the ordinance is aimed, at least in part, toward nuisance algae downstream from Chicago. We agree with the conclusion of the district court that the City can be legitimately concerned with preventing any damage to its neighbors caused by Chicago's actions.

We are now at the stage where we must determine whether the ordinance is a reasonable means of reaching the end desired. We have previously concluded that the burden on interstate commerce that results from this ordinance is slight and the objective of this legislation is legitimate. We hold that the burden is so slight compared to the important and properly local objective that the presumption we discussed earlier should apply. We will accept the City Council's determination that this phosphate ban is a reasonable means of achieving the elimination and prevention of nuisance algae unless we find that the plaintiffs have presented clear and convincing proof to the contrary.

[The opinion reviewed the evidence on whether the phosphate ban would be effective, and concluded, in essence, that (1) it could play a part in an overall strategy that would be effective, and (2) even standing alone, the Chicago ordinance might have a positive effect under some circumstances.]

The case has presented a very difficult constitutional problem. On the basis of the above analysis we have resolved the question in favor of the constitutionality of the ordinance. Accordingly, the judgment of the district court is reversed.

COMMENTARY AND QUESTIONS

1. To balance or not to balance. In an omitted portion of the *Procter & Gamble* opinion, the court discusses the argument that what it called "third-stage" balancing in dormant commerce clause cases is a usurpation of the legislative role. The idea as presented by the opinion stems from the Supreme Court decision in Brotherhood of Locomotive Firemen & Engineers v. Chicago, Rock Island & Pacific Railroad Co., 393 U.S. 129 (1968). A lower court had invalidated an Arkansas full train crew law on the ground that it provided a small increment of safety that was not worth the added cost and burden on interstate commerce. The Supreme Court reversed, finding that the District Court had tried to make public policy and in so doing had "indulged in a legislative judgment wholly beyond its limited authority to review state legislation under the Commerce Clause." In deciding that balancing the benefits of the Chicago phosphate ban against its burdens on interstate commerce would not usurp the legislative role, the *Procter & Gamble* decision distinguished the public policy issue (how much benefit is there from phosphate removal and prevention of nuisance algae?) from the more pragmatic issue (will the ordinance result in any prevention of algae growth?) and said it was limiting its review to the latter question. Is this distinction workable?

In general, the Supreme Court continues to adhere to its approval of balancing under the *Pike* test. Only Justice Scalia has strenuously advocated a break from that position. See CTS Corp. v. Dynamics Corp. of America, 107 S.Ct. 1637, 1652 (1987)(opinion of Scalia, J., concurring); Bendix Autolite v. Midwesco, 108 S.Ct 2218, 2224 (1988)(opinion of Scalia, J., concurring).

2. Applying the *Pike* test. How is the *Pike* test used in *Procter & Gamble*? The court seems to use it to set the standard by which its review of the statute's effectiveness is to be measured. As long as the burden on interstate commerce is slight, the court will give a great deal of deference to the legislative determination that the means it has chosen will work to address the problem it has identified. The court translates that position into an evidentiary burden: a party challenging the law must demonstrate that the law fails to further its purpose by clear and convincing proof. Is that what you would have expected to be the application of the *Pike* test? *Pike* seems to call explicitly for a weighing of burdens and benefits when it says statutes will be upheld "unless the burden imposed on [interstate] commerce is clearly excessive in relation to the putative local benefits."

3. Environmental altruism as a legitimate local purpose. The *Procter & Gamble* court is clearly troubled by the fact that most of the benefits that are generated by Chicago's phosphate ban accrue outside of Chicago, downstream on the Illinois waterway. Why should the court feel that the constitutional analysis is affected by the location of the benefits? On one hand it could be a question of "authority" or "proper public purpose."[24] Or perhaps it goes to the weighing of burdens, since the fact that the benefit is enjoyed elsewhere might reduce the weight to be given to putative local benefits compared with burdens on interstate commerce. Such a scrutiny of local benefits, however, seems to run afoul of the courts' hesitancy to review legislative "public policy" determinations, as referred to above.

Section 3. AVOIDING DORMANT COMMERCE CLAUSE SCRUTINY OF REGULATORY ACTIONS FAVORING IN-STATE INTERESTS

Remembering Philadelphia v. New Jersey and its ban on state exclusions of out-of-state landfill customers, it is easy to see how such parochial legislation gets enacted. It is very popular to legislate preferences that provide local benefits at the expense of out-of-state third parties who are not part of the voting electorate. In a post-Love Canal NIMBY world, moreover, holding threats posed by dumpsite landfills to a minimum is a very popular position. As one waste disposal official said in a federal hearing on the subject, "Everyone wants us to pick up the trash, but no one wants us to put it down."

After the Supreme Court's decision in *Philadelphia*, local banning of out-of-state wastes from landfills became a more difficult – but not impossible – proposition. This section samples a number of statutes that have sought to discriminate against out-of-state waste[25] while avoiding constitutional invalidation. Simultaneously, it provides a vehicle for reviewing some further doctrinal wrinkles in dormant commerce clause jurisprudence.

a. THE MARKET PARTICIPANT DOCTRINE

Swin Resource Systems, Inc. v. Lycoming County
United States Circuit Court of Appeals for the Third Circuit, 1989
883 F.2d 245, cert. denied, 110 S. Ct. 1127

[The operator of a solid waste processing facility brought suit against a county which operated a landfill, challenging, on dormant commerce clause grounds, regulations giving the county residents preference in use of the landfill.]

BECKER, J....

THE MARKET PARTICIPANT DOCTRINE

Swin contends that Lycoming County's attempt to preserve its landfill capacity for local residents by charging a higher price to dispose of distant waste in the landfill (and limiting the volume of distant waste accepted by the landfill) constitutes an impermissible interference with and discrimination against interstate commerce

24. A rather technical legal argument could attack the ordinance, if it provided only extra-territorial benefits, as an illegitimate use of the police power because it is beyond the scope of authority delegated to Chicago. This, however, is a question of state law that must be resolved by looking at what powers Illinois grants to its cities, and whether those powers limit the ability to bestow extra-territorial benefits. This was clearly not what concerned the court. Protection of the city from downstream plaintiffs, moreover, is an affirmative and less altruistic local benefit.

25. Efforts to ban wastes that originate outside the United States are equally subject to dormant commerce clause scrutiny. Recall that the commerce clause addresses foreign commerce as well as interstate commerce. For a case striking down an import ban on hazardous waste generated at Mexican facilities operated by United States companies, see Chemical Waste Management v. Templet, 1991 WL 126254 (M.D.La. July 9, 1991).

in violation of the commerce clause. The district court granted the defendants' motion to dismiss the commerce clause claim on the ground that Lycoming had acted as a "market participant." Under the market participant doctrine, a state or state subdivision that acts as a market participant rather than a market regulator "is not subject to the restraints of the Commerce Clause." White v. Massachusetts Council of Construction Employers, Inc., 460 U.S. 204, 208 (1983)....

For the reasons explained below, we hold that Lycoming County acted as a market participant rather than a market regulator in deciding the conditions under which Swin could use its landfill. It is useful to begin our analysis with a review of the four principal market participant cases.

In Alexandria Scrap Corp. v. Hughes, 426 U.S. 794 (1976) the Supreme Court upheld Maryland's statutory scheme to rid the state of derelict automobiles, even though the scheme entailed two types of discrimination: (1) Maryland paid bounties to in-state scrap auto hulk processors while refusing to pay bounties to out-of-state processors on the same terms, and (2) Maryland paid bounties only for vehicles formerly titled in Maryland. The Court held that the statutory scheme was consistent with the commerce clause on the ground that Maryland was participating in the market rather than regulating it. As the majority put it, "[n]othing in the purposes animating the Commerce Clause prohibits a State, in the absence of congressional action, from participating in the market and exercising the right to favor its own citizens over others." 426 U.S. at 810.

In Reeves, Inc. v. Stake, 447 U.S. 429 (1980), the Court upheld a South Dakota policy of confining the sale of cement by a state-operated cement plant to residents of South Dakota in order to meet their demand during a "serious cement shortage." The Court affirmed "[t]he basic distinction drawn in *Alexandria Scrap* between States as market participants and States as market regulators" and concluded that "South Dakota, as a seller of cement, unquestionably fits the 'market participant' label." 447 U.S. at 436. The Court upheld the South Dakota policy even though Reeves, a Wyoming corporation that had purchased about 95 percent of its cement from South Dakota's state-operated plant for over twenty years, was forced to cut production by over 75 percent as a result of the policy.

In *White*, the Court, deeming the case "well within the scope of *Alexandria Scrap* and *Reeves*," upheld an executive order of the Mayor of Boston requiring all construction projects funded in whole or in part either by city funds or city-administered federal funds to be performed by a work force of at least 50 percent city residents. 460 U.S. at 211, n. 7....

In South-Central Timber Development Co. v. Wunnicke, 467 U.S. 82 (1984), however, a plurality struck down Alaska's requirement that timber taken from state lands be processed in-state prior to export. Adhering to the distinction suggested in *White*, the plurality held that "the limit of the market-participant doctrine must be that it allows a State to impose burdens on commerce within the market in which it is a participant, but [does not] allow it to...impose conditions, whether by statute, regulation, or contract, that have a substantial regulatory effect outside of that particular market." 467 U.S. at 97. The Alaska policy crossed the line distinguishing participation from regulation because the conditions it attached to its timber sales amounted to "downstream regulation of the timber-processing market in which it is not a participant." 467 U.S. at 99....

No court, to our knowledge, has ever suggested that the commerce clause requires city-operated garbage trucks to cross state lines in order to pick up the garbage generated by residents of other states. If a city may constitutionally limit its trucks to collecting garbage generated by city residents, we see no constitutional reason why a city cannot also limit a city-operated dump to garbage generated by city residents. With respect to municipal garbage trucks and municipal garbage dumps, application of the market participant doctrine enables "the people [acting through their local government] to determine as conditions demand...what services and functions the public welfare requires." *Reeves*, 447 U.S. at 438, n. 11. The residents who reside within the jurisdiction of a county or municipality are unlikely to pay for local government services if they must bear the cost but the entire nation may receive the benefit....

DOES A "NATURAL RESOURCE" EXCEPTION APPLY HERE?

Swin's vigorous argument that Lycoming has attempted to harbor a scarce natural resource for its own residents brings us to the potential caveat we mentioned. While the harboring of a scarce manufactured product or human service does not preclude the invocation of the market participant doctrine because it is scarce (in *Reeves* the Supreme Court applied the doctrine to South Dakota's effort to harbor cement for its own residents despite a serious cement shortage), it may be that there is some special rule to be applied to a state's effort to harbor a scarce *natural* resource. Unlike a manufactured product or the provision of a human service, a state does not have the ability to develop a natural resource if it has not had the fortuity to be favored with such a resource. While it may seem fair for South Dakota to favor its citizens in the sale of cement from a state-owned cement plant, for a state to favor its own citizens in selling rights to mine coal or limestone on state-owned lands, for example, or in selling state-owned coal or limestone, would seem less fair, especially if the state happened to be endowed with the bulk of our nation's coal or limestone reserves and the other states were dependent upon it....

Whether there is a natural resource exception to the market participant doctrine is a difficult question, but, fortunately, one which we need not answer at this level of abstraction. First, land, the natural resource at issue here, cannot be used for a landfill without the expenditure of at least some money to prepare it for that purpose. The Lycoming landfill is therefore "not simply happenstance," Sporhase v. Nebraska, 458 U.S. 941, 957 (1982), but is at least to some extent like South Dakota's cement plant in that government funds were needed to construct it. Moreover, since the land upon which the landfill was constructed had to be leased in this case, the land, even prior to development, bore some resemblance to South Dakota's cement plant in that its devotion to public use required the disbursement or promise of future disbursement of government resources....

COMMENTARY AND QUESTIONS

1. The economic unreality of the market participant doctrine. The majority opinion in *Swin* prompted a vigorous dissent by Chief Judge Gibbons. He argued that the market participant doctrine itself arose out of a "peculiar eruption of Dixieism" and is undercut by later Supreme Court decisions.[26] He also attacked the application of the market participant doctrine as premised on economic unreality:

26. Judge Gibbons' intent in this phrase was to attack judicial decisions that promoted states' rights policies by widening the scope of matters in which states could act contrary to federal directives. The principal object of his venom was National League of Cities v. Usery, 426 U.S. 833 (1976) which was decided on the same day and espoused some of the same ideas as *Alexandria Scrap*. *National League of Cities* was subsequently expressly overruled, thereby undercutting, he thought, the purported expansion of states' rights that it had shared with *Alexandria Scrap*.

> The present appeal provides a typical case in point. However much their market might be regulated, private landfill operators still desire to turn a profit. Few, if any, would give a second thought to the origin of the waste filling the space sold. Nor is it likely that any would long stay in business even assuming some highly unusual public commitment to the preservation of that space by locals. Under any realistic view, the Lycoming landfill in private hands would never have hindered its ability to sell space to the highest bidder by erecting a differential rate structure that discriminated against waste the further its point of origin. If anything, it would have created a fee structure that did precisely the opposite. A vendor of landfill space hoping to attract business, as do genuine market participants, would logically attempt to lure large volume purchasers concerned with transportation costs through a discount, especially when it appeared that customers dealing in local waste could not themselves provide sufficient business. As an exercise toward the political end of saving space for county waste, Lycoming County's price structure makes good regulatory sense. As an essay in market participation, it is aberrant and the majority's application of the label "market participant" to Lycoming County is an economic jest. 883 F.2d at 262.

There can be little doubt that Chief Judge Gibbons has correctly analyzed the economically irrational nature of the local preference aspect of Lycoming County's fee schedule, but is the market participant doctrine bottomed on the expectation that governmental entities will act in an economically rational fashion? Isn't a more plausible basis for the doctrine captured in the phrase that the state has "put its money where its mouth is?" The state has entered the market to buy the privilege of running a business irrationally. When it spends its money this way, the state avoids the unfairness of commanding via regulation that someone else, whose assets the state did not purchase in the marketplace, run their business in an irrational way that favors the state's residents and discriminates against interstate commerce.

b. IMPOSITION OF DIFFERENTIAL FEES

Although *Swin* involved the imposition of differential and discriminatory fees, the court paid relatively little attention to the possibility that such a fee schedule can survive dormant commerce clause scrutiny even without the invocation of the market participant doctrine. The principal argument in support of differential fees comes from Baldwin v. Montana Fish & Game Commission, 436 U.S. 371 (1978), in which the Court upheld a 300 percent out-of-state/in-state elk hunting license fee differential. Montana justified the fee differential by pointing out its substantial expenditures on management and support of the elk herd and other natural resources using funds raised from state taxes. In effect, Montana argued that it was evening out the burden of managing the elk herd between in-state resident hunters, who paid via general taxes, and out-of-state hunters who were not subject to Montana's taxing authority. Although the challenges to the Montana fee schedule were not based on the dormant commerce clause,[27] the logic of the decision raises

27. Two constitutional challenges were presented, one claiming denial of equal protection and the other claiming denial of the privileges and immunities of citizenship.

the possibility that a dormant commerce clause challenge could be overcome on similar logic.

Despite the *Baldwin* precedent, differential fees in the interstate waste disposal context have so far not survived dormant commerce clause scrutiny. The brief excerpts from the following case are typical – the fee differentials are clearly discriminatory and thus subject to a stricter level of scrutiny than that given to even-handed regulations; the proffered justifications for the discriminations then fail to survive that analysis.

National Solid Waste Management Association v. Voinovich
United States District Court for the Southern District of Ohio, 1991
763 F. Supp. 244

[As described more fully below, an Ohio statute imposed a higher "tipping fee" for out-of-state waste deposited in Ohio landfills than it did for in-state waste similarly deposited.]

SMITH, J. To resolve the pending motion, the Court must determine if the Act treats interstate and intrastate commerce evenhandedly, and if not, whether the state has articulated a compelling reason for distinguishing in-state wastes from out-of-state wastes. In either instance, the Court may engage in a balance of the state's interests with the burdens the legislation places on interstate commerce. If, however, the Court finds that the statute discriminates against out-of-state wastes without a compelling need to do so, we must find that it is incompatible with the Commerce Clause and strike it down.[28]

It is uncontroverted the provisions of Ohio Rev.Code §3734.57(A) and (B) treat in-state wastes differently than out-of-state wastes. Under Section (A), the tax levied on wastes imported into the State is as much as one dollar more per ton than that placed on in-district wastes. The fee is not discretionary, nor is it based on any factors other than the wastes' place of origin. Likewise, Section (B) authorizes the individual management districts to impose disparate fees. Although the choice to actually impose the Section (B) taxes is left to the discretion of the management districts, if they are levied...the tax on out-of-state wastes is required to be three times that imposed on in-district wastes.

28. Recently, the United States District Court for the Southern District of Indiana addressed a similar constitutional challenge as the case at bar. In Government Suppliers Consolidating Services v. Bayh, 753 F. Supp. 739 (S.D. 1990), the court struck down an Indiana statute which placed onerous burdens on the interstate shipment of solid wastes into Indiana. The statute imposed a "tipping fee" on out-of-state wastes that was greater than that imposed on in-state wastes; required certification that the wastes were not hazardous; and required disclosure of the point of the waste's generation. In striking down the statute, the Indiana court adopted substantially the same reasoning we do here, although rather than requiring the State to come forth with a compelling reason for the facially discriminatory taxing scheme, the court accepted the State's assertion that the provisions were justified as a means to protect the health and welfare of its citizens. The court, however, found that there were less drastic means of achieving that goal and struck down the statute. Our analysis differs in that we believe that [several Supreme Court cases], do not support the notion that anything less than a compelling reason may justify a facially discriminatory taxing scheme. We decline to engage in an analysis which requires us to accept the State of Ohio's asserted reasons for distinguishing between in-state and out-of-state tax rates and then search for less drastic means to validate those reasons. Nonetheless, the *Bayh* decision supports our finding here. Its thrust is that absent a showing of inherent differences between in-state and out-of-state wastes, discriminatory treatment of the latter is violative of the Commerce Clause.

The fact that the Act discriminates on its face requires us to determine if the State of Ohio has articulated a compelling reason for distinguishing in-state and out-of-state wastes....

The State offers three reasons for the need to tax out-of-state wastes at a higher rate. First, it cites the ever-increasing amount of solid wastes that are being shipped into Ohio. In 1988 alone, according to defendants, over two billion tons of out-of-state waste was disposed of in Ohio – approximately 18 percent of the total amount of waste processed in the state. The sheer volume of waste flowing into the state, it asserts, is sufficient in and of itself to tax out-of-state wastes at a higher rate. Second, the State claims that foreign wastes present unique regulatory problems. Unlike wastes generated in the state, foreign wastes cannot be inspected at their point of origin. This allegedly presents financial and logistical problems. The source of the waste and its composition is more difficult and expensive to ascertain at the place of disposal. Finally, the State argues that the increased threat of hazardous waste materials entering Ohio requires the imposition of higher fees. None of these reasons offered by the State is sufficient to justify the distinction between domestic and foreign wastes and require the Court to engage in a balancing of the state's interests with the actual burden the Act places on interstate commerce....

The State's claim that the allegedly higher costs of inspecting out-of-state wastes requires it to treat domestic and foreign wastes differently is without support. The Court does not question the validity of state taxing schemes which place higher fees on foreign articles when the state incurs additional administrative costs in inspecting articles located outside the state. In fact, it appears that the Supreme Court has only found such fees invalid when they explicitly exempt local activities from the obligations imposed on comparable interstate enterprises....

The purpose of §3734.57 is definitively expressed in the section. It goes to great length to describe in detail the nature of the taxing scheme and for what activities the State may generate revenue. Primarily, the section is concerned with raising money to offset the State's obligations under the Comprehensive Environmental Response, Compensation, and Liability Act of 1980. To that extent, the State is authorized to tax activities related to the proper clean up of wastes. Importantly, Section (A) makes no reference to the costs of inspecting wastes that are generated either inside or outside the state. Section (B) authorizes the taxing of wastes for basically the same purposes although it does make reference to the inspection of foreign wastes. The individual management districts may levy fees to pay the costs of "developing and implementing" a program for inspecting out-of-state wastes.

A careful reading of the statute indicates that it is not designed to be a scheme for the inspection of waste. It is a piece of legislation geared toward raising revenue to offset the state's cost of cleaning up its landfills and disposal facilities. Therefore, we cannot lend any credence to the State's proposition that the disparity of fees is warranted by the alleged higher costs of inspecting out-of-state wastes. The challenged section is exhaustive in defining its purpose. It is designed primarily to raise revenue, not to reimburse the State for the costs of inspecting waste. Moreover, other provisions of the Act specifically deal with waste inspection. We express no opinion as to those provisions; however, the State of Ohio has not endeavored to implement such legislation within the structure of §3437.57 and we are without authority to read into a statute provisions which the State has conspicuously omitted.

Even if we were to read the statute as authorizing fees commensurate with the costs of inspection, the State has not produced any evidence whatsoever that the cost of inspecting out-of-state wastes is significantly higher than the inspection of domestic wastes. The affidavits on which the state relies only illustrate the potential difficulties in evaluating waste materials from unknown sources. They provide no data which shows that the inspection of out-of-state wastes costs up to 300 percent more than the inspection of in-state wastes. Even given the latitude which the Court must accord the opposing party in a motion for summary judgment, there is not a modicum of evidence to suggest that inspection costs justify the great disparity in the taxing scheme.

The State's third articulated reason for the discriminatory treatment of out-of-state wastes is the difficulty in policing the transportation of hazardous wastes. The State cites an incident in which it is believed that hazardous materials were illegally shipped into the state and caused an explosion, as well as other problems, in enforcing criminal restrictions for the transportation of hazardous materials. The Court appreciates the need to insure the safe disposal of waste materials, but the State's arguments have little to do with the statute in question. Section 3734.57 is purely a revenue raising provision, and the State has not articulated any connection between policing hazardous wastes and taxing wastes differently on the single basis of their place of origin.

The State has not provided any acceptable reasons or theories for treating in-state wastes differently from out-of-state wastes. Although the State raises numerous legitimate concerns other than those discussed above, they are largely irrelevant. We deal here only with the narrow issue of whether the discriminatory surcharges on out-of-state wastes impose constitutionally impermissible burdens on interstate commerce. The plain unambiguous language of the statute supports only the conclusion that the State is distinguishing between wastes based solely on their place of origin and placing excessively high premiums on out-of-state wastes. Since Ohio has demonstrated no compelling need to impose substantially higher taxes on out-of-state wastes than in-state wastes, the Court cannot engage in a balancing of interests; the actual burden the provision has on commerce is not relevant.

Ohio Rev. Code §3734.57 is a transparent attempt to discourage the shipment of solid wastes into Ohio. On its face, it discriminates against interstate commerce in violation of the constitution's proscription of such burdens. The State cannot solve its waste problems by blocking or rerouting the market's allocation of that waste, for the Commerce Clause can have no tolerance for parochial decisions "by one State to isolate itself in the stream of interstate commerce from a problem shared by all." Philadelphia [v. New Jersey], 437 U.S. at 629. "The peoples of the several states must sink or swim together, even in their collective garbage." L. Tribe, American Constitutional Law, 2nd Ed., §6-8 (1988)(quoting Baldwin v. G.A.F. Seelig, Inc., 294 U.S. 511, 523 (1935)). Accordingly, plaintiff's motion for summary judgment is hereby GRANTED as to Ohio Rev. Code §3734.57....

COMMENTARY AND QUESTIONS

1. Justifying differential tipping fees. Is there any justification for differential tipping fees that will survive careful scrutiny like that given in the instant case? There needs to be some objective reason to impose the higher fees, and unless the depository state has engaged in some sort of pre-treatment of its wastes, it is hard to imagine what makes an in-state pile of garbage different from an out-of-state pile of garbage. Pretreatment could include segregation of waste streams, so that small volume hazardous materials such as household batteries and non-commercial volumes of paints and solvents are absent from the in-state materials being landfilled. The less safe out-of-state waste stream may, in the long run, require more expensive treatment in the depository state than would the safer in-state waste stream.

2. Using *Taylor* to avoid *Philadelphia*-based invalidation of discriminatory tipping fees. One recent decision has reached the conclusion that differential tipping fees are constitutional. In Hunt v. Chemical Waste Management, Inc. No. 1901043 (Ala. S. Ct. July 11, 1991), reported in part at 60 U.S.L.W. 2066 (July 30, 1991), an effort by Alabama to limit the flow of out-of-state hazardous waste to a major facility (the nation's largest) in Emelle, Alabama, was sustained by the Alabama Supreme Court.[29] The fee provisions in the Alabama case called for a base fee of $25.60 per ton for all waste deposited at regulated facilities, and an "Additional Fee" of $72.00 per ton for all waste originating outside of Alabama. On the dormant commerce clause challenge to the tipping fees differential, the court said:

> We next consider whether the additional fee discriminates against interstate commerce in violation of the Commerce Clause. The Commerce Clause does not invalidate all state restrictions on commerce. It has long been recognized that in the absence of conflicting legislation by Congress, there is a residuum of power in a state to make laws governing matters of local concern that in some measure affect interstate commerce, or even, to some extent, regulate it.
>
> The U.S. Supreme Court has not said that hazardous waste is an article of commerce. But for our purposes, we will assume that it is. We recognize that a state may not limit importation of waste to protect health and the environment as a form of simple economic protectionism. We also recognize, however, that in Maine v. Taylor, 477 U.S. 131 (1986), the Supreme Court made it clear that environmental measures are entitled to greater deference than ordinary legislative acts.
>
> The additional fee serves these legitimate local purposes that cannot be adequately served by reasonable, non-discriminatory alternatives: (1) protection of the health and safety of the citizens of Alabama from toxic substances; (2) conservation of the environment and the state's natural resources; (3) provision for compensatory revenue for the costs and burdens that out-of-state waste generators impose by dumping their hazardous waste in Alabama; and (4) reduction of the overall flow of waste traveling on the state's highways, which flow creates a great risk to the health and safety of the state's citizens.
>
> There is no dispute that the waste dumped at Emelle includes known carcinogens and materials that are extremely hazardous and can cause birth defects, genetic damage, blindness, crippling, and death. This court takes

29. Other attempts by Alabama to limit the in-flow of hazardous waste to the Emelle facility have been struck down; see page 528 *infra*.

> judicial notice that there is a finite capacity for storage of hazardous waste at the facility and that the capacity is rapidly being reached. The record reflects that 85 to 90 percent of the tonnage that is permanently buried at the site is from out of state. There is nothing in the Commerce Clause that compels the state of Alabama to yield its total capacity for hazardous waste disposal to other states. To tax Alabama-generated hazardous waste at the same rate as out-of-state waste is not an available non-discriminatory alternative, because Alabama is bearing a grossly disproportionate share of the burdens of hazardous waste disposal for the entire country. Here, the statute that creates the additional fee does not needlessly obstruct interstate trade, nor does it constitute economic protectionism. It is a responsible exercise by Alabama of its broad regulatory authority to protect the health and safety of its citizens and the integrity of its natural resources.

The Chemical Waste Management Company has indicated that it will seek review of the decision by the United States Supreme Court.

c. THE CONGRESSIONAL AUTHORIZATION DOCTRINE

Dormant commerce clause jurisprudence exists in the vacuum created by congressional inaction. Nothing in the doctrine impairs the plenary power of Congress to override the judicially defined dormant commerce clause principles by expressly authorizing what courts would otherwise disallow. Congress has occasionally expressly done so. At least a few environmental and natural resource cases have argued that Congress, by the scheme of its legislation, has impliedly immunized state action from commerce clause scrutiny. Courts have demanded that evidence of such congressional intent be clear and these attempts in the environmental area have been unsuccessful. See South-Central Timber Development Co. v. Wunnicke, 467 U.S. 82 (1984).

In regard to limiting waste importation, Alabama, has also tried (unsuccessfully) to use an argument parallelling the "congressional authorization" approach. The Emelle facility received more than 85 percent of its waste from outside of Alabama, with materials coming from all but two of the other states. In an inventive twist, attempting to limit the flow of hazardous materials into the Emelle facility, Alabama Code §22-30-11 forbade acceptance of out-of-state wastes from any state that had not met certain *federal* compliance requirements for hazardous waste management within its own borders.

In setting its exclusionary conditions, Alabama borrowed the substance of §104(c)(9) of CERCLA as amended by SARA, 42 U.S.C.A. §9604(c)(9). The crux of §104(c)(9) is that it requires all states to have an EPA-approved Assurance of Hazardous Waste Capacity. These assurances amount to having a plan for disposing of at least as much hazardous waste as the state generates. Acceptable plans for disposal include having in-state disposal capacity for all such waste, or formal agreements with states that have excess disposal capacity. Under federal law, the burden of this provision falls on states that need to export some portion of their waste. There is no requirement in federal statutory law that states must agree to accept wastes generated elsewhere.

The Alabama law was challenged by the owner of the Emelle facility and a waste industry association. A district court decision upholding the law, National Solid Waste Management Association v. Alabama Department of Environmental Management, 729 F. Supp. 792 (N.D. Ala. 1990), was reversed on appeal. 910 F.2d 713 (11th Cir. 1990).[30] After finding that the Alabama law was a "protectionist measure" to be scrutinized strictly, the court addressed the congressional authorization argument:

> Defendants contend that SARA's §104(c)(9) effected a redistribution of power over interstate commerce. According to defendants, the SARA amendments to CERCLA gave the states more responsibility for hazardous waste management, including an obligation to develop increased treatment and disposal capacity. But nothing in SARA evidences congressional authorization for each state to close its borders to wastes generated in other states to force those other states to meet federally mandated hazardous waste management requirements. SARA places the burden of making capacity assurances for future hazardous waste management on the generating state and imposes a sanction on that state for failure to satisfy its obligation.[31] Congress has not, in our opinion, authorized Alabama to restrict the free movement of hazardous wastes across Alabama's borders. See State of Alabama v. United States EPA, 871 F.2d at 1555 n. 3. ("Although Congress may override the commerce clause by express statutory language, it has not done so in enacting CERCLA.") If Congress intended to allow the states to restrict the interstate movement of hazardous wastes as Alabama has tried to do, Congress could (and still can) plainly say so.[32] 910 F.2d at 721–22.

d. QUARANTINE OF NOXIOUS MATERIAL

Some efforts to restrict interstate movement of noxious materials – the so-called quarantine laws invoked by Justice Rehnquist in his *Philadelphia* dissent – have had limited success in avoiding dormant commerce clause invalidation. In the field of interstate movement of waste, however, the quarantine doctrine has not been successfully asserted.

Government Suppliers Consolidating Services v. Bayh

United States District Court for the Southern District of Indiana, 1990
753 F. Supp. 739

TINDER, J. ...At the outset, the Governor argues that commerce clause analysis does not even apply because the items that the challenged statutory provisions attempt to regulate, i.e., out-of-state infectious and hazardous waste, are undesirable substances that the state should be able to restrict under the reasoning of the

---

30. This decision was later modified in ways not relevant to the congressional authorization doctrine. 924 F.2d 1001 (1990), and thereafter certiorari was denied, 111 S. Ct. 2800 (1991).

31. The sanction, withholding of funds for remedial cleanups of Superfund sites on the National Priorities List, seems effective because, in March 1989, almost every state had at least one site on this list. See 40 C.F.R. Part 300, App. B (1989).

32. For example, under the Low-Level Radioactive Waste Policy Act, 42 U.S.C.A. §§2021b-2021j (1982 & Supp. V 1987), states are encouraged to enter into regional compacts to provide for the establishment and operation of regional disposal facilities for low-level radioactive waste. 42 U.S.C.A. §2021d. In this Act, which predates SARA, Congress expressly authorized states that enter into such compacts to ban waste shipments from states that neither enter into a compact nor meet federal deadlines for establishing their own facilities. 42 U.S.C.A. §2021e(e)(2), (f)(1).

quarantine cases. See Illinois v. General Elec. Co., 683 F.2d 206, 214 (7th Cir.1982)(noting that the "quarantine cases" treat interstate commerce in "bads" as not commerce at all), cert. denied, 461 U.S. 913 (1983).

Under the quarantine theory, the Supreme Court has recognized the states' authority to restrict or even ban the importation of intrinsically undesirable products. See e.g., Clason v. Indiana, 306 U.S. 439, 442 (1939)(upholding Indiana's prohibition against interstate transportation of dead animals because "obvious purpose of the enactment [was] to prevent the spread of disease and the development of nuisances"). In City of Philadelphia v. New Jersey, 437 U.S. 617 (1978), however, the Supreme Court clearly held that the interstate movement of solid and liquid wastes is commerce. In that case, an out-of-state user of a New Jersey disposal site challenged a New Jersey statute prohibiting the importation of most out-of-state waste. One of the asserted purposes of the New Jersey statute, like the asserted legitimate local purpose for the challenged Indiana provisions, was the protection of the health of the state's citizens. The Court, however, stated that "all objects of interstate trade merit Commerce Clause protection; none is excluded by definition at the outset." City of Philadelphia, 437 U.S. at 622. The Court distinguished the quarantine cases as involving only those items whose "worth in interstate commerce was far outweighed by the dangers inhering in their very movement...." Id. Then the Court concluded that the innate danger of the solid and liquid waste did not outweigh its worth in interstate commerce; therefore, any restriction on such waste was subject to commerce clause analysis. Subsequently, the Seventh Circuit found that the importation of nuclear waste is commerce that does not fall within the quarantine cases, Illinois v. General Elec. Co., 683 F.2d at 214, and the Eleventh Circuit found that the importation of hazardous waste is commerce that does not fall within the quarantine cases, National Solid Wastes Management Assoc. v. Alabama Dep't of Envtl. Management, 910 F.2d 713, 720-21 (11th Cir. 1990).

While it appears that no court has addressed the question of whether the worth of infectious waste in interstate commerce is outweighed by the dangers in its movement so as to bring such waste within the quarantine cases, this court does not conclude that the interstate movement of infectious waste can be distinguished from the interstate movement of nuclear, hazardous or municipal solid waste.[33] The record in this case simply does not support such a conclusion....

If the quarantine cases were applicable here, the commerce effectively stopped by these regulations would be all out-of-state trash shipped into Indiana. Both "safe" and "dangerous" trash is reached. Indiana has not even closed its landfills to all "dangerous" Indiana trash, to say nothing of all "safe" Indiana trash. The purpose of the commerce clause is to prohibit one state from prohibiting or deterring the residents of other states from sharing in the commerce available in that state. Indiana landfills still do a booming business in the disposal of trash. Under the facts

33. The only post-*City of Philadelphia* quarantine case is Maine v. Taylor, 477 U.S. 131, which upheld a total ban on importation of baitfish to prevent the introduction of disease that was not present in the state. Maine v. Taylor is not controlling in this case. Some courts have tried to distinguish, with varying persuasiveness, the holding of Maine v. Taylor in the context of statutory regulations on the importation of waste. See National Solid Wastes Management Assoc., 910 F.2d at 720-21; Industrial Maintenance Serv., Inc. v. Moore, 677 F. Supp. 436, 442-44 (S.D.W.Va.1987). It appears to this court, however, that the Supreme Court simply treats state regulations restricting the disposal of waste as negatively impacting a national problem. Because of the commerce clause, states are not able to erect barriers to the effective functioning of a national economy and, in effect, to isolate themselves from a nationwide concern.

presented to the court, the plaintiffs cannot be restricted from that business. The plaintiffs do not seek to prohibit Indiana from regulating the disposal of hazardous or infectious materials if it is done in a constitutional, evenhanded manner.

Thus, according to the controlling precedent, the quarantine cases do not apply, and the challenged statutory provisions clearly regulate items within interstate commerce. In the following discussion, therefore, this court will apply the appropriate commerce clause test to each of the three provisions of the state statute, beginning with the tipping fee provision.

[The court subsequently struck down the statute.]

e. FACIALLY EVEN-HANDED REGULATORY SYSTEMS

As a matter of doctrine, it is patent that even-handed state environmental regulation that does not discriminate against interstate commerce has a good chance of being upheld against a dormant commerce clause challenge. The more intriguing problem in the area of blocking the importation of out-of-state waste is how to accomplish a discriminatory result using regulations that are facially even-handed. The even-handed laws may still be struck down if their burden on interstate commerce is excessive, but at least they survive to that last stage of constitutional inquiry and may be upheld if their impact on interstate commerce is not too significant.

The most obviously even-handed laws are ones that treat in-state and out-of-state wastes identically. Michigan has enacted a law that approaches that ideal by authorizing its counties to discriminate on the basis of the origin of wastes as either in-county or out-of-county. More specifically, the Michigan Solid Waste Management Act (MSWMA) provides for a state-wide regulatory scheme for disposal of solid waste that delegates much of the responsibility for planning to the individual counties:

> A person shall not accept for disposal solid waste...that is not generated in the county in which the disposal area is located unless the acceptance of solid waste...that is not generated in the county is explicitly authorized in the approved county solid waste management plan.[34]

If a county wants to serve out-of-county disposers of waste it may do so only as part of a state-approved county waste management plan. A dormant commerce clause challenge to the statute was mounted by a landfill operator whose request for county authorization to accept out-of-state waste was denied. As seen in the excerpt that follows, the legislation was held constitutionally permissible.

Bill Kettlewell Excavating, Inc. v. Michigan Department of Natural Resources

United States Circuit Court for the Sixth Circuit, 1991
931 F.2d 413

Kettlewell argues that "in-county, in-state waste is not subject to the Amendments, and thus...is treated differently than all out-of-state waste." This argument ignores the language of Mich. Stat. Ann. §13.29(13a) that "in order...to serve the disposal needs of *another county, state, or country*, [it]...must be explicitly autho-

34. Mich. Stat. Ann. §13.29(13a); Mich. Comp. Laws Ann. §299.413a.

rized in the...plan of the receiving county." (Emphasis added). Thus §13.29(13a) language places in-county and out-of-county waste in separate categories, but it does not treat out-of-county waste from Michigan any differently than waste from other states.

Under all of the circumstances, we find no error in the conclusion of the district court that:

> The MSWMA grants each county discretion in accepting or denying importation of waste from any outside source, including other counties within the State. Although ultimate authority for acceptance of a county's plan resides with a single official under the MSWMA, Mich.Comp.Laws Ann. §§299.425 and 299.429, the plaintiff has not alleged that this official has used this authority to reject county plans proposing the importation of out-of-state waste.

Further, we find no error in the district court's ultimate conclusion that "MSWMA imposes only incidental effects upon interstate commerce, and may therefore be upheld" unless clearly excessive as compared to local benefits under *Pike*. MSWMA does, indeed, as found by Michigan courts and by the district court, provide a "comprehensive plan for waste disposal, through which appropriate planning for such disposal can result." Thus, we conclude that the attack on the facial constitutionality of the Michigan statute in question must fail.

[The opinion went on to uphold the statute as applied in this case where Kettlewell had been denied an application to accept out-of-state solid waste.]

COMMENTARY AND QUESTIONS

1. Localization as a device. The in-county rule adopted by Michigan is not the only form of localization of waste requirement that can be imagined. Citing the dangers of long distance transport of materials, for example, a state could place a twenty-mile limit on transport of waste for landfilling. Such a law will wall out most interstate wastes, but it also means that there will also be a significant number of in-state sites whose wastes are burried.

2. Will local choice plans work to exclude out-of-state waste? The Michigan law has two levels of decision-making: the counties must act affirmatively if they opt to accept out-of-county waste, and then that decision must be confirmed as consistent with the state's requirements by the appropriate state official. How likely is it that all of Michigan's counties will continue to refuse out-of-county waste? Won't some counties seek to profit by selling landfill space? In Government Suppliers Consolidating Services v. Bayh, 753 F. Supp. 739, 766 n.33 (S.D. Ind. 1990) the court observed that typical landfill charges in Indiana were around $12 per ton, but that on the East Coast, charges above $100 per ton were typical. If a county wants to "sell out," can the state refuse to allow it to do so without violating the dormant commerce clause?

3. Disposal pretreatment requirements. As was suggested previously in an effort to justify differential tipping fees, pretreatment requirements can be employed to create a preference for one's own garbage. A state could, for example, ban landfilling of all wastes that had not been sorted or minimized as to volume, and join that requirement with an aggressive in-state program to insure that all in-state waste is treated in that manner. Drawing on the market participant doctrine and Baldwin v. Montana Fish & Game Commission, the state could even subsidize the pretreatment of in-state waste, making it economically difficult for out-of-state entities to meet the even-handed pretreatment standard. The catch here, it might be argued, is that the state is forcing its own citizens to pretreat, or recycle, or whatever the requirement is, as part of its effort to limit the use of its disposal sites. From the environmental perspective, that "drawback" is an obvious advantage.

4. Interstate compacts and their strategic potential. A forward-looking note: environmental law is likely to be the field for continued development of a series of interstate compacts designed to resolve jurisdictional tensions between states and the federal government. A variety of such compacts already exist – in the fields of toxic disposal, transportation planning, energy transmission, radioactive wastes, river basin management, and others.[35]

Compacts are authorized by Article I §10, cl. 3 of the Constitution. They are binding legal agreements between two or more states, with or without federal participation, made with the consent of Congress. See Cuyler v. Adams, 449 U.S. 433 (1981).

Among the virtues of compacts, beyond their utility in coordinating interconnnected transboundary resources and policies, and sharing of management costs, is their status as enforceable *law* in the signatory states. By ratifying a compact, states accept its terms – and all future regulations issued by the compact commission under those terms – as binding police power law in their courts.

There are also significant enhancements of state power inherent in interstate compacts. Taking the Alaska oil case, the oil industry in 1979 attacked the state's rigorous controls protecting the marine environment, using pre-emption arguments, and successfully won a court order striking them down, a loss that helped cause the Exxon-Valdez oilspill.[36] If, however, a compact and the rules issued under it are *federal* law, as the Supreme Court has said,[37] then the pre-emption argument is obliterated.[38] The compact approach bears watching.

35. Northwest Power Council Compact, 16 U.S.C.A. §839 (1980)(seven-state energy council); Columbia River Gorge Comm'n Compact, 16 U.S.C.A. §544 (1986)(two-state resource management plan); Washington Metropolitan Area Transit Compact, D.C. Code §§1-2431 through 2441 (1972)(regional transportation development authority); Yellowstone River Compact Comm'n, Montana Code §8 5-20-101–121 (1953) (three-state water rights compact); Dakota Interstate Low-Level Radioactive Waste Management Compact, S. Dak. Session Law Ch. 287 (1985)(two-state radioactive waste disposal agreement [not yet ratified]).

36. See Alaska Oilspill Commission, Spill: The Wreck of the Exxon-Valdez iv (Report to Alaska Legislature, Feb. 1990); Chevron v. Hammond, (D. Alaska, Sept. 1979, unreported); 726 F.2d 483 (9th Cir. 1984).

37. *Cuyler*, 449 U.S. at 438.

38. The compact and the regulations issued under it thus can, at least theoretically, amend other federal law within the compact's jurisdiction. See Bader, Potential Utility of an Interstate Compact as a Vehicle for Oil Spill Prevention and Response, in Alaska Oil Spill Commission, Spill Report, App. M, 9.2; M. Ridgeway, Interstate Compacts: A Federal Question (1971).

PART FOUR

ENVIRONMENTAL STATUTES AND THE ADMINISTRATIVE STATE

In his study of environmental law quoted in the Preface to this coursebook, Professor Sax bemoaned the "numbing complexity and detail" of modern environmental regulations. But the administrative state is a core reality of modern society and environmental law.

This Part Four of the coursebook begins with a brief primer on administrative law, Chapter 11, which includes several major environmental administrative law cases.

A TAXONOMY OF ENVIRONMENTAL STATUTES

Each subsequent chapter of this Part focuses on one particularly distinctive legislative approach to environmental protection, with most chapters analyzing a single statutory example.

Many statutes and regulatory programs have already been directly or indirectly encountered in the preceding chapters of this coursebook. The statutory chapters that follow are organized around a set of analytical categories designed to facilitate understanding of the complex array of statutes that exists in environmental law, as well as introducing new and expanded coverage of environmental statutory materials.

No one book can cover all environmental statutes – the Clean Air Act, Clean Water Act, or Superfund could each more than fill an entire semester of readings. The compromise chosen here is to study the selected statutes, analyzing their structures, process, and enforcement mechanisms, their successes and failures, and then to generalize from them. Each statutory type emphasizes a particular strategy for implementing environmental quality, each presenting tactical advantages and disadvantages. (Every statute's actual performance, of course, is also affected to a major degree by its ecological context in the politics and economics of its day.)

By understanding a taxonomy of statutory types, environmental lawyers can improve the depth, breadth, and speed of their analysis of new statutes, as well as their command of issues arising in the established statutory fields.

The categories set out in the taxonomy used here, of course, are not air-tight. Much overlapping can be found between different statutory types, and some statutes contain multiple approaches and functions. In Chapter 22, for instance, the Resource Conservation and Recovery Act (RCRA) is presented as a composite of many of the strategies analyzed elsewhere in Chapters 12–23.

The chapter headings for Chapters 12–23 illustrate the major taxonomic headings covered:

Nature is trying very hard to make us succeed, but nature does not depend on us. We are not the only experiment.

— R. Buckminster Fuller, 1978

Chapter 11

THE ADMINISTRATIVE LAW OF ENVIRONMENTAL LAW

A. THE EVOLUTION OF THE ADMINISTRATIVE PROCESS

If one looks back over the history of the administrative process in America, it can be divided analytically into at least six different stages.[1] The first stage might begin at the birth of the republic, or earlier, before the Revolution, when, it can be argued, the private economy was in fact the predominant "government" of America. Many historians argue that the Revolution was more an economic than a political phenomenon. The colonies ripened and then dropped away from Great Britain when they became self-sufficient market entities. State, federal, and local governments initially attended merely to minor governmental chores, and their major early role was to facilitate the private marketplace. Government agencies built roads, canals, and a postal system, and protected national and international trade.

The second stage, the advent of regulatory agencies, can be traced to the 1880s, when federal and state governments reacted to the perceived evils of an unregulated marketplace, including child labor, railroad gouging of farmers and shippers, and the like. Regulatory agencies were invented to implement a bipolar theory of social governance: the marketplace on one hand supplying economic strength, and government on the other protecting its citizens from the excesses of the marketplace in specific regulated areas. Reactions against governmental regulation were immediate and passionate in the 1890s, and continue in much the same rhetorical terms today. From the beginning, however, private regulated interests did not merely oppose governmental regulatory agencies; they also moved to co-opt them. As the Attorney General wrote to the president of a railroad in 1892 in response to the latter's plea for abolition of the Interstate Commerce Commission as a "socialistic" federal regulatory agency:

> The Commission...is or can be made of great use to the railroads. It satisfies the popular clamor for government supervision of railroads, at the same time that the supervision is almost entirely nominal. Further, the older such a commission gets to be, the more inclined it would be found to take the business and railroad view of things. It thus becomes a sort of barrier between the railroad corporations and the people, and a sort of protection against hasty and crude legislation hostile to railroad interests.... The part of wisdom is not to destroy the Commission, but to utilize it.[2]

1. This historical analysis builds upon ideas in Stewart, The Reformation of American Administrative Law, 88 Harv. L. Rev. 1669 (1975).

2. Letter from Richard Olney to Charles Perkins, in Jaffe, The Effective Limits of the Administrative Process, 67 Harv. L. Rev. 1105, 1009 (1954).

In any event, in this era government involvement in the economy remained the exception, not the rule.

The third stage, in the 1930s, marked a shift from regulatory agencies as mere occasional correctives, to the theory that agencies can be given a primary directive role in the economy, at least during national traumas like the Great Depression and the Second World War. The New Deal produced a host of agencies that were managers as well as regulators. It was at this point that the "administrative state" became a tangible entity. The powers of government reached into areas never before regulated. (This is not to say that the process was systematically rational or even that government became the dominant factor in American society. The relatively unfettered private economy remained the pre-eminent force in the daily life of the nation.)

In 1946 a reaction against regulatory agency high-handedness resulted in the passage of the federal Administrative Procedures Act (APA),[3] copied in many states. There had always been a reaction against governmental interference with the marketplace, because so much human energy and passion is invested in private property and income-generating activities, and government tends to get in the way. The APA's clear and dominating purpose was to prevent the exercise of agency pre-emptory power through required procedures and judicial control of the agency process.

Nevertheless the United States, faced with all the postwar complexities of life as a great power, melting pot, social experiment, and economic dynamo, continued to develop its administrative substructure at every level of government. By 1968 the federal agencies comprised more than one hundred thirty agencies and two million civil servants.

The next phase in the evolution of administrative law is quite closely linked to the growth of environmentalism: it was a 1960s shift from the bipolar model – regulatory agency versus regulated industry – to a far more pluralistic model. Citizen outsiders began to use the legal tools created by industry for limiting governmental powers, and deployed them against defendants who now were often government and industry working together (the "Establishment" that was so maligned by 1960s activists). Beginning in 1966, the federal courts in particular began to be much more open to citizens – to environmentalists, consumers, civil rights activists, and so on – and the administrative process, responding to the courts, began to follow suit. From that pluralistic opening-up of the administrative law system came many of the significant social changes of the second half of the 20th century.

The year 1976, however, provided early steps in a trend of retrenchment against pluralistic democratic involvement in the administrative process. The *Vermont Yankee* case at page 581 *infra* is a major contribution to this trend. The Supreme Court has since moved in a variety of ways to limit opportunities for citizens to involve themselves in judicial challenges of agencies and regulated interests, themes echoed in occasional post-1980 campaigns for deregulation.

These stages in the evolution of administrative law overlap one another, so that in modern society one can still simultaneously see a tendency to turn to governmental agencies to handle newly identified societal problems, a reaction against

3. 5 U.S.C.A. §501 et seq. (1946).

governmental agencies, a pluralistic tendency toward a continuing democratization of the administrative process, and counter-tendencies attempting to limit outsider citizen participation.

From this quick excursion through history one can get a sense of how environmental law, which has consistently been shaped by private citizens' activist efforts, reflects major cross-currents in the development of American government. The administrative state, built upon a foundation of common law, forces environmentalists to deal with the varied advantages and disadvantages of the government process.

Because environmentalism has been so ready to rock the boat – persistently trying to force an evasive status quo to confront a broad range of dread new worries about pollution, poisoning, and dwindling resources – environmental law has tended to be on the cutting edge of a wide range of fields, including equity, tort, civil procedure, and others already encountered, and administrative law is another prime example on this list. A modern administrative law course could be taught using environmental cases exclusively.

This chapter, however, does not purport to be a course in administrative law. It is a glimpse at the field, to inform subsequent consideration of various environmental regulatory programs in later chapters.

B. ADMINISTRATIVE LAW IN A NUTSHELL

Practical questions of administrative law boil down to three broad areas of inquiry, analyzing –

- the process by which government agencies (at all levels – local, state, federal, and perhaps even international) receive the powers that they apply in their various regulatory settings;
- the methods by which they exercise their powers in particular cases; and
- how such agency exercises of power can be mobilized, demobilized, directed, overturned, or circumvented (usually by judicial review litigation second-guessing particular agency decisions, but also including the pressuring process in the legislative or executive branches of government, before or after decisions are made).

THE SOURCE OF POWER: DELEGATION

Agencies are just that: agents. Their only reason for existence, since they are not provided for in the federal Constitution or most state constitutions, is that the constitutionally-created branches of government had too much complex work to do than they could conveniently do themselves. The constitutionally-created branches accordingly delegated some of their powers to standing agents in order to spread the workload and drudgery of performing investigations, day-to-day oversight, and the hands-on administrative tasks of running a society.

This reality reflects the utilitarian assumption, common to all modern nations, that government has to take an active part in running a modern society. The market and various social relationships are incapable of managing the full scope and complexity of modern life. Without the external imposition of governmental powers into the market system, some important needs and values would not be adequately addressed. Without government, there would not be adequate machinery for defending our borders against enemies and building roads and schools for all; factories might well be using child labor (which in localized market terms made compelling good sense), and disposing of pollution by dumping it willy-nilly.

Most government programs, therefore, originate in recognition of market failure, when the marketplace and processes of social accommodation have failed to do a job that a politically significant number of people think needs doing. But virtually all such tasks turn out to be too much for the constitutionally-established officials (a couple thousand or so legislators and judges in the federal government, and a handful of executives) to handle. So they create agents. (And then, of course, more can be done, so then even more new tasks can be undertaken by government, so then more agents have to be created, and then... but that's another issue.)

Agencies can be created by each branch of government, acting alone. Courts can set up "special masters" to handle administrative tasks; legislatures can set up their own budget-analysis and investigatory offices (CBO, GAO, OTA); chief executives can set up councils of economic advisors, security advisors, budget advisors, and environmental advisors. But in the vast majority of cases where an agency is set up to manage affairs that directly affect people outside of government, including most agencies affecting the environment, the agency will be created by statute, and will be placed more or less into the bailiwick of the executive branch.

The powers and duties of most agencies, therefore, must be derived from the statutes that create them (their respective "organic acts") and that delegate various powers to them. The agencies hold only subsidiary powers; they can make only subsidiary rules. Their actions must be authorized by and conform to the requirements of the statutes (and, beyond the statutes, to the Constitution).

The requirements of the "delegation doctrine" provide some of the basic inquiries by which agency actions are tested. Did a statute give the agency the particular power it is attempting to exercise? Do the legislature and the chief executive have the right to delegate a particular role or power to an agent? Is the legislature's delegating language too broad or vague to give adequate definition and limitation to the agency's actions? In some few cases delegations to agencies have been voided under the separation of powers theory: the statute has impermissibly delegated legislative or judicial power to an agent that is a nonlegislature or noncourt. In some few cases agency actions have been struck down under the ultra vires ["beyond the powers"] theory: the delegating statute did not grant a power specifically enough or extend it broadly enough to cover the particular kind of thing that the agency is attempting to do. In the vast majority of federal cases, however, the delegation doctrine is only a background constraint on agency action.[4]

---

4. A few federal judges have made occasional forays, trying to use the delegation doctrine to cut down agency programs and decisions they dislike. Industrial Union Dept., AFL-CIO v. American Petroleum Institute, 448 U.S. 607 (1980)(Rehnquist, J., concurring opinion); American Textile Manuf. Inst. v. Donovan, 452 U.S. 490 (1981)(dissent). Their attempts have not caught on, perhaps because they prove too much. What would happen if courts held legislatures to a strict rule that the terms of all statutes must be "as precise as feasible"?

THE EXERCISE OF AGENCY POWERS

An administrative agency is itself an ongoing, functioning organism. As such it exercises a variety of powers, both internally, within the agency, and externally, impacting upon people outside the agency. The external powers include the power to investigate, require submission of information, etc. and these can be important. Day in and day out, however, the primary exercises of an agency's external powers occur in two ways – rulemaking (the issuance of regulations), and adjudication (the process of making operative agency decisions by applying legal standards set out in statutes or regulations to the facts of particular cases). Most agencies are delegated the power to act in both ways, often according to their own choice of how best to proceed.

The life of the administrative state can be tracked through millions of reams of paper each year. The RCRA statute, which is 96 pages long, for instance, has been arduously articulated through 128 pages of regulations. Each rulemaking reflects hundreds of hours of agency process and disputation. Adjudications – applying statutes and rules to tens of thousands of cases each year – multiply the scope of the process geometrically. And a large number of these agency processes are controversial, which makes their details important to lawyers. The federal Administrative Procedure Act ("APA"), 5 U.S.C.A. §501 et seq. (1946, as amended), is the blueprint of modern federal administrative law, and is used almost universally as a model by the states as well. It sets out many (although not all) of the basic definitions and prescriptions for how an agency is to run itself – how to promulgate rules, how to give notice to the public, how hearings examiners (administrative law judges) are to proceed, and so on. Chapter 7 of the APA prescribes the basis for judicial review of challenged agency actions. 5 U.S.C.A. §§701–706.

Both rulemaking and adjudication can be accomplished "formally," that is, they can be done with full trial-type process, discovery, motions, production of evidence, cross-examination, stenographic record, and a decision-maker bound to decide in a reasoned judgment only on the basis of the record produced.

Both can also be undertaken "informally," through less than formal procedures, without full trial-type process. They also can be "hybrid," part trial-type process and part informal procedure. Hybrid procedures are not prescribed in the APA; they are applied when required by some other particular statute, by the voluntary decision of the agency itself, or in some cases by court order.

The following sections of the APA set out partial prescriptions for how these functions will be exercised; state codes have similar provisions:

	RULEMAKING	**ADJUDICATION**
Informal	§553	no prescribed process
(hybrid, in-between)	§553, plus parts of §§556–557	no prescribed process
Formal	§553, plus full §§556–557 (trial-type procedures, "TTP")	§554, plus full §§556–557 (trial-type procedures, "TTP")

Section 553 says that informal rulemaking, when it affects third parties, must at a minimum provide for public notice and opportunity to comment prior to publication of a rule in the Federal Register. Sections 556 and 557 are the add-ons for formal trial-type process- discovery, cross examination, full record, etc. Section 554 is the prescription for formal adjudication, and it always triggers §§556-557. There is no required process for informal adjudications, even though these are certainly the vast majority of agency actions. Where an agency, for example, says "Yes, you may build a house," or "No, you may not drain a swamp," or "Yes, you may treat pollution abatement as a tax-deductible business expense," or "No, you may not file a late application" – all these are typically informal adjudications, applying law to facts without trial-type procedures.

Battles are often fought between agencies and regulated parties or intervening parties about which kind of process the agency should follow, since often there is no express statutory requirement that an agency act through formal or informal rulemaking or adjudication. Sometimes parties want rulemaking rather than adjudication (because then an agency directive can only be prospective). More often parties try to get more formalized trial-type procedures, regardless of whether the agency is proceeding in rulemaking or adjudication. (Attorneys apparently consider that the more procedure they get, the better the ultimate deal they'll get for their clients.)

The arguments for more procedure usually come down to two constitutional issues. Procedural due process is the prime argument, although it is not usually an easy way to force an agency to give procedure it doesn't want to give. The other constitutional argument is grounded upon the basic judicial review jurisdiction of Article III of the federal Constitution: courts should require more procedure in given cases for the sake of the integrity of their own reviewing role, in order to produce a sufficient body of data (on formal or informal agency records) to permit courts exercising judicial review to make an adequately incisive, though deferential, reviews of agency actions.

PRESSURING AGENCY ACTION

Since agencies wield such broad-ranging powers in modern society, pressuring them in one direction or another has become a fundamental task of hundreds of thousands of attorneys and other citizens. There are very few significant legal or economic issues that do not turn, in substantial part, upon the decisions of governmental agencies – local, state, or federal.

Pressure can be applied before or after a particular agency decision in a variety of forums. Agencies respond to lobbying, to the media, to internal or external politicking, and of course to the legislature that created them and annually can cut them down through the budget process, oversight hearings, and amendments to agencies' statutory authority.

JUDICIAL REVIEW

Judicial review, however, is the most visible constraint on agency freedom of action. Disgruntled persons can, in most cases, easily obtain judicial review of particular agency actions, and judicial review can operate to cramp an agency's style even if ultimate reversal of the agency is not usually likely.

Judicial review of federal agency action operates under Chapter 7 of the APA, 5 U.S.C.A. §701 et seq. The challenging party must show standing[5] and reviewability under §702, and fulfill a few other judge-made requirements (ripeness for review, exhaustion of agency remedies, etc.). Section 706 then sets out a catalogue of challenges on the merits:[6] the "arbitrary, capricious, or abuse of discretion" test (for informal rulemaking or adjudication) or the requirement of "substantial evidence" supporting the decision (in the case of most formal proceedings).

Most substantive challenges to agency decisions turn on the latter two standards, reviewing the rather subjective question of whether the agency's decision was reasonable in the circumstances. In some environmental cases, to be sure, challenges to agency action come down to straightforward application and interpretation of statutes: did the agency violate a provision of some particular law? In far more cases, however, the question is not so easy, instead turning on the assertion that the agency has exercised bad judgment. Courts understandably do not usually like to second-guess agencies, instead preferring to defer to agency discretion and expertise. But their Article III constitutional mandate requires them to review cases presented.

DEGREES OF DEFERENCE

Issues arise concerning the "standard of review" to be applied: in challenges to agency findings of fact, the judicial scrutiny can range from the rather minimal "arbitrary" test all the way to judicial takeover of the question (trial de novo). How deeply will the court pry into the particulars of a decision, especially when it realizes that the closer it looks, the more it is second-guessing and taking over the agency's decisional process? In all but the de novo cases, the question usually comes down to the same judicial determination: could a reasonable agency official have reached this decision on this record of facts? The practical difference between various standards of judicial review comes down to differences in degrees and moods of deference to agencies in each case, reflecting different sensitivities to separation of powers issues. In the minuet of contending powers, moreover, courts can use the

5. On threshold battles over standing, see text at page 565, 574 *infra*.

6. **§706**... To the extent necessary to decision and when presented, the reviewing court shall decide all relevant questions of law, interpret constitutional and statutory provisions, and determine the meaning or applicability of the terms of an agency action. The reviewing court shall –

(1) compel agency action unlawfully withheld or unreasonably delayed; and

(2) hold unlawful and set aside agency action, findings, and conclusions found to be –

(A) arbitrary, capricious, an abuse of discretion, or otherwise not in accordance with law;
(B) contrary to constitutional right, power, privilege, or immunity;
(C) in excess of statutory jurisdiction, authority, or limitations, or short of statutory right;
(D) without observance of procedure required by law;
(E) unsupported by substantial evidence in a case subject to sections 556 and 557 of this title or otherwise reviewed on the record of an agency hearing provided by statute; or
(F) unwarranted by the facts to the extent that the facts are subject to trial de novo by the reviewing court."

In making the foregoing determinations, the court shall review the whole record or those parts of it cited by a party, and due account shall be taken of the rule of prejudicial error.

choice of different standards of review – arbitrary for loose review, substantial evidence for tougher – merely to effectuate a result that they personally prefer. Politics and ideology in this way insinuate themselves into judicial review of agency action.

In challenges to agency interpretations of law, the same sort of scale applies, although a bit less predictably. Judges don't seem quite as inclined to defer to agencies' decisions of law (the agencies' interpretations of what statutes or regulations require) as they do to agencies' decisions about questions of fact.

Issues also arise on "scope of review" – how broadly will the court look in scrutinizing the agency action; how much data and "record" will it require; will it allow new evidence to be introduced in court proceedings that was not brought before the agency? Normally the scope of judicial review is limited to the record of whatever was compiled and presented in the challenged agency proceedings. In some cases a court may say that its necessary scope of review requires more evidence to be prepared and presented.

REMEDIES

Finally there are questions of remedies. If the agency action was faulty, what sanction should the reviewing court apply – injunction, declaratory judgment, damages, criminal penalties[7], remand to the agency, or something else?

As this quick excursion should make clear, administrative law and administrative process make up a separate legal ecosystem that is intricately intertwined with hundreds of important environmental issues, and differs in many regards from the standard litigation model that dominates the law school curriculum.

Whatever substantive area of practice a case arises in, it should by now be evident that a familiarity with underlying administrative law problems is a basic requirement of legal literacy. In no area is this truer than environmental law.

C. *OVERTON PARK* – AN ENVIRONMENTAL ADMINISTRATIVE LAW CASE

Introduction: CITIZEN SUITS AND JUDICIAL REVIEW

The administrative agencies are intimately woven into the power fabric of the nation, and accordingly are linked to most of the environmental issues discovered and decried over the past few decades by environmentalists. Within themselves, agencies mirror many of the forces, procedures, and vested interests that cause environmental problems. It therefore comes as no surprise that environmentalists often find themselves launching challenges against agency actions at all three levels of government, federal, state, and local. Because of their political context, citizen

7. One of the authors once briefly researched the possibility of convicting an agency head on a statutory felony charge. Some of the legal reasons, beyond politics, why such attempts are feckless are set out in Smith, Shields for the King's Men: Official Immunity and Other Obstacles to Effective Prosecution of Federal Officials for Environmental Crimes, 16 Colum. J. Envtl. Law 1 (1991).

interventions often get short shrift in the agency process,[8] so citizen activists end up going to court.

In administrative law lawsuits, environmental plaintiffs are usually not asking the court to take over the matter and make the "right" decision itself. Rather, when a court is asked to look at an agency decision, in most cases it is only applying judicial *review*, and that limitation has consequences. Judicial review of agency actions differs from review of decisions made by lower court judges or juries. An agency is a creature of a different branch of government, so more deference is required. Too much deference, however, would mean that courts abdicate their judicial role. So the critical question of administrative law is how, and how much, the court will scrutinize what an official agency has done.

Environmental plaintiffs must first successfully pass all the threshold obstacles to getting judicial review of administrative action – standing, reviewability, ripeness, exhaustion, and others. The reviewing court then turns to scrutiny of the procedural and substantive merits of the government actions being challenged.

Section 1. THE OVERTON PARK CASE

In the following case, note the plaintiffs' array of arguments: that they did not receive adequate procedures, that the agency decision was substantively wrong, and that the Court should extend the most probing, least deferential, level of scrutiny to the agency's factfinding and decisions of law. They lost virtually all of these battle points, but won their war.

A ROAD

I think that I have never knowed, a sight as lovely as a road.
A road upon whose concrete tops, the flow of traffic never stops;
A road that costs a lot to build, just as the City Council willed;
A road the planners say we need, to get the cars to greater speed;
We've let the contracts so dig in, and let the chopping now begin;
Somebody else can make a tree, but roads are made by guys like me.

— Mike Royko[9]

Citizens to Preserve Overton Park, Inc. v. John Volpe, Secretary of Transportation

United States Supreme Court, 1971
401 U.S. 402, 91 S. Ct. 814, 28 L. Ed. 2d 136

[The "Parkland Act," §4(f) of the Department of Transportation Act of 1966 and Section 138 of the Federal Aid to Highways Act of 1968,[10] provides:

> It is hereby declared to be the national policy that special effort should be made to preserve the natural beauty of the countryside and public park and

8. In the *Pigeon River* case, for instance, the citizens were rebuffed by the agency, which considered itself the rightful public representative in deciding whether the forest reserve should be drilled for oil, and they had to face the agency standing alongside the oil company when they went to court. West Mich. Env. Action Council v. NRC, 275 N.W. 2d 538 (Mich. 1979).

9. For further evidence of the inspirational qualities of trees, and the artistic tendencies of West Publishing Co., see Fisher v. Lowe, 333 N.W.2d 67 (Mich. App. 1983).

10. 49 U.S.C.A. §1653(f), and 23 U.S.C.A. §138. The two sections embody exactly the same language.

recreation lands, wildlife and waterfowl refuges, and historic sites. The Secretary of Transportation shall cooperate and consult with the Secretaries of the Interior, Housing and Urban Development, and Agriculture, and with the States in developing transportation plans and programs that include measures to maintain or enhance the natural beauty of the lands traversed. After the effective date of the Federal-Aid Highway Act of 1968, the Secretary shall not approve any program or project which requires the use of any publicly owned land from a public park, recreation area, or wildlife and waterfowl refuge of national, State, or local significance as determined by the Federal, State, or local officials having jurisdiction thereof, or any land from an historic site of national, State, or local significance as so determined by such officials unless (1) there is no feasible and prudent alternative to the use of such land, and (2) such program includes all possible planning to minimize harm to such park, recreational area, wildlife and waterfowl refuge, or historic site resulting from such use.]

MARSHALL, J. The growing public concern about the quality of our natural environment has prompted Congress in recent years to enact legislation designed to curb the accelerating destruction of our country's natural beauty. We are concerned in this case with §4(f) of the Department of Transportation Act of 1966, as amended, and [§138] of the Federal-Aid Highway Act of 1968.

Petitioners, private citizens as well as local and national conservation organizations, contend that the Secretary has violated these statutes by authorizing the expenditure of federal funds for the construction of a six-lane interstate highway through a public park in Memphis, Tennessee. Their claim was rejected by the District Court, which granted the Secretary's motion for summary judgment, and the Court of Appeals for the Sixth Circuit affirmed. After oral argument, this Court granted a stay that halted construction and, treating the application for the stay as a petition for certiorari, granted review. We now reverse the judgment below and remand for further proceedings in the District Court.

Overton Park is a 342-acre city park located near the center of Memphis. The park contains a zoo, a nine-hole municipal golf course, an outdoor theater, nature trails, a bridle path, an art academy, picnic areas, and 170 acres of forest. The proposed highway, which is to be a six-lane, high-speed, expressway, will sever the zoo from the rest of the park. Although the roadway will be depressed below ground level except where it crosses a small creek, 26 acres of the park will be destroyed. The highway is to be a segment of Interstate Highway I-40, part of the National System of Interstate and Defense Highways. I-40 will provide Memphis with a major east-west expressway which will allow easier access to downtown Memphis from the residential areas on the eastern edge of the city.

Although the route through the park was approved by the Bureau of Public Roads in 1956 and by the Federal Highways Administrator in 1966, the enactment of §4(f) of the Department of Transportation Act prevented distribution of federal funds for the section of the highway designated to go through Overton Park until the Secretary of Transportation determined whether the requirements of §4(f) had been met. Federal funding for the rest of the project was, however, available, and the state acquired a right-of-way on both sides of the park. In April 1968, the Secretary announced that he concurred in the judgment of local officials that I-40 should be built through the park. And in September 1969 the State acquired the right-of-way inside Overton Park from the city. Final approval for the project–the route as well as the design – was not announced until November 1969, after Congress had reiterated in §138 of the Federal-Aid Highway Act that highway construction through public parks was to be restricted. Neither announcement approving the route and design of I-40 was accompanied by a statement of the Secretary's factual findings. He did not indicate why he believed there were no feasible and prudent alternative routes or why design changes could not be made to reduce the harm to the park.

Petitioners contend that the Secretary's action is invalid without such formal findings and that the Secretary did not make an independent determination but merely relied on the judgment of the Memphis City Council. They also contend that it would be "feasible and prudent" to route I-40 around Overton Park either to the north or to the south. And they argue that if these alternative routes are not "feasible and prudent," the present plan does not include "all possible" methods for reducing harm to the park. Petitioners claim that I-40 could be built under the park by using either of two possible tunneling methods,[11] and the claim that, at a minimum, by using advanced drainage techniques the expressway could be depressed below ground level along the entire route through the park including the section that crosses the small creek.

Respondents argue that it was unnecessary for the Secretary to make formal findings, and that he did, in fact, exercise his own independent judgment which was supported by the facts. In the District Court, respondents introduced affidavits, prepared specifically for this litigation, which indicated that the Secretary had made the decision and that the decision was supportable. These affidavits were contradicted by affidavits introduced by petitioners, who also sought to take the deposition of a former Federal Highway administrator who had participated in the decision to route I-40 through Overton Park.

The District Court and the Court of Appeals found that formal findings by the Secretary were not necessary and refused to order the deposition of the former Federal Highway Administrator because those courts believed that probing of the mental processes of an administrative decision-maker was prohibited. And, believing that the Secretary's authority was wide and reviewing courts' authority narrow in the approval of highway routes, the lower courts held that the affidavits contained no basis for a determination that the Secretary had exceeded his authority.

We agree that formal findings were not required. But we do not believe that in this case judicial review based solely on litigation affidavits was adequate.

A threshold question – whether petitioners are entitled to any judicial review – is easily answered. Section 701 of the Administrative Procedure Act, 5 U.S.C. §701 provides that the action of "each authority of the Government of the United States," which includes the Department of Transportation, is subject to judicial review except where there is a statutory prohibition on review or where "agency action is committed to agency discretion by law." In this case, there is no indication that Congress sought to prohibit judicial review and there is most certainly no "showing of 'clear and convincing evidence' of a...legislative intent" to restrict access to judicial review. Abbott Laboratories v. Gardner, 387 U.S. 136, 141 (1967).

11. Petitioners argue that either a bored tunnel or a cut-and-cover tunnel, which is a fully depressed route covered after construction, could be built. Respondents contend that the construction of a tunnel by either method would greatly increase the cost of the project, would create safety hazards, and because of increase in air pollution would not reduce harm to the park.

Similarly, the Secretary's decision here does not fall within the exception for action "committed to agency discretion." This is a very narrow exception. The legislative history of the Administrative Procedure Act indicates that it is applicable in those rare instances where "statutes are drawn in such broad terms that in a given case there is no law to apply." S. Rep. No. 752, 79th Cong., 1st Sess., 26 (1945).

Section 4 (f) of the Department of Transportation Act and §138 of the Federal-Aid Highway Act are clear and specific directives. Both the Department of Transportation Act and the Federal-Aid Highway Act provide that the Secretary "shall not approve any program or project" that requires the use of any public parkland "unless (1) there is no feasible and prudent alternative to the use of such land, and (2) such program includes all possible planning to minimize harm to such park...." This language is a plain and explicit bar to the use of federal funds for construction of highways through parks – only the most unusual situations are exempted.

Despite the clarity of the statutory language, respondents argue that the Secretary has wide discretion. They recognize that the requirement that there be no "feasible" alternative route admits of little administrative discretion. For this exemption to apply the Secretary must find that as a matter of sound engineering it would not be feasible to build the highway along any other route. Respondents argue, however, that the requirement that there be no other "prudent" route requires the Secretary to engage in a wide-ranging balancing of competing interests. They contend that the Secretary should weigh the detriment resulting from the destruction of parkland against the cost of other routes, safety considerations, and other factors, and determine on the basis of the importance that he attaches to these other factors whether, on balance, alternative feasible routes would be "prudent."

But no such wide-ranging endeavor was intended. It is obvious that in most cases considerations of cost, directness of route, and community disruption will indicate that parkland should be used for highway construction whenever possible. Although it may be necessary to transfer funds from one jurisdiction to another, there will always be a smaller outlay required from the public purse when parkland is used since the public already owns the land and there will be no need to pay for right-of-way. And since people do not live or work in parks, if a highway is built on parkland no one will have to leave his home or give up his business. Such factors are common to substantially all highway construction. Thus, if Congress intended these factors to be on an equal footing with preservation of parkland there would have been no need for the statutes.

Congress clearly did not intend that cost and disruption of the community were to be ignored by the Secretary. But the very existence of the statute[12] indicates that protection of parkland was to be given paramount importance. The few green havens that are public parks were not to be lost unless there were truly unusual factors present in a particular case or the cost or community disruption resulting

12. The legislative history of both §4(f) of the Department of Transportation Act, 49 U.S.C. §1653(f) (1964 ed., Supp. V), and §138 of the Federal-Aid Highway Act, 23 U.S.C. §138 (1964 ed., Supp. V), is ambiguous. The legislative committee reports tend to support respondents' view that the statutes are merely general directives to the Secretary requiring him to consider the importance of parkland as well as cost, community disruption, and other factors. See, e.g., S. Rep. No. 1340, 90th Cong., 2d Sess., 19; H. R. Rep. No. 1584, 90th Cong., 2d Sess., 12. Statements by proponents of the statutes as well as the Senate committee report on §4(f) indicate, however, that the Secretary was to have limited authority. See, e.g., 114 Cong. Rec. 24033-24037; S. Rep. No. 1659, 89th Cong., 2d Sess., 25. Because of this ambiguity it is clear that we must look primarily to the statutes themselves to find the legislative intent. [This is footnote 29 in the original.]

from alternative routes reached extraordinary magnitudes. If the statutes are to have any meaning, the Secretary cannot approve the destruction of parkland unless he finds that alternative routes present unique problems.

Plainly, there is "law to apply" and thus the exemption for action "committed to agency discretion" is inapplicable. But the existence of judicial review is only the start: the standard for review must also be determined. For that we must look to §706, which provides that a "reviewing court shall...hold unlawful and set aside agency action, findings, and conclusions found" not to meet six separate standards. In all cases agency action must be set aside if the action was "arbitrary, capricious, an abuse of discretion, or otherwise not in accordance with law," or if the action failed to meet statutory, procedural, or constitutional requirements. In certain narrow, specifically limited situations, the agency action is to be set aside if the action was not supported by "substantial evidence." And in other equally narrow circumstances the reviewing court is to engage in a de novo review of the action and set it aside if it was "unwarranted by the facts."

Petitioners argue that the Secretary's approval of the construction of I-40 through Overton Park is subject to one or the other of these later two standards of limited applicability.... Neither of these standards is, however, applicable.

Review under the substantial-evidence test is authorized only when the agency action is... based on a [trial-type] hearing. See 5 U.S.C. §§556, 557. The Secretary's decision to allow the expenditure of federal funds to build I-40 through Overton Park was plainly not an exercise of a rulemaking function. And the only hearing that is required by either the Administrative Procedure Act or the statutes regulating the distribution of federal funds for highway construction is a public hearing conducted by local officials for the purpose of informing the community about the proposed project and eliciting community views on the design and route. 23 U.S.C. §128. The hearing is nonadjudicatory, quasi-legislative in nature. It is not designed to produce a record that is to be the basis of agency action – the basic requirement for substantial-evidence review.

Petitioners' alternative argument also fails. De novo review of whether the Secretary's decision was "unwarranted by the facts" is authorized by §706(2)(F) in only two circumstances. First, such de novo review is authorized when the action is adjudicatory in nature and the agency factfinding procedures are inadequate. And, there may be independent judicial factfinding when issues that were not before the agency are raised in a proceeding to enforce nonadjudicatory agency action. Neither situation exists here.

Even though there is no de novo review in this case and the Secretary's approval of the route of I-40 does not have ultimately to meet the substantial-evidence test, the generally applicable standards of §706 require the reviewing court to engage in a substantial inquiry. Certainly, the Secretary's decision is entitled to a presumption of regularity. But that presumption is not to shield his action from a thorough, probing, in-depth review.

The court is first required to decide whether the Secretary acted within the scope of his authority. This determination naturally begins with a delineation of the scope of the Secretary's authority and discretion. As has been shown, Congress has specified only a small range of choices that the Secretary can make. Also involved in this initial inquiry is a determination of whether on the facts the Secretary's decision can reasonably be said to be within that range. The reviewing court must consider whether the Secretary properly construed his authority to approve the use of parkland as limited to situations where there are no feasible alternative routes or where feasible alternative routes involve uniquely difficult problems. And the reviewing court must be able to find that the Secretary could have reasonably believed that in this case there are no feasible alternatives or that alternatives...involve unique problems.

Scrutiny of the facts does not end, however, with the determination that the Secretary has acted within the scope of his statutory authority. Section 706(2)(A) requires a finding that the actual choice made was not "arbitrary, capricious, an abuse of discretion, or otherwise not in accordance with law." To make this finding the court must consider whether the decision was based on a consideration of the relevant factors and whether there has been a clear error of judgment. Although this inquiry into the facts is to be searching and careful, the ultimate standard of review is a narrow one. The court is not empowered to substitute its judgment for that of the agency.

The final inquiry is whether the Secretary's action followed the necessary procedural requirements. Here the only procedural error alleged is the failure of the Secretary to make formal findings and state his reason for allowing the highway to be built through the park.

Undoubtedly, review of the Secretary's action is hampered by his failure to make such findings, but the absence of formal findings does not necessarily require that the case be remanded to the Secretary. Neither the Department of Transportation Act nor the Federal-Aid Highway Act requires such formal findings. Moreover, the Administrative Procedure Act requirements that there be formal findings in certain rulemaking and adjudicatory proceedings do not apply to the Secretary's action here. See 5 U.S.C. §§ 553(a)(2), 554(a). And, although formal findings may be required in some cases in the absence of statutory directives when the nature of the agency action is ambiguous, those situations are rare. Plainly, there is no ambiguity here; the Secretary has approved the construction of I-40 through Overton Park and has approved a specific design for the project.

Petitioners contend that although there may not be a statutory requirement that the Secretary make formal findings and even though this may not be a case for the reviewing court to impose a requirement that findings be made, Department of Transportation regulations require them. This argument is based on DOT Order 5610.1, which requires the Secretary to make formal findings when he approves the use of parkland for highway construction but which was issued after the route for I-40 was approved. Petitioners argue that even though the order was not intended to have retrospective effect the order represents the law at the time of this Court's decision and under Thorpe v. Housing Authority, 393 U.S. 268, 281-282 (1969), should be applied to this case.

The *Thorpe* litigation resulted from an attempt to evict a tenant from a federally funded housing project under circumstances that suggested that the eviction was prompted by the tenant's objections to the management of the project. Despite repeated requests, the Housing Authority would not give an explanation for its action. The tenant claimed that the eviction interfered with her exercise of First Amendment rights and that the failure to state the reasons for the eviction and to afford her a hearing denied her due process.... While the case was pending in this Court, the Department of Housing and Urban Development issued regulations requiring Housing Authority officials to inform tenants of the reasons for an eviction and to give a tenant the opportunity to reply. The case was then remanded to the state courts [where, the Court subsequently held, the *new*] HUD regulations were applicable to that case.... The general rule is "that an appellate court must apply the law in effect at the time it renders its decision." 393 U.S. at 281.

While we do not question that DOT Order 5610.1 constitutes the law in effect at the time of our decision, we do not believe that *Thorpe* compels us to remand for the Secretary to make formal findings. Here, unlike the situation in *Thorpe*, there has been a change in circumstances – additional right-of-way has been cleared and the 26-acre right-of-way inside Overton Park has been purchased by the State. Moreover, there is an administrative record that allows the full, prompt review of the Secretary's action...without additional delay which would result from having a remand to the Secretary.

That administrative record is not, however, before us. The lower courts based their review on the litigation affidavits that were presented. These affidavits were merely "post hoc" rationalizations, which have traditionally been found to be an inadequate basis for review. Burlington Truck Lines v. United States, 371 U.S. 156, 168-69 (1962). And they clearly do not constitute the "whole record" compiled by the agency: the basis for review required by §706 of the Administrative Procedure Act.

Thus it is necessary to remand this case to the District Court for plenary review of the Secretary's decision. That review is to be based on the full administrative record that was before the Secretary at the time he made his decision. But since the bare record may not disclose the factors that were considered or the Secretary's construction of the evidence it may be necessary for the District Court to require some explanation in order to determine if the Secretary acted within the scope of his authority and if the Secretary's action was justifiable under the applicable standard.

The court may require the administrative officials who participated in the decision to give testimony explaining their action. Of course, such inquiry into the mental processes of administrative decision-makers is usually to be avoided. United States v. Morgan, 313 U.S. 409, 422 (1941). And where there are administrative findings that were made at the same time as the decision, as was the case in *Morgan*, there must be a strong showing of bad faith or improper behavior before such inquiry may be made. But here there are no such formal findings and it may be that the only way there can be effective judicial review is by examining the decision-makers themselves. See Shaughnessy v. Accardi, 349 U.S. 280 (1955).

The District Court is not, however, required to make such an inquiry. It may be that the Secretary can prepare formal findings including the information required by DOT Order 5610.1 that will provide an adequate explanation for his action. Such an explanation will, to some extent, be a "post hoc rationalization" and thus must be viewed critically. If the District Court decides that additional explanation is necessary, that court should consider which method will prove the most expeditious so that full review may be had as soon as possible.

Reversed and remanded.

Separate opinion of BLACK, J., joined by BRENNAN, J.

I agree with the Court that the judgment of the Court of Appeals is wrong and that its action should be reversed. I do not agree that the whole matter should be remanded to the District Court. I think the case should be sent back to the Secretary of Transportation. It is apparent from the Court's opinion today that the Secretary of Transportation completely failed to comply with the duty imposed upon him by Congress not to permit a federally financed public highway to run through a public park "unless (1) there is no feasible and prudent alternative to the use of such land, and (2) such program includes all possible planning to minimize harm to such park...." That congressional command should not be taken lightly by the Secretary or by this Court. It represents a solemn determination of the highest law-making body of this Nation that the beauty and health-giving facilities of our parks are not to be taken away for public roads without hearings, factfindings, and policy determinations under the supervision of a Cabinet officer – the Secretary of Transportation. The Act of Congress in connection with other federal highway aid legislation, it seems to me, calls for hearings – hearings that a court can review, hearings that demonstrate more than mere arbitrary defiance by the Secretary. Whether the findings growing out of such hearings are labeled "formal" or "informal" appears to me to be no more than an exercise in semantics. Whatever the hearing requirements might be, the Department of Transportation failed to meet them in this case. I regret that I am compelled to conclude for myself that, except for some too-late formulations, apparently coming from the Solicitor General's office, this record contains not one word to indicate that the Secretary raised even a finger to comply with the command of Congress. It is our duty, I believe, to remand this whole matter back to the Secretary of Transportation for him to give this matter the hearing it deserves in full good-faith obedience to the Act of Congress. That Act was obviously passed to protect our public parks from forays by road builders except in the most extraordinary and imperative circumstances. This record does not demonstrate the existence of such circumstances. I dissent from the Court's failure to send the case back to the Secretary, whose duty has not yet been performed.

BLACKMUN, J.

I fully join the Court in its opinion and in its judgment. I merely wish to state the obvious: (1) The case comes to this Court as the end product of more than a decade of endeavor to solve the interstate highway problem at Memphis. (2) The administrative decisions under attack here are not those of a single Secretary; some were made by the present Secretary's predecessor and, before him, by the Department of Commerce's Bureau of Public Roads. (3) The 1966 Act and the 1968 Act have cut across former methods and here have imposed new standards and conditions upon a situation that already was largely developed. This undoubtedly is why the record is sketchy and less than one would expect if the project were one which had been instituted after the passage of the 1966 Act....

MR. JUSTICE DOUGLAS took no part in the consideration or decision of this case.

COMMENTARY AND QUESTIONS

1. Threshold administrative law issues in citizen suits. Before plaintiffs can get to the merits of challenges to agency decisions, they must pass through threshold tests:

Reviewability. When challenged by citizen suits, agency attorneys often (as in the *Overton Park* case), initially argue that their challenged agency decisions are unreviewable because they contain discretionary elements. The courts, however, have demonstrated extreme hesitation in finding nonreviewability, often citing the words of *Abbott Laboratories*:

> The enactment of the Administrative Procedures Act...embodies the basic presumption of judicial review to one "suffering legal wrong because of

> agency action...." The legislative material...manifests a congressional intention that it cover a broad spectrum of administrative actions, and this Court has echoed that theme by noting that the...Act's "generous review provision" must be given a "hospitable" interpretation.... Only upon a showing of "clear and convincing evidence" of a contrary legislative intent should the courts restrict access to judicial review. Abbott Laboratories v. Gardner, 387 U.S. 136, 141 (1967)

Sovereign immunity barriers to reviewability of federal agency actions were specifically removed in 1976 by amendments to APA §702.

Standing. In Overton Park, as in many environmental cases, there is no problem with standing.[13] Some or all of the Tennessee plaintiffs would be directly affected by the consequences of the agency decision. It has long been established that plaintiffs' "injury in fact" necessitated by Article III's case-or-controversy requirement does not have to be economic or legal, but can extend to recreational, aesthetic, and other injuries.[14] If particular persons are not injured, or are injured only to the same extent as millions of other citizens, the courts may deny standing. Occasionally, however, in part to allow troublesome environmental questions to be debated, the Supreme Court has allowed fairly broad standing to sue.[15]

Exhaustion of remedies, and ripeness. In *Overton Park*, the legal issues were clearly ready for review when plaintiffs went to court. In some environmental cases it is argued that citizens should exhaust internal remedies within the agency before going to court; in other cases the argument is that an agency decision, though it has been made, is not yet ripe for judicial review because it has not actually been applied or is not yet completely final. These arguments have not generally been successful defenses against environmental litigation. Courts often, but not always, seem to reflect the legal system's interest in resolving important legal questions at an efficient early stage, before major investments and commitments of resources are wasted. Does it seem likely that the *Overton Park* plaintiffs could have succeeded in getting an injunction against the *earlier* highway activities – the condemnation of land and highway construction up to the edge of the Park[16] – as a violation of §4(f)? Probably not. The defense would have been that the issue was not yet ripe, the law not yet violated.[17]

---

13. See Section 1, page 564 *infra*, but compare the text at 574*infra*, showing successful attempts to use standing to avoid citizen enforcement of the law.

14. Sierra Club v. Morton, 405 U.S. 727, 734 (1972), discussed at page 563 *infra*.

15. See, e.g., United States v. SCRAP, 412 U.S. 669 (1973); Duke Power v. Carolina Environmental Study Group, 438 U.S. 59 (1978).

16. Just as the *Overton Park* plaintiffs were able to bootstrap an injunction against the highway based on the thinness of the agency record, the defendants and their allies had attempted physical bootstrapping: prior to the filing of the case, the citizens had attempted to argue for alternative routes north and south of Overton Park. The highway authorities, however, proceeded to condemn homes, bulldoze them, and build the highway right-of-way right up to the boundary of the Park. They also built a multimillion dollar bridge across the Mississippi River on the Park highway alignment. It was only then that they turned to the Secretary to ask approval for the Park route on the grounds that there was no longer any feasible and prudent alternative.

17. A NEPA suit might offer better prospects (see Chapter 12).

2. The administrative law of *Overton Park*: tactics, and results. Note how easily *Overton Park* accepts the plaintiffs' threshold showings, allowing them to get into court. As to procedure, however, the plaintiffs did not succeed in their request for formal findings, nor did they get hearings before the Secretary. Both of these procedures would obviously have been helpful in sharpening their case against the highway through the park and obtaining closer judicial review of the subsequent decision.

As to the substantive standard of review to be applied to the agency's factual decision, the plaintiffs didn't get de novo review, the toughest standard, nor even the substantial evidence test. They only got review under the arbitrary and capricious test, and they never got a judicial ruling that the Secretary had indeed been arbitrary and capricious in approving the parkland route.

So why didn't the Department of Transportation win? While the Court says that "the ultimate standard of review is a narrow one," thus adopting a continued deference to the agency's expertise on fact-finding, it nevertheless recognizes that judges need to see enough facts to "be able to find that the Secretary could reasonably have believed that in this case there are no feasible alternatives...."

If environmental lawyers can convince reviewing judges that the factual evidence considered by an agency would not be enough to allow the judges themselves to make intelligent decisions on critical points, then the judges are likely to send the case back to the agency, even if they are not ready to declare that the agency decision was indeed arbitrary. This invites environmental attorneys to search out points of decision that do not appear to be adequately supported by the agency's formal or informal record, and to leverage these thin areas into an argument for remand. In the tactics of lawyering, a remand on technical points is not as good as a substantive victory, but is far from a hollow victory. The challenger is perceived to have beaten the agency in court, an accomplishment in itself. Additionally, the challenger now gets another bite at the bureaucratic apple, an opportunity for bringing political and public opinion pressures to bear.

3. Interpreting the statutory language: who, and how? In *Overton Park* the Court sent the case back to the lower court because the agency appears to have applied an incorrect interpretation of the statutory words "feasible and prudent." Why didn't the judges defer to the expert agency in its interpretation of law to the same extent they didn't on fact-finding? See subchapter E at page 589 *infra*. In part it may be that judges consider themselves the experts in interpretation of law. Could it also be, as Justice Black implies, that courts will defer less to those agencies that demonstrate institutional resistance to environmental statutes?

Are you satisfied with the Court's interpretation of the statutory language? What weight should be given to statements by individual congressmen on the floor,[18]

18. What weight would you give a sworn declaration by the principal author of a bill, affirming that he had intended one particular interpretation? Just such a declaration was admitted as evidence by the court in Friends of Mammoth v. Mono County, 4 ERC 1593, 1596 (Cal. 1972), where

legislative committees, etc.? Do you find the Court's footnote 29 surprising when it says, "Because of this ambiguity [in the legislative history] it is clear that we must look primarily to the statutes themselves to find the legislative intent"? If the legislative history had been clear, could the Court have saved itself the bother of looking at the statute? On the other hand, isn't it practically always possible to find some ambiguity in the legislative history, particularly if some members of Congress have inserted misleading statements into the record, intending to create ambiguity?

The "plain meaning" rule is an old maxim of statutory interpretation founded upon the assumption that in some cases the words of a statute are unambiguously clear and hence must be effectuated, whatever their results, because each word of a statute (as opposed to common law terms) is binding law. See page 591 *infra* on the plain meaning rule and the courts' role in statutory interpretation.

4. "Arbitrary and capricious"? Like many courts that decide to overturn a particular agency decision, the *Overton Park* court did not want to declare the Secretary's decision arbitrary and capricious, and so it remanded the case for development of a better record supporting the decision. Could it have found the decision "arbitrary"?

The answer depends on what the term "arbitrary" means. The courts have applied the term to a confusingly wide range of substantive and procedural holdings.[19] Applied as a test of the substantive merits of a decision, it is best defined in terms of rationality: "does the agency decision have rational support on the record reviewed by the court?" or "could a rational official have reached that decision on this record?"[20]

Even limited to application as a test of substantive rationality, analytically the arbitrary and capricious test can be applied in at least four different settings:

(a) where the agency has no legal standard to apply to the evidence, or uses an incorrect standard;

(b) where the agency may have had enough evidence back home in its files to support a decision, but just didn't show it to the court;

(c) where the agency did not have enough evidence to support its decision; and

(d) where the agency had enough evidence to support its decision rationally, if it were accurate, but plaintiffs prove that the evidence is wrong.

Assemblyman John T. Knox swore that he had intended the state's environmental impact statement requirement to apply to private developers, and added, "I communicated this intent to other legislators in the course of the legislative process...."

19. See Plater and Norine, Through the Looking Glass of Eminent Domain: Exploring the "Arbitrary and Capricious" Test and Substantive Rationality Review of Governmental Decisions, 16 Envt'l. Aff. L. Rev. 661, 712–722 (1989).

20. Thus, viewed conceptually, the arbitrary and capricious test and the stricter-sounding "substantial evidence" test come down to the same thing; the latter may just require a greater quantum of evidence to prove the point. Id. at pages 716–718.

In Motor Vehicles Mfrs. Ass'n v. State Farm Mutual Life Ins. Co., 463 U.S. 29 (1983), for instance, the Supreme Court declared a Department of Transportation reversal of the prior administration's seat belt and air bag rule arbitrary and capricious because the agency hadn't considered, and failed to present to the Court, evidence supporting the need for a new rule. This would seem to fit the (b) or (c) definitions of arbitrary. Which would have applied to *Overton Park*? The Court could probably have used one or more of the first three of these tests. In other cases, after examining the record basis of agency decisions, plaintiffs can sometimes prove the fourth.[21]

Challenging agency actions under the arbitrary and capricious test, however, is no easy task because judges consider it such a deferential standard of review. In practical terms, in most cases, when a court begins reviewing an agency action under the arbitrary and capricious test, that means that the agency decision is shortly going to be upheld. Even if their case convinces the court, attorneys can reasonably expect that the agency, instead of being declared arbitrary, will receive the kind of face-saving remand that defendants got in *Overton Park* (although that proved to be enough for plaintiffs).

5. "Feasible and prudent" as a public trust standard. The "feasible and prudent" standard captures well the idea of a strong presumption in favor of protection, to be factored into decisions about how parkland public trust resources should be developed. By extension it can be read into the public trust generally. But what does it mean? Does it mean that questions of cost are not to be considered at all? Presumably there is always an alternative, if cost is no object. But "prudent" implies some attention to money factors.[22] If money is to be considered, how is it to be weighed against intangible natural values? Money tends to be an all-or-nothing factor. If you consider cost, going through parks will virtually always be the preferable option, and a test that incorporates the prudence of cost saving negates the protective purpose and effect. The Court suggests that only an "extraordinary magnitude" of expense would justify going through the Park. What would that mean? Is part of the balance of feasible and prudent the question whether the project should be built at all? Might a decision *not* to build an interstate highway through Memphis be a feasible and prudent alternative?

6. The subsequent history of Overton Park. After the Supreme Court's ruling, the case bounced around in the lower courts for a few more years. Finally, after new hearings and an environmental impact statement, Secretary Volpe announced in January, 1973 that he could not find that there was no feasible and prudent alternative to going through the park. The Tennessee Department of Transportation thereupon challenged his decision, demanding that he tell them what the feasible and prudent alternative was, but the Sixth Circuit upheld the Secretary's

21. See Motor Veh. Mfrs. Ass'n of U.S. v. EPA, 768 F.2d 385 (D.C. Cir. 1985)(by granting a methanol use permit based on a failed test, and tests of three dissimilar gas additives, EPA acted arbitrarily).

22. Note that the standard is *feasible* as well as prudent; agencies thus would want to argue that this means economic feasibility, to expand their range of discretion.

ruling as it stood and the Supreme Court denied certiorari.[23] Congress has not disturbed the judicial results, so I-40 will apparently never be built through Overton Park. Today the original interstate highway corridor comes to an ignominious, disruptive halt at the edge of the Park. A loop bypass to the north now carries I-40's through-traffic.

7. Tradeoffs. Memphis had already purchased 160 acres of private land in the northern part of the city to be made into parks to replace the 26 acres of Overton Park used for the highway, and indicated that it would probably acquire still more. Doesn't this mean there would have been a lot more parkland with the highway project through the Park than without it? Should that have ended the analysis?

D. CITIZEN ENFORCEMENT AND JUDICIAL REVIEW

Section 1. THE IMPORTANCE OF CITIZEN ENFORCEMENT

a. THE ECO-POLITICAL CONTEXT

In the Overton Park setting, who would have enforced the federal statute if a bunch of low-income citizens had not rallied to carry the case up through the federal courts? The Federal Highway Administration? The Governor of Tennessee? The Congress that had passed the Parklands Act? No.[24]

Woven through much of this book are examples of the central role of citizen activism (often resisted at each step by public and private entities) in creating and shaping environmental law, whether through common law strategies or the kind of pressuring for public law that produced the wetlands protection statutes, the Chicago phosphate ordinance in *Procter & Gamble*, at page 512 *supra*, or broad statutes like the Michigan environmental protection act. See page 421 *supra*.

Within the administrative processes that constitute the bulk of positive law in the administrative state, citizen efforts have likewise been critically important, although less visible.

Environmentalists operate within the administrative process in two basic ways – by "intervention," formal or informal, in ongoing agency procedures, and by bringing agency actions to court for judicial review. Once a state wetlands act, for instance, is passed on the strength of citizen lobbying, it can be neutered, or strengthened, depending on the regulations and administrative implementation given to it by the administering agency. Agency officials hear persistently and powerfully from regulated vested interests. Within the day-to-day administrative

23. Citizens to Preserve Overton Park v. Brinegar, 494 F.2d 1212 (6th Cir. 1974), cert. denied, Citizens to Preserve Overton Park v. Smith, 421 U.S. 991 (1975).

24. The point is that enforcement of public law provisions by the official organs of government is often highly unlikely. Perhaps the Sierra Club, NRDC, or another national group could have picked up the immense burdens of litigating the case (and in fact national environmental groups did help in the later stages of the litigation), but these organizations' capabilities are severely limited. They litigate only a fraction of the deserving cases referred to them each year. That means that most cases deserving judicial attention either never get launched or drown.

process, agencies now often also hear a great deal from concerned citizen activists. If rigorous, enforceable wetlands regulations are produced, it is altogether likely that citizen expertise and political pressure helped produce them. If environmental groups think that agency regulations subvert the legislative mandate, they can sue, seeking to hold the agency to the original terms of the statute.

Likewise in the federal arena, the federal air and water acts studied in Chapters 18 & 19, for example, were not only created through extraordinary citizen pressures on Congress, spearheaded by a few notable congressional leaders, but their voluminous subsequent anti-pollution regulatory programs have also been fundamentally shaped by citizen groups, through extensive interventions and litigation.[25]

KNOWING THE PLAYERS

In order to understand any administrative process litigation, one has to figure out the respective roles and status of the various competing participants.

The plaintiffs in the *Overton Park* case were exceptional, in that they were a small group of disgruntled neighbors who were able to hold the case together all the way to the Supreme Court of the United States. Far more typical are national environmental citizen organizations designed for sophisticated advocacy in courts, agencies, and the legislature.

Faced with resistance from industry lobbyists and hesitancy on the part of federal regulators, a "shadow government" has sprung up, including notably the Natural Resources Defense Council, the Environmental Defense Fund, the National Wildlife Federation, National Audubon Society, Friends of the Earth, and the Sierra Club Legal Defense Fund[26] – national public interest law groups that commit themselves to monitor, negotiate, litigate, and lobby for rigorous, enforceable regulatory programs. Beginning in 1970, a few young law graduates, many from Yale Law School, laid the foundations for such groups, attempting to hold federal government agencies to the terms of the environmental statutes so painfully won in the halls of Congress. The groups evolved to enroll thousands of subscribing members, with legal staffs and budgets of sufficient depth and strength to allow them to play an oversight role in many important administrative programs. The critical role these organizations have played in the securing of environmental protection in the United States is impressive, and their example is now being followed around the world, as the international environmental law movement begins to develop twenty years behind the American lead. See Chapter 25.

As to defendants, note how in many of these environmental cases there is no clear distinction between the regulatory agency entrusted with the environmental protec-

---

25. For instance, in the early stages of the Clean Air Act, the federal Environmental Protection Agency (EPA) decided over environmental protests to write rules allowing polluting industry to comply with the CAA by moving to clean air states like Wyoming and Idaho that had pristine air quality, thereby spreading pollution around but not abating it. It was only because of citizen litigation and negotiation that a nationwide "non-deterioration" policy was established. Sierra Club v. Ruckleshaus, 344 F. Supp. 253 (D.D.C. 1973), aff'd 412 U.S. 541. (Note in this controversy the interstate replay of a scene from the Tragedy of the Commons.)

26. This list covers most of the most frequent environmental litigation groups; there are other significant groups as well.

tion mandate and the industry and regulated interests that it is assigned to supervise. In the atomic energy field, for instance, the alignment of the Atomic Energy Commission (AEC) with the nuclear industry was so incestuous that Congress ultimately split the agency into two parts, the promotional Energy Research and Development Agency (ERDA), and the ostensibly protective Nuclear Regulatory Commission (NRC). The environmental community does not necessarily believe that such organizational splits end the affinity of regulator and regulatee. In any event, it is noteworthy that the original bipolar design of the regulatory state – with regulated industries on one hand and the public interest defended by government on the other – has now evolved, under pressure from citizen activists, into a highly articulated and energetic pluralistic democracy, where courts and many agencies are open to a wide variety of differing points of view from a potpourri of citizen intervenors.

OF THE IRON TRIANGLE, THE PORKBARREL, AND THE ESTABLISHMENT

The *Overton Park* case reminds environmental observers that environmental quality initiatives, even when they are backed by statutory provisions, run into the opposition of vested interests, public as well as private. Some environmentalists call it the "Porkbarrel," others the "Iron Triangle" – in either case referring to the interlocking structure and political process linking private construction and industrial interests, government agencies that service the industry, and congressional delegations from areas like Memphis that want to attract particular public expenditures into their backyards. The momentum of that combination makes the porkbarrel one of the most consistently powerful and resistant forces of environmental alteration. Environmentalists are often underfinanced, politically powerless neighborhood agitators who come along late in the game seeking to stop the momentum of the good ol' boys' lucrative establishment steamroller.

In the Overton Park setting, for example, it was not only that interstate highways required just 10 percent contribution from state and local government, while 90 percent of costs would be tapped directly from federal taxpayers and the federal Highway Trust Fund. The attraction of parklands to the highway establishment is even more seductive: parklands are already owned by government. If Tennessee contributes 26 acres of parkland to the highway project, it gets to value that parkland as if it were a cash contribution based on its fair market value, the value of 26 acres of downtown urban land. For this reason, parks attract their own destruction, and it is for precisely that reason that environmentalists had found it so necessary to fight to put §4(f) into the highway legislation.[27]

By successfully, against the odds, putting the Parklands Act onto the federal books, environmentalists did not automatically succeed in enlisting the United States Government as a whole on the side of parkland preservation. Quite the contrary, federal program agencies often adopt a recalcitrant posture toward statutes that limit their standard operating procedures. Agencies that measure their success in terms of accomplishing their mission in terms of pouring concrete and building road mileage understandably treat conservation legislation as a technical-

27. Thus the official argument in *Overton Park* for overriding §4(f), based on "prudent" limiting of acquisition costs, replayed the problem that required §4(f) in the first place.

ity, an annoyance, and often as a frustrating and contradictory obstacle that must be overridden in order to do their jobs.

The need to observe and identify the roles, powers and predilections of the contesting parties, needless to say, is a recurring reality in analyses of environmental controversies under both public and private law.

THE "CAPTURE" PHENOMENON

Environmentalists repeatedly identify the problem of governmental agencies' "capture" by market forces as a disturbing backdrop to many administrative process cases. A regulatory agency created in the fervor of a popular movement to regulate some designated problem may begin its life energetically pursuing the overall public interest, but over time its initiative may gradually be eroded into narrower views, intimately linked with the industry and problems it was intended to solve.

Stewart, The Reformation of American Administrative Law
88 Harvard Law Review 1669, 1684-1687 (1975)

Critics have repeatedly asserted...that in carrying out broad legislative directives, agencies unduly favor organized interests, especially the interests of regulated or client business firms and other organized groups at the expense of diffuse, comparatively unorganized interests such as consumers, environmentalists, and the poor. In the midst of a "growing sense of disillusion with the role which regulatory agencies play," many legislators, judges, and legal and economic commentators have accepted the thesis of persistent bias in agency policies. At its crudest, this thesis is based on the "capture" scenario, in which administrations are systematically controlled, sometimes corruptly, by the business firms within their orbit of responsibility, whether regulatory or promotional. But there are more subtle explanations of industry orientation, which include the following:

First The division of responsibility between the regulated firms, which retain primary control over their own affairs, and the administrator, whose power is essentially negative and who is dependent on industry cooperation in order to achieve his objectives, places the administrator in an inherently weak position. The administrator will, nonetheless, be held responsible if the industry suffers serious economic dislocation. For both these reasons, he may pursue conservative policies.

Second The regulatory bureaucracy becomes "regulation minded." It seeks to elaborate and perfect the controls it exercises over the regulated industry. The effect of this tendency, particularly in a regime of limited entry, is to eliminate actual and potential competition and buttress the position of the established firms.

Third The resources – in terms of money, personnel, and political influence – of the regulatory agency are limited in comparison to those of regulated firms. Unremitting maintenance of an adversary posture would quickly dissipate agency resources. Hence, the agency must compromise with the regulated industry if it is to accomplish anything of significance.

Fourth Limited agency resources imply that agencies must depend on outside sources of information, policy development, and political support. This outside input comes primarily from organized interests, such as regulated firms, that have a substantial stake in the substance of agency policy and the resources to provide such input. By contrast, the personal stake in agency policy of an individual member of an unorganized interest, such as a consumer, is normally too small to justify such representation. Effective representation of unorganized interests might be possible if a means of pooling resources to share the costs of underwriting collective representation were available. But this seems unlikely since the transaction costs of creating an organization of interest group members increase disproportionately as the size of the group increases. Moreover, if membership in such an organization is voluntary, individuals will not have a strong incentive to join, since if others represent the interests involved, the benefits will accrue not only to those participating in the representation, but to nonparticipants as well, who can, therefore, enjoy the benefits without incurring any of the costs (the free rider effect). As a somewhat disillusioned James Landis wrote in 1960, the result is industry dominance in representation, which has a "daily machine-gun like impact on both [an] agency and its staff" that tends to create an industry bias in the agency's outlook.

These various theses of systematic bias in agency policy are not universally valid. Political pressures and judicial controls may force continuing agency adherence to policies demonstrably inimical to the interests of the regulated industry.... Moreover, the fact that agency policies may tend to favor regulated interests does not in itself demonstrate that such policies are unfair or unjustified, since protection of regulated interests may be implicit in the regulatory scheme established by Congress. Nonetheless, the critique of agency discretion as unduly favorable to organized interests – particularly regulated or client firms – has sufficient power and verisimilitude to have achieved widespread contemporary acceptance.

b. THE INSTITUTIONALIZATION OF CITIZEN ENFORCEMENT

A major milestone for citizen participation in administrative law and process – involving citizen enforcement of federal statutes, and citizen standing in agency proceedings as well as in subsequent judicial review of agency decisions – occurred in the mid-1960s in the shadow of Storm King Mountain, on the shores of New York's Hudson River.

The Consolidated Edison Company and the Federal Power Commission (FPC) had been planning Con Ed's construction of a "pumped storage" hydroelectric project, cutting a crater reservoir out of the top of Storm King Mountain so that water could be pumped up in hours of slack electricity use, to be released through generator turbines (as "peaking power") when energy needs were greatest. Disturbed by the prospect, a group of local citizens formed the Scenic Hudson Preservation Conference, and began to question the utility company and the agency about the project's negative effects – loss of a beautiful mountain, scour, sedimentation, and other impacts on fish and the river when huge volumes of water were sucked up and down through turbines. Neither Con Ed nor the federal agency wanted the citizens to participate in the various permit procedures required to license the Storm King project. The agency reluctantly allowed the citizens to enter a limited intervention, but excluded several studies on the project's negative consequences from the agency record.

When the Storm King license was granted, the citizens went to court. In a remarkable Second Circuit opinion, Judge Hays had to weigh the project's troubling facts against the agency's demand for deference and defendants' arguments that the citizens had no right to judicial review.

Scenic Hudson Preservation Conference v. Federal Power Commission
United States Court of Appeals for the Second Circuit, 1965
354 F.2d 608, cert. denied 384 U.S. 941 (1966)

HAYS, J. ...The Storm King project is to be located in an area of unique beauty and major historical significance. The highlands and gorge of the Hudson offer one of the finest pieces of river scenery in the world....

Respondents argue that "petitioners do not have standing to obtain review" because they make no claim of any personal economic injury resulting from the Commission's action...." [and thus are not "aggrieved" within the meaning of the administrative law standing requirements.] The Commission takes a narrow view of the meaning of "aggrieved party."... The Supreme Court has observed that the law of standing is a "complicated specialty of Federal jurisdiction, the solution of whose problems is in any event more or less determined by the specific circumstances of individual situations...." The "case or controversy" requirement of Article III §2 of the Constitution does not require that an "aggrieved" or "adversely effected" party have a personal economic interest.... In order to insure that the Federal Power Commission will adequately protect the public interest in the aesthetic, conservational, and recreational aspects power development, those who by their activities and conduct have exhibited a special interest in such areas must be held to be included in the class of "aggrieved" parties under §313(b) [of the Federal Power Act]....

We see no justification for the Commission's fear that our determination will encourage "literally thousands" to intervene and seek review in future proceedings. We rejected a similar contention in Associated Industries v. Ickes, 134 F.2d 694, 707 (1943), noting that "no such horrendous possibilities" exist. Our experience with public actions confirms the view that the expense and vexation of legal proceedings [are] not lightly undertaken.... [The citizens were acting as "private attorneys-general," enforcing the terms of statute in partnership with the agency, and thus should have been given a hospitable reception in the agency.]

A party acting as a "private attorney-general" can raise issues that are not personal to it.... Especially in a case of this type, where public interest and concern is so great, the Commission refusal to receive the [citizens' power study] testimony, as well as proffered information on fish protection devices and underground transmission facilities exhibits a disregard of the statute and of judicial mandates instructing the Commission to probe all feasible alternatives....

In this case as in many others the Commission has claimed to be the representative of the public interest. This role does not permit it to act as an umpire blandly calling balls and strikes for adversary groups appearing before it; the right of the public must receive active and affirmative protection at the hands of the Commission.

[Reasoning that the agency decision was not rationally supported on the record – absent full citizen participation and agency follow-up on the citizens' substantiated concerns – the court set aside the license and remanded the Storm King project to the district court and the Commission, where it died.[28] See pages 984–993 *infra.*]

---

28. A number of books and law review articles have commented on *Scenic Hudson*. See, e.g. A. Talbot, Power Along the Hudson: The Storm King Case & the Birth of Environmentalism (1972). The full case deserves reading by anyone interested in the history of environmental law. For a scathing criticism of the case in terms of its putative anti-democratic élitism see W. Tucker, Environmentalism and the Leisure Class, 255 Harpers Magazine 49–56, 73–80 (Dec. 1977).

As noted earlier, the standing doctrine is one of the threshold tests citizens have to meet in order to obtain judicial review, and the law of standing in recent years has been made largely through environmental cases.

The first major Supreme Court case encouraging citizen participation through expanded judicial standing was Sierra Club v. Morton,[29] where the Walt Disney Corporation sought to develop a ski lodge and winter resort on national forest public lands at Mineral King Mountain in the California Sierras. The environmental plaintiffs, trying to enforce federal conservation statutes, asked to be heard based only on their general interest in environmental protection, with no claim of individual injury.[30] Previously, courts had extended standing only to persons who had a clearly defined economic injury or a constitutionally protected right. The court refused to allow the Sierra Club to proceed without pleading individual harm, but nevertheless greatly expanded the definition of constitutionally-cognizable injuries that could be the basis of citizen lawsuits:

> The complaint alleged that the development "would destroy or otherwise adversely affect the scenery, natural and historic objects and wildlife of the park and would impair the enjoyment of the park for future generations." We do not question that this type of harm may amount to an "injury in fact" sufficient to lay the basis for standing.... The trend of cases arising under the APA and other statutes authorizing judicial review of federal agency action has been toward recognizing that injuries other than economic harm are sufficient to bring a person within the meaning of the statutory language, and toward discarding the notion that an injury that is widely shared is *ipso facto* not an injury sufficient to provide the basis for judicial review.... The interest alleged to have been injured "may reflect aesthetic, conservational, and recreational, as well as economic values...." Aesthetic and environmental well-being, like economic well-being, are important ingredients of the quality of life in our society, and the fact that particular environmental interests are shared by the many rather than the few does not make them less deserving of legal protection through the judicial process. 405 U.S. at 734, 738.[31]

Several years later, a group of law students in Washington D.C. decided to challenge Interstate Commerce Commission rate-making decisions that encouraged use of raw materials over recycled materials by assigning higher transport

29. 405 U.S. 727 (1972)("*Mineral King*").

30. Note that this was part of Scenic Hudson's successful argument for generalized standing, based on the environmentalists' "activities and conduct [exhibiting] a special interest in such areas." One of the more intriguing issues raised in environmental law has been the attempt to extend standing to non-living things. Could the plaintiffs have filed the lawsuit in the name of the Park itself? In a ringing dissent in the *Mineral King* case, Justice Douglas urged the adoption of Professor Chris Stone's argument that standing should be granted to organizations that speak knowingly and will commit resources in defense of inanimate trees, mountains, or wildlife. C. Stone, Should Trees Have Standing? (1974). Why might the Sierra Club have wanted to have the mountain itself as the plaintiff? To some extent such attempts may reflect a philosophical stance, an attempt to focus attention on the real long-term issues. In part such a claim might reflect the fact that members do not always live or hike in areas where citizen enforcement efforts are necessary, as in Arctic tundra threatened by oil drilling, or in outer space where some energy planners suggest dumping radioactive wastes.

31. Citing Assoc. of Data Processing Services v. Camp, 397 U.S. 150, 154 (1970).

tariffs to the latter. U.S. v. Students Challenging Regulatory Agency Procedures (SCRAP), 412 U.S. 669 (1973). The Court found that SCRAP had alleged sufficient individual harm to get standing:

> The challenged agency action in this case is applicable to substantially all of the Nation's railroads.... All persons who utilize the scenic resources of the country, and indeed all who breathe its air, could claim harm similar to that alleged by the environmental groups here. But we have already made it clear that standing is not to be denied simply because many people suffer the same injury.... To deny standing to persons who are in fact injured simply because many others are also injured would mean that the most injurious and widespread Government actions could be questioned by nobody. We cannot accept that conclusion.
>
> But the injury alleged here is also very different from that at issue in *Sierra Club* because here the alleged injury to the environment is far less direct and perceptible.... Here, the Court was asked to follow a far more attenuated line of causation to the eventual injury of which the appellees complained – a general rate increase would allegedly cause increased use of nonrecyclable commodities as compared to recyclable goods, thus resulting in the need to use more natural resources to produce such goods,... resulting in more refuse that might be discarded [along hiking trails used by the students] in national parks in the Washington area....
>
> Of course, pleadings must be something more than an ingenious academic exercise in the conceivable. A plaintiff must allege that he has been or will in fact be perceptibly harmed by the challenged agency action, not that he can imagine circumstances in which he could be affected by the agency's action. And it is equally clear that the allegations must be true and capable of proof at trial....
>
> If proved, [plaintiffs' allegations] would place them squarely among those persons injured in fact by the Commission's action. 412 U.S. at 687-690.

Understandably, *SCRAP* has been viewed as an expansion of citizens' rights to sue against governmental abuses.

STANDING FOR CITIZEN INTERVENTION IN AGENCY PROCEEDINGS

Section 6 of the Administrative Procedures Act, 5 U.S.C.A. §555(b), provides that "so far as the orderly conduct of the public business permits, an interested person may appear before an agency or its responsible employees for the presentation, adjustment, or determination, request, or controversy in [any] proceeding." Section 555(b), however, has not been extensively developed, at least in non-formal, trial-type proceedings. What does the "orderly conduct of public business" limitation mean, and who is legally an "interested" party? *Scenic Hudson* presumed the validity of citizen participation in FPC proceedings. Since *Scenic Hudson*, permission for citizen intervention in agency proceedings seems to have become the norm, if only because agencies realize that judicial review standing has expanded, so that if intervention is denied within agency procedures, court review will nevertheless occur, and be tougher.[32] Some agencies, nevertheless, are known for their resistance to citizen intervention. See In the Matter of Edlow International Co., 3 NRC 563 (Nuclear Regulatory Commission, 1976)(dismissed as moot, NRDC v. NRC, 580 F.2d 698 (D.C. Cir. 1987)).

Intervention is a vital part of citizen involvement in the administrative process, allowing a pluralist debate to begin early in the process rather than later in retrospective judicial review. The future development of APA §555(b) will reflect the evolution of intervention in informal as well as formal proceedings. The arguments of environmentalists to be allowed to intervene in ongoing agency proceedings will continue to be reinforced by the fact that courts in subsequent review often consider that a record made without active participation is not sufficiently comprehensive, and does not cover certain critical features sufficiently to support the agency action in judicial review.

CITIZEN STANDING IN JUDICIAL REVIEW

As to standing in judicial review of agency decisions, the *Mineral King* Court declined to adopt the broad definition of private attorneys-general articulated in *Scenic Hudson. Mineral King* required the Sierra Club to prove particular injuries from the government action proposed.[33] It firmly established, however, that citizens no longer needed to show either economic injury or violation of a Constitutional right.

In the years since *SCRAP,* standing doctrine has shifted from strict to less strict terms, and back again,[34] often, as in *Duke Power,* reflecting the Supreme Court's apparent desire to raise an environmental argument and dispose of it permanently so as to remove uncertainty from the marketplace.[35] In Lujan v. National Wildlife Federation, __U.S.__, 110 S. Ct. 3177 (1990), the Supreme Court applied a restrictive definition of standing to prevent environmentalists from challenging the opening of Western public lands to grazing, timber, and mining operations. See page 575 *infra.*

In many cases, however, Congress has recognized the importance of citizen enforcement, and created direct official standing for citizens to step in and take on the enforcement of statutes when official agencies fail to do so.

In the federal Clean Water Act's §505, for instance, Congress provided that, unless the EPA has previously commenced a civil enforcement action –

§505(a) [A]ny citizen may commence a civil action on his own behalf –

---

32. As a noted administrative law practitioner observed "today, at least in my experience, intervention is seldom denied.... In light of the role that the courts have carved out for intervenors, and the risks inherent in denying interested citizens the right to be heard, intervention has assumed the proportions of a right, even where the applicable statute or rules are phrased permissively." Butzel, Intervention and Class Actions Before the Agencies and the Courts, 25 Admin. L. Rev. 135, 136 (1973).

33. On remand the Club quickly supplied available evidence of direct use of the mountain by its members, and got standing. Were the original pleadings badly designed, or a grab for the brass ring?

34. Duke Power v. Carolina Environmental Study Group, 438 U.S. 59 (1978); Warth v. Seldin, 422 U.S. 490 (1975).

35. 438 U.S. at 78.

(A) ... (1) against any person (including (i) the United States, and (ii) any other government instrumentality or agency...) who is alleged to be in violation of (A) an effluent standard or limitation under this chapter or (B) an order issued by the Administrator or State with respect to such a standard or limitation, or

(2) against the Administrator where there is alleged a failure of the Administrator to perform any act or duty under this chapter which is not discretionary with the Administrator....

§505(b) No action may be commenced –

(1)... (A) prior to sixty days after the plaintiff has given notice of the alleged violation (i) to the Administrator, (ii) to the State in which the alleged violation occurs, and (iii) to any alleged violator of the standard, limitation, or order, or

(B) if the Administrator or State has commenced and is diligently prosecuting a civil or criminal action in a court of the United States or a State to require compliance with the standard, limitation, or order, but in any such action in a court of the United States any citizen may intervene as a matter of right.... 33 U.S.C.A. §1365

[The sixty day waiting period does not apply in cases of toxic and pretreatment standards, or national performance standards.][36]

More than a dozen major environmental statutes include similar grants of standing.[37] The federal courts have been quite attentive to these citizen suit provisions, generally acknowledging the strength of the congressional intent to open up citizen enforcement as a parallel national strategy for achieving implementation of federal regulatory programs.[38] The Supreme Court, however, has occasionally indicated that these statutory grants of standing will be held strictly to their terms.[39]

---

36. Environmentalists have argued that waivers to the sixty-day waiting period should also be granted or liberalized in other settings where the public interest and congressional policy require it. Irvin, When Survival is at Stake: a Proposal for Expanding the Emergency Exception to the Sixty-Day Notice Requirement of the Endangered Species Act's Citizen Suit Provision, 14 Harv. Env. L. Rev. 343 (1990)(the article presents interesting examples of the necessity for citizen enforcement where industry and government remain passive). CWA §505 is discussed at 857 *infra*.

37. See the list of statutory sections at note 44 *infra*.

38. "[Where the] only public entities that might have brought suit...[are] named as defendants...and vigorously [oppose] plaintiffs,...only private citizens can be expected to guard the guardians." La Raza Unida v. Volpe, 57 F.R.D. 94, 101 (N.D. Cal. 1972). The nation's "regrettably slow progress in controlling air pollution is blamed on [both] the scarcity of skilled personnel available to enforce control measures and on a lack of aggressiveness by EPA's predecessor agency.... The public suit seems particularly instrumental in the statutory scheme [in cases forcing agency compliance], for only the public – certainly not the polluter – has the incentive to complain if the EPA falls short...." NRDC v. EPA, 484 F.2d 1331 (1st Cir. 1973).

39. Hallstrom v. Tillamook County, 493 U.S. 20 (1989); Gwaltney of Smithfield v. Chesapeake Bay Found., 484 U.S. 49 (1987). See Chapter 19 at page 857 *infra*. *Gwaltney's* holding – that citizen suits can be filed only where an ongoing violation continues when the lawsuit is filed, but not for past violations – was specifically overridden by Congress as to the Clean Air Act. The 1990 CAA amendments provided for citizen lawsuits upon evidence that past violations have been repeated. Pub. L. 101–549, §707(g)(amending §304(a) of the Clean Air Act, 42 U.S.C.A. 7410).

COMMENTARY AND QUESTIONS

1. The statutory grants of sixty-day notice citizen standing. What is the congressional premise implicit in provisions granting citizen enforcement standing in major environmental statutes? In the legal systems of other industrial nations it would be quite astonishing to find similar provisions. The standing grants seem to assume that industry will not voluntarily comply with federal pollution standards, and that officially-delegated enforcement agencies in many cases will not enforce the standards sufficiently. The presence of the statutory provisions may reflect a "conservative" reaction against federal bureaucracy, as well as "liberal" theories of pluralistic democracy and citizen antidotes to agency "capture."

2. Standing in courts and agencies. In a notable case expanding citizens' rights to intervene in agency proceedings, then-Judge Warren Burger wrote that "all parties seem to consider that the same standards are applicable to determining standing before the Commission and standing to appeal a Commission decision to this court. We have, therefore, used the cases dealing with standing in the two tribunals interchangeably."[40] Judge Burger took note of the expanding law of standing in federal courts, and required expanded intervention standing in the agency. Analytically are the two tribunals the same? They are doing two very different tasks. A citizen's right to intervene in an agency, under 5 APA §555(b) or otherwise, is arguably broader than standing for judicial review, because administrative agency process is not constitutionally limited by Article III's "case or controversy" requirement.

3. The role of an agency when citizens intervene. Note that in the *Scenic Hudson* opinion the court criticized the agency for treating citizen intervention, not as a helpful contribution, but as a resented disruption; the commission had stepped back and acted like "an umpire blandly calling balls and strikes" between the industry and the small ad hoc group of citizen intervenors. Responding to the same problem, Judge Burger roundly criticized the agency proceedings that had followed his prior order on remand:

> The examiner seems to have regarded [the citizen] appellants as "plaintiffs" and the licensee as "defendant," with burdens of proof allocated accordingly.... We did not intend that intervenors representing a public interest be treated as interlopers. Rather...a "public intervenor" is seeking no license or private right and is, in this context, more nearly like a complaining witness who presents evidence to police or a prosecutor whose duty it is to conduct an affirmative and objective investigation.... In our view the entire hearing was permeated by...the pervasive impatience – if not hostility – of the examiner...which made fair and impartial consideration impossible.... The public intervenors, who were performing a public service under a mandate of this court, were entitled to a more hospitable reception in the performance of that function. As we view the record the examiner tended to impede the

40. Office of Communication, United Church of Christ v. FCC, 359 F.2d 994, 1000 (D.C. Cir. 1966).

> exploration of the vary issues which we would reasonably expect the Commission itself would have initiated; an ally was regarded as an opponent.... The administrative conduct reflected in this record is beyond repair. [The agency decision was revoked and the proceedings remanded to the agency.] Office of Communication of United Church of Christ v. FCC, 425 F.2d 543, 546-550 (D.C. Cir. 1969).

4. Citizens' access to information. Information is power. Or, at least, it is clear that without basic specific information, interested parties and intervenors will not be effective. In 1966, Congress, responding to allegations that agency practices presumed that all governmental information requested should be withheld unless there was specific legal authority for its release, reversed the presumption by statute. The Freedom of Information Act (FOIA), 5 U.S.C.A. §552, provides that –

> each agency upon any request for records which...reasonably describes such records and [follows certain simple procedures] *shall make the records promptly available* to any person. §552((a)(3) [emphasis added].

FOIA restricts permissible withholding to nine fairly narrow exceptions. §552(b)(1-9).

Environmentalists have often found FOIA critically helpful in obtaining agency information through formal requests or, perhaps even more usefully, in prompting informal release of information. Federal courts have applied the Act with stringency in a number of environmental cases,[41] although the development of the Act's disclosure mandate, and its provisions for waiving data retrieval fees for requests "primarily benefiting the public interest,"[42] are still evolving.

5. Accountability: "internalizing costs" in public law? In approaching pollution and other environmental harms caused by private individuals and industries, environmental law often follows the strategy of cost internalization, attempting to force private decision-makers to account for environmental costs in their economic market behavior. Is there an equivalent accounting strategy in the public law setting, where decision-makers are not involved in a market enterprise?

To an extent, government decision-makers often seem to share the functional frame of reference of private corporate entrepreneurs. To the minds of promoters, whether private or public, accounting for negative external consequences is dysfunctional, hence to be avoided, because it gets in the way of the enterprise's mission. Development agencies, however, may tend to be institutionally less sensitive to cost-accounting; their projects are paid for with taxpayer dollars.

How are agency officials practically induced to consider consequential public costs in their internal calculus? One approach is political. The currency of the bureau-

---

41. See Soucie v. David, 448 F. 2d. 1067, [2 ERC 1626] (D.C. Cir. 1971). Cf. Nat'l Parks & Conservation Ass'n v. Morton, 498 F. 2d 765 (D.C. Cir. 1974).

42. §552(a)(4)(A). The Act's serious intent to compel an open governmental process is underscored by its provisions for advancing FOIA cases to the top of federal court dockets, §552(a)(4)(D); for award of attorney's fees against the agencies, §552(a)(4)(E); and for personal accountability, see next note.

cratic marketplace is politics – who has power, who has momentum, who is under fire. Agencies can foresee that if they attract severe media criticism, or legislative committee oversight hearings, or negative reactions from an executive office, they will feel the heat, and so they act accordingly. Another internalizing approach is personal accountability, a rarity in government except at the highest levels. FOIA's §552(a) provides that –

> Whenever the court orders the production of any agency records improperly withheld from the complainant...and...issues a written finding that the circumstances surrounding the withholding raise questions whether agency personnel acted arbitrarily...with respect to the withholding, the Special Counsel [of the Civil Service merit system review process] shall promptly initiate a proceeding to determine whether disciplinary action is warranted.... §552(a)(4)(F).

Such personal sanctions catch and hold bureaucratic attention, but are infrequent. Ultimately it is legal constraints – in practical terms this means legal constraints that will be enforced against agencies, in many cases only by citizen efforts – that constitute the backbone of administrative accountability.

6. Beyond intervention and judicial review: Citizen Oversight Councils. Most citizen participation in the administrative process takes place in interventions and in judicial review of agency actions. Citizen oversight councils, built into governmental processes, offer an interesting alternative for environmental law.

Notable examples of the citizen oversight council were created in the aftermath of the Exxon-Valdez oilspill. That disaster, according to the Alaska Oilspill Commission, was an accident waiting to happen, in large part because of pervasive "complacency and neglect" that had dulled the vigilance of the official corporate, state, and federal government managers.[43] The safety and spill response systems, however, would not have been allowed to deteriorate, or to be circumvented for profit-maximization, if people whose livelihoods depended on the waters of Prince William Sound had sat within the official process.

After the spill, three different models of citizen oversight council were put into effect in Alaska.

The Prince William Sound Regional Citizens' Advisory Council (PWS-RCAC) was created in a formal contract brokered between the Alyeska Pipeline consortium and the commercial fishermen, Alaska Natives, and other citizens of the Sound who had long been critical of the pipeline's land and sea operations. It provided for access to corporate data (which makes it more potent than most "advisory" groups), set up a permanent communication and negotiation system, and provided the citizen group with more than $2 million a year in operating funds.

The state legislature, responding to proposals by the Oilspill Commission, also established a statewide Citizens' Oversight Council on Oil and Other Hazardous

43. Alaska Oil Spill Commission, Spill: The Wreck of the Exxon-Valdez iii (1990).

Substances, Alaska Stat. §24.20.160 et seq. (1990). This oversight council, with support from satellite regional councils, was given subpoena power and a directive to maintain vigilant oversight of oil transport and other hazardous substance activities, and agency regulatory efforts.

Then, when the federal government passed its 1990 Oil Pollution Act ("OPA'90"), also in response to the Exxon-Valdez spill, it adopted a suggestion made by the state oilspill commission to provide for the creation of federally recognized RCACs. These federal RCACs are modelled on the Prince William Sound compact and are likewise financed by funds drawn from the industry. 33 U.S.C.A. §2732(d),(k). The PWS-RCAC then shifted from private compact status to the federally-recognized form; another RCAC has since been set up for the Cook Inlet region.

These citizen councils offer valuable advantages in quality control efforts of both private and governmental resource protection activities, and are designed to be relatively immune from co-optation. The PWS-RCDC, first as a private and then as a federal entity, has occasionally been at loggerheads with the oil industry, exchanging threats of lawsuits, but the council continues to provide a unique citizen-industry forum. The state Oversight Council has also encountered fervent opposition from the oil companies and oil-minded public servants, but in spite of budget cuts has maintained an impressive course of impartial investigation, research, mediation and negotiation of regulations (brokering roundtables of industry, government, and environmentalists), public hearings, and citizen complaint proceedings throughout the state. The Cook Inlet RCAC has been likewise effective, with less turmoil. These three experiments bear continuing study as examples of utilitarian pluralism in government.

c. FINANCING CITIZEN ENFORCEMENT

When citizens embark as "private attorneys-general" attempting to enforce existing law in agencies and courts, they often face substantial administrative and financial burdens, and opponents who are either public officials or well-financed corporate entities writing off expenses against revenues. Expert witnesses and attorneys cost money. For plaintiff groups like the citizens in *Overton Park*, this often means having to raise funds through bake sales, raffles, selling logo tee-shirts, or passing the hat. The larger national environmental groups have substantially greater resources, but are confronted with a proportionally broader range of advocacy commitments, and likewise depend upon volunteer contributions. Environmentalists have turned to both the courts and Congress in attempts to win financial recognition of the role played by private attorneys-general.

In court, environmentalists face the "American Rule" of fee-shifting; unlike their counterparts under the English rule, prevailing plaintiffs in American courts generally are unable to recover the costs of litigation from defendants. (In part this explains why punitive damages are often sought in common law litigation.)

The advantages of fee-shifting are obvious, as are the dangers. As some skeptics note, legions of attorneys might turn from ambulance chasing to environmental litigation as a way of gouging the system. Congress, however, evidently did not share such apprehensions in its grants of citizen standing. In a variety of federal statutes authorizing citizen suits,[44] as in the Clean Water Act's §505 noted earlier, Congress consistently inserted a fee recovery provision in terms similar to the following:

> **§505(d) Litigation costs.** The court, in issuing any final order in any action brought pursuant to this section, may award costs of litigation (including reasonable attorney and expert witness fees) to any prevailing or substantially prevailing party, whenever the court determines such award is appropriate. 33 U.S.C.A. §1365(d).

Many environmental groups have successfully recovered litigation fees under the express statutory fee-shifting provisions. The major issues raised in these lawsuits are, first, whether the plaintiffs have prevailed or substantially prevailed, then, if so, the amount to be awarded. Fees are typically assessed on an hourly basis for hours spent on claims successfully litigated; the hourly rate takes account of the difficulty of the case, the controversiality of the action, and other issues.[45]

Environmentalists can also win fees and costs under broad provisions of the Equal Access to Justice Act (EAJA), 28 U.S.C.A. §2412(d).[46] Prevailing parties, in situations where the reviewing court considers the government agencies' position not "substantially justified," can claim expert witness and attorneys fees. EAJA litigation extends the realm of fee-shifting even where enforced statutes do not specifically grant citizens standing.

Where no statute provides for grants of fees, there are several nonstatutory avenues to funding public interest litigation. Under equity principles, American courts have evolved several exceptions to the American Rule, including where defendants act in bad faith, and where the defendants' actions have built up a "common fund" against which plaintiffs' costs can reasonably be assessed, as well as the private attorney-general theory. Several state and federal courts initially expanded the private attorney-general approach by adding a right to recover attorneys and expert witness fees when citizen suits prevailed.[47]

The Supreme Court, however, in a case arising from environmental efforts to halt or improve the safety of the Alaska Oil Pipeline, held that federal courts would

44. See Toxic Substances Control Act §§19(d), 20(c)(2), 15 U.S.C.A. §2618(d), §2619; Endangered Species Act of 1973 §11(g)(4), 16 U.S.C.A. §1540(g)(4); Surface Mining Control and Reclamation Act of 1977, 30 U.S.C.A. §1270(d); Deep Seabed Hard Mineral Resources Act §117(c), 30 U.S.C.A. §1427(c); Clean Water Act (Federal Water Pollution Control Act Amendments of 1972 §505), 33 U.S.C.A. §1365(d); Marine Protection, Research, and Sanctuaries Act, 33 U.S.C.A. §1415(g)(4); Deepwater Port Act of 1974, 33 U.S.C.A. §1515(d); Safe Drinking Water Act §1449(d), 42 U.S.C.A. §300j-8(d); Noise Control Act of 1972 §12(d), 42 U.S.C.A. §4911(d); Energy Sources Development Act, 42 U.S.C.A. §5851(e)(2); Energy Policy and Conservation Act, 42 U.S.C.A. §6305(d); Solid Waste Disposal Act, 42 U.S.C.A. §6972(e); Clean Air Act §304, 42 U.S.C.A. §§7604, 7607(f); Powerplant and Industrial Fuel Act, 42 U.S.C.A. §8435(d); Ocean Thermal Energy Conservation Act, 42 U.S.C.A. §9124(d); Outer Continental Shelf Lands Act, 43 U.S.C.A. §1349(a)(5).

45. See Troutwine, A Primer on Attorneys' Fees Awards: Fee Computation under Federal and State Attorneys' Fees Statutes, in PLI, Court Awards of Attorneys' Fees 99-108 (1987).

46. Robertson & Fowler, Recovering Attorneys' Fees From the Government Under The Equal Access to Justice Act, 56 Tul. L. Rev. 903, (1982).

47. Sierra Club v. Lynn, 364 F. Supp. 834 (W.D. Tex. 1973); La Raza Unida v. Volpe, 57 F.R.D. 94 (N.D. Cal. 1972).

no longer be permitted to grant expert witness or counsel fees to environmental plaintiffs acting as private attorneys-general unless they could prove bad faith, a common fund, or specific statutory authorization for fee awards. Alyeska Pipeline Service Co. v. Wilderness Society, 421 U.S. 240 (1975).[48]

Although federal courts were thus halted in recognizing fee-shifting in most private attorney-general suits, state courts retain the authority to apply their own equity principles, awarding fees to citizens whose efforts enforce the law and defend a public good.[49]

Section 2. RESISTANCE TO CITIZEN ENFORCEMENT

a. REMOVING COURTS' ABILITY TO GRANT RELIEF TO CITIZENS

Department of Interior and Related Agencies Appropriations Act, 1990

Public Law 101-121 (1989)

> §318(g)...[N]o restraining order or preliminary injunction shall be issued by any court of the United States with respect to any decision to prepare, advertise, offer, award, or operate...timber sales in fiscal year 1990 from the thirteen national forests in Oregon and Washington and Bureau of Land Management lands in Western Oregon known to contain northern spotted owls. The provisions of 5 U.S.C.A. §705 [authorizing courts to stay agency actions] shall not apply to any challenge to such a timber sale. *Provided*, that the courts shall have authority to [issue permanent injunctions for timber sales found to be] arbitrary, capricious, or otherwise not in accordance with law....

[Other provisions of this appropriations rider required the agencies to sell off increased annual quotas of timber; restricted the cutting of certain "ecologically significant old growth forest stands" except as necessary to meet the sales quotas; directed the Forest Service to prepare a new spotted owl plan and have it in place by September 30, 1990; insulated from judicial review Forest Service and Bureau of Land Management (BLM) decisions shown to be based on outdated information; and made quasi-judicial findings to reverse two injunctions against timbercutting.[50]]

COMMENTARY AND QUESTIONS

1. The spotted owl appropriations rider. The above provision was inserted into the Department of Interior 1990 appropriations bill in reaction to environmentalists' successes, under a variety of environmental statutes, in protecting the northern spotted owl, an endangered species threatened by clearcutting operations in various

---

48. The federal courts' position on qui tam lawsuits, noted in Chapter 7 at page 324 *supra*, is generally similar.

49. See, e.g., Serrano v. Unruh, 652 P.2d 985 (Cal. 1982).

50. See §§314, 318(b)(6), 103 Stat. at 743, 747. In practice these timber sales typically auction off the public forests at below-cost subsidized prices. Section 318's quasi-judicial findings were held unconstitutional on separation of powers grounds, Seattle Audubon v. Robertson, 914 F.2d 1311 (9th Cir. 1990); cert. granted, 111 S.Ct. 2886 (1991). See pages 674–682 *infra*.

Section 318 is a "rider" because it was tacked onto the on-rolling spending bill. In fact, attaching such substantive law provisions onto appropriations bills violates House Rule 23 and Senate Rule 16, but through parliamentary manoeuvres the rules were not applied.

old-growth Forest Service public lands in the Pacific Northwest. See page 674 *infra*. For now it is sufficient to note that plaintiffs had successfully shown that corporate and agency plans for logging these ancient forests were in violation of law. The appropriations rider was intended to end the citizens' disruption of ongoing practices.

What is the theory of such appropriations riders? They do not repeal or amend laws that stand in the way of promoters' enterprises. (Repeals or amendments are straightforward legislative alternatives available to Congress, and have been used in various settings over the years.)[51] Instead it merely removes the citizens' ability to get preliminary injunctions (and forecloses permanent injunctions except in extraordinary cases where citizens are able to prove on the restricted merits that agency action was arbitrary, capricious, etc.)[52]

Such appropriations riders are effective federal law for only one fiscal year, although when lobbyists successfully add them to an appropriations bill for one year, they tend to reappear thereafter. [53]

Isn't the rider's approach quite revealing? Its obvious rationale is that – absent citizen enforcement – neither the private industry logging the lands nor the two federal agencies supervising the logging will comply with federal law. In order to nullify the law, one doesn't have to repeal it, but only eliminate the citizen enforcers.

Why was this done by appropriations rider rather than by normal congressional legislation? The legislative standing committees with jurisdiction over forests and wildlife generally oppose any such overrides of judicial review. Senators Hatfield and Adams of Washington, Packwood of Oregon, and their timber industry backers went to the appropriations committees instead. Appropriations committees are often thought to be much more closely aligned to vested interests; they wield extraordinary power through the fact that they and they alone hold annual hearings and pass funding legislation for virtually every federal agency program. Once a rider has been attached to a bill by the appropriations committees, there are so many public spending projects linked to them that the bills become almost impregnable, and "veto-proof."

2. The constitutionality of removing court jurisdiction. Provisions of §318 were challenged in several citizen suits. In two related cases, it was declared unconstitutional. The court in Seattle Audubon Society v. Robertson, 914 F.2d 1311 (9th Cir.

---

51. See Chapter 13 at page 670 *infra*.

52. In the timing of such citizen efforts, practically speaking, preliminary injunctions are the entire battle. If preliminary relief staying the agency action is not ordered, the forest is stripped bare before plaintiffs can get to trial on the permanent injunctions.

53. After 458 law professors from 61 schools in 41 states and the District of Columbia sent a letter to leaders of the House and Senate protesting §318 as a "dangerous precedent" for undermining protective federal laws, however, §318 was not re-promulgated for fiscal year 1991. The fight was successfully led by Senators Baucus and Chaffee, who not coincidentally were the ranking members of the standing committees bypassed by the appropriations stratagem, and by the Sierra Club Legal Defense Fund.

1990) did not focus on §318(g), the removal of judicial review jurisdiction, but rather on §318(b)(6) which specifically declared that the courts should find all statutory requirements satisfied in *Seattle Audubon* and a companion case, *Portland Audubon*.[54]

In several other cases, courts have upheld restrictions on judicial review.[55]

Beyond the question of legislating on appropriations bills, is there any constitutional limit to the ability of special interest riders to foreclose judicial review of targeted questions? After a broad-ranging review of such provisions overriding judicial review, a recent study ended its constitutional and statutory analysis with the plaint that "it is crucial that courts apply a heightened standard of review in examining measures that limit judicial review.... Judicial review is fundamental to the 'very essence of liberty' [citing Marbury v. Madison, 5 U.S. 137, 163 (1803)]. The Supreme Court has held that any 'statutory preclusion of judicial review must be demonstrated clearly and convincingly.'"[56]

The *Seattle Audubon* court noted on one hand that if Congress changes the terms of a statute, then the court must follow, and, on the other hand, if Congress attempts to direct a particular judicial decision without changing the statute, it may not do so, because that is the role of the courts. But what about the hidden issue that lies between? If Congress doesn't change the law, but removes judicial jurisdiction to consider violations in whole or in part, does that violate the Article III judicial power and the separation of powers doctrine? Absent a clear constitutional barrier to such legislative shortcuts, special interest attempts to foreclose citizen enforcement will undoubtedly continue, pressuring Congress to write specific exemptions from judicial review so that statutes will go unenforced.

b. THE COURTS' ABILITY TO CONSTRICT STANDING

The evolution of standing, making the administrative and judicial forums open to citizen participation, was noted earlier as an important part of the 1960s' pluralistic expansion of the legal system. The standing doctrine continues to be a threshold question in all litigation, and is not subject to clear objective standards.

Standing is ultimately a judicial doctrine. It is courts that determine when citizens can claim standing and when they cannot, even under statutory grants of standing. Standing principles can be broadened to permit litigation on issues for which judges want to have dispositive determinations, and conversely can be narrowed to nip off challenges that courts would rather not have to decide. In the

54. 712 F. Supp. 1456 (D. Ore. 1989). The Ninth Circuit wrote, "Congress can amend or repeal any law, even for the purpose of ending pending litigation. But Congress cannot prescribe a rule for a decision of a cause in a certain way where no new circumstances have been created by legislation. 914 F.2d 1311, 1315-1317 (9th Cir. 1990) (citing U.S. v. Klein, 80 U.S. 128, 147 (1871)). The Forest Service's request for a writ of certiorari in *Seattle Audubon* was granted. 111 S. Ct. 2886 (1991).

55. See Oregon Natural Resources Council v. Mohla, 895 F.2d 627 (9th Cir. 1990).

56. Sher and Hunting, Eroding the Landscape, Eroding the Laws: Congressional Exemptions from Judicial Review of Environmental Laws, 15 Harv. Envtl L. Rev. 435, 481 (1991) (citing NLRB v. United Food & Comm'l Wkrs. Union, 484 U.S. 112, 131 (1987)).

federal courts, standing turns on several different inquiries: on personal injury-in-fact, which has been held necessary to establish Article III "case or controversy" standing; on the "zone of interests" test, a court-made rule drawn from the APA's §702, requiring that plaintiffs must be within a class that Congress intended to benefit when it passed the law that they are attempting to enforce;[57] and several judge-made "prudential principles" by which courts have denied standing – where plaintiffs attempt to argue the claims of third parties, where the judicial remedy would not relieve the particular injury claimed, etc.[58]

In the following case, the Supreme Court applied the first of these tests stringently to avoid judicial review in a case where the federal agency had presumptively violated the requirements of federal statutes. Is the effect of the Court's decision to permit the violations to go unchallenged?

Manuel Lujan, Jr., Secretary of the Interior v. National Wildlife Federation

United States Supreme Court, 1990

_ U.S. _, 110 S. Ct. 3177, 111 L. Ed. 2d 695

SCALIA, J. In this case we must decide whether respondent, the National Wildlife Federation (hereinafter respondent), is a proper party to challenge actions of the Federal Government relating to certain public lands.

Respondent filed this action in 1985 in the United States District Court for the District of Columbia against petitioners the United States Department of Interior, the Secretary of Interior, and the Director of the Bureau of Land Management (BLM), an agency within the Department. In its amended complaint, respondent alleged that petitioners had violated the Federal Land Policy and Management Act of 1976 (FLPMA), 43 U.S.C.A. §1701 et seq. (1982 ed.), the National Environmental Policy of Act of 1969 (NEPA), 42 U.S.C.A. §4321 et seq., and §10(e) of the Administrative Procedure Act (APA), 5 U.S.C.A. §706, in the course of administering what the complaint called the "land withdrawal review program" of the BLM....

[A variety of federal statutes over the years have given the Secretary of the Interior and President] authority to classify lands for the purpose of either disposal or retention by the Federal Government.[59] In 1976, Congress passed the FLPMA,

57. This is a test that the Supreme Court has often interpreted broadly. See Clarke v. Securities Industry Ass'n, 479 U.S. 388 (1987):

> The [APA] should be construed "not grudgingly but as serving a broad remedial purpose".... The "zone of interest" formula [in *Data Processing,* 397 U.S. 153 (1970)] has not proved self-explanatory, but significant guidance can be drawn from that opinion. First, the Court interpreted the phrase "a relevant statute" in §702 quite broadly (indeed even using a different statute from the one sued under).... Second, the Court approved the "trend...toward [the] enlargement of the class of people who may protest administrative action".... The test is not meant to be especially demanding; in particular there need be no indication of congressional purpose to benefit the would-be plaintiff. 479 U.S. at 395-400.

58. See, e.g., Valley Forge Christian College v. Americans United, 454 U.S. 464 (1982).

59. [The statutes cited by the Court included: 30 U.S.C.A. §22 et seq. (Mining Law of 1872); 30 U.S.C.A. §181 et seq. (Mineral Lands Leasing Act of 1920); the Pickett Act, 43 U.S.C.A. §141, (repealed 1976); Taylor Grazing Act of 1934, 43 U.S.C.A. §315f; the 1964 Classification and Multiple Use Act, 43 U.S.C.A. §§1411-1418. In 1934, President Roosevelt withdrew all unreserved public lands from the disposal process until such time as they were classified, ending the era of giveaways. The Public Land Law Review Commission established by Congress in 1964 to study land policy recommended that Congress should provide for a careful review of all Executive withdrawals and reservations. See Public Land Law Review Commission, One Third of the Nation's Land (1970).]

which repealed many of the miscellaneous laws governing disposal of public land, 43 U.S.C.A. §1701 et seq., and established a policy in favor of retaining public lands for multiple use management. It directed the Secretary to "prepare and maintain on a continuing basis an inventory of all public lands and their resource and other values," §1711(a), required land use planning for public lands, and established criteria to be used for that purpose, §1712. It provided that existing classifications of public lands were subject to review in the land use planning process, and that the Secretary could "modify or terminate any such classification consistent with such land use plans." §1712(d).... Finally it directed the Secretary within 15 years, to review withdrawals in existence in 1976 in 11 western States, §1714(*l*)(1)....[60] The activities undertaken by the BLM to comply with these various provisions constitute what respondent's amended complaint styles the BLM's "land withdrawal review program," which is the subject of the current litigation.

In its complaint, respondent averred generally that the reclassification of some withdrawn lands and the return of others to the public domain would open the lands up to mining activities, thereby destroying their natural beauty. Respondent alleged that petitioners, in the course of administering the Nation's public lands, had violated the FLPMA by failing to "develop, maintain, and, when appropriate, revise land use plans which provide by tracts or areas for the use of the public lands," §1712(a); failing to submit recommendations as to withdrawals in the 11 western States to the President, §1714(*l*); failing to consider multiple uses for the disputed lands, §1732(a), focusing inordinately on such uses as mineral exploitation and development; and failing to provide public notice of decisions, §§1701(a)(5), 1712(c)(9), 1712(f), and 1739(e). Respondent also claimed that petitioners had violated NEPA [by not preparing a "programmatic" environmental impact statement on the land classification program].... Finally, respondent alleged that all of the above actions were "arbitrary, capricious, an abuse of discretion, or otherwise not in accordance with law," and should therefore be set aside pursuant to §10(e) of the APA, 5 U.S.C.A. §706. Appended to the amended complaint was a schedule of specific land status determinations, which the complaint stated had been "taken by defendants since January 1, 1981"; each was identified by a listing in the Federal Register.

In December 1985, the District Court granted respondent's motion for a preliminary injunction prohibiting petitioners from "[m]odifying, terminating or altering any withdrawal, classification, or other designation governing the protection of lands in the public domain that was in effect on January 1, 1981," and from "[t]aking any action inconsistent" with any such withdrawal, classification, or designation. In a subsequent order, the court denied petitioners' motion under Rule 12(b) of the Federal Rules of Civil Procedure to dismiss the complaint for failure to demonstrate standing to challenge petitioners' actions under the APA, 5 U.S.C.A. §702. The Court of Appeals affirmed both orders. NWF v. Burford, 835 F.2d 305 (1987)....

To support the [district court's standing ruling] the Court of Appeals pointed to the affidavits of two of respondent's members, Peggy Kay Peterson and Richard Erman, which claimed use of land "in the vicinity" of the land covered by two of the listed actions. Thus, the Court of Appeals concluded, there was "concrete indication that [respondent's] members use specific lands covered by the agency's

60. [During the Reagan Administration, Secretary James Watt, an adherent of the "Sagebrush Rebellion," began reclassifying many tracts of Western federal lands to open them up to mining, grazing, timber cutting, and other extractive industries.]

Program and will be adversely affected by the agency's actions," and the complaint was "sufficiently specific for purposes of a motion to dismiss."...

Back before the District Court, petitioners again claimed, this time by means of a motion for summary judgment under Rule 56 of the Federal Rules of Civil Procedure (which motion had been outstanding during the proceedings before the Court of Appeals), that respondent had no standing to seek judicial review of petitioners' actions under the APA. After argument on this motion, and in purported response to the court's postargument request for additional briefing, respondent submitted four additional member affidavits pertaining to the issue of standing. The District Court rejected them as untimely, vacated the injunction, and granted the Rule 56 motion to dismiss....

The Court of Appeals reversed. NWF v. Burford, 878 F.2d 422 (1989). It both found the Peterson and Erman affidavits sufficient in themselves, and held that it was an abuse of discretion not to consider the four additional affidavits as well....

We turn...to whether the specific facts alleged in the two affidavits considered by the District Court raised a genuine issue of fact as to whether an "agency action" taken by petitioners caused respondent to be "adversely affected or aggrieved...within the meaning of a relevant statute." We assume, since it has been uncontested, that the allegedly affected interests set forth in the affidavits – "recreational use and aesthetic enjoyment" – are sufficiently related to the purposes of respondent association that respondent meets the requirements of §702 if any of its members do....

We also think that whatever "adverse effect" or "aggrievement" is established by the affidavits was "within the meaning of the relevant statute" – i.e., met the "zone of interests" test.... The only issue, then, is whether the facts alleged in the affidavits showed that those interests *of Peterson and Erman* were actually affected.

The Peterson affidavit averred:

> My recreational use and aesthetic enjoyment of federal lands, particularly those in the vicinity of South Pass–Green Mountain, Wyoming have been and continue to be adversely affected in fact by the unlawful actions of the Bureau and the Department. In particular, the South Pass–Green Mountain area of Wyoming has been opened to the staking of mining claims and oil and gas leasing, an action which threatens the aesthetic beauty and wildlife habitat potential of these lands.

Erman's affidavit was substantially the same as Peterson's, with respect to all except the area involved; he claimed use of land "in the vicinity of Grand Canyon National Park, the Arizona Strip (Kanab Plateau), and the Kaibab National Forest." The District Court found the Peterson affidavit inadequate for the following reasons:

> Peterson...claims that she uses federal lands *in the vicinity* of the South Pass–Green Mountain area of Wyoming for recreational purposes and for aesthetic enjoyment and that her recreational and aesthetic enjoyment has been and continues to be adversely affected as a result of the decision of BLM to open it to the staking of mining claims and oil and gas leasing.... This decision [W-6228] opened up to mining approximately 4500 acres within a two million acre area, the balance of which, with the exception of 2000 acres, has always been open to mineral leasing and mining.... There is no showing that Peterson's recreational use and enjoyment extends to the particular 4500 acres covered by the decision to terminate classification to the remainder of the two million acres affected by the termination. All she claims is that she

> uses land "in the vicinity." The affidavit on its face contains only a bare allegation of injury, and fails to show specific facts supporting the affiant's allegation. 699 F. Supp. at 331.

The District Court found the Erman affidavit "similarly flawed."

> The magnitude of Erman's claimed injury stretches the imagination.... [T]he Arizona Strip consists of all lands in Arizona north and west of the Colorado River on approximately 5.5 million acres, an area one-eighth the size of the State of Arizona....

The Court of Appeals disagreed with the District Court's assessment as to the Peterson affidavit (and thus found it unnecessary to consider the Erman affidavit) for the following reason:

> If Peterson was not referring to lands in this 4500-acre affected area, her allegation of impairment to her use and enjoyment would be meaningless, or perjurious.... [T]he trial court overlooks the fact that unless Peterson's language is read to refer to the lands affected by the Program, the affidavit is, at best, a meaningless document.
>
> At a minimum [sic], Peterson's affidavit is ambiguous regarding whether the adversely affected lands are the ones she uses. When presented with ambiguity on a motion for summary judgment, a District Court must resolve any factual issues of controversy in favor of the non-moving party....

In ruling upon a Rule 56 motion, "a District Court must resolve any factual issues of controversy in favor of the non-moving party" only in the sense that, where the facts specifically averred by that party contradict facts specifically averred by the movant, the motion must be denied. That is a world apart from assuming that general averments embrace the specific facts needed to sustain the complaint....

Respondent places great reliance, as did the Court of Appeals, upon our decision in United States v. Students Challenging Regulatory Agency Procedures (SCRAP), 412 U.S. 669 (1973). The SCRAP opinion, whose expansive expression of what would suffice for §702 review under its particular facts has never since been emulated by this Court, is of no relevance here since it involved not a Rule 56 motion for summary judgment but a Rule 12(b) motion to dismiss on the pleadings....

Respondent alleges that violation of the law is rampant within this program – failure to revise land use plans in proper fashion, failure to submit certain recommendations to Congress, failure to consider multiple use, inordinate focus upon mineral exploitation, failure to provide adequate environmental impact statements. Perhaps so. But respondent cannot seek *wholesale* improvement of this program by court decree, rather than in the offices of the Department or the halls of Congress, where programmatic improvements are normally made....

In the present case, the individual actions of the BLM identified in the six affidavits can be regarded as rules of general applicability (a "rule" is defined in the APA as agency action of "general or particular applicability *and future effect*," 5 U.S.C.A. §551(4)) announcing, with respect to vast expanses of territory that they cover, the agency's intent to grant requisite permission for certain activities, to decline to interfere with other activities, and to take other particular action if requested. It may well be, then, that even those individual actions will not be ripe for challenge until some further agency action or inaction more immediately harming the plaintiff occurs. But it is at least entirely certain that the flaws in the entire "program" – consisting principally of the many individual actions referenced in the complaint, and presumably actions yet to be taken as well – cannot be laid before the courts for wholesale correction under the APA, simply because one of them that is ripe for review adversely affects one of respondent's members.

The case-by-case approach that this requires is understandably frustrating to an organization such as respondent, which has as its objective across-the-board protection of our Nation's wildlife and the streams and forests that support it. But this is the traditional, and remains the normal, mode of operation of the courts. Except where Congress explicitly provides for our correction of the administrative process at a higher level of generality, we intervene in the administration of the laws only when, and to the extent that, a specific "final agency action" has an actual or immediately threatened effect. Such an intervention may ultimately have the effect of requiring a regulation, a series of regulations, or even a whole "program" to be revised by the agency in order to avoid the unlawful result that the court discerns. But it is assuredly not as swift or as immediately far-reaching a corrective process as those interested in systemic improvement would desire. Until confided to us, however, more sweeping actions are for the other Branches....

[The court also held that NWF did not have standing in its own right because no specific agency actions were identified as injuring NWF's ability to inform its members about resource problems.]

BLACKMUN, J., dissenting, joined by BRENNAN, MARSHALL, and STEVENS, JJ.

In my view, the affidavits of Peggy Kay Peterson and Richard Loren Erman, in conjunction with other record evidence before the District Court on the motions for summary judgment, were sufficient to establish the standing of the National Wildlife Federation to bring this suit. I also conclude that the District Court abused its discretion by refusing to consider supplemental affidavits filed after the hearing on the parties' cross-motions for summary judgment. I therefore would affirm the judgment of the Court of Appeals....

The requirement that evidence be submitted is satisfied here: the Federation has offered the sworn statements of two of its members. There remains the question whether the allegations in these affidavits were sufficiently precise to satisfy the requirements of Rule 56(e). The line of demarcation between "specific" and "conclusory" allegations is hardly a bright one. But, to my mind, the allegations contained in the Peterson and Erman affidavits, in the context of the record as a whole, were adequate to defeat a motion for summary judgment....

Peterson alleged that she uses federal lands "in the vicinity of South Pass–Green Mountain, Wyoming," rather than averring that she uses the precise tract that was recently opened to mining. The agency itself has repeatedly referred to the "South Pass–Green Mountain area" in describing the region newly opened to mining. Peterson's assertion that her use and enjoyment of federal lands *have been* adversely affected by the agency's decision to permit more extensive mining is, as the Court of Appeals stated, "meaningless, or perjurious" if the lands she uses do not include those harmed by mining undertaken pursuant to termination order W-6228. To read particular assertions within the affidavit in light of the document as a whole is, as the majority might put it, "a world apart" from "presuming" facts that are neither stated nor implied simply because without them the plaintiff would lack standing. The Peterson and Erman affidavits doubtless could have been more artfully drafted, but they definitely were sufficient to withstand the Government's summary judgment motion.

I also conclude that the District Court abused its discretion in refusing to consider the supplemental affidavits filed by NWF after the hearing on the summary judgment motion.... Prior to the July 22, 1988, hearing on the parties' cross-motions for summary judgment, NWF had been assured repeatedly that its prior submissions were sufficient to establish its standing to sue. In its memorandum opinion granting the Federation's motion for a preliminary injunction, the District Court stated: "We continue to find irreparable injury to plaintiff and reaffirm plaintiff's standing to bring this action." 676 F. Supp. 280, 281.... The District Court's decision to schedule a hearing on the parties' cross-motions for summary judgment provided no hint that previous assurances concerning standing were open to reconsideration.

Certainly the Federation could have submitted additional evidentiary materials in support of its claim of standing, even though it had no reason to believe further submissions were necessary. But it would hardly enhance the efficiency of the adjudicative process to encourage litigants to reargue questions previously settled in their favor....

I would affirm the judgment of the Court of Appeals.

COMMENTARY AND QUESTIONS

1. A Catch-22? Underlying this case on the merits, apparently, is the fact that the Department of Interior had no plan guiding its releases of public lands as the statute required, nor a programmatic environmental impact statement (see Chapter 12). The Court is able to prevent scrutiny of the program by asserting that (absent such a plan, or programmatic EIS), the land reclassifications are not a program, but hundreds of small cases for which challengers have to plead individual injury related to each specific parcel in order to gain standing. Thus NWF is never able to litigate the statutory question whether the land release program is a single programmatic action for purposes of FLPMA and NEPA. The court decides it is not, based on the pleadings, instead of letting it go to trial under FRCP 56(e), as the dissent notes. Could plaintiffs have broken out of this conundrum by filing a class action as representatives of the class of all other specific users of all other past and future reclassified parcels?

2. *Lujan's* legacy. What does *Lujan* do to the law of standing? Will plaintiffs just have to file more specific affidavits? Will it invite more class actions to cover the big administrative issues? Its mood is clearly strict, including its exclusion of the proferred supplemental affidavits in spite of plaintiffs' reliance on the court's earlier acceptance of standing. Is this a political case, where the court uses standing as the only way to avoid having to reverse the agency decisions on the statutory merits?

On the other hand, the Court echoes a common judicial theme, reminiscent of Judge Bergan's preface to the *Boomer* majority opinion, that courts are not the proper forum for contesting broad public policies. Therefore the *Lujan* plaintiffs were directed instead to the halls of Congress and the federal bureaucracy.

Doesn't the assessment of standing in this case depend on whether you consider it a situation requiring legislative oversight, administrative discretion, or statutory enforcement?

Section 3. ENVIRONMENTALISTS' ATTEMPTS TO EXPAND AGENCY PROCEDURES

In *Overton Park*, the plaintiffs were unsuccessful in persuading the courts to grant extended procedural opportunities to challenge the highway project within the agency or to require formal findings. In subsequent years many federal courts, led by the D.C. Circuit, began to expand the procedures owed to citizen challengers – sometimes on claims of individual due process, especially in matters of "Great Public Import," and sometimes based on the review needs of courts. The following case involved both. Note also the tone of the Supreme Court opinion, the political alignments among the various parties, and how the citizen environmentalists focused their arguments on procedural claims as much as, or more than, attacking the substantive agency decision.

Vermont Yankee Nuclear Power Corp. v. Natural Resources Defense Council

United States Supreme Court, 1978
435 U.S. 519, 98 S. Ct. 1197, 55 L. Ed. 2d 460

REHNQUIST, J. In 1946, Congress enacted the Administrative Procedure Act, which as we have noted elsewhere was not only "a new, basic and comprehensive regulation of procedures in many agencies," Wong Yang Sung v. McGrath, 339 U.S. 33 (1950), but was also a legislative enactment which settled "long-continued and hard-fought contentions, and enacts a formula upon which opposing social and political forces have come to rest."...Interpreting [§4 of the Act, now codified as §553] in United States v. Allegheny-Ludlum Steel Corp., 406 U.S. 742 (1972), and United States v. Florida East Coast Ry. Co., 410 U.S. 224 (1973), we held that generally speaking this section of the Act established the maximum procedural requirements which Congress was willing to have the courts impose upon agencies in conducting rulemaking procedures. Agencies are free to grant additional procedural rights in the exercise of their discretion, but reviewing courts are generally not free to impose them if the agencies have not chosen to grant them. This is not to say necessarily that there are no circumstances which would ever justify a court in overturning agency action because of a failure to employ procedures beyond those required by the statute. But such circumstances, if they exist, are extremely rare....

It is in the light of this background of statutory and decisional law that we granted certiorari to review [a judgment] of the Court of Appeals for the District of Columbia Circuit because of our concern that [the court] had seriously misread or misapplied this statutory and decisional law cautioning reviewing courts against engrafting their own notions of proper procedures upon agencies entrusted with substantive functions by Congress. We conclude that the Court of Appeals has done just that...and we therefore remand [the case] to it for further proceedings....

Under the Atomic Energy Act of 1954, as amended, 42 U.S.C.A. §2011 et seq., the Atomic Energy Commission was given broad regulatory authority over the development of nuclear energy. Under the terms of the act, a utility seeking to construct and operate a nuclear power plant must obtain a separate permit or license at both the construction and the operation stage of the project. In order to obtain the construction permit, the utility must file a preliminary safety analysis report, an environmental report, and certain information regarding the antitrust implications of the proposed project. This application then undergoes exhaustive review by the

Commission's staff and by the Advisory Committee on Reactor Safe-guards (ACRS), a group of distinguished experts in the field of atomic energy. Both groups submit to the Commission their own evaluations, which then become part of the record of the utility's application. The Commission staff also undertakes the review required by the National Environmental Policy Act of 1969 (NEPA), 42 U.S.C.A. §4321 et seq., and prepares a draft environmental impact statement, which, after being circulated for comment, is revised and becomes a final environmental impact statement. Thereupon a three-member Atomic Safety and Licensing Board conducts a public adjudicatory hearing, and reaches a decision which can be appealed to the Atomic Safety and Licensing Appeal Board, and currently, in the Commission's discretion, to the Commission itself. The final agency decision may be appealed to the courts of appeals. The same sort of process occurs when the utility applies for a license to operate the plant, except that a hearing need only be held in contested cases and may be limited to the matters in controversy....

In December 1967, after the mandatory adjudicatory hearing and necessary review, the Commission granted petitioner Vermont Yankee a permit to build a nuclear power plant in Vernon, Vt. Thereafter, Vermont Yankee applied for an operating license. Respondent Natural Resources Defense Council (NRDC) objected to the granting of a license, however, and therefore a hearing on the application commenced on August 10, 1971. Excluded from consideration at the hearings, over NRDC's objection, was the issue of the environmental effects of operations to reprocess fuel or dispose of wastes resulting from the reprocessing operations. This ruling was affirmed by the Appeal Board in June 1972.

In November 1972, however, the Commission, making specific reference to the Appeal Board's decision with respect to the Vermont Yankee License, instituted rulemaking proceedings "that would specifically deal with the question of consideration of environmental effects associated with the uranium fuel cycle in the individual cost-benefit analyses for light water cooled nuclear power reactors." The notice of proposed rulemaking offered two alternatives, both predicated on a report prepared by the commission's staff entitled Environmental Survey of the Nuclear Fuel Cycle. The first would have required no quantitative evaluation of the environmental hazards of fuel reprocessing or disposal because the Environmental Survey had found them to be slight. The second would have specified numerical values for the environmental impact of this part of the fuel cycle, which values would then be incorporated into a table, along with the other relevant factors, to determine the overall cost-benefit balance for each operating license.

Much of the controversy in this case revolves around the procedures used in the rulemaking hearing which commenced in February 1973. In a supplemental notice of hearing the Commission indicated that while discovery or cross-examination would not be utilized, the Environmental Survey would be available to the public before the hearing along with the extensive background documents cited therein. All participants would be given a reasonable opportunity to present their position and could be represented by counsel if they so desired. Written and, time permitting, oral statements would be received and incorporated into the record. All persons giving oral statements would be subject to questioning by the Commission. At the conclusion of the hearing, a transcript would be made available to the public and the record would remain open for 30 days to allow the filing of supplemental written statements. More than 40 individuals and organizations representing a wide variety of interests submitted written comments. On January 17, 1973, the Licensing Board held a planning session to schedule the appearance of witnesses and to discuss methods for compiling a record. The hearing was held on February 1 and 2, with participation by a number of groups, including the Commission's staff, the United States Environmental Protection Agency, a manufacturer of reactor equipment, a trade association from the nuclear industry, a group of electric utility companies, and a group called Consolidated National Intervenors which represented 79 groups and individuals including respondent NRDC....

The Licensing Board forwarded its report to the Commission without rendering any decision. The Licensing Board identified as the principal procedural question the propriety of declining to use full formal adjudicatory procedures. The major substantive issue was the technical adequacy of the Environmental Survey.

In April 1974, the Commission issued a rule which adopted the second of the two proposed alternatives described above. The Commission also approved the procedures used at the hearing, and indicated that the record, including the Environmental Survey, provided an "adequate data base for the regulation adopted."... Respondents appealed from both the Commission's adoption of the rule and its decision to grant Vermont Yankee's license to the Court of Appeals for the District of Columbia Circuit.

With respect to the challenge of Vermont Yankee's license, the court first ruled that in the absence of effective rulemaking proceedings, the Commission must deal with the environmental impact of fuel reprocessing and disposal in individual licensing proceedings. The court then examined the rulemaking proceedings and, despite the fact that it appeared that the agency employed all the procedures required by 5 U.S.C.A. §553 and more, the court determined the proceedings to be inadequate and overturned the rule. Accordingly, the Commission's determination with respect to Vermont Yankee's license was... remanded for further proceedings.

Petitioner Vermont Yankee first argues that the Commission should grant a license to operate a nuclear reactor without any consideration of waste disposal and fuel reprocessing. We find, however, that this issue is no longer presented by the record in this case.... Vermont Yankee will produce annually well over 100 pounds of radioactive wastes, some of which will be highly toxic.... Many of these substances must be isolated for anywhere from 600 to hundreds of thousands of years. It is hard to argue that these wastes do not constitute "adverse environmental effects which cannot be avoided should the proposal be implemented," or that by operating nuclear power plants we are not making "irreversible and irretrievable commitments of resources." [Ed. note: these are requirements from NEPA §102].... For these reasons we hold that the Commission acted well within its statutory authority when it considered the back end of the fuel cycle in individual licensing proceedings.

We next turn to the invalidation of the fuel cycle rule. But before determining whether the Court of Appeals reached a permissible result, we must determine exactly what result it did reach, and in this case that is no mean feat. Vermont Yankee argues that the court invalidated the rule because of the inadequacy of the procedures employed in the proceedings. Respondents, on the other hand, labeling petitioner's view of the decision a "straw man," argue to this Court that the court merely held that the record was inadequate to enable the reviewing court to determine whether the agency had fulfilled its statutory obligation....

After a thorough examination of the opinion itself, we conclude that while the matter is not entirely free from doubt, the majority of the Court of Appeals struck down the rule because of the perceived inadequacies of the procedures employed in the rulemaking proceedings. The court first determined the intervenors' primary argument to be "that the decision to preclude 'discovery or cross-examination' denied them a meaningful opportunity to participate in the proceedings as guaranteed by due process." The court then went on to frame the issue for decision thus: "Thus, we are called upon to decide whether the procedures provided by the agency were sufficient to ventilate the issues." The court conceded that absent extraordinary circumstances it is improper for a reviewing court to prescribe the procedural format an agency must follow, but it likewise clearly thought it entirely appropriate to "scrutinize the record as a whole to insure that genuine opportunities to participate in a meaningful way were provided...." The court also refrained from actually ordering the agency to follow any specific procedures, but there is little doubt in our minds that the ineluctable mandate of the court's decision is that the procedures afforded during the hearings were inadequate. This conclusion is particularly buttressed by the fact that after the court examined the record, particularly the testimony of Dr. Pittman, and declared it insufficient, the court proceeded to discuss at some length the necessity for further procedural devices or a more "sensitive" application of those devices employed during the proceedings. The exploration of the record and the statement regarding its insufficiency might initially lead one to conclude that the court was only examining the sufficiency of the evidence, but the remaining portions of the opinion dispel any doubt that this was certainly not the sole or even the principal basis of the decision. Accordingly, we feel compelled to address the opinion on its own terms, and we conclude that it was wrong.

In prior opinions we have intimated that even in a rulemaking proceeding when an agency is making a "quasi-judicial" determination by which a very small number of persons are "'exceptionally affected, in each case upon individual grounds,'" in some circumstances additional [trial-type] procedures may be required in order to afford the aggrieved individuals due process. United States v. Florida East Coast R. Co., 410 U.S. at 242, 245 (quoting from Bi-Metallic Investment Co. v. State Board of Equalization, 239 U.S. 441, 446 (1915)). It might also be true, although we do not think the issue is presented in this case and accordingly do not decide it, that a totally unjustified departure from well-settled agency procedures of long standing might require judicial correction.

But this much is absolutely clear. Absent constitutional constraints or extremely compelling circumstances the "administrative agencies 'should be free to fashion their own rules of procedure and to pursue methods of inquiry capable of permitting them to discharge their multitudinous duties.'" FCC v. Schreiber, 381 U.S. 279, 290 (1965).

We have continually repeated this theme through the years.... [I]n determining the proper scope of judicial review of agency action under the Natural Gas Act, we held that while a court may have occasion to remand an agency decision because of the inadequacy of the record, the agency should normally be allowed to "exercise its administrative discretion in deciding how, in light of internal organization considerations, it may best proceed to develop the needed evidence and how its prior decision should be modified in light of such evidence as develops." We went on to emphasize: "At least in the absence of substantial justification for doing otherwise, a reviewing court may not, after determining that additional evidence is requisite for adequate review, proceed by dictating to the agency the methods, procedures, and time dimension of the needed inquiry and ordering the results to be reported to the court without opportunity for further consideration on the basis of the new evidence by the agency. Such a procedure clearly runs the risk of 'propel[ling] the court into the domain which Congress has set aside exclusively for the administrative agency.' SEC v. Chenery Corp., 332 U.S. 194, 196 (1947)."

Respondent NRDC argues that §[553] of the Administrative Procedure Act merely establishes lower procedural bounds and that a court may routinely require more than the minimum when an agency's proposed rule addresses complex or technical factual issues or "Issues of great Public Import." We have, however, previously shown that our decisions reject this view.... We also think the legislative history, even the part which it cites, does not bear out its contention. The Senate Report explains what eventually became §[553] thus: "This subsection states...the minimum requirements of public rule making procedure short of statutory hearing. Under it agencies might in addition confer with industry advisory committees, consult organizations, hold informal 'hearings,' and the like. Considerations of practicality, necessity, and public interest...will naturally govern the agency's determination of the extent to which public proceedings should go. Matters of great import, or those where the public submission of facts will be either useful to the agency or a protection to the public, should naturally be accorded more elaborate public procedures." S.Rep. No. 752, 79th Cong., 1st Sess., 14-15 (1945)....

The House Report is in complete accord: "The bill is an outline of minimum essential rights and procedures.... It affords private parties a means of knowing what their rights are and how they may protect them.... [The bill contains] the essentials of the different forms of administrative proceedings...." H.R.Rep. No. 1980, 79th Cong., 2d Sess., 9, 16-17 (1946). And the Attorney General's Manual on the Administrative Procedure Act 31, 35 (1947), a contemporaneous interpretation previously given some deference by this Court because of the role played by the Department of Justice in drafting the legislation, further confirms that view. In short, all of this leaves little doubt that Congress intended that the discretion of the *agencies* and not that of the courts be exercised in determining when extra procedural devices should be employed.

There are compelling reasons for construing §[553] in this manner. In the first place, if courts continually review agency proceedings to determine whether the agency employed procedures which were, in the court's opinion, perfectly tailored to reach what the court perceives to be the "best" or "correct" result, judicial review would be totally unpredictable. And the agencies, operating under this vague injunction to employ the "best" procedures and facing the threat of reversal if they did not, would undoubtedly adopt full adjudicatory procedures in every instance. Not only would this totally disrupt the statutory scheme, through which Congress enacted "a formula upon which opposing social and political forces have come to rest," Wong Yang Sung v. McGrath, 339 U.S. at 40, but all the inherent advantages of informal rulemaking would be totally lost.

Secondly, it is obvious that the court in these cases reviewed the agency's choice of procedures on the basis of the record actually produced at the hearing, and not on the basis of the information available to the agency when it made the decision to structure the proceedings in a certain way. This sort of Monday morning quarterbacking not only encourages but almost compels the agency to conduct all rulemaking proceedings with the full panoply of procedural devices normally associated only with adjudicatory hearings.

Finally, and perhaps most importantly, this sort of review fundamentally misconceives the nature of the standard for judicial review of an agency rule. The court below uncritically assumed that additional procedures will automatically result in a more adequate record because it will give interested parties more of an opportunity to participate and contribute to the proceedings. But informal rulemaking need not be based solely on the transcript of a hearing held before an agency. Indeed, the agency need not even hold a formal hearing. See 5 U.S.C.A. §553(c). Thus, the adequacy of the "record" in this type of proceeding is not correlated directly to the type of procedural devices employed, but rather turns on whether the agency has followed the statutory mandate of the Administrative Procedure Act or other relevant statutes. If the agency is compelled to support the rule which it ultimately adopts with the type of record produced only after a full adjudicatory hearing, it simply will have no choice but to conduct a full adjudicatory hearing prior to promulgating every rule. In sum, this sort of unwarranted judicial examination of perceived procedural shortcomings of a rulemaking proceeding can do nothing but seriously interfere with that process prescribed by Congress....

In short, nothing in the APA,...the circumstances of this case, the nature of the issues being considered, past agency practice, or the statutory mandate under which the Commission operates, permitted the court to review and overturn the rulemaking proceeding on the basis of the procedural devices employed (or not employed) by the Commission so long as the Commission employed at least the statutory *minima*, a matter about which there is no doubt in this case.

There remains, of course, the question of whether the challenged rule finds sufficient justification in the administrative proceedings that it should be upheld by the reviewing court. Judge Tamm, concurring in the result reached by the majority of the Court of Appeals, thought that it did not. There are also intimations in the majority opinion which suggest that the judges who joined it likewise may have thought the administrative proceedings an insufficient basis upon which to predicate the rule in question. We accordingly remand so that the Court of Appeals may review the rule as the Administrative Procedure Act provides. We have made it abundantly clear before that when there is a contemporaneous explanation of the agency decision, the validity of that action must "stand or fall on the propriety of that finding, judged, of course, by the appropriate standard of review. If that finding is not sustainable on the administrative record made, then the Comptroller's decision must be vacated and the matter remanded to him for further consideration." Camp v. Pitts, 411 U.S. 138, 143 (1973). The court should engage in this kind of review and not stray beyond the judicial province to explore the procedural format or to impose upon the agency its own notion of which procedures are "best" or most likely to further some vague, undefined public good....

[The procedural obstacles posed by the court of appeals] border on the Kafkaesque. Nuclear energy may some day be a cheap, safe source of power or it may not. But Congress has made a choice to at least try nuclear energy, establishing a reasonable review process in which courts are to play only a limited role. The fundamental policy questions appropriately resolved in Congress and in the state legislatures are not subject to reexamination in the federal courts under the guise of judicial review of agency action. Time may prove wrong the decision to develop nuclear energy,[61] but it is Congress or the States within their appropriate agencies which must eventually make that judgment.

Reversed and remanded.

BLACKMUN and POWELL, JJ., took no part in the consideration or decision of these cases.

---

61. [Eds.: What does this latter clause imply? Cf. Chapter 10 on pre-emption of state nuclear regulations.]

COMMENTARY AND QUESTIONS

1. Tactics. In procedural terms, what was the NRC attempting to do in *Vermont Yankee*? By shifting the safety and radiation waste disposal questions into an informal rulemaking proceeding, thereafter to be published as a regulation that could be simply incorporated by reference, the agency would avoid having to face questioning and cross-examination on the issue in all future licensing adjudications. If the question remained in the contested cases, it would be subject to all the trial type procedures: full notice, full discovery, full cross examination, full right to present contrary evidence. In the rule-making proceeding itself, the agency did give hybrid procedures, more than mere notice and comment rule-making, but it prohibited discovery and much cross-examination. Would those really have made much difference to the agency's ultimate decision? After the *Vermont Yankee* decision, can agencies push environmental intervenors back into the closet, or do the continuing requirements of judicial review keep the intervenors as active players despite Justice Rehnquist's opinion?

2. What was the holding of *Vermont Yankee*? *Vermont Yankee* is a ringing denunciation of the Court of Appeal's requirements of agency procedures to benefit citizen environmental intervenors. Justice Rehnquist successfully argued that the APA's procedural minimum requirements for agencies were now also the maximum procedures that courts could require. Ironically, in doing so he relied on cases like *Wong Yang Sung*, in which the Court had actually granted extended process far beyond statutory requirements in order to protect individuals against agency procedures. What narrow exceptions to the new rule against court-expanded procedures would the Rehnquist opinion allow? He notes several situations in which courts may force agencies to grant more process. See page 584 *supra*.[62]

But note the penultimate paragraph in the *Vermont Yankee* excerpt. The entire case was sent back for further review on the adequacy of the factual record: whether the NRC had shown enough facts so that a court could determine that reasonable NRC officials could or could not have decided as they did. This is a second kind of procedural argument – that for the *courts'* own sake, rather than for citizens, agencies must produce a sufficient formal or informal review record to permit judges to apply whatever standard of substantive review applies to the decision. The needs of judicial reviewers thus can still become the tail that wags the dog (as in *Overton Park*).

Ultimately the NRC prepared a protocol rule with further documentation and research, which was upheld against citizen challenge in Baltimore Gas & Electric v. NRDC, 462 U.S. 87 (1983).

3. The substantive question on the *Vermont Yankee* record. The factual issue that triggered the *Vermont Yankee* remand appears to have been the shakiness of the

62. One he doesn't note is the entire sector of agency adjudications. Since the APA provides no standards for less-than-formal adjudications, courts are not limited by the *Vermont Yankee* rationale in their ability to require that various procedures be added to agencies' informal adjudications.

report by Dr. Pittman, which was the basis of the NRC decision. Dr. Pittman had devoted most of his report to proposed federal repositories for above-ground storage of wastes, and less than two pages to the problem of geologic waste disposal. The NRC subsequently abandoned above-ground storage, and turned to geologic disposal solutions (although these have also been almost impossible to site). The further problem was that the Pittman report, upon which the NRC rule was based, had been produced without an extensive research effort. Might cross examination, if it had been available, have usefully focused on the thinness of this particular piece of evidence?

4. The "hard look" doctrine. Prior to *Vermont Yankee,* and subsequent to the decision as well, federal courts have enunciated what is called the "hard look" doctrine: when Congress has set a statutory standard for agencies to apply, courts must see enough evidence on the record to be satisfied that the agency itself took a "hard look" at all relevant facts and the statutory standards that applied to them. The "hard look" determination is obviously subjective. Does *Vermont Yankee* do anything to dampen the courts' scrutiny of an agency's hard look?

5. Rulemaking/adjudication: tactical considerations. Other settings illustrate other tactical uses of the rulemaking/adjudication distinction. In some cases, unlike the NRC in *Vermont Yankee,* an agency will seek to proceed by adjudication, rather than rule-making, because subsequent courts do not hold agencies to the terms of their adjudicative precedents as strictly as they do to published rules. Conversely, regulated parties sometimes want to have rule-making on a matter because, unlike adjudication, rule-making is prospective and cannot penalize past activities. Regulated parties, on the other hand, sometimes prefer adjudication, because of the formal trial-type procedures that normally accompany agency adjudicative processes.

Yet another twist shows judicial use of the rulemaking/adjudication distinction. In New York v. Thomas, 802 F.2d 1443 (D.C. Cir. 1986), then-Judge Scalia used the argument of mandatory rulemaking to nullify an environmental injunction on acid rain. According to §115 of the Clean Air Act (the result of a strenuous compromise between environmentalists and polluters), once EPA makes a formal determination that transboundary international air pollution is occurring, and that the foreign country (i.e., Canada) grants reciprocal standing to injured Americans, then the EPA must ensure that state air pollution plans[63] take account of such acid precipitation and restrict it. Section 115 was used by Ontario and several downwind states, including New York and Massachusetts, to try to abate acid rain coming from Midwestern states. Just before he left office, President Carter's EPA administrator made a formal finding under §115, dubbed the "Costle hand grenade," requiring certain states to clean up their acid rain emissions. Judge Scalia overturned the trial court's injunction on the ground that what Costle had done was "rulemaking" (because, like a rule under the APA definition, it had "future effect"), and therefore

63. See Chapter 18.

was void because EPA had not gone through notice and comment rulemaking before acting.[64]

Would Judge Scalia's argument overrule *Overton Park*? There the Secretary's §4(f) decision clearly had future force and effect. If indeed the *Thomas* opinion is correct, it is a potent administrative law weapon for environmentalists and polluters alike, requiring any administrative decision that has future effect to go through notice and comment rulemaking, a possibility that could bring government to its knees.

The distinctions between rulemaking and adjudication, and their tactical consequences, emphasize that administrative law is surprisingly young and evolving. Other interesting administrative law issues will arise in later chapters.[65]

E. STATUTORY INTERPRETATION: HOW, BY WHOM?

Section 1. JUDICIAL REVIEW OF AGENCY INTERPRETATIONS OF LAW

Chevron U.S.A., Inc. v. Natural Resources Defense Council
United States Supreme Court, 1984
467 U.S. 837, 104 S. Ct. 2778, 81 L. Ed. 2d 694

[Section 111 of the Clean Air Act,[66] requires that tougher permit standards, based on "best available technology" (see Chapters 18 and 19), must be applied to any "new source" of pollution in areas that violate existing air quality standards. A "source" was defined in the statute as "any building, structure, facility, or installation which emits or may emit any air pollutant." In 1980, the latter statutory phrase had been interpreted by the EPA to mean that every new sub-unit or smokestack of a factory was a source that had to meet those higher standards. In 1981, however, the agency changed its definition, applying a regulatory "bubble"[67] concept: the new regulation defined the statutory term "source" to mean "all of the pollutant-emitting activities which belong to the same industrial grouping, are located on one or more contiguous or adjacent properties, and are under the control of the same person or persons." The result was that the EPA could now view an entire industrial site as a single source. If a company could offset new emissions within a plant by closing old dirtier units, there would be no *net* increase of pollutants coming from within the bubble, so new construction did not count as a new source and did not have to meet the tougher standards. The Natural Resources Defense Council sued.]

64. The Supreme Court has never specified when an agency must proceed by rulemaking as opposed to adjudication. The Scalia opinion found little precedent, and directed most of its analysis to a question not presented, whether policy rulemaking could be done without notice and comment, an argument that presumed the principal question.

65. Chapter 13, for instance, considers whether, when citizen environmentalists have proved a statutory violation, courts may permit violations to continue, based on traditional common law balancing of the equities (i.e. which party's interests and which policy considerations are more important). The Supreme Court, with one dissent, has said that judges can override legislation they consider to be outweighed by other judicial considerations. See page 666–667 infra.

66. 42 U.S.C.A. §7411, as amended in 1977.

67. Air pollution "bubbles" are considered further in Chapter 20, at page 870 *infra*.

STEVENS, J. The question presented by this case is whether EPA's decision to allow states to treat all of the pollution-emitting devices within the same industrial grouping as though they were encased within a single "bubble" is based on a reasonable construction of the statutory term "stationary source."

When a court reviews an agency's construction of the statute which it administers, it is confronted with two questions. First, always, is the question whether Congress has directly spoken to the precise question at issue. If the intent of Congress is clear, that is the end of the matter; for the court, as well as the agency, must give effect to the unambiguously expressed intent of Congress.[68] If, however, the court determines Congress has not directly addressed the precise question at issue, the court does not simply impose its own construction on the statute, as would be necessary in the absence of an administrative interpretation. Rather, if the statute is silent or ambiguous with respect to this specific issue, the question for the court is whether the agency's answer is based on a permissible construction of the statute.[69] "The power of an administrative agency to administer a congressionally created...program necessarily requires the formulation of policy in the making of rules to fill any gap left, implicitly or explicitly, by Congress."

The principle of deference to administrative interpretations has been consistently followed by this Court whenever decision as to the meaning or reach of the statute has involved reconciling conflicting policies, and a full understanding of the force of the statutory policy on the given situation has depended upon more than ordinary knowledge respecting the matters subjected to agency regulations. *Hearst Publications*, 322 U.S. 111 (1944). "...If this choice represents accommodation of conflicting policies that were committed to the agency's care by the statute, we should not disturb it unless it appears from the statute or its a legislative history that the accommodation is not one that Congress would of sanctioned...." United States. v. Shimer, 367 U.S. 374, 382 (1961).

Our review of the EPA's varying interpretations of the word "source" – both before and after the 1977 amendments – convinces us that the agency primarily responsible for administering this important legislation has consistently interpreted it flexibly – not in a sterile textual vacuum, but in the context of implementing policy decisions in a technical and complex arena.... When a challenge to an agency construction of a statutory provision, fairly conceptualized, really centers on the wisdom of the agency's policy, rather than whether it is a reasonable choice within a gap left open by Congress, the challenge must fail. In such a case, federal judges – who have no constituency – have the duty to respect legitimate policy choices made by those who do. Responsibilities for assessing the wisdom of such policy choices and resolving the struggle between competing views of the public interests are not judicial ones: "Our Constitution vests such responsibilities in the political branches." TVA v. Hill, 437 U.S. 153, 195 (1978). Reversed.

---

68. The judiciary is the final authority on issues of statutory construction and must recheck administrative constructions which are contrary to clear congressional intent. If a court, employing traditional tools of statutory construction, ascertains that Congress had an intention on the precise question at issue, that intention is the law and must be given effect [as a matter of the judges' own statutory interpretation]. [This is footnote 9 in the original opinion.]

69. The Court need not conclude that the agency construction was the only one it permissibly could have adopted to uphold the construction, or even the reading the court would have reached if the question had initially arisen in a judicial proceeding.

COMMENTARY AND QUESTIONS

1. Agency rationale for the bubble interpretation. Do you see how a bubble might result in cleaner air, despite allowing lower standards? If an industry is consistently held to the highest standards, how might that affect its ongoing plant investment decisions?

2. Deference to agency interpretations of law. Does *Chevron* set out a principle of general deference to agency interpretations of statutes, or just to agency gap-filling? The Court says that the agency is merely interpreting the term "source" rather than making law, because EPA follows Congress's overall statutory mandate to clean up the air, and there is no evidence of congressional intention on the particular question of bubbling. In what circumstances would the court *not* defer to an agency's legal interpretations? Can a court decide case-by-case whether to step in and apply its own statutory interpretation, or defer to the agency's, depending on a fairly subjective decision about whether Congress has expressed its intent on the "precise question at issue"? How "precise" need a question be?

Courts cite *Chevron* when they wish to defer to an agency's interpretation of a statute. Since *Chevron*, however, even the Supreme Court has demonstrated that it will dictate its own interpretation of statutory meaning, and will not defer to an agency's interpretation if it believes that standard norms of statutory construction, as interpreted by the court, would lead to a different answer. See INS v. Cardoza-Fonseca, 480 U.S. 421 (1987). The line between deference and judicial takeover of the fundamental decision can thus get quite hazy.

3. The "plain meaning" hypothesis? Continuing on that note, it is interesting to see how courts since *Chevron* have avoided deferring to agency interpretations of law when they disagree with them. One of the approaches is the "plain meaning" theory – that if the legal meaning of a term is clear to a court on the face of a statute or regulation, then the court will apply that interpretation regardless of the expert agency's differing opinion.[70] A recent CERCLA case dealt with §120(h) of the 1986 Superfund Amendments and Reauthorization Act (SARA), Pub. L. No. 99-499, which imposed notice and covenant requirements on federal agencies that transfer real property contaminated by hazardous substances. Section 120(h)(1) provides in relevant part that –

> the head of such department, agency, or instrumentality shall include in such contract notice of the type and quantity of such hazardous substance and notice of the time at which such storage, release or disposal took place, to the extent such information is available on the basis of a complete search of agency files.

In its regulations, however, EPA applied the notice requirements of §120(h)(1) only to real property on which hazardous substances were stored, released, or disposed of "during the time the property was owned by the United States." The EPA believed

70. See Murphy, Old Maxims Never Die: The Plain Meaning Rule and Statutory Interpretation in Modern Federal Courts, 75 Colum. L.Rev. 1299 (1975).

that Congress was primarily concerned with federal facilities (chiefly military bases and nuclear weapons facilities) whose own operations involved the storage, release, or disposal of hazardous substances, and that §120(h) therefore was not intended to apply where contamination occurred prior to the government's acquisition of the property. This interpretation, it concluded, was "more appropriate..." and would avoid imposing unfair and unmanageable obligations on federal agencies that had no role in the storage, release or disposal of hazardous substances.

The reviewing court in Hercules v. EPA[71] held differently –

> By its terms, §120(h) requires agencies to disclose all information of the kind specified (namely, the "type and quantity" of hazardous substances on the property and "the time at which [the] storage, release or disposal took place") to the extent the information is contained in the agency's files, and the plain meaning of Congress's words thus extends the government's notice obligations to properties [contaminated] by prior owners.....
>
> Where, as here, the statute's language is plain, "the sole function of the courts is to enforce it according to its terms."[72] We therefore need not look beyond the words of the statute to the legislative history for guidance....

The court nevertheless *did* apparently analyze the legislative history, for it noted that "nothing in that history in any way suggests a congressional intent inconsistent with the plain meaning of the statute's language." The court again continued beyond plain meaning in an extended statutory interpretation of §120 based on a contextual analysis and a policy analysis of congressional intent in the Act, the statute's broad remedial purposes, the limited agency burdens that would be imposed by the notice requirement, and the legislative purpose of dealing fairly with subsequent purchasers.

This typical exercise in statutory interpretation demonstrates how ready courts are to embark on the familiar task of interpreting legal language, going far beyond plain meaning.

Deference to agencies' legal interpretations, on the other hand, is most likely where a legislative scheme seems highly technical, with a wide range of details delegated to the agency's special expertise. *Chevron*, with its intricate air pollution act technicalities, was thus a particularly apt subject for deference to the agency on legal as well as factual matters. The less daunting the legal provisions faced by the courts, the less likely they are to be deferential on questions of law. Within judicial chambers the tendency is to apply the familiar judicial methods to reach an interpretation, then to consider whether the agency's interpretation agrees with the judge's view of the term's meaning, plain or fancy.[73]

---

71. 938 F.2d 276, 280, 281 (D.C. Cir. 1991).

72. United States v. Ron Pair Enterprises, Inc., 489 U.S. 235, 241 (1989)(quoting Caminetti v. United States, 242 U.S. 470, 485 (1917)).

73. See Diver, Statutory Interpretation in the Administrative State, 133 U. Penn. L. Rev. 549, 562 (1985).

4. Bureaucratic relativity? In *Overton Park*, the court refused to accept the agency's interpretation of the statute; in *Chevron*, the court deferred. Might the *Chevron* court be making a distinction between an agency that has been entrusted by Congress with a major environmental statutory mandate, like EPA with the Clean Air Act, and on the other hand an agency like the Department of Transportation in *Overton Park*, for whom the §4(f) parkland environmental protection provision was an unwelcome burr under its bureaucratic saddle?

Section 2. JUDICIAL CONSIDERATION OF POLITICS: THE THREE SISTERS BRIDGE CASE

§23 of the Federal Aid to Highways Act of 1968
Public Law 90-495

> (a) Notwithstanding any other provisions of law or any court's decision or administrative action to the contrary, the Secretary of Transportation and the government of the District of Columbia shall...construct all routes on the interstate system [within the District].... Such construction shall be undertaken as soon as possible after the date of enactment of this Act...and shall be carried out in accordance with all applicable provisions of Title 23[74] United States Code.
>
> (b) Not later than 30 days after the date of enactment...the government of the District of Columbia shall commence work on the following projects: (1) Three Sisters Bridge, Interstate Highway 266....

The foregoing provision was enacted by Congress after citizens successfully halted the Three Sisters Bridge Project – an interstate highway bridge designed to cross the Potomac River from Virginia, through Rock Creek Park, into Washington D.C. – using the §4(f) provisions later litigated in *Overton Park*. D.C. Federation of Civic Associations v. Airis, 391 F.2d 478 (D.C. Cir. 1968). Subsequently the case became the subject of two cycles up and down between trial and appeals courts, with a final bow in the Supreme Court.[75]

The Three Sisters Bridge decisions confronted the clear congressional direction in §23 that the bridge be started immediately, regardless of "any other provisions of law or any court decision or administrative action to the contrary." In both district court opinions, Judge Sirica allowed the bridge project to continue because of the clear statutory directive to go forward, but he also provided more than a dozen pages of history showing the highly-charged politics of the bridge decision. For unclear reasons, Rep. William Natcher, an otherwise obscure congressman from Kentucky who was a subcommittee chairman with control over District of Columbia funding, strenuously wanted the I-266 Three Sisters Bridge built across the river. The federal and District governments didn't want one more bridge adding to traffic congestion, and siphoning money and commerce out of the city, but they desperately wanted a subway system as the second Sirica opinion noted–

74. Note that Title 23 is not the same thing as §23; Title 23 provided for planning requirements, public hearings, and parkland protection as in §4(f) in the *Overton Park* case.

75. D.C. Federation of Civic Assoc. v. John Volpe, 308 F. Supp. 423 (D.C.D.C. 1970, Sirica, J.); 434 F.2d 436 (D.C. Cir. 1970, Skelly Wright, J.); 316 F. Supp. 754 (D.C.D.C. 1970, Sirica, J.); 459 F.2d 1231 (D.C. Cir. 1972, Bazelon, J.); cert. denied, 405 U.S. 1030 (1972, Burger, C.J., concurring).

> The evidence indicates that strong political pressure was applied by certain members of Congress in order to secure approval of the Bridge project. Congressman Natcher stated publicly and made no secret of the fact that he would do everything that he could to withold congressional appropriations for the District of Columbia rapid transit system, the need for which is universally recognized...until the District complied with the 1968 Act [overriding the *Airis* injunction].... Three of the [council] members who voted in favor of the project issued statements that they were doing so, not because of their conviction that the Bridge was necessary or that it would be beneficial to the local community, but as a direct result of the congressional pressure and threats to delete or withold appropriations for the rapid transit system....
>
> A more serious allegation by the plaintiffs is that Secretary of Transportation Volpe...did not base his decision solely on the merits of the project, but was acting in response to congressional pressure regarding the rapid transit appropriations.... The statement issued by the Secretary...indicates that the pressure on rapid transit funds was a consideration at that time. Also in connection with the decision to go ahead with the bridge project, President Nixon, in a letter to Congressman Natcher, dated August 12, 1969, reviewed the actions of the city and the Department...and stated, "I trust that these actions will fullfill the criteria which you set forth in the statement of August 11, 1969." 316 F. Supp. at 762-765.

Judge Sirica nevertheless determined that the statutory command was dispositive, and permitted bridge construction to begin. Two days after construction was underway, Representative Natcher released funds for the Washington Metro subway system. Within a week, however, the citizens went to the Court of Appeals and obtained a stay and ultimately a decision halting the Bridge again. Judge Bazelon wrote –

> The author of this opinion is convinced that the impact of this [political] pressure is sufficient, standing alone, to invalidate the Secretary's action. Even if the Secretary had taken every formal step required by every applicable statutory provision, reversal would be required, in my opinion, because extraneous pressure intruded into the calculus of considerations on which the Secretary's decision was based. 459 F.2d at 1245-1246. [The other members of the panel added the argument that §23 should be interpreted to require full compliance with §4(f) in planning, hearings, and agency decisions, as in *Overton Park*.]

In the Supreme Court, certiorari was denied, but Chief Justice Burger appended a remarkable concurrence, arguing that he accepted the injunction "solely out of considerations of timing" –

> Questions of great importance...are presented by the petition, not the least of which is whether the Court of Appeals has for a second time unjustifiably frustrated the efforts of the Executive Branch to comply with the will of Congress as rather clearly expressed in §23.... If we were to grant the writ, however, it would be almost a year before we could render a decision.... In these circumstances, Congress, may, of course, take any further legislative action that it deems necessary to make unmistakably clear its intentions

> with respect to the [Three Sisters Bridge] project, even to the point of limiting or prohibiting judicial review of its directives. 405 U.S. 1030, 1030-1031 (1970).

COMMENTARY AND QUESTIONS

1. What's good for the goose... If one believes that agencies must respond conscientiously to congressional statutory requirements like the National Environmental Policy Act, the Endangered Species Act, the Freedom of Information Act, and so on, how can one justify the courts' refusal to force the Department of Transportation to build the Three Sisters Bridge?

2. Political pressure as a judicial review factor. Can courts discount agency actions when the administrative history (or legislative history) reveals political pressure? If so, what governmental decisions are *not* at risk?

On the other hand, if courts matter-of-factly accept that the determining reason for particular agency decisions is politics rather than the purported merits,[76] do they diminish the safeguarding role of the judiciary, and convert the factual and legal merits presented by the agency into an elaborate charade?

3. Due process and removal of judicial jurisdiction. Is Chief Justice Burger's concurring opinion a bit surprising in its open invitation to Congress to curb the courts' powers of judicial review? Echoing an earlier question, what would you make of a standard clause inserted in future special interest statutes: "The courts may not review questions concerning the merits or procedures of projects arising under this Act"?

I was always taught as I was growing up that democracy is not something you believe in, not something you hang your hat on; democracy is something you do.

— Abbie Hoffman, closing argument to jury,
in Commonwealth v. Hoffman, et al., Amherst Mass. 1988

76. In *State Farm*, for example, where the Court insisted that the agency provide an adequate factual basis for reversing an earlier protective regulation, Justice Rehnquist's dissent noted in part that, "the agency's changed view of the standard seems to be related to the election of a new President of a different political party." 463 U.S. at 59.

Chapter 12

NEPA, THE NATIONAL ENVIRONMENTAL POLICY ACT: A MANDATORY DISCLOSURE AND STOP AND THINK STATUTE

NEPA, the National Environmental Policy Act,[1] is a statute that provokes a wild diversity of reactions. To some it is a paper tiger, of awesome but toothless aspect. To others it is a ringing statutory declaration of environmental protection and rational human governance, setting a precedent of international significance. To some it is an unproductive attempt to intrude on ongoing public-private enterprises. To others it is a legislative accident (whether fortunate or unfortunate) that was created and continues to evolve by happenstance. As usual, there is probably some truth in each of these perspectives.

Ultimately NEPA's successes may be impossible to measure, in part because its effectiveness includes the anonymous thousands of destructive federal projects which are withdrawn, or never proposed in the first place, in anticipation of NEPA scrutiny.

In taxonomic form, a distinct new model of statutory regulation can be discerned within NEPA's provisions: NEPA is a broad stop-and-think, disclose-to-the-public administrative law. It is general in its statutory commands – a broad, simple set of directives that apply across the board to all federal agencies. Its operative terms require agencies to contemplate the context and consequences of their actions before acting, in effect mandating a particularized process of program planning, supposed to begin early in the administrative genesis of agency decisions. Public disclosure is NEPA's complementary mandate: agencies must produce a publicly reviewable physical document reflecting the required internal project analysis.[2]

The rationality of this requirement – requiring documented formal consideration of negatives and alternatives as well as benefits before acting – may be obvious, but NEPA was its pioneer. Its logic has subsequently been adopted in several dozen international and domestic systems. The potent nonenvironmental forces that NEPA attempts to control, however, have kept up a running resistance to its statutory mandates, with some successes over the years.

The simple plan: That they should take, who have the power, and they should keep, who can. — Meeker v. City of East Orange, 74 A. 379, 385 (N.J. 1909)

---

1. 42 U.S.C.A. §4321 et seq., Pub.L. 91–190 (1970).

2. Other statutes embody one or another of these functions – benefit-cost analysis requirements in the public works process, see page 54 *supra*; EPCRA's community right-to-know chemical disclosure provisions, see page 254 *supra* – but NEPA remains the broadest, most coherent statutory model.

A. NEPA

Here is the text of NEPA, as it was signed into law by Richard Nixon on January 1, 1970. As you read it, note its terms, its style, its poetry, and the regulatory approaches it consciously or unconsciously incorporated:

Public Law 91–190 (1970)

AN ACT: To establish a national policy for the environment, to provide for the establishment of a Council on Environmental Quality, and for other purposes.
Be it enacted by the Senate and House of Representatives of the United States of America in Congress assembled, that this Act may be cited as the "National Environmental Policy Act of 1969."

Title I Declaration of National Environmental Policy

Sec. 101 (a) The Congress, recognizing the profound impact of man's activity on the interrelations of all components of the natural environment, particularly the profound influences of population growth, high-density urbanization, industrial expansion, resource exploitation, and new and expanding technological advances and recognizing further the critical importance of restoring and maintaining environmental quality to the overall welfare and development of man, declares that it is the continuing policy of the Federal Government, in cooperation with State and local governments, and other concerned public and private organizations, to use all practicable means and measures, including financial and technological assistance, in a manner calculated to foster and promote the general welfare, to create and maintain conditions under which man and nature can exist in productive harmony, and fulfill the social, economic, and other requirements of present and future generations of Americans.

(b) In order to carry out the policy set forth in this Act, it is the continuing responsibility of the Federal Government to use all practicable means, consistent with other essential considerations of national policy, to improve and coordinate Federal plans, functions, programs, and resources to the end that the Nation may –

(1) fulfill the responsibilities of each generation as trustee of the environment for succeeding generations;
(2) assure for all Americans safe, healthful, productive, and esthetically and culturally pleasing surroundings;
(3) attain the widest range of beneficial uses of the environment without degradation, risk to health or safety, or other undesirable and unintended consequences;
(4) preserve important historic, cultural, and natural aspects of our national heritage, and maintain, wherever possible, an environment which supports diversity and variety of individual choice;
(5) achieve a balance between population and resource use which will permit high standards of living and a wide sharing of life's amenities; and
(6) enhance the quality of renewable resources and approach the maximum attainable recycling of depletable resources.

(c) The Congress recognizes that each person should enjoy a healthful environment and that each person has a responsibility to contribute to the preservation and enhancement of the environment.

Sec. 102. The Congress authorizes and directs that, to the fullest extent possible:

(1) The policies, regulations, and public laws of the United States shall be interpreted and administered in accordance with the policies set forth in this Act, and

(2) all agencies of the Federal Government shall –

(A) utilize a systematic, interdisciplinary approach which will insure the integrated use of the natural and social sciences and the environmental design arts in planning and in decisionmaking which may have an impact on man's environment;

(B) identify and develop methods and procedures, in consultation with the Council on Environmental Quality established by title II of this Act, which will insure that presently unquantified environmental amenities and values may be given appropriate consideration in decision-making along with economic and technical considerations;

(C) include in every recommendation or report on proposals for legislation and other major Federal actions significantly affecting the quality of the human environment, a detailed statement by the responsible official on –

(i) the environmental impact of the proposed action,
(ii) any adverse environmental effects which cannot be avoided should the proposal be implemented,
(iii) alternatives to the proposed action,
(iv) the relationship between local short-term uses of man's environment and the maintenance and enhancement of long-term productivity, and
(v) any irreversible and irretrievable commitments of resources which would be involved in the proposed action should it be implemented.

Prior to making any detailed statement, the responsible Federal official shall consult with and obtain the comments of any Federal agency which has jurisdiction by law or special expertise with respect to any environmental impact involved. Copies of such statement and the comments and views of the appropriate Federal, State, and local agencies, which are authorized to develop and enforce environmental standards shall be made available to the President, the Council on Environmental Quality and to the public as provided by section 552 of Title 5, United States Code, and shall accompany the proposal through the existing agency review processes;

(D) study, develop, and describe appropriate alternatives to recommended courses of action in any proposal which involves unresolved conflicts concerning alternative uses of available resources;

(E) recognize the worldwide and long-range character of environmental problems and, where consistent with the foreign policy of the United States, lend appropriate support to initiatives, resolutions, and programs designed to maximize international cooperation in anticipating and preventing a decline in the quality of mankind's world environment;

(F) make available to States, counties, municipalities, institutions, and individuals, advice and information useful in restoring, maintaining, and enhancing the quality of the environment;

(G) initiate and utilize ecological information in the planning and development of resource-oriented projects; and

(H) assist the Council on Environmental Quality established by title II of this Act.

Sec. 103. All agencies of the Federal Government shall review their present statutory authority, administrative regulations, and current polices and procedures for the purpose of determining whether there are any deficiencies or inconsistencies therein which prohibit full compliance with the purposes and provisions of this Act and shall propose to the President not later than July 1, 1971, such measures as may be necessary to bring their authority and policies into conformity with the intent, purposes, and procedures set forth in this Act.

Sec. 104. Nothing in Section 102 or 103 shall in any way affect the specific statutory obligations of any Federal agency (1) to comply with criteria or standards of environmental quality, (2) to coordinate or consult with any other Federal or State agency, or (3) to act, or refrain from acting contingent upon the recommendations or certification of any other Federal or State agency.

Sec. 105. The policies and goals set forth in this Act are supplementary to those set forth in existing authorizations of Federal agencies.

[Title II establishes the President's Council on Environmental Quality (CEQ), which must prepare an annual Environmental Quality Report for submission to Congress. The CEQ's additional duties include gathering information and conducting studies on environmental trends and conditions, reviewing federal government programs in light of NEPA's substantive goals, and recommending national policies for environmental improvement. By executive order the CEQ issues regulations for coordinating federal agency compliance with NEPA. E.O. 11514 (1970) as amended by E.O. 11991 (1977).]

COMMENTARY AND QUESTIONS

1. NEPA as paper tiger. Note that NEPA as finally passed contains a great deal of poetic language and precious little that is mandatory. There are ringing hortatory declarations of policy, and wistful commitments to processes of scientific rationality, especially in §101, and in most of §102. Does all this amount to anything? Is there anything in §101, purportedly the primary section of NEPA, that has any legal effect? There is, of course, the small matter of §102(2)(C). Note that even that subsection is filled with vague verbiage; the instrumental words are limited to a couple of dozen out of two hundred. If you parse it carefully, however, §102(2)(C) levies a sole, narrow, statutory requirement: an environmental impact statement (EIS) *shall* be prepared for all major federal actions significantly affecting the quality of the human environment. That deceptively simple requirement has produced virtually all NEPA caselaw. Nevertheless, even though there may be an enforceable impact statement requirement, it seems merely procedural and does not purport to dictate substantive results. Observing the course of application of NEPA to the intricate internal mechanisms of federal agencies and the market forces with which they are linked, many observers have said that this procedural restraint is relatively meaningless. As Professor Sax wrote about NEPA, "I think the emphasis on the redemptive quality of procedural reform is about nine parts myth and one part coconut oil...."[3] A sustained process in some federal courts and many federal agencies over the years has held NEPA to purely procedural terms and minimal formal compliance.

Continuing through these NEPA materials, therefore, one should note that they may chronicle a statutory program that some consider a symbolic assurance sham, not worth the extensive time and energies invested in it.

2. NEPA as international milestone. NEPA can also be categorized as a remarkable, internationally-pioneering declaration of a national policy of environmental sensitivity. Beyond the high principle of its declaration of policy, moreover, NEPA's environmental impact statement requirement is a novel strategic assertion of an all-too-obvious truth: Government agencies, like all other human actors, are prone to tunnel vision. The realities of a complex world require an institutionalized comprehensive stop-and-think review process within the governmental system itself. The NEPA model has been greeted and adopted as a welcome rationality mechanism by a variety of countries and multi-lateral organizations in Europe and the third world, as well as by a number of American state governments. In following the NEPA model, these other governmental entities have treated the impact statement process as an apt mechanism for achieving practical enforcement of the broad declarations of environmental policy that accompany it, and as a caveat to the administrative state that it look before it leaps.

3. NEPA as accidental legislation. The political reality underlying NEPA's legislative history was an extraordinary post-Silent Spring late-1960s groundswell of popular attention to problems of environmental quality. Facing upcoming by-elections, Congress and President Nixon hastened to adjust to the issue. "The 1970s must be the years that America pays its debts to the past by reclaiming the purity of its air, its water, and our living environment. It is literally now or never," said Nixon. A number of legislative details, however, reveal the moderate intent of the President and Congress. As the various draft bills that became NEPA moved through the legislature in 1969 (as S.1075 and H.R.12549, 91st Congress), they initially were quite innocuous. §101 read then much as it does now; §102 merely called for governmental funding for environmental studies. Where teeth seemed to exist, they were pulled. Section 101(c) originally read: "The Congress recognizes that each person has a fundamental and inalienable *right* to a healthful environment..." and that was changed. Rep. Wayne Aspinall of Colorado, a stalwart friend of the mining and lumber industries, was able to insert a provision into the House bill that "Nothing in this act shall increase, decrease, or change any responsibility or authority of any federal official or agency created by other provision of law...." What would have been the effect of this provision? (It was changed in conference committee to read as in §§103-105, over Aspinall's objection.) And what does the actual title of the act tell you?

---

3. Sax, The (Unhappy) Truth about NEPA, 26 Okla. L.R. 239 (1973).

On April 16, 1969, however, in one of a seemingly endless series of small committee hearings, Professor Lynton Caldwell, a political scientist from Indiana University, mentioned in testimony before Senator Jackson's Interior Committee that he "would urge that in the shaping of such policy it have an action-forcing, operational aspect...." Chairman Jackson, to the surprise of his staff, picked up on this: "I agree with you that realistically what is needed in restructuring the governmental side of this problem is to legislatively create those situations that will bring about an action-forcing procedure that departments must comply with. Otherwise these lofty declarations are nothing more than that.... I am wondering if I may broaden the policy provision in the bill so as to lay down a general requirement that would be applicable to all agencies...."[4] Based on this brief interchange, Caldwell sat down with a couple of staffers and drafted the text of the present §102. The underlying mood of Congress continued to be felt, however. Jackson accepted an amendment inserting the phrase "to the fullest extent possible" into §102, words apparently intended to modify the otherwise strict command of its first sentence. In subsection (2)(C), Jackson's language originally read that there had to be an environmental *finding* by the responsible official, a term that was amended to read "statement," apparently to avoid the implication that there might be required findings of fact that would be judicially reviewable.[5]

Imagine the shock of Richard Nixon and many members of Congress when, early in 1970, they discovered that these apparently innocuous words of §102 could be the basis of very real lawsuits. §102, like a snake in the grass, contained the hidden but potent impact statement requirement. There have subsequently been hundreds of NEPA lawsuits, affecting federal projects and programs running into billions of dollars. Why didn't Congress recognize this potential? If Congress didn't recognize NEPA's potential, can courts nevertheless enforce the statute to give it precisely the judicial effect that Congress had tried to eliminate?

In the years immediately following NEPA's passage almost two hundred bills were introduced to weaken or repeal it. None passed. This indicates that, once passed, a "motherhood" statute is no less sacred for having been unintended. Isn't it likely, however, that Congress would have passed almost any proposed environmental statute, and that it was only an accident of the legislative process that produced a statute with some teeth? What does that say about the process?

4. NEPA's de facto statutory strategy. Despite NEPA's unintended, rather serendipitous legislative history, one can still analyze the provisions that emerged from Congress as embodying a novel de facto statutory strategy, as noted earlier.

First, whatever NEPA requires is government-wide, not a series of directives specifically tailored to any particular governmental agency. This umbrella ap-

---

4. National Environmental Policy, 1969: Hearings on S.1075, S. 233, and S.1752 before the Senate Committee on Interior and Insular Affairs, 91st Cong., 1st Sess. 116-117 (1969)(stataement of Lynton Caldwell, professor of Government, University of Indiana).

5. For a complete history of NEPA's legislative genesis, see R.N.L. Andrews, Environmental Policy and Administrative Change (1976).

proach provides strengths as well as weaknesses.

Second, NEPA asserts a strong general declaration of policy that might be made relevant to a wide range of substantive interpretations and applications of various statutes, although this has not noticeably been the case.

Third, the impact statement procedure requires an internal process of overview accounting, specifying a detailed analysis of agency proposals. It pins down this required process with the EIS, a specific workproduct that provides tangible reviewable evidence of the agency's compliance. The notion, moreover, that the EIS will accompany proposals through the decisional process may impose a practical timing requirement bringing environmental impact accounting into the earlier project stages.

However, there is no enforcement mechanism on the face of NEPA. Caldwell and the committee staff presumed that NEPA would be actively enforced by the President, acting through OMB and CEQ, and by Congress. In reality, as we shall soon see, enforcement, if it was to come, had to come from somewhere else.

Nevertheless, the statutory framework can be viewed as incorporating a coherent and quite novel regulatory logic. Through its provisions, even low-visibility agency decisions that might significantly impact the environment would have to be "ventilated" within and outside the agency, and made accessible in published form to the President, Congress, and the public for their review and response.

5. The political science of NEPA. Note that the only legally-specific section of NEPA targeted its environmental protection efforts upon the federal agencies, not upon the corporate polluters who previously had been the primary focus of public attention. Federal agencies, however, happen to be intimately involved with a host of major production and development activities across the face of the economy and the territory of the United States. Federal agencies are involved in the logging of national forests, in water resources, minerals and mining, the construction of highways and airports, urban redevelopment, the oil industry and offshore oil development, and the like. As the extent of potential NEPA litigation has become more obvious, the targeting of NEPA on federal agencies has provided a broad handle on a very broad range of environmental problems.

6. The role of citizens. The history of each statute is unique. NEPA was written in broad terms, achieved support, and passed through Congress, as a product of its unique times. It is impossible to overestimate the importance of public opinion in pushing NEPA into law. NEPA would never have moved beyond its first drafts without the environmental fervor of hundreds of thousands of citizens in the late 1960s.

Even more than most statutes, however, NEPA was only an incipient force when it was signed in January 1970. Its growth and development once again depended upon citizens' efforts, this time in the courts. Turning to NEPA in the courts, it is important to remember a basic irony: when the terms of a statute require interpretation, courts put their primary reliance upon the intention of the legislature, but in the case of NEPA's §102, there really *wasn't* any.

7. NEPA compliance and enforcement. According to CEQ records,[6] federal agencies filed a total of 430 EISs in 1988. Four agencies filed the majority of these EISs– the Department of the Interior (mainly in connection with parks, wilderness areas, national seashores, wildlife refuges, hatcheries, mining, and forest management); the Department of Transportation (mainly for road construction); the Army Corps of Engineers (primarily with regard to watershed protection, flood control, and navigation); and the Department of Agriculture (mainly in connection with parks, wilderness areas, national seashores, forestry and range management, and pesticide use). The same four agencies, viewed together, comprised the targets for 62 out of the total of 91 NEPA cases filed against federal agencies in 1988. The most common complaint advanced by plaintiffs in these cases was that the agency had neglected to prepare an EIS where it should have done so. The second most common complaint was that the agency prepared an EIS that was inadequate. The majority of NEPA plaintiffs are individual or citizen groups, or environmental organizations.

Note that agencies such as the Department of Commerce, the Department of Housing and Urban Development, the General Services Administration, the Nuclear Regulatory Commission, the Tennessee Valley Authority, the ICC, and the National Aeronautics and Space Administration each filed fewer than four EISs during 1988 (some of these filed none).

Is it likely overall that federal agencies are undertaking so few projects with significant environmental effects? Or does the reality of NEPA compliance and enforcement fall short of NEPA's broad directives?

B. NEPA GOES TO COURT

Whenever a new statute is legislated, an elaborate series of further questions must be answered. Has it created a new cause of action? If so, who can file lawsuits? Against what defendants? What is the statute of limitations? What actions can be attacked? What are potential defendants required to do under the Act? What do plaintiffs have to show in their complaint and at trial? What defenses are available? What remedies are provided for? The evolving answers to these questions create a common law of the statute. Depending upon how they are answered in court, a statute can flourish or wither on the vine.

NEPA litigation has from the beginning focussed upon the one clear requirement of the Act - major federal actions significantly affecting the environment must have an EIS. Tracing some of the issues raised in the cases over the years not only clarifies the law of NEPA but also illuminates the process by which courts shape the flight of the statutory "missile" after the legislature launches it. In the case of NEPA's

6. President's Council on Environmental Quality, 20 Environmental Quality 391-99 (1990).

environmental impact statement requirement, the fact that Congress pretty clearly did not intend to create any new cause of action has had remarkably little effect on the growth of the statute in court cases over time.

SECTION 1. NEPA IN THE JUDICIAL PROCESS: THE CHICOD CREEK CONTROVERSY – A CHRONOLOGICAL ANALYSIS OF A CLASSIC NEPA CASE

No case can be a "typical" NEPA case, because of the remarkable diversity of NEPA lawsuits over the years. The legal and practical elements of the Chicod Creek decisions, however, offer a broadly instructive blueprint of NEPA litigation generally, as well as a fascinating example of how NEPA, which was not intended to be litigable, quickly became a highly functional cause of action when plaintiffs dragged it before federal judges.

Natural Resources Defense Council v. Grant *(Chicod Creek)*

U.S. District Court, Eastern District of North Carolina, 1972
341 F. Supp. 356

LARKINS, District Judge...Chicod Creek Watershed, located in mideastern North Carolina, covers an area of 35,100 acres of which 29,625 acres are in Pitt County and 5,475 acres in Beaufort County. Plans for solving flooding, water management, and other resources problems have been prepared with the concurrence of local sponsors and with federal assistance under the the provisions of P.L. 566. The sponsoring local organizations are the Pitt Soil and Water Conservation District, Beaufort Soil and Water Conservation District, Pitt County Board of Commissioners, and Pitt County Drainage District Number Nine. Under the Chicod Creek Watershed Work Plan and Supplements, the local organizations assume all local responsibilities for the installation, operation and maintenance of planned structural works.

The topography of the watershed is nearly level to gently sloping. The outer perimeter is flat and well drained and the flood plains are broad swamps. Land use in the watershed consists of 15,600 acres of cropland; 15,550 acres of woodland; 350 acres of grassland; and 3,600 acres of miscellaneous uses. Approximately 10,000 acres of crop and pasture land are subject to flooding.... A loss of at least 50 percent is sustained on the crops grown on land subject to flooding about once each five years. [Such flooding] causes interrupted traffic, blocked school bus and mail delivery routes, interrupted feeding schedules of farm animals, and additional maintenance and repair on the roads. Excessive rainfall and flooding create a health hazard. Septic tanks, nitrification lines, and approved pit-privies overflow to the surface of the soil after excessive rainfall. Poor drainage often results in low quality crops and high unit cost of production.

The population of the watershed is approximately 3,000 people. The entire population is classified as rural with 25 percent being non-farm. Agriculture is the principal enterprise in the watershed. The chief cash crops are tobacco, corn, soybeans, and cotton. Livestock production, consisting of beef cattle and swine, make up ten percent of the cash farm receipts. Value of farm products sold was under $10,000 for 77.6 percent of the 250 farms in the watershed. Fifty-five percent of the families make less than $3,000 income per year.

Chicod Creek originates about 6 miles south of Grimesland and flows generally (about 10 miles) north to its confluence with the Tar River. Cow Swamp and Juniper

Branch are the two largest tributaries and they enter Chicod Creek from the west. Chicod Creek and the surrounding area has significant value for numerous waterfowl, fur bearers and other wetland wildlife species. The streams have substantial resident fish population and support a significant spawning run of herring during the spring.

The project was developed for the purposes of flood prevention, drainage, and conservation, development, and improvement of agricultural tracts of land. These objects are to be achieved by land treatment measures and structural measures. The land treatment measures will include conservation cropping systems, cover crops, crop residue use, minimum tillage, grasses and legumes, and tile and open drains. Also, 300 acres of open land will be reforested, while 1,350 acres of land will be subject to thinning and removal of trees. Structural improvements will consist of approximately 66 miles (comprising the main stream and all the various tributaries) of channel enlargement or "stream channelization." Mitigation measures to reduce the adverse effects on fish and wildlife resources are (1) 73 acres of wildlife wetland preservation area. (2) a 12 acre warm-water impoundment area, (3) 11 channel pools, and (4) 30 swamp drainage control structures. These mitigation measures are designed to mitigate for the disruption to the fish caused by the construction of the channels and to offset the wildlife habitat destroyed by the channels and spoil areas. Certain groups feel that these mitigation measures do not sufficiently lessen the adverse effects of the project on the environment. A letter written to Mr. Jesse Hicks, State Conservationist, Soil Conservation Service, from Mr. Ernest C. Martin, Acting Regional Director of the Fish and Wildlife Service, dated September 10, 1971, reflects such an opinion:

> It is the opinion of the Service that the original mitigation measures plus the additional measures do not significantly lessen the adverse effects of the project on the ecosystem of the watershed.

The Watershed Work Plan and an agreement for the implementation thereof were executed on behalf of [the local] Soil and Water Conservation District... organizations, who are parties to the agreement and plan, and before execution by the Soil Conservation Service, the plan was reviewed by the Corps of Engineers of the Unites States Department of the Army and the United States Department of the Interior, and other federal Agencies. The plan was submitted to and approved by the Committee on Agriculture of the United States House of Representatives on August 23, 1966 and by the committee on Agriculture of the United States Senate on August 3, 1966....

Pursuant to the provisions of the National Environmental Policy Act and the Council on Environmental Quality Guidelines,[7] the Administrator of the Soil Conservation Service, through the issuance of Environment Memorandum 1 and Watersheds Memorandum 108, the Chicod Creek Watershed project was placed in Group 2, i.e., those projects having some adverse effect which can be eliminated by minor project modification. Consultations were had with the North Carolina Wildlife Resources Commission and the Fish and Wildlife Service of the United States Department of the Interior. These consultations for the consideration of environmental impact were in addition to considerations based on the expertise of

7. The 1971 guidelines are now formalized as regulations on NEPA implementation. 40 CFR Ch. V, §1500 et seq. These regulations evolved in varying degrees over the course of the Ford, Carter, Reagan, and Bush presidencies.

the Soil Conservation Service in the area of fish and wildlife preservation. As a result of the above actions the project was modified to provide for further mitigation of adverse environmental effects. The modifications were incorporated by Supplemental Agreement 2 [in 1971]. After consideration of environmental concerns, including the unfavorable comments of the Fish and Wildlife Service, officials of the Soil and Conservation Service determined that the project as modified was not a major federal action significantly affecting the quality of human environment and that the project should proceed.

The present action was instituted to enjoin the defendants from financing and participating in the construction of the Chicod Creek Watershed Project. The total installation cost of the project is estimated to be $1,503,831. Public Law 566 funds are to pay $706,684 and other funds will provide $797,147.

There has been extensive preparation by the defendants and the intervenors for this project. The landowners have incurred approximately $13,000 of debts to create the drainage district. Easements and rights-of-way have been obtained on 282 tracts of land involving 230 landowners. The local sponsors have procured a Farmers Home Administration loan. The Soil Conservation Service has incurred substantial expenses on the project, having expended $50,000 for planning and $159,176 for engineering, design, and land treatment. The Soil Conservation Service will suffer expenses as a result of the delay caused by this action. The projected cost of delay amounts to $7,650 per month, representing salaries and increased construction costs. The cost of preparing impact statements is approximately $7,500 per project....

COMMENTARY AND QUESTIONS (ON *CHICOD CREEK* TO THIS POINT)

1. The factual setting. Can you figure out what is going on here? Physically, these Soil Conservation Service (SCS) channelization projects involve cutting a swath of trees (here about 10 percent of the area's woodland) along a watercourse, then, using power-scoopers called "draglines," cutting a wide open-banked canal in a straight line through the watershed. The natural meandering stream is thus replaced by a broad ditch. The judge does not seem particularly aware of what "adverse effects" might result. What kind of ecological evidence would you have brought to the hearing on a preliminary injunction to demonstrate the facts?

What were the purposes of the project? "Flood prevention" clearly does not mean protection of lives and property from rampaging floodwaters. Rather, the flood problem appears to be drainage, and the purpose of the project is largely to promote agriculture (although traffic and sanitation consequences are mentioned). By channelizing the watershed and adding open ditches and tile drains, the project would not only have reduced seasonal drainage problems but also have created new arable land out of "useless marshes." About 17 percent of the benefited acreage is owned by the Weyerhaeuser Lumber Company.

Economically, it is Public Law 566 that pushes the project along. Watershed Protection Act, 16 U.S.C.A. §§1001-1009 (1970). The court notes that $706,684 out of the $1,503,831 total cost is to be contributed by federal taxpayers. The "local" contribution is typically not wholly paid in dollars. By donating land rights (i.e., easements of access for the dragline, rights-of-way for ditches), landowners are

KARL SCHURR

Stream channelization involves bulldozing or draglining the natural contours and meanders of a stream into straight-line trapezoidal cross-section ditches. The trees and shrubs naturally clustered along the streambanks are stripped away and burned or left in spoils piles. Water flows change dramatically from natural flows in terms of temperature, volume, velocity, erosion, and water quality. The pre-existing populations of fish and other aquatic life typically decline severely. In this photograph, the dragline is re-dredging a silted-in channelization done approximately five years prior.

credited with economic contributions toward the local share. The remainder is made up by assessments in the drainage district. As a result, local agriculture gets a construction project subsidy five to ten times its own dollar outlay (the federal contribution rate varies depending upon how much can be called "flood protection" (75 percent) rather than drainage (50 percent)). Does the fact that the private market does not build these projects on its own show that they are not cost-effective without federal subsidies?

2. The political setting. The political organization of SCS projects is part of the NEPA story. Originally the SCS was an erosion-control agency whose motto was "stop the raindrop where it falls" through contour plowing and other methods. The agency was so successful that it worked itself out of a job. Accordingly, the SCS shifted its focus to carrying water away from the land, an about-face that naturally brought it into the business of managing small streams, as the Corps had carved out its jurisdiction over rivers. Annually, huge sums of federal money are appropriated by the congressional agricultural appropriations subcommittees for distribution around the nation to SCS projects. At the local level, agribusiness and individual farmers who will ultimately benefit from the subsidies are organized into Drainage Districts through the efforts of the county or regional agent who administers the local-level SCS Soil Conservation District. The drainage districts are basically state-chartered quasi-governmental units with the power to contract for construction, and to assess fees. A project is proposed by one of the participants (often the local SCS agent, whose career advancement typically is linked to success in getting such projects underway). A majority of affected landowners (measured by acreage rather than per capita) must approve the project; if approved, all must subsequently contribute. The project is then transmitted by the SCS's "State Conservationist" to Washington where it is "authorized" for construction by the SCS and the FHA, and the Secretary of Agriculture. (The SCS and the TVA are rare examples of agencies that have been given extraordinary powers to self-authorize projects without a congressional vote). Appropriated money is then released to the District for sequential planning, design, and construction. Low interest loans, moreover, are granted to finance part of the local share. The participants throughout this process are linked in an identity of interests. The SCS owes its existence to the continuation of the drainage function; the Congressional appropriations committees derive their political power from the ability to deliver dollars throughout the country; the Department of Agriculture and its subdepartments likewise; state and local government officials may be incorporated into the District funding process; and private individuals receive direct financial benefits, some from the project's subsidized land modifications, others from the award of construction contracts (in the *Ray* case at page 421 *supra*, the ditching contractor appears to have been the brother of the local contracting officer). The various private and public participants have their nationwide organizations, with annual conventions, newsletters, and Washington-based lobbyists, all to assure the system's smooth functioning.

Outside the network of drainage-oriented interests are other public and private bodies. The state Wildlife Commission had received a report from its expert, George Burdick, noting the drastic ecological effects of channelization, and had tried to persuade the SCS to terminate the program. The SCS told the state agency that Chicod Creek was being pushed by local landowners and was beyond SCS control. ("Meantime," said one state official, "the SCS agents were whooping it up with the local people telling them what they wanted where.") In controversial matters like this, a state agency will usually not sue to achieve its objectives, nor even complain administratively over the SCS officer's head. The state commission did not insist on its position, but did take part in some planning "at a time when the SCS had already established the design"; it did follow the litigation closely, however, and participated in subsequent negotiations. The federal Fish and Wildlife Service volunteered the letter cited, noting adverse effects. Because, however, Congress's Agriculture committees had exempted the SCS from the Fish and Wildlife Coordination Act, the FWS had no legal basis to participate in the decision even if it had wanted to interfere with a sister agency. In sum, from top to bottom, no governmental body existed to defend environmental interests. This gap left things up to the local sporting and conservation groups, which happened to find out about the project and got organized in time to persuade the National Resources Defense Council, a private entity, to take on the expensive task of litigating this, out of hundreds of other potential cases.

3. Judicial attitudes towards NEPA challenges. How do you interpret the mood of Judge Larkins at this stage of the case? Do you notice the inevitability implied in the phrasing (so common in NEPA cases) that "1350 acres of land *will be* [deforested]," etc.?

4. Financial commitments and delay costs. The judge notes the amounts of money committed to date and the cost of delay if an injunction were granted. This information is regularly emphasized by environmental defendants to show that too much project expenditure has occurred before trial to permit the project reasonably to be stopped. Has the $130,000 been *spent*? Were easements paid for? Can the FHA loan be returned? Do any of the SCS expenditures, for "land treatment," etc., have value irrespective of project completion? How much of this financial commitment took place after NEPA became law in January 1970? As to delay, is it relevant that the majority of costs that would inflate over the course of the suit would ultimately be paid in federal tax dollars that have likewise inflated in revenue terms? In light of the $7,500 cost of an SCS environmental impact statement, what relevance do all these numbers seem to have for the judge?

NRDC v. Grant, 341 F. Supp. 356, continued...

Conclusions of Law: Jurisdiction

This Court has jurisdiction of this matter pursuant to 28 U.S.C.A. §1331 (federal question) and 5 U.S.C.A. §702 (Administrative Procedure Act).

NATIONAL ENVIRONMENTAL POLICY ACT

The National Environmental Policy Act of 1969, 42 U.S.C.A. §4321 et seq., requires all federal agencies, in performing their respective functions, to be responsive to possible environmental consequences of their actions. The Act makes it the "continuing" responsibility of the federal government to "use all practicable means and measures" to carry out the national policy of restoring and maintaining a quality environment....

RETROACTIVITY

The effective date of NEPA was January 1, 1970. It is contended here that NEPA is not applicable to projects planned and approved before this date. Some courts have held that NEPA is not to be given retroactive application. In so holding these courts have focused upon a specific federal action or action which occurred on a particular date or dates, and if this action(s) was taken prior to the effective date of NEPA, the Act was held inapplicable to that project.... In Environmental Defense Fund v. Corps of Engineers, 325 F. Supp. 749 (E.D. Ark. 1971) the court applies NEPA to...the construction of a dam across the Cossatot River, even though the project was approved in 1958 and construction of the project, but not the dam, was begun in 1963. The court states:

The language and legislative history of NEPA indicate that Congress intended that it apply to such situations as presented here. The act clarifies congressional policy and imposes an obligation upon the defendants to protect the environment in planning and in conducting their lawful activities. §101(a) of the act declares it to be 'the continuing policy of the federal government' to protect the environment, and §101(b) declares it to be 'the continuing responsibility of the federal government to...improve and coordinate federal plans, functions and resources to accomplish that objective'. So, while new plans and programs must be structured from the outset in accordance with the requirements of NEPA, it is also clear that the act requires the defendants to 'improve' or upgrade existing plans and programs to meet those requirements.

Also, the Interim Guidelines for the enforcement of NEPA issued by the council on Environmental Quality on April 30, 1970, provide that NEPA applies to ongoing projects:

> ...the §102(2)(C) procedure should be applied to further major Federal actions having a significant effect on the environment even though they arise from projects or programs initiated prior to the enactment of the Act on January 1, 1970. 35 Fed. Reg. 7390, 7392, no. 11.

The Chicod Creed Watershed Project received congressional approval in 1966, and much planning and preparation has occurred prior to January 1, 1970. However, a construction contract remains to be let and construction upon the installation of the projects has yet to begin. NEPA is applicable to the Chicod Creek Watershed Project as it is an ongoing federal project on which substantial actions remain to be taken.

REQUIREMENTS OF §102(2)C OF NEPA

§102(2)(C) directs all agencies of the federal government to prepare an environmental impact statement for every major federal action significantly affecting the environment. The defendants contend that even though they have not filed an environmental impact statement, "a particular form," that in substance they have fulfilled all of the requirements of §102(2)(C). In support they assert that a detailed statement has been prepared and circulated; that the environmental impact has been considered by the Soil Conservation Service and agencies of both state and federal government; that adverse effects which cannot be avoided have been considered and weighed against the total benefit of going on with the project; that alternatives have been considered and some have been adopted; that there have been consultations with other federal agencies and with state and local agencies; and that the project has been open to and has received public comment. According to the record and the testimony received at the motion hearing on January 5, 1972, this cannot be disputed. But the fact remains that an environmental impact statement has not been prepared and filed for the Chicod Creek Watershed Project. Mr. Hollis Williams, Deputy Administrator of Watersheds, Soil Conservation Service at the motion hearing testified to the effect: "We had the belief and still do, that an environmental impact statement is not needed in the Chicod Creek Project." An environmental impact statement must be filed for every major federal action significantly affecting the quality of the human environment. The District of Columbia Circuit noted in Calvert Cliffs v. AEC, 449 F.2d 1109 (D.C. Cir. 1971) that "...the §102 duties are not inherently flexible. They must be complied with to the fullest extent, unless there is a conflict of statutory authority. Considerations of administrative difficulty, delay or economic cost will not suffice to strip the section of its fundamental importance." In Environmental Defense Fund v. Corps of Engineers, *supra*, the court held that agencies might use different procedures for preparing impact statements for both new and old projects:

> The court is of the opinion that the defendants may approach the problem of the ongoing project differently from a new project, but the end product should be essentially the same in both cases. For instance, the evidence indicates that the defendants will require, by their own regulations and policies, elaborate hearings

spaced out over a long period of time (indeed, several years) with respect to the environmental impact of new projects. NEPA would not require the same approach with respect to ongoing projects. Any procedure would be adequate so long as the 'detailed statement' requirements of the Act, along with the other applicable provisions of §102 are complied with.

Therefore, an environmental impact statement is required for every major federal action significantly affecting the the quality of the human environment.

ADMINISTRATIVE DISCRETION

It is contended that the determination of whether a project is (1) "a major Federal action" and (2) "significantly affecting the quality of the human environment" is within the discretion of the Administrator of the Soil Conservation Service, and that an administrative determination should not be reversed by this Court in the absence of a strong showing that it was arbitrary, capricious, or clearly erroneous. In the case at bar the administrator, with the advice of scientists and specialists, made the determination that the project as modified could not significantly affect the quality of the human environment within the meaning and intent of NEPA, and as such "going forward with the project as modified" was in compliance with the requirements of NEPA. Certainly, an administrative agency like the Soil Conservation Service may make a decision that a particular project is not major, or that it does not significantly affect the quality of the human environment, and, that, therefore, the agency is not required to file an impact statement. However, when the failure to file an impact statement is challenged, it is the court that must construe the statutory standards of "major federal action" and "significantly affecting the quality of the human environment," and having construed them, then apply them to the particular project, and decide whether the agency's failure violates the Congressional command.

STATUTORY STANDARDS

A "major federal action" is federal action that requires substantial planning, time, resources, or expenditure. The Chicod Creed Watershed Project is a "major federal action." This project calls for sixty-six miles of channelization and the expenditure of $1,503,831, $706,684 of which is to be federally funded. The project has been in the planning and preparation stages for several years. Many persons and agencies have become involved and concerned with this project, and the construction of this project will require a substantial amount of time and labor. Certainly this can be considered to be a "major federal action."

The standard "significantly affecting the quality of the human environment" can be construed as having an important or meaningful effect, direct or indirect, upon a broad range of aspects of the human environment. The cumulative impact with other projects must be considered. Any action that substantially affects, beneficially or detrimentally, the depth or course of streams, plant life, wildlife habitats, fish and wildlife, and the soil and air "significantly affects the quality of the human environment." This project will require sixty-six miles of stream channelization. As a result of such channelization there will be a substantial reduction (ninety percent) in the fish population. As a result of drainage and the clearing of right of ways, there will be significant lossage in wetland habitat which is vital to waterfowl and forest game. The Chicod Creek Watershed Project as presently proposed will have a cumulative effect upon the environment in the eastern plains of North Carolina. There are a total of forty Soil Conservation projects either authorized for construction, under construction, or completed, representing 1562 miles of stream channelization, affecting over 100,000 acres of wetlands, and having very serious repercussions upon fish and wildlife in the Coastal Plains of North Carolina. The Chicod Creek Watershed Project "significantly affects the quality of the human environment."

It is interesting to note that one of the Soil Conservation Service's own biologists, prior to the implementation of any mitigation, concluded that this project would have significant effects upon the environment. Also noteworthy is the fact that subsequent to Watersheds Memorandum 108, the Soil Conservation Service placed this project in Group 2, a category established by the Watersheds Memorandum indicating that projects placed in this group could have some adverse effect upon the environment. After certain mitigation measures were implemented, this project was placed in Group 1, signifying minor or no known adverse effect upon the environment. It is the opinion of this Court that an environmental impact statement should have been issued when this project was placed in Group 2.

STANDING

It is contended that the plaintiffs lack standing to pursue this action on the grounds that they have not suffered a legal wrong and have not been adversely affected by agency action....

The plaintiffs have standing to maintain this action as they have alleged injury to conservational interests and that such interests are within the zone of interests protected by NEPA.

IMPAIRMENT OF CONTRACT

The intervenors contend that NEPA cannot apply to pre-existing contracts as it would serve to impair the obligation of contract. At this time the intervenors have failed to show that the application of NEPA to the project entails any taking or deprivation of property or impairment of contract. NEPA merely requires the federal agencies to consider the environmental consequences of their acts and to prepare detailed environmental impact statements.

LACHES

The mere lapse of time does not constitute laches. Lache is determined in light of all the existing circumstances and requires all delay to be unreasonable and cause prejudice to the adversary. This project has been in the planning and preliminary stages for several years. However, NEPA became effective only on January 1, 1970. The plaintiffs instituted this action on November 30, 1971. At that date no construction contract had been let or had any construction on the installation of the project taken place. Therefore, it appears to this Court that there was no unreasonable delay in the commencement of this action, and even assuming such, there does not appear to be any prejudice to the defendants or intervenors as construction of the project has yet to begin.

INJUNCTION

The plaintiffs seek a preliminary injunction to enjoin construction of the Chicod Creek Watershed Project on the grounds that an environmental impact statement has not been issued as required by NEPA. The tests for granting such relief were recently restated by the Fourth Circuit:

> In the exercise of its discretion (to issue a preliminary injunction) it is sufficient if a court is satisfied that there is a probable right and a probable danger and that the right may be defeated, unless the injunction is issued, and considerable weight is given to the need of protection to the plaintiff as contrasted with the probable injury to the defendant.... W. Virginia Highlands Conservancy v. Island Creek Coal, 441 F. 2d 232, 235 (4th Cir. 1971).

In summary, the movants are entitled to preliminary injunctive relief if they demonstrate (a) a substantial likelihood that they will prevail on the merits, and (b) that a balancing of the equities favors the granting of such relief. Here, the plaintiffs have shown more than a substantial likelihood that they will prevail on the merits upon final determination of their NEPA environmental impact statement claim as NEPA requires that an environmental impact statement be filed for "major federal actions significantly affecting the quality of the human environment." The plaintiffs have shown that this project is a "major federal action significantly affecting the quality of the human environment," and that an impact statement has not been filed.

The question as to the balancing of the equities gravely concerns this Court. Basically, there are three different interests represented in this action: the conservationists, the Soil Conservation Service, and the landowners. In considering the various interests the public interest is a relevant consideration. This project was designed to enable the landowners to control severe drainage problems and to increase farm productivity. These farmers have spent much time, effort, and money in preparation for this project with the expectation of federal aid. This has been no easy task for farmers in an area in which fifty-five percent of the families make less than $3,000 income per year. These farmers have given up much in expectation of innumerable benefits resulting from the project. Truly, this project has progressed slowly since it was approved by the Soil Conservation Service in 1966. Much of this delay is accountable to the fact that it has taken time for the local sponsors and farmers to organize and make initial preparations. It was only when the preparations had been made and construction ready to begin that this action was initiated to enjoin the project. The Soil Conservation Service is the federal agency responsible for the planning and funding of this project. Its primary concern in this action seems to be that if it has to issue an impact statement for this project, it will have to do the same for many other ongoing projects. This will cause delay and, in many cases, duplicity [sic]. The projected cost per project for issuing an impact statement is approximately $7,500. This cost is minute indeed in comparison to the equity of the farmers and the effect that this project will have on the environment. The conservationists are organizations dedicated to the laudable cause of conservation and preservation of our environment. They have shown that this project will have a significant effect on the environment. It is to the public's welfare that any project significantly affecting the environment comply with the procedures established by NEPA so there can be assurance that the environmental aspects have been fully considered. It would constitute irreparable damage for this project to proceed without the environmental aspects being properly considered as required by NEPA. Therefore, the equitable considerations favor the environment, the public, and the plaintiffs and require that the construction of the Chicod Creek Watershed Project be enjoined until the requirements of NEPA are satisfied.

The defendants shall have thirty days within which to prepare and file a "full disclosure" environmental impact statement. The preliminary injunction shall remain in effect thereafter until all of the procedures of NEPA have been complied with. The plaintiffs shall file a bond for the payment of costs and damages as may be suffered by any party who is found to have been wrongfully restrained herein. The amount of bond shall be commensurate to the possible damages incurred by the defendants and the intervenors as a result of the injunction. Over $200,000 has already been expended on this project by the Soil Conservation Service and $130,000 of debt has been incurred by the intervenors. The projected cost of delay to the Soil Conservation Service resulting from the institution of this suit is approximately $7,650 per month. Taking into consideration the amounts that have been expended, the costs of delay, and that other amounts are obligated, this Court sets the bond at $75,000.

NOW THEREFORE, in accordance with the foregoing, it is

ORDERED, that the defendants and their agents, employees, and persons in active concert and participation with them who receive actual notice hereof, be and the same are hereby restrained and enjoined from taking any further steps to authorize, finance, or commence construction or installation of the Chicod Creek Watershed Project until an environmental impact statement is filed and circulated according to the requirements of the National Environmental Policy Act of 1969; and,

FURTHER ORDERED, that the defendants prepare and file a "full disclosure" environmental impact statement within thirty (30) days from the filing of this Order; and,

FURTHER ORDERED, that plaintiffs file a bond for the payment of costs and damages as may be suffered by any party who is found to have been wrongfully or unlawfully restrained herein, in the amount of, or security equivalent to, $75,000....

Let this Order be entered forthwith.

COMMENTARY AND QUESTIONS

1. Standing. Note how little trouble the court has in finding standing to challenge agency action, despite the fact that NEPA had not given citizens such a right.

2. A cause of action? The court *presumes,* with the other courts that encountered NEPA, that §102 *must* be actionable, because it plainly set up a legal duty – all agencies shall prepare statements – that sounds enforceable, and if Congress had not meant that as a requirement, surely it would not have said that. This amounts to the principle of statutory interpretation that "the Emperor *must* be wearing clothes."

3. Laches. Owing to its casual congressional history, NEPA had no statute of limitations; the equitable doctrine of laches will prevent injunction suits that are "unreasonably delayed." Here, would the judge have decided differently if a construction contract *had* been let? Should the doctrine of laches be waived for public interest plaintiffs?

4. Time limitations: "retroactivity." Can NEPA and other similiar environmental statutes be applied to projects that were started prior to their effective dates? This is the so-called "retroactivity" issue. In the early 1970's many ongoing federal projects were continued from pre-NEPA days. (Even today, there are uncompleted federal projects initiated prior to 1970!) The courts have generally followed the line of reasoning reflected in this case. If there is significant further action that remains to be taken, which could in part or whole be affected by the environmental impact review process required by Congress, then an EIS must be done. In litigation, it is wise for plaintiffs to call this "applying current law to ongoing projects" rather than "retroactive" application of a law. Note that this latter argument in NEPA cases builds upon the interpretive presumption that Congress intended the EIS process to have real force and benefit in controlling federal activities.

5. The bureaucratic temptation to minimize. NEPA's enforceability was initially unclear, and some construction agencies tended to minimize its requirements. The following is reportedly the text in its entirety of an impact statement as it was first published by the Bureau of Reclamation in satisfaction of NEPA:

> Palmetto Bend Project, Jackson County, Tex. Proposed construction of a 12.3-mile long, 64-foot high earthfill dam on the Navidad River. The purpose of the project is the supply of industrial and municipal water. Approximately 18,400 acres (11,300 of which will be inundated) will be committed to the project; 40 miles of free-flowing stream will be inundated; nine families will be displaced; fresh water inflow to the Matagorda estuary will be altered; fish and shellfish nursery areas will be impaired; habitat for such endangered species as the Texas red wolf, the American alligator, the Southern bald eagle, the Peregrine falcon, and the Attwater prairie chicken will be lost.

(The Bureau subsequently realized that more was required, and the project was ultimately subjected to a full formal EIS preparation and review process.)

6. The classic *Calvert Cliffs* case. Part of the legal backdrop to Judge Larkins' review of the Chicod Creek case was a forceful decision from the District of Columbia Court of Appeals that became the most important of all early NEPA cases. Calvert Cliffs Coordinating Committee v. AEC, 449 F.2d 1109 (D.C. Cir. 1971), confronted the Atomic Energy Commission's refusal to consider environmental issues in its nuclear construction program until after projects were under construction. The AEC, Judge Wright wrote, must proceed to implement NEPA's requirements "at a pace faster than a funeral procession." Otherwise, "the NEPA procedures, viewed by the Commission as superfluous, will wither away in disuse." *Calvert Cliffs* set out the guiding theory of NEPA reviews. Congress must have meant what it said when it made NEPA into law, and now courts must see to it that environmental considerations become "to the fullest extent possible" a true part of federal agency decisionmaking.

As a 1980 treatise on NEPA noted:

> ...the *Calvert Cliffs* decision can be approached from three different perspectives. First, it goes step by step through the major provisions of NEPA and, in dicta of the grandest style, specifies how they should be interpreted:
>
> (1) "NEPA...makes environmental protection a part of the mandate of every federal agency and department"; (2) "NEPA mandates a rather finely tuned and 'systematic' balancing analysis in each instance"; (3) "Of course...§102 duties are qualified by the phrase 'to the fullest extent possible.' We must

stress as forcefully as possible that this language does not provide an escape hatch for footdragging agencies; it does not make NEPA's procedural requirements somehow 'discretionary'"; and (4) "The reviewing courts probably cannot reverse a substantive decision on its merits under §101 unless it be shown that the actual balance of costs and benefits that was struck was arbitrary or clearly gave insufficient weight to environmental values."

Calvert Cliffs was the D.C. Circuit's first comprehensive interpretation of NEPA. It laid the groundwork for scores of other NEPA cases decided by the court including *SIPI*, *Vermont Yankee*, and NRDC v. Morton,[8] and hundreds of other cases decided by district and appellate courts.

The opinion can also be read, not for what it specifically says about NEPA's major provisions, but for the tone it uses to describe agencies' and courts' responsibilities under the statute. "[The duty of our court] is to see that important legislative purposes, heralded in the halls of Congress, are not lost or misdirected in the vast hallways of the federal bureaucracy." "We believe that the Commission's crabbed interpretation of NEPA makes a mockery of the Act." "[W]e conclude that §104 of NEPA does not permit the sort of total abdication of responsibility practiced by the Atomic Energy Commission." The decision was a call to action, a battle cry. Its tone left no doubt in observers' minds about whether the court would enforce strict compliance with NEPA's provisions. Orloff and Brooks, The National Environmental Policy Act, 354-355 (1980).[9]

7. What is a "major federal action"? Is the Chicod Creek channelization project federal? The entire project is to be undertaken by the local District. Yet federal dollars are being spent and "many persons and agencies have become involved." Does that mean that every expenditure of federal revenue-sharing funds requires an EIS?

Note the following excerpt from the CEQ regulations on the meaning and implementation of NEPA[10] –

§1508.18 Major Federal Action. "Major Federal action" includes actions with effects that may be major and which are potentially subject to Federal control and responsibility. Major reinforces but does not have a meaning independent of significantly (§1508.27). Actions include the circumstance where the responsible officials fail to act and that failure to act is reviewable by courts or administrative tribunals under the Administrative Procedure Act or other applicable law as agency action.

(a) Actions include new and continuing activities, including projects and programs entirely or partly financed, assisted, conducted, regulated, or approved by federal agencies; new or revised agency rules, regulations, plans,

8. [See *SIPI*, page 638 *infra*; *Vermont Yankee*, page 581 *supra*; NRDC v. Morton, page 632 *infra*.]

9. The *Calvert Cliffs* decision addressed the AEC's regulations, and found them unlawful under NEPA in four respects: (1) permitting hearing board members not to consider environmental issues; (2) prohibiting nonradiological environmental issues from being raised at hearings noticed before March 4, 1971; (3) deferring to certifications from other environmental agencies; and (4) waiting until the operating license stage for the NEPA analysis of projects already under construction.

10. All references to CEQ regulations are from the July 1, 1990 edition, codified at 40 CFR Ch. V, §1500 et seq.

> policies, or procedures; and legislative proposals. Actions do not include funding assistance solely in the form of general revenue sharing funds, distributed under the State and Local Fiscal Assistance Act of 1972, 31 U.S.C.A. §1221 et seq., with no Federal agency control over the subsequent use of such funds. Actions do not include bringing judicial or administrative civil or criminal enforcement actions.

In addition, §1508.18 explains that federal actions tend to involve the adoption of official policy, formal plans, or programs, or the approval of specific projects. Courts also have held federal permits, licenses, or leases given to private parties to be federal actions.

As to whether it is a "major" action, isn't the Chicod Creek project's $706,684 cost a trifling amount in the federal context? Conceptual rather than financial definitions obviously are part of the decision, which depends on an analysis of surrounding circumstances. Is an armed forces plan to launch an amphibious practice assault on a beach in Marine's Acadia National Park a "major" action? Is the installation of an incinerator on a federal hospital? The courts answered "no" and "yes," respectively, perhaps making a distinction based upon short-term versus long-term actions. If Chicod Creek were only 4 miles long, would the project be "major"? Can you take notice of *cumulative* effects in order to judge whether an action is "major" or of significant effect? See §1508.27, beginning on the next page *infra*, at (b)(7).

8. The "small handle" problem. Consider this not-so-hypothetical: several Japanese and Korean corporations plan to open seventeen woodchipping installations throughout the southeastern United States, designed to process trees and vegetation stripped from hundreds of thousands of acres of private forests, and ship the chips by barge and freighter to the Far East, as raw material for paper and laminates. This activity would affect the biological and climatalogical character of major portions of six southern states. Assume that the only federal permit required is a Corps of Engineers wharf-building permit for the barge-loading facilities. With that federal permit, the operation will take place; without it, it will not. The corporate proponents and the Corps can argue, however, that a barge wharf is too minor a structure to require an EIS.

This is the small handle problem. Courts disagree on whether, in such cases, the NEPA EIS requirement is triggered by the entire factual consequences of a federal action or focuses exclusively on the effects of the federal component of the project. In Winnebago Tribe v. REA, 621 F.2d 269 (8th Cir. 1980), the court held that a federal river-crossing permit necessary for construction of a 67-mile high-tension power line was not sufficient federal involvement to require an EIS. Some courts have been more willing to note the actual effect of federal actions. Colorado River Indian Tribes v. Marsh, 605 F. Supp. 1425 (C.D.Cal. 1985), held that a Corps permit for riverbank re-inforcement (a practical precondition for a proposed large rural commercial and residential development) required an EIS covering the entire actual impact deriving from the federal action. NEPA, the court held, implicitly incorporates reasonable forecasting of consequential and environmental effects. In a Maine case, where construction of a major oil terminal on Sears Island depended upon grant of a Corps permit for an access road causeway, the court required an EIS covering the entire development, taking into account the "reasonably foreseeable indirect effects" of consequential industrial development, because the causeway was a necessary part of the larger plan. Sierra Club v. Marsh, 769 F.2d 868, 877 (1st Cir. 1985).

9. **"Significantly affecting the human environment."** This standard echoes the preceding issues. "Significance" similarly varies according to context. What if the project allegedly has net *beneficial* effects? One SCS official argued that this was so in stream channelization cases, adding that "Conservation is our middle name!" NEPA is clearly aimed at *adverse* environmental effects (and the present CEQ regulations so direct the EIS procedure); if adverse effects exist, the courts have generally not permitted the counterbalancing of alleged benefits to avoid NEPA.[11]

The CEQ regulations describe "significantly" in terms of "context" and "intensity:"

> §1508.27 "Significantly." "Significantly" as used in NEPA requires considerations of both context and intensity:
>
> (a) *Context.* This means that the significance of an action must be analyzed in several contexts such as society as a whole (human, national), the affected region, the affected interests, and the locality. Significance varies with the setting of the proposed action. For instance, in the case of a site-specific action, significance would usually depend upon the effects in the locale rather than in the world as a whole. Both short- and long-term effects are relevant.
>
> (b) *Intensity.* This refers to the severity of impact. Responsible officials must bear in mind that more than one agency may make decisions about partial aspects of a major action. The following should be considered in evaluating intensity:
>
> (1) Impacts that may be both beneficial and adverse. A significant effect may exist even if the Federal agency believes that on balance the effect will be beneficial.
>
> (2) The degree to which the proposed action affects public health or safety.
>
> (3) Unique characteristics of the geographic area such as proximity to historic or cultural resources, park lands, prime farmlands, wetlands, wild and scenic rivers, or ecologically critical areas.
>
> (4) The degree to which the effects on the quality of the human environment are likely to be highly controversial.
>
> (5) The degree to which the possible effects on the human environment are highly uncertain or involve unique or unknown risks.

11. After an agency has complied with NEPA, issuing an adequate EIS, it may still decide to proceed based on a balance of environmental and nonenvironmental issues (unless going forward can be shown to be "arbitrary").

(6) The degree to which the action may establish a precedent for future actions with significant effects or represents a decision in principle about a future consideration.

(7) Whether the action is related to other actions with individually insignificant but cumulatively significant impacts. Significance exists if it is reasonable to anticipate a cumulatively significant impact on the environment. Significance cannot be avoided by terming an action temporary or by breaking it down into small component parts.

(8) The degree to which the action may adversely affect districts, sites, highways, structures, or objects listed in or eligible for listing in the National Register of Historic Places or may cause loss or destruction of significant scientific, cultural, or historical resources.

(9) The degree to which the action may adversely affect an endangered or threatened species or its habitat that has been determined to be critical under the Endangered Species Act of 1973.

(10) Whether the action threatens a violation of Federal, State, or local law or requirements imposed for the protection of the environment.

10. FONSIs. The *Chicod Creek* case offers an example of another tack: The SCS Administrator made a "negative declaration" or "FONSI" ("finding of no significant impact"), a declaration that the project would cause no significant environmental effect. A FONSI must be based upon an initial Environmental Assessment, or "EA," in which the agency briefly discusses the need for the proposal as well as the environmental impacts of and alternatives to the proposal. An EA is a threshold document, and is held to a lower degree of analysis than an EIS. Typically, a court will defer to the agency's decision unless the citizens can show that it is arbitrary and capricious. FONSIs are tactically attractive to many federal project directors because they permit the agency to circumvent EIS requirements. How did Judge Larkins avoid deference to the agency's FONSI claim, taking on the decision himself?

A corollary question, raised in *Chicod Creek* and subsequent cases, is whether agencies can base negative declaration FONSIs on the claim that their projects will produce environmental benefits as well as detriments – or that agency mitigation efforts will substantially lessen the impacts – so that on balance there will be no *net* significant impact. This claim, which would make EIS compliance subject to self-serving agency estimates of project benefits and detriments, has not fared well in the courts.[12]

11. Formal compliance vs. "functional equivalence." The judge scarcely listened to the SCS's claim that even though it had not filed a formally-prepared EIS, it had substantially complied with the various requirements of an EIS; yet Congress appears to have drafted the phrase "statement" instead of "formal finding" precisely

12. The statutory term "significantly" does not distinguish between positive and negative impacts, which argues against an interpretation of net negative impact as the trigger for the EIS.

in order to avoid formal requirements. This court simply says, however, that "an environmental impact statement has not been prepared and filed for the Chicod Creek Watershed Project."

In several early NEPA cases polluters tried to use the statute against EPA itself, and courts began to develop an exception for environmental protection agencies whose procedures provide the "functional equivalent" of NEPA. "[The courts have seen] little need in requiring a NEPA statement from an agency whose raison d'etre is the protection of the environment and whose decision...is necessarily infused with the environmental considerations so pertinent to Congress in designing the statutory framework. To require a 'statement,' in addition to a decision setting forth the same considerations, would be a legalism carried to the extreme." International Harvester Co. v. Ruckelshaus, 478 F. 2d 615, 650 n. 130 (D.C. Cir. 1973); Texas Committee on Natural Resources v. Bergland, 573 F.2d 201, 207 (5th Cir. 1979). How similar to the EPAprocedures do agency procedures need to be in order to be deemed "functionally equivalent" to NEPA? Does the expansion of this judge-made doctrine undermine NEPA's express requirement that *all* federal agencies shall prepare environmental impact statements?

In State of Alabama ex rel. Siegelman v. EPA, 911 F. 2d 499 (11th Cir. 1990), the EPA issued a permit to allow the ChemWaste company to open the nation's largest hazardous waste disposal facility at Emelle, Alabama, without preparing an EIS. EPA asserted that the RCRA permit process was the functional equivalent of an EIS. The court held that:

> NEPA is [a] general statute forcing agencies to consider the environmental consequences of their actions and to allow the public a meaningful opportunity to learn about and to comment on the proposed actions. If there were no RCRA, NEPA would seem to apply here. But RCRA is the later and more specific statute directly governing EPA's process for issuing permits to hazardous waste management facilities. As such, RCRA is an exception to NEPA and controls here.
>
> Petitioners complain, and EPA agrees, that RCRA does not require EPA to consider every point the agency would have to consider in preparing a formal EIS under NEPA; thus, NEPA and RCRA conflict. Still, RCRA is the functional (though not the structural or literal) equivalent and more specific counterpart of NEPA. RCRA is comprehensive in its field of application. RCRA's substantive and procedural standards are intended to ensure that EPA considers fully, with the assistance of meaningful public comment, environmental issues involved in the permitting of hazardous waste management facilities. The RCRA permitting procedures "strike a workable balance between some of the advantages and disadvantages of full application of NEPA." *Portland Cement*, 486 F.2d at 386 (finding section III of Clean Air Act functionally equivalent to NEPA)....
>
> NEPA's environmental impact statement is merely an implement devised by Congress to require government agencies to think about and weigh environmental factors before acting. Considered in this light, an organization like

> EPA whose regulatory activities are necessarily concerned with environmental consequences need not stop in the middle of its proceedings in order to issue a separate and distinct impact statement just to be issuing it. 911 F. 2d at 505.[13]

The procedures mapped out in the CEQ's NEPA regulations include extensive provisions requiring agencies to make diligent efforts to solicit information from the public and from other agencies with relevant expertise, to provide adequate notice of NEPA-related hearings, and to respond to comments in the final EIS. Does the "functional equivalence" doctrine adequately address the role of public involvement and comment in the EIS procedure under NEPA? Is it clear that EPA examined alternatives or considered the environmental consequences of issuing a permit to the Emelle facility? What standards would be applied to the SCS channelization process if the Chicod Creek case were brought today?

12. Conflicting statutory mandates. Courts have recognized a narrow exception to NEPA's EIS requirement where compliance with NEPA would result in a "clear and fundamental conflict of statutory duty." Flint Ridge Dev. Co. v. Scenic Rivers Ass'n., 426 U.S. 776, 791 (1976). In *Flint Ridge*, the court held that the Secretary of HUD was not required to prepare an EIS before allowing disclosure notices for large-scale rural subdivisions to be filed, even if the developments would significantly affect the environment. Because the Interstate Land Sales Full Disclosure Act required the Secretary to allow accurate and complete notices to go into effect within 30 days of filing, the Court found that it would be impossible simultaneously to prepare an EIS and to respond adequately to comments. While acknowledging that NEPA requires that agencies comply "to the fullest extent possible," the Court reasoned that NEPA was not intended to "repeal by implication any other statute." The Court also, however, quoted statements from House Conferees involved in drafting §102, providing that "no agency shall utilize an excessively narrow construction of its existing statutory authorization to avoid compliance [with NEPA]."

Courts have been unwilling to apply the *Flint Ridge* exception liberally. In Jones v. Gordon, 621 F. Supp. 7 (D. Alaska 1985), the district court held that the National Marine Fisheries Service (NMFS) could not issue a permit for the taking of up to 100 Orca whales without preparing an EIS. The court rejected the argument that the 90-day time limit for issuing such permits under the Marine Mammal Protection Act rendered NMFS compliance with NEPA impossible. Instead, the court held that "in the rare cases where an EIS may be required, the NMFS can create time in the application process by delaying initial publication of the notice of the application in the Federal Register." The court found the conflict between statutes in this case to be minor and ultimately reconcilable.

---

13. See Merrell v. Thomas, 807 F.2d 776, 778, 779 (9th Cir. 1986)(NEPA inapplicable where Federal Insecticide, Fungicide, and Rodenticide Act provided more specific registration requirements). See generally Busic v. United States, 446 U.S. 398, 406 (1980)(more specific statute is given precedence over more general one, regardless of temporal sequence).

13. "Significantly affecting the *human* environment." What does that phrase mean? Chicod Creek is not human, but without much questioning courts have interpreted the phrase to cover natural environmental qualities that affect humans. What about an Army decision to close down a military depot, which will have major socio-economic dislocation impacts on humans? See Breckinridge v. Rumsfeld, 537 F.2d 864 (6th Cir. 1976)(No compliance necessary).

The Supreme Court confronted the question about NEPA's application to the human environment in Metropolitan Edison v. PANE, 460 U.S. 166 (1983). The worst nuclear accident Americans have yet experienced occurred on March 28, 1979, at Three Mile Island, south of Harrisburg, Pennsylvania. After the accident, the two nuclear reactors at the plant were shut down. Only one of them, however, had been damaged in the accident. After a lengthy investigation and public hearings, the NRC decided to allow restart of the undamaged reactor (TMI-1). During the hearings, the commission consistently refused to consider neighboring residents' claims that NEPA requires it to study the psychological distress that would allegedly accompany the restart. People Against Nuclear Energy (PANE), a group composed primarily of neighbors of TMI, sought judicial review.

Note the definition of "Human Environment" articulated in the CEQ regulations:

> §1508.14 Human environment. Human environment shall be interpreted comprehensively to include the natural and physical environment and the relationship of people with that environment...This means that economic or social effects are not intended by themselves to require preparation of an environmental impact statement. When an environmental impact statement is prepared and economic or social and natural or physical environmental effects are interrelated, then the environmental impact statement will discuss all of these effects on the human environment.

The NRC argued that NEPA requires only that effects on the "natural environment" must be studied. Psychological stress in this case is a product of area residents' fear of a second accident at Three Mile Island, and is not a product of physical changes in the environment. "Peoples' anxiety has very little to do with the environment," the NRC said. Did the psychological effects of restarting the reactor mean that it would be an "action significantly affecting the human environment?"

Justice Rehnquist answered that the NRC need not consider PANE's contentions. His argument for the majority was that:

> First, §102(2)(C) does not require an agency to assess every impact or effect of its proposed action, but only impacts or effects on the environment. The statute's context shows that Congress was talking about the physical environment. Although NEPA states its goals in sweeping terms of human health and welfare, these goals are ends that Congress has chosen to pursue by means of protecting the physical environment.

> Second, NEPA does not require agencies to evaluate the effects of risk *qua* risk. The terms "environmental effects" and "environmental impact" in §102(2)(C) should be read to include a requirement of a reasonably close causal relationship between a change in the physical environment and the effect at issue. Here, the federal action that affects the environment is permitting renewed operation of TMI-1. The direct effects of this action include release of low-level radiation, increased fog, and the release of warm water into the Susquehanna River, all of which are effects the NRC has considered. The NRC has also considered the risk of a nuclear accident, but a risk of an accident is not an effect on the physical environment. In a causal chain from renewed operation of TMI-1 to psychological health damage, the element of risk and its perception by PANE's members are necessary middle links. That element of risk lengthens the causal chain beyond NEPA's reach. Regardless of the gravity of the harm alleged by PANE, if a harm does not have a sufficiently close connection to the physical environment, NEPA does not apply.
>
> Finally, the fact that PANE's claim was made in the wake of the accident at TMI-2 is irrelevant. NEPA is not directed at the effects of past accidents and does not create a remedial scheme for past federal actions.

Are these conclusions self-evident? What happened to the word "human" in the phrase "human environment"? Is the opinion nevertheless correct in holding that there must be some limits upon NEPA coverage of effects that occur far down a chain of indirect causation? Or does the gravity of potential harms, or NEPA's logic in general, argue for consideration of all real consequential effects? Compare the *Pruitt* case's consideration of long-distance liability in the Kepone affair, at page 160 *supra*.

14. The injunction. Quite simply, the Chicod Creek project had no EIS, so NEPA was violated. Note, however, that injunctive relief was not automatic; the court traditionally balances the equities before deciding to issue an injunction. How does the judge weigh the value of NEPA compliance against the financial costs involved? In some NEPA cases, judges have permitted the agency to continue construction while preparing an EIS on the question of whether the project should be built. EDF v. Ellis Armstrong, 487 F.2d 814 (9th Cir. 1973)(New Melones Dam). How does a court determine whether an injunction is justified for an ongoing project that does not have an EIS?[14] In another context, the Supreme Court has said that, once having found a statutory violation, it had no discretion but to see that the law was complied with. TVA v. Hill, 437 U.S. 153 (1978). As to NEPA violations, however, the Court

14. In Boston v. Volpe, the 1st Circuit confronted an ongoing airport construction project which would destroy wetlands, for which an EIS had not been completed. The court wrote that "The concept of [NEPA] was that responsible officials would think about environment *before* a significant project was launched; that what would be assessed was a *proposed* action, not a fait accompli." For projects under construction without EISs, "a full statement is required 'if an irrefutable showing cannot be made that [environmental] consequences were fully evaluated at the time of initial...funding,'" [quoting DOT regulations] despite the fact that "a belated effort to comply with NEPA may or may not prove to be as unlikely an enterprise as adding yeast to an unleavened loaf." 464 F.2d 254, 257 (1st Cir. 1972)(an injunction against state agency defendants, however, was denied).

has appeared less ready to hold defendants strictly to compliance. Amoco Prod. Co. v. Village of Gambell, 480 U.S. 531 (1987); cf. Sierra Club v. Marsh, 872 F.2d 497, 500 (1st Cir. 1989). Does failure to consider environmental consequences in agency decisionmaking constitute irreparable harm? Or must there be an imminent threat of serious injury to justify the granting of injunctive relief? See pages 666–669 *infra*.

Lower courts have been increasingly reluctant to find NEPA violations and to issue injunctive relief when NEPA violations occur. CEQ records reflect that courts granted only 3 injunctions out of 80 NEPA cases filed in 1987, as compared to 202 injunctions granted out of the 938 NEPA cases filed in 1977. This represents a decrease from 22 percent to 4 percent in the granting of injunctions in NEPA cases.[15] To some extent, of course, this may reflect a substantial improvement in agencies' compliance with EIS requirements.

15. A bond requirement? Finally, having won everything at issue, the citizens unexpectedly were faced with Judge Larkins' requirement of a $75,000 bond. Such bonds are common in commercial litigation. Why not here?

NRDC v. Grant

U.S. Court of Appeals for the Fourth Circuit, 1972
(unreported) 2 ELR 20,555 (Sept. 5, 1972)(No. Misc. 979)

ORDER

HAYNSWORTH, J. In this ecology case, the District Judge issued a preliminary injunction because no environmental impact statement had been filed. It was conditioned, however, upon the filing by the plaintiffs of a bond in the amount of $75,000. The bond was not filed, and the District Judge withdrew the preliminary injunction on that account. Meanwhile, however, an environmental impact statement had been filed, substantially changing the posture of the case.

The controversy is far from ended. The plaintiffs intend to attack the adequacy of the environmental impact statement and they seek a continuing injunction against commencement of the project until that question is determined. That is a question initially for the District Court, not for us, but the plaintiffs, organizations interested in conservation and having no financial interest in this controversy, are fearful that any further injunctive order will again be conditioned upon their posting a large bond.

Thus, they seek to prosecute an appeal and have requested a stay of the order dissolving the injunction. The defendants have countered with a suggestion of mootness.

Under all the circumstances, we think an immediate remand of this case to the District Court appropriate.

Any further preliminary injunctive order should not be issued unless the District Judge, after examination of the environmental impact statement, is of the opinion that it is probably deficient, and that the plaintiffs more likely than not will

15. See Blumm, The National Environmental Policy Act at Twenty: A Preface, 20 Envt'l L. 447, 451, n.18, citing CEQ, Envt'l Quality 209-10 (1979); CEQ, Envt'l Quality 409 (1978).

prevail. If he satisfies himself on that score, there seems little or no reason for requiring more than a nominal bond of these plaintiffs, who are acting much as private attorneys general. If he finds no apparent deficiencies in the statement and little probability that the plaintiffs will ultimately prevail, he should deny all interim relief and await the conclusion of the hearing on the merits.

COMMENTARY AND QUESTION

1. The bond. Note the court's discussion of the only point the citizens care about, the possibility of another $75,000 bond. Does Judge Haynsworth's opinion reflect economic reality? On the other hand, what would be the result of a blanket requirement that environmental plaintiffs seeking to enforce federal laws must post bonds sufficient to cover potential damages to defendants wrongfully restrained?[16]

The case then went back to Judge Larkins' court for review of the SCS's newly-prepared EIS. The citizen plaintiffs again sued for a preliminary injunction, alleging that even though there now was an EIS, it was inadequate under the terms of NEPA.

NRDC v. Grant

U.S. District Court, Eastern District of North Carolina, 1973
355 F. Supp. 280

LARKINS, District Judge:

"The River...is the living symbol of all the life it sustains or nourishes – fish, aquatic insects, water ouzels, otter, fisher, deer, elk, bear, and all other animals, including man, who are dependent upon it or who enjoy it for its sight, its sound or its life." Justice William O. Douglas, dissenting in Sierra Club v. Morton, 405 U.S. 727 (1972).

Now comes this cause before this Court on the Plaintiffs' Motion for Preliminary Injunctive Relief to enjoin the Defendants from inviting any further bids and from taking any further steps to authorize, approve, fund, finance, sponsor, initiate, contract for, or commence construction or installation of the Chicod Creek Watershed Project pending final hearing upon the Plaintiffs' claims.... This is an action to permanently enjoin the construction of the Project because construction of this 66-mile stream channelization project allegedly would violate the Watershed Protection and Flood Prevention Act, P.L. 83-566, 16 U.S.C.A. §100-1009 (1970), the National Environmental Policy Act of 1969, 42 U.S.C.A. §4321 et seq. (1970), the rules and regulations of the Soil Conservation Service, United States Department of Agriculture, and §13 of the Rivers and Harbors Act of 1899 (Refuse Act) 33 U.S.C.A. §407 (1899)....

FINDINGS OF FACT AND CONCLUSIONS OF LAW

1. There is a Substantial Probability that the Provisions of NEPA are Not Satisfied by the Chicod Creek Watershed Environmental Statement

---

16. See Calderon, Bond Requirements Under FRCP 65(c): an Emerging Equitable Exemption for Public Interest Litigants, 13 Envt'l Aff. L. Rev. 125 (1985).

a. Scope of Judicial Review of the Environmental Impact Statement

As the Court views this case, the ultimate decisions must not be made by the judiciary but by the executive and legislative branches of our government. This court does not intend to substitute its judgment as to what would be the best use of Chicod Creek and its environs for that of the Congress or those administrative departments of the executive branch which are charged by the Congress with the duty of carrying out its mandate. The Court's function is to determine whether the environmental effects of the proposed action and reasonable alternatives are sufficiently disclosed, discussed, and that conclusions are substantiated by supportive opinion and data. Environmental Defense Fund v. Corps of Engineers, 325 F. Supp. 749 (E.D. Ark. 1971); Natural Resources Defense Council v. Morton, 458 F.2d 827 (D.C. Cir. 1972).

b. Requirements of NEPA

§102(2)(C) of NEPA requires, first, that federal agencies make full and accurate disclosure of the environmental effects of proposed action and alternatives to such action; and, second, that the agencies give full and meaningful consideration to these effects and alternatives in their decision-making. Natural Resources Defense Council v. Morton, *supra*. In Environmental Defense Fund v. Corps of Engineers, *supra* at 759, Judge Eisels wrote: "At the very least, NEPA is an environmental full disclosure law...intended to make...decision-making more responsive and responsible. The 'detailed statement' required by 102(2)(C) should, at a minimum, contain such information as will alert the President, the Council on Environmental Quality, the public, and indeed, the Congress to all known possible consequences of proposed agency action."

But NEPA requires more than full disclosure of environmental consequences and project alternatives. NEPA requires full consideration of the same in agency decision making. Calvert Cliffs Coordinating Committee v. Atomic Energy Commission, 449 F.2d 1109 (D.C. Cir. 1971).

The environmental impact statement "must be written in language that is understandable to the nontechnical minds and yet contains enough scientific reasoning to alert specialists to particular problems within the field of their expertise." Environmental Defense Fund v. Corps of Engineers, 348 F. Supp. 916 W.D. Miss. 1972).

C. The Final Statement Omits and Misrepresents a Number of Important Environmental Effects of the Project.

(1)*The Statement Misrepresents the Adverse Environmental Effects of the Project upon Fish Habitat*

The final Statement concedes that the Project will greatly increase the quantities of sediment carried downstream from the project area into the lower reaches of Chicod Creek and the Tar River. Immediately after construction, annual sediment deposit in the lower Chicod will be 11,670 tons. Sediment yield at the confluence of the Tar River is expected to be 730 tons annually. On the assumption that the banks will stabilize in two years, sedimentation will still be increased to 4,010 tons deposited annually in Chicod Creek and 250 tons in the Tar River. The present annual yield in the Tar River is 50 tons.

While disclosing the fact of this increase in sediment load, the statement contains no discussion of its downstream effects. The statement merely concludes, without supportive scientific data and opinion that "No significant reduction in quality of the waters of the Tar River, Pamlico River, and Pamlico Sound is expected." Credible evidence suggests the opposite conclusion. Having conceded a massive increase in sedimentation, the Statement disposes of its environmental effects in one conclusory statement unsupported by empirical or experimental data, scientific authorities or explanatory information of any kind.

Where there is no reference to scientific or objective data to support conclusory statements, NEPA's full disclosure requirements have not been honored.

(2)*The Statement Misrepresents the Effect of the Project upon Fish Resources*

The Statement is not at all clear on the effect of the Project on the fishery resources in Chicod Creek. It suggests that there will be effects upon the resident and anadromous fish in Chicod Creek, but the Statement does not define the effects. Yet the Statement without any supportive data declares "Most of the fishery resources within the watershed will not be affected by the project's works of improvement or will be mitigated." This falls far short of the standards of NEPA.

(3)*The Statement Ignores the Effect of the Project on Potential Eutrophication Problems in the Tar-Pamlico Estuary*

Eutrophication problems occur in waterways which accumulate an excess of nutrients such as nitrogen and phosphorous. Nutrients may be introduced in the waterways form several sources including agricultural runoff and swamp drainage. At the present time the nearby Chowan River is suffering from a very serious eutrophication problem. Also, other rivers in coastal North Carolina face potential eutrophication problems. Indeed, the Interim Report of Chowan River Water Quality Study states:

> In that connection, while the Chowan River is the first in North Carolina to show the beginning of a state of eutrophication, it probably will not be the last.... Of particular concern, the lower Pamlico and Neuse Rivers are already showing evidence of over-fertilization, and deterioration to a eutrophic condition appears imminent. Development and rigid enforcement of a comprehensive water management plan based on extensive and continuing studies, is vitally needed if the coastal waters of North Carolina are to remain an asset rather than become a liability to the people of the State.

Eutrophication is a problem that needs extensive study and research. Yet the Statement is silent on eutrophication. This is a violation of the "full disclosure" requirements of NEPA.

(4)*The Statement Fails to Disclose the Maintenance History of P.L. 566 Projects*

The sponsors of the Project, the local drainage district, are responsible for the operation and maintenance of the structural measures of the Project. Evidence indicated that local sponsors have failed to adequately perform their maintenance responsibilities in the past. Although here there are agreements defining the responsibilities and duties of the local sponsors, this Court is concerned by the history of past projects as the success of a project is dependent upon the operation and maintenance of the project after it is completed. The Statement should disclose the history of success and failure of similar projects.

(5)*The Statement Ignores the Serious Environmental Consequences of the Proposed Use of Kudzu*

Although one may not know what it is called, a person does not have to be a scientist to recognize kudzu. One can frequently see kudzu along roads and highways. Most likely it can be seen growing on banks, stretching over shrubs and underbrush, engulfing trees, small and large, short and tall, slowly destroying and snuffing out the life of its unwilling host. Even manmade structures are susceptible to the vine – the tall slender green tree may be your telephone pole. However, if controlled, kudzu may have erosion preventing value. The defendants propose to plant one row of kudzu at the top edge of the channel slope in cultivated areas – along 23.5 miles of the new channels. As to the use of kudzu, the Statement merely discloses; "one row of kudzu will be planted at the very top edge of the channel slope through cultivated areas. The growth of kudzu will be controlled by mechanical methods." The Statement fails to disclose *how* the growth of kudzu can be controlled by mechanical or any other methods and in this respect fails to satisfy the requirements of NEPA.

(6)*The Statement Misrepresents and Fails to Disclose Other Important Environmental Effects of the Project*

The Statement fails to disclose that over 17 percent of the acreage to be benefited by the Project is held by the Weyerhaeser Company, a large lumber company.

The Statement does not contain an adequate discussion of the possible adverse effects of the Project upon downstream flooding.

d. The Statement Does not Disclose or Discuss the Cumulative Effects of the Project.

In the Memorandum Opinion and Order filed March 16, 1972, this Court found that the Chicod Creek Watershed Project as proposed would have a cumulative effect upon the environment in the eastern plains of North Carolina. The Guidelines of the Council of Environmental Quality focus attention upon the "overall cumulative impact of the action proposed (and further actions contemplated)," since the effect of decision about a project or a complex of projects "can be individually limited but cumulatively considerable," 36 Fed. Reg. 7724, April 23, 1971. Yet, the Defendants have failed to consider fully in the final Statement the cumulative impact of the Chicod Creek Watershed Project and other channelization projects on the environmental and economic resources of Eastern North Carolina. The only reference whatsoever to cumulative impact relates solely to the "South Atlantic Flyway for migratory waterfowl." With respect to all other resources affected by the Project there was no disclosure of consideration of cumulative effect. The cumulative effect of sedimentation is ignored in the Statement. There is no discussion of the potential adverse effects of long-term accumulation of nutrients caused by this and other channelization projects in the Tar-Pamlico River Basin. There is no discussion of the cumulative impact of drainage projects upon hardwood timber or groundwater resources. As stream channelization projects have cumulative effects upon a number of the major resources of the North Carolina coastal plains, such effects should be assessed and disclosed in the environmental impact statement.

e. The Statement Does Not Fully Disclose or Adequately Discuss Alternatives to the Project.

The "full disclosure" impact statement required by NEPA must contain a full and objective discussion of (1) reasonable alternatives to the proposed project and (2) the environmental impacts of each alternative. The Statement falls far short of satisfying these important and essential standards. Several critical reasonable alternatives are not discussed at all in the Statement. The recommendation of the Bureau of Sport Fisheries and Wildlife that seven miles of channelization be deleted from the most productive portion of the Chicod ecosystem is not discussed as an alternative to the Project. The Statement fails to discuss the alternative of deferral of the Project. Deferral is particularly appropriate in view of the differing opinion about the environmental effects of the Project and Section 102(2)(A) of NEPA which "makes the completion of an adequate research program a prerequisite to agency action." Environmental Defense Fund v. Hardin, 325 F. Supp. 1401 (D.D.C., 1971). Many of the conclusions in the Statement as to the potential adverse effects of the Project are not supported by references to scientific or other sources. The Statement omits any discussion of the recommendation of the North Carolina Department of Natural and Economic Resources that vertical drainage and water level control structures be discussed in the alternatives section, specifically as they mitigate any adverse ground water effects of the proposed project.

Alternatives are discussed only superficially, and nowhere are the environmental impacts of the alternatives discussed. The Statement thus does not provide "information sufficient to permit a reasoned choice of alternatives so far as environmental aspects are concerned." Natural Resources Defense Council v. Morton, *supra*. It is not the "full disclosure" statement required by NEPA.

f. Conclusions

This Court finds as a fact that the final Chicod Creek Watershed Environmental Statement does not fully and adequately disclose the adverse environmental effects of the Chicod Creek Watershed Project; nor does the Statement adequately disclose or discuss reasonable alternatives to the Project; and, therefore, there is a substantial probability that the Plaintiffs will be able to demonstrate at trial on the merits that the final Statement is not the "full disclosure" statement required by this Court's Order of March 16, 1972, and NEPA. A preliminary injunction barring further action on the Project pending a full hearing on the merits is thus appropriate....

COMMENTARY AND QUESTIONS

1. Agencies and EISs – a shotgun marriage? What apparently was the nature and tone of the Chicod Creek EIS? Most agencies have an understandable inclination to build their projects as conveniently as possible, and EISs do not serve this end. The central problem of the §102 EIS requirement is that it presents federal agencies (especially "construction" agencies and regulatory agencies with a high level of market involvement like the Nuclear Regulatory Commission, the Department of Agriculture, etc.) with conflicting mandates. On one hand, they have specific statutory missions, backed by the elaborate reward structure of supportive congressional committees, money, and the support of the related private industries and organizations with which they work. On the other hand, they have the vague generalized values and directives of NEPA, for which there is no affirmative administrative reward system (beyond the satisfaction of a job well done in environmental terms). At the end of a year, agency officials tend to measure their accomplishments in terms of how many miles of river were dammed or channelized, or how many reactors licensed – it must be harder to measure institutional success in terms of how many wetlands have *not* been disrupted, or how many rivers left as they are. Yet EISs, by illuminating facts and concerns that previously had no legal place in the institutional decisionmaking process, now can show in some cases that the country would be better off without the agency's projects. A straightforward EIS may militate against building the project at all, or may indicate a less destructive way of constructing it, for the sake of newly-declared ecological values that do not square with the agency's own specific mandate.

Little wonder, then, that there is a marked tendency to write EISs in a manner that is consistent with agencies' program missions. Pick up any recent environmental impact statement, review its prose, and you will probably be confronted with the predictable agency reaction to contradictory statutory mandates.

So the temptation is great to make the EIS a "post hoc rationalization" which is supportive of the decision the agency has already effectively made. Project benefits are stressed, negative effects are briefly noted and rated "manageable," and alternatives are cursorily noted and dismissed.

Courts rarely mention the reality of this administrative inclination to write self-justifying impact statements, but in the Chicod Creek case the court seems skeptical. In judicial review of agency decisions under NEPA and other environmental laws, can environmental lawyers ask judges to take account of political science and be *less deferential*, where applicable laws were designed to constrain the agencies' singlemindedness? Do they already do so implicitly?

2. Judicial psychology. Do you detect a change in Judge Larkins' tone? What happened? There is no mention now of the alleged project benefits to small farmers; rather the opinion is a catalog of the project's negative effects. Can you discern which pieces of evidence at trial got through to the judge most dramatically? How sophisticated would the various pieces of plaintiff's evidence have to be on eutrophication, sedimentation, fisheries, and kudzu? What about Weyerhaeser's ownership? Problems of past maintenance? How do environmental plaintiffs get around a judge's natural inclination to defer to official expertise?

3. Epilogue to *Chicod Creek*. What did finally happen in our North Carolina case? As one state official put it, "Old John Larkins saw he was going to make some enemies either way he decided this thing, so he called in the attorneys for both sides and said 'Boys, we've gone through this stuff long enough now, why don't you go settle it between yourselves?' And because the handwriting was on the wall, the SCS agreed to a compromise." [Confidential interview, February 1981]. No channelizing, channel straightening, or major treecutting was allowed; silt removal was permitted in the upper stretches. The lower six to seven miles of the creek were cleaned of snags and silt, but no draglines were permitted. As a result, the stream and its tributaries were to a great degree returned to the quality of the days before intensive agriculture, with a meandering wooded course and restored swimming holes. The redesigned project was so successful that the North Carolina legislature passed a Stream Restoration Act in 1979 mandating consultation with the State Wildlife Resources Commission for all such projects. Is this a success story? What about the poor families that Judge Larkins wrote of in his first opinion? No new subsidized farmland was created. Is this another example of élite conservationism oppressing poor folks?

Section 2. THE JUDICIAL DEVELOPMENT OF NEPA

Especially when a statute is written in such general and enigmatic terms as NEPA, and passed with so little relevant legislative history, it is inevitable that a parade of questions will have to be answered before the statute's shape and substance become clear in practice. The position to which NEPA has evolved over the years, almost entirely as a function of citizen litigation, was certainly not preordained. As the *Chicod Creek* case demonstrated, NEPA could have become merely a footnote of judicial deference to agency action, but didn't. With few exceptions, the federal courts took NEPA seriously. NEPA could also have become a super-statute, imposing strict court-enforced substantive controls on the administrative process. That didn't happen either.

The following materials review some of the basic questions raised in the judicial implementation of NEPA. In the course of this development, NEPA became what it is today – a useful, mixed proposition, a milestone statute in the emerging evolution of national (and international) environmental policy.

a. ISSUES IN IMPLEMENTING THE IMPACT STATEMENT REQUIREMENT

THE EIS: WHAT MUST IT CONTAIN?

Note the array of requirements for the preparation of EISs set out in §102 as it was drafted by Professor Caldwell. Is there any real difference between (i) "environmental impacts," (ii) "adverse environmental effects which cannot be avoided," (iii) "the relationship between short-term uses and maintenance of long-term productivity(?)"; and (iv) "irretrievable commitments of resources"? Some EISs dutifully separate out multiple sections to cover each of these, but analytically it seems that §102 just requires a statement of *effects,* (§102(2)(C) i , ii, iv, & v), and *alternatives* (C(ii) and D), prepared in consultation with other relevant agencies.

Judge Larkins' opinion follows this approach – it looks at only two categories, effects and alternatives. Note the kinds of effects that were left out, insufficiently disclosed, or, worse, "misrepresented" in the EIS. What effects must be discussed, and to what extent, in order to comply with whatever it is that §102 is supposed to do? Effects on human sport? The aesthetics of a scraped-off linear canal? Slight thermal changes in the local micro-climate? Is a short description of sedimentation enough to disclose the existence of a problem to whomever is intended by NEPA to read the EIS? Judge Larkins requires the EIS to consider cumulative effects of this and other projects. Is this supported by the implied intention of NEPA? Another "effect" of the project is to violate our old friend the Refuse Act. Is this itself a §102 "effect" or merely evidence of water quality effects? What if the plaintiffs claim that the project will have an effect that is not clearly provable, like increasing the likelihood of earthquakes? The courts have generally held that if the alleged adverse effect is not purely speculative or minimal, and is supported by some responsible scientist's opinion, then the EIS must deal with it.

But this presents a paradox: in order to convince a court of substantial doubts attending an agency project, plaintiffs must find out in advance much of the information they are asking the agency to develop in an EIS. This requires private plaintiffs to come up with a lot of expensive expert testimony, and to some extent mixes up the players' roles.

To what extent must environmental effects be analyzed and discussed in the EIS? The Chicod Creek EIS discussed eutrophication, for example, but not extensively enough for Judge Larkins. If, as some courts have said, the purpose is to bring the project's consequences to the attention of the agency decision-maker, mere disclosure may be enough. If, on the other hand, the EIS is intended to demonstrate to a court that the agency gave "full consideration" to the impact, *Calvert Cliffs*, 449 F.2d at 1128, then more analysis must be reflected in the EIS itself. A middle ground definition was given by the Ninth Circuit: "reasonably thorough discussion of the significant aspects of the probable environmental consequences is all that is required by an EIS," said the court in Trout Unlimited v. Morton, 509 F.2d 1276, 1283 (1974)(the decision that allowed the construction of the Teton Dam in spite of environmentalists' safety warnings; the dam collapsed, killing more than 100 people).

ALTERNATIVES

Alternatives have been part of our environmental analysis from the beginning of this book, and are a critical part of NEPA's EIS requirement. In some SCS EISs, and those of other agencies, the agency refused to consider the "do-nothing," "no-action," or "zero" alternative. Why? Other agencies refused to consider any alternatives that they themselves could not build or manage. NRDC v. Morton, 458 F.2d 827 (D.C. Cir. 1972) set those arguments to rest: the Interior Department had to consider all practical alternative sources of energy, regardless of whether they were within the agency's control, before deciding to lease offshore oil deposits.

Note the relationship between discussions of alternatives and of environmental consequences required by the following CEQ regulations:

> §1502.14 Alternatives including the proposed action. This section is the heart of the environmental impact statement...[I]t should present the environmental impacts of the proposal and the alternatives in comparative form, thus sharply defining the issues and providing a clear basis of choice among options by the decision maker and the public. In this section agencies shall:
>
> (a) Rigorously explore and objectively evaluate all reasonable alternatives and for alternatives which were eliminated from detailed study, briefly discuss the reasons for their having been eliminated.
>
> (b) Devote substantial treatment to each alternative considered in detail including the proposed action so that reviewers may evaluate their comparative merits.
>
> (c) Include reasonable alternatives not within the jurisdiction of the lead agency.
>
> (d) Include the alternative of no action....
>
> §1502.16 Environmental consequences. ...The discussion will include the environmental impacts of the alternatives including the proposed action, any adverse environmental effects which cannot be avoided...and any irreversible or irretrievable commitments of resources which would be involved in the proposal should it be implemented....

§1502.16 also provides that the EIS will include discussions of direct and indirect effects and their significance; possible conflicts between the proposed action and the objectives of land use plans, policies, and controls for the area concerned; and the energy and resource requirements and conservation potential of the various alternatives. An EIS also must address urban quality, historic and cultural resources, and measures to mitigate adverse evironmental impacts.

If courts do not require consideration of rational alternatives, the stop-and-think process would be neutralized. In Citizens Against Burlington v. Busey, for instance, 938 F.2d 190 (D.C. Cir. 1991)(request for cert. filed, Sept. 9, 1991) an air freight carrier wanted permission to shift its operations 80 miles from Fort Wayne to a Toledo air field, increasing night traffic there from 400 to more than 11,700 flights per year, in order to save operating expenses. The Federal Aviation Administration's EIS considered only the two options advanced by the corporation – the proposed facility, or nothing – ignoring the citizens' evidence that operations could be improved at the original facility. Writing for the D.C. Circuit, Judge Clarence Thomas permitted this circumscribing of EIS alternatives.[17] Writing in dissent, Judge James Buckley, a conservative Reagan appointee, complained that the Thomas opinion allowed nonfederal parties "to define the limits of the EIS inquiry and thus to frustrate one of the principal safeguards of the NEPA process, the mandatory consideration of reasonable alternatives." 938 F.2d at 209.

SEGMENTATION

One agency strategy for avoiding the effect of NEPA has been segmentation. If an entire project raises major environmental questions, divide it into smaller segments, and build the least destructive segment first, with an EIS (or less, an EA with a FONSI) limited to that segment. Then the later segments will draw momentum from the approval and construction of the first. Some courts have rejected these EISs, on the grounds that the segmentation did not have "independent utility" or, implicitly, that this was an attempt to evade NEPA through coercive construction "bootstrapping." Other courts have allowed the strategy. Swan v. Brinegar, 542 F.2d 364 (7th Cir. 1976); Sierra Club v. Callaway (Wallisville Dam), 499 F.2d 982 (5th Cir. 1974); Indian Lookout Alliance v. Volpe, 484 F.2d 11 (8th Cir. 1973).

Would it be legal for the builders of a highway to take one portion of the project that is environmentally destructive – say the portion of the highway that runs through a wetlands – and have the state road department build that without federal dollars, thereby trying to "defederalize" the wetlands stretch of road, avoiding an EIS that would reveal major negative impacts?

INTERAGENCY CONSULTATION

Section 102(2)(C) does not merely require EIS preparation; it also requires that, in this case, the SCS "consult with and obtain the comments of any Federal agency [involved relevant to environmental issues]," and those comments must "accompany the proposal through existing agency review processes." This requirement may have tactical importance, e.g. if the Department of Interior's Fish and Wildlife

17. The Court also declined to require noise mitigation measures required under §509(b)(5) of the Airport & Aviation Import Act (AAIA), 494 U.S.C.A. §2298(b)(5).

Service wants to raise serious questions about habitat destruction, but has no direct power over its sister agency, what can plaintiffs make of the fact that this EIS does not reflect much of an interagency consultation process? If the SCS tried to solicit comments of other agencies, but received none, can the plaintiffs demand an injunction until such consultation does occur?

WHO REALLY PREPARES THE EIS?

Who prepares the EIS? NEPA says "the responsible official," and in a number of early cases the courts had to deal with EISs that were drafted at the local level by state officials or other project proponents and merely adopted by the relevant federal agencies. Citizen plaintiffs successfully urged the courts to require the EISs to be prepared by the federal agencies themselves, on the ground that NEPA was designed to inform the federal decision as it was being made. Greene County Planning Board v. FPC, 455 F.2d 412 (2d Cir. 1972), *cert. denied*, 409 U.S. 849 (1972). What premises are reflected in such lawsuits about the relative bias within and outside the federal agency? Congress amended NEPA in 1975 to permit preparation of the EIS by state agencies that receive federal grants for particular projects. Here the EIS was prepared by the SCS; from whom do you suppose the SCS got its information, and who probably wrote the first draft?

ARE AGENCY PROMISES IN AN EIS ENFORCEABLE?

What if an agency prepares an EIS that promises extensive mitigation work (setting up new wetland reserves, wildlife enchancement, etc.) to offset negative project effects, defeats a citizen lawsuit on this basis, and then announces that it will not undertake the promised work (because it has insufficient funds or whatever)? The lower courts have reviewed a few of these cases, and uniformly have said that the citizens have no remedy. NOE v. Metro. Atlanta Transit Auth., 485 F. Supp. 501 (N.D. Ga. 1980); Ogunquit Village Corp. v. Dagis, 553 F. 2d 243 (1st Cir. 1977). Even if the plaintiffs prove agency bad faith, a court will weigh the value of the requested compliance against the costs. EDF v. Marsh, 651 F. 2d 983 (5th Cir. 1981). But the CEQ regulations imply a different answer.

> §1505.2 Record of decision in cases requiring environmental impact statements. At the time of its decision... each agency shall prepare a concise public record of decision. The record, which may be integrated into any other record prepared by the agency...shall (a) State what the decision was...[and] (c) State whether all practicable means to avoid or minimize environmental harm from the alternative selected have been adopted, and if not, why they were not. A monitoring and enforcement program shall be adopted and summarized where applicable for any mitigation.
>
> §1505.3 Implementing the decision. Agencies may provide for monitoring to assure that their decisions are carried out and should do so in important cases. Mitigation and other conditions established in the environmental impact statement or during its review and committed as part of the decision shall be implemented by the lead agency.... The lead agency shall: (a) Include appropriate conditions in grants, permits or other approvals. (b) Condition funding of actions on mitigation. (c) Upon request, inform cooperating or

commenting agencies on progress in carrying out mitigation measures which they have proposed or which were adopted by the agency making the decision. (d) Upon request, make available to the public the results of relevant monitoring.

THE POWERS OF THE CEQ

The President's Council on Environmental Quality (CEQ), remember, was created by NEPA's Title II. It has no enforcement power, but its guidelines and regulations have had recurrent persuasive power for the courts on NEPA interpretation. Facing the increasing complexity of NEPA caselaw and EIS compliance, the CEQ regulations have tried to streamline the process, including "scoping" overview of the process, page limitations (150 pages or, in the case of complex proposals, 300 pages), and an interagency teamwork approach under the direction of a lead agency. See Yost, Environmental Regulation Myths, Realities, and Reform, 1 Env'tl Prof. 256, 258–59 (1979).

RATIONAL DECISIONMAKING AND NEPA'S SUBSTANTIVE EFFECT?

The earliest chapters of this book set out the analytical basis of questions now raised by NEPA: a sound, rational decision requires consideration of all the significant *effects* of a proposal, and of its *alternatives,* as well as its real benefits. When these have finally been disclosed in an adequate EIS, however, can a court force the agency to make its substantive decision consistent with the EIS? Could Judge Larkins, for example, forbid the Chicod Creek project if the final EIS showed major sedimentation, eutrophication, wildlife and drainage disruption, and showed that the countervailing benefits to farming were estimated at less than $100 per acre?

Put another way, does NEPA have an enforceable substantive requirement – i.e. that agency decisions must be environmentally sound – as well as the bare procedural requirement that an EIS be prepared and circulated? If it is only the latter, then NEPA appears superficial, allowing an agency to go ahead with major destructive projects if only it first accurately catalogs the destructive effects in an EIS document. If, on the other hand, courts can enforce a substantive application of NEPA's broad principles upon an unwilling agency, what limit is there to the judicial power? Suppose Judge Larkins is deeply convinced at the end of the trial on the merits that the Chicod Creek case is ludicrously negative on an overall balance of effect. What can he do? Section 101, of course, is written in substantive terms. It is "the continuing responsibility of the Federal Government to use all practicable means" to achieve environmental quality. Using this language, some courts state that direct "judicial action might be required if there was a significant potential for subversion of the substantive policies in NEPA." Sierra Club v. Froehlke, 309 F Supp. 1289, n. 200, (S.D. Texas 1973)(which required that the Corps of Engineers actually implement a mitigation plan). Justice Rehnquist, however, writing for the Supreme Court in *Vermont Yankee,* 435 U.S. at 558, stated that while NEPA "establishes significant substantive goals for the Nation," its actual requirements for the agencies are "essentially procedural."

JUDICIAL REVIEW: THE ARBITRARY AND CAPRICIOUS TEST?

Even if courts do not have a direct substantive review power under NEPA, they have some ability to review the decisions of federal agencies under the Administrative Procedures Act's §706, which prohibits actions that are "arbitrary, capricious, or an abuse of discretion" (studied further in Chapter 11). What does this test mean? There have been several interpretations in NEPA cases:

> The test is whether the balance of cost and benefits that was struck was arbitrary or clearly gave insufficient weight to environmental values. *Calvert Cliffs*, 449 F.2d at 1115;
>
> Our review will perforce be a narrow one, limited to ensuring that the Commission has adequately explained the fact and policy concerns it relied on [and that these] considerations could by themselves lead a reasonable person to make the judgment that the Agency has made. NRDC v. SEC, 606 F.2d 1031, 1053 (D.C. Cir. 1979);
>
> [The role of the court is to assure that the agency made a] good faith [balancing of environmental benefits and costs.] EDF v. TVA, 339 F. Supp. at 810 (1972);
>
> [The reviewing court must insure that the agency] has taken a "hard look" at environmental consequences. Kleppe v. Sierra Club, 427 U.S. 390, 410 n. 21 (1976).

Each of these tests permits a court to review the agency's substantive decision to some degree. Strycker's Bay Neighborhood Council v. Karlen, 444 U.S. 223 (1980), however, considerably clouded the issue. A low-income housing unit that was determined to have serious environmental consequences (including social and economic ghettoization – urban NEPA issues?) was proposed for a site in Manhattan. The EIS showed alternative sites available which did not have such adverse environmental effects, but each alternative would have required a two-year delay to shift the project. The agency chose to build as planned to save time. The Court of Appeals for the Second Circuit said that in light of NEPA's policy, the two-year time factor could not be treated as "an overriding factor"; "environmental factors...should be given determinable [sic] weight." 590 F.2d at 44. The Supreme Court reversed, saying "once an agency has made a decision subject to NEPA's procedural requirements, the only role for a court is to insure that the agency has *considered* the environmental consequences." What then is the test? The Court cannot mean that an agency can ignore the environmental evidence after considering it. Even the defendant agency conceded that their decision would be arbitrary if it gave little or no decisional weight to environmental factors. Because of the high court's opinion, however, the lower court could no longer give superior weight to environmental factors. So how about equal weight? Does that simplify the question? If the costs of a two-year delay closely balance the negative environmental effects, the agency can be expected to tilt in favor of its original plans, and that decision will not be "arbitrary." But who is to say the opposing factors (apples and oranges?) are or are not closely balanced? If the courts can do so, are they necessarily making part of the substantive decision?

b. THE EIS PROCESS: QUESTIONS OF TIMING AND SCOPE

INTERNAL AGENCY TIMING

The CEQ regulations prescribe basic time parameters for the preparation of an EIS. These timing requirements are minimal, however, reflecting CEQ's view that comprehensive agency scheduling requirements would be too inflexible.

The standard course of the EIS's production as a public document follows the APA rulemaking model: the agency prepares a Draft EIS ("DEIS," analogous to a notice of proposed rulemaking); the DEIS is opened for public comment; the agency prepares the Final EIS ("FEIS," analogous to a final rulemaking) with an appendix of comments received on the draft and the agency's responses thereto. 40 CFR §1506. (Note that there is no requirement that agencies hold hearings on draft or final EISs.)

Once EPA has published notice that an EIS has been filed, an agency cannot make a decision sooner than 90 days after publication, for a draft EIS, or 30 days after publication, for a final EIS. If the periods overlap, the later of the two cut-off dates applies. Agencies must allow at least 45 days for comments on draft statements. 40 CFR §1506.11. The lead agency may set time limits consistent with these parameters. In setting such time limits, the regulations suggest that the agency consider factors such as the scope of the action, the potential environmental risks, the consequences of delay, and the degree to which the proposed action is controversial.

Are these time parameters realistic, given the long lead time customarily involved in planning agency projects, not to mention the length and complexity of modern EIS preparation?

The CEQ regulations suggest that the EIS should indeed be a decision-making tool:

> §1502. 1 Purpose. The primary purpose of an environmental impact statement is to serve as an action-forcing device to insure that the policies and goals defined in [NEPA] are infused into the ongoing programs and actions of the Federal Government.... *An environmental impact statement is more than a disclosure document. It shall be used by Federal officials in conjunction with other relevant material to plan actions and make decisions.* (emphasis added).
>
> §1505.1 Agency decisionmaking procedures. Agencies shall adopt procedures to ensure that decisions are made in accordance with the policies and purposes of the Act. Such procedures shall include... (d) Requiring that relevant environmental documents, comments, and responses accompany the proposal through existing agency review processes *so that agency officials use the statement in making decisions.* (emphasis added)
>
> §1502.2 Implementation.... (f) Agencies shall not commit resources prejudicing selection of alternatives before making a final decision.
>
> §1502.5 Timing. The [EIS] shall be prepared early enough so that it can serve practically as an important contribution to the decision making process and

will not be used to rationalize or justify decisions already made.[18]

SCOPING

The NEPA regulations also introduce the process of "scoping." 40 CFR §1501.7 At an early stage in the decisional process an agency must review the breadth of project effects and alternatives, invite comments from the public and other governmental agencies, and prepare a comprehensive plan for addressing all significant issues. The intent is clearly to facilitate EIS preparation. What would its effect have been on the Chicod Creek EIS?

When in a project's life history should the EIS be prepared?

The *SIPI* case, Scientists Institute for Public Information v. Atomic Energy Commission, 481 F.2d 1079 (D.C. Cir. 1973), presented a demand for an EIS for the federal breeder reactor research program, a sequentially evolving enterprise with millions of dollars in present expenditures, leading to billions in future expenditures, with great potential environmental costs. The question of when in this process an EIS must be presented was poignantly put in the trial judge's question:

> There comes a time, we start with $E=MC^2$, we both agree you don't have to have the impact statement then. Then there comes a time when there are a thousand of these breeder plants in existence all over the country. Sometime before that, surely...there has to be an impact statement, and a long time before that, actually. But the question is, exactly where in this chain do we have to have an impact statement? 481 F.2d at 1093.

The appeals court set up a four-factor balancing test, designed to require an EIS at the point where binding decisions are being made. The factors: (1) the program's likelihood of practical feasibility, and how soon; (2) the availability of data on the technology and its alternatives, and their effects; (3) the likelihood that irretrievable commitments are being made and options foreclosed as the program continues; and (4) the potential seriousness of environmental effects. Based on these criteria, the Court of Appeals required an EIS, which exposed the issues of plutonium radiation hazards and runaway costs, and led to Congress' deauthorization of the reactor. What was *SIPI's* premise? That if an EIS is truly to inform governmental decision-making, it has to occur sufficiently early in the process to make a meaningful difference, rather than as a last-step afterthought. As §102(2)(c) says, the draft EIS "shall accompany the proposal through the existing agency review [decision-making?] process."

PROGRAMMATIC IMPACT STATEMENTS

The reality of agency behavior is that individual projects are often part of broad ongoing programs. The CEQ regulations provide two rationales underlying the

18. In the *Chicod Creek* case the EIS was drafted after the SCS had decided exactly what it wanted to do. Should Judge Larkins have ordered the SCS to reopen the entire question while the EIS was being drafted? If NEPA is interpreted as a directive to include environmental concerns in the actual decision-making process, that question necessarily arises. If NEPA is primarily considered a disclosure requirement (to whom? Congress, the President, the public, the courts?) then courts need not pretend that it will change the minds of agencies, but rather can insist on full EISs for reasons external to the agency process.

requirement that agencies prepare "programmatic" EISs where appropriate. §1502.4, 1502.20. For the agency, preparation of a programmatic EIS can greatly streamline the EIS process for all of the subsequent specific projects that derive from it. A programmatic EIS on nuclear waste disposal, for example, can be done once and for all, and then merely incorporated by reference in subsequent nuclear powerplant EIS proceedings. For environmentalists, a timely programmatic EIS can raise fundamental issues and shape basic agency decisions at a sufficiently early stage to improve or block a program before it is cast in bureaucratic stone.

The Supreme Court later, in a very different setting, had the opportunity to consider both questions – of programmatic EISs and the timing of EISs in evolving agency processes.

Kleppe v. Sierra Club
United State Supreme Court, 1976
427 U.S. 390, 96 S.Ct. 2718, 49 L.Ed.2d 576

POWELL, J.... Respondents, several organizations concerned with the environment, brought this suit in July 1973 in the United States District Court for the District of Columbia. The defendants in the suit, petitioners here, were the officials of the Department [of Interior] and other federal agencies responsible for issuing coal leases, approving mining plans, granting rights-of-way and taking...other actions necessary to enable private companies and public utilities to develop coal reserves on land owned or controlled by the Federal Government. Citing widespread interest in the reserves of a region identified as the "Northern Great Plains region," and an alleged threat from coal-related operations to their members' enjoyment of the region's environment, respondents claimed that the federal officials could not allow further development without preparing a "comprehensive environmental impact statement" under §102(2)(C) on the entire region.... [Plaintiffs lost in the District Court, but the Court of Appeals reversed and granted an injunction.]

The "Northern Great Plains region" identified in respondents' complaint encompasses portions of four States – northeastern Wyoming, eastern Montana, western North Dakota and western South Dakota. There is no dispute about its richness in coal, nor about the waxing interest in developing that coal, nor about the critical role the federal petitioners will play due to the significant percentage of the coal to which they control access. The Department has initiated, in this decade, three studies in areas either inclusive of or included within this region....

While the record does not reveal the degree of concern with environmental matters in the first two studies, it is clear that the NGPRP [Northern Great Plains Resources Program] was devoted entirely to the environment. It was carried out by an interagency federal-state task force with public participation, and was designed "to assess the potential, economic and environmental impacts" from resource development in five States – Montana, Wyoming, South Dakota, North Dakota, and Nebraska....

In addition, since 1973 the Department has engaged in a complete review of its coal leasing program for the entire Nation.... The purpose of the program review was to study the environmental impact of the Department's entire range of coal-related activities and to develop a planning system to guide the national leasing program. The impact statement, known as the "Coal Programmatic EIS," went through several drafts before issuing in final form on September 19, 1975 – shortly before the petition for certiorari was filed in this case....

The major issue remains the one with which the suit began: whether NEPA requires petitioners to prepare an environmental impact statement on the entire Northern Great Plains region. Petitioners, arguing the negative, rely squarely on the facts of the case and the language of §102(2)(C) of NEPA. We find their reliance well placed....

Respondents can prevail only if there has been a report or recommendation on a proposal for major federal action with respect to the Northern Great Plains region. Our statement of the relevant facts shows there has been none; instead, all proposals are for actions of either local or national scope....

The District Court, in fact, expressly found that there was no existing or proposed plan or program on the part of the Federal Government for the regional development of the area described in respondents' complaint. It found also that the three studies initiated by the Department in areas either included within or inclusive of respondents' region...were not parts of any plan or program to develop or encourage development of the Northern Great plains. That court found no evidence that the individual coal development projects undertaken or proposed by private industry and public utilities in that part of the country are integrated into a plan or otherwise related. These findings were not disturbed by the Court of Appeals, and they remain fully supported by the record in this Court....

The Court of Appeals, in reversing the District Court, did not find that there was a regional plan or program for development of the Northern Great Plains region. It accepted all of the District Court's findings of fact, but concluded nevertheless that the petitioners "contemplated" a regional plan or program....

Even had the record justified a finding that a regional program was contemplated by the petitioners, the legal conclusion drawn by the Court of Appeals cannot be squared with the Act. The Court recognized that the mere "contemplation" of certain action is not sufficient to require an impact statement. But it believed the statute nevertheless empowers a court to require the preparation of an impact statement to begin at some point prior to the formal recommendation or report on a proposal. The Court of Appeals accordingly devised its own four-part "balancing test" for determining when, during the contemplation of a plan or other type of federal action, an agency must begin a statement. The factors to be considered were [based on *SIPI*:] the likelihood and imminence of the program's coming to fruition, the extent to which information is available on the effects of implementing the expected program and on alternatives thereto, the extent to which irretrievable commitments are being made and options precluded "as refinement of the proposal progresses," and the severity of the environmental effects should the action be implemented....

The Court's reasoning and action find no support in the language or legislative history of NEPA. The statute clearly states when an impact statement is required, and mentions nothing about a balancing of factors. Rather...the moment at which an agency must have a final statement ready "is the time at which it makes a recommendation or report on a *proposal* for federal action." The procedural duty imposed upon agencies by this section is quite precise and the role of the courts in enforcing that duty is similarly precise. A court has no authority to depart from the statutory language and, by a balancing of court-devised factors, determine a point during the germination process of a potential proposal at which an impact statement *should be prepared.* Such an assertion of judicial authority would leave the agencies uncertain as to their procedural duties under NEPA, would invite judicial involvement in the day-to-day decision making process of the agencies, and would invite litigation....

Respondents [further] insist that, even without a comprehensive federal plan for the development of the Northern Great Plains, a "regional" impact statement nevertheless is required on all coal-related projects in the region because they are intimately related....

We begin by stating our general agreement with respondents' basis premise that §102(2)(C) may require a comprehensive impact statement in certain situations where several proposed actions are pending at the same time.... Thus, when several proposals for coal-related actions that will have a cumulative or synergistic environmental impact upon a region are pending concurrently before an agency, their environmental consequences must be considered together[19]....

Respondents conceded at oral argument that to prevail they must show that petitioners have acted arbitrarily in refusing to prepare one comprehensive statement on this entire region, and we agree. The determination of the region, if any, with respect to which a comprehensive statement is necessary requires the weighting of a number of factors, including the extent of the interrelationship among proposed actions and practical considerations of feasibility. Resolving those issues requires a high level of technical expertise and is properly left to the informed discretion of the responsible federal agencies. Absent a showing of arbitrary action, we must assume that the agencies have exercised this discretion appropriately. Respondents have made no showing to the contrary.

MARSHALL, J., concurring in part and dissenting in part.

While I agree with much of the Court's opinion, I must dissent from [that part] which holds that the federal courts may not remedy violations of [NEPA] – no matter how blatant – until too late for an adequate remedy to be formulated. As the Court today recognizes, NEPA contemplates agency consideration of environmental factors throughout the decisionmaking process. Since NEPA's enactment, however, litigation has been brought primarily at the end of that process – challenging agency decisions to act made without adequate environmental impact statements or without any statements at all. In such situations, the courts have had to content themselves with the largely unsatisfactory remedy of enjoining the proposed federal action and ordering the preparation of an adequate impact statement. This remedy is insufficient because, except by deterrence, it does nothing to further early consideration of environmental factors. And, as with all after-the-fact remedies, a remand for the preparation of an impact statement after the basic decision to act has been made invites *post hoc* rationalizations, rather than the candid and balanced environmental assessments envisioned by NEPA. Moreover, the remedy is wasteful of resources and time, causing fully developed plans for action to be laid aside while an impact statement is prepared.

19. At some points in their brief respondents appear to seek a comprehensive impact statement covering contemplated projects in the region as well as those that already have been proposed. The statute, however, speaks solely in terms of *proposed* actions; it does not require an agency to consider the possible environmemental impacts of less imminent actions when preparing the impact statement on proposed actions. Should contemplated actions later reach the stage of actual proposals, impact statements on them will take into account the effect of their approval upon the existing environment; and the condition of that environment presumably will reflect earlier proposed actions and their effects. [This is footnote 20 in the original.]

Nevertheless, until this lawsuit, such belated remedies were all the federal courts had had the opportunity to impose under NEPA. In this case, confronted with a situation in which, according to respondents' allegations, federal agencies were violating NEPA prior to their basic decision to act, the Court of Appeals...seized the opportunity to devise a different and effective remedy....

The Court begins its rejection of the [Court of Appeals'] four-part test by announcing that the procedural duty imposed on the agencies by §102(2)(C) is "quite precise" and leaves a court "no authority to depart from the statutory language." Given the history and wording of NEPA's impact statement requirement, this statement is baffling. A statute that imposes a complicated procedural requirement on all "proposals" for "major federal actions significantly affecting the quality of the human environment" and then assiduously avoids giving any hint, either expressly or by way of legislative history, of what is meant by a proposal for a "major federal action" can hardly be termed precise. In fact, this vaguely worded statute seems designed to serve as no more than a catalyst for development of a "common law" of NEPA. To date, the courts have responded in just that manner and have created such a "common law." Indeed, that development is the source of NEPA's success. Of course, the Court is correct that the courts may not depart from NEPA's language. They must, however, give meaning to that language if there is to by anything in NEPA to enforce at all. And that is all the Court of Appeals did in this case.

COMMENTARY AND QUESTIONS

1. Tiering of EISs. Plaintiffs-respondents wanted a full complement of impact statements on the federal coal-leasing program: a national (programmatic, or generic) EIS; a regional EIS; and impact documents for each local coal lease and right-of-way granted by the Department. This hierarchy of impact documents is called "tiering." See CEQ regulations, §1508.28. How informative can the national EIS and the local impact statements be without a regional EIS integrating them? Is the Court suggesting that the NGPRP was the "functional equivalent"of an EIS? Thus far, courts have restricted the functional equivalency doctrine to EPA actions. Should it be extended to Interior's activities? Do the Bureau of Mines and the Fish and Wildlife Service (two sub-agencies in Interior), for example, always agree on development proposals?

2. To plan or not to plan. Is the *Kleppe* decision a disincentive to comprehensive planning? After all, from the standpoint of a federal agency, if you don't plan, you then don't have to go public with an EIS, thus avoiding public controversy until the action has become a self-fulfilling prophecy. If this is so, doesn't *Kleppe* contradict NEPA's emphasis on early planning in order to forestall irretrievable commitments of resources to environmentally damaging projects?

3. When is there a proposal? *Kleppe* stands for the rule that a proposal only comes into existence when the agency declares it, unless the agency has been arbitrary and capricious in not making a proposal. The CEQ regulations (§1508.23) state that a proposal may exist in fact even if it is not explicitly made. Should CEQ or the Court have the the last word in interpreting NEPA? On one hand, courts should defer to an agency's interpretation of its own enabling act, but this presumption does not apply where the agency interpretation violates the plain language of the statute (see page 591 *supra*). Do you agree with Justice Powell or Justice Marshall about how strictly the language of NEPA should be interpreted?

In effect, the *Kleppe* Court holds that the agency itself must determine when a "proposal" is being made, and a court should only overturn this decision if it is arbitrary. Under the *Kleppe* ruling, environmental plaintiffs find it difficult to establish the existence of "de facto proposals." (cf. CEQ regulation §1508.23) Is the *Kleppe* interpretation consistent with NEPA's goal of factoring environmental analysis into federal agency planning at the earliest possible time? What could the NRC now do in a *SIPI* situation if it wanted to begin a breeder reactor research program with minimal public scrutiny?

How successful do you think you would be in contending in court that an agency has been arbitrary and capricious because it *hasn't* done something that you claim it should have done?

4. Cumulative impacts and NEPA. Do you agree with the Court that the cumulative impacts of potential activities in the surrounding area cannot be considered in impact documents until the activities have actually been proposed? Doesn't this lead to fragmented, reactive planning? Even if you only consider the impacts of proposed projects, how helpful is it to consider them in each local, site-specific impact document? Once again, the CEQ regulations appear to conflict with the Supreme Court's interpretation of NEPA. (see §1508.28).

5. Hard cases make bad law. Should the Sierra Club have decided not to file this action under this set of facts? After all, it's not as if the Department hadn't done any planning for utilization of the Northern Great Plains coal reserves. The Sierra Club simply disagreed with Interior about what the relevant planning area should have been.

6. NEPA as post-hoc rationalization. Is Justice Marshall correct when he charges that a NEPA lawsuit usually comes too late in the agency decision-making process to be effective? Has the agency already invested too much money and political capital to change its plans? Or, on the other hand, does the spectre of a NEPA suit that would expose substantial waste and shoddy planning inspire agency officials to give prudent consideration to environmental problems early in the process? Is Justice Marshall's reservation about NEPA answered by the CEQ's "scoping" suggestions? (§1501.7.) Note that if the agency doesn't scope, its failure to do so can't be raised until after the final EIS has been released.

7. Where is NEPA's overview? Observing the scene that has followed the *Kleppe* decision, Professor Oliver Houck has commented that –

> NEPA is missing the point. It is producing lots of little statements on highway segments, timber sales, and other foregone conclusions; it isn't even present, much less effective, when the major decisions on a national energy policy

> and a national transportation policy are made. On the most pivotal development questions of our time, NEPA comes in late in the fourth quarter, in time to help tidy up.[20]

The question of when a programmatic EIS can be required after *Kleppe* is obviously a strategic issue.

C. FURTHER ISSUES IN NEPA'S JUDICIAL EVOLUTION

In two cases from the Northwest decided in 1989, The Supreme Court raised a variety of questions, in opinions that help to chronicle the continuing evolution of NEPA:

- When does an agency have to prepare a Supplementary EIS (SEIS) before it can proceed?
- By what standard of review does a court scrutinize agency actions implementing NEPA?
- Must an EIS include a "worst-case analysis" of what may result from a project, in situations where the agency claims that scientific data is insufficient or uncertain?
- Must an agency provide for mitigation efforts to eliminate negative environmental effects (note that this involves a form of substantive compliance requirement)?

John Marsh, Secretary of the Army v. Oregon Natural Resources Council
United States Supreme Court, 1989
490 U.S. 360

STEVENS, J. This case... arises out of a controversial decision to construct a dam at Elk Creek in the Rogue River Basin in Southwest Oregon.... In 1961 a multi-agency study recommended the construction of three large dams: the Lost Creek Dam on the Rogue River, the Applegate Dam on the Applegate River, and the Elk Creek Dam on the Elk Creek near its confluence with the Rogue River. The following year, Congress authorized the Army Corps of Engineers (the Corps) to construct the project in accordance with the recommendations of the 1961 study. The Lost Creek Dam was completed in 1977 and the Applegate Dam was completed in 1981.

Plans for the Elk Creek Dam describe a 238-foot-high concrete structure that will control the run-off from 132 square miles of the 135-square-mile Elk Creek watershed. When full, the artificial lake behind the dam will cover 1,290 acres of land, will have an 18-mile shoreline, and will hold 101,000 acre-feet of water. The dam will cost approximately $100 million to construct and will produce annual benefits of almost $5 million. It will be operated in coordination with the nearby Lost Creek Dam, where the control center for both dams will be located. Its

20. Letter to Michael Deland, Chairman, CEQ, 19 Feb. 1991. Houck urges that CEQ not focus on making each EIS "a 'succinct review for a single project'...[but] rather, to make NEPA work for legislative proposals and for programs that all but conclusively determine what the subsequent projects will be."

"multiport" structure, which will permit discharge of water from any of five levels, makes it possible to regulate, within limits, the temperature, turbidity, and volume of the downstream flow. Although primarily designed to control flooding along the Rogue River, additional project goals include enhanced fishing, irrigation, and recreation.

In 1971, the Corps completed its EIS for the Elk Creek portion of the three-dam project and began development by acquiring 26,000 acres of land and relocating residents, a county road, and utilities. Acknowledging incomplete information, the EIS recommended that further studies concerning the project's likely effect on turbidity be developed. The results of these studies were discussed in a [Final EIS Supplement (FEISS)] completed in 1975....

Because the Rogue River is one of the Nation's premier fishing grounds, the FEISS paid special heed to the effects the dam might have on water quality, fish production, and angling. In its chapter on the environmental effects of the proposed project, the FEISS explained that water quality studies were prepared in 1974 and in 1979 and that "[w]ater temperature and turbidity have received the most attention."...

In October 1985, four Oregon nonprofit corporations filed this action in the United States District Court for the District of Oregon seeking to enjoin construction of the Elk Creek Dam. Their principal claims were that the Corps FEISS violated NEPA by failing (1) to consider the cumulative effects of the three dams on the Rogue River Basin in a single EIS; (2) adequately to describe the environmental consequences of the project; (3) to include a "worst case analysis" of uncertain effects; and (4) to prepare a second supplemental EIS to review information developed after 1980.

After conducting a hearing on respondents' motion for a preliminary injunction, the District Judge denied relief on each of the NEPA claims. 628 F. Supp. 1557 (Ore. 1986). He first held that courts must employ a standard of "reasonableness" in reviewing an agency's compliance with NEPA. Under this standard of review, the court must "'make a pragmatic judgment whether the EIS's form, content and preparation foster both informed decision-making and informed public participation.'" Id., at 1562 (quoting California v. Block, 690 F.2d 753, 761 (CA9 1982)). Applying this standard, the District Judge concluded that a "worst case analysis" was not required because other Corps used state-of-the-art mathematical models, thus avoiding scientific uncertainty and the need to fill gaps in information with a worst case scenario. Id., at 1567. Finally, the District Court held that the Corps' decision not to prepare a second supplemental EIS to address new information was "reasonable."

The new information relied upon by respondents is found in two documents. The first, an internal memorandum prepared by two Oregon Department of Fish and Wildlife (ODFW) biologists based upon a draft ODFW study, suggested that the dam will adversely affect downstream fishing, and the second, a soil survey prepared by the United States Soil Conservation Service (SCS), contained information that might be taken to indicate greater downstream turbidity than did the FEISS. As to both documents, the District Judge concluded that the Corps acted reasonably in relying on the opinions of independent and Corps experts discounting the significance of the new information...

The Court of Appeals reversed. 832 F.2d 1489 (CA9 1987). Applying the same "reasonableness" standard of review employed by the District Court, the Court of Appeals reached a contrary conclusion, holding that the Corps had not adequately evaluated the cumulative environmental impact of the entire project. Id., at 1497. Since the Corps did not seek review of that holding, we do not discuss it. The court also held that the FEISS was defective because it did not include a complete mitigation plan and because it did not contain a "worst case analysis." Id., at 1493-1494, 1496-1497. These holdings were erroneous for the reasons stated in our opinion in Robertson v. Methow Valley Citizens Council, 109 S.Ct. 1835 (1989) [see next case, *infra*]. With regard to the failure to prepare a second supplemental EIS, the Court of Appeals concluded that the ODFW and SCS documents brought to light "significant new information" concerning turbidity, water temperature, and epizootic fish disease; that this information, although "not conclusive," is "probably accurate"; and that the Corps' experts failed to evaluate the new information with sufficient care. 832 F.2d, at 1494-1496. The court thus concluded that a second supplemental EIS should have been prepared. Judge Wallace, writing in dissent, took issue with the majority's analysis of the new information. In his view, it was reasonable for the Corps to have concluded, based on its own expert evaluation, that the information contained in the ODFW document was inaccurate and the information contained in the SCS document was insignificant. Id., at 1500 (opinion concurring in part and dissenting in part).

The subject of post-decision supplemental environmental impact statements is not expressly addressed in NEPA. Preparation of such statements, however, is at times necessary to satisfy the Act's "action-forcing" purpose. NEPA does not work by mandating that agencies achieve particular substantive environmental results. Rather, NEPA promotes its sweeping commitment to "prevent or eliminate damage to the environment and biosphere" by focusing government and public attention on the environmental effects of proposed agency action. 42 U.S.C.A. §4321. By so focusing agency attention, NEPA ensures that the agency will not act on incomplete information, only to regret its decision after it is too late to correct. [citing *Robertson*]. Similarly, the broad dissemination of information mandated by NEPA permits the public and other government agencies to react to the effects of a proposed action at a meaningful time. It would be incongruous with this approach to environmental protection, and with the Act's manifest concern with preventing uninformed action, for the blinders to adverse environmental effects, once unequivocally removed, to be restored prior to the completion of agency action simply because the relevant proposal has received initial approval. As we explained in TVA v. Hill,[21] although "it would make sense to hold NEPA inapplicable at some point in the life of a project, because the agency would no longer have a meaningful opportunity to weigh the benefits of the project versus the detrimental effects on the environment," up to that point, "NEPA cases have generally required agencies to file environmental impact statements when the remaining governmental action would be environmentally 'significant'."

This reading of the statute is supported by Council on Environmental Quality (CEQ) and Corps regulations, both of which make plain that at times supplementation is required. The CEQ regulations, which we have held are entitled to substantial deference, *see Robertson*, impose a duty on all federal agencies to prepare supplements to either draft or final EISs if there "are significant new circumstances or information relevant to environmental concerns and bearing on the proposed action or its impacts." Similarly, the Corps' own NEPA implementing regulations require the preparation of a supplemental EIS if "new significant impact information,

21. 437 U.S. 153, 188, n. 34.

criteria or circumstances relevant to environmental considerations impact on the recommended plan or proposed action."

The parties are in essential agreement concerning the standard that governs an agency's decision whether to prepare a supplemental EIS. They agree that an agency should apply a "rule of reason," and the cases they cite in support of this standard explicate this rule in the same basic terms. These cases make clear that an agency need not supplement an EIS every time new information comes to light after the EIS is finalized. To require otherwise would render agency decisionmaking intractable, always awaiting updated information only to find the new information outdated by the time a decision is made. On the other hand, and as the Government concedes, NEPA does require that agencies take a "hard look" at the environmental effects of their planned action, even after a proposal has received initial approval. Application of the "rule of reason" thus turns on the value of the new information to the still pending decisionmaking process. In this respect the decision whether to prepare a supplemental EIS is similar to the decision whether to prepare an EIS in the first instance: If there remains "major Federal actio[n]" to occur, and if the new information is sufficient to show that the remaining action will "affec[t] the quality of the human environment" in a significant manner or to a significant extent not already considered, a supplemental EIS must be prepared. Cf. 42 U.S.C.A. §4332(C).

The parties disagree, however, on the standard that should be applied by a court that is asked to review the agency's decision...

Respondents contend that the determination of whether the new information suffices to establish a "significant" effect is either a question of law or, at a minimum, a question of ultimate fact and, as such, "deserves no deference" on review. Apparently, respondents maintain that the question for review centers on the legal meaning of the term "significant" or, in the alternative, the predominantly legal question of whether established and uncontested historical facts presented by the administrative record satisfy this standard. Characterizing the dispute in this manner, they posit that strict review is appropriate under the "in accordance with law" clause of §706(2)(A) or the "without observance of procedures required by law" provision of §706(2)(D). We disagree.

The question presented for review in this case is a classic example of a factual dispute the resolution of which implicates substantial agency expertise. Respondents' claim that the Corps' decision not to file a second supplemental EIS should be set aside primarily rests on the contentions that the new information undermines conclusions contained in the FEISS, that the conclusions contained in the ODFW memorandum and the SCS survey are accurate, and that the Corps' expert review of the new information was incomplete, inconclusive, or inaccurate. The dispute thus does not turn on the meaning of the term "significant" or on an application of this legal standard to settled facts. Rather, resolution of this dispute involves primarily issues of fact. Because analysis of the relevant documents "requires a high level of technical expertise," we must defer to "the informed discretion of the responsible federal agencies." Kleppe v. Sierra Club, 427 U.S. 390 (1976).[22] Under these circumstances, we cannot accept respondents' supposition that review is of a legal question and that the Corps' decision "deserves no deference." Accordingly, as long as the Corps' decision not to supplement the FEISS was not "arbitrary or capricious," it should not be set aside....

---

22. See also Baltimore Gas & Electric Co. v. NRDC, 462 U.S. 87 (1983)("When examining this kind of scientific determination...a reviewing court must generally be at its most deferential").

Respondents' argument that significant new information required the preparation of a second supplemental EIS rests on two written documents. The first of the documents is the so-called "Cramer memorandum," an intra-office memorandum prepared on February 21, 1985 by two scientists employed by ODFW. The Cramer Memorandum, in turn, relied on a draft ODFW study describing the effects of the Lost Creek Dam on fish production. The second document is actually a series of maps prepared in 1982 by SCS to illustrate the composition of soil near the Elk Creek shoreline. The information was provided to the Corps for use in managing the project. Although respondents contend that the maps contained data relevant to a prediction of the dam's impact on downstream turbidity, the maps do not purport to shed any light on that subject. Nor do they purport to discuss any conditions that had changed since the FEISS was completed in 1980. The Corps responded to the claim that these documents demonstrate the need for supplementation of the FEISS by preparing a formal Supplemental Information Report, dated January 10, 1986. See U.S. Army Corps of Engineers, Portland District, Elk Creek Lake Supplemental Information Report No. 2, p. 7a (hereinafter SIR). The SIR explained, "([w]hile it is clear based upon our review that this information does not require additional NEPA documentation, Corps regulations provide that a Supplemental Information Report can be used to disseminate information on points of concern regarding environmental impacts set forth in the EIS."

The significance of the Cramer Memorandum and the SCS survey is subject to some doubt. Before respondents commenced this litigation in October 1985, no one had suggested that either document constituted the kind of new information that made it necessary or appropriate to supplement the FEISS....

The Court of Appeals attached special significance to two concerns discussed in the Cramer Memorandum: the danger that an increase in water temperature downstream during fall and early winter will cause an early emergence and thus reduce survival of spring chinook fry and the danger that the dam will cause high fish mortality from an epizootic disease. Both concerns were based partly on fact and partly on speculation.

With respect to the first, the Cramer Memorandum reported that the authors of the draft ODFW study had found that warming of the Rogue River caused by the Lost Creek Dam had reduced the survival of spring chinook fry; however, the extent of that reduction was not stated, nor did the memorandum estimate the extent of warming to be expected due to closure of the Elk Creek Dam....

The Corps' response to this concern in its SIR acknowledged that the "biological reasoning is sound and has been recognized for some time," but then explained why the concern was exaggerated. The SIR stressed that because the model employed by ODFW had not been validated, its predictive capability was uncertain.

With respect to the second concern emphasized by the Court of Appeals, the Cramer Memorandum reported the fact that "an unprecedented 76 percent of the fall chinook in 1979 and 32 percent in 1980 were estimated to have died before spawning" and then speculated that the Lost Creek Dam, which had been completed in 1977, was a contributing cause of this unusual mortality. The Corps responded to this by pointing out that the absence of similar epizootics after the closure of the Applegate Dam and the evidence of pre-spawning mortality in the Rogue River prior to the closing of the Lost Creek Dam were inconsistent with the hypothesis suggested in the Cramer Memorandum. In addition, the Corps noted that certain diseased organisms thought to have been the cause of the unusually high mortality rates were not found in the outflow from the Lost Creek Dam....

There is little doubt that if all of the information contained in the Cramer Memorandum and SCS survey was both new and accurate, the Corps would have been required to prepare a second supplemental EIS. It is also clear that, regardless of its eventual assessment of the significance of this information, the Corps had a duty to take a hard look at the proffered evidence. However, having done so and having determined based on careful scientific analysis that the new information was of exaggerated importance, the Corps acted within the dictates of NEPA in concluding that supplementation was unnecessary. Even if another decisionmaker might have reached a contrary result, it was surely not "a clear error of judgment" for the Corps to have found that the new and accurate information contained in the documents was not significant and that the significant information was not new and accurate. As the SIR demonstrates, the Corps conducted a reasoned evaluation of the relevant information and reached a decision that, although perhaps disputable, was not "arbitrary or capricious"....

In *Robertson*, decided the same day as *Marsh*, the Court spoke on "worst-case analysis " under NEPA, and on mitigation requirements:

Dale Robertson, Director of U.S. Forest Service
v. Methow Valley Citizens' Council
United States Supreme Court, 1989
490 U.S. 332

[Early Winters is a ski resort being built by a private entrepreneur on Sandy Butte in the Forest Service's Okanogan National Forest in Washington.]

STEVENS, J. ...The Court of Appeals...concluded that the Forest Service had an obligation to make a "worst case analysis" if it could not make a reasoned assessment of the impact of the Early Winters project on the mule deer herd. Such a "worst case analysis" was required at one time by CEQ regulations, but those regulations have since been amended. Moreover, although the prior regulations may well have expressed a permissible application of NEPA, the Act itself does not mandate that uncertainty in predicting environmental harms be addressed exclusively in this manner. Accordingly, we conclude that the Court of Appeals erred in requiring the "worst case" study.

In 1977, President Carter directed that CEQ promulgate binding regulations implementing the procedural provisions of NEPA. Pursuant to this presidential order, CEQ promulgated implementing regulations. Under §1502.22 of these regulations – a provision which became known as the "worst case requirement" – CEQ provided that if certain information relevant to the agency's evaluation of the proposed action is either unavailable or too costly to obtain, the agency must include in the EIS a "worst case analysis and an indication of the probability or improbability of its occurrence." 40 CFR §1502.22 (1985). In 1986, however, CEQ replaced the "worst case" requirement with a requirement that federal agencies, in the face of unavailable information concerning a reasonably foreseeable significant environmental consequence, prepare "a summary of existing credible scientific evidence which is relevant to evaluating the...adverse impacts" and prepare an "evaluation of such impacts based upon theoretical approaches or research methods generally accepted in the scientific community." 40 CFR §1502.22(b)(1987). The amended regulation thus "retains the duty to describe the consequences of a remote, but potentially severe impact, but grounds the duty in evaluation of scientific opinion rather than in the framework of a conjectural 'worst case analysis'." 50 Fed. Reg. 32237 (1985).

The Court of Appeals recognized that the "worst case analysis" regulation has been superseded, yet held that "this rescission...does not nullify the requirement...since the regulation was merely a codification of prior NEPA case law." 833 F.2d, at 817, n. 11. This conclusion, however, is erroneous in a number of respects. Most notably, review of NEPA case law reveals that the regulation, in fact, was not a codification of prior judicial decisions. The cases cited by the Court of Appeals ultimately rely on the Fifth Circuit's decision in Sierra Club v. Sigler, 695 F.2d 957 (1983). *Sigler*, however, simply recognized that the "worst case analysis" regulation codified the "judicially created principl[e]" that an EIS must "consider the probabilities of the occurrence of any environmental effects it discusses." Id., at 970-971. As CEQ recognized at the time it superseded the regulation, case law prior to the adoption of the "worst case analysis" provision did require agencies to describe environmental impacts even in the face of substantial uncertainty, but did not require that this obligation necessarily be met through the mechanism of a "worst case analysis." See 51 Fed.Reg. 15625 (1986). CEQ's abandonment of the "worst case analysis" provision, therefore, is not inconsistent with any previously established judicial interpretation of the statute....

CEQ explained that by requiring that an EIS focus on reasonably foreseeable impacts, the new regulation "will generate information and discussion on those consequences of greatest concern to the public and of greatest relevance to the agency's decision," 50 Fed. Reg. 32237 (1985), rather than distorting the decision making process by overemphasizing highly speculative harms, 51 Fed. Reg. 15624-15625 (1986); 50 Fed.Reg. 32236 (1985). In light of this well-considered basis for the change, the new regulation is entitled to substantial deference. Accordingly, the Court of Appeals erred in concluding that the Early Winters Study is inadequate because it failed to include a "worst case analysis."

The Court of Appeals also held that the Forest Service's failure to develop a complete mitigation plan violated [NEPA]....

The court held that the Forest Service could not rely on "the implementation of mitigation measures" to support its conclusion that the impact on the mule deer would be minor "since not only has the effectiveness of these mitigation measures not yet been assessed, but the mitigation measures themselves have yet to be developed." Id., at 817....

The court found a similar defect in the EIS's treatment of air quality. Since the EIS made it clear that commercial development in the Methow Valley will result in violations of state air quality standards unless effective mitigation measures are put in place by the local governments and the private developer, the Court of Appeals concluded that the Forest Service had an affirmative duty to "develop the necessary mitigation measures *before* the permit is granted." Id., at 819 (emphasis in original)(footnote omitted). The court held that this duty was imposed by both the Forest Service's own regulations and §102 of NEPA. Ibid. It read the statute as imposing a substantive requirement that "action be taken to mitigate the adverse effects of major federal actions." Ibid. (quoting Stop H-3 Assn. v. Brinegar, 389 F. Supp. 1102, 1111 (Haw.1974), rev'd on other grounds, 533 F.2d 434 (CA9), cert. denied, 429 U.S. 999 (1976)). For this reason, it concluded that "an EIS must include a fair discussion of measures to mitigate the adverse environmental impacts of a proposed action."

"The importance of the mitigation plan cannot be overestimated. It is a determinative factor in evaluating the adequacy of an environmental impact statement. Without a complete mitigation plan, the decisionmaker is unable to make an informed judgment as to the environmental impact of the project – one of the main purposes of an environmental impact statement." Id., at 820....

The sweeping policy goals announced in §101 of NEPA are...realized through a set of "action-forcing" procedures that require that agencies take a "'hard look' at environmental consequences," *Kleppe, supra,* 427 U.S., at 410, n. 21, and that provide for broad dissemination of relevant environmental information. Although these procedures are almost certain to affect the agency's substantive decision, it is now well settled that NEPA itself does not mandate particular results, but simply prescribes the necessary process. [citing *Strycker's Bay* and *Vermont Yankee*] If the adverse environmental effects of the proposed action are adequately identified and evaluated, the agency is not constrained by NEPA from deciding that other values outweigh the environmental costs. In this case, for example, it would not have violated NEPA if the Forest Service, after complying with the Act's procedural prerequisites, had decided that the benefits to be derived from downhill skiing at Sandy Butte justified the issuance of a special use permit, notwithstanding the loss of 15 percent, 50 percent, or even 100 percent of the mule deer herd. Other statutes may impose substantive environmental obligations on federal agencies, but NEPA merely prohibits uninformed – rather than unwise – agency action.

To be sure, one important ingredient of an EIS is the discussion of steps that can be taken to mitigate adverse environmental consequences. The requirement that an EIS contain a detailed discussion of possible mitigation measures flows from both the language of the Act and, more expressly, from CEQ's implementing regulations. Implicit in NEPA's demand that an agency prepare a detailed statement on "any adverse environmental effects which cannot be avoided should the proposal be implemented," 42 U.S.C.A. §4332(C)(ii), is an understanding that the EIS will discuss the extent to which adverse effects can be avoided. More generally, omission of a reasonably complete discussion of possible mitigation measures would undermine the "action-forcing" function of NEPA. Without such a discussion, neither the agency nor other interested groups and individuals can properly evaluate the severity of the adverse effects. An adverse effect that can be fully remedied by, for example, an inconsequential public expenditure is certainly not as serious as a similar effect that can only be modestly ameliorated through the commitment of vast public and private resources. Recognizing the importance of such a discussion in guaranteeing that the agency has taken a "hard look" at the environmental consequences of proposed federal action, CEQ regulations require that the agency discuss possible mitigation measures in defining the scope of the EIS, 40 CFR §1508.25(b)(1987), in discussing alternatives to the proposed action, §1502.14(f), and consequences of that action, §1502.16(h), and in explaining its ultimate decision, §1505.2(C).

There is a fundamental distinction, however, between a requirement that mitigation be discussed in sufficient detail to ensure that environmental consequences have been fairly evaluated, on the one hand, and a substantive requirement that a complete mitigation plan be actually formulated and adopted, on the other. In this case, the off-site effects on air quality and on the mule deer herd cannot be mitigated unless nonfederal government agencies take appropriate action. Since it is those state and local governmental bodies that have jurisdiction over the area in which the adverse effects need be addressed and since they have the authority to mitigate them, it would be incongruous to conclude that the Forest Service has no power to act until the local agencies have reached a final conclusion on what mitigating measures they consider necessary. Even more significantly, it would be inconsistent with NEPA's reliance on procedural mechanisms – as opposed to substantive, result-based standards – to demand the presence of a fully developed plan that will mitigate environmental harm before an agency can act. Cf. Baltimore Gas & Electric Co., 462 U.S. at 100 ("NEPA does not require agencies to adopt any particular internal decisionmaking structure").

We thus conclude that the Court of Appeals erred, first, in assuming that "NEPA requires that 'action be taken to mitigate the adverse effects of major federal actions'," 833 F.2d, at 819 (quoting Stop H-3 Assn. v. Brinegar, 389 F.Supp., at 1111), and, second, in finding that this substantive requirement entails the further duty to include in every EIS "a detailed explanation of specific measures which *will* be employed to mitigate the adverse impacts of a proposed action," 833 F.2d, at 819 (emphasis supplied).

COMMENTARY AND QUESTIONS

1. NEPA and the Supremes. Analyzing these Supreme Court NEPA cases, how do you read the Court's mood in applying the statute? Has the continuing life of NEPA been largely attributable to the lower federal courts?

How do the foregoing opinions clarify the NEPA issues they debate? When would the Court require the agencies to prepare an SEIS? The *Marsh* opinion says that "if all the information contained in the Cramer Memorandum and SCS survey was both new and accurate, the Corps would have been required to prepare a...supplemental EIS." Doesn't this imply that the Court would have applied its own interpretation of the legal term "significant" (new information) to the new facts, even if the agency decided that the data was not significant? This interpretation substantially changes the tone of the Court's deference under the arbitrary and capricious test. The Court also said that "regardless of its eventual assessment of the significance of this information, the Corps had a duty to take a hard look at the proffered evidence," which is again a court-enforced review standard.

Robertson holds that an EIS need not include a formal "worst-case analysis" in situations of "highly speculative" uncertainty. On the other hand the EIS must "describe the consequences of...remote but potentially severe [reasonably foreseeble]" impacts, even where probability of occurence cannot be shown. Does this mean that the substance of a worst-case analysis will be required in appropriate situations, if not a formal analysis?

As to mitigation efforts, it is clear now that in the eyes of the Court NEPA is basically procedural, not dictating substantive actions (except the creation of required EISs). Paraphrasing the *Robertson* decision, however, if it were shown that "the benefits to be derived from downhill skiing at Sandy Butte" were rather minimal, with several other existing ski areas nearby, and development would cause "the loss of...100 percent of the mule deer herd," would the courts be bound by the agency's (procedurally proper) decision? At some point the arbitrariness test and the hard look doctrine must import substantive elements that can lead a court to strike down agency decisions, or alternatively to order mitigation.

2. Applying NEPA to federal agencies' international actions. To what extent does NEPA apply to agency actions overseas? In many cases American agencies plan, fund, or participate in international projects that pose significant environmental risks – dams and other projects displacing indigenous peoples, unique habitats, or endangered species; building nuclear reactors; and the like. To the extent that NEPA can be applied to such actions it serves as a longarm protection and model for conservation in other nations. See Chapter 25 on international environmental law.

3. Emergency Exemptions from NEPA. To what extent can agencies ignore NEPA in situations they deem to be "emergencies," (recognizing that such a loophole could invite selfserving agency evasions of its mandate)? The CEQ on its own authority issued a regulation, 40 CFR §1506.11, providing that the requirements of NEPA could be bypassed in emergencies. In Crosby v. Young, 512 F. Supp. 1363 (E.D. Mich. 1981), a district court upheld the claim that Detroit's use of federal funds to raze the Poletown community to build a Cadillac plant (studied in Chapter Nine, at page 432) was an emergency necessity. That exemption had been, surprisingly, approved by the Carter CEQ and supported by the litigation efforts of David Sive, an eminent attorney-environmentalist. The same result occurred in Hester v. Nat'l Audubon Soc., 801 F.2d 405 (9th Cir. 1986), where the U.S. Fish and Wildlife Service was granted leave to capture the last of 26 surviving California condors for zoo propagation in the face of imminent extinction without an EIS. Although common sense indicates that in some situations the requirements of NEPA must be inapplicable, how do courts or the CEQ fashion such exceptions to a clear legislative mandate?

4. NEPA and national security. NEPA does not provide for a national security exception. The Supreme Court, however, has refused to review Defense Department compliance with NEPA, where to do so inevitably would result in the disclosure of confidential matters regarding national security. Weinberger v. Catholic Action of Hawaii, 454 U.S. 139 (1981) involved a NEPA challenge to the Navy's construction of nuclear-capable storage structures and the possible storage of nuclear weapons in those facilities. The Navy's regulations prohibited it either to admit or to deny that nuclear weapons were actually stored at the facility. The complaint claimed that the Navy's determination that no significant environmental hazards were present failed to take into account the enhanced risks of a nuclear accident and the potential effects of radiation from the storage of nuclear weapons in a populated location. The Court distinguished between NEPA's role in the decisionmaking process and NEPA's public disclosure goals:

> The decision-making and public disclosure goals of §102(2)(C), though certainly compatible, are not necessarily coextensive. Thus, §102(2)(C)

> contemplates that in a given situation a federal agency might have to include environmental considerations in its decisionmaking process, yet withhold public disclosure of any NEPA documents, in whole or in part, under authority of a FOIA exemption....[23]
>
> Since the public disclosure requirements of NEPA are governed by FOIA, it is clear that Congress intended that the public's interest in ensuring that federal agencies comply with NEPA must give way to the Government's need to preserve military secrets. In the instant case, an EIS concerning a proposal to store nuclear weapons at West Loch need not be disclosed. ...If the Navy proposes to store nuclear weapons at West Loch, the Department of Defense's regulations can fairly be read to require that an EIS be prepared solely for internal purposes, even though such a document cannot be disclosed to the public. The Navy must consider environmental consequences in its decisionmaking process, even if it is unable to meet NEPA's public disclosure goals by virtue of FOIA Exemption 1....
>
> It is the proposal to *store* nuclear weapons at West Loch that triggers the Navy's obligation to prepare an EIS. Due to national security reasons, however, the Navy can neither admit nor deny that it proposes to store nuclear weapons at West Loch. In this case, therefore, it has not been and cannot be established that the Navy has proposed the only action that would require the preparation of an EIS dealing with the environmental consequences of nuclear weapons storage at West Loch.
>
> Ultimately, whether or not the Navy has complied with NEPA "to the fullest extent possible" is beyond judicial scrutiny in this case. In other circumstances, we have held that "public policy forbids the maintenance of any suit in a court of justice, the trial of which would inevitably lead to the disclosure of matters which the law itself regards as confidential, and respecting which it will not allow the confidence to be violated."...We confront a similar situation in the instant case. 454 U.S. at 143–47.

Subsequent cases have held that some NEPA claims involving National Security are justiciable. In No GWEN Alliance of Lane County, Inc. v. Aldridge, 841 F.2d 946 (9th Cir. 1988), the appeals court held that a lawsuit claiming that the Air Force did not discuss environmental impacts of installing radio towers designed to send war messages to U.S. strategic forces in the event of nuclear war raised justiciable questions. See also Romer v. Carlucci, 847 F.2d 463 (8th Cir. 1988)(review of EIS for compliance with NEPA is justiciable under political question doctrine, in connection with proposed deployment and peacetime operations of MX missiles in minuteman silos). Note that while both the eighth and ninth circuits pointed out that there is no national security exemption from NEPA, the *Carlucci* court refused to require the Army EIS to discuss alternative basing modes or alternative weapons systems, as such strategic considerations would "involve review of intricate and sensitive defense policy information." 847 F.2d at 454. In addition, the *No GWENN* court ultimately did not require the Air Force to prepare an EIS on

23. FOIA's Exemption 1, 5 U.S.C.A. §552(b)(1) in conjunction with Executive Order 12065, 3 CFR 190 (1978 - 79) authorizes classifying and keeping secret information that would threaten national security if released. See *Weinberger*, 454 U.S. at 144.

the grounds that their EA adequately addressed non-nuclear effects and that the nexus between constructing the radio towers and nuclear war was too attenuated to trigger NEPA requirements of discussing environmental effects of nuclear war. 841 F.2d at 1386–87.

5. Has NEPA been worth the effort? In The (Unhappy) Truth about NEPA, 26 Okla. L.R. 239 (1973), where he argued that NEPA's procedural reform is "nine parts myth and one part coconut oil," Joseph Sax argued that the Act was unlikely to change the nature of agency decisionmaking. Here are his five basic rules of the game:

1. Don't expect hired experts to undermine their employers.
2. Don't expect people to believe legislative declarations of policy. The practical working rule is that what the legislature will fund is what the legislature's policy is.
3. Don't expect agencies to abandon their traditional friends.
4. Expect agencies to back up their subordinates and professional colleagues.
5. Expect agencies to go for the least risky option (where risk means a chance of failing to perform their mission).

Consider the *Chicod Creek* case, however. Does NEPA have a useful tactical role to play even if it does not change administrative minds?

6. NEPA as a role model. As of 1984, at least twenty-four states had adopted requirements for preparation of environmental impact statements or for environmental reviews.[24] These state environmental policy acts (SEPAs) often go further than NEPA in imposing substantive controls on agency actions. *See, e.g.,* California Environmental Quality Act (CEQA), Cal. Pub. Res. Code §§21000–21176.

NEPA also has had remarkable international significance as a "look before you leap" statute. Australia, Canada, France, Germany, and the United Kingdom now have procedures for environmental impact assessment, while many other countries in Europe and in Asia and a variety of multi-lateral development agencies are considering adopting such regulations.[25]

7. Coda. What is NEPA coming to? Where would we be without it? And what would NEPA's dramatic declaration of national environmental purpose have accomplished without the rather accidental existence of subsection §102(2)(C)?

I know of no safe repository of the ultimate powers of the society but the people themselves; and if we think them not enlightened enough to exercise their discretion, the remedy is not to take it from them, but to inform their discretion.

— Thomas Jefferson to William Charles Jarvis, September 28, 1820

24. See Renz, The Coming of Age of State Envtl Policy Acts, 5 Pub. Land L. Rev. 31 (1984).

25. See Blumm, The Nat'l Envtl Policy Act at Twenty: A Preface, 20 Envtl L. 447, 451 n. 18 (1990).

Chapter 13

SUBSTANTIVE ROADBLOCKS: SECTION 7 OF THE ENDANGERED SPECIES ACT OF 1973, A STARK PROHIBITION STATUTE

Introduction: Roadblock Statutes

There are times when a problem is so complex, so incapable of careful measurement and fine tuning, so emotional, or so politically difficult to approach in piecemeal fashion, that the legislature decides to pass a highly particularized flat prohibition. There are a number of such statutes in the environmental realm – the "Delaney clause" in the Food and Drug Act, for instance, prohibiting sale for human consumption of any compound that causes cancer in test animals, 21 U.S.C.A. §348(c)(3)(A) – and other prohibitions that contain very limited exceptions, like Title II of the Clean Air Act prohibiting auto emissions beyond 10 percent of 1970 levels (see Chapter 17), *Overton Park's* federal highway act §4(f) provision, and the like.

As these examples demonstrate, "roadblock" prohibition statutes have great potential because of the directness of their prohibitions and their lack of ambiguity. For the same reason, however, they may be especially subject to the problems of the unguided missile. The tradeoff for decisiveness is the risk that they may hit too hard, in not exactly the right place, or with disruptive consequences that weren't predicted.

Section 7 of the 1973 Endangered Species Act (ESA), which provides the focal point of this chapter, in fact contained a strict roadblock. Like NEPA, §7 permitted unexpected environmental lawsuits challenging a variety of federal agency actions. Unlike NEPA, however, §7's provisions were substantive, specific, and mandatory, providing a useful case study of the strengths and drawbacks of the roadblock approach. In reaction to §7's tough potential effects, Congress in 1978 passed a flexibility amendment, considered later in the chapter, demonstrating further interesting issues of law and policy.

A. THE ENDANGERED SPECIES ACT

The Endangered Species Act of 1973 (ESA)[1] was a revolutionary legal document. It was the first major piece of legislation in any legal system that sought to put teeth

1. 16 U.S.C.A. §1531 et seq. (1973, as amended). The text is adapted in part from an article, Plater, In The Wake of the Snail Darter: An Environmental Law Paradigm and its Consequences, 19 J. Law Ref. 805 (1986). A governmental account of the subjects covered in Part B can be found in U.S. Dep't of Interior, Tellico Dam and Reservoir – Staff Report to the [Cabinet-level] Endangered Species Committee, 19 Jan. 1979. See also Plater, Reflected in a River: Agency Accountability and the TVA Tellico Dam Case, 49 Tenn. L. Rev. 747, 779-780 (1982).

into the protection of endangered species domestically and internationally, and has been a model for subsequent wildlife conservation efforts throughout the world. The Act has a triple approach to the problem of conserving species threatened with extinction.

First, it provides a partial answer to the threats posed by the worldwide market in endangered wildlife by closing down the United States market. The free market fails to protect endangered species that have market value, such as leopards, turtles, rare birds for feathers, elephants for ivory, cactuses, and the like. Indeed, the market encourages the complete destruction of any endangered species that has market value by *raising* the value of each animal as it approaches extinction. As the market price per skin or rhino horn skyrockets, exploitation of the endangered species becomes almost impossible to stop. Either the Third World countries of origin cannot afford to halt the lucrative trade, or high prices create poaching pressures that can subvert any local enforcement efforts. The only way to prevent the elimination of the species is by shutting down the market in developed countries. The United States was a major market for such endangered species. To the extent that it has closed down that market, the ESA has eliminated the pressures on animals hunted to provide fur coats and other luxuries for the American fashion world's cosmopolitan tastes.

The Act's second strategy is a prohibition against "taking" any endangered species, a prohibition that attaches heavy criminal sanctions to the act of killing or capturing endangered animals. The taking provision, which generally does not apply to plants, was further strengthened by a definition that interprets "take" to mean "harass, harm, pursue, hunt, shoot, wound, kill, trap, capture, or collect, or to attempt to engage in any such conduct."[2] As a result, protection is extended not only to exotic species but to all endangered and threatened species within the jurisdiction of the United States.

The third, less-heralded strategy of the Act lay latent within §7 of the ESA of 1973, and forms the basis of this chapter's analysis of a direct congressional prohibition as it develops in court and in practice. Section 7 of the ESA of 1973 was certainly not identified as a "prevention of destructive federal projects" provision. Labelled "Interagency cooperation," §7 lay camouflaged. It focuses on federal agencies, often major actors in the developmental forces of the United States, and when parsed carefully its words absolutely prohibit harmful federal actions. As you read through the words of §7, underline the few words which carried a substantive mandate, while noting the prose style that made it unlikely that many members of Congress knew what they were passing.

Section 7 of the Endangered Species Act of 1973, 16 U.S.C.A. §1536 (1973):

§7. INTERAGENCY COOPERATION

> The Secretary [of Interior] shall review other programs administered by him and utilize such programs in furtherance of the purposes of this chapter. All other Federal departments and agencies shall, in consultation with and with the assistance of the Secretary, utilize their authorities in furtherance of the

2. 16 U.S.C.A. §§1532(19); 1538(a)-(b)(1982); 50 CFR §17.3 (1985).

> purposes of this chapter while carrying out programs for the conservation of endangered species and threatened species listed pursuant to section 1533 of this title and by taking such action necessary to insure that actions authorized, funded, or carried out by them do not jeopardize the continued existence of such endangered species and threatened species or result in the destruction or modification of habitat of such species which is determined by the Secretary, after consultation as appropriate with the affected States, to be critical.

The strategic resemblance between ESA §7 and NEPA is remarkable. Both statutes possess effective widespread strength because they target the actions of federal agencies. Both statutes contain action provisions that originally came as a surprise to most members of Congress who voted for them. NEPA, however, only requires procedural compliance; §7 contained a flat substantive prohibition.

Another strength of §7 was, and is, that it reaches one of the major causes of the extinction of species on the face of the earth: habitat destruction. Over the years, habitat destruction has been a far more important cause of extinction than hunting and killing because the largest number of endangered species are "nonmarket species." They lack currently quantifiable market value. They are the often anonymous constituent parts of various food chains and ecological webs that are disrupted when a desert becomes developed for irrigated farms, a prairie is destroyed for residential development or agribusiness, a swamp is drained to produce a parking lot, and so forth. Section 7's provisions were the first statutory prohibitions directly applicable to the problem of habitat destruction. The ESA, moreover, specifically authorizes enforcement by citizens acting as private attorneys-general, §1540.

RATIONALES FOR ENDANGERED SPECIES PROTECTION

Given the ESA's strengths, both patent and latent, it might well be asked why a nation might consider it sufficiently important to pass such a statute in an abstract area of natural science. The question is made all the more pointed by the fact that protection of endangered species inevitably causes a head-on confrontation with the forces of the marketplace. The effort to prohibit the sale of valuable endangered species confronts a worldwide trade involving large amounts of money. Moreover, protecting the habitat of various endangered species completely lacking in market value can impose major market costs upon government and private development projects.

It is easiest to say that the ESA of 1973 was passed to satisfy a popular clamor, beginning in the 1960's, to conserve natural resources. Endangered species had the good fortune to be represented by such mediagenic figures as the bald eagle, the polar bear, whales, and whooping cranes, all of which were sentimentally appealing, fairly remote from market considerations affecting most people, and dramatic or beautiful. Further, there were international conventions ratified by the United States which in broad, hortatory terms expressed an international intention to conserve such species and all endangered and threatened wildlife. Part of the impetus came from the well-organized nationally-based conservation groups that have long made the United States a leader in international conservation.

But political pressure and aesthetics alone do not represent a sufficient explanation for why the ESA of 1973 became domestic law. The argument for protection of endangered species represented not only protection of the aesthetic beauties of certain species, but also ecological and philosophical principles asserting the value of the survival of the widest possible number of species, some of them quite homely, in the context of the continuing loss each year of hundreds of species worldwide. The utilitarian position holds that preserving endangered species is in some way directly or indirectly important for the continued survival of human beings. An endangered species may possess chemical or medical properties that will never be discovered if the creatures are rendered extinct. We preserve species because of lessons they may teach us in the future; at some point, "they may reveal a cure for cancer."[3] Another argument is that the more diversity that exists in the natural world, the more adaptable that world is to continuing stresses. This argument reflects a fundamental law of ecology that the more diverse a gene pool or ecosystem, the greater the natural bank of adaptive diversity upon which society can draw.

Unfortunately, as repeatedly demonstrated in subsequent hearings on the Act, it is very difficult to show the utility of many species, especially species previously unknown that happen to confront a specific valuable development project. Therefore, beyond the strict utility argument, endangered species protection often draws upon a variety of quasi-religious principles emphasizing the sanctity of life. This latter philosophical principle was the most difficult to articulate amidst congressional hearings or agency proceedings, but it reflects an important thread running through the endangered species cases – humans are stewards of their natural environment and ultimately are only constituent members of the community of life of the globe. The ESA, which made no distinction between species that have a commercial value or direct human utility and those that do not, affirmed a variety of abstract interests in protecting species because they were endangered. The statute gave legal value to an abstraction. The survival of species, insofar as possible, was declared a valid and important national goal.

THE SNAIL DARTER – AND THE TELLICO DAM CASE

The Tennessee Valley Authority's (TVA) Tellico Dam case was a classic environmental conflict between a citizens group, including farmers, sportsmen, archaeologists, and the Cherokee Indians on one hand, and on the other a pork-barrel group comprising a federal construction agency allied with private business interests, primarily real estate. The case started in the early 1960s and decided the fate of the last remaining undammed segment of the Little Tennessee River.[4]

As reported during the 1970s, the story consistently came down to a simple caricature: the snail darter, a two-inch minnow, discovered at the last possible moment and misused by extremist environmentalists, halts completion of a massive $150,000,000 hydroelectric dam. On the factual record virtually every

3. See pages 12-15 *supra* on environmental ethics.

4. The case background, because it occupied six years of efforts by one of the authors from 1974 to 1980, is set out here with more detail than usual.

element of that story was wrong. The Tellico Dam was small with no generators, and was only a fractional part of a quixotic federal land development project that subsequently fell of its own weight. The river valley itself, without the dam, held the potential to produce more public profits than the project. And far from discovering the snail darter at the last moment, TVA knew about the endangered fish in 1973, but ignored the law and spent most of its budget after 1973 in an accelerated effort to foreclose alternatives to the reservoir. The perceived media reality, however, had an immutable force of its own, possessing more importance than the facts on the record. In that irony lies one of the important lessons to be drawn from the case.

THE LITTLE TENNESSEE VALLEY AND ITS LEGAL HISTORY

The valley of the Little Tennessee River (the "Little T"), where it flows out of the Great Smoky Mountains, was settled more than 10,000 years ago. The river's waters ran cool, highly oxygenated, fertile, and filled with fish. The valley lands were rich beyond belief, high-grade topsoil to a depth of twenty feet or more. The Cherokees became a people here over the last millennium. Their most sacred places and Chota, their holy city of refuge, were located here. The first Anglo colonists entered the valley in the 18th century, building Fort Loudon as their southwestern-most redoubt to protect them and their Cherokee allies from the French and other Indian tribes. In the 1830's, responding to the land demands of the white settlers, Andrew Jackson drove the Cherokees off their lands in the Little T Valley in a forced emigration, which culminated in the Trail of Tears to Oklahoma. The white settlers immediately moved in to take over the vacated Cherokee lands. Fort Loudon and many of those early families were still there 200 years later when the TVA arrived and began building dams.

The TVA first hypothesized the Tellico Dam in a 1936 compilation of all dammable sites in the Tennessee Valley system. The Authority gave the site, located at the mouth of the Little Tennessee River where it flows into the Big Tennessee, lowest priority on the list of approximately seventy dam sites because of its marginal cost justification. It remained only a hypothetical site over the years while the TVA built hydroelectric dams and flood control structures elsewhere throughout the river system. All dams justifiable in terms of flood control, navigation, and power – more than forty – had been built by 1950. The Authority continued building dams, however, stretching to justify each on grounds such as "economic development demonstrations." By 1960, more than sixty dams had been built, and the TVA finally turned to the few remaining sites, including Tellico. By then what had always been a treasure had also become unique. The remnant thirty-three-mile stretch of the Little T, flowing with all its ancient qualities of richness and clarity, was the last such stretch of river left.

Congress at first refused to permit the dam to be built, but, faced with repeated TVA requests, in 1966 the House Appropriations Committee finally passed an appropriations bill providing funds for the project. Its primary stated purposes were not hydroelectric. They were (1) to provide recreation and (2) to promote industrial development through the sale of large blocks of condemned farmlands. To support the benefit-cost justification claims, the TVA projected extraordinary net recreation increases, although by this time the Little T was the last remaining stretch of high-quality recreational flowing river, with twenty-four other reservoirs within a fifty-mile radius. TVA hypothesized extensive shoreland development based on a model industrial city to be called "Timberlake," which theoretically would be attracted to the project area, with a series of factories requiring hundreds of acres for industrial development.

But more than 300 farm families then lived in the valley; hundreds of fishermen and canoeists loved it as the last, best remaining stretch of clean flowing river in the region; and the valley of the Little T was sacred to the Cherokees, whose most revered places would be destroyed by a reservoir. A rough citizen coalition, "The Association for the Preservation of the Little Tennessee River," was formed in 1964, and attempted to resist the project in Congress and through local political opposition. Faced with a solid linkage between the TVA, the pork-barrel congressional committees, local politicians, and land speculators, however, the citizens had no realistic chance, legally or on the merits, to stop the project during the 1960s. The concrete part of the dam structure was built in 1968, costing somewhat less than five million dollars, that would not impound any part of the river until later, with the construction of earthen dikes. In 1970, however, NEPA gave the citizens a new lease on life, and they filed suits to stop the project.

Litigation under NEPA produced an injunction, which held for two years but ultimately was dissolved in 1973 when the Authority produced an adequate statement of the project's negative consequences. In the same year, Dr. David Etnier, a University of Tennessee ichthyologist, discovered a small endangered perch living in the midst of the Tellico project area, and a new round of litigation began. Section 7 of the ESA apparently prohibited federal agencies from taking any action that jeopardized the existence of an endangered species or modified a critical habitat. The Tellico project would do both. The fish was endangered and required the clean flowing river habitat that the dam would destroy. No federal statutes permitted a straightforward challenge to the dam project; the snail darter and §7 offered a "handle" to raise the challenge indirectly. Armed with the clear statutory violation, the dam's citizen opponents formed an ad hoc litigation group, filed administrative petitions in 1974 under the terms of the Endangered Species Act, and began court proceedings in 1975. TVA, meanwhile, began working three shifts, night and day, to moot the case before an injunction could issue.

TELLICO'S "ENVIRONMENTAL" CASE

In the case of the Tellico Dam, the project's environmental opponents had determined early that they would have to do more than merely oppose the dam and reservoir using §7's roadblock terms. Instead, as so often occurs in environmental cases, to have a realistic chance of prevailing in the long run, they had tc back up their legal argument with a rational benefit-cost-alternatives accounting. On one hand, the Tellico citizens group reviewed the purported benefits of the reservoir – recreation, industrial development on condemned lands, and various vestigial benefits in water supply, flood control, and hydroelectric capacity – and found that on the objective record, viewed in businesslike terms, the economic case for the dam project was a fantasy. They then looked at the purported costs of the project, arguing that the *true* costs extended beyond the Authority's costs for cement, fill dirt, land condemnation, and roads and bridges. A realistic accounting of the true social costs would have to include the loss of all the special qualities of the river valley that had made it a treasure over the centuries. The river was a major recreational resource on its own terms, even before it had been rendered a virtually unique resource by the impoundment of 2500 linear miles of river in the surrounding region. The agricultural soils of the valley were of great economic value, the historic resources held great public value in their own right and could be capitalized monetarily in a tourist-based development if the valley's central portion was not flooded, and a major parcel of upriver project lands had particular potential for use as an access and overflow management area for the Great Smoky Mountains National Park. The citizens' benefit-cost accounting thus included extensive consideration of development alternatives. With increasing sophistication over the years they argued for a comprehensive river-based development project, allowing displaced families to go back onto most of the rich agricultural lands of the valley, developing a tourist highway through the valley to the Park, developing recreation to promote canoe float trips and other water-based sports, improving access to the superb trout fishing resource, and providing for two industrial parks along the river at locations where they would not disturb the other qualities of the valley. The citizens' analysis of the project consistently proved more accurate than the TVA's projections in every subsequent expert review that took place during the course of the controversy.

The availability of the snail darter, the citizens argued, was not a cynical fortuity. The precarious existence of the endangered fish in the Little T constituted a barometer of endangered human and economic values in this last remaining stretch of high quality river. The snail darter in the Little T was a "canary in a coal mine."

The trial court judge found that the dam would destroy the canary but declined to issue an injunction. The Sixth Circuit Court of Appeals corrected the trial judge's omission, and the case went to the Supreme Court of the United States.[5]

Tennessee Valley Authority v. Hiram Hill, et al.
United States Supreme Court, 1978
437 U.S. 153, 98 S. Ct. 2279, 57 L. Ed. 2d 117

BURGER, C.J. We begin with the premise that operation of the Tellico Dam will either eradicate the known population of snail darters or destroy their critical habitat. Petitioner does not now seriously dispute this fact.

Starting from the above premise, two questions are presented: (a) would TVA be in violation of the Act if it completed and operated the Tellico Dam as planned? (b) if TVA's actions would offend the Act, is an injunction the appropriate remedy for the violation? For the reasons stated hereinafter, we hold that both questions must be answered in the affirmative.

It may seem curious to some that the survival of a relatively small number of three-inch fish among all the countless millions of species extant would require the

5. Hill v. TVA, 419 F. Supp. 753 (E.D. Tenn. 1976), 549 F.2d 1064 (6th Cir. 1977).

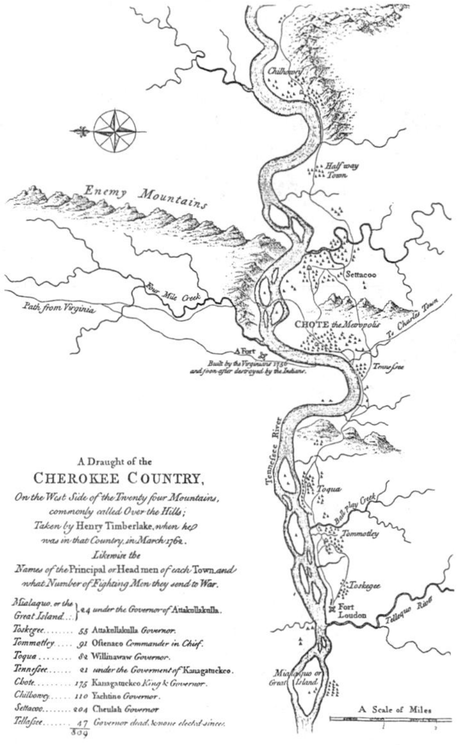

SNAIL DARTER LITHOGRAPH (EXHIBIT 12 AT TRIAL) BY DOLORES ROBERSON

The Little Tennessee River Valley, the dam, and the snail darter. The river and valley were sacred to the Cherokee, whose towns and sanctuaries appear on the 1762 colonial map. Prior to the Tellico case, TVA had eliminated the river above the Enemy (Smoky) Mountains. Tellico dam, located 14 miles downriver from the bottom of the map, destroyed all of the remainder of the freeflowing river. The dam structure, as shown, is small (note size of adjacent trees), costing less than $5 million. The darters lived on a broad shallow shoal below the Great Island.

permanent halting of a virtually completed dam for which Congress has expended more than $100 million....

One would be hard pressed to find a statutory provision whose terms were any plainer than those in §7 of the Endangered Species Act. Its very words affirmatively command all federal agencies "to insure that actions authorized, funded, or carried out by them do not jeopardize the continued existence" of an endangered species or "result in the destruction or modification of habitat of such species...." This language admits of no exception. Accepting the Secretary's determinations, as we must, it is clear that TVA's proposed operation of the dam will have precisely the opposite effect, namely the eradication of an endangered species.

Concededly, this view of the Act will produce results requiring the sacrifice of the anticipated benefits of the project and of many millions of dollars in public funds, but close examination of the language, history, and structure of the legislation under review here indicates beyond doubt that Congress intended endangered species to be afforded the highest of priorities.

"The dominant theme pervading all Congressional discussion of the proposed [ESA] was the overriding need to devote whatever effort and resources were necessary to avoid further diminution of national and worldwide wildlife resources. Much of the testimony at the hearings and much debate was devoted to the biological problem of extinction. Senators and Congressmen uniformly deplored the irreplaceable loss to aesthetics, science, ecology, and the national heritage should more species disappear." Coggins, Conserving Wildlife Resources: An Overview of the Endangered Species Act of 1973, 51 N.D.L. Rev. 315, 321 (1975).

The legislative proceedings in 1973 are, in fact, replete with expressions of concern over the risk that might lie in the loss of any endangered species. Typifying these sentiments is the Report of the House Committee on Merchant Marine and Fisheries on HR 37, a bill which contained the essential features of the subsequently enacted Act of 1973; in explaining the need for the legislation, the Report stated:

> As we homogenize the habitats in which these plants and animals evolved, and as we increase the pressure for products that they are in a position to supply (usually unwillingly) we threaten their and our own-genetic heritage. The value of this genetic heritage is, quite literally, incalculable. From the most narrow possible point of view, it is in the best interests of mankind to minimize the losses of genetic variations. The reason is simple: they are potential resources. They are keys to puzzles which we cannot solve, and may provide answers to questions which we have not yet learned to ask. To take a homely, but apt, example: one of the critical chemicals in the regulation of ovulations in humans was found in a common plant. Once discovered, and analyzed, humans could duplicate it synthetically, but had it never existed – or had it been driven out of existence before we knew its potentialities – we would never have tried to analyze it in the first place. Who knows, or can say, what potential cures for cancer or other scourges, present or future, may lie locked up in the structures of plants which may yet be undiscovered, much less analyzed?.... Sheer self-interest impels us to be cautious. The institutionalization of that caution lies at the heart of HR 37.... HR Rep. No. 93-412.

As the examples cited here demonstrate, Congress was concerned about the unknown uses that endangered species might have and about the unforeseeable place such creatures may have in the chain of life on this planet.

In shaping legislation to deal with the problem thus presented, Congress started from the finding that "[t]he two major causes of extinction are hunting, and destruction of natural habitat." Sen. Rep. No. 93-307,2 (1973). Of these twin threats, Congress was informed that the greatest was destruction of natural habitats.

It is not for us to speculate, much less act, on whether Congress would have altered its stance had the specific events of this case been anticipated. In any event, we discern no hint in the deliberations of Congress relating to the 1973 Act that would compel a different result than we reach here.

One might dispute the applicability of these examples to the Tellico Dam by saying that in this case the burden on the public through the loss of millions of unrecoverable dollars would greatly outweigh the loss of the snail darter. But neither the Endangered Species Act nor Article III of the Constitution provides federal courts with authority to make such fine utilitarian calculations. On the contrary, the plain language of the Act, buttressed by its legislative history, shows clearly that Congress viewed the value of endangered species as "incalculable." Quite obviously, it would be difficult for a court to balance the loss of a sum certain – even $100 million – against a congressionally declared "incalculable" value, even assuming we had the power to engage in such a weighing process, which we emphatically do not.

Having determined that there is an irreconcilable conflict between operation of the Tellico Dam and the explicit provisions of §7 of the Endangered Species Act, we must now consider what remedy, if any, is appropriate. It is correct, of course, that a federal judge sitting as a chancellor is not mechanically obligated to grant an injunction for every violation of law.

Once Congress, exercising its delegated powers, has decided the order of priorities in a given area, it is for the Executive to administer the laws and for the courts to enforce them when enforcement is sought.

Here we are urged to view the Endangered Species Act "reasonably," and hence shape a remedy "that accords with some modicum of common sense and the public weal." But is that our function? We have no expert knowledge on the subject of endangered species, much less do we have a mandate from the people to strike a balance of equities on the side of the Tellico Dam. Congress has spoken in the plainest of words, making it abundantly clear that the balance has been struck in favor of affording endangered species the highest of priorities, hereby adopting a policy which it described as "institutionalized caution."

Our individual appraisal of the wisdom or unwisdom of a particular course consciously selected by the Congress is to be put aside in the process of interpreting a statute. Once the meaning of an enactment is discerned and its constitutionality determined, the judicial process comes to an end. We do not sit as a committee of review, nor are we vested with the power of veto. The lines ascribed to Sir Thomas More by Robert Bolt are not without relevance here:

> The law, Roper, the law. I know what's legal, not what's right. And I'll stick to what's legal.... I'm not God. The currents and eddies of right and wrong, which you find such plain-sailing, I can't navigate. I'm no voyager. But in the thickets of the law, oh there I'm a forester.... What would you do? Cut a great road through the law to get after the Devil?.... And when the last law was down, and the Devil turned round on you, where would you hide, Roper, the laws all being flat?.... This country's planted thick with laws from coast to coast – Man's laws, not God's – and if you cut them down...d'you really think you could stand upright in the winds that would blow then? Yes, I'd give the Devil benefit of law, for my own safety's sake. R. Bolt, A Man for All Seasons, Act I, 147 (Heinemann ed. 1967).

We agree with the Court of Appeals that in our constitutional system the commitment to the separation of powers is too fundamental for us to pre-empt congressional action by judicially decreeing what accords with "common sense and the public weal." Our Constitution vests such responsibilities in the political branches. Affirmed.

POWELL, J., joined by BLACKMUN, J., and REHNQUIST, J., wrote separate opinions

COMMENTARY AND QUESTIONS

1. An "environmental" opinion? Much of the snail darter majority opinion looks at the Endangered Species Act only to determine, via statutory construction, the bald question of whether it applied to the dam, and whether a court had to obey the statute. The court does not mention any of the plaintiffs' evidence on overall environmental-economic balancing, or on rational development alternatives. Justice Burger does echo congressional declarations of the high purposes of endangered species preservation, and "institutionalized caution," a critical environmental principle, but in his oral presentation of the decision he invited Congress to repeal protection for the fish. And the media predictably chorused the "little fish bites dam" theme, casting the case and plaintiffs in damaging terms of extreme environmentalism. On balance, did the snail darter litigation aid the cause of conservation, or undercut it?

2. A tactical footnote on ESA legislative history. Would it change your view of §7 of the 1973 ESA if you were told that it had been consciously drafted by a legislative aide and an ardent wildlife advocate in a form that would avoid its being recognized as a substantive roadblock statute? If §7, which has become one of the landmark environmental protections in federal law, would never have been passed without a virtually impenetrable verbal camouflage, what does that say about Congress and the legislative process? What does it say about the ethics of the drafters of the provision who successfully slipped it into federal law? It is not a satisfactory excuse, for many environmentalists, that the opponents of environmental protection regularly slip exceptions and destructive undercutting amendments into ongoing legislation.

The tactical questions that arise when environmentalists actively participate in the legislative process continually force thoughtful people to reconsider their philosophy of government, of public interest advocacy, and ethics.

And the text virtually admits that the plaintiffs used the snail darter as a convenient "handle" to raise public issues about farmland, historic values, river recreation, and economics. Isn't this a misuse of the law, one that, moreover, selfishly risks the destruction of the ESA itself?

3. The clash between stark roadblocks and pressures for flexibility. Stark "roadblock" prohibitions clearly have a potent ability to effectuate their terms. Section 7 helped make the ESA a high-profile and credible governmental protective program. But strict prohibitions are not always rational when applied in the realities of a complex world. Inevitably there will be circumstances in which they may require modification. In every case there will be regulated and affected parties who argue strongly for eliminating the roadblock, or opening it up with a variety of discretionary or bureaucratic flexibility devices. How can and should flexibility be considered?

4. Flexibility: statutory violations and equitable balancing. One way for a roadblock to gain flexibility is if appellate courts say that it need not be enforced if violated. Justice Burger's opinion, however, declared a ringing endorsement of the environmentalists' proposition (and the basis of their empowerment strategy) that if citizens are able to prove a statutory violation, the court must enforce the law without equitable balancing, and transfer the debate to the legislative forum. This was a fairly conservative, non-activist theory of judicial review. It distinguished the traditional three areas of equitable balancing,[6] and argued that where statutory

6. Noted earlier in Chapter 3's consideration of equitable remedies, page 142 *supra*.

violations are concerned, the scope of equitable balancing is restricted to threshold questions (of laches, clean hands, etc.) and to the question of which remedy is necessary to effectuate the legislature's substantive prohibition. It does not extend to second-guessing what actions should be prohibited.

Justice Rehnquist wrote a scathing dissent in *Hill* arguing that trial judges, as in this case, should have equitable discretion to permit projects to go on despite statutory violations. This activist argument raises a basic question about roadblock statutes. When they are violated, who should be able to grant the necessary flexibility, a trial judge "balancing the equities," or the Congress? The plaintiffs argued throughout the case that it was perfectly proper for Congress to consider such exemptions. In that way citizens might win the opportunity to have full, rational legislative hearings on the issue, based on the tactical leverage of the injunction.[7]

The citizens thus argued that, as in Hecht Co. v. Bowles, a leading equity case,[8] courts remained free to deny injunctions or modify injunctions as necessary so long as they accomplished whatever the statute required or prohibited. The second balance, however, as to whether the defendant's activity should in fact be prohibited, was pre-empted by statute. In *Hecht*, the Supreme Court had made a much-quoted declaration of a court's continuing power to balance the equities when confronted with a petition for an injunction. But in that case it had been established that the defendant would no longer violate the statutory price-fixing prohibition. The injunction was not necessary because the legislature's wish was being obeyed.

In a case soon after *Hill*, the Supreme Court had to apply the strict enforcement principle to a controversy between Puerto Rico and the Navy. The Governor of Puerto Rico, joined by fishermen, environmentalists, and other disaffected citizens, attempted to halt the United States Navy's practice bombing on and around the inhabited island of Vieques. Weinberger v. Romero-Barcelo, 456 U.S. 305 (1982). The Navy's action threatened the safety and peace of several hundred people living close to the area where bombs were dropping every day. In this case, as with the snail darter, the citizen plaintiffs were desperately seeking a legal "handle" by which they could halt the government action and negotiate a compromise. Absent some statutory authority, it was clear they would lose. Political pressure and public petitions had proved useless in obtaining concessions from the Defense Department. The Governor and the citizens found several relevant statutory provisions; the most direct was a violation of the Clean Water Act. According to the clear statutory provisions and legislative history of the Act, Congress had made it illegal to dump munitions into the waters of the United States without a permit. To make it even clearer that this provision of the Act applied to the military, the statute included a waiver provision for cases of military necessity – the President could issue an executive exemption to permit particular activity to continue. In the circumstances, the citizens thought that they would at the least get an opinion from the Supreme Court requiring the President to issue such a waiver. This would have

7. See Plater, Statutory Violations and Equitable Discretion, 70 Cal. L. Rev. 524, 583-588 (1982).
8. 321 U.S. 321 (1944).

forced the President to acknowledge their problem publicly, and perhaps would have stimulated negotiations.

In both *Hill* and *Romero-Barcelo*, the citizens would have been delighted if the defendants would have voluntarily complied with statutory requirements absent an injunction. In both cases, however, government agencies took the position that they would not comply with the law unless a court forced them to do so. In such circumstances, the citizens argued, the courts' discretion had to be exercised to achieve compliance with the law.

The Puerto Ricans' argument stressed the dangers to separation of powers if activist courts could override legislative pronouncements. In the circumstances, they understandably expected that the Court would apply the statute as written, especially because the statute provided for the flexibility of a presidential waiver. The expectations of the citizens, scholars, and analysts watching the case were derailed when the Supreme Court, in an eight-to-one vote, bypassed the statutory mandate. The Court declared, citing *Hecht*, that equitable jurisdiction meant that courts could always balance all the equities, even in the case of specific statutory prohibitions. The Court thus asserted that judges could override statutory violations when, in the exercise of their discretionary judgment, they considered the statute unwise as applied to a particular case. This is, needless to say, an extremely "activist" stance, indicating that judicial passivity in other cases may be less a matter of principle than a pragmatic basis for reaching organic decisions.

But the *Romero* Court had to deal with the snail darter. The majority declared that the Tellico case had been special, one of those rare cases in which Congress had legislated a clear, decisive protection and intended it to be stringent. This reasoning was especially bemusing because most observers would agree that Congress had no idea what it was doing when it initially passed §7. The Court stated the presumption that statutes implicitly include recognition of the judiciary's power to override violations through a traditional common law balancing of equities. Only when a statute clearly abjures such judicial power is a court restricted in its rewriting of legislation.[9]

In lonely dissent, Justice Stevens tracked the citizens' argument in detail, recognizing that the majority was overlooking some very important organic issues reaching beyond the question of equitable jurisdiction per se. The majority's decision, he argued, was "premised on a gross misunderstanding of the statutory scheme" of the Clean Water Act and lacked the "profound respect for the law and the proper allocation of lawmaking responsibilities in our Government" reflected in the TVA v. Hill opinion.

The debate – whether courts are bound to enforce statutes when citizens prove

9. Does this holding in *Romero-Barcelo* amount to a declaration that Congress, when passing a regulatory statute, must say: (1) "it is hereby prohibited to do A, B, and C" and (2) "we really mean it!"?

violations – continues. Amoco Prod. Co. v. Village of Gambell, 480 U.S. 531 (1987);[10] cf. Sierra Club v. Marsh, 872 F.2d 497, 500 (1st Cir. 1989).

5. Flexibility through statutory interpretation? The Supreme Court's opinion in TVA v. Hill also included an extensive analysis rejecting the agency's arguments that the statute should be interpreted not to cover the snail darter and the dam – primarily arguments based on retroactivity, implied amendment, and "common sense."

The retroactivity argument urged that since the concrete part of the dam, worth $5 million of the $150 million total, had been built before the Endangered Species Act was passed, the project could continue even if it would eliminate the endangered species. The Court upheld the citizens' argument that a statute should be applied if it prohibits actions which would cause, as in Justice Holmes's dictum, "the evils that the legislature intended to address." Further, governmental agencies have no civil right or vested right to proceed with favorite projects in spite of subsequent federal legislation (see *Thorpe*, noted in the *Overton Park* discussion at page 550 *supra*).

TVA had continued to receive funding for the dam project from the porkbarrel appropriations committees year after year despite the committee's knowledge of the endangered species statutory violation. The agency and appropriations committees also added phrases to the annual funding bills stating the committees' opinion that the Act did not apply, that the Act was frivolous in this setting, and that the importance of the project so exceeded the importance of the endangered species that the project should continue irrespective of any possible statutory violation. TVA argued that continued funding, plus this legislative intent, constituted an implied amendment, implied repealer, or implied statutory exception to the Act. The Supreme Court disagreed, noting a long line of cases declaring that repeals by implication are suspect, particularly if they are found in appropriations bills, which typically deal with budgetary and financial matters rather than substantive law.

As to common sense in statutory interpretation, at many stages during the course of the litigation, and in the halls of Congress and the agencies, it was argued that a statute should not be applied if it would lead to what the particular observer considered an "absurd" or "extreme" result. As Justice Powell said –

> In my view §7 cannot reasonably be interpreted as applying to a project that is completed or substantially completed when its threat to an endangered species is discovered. Nor can I believe that Congress could have intended this Act to produce the "absurd result" – in the words of the District Court – of this case. 437 U.S. at 196.

The Supreme Court held, however, that even when a statute led to what a court might think was an absurd result, if the facts fit the law, the statute was to be applied as it was written.

---

10. *Gambell* holds that a court may balance the equities so as to allow a violation to continue, although it includes language that:

> Environmental injury, by its nature, can seldom be adequately remedied by money damages and is often permanent or at least of long duration, i.e., irreparable. If such injury is sufficiently likely, therefore, the balance of harms will usually favor the issuance of an injunction to protect the environment. 480 U.S. at 545.

6. Flexibility: remand to Congress. Throughout the Tellico Dam case, the environmentalists had argued that courts should merely enforce the statute, and the matter then would necessarily be transferred to the legislature, where for the first time they could obtain public review of the controversy on the factual and economic merits.

The case by no means ended with the Supreme Court decision, given the cantankerousness of the contending parties. Congress responded with three series of hearings in the relevant substantive committees, considering whether this extreme application of the law should be reversed. Three times the committees were convinced, much to their surprise, that preservation of the river was not an example of environmental irrationality; and no Tellico amendment was passed. The media, however, remained fixed upon its "fish bites dam" characterization of the case.

7. 1978 ESA amendments, §7, and a God Committee. Ultimately, however, the Congress was persuaded in late 1978 to create a new statutory flexibility device to calm the avalanche of criticism levied against the "extremism" of the Act revealed by the snail darter decision.

An exemption procedure was added to §7, providing that a Cabinet-level review board (dubbed the God Committee) could allow the extinction of a species if it found by special majority that:

(a) the federal project is of regional or national significance,

(b) there is no "reasonable and prudent alternative," and

(c) the project as proposed "clearly outweighs the alternatives."

If exemption is granted, the agency must implement the best possible mitigation plan. Was this amendment ultimately a tragic watering-down of the ESA?

8. Administrative flexibility in practice: the God Committee. In the 1978 ESA amendments, Congress required that the Tellico project be reviewed by the God Committee for exemption. This was the plaintiffs' first chance to argue their full case before a legal forum that would (unlike the courts) have to make a comprehensive judgment.

On January 23, 1979, the God Committee unanimously denied an exemption for Tellico, specifically on economic, rather than ecological, grounds. "I hate to see the snail darter get the credit for stopping a project that was ill-conceived and uneconomic in the first place," said Chairman Andrus. The reservoir project, the committee said, deserved to be killed on its own merits. As Charles Schultze, then-Chairman of the Council of Economic Advisers and a member of the Committee said, "Here is a project that is 95 percent complete, and if one takes just the cost of finishing it against the [total project] benefits, and does it properly, it doesn't pay, which says something about the original design." A remarkable feature of the last phase of the Tellico case was that at this stage the river defenders had to make their arguments on the basis of tangible economic values rather than "intangible" ecological values, and still, despite the expenditure of millions of dollars, the non-

dam alternatives compared favorably to the dam plan. The river's non-dam development alternatives, with a host of nonquantifiable social values, were largely ignored in the governmental process and the media.

The citizens had been vindicated on the merits in every element of their long-running campaign against the project. The possibility lay open for an innovative redevelopment of the valley and its river resource, demonstrating to the nation what could be done with coordinated management of prime agricultural lands and a valley's historic, recreational, touristic, and ecological assets.

9. Denouement for the snail darter. For the next four and a half months after the God committee decision, the citizens worked desperately to begin implementation of alternative planning for the river and the valley. Despite some reforms in TVA's stonewalling behavior, however, the agency declined to talk with the farmers or environmentalists, and nothing happened. Into the vacuum, on June 18, 1979, stepped Senator Howard Baker and John Duncan, a local Tennessee congressman. Through a parliamentary maneuver engineered by the porkbarrel appropriations committee, Duncan, in 42 seconds, slipped a rider onto the ongoing House appropriations bill explicitly overriding the Supreme Court decision and all other federal or state protective laws as they applied to Tellico and ordering the reservoir's immediate completion. Because the amendment was not read in the empty chamber, none of the few congressmen on the floor other than the committee members knew what was being done. Ultimately the rider passed through the Senate with Baker's decisive help. President Jimmy Carter threatened to veto, then signed the bill with an abject telephone call apology to plaintiffs on October 4, 1979.

The Cherokees filed another lawsuit based upon the constitutional rights that would be infringed if their most sacred places were destroyed by the reservoir. (Was this an "environmental" suit?) The case died in the courts when an injunction was denied on grounds that the Indians could not assert religious rights on land they did not own, and TVA closed the gates to start flooding the valley on November 28, 1979. Ammoneta Sequoyah v. TVA, 480 F. Supp. 608 (E.D. Tenn. 1979), 620 F.2d 1159 (6th Cir. 1980), cert. denied, 449 U.S. 953 (1980).

Of the last major population, 25,000 darters that had lived in the Little Tennessee prior to dam construction, none has survived. Small relict populations have been discovered in several sites downstream, and at two other sites, and the Department of Interior has downlisted the darter to "threatened" status.[11] The condemned valley lands produced no model industrial city, and little economic development.[12]

11. A side note: both Hiram Hill, the student-plaintiff who discovered the potential for this endangered species litigation while writing an environmental law term paper, and the Senate aide who drafted the tough "clearly outweighs" God Committee test, had studied environmental law using an earlier version of this coursebook.

12. TVA strove to sell the condemned lands for development, but without much success. The first major development proposal after two years of stagnation was to create regional toxic waste landfills on the valley lands; the citizens quashed it. Subsequently a small industrial park (smaller than the industrial park included as part of the citizens' non-dam alternative plan) attracted several small businesses. To achieve more development, TVA then transferred a substantial portion of the valley, on a subsidized basis, to a second-home vacation housing developer.

10. ESA procedures: consultation. The §7 roadblock provision in its original form contained a bare requirement for endangered species "consultation" between Interior and other agencies. When it became clear that §7 was strictly enforceable, the consultation process evolved quickly in agency practice to mediate conflicting interests. By 1979, Department of Interior records showed that more than 4500 potential conflicts between endangered species and federal projects had arisen, and in all but four cases[13] the agencies were able to adjust project design, timing, or location to accommodate the ESA protections.

When §7's strict prohibition was modified to include the God Committee exemption possibility, the consultation process was further articulated by statute and rule. 50 C.F.R. Pt. 402; 16 U.S.C.A. §1536(b)(3)(1978). A request for consultation triggers a strict time schedule. FWS undertakes active consultation, and must issue a "biological opinion," analyzing the conflict and suggesting alternatives, if necessary, within 90 days. The consultation process and biological opinions are held to good faith and best available data.[14]

11. Critical habitat. In the snail darter case, designation of critical habitat was pro forma. In subsequent cases, however, critical habitat listing has been hotly contested, in part because it automatically requires at least minimal review of any federal actions within the habitat areas. Public and private project proponents often view it in more drastic terms, as a "power grab" (as when Interior considers listing broad geographical areas[15]), and a nefarious part of protectionists' "agenda to lock up all public lands as de facto wilderness."[16]

The Interior Department is often diffident about declaring critical habitat. Only half of listed endangered species have critical habitat listings.[17] Critical habitat protection lawsuits are accordingly rare.

12. Agencies' affirmative conservation duties? Section 7's vague hortatory provision urging agencies to "carry...out programs for the conservation of endangered species" may become a litigable requirement. In Carson-Truckee Water Conservacy

---

13. The exceptions were, according to Interior testimony, attributable to agency intransigence rather than irresolvability – TVA's Tellico Dam, the FHWA's insistence on putting Interstate-10 through a sandhill crane habitat, the Corps of Engineers' Meramec Dam, and the Corps and REA's Greyrocks Dam. See Endangered Species Oversight Hearings, Senate Committee on Environment and Public Works, No. 95-H33, 62-75, 79-91 (1977). Of these, all but Tellico were settled through negotiation after citizen litigation. Greyrocks' settlement was incorporated into a God Committee ruling under the 1978 ESA amendments. The Administration's data for the hearings was compiled by Mardi Hatcher and Deborah Labelle, working in the federal archives as student volunteers from the Wayne Environmental Law Society.

14. Bob Marshall Alliance v. Hodel, 852 F.2d 1223 (9th Cir. 1988); Village of False Pass v. Watt, 733 F.2d 605 (9th Cir. 1984); Roosevelt Campobello Int'l Park v. EPA, 684 F.2d 1041 (1st Cir. 1982).

15. This is especially so when Interior proposes designating habitat in ranchland or other developed areas where a predator endangered species has been exterminated but may be re-introduced.

16. Murray, The Act Will Work – If They Let It, 7 Envt'l Forum 32 (July 1990).

17. Illustrating this diffidence, the regulations provide for habitat listing "to the maximum extent *prudent* and *determinable*." (emphasis added). Those mitigating adjectives are complemented by a requirement that FWS "tak[e] into consideration the probable economic and other impacts...," 50 C.F.R. §424.12, and "exclude any...area from the critical habitat if the benefits of such exclusion outweigh the benefits of [inclusion]." §424.19.

District v. Clark,[18] for example, the court held that the Department of Interior was required not only to protect existing habitats and endangered species, but also to "use programs administered by [the Department] to further the conservation purposes of [the Endangered Species Act]." The Department must "conserve threatened and endangered species to the extent that they are no longer threatened" and "halt *and reverse* the trend toward species extinction, whatever the cost." 741 F.2d at 262 (the emphasis is the court's).

13. Extending ESA habitat protection to private property. Section 7 prohibits only federal agencies from jeopardizing the existence of a species or modifying critical habitat. But ESA §9 potentially goes even further when it provides that no one can "take" an endangered species. The most obvious intent is to prevent the killing or capturing of endangered species, but the statutory and regulatory definitions of "take" extend beyond acts that result in the killing of endangered wildlife to include "harass," "harm," causing "significant habitat modification or degradation," and acts that alter endangered species' breeding, feeding, or sheltering patterns.[19]

If §9's statutory prohibition against taking endangered species is interpreted to include conscious disruption – bulldozing, killing, displacing – of species, or destruction of their habitat, then the prohibitions of the statute can reach out to private and state government actors as well. Thus developers planning to fill a mangrove swamp containing an eagle's nest in order to build a condominium project might find their enterprise halted by a conflict with the ESA, enforced by the stringencies of civil and criminal penalties or injunction. A fascinating case raising this and other endangered species issues is the Hawaiian litigation concerning a little brown bird, Palila v. Hawaii DLNR, 471 F. Supp. 985 (D. Ha. 1979), aff'd 639 F. 2d 495 (9th Cir. 1981). Given the widespread destruction of habitat that accompanies the day-by-day development of land and water resources in America, this provision may come to be the Act's next cause célèbre.

14. Statutory exceptions for "incidental taking" of species. The 1982 amendments gave the Secretary authority to permit "incidental takes" where the harm to the species is "not the purpose of...an otherwise lawful activity." §1539(a)(1)(B). This seemingly permissive loophole is considerably tightened by subsequent subsections, requiring a strict series of findings and protective actions. §1539(a)(2)(A,B,C).[20] To date, agency implementation and court review of the incidental taking provisions have appeared to be quite punctilious.[21] Because of the political avalanches that descend upon any endangered species that stands in the way of market decisions, however, further pitched legal battles over incidental taking permits are inevitable.

18. 741 F.2d 257 (9th Cir. 1984), cert. denied 105 S. Ct. 1842 (1985).

19. 15 U.S.C.A. §§1532(19); 1538(a-b)(1982); 50 CFR §17.3 (1985).

20. The incidental taking exception can also be applied to facilitate species conservation actions. See Las Vegas v. Lujan, 891 F.2d 927 (D.C. Cir. 1989).

21. See Friends of Endangered Species v. Jantzen, 760 F.2d 976 (9th Cir. 1985). This is the case of California's Mission Blue butterfly, an interesting confrontation where an incidental take permit was issued after extensive biological study and mitigation.

B. THE SPOTTED OWL AND ANCIENT FORESTS

Seattle Audubon Society v. John L. Evans (U.S. Forest Service) and Washington Contract Loggers Assoc.

United States District Court, Western District of Washington, 1991
771 F. Supp. 1081[22]

DWYER, J. ...Plaintiffs Seattle Audubon Society, et al. have moved for a permanent injunction prohibiting the sale of logging rights in northern spotted owl [strix occidentalis caurina] habitat areas until the Forest Service complies with the National Forest Management Act ("NFMA"), 16 U.S.C.A. §1600 et seq. and its regulations by adopting standards and guidelines to assure that a viable population of the species is maintained in the forests....

The national forests are managed by the Forest Service under NFMA. Regulations promulgated under that statute provide that fish and wildlife shall be managed to maintain viable populations of existing native and desired non-native vertebrate species in the planning area. 36 CFR §219.19. A viable population is "one which has the estimated numbers and distribution of reproductive individuals to insure its continued existence is well distributed in the planning area." Id. To insure viability, habitat must be provided to support at least a minimum number of reproductive individuals.... Since not every species can be monitored, "indicator species" are observed as signs of general wildlife viability. Id. §219.19(a)(1). The northern spotted owl is an indicator species....

In recent years logging and development have steadily reduced wildlife habitat in the Pacific Northwest. At the same time many local mills have experienced log shortages. The result is an intensified struggle over the future of the national forests....

[The court discusses the Forest Service's multiple use mandates, studied in Chapter 14 *infra,* and the §318 appropriations rider studied at page 572 *supra.*]

The court of appeals ruled that §318 was...an unconstitutional attempt to adjudicate rather than legislate. The requirements of §318 were thus held to be in addition to, and not in lieu of, those of the general environmental statutes....

In June 1990, the Fish and Wildlife Service, having completed its listing process [under court order,[23] after having initially declined to do so] listed the owl as a threatened species under the Endangered Species Act. Determination of Threatened Status for the Northern Spotted Owl, 55 Fed. Reg. 26114....

On February 26, 1991, Judge Zilly ruled [in Northern Spotted Owl v. Lujan, 758 F. Supp. 621, 629 (W.D. Wash. 1991)] that the FWS had again failed to comply with the law, stating:

> Upon the record presented, this Court finds the Service has failed to discharge its obligations under the Endangered Species Act and its own administrative regulations. Specifically, the Service, acting on behalf of the Secretary of the Interior, abused its discretion when it determined not to designate critical habitat concurrently with the listing of the northern spotted owl, or to explain any basis for concluding that the critical habitat was not determin-

---

22. On remand from the Ninth Circuit., 914 F.2d 1311 (9th Cir. 1991); cert. granted, 111 S. Ct. 2886 (1991).

23. Northern Spotted Owl v. Hodel, 716 F.Supp. 479 (W.D. Wash. 1988).

able. These actions were arbitrary and capricious, and contrary to law. 758 F. Supp. at 629.

The Forest Service's argument in this case that it was relieved of its NFMA duty to plan for the spotted owl's viability once the species was listed by the FWS as "threatened" [is] rejected.... The Forest Service has understood at all times that its duties under NFMA and ESA are concurrent.

The Forest Service did not comply by the deadline of September 30, 1990 – or at all – with §318's requirement that it adopt a revised plan to ensure the owl's viability....

[In September 1990, without notice, hearing, environmental impact statement, or other rule-making procedures, the Forest Service announced that it was proceeding with the timber sales, and this court issued a preliminary injunction. A full trial followed.]

FINDINGS OF FACT...

Background Findings

1. The fate of the spotted owl has become a battleground largely because the species is a symbol of the remaining old growth forest. As stated in the [April 1990] ISC Report:[24]

> Why all the fuss about the status and welfare of this particular bird? The numbers, distribution, and welfare of spotted owls are widely believed to be inextricably tied to mature and old-growth forests. Such forests have been significantly reduced since 1850 (mostly since 1950) by clearing for agriculture, urban development, natural events such as fire and windstorms, and most significantly, by logging in recent decades. Nearly all old growth has been removed on private lands. Most of the remainder is under the management of the BLM, FS, and NPS on Federal lands. As its habitat has declined, the owl has virtually disappeared from some areas and its numbers are decreasing in others.

2. An old growth forest consists not just of ancient standing trees, but of fallen trees, snags, massive decaying vegetation, and numerous resident plant and animal species, many of which live nowhere else.

3. A great conifer forest originally covered the western parts of Washington, Oregon, and Northern California, from the Cascade and Coast mountains to the sea. Perhaps ten percent of it remains. The spaces protected as parks or wilderness areas are not enough for the survival of the northern spotted owl.

4. The old growth forest sustains a biological community far richer than those of managed forests or tree farms. As testified by Dr. William Ferrell, a forest ecologist:

> The most significant implication from our new knowledge regarding old-growth forest ecology is that logging these forests destroys not just trees, but a complex, distinctive, and unique ecosystem.

5. The remaining old growth stands are valued also for their effects on climate, air, and migratory fish runs, and for their beauty. A 1984 Forest Service document summed up the controversy:

24. [The Interagency Scientific Committee (ISC), chaired by Jack Ward Thomas of the Forest Service, recommended setting aside 20–30 percent of the available old growth in public forests to protect the owls.]

> There are at least three main reasons cited for maintaining old growth: wildlife and plant habitat, ecosystem diversity, and preservation of aesthetic qualities. Those opposed to the retention of old growth are primarily concerned with economic factors and urge rapid conversion of the existing old growth to managed forests of productive, young age classes. Forest Service, Regional Guide for Pacific Northwest Region 3-40 (May 1984).

6. Through most of the country's history there was little or no logging in the national forests. Intensive logging began with World War II and has accelerated....
8. Despite increasing concern over the environment, logging sales by the Forest Service have continued on a large scale....
9. ...Many small mills and logging companies depend in whole or in part on federal timber.
10. Mill owners and loggers, and their employees, especially in small towns, have developed since World War II an expectation that federal timber will be available indefinitely, and a way of life that cannot be duplicated elsewhere.
11. The region's timber industry has been going through fundamental changes. The most important is modernization which increases productivity and reduces the demand for labor (i.e., the jobs available). There have also been recent changes in product demand, in competition from other parts of the country and the world, and in the export of raw logs for processing in the Far East. The painful results for many workers, and their families and communities, will continue regardless of whether owl habitat in the national forests is protected.

STATUTORY VIOLATIONS

12. The records of this case...show a remarkable series of violations of the environmental laws.... In...the fall of 1990 the Forest Service admitted that [its 1988 protocol for logging old growth national forests] was inadequate after all – that it would fail to preserve the northern spotted owl. In seeking a stay of proceedings in this court in 1989 the Forest Service announced its intent to adopt temporary guidelines within thirty days. It did not do that within thirty days, or ever. When directed by Congress to have a revised ROD [record of decision] in place by September 30, 1990, the Forest Service did not even attempt to comply....
13. The reasons for this pattern of behavior were made clear at the evidentiary hearing. [A Forest Service wildlife biologist testified that the agency process had been diluted] –

> because in every instance there was a considerable – I would emphasize considerable – amount of political pressure to create a plan which was an absolute minimum. That is, which had a very low probability of success and which had a minimum impact on timber harvest.... [Other testimony showed repeated political amendments to the spotted owl plan made in executive offices in Washington.]

20. The Forest Service now has advantages it lacked in early 1990. Much of the research and analysis has been done.... The agency...has the benefit of an [endangered species consultation] opinion letter from the FWS...commenting at length on the ISC strategy and giving recommendations.
21. With the knowledge at hand, there is no reason for the Forest Service to fail to develop quickly a plan to ensure the viability of the spotted owl in the national forests. Coordination with the FWS need not be an obstacle; the agencies have coordinated their efforts on other species, and can on this one....

PROBABILITY OF IRREPARABLE HARM

22. The northern spotted owl is now threatened with extinction. The ISC Report states:

> We have concluded that the owl is imperiled over significant portions of its range because of continuing losses of habitat from logging and natural disturbances. Current management strategies are inadequate to ensure its viability. Moreover, in some portions of the owl's range, few options for managing habitat remain open, and available alternatives are steadily declining throughout the bird's range. For these reasons, delay in implementing a conservation strategy cannot be justified on the basis of inadequate knowledge.

23. The population of northern spotted owls continues to decline. "We're going to have to arrest that decline and reverse it," as Dr. Thomas testified.
24. "Spotted owl habitat," also called "suitable habitat," is defined as follows by FWS:

> Suitable owl habitat has moderate to high canopy closure (60 to 80 percent); a multi-layered, multi-species canopy dominated by large (> 30 inches in diameter at breast height (dbh)) overstory trees; a high incidence of large trees with various deformities (e.g., large cavities, broken tops, dwarf-mistletoe infections, and other evidence of decadence); numerous large snags; large accumulations of fallen trees and other woody debris on the ground; and sufficient open space below the canopy for owls to fly. 55 Fed. Reg. 26114, 26116 (1990).

25. The Forest Service estimates that an additional 66,000 acres of spotted owl habitat would be destroyed if logging went forward to the extent permitted by the ISC Report over the next sixteen months. That would be in addition to about 400,000 acres of habitat logged in the seven years since the agency began preparing these guidelines, all without having a lawful plan or EIS for the owl's management in place.
31. The ISC Report has been described by experts on both sides as the first scientifically respectable proposal regarding spotted owl conservation to come out of the executive branch. However...to have a chance of success, the strategy would have to be adopted and followed by the agencies concerned. So far it has not been adopted by any....
35. The logging of 66,000 acres of owl habitat, in the absence of a conservation plan, would itself constitute a form of irreparable harm. Old growth forests are lost for generations. No amount of money can replace the environmental loss.
36. ...There is a substantial risk that logging another 66,000 acres, before a plan is adopted, would push the species past a population threshold from which it could not recover. Dr. Gordon Orians, an expert in avian populations and ecology, has testified:

> ...I recommend a cessation of logging of owl habitat in the short run because I think the risk that the population crosses a very significant viability threshold is increased significantly by continued loss of its habitat. This will reduce the options to maintain viability in the future.... "Significant probability" means, in this context, that given the threats that exist on the owl now...implementing the plan in a manner that continues to lose significant amounts of habitat during a transition period poses very significant risks to

the spotted owl population; that is, a reasonably high probability that it would cross such a threshold line....

ECONOMIC AND SOCIAL CONSEQUENCES

37. ...The difference between protecting and not protecting habitat until the Forest Service develops its plan would...be between 1.03 and 1.34 billion board feet during fiscal year 1991 and between 1.04 and 1.59 billion board feet during fiscal year 1992.
38. The injunction would not prohibit the logging of existing sales, but rather the sale of additional logging rights in owl habitat areas while the Forest Service was in the process of adopting a plan. Thus, timber sale reductions do not translate directly into harvest reductions. [There are] 4.778 billion board feet of uncut timber already under contract in the "spotted owl" forests....
41. Additional timber supplies from private lands can reasonably be expected to enter the market if the price of timber stumpage increases, as it probably will do if Forest Service sales decline. In addition, some timber now exported will probably be diverted to the domestic market.
42. To the extent that Pacific Northwest mills have had supply shortages, the problem has been exacerbated by the export of raw logs...to Japan, China, or Korea....
43. While some mills may experience log shortages during the period of an injunction, that would occur to some degree regardless of whether owl habitat is protected, and there is no way of assuring that the mills most in need of logs would get them if the Forest Service proposal were adopted.
44. Over the past decade many timber jobs have been lost and mills closed in the Pacific Northwest. The main reasons have been modernization of physical plants, changes in product demand, and competition from elsewhere. Supply shortages have also played a part. Those least able to adapt and modernize, and those who have not gained alternative supplies, have been hardest hit by the changes....
45. Job losses in the wood products industry will continue regardless of whether the northern spotted owl is protected. A credible estimate is that over the next twenty years more than 30,000 jobs will be lost to worker-productivity increases alone.
46. A social cost is paid whenever an economic transformation of this nature takes place, all the more so when a largely rural industry loses sizeable numbers of jobs. Today, however, in contrast to earlier recession periods, states offer programs for dislocated workers that ease and facilitate the necessary adjustments.
47. Counties in timber-dependent communities derive revenues from the harvest of national forest timber....
48. The timber industry no longer drives the Pacific Northwest's economy. In Oregon, for example, the level of employment in lumber and wood products declined by seventeen percent between 1979 and 1989. In the same period, Oregon's total employment increased by twenty-three percent.
49. The wood products industry now employs about four percent of all workers in Western Oregon, two percent in Western Washington, and six percent in Northern California. Even if some jobs in wood products were affected by protecting owl habitat in the short-term, any effect on the regional economy probably would be small.
50. The remaining wilderness contributes to the desirability of this region as a site for new industries and their employees. The resulting economic gains, while hard to measure, are genuine and substantial. The FWS has recently noted that preservation of old growth brings economic benefits and amenities "of extremely high value." 56 Fed. Reg. 20816, 20822 (May 6, 1991).

© 1988 GARY BRAASCH

The winged blur in the center right of this ancient forest clearing is a rare daylight image of the northern spotted owl (Strix occidentalis caurina), perhaps about to strike a red-backed vole. The background shows a fallen "nurse log" which opens a hole in the canopy for sunlight to reach the forest floor, allowing new trees to grow up from the nurse log's decomposing organic matter. The lushness of the decomposition and growth processes in the natural old-growth forests of the Pacific Northwest is supported by rhizoform fungus nodules in the forest's root systems. The fungi provide nutrients and water retention to balance forest moisture throughout the low-precipitation summer season. Red-backed voles live in the nurse logs and specialize in eating the subsoil fungal truffles. The owls eat the voles. The fungi are then transplanted through the forests in owl pellet droppings. Without the owl, the forest's balances of life and water are disrupted.

THE PUBLIC INTEREST AND THE BALANCE OF EQUITIES

The court must weigh and consider the public interest in deciding whether to issue an injunction in an environmental case. See, e.g., Sierra Club v. Penfold, 857 F.2d 1307, 1318 (9th Cir. 1988); Northern Alaska Environmental Center v. Hodel, 803 F.2d 466, 471 (9th Cir. 1986). It must also consider the balance of equities among the parties. *Village of Gambell*, 480 U.S. at 545.

The problem here has not been any shortcoming in the laws, but simply a refusal of administrative agencies to comply with them.... This invokes a public interest of the highest order: the interest in having government officials act in accordance with law. See Olmstead v. United States, 277 U.S. 438, 485 (1928)(Brandeis, J., dissenting). The public also "has a manifest interest in the preservation of old growth trees." Pilchuck Audubon Soc'y v. MacWilliams, 19 ELR 20526, 20529 (W.D. Wash. 1988) This is not the usual situation in which the court reviews an administrative decision and, in doing so, gives deference to agency expertise.... The

Forest Service here has not taken the necessary steps to make a decision in the first place – yet it seeks to take actions with major environmental impact.

The loss of an additional 66,000 acres of spotted owl habitat, without a conservation plan being in place, and with no agency having committed itself to the ISC strategy, would constitute irreparable harm, and would risk pushing the species beyond a threshold from which it could not recover.

Any reduction in federal timber sales will have adverse effects on some timber industry firms and their employees, and a suspension of owl habitat sales in the national forests is no exception. But while the loss of old growth is permanent, the economic effects of an injunction are temporary and can be minimized in many ways....

To bypass the environmental laws, either briefly or permanently, would not fend off the changes transforming the timber industry. The argument that the mightiest economy on earth cannot afford to preserve old growth forests for a short time, while it reaches an overdue decision on how to manage them, is not convincing today. It would be even less so a year or a century from now.

For the reasons stated, the public interest and the balance of equities require the issuance of an injunction directing the Forest Service to comply with the requirements of NFMA by March 5, 1992, and preventing it from selling additional logging rights in spotted owl habitat until it complies with the law.

COMMENTARY AND QUESTIONS

1. The ESA and the owl. Note that *Seattle Audubon* is not an Endangered Species Act case. The endangered species issues – reflected in parallel litigation proceeding in the Oregon and Washington district courts[25] – provided the backdrop for *Seattle Audubon*'s NFMA injunction. Judge Dwyer's excerpted opinion reveals the conflicting pressures within the federal agencies about the listing of the owl and its critical habitat.

According to the data of the ISC Report, the spotted owl's survival would probably *not* be threatened by cutting the 4 billion board feet of timber already sold, but probably would be by further cutting thereafter. Thus §7's prohibitions will kick in only when the owl's habitat is knowingly brought to the brink of endangerment. Do §7's affirmative conservation provisions provide for earlier anticipatory protective efforts?

Facing the inevitability of a §7 injunction action, in October 1991 Interior Secretary Lujan and Forest Service Director Jamison called for a God Committee exemption process, the first since the snail darter's Tellico Dam and its companion case.[26]

2. Owl politics. *Seattle Audubon* describes much of the political backdrop of the spotted owl controversy. The privately-owned old growth forests have long since

25. Lane County Audubon v. Jamison, No. 91-6123 (D. Ore. Sept. 11, 1991, Jones, J.); Northern Spotted Owl v. Hodel and Northern Spotted Owl v. Lujan, 716 F. Supp. 478 and 758 F.Supp. 621 (W.D. Wash. 1988 and 1991, Zilly, J.).

26. See page 662 *supra*. In spotted owl exemption process proceedings, the detail in which the factfinding review process examines the economics is critical. Economic consideration of proposed logging and its alternatives can squarely present the subsidy issue, or obscure it, in which case court challenge under the substantial evidence test is inevitable.

been largely eliminated, replaced with monoculture (single species) tree farms that are less productive in terms of biomass and have not served to maintain the industry (as well as drastically reducing plant and wildlife ecosystem diversity). Timber companies have thus turned to the remaining old growth public forests to maintain their prosperity, in large part through exports of raw timber to Japan and Korea.

The coalition against the owl is led by the forests products industry's national associations, with its public positions vocally presented in the media by loggers whose jobs appear threatened.[27] The spotted owl issue is often portrayed in the media as a "jobs vs. owls" conflict, but the actual tradeoff is more subtle: the historical backdrop is the timber industry's past broad-scale cutting of private lands, and more than two-thirds of the marketable public forests, with inadequate reforestation. The economic reality of the conflict, moreover, is a massive program of latent federal subsidies.

Federal taxpayers subsidize the timber industry in four major ways. The Forest Service (in ascending order):

- sells timber from national forests below regular market price;[28]
- spends several hundred million dollars per year on building and maintaining logging roads in rugged terrain (to date the Service has built 7 times more road mileage than the entire Interstate highway system) and providing other free services to the industry. Thus the timber itself is even sold in many cases below the Government's own out-of-pocket cash flow costs. From 1979-91, the Service sold 124 billion board feet at a loss of $3.5 billion dollars;[29]
- pays 25 percent of its gross timber receipts to local communities as payments in lieu of property taxes;[30]
- and, fourth, the largest subsidy (unaccounted for in economic analyses) is the ecological subsidy – the permanent sacrifice of thousands of acres of diverse

27. The Northwest's loggers have taken a yellow ribbon tied to the truck antenna as their totem, arguing forcefully against environmental accounting and cuts in public subsidies, and informally advocating extermination of the spotted owl. With mass gatherings of logging trucks on the roads and in the capitals of the Northwest, the yellow-ribbon timbercutters have forcefully argued their special perspective on timbering, "Shoot an owl, save a job." "I love spotted owls... *fried*; "If it comes down to my family or that bird, that bird's going to suffer." Time, 25 June 1990 at 60. See Plater, Political Tribalism in Natural Resources Management, 11 Pub. Land L.Rev. 1, 11 (1990).

28. The Forest Service sets its auction base price with reference to the *average* potential buyer, rather than the normal appraisal standard of the price that would be paid by a willing buyer to a willing private market seller. See Wolf, National Forest Timber Sales and the Legacy of Gifford Pinchot: Managing a Forest and Making it Pay, 60 Univ. of Colo. L. Rev. 1037 (1989); and Wolf's resource analyses prepared at the request of the House Governmental Operations Subcommittee on Environment, Energy, and Natural Resources, 102d Cong., 1st Sess., Fall 1991.

29. If interest is figured in, this is a loss of $6.3 billion. Other services besides providing logging roads include surveying and inventorying timberlands, fire protection, staff personnel and structures, mapmaking, and disease control. Under cost-accounting analysis, most of the 122 national forests have never earned a penny on timber; in 1990 only 15 showed a cash flow profit. Wolf, preceding note; Knize, The Mismanagement of the National Forests, 268; The Atlantic Monthly Oct. 1991 at 98–101.

30. In 1990 this amounted to $327 million. The theory of these payments is that the federal government ought to contribute because it is exempt from state and local property taxation. The Service does not reckon these and many other public costs against revenues in figuring net revenues. Id.

natural forests, often on fragile, high-elevation steep slopes – that otherwise would be available for multiple non-logging public uses. The logging of old-growth forests leads to severe erosion, wildlife losses, water quality degradation, a ten-fold drop in the ecosystem's diversity of species, and other serious long-term effects.[31]

3. Protecting biodiversity. The spotted owl is an indicator of the declining health of the old-growth ecosystem, which is characterized by unparalleled biodiversity. If we want to preserve biodiversity, why don't we simply set aside bioreserves[32] instead of indirectly attempting to preserve ecosystems through endangered species protection? The ESA, perhaps mistakenly, wasn't primarily intended to preserve habitat, although habitat loss is the major cause of species extinction. Are we being fair, not only to ourselves, but to the spotted owls and snail darters of the world, when we use indicator species as legal "handles" to preserve critical ecosystems? Or does our political system, which functions to muddle through and "satisfice" conflicting demands, militate against attacking the habitat issue directly? Is the ESA only a stopgap measure while we build a political constituency for bioreserve protection?

4. Canaries in a coal mine: the practical utility of endangered species. Whatever the moral and philosphical arguments for species protection, it is clear that the everyday logic of the political process responds far more readily to practical economic self-interest than to abstract principle.

Accordingly many of the policy arguments for endangered species protection are pitched beyond ethics and aesthetics to stress the utilitarian importance of protecting endangered species.[33] Thus in the spotted owl debates it has been useful to emphasize the useful function played by the owl in maintaining the ecological and water-cycle balance in the Northwest forests.[34] The Pacific yew tree (Taxis brevifolia), for instance, a slow-growing endangered plant living under the ancient forest canopy, is the only known source of taxol, one of the most promising new drugs for treating ovarian and breast cancer. Protection of endangered species' habitat thus protects the critical sources of useful medicines and other products, some of which will remain unknown until future scientists find them, if the trees survive.

But the utilitarian arguments go further. Like the canaries that were carried into coal mines earlier in this century (because the birds were sensitive to coal gas, so that when they began to asphyxiate, it was time for miners to flee) endangered species can be vivid living indicators of threats to humans. In the snail darter case, for

---

31. See Young, Tree Slaughter: Your Taxes at Work, Wash. Post, Aug. 13, 1989, at B3; Barlow, Evolution of the NFMA, 8 Envt'l Law 539 (1978).

32. This is the approach taken by a bill in the 102d Congress, The National Biological Diversity Conservation and Environmental Research Act, H.R. 2082 and S. 58, authored by Rep. Gerry Studds and Sen. Daniel Moynihan.

33. See Chapter 1, at page 12 *supra*. Why do we protect endangered species even in cases in which they cannot conceivably help human prosperity?

34. D. Kelly and G. Braasch, Secrets of the Old Growth Forest 32 (1988).

example, when Justices, reporters, or TVA's minions asked, "What good is the snail darter?" the citizens responded that it was a sensitive barometer of the highly specific qualities of its habitat – the Southeast's last cool, clean, highly-oxygenated big river, flowing through a rich, unpolluted valley. The little fish was endangered because all other portions of its prior range, 2500 linear miles of river valley, had been destroyed by muddy reservoirs, so that this was the last such place left in the Southeast for humans as well. Although the answer seemed too complex for many questioners, the endangered species' barometer function is often an applicable rationale in endangered species cases.

5. ESA implementation. The courts since 1979 have generally been more attentive to the Act's requirements than the national administration.[35] In case after case after TVA v. Hill, courts strictly interpreted the Endangered Species Act to the detriment of powerful market forces. Oil well leases have been delayed, a major East Coast refinery was scuttled, in part because of endangered species problems, western water reclamation allocations have been changed to favor species protection over industrial and municipal use, and the courts have written these opinions without reference to the "significance" of the species concerned. How strong would the courts have been in these cases had not the Supreme Court held such a strong line in a highly publicized case posing an "insignificant" species against a purported multimillion dollar project? Judicial experience to date thus offers indications that future cases will be held to a high level of species protection. The snail darter itself may be subject to continued disparagement, and did not fare well in congressional politics, but its precedential position seems to have secured protections to its comrades throughout the natural world. Endangered species protection seems likely to be with us for a long time.

6. The "roadblock" statutory approach. In terms of statutory taxonomy, what do you think of the wisdom of absolute roadblocks? The original §7 permitted no flexibility. Proof of potential jeopardy to a species raised an absolute bar to continuation of federal projects. Was this extreme? naïve? necessary? Flexibility, of course, can always be imposed upon strict roadblock statutes by taking them back to Congress for specific amendments, as ultimately occurred in the darter case. If extinction is to be decreed, perhaps it is most appropriate that this be done in the nation's most democratic forum, after debate by elected officials, considering all factors and balancing all tradeoffs. Or is the legislature *not* such an ideal forum for micro-management? Are statutory adjustments via legislative amendments not certain to be made in an atmosphere of thoughtful trusteeship? Are the protective standards of an environmental statute better entrusted to a system of flexible adjustment by courts, or administrative agencies, with a more or less formal agency

---

35. During the 1980s, the Administration was unenthusiastic about endangered species protection. When he was Vice-President, George Bush initially made the endangered species regulatory process a target of the anti-regulation commission he headed. Subsequently, unable to convince Congress to back away from the terms of the Act, the Administration resorted to an administrative slowdown, drastically curtailing the rate at which new species were listed and species protection programs funded in the field. In the later 1980s, however, implementation improved somewhat.

process for definition, investigation, application, and enforcement, subject as always to some judicial review? That is now the situation of §7 of the ESA after the 1978 amendments: the God Committee can theoretically order the extinction of a species when it determines after stringent administrative process that the federal action is overwhelmingly necessary to meet human needs. Does this mean that the original absolute bar in §7 was misguided? Is it likely that the stringencies of the God Committee amendments would have been achievable legislatively, if there had never been an (accidental) absolute in the original 1973 version establishing a strong legal beachhead against federal projects that threaten extinction?

In light of the statute's political situation, it may well be said that had the statute *not* received such a flexibility mechanism it might have been repealed. Instead, §7 has been secured in an overtly stringent form. The God Committee procedure secures §7's protections, subject to an exemption process so rigorous that agencies have subsequently been unwilling to undertake the difficulties of obtaining one. The net result is more than a pragmatic compromise. It leaves the United States with the strongest enforceable legal provisions protecting endangered species that exist anywhere today.

7. Endangered species in national governance. It will be interesting to see in the controversies ahead how much we have learned from the whooping crane, the snail darter, and the spotted owl. Will endangered species be listened to as early warning devices serving to identify larger governance issues at stake, or will they be cast in the narrowed caricature of localized tradeoffs – "what do you want, owls or jobs?" When the pumps that divert water from northern California's Sacramento River to farms and cities in California's arid south threaten to eliminate the delta smelt (Hypomesus transpacificus),[36] will the question be cast as another "worthless little minnow" versus jobs and progress, or an occasion to raise sensible questions about where most of the water now goes – to massive fiscal and water subsidies for inappropriate agriculture. One such basic question: "Why should we be subsidizing California farmers to grow rice and other water-intensive crops in the middle of the desert?"

Like so much of environmental law, endangered species protections can serve as triggering opportunities for reviewing long-term necessities of rational social governance, or can be overwhelmed by the concentrated forces of short-term selfaggrandizement.[37] If the decisional processes ultimately turn on the merits rather than political ploys, endangered species will continue to play their socially useful role – as well as continuing to be prime symbols of a national environmental ethic.

---

36. See Gross, A Dying Fish May Force California to Break Its Water Habits, N.Y. Times, Oct. 27, 1991 A16.

37. Illustrating such obstacles, a May 1, 1990 Forest Service – Bureau of Reclamation study indicating that management of Northwest forests to protect the spotted owl could actually create more than 15,000 new jobs for former timber workers was suppressed and recalled by the Administration. Leaked copies available: Assoc. of Forest Service Employees for Environmental Ethics (AFSEEE), POB 111615, Eugene, OR 97440.

Chapter 14

PUBLIC RESOURCE MANAGEMENT STATUTES

Introduction

Public resources, whether natural or man-made, are owned by, or held in trust for, all members of a broad community, some of whom actually use the resources and some of whom do not. Public libraries, beds and banks of navigable waterbodies, and public parks are examples of public resources. In order to prevent the tragedy of the commons that threatens resources to which the public has unlimited access, various governmental institutions are capable of imposing resource management controls, in Hardin's terms "mutual coercion, mutually agreed upon."[1] The primary source of such coercion in practice lies in public resource management statutes that delegate responsibility, through enabling or organic legislation, to administrative agencies in order to regulate public access and use consistent with legislative goals and requirements.

In each case, subtle and contentious issues are woven into the legal management regime of public resources: Are the resources a legacy for the future or assets for maximization of current economic revenues? Are they appropriately consigned to one dominant use, or to be managed for a diversity of uses? Are local citizens specially privileged to use them, or are they for all Americans? What if the activity of one class of resource users interferes with the uses of others? And how are these recurrent political and theoretical questions to be resolved?

This chapter focuses on the Federal Land Policy and Management Act ("FLPMA," pronounced "Flipma"),[2] and the federal Bureau of Land Management (BLM), an agency within the United States Department of the Interior. Part A of the chapter introduces the federal public lands. Part B presents a brief history of grazing on the public lands and a description and analysis of FLPMA. Part C examines a number of issues raised by one of the keystone public land law cases, Kleppe v. New Mexico, 426 U.S. 529 (1976), analyzing BLM's authority to regulate wild horses on federal land in New Mexico. Part D develops a case study of off-road vehicle use on BLM lands. The resource commons can be destroyed by unlimited recreational use, as well as by grazing and other consumptive uses, and the BLM and other federal land management agencies are increasingly called upon to allocate access to their lands among competing recreational groups.

As you read this chapter, consider its close relationship to the two preceding chapters on NEPA and the ESA. Those two statutes do, to some extent, apply to

1. See page 37 *supra*.

2. 43 U.S.C.A. §1701 et seq.

activities on private lands, e.g. a Corps of Engineers permit to dredge and fill wetlands on private land, or the arrest of a rancher for shooting a grizzly bear on his own property (in a non-self-defense situation). For the most part, however, NEPA and ESA cases concern activities planned by federal agencies or their private permittees, often on federally-owned lands. Moreover, land-use planning for federal lands, such as that required by FLPMA, is inextricably connected to the preparation of the environmental impact documents and mandatory endangered species consultation. In most cases, the land-use plan, the negative declaration or environmental impact statement, and the ESA biological assessment are contained in a single document.

A. THE PUBLIC LANDS

The most extensive public resource in the United States is the federal public land system. Almost one-third of the nation's land (over 700 million acres, particularly in the West and Alaska) is owned by the federal government. The federal government owns roughly one-half of all the land in the eleven contiguous western states, including eighty-five percent of the State of Nevada and sixty-three percent of the State of Utah.[3] These massive federal landholdings persist despite the federal government's spirited attempts, during most of the nineteenth and twentieth centuries, to dispose of the lands obtained in treaties with Great Britain, France, Spain, Russia, and Indian tribes. Between 1781 and 1985, over one billion acres of federal public land were sold or granted to homesteaders (287 million acres), railroads (100 million acres), states (72 million acres in the western states), and other persons and entities. The remaining federal public lands are managed, more or less successfully, by numerous federal agencies, some located in different departments of the federal government, with different enabling acts, goals, management philosophies, levels of support and supervision from Congress, and political alliances.

The BLM administers 170 million acres of arid or semiarid federal land in the eleven western states pursuant to the congressional directives included in FLPMA. There are several reasons for this chapter's concentration on FLPMA and the BLM:

- FLPMA is the most recent, most unified, and most comprehensive organic management legislation governing the activities of any federal resource management agency;
- the BLM range lands exhibit a classic tragedy of the commons (destructive overgrazing) caused by the "capture" of a regulatory agency by a single user group and its political allies; and
- FLPMA adopts a "multiple use, sustained yield" management standard, the standard that prevails with regard to most of the federal public lands, including the roughly 200 million acres administered by the National Park Service (NPS) also located within the Department of Interior, and the U.S. Forest service in the Department of Agriculture.

3. See Coggins and Wilkinson, Federal Public Land and Resources Law 13 (2d ed. 1987) (hereafter Coggins and Wilkinson), an invaluable reference work for the study of public land law.

The BLM lands have traditionally been managed for grazing of private livestock. In 1974, approximately 23,000 western ranches held BLM permits or leases to graze 3.5 million cattle and horses and 4.5 million sheep and goats on BLM lands.[4] This five percent of all American ranchers using approximately three percent of national livestock forage production has had an inordinately strong impact on congressional and BLM policy regarding BLM lands. Some of the reasons for the extraordinary political influence of this segment of the livestock industry are its entrenchment in American mythology, historic dominance over the BLM, consistent single-mindedness, abundant financial resources, and close proximity to information and the BLM field personnel who manage the resource.[5] Locally prominent individuals and interest groups typically have supported the demands of the local livestock industry. Since grazing permits are comparatively permanent privileges, they add great economic value to the ranchers' private "base properties" contiguous to federal permit grazing lands. Consequently, local financial institutions that loan money to ranchers with grazing permits as security, actively oppose proposals that might have negative effects on the short-term profit margins of local ranchers – such as cutbacks in grazing allotments in order to revive overgrazed range.

Western state governments also constitute a "public" deeply concerned about BLM management of federal public lands. Because states cannot impose property taxes on federal property,[6] they have persuaded Congress to provide annual federal reimbursement payments in lieu of property taxes. These "in lieu payments" are themselves paid from funds generated by fees on private use of federal lands. Western states, for example, receive 12.5 percent of BLM income from grazing fees.[7] Thus, state officials also support continued heavy grazing on BLM lands out of their own institutional fiscal imperatives.

Since the 1960s, however, public land law has been revolutionized by the emergence of powerful conservationist and preservationist organizations:

> It is not possible to delineate precisely just who the new parties are or what they represent. In some cases, private landowners have rejected economic benefit to themselves by various forms of development on or adjacent to their property.... Allied to new landowner attitudes is a new aggressiveness on the part of non-consumptive economic users of public lands. Resorts, guides, river outfitters, backpacking equipment manufacturers, and so forth have resisted development of a resource valuable to them as primitive real estate....
>
> Many of the largest changes have come about through institutional strategies and actions by established and new environmental organizations.

4. Coggins, Evans, and Lindeberg-Johnson, The Law of Public Rangeland Management I: The Extent and Distribution of Federal Power, 12 Env. Law 536–621, 559 (1982)(hereafter cited as "Coggins I").

5. As with the "capture" phenomenon studied earlier at page 560 *supra*, it is common for governmental personnel who live closely amongst members of a particular political culture to assimilate the mores of that culture.

6. Coggins and Wilkinson, 182–191.

7. Coggins and Lindeberg-Johnson, The Law of Public Rangeland Management II: The Commons and the Taylor Act, 13 Envt'l L. 1, 11 (1982)(hereafter cited as "Coggins II").

> Among the most active an effective organizations are the oldline Sierra Club and Wilderness Society, and three newcomers, the Environmental Defense Fund (EDF), the Natural Resources Defense Council (NRDC), and the National Wildlife Federation. Even the traditionally apolitical Audubon Society has found itself lobbying and litigating. These organizations alone – and there are dozens of similar if less visible groups – have wrought legislative change, pursued hundreds of lawsuits...and mobilized considerable public support.[8]

This new "non-consumptive use" public, while generally sharing basic preservationist goals, is not monolithic. Local river rafting outfitters, for instance, have occasionally faced off against national kayaking groups over National Park Service allocations of permits for trips down the Colorado River.[9]

B. THE BLM, FLPMA, AND GRAZING ON THE PUBLIC LANDS

During the years between 1789 and 1976, when the federal government pursued a policy of disposing of western public lands, a concurrent federal policy was to forestall monopolies by large landholders. Given the relatively unproductive character of the western range, the disposal and antimonopoly policies came into conflict, causing legendary fraud and corruption as well as overgrazing of small holdings.

> Federal land was given to five distinct classes of beneficiaries, but in parcels too small or too scattered to overcome the inherent problems of low vegetative productivity in much of the West. States, railroads, miners, farmers, and ranchers received most of the federal largess.
>
> The federal government gave an enormous amount of public land to the states...estimated to be 72 million acres in the eleven western states.... Those lands are often still arbitrarily interspersed among private and federal lands.... The railroad land grants continue to obstruct integrated management because they are frequently checkerboarded section-by-section with the public lands.[10] Mining claims are also interspersed, but more randomly. Prospectors who locate a valuable mineral discovery are allowed to take title to the land on which the mineral is found. Agrarian homesteaders claimed hundreds of millions of acres under the various disposition laws, all of which limited the number of acres that could be granted to one individual. Homesteading policy was liberalized many times to accommodate rancher desires for more land, but the effort proved futile in the end: profitable ranching in the Intermountain West required more land per operation than Congress was willing to grant.[11]

---

8. Coggins and Wilkinson, 6–7.

9. See Wilderness Public Rights Fund v. Kleppe, 608 F.2d 1250 (9th Cir. 1979), cert. denied, 446 U.S. 982 (1980).

10. Ed. note: As an incentive to build the transcontinental railroads, railroad companies were given odd-numbered sections of land within 20 miles on both sides of their rights-of-way. These odd-numbered sections were later sold to private parties, creating a "checkerboard pattern" of landownership with the even-numbered federally-retained sections.

11. Coggins II, 5–6.

The lands retained by the federal government were those that, as Professor Coggins puts it, "Nobody was willing to buy or steal." Nevertheless, these huge expanses of federal land became immensely valuable as supplementary grazing land to landholders who discovered that their arid lands were profitable only for grazing cattle, and that the relatively small size of their holdings precluded successful ranching operations.

Until 1934, the federal government maintained a laissez-faire attitude toward the public lands, perpetuating an unregulated commons that deteriorated into a severely overgrazed range. A combination of drought and the New Deal prompted a re-evaluation of federal range policy, resulting in the Taylor Grazing Act of 1934.[12] Congress had two avowed purposes in enacting the Taylor Act – to end overgrazing and to stabilize the livestock industry. Once again, federal policies that appeared laudable in theory were inconsistent in practice; the Taylor Act did stabilize the livestock industry, but did little to alleviate range deterioration.

The Taylor Act had three main components: (1) it authorized the Secretary of the Interior to withdraw the unappropriated public lands from homesteading and organize them into grazing districts; (2) it gave preference in obtaining and renewing grazing permits to adjacent landowners; and (3) it established district advisory boards, composed mainly of ranchers, that had to be consulted before management decisions were made. The unfortunate result was a "captured agency," in which large adjacent ranchers dominated an understaffed Grazing Division (the BLM's predecessor) through advisory boards, gaining for themselves excessive grazing allotments at fees far below market value:

> The first round of grazing permit decisions set a pattern for the next four decades. Adjacent ranchers first received temporary one-year permits. Later hearings to determine carrying capacity for purposes of permit adjustments were conducted by the ranchers through the advisory boards. Ten-year permits – the maximum allowed by statute – soon became the norm.
>
> By early 1936, board representatives and the Grazing Division (which had already issued thousands of permits) worked out rules for preference and fees.... The Division set grazing fees at five cents per month for cows and one cent for sheep. The permits were theoretically limited to "carrying capacity." That term, however, turned out to have a different meaning in practice than in science because capacity was determined (primarily by the stockmen) within the first year of two of Taylor Act administration without benefit of survey or biological opinion. In most districts permits had been issued for many more livestock than the range could properly support. When later scientific information, however inadequate, indicated the need for downward revision, ranchers often effectively opposed cuts.[13]

Instead of affording security to the livestock industry in exchange for responsible grazing practices on public lands, the Taylor Act provided further subsidies to ranchers – primary access to the public lands, preferential permits, federal funds for

12. 43 U.S.C.A. §315 et seq. See Coggins and Wilkinson 153–160.

13. Coggins II, 58-59.

"range improvements" (fencing, revegetation, etc.), and low grazing fees – to continue their traditional despoliation of the federal range resource.

In 1946, the Grazing Division was merged with the General Land Office (an agency with strong disposal inclinations) to form the BLM. There was little change in BLM range policies until 1974, despite a 1970 report of the Public Land Law Review Commission recognizing the deteriorated condition of a substantial amount of BLM lands and recommending that grazing allotments should be consistent with the productivity of the land.[14] In 1974, a NEPA lawsuit, NRDC v. Morton, transformed federal range management. 388 F. Supp. 829 (D.C.D.C. 1974). BLM had prepared a programmatic environmental impact statement on its grazing program after the enactment of NEPA in 1970. The NRDC sued, alleging that the programmatic EIS was inadequate because it did not address the site-specific impacts of grazing. The federal district court sided with NRDC, ordering BLM to prepare EISs for each grazing district. Compelled to study rangeland conditions openly and "go public" with its findings, BLM "has had no choice but to reduce allotments down to carrying capacity."[15] NRDC v. Morton also alerted Congress to the deplorable condition of the BLM lands and the failure of the Taylor Act, leading directly to passage of the Federal Land Policy and Management Act of 1976.

Coggins, The Law of Public Rangeland Management (IV): FLPMA, PRIA, and the Multiple Use Mandate

14 Environmental Law 1, 5-6 (1983)[16]

FLPMA does not repeal the major Taylor Act provisions. Instead, the 1976 Act superimposes a new management system, with more diverse goals and emphases. FLPMA requires the multiple use, sustained yield that the BLM has long claimed to practice. The 1976 Act mandates intensive planning; of equal importance, specific management decisions made after the land use plans are completed must accord with the plans. The Act also protects grazing permittees to a limited extent. On the whole, however, FLPMA represents a condemnation of past stewardship and requires that the BLM utilize a broader approach to public rangeland management....

FLPMA resolves two fundamental issues: Congress decided to retain the public lands in public ownership and to manage the lands in ways that avoid the "unnecessary or undue degradation" so common in the past.

The framework of FLPMA apparently originated in the 1970 report of the Public Land Law Review Commission (PLLRC). Senator Henry Jackson later claimed that FLPMA embodies the enactment of over 100 PLLRC recommendations into law. In the area of range management, however, the dissimilarities between the report and the final legislation are at least as prominent. The PLLRC recommended that Congress authorize the sale to permittees of lands chiefly valuable for grazing, give ranchers greater security of tenure while requiring them to pay higher fees to use the retained lands, and make livestock grazing the "dominant use of retained lands where appropriate." FLMPA secures permittee tenure in some ways and holds down grazing fee increases, but Congress rejected the generous PLLRC attitude toward

14. One Third of the Nation's Land, 106–108.

15. Coggins I, 555.

16. Hereafter cited as "Coggins IV."

ranchers in those other respects. FLMPA adopts the PLLRC recommendations that sought consistency between grazing and land "productivity," that put "priority on the rehabilitation of deteriorated rangeland where possible," that required more administrative flexibility, and that paid more attention to public values, including wildlife. Congress arguably stopped short of adopting the PLLRC recommendation to exclude livestock from "frail lands" and did not make the permittee responsible for the frail condition of the land....

Section 1701(a) of FLPMA declares thirteen sweeping policies. Although it contains some apparent inconsistencies, the section is Congress' most thorough and unambiguous statement of public land policy. The statement is qualified by the proviso in §1701(b) that FLPMA policies are not "effective" until specifically enacted in the Act itself or elsewhere. The courts faced with questions involving §1701(a), however, have uniformly assumed that the policies are binding and effective in the absence of contrary provisions. Whatever their precise legal status, the congressional policies ought to serve as fundamental range management guidelines.

Congress first stated that the public lands will remain in federal ownership unless planning determines that the "national interest" requires disposal of "a particular parcel."...

The second policy is that "the national interest will be best realized if the public lands and their resources are periodically and systematically inventoried and their present and future use is projected through a land use planning process coordinated with other Federal and State planning efforts."...

[Policies three to six involve reviews of existing federal land classifications, restraints on executive withdrawls, encouragement of public participation in BLM decisionmaking, and judicial review of public land adjudications.]

The seventh congressional statement should be, but has not yet become, the touchstone of public rangeland management. Congress declared that "goals and objectives be established by law as guidelines for public land use planning, and that management be on the basis of multiple use and sustained yield unless otherwise specified by law." Congress specifically enacted these general requirements, but the BLM has neither understood nor carried out these commands.

The eighth statement of policy is a radical departure from all prior rangeland management understanding. Congress required that:

> the public lands be managed in a manner that will protect the quality of scientific, scenic, historical, ecological, environmental, air and atmospheric, water resource, and archeological values; that, where appropriate, will preserve and protect certain public lands in their natural condition; that will provide food and habitat for fish and wildlife and domestic animals; and that will provide for outdoor recreation and human occupancy and use.

Whether or to what extent Congress specifically enacted this goal is unclear. Some sections of FLPMA and other statutes support an argument that this policy binds public land managers, but all the statutory provisions are qualified in some way.

In its ninth policy, Congress sought "fair market value" for public land uses and resources "unless otherwise provided by statute." This policy is definitely not law; not only are grazing fees set at a fraction of market value, but the United States probably does not receive full value for any of the nation's resources.

Congress's tenth policy statement calls for uniform procedures for disposal, exchange, or acquisition of public lands. This policy was enacted in other FLPMA sections. The eleventh policy seeks rapid protection of "areas of critical environmental concern"; the statute provides that protection.

The twelfth congressional policy balances or counteracts the eighth by emphasizing use instead of preservation. Congress required that "[t]he public lands be managed in a manner which recognizes the Nation's need for domestic sources of minerals, food, timber, and fiber from the public lands."... The thirteenth and final policy calls for equitable reimbursement to states for the local tax burden caused by federal immunity from taxation.

This policy was enacted in the Payment in Lieu of Taxes Act of 1976.[17]...

For the first time, the BLM is forced by law to develop land use plans in fairly precise ways and, after the plans are promulgated, to act in accordance with the guidelines established in the plans. Section 1711 commands a detailed inventory of all public land resources, and §1712 requires preparation of land use plans for all public land areas.... Section 1732(a) negates any implication that the plans are to be just public relations make-work by making the plans binding on all subsequent multiple use decisions....

FLPMA emphatically rejects the grazing-as-dominant-use tradition in public rangeland management in favor of multiple use, sustained yield principles....In theory, the standard requires the agency to give all listed resources roughly equal consideration and weight in all decisionmaking. Multiple use, sustained yield is basically a utilitarian principle requiring high-level annual production of all resources in combination.[18] Congress defined both multiple use and sustained yield in sweeping terms. Apparently, however, the legislature never debated precisely how those management concepts were to be applied. Congress assumed instead that the standard was a significant, environmentally-oriented advance over existing authorities. Contrary to the opinions of several commentators, and to BLM predilections, multiple use and sustained yield are more than idle slogans allowing the agency to do as it professionally pleases. If courts begin reviewing multiple use decisions with any depth or insight, the standard as applied through planning processes will reverse the course of public rangeland management....

Before investigating the limitations on management discretion inherent in the multiple use standard, the uses or resources themselves should be defined. In the Multiple Use – Sustained Yield Act (MUSY),[19] the "renewable surface resources" include only "outdoor recreation, range, timber, watershed, and wildlife and fish purposes." In 1976, Congress broadened the list of uses to "renewable and nonrenewable resources including, but not limited to, recreation, range, timber, minerals, watershed, wildlife and fish, and natural scenic, scientific, and historical values."...

Most of the listed resources are "renewable," meaning that they regenerate in some biological or climatological fashion. Although minerals are now included in the list, both hardrock mining and mineral leasing remain primarily governed by other statutes that have given mineral exploitation legal or de facto priority over other uses. Water itself, the key resource, was omitted,[20] probably because water

17. 31 U.S.C.A. sections 1601 et seq.

18. Ed. note: Multiple use sustained yield standards do not necessarily apply to each management unit where multiple use would be inconsistent with the nature of the resource base. In such cases, multiple use sustained yield must be maintained on the level of some larger, more inclusive planning unit.

19. Ed. note: The Multiple-Use, Sustained-Yield Act of 1960, 16 U.S.C.A. §528 et seq., along with other statutes, governs the activities of the United States Forest Service.

20. Ed. note: Watershed protection, in multiple use legislation, means preservation of the soil and vegetation conditions necessary to provide adequate supplies of clean water.

allocation was seen as a state function. Wilderness, or "preservation," is not specifically listed, but is supplied in §1782....

The key to multiple use, sustained yield management as a land management system is in the statutory definition of the two phrases. FLPMA borrows heavily from the MUSY Act:

> 43 U.S.C.A. §1702...(c) the term "multiple use" means the management of the public lands and their various resource values so that they are utilized in the combination that will best meet the present and future needs of the American people; making the most judicious use of the land for some or all of these resources or related services over areas large enough to provide sufficient latitude for periodic adjustments in use to conform to changing needs and conditions; the use of some land for less than all of the resources; a combination of balanced and diverse resource uses that takes into account the long-term needs of future generations for renewable and nonrenewable resources,...and harmonious and coordinated management of the various resources without permanent impairment of the productivity of the land and the quality of the environment with consideration being given to the relative values of the resources and not necessarily to the combination of uses that will give the greatest economic return or the greatest unit output....
>
> (h) The term "sustained yield" means the achievement and maintenance in perpetuity of a high-level annual or regular periodic output of the various renewable resources of the public lands consistent with multiple use.

The main differences between the 1960 and 1976 definitions, apart from the inclusion of additional resources and values in 1976, are the congressional emphasis on intergenerational equity, the clear directive to achieve long-term conservation, and the requirement of environmental nonimpairment....

[After discussing the numerous discretionary aspects of these statutory definitions, Professor Coggins comments on what he considers to be their enforceable aspects: (1) avoiding impairment of productivity of land and the quality of the environment; and (2) managing for sustained yield.]

This [nonimpairment] standard is fairly precise, and it ought to be enforceable. In a sense, the limitation is a restatement of the watershed value because rangeland productivity requires both water to grow grass and grass to keep the soil in place. "Productivity" is the capacity of the land to support flora and fauna and to furnish "the various renewable resources" in the future. The two key elements in production are soil and water. Therefore, soil and water quality and quantity should be the central focus of public rangeland management attention, but that has not been the case so far.

If the manager were to allow a practice, such as prolonged overgrazing, that causes permanent reductions in future grass production, the nonimpairment limitation would make that action illegal as well as arbitrary. Moreover, when enjoyment of a listed use depends on a rare or unique attribute of an area, the manager must safeguard (or preserve) that attribute to ensure nonimpairment. For example, if a particular vista is especially attractive for hikers or tourists (the "outdoor recreation" resource), actions that seriously and permanently interfere with those scenic qualities arguably violate the nonimpairment standard... The nonimpairment standard is clear, mandatory and nondiscretionary....

The most significant management limitation in FLPMA is the definition of "sustained yield" in §1702(h). The phrase means *perpetual, high level* annual resource outputs of *all* renewable resources. Sustained yield is a separate, binding standard that makes continuing resource productivity the highest management criterion. The plain meaning of sustained yield...is that administrators may not sacrifice the future output of any renewable resource in present resource allocations. The "permanent" impairment provision qualifies the sustained yield limitation by ensuring that only serious, longlasting damage is prohibited.... In other words, the agency must plan to accommodate recreation, timber, watershed, wildlife, and natural values, as well as grazing, at high levels in perpetuity, and then act according to that plan....

The search for compatible use combinations at optimum production levels will encounter more conflict than harmony. The main point of multiple use decisionmaking is conflict resolution, with all of the political problems that phrase implies. The manager must try to accommodate all resource uses to the extent possible, giving priority to none – at least on the broad scale – and consideration to all. Sustained yield in compatible combinations does resolve conflicts by theoretically forbidding the optimization of one resource at the expense of others. Such optimization of one resource could leave multiple use decisions vulnerable to attack on sustained yield grounds....

Multiple use, sustained management was meant to be more than a "succotash syndrome." Inherent in the concept are detailed and comprehensive commands to force thinking before acting and to mold individual actions into a long-range scheme for the public benefit. FLPMA does not allow the manager to do whatever appears politic or expedient at the time....

COMMENTARY AND QUESTIONS

1. Public land constituencies. Whom does Congress serve when it legislates regarding the public lands? In a political sense, there is no homogeneous "public" for any major decision regarding the allocation of public resources. We can only speak of various "publics" that have different geographical configurations, numbers of members, quantities of financial resources, attention spans, degrees of cohesiveness, kinds of interests, avenues and intensities of political influence, etc. Imagine the conflicting constituencies and political strategies involved in an issue such as whether to open the Arctic National Wildlife Refuge for oil and mineral extraction.

2. Public land management philosophies. Multiple use, sustained yield is the management philosophy that applies to BLM lands and national forests managed by the USFS. Its major rival is "dominant use," a standard recommended by the Public Land Law Review Commission for the BLM lands. In a dominant use management system, a primary use is selected for a portion of the public lands; after that, only those secondary uses that are compatible with the dominant use will be allowed there. Where grazing or mining are set as dominant uses, environmental values would be broadly precluded. Another, somewhat more benign, example of a dominant use statute is the National Wildlife Refuge Administration Act (16 U.S.C.A. §668dd et seq.), under which the Secretary of the Interior, through the Fish and Wildlife Service (FWS) which manages refuges, may "permit the use of any area within the System for any purpose, including but not limited to hunting, fishing, public recreation and accommodations, and access whenever he determines that such uses are compatible with the major purposes for which such areas were established." 16 U.S.C.A. §668dd(d)(1). Is hunting appropriate in a wildlife refuge? What about ORV use? Would dominant use justify opening a wildlife refuge for oil recovery operations that impinge on only a small part of the surface area, but drain a pool of oil that underlies the entire refuge? For a series of decisions overturning FWS regulations permitting motorboating in a wildlife refuge, see Defenders of Wildlife v. Andrus, 11 ERC 2098 (D.C.D.C. 1978), and 455 F. Supp 446 (D.C.D.C. 1978).

If, as Professor Coggins argues, FLPMA's nonimpairment of land productivity and environmental quality standards are enforceable, is there any operational difference between multiple use sustained yield and dominant use? One commentator concludes that the only real difference between them is the geographic scale of management units, and that a compromise between multiple use sustained yield and dominant use would provide for the most efficient and equitable management of public lands. See Daniels, Rethinking Dominant Use Management in the Forest-Planning Area, 17 Envtl. L. 483 (1987).

3. Wilderness preservation. Perhaps the most important and well-known dominant use statute is the Wilderness Act of 1964 (16 U.S.C.A. §1131 et seq.). Under the express terms of this statute, all commercial logging and permanent roads and most structures and installations, temporary roads, commercial enterprises, and motorized equipment and forms of transportation are prohibited, but the following secondary uses are explicitly permitted: logging to control insect infestations and fires; mineral exploration; mining claims, mineral leases, and grazing permits obtained before January 1, 1964, subject to reasonable environmental regulations; water resource projects approved by the President; commercial services provided by guides, packers, and river runners; and hunting and fishing. Are these permitted secondary uses compatible with a wilderness area, which is defined by the Act as "an area where the earth and its community of life are untrammeled by man, where man is himself a visitor who does not remain"? 16 U.S.C.A. §1131(c).

The Wilderness Act of 1964 established a process for designating wilderness areas in national forests, parks, and refuges. It did not apply to the BLM lands. The USFS wilderness designation process has proceeded through three phases – Roadless Area Review and Evaluation (RARE) I, II, and III – at a painfully slow pace, impeded by political controversy and negative court decisions.[21]

> The BLM seems destined to suffer even more travail. The BLM lands were not included in the initial Wilderness Act inventory, but the congressional oversight was corrected by FLPMA in 1976. Before 1976 the BLM had set aside 170,000 acres in "primitive" areas. However, because the BLM's initiatives in this sphere were miniscule compared to the Forest Service's prelegislation actions [over nine million acres designated as "wild," "wilderness," and "canoe" areas], the agency's commitment to preservation was often questioned – most severely by its own employees.

21. See Coggins and Wilkinson, 995–1019.

> Post-1976 developments have given credence to the critics. The BLM has been laggard in its wilderness designation process and legal trouble bodes. The agency first attempted to exclude about eighty-six percent of its technically eligible holdings from study. The Forest Service experience indicates that courts as well as legislatures would find that decision arbitrary....[22]

Since BLM is in the midst of its wilderness review process, litigation to date has involved the requirements in FLPMA §603(c) that BLM manage lands under wilderness review "in a manner so as not to impair the suitability of such areas for preservation as wilderness," and that BLM "take any action required to prevent unnecessary or undue degradation of the lands and their resources or to afford environmental protection." See, e.g., Rocky Mountain Oil and Gas Association v. Watt, 696 F.2d 734 (10th Cir. 1982)(upholding BLM's application of the nonimpairment standard to mineral leases on BLM wilderness study lands). For a discussion of FLPMA's general requirement that BLM prevent "unnecessary or undue degradation" to the public lands, see Mansfield, On the Cusp of Property Rights: Lessons from Public Land Law, 18 Ecol. L.Q. 43 (1991).

4. Unenforceable policies and mixed mandates. FLPMA, like almost every other federal and state statute, has a section (§102) entitled "Declaration Of Policy." Section 102(b) states that "[t]he policies of this Act shall become effective only as specific statutory authority for their implementation is enacted by this Act or by subsequent legislation...." As the above excerpt points out, some of FLPMA's policies have been enacted, some have been conditionally enacted, some have not been enacted, and some – e.g., the "fair market value" policy – are being ignored by the BLM. Moreover, FLPMA §102 contains policies encouraging both preservation and consumption. What are the functions of legislative policy statements such as these? Are they intended to mislead an unwary public? Are they media "sound bites"? Do they serve to mollify interest groups that haven't received all they wanted? Or are they statements of long-term goals that may or may not now be practicable? In fact, all of these concerns, among others, motivate draftspersons when drafting statutory declarations of policy. Consequently, in reading statutes, one must be sensitive to the difference between hortatory, emotive, and political statements, on the one hand, and enforceable commands on the other.

5. FLPMA as an organic act. Before 1976, BLM's legislative authority was scattered and vague. Section 303(a) of FLPMA gives the Secretary of the Interior the authority to "issue regulations necessary to implement the provisions of this Act with respect to the management, use, and protection of the public lands, including the property located thereon." Pursuant to section 310, the Secretary "shall promulgate rules and regulations to carry out the purposes of this Act and of other laws applicable to the public lands...." This broad organic authority may, however, be merely symbolic assurance in light of the BLM's meager enforcement resources:

22. Coggins, The Law of Public Rangeland Management III: A Survey of Creeping Regulation at the Periphery, 1934–1982, 13 Envtl. L. 295, 304 (1983)(hereafter cited as "Coggins III").

> In sum, the Secretary has adequate legal authority to promulgate regulations to carry out the purposes of the Act. The penalties for violations are also adequate. The true difficulty is both deeper and subtler. The BLM lacks sufficient personnel to police its domain in anything more than a cursory fashion.[23] The offenses by nonpermittees – such as taking off-road vehicles into closed areas – are likely to go unpunished for that reason and because the relative triviality of the transgression will discourage use of the prosecutorial apparatus. Rancher-permittees also may have practical immunity, even though the potential sanctions against them are more immediate and more efficient, because of the agency's traditional reluctance to penalize its clientele.[24]

Would making grazing permittees responsible for restoring range illegally grazed, as the PLLRC recommended, be a sufficiently strong sanction to counteract the BLM's enforcement deficiencies?

Do the ranchers and their political friends lobby for or against greater funding for BLM enforcement? Can BLM plead lack of resources as a defense to an action attempting to compel it to perform its FLPMA duties? See NRDC v. Morton, above, where the Court rejected BLM's pleas of poverty in a NEPA case.

6. Mining on public lands. Hardrock mining on public lands represents an extreme form of dominant use. It is still governed primarily by the General Mining Law of 1872, which declares all unreserved public lands open to mineral exploration and extraction.[25] Under this statute, a prospector locating valuable minerals can stake her claim without notifying or obtaining permission from the federal land management agency, exclude other prospectors and interfering recreationists, and use whatever natural resources present on the claim that she needs for mining purposes. After several years of negligible work and payment of a modest fee, the locater can be granted a federal patent that will entitle her to outright ownership of the former mining claim. Once a claim has been patented, the owner can do whatever she wants with the claim, including use it or sell it for non-mining purposes. At no time is the locater-patentee required to pay rent or a royalty to the United States. Moreover, until relatively recently, federal agencies claimed to possess no statutory authority to regulate the environmental abuses caused by hardrock mining. In addition to requiring, for the first time, recordation of unpatented mining claims, FLPMA clearly gives BLM authority to "prevent unnecessary or undue degradation of the public lands."

States and municipalities may impose reasonable environmental regulations on hardrock mining on federal lands, as long as these regulations do not effectively prohibit the mining. See *Granite Rock*, 480 U.S. 572 (1987), at page 499 *supra*.

---

23. Some range managers, for instance, are individually responsible for overseeing activities on a million or more acres.

24. Coggins IV, 30.

25. 30 U.S.C.A. §22–39.

In the Mineral Leasing Act of 1920[26], Congress removed fuel minerals from the ambit of the General Mining Law and established a leasing system, including provisions that would authorize the BLM (which also oversees mineral leases on federal lands) to insert environmentally protective provisions in mineral leases.

Other federal mineral leasing systems can be found in the Outer Continental Shelf Lands Act of 1953 (43 U.S.C.A. §1331 et seq.), the Geothermal Steam Act of 1970 (30 U.S.C.A. §1001 et seq.), and the Federal Coal Leasing Amendments of 1975, (30 U.S.C.A. §1201 et seq.).

7. **Water rights**. Water is the key to other land-uses in the arid West, but water allocation is not listed as one of FLPMA's multiple uses because water allocation on federal land has traditionally been governed by state law. West of the Mississippi River, state water allocation laws are based on the prior appropriation principle ("first in time is first in right"). Where federal lands have been reserved from the public domain for a particular purpose, however, such as Indian reservations or national parks, the federal government is presumed to have reserved sufficient water to carry out the primary purposes of the reservation. These federal reserved water rights, a feature of federal law, take priority as of the dates of reservation, and prevail over subsequently perfected state water rights. See J. Sax, R. Abrams, and B. Thompson, Legal Control of Water Resources, (2d. Edition,1991). In Sierra Club v. Block, 622 F. Supp 842 (D. Col. 1985), vacated on other grounds (ripeness), Sierra Club v. Yeutter, the court held that federal reserved water rights are created by the Wilderness Act of 1964, but that USFS officials are not legally obligated to assert reserved water rights claims for wilderness areas in state stream adjudications. For an argument that federal officials must aggressively assert federal reserved water rights, see Abrams, Water in the Western Wilderness: The Duty to Assert Reserved Water Rights, 1986 U. Ill. L. Rev. 387 (1986). The court also remarked, in dicta, that FLPMA does not effect withdrawal and reservation of lands so as to create reserved water rights, although this conclusion, presumably, does not apply to BLM-designated wilderness areas. See also Sierra Club v. Watt, 659 F.2d 203 (D.C. Cir. 1981)(no reserved rights attach to BLM lands). These decisions present the anomalous situation that reserved rights attach to national forest lands,[27] which are also managed under multiple use sustained yield standards, but not to BLM lands.

8. **The public trust and the public lands**. Does the public trust doctrine (see Chapter 8) impose obligations on federal land managers supplementary to those found in their management statutes? Compare Sierra Club v. Department of the Interior, 376 F. Supp. 90 (D.N.D. Cal. 1974) and Sierra Club v. Department of the Interior, 398 F.Supp 284 (D.N.D. Cal. 1975)(the public trust doctrine applies to the activities of the National Park Service with regard to the management of Redwood National Park), with Sierra Club v. Block (holding where Congress has set out statutory

---

26. 30 U.S.C.A. §181 et seq.

27. United States v. New Mexico, 438 U.S. 696 (1978)(reserved rights attach to national forest lands for timber and watershed purposes but not for wildlife protection).

duties, they comprise all the responsibilities of a federal land management agency). Is the doctrinal difference between these cases due to the relative specificity of the Wilderness Act construed in *Block* as contrasted with the vagueness and ambiguity of the Redwood National Park Act (16 U.S.C.A. §79(a) et seq.)(Secretary is authorized to "afford as full protection as reasonably possible to the timber, soil, and streams within the boundaries of the park")? Should the public trust doctrine apply where the statutory mandate is mixed, as in the National Park Service Act of 1916 (16 U.S.C.A. §1 et seq.)(the National Park Service (NPS) is directed to "promote and regulate the use of the Federal areas known as national parks, monuments, and reservations" in order to "conserve the scenery and the natural and historic objects and the wild life therein and to provide for the enjoyment of the same in such manner and by such means as will leave them unimpaired for the enjoyment of future generations")? See Friends of Yosemite v. Frizzell, 420 F. Supp. 390 (D.N.D.Cal.1976)(plaintiffs' allegation that NPS was breaching the public trust by overcommercializing Yosemite National Park rejected because NPS was not violating a statutory duty).

9. Subsequent grazing legislation. In the Public Rangelands Improvement Act of 1978, 43 U.S.C.A. §1901 et seq., (PRIA), Congress found that "[v]ast segments of the public rangelands" were "producing less than their potential" for the multiple uses detailed in FLPMA. For this reason, Congress found that these vast areas were in "an unsatisfactory condition." Congress recognized the need for additional funding to reclaim the damaged lands and expressed a commitment to "intensive" maintenance, management, and improvement programs. PRIA also includes a congressional directive that "the goal of [BLM] management shall be to improve the range conditions of the public rangeland so that they become as productive as feasible in accordance with the rangeland management objectives established through the land use planning process...." One of the range improvement techniques explicitly recognized by PRIA is the discontinuance of grazing on certain stressed lands. Coggins[28] argues that in PRIA, "Congress has unambiguously established a single management priority [i.e., range improvement] to which all other objectives must be related and subordinated." Is PRIA unambiguous on this score? If Coggins is correct, is range management once again subject to a dominant use, albeit a different dominant use than the one that BLM has traditionally encouraged?

PRIA also directed the Secretary to select areas of the public lands with representative conditions, trends, and forages, and to concentrate on these areas in order to "explore innovative grazing management policies and systems which might provide incentives to improve range conditions." BLM relied on this experimental stewardship clause to promulgate regulations establishing a Cooperative Management Agreement (CMA) program authorizing BLM to enter into special permit arrangements with selected ranchers who had demonstrated "exemplary rangeland management practices." "Exemplary practices" were not defined in the regulation; their selection was left to BLM discretion. The purpose of this program was to allow

28. Coggins IV, 117.

these exemplary ranchers to "manage livestock grazing on the allotment as they determine appropriate" for a period of ten years. The agreements were not required to contain performance standards or any limiting terms or conditions. If a permittee did not comply with the nebulous goals of the program, BLM's only remedy was to deny renewal of the agreement after its ten year term had elapsed. In NRDC v. Hodel, 618 F. Supp. 848 (D.E.D.Cal. 1985), the court, finding that "the CMA program is *not* an experiment, but is a permanent system of permit issuance aimed at a group of favored permittees," struck down the CMA regulations as inconsistent with BLM's duties under the Taylor Act, FLPMA, and PRIA to "prescribe the manner in and extent to which livestock practices will be conducted on public lands."

C. FEDERAL-STATE ISSUES ON THE PUBLIC LANDS

The following Supreme Court decision is the most significant development in over a century of vitriolic litigation regarding federal versus state power on the public lands and reflects a chapter in the anti-federal "sagebrush rebellion." As you read the opinion, consider which legal questions have been definitively settled and which are still open.

Kleppe v. New Mexico

United States Supreme Court, 1976
426 U.S. 529, 96 S.Ct. 2285, 49 L.Ed. 2d. 34

MARSHALL, J. At issue in this case is whether Congress exceeded its powers under the Constitution in enacting the Wild Free-Roaming Horses and Burros Act.

The Wild Free-Roaming Horses and Burros Act (the Act), 16 U.S.C.A. §§1331–1340, was enacted in 1971 to protect "all unbranded and unclaimed horses and burros on public lands of the United States" from "capture, branding, harassment, or death." The Act provides that all such horses and burros on the public lands administered by the Secretary of the interior through the Bureau of Land Management (BLM) or by the Secretary of Agriculture through the Forest Service are committed to the jurisdiction of the respective secretaries, who are "directed to protect and manage [the animals] as components of the public lands...in a manner that is designed to achieve and maintain a thriving natural ecological balance on the public lands." If protected horses or burros "stray from public lands onto privately owned land, the owners of such land may inform the nearest Federal marshall or agency of the Secretary, who shall arrange to have the animals removed."[29]

Section 6 of the Act authorizes the Secretaries to promulgate regulations and to enter into cooperative agreements with other landowners and with state and local governmental agencies in furtherance of the Act's purposes. On August 7, 1973, the Secretaries executed such an agreement with the New Mexico Livestock Board (the Livestock Board), the agency charged with enforcing the New Mexico Estray Law. The agreement acknowledged the authority of the Secretaries to manage and

29. The landowner may elect to allow straying wild free-roaming horses and burros to remain on his property, in which case he must so notify the relevant Secretary. He may not destroy such animals, however.

protect the wild free-roaming horses and burros on the public lands of the United States within the State and established a procedure for evaluating the claims of private parties to ownership of such animals.

The Livestock Board terminated the agreement three months later. Asserting that the Federal Government lacked power to control wild horses and burros on the public lands of the United States unless the animals were moving in interstate commerce or damaging the public lands and that neither of these bases of regulation was available here, the Board notified the Secretaries of its intent

> to exercise all regulatory impoundment and sale powers which it derives from the New Mexico Estray Law, over all estray horses, mules, or asses found running at large upon public or private lands within New Mexico.... This includes the right to go upon Federal or State lands to take possession of said horses or burros, should the Livestock Board so desire.

The differences between the Livestock Board and the Secretaries came to a head in February 1974. On February 1, 1974, a New Mexico rancher, Kelley Stephenson, was informed by BLM that several unbranded burros had been seen near Taylor Well, where Stephenson watered his cattle. Taylor Well is on federal property, and Stephenson had access to it and some 8,000 surrounding acres only through a grazing permit issued pursuant to the Taylor Grazing Act. After BLM made it clear to Stephenson that it would not remove the Burros and after he personally inspected the Taylor Well area, Stephenson complained to the Livestock Board that the burros were interfering with his livestock operation by molesting his cattle and eating their feed.

Thereupon the Board rounded up and removed 19 unbranded and unclaimed burros pursuant to the New Mexico Estray Law. Each burro was seized on the public lands of the United States, and, as the director of the Board conceded, each burro fit the definition of a wild free-roaming burro under the Act. On February 18, 1974, the livestock Board, pursuant to its usual practice, sold the burros at public auction. After the sale, BLM asserted jurisdiction under the Act and demanded that the Board recover the animals and return them to the public lands.

On March 4, 1974, appellees [New Mexico public officials] filed a complaint in the United States District Court for the District of New Mexico seeking a declaratory judgment that the Wild Free-Roaming Horses and Burros Act is unconstitutional and an injunction against its enforcement....

Following an evidentiary hearing, the District Court held the Act unconstitutional and permanently enjoined the Secretary of the Interior (the Secretary) from enforcing its provisions. The court found that the Act "conflicts with...the traditional doctrines concerning wild animals," and is in excess of Congress' power under the Property Clause of the Constitution, Art. IV, §4, cl. 2. That clause, the court found, enables Congress to regulate wild animals found on the public land only for the "*protection* of the public lands from damage of some kind." Accordingly, this power was exceeded in this case because "the statute is aimed at protecting the wild horses and burros, not at protecting the land they live on." We noted probable jurisdiction, and we now reverse.

The Property Clause of the Constitution provides that "Congress shall have Power to dispose of and make all needful Rules and Regulations respecting the Territory or other Property belonging to the United States." In passing the Wild Free-Roaming Horses and Burros Act, Congress deemed the regulated animals "an integral part of the natural system of the public lands" of the United States, and found that their management was necessary "for the achievement of an ecological balance on the public lands." According to Congress, these animals, if preserved in their native habitats, "contribute to the diversity of life forms within the Nation and enrich the lives of the American people." Indeed, Congress concluded, the wild free-roaming horses and burros "are living symbols of the historic and pioneer spirit of the West." Despite their importance, the Senate Committee found that these animals

> have been cruelly captured and slain and their carcasses used in the production of pet food and fertilizer. They have been used for target practice and harassed for "sport" and profit. In spite of public outrage, this bloody traffic continues unabated, and it is the firm belief of the committee that this senseless slaughter must be brought to an end.

For these reasons, Congress determined to preserve and protect the wild free-roaming horses and burros on the public lands of the United States. The question under the Property Clause is whether this determination can be sustained as a "needful" regulation "respecting" the public lands. In answering this question, we must remain mindful that, while courts must eventually pass upon them, determinations under the Property Clause are entrusted primarily to the judgment of Congress.

Appellees argue that the Act cannot be supported by the Property Clause. They contend that the Clause grants Congress essentially two kinds of power: (1) the power to dispose of and make incidental rules regarding the use of federal property; and (2) the power to protect federal property. According to appellees, the first power is not broad enough to support legislation protecting wild animals that live on federal property; and the second power is not implicated since the Act is designed to protect the animals, which are not themselves federal property, and not the public lands. As an initial matter, it is far from clear that the Act was not passed in part to protect the public lands of the United States[30] or that Congress cannot assert a property interest in the regulated horses and burros superior to that of the State.[31] But we need not consider whether the Act can be upheld on either of these grounds, for we reject appellees' narrow reading of the Property Clause....

In brief...appellees have presented no support for their position that the [Property] Clause grants Congress only the power to dispose of, to make incidental rules regarding the use of, and to protect federal property. This failure is hardly surprising, for the Clause, in broad terms, gives Congress the power to determine what are "needful" rules "respecting" the public lands. And while the furthest reaches of the power granted by the Property Clause have not yet been definitively resolved, we have repeatedly observed that "the power over the public land thus entrusted to Congress is without limitations." United States v. San Francisco, 310 U.S. 16, 29 (1940).

The decided cases have supported this expansive reading. It is the Property Clause, for instance, that provides the basis for governing the territories of the United States. And even over public land within the States, "the general government doubtless has a power over its own property analogous to the police power of the several states, and the extent to which it may go in the exercise of such power

---

30. Congress expressly ordered that the animals were to be managed and protected in order to "achieve and maintain a thriving natural ecological balance on the public lands."

31. The Secretary makes no claim here, however, that the United States owns the wild free-roaming horses and burros found on public land.

is measured by the exigencies of the particular case." Camfield v. United States, 167 U.S. 518, 525 (1897). We have noted, for example, that the Property Clause gives Congress the power over the public lands "to control their occupancy and use, to protect them from trespass and injury, and to prescribe the conditions upon which others may obtain rights in them...." Utah Power & Light Co., v. United States, 243 U.S. 389, 405 (1917).... In short, Congress exercises the powers both of a proprietor and of a legislature over the public domain. Although the Property Clause does not authorize "an exercise of a general control over public policy in a State," it does permit "an exercise of the complete power which Congress has over particular public property entrusted to it." United States v. San Francisco, 310 U.S., at 30. In our view, the "complete power" that Congress has over public lands necessarily includes the power to protect the wildlife living there.

Appellees argue that if we approve the Wild Free-Roaming Horses and Burros Act as a valid exercise of Congress' power under the Property Clause, then we have sanctioned an impermissible intrusion on the sovereignty, legislative authority and police power of the State and have wrongfully infringed upon the State's traditional trustee powers over wild animals. The argument appears to be that Congress could obtain exclusive legislative jurisdiction over the public lands in the State only by state consent, and that in the absence of such consent Congress lacks the power to act contrary to state law. This argument is without merit....

While Congress can acquire exclusive or partial jurisdiction over lands within a State by the State's consent or cession [under the so-called Enclave Clause of the Constitution, Article I, §8, cl. 17], the presence or absence of such jurisdiction has nothing to do with Congress' powers under the Property Clause. Absent consent or cession a State undoubtedly retains jurisdiction over federal lands within its territory, but Congress equally surely retains the power to enact legislation respecting those lands pursuant to the Property Clause. And when Congress so acts, the federal legislation necessarily overrides conflicting state laws under the Supremacy Clause. As we said in Camfield v. United States, 167 U.S., at 526, in response to a somewhat different claim, "A different rule would place the public domain of the United States completely at the mercy of state legislation."...

Appellees' fear that the Secretary's position is that "the Property Clause totally exempts federal lands within state borders from state legislative powers, state police powers, and all rights and powers of local sovereignty and jurisdiction of the states," is totally unfounded. The Federal Government does not assert exclusive jurisdiction over the public lands in New Mexico, and the State is free to enforce its criminal and civil laws on those lands. But where those state laws conflict with the Wild Free-Roaming Horses and Burros Act, or with other legislation passed pursuant to the Property Clause, the law is clear: the State laws must recede....

Appellees are concerned that the Act's extension of protection to wild free-roaming horses and burros that stray from public land onto private land will be read to provide federal jurisdiction over every wild horse or burro that at any time sets foot upon federal land. While it is clear that regulations under the Property Clause may have some effect on private lands not otherwise under federal control, Camfield v. United States, 167 U.S. 518 (1897), we do not think it appropriate in this declaratory judgment proceeding to determine the extent, if any, to which the Property Clause empowers Congress to protect animals on private lands or the extent to which such regulation is attempted by the Act....

COMMENTARY AND QUESTIONS

1. The statutory policy. The Wild Free-Roaming Horses and Burros Act is a statute that causes mixed feelings amongst both ranchers and environmentalists. On one hand these animals, brought from Europe by Spanish and English pioneers, are living symbols of the historic or mythical frontier West, and creatures that deserve humane treatment. On the other, they have multiplied so successfully in some niches of their transplanted habitat that they destroy the forage and threaten the survival of native species in the western ecosystem, like antelope and black-footed ferrets, as well as private livestock.

A vivid, highly-focused citizens' campaign – using video footage of dog food suppliers stampeding and butchering terrified wild horses – pushed the statute through Congress, and as law it must be enforced by federal land managers. But the statute does not confront the policy contradictions it presents, with endangered species laws, for instance. Some environmentalists have suggested the compromise of inserting IUDs in wild horses and burros (as birth control pigeon food has been advocated in somewhat analogous urban settings), but the issues are likely not to be so easily resolved.

2. Public land and private land. Consider a situation where a herd of free-roaming horses and burros strays from public land onto adjacent private land, the rancher informs the BLM, and the BLM fails to remove the animals. Can the rancher sue the BLM for violation of a statutory duty? The Act specifies that the Secretary "shall arrange to have the animals removed," but it contains no time limitation for BLM action. If the animals are not removed, and they decimate the private range, can the rancher sue the federal government in inverse condemnation? The result may depend upon whether the rancher's property can sustain another economically substantial use. (See Chapter 9.) The federal government may argue, as a defense to an inverse condemnation action, that it cannot have constructively taken the adjacent land because it doesn't own the horses and burros. (The doctrine of state ownership of wildlife was disavowed in Hughes v. Oklahoma, 441 U.S. 322 (1979), but it wasn't replaced by a doctrine of federal ownership.) Does the New Mexico Estray Law apply to a herd that lives most of the year on the adjacent ranch but wanders onto public lands only when forage is scarce? Can the rancher legally drive the herd from his range onto public land? Consider questions such as these with regard to wildlife that, unlike wild horses and burros, is not specifically protected by a special federal statute like the Wild Free-Roaming Horses and Burros Act. See Fallini v. Hodel, 725 F. Supp. 122 (D. Nev. 1989). Can a Montana rancher legally shoot a bison that has wandered out of Yellowstone National Park onto his range? Does the result depend on whether the National Park Service has promulgated a relevant regulation? What if the bison is an endangered or threatened species?

3. Helpless giants? Does the property clause give the federal government the authority to regulate activities on private lands within ("inholdings") or outside federal landholdings when the private activities are interfering with the uses of the federal lands? For example, assume that the Fish and Wildlife Service seeks an injunction that forbids a promotor from holding rock concerts just outside a wildlife refuge, or that the National Park Service wants to prevent the construction of a hideously ugly commercial structure adjacent to, and painfully visible from, a national battlefield. Camfield v. United States, cited frequently in Kleppe v. New Mexico, would appear to authorize the federal government to protect its property against external threats. In *Camfield*, an owner of alternate, odd-numbered sections (purchased from a railroad) effectively fenced-off 20,000 acres of federal land by building a zigzag fence on his own property. Declaring that the federal government has the constitutional power to protect its land against nuisances, the Supreme Court held that the fence was a violation of a federal statute forbidding enclosures of public lands. *Camfield* was followed by United States v. Alford, 274 U.S. 264 (1927), upholding a statute prohibiting unauthorized fires "in or near" national forests. In Minnesota v. Block, 660 F.2d 1240 (8th Cir.1981), the Eighth Circuit Court of Appeals upheld a federal ban on the use of power boats and snowmobiles on state-owned lands within the Boundary Waters Canoe Area Wilderness in Minnesota, reasoning as follows:

> Under [the Property Clause], Congress' power must extend to regulation of conduct on or off the public land that would threaten the designated purpose of federal lands. Congress clearly has the power to dedicate federal land for particular purposes. As a necessary incident of that power, Congress must have the ability to insure that these lands be protected against interference with their intended purposes. 660 F.2d at page 1249.

Should a different legal rule apply to federal regulation of conduct on inholdings, as in Minnesota v. Block, than to activities on external lands? Despite the ostensibly adequate legal authority to regulate both internal and external threats to federal lands, the federal land management agencies have been unenthusiastic about exercising these powers. See Sax, Helpless Giants: The National Parks and the Regulation of Private Lands, 75 Mich. L. Rev. 239 (1976). If the federal government has the power to regulate external activities, how far does this regulatory power extend? Can the National Park Service promulgate a regulation requiring a large agricultural operation, fifty miles upriver of a park, to cease discharging nutrients because the nutrients are causing the river in the park to become eutrophic (prematurely aged)? If it can't promulgate such a regulation, can the NPS bring a nuisance action in federal court under the federal common law of nuisance? (See page 313 *supra*.) What about a state private or public nuisance action? (See Chapter 3.)

4. Access problems. On checker-board land grants, can private owners of alternate, odd-numbered sections deny access to recreationists traveling on a BLM-constructed road through sections 14, 22, and 16 in order to reach a federal reservoir, even though the public road only touches their sections 15, 21, and 23 at the corners? In Leo Sheep Company v. United States, 440 U.S. 668 (1979), the Supreme Court rejected express or implied easements across private lands, thus requiring the BLM to purchase or condemn a road easement. Justice Rehnquist, writing for the majority, distinguished *Camfield* in unconvincing fashion. Isn't the Leo Sheep Company really enclosing public lands? In a condemnation proceeding, should the fair market value of Leo Sheep's land include its proximity to the water and recreation provided by the federally-funded reservoir? For a discussion of access cases, see Coggins and Wilkinson's Chapter 2.

5. The "Sagebrush Rebellion." Problems caused by interspersed federal and private lands, exacerbated by FLPMA's declaration that the federal public lands will generally remain in federal ownership and be managed for multiple use and sustained yield, generated a reaction known as the "Sagebrush Rebellion," one outgrowth of which led a number of western states to contest the constitutionality of federal ownership of the public lands. In 1978, the State of Nevada sued the federal government, claiming that federal land ownership was a violation of both Nevada's Tenth Amendment rights and its right to be admitted to the Union on an "equal footing" with the original thirteen states, in which there is comparatively little federal land. These claims were denied in Nevada Ex Rel. Nevada State Board of Agriculture v. United States, 512 F. Supp.166 (D.Nev.1981), affd. on other grounds, 699 F.2d 486 (9th Cir.1983). But, as a policy matter, would selling the public lands to the highest private bidders protect those lands by ending the tragedy of the commons that frequently prevails with regard to public lands? Privatization would most likely only reinstate the "cut and run" attitude that has traditionally prevailed toward natural resources in the United States because the highest bidders in such an auction would probably be those interests with the strongest financial positions, i.e., the extractive interests. Public interest groups and representatives of future generations would be hopelessly disadvantaged in the bidding process. Thus, privatization of public resources would, in effect, create a dominant use system with extraction as the primary use.

6. Land as an ecosystem. The Wild Free-Roaming Horses and Burros Act, which deems these animals to be "an integral part of the natural system of the public lands," is Congress' clearest acceptance to date of Aldo Leopold's concept of land as an ecological community rather than a commodity. According to Congress, these animals, if preserved in their native habitats, "contribute to the diversity of life forms within the Nation and enrich the lives of the American people." Increasingly, Americans are looking beyond preservation of particular species or resources (e.g., endangered species or wild and scenic rivers), which is based on a variety of "zoo" mentality, toward preservation of entire ecosystems in so-called "bioreserves."

For a critique of the resource-by-resource preservation approach, in the context of the Endangered Species Act, and an exploration of the potential legal means of protecting biological diversity, see Doremus, Patching the Ark: Improving Legal Protection of Biological Diversity, 18 Ecol. L. Q. 265 (1991).

7. Agency organization and jurisdiction. The federal land management agencies possess jurisdiction based on historical accident (the BLM manages those lands that nobody wanted), intentional reservation for human uses (the NPS manages the national parks for public recreation), or resource type (by and large, the USFS manages only forested areas). Furthermore, there has traditionally been tension among these agencies: the USFS, with a strong sense of professionalism and located in the United States Department of Agriculture, has frequently been at odds with the more disposal-minded BLM, located in the United States Department of the Interior. Among the Interior agencies, the BLM has often clashed with the more preservationist NPS and FWS. Is the existing organization of federal land management agencies an anachronism? Given a clean bureaucratic slate, how would you reorganize the federal government to best manage the federal lands?

D. THE BLM AND OFF-ROAD VEHICLES: A CASE STUDY

D. Sheridan, Off-Road Vehicles on Public Lands
7-12 (1979)

[Off-road vehicles] (ORVs) have damaged every kind of ecosystem found in the United States: sand dunes covered with American Beach grass on Cape Cod; pine and cyprus woodlands in Florida; hardwood forests in Indiana; prairie grasslands in Montana; chaparral and sagebrush hills in Arizona; alpine meadows in Colorado; conifer forests in Washington; arctic tundra in Alaska. In some cases the wounds will heal naturally; in others they will not, at least for millennia....

Federal lands have borne a disproportionate share of the damage. State lands are far less extensive; in addition, some states have either prohibited ORV use on their lands (Indiana) or have restricted their use to designated trails (Massachusetts). And the federal government has been more willing to open the lands which it manages for the American public to ORVs than have private landowners....

The ready availability of federal land has profoundly shaped the ORV phenomenon. Per capita ownership of ORVs is significantly higher in areas that possess a lot of public land. The reason is simple: a person is more likely to buy an ORV if he has some place to drive it.... Thus federal land policy has been an important stimulant to ORV growth. Because the federal government has allowed ORVers to consume public resources free of charge, the general public has in a sense subsidized the ORV phenomenon.

A second consequence of federal land policy has been to discourage private enterprise from meeting ORVers demand for land. Commercially developed ORV areas are extremely rare....

First and foremost [among environmental costs of ORV use], ORVs eat land. It is because ORVs attack that relatively thin layer of disintegrated rock and organic material to which all earthly life clings – soil – that they can have such a devastating effect on natural resources....

There seem to be two basic soil responses to ORV use. One, sandy and gravelly soils are susceptible to direct quarrying by ORVs, and when stripped of vegetation they are susceptible to rapid erosion processes – usually by rill and gully erosion. Near Santa Cruz, California, for example, ORV trails used for about 6 years are now gullies 8 feet deep. Two, more clay-rich soils are less sensitive to direct mechanical displacement by ORVs, but the rates of erosion of stripped clay-rich soil are much higher under ORV use than under natural conditions. Furthermore, ORV pounding of clay-rich soil causes strong surface seals to form, thereby reducing the infiltration of water. This, in turn, leads to greater rainwater runoff, which causes gullying lower in the drainage.

Once massive soil erosion begins, it will stop only after ORV riding stops and the native vegetation has had a chance to reestablish itself and stabilize the soil. In arid and semiarid areas, recovery is very slow. The same holds true for hilly or mountainous areas which receive heavy rainfall, such as Appalachia or northern California....

In flat, dry areas ORVs expose the soil to another powerful erosional force – the wind. In damp flat areas such as wet prairies or meadows, ORV ruts can turn into drainage ditches – siphoning off water held in the surrounding area....

ORVs destabilize sand dunes, making them more vulnerable to wind erosion and, in the case of coastal dunes, to sea erosion....

A major difficulty with ORVs...is that the terrain which truly challenges the capability of these machines, and which is therefore most attractive to many ORV operators, is exactly that which is most highly sensitive to erosional degradation. This open contradiction between machine capability and land sensitivity is a key issue.

Aside from tearing up soils, ORVs also damage vegetation. They kill plants in several ways. By direct contact – the ORV runs over the plant or brushes against it, breaking off limbs or branches. Sometimes ORV use around a plant so badly erodes the soil that the plant simply collapses from lack of anything to hold onto. Also, ORV soil compaction injures root systems and larger perennials eventually die. In addition, ORVs crush seedlings beneath their wheels or treads as well as seeds germinating on or within the ground. Lastly, on slopes, soil eroded because of ORV use washes to the bottom where it smothers plants that are growing there.

ORVs also disrupt animal life.... They collide with animals, especially smaller mammals and reptiles. By destroying vegetation, they are also destroying animal food and shelter.

In addition, ORVs afford hunters and fishermen access to remote, heretofore untouched areas, thereby dramatically increasing the fish and game kills in those areas.

The effects of ORV noise on animals, although imperfectly understood, is thought to be very damaging....

CONFLICTS WITH OTHER USERS...

ORV and snowmobile use of the land conflicts with other human uses of the land [and] the conflicts engendered by these machines can be quite bitter.

Reports from public land managers in nine western states indicate that conflict occurs, upon occasion, between commercial users of the land, such as ranchers, and ORV recreationists. The conflict with grazing, in fact, seems to be more common than with logging or mining. For example, New Mexico BLM director Arthur W. Zimmerman notes that complaints from ranchers have been received concerning trespass, cut fences, broken gates, polluted livestock water, new jeep roads, noise, gully erosion caused by hill climbs, and interference with their livestock operations. The less frequent complaints received from loggers and miners usually concern vandalism of their equipment and property by ORVers.

The most serious conflict arises between ORV operators and nonmotorized picnickers or campers, hikers, backpackers, sightseers, and so on – or between ORVers and persons using the land for educational purposes – students, teachers, researchers.

Nonmotorized recreationists do not enjoy their encounters with motorcycles, dune buggies, and four-wheel drive vehicles, numerous studies have shown. The

ORV operator, on the other hand, is often quite tolerant, even oblivious, of the person on foot or on horseback.

ORVs, in other words, impair other people's enjoyment or understanding of the outdoors on public land. In terms of public policy, this is a problem equal in importance to ORV damage of the environment.

To the BLM's credit, it was the first federal agency that recognized the magnitude of the ORV problem on public lands and attempted to do something about it. In 1968, the California state office of the BLM and the Western Regional office of the National Park Service published a document detailing the damage caused by ORVs in the California Desert and recommending that BLM develop special ORV centers where environmental damage could be kept to a minimum. In 1969, the BLM in California convened an Off-Road Advisory Council composed of ORV organization representatives, environmentalists, ranchers, and businessmen. Despite heated internal disputes, the Council recommended that ORV use not be permitted on highly erodable lands; sites unique for historic, ecological, or archaeological value; or lands typically used for other kinds of public recreation. Apparently, these recommendations led the ORV organizations to withdraw their support for the Advisory Council Process and use their contacts in the Interior Department for their own self-interest. In 1971, the Secretary of the Interior formed an ORV task force that whitewashed the ORV problem, recommending further study, state regulation of ORV use, and the development of private ORV facilities (with no mention of increased federal regulation or subsidies to stimulate the private sector).

By 1972, however, environmental abuse of the public lands by the burgeoning ranks of ORV users was becoming so pronounced that President Nixon issued Executive Order 11644 calling for a unified federal policy toward ORVs on the public lands. E.O. 11644 established a presumption that public lands should be closed to ORV use unless specifically opened by agency regulation, after findings are made under the following criteria:

> (1) Areas and trails shall be located to minimize damages to soil, watershed, vegetation, or other resources of the public lands.
>
> (2) Areas and trails shall be located to minimize harassment of wildlife or significant disruption of wildlife habitats.
>
> (3) Areas and trails shall be located to minimize conflicts between off-road vehicle use and other existing or proposed recreational uses of the same or neighboring public lands and to ensure the compatibility of such uses with existing conditions in populated areas, taking into account noise and other factors.
>
> (4) Areas and trails shall not be located in officially designated Wilderness Areas or Primitive Areas. Areas and trails shall be located in areas of the National Park system, Natural Areas, or National Wildlife Refuges and Game Ranges only if the respective agency head determines that off-road vehicle use in such locations will not adversely affect their natural, aesthetic, or scenic values.

© 1989 HOWARD WILSHIRE

ORV use on public lands. This ridge in California's Jawbone Canyon has been stripped of vegetation by heavy ORV recreational use. The plume of dust marks the uphill run of an all-terrain motorcycle. In the desert, even in cases of low-volume ORV use, noise levels can be deafening, and the tire track ruts made by one machine in one 15-minute run through the fragile ecology of the desert floor may remain visible for more than 50 years.

The BLM regulations implementing E.O. 11644, however, established the opposite presumption, that public lands should be open to ORV use until closed by the management agency because of environmental damage or conflict with other users.[32]

In National Wildlife Federation v. Morton, 393 F. Supp. 1286 (D.D.C. 1975), a federal district court overturned the BLM regulations as inconsistent with E.O. 11644, remarking that "BLM has significantly diluted the standards emphatically set forth in Executive Order 11644."

32. In other words, whereas E.O. 11644 minimized false negatives (was proactive), the BLM regulations minimized false positives (were reactive).

FLPMA, enacted in 1976, was primarily addressed to the grazing issue, and its treatment of ORV use was cursory. Section 601 of FLPMA established a planning process for the 12 million-acre California Desert Conservation Area, one objective of which was that

> [§601(4)] the use of all California desert resources can and should be provided for in a multiple use and sustained yield management plan to conserve these resources for future generations, and to provide present and future use and enjoyment, particularly outdoor recreation uses, including the use, where appropriate, of off-road recreational vehicles.

In other words, ORVs were perceived by Congress as just another one of the multiple uses to be accommodated on public lands.

In response to the hesitancy of federal agencies to control ORV use and implement E.O. 11644, President Carter issued E.O. 11989 in 1977.[33] E.O. 11989 reiterated many of the provisions of E.O. 11644, but, in addition, ordered agency heads (1) "to develop and issue regulations [governing the] designation of the specific areas and trails on public lands on which the use of off-road vehicles may be permitted," and (2) to immediately ban ORVs where ORV use "will cause or is causing considerable adverse effects." Nevertheless, two days after President Carter signed E.O. 11989, the Interior Department issued a press release[34] interpreting the order as applying only to "fragile areas which are actually threatened with serious damage," disclaiming a general ban on ORV use on public lands, and stressing voluntary action on the part of ORV users. E.O. 11644 had declared that "areas and trails shall be located to minimize [environmental] damages," a highly protective standard; as for closure of *existing* trails, E.O. 11989 required the agency to prove "considerable adverse effects." The BLM, in its California Desert Conservation Area Plan, applied the latter order's looser closure standard, instead of the more protective minimization standard, in its designation of new trails, thus making it far easier to designate ORV routes. This aspect of the plan was struck down in American Motorcyclist Association v. Watt, 543 F. Supp. 789 (D.C.D. Cal. 1982).

Sierra Club v. Clark

United States Court of Appeals for the Ninth Circuit, 1985

756 F.2d 686

POOLE, J. Plaintiffs...filed this action seeking review under the Administrative Procedure Act, 5 U.S.C.A. §706(1), of the failure of the defendants Secretary of the Interior, Director of the Bureau of Land Management ("BLM"), and California State Director of BLM ("Secretary") to close Dove Springs Canyon to off road vehicle ("ORV") use. Sierra Club appeals from the district court's denial of their motion for summary judgment, and the grant of the Secretary's motion for summary judgment. We affirm.

Dove Springs Canyon is located in the California Desert Conservation Area ("Desert Area").... The Desert Area covers approximately 25 million acres in

33. Bleich, Chrome on the Range: Off-Road Vehicles on Public Lands, 15 Ecol. L. Q. 159, 166–67 (1988).

34. Sheridan, *supra*, Appendix 4.

southeastern California, approximately 12.1 million of which are administered by the BLM. Dove Springs Canyon is comprised of approximately 5500 acres; 3000 acres are designated "open" for unrestricted use of ORVs.

Dove Springs Canyon possesses abundant and diverse flora and fauna. Over 250 species of plants, 24 species of reptiles, and 30 species of birds are found there. It also offers good habitat for the Mojave ground squirrel, the desert kit fox, and the burrowing owl. Because the rich and varied biota is unusual for an area of such low elevation in the Mojave Desert, the canyon was once frequented by birdwatchers and naturalists, as well as hikers and fossil hunters.

Recreational ORV usage of Dove Springs Canyon began in 1965 and became progressively heavier in the ensuing years. By 1971, the Canyon was being used intensively by ORV enthusiasts. It became especially popular because the site's diverse terrain, coupled with relatively easy access, provides outstanding hill-climbing opportunities. By 1979, up to 200 vehicles used the Canyon on a typical weekend; over 500 vehicles used it on a holiday weekend. In 1973, the BLM adopted the Interim Critical Management Program for Recreational Vehicle Use on the California Desert ("Interim Program") which designated Dove Springs Canyon as an ORV Open Area, permitting recreational vehicle travel in the area without restriction.

Extensive ORV usage has been accompanied by severe environmental damage in the form of major surface erosion, soil compaction, and heavy loss of vegetation. The visual aesthetics have markedly declined. The character of the Canyon has been so severely altered that the Canyon is now used almost exclusively for ORV activities.

In July of 1980 Sierra Club petitioned the Secretary of the Interior to close Dove Springs Canyon to ORV use under the authority of Executive Order No. 11644 as amended by Executive Order No. 11989, because of "substantial adverse effects" on the vegetation, soil and wildlife in the Canyon. The Secretary responded that the matter would be addressed in the California Desert Conservation Plan and Final Environmental Impact Statement ("the Final Plan").

The Final Plan approved by the Secretary in December 1980 maintained unrestricted ORV use in Dove Springs of 3000 of the 5500 acres. Sierra Club filed this action on January 6, 1981, alleging that the Secretary's failure to close Dove Springs violated Executive Order No. 11644, as amended by Executive Order No. 11989, and 43 U.S.C.A. §1732(b) [FLPMA], which requires the Secretary to prevent "unnecessary or undue degradation of the lands;" and §§1781(b) and (d), which require the Secretary to maintain and conserve resources of the Desert Area under principles of "multiple use and sustained yield."...

The Secretary interprets "considerable adverse effect" to require determining what is "considerable" in the context of the Desert Area as a whole, not merely on a parcel-by-parcel basis. The Secretary contends such a broad interpretation is necessary and is consistent with §1781(a)(4) which expresses a congressional judgment that ORV use is to be permitted "where appropriate."

Sierra Club argues against the Secretary's interpretation. Sierra Club contends that the interpretation of the Executive Orders set forth by the Council on Environmental Quality (CEQ) in its August 1, 1977 memorandum is entitled to great deference, and that the CEQ's interpretation requires the closure of the canyon. This argument fails on two grounds.

First, the CEQ's interpretation of the Executive Order does not directly conflict with the Secretary's interpretation of the regulation. While it states that "the term 'considerable' should be liberally construed to provide the broadest possible protection reasonably required by this standard," it does not purport to decide whether the term "considerable adverse effects" should be analyzed in the context of the entire Desert Area, or on a site-specific basis. Moreover, the memorandum acknowledges that the responsibility for closing particular areas rests with "responsible federal officials in the field" "[b]ased on their practical experience in the management of the public lands, and their first-hand knowledge of conditions 'on-the-ground.'"

Second, the authority of the CEQ is to maintain a continuing review of the implementation of the Executive Order. The authority of the Secretary, on the other hand, is to promulgate regulations to provide for "administrative designation of the specific areas and trails on public lands on which the use of off-road vehicles may be permitted, and areas in which the use of off-road vehicles may not be permitted." Discretion rests with the Secretary, therefore, to determine whether and to what extent specific areas should be closed to ORV use. Thus, it is the Secretary's interpretation which is entitled to our deference.

Sierra Club argues that even if the CEQ's interpretation of the closure standard is not controlling, the Secretary's interpretation should not be adopted because it is unreasonable. Sierra Club insists that the sacrifice of any area to permanent resource damage is not justified under the multiple use management mandate of §1702(c) that requires multiple use "without permanent impairment of the productivity of the land and the quality of the environment." In further support of its position Sierra Club adverts to the requirement in the Act that the Secretary prevent "unnecessary and undue degradation" of the public lands. In addition, Sierra Club contends, when Congress established the Desert Area it intended the Secretary to fashion a multiple use and sustained yield management plan "to conserve [the California Desert] resources for future generations, and to provide present and future use and enjoyment, particularly outdoor recreational uses, including the use, where appropriate, of off-road recreational vehicles." Sierra Club argues that it is unreasonable for the Secretary to find ORV use "appropriate" when that use violates principles of sustained yield, substantially impairs productivity of renewable resources and is inconsistent with maintenance of environmental quality.

We can appreciate the earnestness and force of Sierra Club's position, and if we could write on a clean slate, would prefer a view which would disallow the virtual sacrifice of a priceless natural area in order to accommodate a special recreational activity. But we are not free to ignore the mandate which Congress wrote into the Act. Sierra Club's interpretation of the regulation would inevitably result in the total prohibition of ORV use because it is doubtful that any discrete area could withstand unrestricted ORV use without considerable adverse effects. However appealing might be such a resolution of the environmental dilemma, Congress has found that ORV use, damaging as it may be, is to be provided "where appropriate." It left determination of appropriateness largely up to the Secretary in an area of sharp conflict. If there is to be a change it must come by way of Congressional reconsideration. The Secretary's interpretation that this legislative determination calls for accommodation of ORV usage in the administrative plan, we must conclude, is not unreasonable and we are constrained to let it stand....

Under the California Desert Conservation Area Plan, approximately 4 percent (485,000 acres) of the total acreage is now open to unrestricted ORV use. Dove Springs itself constitutes only 0.025 percent of BLM administered lands in the Desert Area. Although all parties recognize that the environmental impact of ORV use at Dove Springs is severe, the Secretary's determination that these effects were not "considerable" in the context of the Desert Area as a whole is not arbitrary, capricious, or an abuse of the broad discretion committed to him by an obliging Congress....

COMMENTARY AND QUESTIONS

1. Straw man in the desert. Do you agree that application of the closure standard to specific areas rather than the Desert Area as a whole would inevitably result in the total prohibition of ORV use in violation of statute? Doesn't this argument assume that there are no qualitative differences among desert areas? Indeed, Sierra Club was making the argument that Dove Springs had been a unique ecological resource. (Note the poignancy of the court's use of the past tense in "the Canyon was once frequented by birdwatchers, naturalists, hikers, and fossil hunters.") Do you think that the court might have been implicitly reacting to a perception that the Canyon was already too far gone to save?

2. Multiple use reconsidered. What do you now think of Professor Coggins' conclusion at page 694, *supra*, that multiple use, sustained yield is not a "succotash syndrome" but a substantive standard that requires federal officials to manage for nonimpairment of land productivity and environmental quality as well as for sustained yield? The Sierra Club v. Clark court, applying the deferential "arbitrary and capricious" criterion, suggests that Congress might specify more clearly what it means by multiple use, sustained yield and "appropriateness" of ORVs in the California Desert; but it is often in Congress's political interest to be vague with regard to controversial issues. One way of escaping this dilemma would be for Congress to designate especially sensitive areas such as the California Desert as national parks, monuments, or reserves. But will "critical area" treatment (see Chapter 23) do any good if Congress doesn't appropriate more funds for enforcement by federal land management agencies? Should ORV users pay user fees to the federal government, the proceeds of which would be earmarked for administration and enforcement?

3. The BLM reconsidered. As with its implementation of the grazing permit program, the BLM, in its handling of the ORV situation, has become the representative of a financially and politically powerful interest group – the ORV lobby. The BLM has been so intransigent on the ORV issue that it appears to defy executive orders. Might it be that the BLM's "agency culture" is simply antithetical to a multiple use, sustained yield outlook? How could such attitudes be changed? Possibilities for reform of the BLM do exist. Presidential appointment of individuals other than ranchers to head the agency is an option. Congressional funding for the BLM could be conditioned on better environmental performance. Alternatively, the BLM could be merged with another federal agency, like the Fish and Wildlife Service, that possesses a broader focus. Some environmentalists have concluded that it is time to "break up the BLM."

4. ORVs and the national parks. The National Park Service has also been involved in ORV litigation, particularly with regard to ORV use on the Cape Cod National

Seashore in Massachusetts. See Bleich, Chrome on the Range: Off-Road Vehicles on Public Lands, 15 Ecol. L. Q., 159,170-177 (1988). In Conservation Law Foundation v. Secretary of the Interior, 864 F.2d 954 (1st Cir. 1989), the ORV component of the NPS's Management Plan for the seashore was upheld against claims that it violated the Cape Cod National Seashore Act, 16 U.S.C.A. §459b et seq. ("the Secretary may develop [the seashore] for appropriate public uses") and the ORV-related executive orders. Obviously impressed by the NPS's technical research and consequent limitations on ORV routes, the Court held that NPS's ORV policy was not arbitrary and capricious or a violation of the Act. The court noted that "the National Park Service has added a number of rangers to improve patrol of the Seashore." In light of decisions like the *Dove Canyon* and *Cape Cod National Seashore* cases, are conservationist lawsuits that contest ORV components of public land-use management plans quixotic? If nothing more, they raise the visibility of certain issues so that agencies like BLM may be forced to enlarge their perspectives, and agencies like the NPS are encouraged to conduct further studies documenting environmental damages.

5. Theoretical dilemmas underlying public resource management. This chapter has not provided clear answers to the generic questions with which it began: are public resources to be a continuing legacy or current profit-maximizers, assigned to single or multiple uses, used for local or nationwide benefit, precluding or harmonizing various competing interests?

Statutes like the Wilderness Act and FLPMA attempt to establish long-term basic principles to guide resource management, which inevitably collide with the pressures of economic interests that focus, as we all do, on the short-term specific.

It doesn't make much difference to the mayor of a small Northwest logging town whether the surrounding mountains are public or private; the old growth forests that remain there are a source for a half dozen more years of economic life for the community on the only terms that are available – clearcutting according to prevailing market practice. For as long as these last forests are allowed to be cut, by just so long will local citizens be able to pay their mortgages and taxes, and avoid having to go on welfare or move away. The practices of the timber industry, and its failures to implement successful long-term renewable, sustainable timber supply, are matters beyond the control of the community.

And what is lost when an ancient forest is gone, beyond a localized depreciation of natural environment? Are there public losses other than those that occur in terms of recreation, tourism, water quality, etc.? A few years ago it was reported that a geography professor on a summer grant project had found the oldest living thing on the face of the earth, a bristle-cone pine tree in a federal forest reserve. Bristle-cone pine trees are not majestic monoliths, but rather small scraggly survivors, twisted and gnarled with the storms of time, clinging to ridges in a remote region of eastern Nevada. The professor, however, did not know about modern coring techniques for dating trees; the only way he knew to determine a tree's age was to cut it down and count the cross-section rings. So with the approval of the government official in charge of the forest, he found the oldest living thing, dubbed it "Methuselah," and dated it the only way he knew. It was 4990 years old. To be certain he had found the real Methuselah, moreover, he also cut down and dated the next two oldest bristle-cones. What did we lose thereby? Since another bristle-cone pine was automatically made the oldest living thing by the professor's actions, what difference did it make?

Such questions become even more abstract when it isn't the oldest single tree, or the last carrier pigeon, but thousands of acres comprising the last 5 per cent of our original natural forest – or when human actions do not destroy the resource, but change its setting. Joe Sax once was startled as he climbed up a tortuous ridge in Tennessee to look out over a sprawling, forested, mountain-girded gulf in the Great Smokies National Park, and see a white high-rise Sheraton hotel thrusting up in the middle distance of the valley, built on an inholding within the Park.[35] Like the tower at the Gettysburg battlefield, what kind of experiential or aesthetic issues does this commercial intrusion raise? What is a "wilderness experience"?[36]

Or, for another example raising a composite of these issues, consider the re-introduction of wolves, grizzlies, and other endangered predator species to areas from which they had previously been exterminated. Montana, Wyoming, Minnesota, and other northern tier states have seen a number of attempts to restore large predators on public lands, especially national parks. For ranchers grazing cattle on nearby public and private rangelands, these ecological experiments represent the height of public policy folly. Killing bears, mountain lions, and wolves[37] seems to be an atavistic human instinct, aggravated by a farmer's vivid sense of emotional and economic injury upon finding a calf slaughtered in an early morning meadow. Doesn't a policy to bring back the predators seem irrational? To shoot the animal that killed your calf, however, runs the risk of a $25,000 fine and imprisonment.[38]

At the very least we owe future generations an attempt to clarify what our national public resources policies are.

---

35. From several such experiences came Sax, Mountains Without Handrails: Reflections on the National Parks (1980); Helpless Giants: The National Parks and the Regulation of Private Lands, 75 Mich. L.Rev. 239 (1976); and a number of other works on parks and resource policy.

36. To what extent, for instance, is motorized transportation a hindrance or a help to managing and experiencing a wilderness area? Friends of the Boundary Waters Wilderness v. Robertson, __ F. Supp. __, [1991 WL 155184 (D. Minn. 1991)]

37. See Aldo Leopold, at page 11 *supra*; Keiter and Holscher, Wolf Recovery under the Endangered Species Act: a Study in Contemporary Federalism, 11 Public Land L. Rev. 19 (1990).

38. ESA §11, 16 U.S.C.A. §1540(a)(1). It makes no difference to farmers and ranchers whether the grazing lands have been recently cut out of the forests, thus impinging on wild habitat, or have been grazed for generations. Proportionality of losses is not a test; one farmer who lost "one or two" cows was able to persuade the government to kill 41 wolves to protect his interests. Coggins and Evans, Predators' Rights and American Wildlife Law, 24 Ariz. L.Rev. 821, 864 (1982).

Another setting that raises similar hackles is the Forest Service's recent "let burn" policy for public forests, that seeks to restore the natural cycle of regularly-recurring moderate fires, in order to permit natural regeneration processes and avoid the buildup of so much unburned woody litter in the forests that fires, when they do occur, become devastating conflagrations. See Wiener, Uncle Sam and Forest Fires: His Rights and Responsibilities, 15 Envt'l Law 623 (1985)(arguing that the government should be liable for injuries to private property caused by such policies).

Chapter 15

TRADITIONAL REVIEW-AND-PERMIT PROCESS, AND A SURVEY OF MODERN STANDARD-SETTING APPROACHES

A. EARLY PUBLIC AGENCY OVERSIGHT OF HEALTH AND ENVIRONMENT

Beginning early in the twentieth century, a number of American state and municipal governments took preliminary steps toward controlling environmental pollution. Local public health departments typically had been delegated the authority to sue for abatement of public nuisances that might be injurious to health. This reactive form of pollution control was, in a few localities, supplemented by legislation specifying regulatory standards for declaring various amounts of pollution to be violations of law. Most often, this legislation took the form of smoke control air pollution ordinances.[1] These ordinances made it illegal to emit smoke of a certain color or density, and in some instances forbade the burning of high sulfur coal.[2]

These prohibitory laws were not always easy to enforce. In some cases it was difficult to prove that smoke violated the standards set by the ordinance. There was no smokestack sampling, and technical measurements were primitive. Under even the most sophisticated of these early laws, violations were (and still are in some areas) judged by the eye of the inspector, who visually compares the smoke as it comes out of the stack to samples on a "Ringelmann" chart. The chart is little more than a printed strip of numbered blotches, not wholly dissimilar from paint samples, ranging from an unblemished white hue, progressively through the grays, to black. In addition, defendants typically argued that the visual readings were arbitrary, and that there was no proof that violations caused any harm. Although proof of harm was not an element of the ordinances, the influence of nuisance law and its focus on harm often influenced judges to undercut the law. By the late 1950s those arguments were usually rejected, but their staying power testified to the slow acceptance of pollution control as a social norm.

Smoke control ordinances and public nuisance prosecutions were no match for the deteriorating environmental quality conditions in America's cities caused by increasing urbanization and industrialization. More effective regulatory regimes were needed. The standard approach to pollution control then became a permit-

---

1. Smoke control ordinances have a long history, dating back to thirteenth-century London.

2. See generally Laitos, Legal Institutions and Pollution: Some Intersections Between Law and History, 15 Nat. Res. J. 423 (1975).

issuing statutory program, requiring that polluters whose actions posed threats to public health obtain a governmental permit to dump their wastes into the air or water. Under the simple permit system, the agency (still the local public health department in many places) would review applications from sources of potentially injurious pollution, and issue permits to them. Permits could be denied if the agency found that permit issuance would be detrimental to public health. Operating without a permit was either a civil or criminal offense, usually punishable by a small fine. Repeated offenses could, in theory, provide a basis under which a prosecutor could maintain a public nuisance action that might, if a judge agreed, force closure of the plant. Likewise, the threat of permit denial presumably provided these agencies with leverage to require that the regulated entities improve their operations in a way that would reduce the danger to public health.

Even these simple permit systems were difficult to enforce. Major pollution sources were frequently major employers and politically powerful entities. They opposed stringent regulation and complained about the expense of pollution control, or made the lack of proof of violation and lack of harm arguments referred to above. Even if those arguments lacked legal merit, they certainly had an influence on local public officials whose efforts at pollution control did not enjoy a vigorous political mandate. The pollution standards that were set were typically quite permissive, and enforcement had a haphazard and ineffectual quality about it. Most violations went either unnoticed, or unpunished; punishments actually imposed were generally trifling.

Following World War II, the use of review and permit systems as a means of pollution control continued and was greatly expanded. In the 1950s and early 1960s, there was sufficient awareness of the limited pollution assimilation capacity of the nation's airsheds and rivers to generate momentum for more thorough efforts at pollution control. The review and permit process was the most common regulatory approach, and it increasingly incorporated a specialized agency staff, a greater sense of purpose, and a somewhat more credible political mandate.

The typical review and permit system had several features. The statutes creating them (1) erected a permit requirement as a condition precedent to discharges of air or water pollution, and set forth penalties for operating without a permit; (2) created the special administrative agency or commission whose principal function was the operation of the pollution control permit system; (3) delegated to that agency the authority to operate such a system; and (4), directed the agency to exercise its discretion in administering the system "in a manner consistent with the public good" or "in furtherance of the public welfare." Most of these systems authorized the agency to grant conditional permits and, most important, provided sanctions for non-compliance with permit terms.

What this post-war generation of review and permit statutes generally did not do was to consider the very difficult question of standards. It often wasn't at all clear how permit standards were to be designed and applied – was it in terms of general parts-per-million levels set statewide, or total weight limits of discharge per day, or standards based on each factory's local air or water quality, or in terms of manufacturing procedures to be followed, etc.[3] – and how in each case was the agency to draw the line between what was allowable and what was illegal? The general public welfare language noted above served as the only guide for how rigorous an effort at pollution control was intended.

COMMENTARY AND QUESTIONS

1. Anticipating the problems of typical review and permit statutes. Can you identify the various ways in which review and permit systems having the general characteristics described above are likely to be subverted or stymied by industrial polluters? Some predictable problems might be described as institutional, political, or economic. The agency charged with pollution control, if it acts with great vigor to require major changes in the status quo, places itself in a vulnerable position. The legislature, having passed the legislation, has probably let its attentiveness lapse. If anything, once the initial legislation is in place, it probably is polluters who have the legislature's ear. The regulated polluters are, in the main, the economic bulwarks of the community, providing employment and other benefits to the community and important political support to friendly legislators. In the pre-Earth Day atmosphere of the 1950s and early 1960s, moreover, there was insufficient community and general public concern to offset the economic and political clout of the regulated interests.

On the more technical side, the mandate given to the pollution control agencies was often, as noted, too general to be translated directly into specific, enforceable standards. This left the agencies with the monumental task of devising rational health and technological standards based on scientific and engineering data that the agencies were generally ill-equipped to assemble due to their lack of expert staff and other technical resources. Despite the near-impossibility of the technical task under those circumstances, the agencies were given only vague directions, along with broad discretion to fashion standards. When matched against a formidable and focused opposition – the regulated community of polluters – the discretion that might have provided agencies with the flexibility necessary to manage pollution problems instead tended to function as a one-way ratchet that weakened the agencies' pollution control efforts.

B. A CASE STUDY IN NON-ENFORCEMENT UNDER A TYPICAL REVIEW AND PERMIT STATUTE

Section 1. MICHIGAN'S WATER POLLUTION STATUTE: A TYPICAL REGULATORY MODEL

The Michigan Water Resources Commission Act, as it stood from 1949 to the

3. The nature of the regulatory measure makes a great deal of difference. You can discharge 75 pounds a day of arsenic almost imperceptibly on a parts-per-million (ppm) basis if you dilute it enough with air, steam, or water, and that may not avoid its toxicity. Similarly, the quality and retentiveness of the "receiving body" of local air, water, or humans makes a difference in long- and short-term effects. And if the permit chooses the very different approach of dictating manufacturing procedures and controls ("available technology," Chapter 19, *infra*), what set of minimum requirements will be chosen?

early 1970s,[4] was a typical example of a state review and permit statute in the pollution control area and provides the basis for analyzing an industrial case study taken from agency files, set out at page 723–726 *infra*.

Derived from a public health statute, the Michigan statute established a seven-member, part-time commission (WRC) to make and enforce water pollution law. The composition of the commission was spelled out in the legislation, and in 1949 comprised:

> the director of the department of natural resources, the director of the department of public health, the director of the department of state highways, the director of the department of agriculture, and 3 citizens of the state to be appointed by the governor, by and with the advice and consent of the senate, 1 from groups representative of industrial management, 1 from groups representative of municipalities, and 1 from groups representative of conservation associations or interests, for terms of 3 years each. Mich. Comp. L. Ann §323.1 (1949).

The statutory charge given to the WRC was ambitious. The preamble spoke of "a water resources commission to protect and conserve the water resources of the state" that would "prohibit the pollution of any waters of the state."[5] In literal terms, the legislation delivered on those promises by establishing the WRC and giving it the needed authority to accomplish those purposes in almost exactly the same broad terms:

> The commission shall organize and make its own rules and procedure and shall meet not less than once each month and shall keep a record of its proceedings. The commission shall protect and conserve the water resources of the state and shall have control of the pollution of surface or underground waters of the state and the Great Lakes, which are or may be affected by waste disposal of municipalities, industries, public or private corporations, individuals, partnership associations, or any other entity.... The commission shall enforce this act and shall promulgate rules as considered necessary to carry out its duties under this act. Mich. Comp. L. Ann. §323.2(1).

To go along with its broad mandate, the WRC was given investigatory power and the power to bring actions at law and in equity to enforce the water pollution laws of the state.[6] There were not many water pollution control laws to be enforced at that time, so the legislation prohibited discharges that harmed public health or destroyed fish life in the water.[7] The statute also granted the WRC the power to regulate discharges into the state's waters by setting and enforcing pollution standards, in terms common to other review and permit programs noted earlier:

> The commission shall establish such pollution standards for lakes, rivers, streams and other waters of the state in relation to the public use to which they are or may be put, as it shall deem necessary.... It shall have the authority

4. The Act has since been amended to satisfy the more rigorous requirements of the federal Clean Water Act. See Act 293 of Pub. Acts of 1972, Mich. Comp. Laws §16.357.

5. Michigan P.A.1929, No. 245, as amended.

6. Mich. Comp. L. Ann. §323.3–4.

7. Mich. Comp. L. Ann. §323.6.

> to make rules and orders restricting the polluting content of any waste material or polluting substance discharged or sought to be discharged into any lake, river, stream or other waters of the state. It shall have the authority to take all appropriate steps to prevent any pollution which is deemed by the commission to be unreasonable and against public interest in view of the existing conditions in any lake, river, stream or other waters of the state. Mich. Comp. L. Ann. §323.5.

The broad terms of the review and permit process were set out in the 1949 version of the WRC Act. Although the standard setting provision originally enacted had included the power to make orders (permits) that would limit discharges, the WRC had the burden of initiating standard-setting and permitting procedures. If it did not make standards and apply them to specific polluters, there was no need for the polluters to seek WRC approval of their practices. In 1949, *as to new or increased discharges only*, a mandatory review and permit process was added:

> It *shall* be the duty of any person...requiring a new or substantial increase over and above the present use now made of the waters of the state for sewage or waste disposal purposes, to file with the commission a written statement setting forth the nature of the enterprise or development contemplated, the amount of water required to be used, its source, the proposed point of discharge of said wastes into the waters of the state, the estimated amount so to be discharged, and a fair statement setting forth the expected bacterial, physical, chemical and other known characteristics of said wastes. Within 60 days of receipt of said statement, it shall be the duty of the commission to make an order stating such minimum restrictions as in the judgment of the commission may be necessary to guard adequately against such unlawful uses of the public waters.... Mich. Comp. L. Ann. §323.8(b)(emphasis added).

COMMENTARY AND QUESTIONS

1. The evolution of the state Water Resources Commission. From its creation in 1929 as a statewide water pollution control agency, the WRC's mission and mandate continued to grow. Initially, the WRC was to address problems of public health and fish kills resulting from water pollution on a statewide basis. With the 1949 addition of a mandatory permit system, the broader language of the original mandate seemed to come to the fore – the WRC was to become engaged in broad proactive control of pollution. Later amendments, which required compliance with federal Clean Water Act norms, expanded the regulatory mandate even further, including systematic regulation of *all* point source and municipal dischargers, not merely new and increased sources.

2. The 1949 mandatory permit system. Why did the legislature decide to require a mandatory permit system in 1949? One explanation, having some support in the amendatory process itself, was that the cumulative effects of pollution on aquatic ecosystems were then becoming a concern, as was the economic impact of deteriorating water quality on all forms of water use. As an indication of legislative concern in those areas, a natural resources section was extensively updated in 1949. Section 323.6 was expanded from a concern with pollution that endangered public health and fish kills to include pollution that would harm "any fish or migratory bird life or any wild animal or aquatic life." The language formerly addressed to public health alone was expanded to prohibit any water use "which is injurious to the public health or to the conducting of any industrial enterprise or other lawful occupation."

3. A non-comprehensive permit requirement. Why was the 1949 mandatory permit process imposed only on new and increased sources? Assuming that existing pollution was already severe enough to be causing undesirable effects, it seems irrational to exclude all existing sources from the permit system. Political realities may have required that compromise.

4. Section 8(b) as a review and permit process. The process calls for the polluter (the applicant) to furnish information about its anticipated discharge (the application); the WRC must then issue an order that includes restrictions on the discharge (a permit). In omitted portions of the section, the permit process is subject to subsequent judicial review.

5. The standards to be applied by the WRC. What standards are to be applied by the WRC in acting on permit applications? The principal legislated standard relates to pollution that is unlawful under §323.6. Under that section, as it stood in 1949, pollution could not be permitted if it would injure public health and welfare or the aquatic ecosystem. In addition, "any pollution which is deemed by the commission to be unreasonable and against public interest" was prohibited under §323.5. Are these standards likely to obtain effective protection of water quality? The standards' generality poses two different obstacles to preventing pollution.

The first obstacle is interpretive – to the extent that the standards are vague (e.g. "injurious to public health or the conducting of any industrial enterprise"), the WRC had to provide more precise definitions. Recalling that the WRC was not a politically powerful agency – and by its very composition was somewhat sympathetic to industrial and commercial interests – suggests that it would tend not to interpret those terms stringently. Only the clearest cases of injury would be defined by the WRC as violating the threshold of harm that triggered its regulatory powers.

The second obstacle lies in the steps required in going from a case of probable unlawful discharge (i.e. a finding that the application, if granted without conditions, would result in an unlawful discharge) to the regulatory application of adequate permit conditions to prevent the proscribed harm from occurring. The WRC was, for political reasons already described, hesitant to deny permit applications outright. In general, the WRC could be expected to insert permit conditions that would allow the discharger to go forward with the overall project, but require that the effluent be treated in some manner before discharge. Here the WRC's lack of staff and technical expertise was a major barrier to effective operation. Industrial applicants for permits necessarily have engineering expertise commensurate with the nature of their projects and can call on that capacity in negotiating permit conditions. The WRC, and most similar agencies or commissions, were, in the period under discussion, simply overmatched in that process.

The Michigan WRC Act – a typical review and permit statutory program – produced a weak system of water pollution control. Pre-1949 sources were exempt from the mandatory permit process at their original levels of discharge. This was not a trivial loophole because by 1949 the state's streams and lakes were already severely polluted. The regulation of new and increased sources under the review and permit system, moreover, had two strikes against it because of the generality of the statute and the WRC's lack of technical resources that meant it could not discuss permit conditions with permitees on an even footing.

The third strike against the WRC Act was its under-enforcement.

Section 2. UTILEX: A WATER POLLUTION CASE STUDY

As part of a project undertaken by the University of Michigan Environmental Law Society in the early 1970s, a case file involving a WRC permit was studied. (The file has been revisited to update the study.) The file involved an electroplating shop, the Utilex Company of Fowlerville, Michigan. The partial chronology that follows tells its own story.

UTILEX-HOOVER BALL BEARING

Michigan Department of Natural Resources File No. MI 0003727

Digest of file entries:

December, 1952:	Utilex Company requests "new use" permit to allow dumping of cyanide, copper, zinc, nickel and other matter, in connection with new plating operations, into the adjoining Looking-glass River.
January, 1953:	WRC makes order granting permit, attaching [weak] standards for water quality.
July, 1953:	Staff field report: effluent violates permit standards.
September, 1953:	Staff field report: effluent violates permit standards.
September, 1954:	Staff field report: effluent violates permit standards.
March, 1955:	Staff field report: effluent violates permit standards. Staff writes letter to company suggesting new control equipment.
March, 1956:	Staff field report: effluent violates permit standards.
November, 1956:	Staff field report: effluent violates permit standards.
June, 1957:	Violation noted for nickel only.
June, 1959:	Staff field report: effluent violates permit standards in all categories.
January, 1960:	Staff field report: effluent violates permit standards in all categories.
October, 1960:	Staff field report: effluent violates permit standards in all categories.
May, 1961:	Staff field report: effluent violates permit standards in all categories. Biological test shows long-term toxic effect; fifteen river miles required for recovery of water quality in river.

June, 1963:	Staff field report: effluent violates permit standards.
September, 1963:	Staff field report: effluent violates permit standards.
January, 1964:	Biological test shows no sign of life to three and one-half miles downstream; near-lethal cyanide levels.
October, 1964:	WRC writes company that controls would be "most desirable."
November, 1965:	Staff field report: concentrations exceeding standards 9.3 miles downstream.
September, 1966:	Citizen complaints [others have apparently been received, but are not copied in file] lead to staff field report: effluent violates permit standards.
November, 1966:	University biological test shows complete eradication of life to 4.7 miles downstream.
March, 1968:	Staff field report: excess effluents in all categories.
May, 1968:	In response to public environmental concern, WRC asks company for stipulation of new standards; company accepts, "prefers to have voluntary stipulation"; no mention of previous violations of permit.
December, 1968:	Excess effluents; company submits plans for control equipment to meet new standards by April, 1969.
July, 1969:	Company fails to install equipment by promised date due to "changed engineering plans." WRC sets new due date: April, 1970.
February, 1970:	Staff field report: effluent violates both old and new standards.
April, 1970:	Staff field report: effluent violates both old and new standards; no equipment installed by due date.
June, 1970:	Company requests postponement of due date; WRC notes the company "is moving expeditiously."
September, 1970:	Equipment installed.
October, 1970:	Staff field report: excess heavy metals in violation of 1953 standards.
December, 1970:	Staff field report: effluent violates permit standards.
Spring, 1971:	Environmental Law Society has been investigating WRC files; WRC passes resolution limiting citizen access to its files.
March, 1972:	Staff field report: effluents exceed standards up to two miles downstream. Company writes letter explaining difficulty of cleaning up. Effluents do not meet 1953 permit standards.
[October 1972:	Congress passes Federal Water Pollution Control Act Amendments (Clean Water Act, see Chapter 19) requiring states in the National Pollution Discharge Elimination System (NPDES) program to upgrade their state pollution regulatory systems.]

February 28, 1974:	NPDES discharge permit issued; includes stricter standards.
August 9, 1974:	NPDES discharge permit issued on 02/28/74 found to be in error.
January 8, 1976:	Monitoring requirements are revised. Verification that cadmium was no longer present in detectable quantities; cadmium monitoring requirement could be deleted.
January 20, 1977:	New NPDES permit is issued to Utilex on nickel and chromium discharges.
January 22, 1977:	Utilex files application with Air Pollution Control Commission regarding a blower-scrubber combination unit for ventilating copper cyanide plating bath.
January 28, 1977:	Utilex receives an "I" rating for inadequate permit compliance; effluent violates permit.
February 7, 1977:	A waste water treatment construction project is begun at Utilex.
June 22, 1977:	A sulfuric acid spill occurs at Utilex.
June 30, 1977:	Revised draft permit for Utilex. Standards of original permit based on Michigan Waste Criteria were more stringent than EPA guidelines. WRC agrees to loosen standards.
July 11, 1977:	Completion of waste water treatment system at Utilex.
July 13, 1977:	A letter from Utilex explaining corrective actions taken in response to the acid spill of 06/22/77. Utilex installed a lining for a retaining wall and replaced storage tanks.
July 29, 1977:	Completion of water waste treatment project is confirmed.
September 13, 1977:	Field waste water survey done; shows violations.
October 4, 1977:	Notice of non-compliance and Order to Comply sent to Utilex. Utilex found to have exceeded both its chromium and oil & grease maximums during July. Letter of explanation requested.
October 12, 1977:	Utilex writes that the parameters set forth by the permit have been attained.
October 12, 1977:	Utilex explains, as requested in the notice of non- compliance issued on 10/04/77, that the excesses of chromium and grease & oil were the result of a change in cleaning solutions.
November 8, 1977:	Utilex exceeds permit limits on ph acidity, zinc, and copper.
November 9, 1977:	Utilex writes that DNR limits for chrome, acid, and nickel had been exceeded due to a crack in a pipe sustained during demolition and replacement of roof.
December 6, 1977:	Letter from Water Quality Division stating that waste water survey of 09/13/77 indicated that limits on NPDES permit had been exceeded. A letter of explanation is requested.

December 21, 1977: Application to Air Pollution Commission for new pollution control system.

December 22, 1977: Notice of non-compliance with permit issued on 01/20/77. Chromium and nickel levels exceeded limits during the period from 10/14 to 10/25/77.

1978: Utilex closes, still in violation of standards.

COMMENTARY AND QUESTIONS

1. The WRC explanation of under-enforcement. When asked about the Utilex file in 1972, the WRC Executive Director complained that he "didn't have sufficient manpower and budget to enforce the law" and that his agency also lacked sufficient legal authority. The manpower and budget complaints were, to some extent, well-founded. By 1972, the WRC was administering thousands of permits with a mere handful of staff, although there had been enough staff to do almost 20 years of violation reports. The claim of insufficient legal authority seems to be contradicted by the broad grant of enforcement authority set forth in the WRC Act. The WRC, however, had no legal counsel on its own staff, and its only method of seeking enforcement was to refer cases to the offices of the attorney general or local county prosecutors for action. Perhaps ironically, a number of cases like Utilex were not referred for prosecution because the WRC staff had the erroneous belief that legally they had to be able to prove fish kills to mount a prosecution, and, as one field inspector said, "all of the fish were poisoned out of there in the 1950s."

2. Improving the system. The WRC case study and the Utilex file are paradigms of why enforcement of pollution control laws was weak during the pre-1970 years of traditional review and permit statutes. What is needed to improve the control of pollution by administrative agencies? A move toward more definite standards is surely one possibility. The next chapters in this book, especially Chapters 17 to 19, consider alternative approaches to standards and standard-setting. A further change is the development of technical expertise by pollution control agencies. The WRC staff was originally drawn from its base in the Department of Natural Resources (DNR), which historically was concerned with fish and game management, not pollution control. Over time, DNR and similar agencies throughout the nation have added staff with the necessary engineering and other technical backgrounds.

C. ALTERNATIVE APPROACHES TO STANDARD SETTING IN ENVIRONMENTAL PROTECTION LAWS

The Utilex case study presents an unflattering picture of environmental enforcement under a typical review and permit statute. The experience nationwide paralleled that of Michigan, and environmental quality seemed to be on a downward spiral despite the existence of state permit programs. Exacerbating local pressures for non-enforcement of environmental laws was the ominous threat of industrial flight from states that vigorously enforced environmental protection laws. As the national infrastructure and methods of transport of commodities improved, industries could convincingly threaten to relocate to avoid local conditions that were unfavorable – e.g. high taxes, high labor costs, unionization, or environmental controls that imposed high pollution control costs. States wishing to attract industries to bolster their local economies competed to attract firms by engaging in what some observers called "the race of laxity" in environmental protection laws.

A breakthrough was needed, and it came in the early 1970s in the form of major federal statutes that simultaneously addressed some of the structural failings of traditional review and permit statutes and removed much of the latitude for interstate industrial flight as a way of avoiding stringent pollution control laws. These new federal laws, the Clean Air Act (CAA) and the Clean Water Act (CWA), curbed the race of laxity by setting uniform national minimum pollution standards that all states must meet, or at their option, exceed. These new laws also focused on the problem of how to define and apply standards. The vague public welfare standards of traditional state review and permit laws were replaced by a new variety of more concrete national standards.

These new standards, and environmental standards more generally, can be grouped into two general types: *specification standards* and *performance standards*. Specification, or "available technology," based standards are requirements by legislatures or administrative agencies specifying the particular manufacturing control technology that must be installed and maintained by a pollution source. Specification standards possess the virtue of being very precisely defined, and compliance with them is easy to measure and enforce. Specification standards, however, tend to freeze existing technology and inhibit the development of new pollution control devices. Specification standards are often criticized as being inefficient both because they offer no room for the employment of lower-cost technologies and take no account of local variations.

Performance standards, on the other hand, specify the maximum permitted levels of pollution that sources can legally discharge. A source's operator may choose the most economically efficient and technologically accessible mix of controls to meet the relevant performance standard. If, for example, a fossil-fueled electric power plant has a sulfur oxides emission limitation of 1,000 pounds per hour,[8] it can seek to achieve it by burning low-sulfur coal, washing high-sulfur coal, installing technological devices such as baghouse units and wet scrubbers, or combining a number of these methods.[9] Under a "command and control" regulatory system, sources that exceed the performance standards will be subject to enforcement sanctions imposed by an administrative agency or court. Under an "economic incentive" system (see Chapter 20), violating sources would be required to pay an effluent tax, or purchase pollution rights from another source that has reduced its pollution below permit levels.

---

8. Such a permit limit might be averaged over 24 hours, and be backed up by a parts-per-million (ppm) and/or a pounds per million BTU measure.

9. The 1990 amendments to the Clean Air Act added the possibility that a plant can satisfy the performance standard by purchasing credits for reductions in emissions from another plant. This emissions trading is discussed in detail in Chapter 20.

The use of specification or performance standards in environmental laws usually occurs within the context of a particular type of approach to the problem of controlling pollution. Among other methods of addressing problems of air and water pollution, in the Clean Air Act of 1970 and Clean Water Act of 1972, Congress employed three fundamentally different approaches to the use of standards and the process of standard setting. First, in the CAA's Title II, Congress directly legislated numerical performance standards for motor vehicle exhaust emissions that were not capable of being met by existing technology.[10] Second, Congress, acting through the EPA, mandated the establishment of harm-based National Ambient Air Quality Standards (NAAQS) that must be met nationwide. The NAAQSs were to be set at levels that avoided injuries to human health and welfare.[11] Third, in the CWA, Congress and EPA created specific technology-based standards requiring polluters to employ particular pollution control equipment and processes.[12]

Although these three types of standards are the focus of Chapters 17 to 19, an advance thumbnail description of each of the approaches is helpful. In technology-forcing, government deliberately sets performance standards at a level higher than can be achieved using currently available equipment. In the Clean Air Act's regulation of pollution from new motor vehicles, Congress set specific emissions limitations (through percentage reductions from existing emissions) for pollutants produced by new motor vehicles. Presumably, if the auto manufacturers could not meet these performance standards by the statutory deadlines, they would not be able to sell new vehicles.[13] Merely to state this possibility is to suggest the impracticality of technology-forcing. In fact, technology-forcing is rarely employed, and even where it is utilized, its potentially drastic effects are tempered by statutory variances and congressional oversight. Congress, when it enacted the auto emissions rollback, was not engaging in pure technology-forcing. The catalytic converter – the device that actually did enable auto manufacturers to meet the congressional performance standards – had been demonstrated to be a viable technology for obtaining needed emissions reductions, although it had not been tested on a widespread basis when Congress enacted the legislation. Moreover, Congress included variance clauses in the statute that permitted postponement of compliance for up to two years if manufacturers could show that it was impossible despite their good faith efforts. Congress amended the Clean Air Act in 1977 to further delay the compliance dates.

---

10. See Chapter 17.

11. See Chapter 18.

12. See Chapter 19. These types of standard setting approaches, although distinctive, can be used alone or in combination. Some federal environmental statutes adopt only one of these methods, for example, the Safe Drinking Water Act is purely technology-based. Other statutes utilize two of these approaches or even, as with the Clean Air Act, all three.

13. Alternative sanctions, such as a per-vehicle monetary penalty, can be imagined. The effort to induce the automakers to embrace fuel efficient vehicles uses the penalty approach. Automakers pay a predetermined fine if vehicles they sell fail to satisfy the corporate average fuel efficiency (CAFE) standards. 15 U.S.C.A. §2002 et seq. The CAFE standards are not technology-forcing in the absolute sense. Carmakers can meet them by building smaller cars employing existing technology. If carmakers wish to continue to market as large a proportion of larger cars, however, technological innovation will be needed.

Harm-based performance standards are set at ambient levels that are devised to protect human health and the environment from the adverse effects of certain pollutants. After national ambient quality standards have been set, each state government allocates pollutant loads among sources, based on environmental quality modelling, in amounts that in the aggregate will not violate ambient quality standards. The uncertainties involved in setting ambient standards and allocating pollution loads renders the harm-based approach extremely difficult to administer. Harm-based regulation tends to be inequitable, moreover, in that identical pollution sources can receive different pollution allocations depending on their respective locations (e.g. factors relating to the current distribution of pollutants in the receiving medium or its meteorology or hydrology). On the other hand, the harm-based approach is economically efficient because duplicative reductions are avoided. The harm-based approach is essentially reactive with regard to scientific uncertainty (i.e. it minimizes false positives – see Chapter 2). It assumes that each environmental medium possesses an "assimilative capacity" that can neutralize certain levels of pollution. The burden of going forward to show the abuse of a particular medium's assimilative capacity is on government. Only discharges in excess of assimilative capacity are intolerable. Ambient standards are set based on current knowledge, and pollution is tolerated up to those standards, under the tacit assumption that future findings will be "good news," or that current levels of pollution can be reduced in the future if necessary. In order to compensate for the reactive nature of the harm-based approach, the Clean Air Act, for example, provides that ambient air quality standards must be set based on exposure levels experienced by the most sensitive populations, and that these standards must include an "adequate margin of safety."

The technology-based approach, on the other hand, is essentially proactive (i.e. it minimizes false negatives). Its underlying assumption is that all pollution is bad, but that immediate cessation of pollution is undesirable because economically achievable technology is not currently available to eliminate the pollution. Technology-based statutes, such as the Clean Water Act, typically require that pollution sources install the best available technology economically achievable (BAT), regardless of each source's particular location. Government is required to tighten technology-based standards when control technology improves, so that eventually BAT will theoretically be equivalent to "zero discharge." The technology-based approach is far easier to administrate than the harm-based approach because the latter's problematic environmental modelling and wasteload allocations are unnecessary. Moreover, the technology-based approach often seems more equitable because identical pollution sources must install identical control equipment. This also avoids any race of laxity. That same even-handedness in the treatment of pollution sources regardless of location also means that the technology-based approach tends to be economically inefficient. Costs are incurred to prevent pollution that is not harmful under the particular circumstances prevailing in some locations. Further objection to the technology-based approach is that it permanently enshrines existing technology, because polluters have no incentive to improve control technology, and government is loath to force technology in order to improve the state of the art.[14] Other critics of this approach charge that setting standards based on BAT, like harm-based standards, can lead to the degradation of currently pristine environments. For this reason, environmental standard-setting statutes generally contain "antideterioration" clauses.

Environmental standards are still usually linked to the polluters they regulate through permits issued by federal, state, or local agencies. At the present time, most permits are issued by state governmental agencies under federal-state partnerships, sometimes called cooperative federalism. In these programs EPA sets ambient quality or technology-based standards in the first instance, but authorizes state agencies to apply the standards to individual pollution sources. EPA customarily provides states that have accepted the primary permitting role with program grants, technical assistance, and backup monitoring and enforcement capability. If a state mismanages its permit program, EPA can veto individual permits, enforce statutes and permit requirements independently of the state, or, in extreme cases, cancel a state's primary enforcement authority.

Most permits contain three major parts: the standards themselves, compliance schedules, and monitoring and reporting requirements. Compliance schedules are often subdivided into enforceable chronological steps: e.g. contracts for purchase of pollution control equipment must be executed by date X; installation must be substantially complete by date Y; and standards must be met by date Z. Permits often include subsidiary clauses such as "upset clauses" (dealing with violations caused by unpredictable human or natural factors) or "reopener clauses" (dealing with supervening stricter standards imposed before the permit's expiration date). Permits may be canceled because of frequent or serious violations. A permit is, in effect, a contract between a governmental agency and a source that confers a temporary privilege to discharge[15] under certain stipulated conditions and subject to certain enforcement sanctions for violation. Weak or flawed permits properly can be condemned as being "licenses to pollute."

Most environmental permits are first issued in draft form for comment by the dischargers and public interest groups. Quasi-legislative "public" hearings are often provided on controversial draft permits. After a final permit has been issued, an objecting source or qualified environmental group may request a trial-type ("quasi-judicial") administrative hearing on the record. Cross-examination, limited discovery, and formal findings are common elements of such trial-type hearings. At the conclusion of a formal hearing, the hearing examiner reports her recommendations to the agency head, who makes the final decision. Final agency actions can then be presented to a court for judicial review (see Chapter 11).

Environmental standards contained in permits face a fundamental problem relating to "cumulative impacts" or, as Professor Sax calls it, the "nibbling effect." With the exception of permits based on ambient standards, where cumulative impacts are of the essence, each permittee's pollution load tends to be considered

14. Available-technology standards do create incentives for innovation by the small-but-growing pollution control industry, however.

15. E.g. Clean Water Act permits remain in effect for five years and until renewal, assuming timely renewal application.

in a vacuum. This can lead to undesirable cumulative impacts, especially because standards included in one permit become informal precedent for those in later, similar permits. Applications for permits to discharge dredged and fill material in wetlands under §404 of the Clean Water Act, for example, are considered case-by-case without regard to the regional effects of other granted, proposed, or potential §404 permits in nearby wetlands. In this manner valuable wetlands can be filled on a piecemeal basis without regard to the inevitable effect of overall wetlands decimation. In another example of the problems of cumulation, allocations of sulfur oxide emissions limitations based on an area's ambient air quality standard for sulfur oxides may ignore the synergistic reactions of those emissions and other uncontrolled pollutants in creating sulfates, which are not regulated "criteria pollutants." The cumulative mix can cause downwind acid precipitation. Thus in order to achieve environmental protection, standard-setting and permitting must be coordinated with a comprehensive system of environmental planning and management, preferably imposed on a regional basis (i.e. by airshed, watershed, etc.), including controls on land use.

D. MODERN PERMIT PROCESSES

There can be no single description of the modern permit process, because permits are used in so many aspects of American government. Within the range of activities that frequently have environmental impacts, almost all involve some sort of permitting process. Many land use regulations, for example, are enforced by boards that are authorized to issue permits for specified land uses. Similarly, most major emissions of effluents into either air or water are now the subject of permit processes.

Permit systems can be quite simple. In some communities, a local resident can write a letter to a local zoning board or planning agency requesting permission to engage in some activity. The board, usually an elected body, is almost universally required to provide some minimal notice of its agenda. Notice is given, a meeting is held, a vote is taken, and the permit may be granted.

Permit systems can also be quite complex. The first chart that follows is a graphic representation of the steps taken in considering an air emissions permit in Michigan in the mid-1980s.[16] The permits rendered under that system are part of Michigan's State Implementation Plan (SIP) under the Clean Air Act. The relevant portions of the CAA are the subject of more detailed study in Chapter 18.

For now, a brief summary of the way in which this part of the CAA operates is sufficient to understand the steps in the processing of a permit. Under the CAA, the EPA is required to set air quality standards setting an upper limit for a number of common air pollutants. The standards are set at levels calculated to prevent injury to human health and welfare, and are expressed as maximum concentrations of

16. The source of this chart and the supporting text is R. Abrams, American Legal Controls of Transboundary Pollution Affecting the Essex (Ontario) Region (monograph prepared for the Great Lakes Institute)(1984).

AIR PERMITS

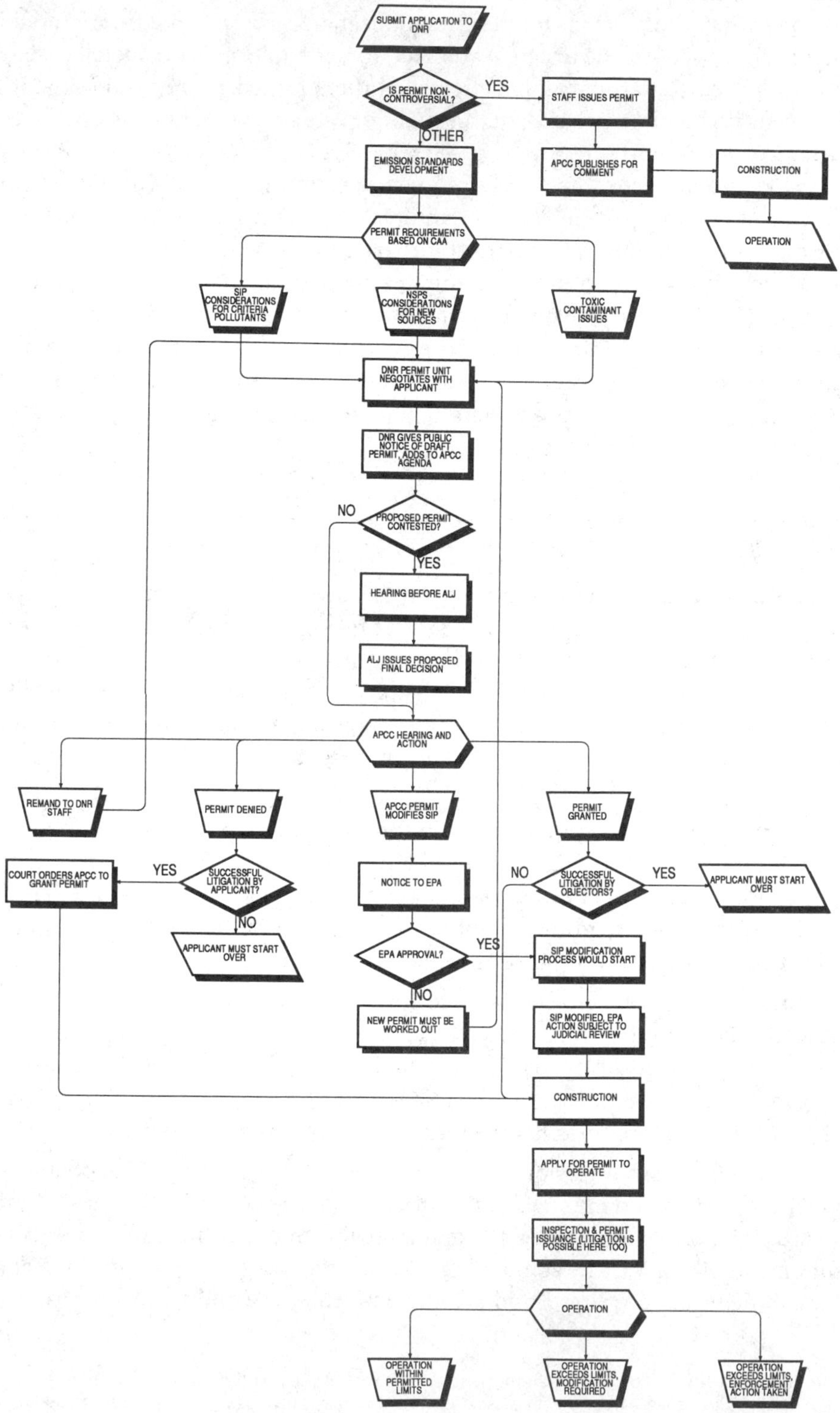
SUBMIT APPLICATION TO DNR
IS PERMIT NON-CONTROVERSIAL?
YES
STAFF ISSUES PERMIT
OTHER
EMISSION STANDARDS DEVELOPMENT
APCC PUBLISHES FOR COMMENT
CONSTRUCTION
OPERATION
PERMIT REQUIREMENTS BASED ON CAA
SIP CONSIDERATIONS FOR CRITERIA POLLUTANTS
NSPS CONSIDERATIONS FOR NEW SOURCES
TOXIC CONTAMINANT ISSUES
DNR PERMIT UNIT NEGOTIATES WITH APPLICANT
DNR GIVES PUBLIC NOTICE OF DRAFT PERMIT, ADDS TO APCC AGENDA
NO
PROPOSED PERMIT CONTESTED?
YES
HEARING BEFORE ALJ
ALJ ISSUES PROPOSED FINAL DECISION
APCC HEARING AND ACTION
REMAND TO DNR STAFF
PERMIT DENIED
APCC PERMIT MODIFIES SIP
PERMIT GRANTED
COURT ORDERS APCC TO GRANT PERMIT
YES
SUCCESSFUL LITIGATION BY APPLICANT?
NO
APPLICANT MUST START OVER
NOTICE TO EPA
NO
SUCCESSFUL LITIGATION BY OBJECTORS?
YES
APPLICANT MUST START OVER
EPA APPROVAL?
YES
SIP MODIFICATION PROCESS WOULD START
NO
NEW PERMIT MUST BE WORKED OUT
SIP MODIFIED, EPA ACTION SUBJECT TO JUDICIAL REVIEW
CONSTRUCTION
APPLY FOR PERMIT TO OPERATE
INSPECTION & PERMIT ISSUANCE (LITIGATION IS POSSIBLE HERE TOO)
OPERATION
OPERATION WITHIN PERMITTED LIMITS
OPERATION EXCEEDS LIMITS, MODIFICATION REQUIRED
OPERATION EXCEEDS LIMITS, ENFORCEMENT ACTION TAKEN

INSTALLATION PERMIT APPLICATION (IPA)

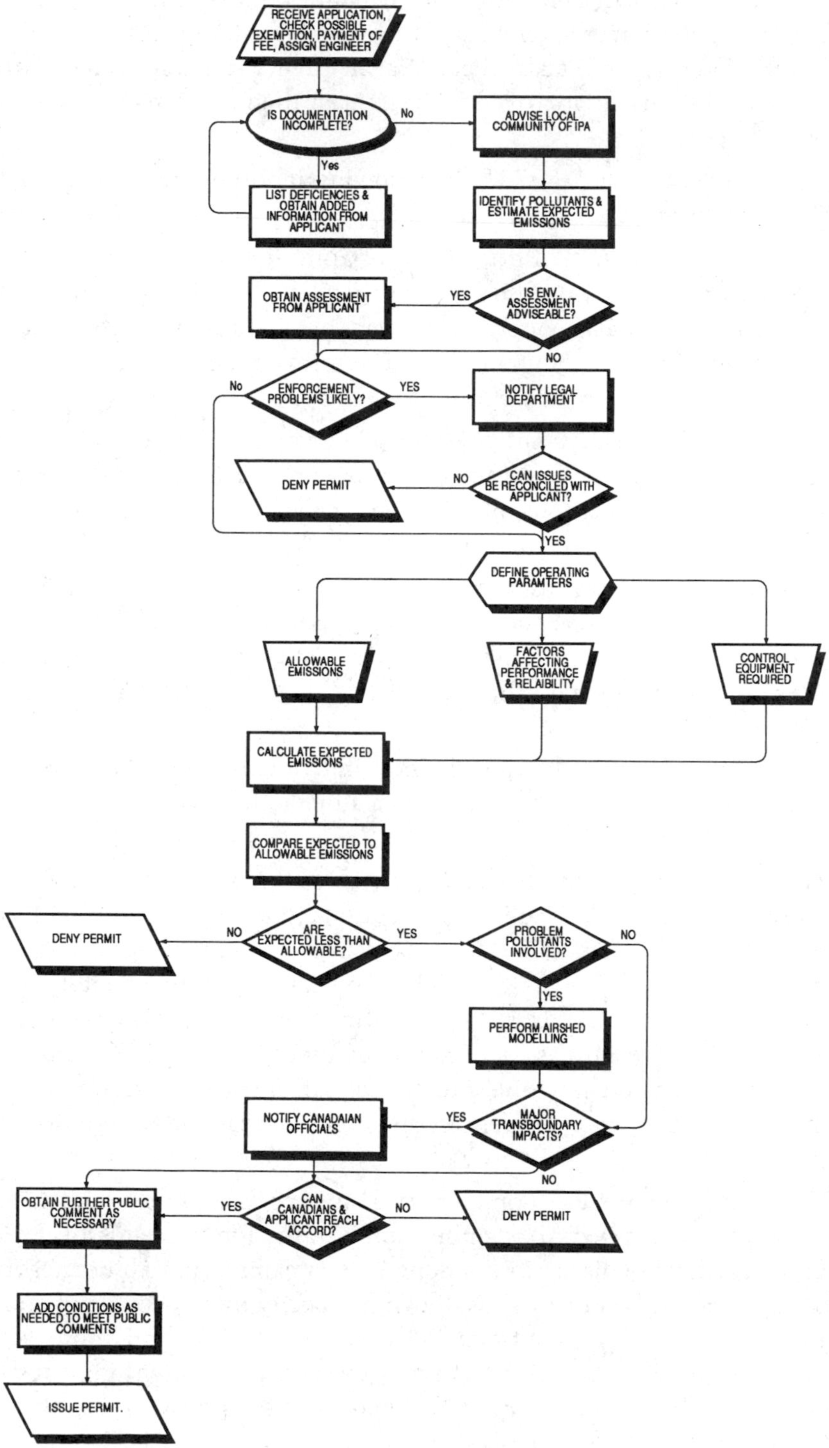

pollution, usually as a number of parts per million for each of the pollutants. States that elect to take on the regulatory burdens of the CAA (all states have done so) are required to come up with a plan for limiting pollution from all stationary sources (factories, etc., but not motor vehicles) that, in total, produce a resulting air quality that is as clean as that required by the federal air quality standards. That plan is the SIP, and it must be initially approved by the EPA; SIP modifications must also obtain EPA approval.

In reading the chart on page 732, the following annotated descriptions of terms and abbreviations will be helpful.

APCC is the Michigan Air Pollution Control Commission. As with the Michigan Water Resources Commission Act that was described previously in this chapter, the APCC is designed in a way that insures the representation of a number of varied points of view. The terms of commissioners and their qualifications are set by statute.

DNR is the Michigan Department of Natural Resources. The DNR is the overall agency charged with administering the air permit program. Many major policymaking decisions, however, are made by the APCC, rather than the DNR.

EPA is the United States Environmental Protection Agency. EPA's role in acting on individual permit applications is limited to cases involving SIP revisions, but its larger role in initially setting air quality standards fixes the baseline against which the cumulative effect of all permitting decisions must be measured.

ALJ is an administrative law judge. These individuals are DNR employees who sit as judges in cases contesting regulatory actions taken by the agency or by the APCC.

Assume that an applicant corporation wants to build a new "stationary source" installation that will produce added air pollution emissions. It begins by seeking a permit to install a new or modified stationary source. The application is directed to the air quality division of DNR, which immediately makes a vital threshold decision. A finding that the impact of granting the application would be "non-controversial" leads to a bypass of all subsequent pre-construction scrutiny of the proposal. The intent here is to divert matters having little or no air quality impact from the delay and expense inherent in the more elaborate procedure reserved for more significant cases.

Applications that are not "non-controversial" are then put through an administrative process that appears to be rather simple. Emission standards are developed and, through a series of discussions among DNR personnel and a bit of negotiation with the applicant, a draft permit is drawn up specifying a schedule of allowable emissions under the permit. (As you will see later from a second, more elaborate flow chart at page 734 *infra*, this part of the process is in fact anything but simple.) The draft permit is placed on the APCC agenda for its approval or denial.

After the APCC takes initial action, if either the applicant or a party objecting to the permit contests the agency's action on the draft permit, the matter is referred to an ALJ. The ALJ reviews the file, in some cases may hear additional evidence, and then makes a recommendation that goes back to the APCC for hearing and final decision.

The APCC again considers the draft permit, voting to grant, deny, or approve it with conditions or amendments. If it grants a permit that would result in a modification of Michigan's SIP, the matter is referred to EPA, which makes its own determination regarding whether the SIP modification can be allowed consistent with the requirements of the CAA. An EPA veto sends the process back to the agency staff to work out a new, more restrictive permit. Assuming that APCC, and if necessary EPA, approve permit issuance, their decisions are subject to judicial review in the regular judicial system. Assuming that the courts find nothing amiss, the permit to install is finally effective.

The remainder of the process is, in large measure, routine. When installation of the new equipment is completed, a permit to operate the facility must be obtained. This second permit process, however, is more in the nature of an engineering reality check. The system is inspected to insure that it was built in accordance with the permit. Then it is tested to insure that it performs as predicted. Although it is possible to attack the issuance of an operating permit, it is generally unavailing in the air pollution context. What remains is the possibility that the source will have to make further modifications in order to get operational emissions down to levels allowed by the permit.

As pointed out above, the steps going from permit application to draft permit seem simple, but are not. The flow chart on the facing page is a simplified version of one drawn by the Wayne County, Michigan, Board of Health's Air Pollution Control Division (APCD), describing its processing of commercial Installation Permit Applications (IPAs). The process resembles the typical internal chronology of state air pollution agencies.[17]

Some highlights of the APCD process stand out. Notice is given to potentially affected community residents very early in the process. The community is involved even before APCD has scrutinized the merits of the application. Similarly, APCD makes an early estimate of emissions to determine if a more complete environmental assessment should be obtained from the applicant before proceeding further.

The stage at which operating parameters are determined is the stage at which the most critical engineering analysis begins. The first element is determining what emissions are allowable. This is at times a very difficult determination. The APCD must limit the total concentration of pollutants in the airshed to levels below those set as standards by EPA under the CAA. The APCD has a very elaborate system of air quality monitoring already in place, so it has a clear sense of how badly polluted the air is at any given time. That same data provides a measure of what additional concentrations of pollution can be added to the air without violating the national

17. Michigan, owing to the early entry of the City of Detroit and Wayne County (comprising the greater Detroit area) into serious air pollution control efforts, has a unique system of bifurcated air pollution permitting responsibility. Permits for the metropolitan Detroit area are issued by the APCD with some DNR involvement, while permits for the rest of the state are issued by the DNR/APCC process outlined above.

requirements. It is often difficult to determine the effects on ambient air quality of new emissions that are sought in the permit application. This is an engineering problem, but may also be an allocational problem. Assuming that there remains some leeway for additional emissions, how much of that limited pollution disposal capacity is to be granted to this particular applicant via the issuance of a permit? Once the allowable emissions are determined, the applicant's engineering scheme is reviewed and the APCD makes its own independent assessment of the likely emissions from the proposed operation, as well as estimates of equipment performance and reliability. These calculations have to be made for each of several regulated pollutants.

If the applicant wishes to emit a pollutant that the APCD is having difficulty controlling,[18] modelling may be necessary. Modelling is a computer-based exercise in which data representing expected emissions for this and all other sources in the area are fed into a computer programmed to try to predict the resulting air quality outcomes. The program takes into account items such as topography, wind patterns, precipitation patterns, stack height, and a host of other variables. If the model predicts that problems will arise from granting the permit, the applicant is contacted and the problems are addressed.

By now, the process has developed to the point where all remaining applications that have not been denied have a realistic chance of meeting the legal requirements of the Clean Air Act as to the impact of emissions on local air quality. Here the Wayne County APCD process takes a special turn, due to the location of Canada just downwind to the east, across the Detroit River. A series of steps are added to allow for consultation with the Ontario Ministry of the Environment in order to take Canadian concerns into account. Thereafter the issue of further public involvement is taken up. IPAs that seem to have little or no effect on air quality or on the community are passed into the final permitting process, but all others are made the subject of either a formal public hearing or a formal written comment period. Based on public input, further modifications may be in order. As at many of the earlier stages of the process, an irreconcilable problem may result in permit denial.

The last point in the process is the drafting of the actual permit, with or without conditions. The conditions often address methods of operation (e.g. hours of operation, staffing, maintenance schedules), rather than more technical matters of engineering design that have been thrashed out along the way.

COMMENTARY AND QUESTIONS

1. The role of the public. The agencies involved are the primary representatives of the public interest in the permitting process. After all, as in many state laws, like the WRC Act, a mandate to protect the public interest is part of the typical agency's statutory charge. Is that an adequate guarantee that the public interest will be vindicated? If not, how extensive are the opportunities for public input into agency decisionmaking? The APCC flow chart does not even provide for any public input

18. The APCD's term "problem contaminant," although it is a general term, is directed primarily at pollutants as to which the national ambient air quality standards are not yet being met in the region. These problems of "non-attainment" are considered more fully in Chapter 18.

before the draft permit issues from the staff. Assuming that the staff did not solicit public input prior to that stage, why is subsequent public input likely to be viewed by the agency as hostile and counter-productive? Looking at the IPA procedure of the Wayne County APCD, is the public hearing or public comment period just prior to issuing the permit (with or without conditions) still timely? The fear is that the agency staff, after working out so many compromises with the applicant, will have become convinced that the permit as drawn has already addressed the interests of the public. What can interested citizens do? The answer is to become involved in the permit process during the period when the permit is in its formative stages. In the APCD setting, that means immediately after the initial notice that a permit is under consideration. How will citizens obtain the technical and financial resources needed to be full participants in the permit process? Doesn't this ask a lot of citizen volunteers?

2. The judicial role. What is the judicial role in the permit process? The ALJ procedure is a part of the administrative process, resembling a magistrate's hearing, and is not usually referred to as a "judicial" function. Judicial review, as described previously in Chapter 11, is highly deferential to the agency, in most circumstances upholding agency action unless that action is arbitrary and capricious. This, too, militates for public intervention in the early stages of the administrative process.

3. Pro forma permits to operate. The text describes the permit to install as the key decision and the permit to operate as more like an audit checking that the facility is built and will perform as planned. What is the justification for this arrangement? The basic answer is one regarding protection of sunk investment. It would be wasteful to have to build a project and then obtain the bad news that it will not be allowed to operate, rather than being told in advance that the plant as planned is inadequate. If that is the rationale, however, why have the second permit process at all? Why not simply make it a violation of law to construct a facility other than in accordance with its permit to install? One justification for the second permit is that it provides an opportunity to obtain a reliable indication (more reliable than mere engineering calculations) that the effluents from the plant will be as claimed. Operational testing also provides data for use in assessing other permit applications involving similar design characteristics.

Questions of standard-setting, at both macro and micro levels, recur throughout the succeeding chapters.

Chapter 16

REGULATORY CONTROL OF MARKET ACCESS: PESTICIDES AND TOXICS

Environmental protection in the United States is currently in a transition stage from regulatory strategies oriented toward pollution cleanup to strategies based on pollution prevention. It has become clear that waiting for problems to occur before acting (a strategy dominated by a desire to minimize "false positives") has resulted in serious and widespread damage to human health and the environment, as well as abandoned hazardous waste sites that can only be cleaned up at a cost running into many billions of dollars.

At the other end of the regulatory continuum, an unqualified minimization of false negatives (the pure preventive approach, through stringent precautionary control of a chemical's market access) would prohibit the introduction of new products, or the further sales of existing products, where they might conceivably be hazardous to human health or the environment. Such broad denials of market access based exclusively on speculative environmental damage would have a disabling effect on our system of market enterprise, especially in light of increasing foreign competition. There are many products, moreover, whose palpable economic and environmental benefits outweigh their uncertain environmental costs.

With one exception, federal environmental protection statutes adopting a market access strategy have attempted to achieve a balance between the environmental benefits and economic costs of denying market access to a particular product. The single exception is the so-called "Delaney Clause" of the Federal Food, Drug, and Cosmetic Act which prohibits the sale of any food additive that "is found to induce cancer when ingested by man or animal...."[1]

The two most important federal environmental market access statutes are the Federal Insecticide, Fungicide, and Rodenticide Act (FIFRA)[2] and the Toxic Substance Control Act (TSCA, or ToSCA).[3] Although these statutes take a similar approach to environmental regulation of toxics, they present instructive differences in practice because of their disparate approaches to the triggering mechanisms for regulation and enforcement. To a great extent, FIFRA places the burden of going forward – collecting data, establishing testing protocols, testing, and proving safety – on the industry itself under threat of potentially severe legal sanctions. ToSCA

---

1. 21 U.S.C.A. §348(c)(3)(A). The "Delaney Clause" is such a crude regulatory device that the Food and Drug Administration (FDA) has only applied it in a limited number of situations where certain explicit toxicological criteria have been satisfied, e.g., an increased risk of fatality, of "one in a million" (see Chapter 2).

2. 7 U.S.C.A. §135 et seq.

3. 15 U.S.C.A. §2601 et seq.

leaves most of this up to EPA. As you consider these laws, analyze which approach is more likely to be effective.

A. PESTICIDES: THE FEDERAL INSECTICIDE, FUNGICIDE, AND RODENTICIDE ACT

M. Miller, Federal Regulation of Pesticides, Environmental Law Handbook 473–483 (1989)

The benefits of pesticides, herbicides, rodenticides, and other economic poisons[4] are well known. They have done much to spare us from the ravages of disease, crop infestations, noxious animals, and choking weeds. Over the past two decades, however, beginning with Rachel Carson's Silent Spring, there has been a growing awareness of the hazards, as well as the benefits of these chemicals, which may be harmful to man and the balance of nature. The ability to balance these often conflicting effects is hampered by our lack of understanding of adverse side effects, a problem which will become even more acute during the next few years as the Congress in 1988 approved legislation calling for accelerated reviews by EPA of hundreds of chemicals registered before the stricter 1972 pesticide law.

Although pesticides have been subject to some degree of federal control since the Insecticide Act of 1910, relatively insignificant pesticide usage before World War II made regulation a low priority. This act was primarily concerned with protecting consumers from ineffective products or deceptive labeling, and contained no federal registration requirements or significant safety standards.

The war enormously stimulated the development and use of pesticides. The resulting benefits to health and farm production made pesticides a necessity and transformed the agricultural chemical industry into an influential sector of the economy. In 1947 Congress responded to the situation by enacting the more comprehensive Federal Insecticide, Fungicide, and Rodenticide Act (FIFRA) requiring that pesticides distributed in interstate commerce be registered with the United States Department of Agriculture (USDA), and containing a rudimentary labeling provision. The act, like its predecessor, was more concerned with product safety, but the statute did declare pesticides "misbranded" if they were necessarily harmful to man, animals, or vegetation (except weeds) even when properly used.

Three major defects in the new law soon became evident. First, the registration process was largely an empty formality since the Secretary of Agriculture could not refuse registration even to a chemical he deemed highly dangerous. He could register "under protest," but this had no legal effect on the registrant's ability to manufacture or distribute the product. Second, there was no regulatory control over the use of a pesticide contrary to its label, as long as the label itself complied with statutory requirements. Third, the secretary's only remedy against a hazardous product was a legal action for misbranding or adulteration, and – this was crucial – the difficult burden of proof was on him....

In 1964 the USDA persuaded Congress to remedy two of these three defects: the registration system was revised to permit the secretary to refuse to register a new

*Mr. Miller is a partner in the Washington D.C. firm of Baker and Hostetler.

4. Ed. note: The term "economic poisons" has been applied to pesticides since the 1940s. It reflects the "necessary evil" character of these substances, which FIFRA expresses in its weighing of benefits against costs.

product or to cancel an existing registration, and the burden of proof for safety and effectiveness was placed on the registrant. This considerably strengthened the act but made little difference in practice. The Pesticide Registration Division, a section of USDA's Agricultural Research Service, was understaffed...and the division was buried deep in a bureaucracy primarily concerned with promoting agriculture and facilitating the registration of pesticides. The cancellation procedure was seldom if ever used, and there was still no legal sanction against a consumer's applying the chemical for a delisted use.

The growth of the environmental movement in the late 1960s, with its concern about the widespread use of agricultural chemicals, overwhelmed the meager resources of the Pesticide Division. Environmental groups filed a barrage of law suits demanding the cancellation or suspension of a host of major pesticides such as DDT, Aldrin-Dieldrin, and the herbicide 2,4,5-T. This hectic and bewildering situation demanded a new approach to pesticide regulations.

On December 2, 1970, President Nixon signed Reorganization Order No. 3 creating the Environmental Protection Agency (EPA) and assigned to it the functions and many of the personnel previously under Interior, Agriculture, and other government departments. EPA inherited from USDA not only the Pesticides Division but also the environmental law suits against the Secretary of Agriculture....

The Federal Insecticide, Fungicide, and Rodenticide Act (FIFRA), as amended by the Federal Environmental Pesticide Control Act (FEPCA) of October 1982 and the FIFRA amendments of 1975, 1978, 1980, and 1988, is a complex statute. Terms have a meaning different from, or even directly contrary to, normal English usage. For example, the term "suspension" really means an immediate ban on a pesticide, while the harsher-sounding term "cancellation" indicates only the initiation of administrative proceedings which can drag on for years....

All new pesticide products used in the United States, with minor exceptions, must first be registered with EPA. This involves the submittal of the complete formula, a proposed label, and "full description of the tests made and the results thereof upon which the claims are based." The administrator must approve the registration if the following conditions are met:

(A) its composition is such as to warrant the proposed claim for it;

(B) its labeling and other materials required to be submitted comply with the requirements of this act;

(C) it will perform its intended function without unreasonable adverse effects on the environment; and

(D) when used in accordance with widespread and commonly recognized practice it will not generally cause unreasonable adverse effects on the environment.

The operative phrase in the above criteria is "unreasonable adverse effects on the environment," which was added to the act in 1972. This phrase is defined elsewhere in FIFRA as meaning "any unreasonable risk to man or the environment, taking into account the economic, social, and environmental costs and benefits of the use of the pesticide."...

The registration is not valid for all uses of a particular chemical. Each registration specifies the crops and insects on which it may be applied, and each use must be supported by research data on safety and efficacy. Registrations are for a five-year period, after which they automatically expire unless an interested party petitions for renewal, and, if requested by EPA, provides additional data indicating the safety of the product. For the past few years, pre-EPA registrations have been coming up for renewal under much stricter standards than when originally issued....

Until 1972 the government had no control over the actual use of a pesticide once it had left a manufacturer or distributor properly labeled. Thus, for example, a chemical which would be perfectly safe for use on a dry field might be environmentally hazardous if applied in a marshy area, and a chemical acceptable for use on one crop might leave dangerous residues on another. EPA's only recourse...was to cancel the entire registration – obviously too unwieldy a weapon to constitute a normal means of enforcement. A second problem was that a...chemical might be too dangerous for general use but could be used safely by trained personnel. There was, however, no legal mechanism for limiting its use only to qualified individuals.

Because of these problems, both environmentalists and the industry agreed that EPA should be given more flexibility than merely the choice between cancelling or approving a pesticide. Congress therefore provided for the classification of pesticides into general and restricted categories, with the latter group available only to Certified Applicators....

While the registration process may be the foundation of the FIFRA, cancellation represents the cutting edge of the law and attracts the most public attention. Cancellation is used to initiate review of a substance suspected of [posing] a "substantial question of safety" to man or the environment. During the pendency of the proceedings the product may be freely manufactured and shipped in commerce. A cancellation order, although final if not challenged within thirty days, usually leads to a public hearing or scientific review committee, or both, and can be quite protracted – a matter of years rather than months. A recommended decision from the agency hearing examiner (now called the administrative law judge) goes to the administrator or his delegated representative, the chief agency judicial officer, for a final determination on the cancellation....

A suspension order, despite its misleading name, is an immediate ban on the production and distribution of a pesticide. It is mandated when a product constitutes an "imminent hazard" to man or the environment, and may be invoked at any stage of the cancellation proceeding or even before a cancellation procedure has been initiated....

The purpose of an ordinary suspension is to prevent an imminent hazard during the time required for cancellation or change in classification proceedings. An ordinary suspension proceeding is initiated when the administrator issues notice to the registrant that he is suspending use of the pesticide and includes the requisite findings as to imminent hazard. The registrant may request an expedited hearing within five days of receipt of the administrator's notice. If no hearing is requested, the suspension order can take effect immediately thereafter and the order is not reviewable by a court....

The emergency suspension is the strongest action EPA can take under FIFRA and immediately halts all uses, sales, and distribution of the pesticide. An emergency suspension differs from an ordinary suspension in that the registrant is not given notice or the opportunity for an expedited hearing prior to the suspension order taking effect. The registrant is, however, entitled to an expedited hearing to determine the propriety of the emergency suspension. The administrator can only use this procedure when he determines that an emergency exists which does not allow him to hold a hearing before suspending use of a pesticide. This action has only been taken a few times....

Environmental Defense Fund v. Environmental Protection Agency
United States Court of Appeals for the District of Columbia Circuit, 1972
465 F.2d 528

LEVENTHAL, C.J. On December 3, 1970, petitioner Environmental Defense Fund (EDF), a non-profit New York Corporation, petitioned the Environmental Protection Agency under the Federal Insecticide, Fungicide, and Rodenticide Act, for the immediate suspension and ultimate cancellation of all registered uses of aldrin and dieldrin, two chemically similar chlorinated hydrocarbon pesticides. On March 18, 1971, the Administrator of the EPA announced the issuance of "notices of cancellation" for aldrin and dieldrin because of "a substantial question as to the safety of the registered products which has not been effectively countered by the registrant." He declined to order the interim remedy of suspension, pending final decision on cancellation after completion of the pertinent administrative procedure, in light of his decision that "present uses [of aldrin and dieldrin] do not pose an imminent threat to the public such as to require immediate action." EDF filed this petition to review the EPA's failure to suspend the registration....

The EPA's Statement points out that whereas a notice of cancellation is appropriate whenever there is "a substantial question as to the safety of a product," immediate suspension is authorized only in order to prevent an "imminent hazard to the public," and to protect the public by prohibiting shipment of an economic poison "so dangerous that its continued use should not be tolerated during the pendency of the administrative process." The EPA describes its general criteria for suspension as follows:

> This agency will find that an imminent hazard to the public exists when the evidence is sufficient to show that continued registration of an economic poison poses a significant threat of danger to health, or otherwise creates a hazardous situation to the public, that should be corrected immediately to prevent serious injury, and which cannot be permitted to continue during the pendency of administrative proceedings. An "imminent hazard" may be declared at any point in a chain of events which may ultimately result in harm to the public. It is not necessary that the final anticipated injury actually have occurred prior to a determination that an "imminent hazard" exists. In this connection, significant injury or potential injury to plants or animals alone could justify a finding of imminent hazard to the public from the use of an economic poison. The type, extent, probability and duration of potential or actual injury to man, plants, and animals will be measured in light of the positive benefits accruing from, for example, use of the responsible economic poison in human or animal disease control or food production.

Part II of the Statement of Reasons, captioned "Formulation of Standards," begins with the general standards deemed pertinent to the administration of FIFRA.

EPA points out that, in general, economic poisons, including those under present consideration, are "ecologically crude" – that is, by reason of technology limitations, [they] are toxic to non-target organisms as well as to pest life. Thus continued registration for particular ecologically crude pesticides "are acceptable only to the extent that the benefits accruing from use of a particular economic poison outweigh" the adverse results of effects on non-target species. EPA cites "dramatic steps in disease control" and the gradual amelioration of "the chronic problem of world hunger" as examples of the kind of beneficial effect to be looked for in balancing benefits against harm for specific substances. But it cautions that "triumphs of public health achieved in the past" will not be permitted to justify future registrations, recognizing that fundamentally different considerations are at work in evaluating use of a dangerous pesticide in a developed country such as the United States rather than in a developing non-industrial nation....

Laboratory tests with some substances have raised serious questions regarding carcinogenicity that "deserve particular searching" because carcinogenic effects are generally cumulative and irreversible when discovered. Threats presented by individual substances vary not only as to observed persistence in the environment but also as to environmental mobility – which in turn depends in part on how a particular pesticide is introduced into the environment either by ground insertion or by dispersal directly into the ambient air or water.

Based on the discussion of these general considerations, the EPA concludes that individual decisions on initial or continued registration must depend on a complex administrative calculus, in which the "nature and magnitude of the foreseeable hazards associated with use of a particular product" is weighed against the "nature of the benefit conferred" by its use....

The EDF's main argument [is that] while the Statement of Reasons sets forth, as a matter of EPA policy, that suspension decisions would be made only after the Administrator makes a preliminary assessment of imminency of hazard that includes a balancing of benefit and harm, yet when the EPA discussed aldrin and dieldrin, it inconsistently failed to identify any offsetting benefits, and limited itself to the reference to certain hazards.

The EPA concedes that the "thrust" of the Administrator's analysis related to the absence of any short run major hazards. But it parries that he "did refer to the purposes for which aldrin and dieldrin are used."

In light of his findings with respect to the absence of any foreseeable hazard, there was little need for the Administrator to go into detail in considering – as he had indicated he would do in suspension decisions... – "the positive benefits."

We are not clear that the FIFRA requires separate analysis of benefits at the suspension stage. We are clear that the statute empowers the Administrator to take account of benefits or their absence as affecting imminency of hazard. The Administrator's general decision to follow that course cannot be assailed as unreasonable. The suspension procedures of this agency, though in the abstract designed for emergency situations, seem to us to resemble more closely the judicial proceedings on a contested motion for a preliminary injunction, to prevail during the pendency of the litigation on the merits, rather than proceedings on an ex parte application for an emergency temporary restraining order. The suspension decision is not ordinarily one to be made in a matter of moments, or even hours or days. The statute contemplates at least the kind of ventilation of issues commonly had prior to decisions by courts that govern the relationships of parties pendente lite, during trial on the merits.

Judicial doctrine teaches that a court must consider possibility of success on the merits, the nature and extent of the damage to each of the parties from the granting or denial of the injunction, and where the public interest lies. It was not inappropriate for the Administrator to have chosen a general approach to suspension that permits analysis of similar factors. By definition, a substantial question of safety exists when notices of cancellation issue. If there is no offsetting claim of any benefit to the public, then the EPA has the burden of showing that the substantial safety question does not pose an "imminent hazard" to the public.

EDF is on sound ground in noting that while the EPA's general approach contemplates a decision as to suspension based on a balance of benefit and harm, the later discussion of aldrin and dieldrin relates only to harm.

The Administrator's mere mention of these products' major uses, emphasized by the EPA, cannot suffice as a discussion of benefits, even though the data before him...reflected the view that aldrin-dieldrin pesticides are the only control presently available for some twenty insects which attack corn and for one pest which poses a real danger to citrus orchards....

The interests at stake here are too important to permit the decision to be sustained on the basis of speculative inference as to what the Administrator's findings and conclusions might have been regarding benefits....

Our conclusion that a mere recitation of a pesticide's uses does not suffice as an analysis of benefits is fortified where, as here, there was a submission, by EDF, that alternative pest control mechanisms are available for such use. The analysis of benefit requires some consideration of whether such proposed alternatives are available or feasible, or whether such availability is in doubt.

The importance of an EPA analysis of benefits is underscored by the Administrator's flexibility, in both final decisions and suspension orders, to differentiate between uses of the product. Aldrin and dieldrin are apparently not viewed by the EPA as uniform in their benefit characteristics for all their uses. The Administrator had previously stopped certain uses of the pesticides in question in house paints, and in water use. These actions presumably reflected some evaluation of comparative benefits and hazards. The Administrator's reliance on the "pattern of declining gross use" itself indicates that for some purposes aldrin and dieldrin are or will soon become non-essential. Even assuming the essentiality of aldrin and dieldrin, and of the lack of feasible alternative control mechanisms for certain uses, there may be no corresponding benefit for other uses, which may be curtailed during the suspension period....

We do not say there is an absolute need for analysis of benefits. It might have been possible for EPA to say that although there were no significant benefits from aldrin-dieldrin, the possibility of harm – though substantial enough to present a long-run danger to the public warranting cancellation proceedings – did not present a serious short-run danger that constituted an imminent hazard. EPA's counsel offers this as a justification for its action.

If this is to be said, it must be said clearly, so that it may be reviewed carefully. Logically, there is room for the concept. But we must caution against any approach to the [statutory] term "imminent hazard"...that restricts it to a concept of crisis. It is enough if there is substantial likelihood that serious harm will be experienced during the year or two required in any realistic projection of the administrative process. It is not good practice for an agency to defend an order on the hypothesis that it is valid even assuming there are no benefits, when the reality is that some conclusion of benefits was visualized by the agency. This kind of abstraction pushes argument – and judicial review – to the wall of extremes, when realism calls for an awareness of middle ground.

COMMENTARY AND QUESTIONS

1. The subsequent suspension of aldrin and dieldrin. The court remanded the matter to EPA for further study. After considering the Advisory Committee Report and further public comments, EPA affirmed its previous decisions to cancel without interim suspension. Twelve months into the cancellation proceeding, the Administrator issued a notice of intent to suspend, and the suspension became final on October 1, 1974. EPA's suspension decision was substantially upheld in EDF v. EPA, 510 F.2d 1292 (D.C. Cir. 1975), where Judge Leventhal, emphasizing that "the responsibility to demonstrate that the benefits outweigh the risks is upon the proponents of continued registration," upheld EPA's finding that alternatives to aldrin-dieldrin were currently available. See also EDF v. EPA, 548 F.2d 998 (D.C. Cir. 1976) (heptachlor and chlordane).

2. Emergency suspension. The aldrin-dieldrin case was an ordinary suspension rather than an emergency suspension. EPA first used the emergency suspension procedure in 1979 when it suspended many uses of 2,4,5-T and Silvex. In Dow Chemical Co. v. Blum, 469 F. Supp. 892 (E.D. Mich. 1979), a federal district court, upholding EPA's emergency suspension, concluded that whereas an ordinary suspension proceeding is similar to a motion for a preliminary injunction during a lawsuit, the emergency suspension proceeding is similar to an application for a temporary restraining order. An emergency suspension order will be upheld if there is "minimal evidence in the record to support EPA's decision." But see Love v. EPA, 838 F.2d 1059 (9th Cir. 1988), where the emergency suspension of dinoseb in the Northwest was overturned because "EPA's evaluation of the relevant factors under FIFRA was incomplete and rushed and...simply not adequate to justify the emergency suspension...." Registration of dinoseb was later cancelled, but existing stocks were permitted to be used for limited purposes. See Northwest Food Processors Ass'n. v. EPA, 886 F.2d 1075 (9th Cir. 1989). Should a reviewing court be more or less deferential to an EPA decision on an ordinary suspension because of the existence of the emergency suspension device?

3. Imminent hazards. FIFRA operates as a threshold preventive, in that it applies "up front" before a potentially dangerous pesticide is introduced into commerce. On the other hand, FIFRA's standards are not pure safety criteria because the economic benefits and costs of regulation are weighed at the registration, cancellation, and suspension stages. Does the "imminent hazard" standard serve as a margin of safety where economic benefits are tangible, and potential environmental harms are uncertain? EPA's interpretive statement on "imminent hazard" is highly precautionary, justifying action whenever there is "significant injury or potential injury to plants or animals alone...." Another administrative mechanism for erring on the side of safety is EPA's "Special Review" process (formerly called "Rebuttable Presumption Against Registration," or RPAR), in which evidence developed by EPA or a third party that a pesticide exceeds specified "risk criteria" will raise a presumption against registration or in favor of cancellation or suspension. 40 CFR Part 154. Moreover, the EDF v. EPA court adds that once a notice of cancellation is issued – if there is no offsetting claim of benefits – then "EPA has the burden of showing that the substantial safety question does not pose an 'imminent hazard' to the public." It seems clear, as the court points out, that "imminent hazard" does not mean "crisis." Operationally it means that the greater the amount of credible evidence EPA has about potential dangers posed by a registered pesticide, the more quickly and easily its use can be discontinued, and the more pronounced benefits must be in order to justify its continued use. Recalling the Huber excerpt in Chapter 2, at page 81 *supra*, would Huber approve of a regulatory scheme that allows a product to be marketed, but makes quick protective withdrawal possible once negative evidence appears?

"Imminent hazard" is one of those all-important statutory terms that defy precise analysis but facilitate administrative and judicial determinations regarding uncertainty and burdens of proof, creating the "common law" of particular statutes. The "imminent hazard" phrase serves a similar function in CERCLA (see Chapter 21) and RCRA (see Chapter 22). Another such term is "endanger." See Ethyl Corp. v. EPA, 541 F.2d 1 (D.C. Cir. 1976).

4. The role of benefits in a suspension proceeding. Must benefits be analyzed in a suspension proceeding? Judge Leventhal's opinion is not consistent on this point. Does it depend on whether evidence of available alternatives has been introduced? If there is no short-term danger, why bother analyzing benefits at all? Is it possible to distinguish clearly between short and long-term hazards?

5. Registration of exports. Whereas imported pesticides are subject to FIFRA registration requirements, exports are excluded from the regulatory provisions of the Act; e.g., Kepone was unregulated because it was not intended for domestic use. Should DDT be permitted to be exported to a developing nation where malaria is a serious problem, if DDT is the only affordable malaria-control alternative? To what extent should the transboundary character of pollution from persistent pesticides be considered in such judgments?

6. Paying for suspension. A controversial provision of the 1972 amendments required EPA to indemnify registrants, formulators, and end users of cancelled or suspended pesticides for remaining stocks that were not permitted to be exhausted. Needless to say, this provision had a chilling effect on cancellations and suspensions. In the 1988 FIFRA amendments, the indemnity requirement was deleted except for end users (farmers and applicators).[5]

7. FIFRA and pre-emption. There are three issues involved here. First, do FIFRA's labeling requirements pre-empt state common law tort suits based on inadequate labeling ("failure to warn")? Courts are split on this issue, although the general rule is that a license or permit will not insulate a defendant from obligations imposed by common law or other statutes. Thus, FIFRA registration is ordinarily no defense to a tort action or to an action demanding compliance with NEPA.[6] The second issue is whether states can impose labeling and packaging requirements stricter than

5. Pub. L. 100–532 §501.

6. Compare *Ferebee*, page 193 *supra* (state suit not pre-empted) with Pappas v. Upjohn, 32 ERC 1815 (11th Circuit 1991)(state suit pre-empted); Save Our Ecosystems v. Clark, 747 F.2d 1240 (9th Cir. 1984)(FIFRA does not avoid duty to comply with NEPA). See also Howarth, Pre-emption And Punitive Damages: The Conflict Continues Under FIFRA, 136 U. Pa. L. Rev. 1301 (1988) (favoring pre-emption).

those imposed by EPA under FIFRA. Thus far, courts have upheld more restrictive state pesticide registration requirements.[7] Finally, can municipalities ban or limit the use of pesticides registered under FIFRA? The Supreme Court resolved a conflict among the federal circuits by unanimously holding, in Wisc. Public Intervenor v. Mortier, 111 S. Ct. 2476 (1991), noted at page 478 *supra*, that municipalities are not pre-empted by FIFRA from controlling pesticide use:

> FIFRA nowhere seeks to establish an affirmative permit scheme for the actual use of pesticides. It certainly does not equate registration and labeling requirements with a general approval to apply pesticides throughout the Nation without regard to regional and local factors like climate, population, geography, and water supply. Whatever else FIFRA may supplant, it does not occupy the field of pesticide regulation in general or the area of local use permitting in particular. 111 S. Ct. at 2486.

Although the local ordinance upheld in the *Mortier* case involved the legality of a permit requirement for aerial spraying on private lands, the opinion appears to condone local pesticide bans as well.

8. FIFRA as a licensing statute. FIFRA, as commentators have noted, creates a unique form of licensing system. As Professor Applegate has written:

> If as a general rule manufacturers can develop toxicology information more cheaply than EPA, or if the cost is more efficiently or equitably borne by them and their customers, then it makes sense to assign the burden of proof to the manufacturer. In regulatory systems, shifting the burden of proof from the government to industry is typically accomplished by enacting a licensing or screening system. In the case of toxic substances, chemical producers would have to demonstrate the safety of their products before these products could be introduced into commerce. Licensing, therefore, not only provides an incentive to development of new information; it also shifts the cost of development away from government to a group that in theory has the capacity to absorb and spread the loss.
>
> Of the toxics statutes, only FIFRA has a true licensing scheme. Before pesticides can be sold, they must be registered and EPA must determine that they do not present an unreasonable risk. The registrant has the initial and continuing burden of demonstrating safety, though EPA has an initial burden of production in a cancellation proceeding and must ultimately be able to support its conclusions by substantial evidence. By placing the burden on the registrant, EPA is able to obtain whatever information it deems necessary to assess whether the chemical poses an unreasonable risk through the simple expedient of specifying data requirements for registration. EPA needs only the most general justification for these requirements, given the breadth of factors relevant to the unreasonable risk determination. Furthermore, the data requirements apply to all pesticides, eliminating the need to demand

7. See Nat'l Agric. Chem. Ass'n. v. Rominger, 500 F. Supp 445 (E.D. Cal. 1980) and N.Y. State Pesticide Coalition v. Jorling, 874 F.2d 115 (2d Cir. 1989); see also Stever, Law of Chemical Regulation and Hazardous Waste §3.08 (1991) for an interesting discussion of this question.

> data on a chemical-by-chemical basis. This technique obviously brings the full profit motive to bear in developing adequate data in an expeditious manner.[8]

Nevertheless, FIFRA, like all licensing statutes, has two major disadvantages:

> First, the premarket phase of product development is the time when the least information is known about a chemical's long-term effects. Without indications of chronic toxicity, it is hard to justify lengthy, expensive bioassays. Second, a licensing scheme intercepts only new or prospective risks. Since older chemicals are likely to be less well-tested relative to more recently licensed chemicals, the lack of data on existing chemicals constitutes a major gap in an information generation system. This problem can be resolved by a retroactive licensing arrangement like FIFRA's re-registration process.... Recognizing that licensing fails to generate any information for existing chemicals or post-license information for new ones, FIFRA established a five-year registration period after which reconsideration is necessary. This provision has not generated large amounts of data, however, because EPA has never used the five-year period aggressively for this purpose. Indeed, EPA has lacked sufficient resources to do much more than keep current on new registrations and cancellations.[9]

These drawbacks in the FIFRA licensing system further emphasize the importance of the cancellation and suspension mechanisms. Ultimately, the best way to prevent pesticide pollution is probably Integrated Pest Management (IPM) – placing primary reliance on biological and management controls, with limited applications of pesticides permitted only when absolutely necessary and where least likely to cause environmental damage. Genetic engineering also shows promise in redesigning plants for immunity to traditional pests.

B. REGULATING MARKET ACCESS OF TOXICS: THE TOXIC SUBSTANCES CONTROL ACT

The Toxic Substances Control Act of 1976 (ToSCA) extended the market access concept to most new and existing chemicals. Both environmental and industry groups lobbied heavily during congressional deliberations over ToSCA. The result is perhaps the most complex, confusing, and ineffective of all our federal environmental protection statutes.

R. Druley and G. Ordway, The Toxic Substances Control Act, 1–4 (1977)

As summarized by the House Interstate and Foreign Commerce Committee Report, major provisions of the Act:

- Require manufacturers and processors of potentially harmful chemical substances and mixtures to test the substances or mixtures, as required by rules

8. Applegate, The Perils of Unreasonable Risk: Information, Regulatory Policy, and Toxic Substances Control, 91 Colum. L. Rev. 261, 308–309 (1991)(hereafter "Applegate").

9. Id., 312–313.

issued by the Administrator of [EPA], so that their effect on health and the environment may be evaluated.

- Require manufacturers of new chemical substances and manufacturers and processors of existing chemical substances for significant new uses to notify the Administrator ninety days in advance of commercial production.
- Authorize delays or restrictions on the manufacture of a new chemical substance if there is inadequate information to evaluate the health or environmental effects of the substance and if in the absence of such information, the substance may cause or significantly contribute to an unreasonable risk to health or the environment.
- Authorize the Administrator to adopt rules to prohibit the manufacture, processing, or distribution of a chemical substance or mixture, to require labeling, or to regulate the manner of disposal of a chemical substance or mixture for which there is a reasonable basis to conclude that it causes or significantly contributes to an unreasonable risk to health or the environment.
- Authorize the Administrator to obtain injunctive relief from a United States district court to protect the public and the environment from an imminently hazardous chemical substance or mixture.
- Authorize the Administrator to require manufacturers and processors to submit reports and maintain records respecting their commercially produced chemical substances and mixtures, to maintain records respecting adverse health or environmental effects of such substances and mixtures, and to provide available health and safety data on them.
- Require manufacturers and processors of chemical substances and mixtures to immediately notify the Administrator of information indicating that one of their substances or mixtures causes or contributes to a substantial risk to health or the environment.
- Permit administrative inspections to enforce the bill and authorize court actions for seizures of chemical substances and mixtures which have been manufactured or distributed in violation of the requirements of the bill or of rules and orders promulgated under it.
- Permit citizens to bring suits to obtain compliance with the bill.
- Permit federal district courts to order the Administrator to initiate rulemaking proceedings in response to citizen petitions.
- Set up procedural mechanisms to insure that all interested persons have an opportunity to participate in the agency rulemaking proceedings.
- Provide protection for employees who cooperate in the enforcement of the bill.
- Provide for evaluation on a continuing basis of the effects on employment of actions taken under the bill....

TESTING AND PREMARKET NOTIFICATION...

Under the act, EPA cannot require testing of every chemical. EPA must first find that there may be a risk or that there may be extensive human or environmental exposure and that information is lacking and testing is necessary. Given these findings, EPA must issue a rule requiring a manufacturer to perform testing and specifying the actual form of testing.

EPA is to issue its testing rules with the advice of an inter-agency committee, which will recommend testing priorities. Although the committee's advice is not binding, EPA is required to publish reasons for not requiring testing of certain specially designated compounds given high priority by the committee.

One of the key provisions of the Act is the section requiring manufacturers to provide EPA with data in advance of marketing. Chemical manufacturers must provide at least a 90-day notice before starting the manufacture of a new chemical or marketing a chemical for a new use as prescribed by EPA.

In order to determine what constitutes a new chemical that must be reported to EPA, EPA must publish an inventory list of chemicals known to be manufactured in the U.S. If a substance is not listed, it is to be considered a new chemical, and its planned production must be reported.

Under certain circumstances EPA can block the marketing of a chemical product pending the completion of testing. If a test order has been issued, test data must be submitted at the same time as the pre-market notification. Because testing may often require several years, this is a much more stringent requirement than simple 90-day notification.

EPA may also publish a hazardous substance list and can even do so by generic names. A manufacturer planning to market a substance included in the list must submit data to show that it is not a hazard for health or the environment.

Finally, if EPA determines upon notification that it has insufficient data on which to base a safety judgment, it may issue a proposed order to block production until testing is completed. The manufacturer may protest this order, and in this case EPA must apply to a federal district court for an injunction in order to block production.

Experimental and research chemicals produced in small quantities are exempt from the premarket notification requirements of the Act.

[ToSCA also does not apply to the following products regulated under other federal laws: firearms and ammunition; food, food additives, drugs and cosmetics; meat and meat products; eggs and egg products; poultry and poultry products; pesticides; tobacco or tobacco products; and nuclear materials.]

Chemical Manufacturers Association v. Environmental Protection Agency
United States Circuit Court of Appeals for the D.C. Circuit (1988)
859 F.2d 977

WALD, C.J. Petitioners, Chemical Manufacturers Association and four companies that manufacture chemicals (collectively "CMA"), seek to set aside a rule promulgated by the Environmental Protection Agency. This Final Test Rule was promulgated under §4 of the Toxic Substances Control Act. The final test rule required toxicological testing to determine the health effects of the chemical 2-ethylhexanoic acid ("EHA")....

We uphold EPA's interpretation of TSCA as empowering the Agency to issue a test rule on health grounds where it finds a more-than-theoretical basis for suspecting that the chemical substance in question presents an "unreasonable risk of injury to health." This, in turn, requires the Agency to find a more-than-theoretical basis for concluding that the substance is sufficiently toxic, and human exposure to it is sufficient in amount, to generate an "unreasonable risk of injury to health." We hold, further, that EPA can establish the existence and amount of human exposure on the basis of inferences drawn from the circumstances under which the substance is manufactured and used. EPA must rebut industry-supplied evidence attacking those inferences only if the industry evidence succeeds in rendering the probability of exposure in the amount found by EPA no more than theoretical or speculative. The probability of infrequent or even one-time exposure to individuals can warrant a test rule, so long as there is a more-than-theoretical basis for determining that exposure in such doses presents an "unreasonable risk of injury to health." Finally, we hold that the Agency correctly applied these standards in this case and that its findings are supported by substantial evidence. Consequently, we affirm the Final Test Rule.

TSCA provides for a two-tier system for evaluating and regulating chemical substances to protect against unreasonable risks to human health and the environment. Section 6 of the Act permits EPA to regulate a substance that the Agency has found "presents or will present an unreasonable risk of injury to health or the environment." Section 4 of the Act empowers EPA to require testing of a suspect substance in order to obtain the toxicological data necessary to make a decision whether or not to regulate the substance under §6. The Act provides, not surprisingly, that the level of certainty of risk warranting a §4 test rule is lower than that warranting a §6 regulatory rule. EPA is empowered to require testing where it finds that the manufacture, distribution, processing, use or disposal of a particular chemical substance "may present an unreasonable risk of injury to human health or the environment." The Agency's interpretation of this statutory standard for testing is the central issue in this case.

One of the chief policies underlying the Act is that adequate data should be developed with respect to the effect of chemical substances and mixtures on health and the environment and that the development of such data should be the responsibility of those who manufacture and those who process such chemical substances and mixtures.

The statute establishes an Interagency Testing Committee, comprised of scientists from various federal agencies, to recommend that EPA give certain chemicals "priority consideration" for testing. Under §4, the Agency "shall by rule require that testing [of a particular chemical] be conducted" if three factors are present: (i) activities involving the chemical "may present an unreasonable risk of injury to health or the environment"; (ii) "insufficient data and experience" exist upon which to determine the effects of the chemical on health or environment; and (iii) testing is necessary to develop such data. The companies that manufacture and process the substance are to conduct the tests and submit the data to the Agency. Costs of the testing are to be shared among the companies, either by agreement or by EPA order in the absence of agreement.

A test rule promulgated under §4 is subject to judicial review in a court of appeals.... A test rule may be set aside if it is not "supported by substantial evidence in the rulemaking record...taken as a whole."

EHA is a colorless liquid with a mild odor. It is used exclusively as a chemical intermediate or reactant in the production of metal soaps, peroxy-esters and other products used in industrial settings. EHA itself is totally consumed during the manufacture of these products; as a result, no products offered for sale to industry or to consumers contain EHA.

The Interagency Testing Committee first designated EHA for priority consideration for health effects tests on May 29, 1984. The Committee based its recommendation in part on the structural similarity of EHA to chemicals known to cause cancer in test animals and on its finding that insufficient information existed concerning the chronic health effects of EHA. Subsequently, EPA held two public meetings on EHA. During these meetings, in which persons representing the petitioners made appearances, EPA sought information on a variety of issues relating to EHA uses, production and human exposure.

EPA issued a proposed test rule on May 17, 1985. The rule proposed a series of tests to ascertain the health risks of EHA, and it set out proposed standards for the conduct of those tests. EPA based the Proposed Test Rule on a finding that EHA "may present an unreasonable risk" of subchronic toxicity (harm to bodily organs from repeated exposure over a limited period of time), oncogenicity (tumor formation) and developmental toxicity (harm to the fetus). As to subchronic toxicity, EPA cited studies suggesting that both EHA and chemicals structurally similar to it cause harm to the livers of test animals. As to oncogenicity, EPA cited studies suggesting that chemicals structurally analogous to EHA cause cancer in laboratory animals. As to developmental toxicity, EPA cited studies indicating that both EHA and its chemical analogues have produced fetal malformations in test animals.

The Proposed Test Rule also addressed the question of whether humans are exposed to EHA, a question of critical importance to this case. The Agency acknowledged that, since no finished products contain EHA, consumer exposure is not a concern. It likewise discounted the dangers of worker exposure to EHA vapors. The Agency based its Proposed Test Rule solely on the potential danger that EHA will come in contact with the skin of workers. As evidence of potential dermal exposure, the Agency noted that approximately 400 workers are engaged in the manufacture, transfer, storage and processing of 20 to 25 million pounds of EHA per year. Further, rebutting claims by industry representatives that gloves are routinely worn during these activities, EPA noted that worker hygiene procedures "can vary widely throughout the industry," that workers are not required by existing federal regulations to wear gloves, and that the industry had not monitored work sites for exposure to EHA.

A public comment period commenced with the publication of the Proposed Test Rule and ended on July 16, 1985. EPA held a public meeting on October 8, 1985, to discuss issues related to the Proposed Test Rule. Industry representatives submitted extensive comments on July 15, 1985, and January 17, 1986. Before publication of the Final Test Rule, EPA received notice of a new study purporting to present further evidence of the potential developmental toxicity of EHA....

EPA published the Final Test Rule for EHA on November 6, 1986. The Rule required a 90-day subchronic toxicity test, a developmental toxicity test, and a pharmacokinetics test....The pharmacokinetics study required by the rule entailed the oral and dermal administration of EHA to experimental animals at low and high doses. The subchronic toxicity study involved administering EHA to animals in graduated daily doses over a period of 90 days. The developmental toxicity tests entailed administering EHA orally in various doses during the pregnancy of experimental animals. All studies were to be conducted in accordance with EPA standards. Results were to be submitted by certain deadlines, the last of which was 18 months after the effective date of the Final Test Rule....

The Toxic Substances Control Act requires EPA to promulgate a test rule under §4 if a chemical substance, *inter alia*, "may present an unreasonable risk of injury to health or the environment." The parties both accept the proposition that the degree to which a particular substance presents a risk to health is a function of two factors: (a) human exposure to the substance, and (b) the toxicity of the substance. See Ausimont U.S.A., Inc. v. EPA, 838 F.2d 93, 96 (3d. Cir. 1988). They also agree that EPA must make some sort of threshold finding as to the existence of an "unreasonable risk of injury to health." The parties differ, however, as to the manner in which this finding must be made. Specifically, three issues are presented.

The first issue is whether, under §4 of TSCA, EPA must first find that the existence of an "unreasonable risk of injury to health" is more probable than not in order to issue a test rule. CMA argues that the statute requires a more-probable-than-not finding. EPA disagrees, contending that the statute is satisfied where the existence of an "unreasonable risk of injury to health" is a substantial probability – that is, a probability that is more than merely theoretical, speculative, or conjectural.

The second issue is whether, once industry has presented evidence tending to show an absence of human exposure, EPA must rebut it by producing direct evidence of exposure. CMA claims that, when industry evidence casts doubt on the existence of exposure, the burden of production shifts back to EPA, which must produce direct evidence documenting actual instances in which exposure has taken place. EPA, on the other hand, argues that it can make the requisite finding of exposure based solely on inferences drawn from the circumstances under which a chemical substance is manufactured and used.

The third issue is whether the Agency has authority to issue a test rule where any individual's exposure to a substance is an isolated, non-recurrent event. CMA argues that, even if EPA presents direct evidence of exposure, the Act precludes issuance of a test rule where exposure consists only of rare instances involving brief exposure. EPA contends, on the other hand, that the Act does not require in all circumstances a risk of recurrent exposure....

As to the first issue in this case,...[b]oth the wording and structure of TSCA reveal that Congress did not expect that EPA would have to document to a certainty the existence of an "unreasonable risk" before it could require testing. This is evident from the two-tier structure of the Act. In order for EPA to be empowered to *regulate* a chemical substance, the Agency must find that the substance "presents or will present an unreasonable risk of injury to health or the environment." The *testing* provision at issue here, by contrast, empowers EPA to act at a lower threshold of certainty than that required for regulation. Specifically, testing is warranted if the substance "*may* present an unreasonable risk of injury to health or the environment." Thus, the language of §4 signals that EPA is to make a probabilistic determination of the presence of "unreasonable risk."

The legislative history of TSCA compels a further conclusion. It not only shows that "unreasonable risk" need not be a matter of absolute certainty; it shows the reasonableness of EPA's conclusion that "unreasonable risk" need not be established to a more-probable-than-not degree.

A House Report on the version of the bill that eventually became TSCA underscores the distinction between the §6 standard and the §4 standard. To issue a test rule, EPA need not find that a substance actually does cause or present an "unreasonable risk."

> Such a finding requirement would defeat the purpose of the section, for if the Administrator is able to make such a determination, regulatory action to protect against the risk, not additional testing, is called for. H.R. Rep. No.1341, 94th Cong., 2d Sess. 17–B. Toxics: Tosca18 (1976).

The House Report also contains signals indicating that Congress expected EPA to act even when evidence of "unreasonable risk" was less than conclusive. According to that report, the word "may" in §4 was intended to focus the Agency's attention on chemical substances *"about which there is a basis for concern, but about which there is inadequate* information to reasonably predict or determine the effects of the substance or mixture on health or the environment." Id. at 17 (emphasis added). The Conference Committee Report re-emphasized that the statutory language focused the Agency's attention on substances "about which there is a basis for concern." H.R. Conf. Rep. No. 1679, 94th Cong., 2d Sess. 61 (1976).

These indications of congressional intent illustrate that EPA's reading of TSCA is a permissible one. Congress intended to authorize testing where the existence of an "unreasonable risk" could not yet be "reasonably predicted." The Agency's determination that it is empowered to act where the existence of an "unreasonable risk" cannot yet be said to be more probable than not is entirely consistent with that expression of intent. The EPA interpretation is likewise consistent with the level of certainty suggested by the phrase "basis for concern." To accept the CMA's position would require the Agency to gather "adequate" information to make a reasonable prediction or determination of risk before issuing a test rule. To say the least, this is not mandated by the statutory history, which indicates Congress's desire that EPA act on the basis of rational concern even in the absence of "adequate" information that an unreasonable risk existed. Section 4 may permissibly be read to authorize issuance of a test rule on the basis of less than more-probable-than-not evidence about a potentially unreasonable risk to health.

This conclusion is further bolstered by the legislative history underlying §6. If CMA were correct that EPA must make a more-probable-than-not finding of risk under §4's "may present" language, then it would logically follow that §6 – which contains the term "presents or will present an unreasonable risk" – must require an even stronger than more-probable-than-not demonstration of "unreasonable risk." Yet neither §6 nor its legislative history indicate any such super-requirement of certainty. Indeed, §6 states expressly that the Agency need only find a "reasonable basis" to conclude that an "unreasonable risk" exists. A "reasonable basis" requirement is certainly no more demanding than a more-probable-than-not requirement; indeed the phrase suggests a less demanding standard. This interpretation is confirmed by the House Report, which states that an EPA finding of "unreasonable risk" under §6 is not expected to be supported by the same quantum of evidence as is customary in administrative proceedings.... In sum, the standard Congress set for §6 regulation, that the chemical "will present an unreasonable risk," is no more rigorous (and arguably is less rigorous) than a more-probable-than-not finding. It follows as a matter of course that §4's "may present" language demands even less.

Of course, it is also evident from the legislative history that Congress did not intend to authorize EPA to issue test rules on the basis of mere hunches. The House Report states:

> The term "may"...does not permit the Administrator to make a finding respecting probability of a risk on the basis of mere conjecture or speculation, i.e., [that] it may or may not cause a risk. H.R. Rep. No.1341, at 18.

Congress obviously intended §4 to empower EPA to issue a test rule only after it had found a solid "basis for concern" by accumulating enough information to demonstrate a more-than-theoretical basis for suspecting that an "unreasonable risk" was involved in the use of the chemical....

Relying on the "more-than-theoretical-basis" test, the court then rejected CMA's other two arguments regarding use of inferences versus direct evidence of exposure and rare versus recurrent exposure. Finally, the court analyzed the evidence submitted by EPA for the Final Test Rule and held that the Agency had "produced substantial evidence to demonstrate not fact, but doubt and uncertainty."[10]]

COMMENTARY AND QUESTIONS

1. An exceptional case. *Chemical Manufacturers* is an unusual example of ToSCA working smoothly with regard to the promulgation of test rules for existing chemicals. When ToSCA was enacted, some commentators predicted that the statute would be unenforceable because it had been so compromised during the legislative process. See Gaynor, TSCA: A Regulatory Morass, 30 Vand. L. Rev. 1149 (1977), and Reynolds, TSCA: An Introductory Background and Analysis, 4 Colum. J. Envt'l L. 35 (1977). Unfortunately, these dire predictions have often been borne out. ToSCA's requirements that EPA promulgate test rules through notice and comment rulemaking and support them by substantial evidence, combined with the inadequacy of EPA's budget for ToSCA implementation and intense lobbying by industry, have militated against EPA promulgation of test rules. "By the end of fiscal year 1989, EPA had received full test data for only six chemicals and had not completed review of the data for any."[11] EPA did not perform its mandatory duty to respond to Interagency Testing Committee (ITC) recommendations until compelled to do so by court order. NRDC v. Costle, 14 ERC 1858, 10 E.L.R. 20274, 11 E.L.R. 20202 (1980). Moreover,

> EPA has historically rarely imposed a testing rule.... The agency has more often found reasons for declining to follow the ITC's testing recommendations. In addition, EPA has followed an administrative practice of entering into Negotiated Testing Agreements (NTAs) with industry trade associations in lieu of issuing test rules, wherever possible.[12]

The NTA program was struck down in NRDC v. EPA, 595 F. Supp 1255 (S.D. N.Y. 1984), partly because it excluded public interest groups. A new process called "testing consent agreements," which provides for public participation, is currently in effect. But ToSCA's cumbersome test rule procedures give EPA and the public little leverage in negotiations with industry.

2. ToSCA and new chemicals. ToSCA is no more effective with regard to the introduction of new chemicals into commerce. EPA cannot require the testing of all new chemicals under ToSCA. Unless a test rule is in effect for a component of a new chemical compound, or that component is included on EPA's §5(b)(4) "suspect list,"

10. Quoting from Ausimont U.S.A., Inc. v. EPA, *supra*, 838 F.2d 93, 96 (3d Cir. 1988).

11. Applegate, at 319, citing Comptroller-General, EPA's Chemical Testing Program Has Made Little Progress (April, 1990).

12. Stever, The Law Of Chemical Regulation And Hazardous Waste 2–8 (1991).

a manufacturer need not submit health and environmental test data unless it has independently developed these data or they are generally available elsewhere. Perhaps half of all premarket notifications (PMNs) submitted under ToSCA contain any toxicity information at all, and less than twenty percent include data on long-term toxicity.[13] Does ToSCA actually discourage premarket testing and encourage concealment of information? Or would a manufacturer most likely test a substance prior to manufacture in order to forestall tort liability? For a negative answer to the latter question, see Applegate at 299 ("industry has real incentives to *avoid* either creating toxic risk data or disclosing the data it already has"), and Lyndon, Information Economics and Chemical Toxicity: Designing Laws to Produce and Use Data, 87 Mich. L. Rev. 1795 (1989).

If EPA does not act to require testing before the expiration of the 90-day PMN period plus an optional additional 90 days, the manufacturer may commence manufacture or distribution. On the other hand, if after receipt of a PMN EPA finds that it has insufficient information on which to base an evaluation of the chemical substance, it may propose a test rule or, after making findings similar to those in §4, it may issue a proposed order to prohibit or limit the production of the substance. If the manufacturer formally objects to the proposed order, EPA must seek an injunction in federal district court under §5(e). The strictness of these time constraints and the necessity of resorting to judicial action if a test rule cannot be proposed in time virtually guarantees agency inaction.

3. FIFRA and ToSCA. In the congressional proceedings leading to the passage of ToSCA, the Senate preferred a licensing system similar to FIFRA, while the House favored allowing new chemicals to be marketed without notification or registration unless the chemicals or their components appeared on EPA's "suspect list." The emergent ToSCA compromise was based on notification and discretionary intervention by EPA. According to Professor Lyndon, the FIFRA presumption that a substance is unsafe unless the manufacturer proves safety has, in ToSCA, been transformed into a presumption that a substance is safe unless EPA can prove that it is unsafe:

> TSCA's requirement that the EPA issue a rule before requiring testing distinguishes it from food, drug, and pesticide regulations, which mandate production of safety data prior to marketing. The TSCA standard essentially establishes a presumption of safety, which the agency must overcome before it may require further testing of a chemical. Thus, the TSCA's use of strict rulemaking standards inhibits the very information production the statute was written to encourage.[14]

There is a fundamental ToSCA paradox in regulatory information-gathering. Where is EPA to procure the information that it needs to require manufacturers – who have every incentive to suppress information – to produce health and safety data

---

13. Applegate, at 303, citing Office of Technology Assessment, The Information Content of Premanufacture Notices (1983).

14. Lyndon, 87 Mich. L. Rev. at 1824.

regarding new and existing chemicals? Does EPA have to know already what it needs to know in order to ask for information about it?

4. Regulation and the common law. CMA's arguments in opposition to the Final Test Rule were based on common law analogues: (1) the more-probable-than-not test is similar to the "preponderance of the evidence" standard in common law litigation; (2) the criticism of EPA's inferences regarding modes of EHA use reflects the burden placed on a common law plaintiff to prove causation-in-fact by a preponderance of the evidence; and (3) the objection to EPA's regulating non-recurrent exposures echoes a common law defendant's argument that an injunction should not be granted because there is an adequate remedy at law (damages) if the event is unlikely to recur. Administrative agencies, however, are not limited by these common law constraints, as the court reaffirmed in its rejection of CMA's arguments.

5. The more-than-theoretical-basis test. Could this standard be used to support a test rule where EPA has not yet explored the toxicity of a chemical, but suspects, based on an educated guess, that the substance may be toxic? The more-than-theoretical-basis test could probably not be extended this far, but another section of ToSCA might cover such a situation. Section 4(a)(1)(B) provides that EPA may require testing where

> a chemical substance or mixture is or will be produced in substantial quantities, and (i) it enters or may reasonably be anticipated to enter the environment in substantial quantities or (ii) there is or may be significant or substantial human exposure to such substance or mixture.

In Chemical Manufacturers Association v. EPA, 899 F.2d 344 (5th Cir. 1990)(frequently referred to as *Chemical Manufacturers II*), EPA contended that

> while there is a need to show a potential for exposure in order to make a §4(a)(1)(A) finding ["may present an unreasonable risk of injury to health or the environment"], the exposure threshold is much lower than that under §4(a)(1)(B). This is because the former...finding was intended to focus on those instances where EPA has a scientific basis for suspecting potential toxicity and reflects that the potential for risk to humans may be significant even when the potential for exposure seems small, as, for example, when the chemical is discovered to be hazardous at very low levels. In contrast, the §4(a)(1)(B) finding was intended to allow EPA to require testing, not because of suspicions about the chemical's safety, but because there may be a substantial or significant human exposure to a chemical whose hazards have not been explored. 899 F.2d at 358, n. 20.

The language of §4(a)(1)(B), however, is so ambiguous that this section is of doubtful utility. In *Chemical Manufacturers II,* the Court remanded the test rule to EPA to explain what it meant by "substantial" quantities and human exposure.

6. The role of economics. All ToSCA regulatory decision-making must balance economic costs against environmental benefits under the "unreasonable risk" standard imported from FIFRA. In addition, §2(c) provides that EPA "shall consider the environmental, economic, and social impact of any action" taken by it under

ToSCA. Section 2(b) declares a policy that "authority over chemical substances...be exercised...so as not to impede unduly or create unnecessary economic barriers to technological innovation." Pursuant to §4(b), in specifying tests to be carried out, the EPA shall consider "the relative costs of the various test protocols and the methodologies which may be required." Is it fair to balance tangible and predictable economic costs against intangible and uncertain environmental benefits? The human mind naturally prefers the certain to the uncertain, leading to a "fallacy of numeration." (See Chapter 2.) Should the "unreasonable risk" balance be weighted on the side of the environment? Going even further, Professor Applegate recommends that the "unreasonable risk" standard be eliminated from §4:

> Unreasonable risk should be replaced in the §4 context by a more readily satisfied, less complex standard – something, in short, with less baggage. The term "unreasonable" should be dropped. The appropriate level (as opposed to existence) of risk is a policy question and more suitable in the standard-setting stage than in data collection. Under §4, EPA should be exploring policy options, not setting policy. Reasonable restraint by EPA can be assured by the existing provision requiring cost-effective testing and by the usual understanding that the term "risk" standing alone does not include de minimis risks.[15]

But is it likely that Congress will repudiate "unreasonable risk," even as to data collection?

7. ToSCA §6. Under §6 of ToSCA, discussed in *Chemical Manufacturers*, "if the Administrator finds that there is a reasonable basis to conclude that the manufacture, processing, distribution in commerce, use, or disposal of a chemical substance or mixture, or that any combination of such activities, presents or will present an unreasonable risk of injury to health or the environment, the Administrator shall by rule" impose one of the following measures: a prohibition or limitation on the manufacture, processing, or distribution of a substance in general or for specific uses, or an imposition of concentration limits; a requirement as to labeling, public warning, recall, or recordkeeping; or a ban or limitation on a particular form of use or disposal. All other things being equal, however, EPA must regulate under another statute rather than ToSCA §9(b). Although §6, like §4, has not been utilized very often,[16] it does represent a "catchall" or residuary pollution control statute, providing authority to regulate substances or uses that cannot be controlled under other federal pollution control statutes. EPA, for example, initially moved to regulate leaking underground storage tanks under ToSCA §6 until Congress enacted the 1984 RCRA amendments. (See Chapter 22.) EPA has also relied on §6 to set soil concentration limits for land application of dioxin-containing pulp and paper sludge. See 56 Fed. Reg. 21802 (May 10, 1991).

Section 6(e) contains a ban on the manufacture, distribution, and use of PCBs other than in a totally enclosed manner, although EPA may grant exemptions. See EDF v.

15. Applegate, at 320.

16. USGAO, Toxic Substances: Effectiveness Of Unreasonable Risk Standards Unclear 1–2 (1990).

EPA, 636 F.2d 1267 (D.C. Cir. 1980) (EPA's PCB regulations overturned and remanded). After initial doubt about whether a genetically-engineered organism can be considered a "chemical substance or mixture," EPA decided to require PMNs for environmental releases of these organisms. EPA regulates bioengineered pest-control products under FIFRA. For a description and critique of the federal regulatory response to biotechnology, see Fogleman, Regulating Science: An Evaluation of the Regulation of Biotechnology Research, 17 Envtl. L. 183 (1987).

8. Market access statutes and confidentiality. Given industry's desire to protect trade secrets from competitors, and potential tort plaintiffs' eagerness for access to health and safety testing data, both FIFRA and ToSCA contain extensive provisions regarding confidentiality of information disclosed to EPA. With regard to FIFRA, see Ruckleshaus v. Monsanto, 467 U.S. 986 (1984); as to ToSCA, see McGarity and Shapiro, The Trade Secret Status of Health and Safety Testing Information: Reforming Agency Disclosure Policies, 93 Harv. L. Rev. 837 (1980), and Chevron v. Costle, 443 F. Supp 1024 (N.D. Cal.1978).

9. The future of ToSCA. Although ToSCA is currently in eclipse, several commentators agree that it has tremendous potential for achieving environmental protection. Professor Guruswamy sees §3(5) of ToSCA, which defines the term "environment" to include "water, air, land, and the interrelationship which exists among and between water, air, and land and all living things," as the statutory lever for integrating our fragmented, media-specific pollution control statutes. Guruswamy, Integrating Thoughtways: Re-Opening of the Environmental Mind?, 1989 Wis. L. Rev. 463, 523–525 (1989). Professor Applegate envisions an amended ToSCA as the key to coordinating and enhancing federal information-acquisition regarding toxic substances. In a gloomier vein, Professor Flournoy condemns the basic approaches of all agency decision making with regard to environmental protection, and recommends that Congress enact a more sophisticated structure. Flournoy, Legislating Inaction: Asking the Wrong Questions in Protective Environmental Decisionmaking, 15 Harv. Envtl. L. Rev. 327, 382–391 (1991).

Statutes like ToSCA fail because there is an insufficient political consensus (1) to include provisions that are sufficiently clear and mandatory to be enforceable, and (2) if statutes are indeed clear and enforceable, to fund and enforce them once enacted. Congress is expert in enacting compromise legislation that appears to decide disputes between contending interest groups but does little to change the status quo. Agencies are expert at taking refuge in nonenforcement or "moderated" enforcement of statutes. ToSCA has failed for both reasons. Thus the real problem with ToSCA is not legal, as some commentators appear to suggest, but political. The dilemma that besets ToSCA has not changed since its congressional evolution during the 1970s: as a nation we have been, and still are, unwilling to institutionalize a fully preventive approach to pollution control in the face of the pervasive uncertainty that characterizes environmental decision-making. This dilemma recurs in discussions of recent policy shifts toward "pollution prevention." See Pollution Prevention Act of 1990, 42 U.S.C.A. §13101 et seq., noted at page 1037 *infra*.

Chapter 17

DIRECT LEGISLATION OF SPECIFIC POLLUTION STANDARDS, AND TECHNOLOGY-FORCING: AUTOMOBILE AIR POLLUTION

In this chapter, we examine how the Congress dictated direct, highly-specific statutory standards to clear the air, implementing a statutory tactic of technology-forcing.[1] While technology-forcing can be highly effective, it also can be a crude blunt instrument, raising difficult methodological and enforcement problems.

A. AUTOMOBILE AIR POLLUTION AND THE 1970 CLEAR AIR ACT'S TITLE II

While the American public has had a century-long love affair with the automobile, by the late 1960s it had become clear that American's cars are a mixed blessing. Before the 1970 Clean Air Act Amendments (CAA), auto emissions were responsible for approximately 60 percent of all air pollutants (by weight), and 30 to 60 percent of the three main pollutants – hydrocarbons, carbon monoxide, and nitrogen oxides. A 1967 study linked air pollution to diseases such as respiratory cancer, chronic bronchitis, acute bronchitis, pneumonia, emphysema, asthma, and the common cold – diseases that were costing $680 million annually in expenses from health care, lost productivity, and death.[2] In 1988, that figure was $40 billion.[3]

Despite the severity of the air pollution problem caused by automobile emissions, Congress prior to the 1970 CAA had taken a relatively innocuous approach to correcting it, primarily stressing research in auto technology. Faced with strenuous industry denials that automobiles caused smog pollution, regulation was extremely controversial. In 1955, Congress passed a five-year Air Pollution Act that had no practicable regulatory provisions. When it expired, the weak Motor Vehicle Exhaust Study Act of 1960 was enacted. The state of California then decided to move ahead, imposing its own strict emission standards. The first federal Clean Air Act was enacted in 1963, followed by the Motor Vehicle Air Pollution Control Act of 1965, which basically authorized more study. The Air Quality Act of 1967 contained few substantive restrictions, but it pre-empted state regulation of auto

1. The initial draft of this chapter was prepared by Carole LoConte, Esq., Boston College Law School Class of 1992.

2. D. Dewees, Economics and Public Policy: The Automobile Pollution Case, 34 (1974)(hereafter Dewees).

3. M. Renner, Rethinking the Role of the Automobile, Worldwatch Paper No. 84, 35 (1988)(hereafter Renner).

emissions. It specifically permitted California, however, to impose stricter standards, recognizing the regulatory effort California had undertaken in attempting to solve its serious smog problems. Primarily, though, these statutes served as research authorizations and exhortations to the auto industry to reduce emissions voluntarily. They did very little to remedy the growing problem of auto air pollution.[4] By 1969, it had become quite clear that the auto industry was dragging its feet, and that cleaner technologies would not be developed or installed voluntarily. As a result, Congress felt compelled to impose drastic measures to force change.

Before the 1970 CAA Amendments were passed, there was debate in Congress on a proposal to ban all internal combustion engines by 1985. While the proposal failed, the fact that it was debated at all demonstrates the extreme options Congress was willing to consider as remedies for the problem of air pollution. Although the 1970 enactments were supposedly only amendments to the Clean Air Act, Congress in fact rewrote the Act. The new law demonstrated a major shift in policy: instead of stressing improvements in available technology, the new standards forced the development of new technologies capable of meeting the strict requirements of the law.

Section 1. TITLE II OF THE 1970 CAA

In the following excerpts from the Clean Air Act Amendments of 1970 and 1977,[5] note the specificity and severity of the standards that Congress imposed on automobile manufacturers:

Title II. MOTOR VEHICLE EMISSION AND FUEL STANDARDS

§202(a) Except as otherwise provided in subsection (b) –

(1) The Administrator [of EPA] shall by regulation prescribe (and from time to time revise) in accordance with the provisions of this section, standards applicable to the emission of any air pollutant from any class or classes of new motor vehicles or...engines, which in his judgment causes or contributes to, or is likely to cause or contribute to, air pollution which endangers the public health or welfare. Such standards shall be applicable to such vehicles and engines for their useful life....

(2) Any regulation prescribed under this subsection...shall take effect after such period as the Administrator finds necessary to permit the development and application of the requisite technology, giving appropriate consideration to the cost of compliance within such period.

(b)(1)(a) The regulations under subsection (a) applicable to emissions of carbon monoxide and hydrocarbons from light duty vehicles and engines manufactured during or after model year 1975 shall contain standards which require a reduction of at least 90 per centum from emissions of carbon monoxide and hydrocarbons allowable under this section applicable to light duty vehicles and engines manufactured in model year 1970.

4. Merson, BNA Monograph No. 31, Environmental Regulation of the Automobile (December 17, 1982)(hereafter Merson).

5. Pub. L. 91-604, 42 U.S.C.A. §7521 (1970), (formerly 42 U.S.C.A. §1857 et seq.); Pub. L. 95-95 (1977) 42 U.S.C.A. §7521 (1977), (formerly 42 U.S.C.A. §7401 et seq.).

(b)(1)(b) [Equal reductions in emission averages are required for oxides of nitrogen one year later.] Such averages of emissions shall be determined by the Administrator on the basis of measurements made by him....

(d) The Administrator shall prescribe regulations under which the useful life of vehicles and engines shall be determined for purposes of subsection (a)(1) of this section....Such regulations shall provide that useful life shall –

(1) in the case of light duty vehicles and light duty engines, be a period of use of five years or fifty thousand miles, whichever first occurs....

In 1977,[6] Congress included even more specific standards for §202(b)(1)(A):

The regulations under subsection (a) of this section applicable to emissions of carbon monoxide and hydrocarbons from light-duty vehicles and engines manufactured during model years 1977 through 1979 shall contain standards which provide that such emissions from such vehicles and engines may not exceed 1.5 grams per vehicle mile of hydrocarbons and 15.0 grams per vehicle mile of carbon monoxide. The regulations...applicable to emissions of carbon monoxide from light-duty vehicles and engines manufactured during the model year 1980 shall contain standards which provide that such emissions may not exceed 7.0 grams per vehicle mile. The regulations...applicable to emissions of hydrocarbons from light-duty vehicles and engines manufactured during or after model year 1980 shall contain standards which require a reduction of at least 90 percent from emissions of such pollutant allowable under the standards under this section applicable to light-duty vehicles and engines manufactured in model year 1970. [Carbon monoxide got an extra year, to 1981, and the possibility of a waiver under §5].

(1)(B) The regulations...applicable to emissions of oxides of nitrogen from light-duty vehicles and engines manufactured during models years 1977 through 1980 shall contain standards which provide that such emissions from such vehicles and engines may not exceed 2.0 grams per vehicle mile. The regulations...applicable to emissions of oxides of nitrogen from light-duty vehicles and engines manufactured during the model year 1981 and thereafter shall contain standards which provide that such emissions from such vehicles and engines may not exceed 1.0 grams per vehicle mile....

§206(a)(1) The Administrator shall test, or shall require to be tested in such manner as he deems appropriate, any new motor vehicle or...engine submitted by the manufacturer to determine whether such vehicle or engine conforms with the regulations prescribed under §202 of this Act. If such vehicle or engine conforms to such regulations, the Administrator shall issue a certificate of conformity upon such terms, and for such period of time (not in excess of one year) as he may prescribe.

(a)(2) The Administrator shall test any emission control system incorporated into a motor vehicle or...engine submitted by any person, in order to determine whether such system enables such vehicle or engine to conform with the standards required to be prescribed under section 202 (b) of this Act. If the Administrator finds on the basis of such tests that such vehicle or

6. Pub. L. 95–95 (1977).

engine conforms to such standards, the Administrator shall issue a verification of compliance with emission standards....[7]

COMMENTARY AND QUESTIONS

1. The stark specificity of Title II's legislated standards. Do the terms of §202(b) strike you as reasonable? How frequently does Congress set out strict, specific numerical requirements, especially in areas which are highly technical and complex, and even more, where there is pitched political controversy? Far more typical are the terms of §202's subsection (a); what would have happened if Congress had stopped at (a)?

Congress didn't stop there, however, and the seemingly broad grant of agency discretion – delegating authority to shape and apply regulatory standards in terms that in many other pollution contexts had led to years of industry footdragging and political dilution of enforcement efforts – was nailed down in excruciating detail in subsection (b). If cars did not meet §202(b) standards, under §203(a) they couldn't be sold in the U.S.. [8]

2. Technology-forcing. Title II's standards were not only quantitatively specific. They were also very tough. A 90 percent rollback in emissions in a five-year horizon was a drastic order. The congressionally-dictated standards were patently defined to be "technology-forcing." The industry had argued strenuously during the hearings that these low levels of auto emissions in hydrocarbons (HC), carbon monoxide (CO), and oxides of nitrogen (NOX) were technically impossible to achieve given existing technology. In Title II, Congress commanded that the automakers come up with new technology or stop selling cars, unless they could win one year waivers from EPA under §203. As with Judge Jasen's dissent in *Boomer*, the hypothesis was that where there's enough will, there'll be a way.

3. Strictly Unfair? The automakers reacted to Title II as an aggressive intrusion upon an American industry that had never before needed regulation, and that was directly or indirectly linked to one out of every six jobs in the U.S. economy (echoing arguments made three years before against the Nader-inspired auto safety bill). But didn't Title II incorporate some basic unfairness or irrationalities? What effect did its 90 percent emissions rollback have on (a) a company that had voluntarily tried to clean up its cars prior to 1970, and (b) a company that had steadfastly avoided efforts to control its cars' emissions?[9] Further, the 90 percent rollback numbers were based on the smog conditions of Los Angeles and a few other cities, yet all cars in America had to meet those standards. Within Los Angeles, the requirements were probably not strict enough. Therefore, weren't they unnecessary?

---

7. In addition to setting Title II's strict emissions standards, in §212 Congress employed explicit economic incentives by authorizing federal vehicle fleets to purchase low-emissions vehicles even if they were up to twice as expensive, although in practice this carrot was much smaller than the stick of §202.

8. Subject to possible one-year extensions of the deadline under tight statutory exceptions in §202(b)(5)(D).

9. In fact, automakers were generally in the latter pool. See notes following.

4. Waivers. Title II did allow the possibility of last minute extension waivers:

> §203(b)(5)(D) the Administrator may grant such a waiver if he finds that the protection of the public health does not require attainment of such 90 percent reduction for carbon monoxide for the model years to which such waiver applies in the case of such vehicles and engines and if he determines that –
>
> (i) such waiver is essential to the public interest or the public health and welfare of the United States;
>
> (ii) all good faith efforts have been made to meet the standards established by this subsection;
>
> (iii) the applicant has established that effective control technology, processes, operating methods, or other alternatives are not available or have not been available with respect to the model in question for a sufficient period of time to achieve compliance prior to the effective date of such standards, taking into consideration costs, driveability, and fuel economy; and
>
> (iv) studies and investigations of the National Academy of Sciences...and other information available to [the Administrator] has not indicated that technology, processes, or other alternatives are available (within the meaning of clause (iii)) to meet such standards.

Chrysler successfully petitioned for the first waiver, in 1973. EPA Administrator William Ruckelshaus had clear evidence that Chrysler had not tried in good faith to comply, but faced with the imminent loss of 20,000 jobs, he granted the waiver and prayed that no environmental group would sue. None did.

5. Draconian technology forcing. A tight waiver provision fails to alleviate very tight deadlines for statutory compliance. In the case of Title II, American automakers had such monolithic production establishments that five years was an impossibly short lead time to design new technology. The strict technology-forcing schedule practically boxed the industry in to a strategy of tinkering with the old style engines rather than innovating with cleaner-burning engine designs.

Why didn't the waiver provision provide necessary flexibility? The practical answer lay with the tough requirements for a waiver, the uncertainty that it would be granted, its last minute timing only when a model year was close to production, and its short one-year term with no guarantee of renewal.

Section 2. THE POLITICAL CONTEXT OF TITLE II: CONGRESSIONAL REACTION TO INDUSTRY STONEWALLING

To understand how Congress was motivated to impose Title II's double stringency – rigorous congressional requirements, setting limits that surpassed existing technology – one must understand that Congress thought it had good historical reasons to doubt the automakers' good faith. The background was set out in a confidential 1968 Department of Justice memorandum:[10]

10. Confidential Memorandum, U.S. Department of Justice, (undated, prepared prior to January 10, 1969), printed in Congressional Record, May 18, 1971 H4063–4074.

> In early 1951, Dr. Arte J. Haagen-Smit...at the California Institute of Technology, discovered that when oxides of nitrogen, ozone and gasoline (hydrocarbon) vapors were introduced into a plexiglass test chamber and exposed to ultraviolet light (artificial sunlight), an irritating haze with all the properties of natural smog was formed.... Following the publication and general acceptances of the Haagen-Smit theory, the automobile industry finally acknowledged that motor vehicles contributed to air pollution, which it had steadfastly denied prior thereto. The problem of how to control motor vehicle emissions was then turned over by the industry to the Automobile Manufacturers Association...a trade association whose members manufacture 99 percent of the cars, trucks and buses produced annually in the United States.... From the very outset the industry realized that air pollution control devices to do not help sell automobiles.
>
> The AMA Board...formed the Vehicle Combustion Products Committee (VCP) to direct all industry efforts on a noncompetitive basis.... An AMA internal memorandum prepared for presentation at VCP and Engineering and Advisory Committee (EAC) meetings disclosed that...dilatory tactics prevailed:
>
> "On the basis of the facts the industry is not convinced that exhaust emissions devices or systems are necessary for nationwide application to motor vehicles, but believes instead that they will be an economic and maintenance burden on motorists. It is therefore not prepared or desirous to initiate any voluntary program to impose these systems or devices...."

The Justice investigation revealed the existence of an AMA cross-licensing agreement designed to eliminate competitive incentives to develop emissions technology.

> The AMA cross-licensing agreement placed the automobile producers in a position where they did not have to fear that a competitor would develop an effective device or system for its exclusive use which might become required equipment and thus put the others at a competitive disadvantage.

Further, Justice found that the automakers had agreed not to purchase or utilize any device developed by a nonsignatory to the cross-licensing agreement.

> Failure on the part of the manufacturers to purchase devices of independent companies, produced at costs of millions of dollars, discouraged such independents from further research, development, or manufacture of control devices to the great detriment of the American people, science and industry.

The investigation led to the filing of a major antitrust suit against GM, Ford, Chrysler, and AMC in 1968 in the final weeks of the outgoing Democratic administration.

The industry's strategy played out revealingly in the state of California's smog control initiatives. California, impatient with federal inaction, had passed its auto emissions law in 1960,[11] setting tough emissions limits despite industry protests that the limits were technologically impossible to meet. It provided that when any two control devices were developed and certified by the state Motor Vehicle Pollution Control Board (MVPCB) as effective emissions controls, all new cars in California would have to install emissions controls within one year.

11. Cal. Health & Safety Code §§24378–24398.

> The MVPCB of California [in 1964] approved four devices developed by independent manufacturers which...made the installation of pollution control equipment mandatory on 1966 production. Instead of utilizing any of the approved devices [the] auto companies utilized devices or systems which they themselves developed.

It turned out, moreover, that the combustion-control and catalytic systems installed in the AMA members' California cars in 1966 (under their cross-licensing agreement) had long been known or even patented by the automakers, in some cases since the 1930s. Given this history, Congress was in no mood to yield to Detroit's handwringing about unaccomplishable technology-forcing.

Although the incoming Nixon administration quickly settled the antitrust case shortly after it took office, with a promise by the industry that it would go and sin no more,[12] the case diminished the automakers' lobbying strength in Congress, and paved the way for Title II.

B. STATUTORY OVERKILL?

RESULTS, AND CONTINUED PROBLEMS

At the time the 1970 amendments were enacted, automobile industry spokespersons characterized the emission standards as "a classic case of regulatory overkill."[13] Whether they were right or not about overkill, it is undeniable that Title II's strictness did force change, and did improve air quality. Between 1970 and 1987, hydrocarbons and carbon monoxide emissions in new cars dropped by 96 percent, and oxides of nitrogen by 76 percent.[14]

Alterations in auto technology brought about other beneficial changes as well. Use of the catalytic converter, for example, required that fuel companies develop unleaded gasoline, since leaded fuel "poisons" the converter and makes it ineffective as a pollution control device. As a result, lead emissions fell 94 percent between 1976 and 1986, and, correspondingly, lead levels in Americans' blood dropped one-third.[15] Note the reductions reflected in the table on the following page, compiled by EPA.

But at what cost? Although air quality on the highways and in congested urban areas has improved since the 1970 Amendments, the goal of eliminating auto-caused pollution is still far away. Los Angeles is still among the most polluted American cities, and its air quality violated federal standards on 143 occasions between 1985 and 1987. Fifty-nine American cities still do not meet the Act's carbon monoxide standards. One-third of these cities are unlikely *ever* to meet the standards. As Michael Renner of Worldwatch Institute notes pessimistically,

---

12. There is at least some argument that cooperation between the now-chastened automakers in their research efforts might have hastened and improved emission control results, but the industry's history of collusion to avoid cleaner technology tainted that argument fatally.

13. The remark is attributed to GMC Chairman Richard Gerstenberg.

14. F. Alan Smith, "Autopower in the '90s," *Automotive News*, November 29, 1989.

15. Renner at 37.

LEVELS OF MAJOR AUTO EMISSION POLLUTANTS 1970–1987
(in total pounds per year)

YEAR	NITROGEN OXIDES (millions)	VOLATILE ORGANIC COMPOUNDS (millions)	CARBON MONOXIDE (millions)	LEAD (thousands)
1970	6.1	9.8	64.2	156.0
1975	7.2	8.0	55.4	118.1
1978	7.8	7.4	53.8	108.2
1979	7.5	6.8	49.8	90.8
1980	7.4	6.2	46.2	56.4
1981	7.5	6.0	45.2	43.9
1982	7.2	5.7	43.0	44.4
1983	6.8	5.6	42.9	38.7
1984	6.8	5.5	40.5	32.6
1985	7.0	5.2	38.3	14.5
1986	6.6	4.9	35.6	3.3
1987	6.6	4.7	33.4	2.8

> There is little hope that air quality standards can be improved with current measures. While U.S. standards are still serving as a roadmap for emission controls in other countries, they are clearly not tight enough to chart the course toward clean air. The average new gasoline-powered car could already meet considerably more stringent norms than those in force today. Yet there are no in-use standards for older cars, even though these often pollute far more than permitted by new-car standards.[16]

It is clear that Title II has not brought about an end to dangerous levels of automobile pollution. Despite strict statutory standards, the volume of traffic and lax enforcement have undermined improvements. Since 1970, moreover, grave new air pollution consequences connected to auto emissions have come to the attention of the American public, including dangerously high levels of ground level ozone, dangerously low levels of stratospheric ozone, acid deposition, and the greenhouse effect.[17]

EPA enforcement and congressional fortitude have been occasional. In part the problem has been political, with a lack of commitment in the corridors of the bureaucracy and the Congress in the face of industry economic arguments. In 1974, during the first Arab Oil embargo, Congress approved new amendments to the CAA, which delayed until 1976 the effective date of all tailpipe standards and allowed the EPA administrator to delay these standards an additional year.[18] The agency, fearing that catalytic converters would emit noxious emissions of sulfur dioxide, granted a delay of carbon monoxide and hydrocarbon requirements until 1978.[19] Further, the

16. *Id.* at 42.
17. Renner at 41.
18. Pub. L. 93–319 (1974).
19. Merson

CAA amendments of 1977 delayed compliance with percentage reductions for hydrocarbon and carbon monoxide, and delayed and relaxed the standard for nitrogen oxides.[20] While waiver provisions are probably necessary adjuncts to Title II's strict technology-forcing structure, their too-frequent application has served to soften the bite of the Act. In 1981-1982, for example, 30 percent of the automobiles produced in the U.S. were granted waivers.[21]

The EPA, moreover, developed a regulatory loophole in its selective enforcement auditing (SEA) program. Under SEA, cars are tested for emissions at the end of the assembly line, and calculations are made to extrapolate emission levels as they will be at the end of the automobile's useful life. The regulations require that no more than 40 percent of the tested automobile models fail to meet the standards. The EPA considers this 40 percent failure rate to be an "acceptable quality level," and autos meeting this generous standard are awarded an EPA certificate of conformance.[22] Given this leeway, it is not surprising that auto emissions are still causing grave air pollution problems. What would happen if the EPA were to require an 80 percent passing rate? a 99 percent passing rate?

Nevertheless, irrespective of bureaucratic and congressional wavering, the problems of effective auto air pollution control may be insoluble under current approaches. Even if actual tailpipe emissions from the average gasoline-powered car were cut by 60 percent, for example, the ever-increasing number of of drivers and total mileage driven in America and around the world would quickly nullify the gains. Future improvements in this undoubted public health environmental problem area may require fundamental changes in something.

FUTURE ROUTES FOR AUTO POLLUTION CONTROL

What strategies will guide future efforts to alleviate auto-caused air pollution? A fundamental problem is that although Americans have grown increasingly concerned about environmental problems, we (and this probably includes most environmentalists) are unwilling to sacrifice our automobility. According to F. Alan Smith, chairman of the Highway Users Federation and Executive Vice President of GM, there are 824 cars for every 1000 Americans, as compared to 561 cars per 1000 in Japan; 85 percent of Americans commute to their jobs in private cars. Addicted to the freedom, comfort, and convenience they sometimes represent, we drive our cars more often and over longer distances than any other country in the world, suggesting that lessons learned during past oil crises are largely forgotten.[23] Former EPA Administrator Lee Thomas suggested that perhaps the only way to deal with the smog problem is to reduce the number of cars on the road, and restrict the miles Americans may drive. Such regulations would doubtless be met with enormous outcry, although they have successfully been imposed in cities like Athens and Budapest which suffer from extremely serious air pollution.[24] Until non-petroleum

20. Pub. L. 95–95 (1977).

21. Merson

22. *Id.*

23. Smith, *Automotive News*, November 29, 1989.

24. Renner at 42.

based fuels such as methane, hydrogen and electricity are developed and used on a large scale, there may be few options other than discouraging use of the automobile.

Environmentalists and industry people alike have begun looking beyond the gasoline-fired internal combustion engine for solutions to the air pollution crisis we are now facing.

There are theoretically a number of promising avenues. Some lie in the realm of better fuels, but these are not panaceas. Grain-based ethanol fuels burn cleanly, but are expensive and erode engine seals. Methanol is being pushed by the California MVPCB, and dramatically reduces hydrocarbons, but produces 2 to 5 times as much carcinogenic formaldehyde as regular gasoline. Natural gas is more efficient but appears to produce more nitrogen oxides.[25] Electric cars are only as efficient and clean as the fuel that generates their charge. Probably the best all-around future prospect is hydrogen. It is 15–45 percent more efficient, produces no carbon monoxide or unburnt hydrocarbons, and very little oxides of nitrogen. Production of hydrogen, however, would require major retooling in the energy industry, and under current technology would be prohibitively expensive.

New automobile propulsion designs are also possible, building new concepts of energy use systems and control systems into engines of the future. Innovative versions of the stratified charge engine, fuel reactor systems, superefficient motors using flywheel energy banks, and other innovations are possible. California, ever the leader, has recently passed regulation requiring introduction of the currently theoretical "zero-emission" car to California by 1998, with a target of 10 percent of the state's cars reaching zero emissions by 2003.[26]

If these technological fixes prove impracticable, other measures will have to be tried. Remember the drastic measures considered in the 1969 debates (e.g. banning the internal combustion engine). As a lesser measure, Congress could establish a mileage rationing system, restricting the number of miles Americans can drive, with all the snafus such systems entail. Or the price of gas could be raised to $10 a gallon, or taxes imposed for each mile driven beyond a certain base limit. The mixed economic, social, and environmental values of the American public and American automakers guarantee that such drastic measures would produce a Donnybrook. So most of us implicitly sit waiting for a technological breakthrough.

LESSONS FROM A CRUDE BLUNT INSTRUMENT

If reliance on future technology is the primary strategy, the question remains: how do we get from here to there? Should we wait for the industry – or perhaps even an upstart – voluntarily to develop these technologies on their own, while we continue to retrofit our standard gasoline-powered cars? Or, following Title II's stark precedent, should Congress impose a draconian near-term requirement on the industry for the development and widespread use of innovative technologies, or else, as California is attempting to do?

25. Renner at 42.
26. Title 13, California Code of Regulations, §1960.1

While the technology-forcing design of Title II was useful in effecting major changes in auto pollution control, it was a painful means of doing so: painful for the auto manufacturers, in that they were forced to expend enormous sums for rapid research and development; painful for consumers, who faced sharp increases in new car costs due to the installation of pollution control devices; and painful for taxpayers, who underwrote the expensive administration of the regulations. And how appropriate was it for Congress to strip EPA of the discretion usually afforded agencies in formulating regulations? Who is more qualified to make standard-setting determinations, legislators or agency officials? Were there other less drastic statutory mechanisms which Congress could have used to achieve the same ends?

Although much of the apparent success of Title II in getting the industry to move can be attributed to its strictness, the rigidity of the regulation also served to blunt its effectiveness in some areas. The technology-forcing structure of Title II was intended to encourage automakers to develop alternatives to the internal combustion engine. Several "cleaner" possibilities existed, including the Wankel turbine engine, the stratified charge engine, the ceramic engine, and various alternative-fuel systems, including steam, electric, natural gas, and alcohol-powered systems. In order to make such alternatives operational, though, auto manufacturers would have had to build new plants, acquire new machinery, and retrain personnel. Overhauling the auto industry in this way would have cost enormous sums of money, and would have taken years of experimentation, development, and production retooling to accomplish – time and flexibility which Title II did not provide. Foreign manufacturers, who had smaller production volumes, more flexible managements, and shorter lead times for getting ideas onto the road, were able to certify new cleaner engine designs, including Japan's stratified charge engine block and several German innovations.

American automakers, on the other hand, invested their time and money in developing more advanced add-on pollution control devices, like the catalytic converter, rather than developing new, non-polluting systems. The pollution control mechanisms which the auto manufacturers preferred had pollution problems of their own. Catalytic converters were extremely unreliable in early testing, and could be easily rendered ineffective by leaded fuel. Converters today are vastly improved. They cut average hydrocarbon emissions by about 87 percent, carbon monoxide by 85 percent, and nitrogen oxides by 62 percent. When new, they have the capacity to reduce hydrocarbons by 93 percent, carbon monoxide by 98 percent, and nitrogen oxides by 76 percent. But in the process of converting hydrocarbons and carbon monoxide into water and harmless gases, the devices increase carbon dioxide and sulfur dioxide emissions somewhat.[27] In 1975 the EPA Administrator granted a one-year suspension of the 1977 emission standards because of problems with the catalytic converter. In Senate subcommittee hearings, he expressed his fear that sulfuric acid emissions from cars with catalytic converters could pose a "localized public health problem in the vicinity of heavily traveled freeways," and that "prudence dictated caution in not exposing the public to unacceptable levels of a pollutant which possibly could prove more dangerous than those being

27. Renner at 38.

A modern urban scene with air pollution caused by automobile emissions. This could be any one of the more than four dozen American cities that are consistently in violation of federal air quality standards due to hydocarbons, nitrogen oxides, and carbon monoxide produced by automobiles.

FUND FOR PUBLIC INTEREST RESEARCH

controlled."[28] Since that time, devices such as the three-way catalyst have corrected the sulfur problem. While the reliability and safety of the converter in reducing emissions have improved over the years, however, consistent professional inspection and maintenance are required to insure its effectiveness.[29] And the basic engine on American-designed cars still continues to be the 1970 motor with a jungle of little pipes and sensors piled on to try to clean up the old baby's emissions.

COMMENTARY AND QUESTIONS

1. A verdict on Title II's stark technology-forcing? Was Title II's tactic of imposing strict legislated technology-forcing standards a good one for then, and for now? If it is, its application potentially extends far beyond the area of auto emissions.

Observers disagree passionately about the Title II track record.

Larry White, an ardent critic of governmental regulatory highhandedness, estimates that the 1981 costs of the program exceeded 14 billion dollars.[30] For White, such a large price tag raises the question of whether the automotive program is an efficient (low-cost or least-cost) way of achieving overall emissions reductions. He writes:

28. Merson.
29. Renner at 39.
30. L. White, The Regulation of Air Pollutant Emissions from Motor Vehicles, 64 (1982).

> ...one can simply take the ultimate benefits from the emissions reductions achieved by the automotive standards as given. There are, however, alternative ways of achieving those emissions reductions. Other industries emit the same pollution from stationary sources. Greater emissions reductions by those sources could achieve the same result as that achieved by the automotive standards...if the various emissions reductions are going to be achieved in any event, the automotive standards are a low-cost way of achieving them. But...there are less costly ways of achieving them. [31]

F. Alan Smith, executive vice president of GM, spoke for the entire auto industry when he wrote that "we applaud the Bush administration's effort to use market incentives for cleaner air, rather than the government 'command and control' system, which works against the free market rather than for it."[32] GM has insisted that many major auto improvements, like increased fuel economy were the result of market forces – like fuel shortages and corresponding high prices – rather than government regulation.[33]

Michael Walsh, a Washington D.C. consultant who was former EPA Director of Motor Vehicle Emission Regulation argues that –

> Title II was blunt, but it was the only thing that would work in practical policy terms. Since it was first passed we have gone through the '70s and '80s with no further tightening. Industry has come up with no new technology. Look at California's response: it has again adopted very tight controls, mandating introduction of zero-emission cars. Forcing technological development through a "regulatory hammer" has been and continues to be the only demonstrated way to succeed. Telephone interview, Oct. 16, 1991.

2. Pragmatic tradeoffs. How heavily should concern for the national economy weigh against concern for the environment? In drafting Title II, Congress seemed to have made a decision that the costs of reducing auto emissions and improving air quality were worth the price. There was therefore only minimal consideration of economic factors in the language of the Act. Automakers stress, however, that one-third of the annual $150 billion balance of trade deficit is attributable to imported automobiles, and we must do all we can to keep the American car industry rolling on its own terms.[34] Are we perhaps, however, reaching a point in our nation's and planet's history where the social costs of our automobility outweigh its social benefits?

3. The Title II precedent. Reviewing the ambivalent history of Title II – its successes and shortcomings, its costs, benefits, and alternatives – are there other regulatory situations in which such congressional technology-forcing standard-setting of the magnitude found in Title II would be useful and appropriate?

---

31. *Id.* at 85-86.
32. Smith, *Automotive News*, November 29, 1989.
33. Abrahamson, "A Storm of Protest," *AutoWeek*, July 24, 1989.
34. *Id.*

Chapter 18

ADMINISTRATIVE STANDARD-SETTING STATUTES: THE CLEAN AIR ACT'S HARM-BASED AMBIENT STANDARDS

This Chapter explores the use of pollution standards that are set initially, and then later enforced, by reference to the "ambient" measured quality of the receiving environment, e.g. of the air or water in the particular locality of the source. Such regulatory standards are based on the overall quality of the relevant airshed or water body into which pollution is discharged. A prime example of this regulatory technique is the federal Clean Air Act (CAA)[1] in its regulation of conventional air pollution for sulfur dioxide, nitrogen dioxide,[2] suspended particulates, carbon monoxide, ozone and lead. The CAA establishes National Ambient Air Quality Standards (NAAQS) applicable on a nationwide basis. The standards are called "harm-based" here because the mandated quality levels are set by reference to ambient levels of pollutants that would result in harm to human health and the environment.

The Clean Air Act, as enacted in 1970 and significantly amended in 1977 and 1990,[3] embodies a combination of four distinct statutory techniques:

- Sections 107, 108, 109, and 110, taken together created the broad basic workhorse regulatory system for control of the most commonly-produced and significant air pollutants. These sections apply a harm-based ambient quality regulatory approach which constitutes this chapter's primary focus.
- Title II, already discussed in the preceding chapter, set specific strict congressional standards for across-the-board rollbacks in automobile and truck tailpipe emissions.[4]
- Section 111, which applies to "new sources" of air pollution, establishes a system of "best-technology" emissions requirements, following a technol-

1. 42 U.S.C.A. §7401 et seq.

2. In regard to sulfur dioxide and nitrogen dioxide, the ambient quality approach described in this chapter has been supplemented by the 1990 CAA amendments to include a tradeable emissions credit program intended to reduce long-range acid deposition problems. This alternative regulatory approach is considered in detail in Chapter 20.

3. More technically, the legislation now known as the Clean Air Act was actually the Clean Air Act Amendments of 1970. The prior federal statute had relied almost exclusively on voluntary state efforts to control air pollution. 69 Stat. 322 (1955). The 1970 legislation amended it beyond recognition. Pub.L. 91-604 (1970). The 1970 statute continues to be the basis for the current law. The major amendments have been Pub.L. 95-95 (1977) and Pub.L. 101–549 (1990).

4. The auto pollution standards were set to some degree based on the degree of rollback thought necessary to prevent smog in the worst urban air quality areas, e.g. Los Angeles. In this sense they are "harm-based" uniform national (i.e. not local ambient) standards. In another sense, the auto emissions limits were "politics-based" standards.

ogy-based standard-setting approach. (The technology-based regulatory technique is explored more fully in Chapter 19, using the Clean Water Act as its principal example.)

- Section112 originally called for uniform harm-based national emission standards for hazardous air pollutants.[5] This effort, based on attempts to weigh relative hazards to health, proved wholly unsatisfactory. In 1990 Congress shifted §112 to a technology-based strategy for regulating hazardous air pollutants.

The Clean Air Act thus enjoys the ambiguous honor of having been a statutory laboratory for a variety of different command and control pollution regulation approaches.

A. AMBIENT STANDARDS, THE COMMONS AND AMERICAN FEDERALISM

Both air and water are sometimes referred to as "pollution sinks," implying that airsheds and water bodies are like large vats into which pollutants can be thrown as a form of disposal. Despite much innuendo to the contrary, there is more than a grain of truth in that image. Both air and water have an ability to assimilate some man-induced pollution without significant detriment to the natural systems of which the air and water are a part. The determination of the amount of effluent that can safely be assimilated is, of course, a complex and difficult scientific (not to mention political) question. The conventional air pollutants, other than lead, are all examples of pollutants that can be discharged into the air in reasonable amounts without severe environmental consequences.

From the foregoing observations, it is possible to forge a pollution regulatory technique that allows some pollution to occur. To do so is eminently sensible, for it avoids the unnecessary social cost of treating or eliminating discharges that do not harm the environment. Simultaneously, that same strategy forbids excessive pollution, limiting total emissions below the threshold level at which undesirable environmental or public health effects are felt.

The fulcrum on which this system of permissible levels of pollution rests is the concept of ambient receiving body quality standards. These standards do not exist in a vacuum – they are a function of the purposes for which the resource base is to be used. Although the bulk of the material in this Chapter focuses on the use of ambient standards in the Clean Air Act, the link between ambient quality standards and intended use of the resource complex is more easily grasped by an example involving water as the pollution sink. Water in a receiving body can be used for a variety of purposes, such as drinking, bathing, supporting aquatic life, pleasure boating, industrial process source water, commercial navigation, effluent transport and so on. The quality of the water necessary to support the aforementioned uses

5. The §112 standards for hazardous air pollutants were primarily harm-based; they were not ambient standards because they were based on uniform nationwide limits set without regard to localized conditions. They measured allowable concentrations of pollutants in the waste stream itself, i.e. in the smokestack.

varies greatly and, therefore, the ambient receiving body water quality standards that would be erected would also vary greatly.

There is a sense in which the attendant standards can all be thought of as harm-based. Water used for drinking that causes illness or death if ingested causes harm to the intended user. A harm-based ambient quality standard, therefore, will be set at a level that is sufficient to avoid the harm that would ensue to the intended use or user. The standards are a function of the intended use. For example, water that is intended only for commercial navigation need not be totally free of some hazardous pollutants that would be injurious to health if someone were to drink the water, nor need the concentrations of conventional pollutants be as low as might be required for full-body contact with the water, and so on.

The resort to ambient receiving body quality standards can be understood as a form of response to the tragedy of the commons. Here, imagine that the commons is a receiving body, such as a lake surrounded by several industrial facilities that emit effluents into the lake. To any one industrialist, the cost of avoiding pollution of the lake creates an incentive to pollute the lake. To forego pollution might avoid costs of reduced receiving body quality, such as the need to treat water drawn from that source for industrial use, but the common pool nature of the receiving body vitiates that possible benefit of avoiding pollution. In the absence of regulatory intervention or comprehensive private agreement, there is no guarantee that the benefit of cleaner water will be obtained because other polluters may elect to dump their wastes into the commons.

Setting and maintaining ambient quality levels attacks the commons problem by outlawing the untoward result of unacceptable (harmful) deterioration in quality. In this way, an ambient standards approach initially addresses the problem of the commons at a collective level – it defers the intractable problem of translating a prescription about collective results into a series of controls on the behavior of individuals. It is important to emphasize that the choice of means for controlling the individual contributions to ambient quality is wholly independent of adopting an ambient standards approach. From an environmental quality standpoint, as long as the desired ambient quality level is achieved, the choice between a rule that requires zero discharge by all polluters born under the sign of Gemini as opposed to a rule requiring 15 percent reductions in emissions by all emitters is a matter of indifference. More realistically, however, the choice among possible means of individual control is important because of the economic and political ramifications of that choice.

Historical context helps to explain the important role assigned to harm-based ambient standards in the Clean Air Act of 1970. Environmental regulation in the United States was traditionally the province of the several states as an incident of their police power regulation of health and safety. As noted in previous materials discussing the revolutionary changes in perspective that came to the fore at the time of the first Earth Day in 1970, state efforts at pollution control and a relatively passive federal role in the field had not preserved environmental quality in the United States at an acceptable level. Pre-1970 federal activity primarily focused on providing funds to defray the large capital costs of pollution control facilities, and on providing various forms of technical expertise. See, e.g., Air Pollution Control Act of 1955, 42 U.S.C. §§1857 et seq. Upon a finding of interstate impact, the federal government sometimes had enforcement authority, but again this usually consisted of requesting state enforcement of relevant state laws. In short, there was little federal involvement in direct pollution control. The dramatic escalation in environmental concern required a new approach on the part of the federal government.

The historic primacy of the several states in the pollution regulation field came under attack. The sorry state of the environment was irrefutable testimony to the failure of the states to control emissions, and there were few indications that the states would, or could, rise to the occasion and alter their longstanding policies of ineffective pollution control. Most centrally, the economic incentives at work at the state level pointed in the wrong direction. Industrial development and the associated concentration of pollution was not evenly dispersed throughout the nation. Calls for more stringent pollution control in the nation's heavily industrialized areas were met with threats of industrial relocation by the polluters who, simultaneously, were being wooed to relocate by less developed areas willing to trade environmental amenity values for the economic benefits of increased economic development. A resultant "race of laxity" ensued, in which states having more stringent pollution control standards found themselves disadvantaged in the competition for economic development.[6]

In areas other than health and safety, the primacy of the states as regulators had eroded substantially during the middle third of the twentieth century. Beginning with massive federal intrusion into economic fields as a cure for the Great Depression, continuing with the centralized planning of materials allocation for the war effort and culminating in the civil rights struggle of the 1960s, the national government became a more active and even dominant partner in the regulation of American life. An aggressive move by the federal government into active regulation of the environment no longer seemed unthinkable; to the contrary, it seemed appropriate once environmental quality had emerged as a widespread concern. As a part of its new posture, the federal government mandated that all of the air in the nation had to meet quality standards that it set. These standards are the NAAQS for conventional air pollutants mentioned at the beginning of this chapter.

Relying on what is now termed "cooperative federalism," the federal government offered the states a partnership in the new regulatory regime for clean air. States could retain their longstanding primacy as regulators of the local entities that caused air pollution by adopting state implementation plans (SIPs) that would assure attainment of the NAAQS. The federal government's role would be threefold: first, it would set the standards that must be met; second, it would review SIPs to insure that plans would result in the attainment of the mandated degree of air quality; and third, it would supplant the states as primary regulators if the states failed to act, or acted in a way that would not insure attainment.

6. The sweetheart deals offered to industrial concerns willing to site facilities in particular locations continue to the present time, although nationwide pollution control laws have done much to level the playing field on that score. See *infra* at page 819. Contemporary inducements include tax breaks, infrastructure improvements and, occasionally, use of the governmental power of eminent domain to consolidate parcels for development.

Harm-based ambient standards are perfectly matched to the vision of cooperative federalism. The federal government could set the goal with reference to relatively objective criteria – what level of pollution causes harm to human health (the NAAQS primary standards) and what level of pollution causes harm to welfare and the environment (the NAAQS secondary standards). The states, more familiar with their own needs and the capabilities of the polluters within their borders, would have the freedom and the responsibility to make the difficult and multifaceted determinations about how to limit pollution to the allowable upper bound. The national need is served because unacceptable harm to health and welfare is eliminated. The states retain their sovereign prerogatives in managing and accommodating the competing interests of their constituents.

COMMENTARY AND QUESTIONS

1. Air, water and what else? Would harm-based ambient standards be a valuable regulatory technique in fields other than air and water pollution? Harm-based standards are ubiquitous in other fields of regulation involving, for example, product safety for consumer goods and drugs, but there is no commons involved and therefore no concern with ambient standards. Noise regulation that relies on setting maximum allowable levels is probably another example of a harm-based ambient standard.

2. State responsibilities. The principal sections of the Clean Air Act that erect the harm-based ambient standards program are §§107–110, 42 U.S.C.A §§7407–7410. Section 107(a) admirably summarizes the overall concept:

> Each State shall have the primary responsibility for assuring air quality within the entire geographic area comprising such State by submitting an implementation plan for such State which will specify the manner in which national primary and secondary standards will be achieved and maintained within each air quality control region in such State.

3. State primacy. Why should "primary responsibility" for air quality be lodged with the states? Does the national interest in the solution of the problem of air pollution end with the attainment of acceptable ambient quality? It would seem that the national interest might be affected by the ways in which the states choose to achieve and maintain air quality. A decision by an upwind state to require tall smokestacks and location of polluting facilities near the downwind state line might result in satisfactory ambient air quality in the upwind state, but it hardly seems consistent with sound national policy. The national interest can be protected in this sort of a case by the power of the federal government to reject that sort of an implementation plan as inadequate. The statutory devices directed toward the concerns of downwind states are considered at the conclusion of this Chapter, *infra* at page 821.

Despite the statutory language regarding state primacy, who is really in control, the states or the federal government? Recalling the concept of federal supremacy, this is a game which the states have no choice but to play. The third prong of the federal role, taking over for states that do not undertake conforming regulation, is anathema to the states. No state would want the federal bureaucracy making decisions that may have calamitous economic repercussions in their states, such as forcing major manufacturing facilities to shut down or relocate due to the imposition of stringent pollution control requirements. Moreover, the federal government, through its power to refuse to approve SIPs, can influence how any SIP is drawn. This point will be more easily understood after you have studied the materials in Part D of this chapter that demonstrate EPA's power to insist on various forms of compliance with its dictates by both states and polluters.

4. A different view of the race of laxity. What is so bad about the race of laxity? After all, although pollution may be deplorable from an aesthetic or environmental viewpoint, living in a degraded environment can reflect a reasoned choice. Few among us would insist on absolutely no emissions of pollution, preferring instead some level of human-induced pollution and material comforts such as heat in the winter, refrigeration for food, automobiles and the like. Why should citizens of the State of Filth be denied the economic prosperity of a booming economy and dirty environment if that is their wish? Is concern for the health of Filth's citizens a sufficient ground for federal standard-setting if the residents of Filth decide to forego a safe environment? Whatever the force of the argument against national standards as an invasion of Filth's 'right' to be filthy, the argument's force wanes dramatically should Filth's filth fail to "stay at home." The air and water into which most industrial effluents are discharged circulate and carry pollutants downwind and downstream, imposing social costs on people far from those living in the state of origin. If the external costs of Filth's filth can be controlled, beyond concern for the health of Filth's citizens, a second national interest that justifies imposing national ambient air quality standards is avoiding the race of laxity. As America moves away from reliance on heavy industry as the driving force in the economy toward an economy driven by the high-technology and service sectors, is the race of laxity still of major importance?

5. Ending the race of laxity. Do harm-based ambient standards eliminate the race of laxity among the states? Areas with cleaner-than-required air can still run in the race and attract new industry with lax pollution control programs. Their race, however, will be a short one, and their victory will be incomplete. Ambient air quality will fall in states that are apparent initial winners in the race of laxity. Once their air reaches the pollution levels permitted by the NAAQS, those states too will have to adopt pollution control measures or see their economic development stagnate because no additional pollution can be allowed through the introduction of additional sources. Fearing this boom and then bust pattern of growth, most states will regulate pollution. Some competition for laxity will still exist – states with cleaner air initially might be tempted to offer laxer regulation knowing that there is, in effect, more clean air to be consumed in their state than in others.[7] Another

7. If water is the medium involved, the differences in receiving body characteristics can be far more extreme. Compare the effect of an ambient quality standard on the Atlantic Ocean near the terminus of the Hudson River as receiving body and some small western creek. The inability of water-poor states to compete for industrial location if only ambient standards are employed is one of several factors that led to the subordinate position of harm-based ambient standards in the Clean Water Act.

check on the length of the race of laxity under the CAA is the prevention of significant degradation (PSD) program. It is described *infra* at page 819.

B. HARM AS THE THRESHOLD OF REGULATION

In the absence of identifiable or threatened harm, there is no warrant for regulating conduct under most contemporary theories of social and political organization. In general, there is no social benefit to be had in the regulation of such conduct and it bears a cost in terms of both loss of individual autonomy and whatever resources are devoted to enforcement of the prohibition or regulation. There is also little disagreement that government is authorized to act to prevent widespread harms caused by the activities of its citizens – to apply Hardin's "mutual coercion, mutually agreed upon." The two controversial threshold decisions that must be made in adopting harm-based ambient standards involve (1) what harms are significant enough to justify the subsequent burden of regulation,[8] and (2) the correlation of cause and effect – i.e., the linkage of a particular ambient quality level with the avoidance of harm.[9]

In regard to setting harm-based ambient standards for a medium like air or water, the fact that the common resource is a composite substance that can contain many things adds additional difficulty. There is no single litmus of what classifies air or water as benign or harmful. As previously mentioned, the Clean Air Act has approached the multiplicity of harmful agents that might be present in the air by regulating a small number of pollutants that are labelled "criteria pollutants" under an ambient standards approach, having switched to a technology-based source control approach to the regulation of toxic pollutants. Here our concern is solely with the criteria pollutants.

The term "criteria pollutants" is traceable to the halting pre-1970 federal air pollution control legislation. A series of statutes mandated federal study of the causes of air pollution and its health effects. One of those enactments assigned to the Secretary of Health, Education and Welfare the responsibility to "compile and publish *criteria* reflecting accurately the latest scientific knowledge useful in indicating the kind and extent of [harm] which may be expected from the presence of [an] air pollution agent (or combination of agents) in the air in varying quantities."[10] The choice of members for the set of criteria pollutants thus reflected the patterns that had evolved in scientific studies of the harms caused by air pollution. Not surprisingly, the criteria pollutants included many of the most common and widely generated pollutants, principally those emitted by the combustion of fossil

8. A related issue here is the more general benefit-cost concern that compares the cost of harm prevention with the benefits of harm avoidance.

9. A related issue in this arena is the concurrence of multiple causes. For example, lead exposure comes from multiple sources, not air pollution alone.

10. Pub.L. 88-206, §3(c)(2)(1963)(emphasis supplied). The term "criteria" is also used in distinction to the term standards. Criteria are scientific data-oriented matters, concerned with the causal nexus between ambient concentrations and harmful effects. Standards are set with reference to the information adduced by the criteria studies, but standard-setting may also include consideration of technical and economic issues.

fuels. The Clean Air Act in §108(a)(1)(a-b) defined criteria pollutants generically as those that "cause and contribute to air pollution which may reasonably be anticipated to endanger public health or welfare; the presence of which in the ambient air results from numerous or diverse mobile or stationary sources." The statute required the Environmental Protection Agency (EPA) to revise the list of criteria pollutants on a periodic basis.

Natural Resources Defense Council v. Train
United States Circuit Court for the Second Circuit, 1976
545 F.2d 320

SMITH, J. The Environmental Protection Agency and its Administrator, Russell Train, appeal from an order of the United States District Court for the Southern District of New York...requiring the Administrator of the EPA, within thirty days, to place lead on a list of air pollutants under §108(a)(1) of the Clean Air Act.... We affirm the order of the district court....

The relevant section of §108 reads as follows:

> (a)(1) For the purpose of establishing national primary and secondary ambient air quality standards, the Administrator shall within 30 days after December 31, 1970, publish, and shall from time to time thereafter revise, a list which includes each air pollutant -
>
> (A) which in his judgment has an adverse effect on public health or welfare;
>
> (B) the presence of which in the ambient air results from numerous or diverse mobile or stationary sources; and
>
> (C) for which air quality criteria had not been issued before December 31, 1970, but for which he plans to issue air quality criteria under this section.

Once a pollutant has been listed under §108(a)(1) by EPA, §§109 and 110 of the Act are automatically invoked. These sections require that for any pollutant for which air quality criteria are issued under §108(a)(1(C) after the date of enactment of the Clean Air Amendments of 1970, the Administrator must simultaneously issue air quality standards. Within nine months of the promulgation of such standards, states are required to submit implementation plans to the Administrator. §110(a)(1). The Administrator must approve or disapprove a state plan within four months. §110(a)(2). If a state fails to submit an acceptable plan, the Administrator is required to prepare and publish such a plan himself. §110(c). State implementation plans must provide for the attainment of primary ambient air quality standards no later than three years from the date of approval of a plan. §110(a)(2)(A)(i). Extension of the three-year period for attaining the primary standard may be granted by the Administrator only in very limited circumstances, and in no case for more than two years. §110(e).[11]

---

11. It is irrelevant that the current state of scientific knowledge may make it difficult to set an ambient air quality standard. The Administrator must proceed in spite of such difficulties:

> The Committee is aware that there are many gaps in the available scientific knowledge of the welfare and other environmental effects of air pollution.... A great deal of basic research will be needed to determine the long-term air quality goals which are required to protect the public health and welfare from any potential effects of air pollution. *In the meantime, the Secretary will be expected to establish such national goals on the basis of the best information available to him.* (emphasis added). S. Rep. No. 91–1196 on S. 4358.

The EPA concedes that lead meets the conditions of §§108(a)(1)(A) and (B) – that it has an adverse effect on public health and welfare, and that the presence of lead in the ambient air results from numerous or diverse mobile or stationary sources. The EPA maintains, however, that under §108(a)(1)(C) of the Act, the Administrator retains discretion whether to list a pollutant, even though the pollutant meets the criteria of §§108(a)(1)(A) and (B). The Agency regards the listing of lead under §108(a)(1) and the issuance of ambient air quality standards as one of numerous alternative control strategies for lead available to it. Listing of substances is mandatory, the EPA argues, only for those pollutants for which the Administrator "plans to issue air quality criteria." He may, it is contended, choose not to issue, i.e., not "plan to issue" such criteria, and decide to control lead solely by regulating emission at the source, regardless of the total concentration of lead in the ambient air. The Administrator argues that if he chooses to control lead (or other pollutants) under §211, he is not required to list the pollutant under §108(a)(1) or to set air quality standards.

The EPA advances three reasons for the position that the Administrator has discretion whether to list a pollutant even when the conditions of §§108(a)(1)(A) and (B) have been met: the plain meaning of §108(a)(1)(C); the structure of the Clean Air Act as a whole; and the legislative history of the Act.

The issue is one of statutory construction. We agree with the district court and with appellees, National Resources Defense Council, Inc., et al., that the interpretation of the Clean Air Act advanced by the EPA is contrary to the structure of the Act as a whole, and that if accepted, it would vitiate the public policy underlying the enactment of the 1970 Amendments as set forth in the Act and in its legislative history. Recent court decisions are in accord, and have construed §108(a)(1) to be mandatory if the criteria of subsections A and B are met.

Section 108(a)(1) contains mandatory language. It provides that "the Administrator *shall*...publish...a list..." (emphasis added). If the EPA interpretation were accepted and listing were mandatory only for substances "for which [the Administrator] plans to issue air quality criteria...", then the mandatory language of §108(a)(1)(A) would become mere surplusage. The determination to list a pollutant and to issue air quality criteria would remain discretionary with the Administrator, and the rigid deadlines of §108(a)(2), §109, and §110 for attaining air quality standards could be bypassed by him at will. If Congress had enacted §211 [relating to regulation of fuel additives, such as lead] as an alternative to, rather than as a supplement to, §§108–110, then one would expect a similar fixed timetable for implementation of the fuel control section. The absence of such a timetable for the enforcement of §211 lends support to the view that fuel controls were intended by Congress as a means for attaining primary air quality standards rather than as an alternative to the promulgation of such standards....

When a specific provision of a total statutory scheme may be construed to be in conflict with the congressional purpose expressed in an act, it becomes necessary to examine the act's legislative history to determine whether the specific provision is reconcilable with the intent of Congress. Because state planning and implementation under the Air Quality Act of 1967 had made little progress by 1970, Congress

---

National Quality Standards Act of 1970, "Report of the Committee on Public Works, United States Senate," 91st Cong., 2d Sess. at 11; A Legislative History of the Clean Air Amendments of 1970, Vol. I at 411 (1974)(hereafter Legislative History, Clean Air Amendments).

reacted by "taking a stick to the States in the form of the Clean Air Amendments of 1970...." Train v. NRDC, 421 U.S. 60, 64 (1975). It enacted §108(a)(1) which provides that the Administrator of the Environmental Protection Agency "shall" publish a list which includes each air pollutant which is harmful to health and originates from specified sources. Once a pollutant is listed under §108(a)(1), §§109 and 110 are to be automatically invoked, and promulgation of national air quality standards and implementation thereof by the states within a limited, fixed time schedule becomes mandatory.

The EPA contention that the language of §108(a)(1)(C) "for which [the Administrator] plans to issue air quality criteria" is a separate and third criterion to be met before §108 requires listing lead and issuing air quality standards, thereby leaving the decision to list lead within the discretion of the Administrator, finds no support in the legislative history of the 1970 Amendments to the Act. The summary of the provisions of the conference agreement furnished the Senate by Senator Muskie contained the following language:

> The agreement requires issuance of remaining air quality criteria for major pollutants within 13 months of date of enactment.... Within the 13-month deadline, the Congress expects criteria to be issued for nitrogen oxides, fluorides, lead, polynuclear organic matter, and odors, though others may be necessary....[12]

While the literal language of §108(a)(1)(C) is somewhat ambiguous, this ambiguity is resolved when this section is placed in the context of the Act as a whole and in its legislative history. The deliberate inclusion of a specific timetable for the attainment of ambient air quality standards incorporated by Congress in §§108-110 would become an exercise in futility if the Administrator could avoid listing pollutants simply by choosing not to issue air quality criteria. The discretion given to the Administrator under the Act pertains to the review of state implementation plans under §110, and to §211 which authorizes but does not mandate the regulation of fuel or fuel additives. It does not extend to the issuance of air quality standards for substances derived from specified sources which the Administrator had already adjudged injurious to health....

The structure of the Clean Air Act as amended in 1970, its legislative history, and the judicial gloss placed upon the Act leave no room for an interpretation which makes the issuance of air quality standards for lead under §108 discretionary. The Congress sought to eliminate, not perpetuate, opportunity for administrative foot-dragging. Once the conditions of §§108(a)(1)(A) and (B) have been met, the listing of lead and the issuance of air quality standards for lead become mandatory.

The order of the district court is affirmed.

COMMENTARY AND QUESTIONS

1. The criteria pollutants. There are currently six criteria pollutants under the Clean Air Act: sulfur dioxide, nitrogen dioxide, suspended particulates, carbon monoxide, ozone, and lead. In light of the generic statutory definition and the mandatory nature of EPA's obligation to add new criteria pollutants, does the brevity of the list surprise you? In part the small number reflects the fact that hazardous air pollutants are regulated separately by §112 of the Act, 42 U.S.C.A. §7412.

---

12. Legislative History, Clean Air Amendments, Vol. 1 at 430, 432 (1974). [This is note 9 in the original.]

2. EPA's better way to control lead emissions. EPA raised two types of arguments against the addition of lead as a criteria pollutant, arguments that vested EPA with general discretion in the selection of criteria pollutants and what might be termed "lead-specific" arguments. The claims for a general discretion may have seemed a bit lame, but EPA had what it felt were strong reasons in support of its lead-specific argument. EPA studies had shown that almost 90 percent of lead emissions into the environment were traceable to motor vehicles, an air pollution source that EPA was empowered to regulate both directly and through the regulation of fuel additives. EPA felt the most effective means for limiting lead emissions to safe levels was to force the removal of lead from gasoline. Might EPA's position make good sense, but still be a violation of the statutory command?

The Clean Air Act requires EPA to follow the listing of a criteria pollutant with the promulgation of both primary and secondary National Ambient Air Quality Standards (NAAQS). The Act in §109(b)(1-2) defines the qualitative effect that adherence to the standards will have:

> National primary ambient air quality standards...shall be [ones] the attainment and maintenance of which in the judgment of the Administrator [of EPA], based on such criteria and allowing an adequate margin of safety, are required to protect the public health.
>
> Any national secondary ambient air quality standard...shall specify a level of air quality the attainment and maintenance of which in the judgment of the Administrator [of EPA], based on such criteria, is requisite to protect the public welfare from any known or anticipated adverse effects associated with the presence of such air pollutant in the ambient air.

Standard setting requires judgments about the causal effects of exposure to varying concentrations of pollutants. Returning to lead as an example, the addition of lead as a criteria pollutant was followed by promulgation of primary and secondary ambient standards. A court challenge to those standards ensued.

Lead Industries Association v. Environmental Protection Agency
United States Circuit Court of Appeals
for the District of Columbia Circuit, 1980
647 F.2d 1130, cert. denied 449 U.S. 1042 (1980)

J. SKELLY WRIGHT, Chief Circuit Judge.

[The court's very lengthy opinion upheld the primary and secondary NAAQS for lead, which were attacked by St. Joe Minerals Corporation and the Lead Industries Association (LIA), among others. After examining the statutory requirements, the criteria document, the proposed and final ambient standards, and the standard of judicial review to be applied to review the rule-making, the court addressed the key claims.]

The petitioner's first claim is that the Administrator exceeded his authority under the statute by promulgating a primary air quality standard for lead which is more stringent than is necessary to protect the public health because it is designed to protect the public against "sub-clinical" effects which are not harmful to health. According to petitioners, Congress only authorized the Administrator to set primary air quality standards that are aimed at protecting the public against health effects which are known to be *clearly harmful*. They argue that Congress so limited the Administrator's authority because it was concerned that excessively stringent air quality standards could cause massive economic dislocation....

Where Congress intended the Administrator to be concerned about economic and technological feasibility, it expressly so provided. For example, Section 111 of the Act directs the Administrator to consider economic and technological feasibility in establishing standards of performance for new stationary sources of air pollution based on the best available control technology. S. Rep. No 91-1196, 91st Cong. 2d Sess. 416 (1970). In contrast, §109(b) speaks only of protecting the public health and welfare. Nothing in its language suggests that the Administrator is to consider economic or technological feasibility in setting ambient air quality standards.

The legislative history of the Act also shows the Administrator may not consider economic and technological feasibility in setting air quality standards; the absence of any provision requiring consideration of these factors was no accident; it was the result of a deliberate decision by Congress to subordinate such concerns to the achievement of health goals. Exasperated by the lack of significant progress toward dealing with the problem of air pollution under the Air Quality Act of 1967, 81 Stat. 485, and prior legislation, Congress abandoned the approach of offering suggestions and setting goals in favor of "taking a stick to the States in the form of the Clean Air Amendments of 1970..." Train v. NRDC, Inc. 421 U.S. 60, 64 (1975); see Union Electric Co. v. EPA, 427 U.S. 246, 256-257 (1976). Congress was well aware that, together with Sections 108 and 110, Section 109 imposes requirements of a "technology-forcing" character....

It may well be that underlying St. Joe's argument is its feeling that Congress could not or should not have intended this result, and that this court should supply relief by grafting a requirement of economic or technological feasibility onto the statute. The Supreme Court confronted a similar suggestion in the Tellico Dam case. TVA v. Hill, 437 U.S. 153 (1978). There TVA argued that the Endangered Species Act should not be construed to prevent operation of the dam since it had already been completed at a cost of approximately $100 million, Congress had appropriated funds for the dam even after the Act was passed, and the species at risk – the snail darter – was relatively unimportant and ways might ultimately be found to save it. The Court rejected the invitation to "view the...Act 'reasonably,' and hence shape a remedy that 'accords with some modicum of common sense and the public weal.'" 437 U.S. at 194.

According to LIA, Congress was mindful of the possibility that air quality standards which are too stringent could cause severe economic dislocation. For this reason it only granted the Administrator authority to adopt air quality standards which are "designed to protect the public from adverse health effects that are clearly harmful." LIA finds support for its interpretation of congressional intent in various portions of the legislative history of the Act. For example, it notes that the Senate Report on the 1970 legislation states that EPA "would be required to set a national *minimum* standard of air quality," S. Rep. No 91-1196 at 10 (emphasis added).... LIA then argues that the Administrator based the lead air quality standards on protecting children from "subclinical" effects of lead exposure which have not been shown to be harmful to health, that in so doing the Administrator ignored the clear limitation that Congress imposed on his standard-setting powers, and that the Administrator's action will in fact cause the very result that Congress was so concerned about avoiding.

LIA's argument appears to touch on two issues. The first concerns the type of health effects on which the Administrator may base air quality standards, i.e., the point at which the Administrator's regulatory authority may be exercised. This issue, as LIA suggests, does concern the limits that the Act, and its legislative history, may place on the Administrator's authority. The second issue appears to be more in the nature of an evidentiary question: whether or not the evidence in the record substantiates the Administrator's claim that the health effects on which the standards were based do in fact satisfy the requirements of the Act. Although these two issues are closely related, they are conceptually distinct, and they are best examined separately.

Section 109(b) does not specify precisely what Congress had in mind when it directed the Administrator to prescribe air quality standards that are "requisite to protect the public health." The legislative history of the Act does, however, provide some guidance. The Senate Report explains that the goal of the air quality standards must be to ensure that the public is protected from "adverse health effects." S. Rep. No. 91-1196 at 10. And the report is particularly careful to note that especially sensitive persons such as asthmatics and emphysematics are included within the group that must be protected. It is on the interpretation of the phrase "adverse health effects" that the disagreement between LIA and EPA about the limits of the Administrator's statutory authority appears to be based. LIA argues that the legislative history of the Act indicates that Congress only intended to protect the public against effects which are known to be *clearly harmful* to health, maintaining that this limitation on the Administrator's statutory authority is necessary to ensure that the standards are not set at a level which is more stringent than Congress contemplated. The Administrator, on the other hand, agrees that primary air quality standards must be based on protecting the public from "adverse health effects," but argues that the meaning LIA assigns to that phrase is too limited. In particular, the Administrator contends that LIA's interpretation is inconsistent with the precautionary nature of the statute, and will frustrate Congress' intent in requiring promulgation of air quality standards.

The Administrator begins by pointing out that the Act's stated goal is "to protect and enhance the quality of the Nation's air resources so as to promote the public health and welfare and the productive capacity of its population." Section 101(b)(1). This goal was reaffirmed in the 1977 Amendments. For example, the House Report accompanying the Amendments states that one of its purposes is "[t]o emphasize the preventive or precautionary nature of the act, i.e., to assure that regulatory action can effectively prevent harm before it occurs; to emphasize the predominant value of protection of public health." H.R. Rep. No. 95-294, 95th Cong., 1st Sess. 49 (1977). The Administrator notes that protecting the public from harmful effects requires decisions about exactly what these harms are, a task Congress left to his judgment. He notes that the task of making these decisions is complicated by the absence of any clear thresholds above which there are adverse effects and below which there are none. Rather, as scientific knowledge expands and analytical techniques are improved, new information is uncovered which indicates that pollution levels that were once considered harmless are not in fact harmless. Congress, the Administrator argues, was conscious of this problem, and left these decisions to his judgment partly for this reason. In such situations the perspective that is brought to bear on the problem plays a crucial role in determining what decisions are made. Because it realized this, Congress, the Administrator maintains, directed him to err on the side of caution in making these judgments. First, Congress made it abundantly clear that considerations of economic or technological feasibility are to be subordinated to the goal of protecting the public health by prohibiting any consideration of such factors. Second, it specified that the air quality standards must also protect individuals who are particularly sensitive to the effects of pollution. Third, it required that the standards be set at a level at which there is "an absence of adverse effect" on these sensitive individuals. Finally, it specifically directed the Administrator to allow an adequate margin of safety in setting primary air quality standards in order to provide some protection against effects that research has not yet uncovered. The Administrator contends that these indicia of congressional intent, the precautionary nature of the statutory mandate to protect the public health, the broad discretion Congress gave him to decide what effects to protect against, and the uncertainty that must be part of any attempt to determine the health effects of air pollution, are all extremely difficult to reconcile with LIA's suggestion that he can only set standards which are designed to protect against effects which are known to be *clearly harmful to health*....

It may be...LIA's view that the Administrator must show that there is a "medical consensus that [the effects on which the standards were based] are harmful..." If so, LIA is seriously mistaken. This court has previously noted that some uncertainty about the health effects of air pollution is inevitable. And we pointed out that "[a]waiting certainty will often allow for only reactive, not preventive regulat[ory action]." Ethyl Corp. v. EPA, 541 F.2d 1, 25 (D.C. Cir. 1976). Congress apparently shares this view; it specifically directed the Administrator to allow an adequate margin of safety to protect against effects which have not yet been uncovered by research and effects whose medical significance is a matter of disagreement. This court has previously acknowledged the role of the margin of safety requirement. In EDF v. EPA, 598 F.2d 62, 81 (D.C. Cir. 1978), we pointed out that "[i]f administrative responsibility to protect against unknown dangers presents a difficult task, indeed, a veritable paradox...calling as it does for knowledge of that which is unknown...then, the term 'margin of safety' is Congress' directive that means be found to carry out the task and to reconcile the paradox." Moreover, it is significant that Congress has recently acknowledged that more often than not the "margins of safety" that are incorporated into air quality standards turn out to be very modest or nonexistent, as new information reveals adverse health effects at pollution levels once thought to be harmless. See H.R. Rep. No. 95-294 at 103-117. Congress' directive to the Administrator to allow an "adequate margin of safety" alone plainly refutes any suggestion that the Administrator is only authorized to set primary air quality standards which are designed to protect against health effects that are known to be clearly harmful....

As we read the statutory provisions and the legislative history, Congress directed the Administrator to err on the side of caution in making the necessary decisions. We see no reason why this court should put a gloss on Congress' scheme by requiring the Administrator to show that there is a medical consensus that the effects on which the lead standards were based are "*clearly harmful to health*." All that is required by the statutory scheme is evidence in the record which substantiates his conclusions about the health effects on which the standards were based. Accordingly, we reject LIA's claim that the Administrator exceeded his statutory authority and turn to LIA's challenge to the evidentiary basis for the Administrator's decisions....

[The opinion went on to uphold ambient air quality standards designed with reference to adverse health effects in children (a particularly lead-sensitive population) when they suffer elevated blood lead levels.[13] The court found that the Administrator's methodology provided an ample margin for safety and was not impermissibly redundant nor overly conservative.]

COMMENTARY AND QUESTIONS

1. The NAAQS. As a point of reference for future discussions, you should be aware that ambient air quality standards are described in terms of maximum concentrations, that are applicable for various time periods and that are not to be exceeded more than a specified number of times (usually once, if at all) on an annual basis. The current standards are set forth in 40 CFR §§50.4-50.12.

Does the difficulty of translating concern for health and welfare into ambient air quality standards, and the subsequent step of translating those standards into source-specific emissions limitations spell doom for a harm-based ambient quality approach? After seeing the difficulty EPA encounters in establishing NAAQSs for each criteria pollutant, is it surprising that EPA is in no great hurry to add additional pollutants to the CAA's short list? That hesitancy is multiplied at least fifty-fold when you consider that every state must have a SIP in place for the control of each criteria pollutant, designed to assure that each NAAQS will be met. The litigation over SIPs has been intense and protracted. See, e.g., the *Cleveland Electric* case, *infra*, at page 801.

2. Primary and secondary standards. The CAA treats primary and secondary NAAQS identically in the promulgation process that EPA must follow. In contrast §110 describing the necessary elements of SIPs, sets different timetables for attainment. Section 110(a)(2)(A) requires that SIPs must be able to meet primary standards "as expeditiously as practicable but...in no case later than three years from the date of [EPA] approval of such plan" whereas SIPs need only "specif[y] a reasonable time at which such secondary standard will be attained." This difference in treatment has had the practical effect of making the secondary standards more of a desideratum than an enforceable part of the Act. States have been slow to propose means for attaining the secondary standards and EPA has not forced them to set a time certain for attainment. In his article Clean Air: From the 1970 Act to the 1977 Amendments, 17 Duq. L. Rev. 33, 35-36 (1978–79), Samuel Hayes describes EPA's lack of aggressiveness in pursuing compliance with secondary standards:

> The secondary standards have not been enforced so strictly as the primary ones, especially in the case of sulfur dioxide. One could argue that the entire clean air program has been influenced overwhelmingly by health effects and, in the process of day-to-day administration, agencies slowly drifted toward a preoccupation with the correction of health problems to justify an action. One of the first major judicial decisions involved a challenge by the smelting

13. Eds: The industry had challenged EPA's correlation of ambient air lead levels to blood lead levels, which had formed the basis for translating health-based effects into an air quality standard.

industry to the secondary sulfur dioxide annual average standards. The case was remanded by the court to the EPA for further consideration, and it has never reemerged.

As a matter of administrative performance this result should be unsurprising – there is no institutional incentive to tackle the problem and no enforceable legal command that it be tackled. The timetable is committed to EPA discretion by the Act, so a lawsuit will find no mandatory duty that can be forced upon EPA. EPA has chosen to expend its limited air pollution control resources for what Congress has determined is the more pressing objective, attainment of the primary NAAQS. EPA also avoids the unpleasantness of confrontation with the states over amending their SIPs to include attainment of secondary NAAQS by a date certain. The states are loathe to adopt SIPs that will force them through the painful process of imposing additional regulations on the sources of pollution because of the adverse impact of additional pollution control costs on the economic development within the state (the old race of laxity problem).

Shouldn't Congress have foreseen institutional reluctance to enforce the secondary standards and legislated a deadline for attainment? Put differently, as a matter of statutory design, what explains the different treatment of primary and secondary standards? The hierarchical structure of the NAAQS that links primary standards to protection of public health and secondary standards to public welfare and environment may seem self-evident, especially in light of the anthropocentric view of environmental issues that has so long prevailed in this country's majority culture. In the same fashion, public perception of risk is disproportionately influenced by matters of bodily security and public health. See page 79 *supra*. Still, it is worth asking whether the hierarchy is in all instances rational. For example, what if the human health protective standard for sulfur dioxide permits sufficiently high ambient concentrations of that pollutant to remain in the atmosphere to cause widespread destruction of aquatic and plant life? That scenario is, more or less, a principal cause of acid rain. Sulfur dioxide and water vapor react in the atmosphere to form dilute sulfuric acid that is then deposited by precipitation, damaging the ecology of downwind lakes and forests. Is the example a cogent criticism of the subordination of "welfare" protection, or does the Clean Air Act still leave EPA enough power to insist on attainment of both primary and secondary standards in those cases where "mere" welfare is of vital concern?

A second plausible explanation of this double standard was Congress' fear that the burdens of compliance with the more stringent secondary standards would have been too great a blow for the affected polluting entities to absorb. There is no doubt that pollution control requirements have put some marginal firms out of business. Moreover, from a global perspective, the race of laxity still exists, in that most nations have significantly less stringent air pollution laws than the United States. Consider also that Congress has the power to revisit the issue and adopt a fixed date when it believes that policy is warranted. Looking at the history of federal environmental regulation since 1970, it is apparent that Congress has on several occasions amended its major regulatory efforts to make them more stringent, although it has also acted to relax standards or postpone deadlines. As an example, Hayes, continuing the analysis excerpted above, notes:

> Visibility as a specific element of an aesthetic air quality standard was not taken seriously by EPA. It did appear in a number of state programs, and the 1977 amendments explicitly incorporated visibility into the federal program for most national parks and wilderness areas. Thus, the 1977 amendments attempted to capture a broader spectrum of objectives in standard setting, as originally outlined in the 1970 Act. 17 Duq. L. Rev. 36.

3. Risk and uncertainty. What is allocation of risk under conditions of uncertainty in a harm-based standards approach? As a general matter, the risk of uncertainty is borne by the public. Demonstrating that there will be harm at a particular level of pollution is part of the burden that government must carry in order to justify regulation. This approach may be said to minimize the chance of regulating false positives, that is, it minimizes the likelihood that regulation will be imposed on conduct that is in fact harmless. This approach is frequently contrasted to the use of technology-based standards, like the CWA norms studied in the next chapter. That technique is said to minimize the occurrence of false negatives, i.e., the likelihood that harmful conduct will go unregulated owing to an absence of proof that it is indeed harmful. Is one approach *a priori* preferable to the other?

In the case of setting the NAAQS for lead, how did the EPA approach matters of risk to public health and scientific uncertainty? LIA complains of the cautious assumptions that EPA made. What would have been the result had EPA been less conservative – would public interest groups have had any greater success in challenging EPA's methodology? Assuming that the answer is no, agency methodology becomes the final word on how risk and uncertainty is to be regarded in making important public health decisions. Congress can always control the agency through appropriate legislation, but Congress is ill-equipped to do so and has shown little inclination to involve itself in scientific matters. If Congress does not set agency policy by specific legislative guidance, who controls the agency policy-making process?

4. Cost and feasibility in standard-setting. Can a harm-based ambient standards statute, as a whole, ignore the economic and technological feasibility of meeting its standards? The *Lead Industries* case makes clear its view that cost and feasibility have no role to play in the standard-setting process. Despite the whimsical adage that rules and laws are made to be broken, it would be a poor statutory design that did not make compliance with its ultimate requirements not only possible, but probable. The Clean Air Act plainly seeks and expects compliance, although it does make express provision for the problem of non-attainment of the desired quality level. See page 811 *infra*. The more vital general inquiry is one of statutory design – how do you allow matters of economic and technological feasibility to be a part of the harm-based ambient standards regulatory regime without allowing concessions to those imperatives to block the necessary improvement to environmental quality? In places, the Clean Air Act is openly seeking to force technological innovation, but that seems a slender reed on which to balance a threat of massive economic dislocation. Although EPA's discretion is circumscribed in the standard setting process, there is a degree of discretion allowed in the power to approve SIPs. As will be seen in the *Union Electric* case, *infra*, there are CAA contexts in which cost and feasibility may be considered.

C. HARM-BASED STANDARDS FOR HAZARDOUS AIR POLLUTANTS[14]

Hazardous air pollutants are defined as pollutants, other than criteria pollutants, the exposure to which is "reasonably anticipated to result in an increase in mortality, or an increase in serious irreversible, or incapacitating irreversible illness." §7412(a)(1). Until the 1990 amendments to the Act, hazardous air pollutants, in a fashion similar to the criteria pollutants, were regulated by a harm-based device. Unlike the Act's treatment of conventional pollutants, §112 did not rely on the NAAQS process. Instead, EPA was required to compile a list of hazardous air pollutants and promulgate emission standards directly applicable to sources that emitted the hazardous pollutants in question. Those standards were to be set at a level that in the judgment of EPA "provides an ample margin of safety to protect the public health from such hazardous air pollutant." §7412(b)(1)(B).

Experience has shown that a harm-based standards approach is not easily applied to the problems of hazardous air pollutants. In general, these pollutants hold the threat of causing very grave health effects at minimal exposure levels. Many are considered to be "non-threshold" pollutants, meaning that no human exposure to them is safe. Despite agreement on the danger of even low exposures, the task of establishing standards for exposure is one that tends to be shrouded in uncertainty because the available data on exposure and response tend to be quite sketchy.[15] Thus, as a first level problem, the setting of standards is both difficult and uncertain.

Even after a "safe" exposure (ambient concentration) level is established for hazardous pollutants, the problem of meeting the standard will frequently be monumental. Some ambient standards will be so stringent, due to the low levels of allowable exposure, that the controls needed to achieve the standard will be exceedingly expensive. In some cases, control technologies that would prevent excessive emissions are not yet known. In either event, the enforcement of emission standards for hazardous air pollutants holds a significant possibility of causing economic dislocation, either through the cost or impossibility of compliance. The desire to avoid those consequences is heightened in cases where scientific uncertainty undermines confidence that the standard need be set at so stringent a level.

EPA, perhaps understandably, was slow to embark on the hazardous pollutant standard-setting task Congress had set for it. When it did come forth with

---

14. The program to set national emissions standards for hazardous air pollutants is frequently referred to by the acronym NESHAPs.

15. The difficulty of obtaining reliable data on human exposure to hazardous air pollutants rests in part on the obvious impossibility of making controlled tests and in part on the general problem of uncertainty that attends establishing causal links in exposure-response relationships. These matters are considered more fully in Chapter 4, *supra*.

regulations, they were immediately attacked on both sides – industry groups found the standards too exacting and expensive, public interest advocates claimed that the standards failed to provide the statutorily mandated "ample margin for safety." The most interesting litigation arose in relation to the standards set for vinyl chloride. Initially, EPA, while noting that vinyl chloride was "an apparent non-threshold pollutant," claimed that scientific uncertainty, due to the unavailability of dose-response data, made it impossible to establish any definite threshold level of adverse effects to human health. EPA therefore adopted a technology-based approach, calling for the employment of Best Available Technology (BAT).[16] This position was challenged by the Environmental Defense Fund and a settlement of that litigation was reached that required EPA to propose more stringent limitations with a zero emissions goal.

In 1977 EPA proposed new regulations for vinyl chloride in accordance with its agreement, setting lower allowable concentrations than it had in its previous proposal. EPA went on to add that the inability to identify a safe threshold level did not require a ban of all emissions. In EPA's view, that inability would justify using a BAT approach.[17] EPA then accepted public comment on its revised proposed vinyl chloride rule. It received a host of comments and thereafter failed to act, either to promulgate the rule or revise it, for the next eight years. Finally, in 1985, EPA changed its position. Claiming that some facets of the proposed regulations imposed unreasonable costs and that no demonstrated control technology consistently met the proposed standard, EPA concluded that it should abandon the 1977 proposals and adopt in their place a slightly revised version of the 1976 regulations.[18]

This action was challenged by the Natural Resources Defense Council. Being well aware of the deference given by courts to EPA, the attack was limited to a claim that EPA considered statutorily impermissible factors when it relied on cost and technological feasibility as the basis for its action. The District of Columbia Circuit Court of Appeals issued two opinions in the case, both authored by Judge Bork, initially writing for a three judge panel and later writing for the court en banc.[19] In his initial opinion, Judge Bork wrote:

> We believe that the agency in this case has made a reasonable interpretation.... [T]he EPA has not taken the position that it may consider cost and technological feasibility to set a standard that allows a level of emission at or above which evidence has indicated adverse health effects to occur. Perhaps if the evidence positively demonstrated that a given substance had ill effects and endangered the public health in trace amounts, the EPA could permit no emissions of that pollutant. Only when an area of uncertainty exists does the Administrator "reconcile the paradox" of having to protect against dangers he cannot know by setting standards as strict as possible given both available technology and the requirement that the cost of reduction not be grossly disproportionate to the level achieved. That the area

16. 40 Fed.Reg. 59,532 and 59,534 (1975).

17. 42 Fed.Reg 28,154 (1977).

18. 50 Fed. Reg. 1182, 1184 (1985).

19. Natural Resources Defense Council v. EPA, 804 F.2d 710 (1986); Natural Resources Defense Council v. EPA, 824 F.2d 1146 (1987).

of uncertainty, as with vinyl chloride, covers all non-zero levels of emission does not alter our conclusion.

Since the Administrator has no way of knowing health effects in the range of uncertainty, such considerations as technological and economic feasibility seem natural, perhaps inevitable, choices to inform the Administrator's decision whether he has amply provided for a reasonable degree of safety from the unknown. By emphasizing available technology, the EPA has ensured the maximum regulation against uncertainty without the economic and social displacements that would accompany the closing of an industry or any substantial part of an industry. By ensuring that costs do not become grossly disproportionate to the level of reduction achieved, the EPA guarantees that the consuming public does not pay an excessive price for the marginal benefits of increasing increments of protection against the unknown. We cannot say that this represents an unreasonable weighing of values, especially when no other value readily suggests itself and petitioner supplies none apart from health effects, which in the range of uncertainty are by definition unknowable. 804 F.2d at 722-23.

In the en banc rehearing, NRDC persisted in its argument that cost and technological feasibility were impermissible considerations in §112 standard setting. EPA took the position that it was allowed to set an emission level for non-threshold hazardous pollutants at the level achievable by BAT whenever that level is below the level of demonstrated harm and the cost of setting a lower level is grossly disproportionate to the benefits of removing the remaining risk. Writing for the court, Judge Bork rejected both positions as well as that of his own previous opinion. The final opinion held that unlike §109 and 110 where prior cases had limited EPA consideration of cost and technological feasibility,[20] §112 allowed EPA to consider those factors in setting emissions standards, but only after determining what is "safe" "based solely on the risk to health." The EPA methodology under review had failed to make a determination of what was safe; EPA had exceeded its allowable discretion by substituting a technology-based approach for the harm-based approach that Congress had established as the primary technique for the regulation of hazardous air pollutants.

Even after the vinyl chloride decision, EPA activity in the NESHAPs area continued at a crawl. The agency, by 1990, had managed to promulgate standards for only eight hazardous air pollutants, had listed and was in the process of proposing standards for a handful of additional substances, and was proposing to list another ten. In 1990 Congress largely abandoned a harm-based approach to hazardous air pollutants and substituted a technology-based approach that called for the employment of the "maximum available control technology (MACT)." The legislation identified almost 180 substances to be regulated by that method. Emitting sources were given eight years to install MACT, with EPA thereafter obligated to enact further measures to avoid unacceptable residual risks. This latter provision is, of course, a return to a harm-based approach. Whether EPA will be better able to make

---

20. See Union Electric Co. v. EPA, 427 U.S. 246 (1976)(§110); Lead Industries Ass'n. v. EPA, 647 F.2d 1130 (D.C.Cir.), *cert. denied*, 449 U.S. 1042 (1980)(§109).

significant progress in controlling hazardous air pollution under this altered methodology remains to be seen.

COMMENTARY AND QUESTIONS

1. The reluctance to tackle NESHAPs regulation. What makes hazardous pollutants so much more difficult to regulate than criteria pollutants? Is it uncertainty of the scientific data alone? It is almost always going to be the case that data concerning the health effects of exposure to criteria pollutants will be far more readily available. Large numbers of people in specific locales are exposed to ascertainable concentrations of criteria pollutants and epidemiological data therefore can be used in establishing the health effects of exposure levels. With a few exceptions, such as workers in the asbestos industry, there is not parallel data for hazardous pollutants.

From EPA's perspective, the NESHAPs program was a very inefficient use of its resources. Setting a §112 standard invariably engaged the agency in protracted hearings and subsequent litigation due to the proof problems that arose in regard to quantifying risks associated with low-level, long-term exposures to hazardous substances. Moreover, it was (and remains) single-substance regulation in relation to a universe of hazardous substances that has hundreds or even thousands of members, some of which react with one another (either synergistically or antagonistically) to form new harmful compounds.

2. Cost and feasibility in standard-setting, revisited. As a matter of logic and policy (and not as a matter of statutory interpretation) which of Bork's two positions on cost and technological feasibility is more compelling? In the first opinion he presumes that EPA, in the face of scientific uncertainty, may (should?) seek to impose cost-effective regulations, that is, regulations whose cost of implementation is exceeded by the public health benefits that are produced. In that calculation EPA is allowed to assume that the value of the unknown benefit of regulation more stringent than that afforded by BAT is not greater than the cost of still more effective emissions controls. In contrast, he seems to suggest that cost effectiveness of NESHAPs regulation may not be a consideration where no uncertainty is present. Is cost-ineffective regulation a wiser course to pursue when it is certainly occurring? Does §112 and the remainder of the Clean Air Act require so odd a position? Does that explain Bork's second opinion? That later opinion divorces the determination of what is safe from the subsequent decision of whether pursuing safety is worthwhile under the particular circumstances.

Does the Bork opinion satisfactorily distinguish the *Lead Industries* case? Judge Wright wrote a dissenting opinion in the final vinyl chloride case to the effect that EPA was limited by the statute itself in regard to what factors it could consider, and cost and feasibility were not among the permissible factors to be used in standard setting. Are the positions of EPA in the two cases inconsistent – arguing the irrelevance of cost and feasibility in regard to criteria pollutants and the opposite in the case of hazardous air pollutants? Does EPA have its arguments reversed in that the threat from hazardous air pollutants, arguably, is greater and therefore cost and feasibility ought to be less important rather than more important?

D. TECHNOLOGICAL FEASIBILITY AND THE STATES AS BROKERS

The *Lead Industries* case, *supra*, at page 783, was emphatic in ruling that economic feasibility had no role to play in the standard-setting process under a harm-based ambient quality approach. It is almost axiomatic that the feasibility of compliance with the standard has nothing at all to do with how clean the air must be to avoid the harm. This understanding, despite the interpretation given to §112 in the vinyl chloride case, is a basic precept of harm-based ambient quality standards.

Once the court has identified the approach as harm-based, it has no authority to inject the pragmatic concerns that economic and technologic feasibility embody. The reason for this limit on the court is simultaneously simple and politically sophisticated – because Congress said so. The deference to Congressional intent is constitutionally required because Congress is the lawmaker under the American system. By ascribing the decision to Congress, the court, as well as EPA, is without discretion to change the rule.

One factor in ascribing so inflexible an intent to Congress on the standard-setting issue is the existence in the Clean Air Act of other places where arguments regarding cost and feasibility are relevant. The following case, while resulting in yet another holding that EPA is not allowed to consider cost and feasibility, does so in a very narrow context. The case arose as a challenge to EPA's approval of Missouri's SIP, a SIP that itself did not include cost and feasibility as a consideration. As you will see, had Missouri taken cost and feasibility into account in designing its SIP, that approach would have been permissible as long as EPA determined that the SIP was likely to result in the attainment of the NAAQS.

Union Electric Company v. Environmental Protection Agency

United States Supreme Court, 1976
427 U.S. 246, 96 S.Ct. 2518, 49 L.Ed.2d 474

Mr. Justice MARSHALL delivered the opinion of the Court.

After the Administrator of the Environmental Protection Agency (EPA) approves a state implementation plan under the Clean Air Act, the plan may be challenged in a court of appeals within 30 days, or after 30 days have run if newly discovered or available information justifies subsequent review. We must decide whether the operator of a regulated emission source, in a petition for review of an EPA-approved state plan filed after the original 30-day appeal period, can raise the claim that it is economically or technologically infeasible to comply with the plan....

On April 30, 1971, the Administrator promulgated national primary and secondary standards for six air pollutants he found to have an adverse effect on the public health and welfare. Included among them was sulfur dioxide, at issue here. After the promulgation of the national standards, the State of Missouri formulated its implementation plan and submitted it for approval. Since sulfur dioxide levels exceeded national primary standards in only one of the State's five air quality regions, the Metropolitan St. Louis Interstate region, the Missouri plan concentrated on a control strategy and regulations to lower emissions in that area. The plan's emission limitations were effective at once, but the State retained authority to grant variances to particular sources that could not immediately comply. The Administrator approved the plan on May 31, 1972.

Petitioner is an electric utility company servicing the St. Louis metropolitan area, large portions of Missouri, and parts of Illinois and Iowa. Its three coal-fired generating plants in the metropolitan St. Louis area are subject to the sulfur dioxide restrictions in the Missouri implementation plan. Petitioner did not seek review of the Administrator's approval of the plan within 30 days, as it was entitled to do under §307(b)(1) of the Act, 42 U.S.C. §1857h–5(b)(1), but rather applied to the appropriate state and county agencies for variances from the emission limitations affecting its three plants. Petitioner received one-year variances, which could be extended upon reapplication. The variances on two of petitioner's three plants had expired and petitioner was applying for extensions when, on May 31, 1974, the Administrator notified petitioner that sulfur dioxide emissions from its plants violated the emission limitations contained in the Missouri plan. Shortly thereafter petitioner filed a petition in the Court of Appeals for the Eighth Circuit for review of the Administrator's 1972 approval of the Missouri implementation plan.

...We reject at the outset petitioner's suggestion that a claim of economic or technological infeasibility may be considered upon a petition for a review based on new information and filed more than 30 days after approval of an implementation plan even if such a claim could not be considered by the Administrator in approving a plan or by a court in reviewing a plan challenged within the original 30-day appeal period. In pertinent part §307(b)(1) provides: "A petition for review of the Administrator's action in approving or promulgating any implementation plan under section 110...may be filed only in the United States Court of Appeals for the appropriate circuit. Any such petition shall be filed within 30 days from the date of such promulgation, approval, or action, or after such date if such petition is based solely on grounds arising after such 30th day." Regardless of when a petition for review is filed under §307(b)(1), the court is limited to reviewing "the Administrator's action in approving...(the) implementation plan...." Accordingly, if new "grounds" are alleged, they must be such that, had they been known at the time the plan was presented to the Administrator for approval, it would have been an abuse of discretion for the Administrator to approve the plan. To hold otherwise would be to transfer a substantial responsibility in administering the Clean Air Act from the Administrator and the state agencies to the federal courts.

Since a reviewing court regardless of when the petition for review is filed may consider claims of economic and technological infeasibility only if the Administrator may consider such claims in approving or rejecting a state implementation plan, we must address ourselves to the scope of the Administrator's responsibility. The Administrator's position is that he has no power whatsoever to reject a state implementation plan on the ground that it is economically or technologically infeasible, and we have previously accorded great deference to the Administrator's construction of the Clean Air Act. See Train v. NRDC, 421 U.S., at 75. After surveying the relevant provisions of the Clean Air Amendments of 1970 and their legislative history, we agree that Congress intended claims of economic and technological infeasibility to be wholly foreign to the Administrator's consideration of a state implementation plan.

As we have previously recognized, the 1970 Amendments to the Clean Air Act were a drastic remedy to what was perceived as a serious and otherwise uncheckable problem of air pollution. The Amendments place the primary responsibility for formulating pollution control strategies on the States, but nonetheless subject the

States to strict minimum compliance requirements. These requirements are of a "technology-forcing character" and are expressly designed to force regulated sources to develop pollution control devices that might at the time appear to be economically or technologically infeasible.

This approach is apparent on the face of §110(a)(2). The provision sets out eight criteria that an implementation plan must satisfy, and provides that if these criteria are met and if the plan was adopted after reasonable notice and hearing, the Administrator "shall approve" the proposed state plan. The mandatory "shall" makes it quite clear that the Administrator is not to be concerned with factors other than those specified and none of the eight factors appears to permit consideration of technological or economic infeasibility.[21] Nonetheless, if a basis is to be found for allowing the Administrator to consider such claims, it must be among the eight criteria, and so it is here that the argument is focused.

It is suggested that consideration of claims of technological and economic infeasibility is required by the first criterion that the primary air quality standards be met "as expeditiously as practicable but...in no case later than three years . . ." and that the secondary air quality standards be met within a "reasonable time." §110(a)(2)(A). The argument is that what is "practicable" or "reasonable" cannot be determined without assessing whether what is proposed is possible. This argument does not survive analysis.

Section 110(a)(2)(A)'s three-year deadline for achieving primary air quality standards is central to the Amendments' regulatory scheme and, as both the language and the legislative history of the requirement make clear, it leaves no room for claims of technological or economic infeasibility. The 1970 congressional debate on the Amendments centered on whether technology forcing was necessary and desirable in framing and attaining air quality standards sufficient to protect the public health, standards later termed primary standards. The House version of the Amendments was quite moderate in approach, requiring only that health-related standards be met "within a reasonable time." H.R. 17255, 91st Cong., 2d Sess., §108(c)(1)(C)(i)(1970). The Senate bill, on the other hand, flatly required that, possible or not, health-related standards be met "within three years." S. 4358, 91st Cong., 2d Sess., §111(a)(2)(A)(1970).

The Senate's stiff requirement was intended to foreclose the claims of emission sources that it would be economically or technologically infeasible for them to achieve emission limitations sufficient to protect the public health within the specified time. As Senator Muskie, manager of the Senate bill, explained to his chamber:

> The first responsibility of Congress is not the making of technological or economic judgments or even to be limited by what is or appears to be technologically or economically feasible. Our responsibility is to establish what the public interest requires to protect the health of persons. This may mean that people and industries will be asked to do what seems to be impossible at the present time. 116 Cong. Rec. 32901-32902 (1970).

21. Comparison of the eight criteria of § 110(a)(2) with other provisions of the Amendments bolsters this conclusion. Where Congress intended the Administrator to be concerned about economic and technological infeasibility, it expressly so provided. Thus, §§ 110(a), 110(f), 111(a)(1), 202(a), 211(c)(2)(A), and 231(b) of the Amendments all expressly permit consideration, e. g., "of the requisite technology, giving appropriate consideration to the cost of compliance." Section 110(a)(2) contains no such language.

This position reflected that of the Senate committee:

> In the Committee discussions, considerable concern was expressed regarding the use of the concept of technical feasibility as the basis of ambient air standards. The Committee determined that 1) the health of people is more important than the question of whether the early achievement of ambient air quality standards protective of health is technically feasible; and 2) the growth of pollution load in many areas, even with application of available technology, would still be deleterious to public health.

Therefore, the Committee determined that existing sources of pollutants either should "meet the standard of the law or be closed down...." S.Rep. No. 91-1196, pp. 2-3 (1970).

The Conference Committee and, ultimately, the entire Congress accepted the Senate's three-year mandate for the achievement of primary air quality standards, and the clear import of that decision is that the Administrator must approve a plan that provides for attainment of the primary standards in three years even if attainment does not appear feasible. In rejecting the House's version of reasonableness, however, the conferees strengthened the Senate version. The Conference Committee made clear that the States could not procrastinate until the deadline approached. Rather, the primary standards had to be met in less than three years if possible; they had to be met "as expeditiously as practicable." §110(a)(2)(A). Whatever room there is for considering claims of infeasibility in the attainment of primary standards must lie in this phrase, which is, of course, relevant only in evaluating those implementation plans that attempt to achieve the primary standard in less than three years....

Secondary air quality standards, those necessary to protect the public welfare, were subject to far less legislative debate than the primary standards. The House version of the Amendments treated welfare-related standards together with health-related standards, and required both to be met "within a reasonable time." The Senate bill, on the other hand, treated health- and welfare-related standards separately and did not require that welfare-related standards be met in any particular time at all, although the Committee Report expressed the desire that they be met "as rapidly as possible." The final Amendments also separated welfare-related standards from health-related standards, labeled them secondary air quality standards, and adopted the House's requirement that they be met within a "reasonable time." §§109(b), 110(a)(2)(A). Thus, technology-forcing is not expressly required in achieving standards to protect the public welfare.

It does not necessarily follow, however, that the Administrator may consider claims of impossibility in assessing a state plan for achieving secondary standards. As with plans designed to achieve primary standards in less than three years, the scope of the Administrator's power to reject a plan depends on whether the State itself may decide to engage in technology forcing and adopt a plan more stringent than federal law demands.

[The Court then addressed the claim that the power to engage in technology-forcing is available to the states under the CAA. Here the utility's argument was that the second criterion for plan approval allowed plans to contain only such control devices as "may be necessary."]

We read the "as may be necessary" requirement of §110(a)(2)(B) to demand only that the implementation plan submitted by the State meet the "minimum

conditions" of the Amendments.[22] Beyond that, if a State makes the legislative determination that it desires a particular air quality by a certain date and that it is willing to force technology to attain it or lose a certain industry if attainment is not possible such a determination is fully consistent with the structure and purpose of the Amendments, and §110(a)(2)(B) provides no basis for the EPA Administrator to object to the determination on the ground of infeasibility.[23]

In sum, we have concluded that claims of economic or technological infeasibility may not be considered by the Administrator in evaluating a state requirement that primary ambient air quality standards be met in the mandatory three years. And, since we further conclude that the States may submit implementation plans more stringent than federal law requires and that the Administrator must approve such plans if they meet the minimum requirements of §110(a)(2), it follows that the language of §110(a)(2)(B) provides no basis for the Administrator ever to reject a state implementation plan on the ground that it is economically or technologically infeasible. Accordingly, a court of appeals reviewing an approved plan under §307(b)(1) cannot set it aside on those grounds, no matter when they are raised.

Our conclusion is bolstered by recognition that the Amendments do allow claims of technological and economic infeasibility to be raised in situations where consideration of such claims will not substantially interfere with the primary congressional purpose of prompt attainment of the national air quality standards. Thus, we do not hold that claims of infeasibility are never of relevance in the formulation of an implementation plan or that sources unable to comply with emission limitations must inevitably be shut down.

Perhaps the most important forum for consideration of claims of economic and technological infeasibility is before the state agency formulating the implementation plan. So long as the national standards are met, the State may select whatever mix of control devices it desires and industries with particular economic or technological problems may seek special treatment in the plan itself. Moreover, if the industry is not exempted from, or accommodated by, the original plan, it may obtain a variance, as petitioner did in this case; and the variance, if granted after notice and a hearing, may be submitted to the EPA as a revision of the plan. §110(a)(3)(A), 42 U.S.C. §1857c-5(a)(3)(A)(1970 ed., Supp. IV). Lastly, an industry denied an exemption from the implementation plan, or denied a subsequent variance, may be able to take its claims of economic or technological infeasibility to the state courts.

While the State has virtually absolute power in allocating emission limitations so long as the national standards are met, if the state plan cannot meet the national standards, the EPA is implicated in any postponement procedure. There are two ways that a State can secure relief from the EPA for individual emission sources, or classes of sources, that cannot meet the national standards. First, if the Governor

---

22. Economic and technological factors may be relevant in determining whether the minimum conditions are met. Thus, the Administrator may consider whether it is economically or technologically possible for the state plan to require more rapid progress than it does. If he determines that it is, he may reject the plan as not meeting the requirement that primary standards be achieved "as expeditiously as practicable" or as failing to provide for attaining secondary standards within "a reasonable time."

23. In a literal sense, of course, no plan is infeasible since offending sources always have the option of shutting down if they cannot otherwise comply with the standard of the law. Thus, there is no need for the Administrator to reject an economically or technologically "infeasible" state plan on the ground that anticipated noncompliance will cause the State to fall short of the national standards. Sources objecting to such a state scheme must seek their relief from the State.

of the State so requests at the time the original implementation plan is submitted, and if the State provides reasonable interim controls, the Administrator may allow a two-year extension of the three-year deadline for attainment of primary air quality standards if he finds that it is technologically infeasible for the source to comply. §110(e). Second, again upon application of the Governor of the State, the Administrator may allow a one-year postponement of any compliance date in an implementation plan if he finds, *inter alia,* that compliance is technologically infeasible and that "the continued operation of (the emission source) is essential to national security or to the public health or welfare...." §110(f).

Even if the State does not intervene on behalf of an emission source, technological and economic factors may be considered in at least one other circumstance. When a source is found to be in violation of the state implementation plan, the Administrator may, after a conference with the operator, issue a compliance order rather than seek civil or criminal enforcement. Such an order must specify a "reasonable" time for compliance with the relevant standard, taking into account the seriousness of the violation and "any good faith efforts to comply with applicable requirements." §113(a)(4) of the Clean Air Act, 42 U.S.C. §1857c- 8(a)(4)....

In short, the Amendments offer ample opportunity for consideration of claims of technological and economic infeasibility. Always, however, care is taken that consideration of such claims will not interfere substantially with the primary goal of prompt attainment of the national standards. Allowing such claims to be raised by appealing the Administrator's approval of an implementation plan, as petitioner suggests, would frustrate congressional intent. It would permit a proposed plan to be struck down as infeasible before it is given a chance to work, even though Congress clearly contemplated that some plans would be infeasible when proposed. And it would permit the Administrator or a federal court to reject a State's legislative choices in regulating air pollution, even though Congress plainly left with the States, so long as the national standards were met, the power to determine which sources would be burdened by regulation and to what extent. Technology forcing is a concept somewhat new to our national experience and it necessarily entails certain risks. But Congress considered those risks in passing the 1970 Amendments and decided that the dangers posed by uncontrolled air pollution made them worth taking. Petitioner's theory would render that considered legislative judgment a nullity, and that is a result we refuse to reach.

Affirmed.

Mr. Justice POWELL, with whom THE CHIEF JUSTICE joins, concurring. [Opinion omitted.]

COMMENTARY AND QUESTIONS

1. The role of economic and technologic feasibility. The Court rules that EPA cannot disapprove of a SIP on the grounds of infeasibility. This reflects the Court's interpretation of Congress' intent as forcing technological change and/or economic dislocation if that is what it takes to attain the NAAQS. Congress will brook a little delay in attainment, but attainment there must be. If states cut no slack for polluters on feasibility grounds, that is taken as an indication that the state either (1) intends to put its polluters on the spot to innovate or shut down, or (2) cannot draft a SIP that will attain the NAAQS without placing some of its polluters in that uncomfortable position.

Can EPA disapprove of a SIP that does take feasibility into account? Although the Court doesn't say so in those precise words, it is clear that EPA can approve of SIPs that allow some industries relief on feasibility grounds so long as the allowance of feasibility in allocating plant-specific emissions limitations does not prevent attainment of the mandated ambient air quality. In fact, the Court virtually invites the states, as a part of SIP formulation, to take feasibility into account when it points to the state SIP formulation process as the principal forum for feasibility arguments.

Must the EPA approve of SIPs that allow feasibility to be taken into account as long as those SIPs will result in timely attainment of the relevant NAAQS? Technically, the answer is probably not. EPA has discretion to reject feasibility allowances in SIPs if, in EPA's judgment, the SIPs do not achieve attainment as quickly as would still be practicable with lesser allowance for feasibility. EPA will seldom be inclined to refuse approval of a SIP on that basis. As a matter of federalism, to do so would seem to intrude on the primacy of the state that is envisioned in the SIP process. Additionally, such action by EPA would almost surely prompt a court challenge. Owing to the deference that EPA's determination is likely to receive in court, the lawsuit could probably be defended successfully, but the benefit of a slightly advanced date for ambient air quality attainment is not great in relation to the scarce litigation resources that EPA would be forced to consume.

2. States as pollution allocation brokers. What happens when states take advantage of their ability to consider economic and technologic feasibility in SIP formulation? Arguably, they open themselves up to horrific lobbying pressure from their most influential industries, all of whom can probably make a colorable claim that imposing stringent pollution control requirements on them exceeds their financial or technological abilities. Is there anything wrong with this? One argument is that the political allocation of pollution control burdens will almost certainly be sub-optimal in terms of achieving attainment in a least-cost manner. Viewing the grant of dispensations based on feasibility as a sort of political patronage gives rise to the likelihood that political allocation will tend to result in SIPs that try to achieve attainment by the smallest margin possible. After all, what politician would not dole out as much patronage as possible. How cogent are these criticisms if EPA still insists on NAAQS attainment? Does EPA's watchdog role become more difficult when the states are trying to draw SIPs that are as painless as possible? Keep these questions in mind as you read the *Cleveland Electric* case that appears in the next section.

E. REVERSE ENGINEERING TO ACHIEVE AMBIENT QUALITY LEVELS

Although the setting of harm-based ambient standards calls for difficult scientific judgments, an equally difficult problem attends the decisions that must be made in order to write a prescription for attainment of the standards. Under the Clean Air Act these latter decisions are made in the SIPs and in the grant to individual polluting facilities of permits to operate their facilities in a specified manner that results in controlled emission of effluents into the air.

There is little or no magic to the SIP process – it might be described simply as a form of reverse engineering from a desired result to a plan for attaining the result. As a cornerstone for discussion and planning, however, the SIP process relies heavily on the science of fluid dynamics, employing sophisticated computer models that attempt to describe and predict how pollutants are dispersed under the prevailing local topographic, climatic, and atmospheric conditions. A substantial degree of precision is required in order to predict whether a particular set of allowed emissions will satisfy ambient quality standards that relate not only to long-term average concentrations of pollutants, but also ambient pollution levels under short-term extraordinary conditions. The debates over airshed modelling are hotly contested because the choice of the model and the assumptions made in modelling will directly affect the amount of emissions allowed under the SIP. The battlelines are numerous. The affected states usually are at odds with EPA, seeking a model that will allow a higher level of emissions. Individual polluters within the airshed have interests adverse to one another that can be affected by the assumptions made in modelling.

Procedurally, the contours of the SIP process are fixed by the Clean Air Act itself. A good summary of the statutory deadlines and the process by which EPA oversees the states appears near the beginning of the opinion in NRDC v. Train, page 780 *supra*. The key element is a fixed timeline from the time a pollutant is added to the list of criteria pollutants to the time at which a state must have in place a successful program for limiting emissions of that pollutant sufficiently to attain the primary ambient air quality standard. The "hammer" that gives EPA an ability to insist that the states go forward is the threat that EPA itself will adopt a plan should the state fail to meet the statutory requirements.

Most states have managed to draft SIPs that have met with EPA approval. The case that follows is an example of where a state failed to do so and EPA was forced to draft its own implementation plan to control sulfur dioxide emissions in the State of Ohio. A great deal of the case history has been omitted and the court's opinion is summarized in places as an effort to make the excerpt both shorter and more easily followed.[24]

Cleveland Electric Illuminating Co. v. Environmental Protection Agency

United States Circuit Court of Appeals for the Sixth Circuit, 1978
572 F.2d 1150

EDWARDS, Circuit Judge.

...This court now has before it 23 petitions involving 32 companies filed against the United States Environmental Protection Agency which levy a variety of complaints against the federal agency's imposition of a sulfur dioxide (SO_2) pollution control plan for industrial discharges into Ohio's ambient air. The issues, which have been extensively briefed and argued, divide into general legal and procedural complaints which might be applicable to any one of the petitioners and a wider

24. The prior history of litigation concerning sulfur dioxide emission controls in Ohio is set forth in Buckeye Power, Inc. v. EPA, 481 F.2d 162 (6th Cir. 1973)(Buckeye Power I) and Buckeye Power, Inc. v. EPA, 525 F.2d 80 (6th Cir. 1975)(Buckeye Power II).

variety of specific complaints about the application of the EPA controls to particular power-generating or industrial plants. The cases dealt with in this opinion present the major general issues....

The major issues dealt with in this opinion are: 1) intervenor, the State of Ohio, claims that this court should disapprove the federal plan as irrational and arbitrary and rely upon Ohio to come forward with a more rational plan sometime in the future; 2) petitioners claim that the EPA SO_2 plan should be remanded for hearings because the informal rulemaking hearings employed by EPA under 5 U.S.C. §553 (1970 & Supp. V 1975) were inadequate; and 3) petitioners claim that the major model employed by the United States Environmental Protection Agency in establishing specific emission limitations for particular plants is invalid both intrinsically and as applied. This model is termed the "Real-Time Air-Quality-Simulator Model" (hereinafter RAM).[25]

National air quality standards for sulfur dioxide, one of the most important pollutants of the ambient air, were set by EPA in 1973 as follows:

> 40 CFR §50.4 – National primary ambient air-quality standards for sulfur oxides (sulfur dioxide).
>
> The national primary ambient air quality standards for sulfur oxides measured as sulfur dioxide by the reference method described in Appendix A to this part, or by an equivalent method, are:
>
> (a) 80 micrograms per cubic meter (0.03 p.p.m.) – annual arithmetic mean.
>
> (b) 365 micrograms per cubic meter (0.14 p.p.m.) – Maximum 24-hour concentration not to be exceeded more than once per year.

...The federal Clean Air Act program which produced these standards is based primarily upon the adverse effect which air pollution has upon human life and health.

Acute episodes of high pollution have clearly resulted in mortality and morbidity. Often the effects of high pollutant concentrations in these episodes have been combined with other environmental features such as low temperatures or epidemic diseases (influenza) which may in themselves have serious or fatal consequences. This has sometimes made it difficult to determine to what extent pollution and temperature extremes are responsible for the effects. Nevertheless, there is now no longer any doubt that high levels of pollution sustained for periods of days can kill. Those aged 45 and over with chronic diseases, particularly of the lungs or heart, seem to be predominantly affected. In addition to these acute episodes, pollutants can attain daily levels which have been shown to have serious consequences to city dwellers....

There is a large and increasing body of evidence that significant health effects are produced by long-term exposures to air pollutants. Acute respiratory infections in children, chronic respiratory diseases in adults, and decreased levels of ventilatory lung function in both children and adults have been found to be related to concentrations of SO_2 and particulates, after apparently sufficient allowance has been made for such confounding variables as smoking and socioeconomic circumstances. Rall, Review of the Health Effects of Sulfur Oxides, 8 Envt'l Health Perspectives 97, 99 (1974).

---

25. Eds: A further issue was an attack on EPA's failure to adopt a separate implementation plan for secondary air quality standards. That attack failed.

It appears that present national air quality standards have been set with little or no margin of safety. Adverse health effects are set forth in the two following charts; and the minimal or nonexistent margins of safety are vividly portrayed....

The major sources of sulfur dioxide pollution of the ambient air are coal-fired plants – exemplified by power plants operated by some of the petitioners in this case....

DISPOSITION OF THE GENERAL ISSUES

1. The State of Ohio's Petition

On July 13, 1977, the State of Ohio belatedly moved for leave to intervene in this proceeding. Its motion attacked the EPA sulfur dioxide emission control plan as having an adverse impact on the Ohio coal industry, and the Ohio economy as a whole. The motion also asserted that the State was developing a sulfur dioxide plan which would eliminate excessive abatement requirements which Ohio perceived to exist in the federal regulations. This court granted the motion for leave to intervene and has considered the brief and the reply brief filed by Ohio. Under this first disposition heading we consider only Ohio's suggestion that this court reject the United States Environmental Protection Agency's sulfur dioxide control plan and rely upon Ohio's implied promise to promulgate a state sulfur dioxide plan sometime in the future.

We reject this suggestion on the basis of a record of delay and default which has left Ohio in the position of being the only major industrialized state lacking an enforceable plan for control of sulfur dioxide.

It was clearly the intention of Congress to have a plan for control of sulfur dioxide emissions in place in all states in need of such control by the year 1972. Clean Air Act §§109(a), 110(a), 42 U.S.C. §§1857c-4(a), 5(a)(1970 & Supp. V 1975). It was equally clearly the intention of Congress that the preferred mechanism for establishment of such a plan was through the establishment and operation of a state environmental agency. Section 107(a), 42 U.S.C. §1857c-2(a)(1970). [Here the court summarized the history of Ohio's efforts to adopt a sulfur dioxide SIP. The effort began with a claim by Ohio that "there is presently no technologically feasible method of removing from their coal burning emissions an amount of sulfur sufficient to meet the standards." See Buckeye Power, Inc. v. EPA, 481 F.2d 162, 167 (6th Cir. 1973). The litigation led to a remand of the matter to EPA on technical administrative law grounds. During the pendency of the renewed administrative proceedings, Ohio withdrew its SO_2 SIP. Two years later, Ohio presented a second plan to EPA for approval, but that plan too was withdrawn due to a successful state law challenge to its adoption. This left Ohio with no approved SO_2 SIP by mid-1975, and no plan on the table for which EPA approval was being sought. After quoting the text of §110(c)(1)(A) of the Clean Air Act, the opinion continued.]

Clearly, the State of Ohio has failed to submit an implementation plan for sulfur dioxide for which a national ambient air quality primary standard has been prescribed. Equally clearly, five years have now elapsed beyond the date when such an implementation plan was called for under the Clean Air Act. Under these circumstances, we find no warrant, consistent with the purposes of the federal legislation, for giving heed to Ohio's petition for further delay....

2. The Additional Remand and Cross-Examination Issue

The leading brief in this series of cases filed on behalf of the utilities opens its argument for remand as follows:

The Most Appropriate Manner To Resolve The Multitude of Issues Raised Is A Remand To The EPA With Directions To Hold Further Hearings To Reconsider The Significant Issues; Given The Nature Of This Rulemaking, Any Remand Should Incorporate Procedural Safeguards Such As Right To Cross-Examine Or Question EPA.

Admittedly, there is no statutory requirement that EPA afford the regulated the opportunity to confront its decision makers through adjudicative-type hearings. See Buckeye Power, Inc. v. EPA, 481 F.2d 162 (1973).

However, this EPA promulgation contains so many specific findings and actions that the normal comment period has not been sufficient to expose and evaluate all of the important facts before this Court. EPA has promulgated emission limits specific to a plant, has applied specific diffusion models specific to a plant, and has reached specific conclusions regarding economics specific to a plant. Each decision is based on fact upon fact and conclusion upon conclusion. In essence and in operation, this plan and its formulation smack of the issuance of an order as defined by EPA....

[The court reviewed its previous rulings on the procedures to be followed by EPA and then quoted at length from both a "discussion of the issue now before us in the unanimous opinion in United States v. Allegheny-Ludlum Steel Corp., 406 U.S. 742, 92 S. Ct. 1941, 32 L.Ed.2d 453 (1972)" and a later Supreme Court opinion on the same topic, United States v. Florida East Coast R. Co., 410 U.S. 224, 238, 93 S. Ct. 810, 35 L.Ed.2d 223 (1973).]

Taking those precedents into account, it seems clear to us that the legislative-type hearings conducted by the United States EPA concerning the Ohio SO_2 control plan were consistent with the provisions of the Clean Air Act and the Administrative Procedure Act, and we further conclude that the hearings are not inconsistent with the due process clause of the Fourteenth Amendment. As pointed out in the quotation from *Buckeye Power #1, supra*, Congress did not insert into the Clean Air Act the language requiring the Administrator to make determinations "on the record after an opportunity for an agency hearing" which the Supreme Court has held to trigger the requirement of an adjudicative hearing. And if there was a legitimate due process complaint arising from the fact that petitioners had not had a chance to comment upon the RAM model as employed by United States EPA in its Ohio SO_2 control plan, we believe it was surely cured by this court's remand for reopening of the administrative record and United States EPA's reconsideration thereafter....

3. The RAM Model

The petitioners in these cases center most of their criticisms upon the United States EPA's use of the Real-Time Air-Quality-Simulation Model ("RAM") which was employed by the agency in preparation of the Ohio sulfur dioxide control plan. RAM is a dispersion model which evaluates the interaction of a variety of facts in order to make predictions concerning the contribution to the pollution of the ambient air by specific plants. Its formula takes into account the capacity of each plant on a stack-by-stack basis and adds thereto smokestack height, surrounding terrain, and weather conditions. The model is operated on the assumption that the plants concerned operate 24 hours a day at full capacity and predictions are made for every day of the year. The ultimate standards are set according to the predicted second-worst day in terms of pollution results shown.

In comparison to all other prior methods of controlling pollution, RAM starts with a solid, ascertainable data base. This is the established design capacity of the power plants in question related to the sulfur content of the fuel used by each. From these factors the "emissions data" for each plant are developed.

When stack height, wind, weather, terrain, land use, etc., are figured in, the RAM model has the additional value of allowing its user to predict with considerable accuracy the relative contributions of specific power plant stacks to the points of maximum concentration of pollution of the ambient air.

The RAM model was actually developed as a result of the United States EPA's public hearings on the proposed plan for Ohio after five days of hearings on said proposed plan in Columbus, Cleveland, Cincinnati, and Steubenville at which petitioners involved in this current litigation were given an opportunity (which most accepted) to appear, testify, or submit comments. At those hearings the major source of criticism from industries, including some of the present petitioners, was that the plan then under consideration did not determine limitations by individual stacks to a sufficient degree. EPA in its brief in this case compares the "rollback" model employed in the preparation of the first Ohio plan to dispersion models like RAM, which is now the source of present controversy.

Unlike the rollback model, the dispersion models used in developing the promulgated plan allow a determination of the cause-effect relationship between the SO_2 emissions of the pollution sources in an area and the resulting ambient air quality. Therefore, it is possible to determine the proportion by which each source must reduce emissions to meet ambient standards. With the use of the rollback model, in contrast, each source's emissions in the region, whether or not they contributed to a pollution problem, were required to be reduced. Through dispersion modeling, emission limitations can now be set with increased precision. Overcontrol is minimized, so that the plan will still insure attainment and maintenance of the air quality standards, but at a much reduced cost to the sources. This is most clearly demonstrated by comparing emission limitations for power plants under the various plans. Power plants account for approximately 80 percent of the sulfur dioxide emissions in the State.

However, achievement of this added precision requires a massive analytical task. Tremendous amounts of data are required for each source analyzed. In addition to the emissions data for each source, dispersion modeling requires detailed information on all the factors that affect the dispersion of emissions. These include the height of the source's stack (or usually stacks), the spatial orientation of the sources to each other, the topography of the area and the effects it will have on dispersion, and, of crucial importance, detailed weather data for the area.

All this information is needed so that the computer analysis reflects actual conditions. For example, a gaseous pollutant emitted over a grassy field will disperse much differently than if the pollutant is emitted over a large urban area. There the dispersion will be affected not only by the local weather conditions but also by the greater turbulence caused by the different types of surface areas and heat sources throughout a city.

EPA goes on to point out that there are more than 1,000 point sources in the State of Ohio and more than 2,000 area sources,[26] and that in relation to emission data, United States EPA utilized (among other sources) the data base on sulfur dioxide required to be reported to the State of Ohio under Ohio Rev. Code Ann. §§3704.03(I), 3704.05(C)(Page 1971 & 1976 Supp.).

26. An area source is a small source of emissions that is not a large industrial facility. Examples include dry cleaning establishments, gasoline stations, wood-burning stoves and, most relevant in this case, small combustion units.

It is, of course, no part of the responsibility of this court to determine whether the RAM model represents the best possible approach to determining standards or the control of sulfur dioxide emissions. Our standard of review of the actions of United States EPA is whether or not the action of the agency is "arbitrary, capricious, an abuse of discretion, or otherwise not in accordance with law." Thus, we are required to affirm if there is a rational basis for the agency action and we are not "empowered to substitute [our] judgment for that of the agency." Citizens to Preserve Overton Park v. Volpe, 401 U.S. 402, 416, 91 S.Ct. 814, 824, 28 L.Ed.2d 136 (1971).

Our review of this record convinces us that we cannot properly hold that United States EPA's adoption of the RAM model for predicting sulfur dioxide emissions and for fixing maximum levels of sulfur dioxide emissions by specific sources was arbitrary and capricious or beyond the agency's authority under the Clean Air Act. The factors cited below support EPA's argument that the RAM model is supported by sufficient evidence so that EPA's adoption cannot be held arbitrary and capricious:

1) United States EPA's use of the "rollback" model – the principal basis of its first plan on which five days of public hearings were conducted in Ohio – was strenuously objected to by representatives of many of the present petitioners because it was not source-specific and, as a consequence, tended to require more stringent sulfur dioxide controls than would be required if plant capacity, fuel, population, smokestack height, wind and climate were all taken into account. Thus John R. Martin, of Smith & Singer Meteorologists, Inc., commented on behalf of Ohio utilities on the first United States EPA plan as follows:

> More sophisticated modeling is necessary in all seven of the urban counties that use the proportional rollback. In this way, the Federal air quality standards can be attained without unnecessary SO_2 emission restrictions being imposed upon sources that do not contribute to SO_2 problem... We recommended that new strategies be tested which will more fairly identify and control SO_2 sources that create SO_2 problems.

Similarly, Dr. Howard M. Ellis, of Enviroplan, Inc., said on behalf of Ohio power plants:

> [I]n developing an SO_2 control program for this plant, Region V did not consider economically efficient alternatives to constant uniform emission standards – alternatives such as utilizing a supplementary control system to achieve air quality standards or using separate SO_2 emission standards by stack in accordance with each stack's contribution to ground-level SO_2 concentrations. Separate emission standards by stack can reduce considerably the cost of achieving air quality standards....

2) EPA responded to these arguments favorably by devising and adopting the RAM model which did employ all of these source-specific factors.

3) Further, as shown on [charts that are not reprinted here], the United States EPA 1976-1977 SO_2 control plan (principally based upon the RAM and MAX-24 models) shows less stringent regulation on a county-by-county basis when compared to the Ohio SO_2 control plans originally promulgated in 1972 and 1974. In addition, when the comparison is limited to petitioners involved in this litigation, but including all of their facilities which were subjected to RAM modeling (and which are identified in this record), we find the plan slightly less strict than the Ohio 1974 plan by a count of 23 to 20.

These comparisons do not, of course, necessarily demonstrate RAM's accuracy. Rather, the comparison with Ohio's previous plans (based upon the earlier rollback model which was used and accepted nationwide) tends simply to show that the choice of RAM modeling lay within administrative discretion.

4) While this court has currently before it some 32 petitioners protesting the United States EPA's plan for SO_2 emission control for Ohio, it must be remembered that Ohio is estimated to have over 1,000 point sources and over 2,000 area sources of SO_2 pollution.

5) The RAM model is a general formula which can be applied to many individual sources of pollution to derive specific estimates of SO_2 emission rates for each. It employs a wider, more complete and more accurate data base than any prior model yet employed in devising a sulfur dioxide control strategy for a state or county. The crucial data with which the RAM model starts are the design capacity figure, plus the fuel sulfur content, from which is computed the SO_2 emission rate for each of the heating or power plants sought to be controlled. Thus at the outset the RAM model starts with ascertainable specific figures for each source where disputes can be resolved by inspection of the equipment or fuel concerned. Many of the additional components such as stack height, wind direction, physical relationship of sources to each other, and topography of the area are similarly ascertainable as matters of fact. With the enormous financial stakes involved in this litigation, every effort to avoid disputes about the accuracy of the data base should be made. This record shows that United States EPA's design of the RAM model was brought about at least in large part by Ohio industry's requests for greater specificity and hence lower costs of compliance with National Air Quality Standards.

6) While there may yet be developed (and hopefully will be) a better method of establishing a control strategy for sulfur dioxide emissions than the RAM model, no one has yet come forward with such....

7) We recognize that this record does not present positive proofs of the accuracy of RAM's predictions. Thus far technology has not developed foolproof methods for validating predictions concerning pollution of the ambient air absent years of collection of monitoring data with far more monitors and far more personnel than have thus far been available....

[The court here compared predicted and actual monitor readings for a small number of monitoring sites in Dayton, Ohio.]

Site No.	2d highest 24-hr RAM-predicted concentration in ug per m/3	1972	1973	1974	1975	1976
1	195	*	*	219	*	*
2	201	73	438	181	163	81
3	83	*	*	117	62	57
4	109	*	*	151	109	17
5	161	57	198	*	68	41
6	207	*	13	66	110	73

Our analysis of these data shows that the yearly second-highest concentration of SO_2 pollution (for a 24-hour average) actually recorded on available monitors exceeded the RAM model prediction for each location once in a five-year period at five out of six locations. This analysis certainly falls short of showing RAM's predictive perfection. But it certainly tends to show that the EPA's use of RAM, if conservative, cannot be held to be arbitrary and capricious....

8) Finally, as we pointed out at the beginning of this opinion, SO_2 emissions have a direct impact upon the health and the lives of the population of Ohio – particularly its young people, its sick people, and its old people. If the RAM model did overpredict emission rates, such a conservative approach in protection of health and life was apparently contemplated by Congress in requiring that EPA plans contain "emission limitations.... necessary to *insure* attainment and maintenance" of national ambient air standards. 42 U.S.C.A. §1857c-5(a)(2)(B)(1970). (Emphasis added.)

In summary, we hold that United States EPA's adoption and employment of the RAM model as its general working tool was based upon informal rulemaking which satisfied the requirements of both the Clean Air Act and the Administrative Procedure Act, and the due process requirements of the United States Constitution. Further, the record indicates that the Administrator's control regulations for Ohio through use of the RAM model was a rational choice which was well within the discretion committed to him and his agency. We decline petitioners' requests to set the disputed orders aside on the ground that they are arbitrary and capricious.

OTHER ISSUES

Somewhat half-heartedly the leading brief for the utilities attacks the United States EPA plan for SO_2 controls in Ohio as excessively costly and asserts that the satisfactory operation of Flue Gas Desulfurization machine ("scrubbers") has not been demonstrated.

We note that the United States EPA control strategy for Ohio does not rely heavily upon Flue Gas Desulfurization. (EPA estimates – and petitioners do not dispute – that only six utilities will choose this compliance route.) Alternatives to installation of "scrubbers" are the purchasing and use of low sulfur coals or the employment of coal cleaning or blending techniques. There is no doubt, of course, that SO_2 controls will indeed be costly. EPA estimates capital costs for Ohio industry of well over half a billion dollars and annual costs of 171 million dollars. It also projects these costs as requiring a 3 percent increase in annual electric bills for the consumers who will ultimately pay them – and who will also breathe the less polluted air. Basically the choice of economic burden versus continued deterioration of the air we breathe was made by Congress. In this litigation no issue is raised concerning Congress' power to do so.

We have genuine doubt that this court has the power to review what we regard as petitioners' slightly disguised economic and technological infeasibility arguments. See generally Union Electric Co. v. EPA, 427 U.S. 246, 265-66, 96 S.Ct. 2518, 49 L.Ed.2d 474 (1976). Since this issue does not appear to be definitely resolved as to a United States EPA-designed implementation plan (such as we deal with here), see Union Electric Co. v. EPA, supra at 261 n.7, 96 S.Ct. 2518, we observe that if we did have such power, we would conclude that the technical record compiled in the agency proceeding provides ample support for the economic and technological feasibility of the SO_2 control strategies which United States EPA has promulgated for Ohio....

COMMENTARY AND QUESTIONS

1. Technical complexity and the competence of courts. Can you conclude from a case like *Cleveland Electric* that the technical complexity of the case is so great that a judicial forum is inappropriate? Should there instead be a technological decisionmaking body? The abuse of discretion standard of review provides a significant safeguard that matters of technical expertise will be decided by an expert decisionmaker, subject only to review that no gross misjudgments have been made. Is there any indication that the court is over-matched by the technical matters involved in this case?

2. Does deference include the right to be very wrong? How much stronger would the petitioners' case have been if the chart correlating RAM-predicted pollution concentrations had exceeded actual observed results in every year at every monitoring station? At some degree of error, model failure becomes coextensive with model irrationality.

3. Amending the emissions limitations later. Assume post-implementation monitor readings demonstrate that the RAM over-predicted pollution levels by a significant degree and that EPA is willing to adjust the RAM model to make its predictive capacity more accurate, and revise upward the allowable emission from many of the regulated polluters. Is that a satisfactory method of proceeding? Why will the regulated petitioners claim that is an inadequate remedy? What becomes of their investment in pollution control equipment that is no longer necessary, or their lost profits due to higher operating costs in the interim? The amount of "over-investment" in pollution control might be significant. The opinion pointed out that large sums of money were involved in meeting the EPA-imposed limitations. As a general rule, the cost of emissions reduction is not a linear function. The first few units of reduction are usually inexpensive to achieve, but additional improvements are ever more expensive. Is Ohio harmed in the same way? In the interim its citizens have enjoyed cleaner air and, if it elects to continue emissions controls at their existing levels of stringency on the polluters, it is in a position to introduce new sources of emissions without forcing new cutbacks by the current polluters.

4. Burden of proof on health effects issues. Does the case conform to Hayes' assertion that preoccupation with health is becoming the major concern under the Clean Air Act, *supra*, at page 787? Where should the burden of proof lie, on the EPA to justify the standard or on the opponents (in this case Ohio and the industries involved) to show that the controls are more stringent than demanded by public health? Compare Industrial Union v. American Petroleum Institute 100 S.Ct. 2844 (1980)(discussed *infra* at 846, finding OSHA must prove the efficiency of its work-place health standards).

5. Overriding state sovereignty. The court's opinion is sharply critical of Ohio's foot-dragging in implementing SO_2 standards. In the absence of the federal mandate provided by §110, is it likely that the court's attitude would have been the same?

Can Ohio fairly claim that the federal act has usurped too much of its traditional power to control local matters?

6. State resentment of federally imposed plans. Does *Cleveland Electric* offer an indication of why the states feel threatened by an EPA drafted plan? Due to the economic burdens to be placed on Ohio industries (especially its coal mining and electric generating industries) Ohio seems opposed to any SO_2 control without regard to whose plan it is. The most likely reason for the general state fear of EPA-imposed plans is that EPA might impose the burdens of pollution control in ways that are politically unpopular. For example, EPA has frequently tried to insist that SIPs include regional transportation plans that discourage the use of automobiles by commuters, or reduce emissions by the vehicles that are in service. Limits on available parking spaces, carpool lanes, increased spending on mass transit and mandatory motor vehicle emissions testing and maintenance are all tools in this approach. These programs have proven violently unpopular and their imposition, even though ordered by EPA, have sometimes been the death knell of local political careers. There is a kindred fear that EPA may seek reductions in a way that is insensitive to the needs and ability to pay of local polluting firms.

7. Using tall stacks and intermittent controls to meet NAAQS requirements. In an effort to limit their costs of compliance with the SIP that would eventually emerge, the Ohio utilities were urging Ohio to allow the use of tall smokestacks and intermittent pollution control devices as part of the older (pre-1977) versions of the Ohio SIP. Tall stacks are among the least cost solutions to meeting ambient air quality standards. They operate in two ways to help attain or maintain NAAQS compliance. First, they lead to wider dispersion of the pollutants they emit which means that the concentrations of the pollutant are lower than they would be in areas near the emitting facility if shorter stacks were employed. In effect, the use of taller stack leads to more diluted emissions that cover a wider geographic area. Second, the use of tall stacks makes possible the export of pollution beyond the boundary of the AQCR, turning the pollution into someone else's problem.

Intermittent controls are also a lower cost method of meeting the national standards because they are less expensive than comparable continuous controls. Intermittent controls are employed when receiving body air quality is at or near the allowable NAAQS and these controls are not used when receiving body conditions are favorable, i.e., when there is a low concentration of pollutants in the receiving ambient air. A very simple example of an intermittent control would be a plan that called for turning off an electrostatic precipitator that traps emissions in the stack when the local air is clean. The savings to the firm of this practice result from reduced operating and maintenance costs (because large energy costs are avoided during periods when the precipitator is not needed and the device itself will require less maintenance if it is used less often) and reduced capital costs (because the useful life of the device will be extended). An even more dramatic form of intermittent control is to cease production when receiving body conditions are unfavorable and operate with no controls when receiving body conditions permit. Using intermittent controls as opposed to continuous controls results in an increase in total emissions by allowing greater emissions when conditions permit.

What is objectionable about SIPs that rely on tall stacks and intermittent controls to meet the NAAQS? The export of pollution (externalizing the cost) to another state or AQCR is obviously antithetical to notions of equity and responsibility for one's own deeds. The devices embedded in the CAA to deter export of pollution are discussed *infra*, at page 821. The second objection to tall stacks and intermittent controls turns on the fact that they increase the aggregate amount of pollution that can be emitted without violating the NAAQS. Is that bad? If the NAAQS are set at levels that are sufficiently protective of health, welfare and the environment, the criticism loses part of its force.

The Clean Air Act Amendments of 1977 specifically addressed tall stacks and intermittent controls and limited their attractiveness as control devices. Section §123, 42 U.S.C.A. §7423, explicitly allows firms to increase stack heights and to employ "other dispersion technique[s]" (defined to include intermittent controls), but the degree of emission control attributable to the excessive height of the stack or the use of dispersion techniques does not count toward meeting emission control limitations set by the relevant SIP. For a discussion of this provision and the motivation of Congress in passing it, see Sierra Club v. EPA, 719 F.2d 436, 440–41 (D.C.Cir. 1983). The crux of the arguments for limiting dispersion centered on export and the unreliability and lack of enforceability of intermittent controls.

F. ASSURING ATTAINMENT OF DESIRED QUALITY LEVELS

The Clean Air Act has been in place for more than twenty years and ambient air quality now meets the NAAQS primary standards in most air quality control regions and the secondary standards in many instances as well. There remain, however, a considerable number of areas where even the primary NAAQS remains unmet for one or more of the criteria pollutants. These areas are, quite appropriately, termed non-attainment areas and Congress has addressed special attention to them in post-1970 amendments to the Clean Air Act.

Although there is no systematic study of the characteristics of non-attainment areas, a typical profile would include a densely populated, urbanized area having industrial concentrations. In these non-attainment areas, even stringent air pollution reduction efforts have failed to reduce sufficiently the concentration of the relevant pollutant(s). As noted before, SIP-required efforts to control pollution need not be limited to direct emission controls, such as smokestack flue gas scrubbers. Additional requirements may include fuel switching to cleaner fuels, other process changes, transportation controls to limit the number and type of vehicles, and special limitations on new development.

As a matter of policy, Congress has not chosen to treat non-attainment areas too severely. Congress could, if it desired, order a total ban on all new development as a means of avoiding additional pollution of already unsafe air. So too, Congress could force the discontinuation of existing activities in an effort to provide the desired health benefits. The polluters refrain that was repeated so many times in the Clean Air Act cases, calling for someone to consider economic and technological feasibility, is answered in the political arena. Politically, choices that forbid development, or force closure of too many existing firms, are unpalatable because of their economic and social consequences. Still, as the non-attainment area legislation makes clear, Congress has compromised, but not forsaken, its interest in the promotion of environmental quality and the protection of public health and welfare.

The signal content of the 1977 non-attainment areas legislation, 42 U.S.C.A. §§7501-7508, is the insistence that non-attainment areas make "reasonable further progress" toward attainment. As defined by the statute, those areas must make "annual incremental reductions in emissions of the applicable air pollutant (including substantial reductions in the early years following approval or promulgation of plan provisions...and regular reductions thereafter)...to provide for attainment...by the date set..." §7501(1). (The date set varied depending on what criteria pollutant was involved, but was in no case later than December 31, 1987 for the attainment of the primary NAAQS. See §7502(a).)

The backbone of the regulatory framework remains the SIP process, but for non-attainment areas, EPA must measure SIPs against a series of explicit statutory requirements. §7502(b)(1-11). In the criteria for non-attainment area SIPs, Congress moves away from harm-based ambient standards toward a technique and technology-based approach. For example, the SIP must "... provide for the implementation of all reasonable available control measures as expeditiously as possible...[and] require...reasonable further progress...including such reduction in emissions from existing sources in the area as may be obtained through the adoption, at a minimum, of reasonably available control technology..." New major sources of pollution must "comply with the lowest achievable emission rate [LAER][27]..." §7503(2).

New major sources must also avoid interference with the reasonable further progress toward attainment. Here the key concept is that net emissions of the offending pollutant be reduced. A permit to operate a new major pollution source can be granted only if "by the time the source is to commence operation, total allowable emissions from existing sources in the region, from new or modified sources which are not major emitting facilities, and from the proposed source will be sufficiently less than total emissions from existing sources allowed under the applicable implementation plan...so as to represent reasonable further progress [toward attainment of the NAAQS]." This latter device is called obtaining offsets – the new major source must be able to demonstrate that a sufficient amount of pollution will be eliminated to "offset" its new emissions. As the following case demonstrates, the means for calculating offsets at times seems to frustrate rather than further the goals of the non-attainment provisions.

27. LAER is considered to be an even more stringent technological command than is the employment of best available technology (BAT). BAT is discussed *infra* at 841.

Citizens Against The Refinery's Effects v. EPA
United States Circuit Court of Appeals for the Fourth Circuit, 1981
643 F.2d 183

HALL, Circuit Judge.

Citizens Against the Refinery's Effects (CARE) appeals from a final ruling by the Administrator of the Environmental Protection Agency (EPA) approving the Virginia State Implementation Plan (SIP) for reducing hydrocarbon pollutants. The plan requires the Virginia Highway Department to decrease usage of a certain type of asphalt, thereby reducing hydrocarbon pollution by more than enough to offset expected pollution from the Hampton Roads Energy Company's (HREC) proposed refinery. We affirm the action of the administrator in approving the state plan....

[Before the 1977 amendments][t]he Clean Air Act created a no-growth environment in areas where the clean air requirements had not been attained. EPA recognized the need to develop a program that encouraged attainment of clean air standards without discouraging economic growth. Thus the agency proposed an Interpretive Ruling in 1976 which allowed the states to develop an "offset program" within the State Implementation Plans. 41 Fed. Reg. 55524 (1976). The offset program, later codified by Congress in the 1977 Amendments to the Clean Air Act, permits the states to develop plans which allow construction of new pollution sources where accompanied by a corresponding reduction in an existing pollution source. 42 U.S.C. §7502(b)(6) and §7503. In effect, a new emitting facility can be built if an existing pollution source decreases its emissions or ceases operations as long as a positive net air quality benefit occurs.

If the proposed factory will emit carbon monoxide, sulfur dioxide, or particulates, the EPA requires that the offsetting pollution source be within the immediate vicinity of the new plant. The other two pollutants, hydrocarbons and nitrogen oxide, are less "site-specific," and thus the ruling permits the offsetting source to locate anywhere within a broad vicinity of the new source.

The offset program has two other important requirements. First, a base time period must be determined in which to calculate how much reduction is needed in existing pollutants to offset the new source. This base period is defined as the first year of the SIP or, where the state has not yet developed a SIP, as the year in which a construction permit application is filed. Second, the offset program requires that the new source adopt the Lowest Achievable Emissions Rate (LAER) using the most modern technology available in the industry.

HREC proposes to build a petroleum refinery and off-loading facility in Portsmouth, Virginia. Portsmouth has been unable to reduce air pollution enough to attain the national standard for one pollutant, photochemical oxidants, which is created when hydrocarbons are released into the atmosphere and react with other substances. Since a refinery is a major source of hydrocarbons, the Clean Air Act prevents construction of the HREC plant until the area attains the national standard.

In 1975, HREC applied to the Virginia State Air Pollution Control Board (VSAPCB) for a refinery construction permit. The permit was issued by the VSAPCB on October 8, 1975, extended and reissued on October 5, 1977 after a full public hearing, modified on August 8, 1978, and extended again on September 27, 1979. The VSAPCB, in an effort to help HREC meet the clean air requirements, proposed to use the offset ruling to comply with the Clean Air Act.

On November 28, 1977, the VSAPCB submitted a State Implementation Plan to EPA which included the HREC permit. The Virginia Board proposed to offset the new

HREC hydrocarbon pollution by reducing the amount of cutback asphalt[28] used for road paving operations in three highway districts by the Virginia Department of Highways.[29] By switching from "cutback" to "emulsified" asphalt, the state can reduce hydrocarbon pollutants by the amount necessary to offset the pollutants from the proposed refinery.... [The plan was eventually approved by EPA.]

CARE raises four issues regarding the state plan. First, they argue that the geographic area used as the base for the offset was arbitrarily determined and that the area as defined violates the regulations. Second, CARE contends that EPA should have used 1975 instead of 1977 as the base year to compare usage of cutback asphalt. Third, CARE insists that the offset plan should have been disapproved since the state is voluntarily reducing usage of cutback asphalt anyway. Fourth, CARE questions the approval of the plan without definite Lowest Achievable Emissions Rates (LAER) as required by the statute. We reject the CARE challenges to the state plan....

CARE contends that the state plan should not have been approved by EPA since the three highway-district area where cutback usage will be reduced to offset refinery emissions was artificially developed by the state. The ruling permits a broad area (usually within one AQCR) to be used as the offset basis....

The agency action in approving the use of three highway districts was neither arbitrary, capricious, nor outside the statute. First, Congress intended that the states and the EPA be given flexibility in designing and implementing SIPs. Such flexibility allows the states to make reasoned choices as to which areas may be used to offset new pollution and how the plan is to be implemented. Second, the offset program was initiated to encourage economic growth in the state. Thus a state plan designed to reduce highway department pollution in order to attract another industry is a reasonable contribution to economic growth without a corresponding increase in pollution. Third, to be sensibly administered the offset plan had to be divided into districts which could be monitored by the highway department. Use of any areas other than highway districts would be unwieldy and difficult to administer. Fourth, the scientific understanding of ozone pollution is not advanced to the point where exact air transport may be predicted. Designation of the broad area in which hydrocarbons may be transported is well within the discretion and expertise of the agency.

Asphalt consumption varies greatly from year to year, depending upon weather and road conditions. Yet EPA must accurately determine the volume of hydrocarbon emissions from cutback asphalt. Only then can the agency determine whether the reduction in cutback usage will result in an offset great enough to account for the new refinery pollution. To calculate consumption of a material where it constantly varies, a base year must be selected. In this case, EPA's Interpretive Ruling establishes the base year as the year in which the permit application is made. EPA decided that 1977 was an acceptable base year. CARE argues that EPA illegally chose 1977 instead of 1975.

Considering all of the circumstances, including the unusually high asphalt consumption in 1977, the selection by EPA of that as the base year was within the discretion of the agency. Since the EPA Interpretive Ruling allowing the offset was not issued until 1976, 1977 was the first year after the offset ruling and the logical

28. "Cutback" asphalt has a petroleum base which gives off great amounts of hydrocarbons. "Emulsified" asphalt uses a water base which evaporates, giving off no hydrocarbons.

29. The three highway districts so designated comprise almost the entire eastern one-third of the state. The area cuts across four of the seven Virginia Air Quality Control Regions (AQCR).

base year in which to calculate the offset. Also, the permit issued by the VSAPCB was reissued in 1977 with extensive additions and revisions after a full hearing. Under these circumstances, 1977 appears to be a logical choice of a base year.

For several years, Virginia has pursued a policy of shifting from cutback asphalt to the less expensive emulsified asphalt in road-paving operations. The policy was initiated in an effort to save money, and was totally unrelated to a State Implementation Plan. Because of this policy, CARE argues that hydrocarbon emissions were decreasing independent of this SIP and therefore are not a proper offset against the refinery. They argue that there is not, in effect, an actual reduction in pollution.

The Virginia voluntary plan is not enforceable and therefore is not in compliance with the 1976 Interpretive Ruling which requires that the offset program be enforceable. 41 Fed. Reg. 55526 (1976). The EPA, in approving the state plan, obtained a letter from the Deputy Attorney General of Virginia in which he stated that the requisites had been satisfied for establishing and enforcing the plan with the Department of Highways. Without such authority, no decrease in asphalt-produced pollution is guaranteed. In contrast to the voluntary plan, the offset plan guarantees a reduction in pollution resulting from road paving operations.

LOWEST ACHIEVABLE EMISSIONS RATE

Finally, CARE argues that the Offset Plan does not provide adequate Lowest Achievable Emission Rates (LAER) as required by the 1976 Interpretive Ruling because the plan contains only a 90 percent vapor recovery requirement, places an excessive 176.5 ton limitation on hydrocarbon emissions, and does not require specific removal techniques at the terminal. EPA takes the position that the best technique available for marine terminals provides only a 90 percent recovery and that the 176.5 ton limit may be reduced by the agency after the final product mix at the terminal is determined.

Since the record shows no evidence of arbitrary or capricious action in approving the HREC emissions equipment, the agency determination of these technical matters must be upheld.

In approving the state plan, EPA thoroughly examined the data, requested changes in the plan, and approved the plan only after the changes were made. There is no indication that the agency acted in an arbitrary or capricious manner or that it stepped beyond the bounds of the Clean Air Act. We affirm the decision of the administrator in approving the state plan.

COMMENTARY AND QUESTIONS

1. **Other non-attainment area obligations.** Could the switch from cutback asphalt to emulsified asphalt be considered a "reasonably available control measure" that is required to be a part of a valid hydrocarbon non-attainment plan under §7502(b)(2)? If so, how would that improve CARE's attack on the allowance of the switch as an offset?

2. **Insisting on "reasonable further progress."** Was EPA too permissive with Virginia in this case, so permissive that it violated the statutory "reasonable further progress" requirement? Why, for example, didn't EPA on its own initiative insist on the use of emulsified asphalt when to do so reduces hydrocarbon emissions in the non-attainment area and saves Virginia money at the same time? Here EPA performance seems to be a far cry from the more aggressive posture seen in the

Cleveland Electric case, *supra*. Here too, the standard of judicial review is sufficiently deferential so that the position of the EPA on the issue will be sustained by a reviewing court. Although it is difficult to plumb the motivations of EPA that led it to take such different postures, the cardinal lesson of these cases from a practical standpoint is that cases are won and lost in the agency far more often than in subsequent judicial review.

3. **Offsets pro and con.** Are offsets a good method of accommodating further development while still seeking improvement of ambient air quality in non-attainment areas? In the absence of state intervention in aid of the new source, either like that given in the *CARE* case or in the form of placing tighter controls on existing sources, can you predict which emissions reductions will be realized first? Presumably the operator of the new source will have to purchase the retirement of pollution sources. The least expensive retirements will involve taking marginally profitable enterprises out of production, or paying for pollution control improvements at those sites where the least expenditure produces the greatest reduction. To the extent that practice mirrors the prediction of theory, offsets obtain an apparently optimal result of reducing pollution at the lowest possible cost. Are there social costs that have been overlooked in that assessment? What about the dislocation of workers who lose their jobs when the marginal firms are bought out and closed? It is arguable that for many of them, their firm's survival was unlikely in any event.

4. A Note on bubbles and their similarity to offsets. Bubbles, in Clean Air Act parlance, are the device of treating all of the emitting sources at a single facility as a single point source for the purpose of regulation. For example, a factory having several buildings and multiple smokestacks could be treated as either a series of sources, each having an individual emissions limitation, or as a single entity having a total emissions limitation. The term bubble describes the latter method that treats the group of emitting sources as if all of the emissions occurred in a single bubble and then are released into the atmosphere.

Offsets are a cousin technique to bubbles. The relationship of bubbles to offsets arises when the operator of the facility wants to change operations within the bubble. If increases in emission from one smokestack can be offset by reductions in emission from another stack, there would be no net change in total emissions. If the bubble concept is not employed, increases in emissions from one smokestack would require a modification of that stack's permit. As you might expect, modification of a permit for a major source in a non-attainment area is a major headache. Likewise, if the firm replaces an old part of the facility with a new, less polluting one on the same site, under the bubble concept, no change in the permit would be required. If that new component is considered a new source, in non-attainment areas it is required to employ LAER, and in attainment areas, pursuant to §111, it must employ BAT. In both instances, the applicability of the technology-based standards will usually increase the cost of the improvement and the need for administrative action on permit modifications, or new permits will cause delays, as well as substantial expense.

5. The 1990 Clean Air Act Amendments and the new regime for ending non-attainment. The 1990 revisions of the non-attainment sections of the CAA demonstrate a changed attitude on the part of Congress. The changes in the law impose serious consequences for continued failure to attain the mandated quality levels. The move was prompted in part by the fact that almost one hundred metropolitan areas were still unable to meet the primary NAAQS ozone standard and roughly forty areas still failed to meet the primary carbon monoxide standard. These types of pollution are associated with automobile emissions as well as with various types of chemical use and manufacture.

The 1990 amendments take a multi-faceted approach to insuring reliable and prompt progress toward eventual attainment. As with the basic structure of the harm-based ambient standards system, the amendments rely on the SIP process, but EPA is now required to issue a federal implementation plan (FIP) within two years of a state's failure to submit an adequate SIP.

In regard to ozone non-attainment Congress has differentiated five degrees of non-attainment, calling them marginal, moderate, serious, severe, and extreme.[30] The amendments set increasingly distant dates for compliance, ranging from three years for marginal areas up to twenty years for extreme areas. See §181(a), 42 U.S.C.A. §7511(a). Correlatively, Congress has mandated that SIPs for those areas include an increasingly stringent set of requirements. See §182(a-e), 42 U.S.C.A. §7511a(a-e). Some samples of these requirements include the following: in marginal areas SIPs must include the use of reasonably available control technologies (RACT), vehicle maintenance and inspection programs, and offsets must be obtained in a ratio of at least 1.1 to 1; in moderate areas, mandatory gasoline vapor recovery is added and the offset requirement increases to 1.15 to 1; in serious areas general transportation plans are required and clean-fuel vehicles must be considered as an option, and the offset ratio must be at least 1.2 to 1; in severe areas there must be an enforceable offset for any growth in the number of vehicle miles travelled and mandatory carpool and other vehicle use requirements must be imposed, the offset ratio increases to 1.3 to 1; and in extreme areas major sources are redefined to include much smaller units (10 tons/year of volatile organic compound emissions), switching to cleaner fuels such as natural gas is required for large emitting sources, high polluting vehicles cannot be used during rush hours, and the general offset requirement is 1.5 to 1. To insure that the severe and extreme areas do eventually meet their attainment deadlines, the amendments provide specific enforcement measures that call for penalties of $5,000/ton/yr for excess emissions from major sources if timely attainment does not occur. CAA §185, 42 U.S.C.A. §7511d.[31]

Notice that all of the statutory responses to non-attainment of the harm-based ambient quality standards resort to other techniques. RACT and LAER (for major

30. A similar, but far simpler two-track system of moderate and serious non-attainment is employed in relation to carbon monoxide and particulates and attainment deadlines are set for all of the remaining criteria pollutants. See CAA §§186-192, 42 U.S.C.A. §§7512–7514a.

31. These special sanctions are in addition to the more general power of the Administrator to impose SIP requirements on states that fail to reach timely attainment and the power to withhold federal highway funds. See generally CAA §179, 42 U.S.C.A. §7509.

new sources locating in non-attainment areas) are technology-based standards, mandatory fuel and vehicle switching are forms of legislated pollution control standards akin to technology-forcing. Bans on the use of high-polluting vehicles during periods of heavy traffic volume are in the roadblock category, and so on. Is the application of these other statutory types to address the problem of non-attainment proof that harm-based ambient controls do not work? That view gives too little credit for the majority of instances in which NAAQS are being met, but it is indicative of the fact that harm-based systems are vulnerable to failure and therefore need the support of additional regulatory reinforcement.

G. PROTECTING INTERSTATE AND NATIONAL CONCERNS IN A NATIONWIDE AMBIENT STANDARDS PROGRAM

The implementation of a national harm-based ambient standards approach to protect public health from the dangers of conventional air pollutants requires more than the mere establishment of standards and implementation plans. In a system that relies on *state* implementation plans to achieve the desired results, some special steps need to be taken to insure that national objectives are not sacrificed to the more parochial concerns of the states who play so large a role in drawing most SIPs. First, there are matters of what might be called the growth potential of the dirty air states. Here the principal concern is that even the relatively dirty air areas of the nation need to be able to remain competitive with clean air areas in attracting new economic activity (and therefore additional pollution sources) into their borders. Second, for aesthetic as well as environmental reasons, preserving the cleanliness of existing clean air regions is a significant benefit, even when this increases the cost of pollution control in those regions above what it would be if NAAQS attainment were the only requirement. Finally, and perhaps most obviously, some form of protection must be erected against efforts to control local pollution within a single state by the inexpensive expedient of building tall smokestacks or siting polluting enterprises near the state line and letting the wind blow the pollution problem into another state. In enacting and amending the Clean Air Act, Congress has addressed all three of these concerns.

PERMITTING CONTINUED GROWTH IN DIRTY AIR AREAS

Congress clearly recognized as a national concern the hardship that would be imposed on dirty air areas if they were subjected to a total ban on initiating new industrial activity. To allow those areas to compete for industrial growth and development, as demonstrated in the *CARE* case, the non-attainment area provisions allow new sources to obtain permits so long as they employ LAER (the most demanding technology-based standard) and obtain offsets so that "reasonable further progress" toward attainment is maintained.

At the same time as it made the location of major new sources in non-attainment areas possible, Congress also took steps that lessened the comparative attractiveness of locating a major emitting facility in a clean air area. Congress imposed technology-based standards for pollution controls on all new major emitting sources, wherever they are located through the New Source Performance Standards (NSPS) requirements.[32]

The NSPS program is mandated by §111 of the Act, 42 U.S.C.A. §7411. In general, the NSPS provisions require that all new or modified emitting sources employ the best adequately demonstrated pollution control technology (BADT) for their type of facility. This standard is defined in the Act and commands EPA to take "into consideration the cost of achieving such emission reduction." By requiring a uniform technology to be employed nationwide, the potential for a race of laxity in permitting new sources is greatly reduced, although not entirely eliminated. Major new sources that emit more than a specified tonnage of pollutants are regulated even more tightly, using technology-based standards. In PSD areas (described below) major new emitting sources must employ the best available control technology (BACT)(42 U.S.C.A. §7475(a)(4)), while, as mentioned previously, in non-attainment areas major new emissions sources are subject to even more stringent standards (LAER), and offsets are required as well.

PREVENTION OF SIGNIFICANT DETERIORATION (PSD)

The more novel facet of the Clean Air Act's avoidance of uniformly dirty air is the PSD program that was given much of its detail by the 1977 amendments. See 42 U.S.C.A. §§7470–7491. Although the particularity of the Congressional requirements for the PSD program makes the statute seem incredibly complex, the basic design is rather pedestrian and amounts to little more than limitations on the incremental amount of pollution that is allowed in clean air areas, with smaller increments allowed in areas where there are special national or state interests served by limiting increases in pollution.

The PSD process begins by classifying all attainment air quality control regions (AQCRs), or parts thereof, into three categories. Under the 1977 amendments Class I areas include international and national parks, wilderness areas, and national memorial parks that exceed a prescribed acreage.[33] Class II areas are, in essence, all remaining attainment areas.[34] No Class III areas are established by the legislation, but the states have the ability to redesignate areas according to a process set out in §7474. With classification comes an allowable increment, that is, a statutorily or administratively set upper limit on the amount of increase in ambient concentrations of pollutants that can be added to the region's air. As an example the Class I, II and III allowable increments in the annual geometric mean of particulate contamination are 5, 19, and 37 micrograms per cubic meter respectively.[35]

---

32. Additionally, as will be more fully described below, Congress enacted an affirmative prevention of significant deterioration (PSD) program that is designed to keep clean air areas from becoming as dirty as the NAAQS alone would otherwise allow. The PSD program shortens the race of laxity by limiting the ability of clean air areas to offer lax pollution control as an inducement to attract new firms to locate there.

33. There were additional areas that were classified as Class I under the pre-1977 law. These areas continued as Class I areas, but, if they are not required to be designated Class I by the 1977 amendments, they are subject to redesignation downward under §7474.

34. See 42 U.S.C.A. §7472(b).

35. The primary standard for annual mean concentration of particulates is 100 micrograms per cubic meter. Thus, the PSD increments are, respectively, 5 percent, 19 percent and 37 percent

The next step in the PSD process is to establish the baseline upon which the allowable increment can be added. Conceptually, this would seem to be no more difficult than getting an accurate measure of the current concentration of pollutants. In practice, that measure is not readily available in many locations and due to the difficulty in establishing an accurate baseline, no effort to do so is made until the need arises. Usually this occurs at the time an application for a permit is received from a new major source of emissions. Thereafter, new ambient air quality standards are calculated for the AQCR. In many cases, the new standards are the sum of the baseline concentrations plus allowable increments that are fixed by statute for particulates and sulfur dioxide and by EPA regulation for other criteria pollutants. Particularly in Class III areas, however, the possibility exists that the sum of the baseline concentration plus the increment will exceed the allowable NAAQS limit. In that case, of course, the NAAQS continues as the maximum allowable level of ambient pollution and the AQCR is not allowed to "use" the full amount of the increment.

To provide additional protection for national parks and other areas that obtain Class I designation because of the presence of a federal enclave to which visibility is essential, there are special visibility protection requirements that are even more stringent than the basic PSD provisions. The visibility protection provision even requires the reduction of existing emissions if they interfere with Congressionally announced visibility goals. See §169A, 42 U.S.C.A. §7491.

The PSD provisions are sensitive to the desire of the states to have a substantial degree of control over their own environmental and economic growth policy. As a result, redesignations by states of AQCRs from one classification to another is expressly authorized by the statute. Federal interests are protected in this process by forbidding downward reclassifications of areas of federal concern – the parks, wilderness and other areas of special scenic and recreational significance. The statute also gives Indian tribes authority over the classification of reservation airsheds. Thereafter, however, the states are allowed to reclassify to satisfy state policies. Carte blanche is given to reclassifications upward to Class I. State decisions to promote and preserve higher air quality are encouraged in this fashion. Even downward reclassifications are largely a matter of state choice. EPA approval of such redesignations is required, but may be withheld only if specified procedures are not followed or if statutorily protected interests are adversely affected. For the most part, these are the statutory designations protective of federal land management prerogatives laid out in the classification system itself, but §7474(a)(2)(B) also requires that redesignations "not cause, or contribute to, concentrations of any air pollutant which exceed any maximum allowable increase or maximum allowable concentration...."

---

of the primary standard. This pattern of percentages is not the norm. The Class I increments are usually an even smaller percentage of the NAAQS. A more typical pattern would be roughly 2 percent, 25 percent and 50 percent of the NAAQS as the allowable increments for the three classes. This aspect of the PSD program and its legislative history are thoroughly reviewed in a case successfully challenging EPA's setting of the nitrogen oxides PSD increments. See Environmental Defense Fund v. EPA, 898 F.2d 183 (D.C.Cir. 1990).

COMMENTARY AND QUESTIONS

1. Federalism and PSD. The very nature of the PSD program takes a degree of autonomy away from the states. The level of allowable growth in Class I areas is limited by the stringent PSD increments and the option of redesignation is limited by the presence of various types of federal lands. Should the federal sites of importance, the Yosemites and Grand Canyons, be insulated against loss of amenity value that is at times obtained at the expense of economic development in the host state? Even more generally, the PSD program restricts development in less-developed or later developing states by taking away the potential advantage of less expensive pollution control requirements.

2. Exceeding the federal requirements. The Clean Air Act, although less explicitly than the Clean Water Act's §510, 33 U.S.C.A. §1370, gives the states latitude to do more to limit air pollution than the minimum required by federal law. This is manifest in the PSD reclassification program that allows states to designate all areas other than Indian reservations as Class I areas. Likewise, states in their SIPs and permitting of polluting facilities (except for mobile sources like cars and planes) are free to be as stringent as they like. EPA review will insure only that the SIPs and permits granted thereunder do not fail to meet the NAAQS.

EXPORTING POLLUTION

Exporting pollution as a means of meeting ambient standard requirements can properly be thought of as both a race of laxity problem and an externality problem. As originally enacted in 1970 the Clean Air Act addresses this problem most frontally in 42 U.S.C.A. §§7426 and 7410(a)(2)(D)(i-ii). Notice must be given by the upwind state to the downwind state of new and proposed major sources that will have an effect on the downwind state's ability to meet the NAAQS or will interfere with the downwind state's PSD program. The adversely affected state is given a right to protest to EPA, with EPA becoming the arbiter of the interstate clash of interests. The statute is drawn using language that seems to favor the downwind states. To be approved, an upwind state's SIP must:

> contain adequate provisions (i) prohibiting...any source or other type of emissions activity within the State from emitting any air pollutant in amounts which will (I) contribute significantly to nonattainment in, or interfere with maintenance by, any other State with respect to any such national primary or secondary ambient air quality standard, or (II) interfere with measures required to be included in the applicable [PSD] implementation plan for any other State....

In practice, under the language as it stood prior to the 1990 amendments,[36] the downwind states have won very few concessions from upwind states through the appeal to EPA process. As in virtually all aspects of Clean Air Act administration, those same states have an even worse record in seeking judicial invalidation of upwind activities that have received EPA approval.

36. The 1990 amendments to the section made substantive changes further favoring downwind states by enlarging the classes of upwind sources to be considered.

Air Pollution Control District v. EPA, 739 F.2d 1071 (6th Cir. 1984), a leading case in this area, gives a flavor of the difficulty downwind states have experienced. The case involves sulfur dioxide contributions to the Louisville, Kentucky airshed of a coal-fired power plant located just across the Ohio River in Indiana. For a few months after Indiana and Kentucky had their initial SIPs approved under the then-new Clean Air Act of 1970, the Kentucky and Indiana SIPs required identical sulfur dioxide control efforts for coal fired power plants, an emission limitation of 1.2 pounds of SO_2 per million British thermal units of heat input (MBTU). Indiana almost immediately won EPA approval for a revised SIP that allowed unregulated SO_2 emissions from coal-fired electric generating facilities.[37] Kentucky, on the other side of the river, held firm to the 1.2 lb./MBTU standard and eventually forced Louisville Gas & Electric (LG&E), the primary Kentucky SO_2 producer in the AQCR, to meet that standard. The court described the contrast in an understated way:

> It can therefore be seen that a significant disparity exists between the permissible emission limits of power plants in Jefferson County, Kentucky and the Gallagher plant in Floyd County, Indiana. LG&E, the primary producer of SO_2 in Jefferson County, spent approximately $138 million installing scrubbers to remove SO_2 from its emissions, while just across the river, Gallagher's SO_2 emissions were completely uncontrolled.[38]

Despite Kentucky's SO_2 control efforts in the Louisville AQCR, it remained a non-attainment area even after LG&E had completed installation of all of the needed emission controls. A petition was lodged with the EPA, seeking relief against the interstate effects of SO_2 pollution from the nearby Indiana plant. EPA's record of findings based on its modelling of the airshed concluded that only 3 percent of the Jefferson County, Kentucky SO_2 concentrations that resulted in violations of the NAAQS were attributable to the Gallagher plant. Those same findings also noted, however, that the Gallagher plant contributed large concentrations of SO_2 that were not part of predicted violations of the NAAQS. In particular, Gallagher contributed significantly to the highest second-highest 24-hour and 3-hour predicted concentrations in Kentucky, the amounts being 34.5 percent of the NAAQS primary 24-hour standard and 47 percent of the NAAQS secondary 3-hour standard. EPA's own study of the data observed these impacts have "a far more serious potential for limiting growth in Kentucky..." EPA even stated that by 1985, when controls at the LG&E plant would be fully on line, the Gallagher plant "will be the predominate [sic] influence upon air quality in Louisville, Kentucky."

EPA denied Kentucky's petition and judicial review in the federal court followed. The two central issues in the case were the affirmance of EPA's interpretation of the relevant legislation as (1) prohibiting only interstate pollution that "significantly contributes" to present violations of the NAAQS or an already established PSD program,[39] and (2) meaning that interference with potential growth in the downwind state is not a ground on which relief can be granted in the absence of

---

37. The standard was later revised to 6 lb SO2/MBTU, but that level of emissions was the same rate as uncontrolled emissions for the plant involved in this case.

38. 739 F.2d at 1077.

39. Here, because the relevant Kentucky AQCR was still a non-attainment area, no PSD plan was in place.

interference with an established PSD plan or program. It is hard to be too critical of the EPA position on the first issue. Given the fugitive nature of emissions into the common airshed, it is unlikely in the extreme that Congress meant to forbid all interstate pollution. The statutory language of §7426 suggests as much when it requires notice to downwind states of new sources in the upwind state that "may significantly contribute" to air quality problems in the downwind state. With the EPA data attributing only 3 percent of the non-attainment problem to emissions from the Gallagher plant, EPA's position seems quite reasonable.

The proper accommodation of interstate interests on the margin for growth question presents a more subtle and difficult issue. To grasp the competing positions of Kentucky and the EPA more clearly, imagine what would be the course of events if the Kentucky AQCR involved in the litigation, through additional reductions in emissions, remedies the excessive concentrations of SO_2 in all locations and becomes an attainment area. At that point, Kentucky would be able to adopt a new PSD SIP that allows some new pollution to be introduced if continued compliance with the NAAQS can be maintained. As the facts set forth above showed, EPA's model of the airshed indicated that there are some parts of the AQCR where, but for the Indiana emissions from the Gallagher plant, there would be substantial room for incremental SO_2 emissions without exceeding the NAAQS. On this basis, Kentucky claims that Indiana has "stolen its PSD increment" through the failure to limit Gallagher emissions.

In the case as it was litigated, Kentucky made this argument. EPA's response was formalistic and, in light of its own findings in the case, a bit disingenuous. EPA said there could be no present stealing of a PSD increment, because no PSD baseline could be set in advance of becoming an attainment area. When attainment occurred, the Kentucky concentrations attributable to the Gallagher plant would not then constitute stealing the increment because those concentrations would be part of the baseline. In this way, regardless of terminology, EPA allows Indiana to dispose of significant SO_2 emissions at Kentucky's expense.[40]

While the EPA position seems palpably unfair to Kentucky, it has the administrative advantage of limiting the need to exercise discretion. It avoids the pitfalls of some vague equity-based approach that would inevitably embroil EPA in bitter interstate disputes involving protracted evidentiary matters concerning the precise extent of interstate pollution. The EPA approach also maintains ambient standards as its central technique, whereas an alternative rule that called for equal pollution control efforts on both sides of the state line would rely more on a mandated technology approach. Although these observations hardly amount to a ringing defense of the EPA position, they give it sufficient rationality to be sustained by a reviewing court applying a deferential standard of review.

40. The position of EPA in this case is not an isolated event. In Connecticut v. EPA, 696 F.2d 147 (2d Cir. 1982), EPA allowed (and the court affirmed) the same sort of outcome in a case where New York emissions were raising ambient concentrations in the Connecticut airshed prior to Connecticut's setting of a PSD baseline. There too, it appeared that when the baseline was set there would be no allowable increment left for growth in emissions because the baseline would be so close to the NAAQS, in part as a result of the New York emissions that were challenged by Connecticut under the interstate pollution provisions of the Clean Air Act.

COMMENTARY AND QUESTIONS

1. EPA's dilemma. Do not be too quick to criticize EPA for failing to be more aggressive in these cases. On what principled basis can EPA determine how much pollution can cross state boundaries without constituting an injury to the downwind state? The general movement of air masses and the pollutants they carry is an uncontrollable natural event. For that reason, a zero transboundary emission limit is unattainable and undesirable. To meet that goal, emissions limits in the upwind state would have to be excessively restrictive. Remember that the way the NAAQS are set, with some of the standards being short-term standards and the variability of wind and other atmospheric conditions, virtually all states are both importers and exporters of pollution.

Once EPA is committed to allowing a reasonable amount of pollution to move from a source state to another state, the almost inevitable focus of comparison will be in the relative stringency of regulation of the emissions in the source and recipient state. On that score, the disparity between the uncontrolled emissions at the Gallagher plant and the need to use scrubbers at the LG&E plant may seem to embarrass EPA. Should it? It is possible to argue that EPA is only carrying out the will of Congress. This is a case being resolved using the ambient standards approach that Congress chose for the regulation of conventional air pollutants. The key questions for EPA are whether Indiana is meeting the NAAQS (without need of regulating Gallagher more stringently) and whether Kentucky is being prevented from meeting the NAAQS by Indiana emissions. On the record in the case, there is no warrant for EPA to act because the lax Indiana controls are not undermining the operation of the harm-based ambient standards approach. If Congress had intended EPA to insist on an equivalency of interstate effort in emission control, it could have chosen a technology-based approach, or a system that relied on uniform emissions control efforts nationwide.

2. Interstate transport commissions. As a partial response to the unhappy experience of downwind states with their attempts to use §§110 and 126 to effectively block out-of-state pollution, the 1990 amendments create a new institution called interstate transport commissions. See CAA §176A, 42 U.S.C.A. §7506a. These commissions can be formed at EPA's discretion on EPA's own initiative or following a request from an affected state whenever EPA finds there is a significant interstate transport of air pollutants that significantly contribute to an NAAQS violation. If formed, a commission is comprised of two members from each of the interested states and two EPA officials. The commission then assesses the degree of interstate pollution transport and the strategies for mitigating that pollution and makes recommendations to EPA for SIP provisions that will satisfy the interstate control obligations of §7410(a)(2)(D).

Chapter 19

ADMINISTRATIVE STANDARDS BASED ON AVAILABLE TECHNOLOGY: THE FEDERAL CLEAN WATER ACT

Introduction

The Federal Water Pollution Control Act, 33 U.S.C.A. §1251 et seq., commonly known as the Clean Water Act (CWA), displays an uneasy mix of harm-based and technology-based approaches to pollution regulation: a "federal floor" of nationwide technology-based effluent limitations is overlain by a localized harm-based approach emphasizing water quality-based effluent limitations. In its combination of these two environmental standard-setting methodologies, the CWA attempts to reconcile the significant attitudinal differences between advocates of each:

> Fundamentally, the competing schools disagree on whether uses that pollute water are just another economic activity or a form of moral turpitude. They disagree on whether the norm is an unregulated economy or a pollution-free society. They disagree on whether any regulation should rest heavily on market incentives or retreat confidently to commands and controls. They disagree on whether the costs of pollution control ever should exceed the expected benefits or ever fall below the amount necessary to prevent demonstrable damage. They disagree on whether control costs should be imposed on polluters or assumed by the community. They disagree on whether high uncertainty should be an entreprenurial green light or a regulatory red light. They disagree on who has the burden and the showing necessary to sustain it. W. Rodgers, II Environmental Law Treatise 13 (1986).

The history of American water pollution control law exhibits a tension between the harm-based and technology-based approaches, with first one and then the other gaining ascendency.[1]

In day-to-day administrative practice, the CWA today is predominantly a technology-based statutory program, with the water quality standards (WQS) process left in the background. The following opinion explores the reasons why Congress, in 1972, rejected its previous harm-based water pollution control strategy and replaced it with the technology-based approach:

---

1. See generally Zwick and Benstock, Water Wasteland (1971); Zener, The Federal Law of Water Pollution Control, in Federal Environmental Law (1974); Andreen, Beyond Words of Exhortation: The Congressional Prescription for Vigorous Enforcement of the Clean Water Act, 55 Geo. Wash. L. Rev. 202 (1987); Van Putten and Jackson, The Dilution of The Clean Water Act, 19 U. Mich. J. L. Ref. 863 (1986); Goldfarb, Water Law (2d ed. 1988).

Environmental Protection Agency v. California
United States Supreme Court, 1976
426 U.S. 200, 96 S. Ct. 2022, 48 L. Ed. 2d 578

[In this decision, the Court held that federal facilities were not required to obtain National Pollutant Discharge Elimination System permits from states with approved programs. Congress amended the Clean Water Act in 1977 to require federal wastewater dischargers to procure state permits.[2]]

WHITE, J. Before it was amended in 1972, the Federal Water Pollution Control Act employed ambient water quality standards specifying the acceptable levels of pollution in a State's interstate navigable waters as the primary mechanism in its program for the control of water pollution. This program based on water quality standards, which were to serve both to guide performance by polluters and to trigger legal action to abate pollution, proved ineffective. The problems stemmed from the character of the standards themselves, which focused on the tolerable effects rather than the preventable causes of water pollution, from the awkwardly shared federal and state responsibility for promulgating such standards, and from the cumbrous enforcement procedures. These combined to make it very difficult to develop and enforce standards to govern the conduct of individual polluters.

Some States developed water quality standards and plans to implement and enforce them, and some relied on discharge permit systems for enforcement. Others did not, and to strengthen the abatement system federal officials revived the Refuse Act of 1899, 30 Stat. 1152, 33 U.S.C.A. §407, which prohibits the discharge of any matter into the Nation's navigable waters except with a federal permit.[3] Although this direct approach to water pollution abatement proved helpful, it also was deficient in several respects: the goal of the discharge permit conditions was to achieve water quality standards rather than to require individual polluters to minimize effluent discharge, the permit program was applied only to industrial polluters, some dischargers were required to obtain both federal and state permits, and federal permit authority was shared by two federal agencies.

In 1972, prompted by the conclusion of the Senate Committee on Public Works that "the Federal water pollution control program...has been inadequate in every vital aspect," Congress enacted the Amendments, declaring "the national goal that the discharge of pollutants into the *navigable* waters be *eliminated* by 1985."[4] For present purposes the Amendments introduced two major changes in the methods to set and enforce standards to abate and control water pollution. First, the Amendments are aimed at achieving maximum "effluent limitations on point sources," as well as achieving acceptable water quality standards. A point source is "any discernible, confined and discrete conveyance...from which pollutants are or may be discharged." An "effluent limitation" in turn is "any restriction established by a State or the Administrator [of EPA] on quantities, rates, and concentrations of chemical, physical, biological or other constituents which are discharged from point sources...including schedules of compliance." Such direct restrictions on discharges facilitate enforcement by making it unnecessary to work backward from an overpolluted body of water to determine which point sources are responsible and which must must be abated. In addition, a discharger's performance is now

2. Pub. L. No. 95–217, §61(b).

3. See Chapter 7 for a discussion of the Refuse Act.

4. The Federal Water Pollution Control Act Amendments of 1972, Pub. L. No 92–500.

measured against strict technology-based effluent limitations – specified levels of treatment – to which it must conform, rather than against limitations derived from water quality standards to which it and other polluters must collectively conform. Water quality standards are retained as a supplementary basis for effluent limitations, however, so that numerous point sources, despite individual compliance with [technology-based] effluent limitations, may be further regulated to prevent water quality from falling below acceptable levels.

Second, the Amendments establish the National Pollutant Discharge Elimination System (NPDES) as a means of achieving and enforcing the effluent limitations. Under NPDES, it is unlawful for any person to discharge a pollutant without obtaining a permit and complying with its terms. A NPDES permit serves to transform generally applicable effluent limitations and other standards – including those based on water quality – into the obligations (including a timetable for compliance) of the individual discharger, and the Amendments provide for direct administrative and judicial enforcement of permits. With few exceptions, for enforcement purposes a discharger in compliance with the terms and conditions of an NPDES permit is deemed to be in compliance with those sections of the Amendments on which the permit conditions are based. In short, the permit defines, and facilitates compliance with and enforcement of, a proponderance of a discharger's obligations under the Amendments.

NPDES permits are secured, in the first instance, from EPA.... Consonant with its policy "to recognize, preserve, and protect the primary responsibilities and rights of the States to prevent, reduce, and eliminate pollution," Congress also provided that a State may issue NPDES permits "for discharges into navigable waters within its jurisdiction," but only upon EPA approval of the State's proposal to administer its own program. EPA may require modification or revision of a submitted program but when a plan is in compliance with EPA's guidelines...EPA shall approve the program and "suspend the issuance of permits...as to those navigable waters subject to such program."

The EPA retains authority to review operation of a State's permit program. Unless the EPA waives review for particular classes of point sources or for a particular permit application, a State is to forward a copy of each permit application to EPA for review, and no permit may issue if EPA objects that issuance of the permit would be "outside the guidelines and requirements" of the amendments. In addition to this review authority, after notice and opportunity to take action, EPA may withdraw approval of a state permit program which is not being administered in compliance with the [Amendments]....

COMMENTARY AND QUESTIONS

1. Ineffectuality of prior law. Before 1972, in over two decades only one case alleging violation of federal water pollution control law reached the courts, and in that case over four years elapsed between the initial enforcement conference and the final consent decree.[5] In those benighted days, desired uses were set by individual states, which classified waterways in categories ranging from Class A (swimming) to Class D (agricultural and industrial use). If a state was satisfied that a particular river need only be aesthetically tolerable and fit for commercial navigation, the law did not

5. Congressional Research Service, Library of Congress, A Legislative History of the Federal Water Pollution Control Act Amendments of 1972, 1257 (1973).

afford relief unless the river stank or corroded hulls of ships. One river, the Cuyahoga in Ohio, was not considered legally objectionable until it caught fire in 1969, because the state-designated use of that river was waste disposal. A former EPA Administrator, William Ruckleshaus, reportedly quipped that although our waterways are not yet fishable and swimmable, they are no longer flammable.

If the harm-based prior law had failed so miserably, why did Congress, in the 1972 CWA, adopt both technology-based and harm-based controls, superimposing a level of water quality-based controls on a fundamental level of technology-based controls? The answer has to do with congressional politics. The Senate favored replacing the water quality-based approach with progressively stricter technology-based effluent limitations leading to the ultimate cessation of all discharges. The House of Representatives, however, believed that an improved water quality-based approach was still viable. The resulting compromise entails a dual approach, with a harm-based system applicable only where necessary. A number of commentators believe that the CWA's many ambiguities can be traced to this original, unsuccessful compromise. See Note, The Federal Water Pollution Control Act Amendments of 1972: Ambiguity As A Control Device, 10 Harv. J. Legis. 565, 590 (1973); and Baum, Legislating Cost-Benefit Analysis: The Federal Water Pollution Control Act Experience, 9 Colum. J. Envtl L. 75, 81 (1983) ("conscious ambiguity was substituted for compromise").

Why did Congress move to a primarily technology-based standard-setting methodology in 1972 when it had embraced an almost totally harm-based strategy in the Clean Air Act enacted only two years earlier? The Clean Air Act was, in effect, a statute of the 1960s because it extended and strengthened the harm-based Air Quality Act of 1967, Pub. L. No. 90-148, which, ironically, followed the ambient standard approach earlier established in the 1965 Federal Water Pollution Control Act, Pub. L. No. 89-234. Between late 1970, when the Clean Air Act was being finalized, and the summer of 1971, when the Senate Air and Water Pollution Subcommittee released its technology-based clean water bill (drawn from section 111 of the 1970 Clean Air Act), the burgeoning environmental movement had inspired dissatisfaction with the harm-based approach and its philosophy that there exists a right to discharge up to the assimilative capacity of the environment. Lieber, Federalism and Clean Waters (1975), Chapter 2.

2. Pros and cons of technology-based controls. Critics of the technology-based approach argue that it is: (1) economically inefficient because it frequently demands "redundant treatment" (i.e., greater treatment than necessary to maintain desired uses for waterbodies); and (2) insufficiently technology-forcing, because it does not compel the industry to develop innovative technology. See Stewart, Economics, Environment and the Limits of Legal Control, 9 Harv. Envtl L. Rev. 1 (1985), and Pederson, Turning The Tide on Water Quality, 15 Ecol. L. Q. 69 (1988). Professor Howard Latin responds to the first argument as follows:

> Many control programs initially required marginal harm-based determinations, but they were not successfully implemented. Congress or the EPA

> frequently replaced harm-based regulations with less "efficient" approaches, such as technology-based standards...rather than rely on hazardous effects, because these strategies are more capable of implementation.[6]

As for the second critique, it can be argued that the CWA's technology-based approach, as originally conceived, should encourage the development of new technology by innovators within and outside the manufacturing industrial sector. Although technology-based effluent limitations are based on available technology, EPA must review promulgated effluent limitations every five years with a view toward tightening them to reflect the existence of improved pollution control devices. CWA §301(d). In other words, build a better pollutant trap and the regulated dischargers will be required to beat a path to your door. The CWA's "Zero-Discharge Goal"[7] means that at some future time the best available pollution control technology will entail elimination of residuals, which has already been accomplished by some industries. Unfortunately, EPA has been so preoccupied with developing its initial technology-based standards that it has only just begun its five-year reviews of technology-based effluent limitations, partially as a result of Congressional prodding through §304(m), added by the Water Quality Act Amendments of 1987.[8]

3. Navigable waters. In the CWA, "discharge of a pollutant" means "any addition of any pollutant to navigable waters from any point source." §502(12). "Navigable waters" is generally defined as "waters of the United States." §502(7). It is well-settled that, as far as surface waters are concerned, "waters of the United States" transcends traditional definitions of navigability and is coterminus with the limits of the federal government's commerce clause jurisdiction. U.S. v. Ashland Oil, 504 F.2d 1317 (6th Cir. 1974). Thus, wetlands, drainage ditches, mosquito canals, and even intermittent streams have been held to be waters of the United States. See Annotation, What are Navigable Waters Subject to the Provisions of the FWPCA?, 52 A.L.R. 4th, 788 (1981).[9]

A significant gap in the CWA is that its provisions do not apply to groundwater, at least according to EPA. Compare Exxon v. Train, 554 F.2d 1310 (5th Cir. 1977) (no groundwater is covered by the CWA) with U.S. Steel v. Train, 556 F.2d 822 (7th Cir. 1977)(groundwater is covered if it is hydrologically connected to surface water). See Wood, Regulating Dischargers Into Groundwater: The Crucial Link In Pollution

6. Latin, Ideal vs. Real Regulatory Efficiency: Implementation of Uniform Standards and 'Fine-Tuning' Regulatory Reforms, 37 Stan. L. Rev. 1267, 1313 (1985).

7. Section 101(1) declares, "It is the national goal that the discharge of pollutants into the navigable waters be eliminated by 1985."

8. Pub. L. No. 100–4, §304(m) requires EPA to publish by February 4, 1988, and biennially thereafter, a plan which shall: (1) establish a schedule for the annual review and revision of promulgated effluent guidelines; (2) identify categories of discharges for which effluent guidelines have not been published; and (3) establish a schedule to promulgate, within four years, effluent limitations for categories identified in (2). See NRDC v. EPA, 32 ERC 1969 (D.C. D.C. 1991), where the court, referring to "the well-documented history of agency inertia," overturned EPA's interpretation of §304(m).

9. Ed. note: FWPCA is a rarely used acronym for the CWA. In the 1977 amendments, Congress changed the popular but not the official name of the Act.

Control Under The Clean Water Act, 12 Harv. Envtl L. Rev. 569 (1988) (arguing that "tributary" groundwater is covered by the CWA). Protection of groundwater quality has been attempted through a patchwork of federal and state programs, including the Safe Drinking Water Act. See Goldfarb, Water Law, Ch. 37 (2d ed. 1988), and Glicksman and Coggins, Groundwater Pollution I: The Problem and the Law, 35 U. Kan. L. Rev. 75 (1986).

4. Point source. A "point source" is "any discernible, confined and discrete conveyance, including but not limited to any pipe, ditch, channel, tunnel, conduit, well, discrete fissure, container, rolling stock, concentrated animal feeding operation, or vessel or other floating craft from which pollutants are or may be discharged. This term does not include agricultural stormwater discharges and return flows from irrigated agriculture." §502(14). A "nonpoint source" is any source that is not a point source. In general, a nonpoint source is a diffuse, intermittent source of pollutants that does not discharge at a single location but whose pollutants are carried over or through the soil by way of stormflow processes. As we shall see, another meaningful gap in the CWA is that, to date, it leaves nonpoint sources virtually unregulated. Is there any reason, other than a political reason, for exempting agricultural discharges from being regulated as point sources?

The term "point source" is liberally construed, and has been held to include earth moving equipment in a wetland, Avoyelles Sportsmens' League v. Marsh, 715 F.2d 897 (5th Cir. 1983), and ponded mine drainage that erodes a channel to a river, U.S. v. Earth Sciences, Inc., 599 F.2d 368 (7th Cir. 1979). Are dams, which often cause adverse water quality impacts downstream, to be treated as point or nonpoint sources? See National Wildlife Federation v. Gorsuch, 693 F.2d 156 (D.C. Cir. 1982), upholding EPA's interpretation that dams are nonpoint sources. Because each discharge pipe is a separate point source, "bubbling" is virtually impossible under the CWA. See Chapter 20 for a discussion of "bubbles" under the Clean Air Act.

5. The federal-state partnership. Thirty-nine states administer their own NPDES discharge permit programs with EPA approval. In the other states, EPA regional offices are administering the program. Do you think that the CWA's safeguards, as described in the EPA v. California opinion, are adequate to prevent a state from treating dischargers leniently in order to attract and retain industry? In particular, given EPA's lack of resources, can EPA effectively review draft state permits? Would an EPA threat to withdraw state program authorization be credible? Can EPA meaningfully exercise its backup enforcement authority under §309 of the CWA? Can state pollution control agencies be significantly influenced by EPA's diminishing ability to award program grants, conduct research, and perform technical assistance activities?

6. Types of point source dischargers. Point source dischargers can be either municipal or industrial. Municipal point source dischargers are known as Publicly-Owned Treatment Works or POTWs. Industrial point source dischargers are either direct dischargers, discharging directly into waterbodies, or indirect dischargers that discharge into sewers and into waterbodies through POTWs. Moreover, industrial dischargers can be either existing or new pollution sources. As we will see later on, industrial point source dischargers are further distinguished according to the kinds of pollutants that they discharge.

7. Federal facilities. Subsequent to the 1977 amendment to §313 of the CWA governing federal facility compliance, a number of federal courts held that although federal facilities must procure discharge permits from states with permit-granting authority, federal facilities cannot be subjected to state-imposed civil penalties for violation. See McClellan Ecological Seepage Situation v. Weinberger, 655 F.Supp 601 (E.D. Cal. 1986), and California v. Department of the Navy, 845 F.2d 222 (9th Cir. 1988). More recent decisions, however, have upheld the imposition of state civil penalties on federal facilities violating the CWA and its state counterparts. See Ohio v. Department of Energy, 904 F.2d 1058 (6th Cir. 1990), cert. granted, __U.S.__, 111 S. Ct. 2256 (1991), and Sierra Club v. Interior Department, 931 F.2d 142 (10th Cir. 1991)(citizens may sue federal facilities for civil penalties). The comparable provisions of RCRA and CERCLA regarding federal facility compliance are even more ambiguous than §313 of the CWA. (See Chapters 21 and 22.)

A. WATER POLLUTANTS AND THEIR SOURCES

Before we examine the mechanics of setting technology-based effluent limitations, we should know something about which substances actually pollute our surface waterbodies and where these substances come from.

The Conservation Foundation, State of the Environment: A View Towards the Nineties
87–106 (1987)

The U.S. Geological Survey (USGS) provides comprehensive, nationwide water quality trend information on specific contaminants through their National Ambient Stream Quality Accounting Network (NASQUAN). Ambient monitoring stations located in river basins and subbasins throughout the country have collected information on the same pollutants since 1974, with the number of stations totaling 501 in 1985.... NASQUAN was originally established to measure the quantity of surface flow. Therefore, its monitoring stations generally are located at the downstream end of a watershed. Thus, they are often upstream of, or too far downstream from, major pollution sources to record locally severe problems. NASQUAN stations are limited further because they do not measure all pollutants (including most of the potentially toxic organic chemicals) and because, in many instances, monitoring equipment may not be sophisticated enough to measure pollutants at low concentrations that are nonetheless high enough to be of concern.

DISSOLVED OXYGEN

Dissolved oxygen, usually present in clean waters at levels of 5 ppm [parts per million] or more, is necessary for fish and other aquatic life to survive. The decomposition of organic pollutants, such as those in municipal sewage, or chemicals, such as those in industrial wastes, depletes the natural oxygen level. Temperature can also change the amount of dissolved oxygen by affecting the solubility of oxygen.

Of 369 NASQUAN stations, 17 percent showed improving trends in dissolved oxygen, while 11 percent showed deteriorating trends from 1974 to 1981. The improvement likely reflects the efforts to reduce oxygen-demanding wastes from industries and municipal facilities. Between 1972 and 1982, these waste loads decreased 46 percent from municipal sources and 71 percent from industries.

BACTERIA

Many bacteria are harmless, but the concentration in water of fecal coliform and fecal streptococcus bacteria from human and animal wastes indicate the potential for infection and disease. High bacteria counts force officials to close public swimming beaches and restrict shellfishing in contaminated waters.

Levels of bacteria measured at NASQUAN stations improved notably between 1974 and 1981....

SUSPENDED SOLIDS

Brown, turbid water caused by suspended solids such as soil sediment and other particles can significantly reduce beneficial uses of water by people and can harm aquatic wildlife. These particles also can carry nutrients, pesticides, bacteria, and other harmful substances. Many rivers have always carried high sediment loads because of natural erosion occurring in their watersheds. But erosion from cropland, construction sites, rangeland, and forestland has elevated sediment to a major water pollutant.

NASQUAN stations detected almost the same number of increases as decreases for suspended sediment between 1975 and 1981....

TOTAL DISSOLVED SOLIDS

Dissolved solids are inorganic salts and other substances from natural and human sources after they have dissolved in water. Most commonly these dissolved substances are measured together as total dissolved solids (TDS)....

NASQUAN stations showed increases in TDS at 59 percent of the stations that showed significant trends. The pattern of the trend indicates that irrigation return flow is a major culprit, especially in the semiarid basins of the West and Southwest....

NUTRIENTS

Nutrients, such as phosphorus and nitrogen, can stimulate algae blooms and growth of nuisance water plants, can accelerate eutrophication (the aging of lakes and reservoirs), and can cause problems with oxygen depletion as the plants die and decompose. Nutrients can over enrich water bodies, allowing algal blooms. Such blooms block light from reaching submerged aquatic vegetation, thereby killing off valuable nursery habitat for finfish and shellfish. The primary sources of nutrients are fertilizer runoff from croplands and urban lawns, runoff from feedlots, and discharges from municipal wastewater treatment plants.

Nationwide, nearly as many NASQUAN stations reported decreases as increases in phorphrous concentrations....

Nitrogen concentrations have increased in about three times as many stations as they have decreased. Areas dominated by cropland were most likely to show increases, reflecting the rapid increase in agricultural use of nitrogen fertilizers....

Another significant source of the increased levels of nitrogen is atmospheric deposition of nitrate. In some cases it is the largest nitrogen source in a river basin....

METALS AND TOXIC SUBSTANCES

Probably the most dramatic improvement in surface water quality is the decreased levels of lead.... The explanation for the improvement probably lies more with the reduced use of lead in gasoline imposed by air pollution control requirements than any actions taken under the Clean Water Act....

Trends for other metals are less encouraging. Arsenic concentrations generally increased from 1974 to 1981, most frequently in the Great Lakes and Ohio basins and the Pacific Northwest.... As with lead, atmospheric deposition is probably the main source, with arsenic being emitted in large amounts to the atmosphere by coal-burning electric power plants and nonferrous smelters.

Cadmium measurements also showed predominantly deteriorating trends.... USGS analyses again found that atmospheric deposition was probably a significant source, with fossil fuel combustion being a major contributor.

USGS found few significant trends – either up or down – for the other metals (chromium, iron, manganese, selenium, mercury, and zinc) it measured, and those that it did find showed no particular geographical pattern.

USGS also established a network of 160 to 180 pesticide monitoring network stations to analyze water and sediment samples for 11 chlorinated hydrocarbon insecticides, 7 organophosphate insecticides, and 4 herbicides. Fewer than 1 percent of their water samples showed detectable amounts of these chemicals.... The organochlorine insecticides, which are not water soluble, were much more likely to be found adsorbed onto sediments. Dieldrin, DDD, and DDE (the latter two being degradation products of DDT...), were found in 10 to 20 percent of the sediment samples. DDT itself and chlordane were found in 8 to 10 percent of the samples. EPA banned all three of these in the early to mid 1970s, and USGS found that the frequency of detection gradually decreased from 1975 to 1980....

Some evidence on the prevalence of toxic contamination is provided by state assessments of water quality conditions. State officials listed toxic substances as the fourth most frequent cause of continuing pollution in "waters of concern"; 30 of 35 states cite violations of water quality standards or use impairments resulting from these substances....

MUNICIPAL WASTEWATER DISCHARGES

Municipal wastewater discharges continue to contribute to a significant portion of the pollutants carried in U.S. rivers and streams, in spite of the Clean Water Act amendments in 1972.... In 1982 when ASIWPCA [Association of State and Interstate Water Pollution Control Administrators] asked state officials for the primary reasons why their streams did not support the designated uses, municipal discharges ranked first in 19 states (only nonpoint sources ranked higher) and second in another 20.

Municipal treatment facilities must handle substantial volumes of different types of wastes. In 1986, 172 million people sent 27,692 million gallons of pollutants to 15,438 municipal facilities daily. In addition to normal domestic sewage, wastewater treatment plants must handle a wide variety of toxic and other nonconventional substances disposed of by households and businesses.

A recent EPA study, for instance, identifies about 160,000 industrial and commercial facilities that discharged wastes containing hazardous constituents to POTWs. These businesses discharge an estimated 3,200 million gallons of wastewater, or apoproximately 12 percent of the total POTW flow, daily. This flow contains an estimated 92,000 metric tons of hazardous pollutants annually....

INDUSTRIAL DISCHARGES

EPA's 1984 National Water Quality Inventory blames industrial discharges for impairing the designated use of 10 percent of the nation's lake area and 11 percent of its stream miles. One assessment estimates that they contribute about one-third of the total point source loading of oxygen-demanding wastes....

Another study looked at how industries dispose of the hazardous wastes they generate. It found that the organic chemicals industry, the largest generator of hazardous wastes, discharges half (about 32 million metric tons a year) of its hazardous wastes to surface waters under its water discharge permits....

NONPOINT SOURCES

A more ubiquitous problem than point-source pollution...is presented by nonpoint sources. These include seepage, stormwater runoff from agricultural lands and urban streets, septic tanks, atmospheric deposition, and a number of other sources that do not discharge wastewater through pipes or other structural conveyances. According to a recent Resources For the Future estimate, they are responsible for a majority of many conventional pollutants – nearly 100 percent of sediment, 82 percent of nitrogen, and 84 percent of phosphorous – reaching the nation's surface waters.

Most states have identified nonpoint sources as the primary reasons why their streams do not support their designated uses. Nonpoint sources ranked first in 26 states and second in 13 others. Forty states reported that nonpoint sources need to be controlled if water quality is to continue to improve....

Agriculture is the predominant source of the problem..., contributing most of the sediment, nitrogen, phosphorus, and BOD [Biochemical Oxygen Demand], as well as a large amount of the pesticides, bacteria, and dissolved solids that are degrading U.S. surface waters. State officials identified agriculture as the most widespread source of water pollution in 60 percent of the states, causing problems in 64 percent of the river miles and 57 percent of the acres area assesssed.

COMMENTARY AND QUESTIONS

1. Intermedia pollution. America's pollution control effort has relied on a series of media-specific statutes: e.g., the Clean Air Act for air pollution control; the Clean Water Act for surface water pollution control; and RCRA for control of land and groundwater pollution. However, as the Conservation Foundation selection indicates, we are increasingly recognizing the importance of intermedia effects such as atmospheric deposition of water pollutants. (Intermedia pollution also occurs in reverse when POTWs emit into the air volatile organics that are stripped from wastewater during the municipal treatment process). By and large, intermedia pollution is unregulated by current media-specific statutes, although the 1990 Clean Air Act Amendments regarding control of atmospheric deposition, and hazardous emissions from POTWs are a substantial step in the right direction. (See page 876 *infra*).

This fragmented, media-specific system of legal controls evolved because of congressional dissatisfaction with the broad grants of legislative authority to administrative agencies characteristic of the New Deal, the prevalence of an "incrementalist" political philosophy, competition for environmental credit among members of Congress and presidential candidates, rivalries among congressional committees, the preference of bureaucrats for programmatic administration, and the tendency for politicians and public interest groups to demand quick solutions to perceived environmental crises. Guruswamy, Integrating Thoughtways: Reopening of the Environmental Mind?, 1989 Wis. L. Rev. 463, 492 (1989). What should we now do to address intermedia pollution problems? Should we repeal all of our media-specific statutes and replace them with a single mega-statute that includes all pollution media? If this approach would be too disruptive, can we improve the present system by adopting facility-wide permitting, or are our media-specific statutes so dissimilar that facility-wide permitting would be impossible? Guruswamy believes that a comprehensive, integrative pollution control statute would be politically infeasible at this time. He recommends administrative integration by EPA using existing statutory provisions.

2. Nonpoint Source Pollution. It is a disturbing anomaly that the most widespread sources of water pollution – nonpoint sources – are virtually unregulated by the Clean Water Act. Why is there this gap in the CWA? First, when the CWA was enacted in 1972, water pollution was perceived mostly from the perspective of point source discharges of so-called "conventional pollutants," e.g., BOD, suspended solids, and nutrients. Nonpoint sources and point source dischargers of toxics were not nearly as conspicuous then as they have since become through investigations and pollution events. Second, nonpoint source pollution control involves land-use restrictions that government has been reluctant to impose because of their political sensitivity. See Chapter 23.

B. DEVELOPMENT OF TECHNOLOGY-BASED EFFLUENT LIMITATIONS

The following case is unusual among Clean Water Act effluent limitation cases in that it involves a relatively simple technology and is thus intelligible to readers who lack a background in environmental science or chemical engineering. Because environmental issues arise from competing demands on natural resources, environmental lawyers learn to work closely with scientists, engineers, natural resource managers, planners, policy analysts, and social scientists in formulating multidisciplinary, holistic environmental protection strategies for presentation to courts, legislatures, administrative agencies, private corporations, and the general public.

Rybachek v. EPA
United States Circuit Court for the Ninth Circuit, 1990
904 F.2d 1276

O'SCANNLAIN, J.... Placer mining is one of the four basic methods of mining metal ores; it involves the mining of alluvial or glacial deposits of loose gravel, sand, soil, clay, or mud called "placers." These placers often contain particles of gold and other heavy minerals. Placer miners excavate the gold-bearing material (paydirt) from the placer deposit after removing the surface vegetation and non-gold-bearing gravel (overburden). The gold is then separated from the other materials in the paydirt by a gravity-separation process known as "sluicing."

In the sluicing process, a miner places the ore in an on-site washing plant (usually a sluice box) which has small submerged dams (riffles) attached to its bottom. He causes water to be run over the paydirt in the sluice box; when the heavier materials (including gold) fall, they are caught by the riffles. The lighter sand, dirt, and clay particles are left suspended in the wastewater released from the sluice box.

Placer mining typically is conducted directly in streambeds or on adjacent property. The water usually enters the sluice box through gravity, but may sometimes also enter through the use of pumping equipment. At some point after the process described above, the water in the sluice box is discharged. The discharges from placer mining can have aesthetic and water-quality impacts on waters both in the immediate vicinity and downstream. Toxic metals, including arsenic, cadmium, lead, zinc, and copper, have been found in higher concentration in streams where mining occurs than in non-mining streams.

It is the treatment of the sluice-box discharge water before it re-enters a natural water course that is at the heart of this case.

STATUTORY FRAMEWORK

Congress enacted the Clean Water Act to "restore and maintain the chemical, physical, and biological integrity of the Nation's waters." Under the Act, the EPA must impose and enforce technology-based effluent limitations and standards through individual National Pollutant Discharge Elimination System ("NPDES") permits. These permits contain specific terms and conditions as well as numerical discharge limitations, which govern the activities of pollutant dischargers. Through the Clean Water Act, Congress has directed the EPA to incorporate into the permits increasingly stringent technology-based effluent limitations.

Congress specified a number of means for the EPA to impose and to enforce these limitations in NPDES permits. For instance, it requires the Agency to establish effluent limitations requiring dischargers to use the "best practicable control technology currently available" ("BPT") within an industry. These limits are to represent "the average of the best" treatment technology performance in an industrial category. See EPA v. National Crushed Stone Ass'n., 449 U.S. 64 (1980). The EPA is further required to promulgate limitations both for the discharge of toxic pollutants by mandating that an industry use the "best available technology economically achievable" ("BAT") and for discharge of conventional pollutants by requiring the use of the "best conventional pollution control technology" ("BCT"); the congressionally imposed deadline for promulgation of these limitations was March 31, 1989....

In addition, new pollution sources in an industry must meet a separate set of standards, called new-source performance standards ("NSPS"). These standards limit the discharge of pollutants by new sources based on the "best available demonstrated control technology" ("BDT"). Finally, the EPA is authorized to establish best management practices ("BMPs") "to control plant site runoff, spillage or leaks, sludge or waste disposal, and drainage from raw material storage" in order to diminish the amount of toxic pollutants flowing into the receiving waters.

RULEMAKING HISTORY

On November 20, 1985, proceeding under the Clean Water Act, the EPA proposed regulations for placer mining. For most mines processing fewer than 500 cubic yards of ore per day ("yd³/day"), the EPA proposed BPT effluent limitations of 0.2 millilitres per litre ("ml/l") of discharge for settleable solids and 2,000 milligrams per litre ("mg/l") for total suspended solids. For mines processing more than 500 yd³/day of ore, the EPA proposed more stringent BCT and BAT limitations as well as new-source performance standards (NSPS) prohibiting the discharge of processed wastewater. Twice during the rulemaking process, the Agency published notices of new information and requested public comment on additional financial and technical data.

As a result of its studies, the comments received during the review-and-comment periods, and new studies undertaken in response to the submitted comments, the EPA promulgated final effluent-limitation guidelines and standards on May 24, 1988. The EPA established a BPT limitation, based on simple-settling technology, for settleable solids of 0.2 ml/l for virtually all mines. The final rule also established BAT limitations and NSPS based on recirculation technology, restricting the flow of processed wastewater that could be discharged. In addition, the EPA promulgated five BMPs to control discharges due to mine drainage and infiltration. These regulations were to become effective on July 7, 1988....

The Alaska Miners Association ("AMA") and Stanley and Rosalie Rybachek timely petitioned this court for review of the EPA's regulations. We ordered the petitions consolidated....

THE FINAL RULE

Petitioners make a host of arguments about the content of the final rule. For instance, they attack the EPA's setting of BPT and BAT limitations. They also allege various errors by the EPA in its promulgation of BMPs and its enunciation of new-source criteria....

MERITS OF THE LIMITATIONS

Petitioners challenge the merits of the EPA's regulations on a number of grounds; indeed, virtually every aspect of the regulations is attacked. To the extent the regulations may be divided into component parts (e.g., the BPT limitations, the BAT limitations, and new-source criteria), we address petitioner's arguments along those lines.

DETERMINATION OF BPT

We turn first to petitioners' argument that the EPA erred in its determination that settling ponds are the best practicable control technology currently available (BPT) within the placer mining industry. There is no dispute that settling ponds are currently available pollution control technology; in fact, the AMA concedes that they are now used by almost all miners. Rather, petitioners contend that the EPA failed to use a "cost-benefit analysis" in determining that settling ponds were BPT for placer mining. They also argue that the EPA failed to consider costs when it set forth BPT limitations governing settleable solids for small mines.

The Clean Water Act controls when and how the EPA should require BPT. Under 33 U.S.C. §1311(b)(1)(A), the Act requires "effluent limitations for point sources...which shall require the application of best practicable control technology currently available [BPT]." Under this section, the EPA is to determine whether a technology is BPT; the factors it considers "shall include...total cost of" the technology "in reltion to effluent benefits to be achieved" from it, the age of equipment, engineering aspects, "non-water quality environmental impact...and such other factors as the Administrator deems appropriate."

From this statutory language, it is "plain that, as a general rule, the EPA is required to consider the costs and benefits of proposed technology in its inquiry to determine the BPT." Association of Pacific Fisheries v. EPA, 615 F.2d 794 (9th Cir. 1980). The EPA has broad discretion in weighing these competing factors. It may determine that a technology is not BPT on the basis of this cost-benefit analysis only when the costs are "wholly disproportionate" to the potential effluent-reduction benefits.

We look first to whether the EPA properly considered the costs of BPT and second to whether it properly weighed these costs against the benefits.

First, the record shows that the EPA properly considered costs in conducting the analysis which led to the determination that settling ponds are BPT and to the establishment of BPT effluent limitations for settleable solids. The EPA used a model-mine analysis to estimate the costs to mines of installing settling ponds. The Agency developed several model mines to represent the typical operating and compliance costs that open-cut mines and dredges of various sizes would incur. Commenters attempted to insure that the model-mine analysis reflected actual industry conditions, and the EPA accordingly modified the analysis when it thought it appropriate during the rulemaking. The EPA then determined, for each of its model mines, the incremental costs that would be incurred to construct and operate settling ponds to retain wastewater long enough to achieve a certain settleable solids level. It proceeded to conduct a detailed and complex assessment of the effect of the compliance costs on the mining industry's profits.

The EPA then properly weighed these costs against the benefits of settling ponds. Its data indicated that placer mine wastewater contained high levels of solids and metals that were reduced substantially by simple settling. The upshot of the EPA's analysis was its estimation that installation of settling ponds by open-cut mines industry-wide would remove over four million pounds of solids at a cost of approximately $2.2 million – a removal cost of less than $1 per pound of solids.

We would uphold the EPA's determination of BPT.

DETERMINATION OF BAT: ANALYSIS OF COSTS

We next confront the AMA's challenge to the EPA's determination that recirculation of process wastewater is the best available technology economically achievable (BAT) in the placer mining industry. By definition, BAT limitations must be both technologically available and economically achievable. We conclude that the EPA's BAT limitations were both and therefore uphold them.

The technological availability of recirculating process wastewater is not in dispute; in fact, placer mines commonly practice it. It is recirculation's economic achievability that petitioner's challenge.

In determining the economic achievability of technology, the EPA must consider the "cost" of meeting BAT limitations, but need not compare such cost with the benefits of effluent reduction. The Agency measures costs on a "reasonableness standard"; it has considerable discretion in weighing the technology's costs, which are less-important factors than in setting BPT limitations.

The record demonstrates that the EPA weighed the costs that recirculation would impose on gold placer mining....

TOTAL SUSPENDED SOLIDS LIMITATIONS

We come to petitioner's claim that the EPA has impermissibly established BAT standards to regulate the discharge of total suspended solids. Petitioners argue that total suspended solids are conventional pollutants and therefore subject to BCT (best conventional pollution control technology), rather than BAT, standards. EPA's adoption of recirculation as BAT to control total suspended solids was arbitrary, petitioners contend, because recirculation could not pass the cost-reasonableness test required in determining BCT.

The EPA declined to establish BCT for total suspended solids because test results indicated that settling technology could not consistently control the level of total suspended solids. Moreover, recirculation failed the BCT cost-reasonbleness test.

Petitioners are incorrect in contending that the EPA instead adopted BAT to regulate the level of total suspended solids. The EPA's discussion of BAT in the final rule makes no reference to controlling total suspended solids. Instead, EPA set BAT standards to control the discharge of toxic pollutants – a category which, the parties agree, does not encompass total suspended solids. We therefore reject the contention that the EPA was arbitrary in establishing BAT standards.

SETTLEABLE SOLIDS LIMITATIONS

Petitioners also claim that settleable solids are a component of total suspended solids and that the EPA should have classified settleable solids as a conventional pollutant rather than a nonconventional pollutant. Petitioners contend that the BAT-based effluent limitations are therefore inappropriate for settleable solids. We disagree.

In the Clean Water Act, Congress classified suspended solids as a conventional pollutant. Congress did not classify settleable solids. We must determine, therefore, whether the EPA's classification of settleable solids as a nonconventional pollutant "is based on a permissible construction of the [Clean Water Act]." Chevron U.S.A., Inc. v. EPA, 467 U.S. at 843. This court may not substitute its own construction of the Act if the EPA's interpretation is reasonable.

The EPA argues that because settleable solids were not designated by Congress as either a conventional or a toxic pollutant, they should be considered a nonconventional pollutant under 33 U.S.C.A. §1311(b)(2)(F). This argument is buttressed by the fact that EPA has subjected settleable solids to BAT-level controls in other regulatory areas. And even if settleable solids should more properly be considered a conventional pollutant, we note that the EPA has determined that settleable solids in placer mining effluent are a toxic pollutant indicator and thus may be subject to BAT-level limitations. We find, therefore, that the EPA's decision to treat settleable solids as a nonconventional pollutant and thus subject to BAT standards was both reasonable and permissible....

MANDATING OF TECHNOLOGY

The AMA next claims that by forbidding the discharge of any process wastewater, the EPA is mandating that placer miners use recirculation technology. According to the AMA, the EPA's action violates Congress' intent to avoid dictating technologies and to encourge innovation. While admitting that the wastewater flow standards are currently achievable only through certain technology, the EPA responds that the regulations only prescribe limitations reflecting actually achieved wastewater reduction. We agree with the EPA....

The EPA has not mandated use of a particular technology. The Agency first determined that recirculation is BAT for the control of discharges by placer mines of toxic metals and settleable solids. Based on this determination, the EPA established that Zero discharge of process wastewater is achievable and should be the BAT limitation and new-source performance standard. That the standards and limitations are stringent and currently may be achievable only through certain technology is true. However, nothing in the EPA's regulations specifies the use of any particular technology to meet the BAT limitations and new-source performance standards achievable through recirculation. In fact, the EPA has encouraged miners to employ innovative technologies and to seek compliance extensions and alternative BAT limitations under §301(k) of the Act. We find that the EPA's setting of zero-discharge limitations based on recirculation results was within its mandate under the Clean Water Act.

AVAILABILITY OF VARIANCES

Petitioners claim that EPA has contravened Congress' intent by failing to allow miners to obtain variances for site-specific conditions. We first note that this assertion is flatly contradicted by the final rule's express language allowing miners to apply for fundamentally different factor ("FDF") variances for both the BPT and BAT limitations....

Petitioners argue that the EPA's classification of settleable solids as a toxic pollutant indicator will prevent miners from obtaining a variance. Normally, BAT limitations for nonconventional pollutants (here, settleable solids) are subject to modification under §§301(c) and (g) of the Clean Water Act. In this instance, modifications for settleable solids under these provisions are unavailable because settleable solids are considered an indicator of toxic pollutants. This does not mean, however, that no variance in the BAT limitations for settleable solids is available; miners may still apply for an FDF variance under §301(n) of the Act....

TIME FOR COMPLIANCE

The AMA contends that Alaskan miners were not given sufficient time to comply with the EPA's regulations.... Congress mandated that the BCT and BAT limitations must be achieved no later than March 31, 1989. The EPA does not have discretion to extend this deadline. This does not mean, however, that the EPA must be inflexible in enforcing the regulations.

"Section 309 of the Act provides that, if a discharger fails to comply with a 'final deadline' the [EPA] shall schedule a 'reasonable' time for compliance 'taking into account the seriousness of the violation *and any good faith efforts to comply* with applicable requirements.'" Chemical Manufacturers Ass'n v. EPA, 870 F.2d 177, 242 (5th Cir. 1989), cert. denied, 110 S. Ct. 1936 (1990). It was "Congress' intention that good faith compliance [in appropriate instances] would be accommodated by the

EPA's post-deadline enforcement policy." Id. Thus, while we acknowledge the miner's concerns, we do not think that as a general matter enforcement of the new regulations for the 1989 mining season was unreasonable.

COMMENTARY AND QUESTIONS

1. Evolution of categorical technology-based limitations. When the CWA was enacted in 1972, it contained two phases of technology-based limitations. In the first phase, existing industrial point source dischargers were required to meet effluent limitations based on BPT by 1977. During the second phase, dischargers were to meet effluent limitations based on BAT by 1983. BPT was intended to be primarily "end of pipe" treatment, with process changes required only if they were normal practice within an industry. The factors to be considered in setting BAT limitations were similar to those relied upon in setting BPT-based limitations (and described in the *Rybachek* opinion), except that (1) BAT was originally based on the single best performer within an industry, rather than on an average of "exemplary plants," (2) BAT was based on process changes adopted within the industry or reasonably transferrable from another industry, and (3) BAT involved a consideration only of the cost of achieving such reduction, not comparative benefits and costs. Congress realized that some facilities would be forced to cut back production or even close down as a result of these technology-based limitations. See Chemical Manufacturers Ass'n v. EPA, cited in the last paragraph of *Rybachek*.

EPA adopted a "categorical" approach to setting technology-based effluent limitations. Industries were divided into categories based on products manufactured and subcategories based on processes or raw materials utilized in producing the products (e.g., the dredge-mining subcategory of the placer mining category). Then the BPT and BAT criteria were applied to these categories and subcategories, not to individual plants. EPA's effluent limitation regulations for each industrial subcategory contained maximum daily and monthly average limitations on relevant "parameters" (pollutants) expressed in terms of maximum volume of wastewater, or concentration of parameters in wastewater, per unit of production or other measure of output. These "single number" effluent limitations were uniform for existing plants in a particular subcategory, wherever they are located. EPA cannot establish a subcategory based solely on geographical location. American Iron and Steel Institute v. EPA, 526 F.2d 1027 (3rd Cir. 1975). Hundreds of lawsuits by industry and numerous divergences among circuit courts of appeals were resolved in Dupont v. Train, 430 U.S. 12 (1977), in which the United States Supreme Court upheld EPA's categorical approach, but stipulated that EPA must devise a variance for plants that do not fit within an industrial subcategory. This procedure, known as the "fundamentally different factors" (FDF) variance, was later codified as §301(n) of the CWA. For dischargers receiving an FDF variance (e.g., a placer miner that does not have adequate space for a settling pond), and dischargers for which effluent limitation regulations have not yet been promulgated, effluent limitations are set using "best professional judgment" (BPJ) in light of the statutory criteria. Although abnormal compliance costs cannot be raised by a discharger as a fundamentally different factor, the FDF variance presents a potential loophole in the CWA, especially for large multifacted facilities. See Latin, Ideal Versus Real Regulatory Efficiency: Implementation of Uniform Standards and "Fine-Tuning" Regulatory Reforms, 37 Stan. L. Rev. 1267, 1314–1318 (1985). The water quality of the receiving body of water cannot be considered in setting technology-based effluent limitations. Crown Simpson Pulp Co. v. Costle, 642 F.2d 323 (9th Cir. 1981). Can a discharger dilute its effluent in order to meet effluent limitations? Weyerhaeuser v. Costle, 590 F.2d 1011 (D.C. Cir. 1978) and other cases make it clear that in-plant dilution is not an acceptable solution to pollution under the CWA.

Developers of new sources possess the advantage of being able to build pollution control mechanisms into their original plant designs. Consequently, new sources are required to immediately comply with "new source performance standards" (NSPS) based on "best available demonstrated control technology" (BDT), or zero-discharge where practicable. As in *Rybachek*, NSPS are most often equivalent to BAT. However, having met the relevant NSPS, a new source cannot be required to meet stricter technology-based standards for ten years or the facility's amortization period, whichever comes first. §306.

2. The mid-course corrections of 1977. Between 1972 and 1977 the installation of BPT by industry and the decrease in pollution from POTWs had significantly reduced the loadings of of so-called "conventional pollutants" (BOD, TSS, fecal coliform, etc.) to America's waterbodies. At the same time, Congress had come to the realization that toxic pollutants were far more of a problem than had initially been envisioned. Thus, a mid-course correction was made in 1977 with regard to conventionals and toxics.

In 1977, convinced that the cost of moving to BAT for conventionals was too high, Congress devised a new standard – best conventional pollutant control technology (BCT) – for them. §301(b)(2)(E). BCT includes two cost tests: (1) a comparison between the costs of reducing discharges of conventionals and the resulting water quality benefits; and (2) a comparison between industrial and municipal costs for treating conventionals. §304 (b)(2)(B). The congressional supporters of BCT felt that it would produce effluent limitations falling betweeen BPT and BAT, but in practice BCT is identical to BPT. See generally American Paper Institute v. EPA, 660 F.2d 954 (4th Cir. 1981).

The CWA's original toxic pollutant control mechanism was a cumbersome pollutant-by-pollutant, harm-based system – modelled after §112 of the Clean Air Act – that resulted in little control of toxic water pollutants. See Hall, The Control of Toxic Pollutants Under the Federal Water Pollution Control Act Amendments of 1972, 63 Iowa L. Rev. 609 (1978). Rejecting this exercise in futility, EPA decided to regulate toxic pollutants primarily through BAT-based effluent limitations. EPA's decision was upheld by the famous "Consent Decree of 1976." NRDC v. Train, 8 ERC 2120 (D.C. D.C. 1976). This decree established timetables for EPA to promulgate effluent limitations based on BAT for many industrial categories covering 65 families of compounds, which EPA has broken down into 129 "priority pollutants." EPA can add toxic pollutants to this list by regulation. In 1977, Congress codified this methodology. §§301(b)(2)(C) and 307(a)(1) and (2). As *Rybachek* illustrates, non-toxic pollutants that indicate the presence of toxics ("indicator" or "surrogate" parameters) may be regulated as toxics themselves. 40 CFR §122.44(e)(2)(ii).

In addition to conventional and toxic pollutants, Congress in 1977 created a third class of pollutants called "nonconventional" (or "nonconventional/nontoxic") pollutants. §301(b)(2)(F). Ammonia, chlorine, color, iron, and total phenols are some of the designated nonconventional pollutants. Dischargers of nonconventionals are entitled to apply for two variances, the cost-based §301(c) variance and the harm-based §301(g) variance. In *Rybachek*, petitioners unsuccessfully contested EPA's treatment of settleable solids, ordinarily a nonconventional pollutant, as a toxic pollutant indicator because such treatment would render these variances unavailable to them. Dischargers of toxics, like dischargers of conventionals, may only apply for FDF variances and §301(k) variances for innovative technology.

3. Industrial site BMPs. There is only one nonpoint source of water pollution that can be directly regulated under the CWA. §304(e) authorizes EPA to establish best management practices (BMPs) "to control plant site runoff, spillage or leaks, sludge or waste disposal, and drainage from raw material storage" in order to diminish the amount of toxic pollutants flowing into receiving waters. In *Rybachek*, EPA had promulgated five BMPs to control discharges due to mine drainage and infiltration.

4. Municipal dischargers. POTWs must also possess NPDES permits containing technology-based effluent limitations. They are required to have met effluent limitations based on biological "secondary treatment" (generally defined as 85 percent removal of conventional pollutants) by 1988. §301(b)(B) and 40 CFR §133. Many POTWs are on compliance schedules imposed through EPA's post-deadline enforcement policy, discussed in *Rybachek*.[10]

Between 1972 and 1990, POTWs were entitled to apply for federal subsidies for the construction of sewerage systems and treatment plants. This "Construction Grants Program" (CWA Title II) provided over $50 billion to municipalities and sewerage authorities in 55 percent to 85 percent matching grants for construction and land acquisition. The program has been replaced by federal capitalization grants to state revolving loan funds (SRFs). CWA Title VI. See Goldfarb, Water Law, Chapter 29 (2d ed., 1988). Will municipalities be able to fulfill their present and future water pollution control responsibilities without a federal grants program? One of the problems faced by municipalities in financing new POTWs is that changes in the Internal Revenue Code during the 1980s have made it extraordinarily difficult for municipalities to issue tax-exempt bonds for POTW construction.[11] Would it be possible to "privatize" municipal sewage treatment?

10. For a thorough analysis of enforcement against POTWs, see Gelpe, Pollution Control Against Public Facilities, 13 Harv. Envtl L. Rev. 69 (1989).

11. See EPA, Paying For Progress: Perspectives On Financing Environmental Protection (1990) for discussions of this issue and recommendations for amending the tax code.

5. Indirect dischargers. As pointed out in the Conservation Foundation excerpt in Part A above, up to 40 percent of the toxic pollutants entering America's waterways pass from industries through POTWs. Indirect dischargers are also a major source of toxics that contaminate sewage sludge.

Section 307 of the CWA requires EPA to promulgate "pretreatment standards" for indirect discharges that interfere with POTW operations, contaminate sludge, or pass untreated through the POTW, causing the POTW to violate its discharge permit. The CWA does not compel indirect dischargers to procure discharge permits, although some states do. Under §510 of the CWA, states can be stricter than "federal floor" requirements, but not more lenient.

There are two types of pretreatment standards: "prohibited discharge standards" and "categorical pretreatment standards." 40 CFR §403. Prohibited discharge standards require that pollutants introduced into a POTW not inhibit the POTW's performance. Categorical pretreatment standards set out national discharge limits based on BAT. Major elements of EPA's pretreatment program were struck down in NRDC v. EPA, 790 F.2d 289 (3rd Cir. 1986). The BAT-based pretreatment standards remain in effect but "removal credits" to indirect dischargers for pollution treated by POTWs and sludge disposal guidelines have not yet appeared in final form.

Pretreatment standards are primarily enforced by the POTWs themselves, with the states and EPA retaining backup enforcement authority. This system creates a "fox in the henhouse" situation because POTWs are reluctant to enforce against their own customers unless (1) the indirect discharge disrupts the plant's operations, or (2) the POTW's discharge permit contains toxic effluent limitations, the permit is being violated, and enforcement action is being taken against the POTW – a rare conjunction of circumstances. See Comptroller-General, Improved Monitoring and Enforcement Needed for Toxic Pollutants Entering Sewers (1989), and Houck, Ending the War: A Strategy to Save America's Coastal Zone, 47 Md. L. Rev. 358 (1988). Not only has indirect discharge been a significant loophole in the CWA, but it also has been exacerbated by RCRA's exclusion of indirect discharges from its regulatory ambit. RCRA's "Domestic Sewage Exclusion" can be found at 42 U.S.C.A. §6903 (27).

6. Point source stormwater discharges. Municipal storm sewers that are separate from sanitary sewers discharge directly into waterbodies and can be significant sources of sediment and associated pollutants. Industrial point source stormwater discharges can also degrade waterbodies. In the 1987 CWA Amendments, Congress instituted a phased permit program covering municipal and industrial storm sewers. §402(p). Municipal stormwater permits (1) may be issued on a system or jurisdiction-wide basis (i.e., may be "general permits"), (2) must include a requirement to effectively prohibit nonstormwater discharges into the storm sewers, and (3) must require controls to reduce the discharge of pollutants "to the maximum extent practicable, including management practices, control techniques and system, design, and engineering methods...." Combined sewer overflows (CSOs), which discharge pathogens (bacteria and viruses) and thus cause beach closings, were not addressed by the 1987 Amendments, but EPA is attempting to regulate them through guidance documents. During intense storm events, the capacities of combined storm and sanitary sewers – common in older urban areas – are exceeded and raw sewage is discharged through "overflow points" (some cities have hundreds of them) into waterbodies. CSO-related pollution can be controlled by either delaying the flow in underground or surface retaining structures or installing control devices at overflow points, both of which approaches would be enormously expensive. As with municipal sewage treatment, how can our impoverished cities – in an era of federal fiscal restraint – afford the billions of dollars it will cost to control stormwater discharges?

7. Mandating technology. Do you agree with the *Rybachek* court that the CWA's uniform national technology-based effluent limitations do not mandate use of particular technologies? Is the existence of a standard based on existing technology an incentive to develop new and less expensive technology, or does it "freeze" technological development? If you were an entrepreneur, would you invest in a new technology that promises to achieve improved pollution control by a major industry at substantial savings? Once the innovative technology has been developed, how could you demonstrate it so that EPA might adopt it in order to tighten its effluent limitations guidelines during the 5-year review required by section 301(d)? Do you think that the compliance date extensions and alternative BAT limitations offered to users of innovative technology under §301(k) of the CWA might help to offset the "inertia effect"?

Note that the result of the rulemaking reviewed in *Rybachek* is a validation of the technology-based approach to environmental standard-setting: the regulated industry has achieved zero-discharge of toxic pollutants and their indicators at a relatively modest cost. However, the course of technology-based standard-setting does not always run as smoothly. Implementation of pretreatment standards for the electroplating industry will allegedly cause 20 percent of all facilities to close down, with a loss of 737 firms and 12,000 jobs. Nat'l Ass'n of Metal Finishers v. EPA, 719 F.2d 624 (3rd Cir. 1983). Nevertheless, isn't there a moral and common law obligation to control one's pollution as much as possible?

8. Drinking water protection. Ambient water quality and tap water quality are regulated by different federal statutes. Under the Safe Drinking Water Act, 42 U.S.C.A. §§300f et seq., EPA is required to promulgate national primary and secondary drinking water regulations applicable to "public water systems," defined as systems that have at least 15 service connections or regularly serve at least 25 individuals at least 60 days per year. Primary drinking water regulations identify potential toxic contaminants and for each contaminant set a maximum contaminant level (MCL) if the contaminant can feasibly be measured or a treatment technique if it cannot. Secondary drinking water regulations set MCLs for nontoxic contaminants that affect other parameters, for example, color and taste.

The Safe Drinking Water Act, like the Clean Water Act, relies on technology-based standards. EPA first promulgates "maximum contaminant level goals" (MCLGs), which are nonenforceable health goals for public water systems. MCLGs are to be set at levels at which "no known or anticipated adverse effects on the health of persons occur and which allows an adequate margin of safety." Then, EPA promulgates enforceable primary drinking water regulations, including MCLs and monitoring and reporting requirements for dangerous contaminants. MCLs must be set as close to MCLGs as is "feasible," which means "with the use of the best technology, treatment techniques, and other means, which the Administrator finds are generally available (taking costs into consideration)."

9. The trend toward technology-based regulation. Environmental standard-setting is moving away from harm-based regulation toward a technology-based approach. The clearest example of this trend is the Clean Air Act, which is a harm-based statute upon which technology-based branches have been grafted, culminating in the 1990 amendments requiring MACT for sources of hazardous air pollutants. See Chapter 18. Significant harm-based elements remain in the Clean Air Act, however, as in the NAAQS/SIP approach to controlling criteria pollutants, the system of PSD increments, and the residual risk assessment and regulation required after ten years of MACT implementation. RCRA is another statute where a program that was initially a combination of harm-based and technology-based elements (the "land ban") evolved into a primarily technology-based system. See Chapter 22.

10. The Occupational Safety and Health Act. The Occupational Safety and Health Act (OSHA), 29 U.S.C.A. §651 et seq., combines harm-based and technology-based approaches in a confusing manner. Section 3(8) of the Act defines an occupational safety and health standard as a standard establishing any one of a variety of requirements "reasonably necessary or appropriate to provide safe or healthful employment or places of employment." Section 6(b)(5) of the Act requires the Secretary of Labor to set a standard for any toxic materials "which most adequately assures, to the extent feasible, that no employee will suffer material impairment of health or functional capacity." The Supreme Court interpreted these ambiguous, qualification-riddled provisions as follows:

> We think it is clear that the statute was not designed to require employers to provide absolutely risk-free workplaces whenever it is technologically feasible to do so, as long as the cost is not great enough to destroy an entire industry. Rather, both the language and structure of the Act, as well as its legislative history, indicate that it was intended to require the elimination, as far as feasible, of significant risks of harm.
>
> By empowering the Secretary to promulgate standards that are "reasonably necessary or appropriate to provide safe or healthful employment or places of employment," the Act implies that, before promulgating any standard, the Secretary must make a finding that the workplaces in question are not safe. But "safe" is not the equivalent of "risk free." There are many activities that we engage in every day – such as driving a car or even breathing city air – that entail some risk of accident or material health impairment; nevertheless, few people would consider these activities "unsafe." Similarly, a workplace

> can hardly be considered "unsafe" unless it threatens the workers with a significant risk of harm.
>
> Therefore, before he can promulgate *any* permanent health or safety standard, the Secretary is required to make a threshold finding that a place of employment is unsafe – in the sense that significant risks are present and can be eliminated or lessened by a change in practices.[12]

One might expect a health and safety protection act to be harm-based, but is this true of OSHA? To what extent do the phrases "reasonably necessary and appropriate," "most adequately assures," and "material impairment" qualify the statute's goal of protecting worker health and safety? Does the Supreme Court's requirement of a threshold showing of unsafe-ness mean that OSHA is harm-based? Or is the feasibility criterion an indication that OSHA is essentially technology-based?

Having shown a significant health risk, must the Secretary then perform a benefit-cost analysis, weighing the reduction of health risks against the compliance costs entailed in achieving the desired reductions? See American Textile Manufacturers Institute v. Donovan, 452 U.S. 490 (1981)(benefit-cost analysis unnecessary because "Congress itself defined the basic relationship between costs and benefits, by placing the 'benefit' of worker health above all other considerations save those making attainment of this 'benefit' unachievable.")

What is your opinion of the wisdom of the Supreme Court's interpretation of OSHA in *Industrial Union*? For a searching critique of this decision, see Latin, The Significance of Toxic Health Risks: An Essay on Legal Decisionmaking Under Uncertainty, 10 Ecol. L.Q. 339 (1982). Professor Latin's position is that the Supreme Court's threshold requirement places the burden of uncertainty on the wrong party: "There is...a crucial difference between regulating a substance that presents a risk *known to be insignificant* and regulating a carcinogen whose risk at a given level of exposure is *uncertain*."

11. The future of BAT under the CWA. Although he believes that "BAT under the Clean Water Act has probably been the most effective pollution control program in the world in terms of producing identifiable abatement," Professor Oliver Houck concludes that EPA's technology-based effluent limitation program is faltering with regard to toxic pollutants. Regulation of Toxic Pollutants Under the Clean Water Act, 21 ELR 10528 (September 4, 1991). EPA has not added any priority pollutants or industrial categories to its lists since the consent decree of 1976. According to Houck, "a greater number of individual industries remain unregulated than regulated, and a growing list of toxics have escaped scrutiny and standards." Moreover, in Houck's view,

> discharge standards have emerged unevenly, with a heavy "zero discharge" hand on such unfortunates as seafood canners and placer mine operators, and

12. Industrial Union Department, AFL-CIO v. American Petroleum Institute, 448 U.S. 607, 641–642 (1980). This decision involved the Occupational Safety and Health Administration's permissible exposure level (PEL) for benzene, a known carcinogen.

> a remarkably blind eye to available closed-cycle systems for some of the nation's highest volume dischargers of broad-spectrum toxins [like petroleum refiners, and certain organic chemical producers]. The disparaties in these standards reflect nothing more starkly than a disparity in clout. 21 ELR at 10539.

Skeptical of the water quality-based approach, Professor Houck recommends that Congress either (1) establish specific deadlines for EPA to promulgate new technology-based effluent limitations, with a zero-discharge "hammer" similar to RCRA's land ban (see Chapter 22), or (2) fix timetables, based on relative risk and reasonable lead times, for the elimination of toxic discharges. What are the potential disadvantages of so closely involving Congress in the intricacies of standard-setting? An argument can be made that since Congress possesses a minimum of expertise in the technical aspects of water pollution control, its decisions will be either hopelessly unrealistic or even more politically influenced than EPA's. In other words, under some political scenarios, Houck might be better off with EPA than with Congress.

12. The CWA and the congressional reauthorization process. Over the past several decades it has become common for Congress to attach "sunset" provisions to various statutory programs, so that every five years, say, the statute must be brought back for hearings, review, possible amendment, and reauthorization. If not reauthorized, the program dies.[13] The idea originated in good-government theories emphasizing bureaucratic accountability. Environmentalists often sourly note, however, that it is the "do-good" programs like endangered species protection and environmental quality standards that must fight for their lives on a regular basis, although these bouts sometimes offer the opportunity to strengthen the laws. Mining, damming, public works authorizations, and other resource-exploiting statutes rarely contain the periodic reauthorization requirement.

In the Clean Water Act's 1992 reauthorization review, the major areas of scrutiny and controversy include increased control of non-point source pollution, wetlands protection, reinstituting a grants and public funding program for POTWs, regulation of combined sewer overflows (CSOs), and control of toxic hotspots.

C. HARM-BASED ELEMENTS IN THE CLEAN WATER ACT

Although the CWA's dominant strategy is the technology-based effluent standards approach, the Act contains harm-based elements as well. Stringent water quality-based limitations are to be imposed upon dischargers where water quality is so bad that achievement of technology-based effluent limitations will not result in the attainment of applicable water quality standards. CWA §303 ("water quality-limited" as opposed to technology-based "effluent-limited" stretches). In 1987

13. Congress can keep the program alive, however, dangling from an uncertain thread, by passing a one-year "continuing resolution," which serves as a worrisome sort of probation for the statute and its agency.

CWA Amendments[14], Congress reinvigorated the water quality-based approach by adding §304(l), which presented the basic procedural issue contested in the following case:

Natural Resources Defense Council v. Environmental Protection Agency
United States Court of Appeals for the Ninth Circuit, 1990
915 F.2d 1314

FLETCHER, J.... Congress, in passing the Clean Water Act [of 1972], shifted the focus of the water pollution control laws away from the enforcement of water quality standards and toward the enforcement of technological standards. But Congress recognized that even if all the firms discharging pollutants into a certain stream segment were using the best available technology, the stream still might not be clean enough to meet the water quality standards set by the states. To deal with this problem, Congress supplemented the "technology-based" limitations with "water quality-based limitations."

The water quality standard for a particular stream segment was to be determined in the following manner. First, the state in which the stream segment was located was to designate the uses to which it wished to put the segment. The designations that the states had made prior to the 1972 Clean Water Act were deemed to be the initial designations under that Act; however, states were thereafter to review their designations at least once every three years. CWA §303(c)(1). Pursuant to the statute's policy that the designation of uses "enhance" the quality of water, CWA §303(c)(2), EPA enacted regulations setting limits on the states' ability to downgrade previously designated uses. If a state wished to redesignate a use so that the new use did not require water clean enough to meet the statutory goal of fishable, swimmable water, see CWA §101(a)(2), it had to conduct a "use attainability analysis" as a condition to federal approval of the redesignated use. CWA §303(c)(3), 40 CFR §131.10(j), 131.3(g) (1989). If the result of the "use attainability analysis" was that it was feasible to attain fishable, swimmable waters, EPA would reject the redesignated use.

Second, the state was to determine the "criteria" for each segment – the maximum concentrations of pollutants that could occur without jeopardizing the use. These criteria could be either numerical (e.g., 5 milligrams per liter) or narrative (e.g., no toxics in toxic amounts). The criteria, like the uses, were subject to federal review. The EPA was to reject criteria that did not protect the designated use or that were not based on a "sound scientific rationale." 40 CFR §131.11 (1989).

Under §§301(b)(1)(C) and 402(a)(1), NPDES permit writers were to impose, along with the technology-based limitations, any more stringent limitations on discharges necessary to meet the water quality standards. Although ostensibly they were supposed to impose these more stringent limitations, in practice they often did not.

One explanation for this failure is that the criteria listed by the states, particularly for toxic pollutants, were often vague narrative or descriptive criteria as opposed to specific numerical criteria. These descriptive criteria were difficult to translate into enforceable limits on discharges from individual polluters. As one commentator put it:

14. Called the Water Quality Act of 1987, Pub. L. No. 100-40.

> The descriptive criteria, in particular, call for both expert testimony and a receptive forum to transform, let us say, a general obligation to maintain "recreational" uses into a specific obligation to reduce loadings of phosphorus or nitrogen from a particular source. The decision requires, among other things, judgments about the degree of algal bloom that interferes with "recreational" uses such as swimming or boating, estimates of loadings from all contributing point and nonpoint sources, assumptions about degrees of control elsewhere, and predictions of how a water segment will respond to a hoped-for change of parameters. Rodgers, 2 Environmental Law §4.16 at 250-251 (1986).

The Clean Water Act dealt with the difficulty of these decisions and judgments in various ways, for example by calling for the publication by the EPA of criteria documents spelling out causes and effects of various pollutant loads, see CWA §304(a), and by requiring states to set total maximum daily loads for certain pollutants (but, notably, not for toxic pollutants), CWA §303(d)(1); however, the complexity of these decisions and judgments led many a permit writer to avoid making them altogether. Rodgers, §4.18 at 283-284.

In 1987, Congress reexamined the water pollution laws. It found that the requirement that individual polluters use the best available technology was not sufficient to solve the pollution problem, particularly the problem of toxic pollutants; a renewed enphasis on water quality-based standards was necessary. Congress enacted a number of new provisions. Three are relevant for our purposes.

CWA §319 requires states to submit for federal approval nonpoint source reports and management programs by August 4, 1988, identifying specific nonpoint sources of pollution and setting forth a plan for implementing the "best management practices" to control such sources by 1992. Section 319 does not require states to penalize nonpoint source polluters who fail to adopt best management practices; rather it provides for grants to encourage the adoption of such practices.

CWA §303(c)(2)(B), requires states to adopt "specific numerical criteria" for toxics for which the EPA has published criteria pursuant to §304(a). Those criteria are to be adopted when the state first reviews its water quality standards following the enactment of the 1987 amendments. The requirement of numerical criteria for toxics makes it easier for permit writers to incorporate the water quality standards into individual permits. Permit writers thus no longer have an excuse for failing to impose water quality-based limitations on permit holders.

In addition to requiring the adoption of numerical criteria, Congress enacted new CWA §304(l).... Section 304(l) provides:

> (1) State List of Navigable Waters and Development of Strategies. Not later than 2 years after the date of the enactment of this subsection [February 4, 1987], each State shall submit to the Administrator for review, approval, and implementation under this subsection –
>
> (A) a list of those waters within the state which after the application of effluent limitations required under §301(b)(2) of this Act cannot reasonably be anticipated to attain or maintain (i) water quality standards for such waters reviewed, revised, or adopted in accordance with §303(c)(2)(B) of this Act, due to toxic pollutants....
>
> (B) a list of all navigable waters in such state for which the State does not expect the applicable standard under §303 of this Act will be achieved after

> the [application of technology-based effluent limitations], due entirely or substantially to discharges from point sources of any toxic pollutant listed pursuant to §307(a);
>
> (C) for each segment of the navigable waters included on such lists, a determination of the specific point sources discharging any such toxic pollutant which is believed to be preventing or impairing such water quality and the amount of such toxic pollutant discharged by each such source; and
>
> (D) for each such segment, an individual control strategy which the state determines will produce a reduction in the discharge of toxic pollutants from point sources identified by the State under this paragraph through the establishment of effluent limitations...and water quality standards..., which reduction is sufficient, in combination with existing controls on point and nonpoint sources of pollution, to achieve the applicable water quality standard as soon as possible, but not later than 3 years after the date of establishment of such strategy.
>
> (2) Approval or Disapproval. Not later than 120 days after the last day of the 2-year period referred to in paragraph (1), the Administrator shall approve or disapprove the control strategies submitted under paragraph (1) by any State.
>
> (3) Administrator's Action. If a State fails to submit control strategies in accordance with paragraph (1) or the Administrator does not approve the control strategies submitted by such State in accordance with paragraph (1), then, not later than 1 year after the last day of the period referred to in paragraph (2), the Administrator, in cooperation with such State and after notice and opportunity for public comment, shall implement the requirements of paragraph (1) in such State....

The effect of the individual control strategies is simply to expedite the imposition of water quality-based limitations on polluters – limitations which otherwise would have had to be imposed when the polluters' NPDES permits expired. NPDES permits are issued for periods of no more than five years, although administrative delays can extend de facto the duration of the permits....

[The holding in the case overturned a technical elements in EPA's interpretation regarding the information required to be included in state lists produced under §304(l).]

COMMENTARY AND QUESTIONS

1. Nonpoint sources and §304(1). In a portion of the NRDC v. EPA opinion that is not quoted here, the Court points out that the list required under §304(1)(1)(A)(i) "includes most of the waters on the B list plus waters expected not to meet water quality standards due to pollution attributable entirely or almost entirely to toxic pollution from *nonpoint sources.*" 915 F.2d 1314, 1319. At another point the court admits that:

> the Act thus banned only discharges from point sources. The discharge of pollutants from nonpoint sources – for example, the runoff of pesticides from farmlands – was not directly prohibited. The Act focused on point source polluters presumably because they could be identified and regulated more easily than nonpoint source polluters. 915 F.2d at 1316.

Why require information about nonpoint source pollution if EPA can't regulate nonpoint source polluters or compel the states to do so? Is Congress collecting information for future enactment of a program of mandatory best management practices for nonpoint sources, similar to the technology-based standards program for point sources? Is it fair to impose more stringent individual control strategies (ICSs) on point sources when nonpoint sources remain unregulated? Or is this information intended to encourage the states to regulate their own nonpoint sources? But will an agricultural state, for example, impose mandatory best management practices on its own farmers? Many agricultural states have adopted *voluntary* cost-sharing arrangements for reducing agricultural nonpoint source pollution. In some of the states, such as Wisconsin, having active cost-sharing programs, the worst nonpoint source polluters frequently refuse to participate in the program because it would be an expense to them, even if the state were to provide 60 percent of the funding for best management practices. For an evaluation of the nonpoint source provisions of the Clean Water Act, see Goldfarb, Water Law, Chapter 35 (2d ed., 1988); NRDC, Poison Runoff (1990); Note, State and Federal Land Use Regulation: An Application to Groundwater and Nonpoint Source Pollution Control, 95 Yale L.J. 1433 (1986).

2. Enforceability of §304(l), and the bioassay method. What if a state does not make its submission under §304(l), or EPA does not approve it? Is the threat of EPA implementation of ICSs in the offending state a credible one? What about the threat of losing federal grant funds (which, because of federal budget constraints, have thus far been slow in coming)? If a state is diligent about developing and enforcing ICSs, will it encourage industries located in urban areas to relocate to rural areas or less enthusiastic states? Has Congress' reaffirmation of the harm-based approach undercut its own intention to preclude "forum shopping" by requiring uniform national technology-based effluent limitations?

Do you think that the NRDC v. EPA court, echoing Congress, was being overly optimistic when it wrote the following?

> The requirement of numerical criteria for toxics makes it easier for permit writers to incorporate the water quality standards into NPDES permits. Permit writers thus no longer have an excuse for failing to impose water quality-based limitations on permit holders.

Given the complexity and dynamism of the hydrological and ecological systems involved, will it now be appreciably easier to convert water quality criteria into water quality-based effluent limitations (WQBELs) for individual dischargers, especially in heavily industrialized areas?

A promising development in this area is the emergence of reliable biomonitoring procedures. Biomonitoring (also known as "whole effluent testing" or "bioassay") is essentially a laboratory simulation of the effects of a particular waste stream on a waterbody. In conducting a bioassay, a representative aquatic organism is subjected, either for a shorter ("acute bioassay") or longer ("chronic bioassay") period of time, to a waste stream diluted in a manner that attempts to reproduce existing ambient conditions. The effluent limitation is then set at a certain percentage (providing a margin of safety) of the concentration of the waste stream that causes adverse effects on the organism (e.g., for an acute bioassay, 30 percent of the concentration that kills 50 percent of the organisms over a 96-hour period). Under most state ICSs, if a discharger exceeds its bioassay-based effluent limitation more than twice during a particular period, it must conduct a Toxicity Reduction Evaluation (TRE). Biomonitoring furnishes a useful alternative to "chemical-specific testing" for dealing with mixed waste streams, but there is concern that the science of biomonitoring, especially with regard to chronic bioassays, is not sufficiently well developed to support a regulatory program. See NRDC v. EPA, 859 F.2d 756 (D.C. Cir. 1988) (confirming the legality of a discharge permit containing bioassay requirements).

3. **Antidegradation and attainability**. The NRDC v. EPA 1990 decision quoted above briefly mentioned the issues of antidegredation and attainability. Section 101 of the CWA declares a policy to "restore and maintain" clean water, and antidegradation policies have traditionally been a feature of water pollution control law. See Hines, A Decade of Nondegradation Policy in Congress and the Courts: The Erratic Pursuit of Clear Air and Clean Water, 62 Iowa L. Rev. 643 (1977). Although antidegradation under the CWA is less well developed than its counterpart in the Clean Air Act (see discussion of Prevention of Significant Deterioration in Chapter 18), Congress in 1987 recognized for the first time that antidegradation is an essential part of the Act. §303(d)(4)(B). But the statutory reference to antidegradation is cryptic; it does not clarify what Congress meant by antidegradation, or how this policy is to be implemented. See Snyder, Nondegradation of Water Quality: The Need For Effective Action, 50 Notre Dame L. 890 (1975), which anticipated the problem.

In 1983, EPA promulgated a set of regulations intended to explicate the antidegradation policy. 40 CFR §131.6, 12. These regulations rest on a distinction between "water quality" and "water uses." Each state must adopt an antidegradation policy and identify methods of applying it where waterbodies are of better quality than fishable/swimmable, for example if trout can propagate there. Each state antidegradation policy must contain a prohibition on water quality reductions in segments designated by the state as Outstanding National Resource Waters (ONRWs), such as waters in parks, wildlife refuges, and other "waters of exceptional recreational and ecological significance." On waterbodies not designated as ONRWs, if existing water quality is better than necessary to maintain existing water uses, a state may, after public participation, choose to allow lower water quality where "necessary to accommodate important economic or social development." But existing water uses must be preserved. In other words, these regulations establish a rebuttable presumption that existing water quality, outside of ONRWs, must be maintained, and an irrebuttable presumption that existing water quality in ONRWs and all existing water uses in other waterbodies must be maintained.

Most states have adopted antidegradation policies, but few have meaningful implementation measures. In the first place, most streams that are subject to antidegradation are threated by nonpoint source pollution that EPA does not possess the authority to regulate. In the second place, EPA's antidegradation regulations leave implementation entirely to the states, which may want to attract development with the inducement of unpolluted segments that will be classified as "effluent limited" (i.e., where water quality standards can be met by the imposition of technology-based effluent limitations), thus avoiding the imposition of more stringent water quality-based effluent limitations. EPA can sue a state if the state has not adopted an acceptable antidegradation policy, but it is doubtful whether EPA can enforce antidegradation in a state that has not adopted such an antidegradation policy or is not enforcing its adopted policy. States have a free hand even as to designating and protecting ONRWs. Can EPA object to a state discharge permit that allegedly violates the state antidegradation policy? See American Paper Institute v. EPA, 890 F.2d 869 (7th Cir. 1989)(dismissed for lack of ripeness). Should Congress empower EPA to protect pristine waters where states don't?

Section 101 of the CWA establishes a "national goal that wherever attainable, an interim goal of water quality which provides for the protection and propagation of fish, shellfish, and wildlife and provides for recreation in and on the water be achieved by July 1, 1983." What does "wherever attainable" mean? In contrast to antidegradation, attainability applies where a waterbody is of worse quality than the EPA-required fishable, swimmable condition. Under EPA regulations (40 CFR §131.10), a use is attainable if it is already being attained. Thus, where existing water quality standards specificy designated uses of a lesser nature than those that are presently being attained, the state must revise its standards to reflect the current uses. Second, a use is attainable if it can be achieved by the imposition of technology-based effluent limitations for point sources "and cost-effective and reasonable best management practices for nonpoint source control." Third, a use is deemed attainable unless the state, after a "use attainability analysis," can demonstrate that attaining the fishable, swimmable use is not feasible because of specified natural or intractable man-induced conditions, or that "(c)ontrols more stringent than [the CWA's technology-based effluent limitations] would result in substantial and widespread economic and social impact." How can a definition of attainability be based upon control of nonpoint sources of pollution when EPA has no authority to regulate them or to compel a state to do so? What is "substantial and widespread economic and social impact"? Few states have found it necessary to petition EPA for the removal of fishable, swimmable uses because EPA allows subtle refinements of designated uses. For example, states are permitted to establish designated uses that vary according to season of the year, flow regime, and even according to location on a waterbody. 40 CFR §131.10. Moreover, compliance with water quality standards is not measured at a discharger's outfall pipe, but outside a "mixing zone," thus giving the discharger the benefit of dilution within the mixing zone. 40 CFR §131.35(d)(8). Are "variable water quality standards" and mixing zones inconsistent with the fishable, swimmable requirement and the zero-discharge goal? Can an entire river be designated as a mixing zone? See Ford Motor Co. v. EPA, 567 F.2d 661 (6th Cir. 1977) for a negative judicial response.

4. Other harm-based provisions in the CWA. Heat discharged into a waterbody is a pollutant §502(6). Dischargers of heat must meet effluent limitations based on BAT. Nevertheless, under §316(a) of the CWA, variances based on receiving water quality are available to dischargers of heat. Because of the difficulty of ascertaining the ecological effects of heat, §316(a) has led to a "regulatory breakdown," especially with regard to nuclear power plants seeking to avoid having to install costly cooling towers. See Weyerhaeuser v. Costle, 590 F.2d 1011, 1044 (D.C. Circ. 1978). Other harm-based provisions of the CWA – §301(g)(water quality-based variance for dischargers of nonconventional pollutants), §301(h)(variance for POTWs that discharge into marine waters), and §403 (alternative water quality-based ocean discharge criteria) – have proven to be equally cumbersome. Should Congress repudiate the harm-based approach to water pollution control? See Goldfarb, Water Law, 183–189 (2d ed. 1988); or should it abjure minimum fishable, swimmable uses and allow states to designate and protect whatever uses they desire, with EPA limited to enforcing stringent antidegradation standards with regard to high quality waters? See Gaba, Federal Supervision of State Water Quality Standards Under the Clean Water Act, 36 Vand. L. Rev. 1167 (1983) (Gaba argues that the CWA does not authorize EPA to establish mandatory minimum fishable, swimmable uses.) Another possibility would be to apply §302 of the CWA, which until now has been a dead letter. Entitled "Water Quality Related Effluent Limitations," it allows EPA, after a public hearing, to set stricter effluent limitations on heavily polluted waterbodies unless a discharger can show that it is entitled to a modification of these stricter limitations based on economic inability to comply. EPA and many states have avoided the problems inherent in the harm-based approach by placing water quality-based permitting on the back burner. Whether they can continue to avoid this situation after §304(l) remains to be seen.

5. Land use and water pollution control. Even if it is possible to superimpose a harm-based regulatory system on a technology-based system, can performance standards, however formulated, control water pollution regardless of how intensely developed the watershed is? Will higher levels of development inevitably generate significant water pollution because of cumulative impacts, violations, unregulated activities, breakdowns, spills, and the like? Professor Houck, writing about protecting the coastal zone, might have been discussing the protection of any aquatic ecosystem:

> Regulatory programs have bought us time, and for this reason they need to be defended and applied. But that is all they can do. We must use our time to secure an approach that meets the problem. What is necessary now is for the federal government and coastal states to (1) Declare an overriding public interest in the protection of coastal areas; (2) Exclude certain classes of development including major industrial, commercial, and residential uses; (3) Explicitly permit, on a case-by-case basis, a residuum of more passive economic and other uses sufficient to enable the legislation to survive constitutional attack. Houck, America's Mad Dash to the Sea, Amicus Journal, Summer 1988, 23.

In the future, should water pollution control be supplemented by watershed management with enforceable land-use restrictions?

6. Interstate water pollution. Section 402 of the CWA deals with interstate water pollution in the context of issuing discharge permits. In effect, EPA acts as an arbitrator of interstate disputes. This process was described by the United States Supreme Court in International Paper Company v. Ouellette:[15]

> While source States have a strong voice in regulating their own pollution, the CWA contemplates a much lesser role for States that share an interstate waterway with the source (the affected States). Even though it may be harmed by the discharges, an affected state only has an advisory role in regulating pollution that originates beyond its borders. Before a federal permit may be issued, each affected State is given notice and the opportunity to object to the proposed standards at a public hearing. An affected State has similar rights to be consulted before the source State issues its own permit; the source State must send notification, and must consider the objections and recommendations submitted by other States before taking action. Significantly, however, an affected State does not have the authority to block the issuance of the permit if it is dissatisfied with the proposed standards. An affected State's only recourse is to apply to the EPA Administrator, who then has the discretion to disapprove the permit if he concludes that the discharges will have an undue impact on interstate waters.... Thus, the Act makes it clear that the affected States occupy a subordinate position to source States in the federal regulatory program.

Where an impasse develops between EPA and a source state with an approved permit program, EPA can retake jurisdiction and issue its own permit. See Champion International v. EPA, 850 F.2d 182 (4th Cir. 1988), where EPA intervened, at the behest of Tennessee, to block a North Carolina permit to a paper mill that processed and polluted the entire flow of the Pigeon River, 26 miles above the Tennessee-North Carolina border.

Must a discharger comply with the water quality standards of all affected downstream states? See Oklahoma v. EPA, 908 F.2d 595 (10th Cir. 1990), cert. granted, 111 S. Ct. 1412 (1991)(EPA-approved water quality standards are *federal* law, binding on all permitting authorities; *Ouellette* and *Champion* were distinguished.) A number of interstate water pollution disputes have also been litigated under common law theories.[16]

7. Citizens suits under the CWA. Although all major federal environmental protection statutes except FIFRA and NEPA contain citizen suit provisions, more of these suits have been brought under the CWA's §505 than under any other federal statute:

> Like the majority of citizen suit provisions, §505 allows a citizen to commence suit in two different circumstances. First, a citizen can seek action against "any person" for violating effluent standards set pursuant to

15. 479 U.S. 481, 490–491 (1987).

16. See Chapter 10's discussions of federal common law, at pages 313 *supra*; after *Ouellette*, it is clear that interstate pollution cases can be brought in state or federal court under state common law (applying the doctrinal law of the discharger's state).

the Act. Second, a citizen can bring an action against the Administrator for failure to perform any non-discretionary function.

Citizen suits under this second, bureaucracy-forcing provision have had a major impact on shaping implementation of the environmental statutes. Until 1983, bureaucracy-forcing suits were the primary use of §505 because of the widespread belief that environmental groups could best use their limited resources on actions that would force the EPA to follow its statutory mandate, and thus strengthen the existing act. In 1983, however, the NRDC, perceiving a breakdown in EPA enforcement of Clean Water Act violators, shifted emphasis in its use of §505.

Armed with a small grant to fund enforcement and a small army of enthusiastic student interns, NRDC began a systematic study of major dischargers with repeated violations of their national pollutant discharge elimination system (NPDES) permits in the New Jersey and New York Area. By 1984, NRDC had examined over 1,000 dischargers, issued 131 sixty-day notices of intent to sue, and filed 18 suits. This effort did not go unnoticed by industry or the EPA and, despite their initial outcry, the effort soon spread to other organizations and regions. In 1988, the Bureau of National Affairs reported that over 880 claims had been filed nationwide under §505 since 1983.

The primary reason for the predominance of citizen suits under §505 is the relative ease of uncovering and proving a violation under CWA §402's NPDES program. While the NPDES program allows permitted discharges into navigable waterways, dischargers under the program must routinely file discharge monitoring reports (DMRs) with both state regulatory agencies and the EPA. The discharger must certify the accuracy of each DMR and the CWA imposes substantial penalties for false reports. Each DMR must list the actual quantity of waste discharged, as well as the permitted amount that may be discharged. As a consequence, in many instances spotting permit violations is as easy as comparing two numbers on a printout.

Defendants are usually held strictly liable for NPDES permit violations. Thus, the discharger's good faith and intent are essentially irrelevant. Under the CWA, violators may be subject to civil penalties of up to "$25,000 per day for each violation." The majority of courts have ruled that the DMRs are admissible as evidence of the violations, and have granted summary judgment to citizen plaintiffs based solely on DMRs....

The citizen must give sixty days notice to the alleged violator, the EPA, and the state resource agency prior to filing the suit.[17] Second, citizens are precluded from bringing suits for wholly past violations.[18] Third, although the CWA does not contain a statute of limitations, the courts usually employ

17. The Supreme Court held in Hallstrom v. Tillamook County that this sixty-day notice requirement is a mandatory condition precedent to filing a suit, and that failure to give adequate notice requires dismissal. 110 S. Ct. 304 (1989).

18. Gwaltney of Smithfield v. Chesapeake Bay Fdn., 484 U.S. 49 (1987), held that § 505's language, "alleged to be in violation," requires at least a reasonable likelihood that a past polluter will continue to pollute in the future.

the generic five-year period applicable to suits for civil penalties against violators of a federal law.[19] Fourth, §505(b)(1)(B) precludes citizen enforcement if the EPA or the state is already "diligently prosecuting a civil or criminal action in a court of the United States." Mann, Polluter-Financed Environmentally Beneficial Expenditures: Effective Use or Improper Abuse Of Citizen Suits Under the Clean Water Act?, 20 Environmental Law 176, 182–185 (1990).

Other incentives for bringing citizen suits under §505 are that a "prevailing or substantially prevailing party" can recover reasonable attorney and expert witness fees "whenever the court determines such an award is appropriate," (§505(d), and that effluent data reported to EPA on DMRs are not subject to confidential treatment (§308). Federal courts have the authority to grant injunctive relief as well as "appropriate civil penalties," but no monetary damages can be awarded. Citizen suits frequently result in pre-trial consent decrees, recently including polluter-financed Environmentally Beneficial Expenditures (EBEs), such as donations to environmental organizations to perform studies or purchase critical lands in watersheds where violations have taken place. See Sierra Club v. Electronic Controls Design, 908 F.2d 1350 (9th Cir. 1990) for further discussion of the legality of EBEs.

Why are citizen suits necessary when we have administrative agencies that are supposedly enforcing the law? Do citizen suits disrupt an agency's enforcement priorities, or do they serve as supplements to overburdened agency enforcement efforts? Do 60-day notices distract agencies from more pressing enforcement matters, or do they call attention to violations that agencies, for one reason or another, have ignored? Does the availability of citizen suits vitiate our respect for government or bolster it by making each citizen a "private attorney general"?

Between 1972 and 1985, EPA's record of enforcing the CWA was poor, especially with regard to POTWs. See USGAO, More Efficient Action by the Environmental Protection Agency Needed to Enforce Compliance with Water Pollution Control Discharge Permits (1978), and USGAO, Wastewater Dischargers Are Not Complying with EPA Pollution Control Permits (1983). EPA enforcement has improved significantly since 1985, and especially since Congress, in the 1987 amendments, at last provided the Agency with the authority to levy administrative fines. However, there is evidence that EPA enforcement still falls short of the mark, especially with regard to recovering noncompliance benefits reaped by violators and exercising oversight of state enforcement programs. EPA, Office of the Inspector General, Capping Report on the Computation Negotiation, Mitigation, and Assessment of Penalties under EPA Programs (September 1989).

19. [Ed. Note. See Public Interest Research Group of New Jersey v. Powell Duffryn Terminals, 913 F.2d 64 (3rd Cir. 1990).]

Chapter 20

ECONOMIC INCENTIVE AND ARTIFICIAL POLLUTION MARKET STATUTES

Evaluating each of the regulatory approaches studied here in Chapters 11 to 24 requires a process of double scrutiny. As to each statutory type, one must analyze its practical effectiveness in achieving protection of environmental quality, but also its efficiency and overall cost-effectiveness in terms of the economic and human resources required to implement it.[1] Complaints of environmental regulation's cost-ineffectiveness and inefficiency have been with it from the beginning, most often directed (perhaps with justification) toward the major command and control statutes. These statutes dictate the pollution control measures that industrial polluters must employ in order to limit the total amount of pollution to a governmentally mandated level.

The central thread of the corporate argument in this setting is that the regulatory choice of means to the end of pollution reduction is not necessarily the choice of means that the firms themselves would choose. The criticism is grounded on the rational- choice theory, that corporations, if left free to do so, will naturally adopt the most efficient, least cost methods of reducing pollution.

As suggested in the brief discussion of economics and governmental regulation of polluters which appeared in Chapter 2, if a polluting firm is ordered to install a particular type of control equipment to achieve a 60 percent reduction in emissions of pollutant X and there is a different, less costly, way to achieve the same reduction, the command and control method is inefficient.

When a large number and variety of firms in a given airshed are regulated in an effort to reduce pollution, the command and control method often probably does produce inefficient results. Regulations may call for the installation of specific devices, or require that all firms obtain a specified percentage of emissions reduction. Some firms will have a lower cost of emissions reduction and lower total costs would result if those firms undertook a disproportionately large share of the pollution abatement effort. To avoid unfairness, the high-cost pollution avoiders (who are spared the need to lessen their pollution) could absorb a share of the costs of abatement incurred by the low-cost pollution avoiders. The same net result in emission reduction would be achieved at a lower total cost. This would be far more efficient than the normal command and control approach.

If, control strategies sometimes result in inefficiency because they do not allow regulated firms that would otherwise do so to seek out least cost methods of

---

1. Despite frequent rhetorical attacks on the putative inefficiency of environmental regulation, there are few careful studies of the costs of regulation. One notable exception is Hahn & Hird, The Costs and Benefits of Regulation: Review and Synthesis, 8 Yale J. Regulation 233 (1990).

achieving pollution reduction goals, as a matter of regulatory design, the question becomes how to develop regulatory systems that set environmentally appropriate goals and encourage private market-based decisionmaking to attain those goals in the least cost way.[2] This chapter, after considering the debate between supporters of command and control strategies and proponents of market-oriented strategies, explores several types of devices that can be employed to introduce market decisionmaking into the pollution control process. These include effluent taxes, an array of devices pioneered by the pre-1990 Clean Air Act that include bubbles, netting, offsets and banking, and the tradeable emissions allowances for SO_2 adopted by the 1990 Clean Air Amendments in addressing the problems of acid rain and other airborne acid deposition.

A. DEBATING THE EFFICACY OF REGULATORY STRATEGIES

H. Latin, Ideal Versus Real Regulatory Efficiency: Implementation of Uniform Standards and "Fine Tuning" Regulatory Reforms,
37 Stanford Law Review 1267, 1267–1273 (1985)*

Many environmental, public health, and safety statutes place primary emphasis on the implementation of uniform regulatory standards. In return for benefits that are often difficult to assess, "command-and-control" standards promulgated under such statutes as the Clean Air Act, Occupational Safety and Health Act, and Federal Water Pollution Control Act impose billions of dollars in annual compliance costs on society and also entail significant indirect costs including decreases in productivity, technological innovation, and market competition. As these costs have become increasingly evident, prominent legal scholars such as Bruce Ackerman, Steven Breyer, and Richard Stewart have concluded that command-and-control regulation is inefficient and should be replaced by more flexible strategies. Their principal criticisms may be summarized as follows: Uniform standards do not reflect the opportunity costs of environmental protection,[3] they disregard the

---

2. There are also critical questions about the advisability of allowing more use of market forces to meet pollution control objectives. These questions are in some measure empirical ones: are the potential efficiency gains large enough to be worth achieving, and will the predicted responses to the introduction of markets in pollution conform to the very simple model of behavior that inheres in a reliance on rational choice theory? This chapter does not answer those questions directly because there is not yet enough persuasive data. The focus is on first identifying the mechanics of how market devices can be used in aid of pollution control, and then anticipating the situations in which market-based approaches have the greatest likelihood of working to obtain adequate pollution control results in a least-cost manner.

3. Command-and-control standards often place an absolute priority on environmental protection, with little consideration of competing resource uses that will be foreclosed. Critics of the current approach usually attribute the resulting inefficiencies to public and governmental ignorance about the true social costs of environmental regulation or to the political pressure of extremist special-interest groups. See e.g. B. Ackerman, S. Rose-Ackerman, J. Sawyer & D. Henderson, The Uncertain Search for Environmental Quality 165–207 (1974); M. Douglas & A. Wildavsky, Risk and Culture (1982).

The concept of "opportunity cost" is essential for any comparison of regulatory systems and for any analysis of public policy issues. It means that the real cost of any resource allocation must be measured not by its financial expense alone, but by the value of incompatible resource uses that must be foregone.

individual circumstances of diverse conflicts,[4] they do not achieve environmental protection on a "lowest-cost" basis,[5] and they fail to provide adequate incentives for improved performance.

In response to these alleged deficiencies in the present system, advocates of "regulatory reform" argue that environmental controls should be tailored to particularized ecological and economic circumstances, regulatory benefits weighed against the costs of environmental protection, and increased reliance placed on economic incentive mechanisms, such as taxes on environmentally destructive activities or transferable pollution rights. Professor Stewart, for example, recently advocated "a more individualized or 'fine-tuning' approach to regulation." Critics of command-and-control standards differ on suggested 'fine-tuning' prescriptions, but there is widespread agreement that some alternative must be preferable to the current regulatory system....

The academic literature on "regulatory reform" reflects an excessive preoccupation with theoretical efficiency, while it places inadequate emphasis on actual decisionmaking costs and implementation constraints. Any system for environmental regulation must function despite the presence of pervasive uncertainty, high decisionmaking costs,[6] and manipulative strategic behavior resulting from conflicting private and public interests. Under these conditions, the indisputable fact that uniform standards are inefficient does not prove that any other approach would necessarily perform better. In a "second-best" world, the critical issue is not which regulatory system aspires to ideal "efficiency" but which is most likely to prove effective.[7]

In recognition of severe implementation constraints on environmental regulation there are numerous advantages of uniform standards in comparison with more particularized and flexible regulatory strategies. These advantages include de-

---

Fundamentally, a decision to do one thing implies a decision not to do something else. If we choose to use some of our resources to build a new city hall, then those resources are obviously not available for building a new highway. If we assign our best available engineers to research and development of energy sources, they are not available for work on smog control, or vice versa. An estimate of the cost of any such choice or decision is an estimate of the benefits that would otherwise be obtained. E. Quade, Analysis for Public Decisions 118 (2d ed. 1982).

4. Regulatory standards impose uniform requirements on broad categories of activities. Yet ecological conditions, environmental impacts of human actions, and potential resource uses vary widely at different times and in different locations. The inflexibility of uniform standards leads to "too much" environmental protection in some contexts and "too little" in others....

5. Some regulated parties...will have lower than average abatement costs because of the technological characteristics of their operations or the ecological characteristics of their facility sites. Uniform standards do not discriminate between the differing control capabilities and cost functions of particular polluters, and therefore cannot achieve any given level of environmental protection at the lowest possible cost....

6. Decisionmaking costs are typically high for each environmental conflict because ecological systems are complex, interactions are subtle and may require many years to become evident, people or biospecies are exposed to many potentially harmful agents, relative costs and benefits are difficult to assess, and sharply conflicting values and priorities are the norm rather than the exception. Moreover, many thousands of environmental resource conflicts must be resolved each year; thus, the cumulative costs of environmental decisionmaking would be high even if the cost of each regulatory decision were not. See e.g. A. Kneese & C. Schultze, Pollution, Prices and Public Policy 19, 81, 117 (1975).

7. There are numerous formal economic definitions of efficiency. See e.g. Coleman, Efficiency, Exchange, and Auction: Philosophic Aspects of the Economic Approach to Law, 68 Calif. L. Rev. 221 (1980); Latin, Environmental Deregulation and Consumer Decisionmaking Under Uncertainty, 6 Harv. Envt'l. L. Rev. 187, 191 n.26 (1982). For purposes of this article, the important contrast is between an emphasis on ideal or optimal decisionmaking, which is denoted below by the label "efficiency," and an emphasis on "effective" decisionmaking, which means the achievement of a reasonable congruence between regulatory accomplishments and desired legislative objectives.

creased information collection and evaluation costs, greater consistency and predictability of results, greater accessibility of decisions to public scrutiny and participation, increased likelihood that regulations will withstand judicial review, reduced opportunities for manipulative behavior by agencies in response to political or bureaucratic pressures, reduced opportunities for obstructive behavior by regulated parties, and decreased likelihood of social dislocation and "forum shopping" resulting from competitive disadvantages between geographical regions or between firms in regulated industries. A realistic implementation analysis indicates that "fine-tuning" would prove infeasible in many important environmental contexts; indeed, the effectiveness of environmental regulation could often be improved by reducing even the degree of "fine-tuning" that is currently attempted.

There is more at stake here than academic disagreement and the possible miseducation of a generation of students. When the Reagan Administration took office, it was explicit about its desire for widespread deregulation. After Congress proved generally unwilling to repeal regulatory legislation, the Administration changed its approach and argued that environmental control programs should be made more "efficient." In a letter to the New York Times, for example, an EPA Assistant Administrator claimed that the agency was committed to "clean water," but that the EPA intended to improve regulatory efficiency by: (1) expanding reliance on "cost/benefit analysis"; (2) basing standards on "scientific evidence and not on rumor and soothsaying"; (3) employing "site-specific data"; (4) providing "more flexibility to local governments"; and (5) not imposing regulatory costs unless "a designated [water quality] use is attainable." These are all proposals for increased "fine-tuning." The letter mentioned nothing about Administration initiatives that reduced EPA budgets and manpower, or about information scarcity and "site-specific" collection costs, or about inadequate scientific understanding of many water quality-related problems. Well-intentioned scholars often recommend "fine-tuning" because they focus on ideal efficiency, while Administration officials may advocate "fine-tuning" precisely because they believe it will seldom work in practice and would therefore accomplish *sub rosa* deregulation. Intemperate academic criticisms of command-and-control standards combined with support of unrealistic "fine-tuning" strategies may lend an aura of intellectual credibility to political initiatives designed to achieve less regulation, not better regulation....

Comparison between the *demonstrated inefficiencies* of uniform standards and the *theoretical advantages* of "fine-tuning" cannot lead to the development of a wise regulatory policy.... Uncertainty, high decisionmaking costs, and varying strategic behavior for different regulatory approaches all affect regulatory effectiveness. These constraints would degrade the performance of any environmental protection program, but competing strategies are not all subject to the same kinds of imponderables, expenses, and manipulation, nor are they all vulnerable to the same degree.... The most "efficient" strategies in theory will frequently be the least effective in practice. Moreover, many commentators espouse variations of approaches that have already been tried and found unsatisfactory.... The implementation problems which subverted these approaches in the past remain essentially unchanged, and consequently...most "fine-tuning" proposals reflect wishful thinking rather than a realistic appraisal of present environmental knowledge and regulatory capabilities. Despite its imperfections, command-and-control regulation has fostered significant improvements in environmental quality at a societal cost that has not proved prohibitive.[8] Critics of uniform standards should therefore be required to demonstrate with reasonable assurance that "fine-tuning" approaches can be successfully implemented, and will actually perform better, before the current regulatory system is "reformed."

Bruce Ackerman & Richard Stewart, Reforming Environmental Law,
37 Stanford Law Review 1333, 1333–1340 (1985)*

In 1971, Ezra Mishan brilliantly satirized the views of a Dr. Pangloss, who argued that a world of largely unregulated pollution was "optimal" because cleanup would involve enormous transaction costs. Less than 15 years later, Professor Latin uses the same Panglossian argument to rationalize the current regulatory status quo. He not only accepts but endorses our extraordinarily crude, costly, litigious and counterproductive system of technology-based environmental controls. Like Mishan's Pangloss, he seems to believe that if it were possible to have a better world, it would exist. Since it does not, the transaction costs involved in regulatory improvement must exceed the benefits. Proposals for basic change accordingly are dismissed as naïve utopianism.

What explains this celebration of the regulatory status quo? As critics of the present system, we believe this question to be of more than academic interest. The present regulatory system wastes tens of billions of dollars every year, misdirects resources, stifles innovation, and spawns massive and often counterproductive litigation. There is a variety of fundamental but practical changes that could be made to improve its environmental and economic performance. Why have such changes not been adopted? Powerful organized interests have a vested stake in the status quo. The congressional committees, government bureaucracies, and industry and environmental groups that have helped to shape the present system want to see it perpetuated. But the current system is also bolstered by an often inarticulate sense that, however cumbersome, it "works," and that complexity and limited information make major improvements infeasible.

Professor Latin has performed an important service in providing an articulate, informed, and sophisticated exposition of this view. By developing and making transparent the arguments that might justify the status quo, he has made it easier to assess their merits. If, as we believe, those arguments lack merit, his sophisticated defense of the status quo may ultimately serve to hasten its demise.

We will not respond to all of the groundless charges that Professor Latin levels at the critics of the current system, ourselves included. We focus instead on the major flaws in his defense of existing law and policy. First, Latin's view is based on a Panglossian interpretation of the status quo. The current system does not in fact "work" and its malfunctions, like those of Soviet-style central planning, will become progressively more serious as the economy grows and changes and our knowledge of environmental problems develops. Second, Latin mistakenly treats

---

8. See Costle, Environmental Regulation and Regulatory Reform, 57 Wash. L. Rev. 409, 416 (1982) (estimating that pollution control requirements imposed regulatory costs of about 3.3% of GNP and about 3.1% of total industry expenditures on plants and equipment in 1981; Costle does admit, however, that "the effects [of environmentory costs] on specific industries can be sub-stantial"). Critics of command-and-control regulation contend that current programs "waste" billions of dollars, not that society is incapable of absorbing the aggregate costs if necessary. See e.g., A. Kneese & C. Schultze, Pollution, Prices and Public Policy (1975); Stewart, Regulation, Innovation, and Administrative Law: A Conceptual Framework, 69 Calif. L. Rev. 1256, 1367–68 (1981).

economic incentive systems as a form of regulatory "fine-tuning," rather than recognizing them as fundamental alternatives to our current reliance on centralized regulatory commands to implement environmental goals. Moreover, he completely ignores experience showing that economic incentive systems are feasible and effective. Third, Latin ignores the increasingly urgent need to improve the process by which Congress, the agencies, and the courts set environmental goals. He is mesmerized by decisionmaking costs, ignoring the great social benefits flowing from a more intelligent and democratically accountable dialogue on environmental policy. We deal with each of these points in turn.

I. THE EXISTING SYSTEM

The existing system of pollution regulation, which is the focus of Latin's defense, is primarily based on a Best Available Technology (BAT) strategy. If an industrial process or product generates some nontrivial risk, the responsible plant or industry must install whatever technology is available to reduce or eliminate this risk, so long as the costs of doing so will not cause a shutdown of the plant or industry. BAT requirements are largely determined through uniform federal regulations. Under the Clean Water Act's BAT strategy, the EPA adapts nationally uniform effluent limitations for some 500 different industries. A similar BAT strategy is deployed under the Clean Air Act for new industrial sources of air pollution, new automobiles, and industrial sources of toxic air pollutants. BAT strategies are also widely used in many fields of environmental regulation other than air and water pollution, which are the focus of Latin's analysis.

BAT was embraced by Congress and administrators in the early 1970s in order to impose immediate, readily enforceable federal controls on a relatively few widespread pollutants, while avoiding widespread industrial shutdowns. Subsequent experience and analysis has demonstrated:

1. Uniform BAT requirements waste many billions of dollars annually by ignoring variations among plants and industries in the cost of reducing pollution and by ignoring geographic variations in pollution effects. A more cost-effective strategy of risk reduction could free enormous resources for additional pollution reduction or other purposes.

2. BAT controls, and the litigation they provoke, impose disproportionate penalties on new products and processes. A BAT strategy typically imposes far more stringent controls on new sources because there is no risk of shutdown. Also, new plants and products must run the gauntlet of lengthy regulatory and legal proceedings to win approval; the resulting uncertainty and delay discourage new investment. By contrast, existing sources can use the delays and costs of the legal process to burden regulators and postpone or "water-down" compliance. BAT strategies also impose disproportionate burdens on more productive and profitable industries because these industries can "afford" more stringent controls. This "soak the rich" approach penalizes growth and international competitiveness.

3. BAT controls can ensure that established control technologies are installed. They do not, however, provide strong incentives for the development of new, environmentally superior strategies, and may actually discourage their development. Such innovations are essential for maintaining long-term economic growth without simultaneously increasing pollution and other forms of environmental degradation.

4. BAT involves the centralized determination of complex scientific, engineering, and economic issues regarding the feasibility of controls on hundreds of

thousands of pollution sources. Such determinations impose massive information-gathering burdens on administrators, and provide a fertile ground for complex litigation in the form of massive adversary rulemaking proceedings and protracted judicial review. Given the high costs of regulatory compliance and the potential gains from litigation brought to defeat or delay regulatory requirements, it is often more cost-effective for industry to "invest" in such litigation rather than to comply.

5. A BAT strategy is inconsistent with intelligent priority setting. Simply regulating to the hilt whatever pollutants happen to get on the regulatory agenda may preclude an agency from dealing adequately with more serious problems that come to scientific attention later. BAT also tends to reinforce regulatory inertia. Foreseeing that "all or nothing" regulation of a given substance under BAT will involve large administrative and compliance costs, and recognizing that resources are limited, agencies often seek to limit sharply the number of substances on the agenda for regulatory action.

This indictment is not idle speculation, but the product of years of patient study by lawyers, economists, and political scientists. There are, for example, no fewer than 15 careful efforts to estimate the extra cost burden generated by a wide range of traditional legalistic BAT systems used to control a variety of air and water pollutants in different parts of the country. Of the twelve studies of different air pollutants – ranging from particulates to chlorofluorocarbons – seven indicated that traditional forms of regulation were more than 400 percent more expensive than the least-cost solution; four revealed that they were about 75 percent more expensive; one suggested a modest cost-overrun of 7 percent. Three studies of water pollution control in five different watersheds also indicate the serious inefficiency of traditional forms of command-and-control regulation. These careful studies of selected problems cannot be used to estimate precisely the total amount traditional forms of regulation are annually costing the American people. Nonetheless, very large magnitudes are at stake. Even if a reformed system could cut costs by "only" one-third, it could save more than $15 billion a year from the nation's annual expenditure of $50 billion on air and water pollution control alone.

While Latin entirely fails to address this evidence, he does not seriously contest the economic wastefulness of the current system's excessive compliance costs and penalties on new investment. He simply ignores the last three points in our indictment, even though they have been well developed in the literature. Instead, Latin spends all his time castigating all reform proposals as unrealistic. In his view, reformers characteristically propose utopian efforts at administrative "fine-tuning" that would in practice lead to a bureaucratic nightmare, making the present system seem benign by comparison.

We do not accept this despairing view. To explain why, however, we must correct an analytic deficiency in Latin's critique. The various reforms rejected in his article have little in common with one another – except that they all represent departures from BAT. Indeed, it is a sign of Latin's deep commitment to the status quo that, simply because they depart from BAT, he thinks of them as if they were all variations on the problem of "fine-tuning" that he decries. But "fine-tuning" is much too diffuse a notion on which to base an analysis of the reform agenda. Some of our proposals involve reform of the criteria and procedures which Congress, agencies, and the courts use in *setting environmental goals*; others involve reform of the means by which the goals (whatever they may be) are *implemented* in the real world. Latin's indiscriminate condemnation of "fine-tuning" fails to distinguish systematically between these two types of proposals. In this, as in so much else, his critique is faithful to the BAT system, which also conflates means and ends, preventing the intelligent assessment of either. If, however, we are to move beyond the status quo, it is best to treat these two different kinds of structural reform separately, beginning with the implementation problem and concluding with the question of goal-setting.

COMMENTARY AND QUESTIONS

1. The fuller debate. As is evident, the excerpts reproduced here are only the introductory salvos of these two well-argued articles. Although together the articles exceed one hundred pages in length, they are worth the reading.

2. Separating goals from implementation. Ackerman and Stewart distinguish between environmental goals and the methods suited to accomplish them. This chapter is, for the most part, concerned only with implementation; part D, at the end of the chapter, canvasses in some detail the principal proposal espoused by Ackerman and Stewart, the use of marketable pollution allowances. Before turning to questions of implementing market-based strategies for environmental improvement, however, what would you expect Ackerman and Stewart (and other proponents of economic analysis) to say about environmental goal setting? They first argue that the goals for environmental regulation ought to be expressed in terms of how much pollution reduction is desireable (e.g. a percentage reduction figure) within a given time frame. Perhaps surprisingly, Ackerman and Stewart feel that these are not economic questions to be determined by benefit-cost analysis. Rather they describe these matters as "*the* quintessentially political question that should be answered by the legislative process." Why should such concrete goals be set politically? What is likely to be wrong, in their view, with having an administrative agency collect data and determine appropriate goals on that basis?

Their second proposal in the area of goal-setting, operative in the longer run, is for regional and local differentiation of goals to reflect the differences in the underlying natural systems that are affected by the regulation. This may include especially stringent regulation for pristine areas, or laxer regulation in areas of great waste assimilative capacity. Could it also include a decision to commit some areas to service as pollution havens or national sacrifice areas? The third and final goal-oriented change is to set priorities in the regulatory agenda in a cost-effective way so that the largest gains in environmental quality are realized sooner rather than later. For a less strident criticism of the Ackerman-Stewart prescription, and particularly of the longer-term items, see Mintz, Economic Reform of Environmental Protection: A Brief Comment on a Recent Debate, 15 Harv. Envt'l L. Rev. 149, 160–162 (1991).

B. EFFLUENT TAXES

Effluent taxes are a theoretically elegant economic incentive to improved pollution control. The regulator, simply by taxing emission of effluents, adds to a firm's private cost of pollution. The increased cost of emissions induces polluters to reconsider their polluting behavior. If it is less costly to reduce emissions, the polluter will do so, otherwise the polluter will pay the tax. Each firm is allowed to choose, based on its own specialized knowledge of its situation, the least cost course of action. If the effluent tax is set at the proper amount, the desired reduction in emissions will occur, with the least-cost pollution avoiders opting to reduce emissions and the high-cost pollution avoiders paying the tax. Government thus avoids involvement in the micro-management of the firms' behavior and, as a bonus, collects revenue that can be used to compensate victims of pollution or to invest in further reduction of pollution or environmental remediation.

The elegance of effluent taxes may be more apparent than real. The regulator cannot just slap a tax on pollution and expect the world, efficiently, to become a better place. The amount of the tax matters a great deal. Too low a tax will not spur enough pollution control to obtain the desired environmental improvement. Too high a tax results in over-investment in pollution control. This overinvestment is inefficient as a matter of definition because it makes the environment "too clean." This is not an oxymoron. Recall that there is some degree of pollution that is socially beneficial. To the extent that the regulatory goal was to achieve that optimal level of pollution, any additional investment in pollution control is undesirable. "How clean is clean?" Further, subsequent adjustment of the amount of the effluent charge is not a preferred option because it is inefficient to change the amount of an effluent tax once it has been set and firms have invested in reliance on the amount of the original tax.

To calculate the proper amount of the tax, the regulator must know a great deal. Initially the regulator must fix the goal to be attained. Presumably, the goal will be to attain a quality level for the ambient receiving body – local air or water – that is correlated with health or welfare, i.e. some standard like the NAAQS for conventional air pollutants. Next the regulator must calculate the amount of effluent that is presently emitted by the group of sources that will be subject to the tax and the total amount of reductions that will be needed to produce the desired end result. Thereafter the regulator will have to imagine the cost curves of pollution abatement for each of those firms. This step is every bit as difficult as it seems, involving the regulator in the detailed analysis of the economic and technical processes of all regulated firms. After that, however, the path is far easier. The regulator aggregates the information about the cost of emission reductions into a single function that relates the total amount of pollution reduction to different levels for the tax, and selects the proper tax, perhaps adjusting the amount upward to leave some cushion for growth in emissions in the event that additional firms locate in the area.

Beyond setting the amount of the tax, the measurement of the amount of tax due requires an expensive "real-time" emissions monitoring program or reliance on source by source calculations of what emissions will be under each one's particular production practices (e.g. the type of fuel and other material inputs, design of machinery and other process characteristics). Neither choice is without its drawbacks. Monitoring involves capital cost for equipment and on-going maintenance and personnel outlays, as well as billing and collection of the appropriate tax. Calculating emissions again draws the program into extensive stack-by-stack engineering calculations, this time in a setting where regulated firms have a financial incentive to underestimate their emissions and the regulator has only a small technical staff to oversee the engineering and production resources of the regulated community.

COMMENTARY AND QUESTIONS

1. The non-use of effluent charges in the United States. There is little in the American experience that even vaguely resembles the use of effluent taxes. There is no certain explanation for the failure of effluent taxes to take hold in the United States. In the 1970s – the formative period in modern environmental regulation – effluent taxes were a prominent part of the literature on pollution control. See e.g. F. Anderson, A. Kneese, P. Reed, S. Taylor & R. Stevenson, Environmental Improvement Through Economic Incentives (1977). One suggestion is that the wealth transfer aspects of effluent taxes would lead to strong opposition from the firms that would be subjected to the taxes. See Hahn & Stavins, Incentive-Based Environmental Regulation: A New Era from an Old Idea?, 18 Ecol. L.Q. 1, 8 (1991).

The closest analogs to effluent taxes in the United States are the fees charged for the deposit of hazardous waste at facilities, and the amounts paid for the disposal of other wastes at landfills. These charges are not paid to government, and the levels are not selected with reference to any socially-determined goals, but they do induce firms to reduce their effluents when the cost of waste reduction is less than the cost of disposal. One proposal to reduce the volume of landfill-bound items calls for implementing an incentive system that more nearly resembles effluent charges:

> Simple curbside charges, based on the volume or weight of mixed refuse, provide strong incentives for source reduction, separation of valuable materials, and purchasing of materials that are reusable, recyclable, or less expensive to landfill or incinerate. Another possible option is a highly flexible system of retail charges implemented by entering data on disposal costs into optical scanning cash register systems. This system would facilitate carefully tailored adjustments to individual product prices to reflect disposal costs. If this pricing system were combined with a curbside charge, even greater social benefits could be reaped. Menell, Beyond the Throwaway Society: An Incentive Approach to Regulating Municipal Solid Waste, 17 Ecol. L. Q. 655, 659 (1990).

2. Goals other than ambient quality. The text above suggests that the level of effluent taxes should be reverse-engineered from a goal based on ambient receiving body quality. This is not the only methodology that can be used. Note the descriptions of the German and Chinese use of effluent taxes in the two notes that follow. Consider also the following:

> Most economists agree that a far better way to control pollution than the present method is to impose a tax of a specified amount per unit of effluent discharged. That way the firm would have an incentive to use the cheapest way to keep down the effluent. Equally important, that way there would be objective evidence of the costs of reducing pollution. If a small tax led to a

large reduction, that would be a clear indication that there is little to gain from permitting the discharge. On the other hand, if even a high tax left much discharge, that would indicate the reverse, but also would provide substantial sums to compensate the losers or undo the damage. M. Friedman & R. Friedman, Free To Choose 207 (1980).

Does a high-cost of abatement argue in favor of environmental degradation as an alternative to effluent limitations, as the Friedmans seem to imply in the excerpt?

3. The use of effluent charges in Germany. Effluent taxes, although they function in a somewhat different way than that described in the text above, are employed in parts of Europe, particularly in Germany. On the Emscher River, a tributary of the Rhine, all firms that deposit effluent into the river are assessed a per-unit effluent fee. The fees are used to finance a water treatment plant situated at the mouth of the Emscher that treats the polluted water before discharging it back into the Rhine. The fee is designed to recoup each year's operating and maintenance costs, plus a share of the capital cost of constructing the facility, with each firm being charged in proportion to the number of units of pollution it deposited into the Emscher. Firms have the option of reducing their emissions in order to reduce their share of the annual assessment. Note that this use of effluent fees makes no attempt to control water quality in the Emscher itself; it is effectively treated as an open sewer leading to the treatment plant. It is also important to note that the non-litigious character of German society and the tradition of corporate cooperation with government minimizes the monitoring problem.[9]

4. Effluent charges as a means to other ends. Besides efforts to achieve desired ambient quality goals, are there other applications for which effluent charges would be appropriate? Raising money earmarked for pollution control is one possibility.[10] The fundraising function for effluent taxes does not seem to be widely practiced in the United States, but in many ways this describes the current practice in several larger metropolitan areas of the People's Republic of China. In Beijing, for example, effluent taxes are levied on all pollution in excess of a permitted amount. Of the amount collected, 80 percent is then rebated to firms having excess emissions, with the requirement that the money be spent on pollution control equipment. The remaining 20 percent is used by the Beijing Municipal Environmental Protection Bureau to defray its costs and to construct treatment plants and other facilities. Can you surmise why this system is particularly well adapted to a capital-scarce, highly regulated economy like China's?

5. Pollution-added taxes. An interesting variant on effluent charges is embodied in the idea of a pollution-added tax (PAT). The idea behind the tax is identical to that propounded by the Friedmans: impose a pollution-related tax to increase the cost of pollution and thereby discourage consumers from purchasing as much of the

9. See Plater, Coal Law from the Old World, 64 Ky. L.J. 473, 475, 480–486 (1976).

10. In Ackerman & Stewart, Reforming Environmental Law, 37 Stan. L. Rev. 1333, 1343 (1985), the possibility of auctioning-off transferrable pollution permits is estimated as an immense source of revenue. In their view, a conservative estimate is that $6 to $10 billion could be raised by auctioning such rights in the United States.

product. The special role of a pollution-added tax comes in the context of international pollution reduction efforts, such as those underway to reduce ozone depletion. Several nations can act in parallel fashion by imposing a PAT. To avoid a loss of competitiveness with like products manufactured in non-PAT nations the pollution charge is added to items that are manufactured domestically and then rebated in the event that the item is exported. To equalize competition of domestic goods with imported goods, the PAT is added to the cost of imports. Does the PAT approach seem workable in an international economy in which fewer than all nations are willing to impose the environmentally protective tax? For a more thorough discussion of the concept, see Comment, Proposal: A Pollution Added Tax to Slow Ozone Depletion and Global Warming, 26 Stan. J. Int'l Law 549 (1990).

6. Subsidies. There is a sense in which subsidies that support the installation of pollution control equipment are a form of economic incentive, a sort of inverse effluent tax. The availability of subsidies makes the installation of pollution control devices a lower cost alternative for a firm than would be the case in the absence of the subsidy. What subsidies alone do not do is force the firm to seek a pollution control strategy in the first place. The impetus to reduce pollution must come from some program or source external to the subsidy program. That program can be a command and control system, or an effluent tax system, or anything else that imposes a cost or threat of shutdown if pollution is not controlled. Subsidies for environmental improvement have been most widely used to spur investment in water treatment facilities. For many years the federal government paid up to 85 percent of the construction cost of publicly owned treatment works (POTWs) under the Clean Water Act.

C. BUBBLES, NETTING, OFFSETS, AND BANKING

Bubbles, netting, offsets and banking are four terms that describe different parts of the emissions trading programs that have been used in the first twenty years of the Clean Air Act's existence. It is important to understand that these emissions trading devices, as they have been employed to date, have been used as an adjunct to the Clean Air Act's stationary source emissions control strategies for the standard criteria pollutants. This means that firms engaged in emissions trading are large emitters operating with permits written under state implementation plans (SIPs). As discussed in Chapter 18, *supra*, these permits fix, with considerable precision, allowable maximum emissions limits for each of the criteria pollutants from each source.

Bubbles, netting, and offsets are related activities: each allows a reduction in presently authorized emissions of pollutants to excuse some increase in permitted emissions. Banking, as the name suggests, allows for reductions in pollution to be stored in an "account" which is later drawn upon as part of a bubble, netting, or offset transaction. The central device for emissions trading is the recognition of credit for reducing pollution below the allowable (permitted) levels previously established by the Clean Air Act:

EPA's emissions trading program extends, rather than replaces, the system for regulating emissions of air pollutants established under the Clean Air Act. Emissions trading allows the exchange of emission rights, both externally (between firms) and internally (within a single firm). The commodities exchanged in emissions trading are emission reduction credits (ERCs), which are property rights to emit air pollutants. A firm creates ERCs by reducing its emissions of a specific pollutant below the baseline level allowed by its permit, thereby creating surplus reductions. EPA regulations specify that these reductions must be surplus, enforceable, permanent, and quantifiable in order to qualify as ERCs.[11]

Conceptually, there is very little difference among the three operative programs – bubbles, netting, and offsets. All involve trading reductions in presently allowable pollution in exchange for rights to increase other emissions. As the following excerpt explains, the most vital distinctions among the devices lie in the contexts in which they are applicable and, consequently, the regulatory command and control requirements that can at times be avoided by the use of the emissions trades.

Hahn & Hester, Marketable Permits: Lessons for Theory and Practice,
16 Ecology Law Quarterly 361, 370–372 (1989)

MARKETABLE PERMITS

To understand why different elements of emissions trading vary widely in their performance, it is important to have a working knowledge of what they enable firms to do. As the following summary reveals, the four elements [netting, offsets, bubbles, and banking] differ dramatically: they vary in their provision for external trades, in the types of sources that can participate, and in the locus of administrative control.

Netting allows a modified source to avoid the most stringent emission limits that would be applied to the modification by reducing emissions from another source within the same plant.[12] Thus, netting necessarily involves internal trading only. This reduces the net emission increase to a level below that which is considered significant – hence the term, netting. Netting can result in small net increases in emissions because the cutoff level for treating an emission increase as significant is greater than zero. Netting is controlled at the state level and – subject to individual state restrictions – may be used in attainment and nonattainment areas.[13]

Offsets are used by new and modified sources in nonattainment areas and by certain specified sources in attainment areas. The Clean Air Act specifies that no new emission sources would be allowed in areas that did not meet the original 1975 air quality deadlines. Concern that this provision would stifle economic growth prompted EPA to institute the offset rule in 1976.[14] This rule requires new and modified emission sources in these areas to obtain emission credits from sources in the same area to offset their new emissions.[15] The sources are still subject to the

11. Hahn & Hester, Where Did All the Markets Go? An Analysis of EPA's Emissions Trading Program, 6 Yale J. on Reg. 109, 114 (1989). In support of the passage, Hahn and Hester cite EPA, Emission Trading Policy Statement, General Principles for Creation, Banking and Use of Emission Reduction Credits, Final Policy, 51 Fed. Reg. 43,831 (1986).

12. EPA, Prevention of Significant Air Quality Deterioration, 39 Fed. Reg. 42,510 (1974)(final rule).

13. EPA, Emissions Trading Policy Statement, 51 Fed. Reg. 43,814 (1986)(final policy) [hereinafter EPA Trading Policy].

14. EPA, Emission Offset Interpretive Ruling of Dec. 21, 1976, 41 Fed. Reg. 55,524–25 (1976).

15. 44 Fed. Reg. 3284 (1979).

Table 1: Relation of Emission Limits, by Source Type and Area Class, to Emissions Trading

Source Type	Area Class	Emissions Trading Options	Optional or Mandatory	Applicable Emission Limit[1]	Can Limit be Avoided by Trading?
New	Attainment	Offsets	Optional	BACT	No
New	Non-Attainment	Offsets	Mandatory	LAER	No
Modified	Attainment	Netting	Optional	BACT	Yes
Modified	Non-Attainment	Netting	Optional	LAER	Yes
Modified		Offsets[2]	Mandatory	LAER	No
Existing	Attainment	Bubbles	Optional	State Limits[3]	Yes
Existing		Bubbles	Optional	State Limits[3]	Not Applicable
Existing	Non-Attainment	Bubbles	Optional	RACT	Yes
Existing		Banking[4]	Optional	RACT	Not Applicable

Notes for Table 1:

1. Of these limits, LAER (Lowest Achievable Emission Rate) is the most stringent, Clean Air Act §171(3), 42 U.S.C.A. §7501(3); BACT (Best Available Control Technology) is the next most stringent, id. §169(3), 42 U.S.C.A. §7479(3); and RACT (Reasonably Available Control Technology) is the least stringent, id. §172(3), 42 U.S.C.A. §7502(3). Modified sources that use netting are exempted from BACT or LAER, but may be subject to other limits called NSPS (New Source Performance Standards) that are typically approximately equivalent to BACT. For stringency of state limits, see note 3 below.

2. Offsets are mandatory in nonattainment areas for modified sources that do not use netting. EPA, Emissions Trading Policy Statement, 51 Fed. Reg. 43,830 (1986).

3. There are no specific federally defined emission limits that states must apply to existing sources in attainment areas. States, however, are required to institute measures that assure the maintenance of air quality in attainment areas. Clean Air Act §107(a), 42 U.S.C.A. §7407(a). To do so, states usually employ a permit system as they do in nonattainment areas and impose emission limits on existing sources through that system. While the resulting state limits can vary widely, they are typically no more stringent than RACT, and may be less stringent.

4. Applicable emission limits are used to calculate emission credits for banking, but the use of banking does not, in itself, enable firms to avoid emission limits. See EPA, Emissions Trading Policy Statement, 51 Fed. Reg. 43,835 (1986). The use of their banked credits in other emissions trading activities may enable firms to avoid applicable emission limits, however. [Eds: banked emissions credits can be used for offsets or for netting.]

most stringent emission limits.[16] Offsets may be obtained through internal or external trades.[17] Like netting, offset transactions are controlled at the state level.

Bubbles, first allowed in 1979,[18] are used by existing sources in attainment or nonattainment areas. The name derives from the concept of placing an imaginary bubble over a multi-source plant. The levels of emission controls applied to different sources in a bubble may be adjusted to reduce control costs so long as the aggregate limit is not exceeded. In effect, emission credits are created by some sources within the plant and used by others. Originally, all bubbles had to be submitted by the states to EPA for approval. In 1981 EPA began to approve "generic bubble rules" that enabled states to approve bubbles.[19] Several states now have such rules.

Banking, which was first allowed in 1979,[20] provides a mechanism for firms to save emission credits for future use. EPA has established guidelines for banking programs, but states must set up and administer the rules governing banking.

As the third column in Table 1 shows, different types of sources, classified according to type and location, have different emissions trading options available to them. New sources have the fewest options; the only activity they may engage in is offsets, and the use of offsets is mandatory in nonattainment areas.[21] The stringent emission limits that apply to these sources cannot be avoided thorough trading.[22] Modified sources are faced with similar requirements, except that they may use netting, thus avoiding the most stringent emission limits.[23] Existing sources in nonattainment areas may use bubbles or banking; the former can be used to avoid emission limits that otherwise would apply to individual sources.

These differences in options are crucial to understanding the performance of emissions trading. New and modified sources have the greatest incentive to use emissions trading since they are subject to the most stringent emission limits; however, under the program only modified sources can avoid the stringent emission requirements by doing so. Existing sources enjoy the most flexibility in using emissions trading but have less incentive to do so since they are subject to less stringent emission limits.

COMMENTARY AND QUESTIONS

1. The extraordinary attraction of netting. Netting is popular with firms for good reason. One major attraction of netting is its ability to allow firms to avoid the command and control technology-based standards for modified sources in both

---

16. Clean Air Act §§171, 173(2), 42 U.S.C. §§ 7501, 7503(2)(1982); *see also* EPA, Emission Offset Interpretive Ruling, *supra*, at 55,526.

17. *See* EPA Emission Offset Interpretive Ruling, 44 Fed. Reg. 3,274–76 (1979)(final rule modifying EPA, Emission Offset Interpretive Ruling, *supra*).

18. EPA, Recommendation for Alternative Emission Reduction Options within State Implementation Plans, 44 Fed. Reg. 3,740-42 (1979)(proposed policy statement); id. at 71,780–88 (final policy statement).

19. EPA, Recommendation for Alternative Emission Reduction Options within State Implementation Plans, 44 Fed. Reg. 3,740–42 (1979); Proposed Revision to the New Jersey State Implementation Plan, 45 Fed. Reg. 77,459–60 (1980)(proposed rule and amendment to policy statement)(codified at 40 C.F.R. §52.06 (1987)).

20. EPA, Emission Offset Interpretive Ruling, *supra*, at 3285.

21. Clean Air Act §173(A), 42 U.S.C. § 7503(A) 1982.

22. *See, e.g.,* EPA Trading Policy, *supra*, at 43, 833 (credits from existing sources cannot be used to meet technology-based requirements applicable to new sources).

23. *Id.* at 43,830 (discussing netting for new sources).

attainment and non-attainment areas. Firms realize additional savings by avoiding the costs and delays associated with the permitting process. A review of the quantitative data that attempts to calculate the magnitude of the cost savings of netting appears in Hahn & Hester, Where Did All the Markets Go? An Analysis of EPA's Emissions Trading Program, 6 Yale J. on Reg. 109, 114, 132-136 (1989). They conclude that the average savings on emissions control when a technology-based standard (such as BACT or LAER) is avoided range from $100,000 to $1 million. The savings attributed to avoidance of the permit process is estimated to range from $5,000 to $25,000.

Netting has the most significant environmental downside of the various emissions trading devices. Unlike bubbles and offsets, netting can and often does result in net increases in emissions. The crux of the reasoning that allows emissions to increase is that modifications in emissions that amount to less than the addition of a new major source do not significantly harm air quality. Is this premise defensible? The threshold amount of emissions that qualify as a major source for many facilities is 100 tons per year and may be as great as 250 tons per year. See Clean Air Act §169(1), 42 U.S.C.A. §7479(1).

2. The history of bubbles. Bubbles, and the emissions trading program more generally, were not clearly addressed by the original 1970 Clean Air Act, they were introduced administratively by the EPA. Emissions trading was controversial because it permitted what environmental groups saw as a form of backsliding from the strict technology-based commands of the Clean Air Act. The pivotal legal issue in the bubble controversy became the interpretation given to the statutory term "stationary source." A plantwide definition (or larger) would allow bubbles; if the definition was restricted to a single smokestack, bubbling would not be allowed. EPA's determination to adopt the wider definition (for many, but not all circumstances) was upheld by the Supreme Court in Chevron U.S.A., Inc., v. NRDC, 467 U.S. 837, (1984), at page 589 *supra*.

3. Trading emissions rights in non-attainment areas. Recalling that non-attainment areas are, by definition, areas where the air is not clean enough to protect health (primary NAAQS) or welfare (secondary NAAQS), is it sensible to allow any ERCs to be traded as "surplus" when the air itself is still too dirty? Congress, in the 1977 amendments, took this into account by requiring that offsets exceed new emissions by an amount sufficient to constitute "reasonable further progress" toward attainment. In this way a degree of continued growth was allowed in those regions while air quality improved.

Even in the absence of net reductions in air emissions, trading in non-attainment areas can be defended as efficient: trades make a bad air quality situation no worse, while at least reducing the total social cost of creating the problem. Why is this second argument flawed? Is there a basic flaw in the trading concept, or is it that baselines (the amount of pollution allowed under existing permits) are too generous?

4. Interfirm trading. Robert Hahn and Gordon Hester have been the most vigorous students of emissions trading to date and they have collected considerable empirical evidence about the extent to which trades have taken place. They recount much of that material in Hahn & Hester, Where Did All the Markets Go? An Analysis of EPA's Emissions Trading Program, 6 Yale J. on Reg. 109, 114, 119-32 (1989). As the title suggests, trading has not flourished. Offsets, the only mandatory trading device, were used approximately 2,000 times nationwide in the ten-year period from 1977 to 1986. By 1986, only 42 bubbles had been approved, with a little more than twice that number pending or proposed. Netting has been far and away the most common type of trading, with a probable number of 8,000 instances in the decade from 1974 to 1984. Quite significantly, most of the bubbles, and by definition all netting, is internal to the firm. Likewise, many offsets were also internal rather than external trades among firms. Not surprisingly (given the low volume of interfirm trades), there was very little evidence of active banking.

What explains the low level of interfirm trading? Is it the higher transaction cost of locating an external trading partner in comparison to making internal (intrafirm) changes? Is it the novelty of emissions trading? Is it the lack of true markets in which ERCs are freely bought and sold? Does the EPA requirement that trades involve only emission reductions that are surplus, enforceable, permanent, and quantifiable set too high a threshold for most trades to take place?

5. Offsetting improvements that would take place anyway. Review the *CARE* case that appeared *supra* at page 813 and recall the stringent requirements for non-attainment area SIPs discussed there. Could the switch from cutback asphalt to emulsified asphalt in the *CARE* case be considered a "reasonably available control measure" that is required to be a part of a valid hydrocarbon non-attainment plan under §7502(b)(2)? If so, how would that improve CARE's attack on the allowance of the switch as an offset? Are the ERCs employed here "surplus, enforceable, permanent, and quantifiable."

Was EPA too permissive with Virginia in the *CARE* case – so permissive that it violated the statutory "reasonable further progress" requirement for non-attainment areas? Why, for example, didn't EPA on its own initiative insist on the use of emulsified asphalt when to do so would have reduced hydrocarbon emissions in the non-attainment area and have saved Virginia money at the same time?

6. Offsets pro and con. Are offsets a good method of accommodating further development while still seeking improvement of ambient air quality in non-attainment areas? In the absence of state intervention in aid of the new source, either like that given in the *CARE* case or in the form of placing tighter controls on existing sources, can you predict which emissions reductions will be realized first? Presumably, the operator of the new source will have to purchase the retirement of pollution sources. The least expensive retirements will involve taking marginally profitable enterprises out of production, or paying for pollution control improvements at those sites where the least expenditure produces the greatest reduction. To the extent that practice mirrors the prediction of theory, offsets obtain an apparently optimal result of reducing pollution at the lowest possible cost. Are there social costs that are overlooked in that assessment? What about the dislocation of workers who lose their jobs when marginal firms are bought out and closed? Perhaps it could be argued, for many of them, that the firm's survival was unlikely in any event.

D. USING TRADEABLE EMISSION ALLOWANCES TO REDUCE ACID DEPOSITION

The Clean Air Act Amendments of 1990, Pub. L. 101-549 (1990), revamped the Clean Air Act in many ways. Among the most novel is the establishment of a system of tradeable emissions allowances designed to achieve a 10 million ton per year reduction in SO_2 emissions by the year 2000. This represents more than a 50 percent reduction in the emission of SO_2 for sources so regulated in comparison with 1980 levels. The purpose of the wholesale reduction is to combat acid rain and other forms of deposition.

EPA, Title IV Acid Deposition Program,

in ABA, Implementing the 1990 Clean Air Act: EPA Speaks 51–57
February 21, 1991

SO_2 Allowances – Basic Program. The legislation obtains SO_2 emissions reductions from electric utility plants through the use of a market based system of emission allowances. Under this system, "affected units" (essentially all utility boilers that serve generators larger than 25 megawatts (MW)) are allocated allowances in an amount which is based on their past fossil fuel consumption and the emissions rate required by the legislation. An allowance is defined as an authorization allocated to an affected unit, to emit, during or after a specified calendar year, one ton of SO_2. Any new utility units which commence operation after December 31, 1995 are not allocated allowances and must obtain allowances sufficient to cover their emission by January 1, 2000 and thereafter. Industrial sources may also become affected sources by electing to opt-in to the allowance system.

Allowance Holding Requirement. Affected sources are required to hold sufficient allowances to cover their level of emissions. Allowances may not be used prior to the calendar year for which they are allocated. Sources may not exceed emission limitations provided in the law unless the owner or operator obtains and holds additional allowances to emit excess tons of SO_2. However, the fact that an affected source holds excess allowances does not entitle it to exceed the National Ambient Air Quality Standard limits.

Penalties for Non-Compliance. Sources whose emissions exceed allowances held will be required to pay $2000 per excess ton, and will be required to offset excess tons the following year.

Allowance Usage. Once allocated, allowances can be used by affected sources to cover emissions, banked for future use, or sold to others. Allowances transferred to others are not effective until a written certification of transfer from the parties involved is received and recorded by EPA. No permit alteration is required.

Allowance Tracking. EPA will develop a system for issuing, recording and tracking allowances.

Cap on SO_2 Emissions/Allowances Allocated. Beginning in 2000, the total number of allowances issued by EPA to utility units is, with limited exceptions, not to exceed 8.9 million allowances. This effectively caps emissions and ensures maintenance of the 10 million ton SO_2 reduction....

SO_2 Reduction Program. SO_2 reductions are obtained in two phases.

Phase I Reductions. Phase I reductions are required by January 1, 1995 from 111 plants listed in the legislation. These plants have large units – 100 MWs or more – and have high emission rates – 2.5 lbs/mmBtu or more.[24] There will be approximately 265 affected units in these Phase I plants. Phase I plants are located in 21 eastern and midwestern states.

Phase I Allowance Allocations. Phase I affected units will be issued allowances as reflected in the legislation. The allocation was based on a 2.5 lbs/mmBtu emission rate, multiplied by their "baseline," the average fossil fuel consumed during the years 1985, 1986, and 1987....

Phase II Reductions. In Phase II, which begins on January 1, 2000, the emissions limits imposed on Phase I plants are tightened, and emissions limits are imposed on smaller, cleaner plants as well. In general, all utility plants emitting at a rate above 1.2 lbs/mmBtu will have to reduce their emissions to a level equal to 1.2 lbs/mmBtu multiplied by their baseline....

Special Reserve for EPA Allowance Sales and Auctions. EPA is to create an allowance reserve by tapping each affected source's allocation 2.8 percent during 1995-99, and 2.8 percent of the basic Phase II allocation for each year beginning in 2000. These allowances are to be set aside for EPA allowance sales and auctions.

Allowance Sales. A portion of the allowances in the reserve established above are to be put in a direct sale subaccount and sold by EPA in accordance with EPA regulations. The proceeds of the allowance sales are to be returned to the affected units on a pro rata basis.... Unsold allowances are to be transferred to the auction subaccount (discussed below)....

EPA Direct Allowance Sales. EPA will offer for sale allowances...[in accordance with a schedule[25]]. They shall be offered at a price of $1500 per allowance (CPI adjusted). Sales are to be made on a first come first served basis subject to the priority for Independent Power Producers....

Allowance Auctions. EPA is to establish a subaccount in the allowance reserve for auctions.... Auctions will be open to any person, and will be carried out by sealed bid, with sales based on bid price. No minimum bid will be established. Auction proceeds will be transferred to affected units contributing to the reserve on a pro rata basis, and allowances held for auction which were not sold at the auction will be returned to contributing affected units on a pro rata basis.[26]

---

24. Eds: The emission rates are measured in pounds of SO2 emitted per million British thermal units of heat produced (mmBtu). It is widely conceded that fossil fired power plants can, using widely available techniques and technologies, meet a standard of 1.2 lbs/mmBtu. Some plants using low sulfur fuel can achieve rates as low as .3 lbs/mmBtu.

25. Eds: The schedule calls for advance sale of 25,000 allowances per year for each year beginning in 1993 and spot sales of an additional 25,000 allowances in 2000 and each year thereafter. Spot sale allowances must be used in the year of the sale unless banked. Advance sale allowances may only be used in the 7th year following the sale unless banked.

26. Eds: There is also a schedule for the number of allowances to be offered at auction. Like the direct sales schedule it is bifurcated between spot auction of current year allowances and advance auction of allowances good in the 7th year after the auction. In general, 150,000 allowances are offered in the spot auction in each year beginning in 1995 and 100,000 allowances are offered in the advance auction.

COMMENTARY AND QUESTIONS

1. Untangling the acid deposition program. Before going forward, you must be sure that you understand how Title IV of the 1990 Clean Air Act Amendments creates a market in tradeable emissions allowances for SO_2. The key elements are (1) the allowances, (2) the means by which EPA limits their total number, (3) the initial distribution of the allowances and, (4) the means by which allowances are redistributed.

2. Will the allowance system eliminate acid deposition? The allowance system appears likely to reduce SO_2 emissions substantially. The penalties for excess emissions ($2,000 per ton) may be inconsequential to a large entity such as a power plant, but the offset requirement for the following year means that the offending firm must obtain allowances and apply them against the previous year's excess emissions in addition to paying the fine. Even if this cost is modest, applying the allowances to "retire" the excess means that the total multi-year pollution remains limited to the number of allowances. The larger question of whether the 10 million ton reduction will be sufficient to alleviate the acid deposition problem is somewhat less certain. It is surely a huge step in the right direction.

3. Title IV as prototype. If tradeable emissions allowances work to solve the acid deposition problem, will the same sort of system work with equal facility to reduce the emission of pollutants other than SO_2? There are many ways in which the SO_2 situation is unique. First, the class of major SO_2 emitters regulated by Phase I numbers only 111 and all are in the same business, burning fossil fuels to produce electricity. It is an industry that has been extensively studied and the technological options for emission reduction are all quite well-known and widely available. Most importantly, the net reductions sought are attainable if each plant employs what amounts to BAT (i.e. emissions control that will reduce effluents to 1.2 lbs/mmBTU).

EPA's most successful emissions trading program in the 1980s was its lead trading program that allowed gasoline refiners "greater flexibility in meeting emissions standards during a period when the amount of lead in gasoline was being reduced significantly." Hahn & Stavins, Incentive-Based Environmental Regulation: A New Era from an Old Idea?, 18 Ecol. L. Q. 1, 17 (1991). By producing gasoline with lower lead content than required, refiners earned credits which they could use at a later date for their own products that might exceed the then-current standard, or sell to other refiners. Over half of the nation's refineries participated in the trading program, at an estimated 20 percent savings over costs that would have been incurred without the trading program.[27] To what extent is Title IV of the 1990 Clean Air Act Amendments similar to this lead credit system? First, there is clear definition of the class of potential traders. Second, the credits available for trading can be precisely quantified. Third, There is free transferability of credits without

27. Id., citing EPA, Costs and Benefits of Reducing Lead in Gasoline, Final Regulatory Impact Analysis VIII-31 (1985).

reference to the situs of origin of the credits or their use. The long-term stability of regulatory climate is also important, supporting traders' confidence in their assessment of the value of credits.

4. The cost of Title IV. The Congressional Budget Office estimated in 1986 that achieving the mandated 10 million ton reduction in electric utility SO_2 reductions would increase annual electric costs by $3.2 to 4.7 billion.[28] As a national average, this amounts to an increase in electric costs of between 2 percent and 5 percent. In some midwestern states, however, the average increase in electric cost would be as much as 10 percent.[29] The attractiveness of fuel switching away from high sulfur coal as a means of coping with the new law may cause further social costs in the dislocation of up to 30,000 miners in high sulfur coal areas such as West Virginia, Ohio, and Indiana.

The future costs of maintaining the new status quo will fall disproportionately on new sources of pollution. More stringent control of new sources has always been a hallmark of the Clean Air Act. Under Title IV, new sources coming on line before the turn of the century will receive allowances based on a .3 lbs/mmBtu basis and will be granted allowances for only 65 percent of their designed capacity. Accordingly, new units will immediately be seeking to purchase allowances. Plants coming on linc after the year 2000 will be granted no allowances whatever and will have to seek them in the marketplace.

5. The local/long-distance dichotomy. Acid deposition, the principal target of Title IV, is a long range transport problem. Recall the facts of Air Pollution Control District v. EPA, 739 F.2d 1071 (6th Cir. 1984), discussed at page 822 *supra* . There, the local effects of emissions from coal burning power plants on attainment of the SO_2 NAAQS in the Louisville, Kentucky area was quite minimal. The power plants there (and elsewhere) emitted their effluents through tall stacks that tend to export the pollution far downwind. The bulk of local SO_2 pollution was emitted by other, purely local sources. This situation permits Title IV to be effective without having to include all local sources of pollution in the allowance system. Conversely, units regulated under Title IV, primarily long-distance polluters, are likely to have only minor local impacts on NAAQS attainment. In the event there are local effects, however, non-attainment of NAAQS is not excused by the purchase of additional SO_2 allowances.

6. The marketplace: EPA sales and auctions. The direct sales and the auction programs are both "stocked" with allowances borrowed from "affected units." Why is that the case? Does this resemble a sort of rebate like the previously discussed Chinese effluent charges system? What is the difference between the direct sales program and the auction program? The obvious answer is that the sales take place

---

28. Congressional Budget Office, Curbing Acid Rain: Cost, Budget, and Coal-Market Effects 7 (1986).

29. Congressional Office of Technology Assessment, Acid Rain and Transported Air Pollutants: Implications for Public Policy 14 (1984).

at a predetermined price ($1,500), while the auction price is wholly a function of bids received. If a major motivation of Title IV is to embrace emissions trading as a market method for allocating allowances, what is the role of the fixed price sales? Do they "protect" firms that might be unable to match the prices bid at auction? Should those firms be protected? Do fixed price sales provide a hedge against excessive pollution abatement costs for firms that are risk averse?

How well do you think the new pollution market will work? Do you think that many firms will improve their pollution control equipment beyond the de facto year 2000 norm of 1.2 lbs/mmBtu and seek to market their excess allowances? The answer, of course, depends on the price that other firms are willing to pay for additional allowances. Do the EPA sale and auction programs, by increasing the supply of allowances available for purchase, tend to depress the value of directly marketed allowances? Is that counter-productive? If demand for allowances is thin, the price will fall and firms will lose incentives to reduce pollution. Can environmental groups step in effectively at auction and try to buy allowances for the sake of retiring them without use? The fluidity of the market system has been greatly aided by the Chicago Board of Trade's decision in July 1991 to create a private market in SO_2 emission rights.

7. Distributive consequences. As noted above, the greatest costs of Title IV will fall on the Midwest, a result that is not patently unfair in light of that region's prominence in creating the acid deposition problem. Does the legislation treat those states too leniently? Many politicians in western states took that view. See generally, Recent Developments, The Clean Air Act Amendments of 1990 and the Use of Market Forces to Control Sulfur Dioxide Emissions, 28 Harv. J. on Legis. 235, 245-252 (1991).

A second distributive aspect of Title IV is the intra-utility distribution of allowances. The use of a baseline keyed to actual emissions during the baseline period leads to large emitters being granted a larger number of allowances than cleaner plants. Is that fair? For an answer in the negative, see A. Sholtz & K. Chilton, Acid Rain and Tradeable Permits: How Congress Hobbles the Power of the Marketplace, 14-15 (Paper OP83, Center for the Study of American Business, May 1990).

8. The greater complexity of Title IV. The description of Title IV that appears in these materials has deliberately by-passed much of its rich detail. Its exceptions to the normal rules for allocating allowances, and other interesting twists, have been omitted in an effort to keep the outlines of the mechanism clear. As you might imagine, political log-rolling played an important part in crafting some of the special provisions. Some states, for example, were granted a number of surplus allowances. Firms that do not switch away from eastern high sulfur coal as a fuel were entitled to special consideration, and so on. Another topic addressed in Title IV was control of NO_x (nitrogen oxides, another source of acid deposition) using technology-based standards and an emissions fee like the one employed for excess SO_2 emissions.

9. From emissions credits to free market environmentalism. In a book that is a self-described "Berlitz course in free market environmentalism," a series of anecdotal episodes of market incentives leading to positive environmental outcomes are offered as evidence that "voluntary exchange of property rights between consenting owners...promotes cooperation and compromise...[and] offers an alternative that channels the heightened environmental consciousness into win-win solutions that can sustain economic growth, enhance environmental quality and promote harmony." T. Anderson & D. Leal, Free Market Environmentalism 8 (1991).

At least one commentator thinks that

> Decision-making in environmental markets must [necessarily] be inefficient because decentralized market actors ordinarily lack the environmental information necessary to make choices in line with their preferences. Thus the remedy for inefficient environmental regulation will generally be *better government*, not a reversion to primary reliance on market transactions. Latin, Environmental Deregulation and Consumer Decisionmaking Under Uncertainty, 6 Harv. Envt'l L. Rev. 187, 190 (1982).

Having studied material in this chapter and Chapter 2 on economics and the use of market incentives, is the pollution market approach the cure-all for the future? If not, what areas of environmental law seem best suited for free market approaches?

10. Market incentives in the natural resource setting. The market incentive systems studied in this chapter focus on pollution control. Do they have a place in resource management? During James Watt's tenure at Interior numerous efforts were made to allow market decisionmaking to replace federal resource management planning: proposals for wholesale transfer of parts of the public domain into private ownership, plans to give a freer hand to concessionaires in the National Park system, etc. Although these initiatives were blunted, they were not unprecedented. The federal government has long believed in "privatizing" resources, giving them away or transferring them at rates below market value: mining rights, grazing leases, oil exploration leases, timber rights, and park concessions. In these programs the government is typically driven by non-market political incentives, and as a consequence may be accused even in economic terms of managing the resources in a sub-optimal way. Ongoing federal forest controversies noted at page 680 *supra* may force a rethinking of such programs.

The question remains whether economic incentives and privatization would in any setting be effective methods for managing what are presently public resources administered by federal bureaucracy. What in the resource management field would be a meaningful analogy to effluent taxes or transferrable emissions credits (or other forms of economic incentive program)?

Chapter 21

A STATUTORY SYSTEM FOR MANAGING AND FUNDING ENVIRONMENTAL REMEDIATION: CERCLA (SUPERFUND)

The Comprehensive Environmental Response, Compensation and Liability Act (CERCLA) was studied previously in Chapter 6 as a statutory example for discussing the interplay between common law and legislation. Those materials primarily explored CERCLA's liability rules developed through the judicial process of statutory interpretation. The purpose here is quite different. In this chapter, CERCLA is examined as an administrative system for environmental remediation – removing harmful materials improperly dumped into the environment over past years. In this context, what is important are matters of process and execution: identifying sites in need of environmental cleanups, setting priorities among the needed cleanup efforts, planning what actions are needed on a site-by-site basis, and insuring that planned responses are properly executed. Additionally, owing to the magnitude and expense of the hazardous waste remediation problem, funding the cleanups is a major concern that has shaped both statutory and administrative efforts in the field.

A. IDENTIFYING SITES, FUNDING, AND SETTING THE STANDARDS FOR CLEANUPS

CERCLA is a straightforward statute in many respects (although it will soon become apparent that it proceeds in a cavalcade of bewildering acronyms). CERCLA applies principally to situations in which significant environmental damage has already occurred.[1] It begins with a procedure for identifying and ranking the hazards posed by sites of hazardous materials contamination. On the basis of that hazard ranking system (HRS), CERCLA establishes a national priorities list (NPL) that then functions to ensure that the most dangerous sites are remediated first. CERCLA requires EPA to establish a National Contingency Plan, which is, in essence, a compendium of the standards and procedures for cleanups that will insure an acceptable result. Cleanups are of two kinds: removals are short-term measures taken to minimize the dangers to health and the environment from emergency situations, whereas remedial actions are long-term efforts that attempt to rid the site of dangers on a permanent basis. CERCLA authorizes EPA to arrange for cleanup

---

1. Most CERCLA cases involve cleanups of materials that have already been released into the environment. By its literal terms, §106 authorizes EPA to act via lawsuit or administrative order against "actual *or threatened* release of a hazardous substance...." CERCLA §106(a), 42 U.S.C.A. §9606(a)(emphasis added), but to date, there appear to be few, if any, invocations of §106 that are wholly prospective in character. Instead, §106 is being used to keep past releases from getting worse.

on its own, or to order parties responsible for contamination to undertake cleanups. In the event the EPA undertakes the cleanup, CERCLA establishes a large fund (the Superfund) from which the expenses of cleanup are to be paid, and mechanisms for EPA to sue responsible parties for reimbursement to the fund if they can be identified and have sufficient assets.

The Superfund currently obtains its money from a surtax assessed against large companies (incomes over $2 million per year) and taxes on petroleum and chemical feedstocks. These sums are supplemented by a relatively small amount of general revenue money,[2] plus interest on money held in the fund and money recovered by EPA from potentially responsible parties (PRPs). On a periodic basis, Congress authorizes EPA to make drafts on the fund up to a specified limit. At the end of CERCLA's first decade, that limit stood at $8.5 billion.[3]

This relatively simple statutory mechanism addresses an important public concern. Public perception of the health risks stemming from exposure to hazardous materials ranks that problem as a very serious one. The publicity given to Love Canal and the plight of the families who lived there had galvanized public opinion in favor of a strong cleanup law. The enormity of the cleanup problem, although not fully known at the time of CERCLA's initial passage in 1980, was understood to require a multi-billion dollar effort. The creation of the fund deemphasized issues of cost as an impediment to cleanups. By being able to draw on the fund, EPA was given the ability to act quickly to relieve public health threats at a contamination site – even in cases where the parties who created the problem could no longer be identified, had insufficient means to undertake the cleanup, or were recalcitrant and refused to take the steps desired by EPA. The subsequent reimbursement of the fund by parties responsible for contamination would both replenish the fund and internalize the costs of inadequate hazardous waste disposal back to the parties who had benefitted from those practices.

Generally, CERCLA has worked as expected. The HRS has been used to identify sites and subsequently generate the NPL that serves as the principal means of dictating EPA's cleanup priorities. EPA, through a combination of Superfund money and PRP-funded response and remedial actions, has made progress in the remediation of numerous sites throughout the nation.

CERCLA's major miscalculation has been its gross underestimation of cleanup costs. By 1986, when the Superfund Amendment and Reauthorization Act (SARA) was passed,[4] it was clear that the fund's original $3.5 billion would be insufficient to meet all of EPA's needs. Not only had EPA identified far more NPL sites than had been anticipated in 1980, but the average cost of site remediation had proven to be far more than expected. EPA, moreover, did not have a great deal of success in recouping its cleanup outlays from PRPs. Indeed, recoupment figures for CERCLA's first decade of operation proved alarmingly low. Although it had spent or obligated itself to expenditures totalling more than $4 billion, EPA had successfully recovered

2. CERCLA §111(p), 42 U.S.C.A. §9611(p).
3. CERCLA §111(a), 42 U.S.C.A. §9611(a).
4. Pub. L. 99-499 (1986), 42 U.S.C.A. §§9601–9675 et al. (Supp IV 1986).

only $230 million from PRPs.[5] Congress responded to the situation by reauthorizing the law and providing an increase in funding for the 1986 to 1991 five-year period to $8.5 billion. EPA altered its regulatory methodology to rely more heavily on PRP-funded and performed cleanups; see page 902 *infra*. Even these responses may be insufficient in the face of newer estimates that the total cost for U.S. hazardous waste cleanup will fall in the range of $300 to $700 billion.[6]

In seeking to use CERCLA to obtain private cleanups (and in cases where EPA is seeking reimbursement of the fund), EPA is greatly assisted by broad judicial interpretations of CERCLA's vague statutory liability provisions, studied in Chapter 6. The courts have held that CERCLA relaxes the typical proof of causation requirements associated with tort cases while at the same time imposing strict, joint and several liability for releases on a very broad class of parties. PRPs include past and present generators, transporters, and owners and operators of treatment, storage, and disposal (TSD) facilities. The boundaries of those categories (especially the owner/operator categories) are quite broad, being held to include even parties who loaned money or other assets to a PRP if those parties played an active role in the management of the firm. The definition of a PRP also includes individuals acting within a corporate structure who have the authority to control corporate actions.

For at least the coming decade, an exciting and intensely fought aspect of hazardous materials regulation will be CERCLA cleanups. There are billions of dollars to be paid by PRPs, as thousands of sites of hazardous material releases are remediated. For many lawyers representing PRPs, the problem is less one of environmental law than it is one of engaging in strategic behavior to minimize the share of the cleanup cost allocated to their clients. EPA, too, is engaged in a strategic process, whereby it seeks to accomplish as much of the massive cleanup job as it can with limited human and material resources.

As with most other federal environmental statutes, EPA is the agency principally charged with the administration of CERCLA. Its statutory duties begin under §105 with the creation of the National Contingency Plan (NCP) that serves as the coordinating document of the federal effort to respond to hazardous waste releases. In the NCP, EPA is to "establish procedures and standards for responding to releases of hazardous substances, pollutants, and contaminants...." The statutorily mandated scope of the NCP includes methodologies that will identify sites in need of remediation, analyze the danger to health and the environment posed by releases and threatened releases, determine the scope and extent of needed remedial measures, and insure that remedial actions are cost-effective.[7] The NCP must address such mundane matters as the procurement and maintenance of response equipment, and the qualifications of private cleanup firms that will be engaged to do the cleanup work on Superfund projects. More politically sensitive matters must also be covered by the NCP. These include the division of authority between the

---

5. See J. Acton, Understanding Superfund: A Progress Report 37, 46–47 (1989). Acton reported that EPA had either filed claims for, or sought prosecution by the Department of Justice for, recoveries that would total another $824 million.

6. See Passell, Experts Question Staggering Costs of Toxic Cleanups, New York Times (national edition), Sept. 1, 1991, at page 1.

7. CERCLA §105(a)(1)–(3), (7), 42 U.S.C.A. §9605(a)(1)–(3),(7).

federal, state, and local governments in effectuating the plan, and the standards by which innovative cleanup technologies will be judged.[8]

The required priority ranking of sites in order of hazard (i.e., the HRS/NPL process) is also a part of the NCP. In this area, Congress has provided some general directions for EPA. EPA, for example, is required to revise the NPL to reflect new information about existing and additional sites.[9] Similarly, CERCLA specifies that the relative risk assessment under the HRS should include the extent of the population put at risk by the site, the hazard potential of the substances found at the site, the potential to contaminate groundwater or surface water that is used for either drinking water supply or recreation, the potential for direct human contact, the potential for the destruction of natural resources that affect the human food chain, state preparedness, and "other appropriate factors."[10]

Finally, the statute puts EPA in charge of obtaining the needed cleanups of sites on the NPL in ways that are consistent with the NCP. In this regard, EPA is empowered to (1) undertake cleanups itself, using Superfund monies, and to seek reimbursement from PRPs; (2) issue administrative orders to PRPs directing them to undertake cleanups; (3) seek court orders directing PRPs to undertake cleanups; or (4) use a combination of approaches.

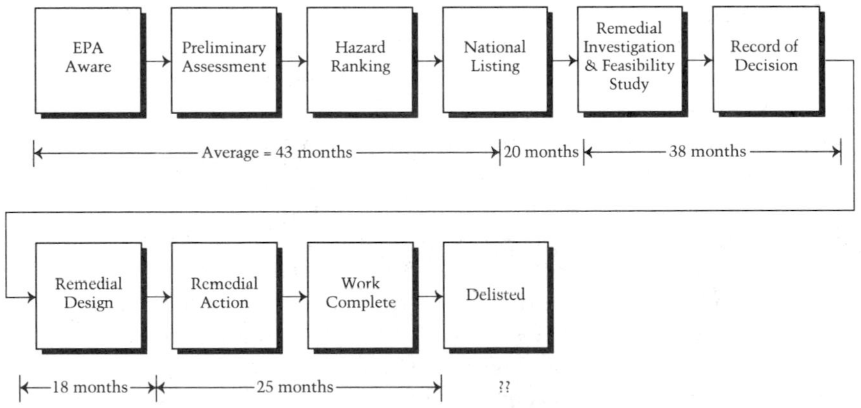

SOURCE: J.P. ACTON, UNDERSTANDING SUPERFUND: A PROGRESS REPORT 16 (RAND CORPORATION INSTITUTE FOR CIVIL JUSTICE, 1989).

Average time between principal steps in the Superfund process

After an uneven start,[11] EPA made extensive efforts to regularize Superfund procedures to insure that all sites receive a thorough investigation and that decisions about remedial actions at each site are made by reference to consistent

8. CERCLA §105(a)(5)–(6), (9)–(10), 42 U.S.C.A. §9605(a)(5)–(6), (9)–(10).

9. CERCLA §105(a)(8), 42 U.S.C.A. §9605(a)(8).

10. CERCLA §105(a)(8)(A), (c)(2), 42 U.S.C.A. §(a)(8)(A), (c)(2).

11. During the Reagan presidency, when extensive government regulation and intervention was ideological anathema, EPA was not allowed to take an active role under Superfund. In fact, Superfund's misadministration by EPA in the early 1980s was a source of scandal, and several EPA officials were criminally prosecuted and convicted. This period in EPA's CERCLA history is recounted in detail in Mintz, Agencies, Congress, and Regulatory Enforcement: A Review of EPA Hazardous Waste Enforcement Effort, 1970-1987, 18 Envtl. Law 683, 715–43 (1988).

principles – focusing in each case on a site study document known as a Remedial Investigation/Feasibility Study (RI/FS). After the study and analysis is complete, EPA issues a record of decision (ROD) that selects the principal remedial actions to be taken. An even more detailed remedial design (RD) is prepared and, finally, remedial activity begins. The diagram on the previous page shows the major steps in the CERCLA process and the average duration of each of those steps.

Starfield, The 1990 National Contingency Plan – More Detail and More Structure, But Still a Balancing Act

20 Environmental Law Reporter 10222, 10228–10229, 10236–10241 (1990)

A ROAD MAP TO THE CERCLA SITE RESPONSE PROCESS

(SUBPART E [OF THE NCP])

Site Discovery. The process begins with the discovery of a release by one of several possible mechanisms (e.g., notification requirements under CERCLA §103(a) or (b) under other laws, a petition from a citizen, etc.). In the case of an emergency (e.g., fire, explosion), a removal action will be taken to stabilize the site.

Removal Assessment. In non-emergency situations, the release is evaluated to determine if a removal action is appropriate based on a removal preliminary assessment (PA) and, if appropriate, a removal site inspection (SI).

Removal Action. Where necessary to protect human health and the environment, the Agency may initiate a removal action to prevent, mitigate, or minimize the threat posed by the release. This may involve removal of surface drums, fencing of the site, the provision of temporary drinking water supplies, etc. Removals may be emergency actions (taken within hours of discovery), time-critical actions, or non-time-critical actions.

Remedial Site Evaluation. A remedial PA (and SI, where appropriate) is conducted on all sites in the CERCLA Information System database (CERCLIS), to see if the site is a priority for long-term remedial response. These evaluations involve the collection of data for scoring the site under the hazard ranking system (HRS) model; sites scoring above the threshold in the HRS are placed on the national priorities list (NPL) for further evaluation and possible remedial action.

Remedial Priorities. The Agency evaluates releases for inclusion on the NPL based on the HRS score or one of the other methods for listing outlined in the NCP. The Agency may spend Fund monies for remedial action only at those sites that are on the NPL. ("Fund-financed remedial action" does not include removal action or enforcement action.)

Remedial Investigation/Feasibility Study. The Agency will undertake a remedial investigation and feasibility study (RI/FS) at sites that are, or appear to be, priorities for action (i.e., that are on, or are proposed for listing on, the NPL). The RI/FS, like any other investigation conducted pursuant to CERCLA §104(b), is a removal action under CERCLA §101(23), despite the word remedial in its name.

During the RI, the nature and extent of the threat posed by the contamination is studied; concurrently, alternative approaches are developed as part of the FS for responding to and managing the site problem.

Preliminary Remediation Goal. The first step in developing alternatives during the FS is the establishment of a preliminary goal for the remediation of the site. This goal is initially based on readily available information, such as chemical-specific applicable, relevant and appropriate requirements of other environmental laws (ARARs), or the "point of departure" in the range of acceptable risk. Alternatives are then developed that are capable of attaining the preliminary remediation goal. (The goal may be modified as additional information is developed.)

Screening of Remedial Alternatives. A broad list of alternatives is then reviewed and screened, with the more extreme, impracticable options being eliminated before the detailed analysis of alternatives begins. Alternatives may be eliminated during screening based on effectiveness, implementability, or "grossly excessive" cost.

Analysis of Alternatives Using the Nine Criteria. The Agency then conducts a detailed analysis of the remaining alternatives (usually three to nine [of them], depending on the complexity of the problem). The advantages and disadvantages of the alternatives are studied and compared using the following nine remedy selection criteria:[12]

- Overall protection of human health and the environment;
- Compliance with (or waiver of) the ARARs of other laws;
- Long-term effectiveness and permanence;
- Reduction of toxicity, mobility, or volume through treatment;
- Short-term effectiveness;
- Implementability;
- Cost;
- State acceptance; and
- Community acceptance.

Selection of Remedy. The nine criteria are then used to select the remedy by evaluating them in three functional categories (threshold, balancing, and modifying criteria), in order to reflect the nature and/or timing of their application. The first two criteria – protectiveness and compliance with ARARs – are identified as threshold criteria; only the alternatives that meet those criteria may be carried forward.

Protective, ARAR-compliant alternatives are then "balanced" (i.e., used to evaluate tradeoffs) based on the middle five criteria (and the two modifying criteria, to the extent they are known). The Agency then attempts to select the remedial alternative that "utilizes permanent solutions and treatment...to the maximum extent practicable," and is "cost-effective" based on a comparison of the appropriate balancing or modifying criteria. Alternatives are judged cost-effective if their costs are "in proportion" to their overall effectiveness; an alternative is found to achieve the maximum permanence and treatment practicable based on a balancing of the seven nonthreshold criteria, with an emphasis on the factors of "long-term effectiveness and permanence" and "reduction in mobility, toxicity or volume through treatment."

EPA and the state then discuss the remedial options and issue a proposed plan, which sets out the lead agency's recommended alternative. Consistent with CERCLA §117, the public is afforded an opportunity to review and comment on the alternatives studied in the FS and the proposed plan. After review of and response to public comments, and formal consideration of the two modifying criteria (state

12. NCP §300.430(e)(9).

and community acceptance), the final remedy selection is documented in a record of decision (ROD).

Remedial Design/Remedial Action and Operation and Maintenance. The lead agency then sets about designing, constructing, and implementing the selected remedy. Often, the remedial action plan set out in the ROD will need to be modified in light of information developed during the design phase (e.g., the Agency may learn that more soil is contaminated and needs to be excavated). If the remedial action to be taken differs "significantly" from the remedy selected in the ROD with respect to scope, performance, or cost, the lead agency will issue an explanation of significant differences (ESD). If the action to be taken "fundamentally alters" the basic features of the remedy selected in the ROD, the lead agency will propose and take comment on a ROD amendment.

Once the remedy is operational and functional (or later, for groundwater restoration remedies), the state undertakes responsibility for funding and carrying out operation and maintenance (O&M) of the remedy.

Deletion From the NPL, Five-Year Review. Once EPA has determined that no further response action is appropriate, the site may be proposed for deletion, or recategorized on the NPL, even where O&M is continuing. Sites at which hazardous substances remain above levels that allow for unlimited use and unrestricted exposure must be reviewed at least every five years after the initiation of the remedy (not merely after completion), consistent with CERCLA §121(c)....

MAJOR ISSUES/CHANGES IN THE 1990 NCP

ARARs Issues. There were several major changes and statements in the final NCP revisions relating to ARARs, the "applicable" or "relevant and appropriate" requirements of other environmental laws. How CERCLA actions comply with ARARs often determines the cleanup standard at a site or certain parameters that the remedial approach must fulfill. Thus, a discussion of major ARARs issues is an important starting point in a review of the final NCP.

Background. As defined in the final rule, "applicable" requirements are cleanup standards, standards of control, and other substantive environmental protection requirements, criteria, or limitations promulgated under federal environmental or state environmental or facility siting laws that specifically address a hazardous substance, pollutant, contaminant, remedial action, location, or other circumstance found at a CERCLA site.

A "relevant and appropriate" requirement is a *promulgated* standard that, while not applicable to the substance, location, or action, addresses problems or situations sufficiently similar to those encountered at a CERCLA site that its use is well suited to the particular site. One example is where a federal requirement has not been adopted by a state authorized to run the federal program. Such requirement may not be applicable in the state, but it could nevertheless be relevant and appropriate to management of the CERCLA waste at issue. In another example, RCRA waste management requirements may be relevant and appropriate to a CERCLA waste that is similar to a RCRA-listed hazardous waste but is not specifically listed in the RCRA regulations (and thus to which RCRA would not independently "apply").

The concept of requiring remedies to attain relevant and appropriate standards (i.e., standards that do not independently apply as a matter of law) is unique to CERCLA and has generated controversy and confusion. (Indeed, it is somewhat counter-intuitive to be required to comply with requirements that do not apply as a matter of law.) To add some consistency to the process, the final rule offers several factors to consider in determining if a requirement is relevant and appropriate under the circumstances of the release (both findings must be made). However, the notion of what standards are appropriate is, almost by definition, a matter of judgment, subject to case-by-case variations. Thus, the Agency retains considerable discretion in making the ultimate decision of what standards a CERCLA remedy should attain based on potential relevance and appropriateness. (Of course, the decision that a remedy must attain a certain standard may be questioned during the comment period of the ROD.) This discretion is even broader in that the Agency may decide that only certain portions of a requirement are relevant and appropriate. The ability to find that a nonapplicable requirement is not appropriate has limited the instances in which statutory waivers are necessary for relevant and appropriate requirements.

There are four conditions that must be met for a requirement to be considered a potential ARAR, based either on applicability or relevance and appropriateness. First, the requirement must be promulgated (i.e., "of general applicability and enforceable"). Second, it must be a substantive – rather than administrative – requirement; CERCLA actions are required to meet only the procedures set out in the NCP (additional procedures of other laws are met where appropriate, as a matter of policy). Third, it must be a requirement of an "environmental" law, as provided in CERCLA §121(d)(2)(A)(i) and (ii); the requirements and procedures of nonenvironmental laws are simply complied with to the extent they apply – they are not considered as part of the ARARs review process under CERCLA. Fourth, ARARs are limited to on-site actions, consistent with CERCLA §121(d)(2)(A); where EPA sends wastes off site, that waste transfer must comply with the substantive and administrative requirements of applicable law (there would be no relevant and appropriate determination, and no waiver option)....

ARARs may be chemical-specific (e.g., an established level for a specific chemical in groundwater), action-specific (e.g., a land disposal restriction for RCRA hazardous wastes), or location-specific (e.g., a restriction on actions that adversely affect wetlands). Thus, the concept is much broader than that of a specific cleanup level for a site....

State ARARs Issues. The SARA amendments added the requirement that CERCLA remedial actions must comply with applicable or relevant and appropriate requirements of state environmental and facility siting laws (as well as federal environmental laws) where those requirements are promulgated, identified in a timely manner, and more stringent than those under federal law....

One of the most difficult state ARARs issues is the determination of whether legislated goals (e.g., nondegradation standards under state law) constitute substantive requirements such that they should be considered ARARs. State laws setting general goals may be considered substantive ARARs if they are promulgated and enforceable, and "directive in intent," either on their face or through regulations. For example, if a state statute prohibits the degradation of surface water below a defined level, it is directive in nature and may be an ARAR. If a state law sets forth an anti-degradation goal without regulations or direction as to how to achieve it, the Agency must decide whether the goal constitutes an ARAR (e.g., is it enforceable), and then may exercise flexibility in determining how to comply with the goal. In any case, even if a remedial response is found not to comply with a state anti-degradation ARAR during the response, an interim action waiver of the state standard may be appropriate if the ARAR will be satisfied upon completion of the total remedy for the site.

RISK ASSESSMENT AND RISK RANGE

The NCP contemplates the use of risk assessments as an integral part of the process for developing remedial alternatives that are protective of human health and the environment.

Risk analysis begins during the early stages of the RI, when a "baseline risk assessment" is performed to evaluate the risk posed by a site in the absence of any remedial action. It is based on a comparison with this no-action risk level that the lead agency will target levels of risk that will be adequately protective of human health for a particular site. The baseline risk assessment also helps to provide justification for performing remedial action at the site.

Concurrently, the lead agency would begin to set a "preliminary remediation goal" as part of the FS. The preliminary remediation goal is an initial statement of the desired endpoint concentration or risk level, and alternatives are developed that are capable of meeting that goal. It is based on readily available information, such as chemical-specific ARARs (e.g., a drinking water standard), concentrations associated with the reference doses or cancer potency factors, or the point of departure for the Agency's acceptable risk range, discussed below....

Where environmental effects are observed, EPA sets remediation goals based on environmental ARARs (where they exist) and levels based on a site-specific assessment of what is protective of the environment. For carcinogens, the establishment of an acceptable level of risk in cases where ARARs do not exist (or are not sufficiently protective) is especially sensitive, because such contaminants arguably pose a risk at almost any level of exposure (although that risk may be large or small depending on the amount and duration of the exposure and the type of carcinogen involved). Under the NCP, when remedies cannot entirely eliminate potential exposure to a carcinogen, the Agency may achieve protection of human health by selecting remedies that pose very small risks (i.e., that are within an acceptable range of risk) based on a review of reliable cancer potency information such as EPA's cancer potency factors.

In the proposed NCP, the Agency had defined the acceptable risk range as being from 10^{-4} to 10^{-7}, meaning that when the excess risk to an individual of contracting cancer due to a lifetime exposure to a certain concentration of a carcinogen falls between approximately 1 in 10,000 and 1 in 10 million, it is judged to be an acceptable exposure.[13] As a measure of additional protection, the proposal provided that there should be a "point of departure" of 10^{-6}, toward the more protective end of the scale, that should be used in setting preliminary remediation goals; if conditions warranted, the final remedy could achieve a level elsewhere within the range.[14]

The final rule maintained the point of departure of 10^{-6}, but narrowed the risk range to 10^{-4} through 10^{-6}.[15] This action was taken in response to public comment and concerns that the Superfund range went below the accepted *de minimis* level used by other EPA programs and those of other federal agencies. It also reflects the limits of available analytical techniques, which cannot effectively verify for many contaminants that concentration levels corresponding to a risk of 10^{-7} have actually been attained.

---

13. 53 Fed. Reg. 51425–26 (Dec. 21, 1988).

14. Exposure factors, uncertainty factors, and technical factors may determine where to set remedial action goals within the risk range. See 55 Fed. Reg. 51426 (Mar. 8, 1990).

15. NCP §300.430(e)(2)(i)(A)(2).

Although this change might appear to be a lessening of protection or a lessening of the Agency's commitment to protect, it is in fact likely to have minimal if any impact on the selection of remedies at Superfund sites for two reasons. First, no CERCLA remedies have selected 10^{-7} as a cleanup level to date (although one or two may have achieved it due to the efficacy of the technology). Second, the Agency has retained the discretion to select a cleanup level outside the range in appropriate circumstances (e.g., where concerns about sensitive populations, synergistic effects among chemical mixtures, etc., suggest that the remedy should attain a level below 10^{-6}).

The use of a range of acceptable risk is general practice for most government programs. As discussed below in the section on role of cost, it affords the Agency the flexibility to take into account different situations, different kinds of threats, and different kinds of technical remedies. If a single risk level had been adopted (e.g., at the more stringent end of the risk range), fewer alternatives would be expected to pass the protectiveness threshold and qualify for consideration in the balancing phase of the remedy selection process....

Role of Cost. The role of cost in remedy selection has been one of the most hotly disputed issues in the Superfund program. Many PRP groups argue that cost must be a major factor in deciding on an appropriate remedy and note that the requirement to select "cost-effective" remedies appears in CERCLA §121(a) and (b). Many environmentalists and some legislators have argued that cost is given too much emphasis in remedy selection and have posited that cost should be considered only in determining the cost-efficient method for implementing a selected remedy. In effect, they argue that the proper cleanup level for a site should be set, and then a remedy should be selected to attain that level, without consideration of cost.

In the preamble to the final rule, EPA discussed the role of cost at great length. The Agency stated that it agrees that cost should not be considered in setting the protective level in situations where a specific ARAR defines the cleanup level that must be achieved at the site (e.g., where an MCLG [maximum contaminant level goal] above zero is available for contaminants in drinkable groundwater). However, where ARARs are not available for the specific contaminants of concern (or where ARARs are not sufficiently protective), the Agency defines protectiveness in terms of the risk range, and several alternative remedial technologies may be capable of achieving protection within that range. Under such circumstances, cost may be one of the factors to consider in choosing among the available technologies.

It is important to note, however, that cost and other factors may be considered only to distinguish among alternatives that have been found to be protective of human health and the environment and in compliance with ARARs (or to have justified a waiver).

Cost is specifically considered during the final balancing process, as the Agency attempts to satisfy two statutory mandates of CERCLA §121(b)(1) by identifying the remedial alternative that utilizes "permanent solutions and treatment ... to the maximum extent practicable" while being cost-effective. These determinations are intended to be made simultaneously; however, for ease of analysis, they are discussed separately in the NCP.

Cost-Effectiveness. The determination whether a proposed remedial alternative is cost-effective is based on an evaluation of several of the nine criteria. First, overall effectiveness is assessed based on: long-term effectiveness and permanence; reduction of mobility, toxicity, or volume through treatment; and short-term effectiveness. The overall effectiveness is then compared to the cost of the alternative to determine if they are "in proportion" to one another (i.e., does the approach represent a reasonable value for the money?). In making this comparison, the decisionmaker is not directed by the NCP to place special emphasis on the factors of "reduction of toxicity, mobility or volume through treatment" and "long-term effectiveness and permanence," as is required during the assessment of permanence and treatment to the maximum extent practicable (as provided in NCP §300.430(f)(1)(ii)(E)). However, because "effectiveness" is measured based on those two factors (plus short-term effectiveness), an alternative that is high in treatment and permanence will be considered more effective and thus can justify a relatively higher cost (high effectiveness and high cost would be in proportion). The comparison of cost to effectiveness is performed for each alternative individually and for all the alternatives in relation to one another. This latter analysis allows the Agency to identify alternatives that produce an incremental increase in effectiveness for a reasonable increase in cost, based on a comparison of corresponding increases for other alternatives. Several alternatives may be found to be cost-effective.

Although the statute requires EPA to select cost-effective remedies, EPA has decided not to consider cost-effectiveness as a threshold criterion on a par with protectiveness and compliance with ARARs. This is based in part on the fact that unlike the "protectiveness" and "compliance with ARARs" determinations, which can be reached for each alternative individually, the cost-effectiveness finding requires a comparison of each alternative in relation to other alternatives and the consideration of several factors during a balancing phase. (The same comment is true of the statutory mandate to utilize permanent solutions and treatment to the maximum extent practicable.) In addition, the preamble to the final rule suggests that reliable information on cost will not be generally available as early in the process as is information on a remedial technology's protectiveness, and thus cost should not be used too early in the final balancing process to eliminate viable alternatives.[16]

Cost and Practicability. The statutory requirement to select the alternative (there is only one) that utilizes permanence and treatment to the maximum extent practicable is fulfilled by selecting the protective, ARAR-compliant alternative that provides the best balance of tradeoffs among alternatives based on a review of all the balancing and modifying criteria (if the latter are known). It is a subjective judgment, but the NCP sets out some parameters to help assure consistency in its application. Specifically, the NCP requires that during the balancing process, the factors of long-term effectiveness and permanence and reduction in toxicity, mobility, or volume should be emphasized, and that the "preference for treatment as a principal element" and the "bias against off-site land disposal of untreated wastes" must be considered. This statutory determination is the final step in the process before a remedy is recommended in the proposed plan.

Although cost, as one of the nine criteria, is considered in making this determination, it is not expected to play a major role. The importance of almost every other criterion to this determination is emphasized by the NCP....

Cost as a Screen. Cost may also be considered during one other aspect of the remedy selection process: screening, when alternatives that are deemed not to be

16. 55 Fed. Reg. 8728 (Mar. 8, 1990). This decision not to use cost as a major factor in eliminating "viable" options prior to balancing is not necessarily inconsistent with the Agency's use of cost during screening, discussed below, to eliminate extreme (nonviable) options with "grossly" excessive cost.

viable are eliminated from more thorough consideration. The use of cost at this early stage has also been the subject of considerable comment. Many were concerned that cost would be used to screen out appropriate remedial technologies early in the process before they were given a fair evaluation and without the benefit of public review and comment.

The final NCP has been revised to narrow the circumstances under which cost may be considered when screening alternatives at the start of the evaluation process. Specifically, the final rule provides that a given alternative may be eliminated during screening if it is determined that the cost of the alternative is "grossly excessive" compared with its effectiveness. This provision will allow the Agency to avoid the need to conduct resource-intensive analyses of extreme and unrealistic options, while at the same time not allowing cost to compromise consideration of viable options that may simply be more expensive than other alternatives....

COMMENTARY AND QUESTIONS

1. The slow pace of CERCLA remediation. Are you surprised at the overall average of 10+ years of time elapsed between EPA's initial discovery of a potential site's existence and completion of cleanup? With the exception of the period of time needed to do the site remediation, all of the stages seem to be longer than necessary, especially the five years that go by at the front end of the process in which the only real activity is making preliminary assessments and obtaining a hazard ranking score. Acton's study (at pages 48-56) suggests a number of factors that may combine to explain the slow pace. These include a lack of aggressiveness by EPA, the complexity of the Superfund program, delays caused while legal interpretations of various portions of the law are obtained, program rigidity, the litigious atmosphere surrounding the program, uncertainty about the efficacy of remedies, and shortages of critical personnel. Do the changes in the 1990 NCP seem likely to quicken the pace at which sites are remediated?

Would the pace of Superfund remediation be improved by EPA's adopting standardized procedures to be used at all of the sites? In an apparent effort in this direction, EPA promulgated model language in 1991 for use in all consent decrees that govern the RI/FS and the RD/RA processes, in an attempt to "reduce transaction time and costs." See 6 Toxics L. Rep. 151 (1991). How does standardized language improve the pace of negotiations? In theory, standardization reduces the number of items which are subject to bargaining and thereby makes it easier for parties to reach agreement. Lawyers for PRPs, however, were quick to criticize the proposals as too one-sided in favor of EPA. They felt that the new terms would deprive PRPs of so many of the benefits of settlement as to have the perverse effect of discouraging settlements.

2. Lead agencies and PRP-led activities. Part of the problem that EPA has faced in administering CERCLA is the burden of too much work to be done by too few people. The NCP addresses this problem by allowing EPA to delegate "lead agency" status to a state, political subdivision of a state, or Indian tribe that EPA finds to have adequate ability and enforcement authority (under state or tribal law) to carry out a NCP-consistent removal or remedial action. EPA is also authorized to allow PRPs to conduct many of the phases of the CERCLA process, including, for example, performing the RI/FS,[17] or doing the actual site remediation work. In instances where PRPs take the lead role, EPA remains the official lead agency. The work is done by the PRPs pursuant to a court or administrative order, or in accordance with an express agreement with EPA.

3. The vital points in the process. While it is probably fair to say that all of the steps in the remediation process are important, the RI/FS and ROD stages stand out as the points at which the site-specific remedy is selected. Remedy selection determines many of the issues that people care most about. For the affected community, the remedy selection determines the extent to which the hazard will be eliminated. For the PRPs, the remedy selection commits the EPA to having a particular type and amount of work done, the cost of which will be borne by the PRPs. By statute, the RI/FS and ROD process is designed to allow input from states and affected communities as well as from PRPs and the EPA itself. Toward that end, the statute authorizes EPA to make grants of up to $50,000 to affected communities for hiring experts to make community participation in the RI/FS and ROD process more effectual.[18]

4. The forces that govern EPA's NCP-based decisionmaking. One commentator has suggested that EPA is driven by several factors in addition to the operating legal criteria of the NCP when it makes its decisions about site remediation. These factors include "(a) the large costs that must be borne by either the fund...or responsible parties if complete and thorough cleanups are to be implemented, (b) pressure from the Office of Management and Budget to minimize the costs to American industry, (c) the political need to proceed more quickly with cleanups at Superfund sites because of the perceived failures of the Reagan Administration, (d) the technical complexity of making decisions about health and environmental harm from contaminants that may be left at the site after cleanup, and, (e) the legal requirements of Superfund that structure how these cleanup standards shall be set." Brown, EPA's Resolution of the Conflict Between Cleanup Costs and the Law in Setting Cleanup Standards Under Superfund, 15 Colum. J. Envtl L. 241 (1990). Assuming that Brown has identified correctly the mix of pressures that govern EPA's decisionmaking, how would they affect remedy selection in a typical case? Using both historical and legal analysis, and an illuminating case study of ROD selection, Brown concludes that the complexity of the technical issues surrounding the post-remedial effects of a remedial plan mask the selection of "remedies that only partially mitigate the impact of the site on the environment" despite legal requirements that the remedy selected must be fully protective of health and environment. Id. at 301. As a cure for this phenomenon, Brown suggests (1) clear congressional definition of "how clean is clean," and (2) allowing RODs that explicitly rely on excessive cost and engineering infeasibility as justifications for

17. See CERCLA §104(a), 42 U.S.C.A. §9604(a).

18. See CERCLA §104(c)(2), §113(k)(2), §117, §121(f); 42 U.S.C.A. §9604(c)(2), §9613(k)(2), §9617, §9621(f).

selecting a remedy that merely mitigates, but does not completely remediate, environmental harm at the site.

5. Challenging EPA's decisions. Congress provided for judicial review of EPA's remedy selection process. The key provisos governing judicial review are a limitation on the scope of review to the administrative record,[19] and setting "arbitrary and capricious" as the standard of review.[20] Interested parties can participate in the building of the administrative record,[21] and EPA must give reasonable notice of the proceeding to identifiable interested parties, including PRPs and the affected community. Do these procedures give interested parties a meaningful opportunity to participate in the remedy selection process? See Friedman, Judicial Review Under the Superfund Amendments: Will Parties Have Meaningful Input to the Remedy Selection Process?, 14 Colum. J. Envtl L. 187 (1989).

6. ARARs (applicable, relevant, and appropriate requirements) as cleanup standards. ARARs function in a very real sense as cleanup standards, defining how thorough the remedial action must be in its efforts to eliminate environmental hazards at the site. Why does the NCP place so heavy a reliance on ARARs? At a minimum, the borrowing of environmental standards from other areas of the law relieves EPA and the NCP of redundant proceedings concerning contaminant issues that have already been fully determined in other environmental regulatory processes. Simultaneously, by employing the ARARs concept, issues of competing applicability of parallel standards do not arise because there is only one standard to apply.

7. The potential paradox of environmentally protective ARARs. One of the more perplexing ARARs problems has been whether the exceedingly stringent land disposal regulations of RCRA, the hazardous wastes management statute (studied in the next chapter), are applicable as ARARs at CERCLA sites. Paradoxically, RCRA's treatment standards can, if applicable as ARARs, require EPA to elect a less complete remedial action due to the great cost associated with treatment in accordance with RCRA standards. Assume, for example, that EPA has a choice between two sufficiently health-protective potential remedial actions – one involving exhuming contaminated soils, treating, and replacing them, and the other merely involving containment of the spread of contamination from the site. In the treatment scenario, the act of placing the treated soil back in its original location would be considered land disposal of that material under RCRA. Pursuant to RCRA §3004(k), however, land disposal restrictions (LDR) forbid the placement of most hazardous wastes in landfills unless they have been treated in accordance with EPA's LDR standards. These standards call for the treatment employing the best demonstrated available technology (BDAT), which is often incineration. Returning to the hypothetical, if RCRA's (BDAT) standard applies to CERCLA remedial actions as an ARAR, contaminated soils that were to be treated on site and replaced at the site as part of a remedial action would have to be treated to the BDAT level, i.e.,

19. CERCLA §113(j)(1), 42 U.S.C.A. §9613(j)(1).
20. CERCLA §113(j)(2), 42 U.S.C.A. §9613(j)(2).
21. CERCLA §113(k), 42 U.S.C.A. §9613(k).

incinerated and then replaced. In choosing a remedial plan for a site, the plan calling for soil treatment would probably be too expensive ("grossly excessive") and EPA would be left with the containment option as the only viable remedial action. To resolve this particular dilemma, EPA has chosen to treat the LDRs as ARARs, but will promulgate a specific BDAT standard for contaminated soils that is tailored to that form of waste rather than the more typical RCRA waste stream. Until that is done, EPA will allow RODs to grant a variance from the LDR ARAR if sufficient justification is present on a case-by-case basis. See Starfield, The 1990 National Contingency Plan – More Detail and More Structure, But Still a Balancing Act, 20 ELR 10222, 10236 (1990).

8. The "Superfund syndrome." In a congressionally mandated study of the Superfund process and experience, the Congressional Office of Technology Assessment (OTA) described what it called the "Superfund syndrome":

> Public fears of toxic waste and toxic chemicals set high expectations for Superfund; site communities perceive substantial risks to their health and environment and they want effective and stringent cleanups from EPA, regardless of cost; but communities have experienced slow, incomplete and uncertain cleanups. EPA tries to limit fund-financed cleanups by getting parties held liable for sites to voluntarily pay for cleanups. However, responsible parties often believe that their liabilities are largely unfair, that risks are not as bad as communities think they are, that cleanup objectives are unnecessarily stringent, and, therefore, that they must work hard to minimize their cleanup costs.[22]

Is this snapshot of differing perspectives and attitudes toward Superfund consistent with the picture of it that you have obtained from the materials and your own experience? Can the syndrome be eliminated by small changes at the margin of the Superfund program, or are major changes needed? OTA concluded that fundamental changes were needed in three broad areas: health and environmental protection priorities and goals; workers and technology; and government management. Does the 1990 NCP seem likely to remedy Superfund syndrome?

9. The staggering cost of "Cadillac" cleanups. In a provocative article, Peter Passell quotes a noted economist as saying, in reference to how thorough hazardous waste cleanups should be, "Everybody wants a Cadillac as long as someone else is paying."[23] To illustrate the impact of that attitude on CERCLA cleanups, Passell gives the example of the options available for remediating one small (in area) Missouri Superfund site. An expenditure of $71,000 could permanently isolate the contaminants at the site and prevent any exposure from ever reaching the community; an expenditure of $3,600,000 could clean up virtually all hazardous material residues and bury any remaining traces under a blanket of clay; an expenditure of

---

22. Congressional Office of Technology Assessment, Coming Clean: Superfund Problems Can Be Solved... 3 (1984).

23. See Passell, Experts Question Staggering Costs of Toxic Cleanups, New York Times (national edition), Sept. 1, 1991, p.1, at 28.

$41,500,000 could remove and incinerate the 14,000 tons of contaminated soil and building materials at the site. EPA selected a mix – incineration of the most severely contaminated materials, and clay-lined on-site disposal of the remainder, at a cost of $13,600,000.

Under the NCP, is each of these options sufficiently protective of health and environment? What are the advantages of the more expensive approaches? The most obvious difference between the low-end and high-end choices is that the high-end choices return the site to suitability for renewed use. As a matter of social policy, is spending $10 million to reclaim a few acres in Missouri a wise investment of resources? Can the predictable local opposition to anything less than a total cleanup (recall Professor Sandman's outrage factor in risk assessment, at page 79 *supra*) be ignored? Two possibilities raised by economists are to make local citizens help pay for "Cadillac" cleanups, or rebate to local communities a percentage of the difference between such a cleanup and a "merely" functional one.

10. Natural resource damage. CERCLA §107(a)(4)(C), reproduced *supra*, at page 261, provides for the recovery of natural resource damage done by the release of hazardous materials. The federal government, the states (and their subdivisions), and Indian tribal governments are designated as trustees empowered to sue for those damages by §107(f). Given the potential breadth and scope of this liability, it could become a major CERCLA battleground. See Breen, CERCLA's Natural Resource Damage Provisions: What Do We Know So Far?, 14 ELR 10304 (1984). To date, however, only a smattering of suits have been filed.

> Several important reasons explain the small number of filings for natural resource damage claims. First, natural resource damage law is a comparatively new area of federal statutory law: damage trustees have little precedent to guide them. Second, until recently economists have not devoted much effort to understanding the value of natural resources to our society. Third, the natural resource damage regulations that DOI [United States Department of the Interior] was supposed to promulgate by 1982 were not finalized until 1988. Fourth, flaws in DOI's damage assessment regulations discourage trustees from using the regulations to assess injuries to natural resources. Fifth, the Act [CERCLA] does not provide trustees with the financial resources necessary to assess injuries to natural resources.[24]

The most prominent flaw in the DOI regulations was the requirement that the valuation be the lesser of (1) the diminution of use values, or (2) the cost of restoration or replacement.[25] Judicial challenges overturned the DOI regulations. In Ohio v. U.S., noted at page 169 *supra*, the "lesser of" rule was held to violate clearly expressed congressional intent. A rigid methodology focused exclusively on market values as the measure of lost use values was also invalidated.

---

24. Woodard & Hope, Natural Resource Damage Litigation Under the Comprehensive Environmental Response, Compensation, and Liability Act, 14 Harv. Env. L. Rev. 189,192–93 (1990).

25. See Anderson, Natural Resource Damages, Superfund, and the Courts, 16 Envt'l Aff. L. Rev. 405, 441–52 (1989); Comment, Natural Resource Damages: Trusting the Trustees, 27 San Diego L. Rev. 407, 416–41 (1990).

The question remains whether suits for natural resource damage will become an important part of CERCLA litigation. If natural resource damage does become a significant part of CERCLA liability, it seems likely that remedial plans will be broadened to include preventiona of future natural resource damage. Further, almost all states now have laws that can base natural resource damage claims beyond the federal regime. See Landreth & Ward, Natural Resource Damages: Recovery Under State Law Compared With Federal Law, 20 ELR 10134 (1990).

11. CERCLA as the model for the Oil Pollution Act of 1990. Galvanized into action by the Exxon Valdez oil spill in 1989, Congress enacted the Oil Pollution Act of 1990 (OPA '90),[26] which integrated and strengthened prior federal law covering liability for and cleanup of oil spills. Modelled on CERCLA, OPA '90 establishes a billion dollar Oil Spill Liability Trust Fund financed by the imposition of a five cents per barrel tax on oil delivered at the refinery. Owners and operators of vessels and onshore and offshore facilities are strictly liable for cleanup and natural resource damages, subject to the defenses of (1) act of God, (2) act of war, or (3) negligence of a third party not associated with the owner or operator. Facilities must develop spill prevention, control, and countermeasure (SPCC) plans, have them approved by EPA or the Coast Guard, and implement them, or face heavy civil and criminal penalties. Single-hull tankers are to be phased out, and licensing and supervision of officers and seamen are strengthened. The OPA '90 explicitly does not preempt state oil spill laws.

B. EPA'S STRATEGY FOR COST RECOVERY AND LOSS ALLOCATION

EPA is charged with many responsibilities in the hazardous waste arena, including its responsibility not only to obtain cleanups at NPL sites, but also to insure that the burden of paying for those cleanups falls on PRPs rather than the Superfund itself. Although it was understood that the Superfund would have to absorb the costs of cleanups of orphan sites where no solvent PRPs could be identified, the mandate to assign the cost of cleanups to the PRPs is a central feature in CERCLA's structure. CERCLA §107 establishes an express cause of action that allows EPA to recover the costs of removal or response actions from PRPs, and CERCLA §106 allows EPA to order PRPs to take action at contaminated sites, thereby relieving the fund of any need to expend its monies.

Through successes in the early years of CERCLA litigation, and with the passage of the Superfund Amendment and Reauthorization Act in 1986, the liability rules that apply in CERCLA cases are extremely favorable to EPA.[27] Strict, joint, and several liability of PRPs and a relaxed standard of causation are the norms. These liability rules make it feasible for EPA to be highly successful when it is forced to pursue cost recovery actions, but even with highly favorable substantive law rules, the job of protecting the Superfund's assets from depletion is more difficult than it

26. Pub. L. No. 101–380 (1990).

27. These developments are discussed in Chapter 6.

may appear. The long drawn out process of litigating cost recovery actions has proved an unavoidable strain on EPA's enforcement and administrative resources. The mere threat of eventual EPA cost recovery has not made PRPs a particularly tractable group. EPA has continued to try to marshall and apply the legal tools provided by CERCLA strategically to undercut "recalcitrant" PRPs. The remainder of this chapter looks into these tactical aspects of the cost recovery and loss allocation processes.

Section 1. THE COSTS OF COST RECOVERY

The problems facing EPA in husbanding the monies of the Superfund and running the cost recovery program can be divided into three distinct categories. Perhaps the most rudimentary problem is cash flow. If the average cleanup spans a ten-year period, and EPA is expending funds at a large number of NPL sites from the investigatory stages onward, the fund may get depleted before §107 cost recovery actions can replenish it.[28] Second, a decade of experience with the cost recovery program has revealed that the program has a surprisingly low rate of recovery. Finally, EPA has a severe staffing problem in both the site management and cost recovery aspects of its operations. The site management staffing problem is simply a lack of sufficient trained and experienced personnel to insure that sites are cleaned up in the proper manner.

The cost recovery staffing problem arises in large part as a result of the nature of CERCLA cases. In most instances, NPL sites involve numerous PRPs with substantial liabilities. The high stakes create a sufficient incentive for PRPs to fight hard to limit their losses on many fronts. They will also be inclined to challenge EPA decisions regarding selection of expensive cleanup measures. PRPs try to minimize EPA's assessment of their contribution to the site, contesting the accuracy of EPA's particular "Waste-In" lists,[29] and the identification of materials found at the site as belonging to them rather than some other PRP. Even though PRPs are almost always held to be jointly and severally liable for cost recoveries,[30] they are given a statutory right of contribution[31] and may join their cross-claims for contribution to EPA's cost recovery suit. The effort to sort out comparative responsibility has the potential to make each of the cost recovery suits a quagmire for all involved. Finally, even when the cost allocation issue is absent, experience in all fields of law has shown that complex multiparty litigation invariably imposes massive burdens on all of the parties involved.

Lawsuits prosecuted under RCRA §7003 and CERCLA §§106 and 107 have proven particularly burdensome and expensive to litigate, to the extent that litigation at

28. By 1991 the NPL included roughly 1,200 sites. Emergency removal actions of some type had been performed at approximately 400 sites, whereas full-scale remedial actions were well underway at only 60 of the sites.

29. A "Waste-In" list is a computer printout generated by EPA after extensive detective work on each site, collecting much data on who dumped what, based on identifiable barrels, trucking invoices, interviews with workers, corporate records, etc. Based on the list, EPA sends out PRP liability notices, sometimes to hundreds of potentially liable addressees.

30. Recall that courts have found that joint and several liability will not be applied in the event that the PRPs can show that the harm is divisible or that there is an appropriate basis on which to apportion liability.

31. CERCLA §113(f), 42 U.S.C.A. §9613(f).

times proves to be counter productive. A great deal of money is spent that might otherwise be directed toward remediation of toxic contamination. The following correspondence provides some enlightening insights:

Letter from John Quarles and William Gardner, counsel for Mobay Chemical Company, to District Court Judge Scott Wright and Special Master Robert Freilich, Filed, United States District Court for the Western District of Missouri, January 7, 1985
Re: UNITED STATES v. CONSERVATION CHEMICAL COMPANY, et al., No. 82-0983-CV-W-5

[The *Conservation Chemical* case involved a typical CERCLA lawsuit to implement a cleanup and to recover response costs expended at the site. The case began with a complaint against a few major corporations that had generated a substantial portion of the materials present on the site, with further claims against another dozen PRPs. Judge Wright ordered the case referred to a Special Master (Professor Freilich) to assist him in his handling of the case. An ambitious litigation schedule was set out for the parties, forcing them to move ahead at a very rapid pace.]

January 4, 1985

Dear Judge Wright and Professor Freilich:

On behalf of our client, Mobay Chemical Corporation, we respectfully request a stay of all proceedings in this matter for a 45-day period to give all parties an opportunity to discuss settlement. This letter reviews several factors of this request for stay, including: (1) sufficient data exist to select a remedy; (2) 1985 litigation costs of outside counsel alone will probably range between 5 and 11 million dollars before the Phase I trial even begins; (3) the time is ripe for the parties to reach a settlement to avoid these litigation costs; and (4) this court has long supported settlement of this case.

Since the order of reference to the Special Master on July 16, this case has been moving at what must be record pace for multi-party litigation. Many of the parties have committed massive resources to date. The proceedings are now at a critical juncture where the interests of judicial economy, the environmental interests in a prompt cleanup, and the general administration of justice would all be served by your giving the parties an opportunity to conduct meaningful settlement negotiations while proceedings are temporarily postponed....

A number of lessons have been learned through extensive experience with Superfund litigation in the last few years. One of the most fundamental of these has been the widespread recognition that, despite the best efforts of parties, Superfund cases are not "ripe" for settlement until adequate facts have been developed about a particular site and the scope of possible remedies and their costs have been reasonably well defined. This means that most cases are not ripe for settlement until the completion of a remedial investigation and a feasibility study.

We are at precisely that stage in this case.... This case is now ripe for settlement. The brief moratorium on discovery and trial preparation which we propose will provide an opportunity for the parties to negotiate and decide upon the appropriate remedial alternative which will meet environmental concerns. Absent this moratorium, however, the parties will be so committed to the conduct of the litigation that there will be no available time to deal with the complexities of settlement discussions....

In support of the urgency we place on the need for this moratorium to permit settlement discussions, we have prepared some cost figures for the 14-week period from January 14 through April 22 in which there will be concentrated multi-track depositions involving expert witness issues, insurance and third-party liability issues, and Phase I trial preparation, and a 19-week period from April 22 through September 1 for the trial of Phase I. While these cost estimates are conservative, they are indeed startling.

We estimate that a lawyer working in this 14-week period will compile billable time charges at a minimum of 40 and quite possibly 50 or more hours each week. We estimate average hourly time charges to be between $100 and $125. Given the seniority of the number of counsel, these estimates are unrealistically low. One lawyer billing 40 hours a week at $100 per hour for 14 weeks will result in legal costs of $56,000. A lawyer billing 50 hours a week at $125 per hour for 14 weeks will generate $88,500 in legal costs.

We then analyzed the number of lawyers involved in this case, for the moment not counting government counsel. The original defendants have, counting liaison counsel, at least eight law firms involved in this case. We estimate each firm will commit two to four lawyers during this period, although based on the concentrated period of discovery prior to Christmas these estimates would fall far short of actual practice. We estimate counsel for CCC and all insurance counsel will number between 10 and 20 lawyers although again, based on the proceedings before Christmas, we suspect this figure is unrealistically low. Of the more than 200 third-party defendants in this case, we estimate the involvement of only 60 to 100 attorneys, although given the level of participation required of some of the more substantial third-party defendants, this figure is also unrealistically low. Thus, the total number of attorneys involved ranges from 86 to 132. No one attorney in a particular firm may spend all of his or her working hours on the case; nonetheless, and on an average basis, each party is estimated to contribute at a minimum this amount of attorney resources.

These totals provide a range of estimated legal counsel time charges of $4,816,000 to $11,682,000. These cost estimates are only a portion of the pre-trial proceedings. (The legal counsel costs of Phase I trial would involve an estimated additional $6,536,000 to $15,675,000.) They do not take into account the government's cost of litigation, in-house client and corporate resource and dollar expenditures, or administrative costs of litigation. Nor do these estimates include the cost of expert witness, out-of-pocket costs, transcripts, travel costs, or living expenses. Much less do they include the millions of dollars expended on this case before third parties were brought in earlier this year. Thus, it is not just legal costs to outside counsel at issue here. It is the full range of litigation costs to all involved.

Juxtaposing these figures against cleanup costs tells, as no words can, why a settlement moratorium is necessary. The remedial investigation and feasibility study prepared by the original defendants proposes a site capping remedy at a cost of approximately $600,000. There also appear to be relatively firm estimates that the site could be completely contained with a slurry wall or grout curtain down to bedrock at a cost of $6,000,000. Thus, it is abundantly clear that litigation costs alone, in just the upcoming 14-week pre-trial period, could very well exceed remedial costs.

We understand preliminary settlement discussions have been taking place but neither Mobay nor any other third-party defendants to our knowledge can apprise you of their status or potential for resolution because we have not been involved.

It is obvious that these discussions have been hindered by the time constraints of the present schedule. We have no doubt the court mandated the accelerated pace of this litigation at least in part to bring about an achievement of the very objective we seek – the prompt effective remediation of the CCC site. We respectfully submit that the Court and Special Master's approval of this initiative will in all likelihood result in remedial action being taken far sooner than if the matter continued on the present schedule....

[The court granted a continuance, and subsequently two more, extending to August 5, 1985, at which point a preliminary settlement was reached between EPA and the four major PRPs – IBM, FMC, Armco Technologies, and AT&T – providing a cap for the site, and construction of a deep slurry wall, interior withdrawal wells, a treatment system for withdrawn water, and a groundwater monitoring system.[32] After a hearing at which non-settling PRPs protested, the court accepted the preliminary agreement. 628 F.Supp. 391 (W.D. Mo. 1985).]

COMMENTARY AND QUESTIONS

1. The likelihood of settlement. How often will settlements of complex groundwater contamination cases be achieved? *Conservation Chemical*'s special facts make it a very likely candidate because the costs of containment (even if they reach $10 million) are relatively small in relation to the costs of litigation, and those costs stand to be shared by a fairly large number of substantial (and solvent) corporate defendants. Are there incentives in addition to the high cost of litigation that might spur parties to settle? Obtaining EPA approval of a PRP-managed cleanup can result in substantial cost savings in comparison to an EPA-managed cleanup. As explored more fully at page 910 *infra*, settling PRPs are protected against additional liability and may seek contribution from non-settling PRPs. See also Bernstein, The *Enviro-Chem* Settlement: Superfund Problem Solving, 13 ELR 10402 (1983).

2. Settlements and administrative orders as cures for Superfund solvency issues and litigation burdens. In order to preclude the cash flow and low recovery rate problems, EPA has tried to reduce outlays of monies from the Superfund by increasing the amount of the cleanup work done by the PRPs (or their contractors) rather than by contractors hired by EPA. One means for shifting the costs to PRPs has been to enter into settlements with PRPs in advance of cleanup that place the full anticipated present and future costs on the PRPs. This method of proceeding has the additional advantage of avoiding two types of staffing problems. PRP-led cleanups require EPA oversight, but that is a far more modest task than managing the cleanup. Similarly, by settling in advance of litigation, the burdens of complex litigation are greatly reduced.[33] A second avenue toward increasing the amount of

32. This remediation program was undoubtedly expensive, which may explain the nonsettling PRPs' dismay with it, but because the site sits in a floodplain over an aquifer used for process water supply, the judge held the expense reasonable. Note that the treated extracted water was not ordered to be re-injected. In part this recognized a need to maintain an inward-flowing groundwater pressure to contain the toxics, in part acceptance of the fact that more legal complexities are raised by re-injecting treated wastes into the site than by discharging them into the river under NPDES standards.

33. Litigation is not wholly avoided. At times, settlements will be reached after litigation is initiated but before it has matured. At other times, settlements will be reached with less than all of the PRPs, leaving EPA to litigate with the remaining PRPs. See, e.g., O'Neil v. Picillo, page 903 *infra*.

cleanup work done by PRPs is to require that PRPs do the work pursuant to administrative order, a power expressly granted to EPA by Congress. This power is limited to cases where a release or threatened release of hazardous material poses "an imminent and substantial endangerment to public health or welfare or the environment...."[34] Given the nature of Superfund sites, few, if any, do not pose such a danger. This option is explored more fully at page 924 *infra*.

3. Congressional guidelines for EPA settlements. Owing to the abuses of the Superfund program in the early years of the Reagan administration, Congress, when it reauthorized CERCLA in 1986, added extremely detailed provisions that were intended to support EPA's pursuit of settlements, while keeping a check on EPA to be sure that the settlement process was administered in an even-handed way. See CERCLA §122, 42 U.S.C.A. §9622. EPA has fully complied with the directive and has promulgated a whole series of guidance documents that announce EPA settlement policies and procedures. These, too, are explored more fully at page 911 *infra*.

4. PRP letters – the invitation to the dance. One of the rituals of Superfund enforcement is the way in which many of EPA's actions are begun. After identifying a site and compiling a list of PRPs, EPA mails letters informing PRPs of their (unhappy) status and inviting them to a forthcoming meeting, usually at a large meeting hall or hotel ballroom near the site. At that meeting, EPA typically presents its waste-in list and a summary of what the agency knows about the site, and then tells the assemblage that they have a few hours to organize themselves into groups for the purpose of negotiating settlements with EPA. The EPA representatives then depart, returning after a few hours to begin discussions with the various newly-formed PRP groups. If settlements are not reached within sixty days, the period for negotiation (unless extended for an additional sixty days by EPA) is over and EPA will file suit or issue administrative orders. Is this reliance on PRPs to organize themselves on such short notice a good procedure to follow in complex Superfund cases? Are brutally short deadlines appropriate and necessary?

Section 2. FAIRNESS AND THE COST RECOVERY PROCESS

Before reading the following excerpt, you may wish to review Chapter 6's material on joint and several liability under CERCLA, at page 292 *supra*.

O'Neil v. Picillo

United States Circuit Court of Appeals for the First Circuit, 1989
883 F.2d 176, cert. denied 110 S. Ct. 1115 (1990)

COFFIN, J. In July of 1977, the Picillos agreed to allow part of their pig farm in Coventry, Rhode Island to be used as a disposal site for drummed and bulk waste. That decision proved to be disastrous. Thousands of barrels of hazardous waste were dumped on the farm, culminating later that year in a monstrous fire ripping through the site. In 1979, the state and the Environmental Protection Agency (EPA) jointly

34. See CERCLA §106(a), 42 U.S.C.A. §9606(a). That same subsection authorizes EPA to initiate litigation seeking injunctive relief to the same effect.

undertook to clean up the area. What they found, in the words of the district court, were massive trenches and pits "filled with free-flowing, multi-colored, pungent liquid wastes" and thousands of "dented and corroded drums containing a veritable potpourri of toxic fluids." O'Neil v. Picillo, 682 F. Supp. 706, 709, 725 (D.R.I. 1988).

This case involves the State of Rhode Island's attempt to recover the clean-up costs it incurred between 1979 and 1982 and to hold responsible parties liable for all future costs associated with the site. The state's complaint originally named thirty-five defendants, all but five of whom eventually entered into settlements totalling $ 5.8 million, the money to be shared by the state and EPA. After a month-long bench trial, the district court, in a thorough and well reasoned opinion, found three of the remaining five companies jointly and severally liable under §107 of CERCLA for all of the State's past clean-up costs not covered by settlement agreements, as well as for all costs that may become necessary in the future. The other two defendants obtained judgments in their favor, the court concluding that the state had failed to prove that the waste attributed to those companies was "hazardous," as that term is defined under the Act.

Two of the three companies held liable at trial, American Cyanamid and Rohm & Haas, have taken this appeal. Both are so called "generators" of waste, as opposed to transporters or site owners. See §107(a)(3), 42 U.S.C. §9607. Neither takes issue with the district court's finding that some of their waste made its way to the Picillo site. Rather, they contend that their contribution to the disaster was insubstantial and that it was, therefore, unfair to hold them jointly and severally liable for all of the state's past expenses not covered by settlements....

JOINT AND SEVERAL LIABILITY: STATUTORY BACKGROUND

It is by now well settled that Congress intended the federal courts to develop a uniform approach governing the use of joint and several liability in CERCLA actions. The rule adopted by the majority of courts, and the one we adopt, is based on the Restatement 2d of Torts: damages should be apportioned only if the defendant can demonstrate that the harm is divisible.

The practical effect of placing the burden on defendants has been that responsible parties rarely escape joint and several liability, courts regularly finding that where wastes of varying (and unknown) degrees of toxicity and migratory potential commingle, it simply is impossible to determine the amount of environmental harm caused by each party. It has not gone unnoticed that holding defendants jointly and severally liable in such situations may often result in defendants paying for more than their share of the harm. Nevertheless, courts have continued to impose joint and several liability on a regular basis, reasoning that where all of the contributing causes cannot fairly be traced, Congress intended for those proven at least partially culpable to bear the cost of the uncertainty.

In enacting the Superfund Amendments and Reauthorization Act of 1986 (SARA), Congress had occasion to examine this case law. Rather than add a provision dealing explicitly with joint and several liability, it chose to leave the issue with the courts, to be resolved as it had been – on a case by case basis according to the predominant "divisibility" rule first enunciated by the *Chem-Dyne* court [572 F. Supp. 802 (S. D. Ohio 1983)]. Congress did, however, add two important provisions designed to mitigate the harshness of joint and several liability. First, the 1986 Amendments direct the EPA to offer early settlements to defendants who the Agency believes are responsible for only a small portion of the harm, so-called *de minimis* settlements. See §122(g). Second, the Amendments provide for a statutory cause of action in contribution, codifying what most courts had concluded was implicit in the 1980 Act. See §113(f)(1). Under this section, courts "may allocate response costs among liable parties using such equitable factors as the court determines are appropriate." We note that appellants already have initiated a contribution action against seven parties before the same district court judge who heard this case.

While a right of contribution undoubtedly softens the blow where parties cannot prove that the harm is divisible, it is not a complete panacea since it frequently will be difficult for defendants to locate a sufficient number of additional, solvent parties. Moreover, there are significant transaction costs involved in bringing other responsible parties to court. If it were possible to locate all responsible parties and to do so with little cost, the issue of joint and several liability obviously would be of only marginal significance. We, therefore, must examine carefully appellants' claim that they have met their burden of showing that the harm in this case is divisible....

REMOVAL COSTS

The state's removal efforts proceeded in four phases, each phase corresponding roughly to the cleanup of a different trench. The trenches were located in different areas of the site, but neither party has told us the distance between trenches. Appellants contend that it is possible to apportion the state's removal costs because there was evidence detailing (1) the total number of barrels excavated in each phase, (2) the number of barrels in each phase attributable to them, and (3) the total cost associated with each phase. In support of their argument, they point us to a few portions of the record, but for the most part are content to rest on statements in the district court's opinion. Specifically, appellants point to the following two sentences in the opinion: (1) "I find that [American Cyanamid] is responsible for ten drums of toxic hazardous material found at the site"; and (2) as to Rohm & Haas, "I accept the state's estimate [of 49 drums and 303 five-gallon pails]." Appellants then add, without opposition from the government, that the ten barrels of American Cyanamid waste discussed by the district court were found exclusively in Phase II, and that the 303 pails and 49 drums of Rohm & Haas waste mentioned by the court were found exclusively in Phase III. They conclude, therefore, that American Cyanamid should bear only a minute percentage of the $995,697.30 expended by the state during Phase II in excavating approximately 4,500 barrels and no share of the other phases, and that Rohm & Haas should be accountable for only a small portion of the $58,237 spent during Phase III in removing roughly 3,300 barrels and no share of the other phases. We disagree.

The district court's statements concerning the waste attributable to each appellant were based on the testimony of John Leo, an engineer hired by the state to oversee the cleanup. We have reviewed Mr. Leo's testimony carefully. Having done so, we think it inescapably clear that the district court did not mean to suggest that appellants had contributed only 49 and 10 barrels respectively, but rather that those amounts were all that could be positively attributed to appellants.

Mr. Leo testified that out of the approximately 10,000 barrels that were excavated during the four phases, only "three to four hundred of the drums contained markings which could potentially be traced." This is not surprising considering that there had been an enormous fire at the site, that the barrels had been exposed to the elements for a number of years, and that a substantial amount of liquid waste had leaked and eaten away at the outsides of the barrels. Mr. Leo also testified that it was not simply the absence of legible markings that prevented the state from identifying the overwhelming majority of barrels, but also the danger involved in handling the barrels. Ironically, it was appellants themselves who, in an effort to induce Mr. Leo to lower his estimate of the number of barrels attributable to each defendant, elicited much of the testimony concerning the impossibility of accurately identifying all of the waste.[35]

In light of the fact that most of the waste could not be identified, and that the appellants, and not the government, had the burden to account for all of this uncertainty, we think it plain that the district court did not err in holding them jointly and severally liable for the state's past removal costs. Perhaps in this situation the only way appellants could have demonstrated that they were limited contributors would have been to present specific evidence documenting the whereabouts of their waste at all times after it left their facilities. But far from doing so, appellants deny all knowledge of how their waste made its way to the site. Moreover, the government presented evidence that much of Rohm & Haas' waste found at the site came from its laboratory in Spring House, Pennsylvania and that during the relevant years, this lab generated over two thousand drums of waste, all of which were consigned to a single transporter. Under these circumstances, where Rohm & Haas was entrusting substantial amounts of waste to a single transporter who ultimately proved unreliable, we simply cannot conclude, absent evidence to the contrary, that only a handful of the 2,000 or more barrels reached the site.[36]

Appellants have argued ably that they should not have been held jointly and severally liable. In the end, however, we think they have not satisfied the stringent burden placed on them by Congress. As to all other issues, we affirm substantially for the reasons set out by the district court. Appellants should now move on to their contribution action where their burden will be reduced and the district court will be free to allocate responsibility according to any combination of equitable factors it deems appropriate. Indeed, there might be no reason for the district court to place any burden on appellants. If the defendants in that action also cannot demonstrate that they were limited contributors, it is not apparent why all of the parties could not be held jointly and severally liable. However, we leave this judgment to the district court. See, e.g., Developments, Toxic Waste Litigation, 99 Harv. L. Rev. 1458, 1535-43 (1986). Affirmed.

COMMENTARY AND QUESTIONS

1. The unfairness of joint and several liability. Although the proofs in the case are riddled with uncertainty, assume for a moment that the amounts actually contributed to the Picillo site by Cyanamid and Rohm & Haas were little more than the

---

35. Appellants contend that the state's record keeping was subpar.... In the context of this case, the state's failure to document its work during Phase I was harmless error since Mr. Leo testified that even when the state made an effort to identify the barrels, it could rarely do so.

36. Even if it were possible to determine how many barrels each appellant contributed to the site, we still would have difficulty concluding that the state's removal costs were capable of apportionment.... Appellants have proceeded on the assumption that the cost of removing barrels did not vary depending on their content. This assumption appears untenable given the fact that the state had to take added precautions in dealing with certain particularly dangerous substances.... Moreover...because there was substantial commingling of wastes, we think that any attempt to apportion the costs incurred by the state in removing the contaminated soil would necessarily be arbitrary.

59 identifiable barrels, and that they were present in only one of the four trenches. Those companies are now liable for all past and future costs at the site not paid by other PRPs. Although the court does not make the point explicitly, the unpaid past costs plus all future costs could amount to millions of dollars beyond the $5.8 million already recovered through settlement with other PRPs. (In fact, Cyanamid and Rohm & Haas were subsequently found liable for $3.5 million in addition to $1.5 million they had already paid.[37]) Both Cyanamid and Rohm & Haas are large, well-financed companies and can pay the amount due. To whatever extent that amount (under the present assumptions of limited contribution of materials to the site) is grossly disproportionate to their responsibility for causing the problems at the site, the operation of joint and several liability seems unfair.

The court refers on several occasions to the possibility that subsequent contribution actions by Cyanamid and Rohm & Haas will remedy the unfairness of being held liable for an overly large share of cleanup costs. This may be disingenuous on the part of the court. The possibility of obtaining contribution in this case was limited because the other parties whom EPA identified as PRPs had settled with the government, and these settlements act as a defense to contribution actions. Cyanamid and Rohm & Haas have filed a contribution action against an additional 17 parties, whom they allege should also be held to be PRPs.[38] The contribution case progressed slowly while O'Neil v. Picillo was still being fought.

2. The unfairness of uncertainty. The unfairness in this case appears to be exacerbated by the actions taken by Rhode Island in cleaning up the site in a way that leaves so much uncertainty about whose wastes were actually present at the site. The court, in essence, answers this complaint by claiming that Congress intended PRPs – as the ones who had benefitted from inadequate disposal practices – to bear the risk of occasionally unfair allocations rather than thrusting that risk onto the Superfund. Does the potential unfairness to PRPs of poorly managed cleanups help to explain why the NCP standards for cleanups are so elaborate?

3. Seeking fairer alternatives. Even if Cyanamid and Rohm & Haas can justly claim unfairness, are there better alternatives to arming EPA with joint and several liability and placing the burden on PRPs to show divisibility of harm? One family of alternatives, the insistence on the traditional rules of liability, seems to leave EPA and the Superfund without any means by which to shift the loss to PRPs. Forcing EPA to meet traditional cause-in-fact standards, for example, would result in minimal cost recoveries whenever a highly accurate "waste-in" list doesn't exist. In the Picillo pig farm case the cost recovery would have been only a small percentage of the total amount expended. In the end this burdens the taxpayers who, comparatively speaking, are surely more "innocent" than any of the PRPs. A more promising avenue is to consider ways in which costs that cannot be attributed to any particular PRP might be shared among the PRP group, rather than thrust upon a

37. The additional liability figure was reported at 5 Toxics L. Rep. 289 (Aug. 1, 1990). The attorney for the two firms, in a conversation with one of the editors, noted the prior payment as well.

38. American Cyanamid Co. v. King Industries, No. 87-0110 (D. R.I. Feb. 27, 1990).

single PRP using joint and several liability. The law has generally made this attempt in regard to contribution actions, which are studied in the materials that follow.

Section 3. CONTRIBUTION AND THE COST RECOVERY PROCESS

In light of strict liability and the difficulty of proving that the toxic cleanup harm can be apportioned, PRPs increasingly are faced with the certainty that, if sued under CERCLA, they will lose and be held jointly and severally liable for all recoverable costs. In the event that a party pays the entire loss, the appropriate course of action is to seek to shift all or part of the loss to other PRPs via contribution.[39]

Congress directs the courts to apply a federal law of contribution under §113(f)(1) of CERCLA "using such equitable factors as the court determines are appropriate." One of several commentators who have addressed this subject summarizes federal practice to date:

> Recent cases suggest that federal courts are creating a federal common law of contribution that follows the Restatement [Second of Torts], §886A, and apportions liability according to a modified comparative fault approach that incorporates equitable defenses as to mitigation of damages, and the multi-factor approach suggested by the [unenacted] Gore Amendment [to CERCLA].[40]

The Restatement (Second) of Torts §886A provides generally that in actions for contribution joint tortfeasors cannot be held liable for more than their equitable share. Its key language provides:

> (2) The right of contribution exists only in favor of a tortfeasor who has discharged the entire claim for the harm by paying more than his equitable share of the common liability, and is limited to the amount paid by him in excess of his share. No tortfeasor can be required to make contribution beyond his own equitable share of the liability.

In its commentary on the "method of apportionment," the Restatement identifies two approaches, either pro rata contribution or something along the lines of a comparative fault determination.

The pro rata (equal shares) approach has its roots in the equitable maxim that, "Equality is equity." A pro rata share, moreover, is easy to calculate. The total

39. Indemnity may also be a possibility. CERCLA itself creates no general right of indemnification in favor of one responsible party against another. Indemnity is available under traditional common law doctrines, such as granting indemnity pursuant to contractual indemnity agreements, or permitting a party that is only passively responsible to seek indemnity from parties that are actively responsible for harm or loss.

40. Comment, Contribution Under CERCLA: Judicial Treatment After SARA, 14 Colum. J. of Envtl. L. 267, 278 (1989). [The Gore Amendment, though never enacted, has nevertheless been applied as persuasive analysis by the courts. Eds.] The factors in the Gore Amendment that facilitate a comparative approach include (1) the extent to which the defendant's level of contribution to the problem can be distinguished, (2) the amount of hazardous waste involved, (3) the degree of toxicity of the hazardous waste involved, (4) the degree of involvement by the parties in the generation, transportation, treatment, storage or disposal of the hazardous waste, (5) the degree of care exercised, taking into account the characteristics of the hazardous materials involved, and (6) the degree of cooperation of the party with public officials in working to prevent harm to public health or the environment. See 126 Cong. Rec. 26,781 (1980). See also Garber, Federal Common Law of Contribution under the 1986 CERCLA Amendments, 14 Ecology L.J. 365 (1987); Dubuc & Evans, Recent Developments Under CERCLA: Toward a More Equitable Distribution of Liability, 17 Envtl. L. Rep. 10197 (1987).

amount paid in the CERCLA case is divided by the number of parties who were found jointly and severally liable.[41] An equal sharing of costs may be fair in some cases, but the typical CERCLA case involves PRPs having markedly different degrees of responsibility for conditions at the site. Some may have minimal volumes of relatively benign wastes at the site while others have been major contributors to the problem. If the PRP selected by EPA to pay the judgment is in the former category, a pro rata recovery on the contribution claim is unsatisfactory.

To obtain a non-pro rata basis for contribution the party seeking that result has to provide the court with a reasonable alternative basis on which to apportion responsibility. Even using the Gore Amendment factors, that task has a Catch-22 quality about it. Recalling that joint and several liability was imposed initially because of the great difficulty of apportioning responsibility among PRPs, PRPs with only a small share of the responsibility face an unpleasant paradox: they could get contribution (on other than a pro rata basis) if the harm could be apportioned, but they are being held jointly liable precisely because the harm cannot be apportioned.

The availability of contribution, even properly apportioned, is not a panacea for PRPs who have paid more than their "fair share." The PRP who pays the judgment to the government will find that co-PRPs who settled with EPA or the state are immune to suits for contribution. In 1986, Congress added §113(f)(2) to CERCLA establishing the effect of settlement on settling parties' subsequent liability for contribution:

> A person who has resolved its liability to the United States or a State in an administrative or judicially approved settlement shall not be liable for claims for contribution regarding matters addressed in the settlement. Such settlement does not discharge any of the other potentially liable persons unless its terms so provide, but it reduces the potential liability of the others by the amount of the settlement.

COMMENTARY AND QUESTIONS

1. Catch-22 revisited. The seemingly empty promise of non-pro rata contribution described in the text overstates to some extent the problem of apportionment among the PRPs in contribution suits. The rationale for creating a de facto presumption that CERCLA site harms are not divisible in government suits for cost recovery is the congressional policy of imposing the cost of cleanups on PRPs rather than on the Superfund. In the contribution suit, no party comes to the court with a preferred position. All of the PRPs are partly responsible for the harm and none is entitled to preferential treatment as a matter of statutory policy; thus the court in the contribution suit will seek to do whatever is most equitable. In that apportionment setting, it is as if no party has the burden of proof on the apportionment issue.[42]

41. If some of the jointly liable parties are unable to pay their shares due to insolvency, the usual rule is that the shares of all remaining parties are increased.

42. If this seems unclear, consider the following analogy of the burden of proof to elections. In the government's action, a PRP seeking to be held liable only on a several basis must, because of the Congressional policy favoring recoveries by the government, win by a clear majority. In the subsequent contest (the contribution lawsuit) among the PRPs, none of whom enjoy a congressionally-favored position, the contest can be won by a mere plurality.

2. Congressional intent on encouraging settlements. Why did Congress grant contribution protection to settling PRPs? The answer has almost nothing to do with contribution and a great deal to do with encouraging settlement. In a settlement, a settling PRP pays only once, an amount that both the PRP and the government think fairly represents the settlor's liability. Absent contribution protection, the settling PRP is at risk of later being held liable for contribution in judgments arising in other subsequent cases, which would reduce the benefits of settling. Settlement without contribution protection would not fix for all time the amount of liability, would not preclude the expense of litigation (e.g., for defense on the merits in contribution actions), and it would not offer any respite from the possibility of greater liability that inheres in litigation.

3. EPA's use of contribution protection as a sword. Can EPA use §113(f)(2) to coerce parties into settlements? Settling PRPs are free of any contribution responsibility, so if EPA enters into "sweetheart" settlements (i.e., settlements that do not recover a fair proportion of the total liability in relation to the responsibility of settling PRPs for expenses at the site), non-settling PRPs will inevitably end up paying a disproportionate share. EPA generally does not want to act in ways that are arbitrary and unfair, but making strategic use of legal rules in furtherance of the legitimate policy of seeking to promote settlement is not arbitrary. As you will see in the next section, EPA has been able to make settlements attractive even without offering over-lenient terms.

4. State law analogies, and pitfalls in obtaining contribution. Although relatively little has been said in this chapter about parallel state cleanup laws – often called spill laws or polluter-pay laws – at times they impose even harsher consequences than CERCLA on parties who pay for cleanups. A recent New Jersey Supreme Court decision dismissed the appeal of the present owner of a parcel who had cleaned up a toluene contamination site under the New Jersey Environmental Cleanup Responsibility Act,[43] a strict liability statute that requires owners to remedy contamination before they can transfer the parcel. The present owner sought contribution from other parties, including the former owner of the parcel who had contributed to the toluene pollution. The owner was not able to invoke the benefits of strict and joint and several liability in its contribution suit against the past owner.[44] Instead, it had to carry the ordinary common law burdens of proof on the issues of causation and severability of harm in order to recover against the former owner. See Superior Air Products v. NL Industries, 522 A.2d 1025 (N.J.Super. Ct. App. Div. 1987), appeal dismissed, No. 32,106 (N.J.S.Ct. Apr. 4, 1991); see also 5 Toxics L. Rep. 1455 (1991).

---

43. N.J. Environmental Cleanup Responsibility Act (ECRA), 13 NJSA § 13:1K-6 (1983).

44. Had the state been prosecuting the cleanup action under the New Jersey Spill Compensation and Control Act, every "discharger" of contaminants would have been jointly and severally strictly liable. This would have included the former property owner.

Section 4. EPA'S STRATEGY: SEEKING SETTLEMENTS

The following excerpt from a long CERCLA decision illustrates EPA's aggressive efforts to encourage settlements. Imagine the choices facing the PRPs who are being confronted by EPA. At the same time, consider what additional or alternative tactics EPA could employ to increase the frequency of settlements.

United States v. Cannons Engineering Corp.

United States District Court for the District of Massachusetts, 1989
720 F. Supp. 1027

[A CERCLA §107 action was brought by the United States and Massachusetts and New Hampshire to recover past and future costs, and to secure the cleanup of remaining hazardous substances at four NPL hazardous waste disposal facilities. The four sites were linked together by the actions of Cannons Engineering, which operated one facility and had large quantities of waste moved from that site to the three others.

The Memorandum and Order excerpted here involve review by the District Court of three groups of settlements, one involving administrative settlement with 300 *de minimis* contributors to the sites, a second involving the entry of a consent decree settling claims against forty-seven major PRPs, and a third involving the entry of a consent decree settling claims against an additional twelve *de minimis* contributors. The settlements were challenged by some of the non-settling PRPs on a variety of grounds. After stating the facts, the court continued with a general discussion of CERCLA §122 and the power it grants to EPA to enter into settlements.]

MEMORANDUM AND ORDER

WOLF, J. Section 122 of CERCLA, which was added to the law by [SARA], identifies several types of settlements which the United States may enter into with potentially responsible parties (PRPs) in a CERCLA action. 42 U.S.C. §9622. Under §122, the United States generally may enter into a Consent Decree which provides for the PRPs to reimburse the United States for response costs incurred, or under which the PRPs agree to undertake response activities themselves. In such settlements, the United States may provide the settling parties with a covenant not to sue concerning their liability; however, except in extraordinary circumstances, that covenant will not extend to liability for unknown conditions discovered in the future. See 42 U.S.C. §9622(f); also see, e.g., Boeing Co. v. Northwest Steel, No. C89-214M, (W.D. Wash., order of July 24, 1991), discussed at 6 Toxics. L. Rep. 340 (1991). Once a settlement has been concluded between a PRP and the United States, that PRP is protected by operation of law from liability to any other PRP who may seek contribution from the settling party. See 42 U.S.C. §9613(f)(2).

Section 122(g) of CERCLA, 42 U.S.C. §9622(g), establishes special terms on which the United States may settle with *de minimis* PRPs. A *de minimis* PRP is one whose contribution is minimal both in the amount and toxicity of the hazardous substances involved. In such settlements, the United States may provide a complete covenant not to sue for all further liability with respect to the facility. §9622(g)(2). PRPs who enter into *de minimis* settlements are also entitled to protection against suits for contribution by other PRPs. §9622(g)(5)....

THE ADMINISTRATIVE DE MINIMIS SETTLEMENT

In 1987 and 1988, the United States and the States made a settlement proposal under the *de minimis* settlement provisions of §122(g) to all the PRPs identified as generators of less than one percent of the waste that was sent to the four sites. The offer was based on a PRP's "volumetric share" – the ratio of the volume of waste that each *de minimis* PRP sent to each of the four sites to the total amount of wastes sent to each of the four sites. A PRP's volumetric share was then multiplied by the estimated total of response costs for each site. Then, the United States and the States offered to settle with each *de minimis* PRP for 160 percent of its volumetric share of the estimated response costs.

The settlement figure of 160 percent of a PRP's volumetric share consisted of two components: (1) a revenue component equal to 100 percent of a PRP's volumetric share of estimated costs of cleanup of all four sites; and (2) a premium component equal to 60 percent of a PRP's volumetric share to cover any unexpected costs or unknown conditions which may be discovered in remediating the four sites. In return for this premium, the participants in this early settlement received a complete covenant not to sue to recover any additional amounts at a time when the plaintiffs had not completed environmental assessments for cleaning up all the sites and thus had not ascertained the final estimate of response costs at the sites. The settling defendants, therefore, obtained a complete limitation on their liability. [The government] plaintiffs, through the settlement premium, received a contribution to possible excess cleanup costs for known conditions and to cleanup costs for conditions which may be discovered at the sites in the future. The settling PRPs also paid an administrative charge.

In a cover letter accompanying the initial *de minimis* administrative settlement offer, the United States warned the eligible PRPs that:

> The government is anxious to achieve a high degree of participation in this *de minimis* settlement. Accordingly, the terms contained in this settlement offer are the most favorable terms that the government intends to make available to parties eligible for *de minimis* settlement in this case.

These terms were accepted by 300 PRPs and raised approximately $13,560,000. None of the 300 PRPs who joined these settlements are parties in this case.

THE MAJOR PRP CONSENT DECREE

The Major PRP Consent Decree requires the settling parties to perform response actions at the Bridgewater, Plymouth and Londonderry sites, and to make payments with respect to the Plymouth and Nashua sites. More specifically, under this proposed settlement, the settling defendants would perform environmental response work at three sites with an estimated value of $15,940,000, and make payments totaling $18,855,000 to the United States, Massachusetts and New Hampshire. The settling defendants have also agreed to assume plaintiffs' costs of overseeing the defendants' response activities. Moreover, an additional $120,000 would be placed in escrow for use if further response actions are needed at the Plymouth site.

In return, the United States, Massachusetts, and New Hampshire have provided a covenant not to sue these parties, qualified by specific re-opener provisions. With respect to response costs at the Bridgewater, Plymouth and Londonderry sites, the United States and the States agree not to sue the settling defendants, except if information or site conditions unknown to the United States at the time of settlement indicate that the remedies provided for by the settlement are not adequate to protect public health and the environment. With respect to the Nashua site, the United States and New Hampshire agree not to sue the settling defendants for response costs, unless plaintiffs spend more than $19,000,000 at that site after January 1, 1988.

Thus, the total liability of the PRPs who have accepted the Major PRP Consent Decree is still uncertain. These PRPs have agreed to accept the risk that the actual costs of cleanup may be higher than currently estimated. They may also be subject to liability for conditions discovered at these sites in the future which are currently unknown.

As indicated earlier, as provided by §113(f)(2) of CERCLA, 42 U.S.C. §9613(f)(2), none of the settling parties may be sued for contribution by other PRPs for the subject matters covered by the settlement.

THE DE MINIMIS PRP CONSENT DECREE

Beginning prior to filing this action, the plaintiffs offered another opportunity to settle to the PRPs who had been eligible to join the administrative *de minimis* settlement, but who had rejected the initial offer. This offer resulted in the *De Minimis* PRP Consent Decree now before the court. As with the administrative settlement, this settlement was offered, under §9622(g), to parties who had sent less than one percent of the volume of hazardous waste to the sites.

Under the terms of the *De Minimis* PRP Consent Decree, eligible [previously non-settling] PRPs may resolve their liability to the plaintiffs by paying 260 percent of their volumetric share of the estimated costs of the response actions at these sites. This settlement figure incorporated the 160 percent figure used in the earlier administrative settlement, increased by a surcharge of 100 percent of a settling PRP's volumetric share. The surcharge was designed to reward and encourage early settlement in this and other CERCLA cases. The surcharge will also further reduce the amounts sought by the plaintiffs from the major PRPs and the non-settling defendants.

Twelve *de minimis* generator defendants have agreed to the *De Minimis* PRP Consent Decree. Under this Consent Decree, the settling *de minimis* PRPs agree to pay a total of $792,000 in return for a covenant not to sue these defendants for response costs with respect to these sites, [and they] are protected against suits for contribution brought by other PRPs.

STATUS OF NONSETTLING DEFENDANTS

Approval of the two pending proposed Consent Decrees, along with the prior administrative settlements, would resolve the claims of the United States, Massachusetts and New Hampshire against 359 PRPs and result in a recovery, including the value of PRP performance and cash payments, with an estimated value of $48,000,000. The precise value of these settlements cannot be ascertained because the actual costs of cleanup for the Bridgewater and Londonderry sites cannot be determined until the agreed-upon remedies are implemented by the settling defendants and until it is determined whether the major PRPs will have financial responsibility for correcting any conditions which are now unknown.

Not all of the money previously spent at the four sites by plaintiffs would be recovered as a result of the settlements now proposed. The United States, Massachusetts and New Hampshire seek to recover the remainder of their past costs incurred from the 25 non-settling defendants in this action, and to obtain a declaratory judgment against those defendants to establish their liability for future costs that are not covered by the re-opener provisions of the Major PRP Consent Decree....

THE MERITS OF THE PROPOSED CONSENT DECREES: STANDARD OF REVIEW

Approval of a proposed consent decree is committed to the discretion of the district court. This discretion is to be exercised in light of the strong policy in favor of voluntary settlement of litigation. The presumption in favor of settlement is particularly strong where a consent decree has been negotiated by the Department of Justice on behalf of a federal administrative agency "specially equipped, trained or oriented in the field...." EPA is such an agency.

In order to approve a consent decree, the court must determine that the settlement is fair, reasonable, and consistent with the Constitution and the mandate of Congress. Protection of the public interest is the key consideration in assessing these factors....

In the instant case, the non-settling defendants challenge the Major PRP Consent Decree only on the basis of fairness and do not oppose approval of the *De Minimis* PRP Consent Decree. Nevertheless, the court must determine that each proposed Consent Decree conforms to all legal requirements and is reasonable....

FAIRNESS

In evaluating the fairness of a proposed consent decree, a court should examine both the procedural and substantive aspects of the decrees. See U.S. v. Hooker Chemical & Plastics Corp., 607 F. Supp. 1052, 1057 (W.D.N.Y.), aff'd, 776 F.2d 410 (2d Cir. 1985) (in determining whether settlement is fair, court should look to factors such as "the good faith efforts of the negotiators, the opinions of counsel, and the possible risks involved in litigation if the settlement is not approved"). Fairness should be examined from the standpoint of signatories and non-parties to the decree. The effect on non-settlers should be considered, but is not determinative in the court's evaluation....

ALLOCATION OF COSTS BETWEEN MAJOR AND DE MINIMIS PARTIES

The non-settling defendants who oppose [the Major PRP Consent Decree] argue that the court should not approve the Major PRP Consent Decree because it ignores the comparative fault of the various defendants by favoring the major PRPs.[45]

Specifically, the non-settling defendants object to the 60 percent premium in the administrative *de minimis* settlement as allegedly being beyond any conceivable calculation of unforeseen costs. They also argue that the proposed *De Minimis* PRP Consent Decree, which charges a 100 percent penalty in addition to the 60 percent premium, constitutes a windfall to the major PRPs because the amount the *de minimis* generators will pay in excess of their volumetric shares will reduce the amount of the major PRPs' liability. Instead, the non-settling defendants seem to be arguing that liability should be based strictly on volumetric share.

---

45. The non-settling defendants have calculated the expected value of the major PRPs' cleanup work and their cash contributions to past costs and suggest that the major PRPs are settling for about 75 percent of their volumetric shares.

STEVEN NOVICK

An EPA aerial survey photograph of a New England toxic waste storage site. Many drums at this and similar sites are unmarked and leaking; site owners lack the resources required to maintain storage integrity or to clean up toxic contamination on the site.

The existence of different types of settlements in a single CERCLA action is not necessarily unfair. See *Seymour Recycling*, 554 F. Supp. at 1339. In *Seymour Recycling*, as in the instant case, there were two groups of defendants. One group agreed under a consent decree to undertake some of the remedial actions necessary at the site. Another group was settling on a "cash-out" basis and receiving a covenant not to sue. The court found nothing unfair in the United States' decision to structure the two settlements in different ways and to make separate settlement offers to different parties. As the court stated:

> While in total the sum being asked from those who are not a party to the Consent Decree is greater than the sum being paid by the 24 who are parties to the Decree, this does not render the government's approach unfair to any parties. Those who are parties to the Consent Decree took upon themselves the obligation to hire the subcontractor and to develop a work proposal by which the surface cleanup is to be completed without management (but with monitoring) by the United States and without respect to cost. Those companies who are not parties to the Decree have a number of choices. They may accept the government's offer for a cash settlement in return for a covenant not to sue; they may try to form a group of their own...or they may choose to litigate with the United States.... 554 F. Supp. at 1339.

See also Acushnet River & New Bedford Harbor: Proceedings re Alleged PCB Pollution, 712 F. Supp. 1019,1032 (D. Mass. 1989)("Nor must this Court ensure that the settlement is perfectly calibrated in terms of shares of liability so long as it is generally fair and reasonable.")

In the instant case, the non-settling defendants' preoccupation with volumetric share is mistaken. In fact, neither Consent Decree is necessarily more attractive than the other. Comparing the settlements solely by volumetric calculation, as the non-settling defendants do, ignores the open-ended nature of the settling major PRPs' commitments under the Major PRP Consent Decree. The settlement contained in the Major PRP Consent Decree is based on requiring a group of parties to be jointly and severally liable for performance of the remedies to the plaintiffs' satisfaction at the Bridgewater, Plymouth and Londonderry sites,[46] as well as paying $17,920,000 toward the cleanup of the Nashua site and an additional $935,000 at the Plymouth site. Actual costs to the major PRPs cannot be ascertained until the cleanups are completed.[47] Remedial work at the Bridgewater and Londonderry sites has not even begun. The settling major PRPs have assumed the risk of encountering unknown environmental conditions or that the plaintiffs will require them to undertake additional cleanup activities which may further drive up the costs.[48] In addition, they run the risk of future transaction and litigation costs if disputes arise as to the re-opener terms of the Major PRP Consent Decree.

---

46. The Major PRP Consent Decree involves a settlement offer made collectively to a group, which could only have been accepted by the group as a whole, or by substantially all of the members of the group. Unlike the *de minimis* settlements, each settling party's share of the "mega-settlement" was not calculated by the plaintiffs. Rather, the settling parties agreed under para. 25 of the Major PRP Consent Decree to be jointly and severally liable for the total obligation of performing the work and making the payments, and entered into separate agreements among themselves as to how they would allocate the costs.

47. This uncertainty in future costs is demonstrated by information submitted to the court since the May 9, 1989 hearing which indicates that the expected value of future costs at the Nashua site – the most advanced of the four clean-up efforts – has increased from $12.13 to $13.77 million.

48. For example, at the Londonderry site the settling parties agreed to meet specified remediation goals concerning the soil and groundwater. They will have to pay for moving soil and pumping

By contrast, under the *de minimis* settlement structure, contained in the initial administrative settlements and in the *De Minimis* PRP Consent Decree, eligible parties have an opportunity to obtain final resolution of liability in this case at a definite cost, which caps their exposure and saves them the cost of continued litigation....

In view of the risks the major PRPs are continuing to assume, the 60 percent premium in the *de minimis* settlements is within the range of being fair and reasonable in order to cover unexpected costs or unknown conditions found at the sites. Indeed, plaintiffs and several major PRPs assert that during settlement negotiations some major PRPs objected that the United States and the States had charged a premium that was too low and made the settlement offer to too many parties.

The non-settling defendants point out that the uncertainty concerning costs could have been reduced if the plaintiffs had waited longer before making the initial administrative settlement offer. However, although the plaintiffs' cost estimates have increased since the time of the original *de minimis* settlement offer, final costs will not be established for many years. The prompt offer of settlement to *de minimis* parties was clearly intended by Congress when it enacted §122(g). In this case, the plaintiffs accepted the recommendation of the *De Minimis* Subcommittee of the Cannons Steering Committee to offer a *de minimis* settlement to 300 *de minimis* parties as quickly as possible. This recommendation of prompt settlement reflects the strong view of most of the *de minimis* parties that finality in this case is extremely valuable and well worth the 60 percent premium. It would have been unfair to delay an administrative settlement that is consistent with congressional intent when 300 other *de minimis* parties wanted the plaintiffs to consummate that settlement expeditiously.

The 100 percent penalty under the *De Minimis* PRP Consent Decree is not unfair and certainly was not unforeseeable. As indicated earlier, in the cover letter accompanying the initial *de minimis* administrative settlement offer, the United States warned the eligible parties:

> The government is anxious to achieve a high degree of participation in this *de minimis* settlement. Accordingly, *the terms contained in this settlement offer are the most favorable terms that the government intends to make available to parties eligible for de minimis settlement in this case.* (Emphasis added.)

This warning was included to advise eligible *de minimis* parties that if they decided to reject the initial *de minimis* offer, they would face risks, particularly the risks of more costly settlements or joint and several liability. The plaintiffs point out that without such an incentive, few eligible parties would have accepted the administrative settlement. Although it is difficult to assess this contention empirically, 300 *de minimis* parties evaluated the risks, determined the initial offer was fair, and

groundwater until those goals are met, regardless of the length of time it takes or the cost. They will also have to pay the cost of EPA's and New Hampshire's overseeing the project. They may have to pay stipulated penalties if their performance is delinquent, and EPA and New Hampshire retain the right to impose additional, and more costly, cleanup obligations if the performance standards are not achieved or if human health and the environment are not adequately protected. The settling parties also agree to indemnify the governments against claims by third parties and assure that their contractors carry insurance. Instead of obtaining finality, these parties have undertaken risk. By contrast, the parties who joined the *de minimis* settlements have no obligation except to pay a specified sum and are protected from claims for future costs.

accepted the settlement. In addition, 12 more *de minimis* generators have accepted the terms of the *De Minimis* PRP Consent Decree. The fact that a meaningful number of parties similarly situated to those who now object have agreed to the *De Minimis* PRP Consent Decree is added evidence of its fairness....

[The court went on to approve all of the partial consent decrees.]

COMMENTARY AND QUESTIONS

1. EPA's official settlement policies. EPA makes no secret of its settlement policies or of its general negotiating strategy. Most matters are set forth in guidance documents that serve as the marching orders for the EPA officials working on CERCLA cases. These documents are publicly available – several have appeared in the Federal Register and others are in the form of Memoranda. See, e.g., EPA, Superfund Program: *De Minimis* Contributor Settlements, 52 Fed. Reg. 24333 (June 30, 1987); EPA Office of Solid Waste and Emergency Response (OSWER), The Superfund Cost Recovery Strategy, OSWER Directive No. 9832.13 (July 29, 1988). A complete list of these materials can be obtained from the CERCLIS database. For anyone undertaking serious work in the CERCLA area, these guidance documents provide essential information.

2. *De minimis* contributor settlements. What makes the status of one PRP *de minimis* and another major? Congress answered that question in CERCLA §122(g)(1)(A-B). For most PRPs the statutory test is that the amount of hazardous substances contributed by that party, and its toxic effect, is minimal in comparison to the total amount of hazardous substances at the site. EPA adds this to the minimal volumetric share criterion:

> The PRP must also have contributed hazardous substances which are not significantly more toxic and not of significantly greater hazardous effect than other hazardous substances at the facility....[49]

EPA announced that its general goal for the *de minimis* settlements program was "to allow PRPs who made minimal contributions to a site to resolve their liability quickly and without need for extensive negotiations with the Government."[50] There is plainly room in this goal for mutual benefit – the PRPs extricate themselves from the case without becoming involved in the immense burdens of protracted litigation, and EPA recovers some of the costs while trimming its own future transaction costs by reducing the number of remaining players.

What are the elements of a *de minimis* settlement? For PRPs the principal objectives of a settlement include a sort of psycho-economic "closure" (i.e., a once-and-for-all certain end to their involvement at the site) at a fixed (and preferably low) cost. This means that PRPs want settlements that fix a price and release them from all further liability. They want contribution protection against other PRPs who may pay a disproportionate share and thereafter seek contribution, and they do not want EPA

---

49. EPA, Superfund Program: *De Minimis* Contributor Settlements, 52 Fed. Reg. 24333, 24337 (June 30, 1987). [Hereinafter cited as "*De Minimis* Guidance."]
50. *Id.*

to be able to "reopen" the matter of their liability to EPA.

EPA's aims are more complex. EPA is responsible for all of the sites on the NPL, a task that strains its resources severely. As a result, EPA must reduce the complexity of each case as much as possible. Getting the *de minimis* contributors out of cases quickly is vital in this regard. EPA, however, as an agent of the national government, is required to treat all of those with whom it deals fairly. For this reason it cannot be perceived as settling too cheaply with *de minimis* PRPs. Moreover, EPA, as protector of the public interest and the long-term solvency of the Superfund, must also be concerned with end results at the site. It cannot enter into settlements that later prove to be inadequate. EPA is therefore concerned that its settlements do not prevent it from being able to charge PRPs for all costs at a site, even those incurred in responding to future discoveries of additional hazards at the site. In this latter regard, Congress has put some limits on the degree to which settlements can "cash out" major PRPs with finality.[51]

EPA has blended its many concerns into a policy that is full of trade-offs. It rewards settling *de minimis* PRPs with the finality that they desire in two ways. First, settlements provide contribution protection to the settlors. This policy was explicitly condoned by Congress in CERCLA §122(g)(5).[52] Second, *de minimis* PRPs may be granted settlements with no reopener clauses in cases where EPA "is able to estimate with a reasonable degree of confidence, the total response costs associated with cleaning up the subject site...."[53] Even in those cases, "in order to protect the Agency against the possibility that a *de minimis* party's full waste contribution to a site has not been discovered, *de minimis* settlements should, in most cases, also include a reservation of rights [allowing EPA to reopen the matter based on major new information]."[54] In exchange for compromising its desire for a broad reopener, EPA charges settling PRPs a "premium" for being allowed to settle on that basis. The premium is, as was seen in *Cannons*, a surcharge calculated as a percentage of a party's allocated share.

3. Calculating settlement amounts. How are settlement amounts calculated for each settling *de minimis* PRP? An EPA guidance document provides the following example:[55]

EXAMPLE

Past Costs: $1,000,000 (removal, RI/FS to date, other pre-remedial costs, enforcement activities, indirect costs and interest)

Future Estimated Costs: $30,000,000 (remaining FS, RD/RA, oversight operation and maintenance, future contingencies)

---

51. See CERCLA §122(f)(6)(A), 42 U.S.C.A. §9622(f)(6)(A).

52. Contribution protection is also regularly granted to other parties settling with EPA. See CERCLA §113(f)(2), 42 U.S.C.A. §9613(f)(2).

53. *De Minimis* Guidance at 24336.

54. *Id.* at 24337.

55. EPA, OSWER Directive No. 9834.7-1B, Methodologies for Implementation of CERCLA Section 122(g)(1)(A) *De Minimis* Contributor Settlements 13 (Dec. 20, 1989).

Premium: 75 percent (based on uncertainties including remedy failure, etc.)

Item	**Generator A**	**Generator B**
volumetric share	0.5%	0.9%
orphan share	0.1%	0.2%
total percentage	0.6%	1.1%
past costs (% x cost)	$6,000	$11,000
future costs (% x cost)	$180,000	$330,000
premium (premium % x future)	$135,000	$247,500
total payment	$321,000	$588,500

The use of premiums has some odd potential consequences. If all of the PRPs were in the *de minimis* mold and all settled, the sum total of the settlements would greatly exceed the estimated cost of cleanup. In the example, the orphan share (although unspecified) can be determined from the figures provided as approximately one-fifth of all waste found at the site. Here, for example, the government would recoup about $52 million to pay for a cleanup that it expects will cost only $31 million. Assuming that EPA is not seeking to profit on site remediation recoveries,[56] once a significant number of parties (*de minimis* or major) settle at a premium, there is a potential windfall to the remaining parties in that their shares may be less than they might otherwise be, barring major cost overruns.

Two observations are important at this point. First, if the parties who don't conclude early settlements do appear to be getting off "too cheaply," settling PRPs can bring contribution suits against them. Second, there is virtually no evidence that EPA has been "overcollecting" from the settling parties. In general, cost estimates have proven too low and costs have wiped out any surpluses from premiums. A major contributor to the higher-than-expected costs has been the longer-term cost of operating and maintaining the remediation systems employed at the sites.

4. Escalating settlement premiums. EPA's use of premiums is not restricted solely to providing for uncertainties. In the *Cannons* case, the most evident EPA tactic for encouraging settlement is its "Pay me now, or pay me significantly more later" approach to premiums in its settlement terms. EPA charged a premium of 60 percent (in excess of their predicted cost share on a volumetric basis) to *de minimis* contributors who settled early, and a 160 percent premium to those who settled nearer the time that suit was filed. Escalating premiums may not matter in cases where the total bill is likely to be small, but the cleanup in *Cannons* is going to cost more than $60 million, so even small shares are costly. For example, one non-settling *de minimis* contributor who complained to the court in *Cannons* was offered an administrative settlement for $390,000 and a judicial settlement for $725,000. These are hardly trifling sums and the premiums are substantial parts of the amounts involved.

56. It is clear that EPA cannot use a §107 suit to seek cost recovery in excess of amounts already recovered from settling parties. Whether additional settlements can lead to recovery in excess of cost presents a slightly different issue.

5. Recalcitrants. "Recalcitrants" is the pejorative label that EPA attaches to non-settling PRPs. There are, no doubt, some instances in which the refusal to settle is justified due to the unfairness of the terms on which EPA is willing to settle. Nevertheless EPA has always adopted a harsh tone toward non-settlors, and in its settlement guidance documents has indicated that it is appropriate to subject non-settlors to a disproportionate share of liability as a form of punishment for their non-cooperation. Do you see why this stance is an important facet of EPA policy? In order to achieve the large number of settlements that it desires, EPA must make settlement more attractive than non-settlement. As the previous materials show, settlements with major PRPs that conform to EPA's need to be protective of the public interest and the fiscal resources of the Superfund tend to be expensive and lack finality because of their reopener clauses.

Despite the importance of making non-cooperation a bitter experience, EPA has not historically been very aggressive about pursuing recalcitrants when full-cost settlements have been obtained, thereby encouraging recalcitrance and discouraging settlements. See Martin, Encouraging Superfund Settlements: The Need to Sanction Free Riders, 2 Toxics L. Rep. 799 (1987). In response to this and similar criticism, EPA has lately filed a number of suits and taken a tough line. In filing two such suits, EPA's Region III administrator James Seif said, "We will negotiate in good faith with those who are willing to accept their legal obligation, and we will pursue vigorously those who are not." Justice Files Suit Against "Recalcitrants" Who Eschewed Settling Superfund Liability, 3 Toxics L. Rep. 178 (1988). Despite the bluster, and the prosecution of a few high visibility cases against recalcitrants, there is not a great deal of evidence that EPA is doing a methodical job of seeking recoveries against non-settlors. Is this surprising? The difficulty of CERCLA litigation and the desire to conserve the government's limited enforcement resources militate against suit. Also, as noted above, attempts at recovery against recalcitrants by EPA may prove futile because CERCLA §107 does not seem to allow for recovery beyond the costs of remedial action.

6. Letting major PRPs do EPA's collection work. What would be the effect of a strategy by which EPA, in effect, held a major solvent PRP (like a General Motors, or a Dow Chemical) responsible for obtaining a cleanup and leaving that party to seek to recoup its costs from the remaining PRPs? The party that cleans up can obtain contribution from all other PRPs who have not settled with EPA as long as the costs incurred were consistent with the NCP. Similarly, although that party can't grant the same kind of contribution protection as EPA, it can offer credible "hold harmless" agreements. That is, other PRPs can settle with the major PRP in exchange for an agreement by the major PRP to pay any subsequent additional CERCLA liability charged to the settling party. Why might a major PRP be willing to incur the transaction costs of negotiating (or coercing by legal action) payments from large numbers of co-PRPs? (Hint: Is there any reason why the major PRP cannot charge its own premium?) Why might EPA be willing to watch from the sidelines? For a *de minimis* PRP, which is better, a "premium" settlement with EPA that has limited reopeners, or a "premium" settlement with General Motors that has an unqualified hold harmless agreement? By letting PRPs take the laboring oar, EPA conserves both the monies of the fund and its own limited enforcement resources.

7. Fairness revisited and judicial review. Should the desire to punish recalcitrants alter the premium policy, or lead to settlements that do not place major emphasis on achieving 100 percent recoveries when there are "recalcitrant" PRPs available for later cost recovery suits to make up the difference? Does that appear to have happened to American Cyanamid and Rohm & Haas in O'Neil v. Picillo, page 903 *supra*, where two PRPs among many ended up paying $5 million while the group of settlors paid only $5.8 million?

Stated more generally, the question is whether EPA can settle "cheap" and sue recalcitrants for the (allegedly disproportionate) remainder. At least one court has seemed to answer that question affirmatively, saying:

> Unfortunately for [the non-settlor], CERCLA, as we read it, is not a legislative scheme which places a high priority on fairness to generators of hazardous waste.[57]

Courts reviewing proposed consent decrees for settlements of site liability have nevertheless taken seriously the issue of fairness to non-settling PRPs. The *Cannons* decision is typical in this regard. The court realized that the contribution protection and limited reopeners would serve to limit the total liability of the settling parties so that any additional cost recovery would come from non-settling PRPs. In *Cannons*, the argument that the settlement was too cheap was highly speculative and EPA had made a good record of the basis for the settlement, including premiums. On appeal the district court's orders were affirmed:

> The consent decrees pass muster from the standpoint of substantive fairness. They adhere generally to principles of comparative fault according to a volumetric standard...[a]nd to the extent they deviate from this formulaic approach, they do so on the basis of adequate justification. In particular, the premiums charged to the *de minimis* PRPs in the administrative settlement, and the increased premium charged...seem well warranted. U. S. v. Cannons Engineering Corp., 899 F. 2d at 88.

What is the scope and standard of judicial review of EPA settlements? Shouldn't it be deferential, giving deference both to EPA's expertise and administrative need to settle the bulk of the cases? In general, the opinions of district courts reviewing settlements have given EPA deference, but they nonetheless engage in a careful review of the fairness of the agreement. One court listed the factors to be considered in judging fairness as including the "volume of contaminants, toxicity, mobility, strength of evidence, parties' ability to pay, litigation risks, public interest considerations, precedential value of case, inequities and aggravating factors." Kelley v. Thomas Solvent Co., 717 F. Supp. 507, 517 (W.D. Mich. 1989). There is some tension in the judicial opinions. Even while giving what appears to be careful scrutiny to the

57. U.S. v. Rohm & Haas Co., 721 F. Supp. 666, 686 (D.N.J. 1989).

fairness of settlements, courts have warned that the government's enforcement resources should not be consumed in extensive litigation over fair share issues. See In re Acushnet River & New Bedford Harbor, 712 F. Supp. 1019, 1027 (D. Mass. 1989); U.S. v. Acton Corp., 749 F. Supp. 616 (D. N.J. 1990).[58]

Does deferential review that shields EPA from excessive litigation of allocation issues give adequate protection to non-settling PRPs? For a powerful argument that courts must superintend settlements more actively to prevent unfairness, see Neuman, No Way Out? The Plight of the Superfund Nonsettlor, 20 ELR 10295 (1990). One decision has offered substantive protection to non-settling PRPs. In U.S. v. Laskin, unreported, 1989 WL 1040230 (N.D. Ohio 1989), the District Court approved entry of a consent decree, but in doing so expressly informed the parties that non-settling parties would be protected against paying a disproportionate share of the total cost in a CERCLA §107 recovery by the government. Consistent with the Uniform Comparative Fault Act (UCFA),[59] the court stated:

> the government's claim against any non-settling defendant shall be reduced by the greater of the amount of the settling defendants' combined equitable share of the obligation or the amount of the settlement. In applying this provision, if the government accepts a settlement of less than the combined equitable share of the settling defendants, the government may not recover the remaining portion of the settling defendant's equitable share from the non-settling defendants. Accordingly, non-settling defendants will not, through the effect of joint and several liability, be required to pay to the government any share of the costs properly attributable to acts of the settling defendants. This Court will use its equitable powers to prevent any grossly unfair allocation of liability and will utilize the concepts of comparative fault of the parties where such application is reasonable.

Is that position sustainable as a matter of statutory interpretation? Most often the list of affirmative defenses set forth in CERCLA §107(b) is considered to exclude all other defenses, including equitable defenses that might include the sort of unfairness raised by inadequate settlements with other PRPs. See, e.g., U.S. v. Kramer, 757 F. Supp. 397 (D. N.J. 1991)(limiting affirmative defenses and viewing the equity issues as appropriate in suits seeking contribution under §113). See also U.S. v. Western Processing, 756 F. Supp. 1424 (W.D. Wash. 1991)(UCFA approach applied to review settlements between PRPs who were being sued by the government and additional PRPs from whom contribution was being sought). For an institutional analysis and a number of process oriented suggestions for assuring fair and responsible administrative action, see Burton, Negotiating the Cleanup of Groundwater Contamination: Strategy and Legitimacy, 28 Nat. Res. J. 105 (1988).

---

58. An additional opinion in the *Acton Corp.* case, with only slight differences, also appears at 733 F. Supp. 869 (D. N.J. 1990).

59. The UCFA is a model statute that may be adopted by states. In this setting, it competes with another uniform law, the Uniform Contribution Among Tortfeasors Act, which does not include a requirement that non-settlors be protected against payment of a disproportionate share.

Section 5. EPA'S OTHER STRATEGY: §106 ADMINISTRATIVE ORDERS

As one means of reducing the burdens on its limited personnel resources, EPA has encouraged PRPs to do more of the removal and remedial work at sites themselves. When a voluntary agreement cannot be reached (or when a previous agreement is breached), EPA may require PRPs to respond, invoking authority granted by CERCLA §106(a). EPA states its policy as follows:

> EPA prefers to obtain private-party response action through the negotiation of settlement agreements with parties willing to do the work. When viable private parties exist and are not willing to reach a timely settlement to undertake work under a consent order or decree, or prior to settlement discussions in appropriate circumstances, the Agency typically will compel private-party response through unilateral orders. If PRPs do not comply with the order, EPA may fund the response or may refer the case for judicial action to compel performance and recover penalties.[60]

Section 106(a) administrative orders cannot be disobeyed without substantial risk. Section 106(b)(1) allows EPA to come to court and seek a fine of up to $25,000 per day against "[A]ny person who, without sufficient cause, willfully violates, or fails or refuses to comply with, any order...." Alternatively, EPA can undertake the action itself and then sue for reimbursement and statutory punitive damages of up to three times the amount of the cost of the government action pursuant to CERCLA §107(c)(3). There is nothing in the statutory language to suggest that EPA cannot seek both the daily penalties and the punitive damages in cases where EPA eventually undertakes the work. See, e.g., U.S. v. Midwest Solvent Recovery, Inc., No. H-79-556 (N.D.Ind.), discussed at 5 Toxics L. Rep. 797 (Nov. 21, 1990).

Administrative orders are even more powerful because they are not subject to pre-enforcement review. CERCLA §113(h) explicitly provides that no federal court has jurisdiction "to review any challenges to...any order issued under §9606(a) [CERCLA §106(a)]...." The jurisdictional proviso lists a number of exceptions, only one of which can take place before the required action has been performed. That one exception is a suit brought by EPA to compel a remedial action. See CERCLA §113(h)(5). Courts interpret the law to prevent pre-enforcement review. In so doing, the courts have rejected constitutional attacks that challenge the Hobson's choice (take expensive action pursuant to an administrative order that you allege to be illegal, or risk a far more costly array of punitive sanctions if your post-cleanup attack on the order fails) as being a denial of due process. See, e.g., North Shore Gas Co. v. EPA, 753 F.Supp. 1413 (N.D.Ill. 1990), aff'd 930 F.2d 1239 (7th Cir. 1991); Aminoil, Inc. v. EPA, 599 F. Supp 69 (N.D.Cal 1984).

Defense of subsequent suits seeking sanctions for non-compliance with §106(a) orders is also difficult. The defendant-violator has the burden of proving that there was "sufficient cause" for non-compliance. This amounts to proving that either (1) the defendant was not a person to whom the order could have been issued (i.e., was not a PRP), or (2) the actions ordered were inconsistent with the NCP. Making the defense even harder to establish, at least one court has ruled that the defendant

60. EPA, OSWER Directive No. 9833.0-1a at page 3 (March 7, 1990).

must, by objective evidence, prove that its belief in the invalidity of the order was held reasonably and in good faith. See Solid State Circuits, Inc. v. U.S., 812 F.2d 383 (8th Cir. 1987).

COMMENTARY AND QUESTIONS

1. Why use consent decrees? Given the formidable §106 power, it might seem strange that EPA does not make administrative cleanup orders its remedial method of choice. Walter Mugdan, EPA Deputy Regional Counsel for Region II, listed six reasons why EPA would still prefer to negotiate consent decrees for remedial (as opposed to removal) actions. These included setting the proper tone for the long-term relationship that is entailed in EPA supervision of a PRP conducted cleanup, rewarding volunteers (by working out fair agreements) and punishing recalcitrants, the Congressional policy favoring settlements, judicial supervision of court orders, the availability of CERCLA §122(l) civil penalties, and the availability of CERCLA §122(e)(3)(B) administrative subpoenas to compel testimony and the production of information. See, Mugdan, The Use of CERCLA Section 106 Administrative Orders To Secure Remedial Action, in ALI-ABA, Study Materials on Hazardous Wastes, Superfund, and Toxic Substances 601-03 (October 25-27, 1990).

2. Punitive treble damages. Despite its presence in CERCLA since original enactment in 1980, the treble damage remedy has not been frequently used. U.S. v. Parsons, 723 F. Supp. 757 (N.D. Ga. 1989), marked the first time that treble damages had been awarded for non-compliance with a CERCLA §106(a) order, although that remedy was being sought in 13 other pending cases.[61] After subsequent litigation over the issue of whether one of the *Parsons* defendants had made a good faith effort at compliance with the order, the court entered judgment for EPA in the amount of $2,260,173.72, based on proven EPA response costs of $753,391.24. EPA sought reconsideration of the award, arguing that it was entitled to both the response costs and the penalty. The District Court ruled against awarding EPA "quadruple" damages. U.S. v. Parsons, 738 F.Supp. 1436 (N.D. Ga. 1990), but was reversed on appeal, U.S. v. Parsons, 936 F.2d 336 (11th Cir. 1991).

3. Agency leverage or abuse of power? The power to seek treble damages for non-compliance with agency orders is, obviously, a powerful tool. How far can the agency go in threatening a treble damage claim as a means to obtain agreement on other matters? A case pending in New Jersey under its spill law raises this question. There the state Department of Environmental Protection (DEP) sought to have Mobil Oil Corp. sign an administrative consent order (ACO) that would govern Mobil's subsequent cleanup responsibilities at the site. Several of the provisions of the ACO were objectionable to Mobil, including limitations on judicial review and stipulated penalties for non-compliance with the order. When Mobil refused to sign the ACO the DEP threatened to interpret that refusal as a violation of a DEP "directive," the New Jersey spill act's equivalent to a §106 administrative order. See

---

61. See "EPA Granted Damages for Company's Failure to Obey 106 Order To Perform Response Action," 4 Toxics L. Rep. 515 (Oct. 4, 1989).

New Jersey v. Mobil Oil Corp., N. J. Sup. Ct., No. 33,408 (Mar. 20, 1991); the proceedings are described at 6 Toxics L. Rep. 1349-50 (Mar. 27, 1991). What is the gravamen of Mobil's legal claim? Being coerced to waive procedural rights certainly played a part.

4. An avalanche of acronyms. At any point in this chapter, did your mind falter under the weight of ARARs, NPLs, HRSs, RI/FSs, OSWERs, PRPs, and their acronym colleagues? If so, consider nevertheless how difficult it would be to discuss a Superfund cleanup without them. Acronyms are a part of the legal coping process. If you managed to work your way through them with your mind and sense of humor intact, however, don't feel smug until you get through the next chapter on RCRA.

The Great Chief in Washington sends word that he wishes to buy our land. How can you buy or sell the sky – the warmth of the land? The idea is strange to us. Yet we do not own the freshness of the air or the sparkle of the water. How can you buy them from us? Every part of this earth is sacred to my people. Every shiny pine needle, every sandy shore, every mist in the dark woods, every clearing and humming insect is holy in the memory and experience of my people.

We know that white man does not understand our ways. One portion of the land is the same to him as the next, for he is a stranger who comes in the night and takes from the land whatever he needs. The earth is not his brother but his enemy, and when he has conquered it he moves on. He leaves his father's graves, and his children's birthright is forgotten.

There is no quiet place in the white man's cities. No place to hear the leaves of spring or the rustle of insect wings. But perhaps because I am savage and do not understand – the clatter only seems to insult the ears. And what is there to life if a man cannot hear the lovely cry of the whippoorwill or the arguments of the frog around the pond at night?

— Chief Sealth [Seattle] of the Duwanish Tribe,
letter to President Franklin Pierce, 1855

Chapter 22

A COMPOSITE APPROACH TO PREVENTING RELEASES OF HAZARDOUS WASTES: THE RESOURCE CONSERVATION AND RECOVERY ACT

Dangerous substances – like PCBs, mercury, arsenic, various petroleum distillates, and a host of others – play vital, even indispensable, roles in producing the material benefits of modern life. They aid in the production of paper, plastics, and other goods; the transmission of electricity; and the powering of motor vehicles. When properly confined, these materials cause little mischief. If released into the environment, however, they pose threats of serious harm to humans, as well as to the plants, animals, and natural systems that make up the ecosphere. As catalogued in Chapter 6 at pages 244–256 *supra*, an array of laws play a role in regulating various aspects of the production, use, and disposal of hazardous materials. Due to monumental difficulties surrounding the cleanup of sites contaminated by hazardous wastes, regulatory strategies that focus on preventing or limiting the release of hazardous materials deserve a very high regulatory priority.

The Resource Recovery and Conservation Act (RCRA)[1] is the major federal law aimed at controlling the release of hazardous materials into the environment. RCRA has become one of the most complex regulatory enactments in contemporary environmental law, employing a variety of statutory techniques as part of its arsenal. This chapter gives an overview of RCRA's regulation of hazardous wastes, analyzing how it uses different regulatory devices explored in the preceding chapters to meet specific regulatory needs. This chapter thus aims to explore the substantive content of RCRA while simultaneously serving as a review of many statutory approaches considered previously. See page 935 *infra*.

It is important to note that this perspective on RCRA inevitably de-emphasizes two vitally important matters. First, although the chapter focuses on hazardous wastes, RCRA as a statute covers much more, including regulation of solid waste generally (a category dominated by non-hazardous industrial waste and municipal waste), underground storage tanks, medical waste, and other categories. Second, although the coverage here focuses solely on the requirements set by federal law, much RCRA enforcement and regulation takes place at the state level.[2] RCRA, like many major federal environmental statutes, encourages the states to take primary

---

1. 42 U.S.C.A. §§6901–6992k.

2. See EPA, The Nation's Hazardous Waste Management Program at a Crossroads: The RCRA Implementation Study 21 (July 1990). As of 1990, forty-four states had taken control of the so-called "base program" and six of those states had taken control of the corrective action program as well.

authority[3] and allows states to adopt programs that are more stringent than the federal minimum.[4] Most of the states have acted to take over primary RCRA responsibilities. In the hazardous waste area, however, federal regulation is quite extensive, and most of the approved state programs do not impose standards that diverge widely from the federal minimum standards.

A. TRACKING AND CONTROLLING THE LIFE CYCLE OF HAZARDOUS WASTE MATERIALS

RCRA's Subtitle C regulating hazardous waste[5] is organized around a pragmatic strategy that can be reduced to the simplest of terms: if I know where hazardous waste material is, and I know the place is secure, I also know that the material is not loose in the environment causing problems.[6] Thus, from the time of generation to the time of its eventual destruction or permanent disposal, hazardous waste is tracked by RCRA. For this reason, RCRA's legislative history and judicial opinions interpreting its provisions have referred to RCRA as "cradle to grave" legislation.[7] In addition to tracking wastes, RCRA and its implementing regulations prescribe waste handling and treatment standards and practices intended to reduce the possibility of escape. This involves equipment, procedure, and design specifications for all parties that play a role in the life cycle of hazardous wastes. In this fashion, generators of waste are regulated, as are transporters, and operators of treatment, storage, and disposal facilities. RCRA even tries to assure that waste handlers are responsible people who can be trusted with a dangerous assignment, and whose long-term stability can be demonstrated. Administrative effort under RCRA, moreover, has increasingly encouraged policies of "waste minimization," under the assumption that there will be fewer releases if there is less hazardous waste to control.[8]

RCRA'S ADMINISTRATIVE THICKET: DEFINING HAZARDOUS WASTES

RCRA has been described, by one judge called upon to interpret it, as a statute of "mind-numbing" complexity.[9] Many forces contributed to RCRA's complexity, but EPA's early failure to implement RCRA is surely among the most prominent. In

3. RCRA §3006(b), 42 U.S.C.A. §6926(b).

4. RCRA §3009, 42 U.S.C.A. §6929. See also Hazardous Waste Treatment Council v. Reilly, 938 F.2d 1390 (1991). A number of states have set up programs even stricter than the federal.

5 RCRA §§3001–3020, 42 U.S.C.A. §§6921–6939a.

6. This can be made to sound more sophisticated by describing it as building upon the scientific principle of the conservation of matter, and logic's law of the excluded middle.

7. Note, however, that RCRA does not track all hazardous materials from creation to disposal, but only during the life cycle of chemical and other *waste* material. Using the cradle-to-grave metaphor, statutes like ToSCA that regulate commercial chemicals and other materials at the stages of manufacture and use (i.e., before they become waste) are forms of pre-natal care.

8. The waste reduction strategy also seeks to limit the need for (1) long-term storage of materials for which treatment methods are not yet available, and (2) disposal of the by-products of treatment that may themselves be hazardous materials (such as ash from incineration). See 42 U.S.C.A. §6902(a)(6)(b). The Pollution Prevention Act of 1990, 42 U.S.C.A. §§13101–13109, confirms and generalizes the waste minimization strategy, applying it to all types of pollution.

9. American Mining Congress v. EPA, 824 F.2d 1177, 1189 (D.C. Cir. 1987)(Starr, J., writing for the majority).

the years immediately following RCRA's appearance in 1976 (in the form of amendments to the ineffectual Solid Waste Disposal Act), the Carter Administration treated it as a low EPA priority, channeling funds and energy into other issues. Successful citizen suits eventually forced EPA to issue regulations just as the Reagan Administration was taking office. The incoming administration, however, made the environmental area one of the prime targets of its deregulation philosophy, and further delayed the promulgation of implementing regulations and the creation of an effective enforcement program. The foot-dragging of EPA in regard to RCRA, coupled with scandals regarding administration of CERCLA, eroded congressional confidence in EPA. This led in 1984 to a major legislative effort requiring more vigorous administration of hazardous waste law, under the Hazardous and Solid Waste Amendments of 1984 (HSWA).[10]

> HSWA represented a turning point in the relationship between Congress and EPA. No longer does Congress rely on the Agency to set regulatory priorities or to exercise a large degree of expert judgment on setting and enforcing requirements. Rather, hammers and limited discretion are likely to characterize environmental legislation for some time to come.[11]

A significant threshold issue under RCRA is defining what materials are to be statutorily regulated as "solid waste," and, further, what solid waste is to be considered "hazardous waste." Congress defined "solid waste" as:

> any garbage, refuse, sludge from a waste treatment plant, water supply treatment plant, or air pollution control facility and other discarded material, including solid, liquid, semisolid, or contained gaseous material resulting from industrial, commercial, mining, and agricultural operations, and from community activities, but does not include solid or dissolved material in domestic sewage, or solid or dissolved materials in irrigation return flows or industrial discharges which are point sources subject to permits under §402 of the Federal Water Pollution Control Act [33 U.S.C.A §1342], or source, special nuclear, or byproduct material as defined by the Atomic Energy Act of 1954 [42 U.S.C.A. §2011 et seq.].[12]

Under this portion of the statute, EPA has promulgated a definition of solid waste that includes abandoned, recycled, and inherently waste-like materials.[13] Abandoned materials are those that have been disposed of, burned, incinerated, or accumulated or stored in lieu of being disposed of, burned, or incinerated.[14] Recycled materials include sludges, by-products, some commercial chemicals, and scrap metals that have been recycled in various ways.[15] The "inherently waste-like" category is a catch-all that includes materials that are usually treated like waste in that they are usually disposed of, burned, or incinerated. Materials are also classified

10. Pub. L. No. 98–616 (1984).

11. Hill, An Overview of RCRA: The "Mind-Numbing" Provisions of the Most Complicated Environmental Statute, 21 ELR 10254, 10256 (1991). A statutory "hammer" is the setting of a deadline by which the agency must act, combined with a harsh legislated standard that will take effect if the agency fails to act. Hammers are considered further at page 940 *infra* .

12. RCRA §1004(27), 42 U.S.C.A. §6903(27).

13. See 40 CFR §261.2(a)(2).

14. See 40 CFR §261.2(b).

15. See 40 CFR §261(c)(1–4).

as inherently waste-like if they contain EPA-listed toxic constituents[16] that are not ordinarily found in the raw materials for which the toxic-bearing material is being used as a substitute.[17] Further, materials like dioxin that may pose a substantial hazard to human health and the environment when recycled are likewise defined as inherently waste-like.[18]

Once material is found to be solid waste, it must further be defined as hazardous waste before the more stringent segments of RCRA are applicable. The statute defines "hazardous waste" as:

> a solid waste, or combination of solid wastes, which because of its quantity, concentration, or physical, chemical, or infectious characteristics may –
>
> (A) cause, or significantly contribute to an increase in mortality or an increase in serious irreversible, or incapacitating reversible, illness; or
>
> (B) pose a substantial present or potential hazard to human health or the environment when improperly treated, stored, transported, or disposed of, or otherwise managed.[19]

A separate section of RCRA[20] directs that EPA promulgate regulations for hazardous wastes taking into account (1) toxicity, persistence, and degradability, (2) the potential of the material to bioaccumulate in plants and animals, and (3) flammability, corrosiveness, and other hazardous characteristics. EPA responded with a dual approach, one that defined material as hazardous waste due to its generic characteristics, and the other listing specifically identified materials or waste streams as hazardous. The characteristics approach relies on four criteria: ignitability, corrosivity, reactivity, and toxicity.[21] Under the specific listing approach, EPA produced three lists, one identifying specific materials that are hazardous without regard to source,[22] another listing materials that are hazardous due to their generation as part of a particular waste stream (e.g., waste from the inorganic chemical industry),[23] and a third for a variety of discarded materials that are acutely hazardous or toxic.[24]

Despite the potential comprehensiveness of the definitions of hazardousness, because RCRA applies only to solid waste, whole categories of potentially hazardous material are not covered by RCRA Subtitle C.[25] The most important exclusions from the solid waste definition include domestic sewage – alone or in combination with other waste material – that passes through publicly owned treatment works, legal point source discharges, irrigation return flows, and material regulated by the Atomic Energy Act of 1954. In addition, EPA regulations also exempt a number of solid wastes from being considered hazardous wastes. The principal exemptions of

16. 40 CFR §261, Appendix VIII.
17. 40 CFR §261(d)(2).
18. Id.
19. RCRA §1004(5), 42 U.S.C.A. §6903(5).
20. RCRA §3001(a), 42 U.S.C.A. §6921(a).
21. See 40 CFR §261.21 –.24.
22. 40 CFR §261.31.
23. 40 CFR §261.32.
24. 40 CFR §261.33.
25. These materials are listed at 40 CFR §261.4.

this type are household waste and agricultural wastes used as fertilizers.[26] Still further exemptions from Subtitle C were established by Congress with regard to five categories of "special wastes."[27] In general, these wastes are high-volume, low-toxicity material, including certain mining materials that remain largely in place throughout the mining process, cement kiln dust, and certain coal and fuel combustion by-products such as fly ash. For each category of special waste, EPA is required to study the matter and determine whether the exemption from Subtitle C should be made permanent. Pending that determination, special wastes are subject to RCRA regulation on the same basis as most non-hazardous solid waste.

REGULATING PARTICIPANTS IN THE HAZARDOUS WASTE LIFE CYCLE

RCRA divides the universe of persons involved in the hazardous waste cycle into three categories: (1) generators of waste; (2) transporters of waste; and (3) owners and operators of treatment, storage, and disposal (TSD) facilities. Of the three groups, only TSD facilities require RCRA permits to operate, but for each of these groups RCRA sets statutory duties that are liberally supplemented by administrative regulation. In general, the very demanding requirements for TSD licensure have limited the number of TSD sites and greatly increased the cost of lawful disposal of hazardous waste.[28]

1. Generators. Generators of hazardous waste are subject to obligations that begin with "recordkeeping practices that accurately identify the quantities...constituents... and the disposition of such wastes."[29] RCRA, and its attendant EPA regulations[30] also require generators to use specific types of containers for hazardous wastes, to label those wastes in a particular fashion, to provide information about the wastes and their characteristics, and to employ a manifest system that tracks the whereabouts of material until its delivery to a permitted TSD facility. The information that must appear on the Uniform Hazardous Waste Manifest includes just what you might expect – the name, address, telephone number, and EPA hazardous waste number of the generator, the transporter, and the TSD facility; a carefully quantified description of the materials and the number and types of containers involved; and a series of descriptive names and codes that identify the waste and its hazards in accordance with EPA regulations. The generator must also certify the accuracy of the manifest and that the material was properly prepared for shipment in addition to signing a certificate that states:

> I have a program in place to reduce the volume and toxicity of waste generated to the degree I have determined to be economically practicable and I have selected the method of treatment, storage, or disposal currently

26. 40 CFR §261.4(b)(1)-(2). The disposal of these materials are subject to the much more lenient provisions of RCRA Subtitle D, discussed briefly, *infra* at pages 937–938.

27. RCRA §3001(b)(2)-(3), 42 U.S.C.A. §6921(b)(2)-(3).

28. To avoid the possibility that generators will seek to avoid the cost of disposal by storing waste on-site, EPA requires that all but a small portion of a generator's hazardous waste must be consigned for delivery to a TSD facility within 90 days after the date of generation. 40 CFR §262.34. A small number of generators have obtained on-site RCRA permits, but the burdens of RCRA regulation and economies of scale have made off-site treatment, storage, and disposal the norm.

29. RCRA §3002(a)(1), 42 U.S.C.A. §6922(a)(1).

30. See generally 40 CFR §262.

> available to me which minimizes the present and future threat to human health and the environment.[31]

The administrative burden of the proper functioning of the manifest system is largely on the generator, who must obtain from the transporter and TSD facility endorsed copies of the manifest that document proper delivery of the material to the TSD facility within 35 days of the time that the material was consigned for delivery. If successful delivery is not documented within 45 days, the generator must file a report with EPA (or the state where the state program is authorized) advising it of that failure and detailing the generator's efforts to locate the waste.[32]

2. Transporters. Transporters are the least heavily regulated actors in the RCRA hazardous waste system.[33] Their basic obligations under RCRA are to facilitate the operation of the manifest system by making sure (as far as possible) that the manifests are accurate and delivering the material in accordance with the manifests. In the event of a spill, transporters come under additional obligations to minimize the spill's effects and to notify local and federal spill response authorities. Transporters can, if they mix dissimilar wastes for shipment in a single container, or accept wastes from sources outside of the country, become liable as generators of wastes for RCRA purposes. Likewise, transporters who store wastes beyond regulatory limits or alter the characteristics of the waste can become subject to regulation as TSD facilities.

3. Treatment, storage and disposal facility owners or operators. TSD facilities are the most extensively regulated parties in the RCRA process. The three components of TSD are defined broadly.

Treatment includes:

> any method, technique, or process, including neutralization, designed to change the physical, chemical, or biological character or composition of any hazardous waste so as to neutralize such waste, or so as to recover energy or material resources from the waste, or so as to render such waste non-hazardous, or less hazardous, safer to transport, store, or dispose of, or amenable for recovery, amenable for storage, or reduced in volume.[34]

Storage includes:

> the holding of hazardous waste for a temporary period, at the end of which the hazardous waste is treated, disposed of, or stored elsewhere.[35]

Disposal includes:

> the discharge, deposit, injection, dumping, spilling, leaking, or placing of any solid waste or hazardous waste into or on any land or water so that such solid waste or hazardous waste or any constituent thereof may enter the environ-

---

31. 40 CFR §262, Appendix.

32. 40 CFR §262.42.

33. Transporters are, however, regulated separately by the United States Department of Transportation (DOT) pursuant to the Hazardous Materials Transportation Act, 49 U.S.C.A. §§1801–1812. DOT has promulgated extensive equipment and materials-handling specifications under this statute.

34. 40 CFR §260.10.

35. Id.

ment or be emitted into the air or discharged into any waters, including ground waters.[36]

The obligations of TSD facilities are again what you might expect. RCRA requires that TSD facilities: (1) treat, store, and dispose of wastes in a manner consistent with EPA directives and standards; (2) maintain records of the wastes treated, stored, or disposed of; (3) comply with the requirements of the manifest system; (4) be built to meet certain EPA specified design and siting requirements that seek to insure safety, such as not being located in flood plains or along earthquake faults; (5) monitor the site for releases of hazardous materials; and (6) take corrective action in the event of a release or threatened release of hazardous materials.[37] Going further, EPA has set standards for continuity of operations, training personnel, and eventual closure of the facility.

RCRA also requires that TSD operators meet qualifications that touch on issues of financial responsibility, past record of regulatory compliance, and freedom from criminal activity. The financial responsibility standards are intended to avoid the dangers associated with "orphan" sites that have been a major problem in the past. The worry is that a presently solvent and viable TSD operation may become insolvent, leaving behind a potential toxic time bomb that becomes a burden on public resources. The good character and compliance record requirements are aimed at excluding organized crime organizations from the industry and also limiting the class of TSD operators to persons and companies having a good history of regulatory compliance.

EPA labels the phases of the TSD facility life cycle as operational, closure, and post-closure. In the operational stage, the site is able to accept wastes, for which fees are charged and from which an income stream is generated. Closure is a six-month period that begins when wastes are no longer accepted at the facility, during which time treatment and disposal operations are completed on all wastes that are not going to be relocated to other operating TSD facilities. Closure also includes dismantling and decontaminating equipment and making needed site improvements, such as applying clay capping over hazardous materials that are to be disposed of on-site. Post-closure is a 30-year period following closure during which the TSD facility operator has continuing monitoring, maintenance, and remediation responsibilities.

Both closure and post-closure costs, including costs for relocation of waste, are substantial and pose a special problem that must be addressed by the financial responsibility regulations. By definition, those costs occur at a time when no additional waste is being accepted at the site and, hence, there is no longer a positive income stream available to meet expenses. Anticipating this situation, as part of

---

36. Id.

37. See generally RCRA §3004, 42 U.S.C.A. §6924. Especially in the early years of RCRA operation, TSD licensing proceeded on a dual track that allowed facilities to obtain "interim" licenses by meeting less stringent standards, and to obtain "permanent" status by meeting the full array of Subtitle C regulation. In the 1984 HSWA, Congress set firm deadlines to retire all interim status facilities, the last of which falls due in 1992. Short-term interim status continues to be a necessary part of the system for facilities that suddenly find themselves possessed of Subtitle C waste due to the expanding list of hazardous wastes.

licensure, a facility-specific closure plan is required and its cost is estimated using a sort of "worst case scenario." This figure is adjusted annually to reflect revisions (if any) in the plan itself, and changes in plan costs due to inflation or other factors. The law requires that the TSD operator give a financial assurance in that amount by establishing a closure trust fund during the operational life of the facility, obtaining a surety bond or irrevocable letter of credit, purchasing closure insurance, or, under certain corporate solvency conditions, giving a corporate guarantee. To alleviate problems of TSD operator insolvency that may occur before closure, a second prong of the financial responsibility regulation requires the purchase of liability insurance, or its equivalent, for both sudden and non-sudden accidental releases of hazardous materials.[38]

RCRA ENFORCEMENT

RCRA enforcement takes a variety of generally unremarkable forms. These are as simple as inspection of the premises and records of regulated entities,[39] or as complicated as issuing administrative orders or bringing lawsuits to abate conditions that are deemed to pose an imminent or substantial danger to health and environment.[40] EPA is also authorized to seek sanctions, both civil and criminal, for failure of a regulated entity to comply with virtually any of its statutory responsibilities.[41] In addition to governmental enforcement, RCRA also provides for a private cause of action to abate imminent and substantial endangerments to health and the environment.[42]

RCRA's penalty provisions are similar to those of many other federal environmental statutes. The law specifically authorizes EPA to issue administrative orders calling for compliance with RCRA and, simultaneously or independently, to assess civil penalties for RCRA violations. Penalties of up to $25,000 per day for violations are allowed by statute.[43] EPA has issued a policy document that explains how it determines the amount of a civil penalty it will seek.[44] The principal determinants of the size of the civil penalty are the "potential for harm" and the "extent of deviation from the requirement" as either "major," "moderate," or "minor" as

38. The policy limits are currently $1M/$2M for sudden releases and $3M/$6M for non-sudden releases (exclusive of legal fees).

39. See RCRA §3007, 42 U.S.C.A. §6927. EPA tries to obtain consent for its inspections. See EPA, RCRA Compliance/Enforcement Guidance Manual 3–3 to 3–8 (1984). Absent consent, EPA is authorized to seek administrative warrants in conformity with standards less stringent than the "probable cause" standard required for the procurement of a search warrant in the typical criminal case. See, e.g., Public Service Co. v. EPA, 682 F.2d 626 (7th Cir. 1982), cert. denied, 459 U.S. 1127 (1983).

40. See RCRA §§3013, 7003, 42 U.S.C.A. §§6923, 6973. As an historical matter, in the early years of RCRA enforcement, §7003 suits for injunctive relief played a major role in obtaining cleanups of hazardous wastes that had escaped containment. This was before the passage of CERCLA §106, which has now become one of EPA's primary tools for obtaining cleanups.

41. See RCRA §3008, 42 U.S.C.A. §6928. In addition, §9006, 42 U.S.C.A. §6991e, posits broad authority to enforce the special underground tank requirements of the Act.

42. RCRA §7002, 42 U.S.C.A. §6972.

43. To assure fairness to alleged violators (and to avoid possible due process objections to its administrative orders under RCRA), EPA by administrative regulation has provided a procedure for hearings on its administrative orders. See generally 40 CFR §22.01 et seq. As an alternative, RCRA §3008(a) authorizes EPA to seek judicial assistance in enforcing administrative orders.

44. See EPA, RCRA Civil Penalty Policy (May 1984).

those terms are defined in the policy document. Multiple independent violations (as at two different sites) are grounds for assessment of multiple penalties; egregious and continuing violations are grounds for seeking multi-day penalties for a violation. To assure deterrence, EPA seeks to make sure that penalties exceed the cost of compliance and profits traceable to non-compliance.

COMMENTARY AND QUESTIONS

1. RCRA's regulatory scheme as a series of statutory types. Recall the variety of statutory types studied in preceding chapters. As discussed so far, what kind of statute is RCRA? Although several facets of RCRA have been mentioned only briefly, or will be more fully described in the remainder of this chapter, RCRA can already be seen to be a composite of many approaches:

- The manifest system is a form of mandatory disclosure;
- The hammer clauses (i.e., the "land ban" considered later in this chapter) is a form of roadblock statute;
- The TSD licensing procedure is, in part, a form of a traditional review and permit statute;
- The financial responsibility requirements are a form of control of market access;
- A number of the congressionally fixed TSD facility design requirements are a form of specific, directly-legislated standards;
- The limitation on land-based disposal, making necessary the development of alternative disposal methods, is a form of technology-forcing;
- The toxic characteristic test used to define some wastes as hazardous[45] is a form of harm-based ambient standard;
- EPA's land disposal waste treatment regulations are, in part, based on BDAT (best demonstrated available technology), a form of technology-based regulation;[46]
- In an oblique way, due to the high cost of dealing with hazardous solid waste under Subtitle C, RCRA rewards and encourages waste reduction, thereby serving as a form of market incentives statute;
- The power of EPA to order corrective action is a form of cleanup statute;
- And, finally, the siting requirements for TSD facilities are a form of land use control.

---

45. Recall that solid wastes exhibiting one of the four characteristics, ignitability, corrosivity, reactivity, or toxicity are hazardous wastes. In deciding whether a waste was characteristically toxic, EPA had to set standards for allowable concentrations of the constituent materials in the waste. In doing so, EPA chose as the standard 100 times the maximum contaminant level established under the Safe Drinking Water Act (42 U.S.C.A. §300f–2) as well as other similar health-based standards for the ingestion of the constituent. See 45 Fed. Reg. 33111 (May 19, 1980); 55 Fed. Reg. 11827 (Mar. 29, 1990).

46. See 51 Fed. Reg. 40572, 40578 (Nov. 7, 1986). Cf. Hazardous Waste Treatment Council v. EPA, 886 F.2d 355 (D.C. Cir. 1989), cert. denied, sub nom., American Petroleum Institute v. EPA, 111 S. Ct. 139 (1990) (remanding due to inadequate explanation of EPA's final selection of a BDAT pre-land disposal rule for treatment of solvents and dioxins rather than the standard that combined BDAT and harm-based tests that had appeared in the proposed regulations).

The wonder is that this spectrum of approaches appears to have evolved into a coherent overall program.

2. RCRA's impact. A 1982 EPA study found that there were in excess of 180,000 facilities at which hazardous waste disposal was occurring prior to RCRA's enactment.[47] By 1986, the number of sites at which legal (RCRA-permitted) disposal of hazardous waste was occurring had dropped below 2,000.[48] Estimates of the amount of hazardous waste generated in the United States vary considerably. EPA's estimate for 1985, based on a census of all waste management facilities, reported that RCRA-regulated hazardous waste totalled 247 million metric tons (MMT). The same EPA study found that 322 MMT of RCRA-exempt hazardous waste were generated in that same year. The reliability of this estimate and many others is open to question.[49]

What is so impressive about the reduction in the number of facilities at which hazardous waste disposal is occurring? Recalling the "if I know where it is, I know that its not somewhere else that's worse" aspect of the RCRA manifest system, it should be clear that herding a substantial portion of the nation's hazardous wastes into RCRA Subtitle C facilities is a vast improvement over past practices. Traditionally, most generators either kept hazardous waste on-site in slag piles, pits, ponds, and lagoons, or shipped it away for disposal at sites that employed the same unsophisticated disposal practices.

3. The cost of RCRA disposal. How expensive has RCRA made the lawful disposal of hazardous waste? Estimates of the cost of building a RCRA-compliant hazardous waste TSD facility range in the tens of millions of dollars for a moderate- to large-sized facility. The process of obtaining a permit alone may cost in excess of $1,000,000. The requirements for obtaining a permit are summarized in C. Schraff & R. Steinberg, 1 RCRA and Superfund: A Practice Guide with Forms ¶ 4.06 (1988).

These costs will, of course, be passed through to firms that send their wastes to TSD facilities. Nevertheless, by 1984 the total national cost for disposal of hazardous wastes was only $2.4 billion. When adjusted to constant dollars, this figure represented a 70 percent increase during the eight-year life span of RCRA. The 1984 cost of disposal represented .106 percent (just over one-tenth of one percent) of the total value of products shipped by the generators of that waste. For chemical and primary metals, the two most affected industries, the percentages were .255 percent and .237 percent, respectively. Even the advent of land disposal restrictions (LDR) (discussed page 940 *infra*) in the 1984 amendments to RCRA were predicted to no more than double the cost of hazardous waste disposal.[50]

What will be the impact of these costs on waste handling practices in the United

47. See EPA, Surface Impoundment Assessment: National Report (Dec. 29, 1982).

48. See United States General Accounting Office, Report to the Chairman, Subcommittee on Environment, Energy, and Natural Resources, Committee on Government Operations, House of Representatives, "Hazardous Waste – The Cost and Availability of Pollution Insurance" 12 (October, 1988). [Hereinafter cited as "GAO Report."]

49. See J. McCarthy & M. Reisch, Hazardous Waste Fact Book 5–19 (Congressional Research Service No. #87–56 ENR, Jan. 30, 1987). [Hereinafter cited as "Fact Book."]

50. All of the cost figures are taken from the Fact Book, *supra*, note 49, pages 46–53.

States? Despite the seemingly small aggregate impact of hazardous waste disposal cost as a percentage of the value of products produced, there appears to be general agreement that the high cost of RCRA disposal is simultaneously an incentive to both dangerous and disruptive illegal dumping and to beneficial waste reduction efforts as well. Firm RCRA disposal price data is hard to obtain, but analogies can be drawn from the CERCLA cleanup context where disposal costs are quite high. An EPA report found, for example, that the cost of depositing 1 cubic yard of gasoline-contaminated soil in a hazardous waste landfill (i.e., a RCRA Subtitle C permitted facility) ranged between $100-$200. A 1991 list of disposal costs provided to one of the authors by an industry source listed PCB-contaminated soil as the most expensive for land disposal, costing $470/ton for disposal.

4. TSD industry characteristics. One of the avowed aims of RCRA was to drive under-capitalized firms from the industry, and seems to have succeeded. A 1988 GAO survey of all non-federal RCRA-permitted land disposal, land treatment, and surface impoundment facilities indicated that the industry had become the province of large firms.[51] Two-thirds of the 1200+ firms responding to the survey had sales in excess of $11 million per year, half had sales of over $50 million per year, one-third had sales of over $100 million per year, and over 20 percent had sales of over $500 million per year.[52]

5. Criticizing RCRA: Under-regulation. More than half of the nation's hazardous waste is outside of the RCRA system. The most significant legal reason for this under-regulation is the series of exemptions noted in the text. Why should those activities and waste streams be exempt from RCRA regulation? Although cost is alleged by some to be the answer, the cost of safe (or at least far safer) disposal is not large in comparison to the value of the finished products of which the wastes are a by-product.

The largest RCRA "loophole" involves industrial waste[53] not legally defined as hazardous:

> There exists a widespread perception that Subtitle D, or nonhazardous waste, is mostly municipal waste. This perception is reinforced by news

---

51. United States General Accounting Office, Hazardous Waste: The Cost and Availability of Pollution Insurance 15 (October, 1989).

52. That same survey found that the purchase of pollution insurance is becoming less common and significantly more expensive for firms choosing that method of satisfying the financial responsibility requirements of RCRA. The number of TSD facilities relying on insurance fell by 12 percent during the four year period from 1982 to 1986. In that same period, premiums increased approximately 600 percent. This escalation of insurance costs for small firms who are unlikely to be able to meet the other financial responsibility standards stands as an additional barrier to entry for those firms.

53. Industrial waste is not specifically defined by RCRA. The category includes more than 90 percent of the waste streams of factories, foundries, mills, processing plants, refineries and slaughterhouses. It also includes sludges and other by-products of in-plant waste treatment and those generated by water pollution control facilities. Many of the compounds that are included in this waste stream have chemical constituents similar to hazardous wastes. As an example, off-specification pesticides containing multiple active ingredients fall into the industrial waste category, as does waste containing concentrations of hazardous materials that fall below the EPA thresholds for hazardousness.

> reports highlighting disposal capacity, ash barges, recycling, and the anticipated publication of EPA's final municipal waste regulations. However, this perception is wrong. Between hazardous waste and municipal waste is a kind of waste that is generated in vastly greater volumes than the other two combined – nonhazardous industrial waste, or simply industrial waste.
>
> The magnitude of the industrial waste problem is overwhelming when it is stated in figures. Nationally, about 211 million tons of municipal waste and approximately 300 million tons of hazardous waste are generated annually. These numbers seem small compared with the 7,600 million tons of industrial waste that are generated and disposed of on-site annually....
>
> Waste that does not meet the legal definition of "hazardous," however, is subject only to EPA's open dump criteria. These criteria apply to only a limited number of waste disposal problems, address many of these problems rather vaguely, and do not apply to treatment, storage, or transportation.[54] RCRA does not expressly require that nonhazardous waste treatment, storage, and disposal facilities be permitted. Generally, Subtitle D treats all nonhazardous waste the same and only includes specific provisions for municipal waste, household hazardous waste, small-quantity generator hazardous waste, and recycled oil. Industrial waste is not given separate attention. The disparity in regulatory control between hazardous and nonhazardous waste is so great that delisting of a hazardous waste means virtual federal regulatory abandonment. Dernbach, Industrial Waste: Saving the Worst for Last?, 20 ELR 10283, 10283-85 (1990).

Dernbach explains in some detail how dangerous wastes can evade RCRA listing as hazardous and concludes that the sharp divergence in regulation is "inappropriate because of the environmental and public health risks posed by industrial waste." Id. at 10285-86.

6. Criticizing RCRA: over-regulation. RCRA is, without question, a giant step forward from unregulated hazardous waste disposal practices, but RCRA inevitably overregulates in a way that has unintended results. Dr. Robert Powitz, the Director of Environmental Health and Safety at Wayne State University, posed the following examples in a lecture to law students:

> Waste acids can often be combined in a chemical reaction with waste bases to form a salt and water. If performed, this reaction would eliminate the need for transport of two hazardous substances (the acid and the base), having changed them to non-hazardous materials. To do so, however, is to perform treatment under RCRA which requires the treater to obtain a TSD license that the University cannot afford to obtain. The University estimates that the cost of mere application for a license is in excess of $1 million. The University's annual disposal costs attributable to materials that could be treated safely on campus without major capital investments is in the $50,000 per year range. The alternative is to ship the hazardous material 80 miles through several heavily populated areas to a licensed TSD facility.

---

54. 40 CFR §257.

> A major chemical facility in the suburbs of Detroit, Michigan produces isocyanate (of Bhopal infamy) as a by-product of plastics production. Isocyanates react readily with water to produce non-toxic by-products. Again, however, to combine them with the water is to engage in treatment and requires a TSD license that the chemical company does not wish to obtain. (Here the hesitancy to seek licensure is less the cost than the desire to avoid being a TSD facility with all of the regulatory burdens that entails.) The lawful disposal requires shipment of isocyanate through residential areas in the vicinity of the plant and highway travel to a facility some 60 miles away.

Do the examples demonstrate that RCRA thwarts its own objectives of increased safety and waste minimization? Should EPA write a blanket exception for safety-enhancing treatment at generators' sites, or promulgate certain categorical exceptions from TSD licensure requirements?

7. Criticizing RCRA: definitional nightmares. One of RCRA's most obvious problems lies in the complex set of definitions and rules that combine to identify what materials qualify as hazardous wastes subject to its stringent regulatory provisions. Some of the complexity is, as described in the text, attributable to the several ways in which substances can be found to be hazardous. Still greater complexity is added by EPA rules that trace the wastes as they move through various stages of a generator's or TSD operator's facilities. The labyrinthine rules are considered in Morriss & Coon, Who's on First, What's on Second, Or a Discussion of the Scope and Potential Misuse of the "Mixture" and "Derived From" Rules and "Contained-In" Policy, 44 Sw. L.J. 1530 (1991).

Another definitional quagmire arises in the determination of how to treat recycling. You will recall that most recycled materials are defined as solid wastes. Does subjecting recycled material (if it meets one of the definitions of hazardous) to rigorous regulation encourage the reuse of those materials, or does it make the use of new raw materials more attractive? To put a damper on recycling would be inconsistent with RCRA's own materials conservation goals. EPA has sought to avoid that dilemma by making its definition of recycled material a term of art that defines some and not other processes as solid waste issues. For example, spreading sludge as fertilizer, using scrap metal as fill material, or adding used oil to boiler fuel are defined as recycling, and the material is therefore solid waste. The principle that places these examples on the regulated side of the solid waste line is that they all involve processes that tend to place material into the environment without treatment. By contrast, reclaimed material intended for reuse in the original primary production process in which it was generated is not solid waste. These distinctions reduce the deterrence to recycling, but do not eliminate it. Another EPA concern is that materials intended for recycling and reuse may not be so used. For example, what if waste oil intended to be resold as boiler fuel finds no buyers due to a dip in energy prices? If that material were not defined as solid waste, its disposal would not be regulated by RCRA. For a more thorough account of the intricacies that confound this area, see Johnson, Recyclable Materials and RCRA's Complicated, Conflicting, and Costly Definition of Solid Waste, 21 ELR 10357 (1991); Gaba, Solid

Waste and Recycled Materials Under RCRA: Separating Chaff From Wheat, 16 Ecology L.Q. 623 (1989).

8. RCRA administrative orders. The language of RCRA §3013, 42 U.S.C.A. §6934 calls for a finding that a site "may present" a "substantial hazard to human health or the environment" as a precondition for the issuance of an EPA order to the site operator to test or monitor for a release of hazardous materials. How, in advance of testing, can EPA know that such a hazard is present? To avoid that conundrum, EPA has taken the position that mere presence of hazardous materials at a site demonstrates that the site is a substantial hazard. Do you think that Congress intended this result? See In re Order Pursuant to §3013(d) RCRA, 550 F. Supp. 1361 (W.D. Wash. 1982).

B. THE "LAND BAN" AND THE USE OF "HAMMERS" TO CONTROL AGENCY ACTION

The Hazardous and Solid Waste Amendments of 1984 (HSWA)[55] made important changes that greatly expanded the reach of federal hazardous waste law. In what may be its most significant feature, the HSWA added stringent regulation of land disposal of hazardous wastes,[56] often referred to as the land ban. In Congress' own words –

> reliance on land disposal should be minimized or eliminated and land disposal, particularly landfill and surface impoundment, should be the least favored method for managing hazardous wastes.... [57]

Fearing undue delay if the implementation of its objectives were left to EPA's discretion, Congress placed stringent time deadlines on EPA for the issuance of regulations. To make sure EPA acted promptly, Congress included "hammer clauses" that amounted to direct Congressional regulation if EPA failed to act in a timely fashion. Congress took a three-pronged approach to land disposal: (1) it made liquids, because of their role in facilitating the migration of hazardous wastes away from disposal sites, a particular focus of regulation;[58] (2) it overhauled the means by which solid wastes could be defined as hazardous; and (3) it set specific standards for landfills and surface impoundments that stressed multiple leachate control mechanisms.[59]

---

55. Pub. L. No. 98–616 (1984). For a discussion of the amendments, see Rosbe & Gulley, The Hazardous and Solid Waste Amendments of 1984: A Dramatic Overhaul of the Way America Manages Its Hazardous Wastes, 14 ELR 10458, 10459 (1984)(hereinafter cited as Rosbe & Gulley).

56. The term "land disposal" as defined by RCRA includes, but is not limited to, "Any placement of...hazardous waste in a landfill, surface impoundment, waste pile, injection well, land treatment facility, salt dome formation, salt bed formation, or underground mine or cave." RCRA §3004(k), 42 U.S.C.A. §6924(k).

57. RCRA §1002(b)(7), 42 U.S.C.A. §6901(b)(7).

58. RCRA §3004(c), 42 U.S.C.A. §6924(c). Uncontainerized liquid hazardous waste was banned from landfills as of May, 1985, the placement of nonhazardous liquids in landfills containing hazardous waste was banned as of November, 1985, and containerized liquid hazardous waste and free liquid in containers containing other hazardous wastes were to be minimized as of February, 1986.

59. Congress required all systems to have at least two liners, a leachate collection system above and between liners in landfills, and groundwater monitoring. RCRA §3004(o)(1), 42 U.S.C.A. §6421(o)(1). EPA was also required to promulgate additional design standards that would require leak detection systems to be present in all types of new facilities.

To insure that EPA did not dally in its assigned regulatory tasks, Congress used the threat of a total nationwide ban on land disposal of hazardous waste as a hammer – EPA could avoid the land ban only by promulgating rigorous disposal standards within the allotted time period. The lists of hazardous wastes were in part developed by Congress and in part by EPA.[60] Before authorizing the land disposal of any listed waste, EPA must first conclude that a ban on the land disposal of that particular hazardous waste is "not required...to protect human health and the environment for as long as the waste remains hazardous." In making that determination, EPA must consider "(A) the long-term uncertainties associated with land disposal, (B) the goal of managing hazardous waste in an appropriate manner in the first instance, and (C) the persistence, toxicity, mobility, and propensity to bioaccumulate of such hazardous wastes and their hazardous constituents."[61] Congress also circumscribed EPA's discretion by stating that land disposal could not be allowed unless EPA finds that wastes have been treated to levels that "substantially diminish the toxicity of the waste or substantially reduce the likelihood of migration of hazardous constituents from the waste so that short-term and long-term threats to human health and the environment are minimized."[62]

The land ban portended far-reaching changes. As one commentary indicated:

> By these Amendments, Congress effectively has required EPA to phase out most, if not all, methods of land disposal of hazardous wastes. To the extent that any method of land disposal might still be allowed, Congress has shifted the burden to EPA to take action before the statutory prohibitions take effect and to industry to urge that EPA act in time. It is doubtful that EPA is capable of meeting the statutory deadlines, even with prodding from industry, unless it can develop simple new procedures for evaluating land disposal methods' protection of health and the environment. Even if EPA develops such procedures, the burden placed on a company to demonstrate "to a reasonable degree of certainty" that there will be "no migration of hazardous constituents" from the unit "for as long as the waste remains hazardous" may be virtually insurmountable. Thus, industry may, instead, elect to invest in incineration and physical-chemical treatment as methods of managing the California list wastes, dioxin-containing wastes, and listed spent solvents rather than attempt to obtain an exception for a method of land disposal for these wastes. With regard to the other listed wastes, industry may decide to focus its efforts on urging EPA to promulgate reasonable treatment standards that would avoid the regulatory prohibitions rather than trying to overcome the burden necessary to obtain an exception. If this happens, Congress will have effectively achieved its goal of forcing the increased use of non-land disposal hazardous waste management methods and the development of

---

60. Congress adopted the so-called "California list" that identifies a number of specific materials at varying concentrations as hazardous. See RCRA §3004(d)(2), 42 U.S.C.A. §6924(d)(2). In addition, Congress required regulation of certain solvents and dioxins. See RCRA §3004(e), 42 U.S.C.A. §6924(e). Finally, EPA was to develop a schedule for reviewing all other EPA-listed hazardous wastes (see RCRA §3001, 42 U.S.C.A. §6921). EPA was given a triparte deadline for completing this process, which led to the description of the EPA regulations as being first third, second third and third third. See RCRA §3004(g), 42 U.S.C.A. §6924(g).

61. RCRA §3004(d), 42 U.S.C.A. §6924(d).

62. RCRA §3004(m), 42 U.S.C.A. §6924(m).

new hazardous waste management technology. Whether the waste disposal industry can respond, within the time allowed, to this new technology-forcing imperative with enough effective treatment and incineration capacity to handle the growing hazardous waste load remains to be seen.[63]

To the surprise of many, EPA met many of the HSWA land ban deadlines.[64] What emerged, though, was not a set of substance-specific treatment standards. Instead, EPA relied on a general treatment standard for hazardous waste that requires treatment using the best demonstrated available technology (BDAT) prior to landfilling of the waste.[65]

The BDAT approach creates a problem of inadequate treatment capacity. Especially in the shorter term, there is insufficient capacity nationwide to treat all of the waste that is in need of land-based disposal. As a result, EPA has been forced to issue variances, because disposal of untreated hazardous wastes in permitted Subtitle C facilities is preferable to storing the materials in other locations until treatment capacity is increased. Over time the supply of BDAT treatment capacity will grow, although that growth has been severely inhibited by the NIMBY phenomenon and the obstacles it presents to siting hazardous waste treatment facilities.

EPA's move to select BDAT treatment as a precondition for land disposal provoked a legal challenge. Generators feared that they would now be faced with the costly prospect of incineration, even in circumstances where putting untreated waste in secure landfills would provide adequate protection of human health and the environment. As described by two commentators:

> Several industry groups sued EPA when it abandoned the risk-based approach. In response to that suit, the D.C. Circuit directed EPA to explain its preference for technology-based treatment standards over the approach based on screening levels.[66] In response, the Agency stated that its "objective is not to require further treatment of prohibited wastes containing threshold levels of hazardous constituents at which listed wastes themselves would no longer be deemed hazardous," but added that it was "presently unable to

---

63. Rosbe & Gulley, *supra* note 55 at 10463.

64. See generally Note, An Analysis of the Land Disposal Ban in the 1984 Amendments to the Resource Conservation and Recovery Act, 76 Geo. L.J. 1563 (1988); Williams & Cannon, Rethinking the Resource Recovery and Conservation Act for the 1990s, 21 ELR 10063 (1991)(hereinafter cited as Williams & Cannon).

65. EPA had initially proposed to set harm-based treatment standards with reference to limiting health effects to what EPA deemed to be acceptable levels. See Hazardous Waste Management System: Land Disposal Restriction, 51 Fed. Reg. 1602 (1986). Under the proposed methodology, EPA would make a comparative risk assessment that compared the risks of commercially available treatment technologies to the risk of land disposal. Only treatments that resulted in lower risk levels could be selected as treatment standards. Moreover, even where treatment was mandated by the comparative risk assessment (i.e., where treatment was found to involve less environmental risk than land disposal), EPA proposed to limit the required treatment if it was unnecessary to protect health or the environment. For this latter calculation, EPA adopted as safe human exposure levels the maximum contaminant levels (MCLs) it had adopted for its Safe Drinking Water Act regulations. After this proposal generated substantial adverse comment, particularly among influential members of Congress, EPA adopted the far less problematic strategy for defining treatment standards by reference to BDAT.

66. Hazardous Waste Treatment Council v. EPA, 886 F.2d 355 (D.C. Cir. 1989), cert. denied, sub nom., American Petroleum Institute v. EPA, 111 S. Ct. 139 (1990).

promulgate such levels."[67] Given its experience with the delisting and characteristic programs,[68] EPA's statement that it is unable to set threshold levels is difficult to understand unless interpreted to reflect the lack of resources for such an effort.[69]

COMMENTARY AND QUESTIONS

1. Hammer clauses. The generally accepted explanation for the presence of hammer clauses in the HSWA (the 1984 amendments to RCRA) is congressional displeasure with the dilatory performance of EPA in the early years of RCRA. Have the hammer clauses proved effective? The short answer is that the hammer clauses and the threat of a true land ban,[70] did force EPA into prompt action to provide an alternative that was less disruptive of on-going economic activity. If the RCRA scenario is to serve as a basis for generalization, it seems that hammer clauses work well as long as the contingent legislative regulation (the hammer) is so stringent that the outcome of administrative process is likely to be more favorable to the regulated community.

Did Congress get what it wanted by using the hammer clauses in the 1984 Amendments? Congress did succeed in getting EPA to adhere to the legislated deadlines, thereby proving the hammer clauses effective as a means of controlling the agency's regulatory agenda and time schedule. Its success led Congress to utilize the same sort of deadline-oriented hammers in various parts of the Clean Air Act Amendments of 1990. See generally Fortuna, The Birth of the Hammer, 7 Envtl Forum (No. 5) 18 (Sept./Oct. 1990). Still, as the notes that follow begin to explore, the BDAT regulations that EPA adopted seem to be shaped more by expedience and administrability than by the policy of minimizing land disposal of hazardous materials, or the goal of cost-effective hazardous waste management.

2. The RCRA Subtitle C universe. In a probing review, EPA identified many trends and problems with its RCRA program. See generally EPA, The Nation's Hazardous Waste Management Program at a Crossroads: The RCRA Implementation Study (July, 1990). EPA described the impact of the HSWA as follows:

> HWSA GREATLY EXPANDED THE REGULATED UNIVERSE
>
> To strengthen the nation's shield against hazardous wastes, HWSA established over 70 statutory requirements (often with very tight deadlines) for EPA's action. They can generally be summarized as follows:
>
> - Move away from land disposal as the primary means of hazardous waste management by requiring the treatment of wastes before their final disposal.

67. 55 Fed. Reg. 6640, 6641 (Feb. 26, 1990).

68. Eds: The delisting of hazardous waste undertaken by EPA and the determination of what wastes are hazardous by virtue of their toxic characteristics are both processes in which EPA can and does promulgate harm-based threshold levels of hazardousness of the materials involved.

69. Williams & Cannon, *supra* note 64 at 10066.

70. See, e.g., RCRA §3004(g)(6)(C), 42 U.S.C.A. §6924(g)(6)(C) (total prohibition on land disposal unless EPA promulgates adequate standards).

- Reduce the environmental and health risks posed by hazardous waste still managed at land disposal facilities by establishing minimum technology requirements.
- Close down facilities that cannot safely manage wastes.
- Decrease and clean up releases to the environment from waste management units by requiring facilities to take corrective action.
- Issue permits for all treatment, storage, and disposal facilities within prescribed time frames.
- Close loopholes in the types of wastes and waste management facilities not covered under RCRA.
- Expand the universe of regulated sources by including generators of small quantities of hazardous wastes.
- Minimize the amount of wastes being produced.

With this comprehensive sweep of hazardous waste issues, HWSA greatly expanded the magnitude of waste types and waste management facilities requiring regulation. Today the RCRA regulated universe consists of 4,700 hazardous waste treatment, storage, and disposal facilities. Within these facilities are approximately 81,000 waste management units, most of which are units that have received hazardous waste and from which contamination may have spread to the soil and ground water. In addition to these 4,700 facilities are 211,000 facilities that generate hazardous waste. Id. at 7.

The same part of the report also predicted that the continuing expansion of the list of hazardous wastes due to the operation of the toxicity characteristic leaching procedure (TCLP) would lead to a further increase in the size of the Subtitle C universe. With more substances considered hazardous, some existing facilities that in the past were not considered to be within RCRA's reach will become covered. The growth in numbers of TSD facilities currently under RCRA regulation is a bit misleading in regard to the longer-term trend. Other data in the report indicate that many of the regulated facilities (almost 3,000) are closed (but still regulated) or in the process of closing rather than meeting RCRA's stringent technology-based standards. Id. at 42–43.

3. Undersupply of TSD capacity. Does the combination of a growing universe of generators and the onerous regulation of TSD facilities threaten a supply and demand imbalance in which more hazardous waste needs to be processed than can be handled by permitted facilities? In the short term, the problem has been finessed by allowing variances to TSD facilities by which they can obtain interim permits even though they are not yet employing BDAT treatment of waste prior to land disposal. Is the variance expedient likely to become a near-permanent fixture in the RCRA program? Another factor in the TSD supply equation is, of course, the NIMBY phenomenon.

Is there any guarantee that there will be adequate disposal capacity? The answer to that question may lie in CERCLA §104(c)(9), 42 U.S.C.A. §9604(c)(9), that threatens to withhold Superfund remedial actions in states that do not provide disposal capacity for wastes generated within their borders. Under that provision, every state was required to submit, by 1989, a capacity assurance plan (CAP) that EPA finds acceptable. These plans must:

> assure the availability of hazardous waste treatment or disposal facilities which – (A) have adequate capacity for the destruction, treatment, or secure disposal of all hazardous wastes that are reasonably expected to be generated within the State during the 20-year period following [the giving of the assurance].

These facilities need not be located in-state, but if a CAP calls for interstate shipment of the hazardous waste for treatment, storage, or disposal, the arrangement with the waste receiving state must be worked out in advance and be evidenced by a formal interstate agreement.

Notice how the CAP requirement is a partial protection for states having RCRA permitted facilities that do not wish to have out-of-state hazardous wastes deposited in their facilities. Unless the prevailing view of the United States Supreme Court changes, the dormant commerce clause will continue to require that out-of-state waste be accepted, see page 504 *supra*, but §104(c)(9) increases the likelihood that most states will develop in-state capacity (or agreements for out-of-state capacity) rather than risk the loss of Superfund money. In the belief that forcing other states to live up to the CAP requirements will slow the flow of hazardous waste into its RCRA permitted facilities, New York has challenged EPA approval of CAPs of other states in the region. New York's challenge attacks CAPs that either rely on New York facilities without having formal agreements with New York, or that rely on planned new sites that have not been constructed due to local opposition. See New York Announces Lawsuit Against EPA for Failure to Enforce Capacity Requirement, 22 BNA Envtl Rep. 1363 (Sept. 27, 1991).

4. Is BDAT bad? In opting for treatment standards founded on BDAT, EPA seems to be locking-in existing treatment methods as the future norm, thereby deterring, rather than spurring, advances in the field. A second major criticism of BDAT as the treatment standard is that it trades a land disposal problem for an air pollution problem. This criticism arises because incineration is the current BDAT for most types of hazardous waste, and even in the best incinerators many hazardous constituents are not fully destroyed. Beyond that, incineration is not a complete treatment insofar as the ash that remains is itself usually a hazardous material in need of subsequent disposal. Still, BDAT is not without some redeeming features, one of which is its clarity. Once a technology is determined to be the BDAT for the treatment of a hazardous substance, generators and TSD facilities alike know what they must do to comply with the law.

5. Rethinking RCRA. In their Dialogue entitled Rethinking the Resource Conservation and Recovery Act for the 1990s, 21 ELR 10063 (1991), Marcia E. Williams and Jonathan Z. Cannon make a series of very technical, but very telling criticisms of

RCRA as it has developed. One of their most fundamental attacks on RCRA can be stated in simplified form – RCRA makes a great deal turn on the division of wastes into the categories of hazardous and non-hazardous, and then draws that line in a fiendishly complicated way. This leads to a multitude of untoward results. First, because the cost of disposal of hazardous waste is vastly greater than the cost of disposal of non-hazardous waste, generators have immense incentives to contest the categorization decisions. In conjunction with the byzantine definitional rules that are currently in force, a disproportionate amount of both regulatory and enforcement effort is directed to issues of coverage that result in little or no environmental benefit. A related criticism is that the definitional distinctions drawn between hazardous and non-hazardous are too often irrational if one keeps in mind RCRA's goal of reducing the release of dangerous substances. Here, the principal examples are the listing of some compounds as hazardous and the non-listing of chemically similar compounds having much the same potential for damaging human health and the environment. Moving from the definitional into the regulatory sphere, Williams and Cannon accuse RCRA of severe under- and over-regulation. The under-regulation occurs in regard to the laxity with which non-hazardous wastes are treated. Their point is that many waste streams that are designated as non-hazardous contain substantial quantities of hazardous materials that find their way into the environment. The over-regulation occurs in practices that overestimate risks (such as assuming that all wastes will be totally mismanaged), or in the adoption of anti-dilution rules that are inflexibly applied as rigid "tracking" rules so that wastes remain legally hazardous, even after treatment that produces a by-product that is non-hazardous according to EPA standards.

A somewhat different perspective on RCRA's future focuses on the failure of Subtitle C to address the larger issues of the solid waste problem posed by the need to safely dispose of such vast quantities of material. Taken together, the severity of regulation under Subtitle C, the expense entailed by detoxification of materials under that portion of RCRA, and the laxity of regulation under Subtitle D, form an unsatisfactory whole. Too little waste is required to be treated, and the waste that is treated is treated in ways that are too expensive to be used for substantial additional quantities of waste. In the end, long-term land disposal of solid waste imposes risks of "creating new environmental problems in the distant future when and if containment breaks down." Pedersen, The Future of Federal Solid Waste Regulation, 16 Colum. J. Envtl L. 109, 110 (1991). Pedersen contends that "since our current approach to the solid waste problem has reached it natural limits, market-based approaches provide the best option to induce further reduction of the quantity and toxicity of wastes disposed on land." His article goes on to suggest such things as a deposit on automobiles and other large-item sources of waste (similar to deposits on beverage containers[71]); taxes on use of virgin (rather than recycled) materials; direct subsidies to support recycled products; taxes on disposal of toxic wastes that present major threats of future harm; and a waste disposal allowance system similar to the tradeable emissions credits of the 1990 Clean Air Act Amendments.

---

71. Professor Menell has made similar proposals. See page 868 *supra* (Chapter 20).

Chapter 23

LAND USE-BASED ENVIRONMENTAL CONTROL STATUTES

Every land-use decision has environmental consequences; most environmental protection measures have land-use consequences. We should thus not expect to find a bright line between environmental law and land-use law. In fact, it is not even clear that they are two separate fields.

In California Coastal Commission v. Granite Rock Co., 480 U.S. 572 (1987), at page 499 *supra*, the Supreme Court attempted to articulate a distinction between land-use regulation and environmental control:

> The line between environmental regulation and land use planning will not always be bright; for example, one may hypothesize a state environmental regulation so severe that a particular land use would become commercially impracticable. However, the core activity described by each phrase is undoubtedly different. Land use planning in essence chooses particular uses for the land; environmental regulation, at its core, does not mandate particular uses of the land but requires only that, however the land is used, damage to the environment is kept within prescribed limits. Congress has indicated its understanding of land use planning and environmental regulation as distinct activities. Congress clearly envisioned that although environmental regulation and land use planning may hypothetically overlap in some instances, these two types of activity would in most cases be capable of differentiation. 480 U.S. at 587–88.

Justice Powell and Justice Stevens, however, found this distinction "unsupportable, either as an interpretation of the governing statutes or as a matter of logic..., a distinction...without a rational difference." 480 U.S. at 601, 603.

For the purposes of this chapter, we will treat the difference between environmental control and land-use regulation as one of degree rather than kind, and analyze several federal and state statutes that emphasize the techniques of land-use regulation, rather than performance standards, for environmental protection.

Although there may be no clear logical or legal distinction between land-use regulation and environmental control, there certainly is a palpable political distinction between the two. The American public reacts in radically different ways to legal controls addressing one or the other. Poll after poll indicates that most people will accept painful sacrifices in the name of environmental protection while they passionately resist added restrictions on the use of their land. Apparently many Americans do not perceive as inevitable the linkage of environmental protection and land-use regulation. They continue to treat land as a commodity rather than as an ecological community.

The American attitude toward land-use is unique. In other parts of the world, land development is not a right but a privilege; private land-use decisions are subordinate to comprehensive land-use plans that represent the interests of all members of the community, including, in some areas, non-human members. In the United States, by contrast, comprehensive land-use planning, outside the context of local zoning, is the exception rather than the rule. Governmental restrictions on the unfettered use of private land are strenuously resisted and even command some degree of constitutional protection, as studied in Chapter 9. In order to avoid stigma, environmental protection agencies at all levels of government often feel compelled to repeat the mantra that they are not regulating land use but protecting the environment.

But the more that environmental and natural resources management policy confronts modern regulatory realities – cumulation of effects, interconnectedness of coastal measures, synergistic causation, and a need for interpretative macroanalysis – the more the regulatory theater of land use becomes a major practical base for future rational overview accounting of short and long-term effects. One challenge to 21st-century environmental law will be to implement reasonable systems of land use-based management controls without disrupting the powerful political consensus that has supported the manifold environmental improvements since 1970.

Land-use controls take a variety of forms, falling along a continuum – ranging from controls that raise a strong presumption of non-development to controls that raise a strong presumption of development, with various intermediate gradations. Siting statutes, for example, presume that certain facilities should be sited but that, in the process, social costs should be kept to a minimum. At the other end of the continuum, critical area protection statutes presume that no development should take place in particularly valuable and vulnerable areas unless it is either clearly innocuous or else necessary to satisfy a paramount public purpose. Zoning, an established but limited method of controlling land-use, falls somewhere between siting and critical area protection legislation on this continuum.

This chapter first studies Congress's most ambitious, but still quite tentative, excursion into explicit land-use legislation – the Coastal Zone Management Act (CZMA) of 1972.[1] The CZMA addresses both siting and critical area protection, but in a way that encourages state planning rather than imposing federal command-and-control over private land-use decisions. Then state hazardous waste facility siting statutes are examined as examples of a type of siting process that is becoming increasingly popular, although fraught with equally grave difficulties. Next, two models of critical area protection statutes are presented: a site-specific permitting model (§404 of the Clean Water Act), and a comprehensive regional planning and control model (the Adirondack Park Agency). Finally, there is a brief discussion of zoning as an instrument of environmental protection.

1. 16 U.S.C.A. §1451 et seq.

A. THE FEDERAL COASTAL ZONE MANAGEMENT ACT

Most federal environmental regulation affects the siting of new development and the protection of critical areas in one way or another. This influence is, for the most part, indirect and implicit. The nonattainment and PSD (prevention of significant deterioration) sections of the Clean Air Act, for example, provide general rules for attaining and maintaining specified ambient air quality standards, but it is up to individual states to determine the mix of sources that will be permitted to use the assimilative capacities of the relevant airsheds. (See Chapter 18.) Federal law establishes visibility requirements to protect sensitive national parks, but it is state public utility commissions that determine the need for fossil-fueled power plants that may interfere with downwind visibility, and state environmental protection agencies that impose performance standards on them. Further down the institutional totem pole, it is local governments that, most often, finally determine whether those sources of air pollution will be permitted to locate in their communities. Only rarely does the federal government directly control private land-use decisions, as in the EPA regulations promulgated under RCRA that prohibit hazardous waste treatment, storage, and disposal facilities from being located in unsuitable, environmentally critical areas such as wetlands and flood plains. 40 CFR 264.18 (1990).

Congress's reluctance to confront private land-use explicitly and directly is a function not only of the American public's apparent aversion to land-use control, but also of Congress's deference to the traditional state police power to regulate private land-use for the public health, safety, and welfare. Under the Tenth Amendment to the United States Constitution, all powers not specifically delegated to the federal government or denied to the states are reserved to the states. This fundamental principle of federalism incorporates the state police power over private land-use, and the federal government has always trod lightly in this area. Only when other public interests have become compelling has Congress enlisted constitutional powers, such as the commerce clause, in aid of regulating land-use, albeit indirectly.

The CZMA does not directly authorize federal land-use controls, but it is explicitly land-use legislation. It is fundamentally a planning statute, in that it authorizes federal matching grants for the purpose of assisting coastal states, including Great Lakes states, in the development of management programs for the land and water resources of their coastal zones.[2] Once the National Oceanographic and Atmospheric Administration (NOAA, the branch of the United States Department of Commerce that administers the CZMA) has approved a state's coastal management program as complying with minimum federal standards, additional federal matching funds become available for the purpose of administering that state's management program. In order to be approved pursuant to §306(d), a coastal state management program must include:

2. Twenty-nine states have approved coastal zone management programs. Six coastal states (Georgia, Illinois, Indiana, Minnesota, Ohio, and Texas) have chosen not to participate.

(1) An identification of the boundaries of the coastal zone subject to the management program;

(2) A definition of what will constitute permissible land uses within the coastal zone which have a direct and significant impact on coastal waters;

(3) An inventory and designation of areas of particular concern within the coastal zone;

(4) An identification of the means by which the state proposes to exert control over the land uses and water uses listed in paragraph (2);

(5) Broad guidelines on priorities of uses in particular areas, including specifically those uses of lowest priority;

(6) A description of the organizational structure proposed to implement such management program, including the responsibilities and interrelationships of local, areawide, state, regional, and interstate agencies in the management process;

(7) A definition of the term "beach" and a planning process for the protection of, and access to, public beaches and other public coastal areas of environmental, recreational, historical, esthetic, ecological, or cultural value;

(8) A planning process for energy facilities likely to be located in, or which may significantly affect, the coastal zone, including, but not limited to, a process for anticipating and managing the impacts from such facilities;

(9) A planning process for assessing the effects of, and studying and evaluating ways to control, or lessen the impact of, shoreline erosion, and to restore areas adversely affected by such erosion.

Under §303(2), state coastal management planning must give "full consideration to ecological, cultural, historic, and esthetic values as well as to needs for economic development." Thus, state coastal planning under the CZMA must balance economic development against environmental protection.

A coastal state may follow one or a combination of three models in designing its coastal management program:

(1) State establishment of criteria and standards for local implementation, subject to administrative review and enforcement;

(2) Direct state land and water use planning and regulation; or

(3) State administrative review for consistency with the management program of all development plans, projects, or land and water use regulations, including exceptions and variances thereto, proposed by any state or local authority or private developer, with power to approve or disapprove....

Although the CZMA is basically a planning statute, it attempts to remedy the major defect of most planning statutes – unenforceability. All too often, governmental planning processes produce abstract documents that collect dust in government libraries because they are not tied to implementation and enforcement. Sometimes, instead of making difficult political choices, governments will temporize by planning or doing studies. Planning statutes can thus be devices for symbolic assurance.

At other times, where governments are genuinely doubtful about the extent of particular problems and possible regulatory responses, planning can develop data bases, alternatives, and preferred regulatory strategies. In order to function as a viable policy tool, a planning statute must be closely integrated with implementation techniques.

The CZMA attempts to assure implementation of state coastal management programs in two ways: (1) authorizing the suspension of federal funding if a coastal state fails to "adhere to its management program" §312(c); and (2) mandating that any federal activity within a state's coastal zone be consistent with that state's approved coastal management program. The following case analyzes the CZMA's "consistency doctrine" in the context of petroleum lease sales on the outer continental shelf.

Secretary of Interior v. California
United States Supreme Court, 1984
464 U.S. 312, 104 S. Ct. 656, 78 L.Ed. 2d 496

O'CONNOR, J. This case arises out of the Department of Interior's sale of oil and gas leases on the outer continental shelf off the coast of California. We must determine whether the sale is an activity "directly affecting" the coastal zone in §307(c)(1) of the Coastal Zone Management Act (CZMA). That section provides in its entirety:

> Each federal agency conducting or supporting activities directly affecting the coastal zone shall conduct or support those activities in a manner which is, to the maximum extent practicable, consistent with approved state management programs. 16 U.S.C. §1456(c)(1).

We conclude that the Secretary of the Interior's sale of outer continental shelf oil and gas leases is not an activity "directly affecting" the coastal zone within the meaning of the statute.

CZMA defines the "coastal zone" to include state but not federal land near the shorelines of the several coastal states, as well as coastal waters extending "seaward to the outer limit of the United States territorial sea." The territorial sea for states bordering on the Pacific or Atlantic Oceans extends three geographical miles seaward from the coastline. Submerged lands subject to the jurisdiction of the United States that lie beyond the territorial sea constitute the "outer continental shelf" (OCS). By virtue of the Submerged Lands Act, passed in 1953, the coastal zone belongs to the states, while the OCS belongs to the federal government.

CZMA was enacted in 1972 to encourage the prudent management and conservation of natural resources in the coastal zone. Congress found that the "increasing and competing demands upon the lands and waters of our coastal zone" had "resulted in the loss of living marine resources, wildlife, nutrient-rich areas, permanent and adverse changes to ecological systems, decreasing open space for public use, and shoreline erosion...."

Once a state plan has been approved, CZMA §307(c)(1) requires federal activities "conducting or supporting activities directly affecting the coastal zone" to be "consistent" with the state plan "to the maximum extent practicable." The

Commerce Department has promulgated regulations implementing that provision. Those regulations require federal agencies to prepare a "consistency determination" document in support of any activity that will "directly affect" the coastal zone of a state with an approved management plan. The document must identify the "direct effects" of the activity and inform state agencies how the activity has been tailored to achieve consistency with the state program. 15 C.F.R §930.34,.39 (1983).

OCS lease sales are conducted by the Department of the Interior (Interior). Oil and gas companies submit bids and the high bidders receive priority in the eventual exploration and development of oil and gas resources situated in the submerged lands on the OCS. A lessee does not, however, acquire an immediate or absolute right to explore for, develop, or produce oil or gas on the OCS; those activities require separate, subsequent federal authorization.

[Over the objections of the California Coastal Commission, Interior placed 115 tracts in the Santa Maria Basin, off the coast of Santa Barbara, up for lease. The Commission argued that some of these tracts should be removed from leasing because oil spills on the OCS in these areas could threaten the range of the Southern Sea Otter within California's coastal zone.]

Respondents filed two substantially similar suits in federal district court to enjoin the sale of 29 tracts situated within 12 miles of the Sea Otter range. Both complaints alleged Interior's violation of §307(c)(1) of CZMA. They argued that leasing sets in motion a chain of events that culminates in oil and gas development, and that leasing therefore "directly affects" the coastal zone within the meaning of §307(c)(1)....

Whether the sale of leases on the OCS is an activity "directly affecting" the coastal zone is not self-evident. [Justice O'Connor interpretted the CZMA's legislative history as excluding certain federal activities on the OCS from consistency determinations because these activities do not "directly affect" the coastal zone.]

Moreover, a careful examination of the structure of CZMA §307 suggests that lease sales are a type of federal agency activity not intended to be covered by §307(c)(1) at all.

Section 307(c) contains three coordinated parts [defining actions that refine consistency review]. Paragraph (1) refers to activities "conduct[ed] or support[ed]" by a federal agency. Paragraph (2) covers "development projects" "undertake[n]" by a federal agency. Paragraph (3) deals with activities by private parties authorized by a federal agency's issuance of licenses and permits. The first two paragraphs thus reach activities in which the federal agency is itself the principal actor, the third reaches the federally approved activities of third parties. Plainly, Interior's OCS lease sales fall in the third category. Section 307(c)(1) should therefore be irrelevant to OCS lease sales, if only because drilling for oil and gas on the OCS is neither "conduct[ed]" nor "support[ed]" by a federal agency. Section 307(c)(3), not §307(c)(1), is the more pertinent provision...[and] CZMA §307(c)(3) definitely does not [apply to] lease sales.... A federal agency may not issue a "license or permit" for an activity "affecting land or water uses in the coastal zone" without ascertaining that the activity is consistent with the state program or otherwise in the national interest. Each affected state with an approved management program must concur in the issuance of the license or permit; a state's refusal to do so may be overridden only if the Secretary of Commerce finds that the proposed activity is consistent with CZMA's objectives or otherwise in the interest of national security. Significantly, §307(c)(3) contained no mention of consistency requirements in connection with the sale of a lease.

In 1976...[s]pecific House and Senate Committee proposals to add the word "lease" to §307(c)(3) were rejected by the House and ultimately by the Congress as a whole. It is surely not for us to add to the statute what Congress twice decided to omit....

COMMENTARY AND QUESTIONS

1. What Congress giveth.... Responding to a strong lobbying campaign by coastal state politicians and environmentalists, Congress overturned the foregoing decision by an amendment to the Omnibus Budget Reconciliation Act of 1990 which requires that *all* federal activities having an effect on the coastal zone be consistent with state management plans. 16 U.S.C.A. §1456(c)(1)(A). It is now clear that such federal actions as fisheries management plans under the Fisheries Conservation and Management Act (16 U.S.C.A. §1853) and the designation of offshore dumpsites under the Marine Protection, Research, and Sanctuaries Act (33 U.S.C.A. §1412(c)), as well as OCS oil exploration leasing, require consistency reviews.

2. Constitutionality of the CZMA. The federal courts, not Congress, have the last word regarding a statute's constitutionality. Is it constitutional for a state to veto a federal activity? Compare Whitney, Johnson & Perles, State Implementation of the Coastal Zone Management Act Consistency Provisions – Ultra Vires or Unconstitutional? 12 Harv. Envtl L. Rev. 67 (1988)(state veto is unconstitutional); and Archer and Bondereff, Implementation of The Federal Consistency Doctrine – Lawful and Constitutional: A Response to Whitney, Johnson, & Perles, 12 Harv. Envtl L. Rev. 112 (1988). Does it matter that the Secretary of Commerce can override a state veto on rather general grounds?

3. Maximal consistency. What does it mean that a federal activity directly affecting the coastal zone must be consistent with a state management plan "to the maximum extent practicable"?

NOAA, perhaps taking its lead from judicial interpretations of similar language in NEPA, requires such federal activities to be "fully consistent" with state programs "unless compliance is prohibited based upon the requirements of existing law applicable to the Federal agency's operations." Deviations from "full consistency" are also permitted under special circumstances. 15 CFR §§930.32(a) and (b). Administrative and judicial resolution of consistency conflicts are analyzed in Eichenberg & Archer, The Federal Consistency Doctrine: Coastal Zone Management and "New Federalism," 14 Ecol. L.Q. 9 (1987).

4. State regulation of federal activities. Can a state regulate activities on federal lands located in the coastal zone, or is the state restricted to its role in consistency review? *Granite Rock*, at page 499 *supra*, held that reasonable state environmental regulations imposed on the operator of an unpatented mining claim located on federally owned land within California's approved coastal zone would be valid, partially because the CZMA does not limit existing state authority. Could a state, using the CZMA, stop the award of a timber contract by the Forest Service in a coastal National Forest? Or would prohibition of a timber sale be, under the

Supreme Court's distinction quoted above, impermissible land-use control rather than environmental protection?

5. The CZMA and the dormant commerce clause. Does the CZMA contain an implied Congressional consent for a state, through its coastal management program, to override the dormant commerce clause? In Norfolk Southern v. Oberly, 822 F.2d 388 (3d Cir. 1987), the Third Circuit answered this question in the negative, concluding that the CZMA neither decreases nor increases state power. Even so, the Court refused to declare unconstitutional a provision of the Delaware Coastal Zone Act that bans all new heavy industry from the state's coastal zone because that prohibition does not discriminate against, or place an undue burden on, interstate commerce.

6. Permissiveness of the CZMA. The CZMA only requires that coastal states receiving federal planning and management funds consider tradeoffs between economic development and environmental protection in their coastal zones; the outcome of any conflict between these two sometimes inconsistent goals is left entirely to state determinations. Thus, the CZMA state veto can lawfully support economic development rather than environmental protection. In Cape May Greene v. Warren, 698 F.2d 179 (3d Cir. 1983), EPA attempted to prohibit a residential development in New Jersey's coastal zone by conditioning a federal construction grant for sewerage facilities on a denial of sewer hookups for the development. However, by including the development in its approved coastal zone management plan, New Jersey was able to veto EPA's development restriction.

America's coastal areas are undergoing profound environmental stress. "Already fifty-three percent of the population of the United States live within fifty miles of the coasts of the Atlantic and Pacific Oceans, the Gulf of Mexico and the Great Lakes. Some estimates project that, by the year 2000, eighty percent of the United States population may live in coastal areas." Archer and Bondereff, 12 Harv. Envtl L. Rev. at 116. For a powerful analysis of our coastal zone problems and a critique of current policies, see Houck, America's Mad Dash to the Sea, Amicus Journal, 21–36 (Summer 1988). According to Houck, "we are expecting state regulation, under the Coastal Zone Management Act, to overcome formidable economic and political pressures without the safeguard of a clear, national mandate."

Is it time for command-and-control legislation governing land-use along America's fragile coastlines?

B. STATE HAZARDOUS WASTE FACILITY SITING STATUTES

All siting statutes presume, to one degree or another, that the facilities involved in the siting process are necessary to society. The purpose of siting statutes is to site these facilities with as little social cost (including environmental cost) and disruption as possible.

Siting facilities for disposal of solid waste, hazardous waste, and nuclear waste, has become extraordinarily difficult because of the way that LULUs (Locally Undesirable Land Uses) trigger the NIMBY (Not In My Back Yard) Syndrome local reaction. Waste management tragedies like Love Canal, New York, and Times Beach, Missouri – along with the close participation of state and federal government officials in the siting and permitting of some of these misplaced and mismanaged facilities (as in *Wilsonville*, at page 68 *supra*) – have created a mood of deep public skepticism about whether waste disposal can be safely performed, and cynicism about whether state or federal governments are sufficiently competent and objective to protect the health and safety of host communities. In addition, local residents harbor reasonable fears that a waste disposal facility will create few jobs, produce little additional tax revenue, overburden local services (e.g., fire, police) and infrastructure (e.g., roads, sewerage facilities), and negatively affect property values. Any proposal to site a waste disposal facility is met by a generally effective combination of zoning prohibitions, political opposition, media denunciation, lawsuits, and civil disobedience. Consequently, America is experiencing a persistent shortfall in waste disposal capacity, especially for the perhaps 100 million metric tons of hazardous waste regulated under RCRA and those CERCLA hazardous wastes that must be disposed of offsite.

Unlike states, municipalities possess no inherent powers. They are capable of exercising only those powers delegated to them by the state governments that created them. Thus even where a state constitution contains a Home Rule provision to the effect that municipalities are responsible for control of land-use within their boundaries, the state can legally override municipal decisions to "zone out" particular waste disposal facilities.

A number of states have enacted hazardous waste disposal facility siting statutes relying on Alternative Dispute Resolution ("ADR," see Chapter 24), with regard to providing compensation for host communities and allaying their safety concerns by establishing environmental monitoring and response mechanisms in addition to those required by federal and state laws. Four state hazardous waste facility siting statutes stand out as contrasting types.[3]

Minnesota law[4] gives the community – broadly defined as the county – control over final siting decisions. Counties volunteer sites by passing non-binding Resolutions of Interest, which may be withdrawn at any time before binding site contracts have been signed. Once a county volunteers an environmentally acceptable site, the Minnesota Waste Management Board simultaneously negotiates a siting contract with the county and searches for a private developer to build and operate a facility on the site. During its negotiations with the Board, the county receives up to $4,000 per month in local government aid. If a siting contract is ultimately signed, the county receives an additional $150,000 per year for two years. These incentives are in addition to any other payments the county may negotiate

3. See generally Schmeidler & Sandman, Getting To Maybe, 276–324 (1988), available from the Environmental Communication Research Program, Rutgers, The State University of New Jersey, New Brunswick, New Jersey 08903. The authors are grateful to Dr. Emilie Schmeidler for her assistance in preparing this section.

4. Minn. Stat. §115A.191.

with the Board, including tax breaks and other forms of state assistance. Extra compensation mechanisms, however, may require legislative approval.

New Jersey law[5] gives the state Hazardous Waste Facility Siting Commission the power to obtain a site by eminent domain and override local zoning where necessary to site a facility. After preparing siting criteria, the Commission searches for the most environmentally acceptable sites. During the latter phases of the siting process, potential host communities are given grant funds to perform their own site suitability studies. Once the site has been chosen, a qualified developer is expected to enter into negotiations with the host community for compensation and safety measures. The host community is entitled to at least five percent of the gross receipts of any facility constructed within its boundaries in order to mitigate the effects of the facility.

In Wisconsin, the developer chooses the site and requests each affected municipality to identify relevant local regulations.[6] The municipality has the choice of whether or not to negotiate with the developer. If the municipality chooses not to negotiate, all applicable local regulations enacted within 15 months of the developer's submission of a site feasibility report are pre-empted. If an affected municipality chooses to negotiate, it must enact a formal siting resolution stating its intent to negotiate and, if necessary, submit to binding arbitration. Arbitrable issues are severely circumscribed. Reimbursement of a community's costs of evaluating a site and participating in the negotiation and arbitration process are limited to $2,500. In the arbitration process, each party immediately submits its final offer, and the arbitrator must choose one of these without modification.

In Massachusetts, all post-siting statutes, local permits, and zoning changes promulgated to exclude particular facilities are pre-empted.[7] The developer initiates the siting process by filing a notice of intent with the state Hazardous Waste Facility Siting Council. The Council may then issue a finding that the proposal is "feasible and deserving" in terms of the developer's financial capability and past management practices, technical feasibility of the proposal, need for the facility, and compliance with state and federal laws. If a feasible and deserving determination is issued, the community, aided by state technical assistance grants, is required to negotiate with the developer and the state. (The state is a party because the negotiations may include state incentives to a host community.) If the negotiations result in impasse, an arbitrator prepares a draft settlement for public comment. The final settlement is submitted to the Council and is subject to judicial review.

COMMENTARY AND QUESTIONS

1. Community veto? Despite these and other sophisticated siting statutes, in point of practical fact no major hazardous waste disposal facility has been sited in any of these four states.[8] In fact, of the twelve states that have enacted hazardous waste disposal facility siting statutes, only Maryland has successfully sited a facility. The

5. N.J. Rev. Stat. §13.1E-52–59.
6. Wis. Stat. §144.44.
7. Mass. Gen. L. 21D §3–15.
8. (This is as of late 1991.)

Maryland facility was constructed and is operated by a state agency. It is located in a highly industrialized, sparsely populated area of South Baltimore, on land owned by the state and city. The homes owned by members of a small neighboring community have been purchased by the state and the population has been relocated. How often are similarly favorable circumstances likely to occur? The design life of the Maryland site, moreover, is only five years.

The Minnesota siting act gives communities ultimate power to accept or reject hazardous waste disposal facilities. Some commentators believe that given the current NIMBY climate and the probable success of communities that oppose LULUs, this is the most viable way to site hazardous waste disposal facilities:

> A community that feels coerced into having a facility is likely to experience too much anger, fear and outrage about the siting process itself to be concerned about examining the content of the proposal. Guaranteeing a community the right to say no to any proposal it found unacceptable would, by freeing it from the threat of coercion, allow it to explore whether having a facility would be a better option than having none. Given the right to say no, a community might weigh the costs, risks, and benefits of hosting a facility and try to negotiate a package that would be more attractive than maintaining the status quo.[9]

On the other hand, one could argue that (1) a community possessing a veto will almost certainly exercise it, (2) a developer will not negotiate with a community possessing a veto, (3) local politicians will never take anything but a "hard line" and then complain that "they made us accept the facility," (4) a community will negotiate only if it believes that the facility is inevitable because the state will override its objections, and (5) a community, which bears the concentrated costs of a facility, will be incapable of recognizing the facility's dispersed, statewide benefits.

The New Jersey statute assumes that communities will not negotiate about compensation and mitigation until after the siting decision has been made. But what leverage does a community possess at that point? Has a community by then become so alienated and defensive that it will only dig in its heels and fight?

2. Choosing the site. There is general agreement that decisions about the need for hazardous waste disposal facilities and appropriate technologies for these facilities are best made at the state level before making site-specific decisions. But states differ in their approaches to choosing sites. In Minnesota, counties volunteer sites and the state determines the best disposal site from among those volunteered. In New Jersey, the state selects the best sites based on predetermined siting criteria adopted with public participation. In Wisconsin, the developer chooses the site and initiates the siting process by notifying affected municipalities. The state then judges each application against minimum state siting criteria, without comparing other potential sites or determining whether better sites exist. Massachusetts follows a similar procedure, except that the developer first notifies the Council by filing a notice of intent.

9. Schmeidler & Sandman, Getting To Maybe, at 48.

Should a developer be permitted to choose a site? Would a developer most likely select a disadvantaged community that is poorly organized and desperate for development? Is it necessarily inequitable to locate LULUs in disadvantaged communities, or is the problem one of unequal access to information and political power? As for information, in New Jersey and Massachusetts state grants are available to communities to assist them in collecting information relative to siting. In Wisconsin, however, the municipality must utilize its own resources to evaluate the proposal, and in arbitration can only recover a maximum of $2,500 to cover all costs of negotiation and arbitration. This system would appear to be unfair to a Wisconsin community that bears the burden of showing, among other things, that there are better sites. In this regard, a state might adopt a "best site" or an "available site" strategy. Does an available site strategy leave too little margin for uncertainty? Will a state cast its net too wide in order to assure that a facility will be sited?

3. Negotiations: who, what, and when? In Minnesota, the county proposes a site and negotiates with the state; the developer is not involved in the negotiations. Is the county the proper institution to represent a host municipality? There is a danger here that the state will "give away the store" in its negotiations with local communities and discourage potential developers. Will other municipalities – especially those whose applications have been rejected – resist the authorization of extraordinary incentives for host communities by opposing the special legislation necessary to enact them?

Negotiation is mandatory in Massachusetts. The state will be part of the negotiations because enhanced state services and benefits are factors that the community and developer may consider. In Wisconsin, an affected municipality is not required to negotiate, but if it does not quickly resolve to negotiate and be subject to arbitration, it loses its power to influence the facility because it cannot "zone out" the facility. (If you were a Wisconsin community, would you swiftly pass a restrictive zoning ordinance and hope that no developer would contact you during the next 15 months?) The developer must negotiate if the municipality resolves to participate in the siting process. Is negotiation that is mandatory (or virtually so as in Wisconsin) a contradiction in terms? Will a party bargain in good faith if it cannot say "no"? The spectre of binding arbitration if a siting agreement is not reached – as is the case in both Massachusetts and Wisconsin – will often spur the parties to negotiate in good faith. As a community or a developer, what would your strategy be in Wisconsin, where the arbitrable issues and judicial review are limited, and the arbitrator must accept either side's "last best offer"? How would that strategy differ in Massachusetts, where the arbitration is wide-ranging and the arbitrator can draft a compromise settlement that is open for public comment and must be approved by the Council, with broad judicial review available?

In Wisconsin, when a community opposes a facility, it passes a siting resolution in order to keep the negotiation option open, but agrees with the developer to hold negotiations in abeyance while the community fights the site on technical and environmental grounds in separate state licensing proceedings. More tractable communities tend to negotiate and participate in the licensing proceeding simultaneously. The Wisconsin process has resulted in numerous completed siting agreements (although none has involved a major offsite hazardous waste disposal facility). Can the success of the Wisconsin siting statute be explained by the fact that its coverage is so inclusive, covering solid waste facilities, on-site facilities, and expansions, as well as new, off-site hazardous waste disposal facilities? Does the familiarity of the process overcome the potential stigma of having a facility sited in a community? Or does the community accept the facility because it hasn't the resources to fight the developer, and the arbitrable issues are so circumscribed? Or is it something about the political culture of Wisconsin? Whatever the reason, Wisconsin communities have accepted waste disposal facilities, negotiating for direct payments, property value protection, disposal privileges, extra monitoring, infrastructure subsidies, and public access for surveillance.

The Massachusetts siting act places extensive technical evaluation of the site and the developer's waste disposal technology at the end of the process, rather than at the beginning or concurrent with negotiations as in Wisconsin. The belated occurrence of technical review has been given as one reason for the apparent failure of the Massachusetts siting act:

> The timing of the process appears to have been a major issue, one which focused repeated controversy on the Council's "feasible and deserving" determination at the beginning of the formal process. For instance, in [one] proposal the community believed it had strong evidence the proposal should be abandoned; however, the Council refused to reject the proposal. The community then argued that it was showing that the proposal was not feasible or deserving, but the Council was unwilling to revoke its "feasible and deserving" determination because these technical issues were to be dealt with more thoroughly [after the completion of negotiations]. The community interpreted the Council's "feasible and deserving" determination to show that the Council was supporting the proposal despite its overwhelming evidence that the proposal was flawed. The Council, in contrast, argued that the determination was only a "coarse screen" to allow the process to begin, and that the careful technical analyses should be done...at the end.[10]

A different drawback of the Massachusetts process is its excessive complexity. At least five state agencies are closely involved. Draft and final reports, public briefings, comment periods, and hearings abound. Multiple time limits intersect and interweave. Negotiations are tripartite rather than bipartite. Must a successful siting process be a relatively simple one, in contrast to the cumbersome Massachusetts system?

4. Other siting statutes. There are three federal siting statutes: the Deepwater Port Act, 33 U.S.C.A. §§1501 et seq. (governing siting of manmade oil transfer ports beyond the territorial sea); the Nuclear Waste Policy Act, 42 U.S.C.A. §§10101 et seq. (establishing a process for siting a repository for disposal of high-level radioactive

10. Schmeidler & Sandman, Getting To Maybe, at 290.

waste); and the Low-Level Radioactive Waste Policy Act, 42 U.S.C.A. §§2021(b) et seq. (instituting a process, emphasizing interstate compacts, for siting regional facilities for disposing of low-level radioactive wastes). Problems of LULU and NIMBY have also beset these statutes, especially the two involving disposal of radioactive wastes. Some states have siting statutes relating to power plants. States can also engage in "back door siting" through lawmaking based on their traditional police powers. Recall how California used its authority over the fiscal aspects of electric generation to defeat proposals to site nuclear power plants. Pacific Gas and Electric v. California Energy Resources Conservation & Development Commission, *supra* at page 483.

5. Begging the question? Do state hazardous waste disposal facility siting statutes assume the continuation of the current levels of hazardous wastes and thus discourage waste reduction and recycling? Surely hazardous waste disposal facilities will continue to be necessary even if we require reasonable steps to effectuate pollution prevention. If fewer facilities will be needed because of pollution prevention measures, perhaps facility siting should be implemented on a regional basis by federal regional siting boards?

C. CRITICAL AREA PROTECTION STATUTES

Section 1. SITE-BY-SITE PERMITTING: SECTION 404 OF THE CLEAN WATER ACT

Section 404 of the Clean Water Act governs the discharge of dredged or fill material into navigable waters. As the following case indicates, the §404 process has profound land-use implications.

Bersani v. Environmental Protection Agency
United States Circuit Court for the Second Circuit, 1988
850 F.2d 36

TIMBERS, J. Appellants...("Pyramid" collectively) appeal from a judgment entered...granting summary judgment in favor of appellees, the EPA and the United States Army Corps of Engineers, and denying Pyramid's motion for summary judgment.

This case arises out of Pyramid [development company's] attempt to build a shopping mall on certain wetlands in Massachusetts known as Sweeden's Swamp. Acting under the Clean Water Act, EPA vetoed the approval by the Corps of a permit to build the mall because EPA found that an alternative site had been available to Pyramid at the time it entered the market to search for a site for the mall. The alternative site was purchased later by another developer and arguably became unavailable by the time Pyramid applied for a permit to build the mall....

Sweeden's Swamp is a 49.5 acre wetland which is part of an 89 acre site near Interstate 95 in South Attleboro, Massachusetts. Although some illegal dumping and motorbike intrusions have occurred, these activities have been found to have had little impact on the site, which remains a "high-quality red maple swamp" providing wildlife habitat and protecting the area from flooding and pollution.

STATUTORY AND REGULATORY FRAMEWORK

One of the sections of the Clean Water Act relevant to the instant case is §301(a), which prohibits the discharge of any pollutant, including dredge or fill materials, into the nation's navigable waters, except in compliance with the Act's provisions, including §404. It is undisputed that Sweeden's Swamp is a "navigable water"...and that Pyramid's shopping center proposal will involve the discharge of dredged or fill materials.

Section 404 of the Act, focusing on dredge or fill materials, provides that the United States Army and EPA will share responsibility for implementation of its provisions. EPA and the Corps also share responsibility for enforcing the Act.

As with virtually all critical areas regulatory programs, applicants seeking permit approval to build a development in the regulated area must submit site plans, various traffic, economic, and environmental analyses, and propose mitigation measures as necessary.

Section 404(a) authorizes the Secretary of the Army, acting through the Corps, to issue permits for the discharge of dredged or fill materials at particular sites. Section 404(b) provides that, subject to §404(c), the Corps must base its decisions regarding permits on guidelines (the "§404(b)(1) guidelines") developed by EPA in conjunction with the Secretary of the Army.

The §404(b)(1) guidelines, published at 40 CFR §230 (1987), are regulations containing the requirements for issuing a permit for discharge of dredged or fill materials. 40 CFR §230.10(a) covers "non-water dependent activities" (i.e., activities that could be performed on non-wetland sites such as building a mall) and provides essentially that the Corps must determine whether an alternative site is available that would cause less harm to the wetlands. Specifically, it provides that "no discharge of dredged or fill material shall be permitted if there is a practicable alternative" to the proposal that would have a "less adverse impact" on the "aquatic ecosystem." It also provides that a practicable alternative may include "an area not presently owned by the applicant which could reasonably be obtained, utilized, expanded, or managed in order to fulfill the basic purpose of the proposed activity." It further provides that "unless clearly demonstrated otherwise," practicable alternatives are (1) "presumed to be available," and (2) "presumed to have less impact on the aquatic ecosystem." Thus, an applicant such as Pyramid must rebut both of these presumptions in order to obtain a permit. Sections 230.10 (c) and (d) require that the Corps not permit any discharge that would contribute to significant degradation of the nation's wetlands and that any adverse impacts must be mitigated through practicable measures.

In addition to following the §404(b)(1) guidelines, the Corps may conduct a "public interest review." 33 CFR §320.4 (1987). This public interest review is not mandatory under §404, unlike consideration of the §404(b) guidelines. In a public interest review, the Corps decision must reflect the "national concern" for protection and use of resources but must also consider the "needs and welfare of the people."

Under §404 of the Act, EPA has veto power over any decision of the Corps to issue a permit. It is this provision that is at the heart of the instant case.

Specifically, §404(c) provides that the Administrator of EPA may prohibit the specification of a disposal site "whenever he determines, after notice and opportunity for public hearings, that the discharge of materials into such area will have an unacceptable adverse effect" on, among other things, wildlife. An "unacceptable adverse effect" is defined in 40 CFR §231.2(e) as an effect that is likely to result in, among other things, "significant loss of or damage to...wildlife habitat...." The burden of proving that the discharge will have an "unacceptable adverse effect" is on EPA.

In short, both EPA and the Corps are responsible for administering the program for granting permits for discharges of pollutants into wetlands under §404. The Corps has the authority to issue permits following the §404(b)(1) guidelines developed by it and EPA; EPA has the authority under §404(c) to veto any permit granted by the Corps. The Corps processes about 11,000 permit applications each year. EPA has vetoed five decisions by the Corps to grant permits....

On appeal, the thrust of Pyramid's argument is a challenge to what it calls EPA's "market entry" theory, i.e. the interpretation by EPA of the relevant regulation, which led EPA to consider the availability of alternative sites at the time Pyramid entered the market for a site, instead of at the time it applied for a permit....

We hold (1) that the market entry theory is consistent with both the regulatory language and past practice; (2) that EPA's interpretation, while not necessarily entitled to deference [because the other federal agency administering §404, the Corps, disagreed with EPA's interpretation], is reasonable; and (3) that EPA's application of the regulation is supported by the administrative record....

THE SWEEDEN'S SWAMP PROJECT [CHRONOLOGY]

The effort to build a mall on Sweeden's Swamp was initiated by Pyramid's predecessor, the Edward J. DeBartolo Corporation. DeBartolo purchased the Swamp some time before April 1982. At the time of this purchase an alternative site was available in North Attleboro (the "North Attleboro site"). Since Massachusetts requires state approval (in addition to federal approval) for projects that would fill wetlands, DeBartolo applied to the Massachusetts Department of Environmental Quality Engineering ("DEQE") for permission to build on Sweeden's Swamp. DEQE denied the application in April, 1982.

Pyramid took over the project in 1983 while the appeal of the DEQE denial was pending. In April 1983, Massachusetts adopted more rigorous standards for approval of permits. The new standards added wildlife habitat as a value of wetlands to be protected and required the absence of a "practicable alternative."...

One of the key issues in dispute in the instant case is just when did Pyramid begin searching for a suitable site for its mall. EPA asserts that Pyramid began to search in the Spring of 1983. Pyramid asserts that it began to search several months later, in September 1983. The difference is crucial because on July 1, 1983 – a date between the starting dates claimed by EPA and Pyramid – a competitor of Pyramid, the New England Development Co. ("NED"), purchased options to buy the North Attleboro site. The site was located upland and could have served as a "practicable alternative" to Sweeden's Swamp, if it had been "available" at the relevant time. Thus, if the relevant time to determine whether an alternative is "available" is the time the applicant is searching for a site (an issue that is hotly disputed), and if Pyramid began to search at a time *before* NED acquired options on the North Attleboro site, there definitely would have been a "practicable alternative" to Sweeden's Swamp, and the Pyramid application should have been denied. On the other hand, if Pyramid did not begin its search until *after* NED acquired options on the North Attleboro site, then the site arguably was not "available" and the permit should have been granted....

In August 1984, Pyramid applied under §404(a) to the New England regional division of the Corps (the "NE Corps") for a permit. It sought to fill or alter 32 of the 49.6 acres of the Swamp; to excavate nine acres of uplands to create artificial wetlands; and to alter 13.3 acres of existing wetlands to improve its environmental quality. Later Pyramid proposed to mitigate the adverse impact on the wetlands by creating 36 acres of replacement wetlands in an off-site gravel pit....

In November, 1984, EPA and FWS submitted official comments to the NE Corps recommending denial of the application because Pyramid's proposal was inconsistent with the the 404(b)(1) guidelines. Pyramid had failed (1) to overcome the presumption of the availability of alternatives and (2) to mitigate adequately the adverse impact on wildlife. EPA threatened a 404(c) review. Pyramid then proposed to create additional artificial wetlands at a nearby upland site, a proposal it eventually abandoned.

In January 1985, the NE Corps hired a consultant to investigate the feasibility of Sweeden's Swamp and the North Attleboro site. The consultant reported that either site was feasible but that from a commercial standpoint only one mall could survive in the area. On February 19, 1985, the NE Corps advised Pyramid that denial of its permit was imminent. On May 2, 1985, the NE Corps sent its recommendation to deny the permit to the national headquarters of the Corps. Although the NE Corps ordinarily makes the final decision on whether to grant a permit, see 33 CFR §325.8 (1982), in the instant case, because of the widespread publicity, General John F. Wall, the Director of Civil Works at the national headquarters of the Corps, decided to review the NE Corps' decision. Wall reached a different conclusion. He decided to grant the permit after finding that Pyramid's offsite mitigation proposal would reduce the adverse impacts sufficiently to allow the "practicable alternative" test to be deemed satisfied. He stated:

> In a proper case, mitigation measures can be said to reduce adverse impacts of a proposed activity to the point where there is no "easily identifiable difference in impact" between the proposed activity (including mitigation) versus the alternatives to that activity.

On May 31, 1985, Wall ordered the NE Corps to send Pyramid, EPA and FWS a notice of its intent to grant the permit. The NE Corps complied on June 28, 1985.

On July 23, 1985, EPA's RA [Regional Administrator] initiated a §404(c) review of the Corps decision....

On May 13, 1986, EPA issued its final determination, which prohibited Pyramid from using Sweeden's Swamp. It found (1) that the filling of the Swamp would adversely affect wildlife; (2) that the North Attleboro site could have been available to Pyramid at the time Pyramid investigated the area to search for a site; (3) that considering Pyramid's failure or unwillingness to provide further materials about its investigation of alternative sites, it was uncontested that, at best, Pyramid never checked the availability of the North Attleboro site as an alternative; (4) that the North Attleboro site was feasible and would have a less adverse impact on the wetland environment; and (5) that the mitigation proposal did not make the project preferable to other alternatives because of scientific uncertainty of success....

As EPA has pointed out, the preamble to the §404(b)(1) guidelines states that the purpose of the "practicable alternatives" analysis is "to recognize the specific value of wetlands and to avoid their unnecessary destruction, particularly where practicable alternatives *were* available in non-aquatic areas to achieve the basic purpose of the proposal." 45 Fed. Reg. 85,338 (1980)(emphasis added). In other words, the purpose is to create an incentive for developers to avoid choosing wetlands when they could choose an alternative upland site. Pyramid's reading of the regulations would thwart this purpose because it would remove the incentive for a developer to search for an alternative site at the time such an incentive is needed, i.e., at the time it is making a decision to select a particular site. If the practicable alternatives analysis were applied to the time of the application for a permit, the developer would have little incentive to search for alternatives, especially if it were confident that alternatives soon would disappear. Conversely, in a case in which alternatives were not available at the time the developer made its selection, but became available by the time of application, the developer's application would be denied even though it could not have explored the alternative site at the time of its decision....

PRATT, Circuit Judge, dissenting: ...

This market entry theory approaches a sensitive environmental problem through a time warp; it ignores the statute's basic purpose and it creates unfair and anomolous results...ignoring the crucial question of whether the site itself should be preserved. Under the market entry theory, developer A would be denied a permit on a specific site because when he entered the market alternatives were available, but latecomer developer B, who entered the market after those alternatives had become unavailable, would be entitled to a permit for developing the same site. In such a case, the theory no longer protects the land but instead becomes a distorted punitive device: it punishes developer A by denying him a permit, but grants developer B a permit for the same property – and the only difference between them is when they "entered the market."

The market entry theory has further problems. In this case, for example, if a Donald Trump had "entered the market" after NED took the option on the North Attleboro site and made it unavailable, under EPA's approach he apparently would have been entitled to a permit to develop Sweeden's Swamp. But after obtaining the permit and the land, could Trump then sell the package to Pyramid to develop? Or could he build the mall and sell the developed site to Pyramid?....

Furthermore, in a business that needs as much predictability as possible, the market entry theory will regretably inject exquisite vagueness. When does a developer enter the market? When he first contemplates a development in the area? If so, in what area – the neighborhood, the village, the town, the state or the region? Does he enter the market when he first takes some affirmative action? If so, is that when he instructs his staff to research possible sites, when he commits money for more intensive study of those sites, when he contacts a real estate broker, when he first visits a site, or when he makes his first offer to purchase? Without answers to these questions a developer can never know whether to proceed through the expense of contracts, zoning proceedings, and EPA applications....

Since Congress delegated to EPA the responsibility for striking a difficult and sensitive balance among economic and ecological concerns, EPA should do so only after considering the circumstances which exist, not when the developer first conceived of his idea, nor when he entered the market, nor even when he submitted his application; rather, EPA, like a court of equity, should have the full benefit of, and should be required to consider, the circumstances which exist at the time it makes its decision. This is the only method which would allow EPA to make a fully informed decision – as Congress intended – based on whether, at the moment, there is available a site which can provide needed economic and social benefits to the public, without unnecessarily disturbing valuable wetlands.

COMMENTARY AND QUESTIONS

1. Timing theories in *Bersani*. Should the "practicable alternative" test be applied at the time of "market entry," permit application, or "time of decision"? There are several problems with Judge Pratt's dissenting "time of decision" test. First, there is the question of which of many decision points is applicable. In this case is it Massachusetts DEQE's original rejection, its subsequent approval, the Corps' original rejection, its subsequent approval, the EPA decision, or the decisions of the two state or two federal courts that considered this matter on judicial review? Second, since the "time of decision" comes rather late in the process, it is doubtful that a developer would take a substantial financial risk in the face of possible permit denial based on distant events that it can neither control nor predict. Third, the developer will have invested so much in project preparation by the time of decision that agencies will be reluctant to deny it a permit based on the availability of a site that has only recently come on the market. How would you resolve the timing problem?

Is §404's "practicable alternative" test a good one? As the dissent points out, this test has nothing to do with the desirability of building in a wetland. Developers are, unfortunately, drawn to wetlands because they are available and relatively inexpensive. Alternative sites may be so much more expensive as to be "impracticable" for the developer. (Under 40 CFR 230.10(a)(2), practicability includes cost considerations.) Once the developer has overcome the presumption of a practicable alternative that has less adverse impact on the aquatic ecosystem, and the Corps approves the permit, the burden is on EPA to prove that the discharge will have an "unacceptable adverse effect." This combination of tests creates an effective presumption in favor of the proposed development. What does "unacceptable" mean? In practice it is apparently tough to prove. When *Bersani* was decided in 1988, EPA had vetoed only five Corps permits out of 11,000 processed each year. Does EPA possess the resources to perform its supervisory role effectively in the §404 permitting process?

2. Mitigation of environmental damage. As you have seen in previous chapters, policies are frequently not uniform within a particular federal agency or among agencies. See Sax, Defending The Environment (1970), Chapters 1 and 2, for case studies illustrating the internal political forces at work that cause these discrepancies. Why, for example, when the Pyramid application was "elevated" to Washington, did General Wall reverse the decision of NE Corps which presumably, was in a better position to assess the prospective effects of the development proposal?

Furthermore, EPA and the Corps disagreed strongly about the merits of this particular proposal, as they have often done over other aspects of §404. (EPA has a mandate to protect the environment, while the Corps has traditionally performed and permitted development activities.) When federal agencies conflict, they usually do not sue each other. (Whom would the Justice Department represent?) Instead their differences are played out against the backdrop of individual permit applications such as this, in political battles between their clienteles and constituencies, and in closed-door negotiations over Memoranda Of Agreement (MOA).

One such MOA was concluded in 1990 between EPA and the Corps over the issue of mitigation of environmental damage, which figured prominently in *Bersani*. See 55 FR 9211, March 12, 1990. Mitigation is defined as 1) avoidance of adverse environmental impacts, 2) minimization of these impacts, and 3) compensation for unavoidable impacts. One dispute between the Corps and EPA was whether the articulated national goal of "no net loss" of wetlands should be applied to each §404 permit or to the §404 program in general. The Corps won this round. EPA, however, won the inclusion of a statement to the effect that "compensatory mitigation may not be used as a method to reduce environmental impacts in the evaluation of the least environmentally damaging practicable alternative...." EPA also won the adoption of a specific process and set of standards for evaluating compensatory mitigation (restoration of existing degraded wetlands or creation of man-made wetlands) proposals, but the Corps won the approval of "mitigation banking" where cash can be paid into a fund to be used for wetland creation or restoration. Environmentalists are skeptical of compensatory mitigation both because of the scientific uncertainties involved in wetlands restoration and creation, and because compensatory mitigation arguably sends the wrong message to the American public about the need for humility and restraint in dealing with the natural world.

3. Section 404 evaluation. Section 404 has not been particularly successful in preserving America's disappearing wetlands: (1) §404 permits are not required for projects involving excavating, draining, clearing, and flooding of wetlands, or performing activities on adjacent non-wetland areas that damage wetlands, where no fill is deposited in the wetlands themselves; (2) the sharing of §404 implementation between the Corps and EPA is cumbersome and contentious; (3) the Corps has been less than zealous in enforcing §404 permits; (4) §404 is replete with statutory exemptions for agricultural, silvicultural, and construction activities; and (5) the Corps has used general permits to limit the scope of its §404 jurisdiction.

See Thompson, Section 404 of the Federal Water Pollution Control Act Amendments of 1977: Hydrologic Modification, Wetlands Protection and the Physical Integrity of the Nation's Waters, 2 Harv. Envtl L. Rev. 264 (1978), Blumm, The Clean Water Act's Section 404 Permit Program Enters Its Adolescence: An Institutional and Programmatic Perspective, 8 Ecol. L.Q. 410 (1980), Want, Federal Wetlands Law: The Cases and the Problems, 8 Harv. Envtl L. Rev. 1 (1984), USGAO, The Corps of Engineers' Administration of the Section 404 Program (1988). Section 404 authorizes the Corps to delegate §404 jurisdiction over inland wetlands to states, but few states have applied for delegation. Several states, including Massachusetts, run wetlands programs that are concurrent with §404. (Massachusetts has instituted a virtual per se prohibition of projects such as Pyramid's proposed mall in Sweeden's Swamp; see Citizens for Responsible Management v. Attleboro Mall, 511 N.E.2d 562 (1987). If you are interested in wetlands preservation, would you be better off with §404 and no state program, with concurrent programs, or with an exclusively state program?

In the introduction to this chapter, a critical area protection statute was defined as one presuming that no development should take place in a valuable and vulnerable area unless the development is environmentally innocuous or necessary for a paramount public purpose. Who bears these burdens with regard to §404? Is the "practicable alternative" test an additional burden for an applicant to bear, or does it substitute for a showing of innocuousness or public need? Was the proposed mall environmentally innocuous? How badly do we need another shopping mall? Does the test presume the predominance of market decisions over wetlands?

4. What is a wetland? Section 404 only applies to delineated wetland areas. Since 1989, EPA and the Corps have been identifying wetlands based on the Federal Manual for Identifying and Delineating Jurisdictional Wetlands ("wetlands manual"). The 1989 wetlands manual defined wetlands in terms of three parameters – hydrology, vegetation, and soils. On August 14, 1991, five federal agencies, including EPA and the Corps, proposed regulations containing revisions to the wetlands manual that would considerably narrow the criteria for wetlands delineation. See 56 FR 40446. For example, the 1989 wetlands manual required inundation by surface water or saturation by groundwater to at least 18 inches of the surface for one week or more during the growing season; in contrast, the proposed regulations required inundation for 15 or more consecutive days, or saturation to the surface for 21 or more consecutive days during the growing season. The ultimate regulatory definition of wetlands will have immediate broad impact.

5. Other site-by-site permitting statutes. Many states have enacted statutes to protect critical areas through site-by-site permitting. In addition to wetlands, some of the resources covered by these statutes are coastal zones, lake and river shorelines, floodplains, wild and scenic rivers, and historic sites.[11]

6. Evaluation of site-by-site permitting. Site-by-site permitting programs, such as §404, can only react to one development proposal at a time. They are insensitive to the cumulative impacts of a proposed project in addition to the impacts of other projects already completed in or planned for the same environmentally vulnerable area, which may transcend political boundaries. Effective critical area protection can only be assured through a preventive land-use planning and management program administered by an institution that possesses jurisdiction over an area that includes the entire resource to be protected.

Section 2. COMPREHENSIVE REGIONAL PLANNING AND CONTROL

Comprehensive regional planning and land-use control systems for environmentally critical areas have emerged sporadically across the United States. Florida

---

11. See Grad, Treatise On Environmental Law II §10.03 (1989) for a list and discussion of these statutes, and cross-references.

established a program for identifying and protecting "areas of critical state concern."[12] Oregon and Vermont exercise state-level development review of projects in designated critical areas based on state land-use plans.[13] Other states have created regional land-use planning and permitting agencies to supervise development along the California Coast, in the Hackensack Meadowlands and Pinelands of New Jersey, and in the Lake Tahoe area.[14]

One of the most successful of these regional land-use planning and management agencies has been the Adirondack Park Agency (APA) in New York.[15] The Adirondack Park encompasses approximately six million acres in northern New York State. Established in 1892, nearly all its state-owned lands have been protected since 1895 by the New York State Constitution that declares them "forever wild." State-owned and nonstate-owned lands are intermingled to a significant degree in the park. About 38 percent of the land is owned by the State, while the remainder is divided into parcels of diverse sizes owned by individuals, corporations, institutions like universities and camps, and municipalities.

Among its outstanding natural resources, the park contains the headwaters of five major river basins. More than 1,200 miles of Adirondack rivers have been designated under New York State's Wild, Scenic, and Recreational Rivers System Act.

In the face of potential development pressure on the Adirondacks, the New York State Legislature, in 1971, passed the Adirondack Park Agency Act, creating the APA and requiring it to prepare a comprehensive management plan for the park's state lands and a land-use and development plan for the nonstate lands in the Adirondacks. The so-called "Private Land Plan" was enacted as a statute in 1973.[16]

The Private Land Plan divides nonstate lands into six land-use areas: (1) hamlets; (2) moderate-intensity-use areas; (3) low-intensity-use areas; (4) rural-use areas; (5) resource management areas; and (6) industrial-use areas. The Plan sets compatible uses and overall density limitations for each land-use area. For example, only 15 residential units per square mile are allowed in a resource management area. Private lands are frequently zoned low-density areas because of their proximity to state lands.

These restrictions are implemented through a project review process involving both the APA and relevant municipalities. The APA has exclusive jurisdiction over shoreland development proposals and proposed large projects of regional significance with potentially serious environmental consequences. Smaller, less environmentally threatening projects of regional concern must be approved by municipalities whose land-use controls have been accepted by the APA as conforming to the Plan. Proposals with only local implications are subject to municipal approval subject to APA review for nonconformity with the Plan.

---

12. Fla. Stat. 380.05.

13. Or. Rev. Stat. §197.040; Vt. Stat. Ann. 10 §6007.

14. Cal. Pub. Res. Code §30601; N.J. Stat. Ann. §13:17–6; Nev. Rev. Stat. §277.200; Cal. Gov't Code §66801.

15. N.Y. Exec. Law §800; N.Y. Const. art. 14 §1. Much of the following discussion is based on Booth, New York's Adirondack Park Agency, in Brower & Carol, eds., Managing Land-Use Conflicts (1987) 140 et seq.

16. N.Y. Exec. Law §805.

Much of the opposition to regional land-use planning and management agencies comes from municipalities that resent being deprived of their traditional "home rule" powers to control land-use within their boundaries. In addition, most municipalities are funded by property taxes, and are typically more concerned with accumulating tax "rateables" than preserving intermunincipal critical areas. Developers oppose the formation of regional agencies because they have more political leverage with municipalities than they would with the newer, larger, and more environmentally sensitive agencies. The following case involving the APA illustrates the legal context in which this opposition to regional land-use agencies arises:

Wambat Realty Corp. v. State of New York

Court of Appeals of New York, 1977
41 N.Y.2d 490, 362 N.E.2d 581

BREITEL, C. J. This is a declaratory judgment action brought against the State, the [Adirondack Park Agency], and related officials to challenge the Adirondack Park Agency Act as violative of the home rule protection afforded local governments in Article IX of the Constitution. Plaintiff, private owner and would-be developer of more than 2,200 acres of land in the Adirondack Park region, appeals directly from a judgment at Special Term declaring the act valid on summary judgment.

The issue is whether comprehensive zoning and planning legislation enacted by the State Legislature to ensure preservation and development of the resources of the Adirondack Park region...is invalid because it encroaches upon the zoning and planning powers of local governments.

There are two subsidiary issues. The first is of long standing in the area of home rule: whether the subject matter of a challenged act, in the instant case the future of a cherished regional park, is a matter of State concern. Put another way, the first subsidiary issue is whether the subject matter relates to "other than the property, affairs or government of a local government" and is thus within the powers which the home rule [constitutional] article expressly reserves to the State. [The second subsidiary issue is one relating to an unusual nuance of New York law that is not of general significance.]

There should be an affirmance. To categorize as a matter of purely local concern the future of the forests, open spaces, and natural resources of the vast Adirondack Park region would doubtless offend aesthetic, ecological, and conservational principles. But more important, such a categorization would give a substantially more expansive meaning to the phrase "property, affairs or government" of a local government than has been accorded to it in a long line of cases interpreting successive amendments to the home rule article....

The land owned by Wambat Realty is situated in the Town of Black Brook, one of numerous local governments within the area known as the Adirondack Park. Although Wambat's proposed land development project, "Valmont Village," was permissible under the pre-existing zoning and planning resolutions of the town, in 1971 the Adirondack Park Agency Act was adopted. Under the act plaintiff was required to seek approval for its project from the Adirondack Park Agency, created by the act to fashion a plan for future use of the public and private lands within the park region. Shortly after receiving a "Notice of Project Application Incompletion" from the agency, Wambat instituted this action for a declaratory judgment challenging the act's validity.

Of particular importance to plaintiff's contention are the 1973 amendments to the act which include adoption of the Adirondack Park land use and development plan and authorization for the filing of an official plan map. Plaintiff argues that these provisions, which set forth a comprehensive zoning and planning program for all of the public and private lands within the park, together with other restrictions on local land use contained in the act, unconstitutionally deprive the Town of Black Brook of its own zoning and planning powers....

Key to plaintiff's contention are subdivisions 6 and 7 of §10 of the [Statute of Local Governments], which grants to cities, villages, and towns "the power to adopt, amend, and repeal zoning regulations" and to all local governments the "power to perform comprehensive or other planning work relating to [their] jurisdiction."...

Defendants, on the other hand, counter that the home rule article's grant of powers to local government is not absolute, but qualified. In pertinent part, §3 of Article IX [of the New York Constitution] provides:

> (a) Except as expressly provided, nothing in this article shall restrict or impair any power of the legislature in relation to: ...
>
> (3) Matters other than the property, affairs or government of a local government.

The reservation of power is largely repeated in §11 of the Statute of Local Governments. Defendants' response to Wambat's contention is, in short, that the subject matter of the Agency Act relates to "other than the property, affairs or government of a local government."...

Turning now to the Adirondack Park Agency Act, application to it of these principles leads inexorably to its validity. Of course, the Agency Act prevents localities within the Adirondack Park from freely exercising their zoning and planning powers. That indeed is its purpose and effect, not because the motive is to impair home rule, but because the motive is to serve a supervening State concern transcending local interests. As ably explained by Mr. Justice James Gibson at Special Term, preserving the priceless Adirondack Park through a comprehensive land use and development plan is most decidedly a substantial State concern, as it is most decidedly not 119 separate local concerns. All but conclusive of this aspect of the issue is the constitutional and legislative history stretching over 80 years to preserve the Adirondack area from despoliation, exploitation, and destruction by a contemporary generation in disregard of the generations to come.

Plaintiff argues that the Agency Act, unlike legislation previously upheld against home rule attacks, does not relate to the life and health of New York's people, and is therefore distinguishable. In the face of increasing threats to and concern with the environment, it is no longer, if it ever was, true that the preservation and development of the vast Adirondack spaces, with their unique abundance of natural resources – land, timber, wildlife, and water – should not be of the greatest moment to all the people of the State. These too relate to life, health, and the quality of life. Indeed, in a larger perspective, it is the teaching of the latter decades that ecological concern with the oceans and the continents has ceased to be a matter only of littoral and national concern.

COMMENTARY AND QUESTIONS

1. Distributive justice, economically speaking. The Town of Black Brook, in a companion case decided with the above, likewise unsuccessfully challenged the APA Act. The Court remarked that the Town "understandably seeks to promote its own development, even, if necessary, at the expense of regional planning for the benefit of all the people and future generations." Is it fair for some municipalities to lose tax rateables because of development controls while other municipalities, outside the critical area, experience developmental and tourism windfalls? Is this a good argument for tax-sharing or other legislation to moderate the windfalls and wipeouts resulting from critical area protection?

2. Impact on private property rights. Wambat Realty's land was developable under the local ordinance that was pre-empted by the APA Act. Was Wambat entitled to compensation for an unconstitutional taking? Would it have made a difference if Wambat had received local development approvals before enactment? How would the establishment of a regional land-use agency affect the balancing of public gain and private loss performed to determine if a taking has occurred?

3. Continuing the success of the APA. During the years since 1973, one factor in the general success of the APA has been its policy of purchasing private lands and conservation easements in critical areas. This policy avoids the difficult takings questions raised where zoning severely diminishes the development potential of particular lands. In these recessionary times, however, New York State voters, concerned about budget deficits, have rejected the conservation bond issues that would have provided funds for APA purchases of open space. Unable to purchase lands or easements in doubtful situations, the APA may be inhibited in its future attempts to preserve the Park.

4. The limited use of regional institutions. To date, fewer than a dozen substate regional, and one interstate, critical area protection institutions have been created. Additionally, some established regional institutions, such as the Delaware River Basin Commission and the South Florida Water Management District, perform land-use planning and management functions with conservation as one of their goals. Why haven't we seen more of these institutions in this era of environmental consciousness? Regional planning and management are often practically necessary for rational resolution of problems that extend beyond village limits, but regional coordination (if it has any teeth) threatens both existing governmental institutions and development interests.[17] There is, moreover, a justifiable fear that new regional institutions will be expensive and cumbersome. Perhaps the American political system – organized as it is by federal, state, and local governments – is simply antithetical to regional governments. It will be interesting to see whether the future brings the formation of other regional land-use institutions, or enhanced state powers over land-use in critical areas.

---

17. The 1970s' campaigns to create regional "councils of governments" (COGs) appear to have foundered on these twin shoals.

D. TRADITIONAL LAND USE CONTROLS AND THE ENVIRONMENT: ZONING, SUBDIVISION REGULATION, ET AL.

In day to day practice, the overwhelming majority of land use management occurs at the local level – predominantly through local government regulation, the focus of this part of the chapter, and at the extremely local level of private land use controls, which offer landowners powerful and elaborate means for regulating the use and development of their own land (see Chapter 5).

Section 1. SUBDIVISION REGULATIONS

There are a variety of environmental problems that arise commonly throughout the United States when subdividers take large parcels of land (often farms or ranches purchased in large blocks) and divide them up legally into many small lots (often a quarter of an acre or less) to be resold off a master recorded deed "plat." The problems posed by subdivisions are often severe. Developers often lack design sophistication, ignoring topography so that various roads and lots lie at steep angles; physical site disruption and other problems occur – erosion, septic overflows, degradation of lakes and rivers from pollution and high density uses.

Subdivision regulations work by focusing on the registration of the master deed plat: before a master plat subdividing a parcel into lots can be recorded, the ordinance requires that it meet a variety of legal requirements – sewerage, road criteria, utilities – often in the form of certificates annexed onto the master plat itself.

To these basic requirements, which have environmental consequences, communities have started adding more sophisticated subdivision requirements – erosion and sedimentation control, dedication of park land and other "exactions" offsetting burdens imposed on the community,[18] certified landscape architects' plans with analysis of groundwater flows, slope analysis, and the like.[19] Subdivision regulations can also require that developers put enforceable restrictive covenants and other private law devices on the master deed, like requirements of open space protection, density controls, and use restrictions specifically enforceable by the local government as third party beneficiary. The more carefully such ordinances are drafted, the more they assure that developments will be harmonious with their surrounding environment; they often produce designs that end up being more profitable.

Section 2. ZONING

By far the most common land use control device in the United States is local zoning, quite different from the proceeding categories because zones actively apply to every square inch of the jurisdiction, and set out a comprehensive set of land use district designations specifying before the fact which uses will automatically be

18. The concept of exactions was accepted by the Supreme Court in the *Nollan* case, at page 474 *supra*.

19. Design standards can encourage site plans that "cluster" residential structures to preserve the maximum amount of amenities and useful space for the inhabitants of the subdivision, rather than cutting up the overall parcel into the maximum number of standardized front, back, and side lots covering the sites like a checkerboard.

WILLIAM CARNEY

A standard design subdivision, laid out with little regard to pre-existing topographical and ecological conditions, causing the maximum amount of site usage with no open common areas or clustering of residential sites.

allowed and which excluded. The most common form of zone ordinance is the "Euclidean" model, named for Village of Euclid v. Ambler Realty Co., 272 U.S. 365 (1926) the case that established zoning's general validity.[20]

Because zoning directly affects private property decisions, from the beginning it has stirred up a hornet's nest of opposition. Nevertheless, because the problems of American communities have become so much more complex and pressured since World War II, zoning has become an unloved but widespread phenomenon. Of major American cities, for instance, only Houston has refused to use zoning, and appears to have paid a chaotic price.

Zoning implicitly incorporates some environmental values. If a zone planning agency knows which way the wind is blowing, it will not locate residential areas downwind from its industrial zone districts. Densities designated for different districts may have direct consequences to local conditions. The districting process, however, must build upon what already exists, and in many cases induces each

20. The Euclidean model requires: a Plan, a comprehensive plan adopted by the community analyzing existing land uses and specifying future community development desires; a separate zone ordinance creating a catalogue of zone district categories, defining the range of permitted uses, densities, and structural characteristics in each category; an official zone map incorporated as part of the ordinance mapping out the districts on the ground; and, finally, a zone enforcement agency, acting to interpret and apply the zone requirements throughout the community, and reviewing and determining enforcement issues, special exceptions, and variances, as required.

community to plan itself like a separate little city-state, each with prime residential areas, industrial zones to capture tax base, and none with a dump, with no coordination on a county or regional basis to determine where larger settlement patterns and economic development patterns should be located.

Over the years, a variety of other kinds of regulations have often been grafted as overlays on top of the basic zoning ordinances, capitalizing upon zoning's established political and legal status. Thus when some communities wanted to protect wetlands or flood plains, they added an overlay category to their zone maps; land in any district that had the characteristics of flood plain or wetland had to comply with the added restrictive requirements. Some communities have added "open space" overlays or green belt requirements, erosion and sedimentation restrictions, historic preservation controls, and similar modern environmental sensitivities to the basic zone ordinance and map.

Over time, as local zoning increasingly reflects the growing sophistication of the land use planning and landscape architecture specialties, more and more environmental sensitivities are incorporated in the initial planning and the subsequent implementation of zone ordinances.

COMMENTARY AND QUESTIONS

1. The local basis of zoning. The federal government, as noted earlier, generally stays far away from regulating land use. State governments also typically avoid direct land use as well, leaving it up to the lowest level of local governments, with a few exceptions.[21] Efforts to set up regional land use controls have largely failed due to the balkanized nature of intergovernmental jealousies and the traditional norms of local government home rule.

Consider the range of problems and turmoil that would be caused by shifting particularized land use control decisions to the state or regional level. How would one draw rational jurisdictional lines? According to river drainage watersheds? Airsheds? Metropolitan-based market areas? Zoning replays a traditional question of democracy: to what extent should single communities be able to operate as isolated individuals?

Along with the drawbacks of fracturing land use controls into tens of thousands of small uncoordinated jurisdictions, there are corresponding advantages. Zoning reflects local knowledge of the community and landscape in which it applies. It can often serve as a useful vehicle for carrying modern environmental ideas into practical land development practice.

2. TDRs: Transfers of Development Rights.[22] An interesting technique built on the foundation of traditional zoning is the concept of transfers of development rights. TDRs occur when a community decides to impose special restrictions on a particular sector of the community. In the *Penn Central* case, page 459 *supra*, for

21. Hawaii and the state of Maine have state based land use regulatory systems that at least in theory cover the entire state.

22. See Costonis, Development Rights Transfer: An Exploratory Essay, 83 Yale L.J. 75 (1973).

instance, New York imposed historic regulations protecting the terminal's facade and preventing the owners from filling the airspace above. Part of the administrative and legal support for the regulation of old buildings in New York's historic districts was the provision that the building rights which otherwise would have applied to the site could be transferred to other sites owned by the same developer, or sold. The mechanism has potential for flexibility and fine tuning of site by site development planning, mitigating the takings effects of regulation.

3. Impact Fees. Another evolving device resembles subdivision exactions. Impact fees respond to the problem that developers often locate high density developments without sufficient regard to the public's costs of providing utilities and amenities. Impact fees are a self-defense mechanism, analyzing the imposed costs and requiring that they be paid in advance – fees for added parks and recreation facilities, schools, drainage and sewer construction, roads and other transportation infrastructure, groundwater recharge facilities and an infinitely expandable range of other imposed costs.[23]

Like other land use devices currently applied at the local level impact fees can mobilize the expertise and defensive instincts of local communities; they hold larger intercommunity and regional potential as well.

We shall never achieve harmony with land, any more than we shall achieve justice and liberty for [all] people. In these higher aspirations, the important thing is not to achieve, but to strive.

— Aldo Leopold, SCA 72

23. See Blasser & Kentopp, Impact Fees: The Second Generation, 38 J. Urban & Contemp. Law 55 (1990).

PART FIVE

TRENDS IN ENVIRONMENTAL LAW

FUTURE GOVERNMENT ENVIRONMENT PROTECTORS of AMERICA
I'M INTERESTED IN PROTECTING THE ENVIRONMENT. CAN I JOIN YOU?
HOLD IT!! ARE YOU ONE OF THOSE "SNAIL DARTER" TYPES?
MEL LAZARUS. 3-19

Chapter 24

ADR: ALTERNATIVE DISPUTE RESOLUTION PROCESSES IN ENVIRONMENTAL CASES

A. WHY USE ALTERNATIVE DISPUTE RESOLUTION?

Environmental law was born and raised in the arena of adversarial combat – the traditional litigation mode in court and agency proceedings. Few would argue, however, that the adversarial litigative process is ideal. Litigation often proves to be a crude mechanism for achieving resolutions, results in antagonistic relationships, and drains scarce resources in terms of time, money, and energy. Because of its obstacles and inefficiencies, ultimately, many disputes never get resolved within the formal mechanisms of the legal system. Because of its practical burdens, the traditional model is often unavailable to those who lack financial and political resources.

Even within traditional adversarial litigation, of course, most disputes are settled out of court through a process of negotiation prior to final judgment. But other options for conflict resolution are increasingly available. A growing movement both within and outside the legal profession has been calling for a shift to ADR – alternative dispute resolution mechanisms like mediation, arbitration, non-litigative negotiation, minitrials, and other procedures. Whether by statutory mandate or pragmatic decision of the parties, many issues that previously would have been handled by litigation or agency enforcement now have the possibility of being resolved through ADR. The trend reemphasizes that the practice of law need not be what many laypersons consider it – an unproductive, insulated mechanism for implementing the more negative elements of human nature – but rather a profession that ultimately tries to make social relationships and civic mechanisms work.

ADR has been increasingly visible in the environmental setting (where it is often referred to as "EDR") only since the late 1970s.[1] Unlike most litigation models, the ADR approach can be forward-looking – designed to anticipate future policy or practical conflicts[2] – as well as retrospective and reactive to existing disputes.

The viability of ADR as an alternative to litigation has been the subject of fierce debate in both the academic and practice communities. Richard Mays, arguing for expanded environmental use of ADR, notes that in standard EPA enforcement cases "the average time between discovery of a violation and settlement might easily be three to five years or more. Even after this delay, [ultimately all but five] percent of

---

1. For an overview of major environmental disputes in which ADR methods were used, see Talbot, Settling Things (1983), and L. Susskind, L. Bacow and M. Wheeler, Resolving Environmental Regulatory Disputes (1983).

2. This mode has been called "front-loading" or anticipatory consensus-building.

EPA's judicial cases are settled rather than tried."[3] Enormous amounts of time and resources spent on such cases could be reduced dramatically if resolutions were reached through negotiation rather than the process or threat of litigation.

Not all cases can or should be settled through ADR. Even proponents like Mays agree that adversarial litigation is necessary and appropriate in some cases – for example if there are important precedential legal issues that need resolution, if injunctions or other court-supervised remedies are necessary and parties lack the time or interest required for negotiating settlements, or if, in light of a party's egregious conduct, the public interest requires an open public trial and punishment. These exceptional cases, they argue, however, make up only a small percentage of the total number of environmental suits filed each year.

Some opponents of alternative remedies claim that ADR's purported savings in time and expense are bought at the cost of accuracy and justice. Edward Brunet, a staunch opponent of ADR, claims that "only formal litigation and adjudication provide a mechanism for accurate determination of facts."[4] Brunet maintains that the informality of ADR procedures makes them "weak since they rely on voluntary party exchange of data and do not have an authority figure equivalent to a judge to prevent discovery abuse." In environmental disputes, Brunet claims, the informality of ADR is particularly dangerous. Given the complexity of environmental disputes, "the 'facts' produced in an environmental mediation are likely to be incomplete and inaccurate."

On the other hand, ADR sometimes presents clear advantages. It can, for example, promote effective joint factfinding techniques producing facts faster and with greater accuracy than traditional discovery. If parties can develop a mutually-acceptable factfinding agenda and methodology, then the traditional "battle of the experts" can be averted and questions shifted from a "position-based" to a broader "interest-based" resolution process on the merits.[5]

Sander, Alternative Methods of Dispute Resolution: An Overview
37 University of Florida Law Review 1 (1985)

Beginning in the late Sixties, American society witnessed an extraordinary flowering of interest in alternative forms of dispute settlement. This interest emanated from a wide variety of sources ranging from the Chief Justice of the United States Supreme Court to corporate general counsel, the organized Bar and various lay groups....

The Sixties were characterized by considerable strife and conflict, emanating in part from the civil rights struggles and the Vietnam War protests. An apparent legacy of those times was a lessened tolerance and a greater tendency to turn grievances into disputes. Also relevant was a significant increase in the statutory

3. Mays, Alternative Dispute Resolution and Environmental Enforcement: A Noble Experiment or a Lost Cause?, 18 ELR 10087, 10088 (1988).

4. Brunet, The Costs of Environmental Alternative Dispute Resolution, 18 ELR 10515, 10516 (December 1988). See also Fiss, Against Settlement, 93 Yale L.J. 1073 (1984), and Out of Eden, 94 Yale L.J. 1669 (1985), arguing that ADR undermines the important law-building, law-applying functions of judicial litigation, and finding other major shortcomings.

5. See L. Susskind and J. Cruikshank, Breaking the Impasse: Consensual Approaches to Resolving Public Disputes (1987); also R. Fisher and W. Ury, Getting to Yes (1981).

creation of new causes of action....

Courts found themselves inundated with new filings, triggering cries of alarm from the judicial administration establishment. This judicial congestion led to the claim that equal access to justice had been denied. Spurred in part by these conditions, parties attempted to resolve some of these disputes through alternative dispute resolution mechanisms.... The Ford Foundation established the National Center for Dispute Settlement and the Institute of Mediation and Conflict Resolution to study dispute resolution mechanisms....

Four goals of the alternatives movement emerged:

1. To relieve court congestion, as well as undue cost and delay.
2. To enhance community involvement in the dispute resolution process.
3. To facilitate access to justice.
4. To provide more "effective" dispute resolution.[6]

These goals might overlap and conflict. Consider, for example, the problem of "excessive" access. If society is too ready to provide access for all kinds of disputes, this will lengthen the queue and aggravate the congestion problem. Similarly, measures aimed at relieving court congestion would take a very different form from measures designed to enhance community control over dispute settlement. Hence, it is essential to think clearly and precisely about the reasons for pursuing ADRMs.

Considering the complex social conditions that have led to court congestion and concomitant delay...the notion that a pervasive use of arbitration and mediation will solve the "court crisis" seems misguided. The principal promise of alternatives stems from the third and fourth goals set forth above. Our primary efforts should be directed toward these two goals. And since the access goal can only be fulfilled by providing access to an ADRM that is appropriate for the particular dispute,[7] the third and fourth goals in effect coalesce....

One could posit a number of plausible criteria for determining the suitability of various dispute mechanisms.... Adjudication typically seeks to make a definitive determination with respect to past events, while mediation attempts to restructure the [present and future] relationship of the disputants.... The open-ended and non-coercive process of mediation is also more likely to teach the parties to recognize and resolve future controversies. Mediation thus gives maximum durability to the settlement....

A significant qualification, however, is presented in the case where the two disputants have substantially disparate bargaining power. In such a case, mediation is either pointless, or worse yet, threatens to take undue advantage of the weaker party. ADRM specialists must learn far more about the optional combination of formal adjudicative and informal mediation processes for this type of case....

What is the proper role of attorneys in alternative dispute resolution mechanisms? First, ADRMs must distinguish between a lawyer's role as a representative of the disputants, and a lawyer's role as a dispute resolver.... Unfortunately, much

6. Although no definitive work has been done with respect to how to measure "effectiveness," presumably to be taken into account are such factors as cost, speed, satisfaction (to the public and the parties) and compliance. At present, it is almost accidental if community members find their way to an appropriate forum other than regular courts.

7. At present, it is almost accidental if community members find their way to an appropriate forum other than regular courts. Several other models of dispute resolution...are available in many communities [but] since they are operated by a hodge-podge of local government agencies, neighborhood organizations, and trade organizations, citizens must be very knowledgeable about community resources to locate the right forum for their particular dispute.

of a law student's training is in adversary dispute settlement rather than accomodative problem-solving. This situation is rapidly changing, however. Increasingly, legal education encompasses mediation and other ADRM training....

B. ENVIRONMENTAL ADR

Section 1. AN ARRAY OF ADR METHODS

National Institute for Dispute Resolution, Paths to Justice: Major Public Policy Issues of Dispute Resolution (1983), in **Administrative Conference of the United States, Sourcebook: Federal Agency Use Of Alternative Means of Dispute Resolution** 5–47 (1987)

Some conflict contributes to and, indeed, is essential to a healthy, functioning society. Social change occurs through dispute and controversy. Some observers attribute the long-term stability of the country to its ability to hear and reconcile the disagreements of its diverse population. Thus one should focus not only on avoiding disputes, but also on finding suitable ways of hearing and resolving those that inevitably arise....

Dispute resolution techniques can be arrayed along on a continuum ranging from the most rulebound and coercive to the most informal. Specific techniques differ in many significant ways, including:

- whether participation is voluntary;
- whether parties represent themselves or are represented by counsel;
- whether decisions are made by the disputants or by a third party;
- whether the procedure employed is formal or informal;
- whether the basis for the decisions is law or some other criteria; and
- whether the settlement is legally enforceable.

At one end of the continuum is adjudication (including both judicial and administrative hearings): parties can be compelled to participate; they are usually represented by counsel; the matter follows specified procedure; the case is decided by a judge in accordance with previously established rules; and the decisions are enforceable by law....

At the other end of the continuum are negotiations in which disputants represent and arrange settlements for themselves: participation is voluntary, and the disputants determine the process to be employed and criteria for making the decision. Somewhere in the middle of the continum is mediation, in which an impartial party facilitates an exchange among disputants, suggests possible solutions, and otherwise assists the parties in reaching a voluntary agreement....

[Here follows a definitional survey of ADR forms:]

Arbitration...involves the submission of the dispute to a third party who renders a decision after hearing arguments and reviewing evidence. It is less formal and less complex and often can be concluded more quickly than court proceedings. In its most common form, binding arbitration, the parties select the arbitrator and are bound by the decision, either by prior agreement or by statute.[8] In last-offer

8. In a somewhat surprising 1990 case, representatives of a Phillips 66 petrochemical plant and citizens of a Texas Gulf Coast community agreed to arbitration to resolve a dispute over the company's discharge of polluted waste water into Linnville Bayou. Under the terms of the

arbitration, the arbitrator is required to choose between the final positions of the two parties....

Court-annexed arbitration, a newer development. Judges refer civil suits to arbitrators who render prompt, non-binding decisions. If a party does not accept an arbitrated award, some systems require they better their position at trial by some fixed percentage, or court costs are assessed against them. Even when these decisions are not accepted, they sometimes lead to further negotiations and pretrial settlement.

Conciliation, an informal process in which the third party tries to bring the parties to agreement by lowering tensions, improving communications, interpreting issues, providing technical assistance, exploring potential solutions and bringing about a negotiated settlement, either informally or, in a subsequent step, through formal mediation. Conciliation is frequently used in volatile conflicts and in disputes where the parties are unable, unwilling or unprepared to come to the table to negotiate their differences.

Facilitation, a collaborative process used to help a group of individuals or parties with divergent views reach a goal or complete a task to the mutual satisfaction of the participants. The facilitator functions as a neutral process expert and avoids making substantive contributions, [helping] bring the parties to consensus....

Fact finding, a process used from time to time primarily in public sector collective bargaining. The fact finder, drawing on information provided by the parties and additional research, recommends a resolution of each outstanding issue. It is typically non-binding and paves the way for further negotiations and mediation.

Med-Arb, an innovation in dispute resolution under which the med-arbiter is authorized by the parties to serve first as a mediator and, secondly, as an arbitrator empowered to decide any issues not resolved through mediation.

Mediation, a structured process in which the mediator assists the disputants to reach a negotiated settlement of their differences. Mediation is usually a voluntary process that results in a signed agreement which defines the future behavior of the parties. The mediator uses a variety of skills and techniques to help the parties reach a settlement but is not empowered to render a decision.[9]

The Mini-trial, a privately-developed method of helping to bring about a negotiated settlement in lieu of corporate litigation. A typical mini-trial might entail a period of limited discovery after which attorneys present their best case before managers with authority to settle and, most often, a neutral advisor who may be a retired judge or other lawyer. The managers then enter settlement negotiations. They may call on the neutral advisor if they wish to obtain an opinion on how a court might decide the matter.[10]

The Multi-door center (or Multi-door courthouse), a proposal [by Professor Sander] to offer a variety of dispute resolution services in one place with a single intake desk

---

agreement assenting to arbitration, a panel of three scientists was given binding authority to determine the extent of pollution in the bayou and to set out the best clean-up method. The decision of the arbitration panel could be appealed only to a retired judge, and appeal was limited to the narrow issue of whether the decision was arbitrary.

9. Mediation has been a particularly successful method for reaching settlement and allocating responsibility among potentially responsible parties in dozens of EPA Superfund toxic waste clean-up cases.

10. Since the mid-1980s, the Army Corps of Engineers has used the minitrial technique in resolving a number of regulatory environmental disputes.

which would screen clients. Under one model, a screening clerk would refer cases for mediation, arbitration, fact-finding, ombudsman or adjudication....

[**Negotiation** is the generic process that recurs in many of these ADR forms. In its simplest incarnation, however, negotiation constitutes discussions between the parties, with no formalized format, groundrules, or third party participation.]

Neighborhood justice centers (NJCs), the title given to... about 180 local centers now operating through the country under the sponsorship of local or state governments, bar associations and foundations.... They are also known as Community Mediation Centers, Citizen Dispute Centers, etc.

Ombudsman, a third party [on the Scandanavian model] who receives and investigates complaints or grievances aimed at an institution by its constituents, clients or employees. The Ombudsman may take actions such as bringing an apparent injustice to the attention of high-level officials, advising the complainant of available options and recourses, proposing a settlement of the dispute or proposing systemic changes in the institution....

Public policy dialogue and negotiation, aimed at bringing together affected representatives of business, public interest groups and government to explore regulatory matters. The dialogue is intended to identify areas of agreement, narrow the areas of disagreement, and identify general areas and specific topics for negotiation. A facilitator guides the process.

[**Reg-neg** is the term given to a process of intensive multiparty negotiations leading to governmental issuance of regulatory rules.]

Rent-a-judge, the popular name given to a procedure, presently authorized by legislation in six states, in which the court, on stipulation of the parties, can refer a pending lawsuit to a private neutral party for trial with the same effect as though the case were tried in the courtroom before a judge. The verdict can be appealed through the regular court appellate system.

Section 2. A CASE STUDY IN EDR

Allan Talbot, The Hudson River Settlement, in Settling Things: Six Case Studies in Environmental Mediation (1983)

Of all the natural resource disputes resolved in recent years through mediation, perhaps none was as complex or as significant as the so-called Hudson River settlement, the conclusion of a 17-year war between and among three environmental groups, four public agencies, and five electric utility companies over the use of the Hudson River for producing electric power.

Storm King Mountain...attracted national attention [with its conflict over] construction of a hydroelectric power facility at the mountain's base [see page 562 *supra*].... After the Federal Power Commission (FPC) granted the license, a U.S. Appeals Court ruled that the FPC must consider the preservation of scenic beauty in its licensing decisions. The court [held] that [Scenic Hudson Preservation Conference,] a citizens' group with no proprietary interest...nonetheless had the right to intervene in...licensing hearings....

In subsequent years, as the FPC reconsidered Consolidated Edison's licensing bid, the issues surrounding Storm King came to involve more than the scenic impact of an immense power station constructed at the base of the mountain. And, among all of the legal, economic, and environmental questions raised by opponents, none proved to be as complicated and as intriguing as the impact of the plant on the fish in thc Hudson River....

An organization called the Hudson River Fishermen's Association (HRFA) pointed out, in November 1964, that the Hudson Highlands were a major spawning ground for anadromous fish, especially striped bass. In fact, the HRFA said, most of the striped bass caught in the Atlantic between Cape Code and the Jersey Shore were spawned in the vicinity of Storm King Mountain. Scenic Hudson, originally concerned merely with the aesthetic aspect of Consolidated Edison's project, quickly seized on the fish issue as well, claiming that the hydroelectric plant would have disastrous consequences for the river's striped bass population.

The question of harm to fish life was posed subsequently by HRFA concerning several other power stations along the river where water was used for cooling. The biggest of these power stations was the Indian Point nuclear complex located in Westchester County some 15 miles south of Storm King [using] river water to cool plant condensers. Water going back into the river was several degrees warmer than when it came out. Many fish are attracted to warm water, especially in the winter, and large numbers of fish were caught on the plant intake screens. The resulting kills were dramatic creating measurable evidence of the dangers to fish life posed by power production.

Less obvious, but in the view of many fish biologists far more serious, was the entrainment of young fish and fish eggs into plant cooling systems.... [A total of six existing power stations using] the waters of the Hudson, and several proposed new units,] each posed some danger to fish life, and the combined effect on the river and the fish was, at best, unclear and therefore in dispute.

Because of its size and its involvement in all the proposed or recently built Hudson River plants, Consolidated Edison bore the brunt of the charges that the utilities were decimating the river's aquatic life. Its initial response at Storm King in FPC's 1964 hearings was to dismiss the issue as irrelevant, and then, in 1967 as the controversy spread to Indian Point, to minimize the problem. Finally, when the FPC held a new round of Storm King hearings in 1968...the utility sponsored some ambitious and expensive fish studies by a variety of consultants. During the 1970s, the utility claims, it spent about three million annually on research into the life cycles and spawning patterns of the Hudson's striped bass, shad, perch, tomcod, and anchovy populations. Consolidated Edison used these data to persuade such licensing agencies as the FPC and the Nuclear Regulatory Commission (NRC) that power production at Storm King and at Indian Point was compatible with survival of the river's fish. Experts retained by the environmental groups invariably disputed these claims. FPC and NRC hearing records contain 20,000 pages of disagreements over probably and acceptable rates of fish kills....

The regulatory agency hearings were a stage for what Ross Sandler, lawyer for the Natural Resources Defense Council (NRDC), a public interest law group, calls "the drama of advocacy science." His legal opponent, Peter Bergen, an attorney representing Con Edison, agrees that the impact on fish life of any power plant "depended on whose experts you were prepared to believe."

Determining the adverse effects of any one power plant was a minor challenge compared to that of assessing the combined effect of all the plants. This was the job facing the EPA when, in 1972, it assumed responsibility for curbing pollution in the Hudson River under the...Clean Water Act. Thermal discharges were among the pollutants the act sought to eliminate or control....

In the spring of 1975, the EPA notified the utilities that the agency was prepared to issue conditional discharge permits requiring that thermal discharges from the [steam] plants be reduced by 90 percent, meaning, for all practical purposes, that the utilities would have to construct cooling towers within five years. The EPA gave the utilities 30 days to challenge its decision, and challenge it, of course, they did.

After reviewing the existing fish studies and retaining its own experts, the EPA staff concluded that cooling towers were the only way to assure that the plants would not do irreparable damage to the Hudson River.... [EPA attorney] Jonathan Strong says that "other industries would be watching to see if we were for real, and we braced ourselves for a fight." This meant getting the necessary budget and cooperation from the U.S. Fish and Wildlife Service to sustain EPA's decisions through what promised to be a lengthy adjudication process.

The utilities' reaction to EPA's position was, predictably, one of dismay. The permit conditions changed long-term operating and construction costs. "We estimated the total cost of the cooling towers to be as much as $350 million..." says Joseph Block, executive vice-president and general counsel of Consolidated Edison....

When the protagonists met, in February 1977, to schedule the presentation of evidence and cross-examination before the hearing examiner, Con Edison attorney Peter Bergen challenged EPA's jurisdiction. He argued, to everyone's surprise and annoyance, that New York State's Department of Environmental Conservation ought to take charge of the permit process [under NPDES]....

While the utilities challenged EPA's [permit] jurisdiction in the courts, EPA attacked the utilities in its adjudication hearings, eventually amassing still another 20,000 pages of records....

"The permit question," Albert Butzel, Scenic Hudson's attorney, says, "could have dragged on for years. And in the background, the FPC awaited the outcome before proceeding with more hearings on the Storm King project."

"It was getting boring," admits Peter Bergen, whose legal involvement in the Hudson River case, just as Butzel's, went back to the 1965 Scenic Hudson decision. He and Butzel had been arguing the same issues for close to 14 years, and there was no end in sight.

In March 1979, Butzel and Sandler met with Bergen to discuss the possibility of some kind of negotiations. "No one would benefit by continuing what amounted to a stalemate," says Butzel.... Bergen agreed that a negotiated settlement probably made sense, and said he would convey Butzel's and Sandler's overture to the other utilities through Joseph Block.

Ending the legal wars on the Hudson River was also on the minds of several utility company executives, especially at Consolidated Edison. Consolidated Edison's readiness to negotiate was attributable, at least partly, to its chairman, Charles Luce, who had come to the company from the U.S. Department of the Interior in 1967, during one of the most difficult periods in Consolidated Edison's history. It was a time of black-outs and shrinking profits. The company found strong opposition wherever it attempted to build new power-generating facilities including, of course, at Storm King. Through management changes, a major capital improvement program, and the establishment of better power interconnections with other utilities, Luce had gradually improved the reliability of Consolidated Edison's generating and distribution system, its financial position, and its corporate image.

"I was close to retirement in 1979," Luce said recently, "and I wanted to settle these outstanding Hudson River cases before I left. I went to the board [members] and asked them for permission to see if they would allow me to pursue some sort of settlement, and they said, 'Go ahead....'"

"Storm King was still an important long-range project for us," says Block, "but no longer a priority." Project costs had soared, and the supplementary power that Storm King was supposed to provide was now coming from gas turbines installed at most of Consolidated Edison's existing power stations during the late 1960s. "The big question," says Block, "was not so much what could be negotiated, but the process: who would be involved and who would mediate it." Block feels that the parties were too numerous and too locked into their positions to be able to stop battling and begin negotiating on their own. "This one needed a neutral third person," he says.

Luce's first choice for a mediator was Laurance S. Rockefeller, who directs the Rockefeller family's conservation interests. Rockefeller declined Luce's invitation, but suggested Russell Train, president of the World Wildlife Fund and a former administrator of the Environmental Protection Agency. Luce like that idea, and asked Rockefeller to approach Train.

Train remembers getting a call, early in April 1979, from George Lamb, an associate of Laurance Rockefeller's, about entering the case. He agreed to do so, Train says, and then he "oozed into the role of mediator." His first step was "to do some quiet checking with the parties involved."

He first contacted Luce, whom he knew personally and with whom he had served in the U.S. Department of the Interior and on the National Water Commission. Luce assured him that the utilities were serious about settling, and that he would be personally delighted if Train intervened. During this and subsequent conversations with Luce, Train became convinced that the Consolidated Edison chairman was committed to a settlement and that he was crucial in getting the participation and continuing cooperation from the other utilities....

Train, who had served on the NRDC board, then contacted John Adams, Ross Sandler's boss at NRDC. Adams told him that NRDC felt that a settlement was possible and that Train was just the person to pull it off.

Getting the EPA to participate was more difficult and time-consuming. EPA's primary activity in this dispute was its insistence on cooling towers [at the steam plants]. It was becoming clear to Train that cooling towers were only one issue to be mediated and might be compromised or traded off in favor of other issues, such as the abandonment of Storm King or the litigation fees of the environmental groups....

Train called Douglas Costle, the EPA administrator at that time, and the two talked about Train as a possible mediator. Costle indicated that mediation was a good idea, but he wanted to check with his staff before committing the agency. Train recalls that about three weeks later he received a call from EPA's general counsel, Joan Z. Bernstein. "She was positive," Train recalls, "but laid down three conditions. EPA's regional office would participate only if the adjudicatory hearings on the cooling towers continued, if the utilities would agree that the cooling towers would have to be considered in a settlement, and if I served as mediator."

The conditions cemented Train's mediator role while also blurring the importance of cooling towers in the discussions. By agreeing to the EPA condition that cooling towers would have to be "considered" in mediation, Train was committing himself to keeping the idea alive. "The essential ambiguity of the word 'considered' also gave us some leeway," Train says.

The formal mediation sessions began on August 28, 1979, at the American Bar Association headquarters on West Forty-fourth Street in New York City. The cast was impressive: 28 people representing 11 groups: Consolidated Edison, Central Hudson, Orange and Rockland Utilities, Niagara Mohawk, the New York State Power Authority, the regional office of the Environmental Protection Agency, the New York State Attorney General's Office, the New York State Department of Environmental Conservation, the Hudson River Fishermen's Association, the Natural Resources Defense Council, and Scenic Hudson.

While all of these organizations had a direct interest in the case, there were really three primary players. Among the public agencies, the EPA was the most critical, since its permit conditions were one of the issues on the bargaining table. Two of the state agencies – the New York State Attorney General's Office and the Department of Environmental Conservation (DEC) – had been involved in the Storm King litigation (by 1978, both had petitioned the Federal Energy Regulatory Commission [FERC] to terminate the license), and DEC was in the potential position of taking over the issuances of discharge permits for the disputed plants. But they didn't have as much at stake, directly, as the EPA.

Consolidated Edison was clearly the major participant among the utilities concerned.... It was generally, and correctly, assumed that other private utilities would follow Consolidated Edison's lead.... Sandler and Butzel, representing the environmental groups, were crucial participants. They saw themselves as the initiators of mediation and were individually committed to making it succeed. They felt they were freer to negotiate than all the other parties, which gave them greater flexibility, and eventually placed them in the role of intermediaries between those parties whose positions, and risks, were more sharply drawn.

The opening session in August was formal, and it was restricted to setting procedures. Train suggested that all press and other inquiries about the mediation effort to be directed to him, and that no participant talk publicly about what was happening. Everyone agreed. Interestingly enough, there never were press inquiries or coverage. It was also agreed that offers or proposals made in mediation would be off the record as far as the adjudicatory hearings or other litigation were concerned. Train also asked the participants to submit written proposals directly to him, which he would distribute to all the parties. He then set September 24 as the date for the next meeting.

Scheduling, always an important part of a mediator's role, was in Train's case especially so. "Russ proved to have a very busy schedule," says Ross Sandler, "and we just had to grab him when he was available." Joseph Block of Consolidated Edison agrees. "Everyone saw him as a busy and important person," says Block. "If he was willing to set a date, then the rest felt that they better go along." This readiness to follow Train's schedule eventually helped keep the mediation effort moving when, during the next 16 months, the parties became discouraged or there was no apparent progress. If Train was willing to press on, the rest of them felt they ought to do the same.

At the September 24 meeting, the environmental groups presented five proposals or issues for discussion. The first, and perhaps most significant, was their willingness to consider what they called a "non-hardware" solution to the fish problem [on the units other than Storm King]. While they wanted further consideration of cooling towers, they were also prepared to consider operational methods of reducing fish kills, for example plant...shutdowns during the spawning season.

Dropping the Storm King plant...was more a demand than a proposal. The three groups also insisted that the land purchased by Consolidated Edison for the project be placed in public ownership to provide permanent protection for Storm King Mountain. They also wanted a moratorium on future power plants in the lower Hudson River Valley. Finally, the environmental representatives asked the utilities to fund a research organization that would develop reliable, long-range information on the river's aquatic life. They also wanted to be reimbursed for their legal costs. This last item raised some eyebrows, and there was, in fact, some disagreement between Sandler and Butzel over whether and how hard they should push for such payment.

The utilities' proposal was some distance from that of the environmentalists. Charles Luce, who presented the utilities' proposal, rejected the idea of periodically closing down the plants. "It raises many practical problems," he said. Luce also ruled out cooling towers. He suggested instead that the utility companies might install elaborate "Ristroph screens," equipped with revolving troughs, that would collect fish impinged in cooling water intakes and deposit them back into the river.... If the cooling tower requirement were dropped and this screen arrangement substituted, Luce said, the utilities would fund a Hudson River fish hatchery, would conduct further research, and would agree to drop Storm King.

The EPA proposal dropped the cooling tower requirement at [one] plant, substituted a Ristroph screen solution in its place and called for periodic closings of the plant during times of heaviest fish entrainment....

While these written positions contained some compromises, they also aggravated suspicions. Some of the EPA representatives sensed that the environmental groups, for example, may have been more interested in killing the Storm King plant than in getting the utilities to construct cooling towers. The absence even of the possibility of cooling towers in the utilities' position seemed, to the EPA, to indicate a lack of good faith. Jonathan Strong, the EPA attorney, recalls that "their throwing Storm King on the table was no concession at all as far as we were concerned." Strong believed that Consolidated Edison really wanted to drop the project anyway, and it was simply looking for an excuse to do so.

Butzel and Sandler were surprised and bothered that Luce's formal statement had so quickly dismissed operating changes as a possible remedy. In fact, much of the September 24 meeting was devoted to persuading the utilities to think about changes in plant operation that might lessen the fish dangers. Luce said he would tell his staff to give it a try. "We then did a 180-degree turn," remembers Block of Consolidated Edison. "We began with hardware solutions, like screens, and in just a month or so we were working on...operating approaches."

During a third meeting, on November 2, 1979, the utilities submitted a significantly expanded proposal, which, in addition to the original offer, included [seasonal plant shutdowns and other operating approaches].... The utilities...outlined the favorable effects of these modifications for reducing fish impingement and entrainment. By the end of December, the utilities had made even further concessions, suggesting that they would reimburse the legal fees of the environmental groups and that they would provide $3 million for an independent research organization.

These offers represented major steps forward in the negotiations. They might even have led to an early agreement except for one major stumbling block. The claims made by the utilities for the reductions in fish mortality proved to be erroneous, or at least dubious....

In January 1980, the mediation effort took a new turn. Rather than continue to deal in claims or charges about fish mortality, the parties now decided to turn over the entire fish question to a smaller technical committee, composed of biologists and other experts retained by the EPA and the utility companies. The committee would devised an operating test [of effects on fish] that all sides could support....

The technical committee struggled valiantly during the winter of 1980 to resolve the complexities.... But, in the end, they could not even agree on how long a suitable test should take. Ross Sandler, who participated in the technical committee sessions, describes them as "confusing and frustrating." "Around April," he says, "I called Joe Block and told him that there was no way that the technical committee would come up with an acceptable testing program. If the negotiations were to succeed, the utilities or the EPA would have to change their positions."

The mediation effort was now in serious trouble. Neither the utilities nor the EPA seemed prepared to budge now that a testing program seemed out of the questions. Rather than dealing in possible solutions, their representatives began trading barbs and insults. As a New York State Power Authority representative put it at one angry meeting, "The whole effort is fruitless." In June, mediator Train asked whether members of the technical committee, together with Butzel and Sandler, might work on some new ideas, not being at all sure what those ideas might be. "My purpose at this point," says Train, "was just to keep the process moving."

The technical committee members included John Lawler and Tom Englert, who were the utilities' fish consultants; John Borman, a consultant to the U.S. Department of the Interior who was serving as the EPA expert; and Robert Henshaw and Edward Horn of the New York State Department of Environmental Conservation. During the summer of 1980, these five people, together with Butzel and Sandler, constituted the heart of the mediation effort. They seemed to perceive that at this stage success or failure depended very much on them. "This period in the mediation," says Butzel, "showed that mediation often requires that the parties involved be separated, including some insulation between the expert consultants and their clients. In this smaller setting, there was a new effort to work something out...."

In late August 1980, Butzel prepared a memorandum summarizing how [a] new combination of [abandoning Storm King and seasonal plant shutdown] outages, together with reduced water withdrawals, the installation of dual-speed pumps at Indian Point, and the construction of a fish hatchery, would substantially reduce fish dangers. The package offered more benefits than the original utility companies' offer, although not to the point of 50 percent of the protection of cooling towers – the minimum objective required by the EPA.

While the utilities seemed ready to back these new ideas, the EPA was not. They did not include cooling towers, nor did they meet the agency's 50 percent standard. While there were still numerous outstanding issues to be argued, such as the size of the research fund and the methods of enforcement, the utilities and the environmental groups now seemed to be moving toward an agreement and, in the process, isolating the EPA. "We were way out on a limb," remembers Jonathan Strong, "and everyone seemed to be sawing it off."

By September 1980, other factors also had undermined the EPA position. Its budget for the case was running low. The New York State Department of Environmental Conservation now indicated its readiness to take over the [NPDES} permit process for the power plants. Bergen, the utilities' lawyer, was back in court arguing that, since EPA's 1975 permits were about to expire, the state surely should assume jurisdiction. Charles Warren, EPA's regional administrator at the time...point[ed] out that the entire permit procedure was, by 1979, proving to be unworkable. "The jurisdictional problem with the state, and the utilities' readiness to appeal the permit conditions, meant that this dispute could have gone on for years. In my view, the striped bass would be better protected by the settlement at hand than they would have been by cooling towers that might never have been built, given the procedural and enforcement problems."

Nonetheless, EPA's enforcement division, and Jonathan Strong in particular, balked at any further mediation attempts. Strong felt that the agency had made concessions, but that there had been no real movement by the utilities....

Faced with this opposition to further mediation, including some obvious conflict within the EPA's regional office, Train called Jeffrey Miller, EPA's assistant administrator for enforcement in Washington, and proposed a meeting where he, Butzel and Sandler, and representatives from the regional office would make their respective cases for and against the EPA's continued participation in negotiations. Train argued in the meeting that an agreement seemed to be a month or so away, that it was an election year, and that a settlement would reflect well on the parties, including the EPA. Train was persuasive. Miller told the EPA regional staff to go back to the bargaining table.

With EPA back in the process, the warring parties now entered the most intensive bargaining period, stretching from late September to mid-December 1980. While the general principles of the potential agreement were by now emerging – the termination of the Storm King project, operating modifications for reduction of fish kills, development of a fish hatchery, establishment of some kind of research fund, and reimbursement of legal fees – there were many details still to be worked out.

Negotiations on such issues as the level of funding and the organization of the research fund, reimbursement of legal fees, and the implementation of the agreement proved to be difficult and often acrimonious. The environmental representatives and the New York State Attorney General's Office were suggesting some very large numbers. "They were taking large bites from the utilities, especially Con Edison," remembers Jonathan Strong of EPA. The utilities started with a $3 million offer for a research fund, but eventually went up to $12 million. They also settled on $500,000 as reimbursement for legal fees.

The utilities, especially the smaller ones, balked at such figures. Consolidated Edison, predictably, ended up paying the most. Block says that his company put up an amount of money roughly equivalent to its "cooling tower exposure": in other words, Consolidated Edison's share of the cooling towers' costs if they had been built.... The utilities also put up, or lost, money in other parts of the agreement. These included an estimated $36 million that Consolidated Edison had invested in Storm King....

While the utilities were concerned by the growing costs of the agreement, they rationalized the price tag as being substantially lower than the $350 million required to construct cooling towers and the $100 million needed annually to operate them. The utilities, of course, also planned to recover these costs through consumer rate increases.

Negotiations became tense indeed when the utilities raised the issue of getting the public service commissions of New York and New Jersey to approve the costs of the agreement before it was executed. Butzel and Sandler knew that the utilities would require legal assurances, such as curtailment of the adjudicatory hearing and the discharge permit conditions, approvals from a variety of environmental review agencies, and the promise from environmental organizations that they would drop their opposition to the plants. But they had not expected that the utilities would want advance approvals from rate regulators. To make matters more difficult, the utilities wanted the environmental organizations to support actively the utilities' bid to pass along the costs of the agreement to consumers.

By December, the parties developed a draft agreement that underwent daily changes. The haggling and bargaining was as intense as ever. Train now pushed everyone to agree on a date, December 18, 1980, on which the arguing would end and something would actually be signed.

Train conducted this formal signing session, attended by the press and representatives from the 11 participants, with a stern hand. There was nervous laughter when he insisted that no one but he would speak until everyone signed the agreement. He says today that he wasn't being funny. There was a real possibility that a fiery speech or an angry word in advance of the signing might have blown apart the whole agreement.

The war on the Hudson ended with Consolidated Edison's agreement to forfeit its Storm King license and to turn the site over to the Palisades Interstate Park Commission. Consolidated Edison and the other utilities promised that they would reduce their plants' water withdrawals through plant outages from May to July for a period of 10 years. They also promised a fish hatchery, new water intakes at Indian Point, a $12 million endowment for a research organization, the reimbursement of legal costs to the environmental groups, and a 25-year moratorium on any new power plants without cooling towers north of the George Washington Bridge. In return, the cooling tower requirements at Indian Point, Roseton, and Bowline were dropped; all litigation and administrative proceedings among the parties ceased; and the environmental groups actively supported the agreement, and its costs, before regulatory agencies.

On December 10, 1981, one year later, New York State issued the necessary [NPDES] discharge permits, which incorporated the terms of the mediated settlement, to the utilities. The research fund had been established, the environmental groups had been reimbursed for their legal fees, and everyone had done what they had agreed to do....

COMMENTARY AND QUESTIONS

1. The determinants of the Hudson River Settlement. Note the ingredients of a successful ADR case, as they are illustrated in this narrative. The choice of method, for example, was apparently well done. Only mediation seems likely to have been viable – the parties would not have accepted binding arbitration, and negotiations without a third party overseer would clearly have come to chaos. Russell Train was also clearly the right mediator for the job, not only as a matter of background skills and temperament, but also because he had ties to all the major players.

Other elements, not present in all disputes, were also crucial: all parties had a genuine interest in accurate factfinding; there was room to compromise in a major arena, power plant operations; a small group of representatives could cover the wider spectrum of interests and commit their respective sides in ongoing negotiations; there were split interests within the different groupings, no monolithic blocks; there was a governmental participant holding a potential hammer; the corporate parties were financially well-secured to fund a compromise; and all representatives had sufficient expertise to speak the same language.

2. Was this one too easy? Although the participants would recoil, could one say this mediation was uncharacteristically soluble? Scrapping Storm King was a ready bargaining chip for the utilities. But what if this case had dealt with Storm King alone? The case shows how ADR can reach out to encompass and resolve a range of somewhat related bargaining items in a way a court could never do. What about the fortuitous presence of Luce and Train, and their special fit with the utilities, environmental attorneys, and governmental reps? What if there had not been such an Ivy League buddy cohort?

3. The role of citizen suit injunctions. What does this case have to say to ADR advocates who deplore those who run to court? What role would the citizen environmentalists have played in the negotiation process (would there have been any such process?) if they had not initially won an injunction in the *Storm King* case? Professor Sander wrote in note 59 of his article that initial adjudication may be required to "equalize the power relationship and bring the more powerful respondent to the bargaining table." Many environmental negotiations involving citizen initiatives therefore necessarily take place "in the shadow of the courts."

4. ADR and democracy. Citizens can indeed be included as central players in ADR, but since ADR processes are frequently a closed-door affair, which citizens get to play, or even to observe? In practice the parties include everyone who can substantially shape, or disrupt, the Deal. Does ADR dilute the rights of minor players, interested nonplayers, or even of the participants themselves? Does a society have a duty to resolve its major public controversies in public?

Section 3. NEGOTIATED RULEMAKING

Susskind & McMahon, The Theory and Practice of Negotiated Rulemaking

3 Yale Journal on Regulation 133, 140–141, 142–146 (1985)

Since the late 1970s, advocates of negotiated approaches to rulemaking have argued that the legitimacy of proposed rules could be restored – and time-consuming court challenges avoided – if informal, face-to-face negotiations were used to supplement the traditional review and comment process.[11] Critics, however, have responded quite negatively to what they perceive as the dangers of "deal-making behind closed doors." Nevertheless, proponents of the innovation have persisted, and during the last few years several federal agencies have experimented with negotiated approaches to rulemaking....

Negotiated rulemaking will only be utilized more broadly if it achieves better results than the traditional rulemaking process.... Each party must feel that the negotiated rule serves its interest at least as well as the version of the rule most likely to be developed through conventional process.... A negotiation should yield realistic commitments from all of those involved. A rule that satisfies everyone in

Susskind and McMahon, The Theory and Practice of Negotiated Rule Making, 3 Yale J. Reg. 133 (1985).

11. [Notable works besides Professor Susskind's include Philip Harter's Negotiated Regulations: A Cure for Malaise, 71 Georgetown L. Rev. 1 (1982) and Perritt, Negotiated Rulemaking Before Federal Agencies, 74 Georgetown L. Rev. 1625 (1986).] The Administrative Conference has published a useful collection: Negotiated Rulemaking Sourcebook (1990).

principle but cannot be implemented is of little use. Not only is the support of the participants important, but so too is the support of any interested party.... The interests of the parties should be so well-reconciled that no possible joint gains are left unrealized. Changes which would help a party without harming another party should not be missed. If a more elegant method of reconciling conflicting interests of the parties is possible, it will probably emerge once the draft of the agreement is publicized.... The agency should be able to demonstrate that it has upheld its statutory mandate, and the public-at-large should feel satisfied that both the process and outcome were fair.... Relationships among the participants in the negotiations should improve, not deteriorate, as a result of their interactions. The parties should be in a better position to deal with their differences in the future.... The negotiated rule should take account of the best scientific and technological information available at the time of the negotiation.

EPA'S REGULATORY NEGOTIATION DEMONSTRATIONS

The notion of using a negotiated approach to rulemaking at EPA first emerged during the Carter Administration.... While the change of Administration slowed the momentum, appointment of Joseph Cannon as Acting Associate Administrator of EPA's Office of Planning and Resource Management in 1981 brought renewed interest.... In February 1983, EPA published a notice in the Federal Register indicating that it intended to pursue the idea of negotiated rulemaking and used solicitation letters to invite interested parties to suggest candidate rules....

In December 1983, David Doniger of the Natural Resources Defense Council (NRDC) formally proposed [rulemaking on CAA motor vehicle emissions] nonconformance penalties [NCPs] as a candidate rule for negotiated rulemaking. Between December 1983 and March 1984, [EPA] found widespread support for negotiating the NCP rule among potential stakeholders. Charles Freed, Director of EPA's Manufacturers Operations Division, the program office responsible for the rule, enthusiastically supported using a negotiated approach, as did the EPA Office of General Counsel and Office of Program Planning and Evaluation. Environmentalists were generally supportive, viewing NCPs as a means to accommodate temporary industry needs while holding industry to technology-forcing standards. Smaller manufacturers were somewhat wary of the costs of participating in a negotiated rulemaking and felt that any NCP rule had to preserve their competitiveness. Larger manufacturers generally supported the proposed process and felt that they had adequate staff to participate in the process. In general, all stakeholders felt that the rule was important enough to merit their involvement and that it did not involve the type of "life and death" value questions that would have made negotiation – an unfamiliar process at any rate – appear less workable.

In an April 1984 Federal Register notice, EPA announced its intention to develop an NCP rule using a regulatory negotiation. At an organizational meeting...some twenty participants met to learn more about the proposed process and to discuss how the negotiations would proceed. At that time, EPA announced the creation of a $50,000 resource pool – a fund that any or all of the participants would be able to draw upon to cover the costs of technical studies or other costs related to their participation.

Negotiations began June 14, 1984, and ended October 12, 1984. In order to develop some structure for the process, a negotiation facilitator opened the June session by asking participants to produce a statement of issues reflecting their interests. A final list of ten issues was synthesized to help organize the work of the negotiating committee. Three work groups were formed....

Five one-day negotiating sessions dealing with substantive aspects of the NCP rule and numerous work group sessions dealing with specific technical and administrative issues were held during a four month period. The NCP negotiating committee used over $10,000 to fund an independent study of a proposed engine testing plan. Other collaborative technical work was done by committee members who designed a micro-computer-based spreadsheet model to test the impacts of parameter changes in the penalty formula.

The negotiations were conducted under a Federal Advisory Committee Act (FACA) charter. Notice of the NCP negotiating committee sessions was given in the Federal Register, and meetings were open to the public. The committee eventually reached consensus on all of the issues it originally identified in the first meeting.

In reaching this consensus, EPA's choice of a facilitator was crucial. The ERM-McGlennon team, which had extensive mediation experience, took the lead in generating agreement on a detailed agenda and work schedule, organizing work group meetings at which components of the final version of the regulation were drafted, and convening the full group to review these work group drafts.... [T]he facilitation team initiated caucuses during and outside of meetings, maintained frequent contact with all participants, and intervened quite actively during several of the sessions.

After the last negotiation session on October 12, 1984, in which all the issues were resolved, a four-member subcommittee – consisting of EPA, state, environmental, and industry representatives – was given the responsibility of translating the tentative agreement into a consensus document. A first draft was circulated in mid-October, and comments were solicited. The subcommittee then used several conference calls to prepare the final draft that was signed by the entire committee in December 1984. With the consensus statement signed by all participants, EPA published its notice of proposed rulemaking on March 6, 1985. Only thirteen comments were received during the comment period, all in support of the committee's proposal. The final rule was promulgated without opposition on August 30, 1985....

COMMENTARY AND QUESTIONS

1. Statutory ADR and regneg. In 1990, Congress formally recognized the utility of ADR and negotiated rulemaking, and made them federal policy. The 101st Congress passed the Administrative Dispute Resolution Act (P.L. 101–552) and the Negotiated Rulemaking Act (P.L. 101–648) as amendments to the adjudication section of the Administrative Procedure Act. Under the ADRA, agencies are required to appoint resolution specialists and to develop policy addressing the potential uses of ADR in that agency. The Act does not force agencies to use ADR mechanisms, but each agency must review its litigation and administrative disputes to determine where ADR techniques may be useful. The second statute explicitly establishes the authority of federal regulatory agencies to use negotiated rulemaking, and permits the use of federal funds to cover the expenses of private party participants. These policies may give ADR methods new legitimacy and force, although temperaments and practical constraints do not automatically change. FRCP Rules 16 and 68 also attempt to promote nonlitigative resolutions in cases filed in federal court.

2. Technical details. The EPA regneg illustrates several technical issues. It is always a question, for instance, who pays – especially where citizen groups are involved. How many participants are too many? Federal rules may well directly affect thousands. What about the records of an ADR process (this issue applies equally to non-regneg cases)? ADR specialists typically try to keep as few records as possible, and get the parties to contract to confidentiality, to avoid the disruptive possibility that information may be subpoenaed to be used in other more litigious forums. (In some jurisdictions a nascent "mediation privilege" is being recognized, analogous to an attorney-client privilege.)

And what about the administrative law consequences? Does regneg violate the delegation doctrine because non-officials effectively make the decision?[12] Do split caucuses in regneg violate the ban on ex parte contacts with agency decisionmakers?[13] Will courts still feel obliged to scrutinize closely to assure that agencies gave a "hard look" to the facts and law?[14]

3. Evaluating ADR. Ultimately, evaluation of ADR depends not only on whether cases reach settlement, but also upon what it is intended to achieve. And different observers have very different views. Justice Burger wanted to unclog the courts. Professor Fiss discerns a questionable political goal "to insulate the status quo from the judiciary."[15] Professor Sander, in the excerpt quoted above, doubted whether comparative efficiency was the point, including "satisfaction" as part of the goal. McThenia & Shaffer likewise focus on more holistic goals, quoting Socrates: "Justice is what we discover – you and I – when we walk together, listen together, and even love one another, in our curiosity about what justice is and where justice comes from."[16] (Fiss says he's as much for love as anybody, but dispute resolution has broader goals and constraints. Id.) Are a governing system's needs adequately fulfilled when the interests of all parties involved in a particular conflict are satisfied, or are there further systemic goals, like establishing precedent?

The law locks up both man and woman
Who steals the goose from off the common,
But lets the greater felon loose
Who steals the common from the goose.

---

12. Susskind argues that it doesn't, because agency officials have the last word. 3 Yale J. on Reg. at 158.

13. Perritt argues that it doesn't, 74 Georgetown L.Rev. 1625, 1697 (1986).

14. Susskind argues that the hard look will be satisfied if the regneg incorporates: notice; equal footing, including funding of citizens; reasonable record; round-robin review of the final draft; full discussion of comments; procedural equality; clear statement of agency negotiation positions; and an opportunity for all parties to sign off on the final rule. 3 Yale J. on Reg. at 164. Cf. Wald, Negotiation of Environmental Disputes: a New Role for the Courts?, 10 Colum. J. Envtl Law 1 (1985).

15. Against Settlement, 94 Yale L.J. 1669, 1670 (1985).

16. For Reconciliation, 94 Yale L.J. 1660, 1665 (1985).

Chapter 25

INTERNATIONAL ENVIRONMENTAL LAW

This coursebook began with the metaphor of Spaceship Earth, emphasizing the interconnectedness of the planet's geophysical, ecological, and human components, and the law. This chapter might properly be called "global environmental law," because environmental law cannot realistically be limited to any set of national boundaries; its challenge is inevitably international in scope.[1] Through an accident of socio-political, economic, and legal history, however (pushed largely by the continuing efforts of non-governmental organizations), the United States took an early lead role in the development of environmental law. In the past decade the rest of the world has begun to take account of the need for such legal protection, often using models drawn from American law.

Global problems of environmental quality are even more daunting than the range of problems encountered in the United States. Slowly circling the globe, an observing eye could catalog a depressingly long list of planetary environmental threats, chronicled in part in the Sancton article in the first chapter.[2] Though most international environmental dilemmas are caused by humans, and virtually all humans act within the jurisdiction of nation states, ecological effects know no boundaries, spilling across political frontiers and causing cumulative effects throughout the global system. The fundamental challenge for international law is to handle problems which exist irrespective of frontiers, in a system of nation states that takes territorial sovereignty as one of its most sacred legal tenets.

---

1. International law is not the same thing as comparative law, although many internationally-focused commentators concern themselves with both. When chemical plants exploded at Seveso, Italy, in 1980, and at Bhopal, India, in 1984, the pollution did not discernably cross any frontiers, so these tragedies did not fit within "international" law (except insofar as they concern international businesses, potential problems facing all developing countries). The tragedies were nevertheless significant for the development of an international consciousness of environmental law.

Comparative law – studying the domestic, or "municipal," law of different countries – is often critically important in determining the possibilities for legal regulation of global environmental problems. Thus, to understand the legal consequences of the Bhopal disaster, one would review the tort liability provisions of Indian common law, and relevant statutes including the Bhopal Gas Leak Disaster (Processing of Claims) Act, passed by the Ragta Sabha on March 18, 1985, Bill No. V-C/1985, as well as the interesting Bhopal litigation filed in the United States, where the government of India itself tried to assert that American jurisdiction was more appropriate for adjudicating liability and damages against the multinational corporate defendant. In re Union Carbide Corp., 809 F.2d 195 (2d Cir. 1987). See Gladwin, A Case Study of the Bhopal Tragedy, in Pearson, Multinational Corporations, Environment, and the Third World (1987). This chapter focuses on transboundary and international legal actions, but concerned students must recognize that learning to be a "quick study" in different nations' legal systems may often be of great importance in coping with environmental disasters of international concern.

2. A superb source for statistics and detailed analysis of global ecological conditions is the World Resources Institute's bi-annual deskbook, World Resources.

TWO PERSPECTIVES: TRANSBOUNDARY AND GLOBAL

This chapter can offer only a glimpse at the field of international environmental law, a field that has been fast-growing over the past few years. For a field so huge, it is nevertheless possible to choose two paradigms that introduce most of the areas of international environmental law concern. First, in terms of historical development, is the issue of transboundary pollution. Over the years a number of international controversies have arisen from injury spilling over from one state's territory into another. Some resemble garden-variety domestic pollution cases, like the classic *Trail Smelter* case noted below,[3] where air pollution fumes and particles happened to cross the international boundary between Canada and the United States. Transboundary pollution has since become more dramatic. One small but vivid example exists because many Nordic women have blond hair: acid rain from England falls on the Scandinavian coast, leaching copper oxides from residential plumbing systems, which has turned the hair of some Norwegian women a pale shade of green. Beyond acid rain, Europe has witnessed the explosion of the Chernobyl nuclear reactor and the Sandoz chemical spill in the Swiss headwaters of the Rhine, both ecological disasters causing great human and economic suffering. Transboundary pollution is often incident- or locality-specific.

The second sector is more straightforwardly planetary: environmental problems imposed on the global commons. Sometimes this means global pollution; at other times, a global perspective on resource depletion. The global commons has suffered a wide variety of impacts – massive extinction of species; global warming and the CO_2 greenhouse effect caused in part by woodburning and fossil fuels; CFC-induced holes in the stratospheric ozone layer; desertification; disruption of traditional peoples and cultures; a distressing lack of nutrition and the spread of disease, especially in overpopulated, high density areas; destruction and vandalization of archaeological sites; destruction of ancient forests; erosion and sedimentation; ocean pollution; toxic contamination of air, water and other resources; international dumping of toxic wastes, contaminated pharmaceuticals and other manufacturers (most often in the third world); DDT in the tissues of living organisms, even in the Arctic and Antarctic; the fundamental stress of overpopulation; a decline in many societies' quality of life – all these and more are problems of global commons, and are not so susceptible as transboundary pollution to discrete limited international law remedies.

THE PLAYERS

As with domestic environmental law, international environmental law involves a variety of players. The actors who cause environmental problems are often private parties – multinational corporations, smaller businesses and private citizens – or quasi-private actors, governmental agencies acting in a corporate proprietary fashion or acting as development agencies. Beyond these, official actors in international environmental law are generally limited to nation states and the international organizations they form. But lurking significantly in the background, as in the

3. See page 1001 *infra.*

domestic American process, are NGOs, the non-governmental organizations that create and advance the political context of "the environmental movement."

A. INTERNATIONAL TRANSBOUNDARY POLLUTION CASES

Section 1. THE RHINE RIVER SPILL

A classic transboundary pollution case: at nineteen minutes after midnight, November 1, 1986, a traffic patrol of the cantonal police saw fire shooting from the roof of Warehouse 956 in the Sandoz Chemical Company's industrial compound near Basel, Switzerland, on the banks of the River Rhine. Within a few minutes, fire brigades began pouring tons of water into the warehouse and extinguished the blaze five hours later. The volume of water greatly exceeded the company's minimal catchbasin capacity around the warehouse. Between 10,000–15,000 cubic meters of water laced with chemicals poured into the Rhine – 11 metric tons of organic mercury compounds and more than 100 tons of insecticides, fungicides, herbicides and other agricultural chemicals. A red toxic tide ultimately coursed 900 kilometers down the Rhine into the Baltic Sea. The Sandoz spill[4] was an ecological catastrophe. Hundreds of thousands of fish and waterfowl were killed; the extinction of living organisms extended to the base of the food chain, eliminating micro-organisms down to the microbe level. While no humans died (though a flock of sheep was lost near Strasbourg, France, when a farmer unwisely led them to drink at the river), the economic and ecological devastation was otherwise extraordinary. Citizen protests took place along the length of the Rhine, 10,000 people marching through the streets of Basel to protest the spill and demonstrating downstream in Germany, France and the Netherlands. Estimates of the direct damages to property downstream from the Sandoz spill exceeded 100 million Swiss francs.

The following text focuses on two sources of international law – customary law and treaties – and their limitations in achieving practical remedies for transboundary pollution.

Schwabach, The Sandoz Spill: The Failure of International Law to Protect the Rhine from Pollution
16 Ecol. L.Q. 443, 454–471 (1989)

INTERNATIONAL LAW RELATING TO THE SANDOZ SPILL

Both customary international law and a treaty regime govern accidents such as that at the Sandoz plant. Unfortunately, customary international law in this area is informed by conflicting theories and approaches. Further, the treaty regime, while apparently solid, is plagued by structural and substantive weakness.

4. Coincidentally, a spill from a nearby Ciba-Geigy chemical plant occurred the day before, and had not been reported; it was detected in the extensive water-testing following the Sandoz spill.

CUSTOMARY INTERNATIONAL LAW OF TRANSBOUNDARY RIVER POLLUTION

Customary international law has its sources in state practice, in the general principles of law that are recognized by civilized nations, and in judicial decisions and the teachings of respected jurists.[5] Examination of the relevant materials from each of these sources reveals a lack of consensus on the law governing pollution of transboundary rivers. There are four major legal approaches to transboundary river pollution, each of which depends on a different conception of sovereignty....

1. Absolute Territorial Sovereignty: The Harmon Doctrine

The absolute territorial sovereignty theory holds that a riparian state is free to do as it chooses with the water within its territory, without regard for the effects on the downstream or co-riparian states. Grotius expressed the theory of absolute territorial sovereignty more than three centuries ago when he stated, "a river, viewed as a stream, is the property of the people through whose territory it flows, or the ruler under whose sway that people is...to them all things produced in the river belong."[6]

A more recent manifestation of this theory is the Harmon Doctrine. In 1895, in response to Mexico's protest of the United States' diversion of water from the Rio Grande, then-Attorney General Judson Harmon stated that "the rules, principles, and precedents of international law impose no liability or obligation upon the United States."[7] The Harmon Doctrine has since become synonymous with the theory of absolute territorial sovereignty.

The absolute territorial sovereignty theory is naturally more appealing to upstream states than to downstream states. The appeal of the theory is somewhat diminished, however, by the fact that most countries are both upper and lower riparians....

The Harmon Doctrine has been almost universally denounced. Although no state formally adheres to the theory of absolute territorial sovereignty with regard to transboundary rivers, an argument can be made that many states continue to base their practice on such a theory, dumping wastes without regard for the welfare of downstream states.

2. Absolute Territorial Integrity

The absolute territorial integrity theory holds that a downstream riparian state may demand the continuation of the full flow of the river from an upper riparian state, free from any diminution in quantity or quality. The theory is the inverse of the absolute territorial sovereignty theory and, as such, appeals to downstream states. The same weakness that plagues the first theory, though, also applies to the second – namely, most states are both upstream and downstream states.

3. Limited Territorial Sovereignty

The limited territorial sovereignty theory holds that a state may make use of the waters flowing through its territory to the extent that such use does not interfere with reasonable use of waters by the downstream states. Decisions of international and domestic tribunals, as well as pronouncements of private and public international bodies, support this approach to transboundary river pollution.

5. Statute of the International Court of Justice, Art. 38, 1978 IJ. Acts & Doc. 77.

6. 2 H. Grotius, De Jure Belli et Pacis, ch. 2 §12 (Kelsey trans. 1925)(7th ed. 1646).

7. Re: Treaty of Guadalupe Hidalgo, 21 Op. Att'y Gen. 274, 283 (1895).

The *Trail Smelter* arbitration expresses the principle that a state has responsibility for environmental damage extending beyond its territorial limits. The arbitral tribunal stated that, under principles of international law,

> no State has the right to use or permit the use of its territory in such a manner as to cause injury by fumes in or to the territory of another or the properties or person therein, when the case is of serious consequence and the injury is established by clear and convincing evidence.[8]

The *Corfu Channel* case, although it did not concern pollution, also supports the general principle of limited territorial sovereignty.[9] The International Court of Justice held in that case that it is "every State's obligation not to allow knowingly its territory to be used for acts contrary to the rights of other States."

The *Lac Lanoux* arbitration[10] also applied this principle [of state responsibility, and extended it explicitly to pollution, although liability was not found]. In that case Spain objected to French hydroelectric plants on the Carol River. France proposed to divert the waters of the Carol, which flows across the border into Spain, in order to generate electricity. Water equal in quantity and quality would be returned to the Carol before it entered Spain. The arbitral tribunal stated:

> When one examines whether France, either during the discussion or in her proposals, has given sufficient consideration to Spanish interests, it must be stressed how closely linked together are the obligation to take into consideration, in the course of negotiations, adverse interests and the obligation to give a reasonable place to these interests in the solution finally adopted.[11]

In other words, the upstream state has an obligation to take into account, in good faith, the interests of the downstream riparians as well as its own interests....

National and international tribunals have also applied the concept of limited territorial sovereignty. In 1938, the Italian Corte de Cassazione asserted in dicta that:

> international law recognizes the right of every riparian state to enjoy, as a participant of a kind of partnership created by the river, all the advantages deriving from it. A State cannot disregard the international duty not to impede or to destroy the opportunity of the other States to avail themselves of the flow of water for their own national needs.[12]

Public and private international organizations have also embraced the limited territorial sovereignty approach. Principle 21 of the United Nations' Stockholm Declaration on the Human Environment provides that states have the "sovereign right to exploit their own resources pursuant to their own environmental policies,"

8. Trail Smelter Case (U.S. v. Can.), 3 R. Int'l Arb. Awards 1905, 1965 (1941), reprinted in 35 Am. J. Int'l 684, 716 (1941); see Read, The Trail Smelter Dispute, 1 Can. Y.B. Int'l L. 213, 215–29 (1963).

[Ed. note: Actually this is pure dicta. The tribunal had authority only to determine the extent of damages, and causation. Trail Smelter Arbitration, 9 Ann. Dig. & Rep. Rub. Int'l Cases 315-316 (1941). *Trail Smelter* is often cited for the customary law principle of state responsibility for pollution, but that proposition requires the application of the two cases following in the text.]

9. Corfu Channel Case (U.K. v. Alb.), 1949 IJ. 4, 21 (Apr. 9, 1949).

10. Affaire du Lac Lanoux (Spain v. Fr.), 12 R. Int'l Arb. Awards 281 (1957), digested in 53 Am. J. Int'l L. 156 (1959).

11. Id. at 317.

12. Judgment of Feb. 13, 1939, Corte Cass., Italy, 64 Foro It. I 1036, 1046, digested in 3 Dig. of Int'l L. 1050–51 (1938–39).

but along with this right comes the "responsibility to ensure that activities within their jurisdiction or control do not cause damage to the environment of other States or areas beyond the limit of national jurisdiction."[13]

The Helsinki Rules promulgated by the International Law Association also assume limited territorial sovereignty. Article IV of the Helsinki Rules states that "each basin State is entitled, within its territory, to a reasonable and equitable share in the beneficial uses of the waters of an international drainage basin."[14]

Articles X and XI of the Helsinki Rules specifically address transboundary river pollution. Article X prohibits "any new form of water pollution or any increase in the degree of existing water pollution in an international drainage basin which would cause substantial injury in the territory of a co-basin State." Article XI provides that a polluting state shall not only be required to cease the polluting activity but must also compensate the injured state.

The limited territorial sovereignty theory is thus the basis for the rules of international law most frequently applied to the pollution of transboundary rivers.

4. The Community Theory

The community theory holds that the water of a drainage basin should be managed as a unit, without regard to national territorial boundaries. The various co-riparians should manage and develop the drainage basin jointly, and share the benefits derived therefrom.

In its judgment with respect to the territorial jurisdiction of the International Commission of the River Oder, the Permanent Court of International Justice went beyond the limited territorial sovereignty theory and expressed some elements of the community theory, stating that –

> the community of interest in a navigable international river becomes the basis of a common legal right, the essential features of which are the perfect equality of all riparian States in the use of the whole course of the river and the exclusion of any preferential privilege of any one riparian State in relation to the others.[15]

Although the community theory is a favorite of legal theorists, it does not yet enjoy widespread acceptance in the practice of states. The community theory is perhaps better thought of as a goal or an ideal toward which international law strives rather than as a rule of practice.

TREATIES GOVERNING POLLUTION OF THE RHINE

In addition to customary international law, several treaties govern the pollution of the Rhine. Some of these date back to the last century, but the most important are two modern treaties: the Berne Convention and the Rhine Chemical Convention.

1. Historical Treaties

The Rhine's problems did not begin with the Sandoz accident. Rhine pollution has been a problem at least since 1834, when Coleridge first asked, "what power divine/Shall henceforth wash the river Rhine?" As early as 1868, the various riparian states of the Rhine agreed by treaty to certain restrictions on the transport of toxic substances on the river. Packages containing arsenic and other toxic

13. Report of the United Nations Conference on the Human Environment, Principle 21, U.N. Doc. A/CONF.48/14/Rev. 1 (1972).

14. ILA, Helsinki Rules on the Uses of the Waters of International Rivers (1966) at 163–71.

15. 1929 P.I.J. (ser. A) No. 23, at 27 (Sept. 10, 1929).

materials were required to bear the warning "poison" in French and German, in clearly legible black oil paint....

Prohibition of pollution of the Rhine from land-based sources dates back at least 120 years to an 1869 fisheries treaty between Switzerland and the Grand Duchy of Baden, which forbade the discharge of industrial wastes into the Rhine or its tributaries between Konstanz and Basel. Despite these early efforts, however, the condition of the Rhine continued to worsen.

2. The Berne Convention

In 1946, the Netherlands delegation to the Central Commission for the Navigation of the Rhine drew attention to the serious problems resulting from the growing pollution of the waters of the Rhine and suggested that the matter be examined at an international conference.

A conference was held, as a result of which the Convention concerning the Commission for the Protection of the Rhine Against Pollution (the Berne Convention) was signed in Berne on April 29, 1963, by Switzerland, West Germany, the Netherlands, France, and Luxembourg and entered into force in 1965. The Convention set up the International Commission for the Protection of the Rhine Against Pollution (International Commission) and gave the Commission three tasks, [to identify pollution sources, identify protective measures, and propose international agreements thereon]....

The rulemaking procedures of the Berne Convention are hardly conducive to decisive action. Decisions under the Berne Convention require unanimity among the Contracting Parties. Each delegation has one vote, with the provision that the European Community can cast a number of votes equal to the number of European Community members who are Contracting Parties; the European Community may not vote in cases where its member states vote, and vice versa. In other words, the European Community may vote, as a bloc, with Switzerland the only country outside that bloc.

A single negative vote, or the abstention of more than one party, negates unanimity and thus prevents the adoption of a resolution. Switzerland, therefore, has effective veto power over any European Community proposal....

3. The Rhine Chemical Convention...

In the summer of 1971, the middle course of the Rhine was entirely without oxygen in an area over 100 kilometers long, a situation that ultimately prompted European governments to take action. On March 22, 1972, the European Community requested that the parties to the Berne Convention design an emergency program for decontaminating the Rhine. On June 20, 1975, the European Parliament passed a resolution calling on those countries that were both parties to the Berne Convention and members of the European Community to agree on "immediate, practical and coordinated measures to avoid the impending disaster." Finally, a conference called by the Netherlands between ministers of parties to the Berne Convention led to the adoption of the Convention on The Protection of the Rhine Against Chemical Pollution (Rhine Chemical Convention).[16]

a. General Provisions of the Rhine Chemical Convention

The Rhine Chemical Convention amends and modifies the Berne Convention by placing additional responsibilities on the International Commission and the

16. Convention on the Protection of the Rhine Against Chemical Pollution, Dec. 3, 1976, I.L.M. 242 (1977).

Contracting Parties. Article I of the Convention sets two goals for improving the water quality of the Rhine: elimination of pollution of the Rhine by certain highly dangerous substances, enumerated in the "black list" of Annex I, and reduction of pollution of the Rhine by substances listed in the "grey list" of Annex II. Among the chemicals listed in Annex I are "organophosphoric compounds" and "mercury and mercury compounds." Chemicals in both of these categories were released into the Rhine by the Sandoz accident. Annex II contains a general category of "Biocides and their derivatives not appearing in Annex 1." This latter category includes most of the other chemicals released into the Rhine by the Sandoz fire....

The bulk of the Convention's provisions deal with deliberate discharges of pollutants.... The limits for discharges of Annex I substances are set by an international body, rather than a national one, albeit by the unanimous agreement of the Contracting Parties.... In contrast, national authorities set the limits for discharges of Annex II substances after mutual consultation within the International Commission....

The Convention contains only minimal provisions regulating accidental discharges, although such discharges are a major source of harm to the Rhine. To prevent accidental discharges, Article 7 of the Convention provides that "The Contracting Parties will take all the legislative and regulatory measures guaranteeing that the storage of Annex I and II substances shall be done in such a way that there is no danger of pollution for the waters of the Rhine...."

b. International Alarm Plan Rhine

Article 11 of the Rhine Chemical Convention also provides for the establishment of an international warning system to handle pollution emergencies.... To implement Article 11 the International Commission set up a network of warning stations known as the International Alarm Plan Rhine....

c. Rulemaking Powers

Under both the Berne Convention and the Rhine Chemical Convention, the International Commission's rulemaking function is purely advisory. The Commission may make recommendations and suggestions but may not make binding substantive rules, with the exception of setting limit values for the discharge of Annex I substances. Any decisions must be made by unanimous consent of the Contracting Parties.

The Convention does, however, place certain binding obligations on the Contracting Parties. It requires them to monitor discharges and to set up water quality testing stations. Of greater significance in the context of the Sandoz spill is the obligation to inform the International Commission and the Contracting Parties, without delay, of any accident which could seriously threaten the quality of Rhine water. [In the Sandoz incident] Switzerland delayed more than twenty-four hours before notifying the downstream states of the danger to the Rhine.

d. Dispute Resolution

Article 15 of the Rhine Chemical Convention provides that any dispute between the Contracting Parties concerning the interpretation or implementation of the Convention that cannot be settled by negotiation shall be submitted to arbitration....

THE FAILURE OF THE RHINE TREATY REGIME...

The ways in which existing law failed to protect the Rhine...illustrate the need for new mechanisms to prevent these disasters in the future.

1. Failure of the International Warning and Alarm Plan Rhine

Although the downstream states accused Switzerland of deliberately concealing information, Switzerland's delay of more than twenty-four hours before notifying the downstream states resulted as much from poor planning as from deliberate secretiveness. Incompatibility between the various alarm systems delayed the response to the crisis.... Although some of the environmental damage caused by the Sandoz spill might not have occurred had adequate warnings been given, the greater part of the damage was inevitable once the chemicals had entered the river....

2. Violation of the Rhine Chemical Convention

The greater part of the environmental damage resulting from the Sandoz spill was caused not by the delay in warning downstream states but by the failure of various safety systems designed to prevent the entry of chemicals into the river in the event of a fire. But for the lack of adequate catchbasins for runoff water from firefighting, the absence of a fire alarm and sprinkler system at Warehouse 956, and the faulty installation of a drainage seal, the catastrophe might have been averted.

Sandoz insists that it broke no laws in storing the chemicals in Warehouse 956, despite the absence of catch basins for runoff water. This assertion appears to be true. If so Switzerland, which otherwise has an excellent record in the area of environmental legislation, failed to fulfill its obligation under Article 7 of the Rhine Chemical Convention to ensure by all necessary legislative and administrative measures that the storage of hazardous substances did not endanger the Rhine.... If Article 7 is given its broadest construction, it creates an affirmative duty on the part of the Swiss administrative authorities to carry out inspections and otherwise police waterfront warehouses to ensure that no danger to the Rhine exists.[17] Under this interpretation of the Convention, Switzerland's failure to fulfill its administrative obligations under Article 7 was extended from the time the permit was granted, in 1979, to the time of the fire.[18]

WHY THE TREATIES FAILED

The Berne convention is purely institutional in nature; it lacks rulemaking powers and enforcement mechanisms.... The three tasks that the Convention sets for the International Commission are investigative rather than preventive in nature. The findings and proclamations of the International Commission are not binding. Switzerland's [possible] violation of Articles 7 and 11 of the Rhine Chemical Convention... is of little import...when one considers that the Convention provides neither incentives for compliance nor sanctions for noncompliance. Without either a carrot or a stick with which to induce the Contracting Parties to comply, the Convention is little more than a "feel-good" document that allows the Contracting

17. See Rhine Chemical Convention, Art. 7: "The Contracting Parties will take all the legislative and regulatory measures guaranteeing that the storage of Annex I and II substances shall be done in such a way that there is no danger of pollution."

Although neither the Swiss government nor the governments of the downstream states have taken any legal actions against Sandoz, private individuals have brought a criminal charge against an unknown party or parties and the public prosecutor has commenced an investigation.

18. An alternative approach is that the Swiss probably violated customary international law. Under the limited territorial sovereignty approach to transboundary pollution, Switzerland violated its duty not to interfere with the reasonable use of the waters of the Rhine by the lower riparians. The same is true under either the community theory or the absolute territorial integrity theory. The lower riparians suffered significant harm as a result of Switzerland's violation of its duty. The fishing industry was virtually wiped out. Alternative sources of drinking water had to be obtained, and the value of the river for recreational use and as a magnet for tourism was decreased.

Parties to voice concern over the deteriorating state of the Rhine without having to face the domestic economic and political sacrifices that a genuine commitment to cleaning up the Rhine would require....

COMMENTARY AND QUESTIONS

1. The problem of sovereignty. One of the River Rhine's fundamental problems is that it flows through six sovereign nations. There is no one government which has responsibility for the river system, and many diverse reasons why no national government along the Rhine wishes to concede any superior position to the others. No country wants to yield a superior legislative, judicial, administrative, or enforcement power to any supra-national river authority. In the River Rhine conventions, for example, note the frequently-encountered requirement that provisions be adopted by unanimous consent, and the further fact that even those provisions typically lack specific mandatory requirements. The understandable perquisites of sovereignty form a fundamental constraint on the growth and application of international environmental law.

2. The international litigation approach. It would seem in many of these transboundary cases that liability is obvious. The corporations or individuals that cause pollution typically do so knowing that it can be transported over long distances by air or water to places where it may cause injury. The fact that the victims are outside the borders of the actor's nation, however, tends to externalize those costs. To what extent is litigation, the first instinct of American environmentalists, a practical possibility in the international realm?

Two threshold questions: what litigation forum could the injury be brought to, and what law applies? The Schwabach essay focuses on sources of law that could be a basis for international litigation on the Rhine spill, drawn from customary law and treaties. As to forum, there is no supra-national court that automatically has jurisdiction over controversies between two nation states. States must themselves decide to be subject to a higher level court, and, even if they do open themselves to adjudication, they typically retain loophole escape clauses for avoiding such jurisdiction.

3. What forum for an accounting of the Rhine pollution damages? What forums exist for after-the-fact resolution of liability issues arising from the Sandoz spill? Ideally, international lawyers instinctively would prefer to turn to a pre-existing supra-national mechanism created by agreement of the different national parties. As Schwabach's article illustrates, however, there usually is no such convention capable of enforcing standards and assigning liability for their breach. Since the Sandoz spill there have been few serious moves in the direction of creating such a mechanism. In 1987, the EC states updated the "Seveso Directive," a Community declaration that was originally issued in 1982 following the Seveso, Italy, chemical poisoning incident.[19] But even with the Sandoz spill fresh in mind, the parties could

---

19. Directive 82/501, 25 O.J. Eur. Comm. (No. L 230) 1 (1982), as modified by 30 Eur. Comm. (No. L 85) 36 (1987).

only agree to establish a better alarm and notification system, a pool of experts to study the problem, improved industrial safety goals, and standards for moving toward a uniform system of transporting and storing hazardous waste.

The absence of liability-assigning mechanisms is again apparent, mitigated in the Sandoz case by the industry's energetic attempts to offer generous private compensation settlements to all potential claimants.

For observers trained in the Anglo-American legal mold, international environmental incidents like the Sandoz spill cry out for some kind of adjudicative mechanism that permits economic accounting to proceed without relying on voluntary compensation or the glacial processes of international diplomacy. Several international adjudicative forums do exist: the International Court of Justice (ICJ) in The Hague, various regional tribunals that may exist by treaty, consensual arbitration panels, and the "municipal" (i.e., national domestic) courts in the various nation states.[20]

In the *Trail Smelter* case, Canada and the United States, after much diplomatic fencing, agreed that it was in their mutual interest to have the matter resolved by a higher authority, and appointed the International Joint Commission (IJC), a treaty body that had been set up to study and advise on transboundary issues, to act as an arbitral tribunal to settle the case. The existence of this kind of forum depends on case by case happenstance, and is quite exceptional.

Many nation states, on the other hand, have accepted the jurisdiction of the ICJ. The ICJ has the advantage that it operates at a supra-national level; it treats a pollution incident like the Sandoz spill at the international level best suited to resolution of transnational issues. But the ICJ jurisdiction has its limitations as well. Many member states have not agreed to full automatic ICJ jurisdiction. Some have agreed to only limited jurisdiction, and some, like the United States in the famous *Nicaragua* case,[21] have asserted their sovereign right to withdraw from their acquiescence to jurisdiction when unwelcome litigation is filed (despite original agreement that jurisdiction required six months notice to withdraw). In such circumstances, it is painfully evident that nation states will not usually be brought into ICJ adjudications when they strenuously do not want to participate, and no judicial enforcement remedy is available. Some limited exceptions exist: the European Court of Justice (ECJ) established in Luxembourg by the European Community (EC) has been granted supra-national adjudicative power within the Community and offers a fascinating potential regional forum, based on treaties between EC member states, although the scope of matters within that jurisdiction is limited and growing only slowly.[22] Switzerland is not a member of the EC.

20. "Municipal" as used in international law refers to the domestic law of a nation, as opposed to international principals and international legal forms such as the ICJ.

21. Nicaragua v. U.S., Merits and Judgment, ICJ Reports 1986 at 14 et seq.

22. See, however, Phillippe Sands, European Community Environmental Law: Legislation and the European Court of Justice, Centre for International Environmental Law Monograph (1991), noting several recent cases strongly affirming environmental principles in interpretations of EC legislation.

As in transboundary suits within the United States, courts in one nation state can often exercise jurisdiction over defendants in other countries through a form of long-arm jurisdictional claim. In some acid rain and transboundary air pollution cases between the United States and Canada, litigants have found practical damage remedies in the municipal courts. Michie v. Great Lakes Steel, 495 F.2d 213 (6th Cir. 1974).

4. Official state or private litigants? There is a further issue whether litigants would be national governments representing their citizens on a parens patriae basis, or injured private parties themselves. A number of commentators have noted the inertia of governmental involvement except in the most dramatic cases. As one commentator[23] said –

> As evidenced by its role in the Basel accident, public international environmental law is nearly impotent, and will probably remain so barring a revolutionary change in the values underlying the distribution of authority in goals of the international system. Private international remedies may offer more effective legal solutions to environmental problems. The basic policy orientation parallels that of public law: the principal questions to be resolved are those of compensation for injury, rather than prevention of pollution. Theoretically, strengthening private remedies could lead to incentives for reduction of injury-creating pollution. If private remedies are frequently used, the cost of pollution will be internalized by the polluter, who may then take greater precautions for future accidents.... Proponents of the use of private rather than public remedies back the approach favored by the Organization for Economic Cooperation and Development (OECD)[24] in its recommendation "Principles Concerning Transfrontier Pollution," and the Scandanavians in their Nordic Convention.[25]

These latter efforts have sought the lowering of barriers for transborder private suits, advocating "equal right of access" and "non-discrimination" in cases of pollution litigation. Agreements for the mutual enforcement of civil judgments in Europe already exist.

Where the transborder polluter is a government agency, however, as in the Chernobyl nuclear disaster, it may be far more difficult to bring effective litigation in the municipal courts of either state. In the Rhine spill example, the transboundary pollution was not caused by governmental action, but nevertheless it was clear that governmental parties would be deeply involved in the legal discussions that followed.[26] When a pollution incident or a course of conduct has become so offensive

23. Darrell, Killing the Rhine: Immoral, But is it Legal?, 29 Virginia J. Int'l L. 421, 454 (1989).

24. OECD Doc. (74) 224, in 114 I.L.M. 242 (1975)

25. Convention on the Protection on the Environment, February 19, 1974, Demark-Finland-Norway-Sweden, in 13 I.L.M. 591 (1974).

26. In only a few cases are citizens of one country able to go directly into the courts of another country to litigate a case of transboundary pollution. Between the United States and Canada, for instance, it has been important that the courts of each are open to citizens of the other filing tort suits. See Michie v. Great Lakes Steel Co., 495 F.2d 213 (6th Cir. 1974). See also §115 of the Clean Air Act Amendments of 1970, and EPA findings thereunder, in Thomas v. N.Y., 802 F.2d 1443 (D.C. Cir. 1986).

that the effected state decides to take on the controversy (by no means a foregone conclusion), the first official stage of international law is typically diplomatic negotiation, which can be a slowmoving morass. As the acid rain experience in northern Europe and North America indicates, nations that produce power plant pollution can be quite unenthusiastic about assuming responsibility for the widespread costs caused by themselves and their citizens, dragging out negotiations and attempted mediations for decades.

5. What law applies? Even if a pollution question can be brought to a judicial or quasi-judicial forum, the question remains, what law applies? Within Europe, for instance, it may be quite difficult to apply a downstream nation's law against an upstream defendant; conflicts of law questions abound in any municipal forum. The European Community, with its legislature in Brussels, represents an ongoing (and atypical) experiment in supra-national jurisdiction and the creation of regional law, but the role of the European Court of Justice in pollution matters is just now beginning to develop. To the extent that the EC has established a supra-national adjudicatory ability, the law of the Community may be applied, but that law is in its infancy as a set of principles governing transboundary pollution. The fascinating feature of EC law is that principles derived from European conventions can be applied in the municipal courts of member nations as well as in the European Court of Justice itself. Most areas of the world, lacking any entity like the European Community, have no such supra-national option available.

If a matter is brought to adjudication between nation states, upon what "law" will it be decided? The ICJ is rigorously limited in the "law" it can apply. The ICJ Statute states –

> **Article 38:** (1) The Court, whose function is to decide in accordance with international law such disputes as are submitted to it, shall apply:
>
> a. international conventions whether general or particular, establishing rules expressly recognized by the contesting states;
>
> b. international custom, as evidence of a general practice accepted as law;
>
> c. the general principles of law recognized by civilized nations;
>
> d. subject to the provisions of Article 59, judicial decisions and the teachings of the most highly qualified publicists of the various nations, as subsidiary means for the determination of rules of law.
>
> (2) This provision shall not prejudice the power of the court to decide a case ex aequo et bono, if the parties agree thereto....
>
> **Article 59:** The decision of the Court has no binding force except between the parties and in respect of that particular case.

Article 38 apparently creates a hierarchy of authorities to be applied as law in international disputes. Needless to say, the easiest of these sources of law to apply is the first, because states have conceded the applicability of terms and standards of treaties and conventions which can then be applied to particular controversies. This source of law, however, depends first upon the accidental coincidence of the petitioning and responding states having ratified a common instrument, and also that the treaty or convention have terms which are crisp and clear enough to imply specific mandatory responsibilities, by no means a sure thing. The treaty texts that get ratified tend not to be very crisp, clear, or mandatory. As noted, both of the Rhine conventions included loopholes and exceptions which frustrated their direct application.

In transboundary cases, if there is no treaty or convention in force, by what combination of other international law principles can the rules of liability and remedy be determined?

Custom? The most frequent attempts by international environmental lawyers to define legal responsibilities for transboundary pollution are based on arguments of alleged custom. The trouble is that there is no generally agreed upon set of customary principles of international environmental law. As the Schwabach text indicates, there are a variety of competing theories. Publicists (eminent legal scholars working privately or for international governing organizations) either arrive at such vague generalities as to be meaningless, in protecting each nation's jealous sense of sovereignty, or attempt to assert specific mandates in a form that deters sovereign nations from wanting to acquiesce in these principles.

What is a principle of international custom to be based upon? It cannot be based upon the myriad Declarations, Resolutions, Protocols and other non-binding statements produced in a succession of wishful conferences held by various scholarly groups and IGOs (intergovernmental organizations). The dramatic 1972 Stockholm Declaration, for instance, produced at a conference held under the aegis of the United Nations, declared a series of fairly strong environmental principles.[27] Principles 21 and 22 stated –

> 21. States have, in accordance with the Charter of the United Nations and the principles of international law, the sovereign right to exploit their own resources pursuant to their own environmental policies, and the responsibility to ensure that activities within their jurisdiction or control do not cause damage to the environment of other States or of areas beyond the limits of national jurisdiction. [Note the ambivalent mandates – Eds.]
>
> 22. States shall cooperate to develop further the international law regarding liability and compensation for the victims of pollution and other environmental damage caused by activities within the jurisdiction or control of such States to areas beyond their jurisdiction.

Virtually nothing official, however, has been done since 1972 to develop an international law of liability and compensation.[28]

---

27. The Declaration included much ambiguity and many potential escape clauses. Stockholm Declaration on the Human Environment, U.N. Doc. A/Conf. 4/8/14, in 11 I.L.M. 1416 (1972).

28. Phillippe Sands, Chernobyl: Law and Communication 23 (1988).

One common line of argument for a customary rule of liability is the "due diligence" doctrine, which holds that there is "a custom-based rule of due diligence imposed on all States in order that activities carried out within their jurisdiction do not cause damage to the environment of other states." OECD, Report by the Environment Committee: Responsibility and Liability of States in Relation to Transfrontier Pollution (1984).

But what is due diligence? Many commentators try to define due diligence by reference to the familiar old common law nuisance principle sic utere tuo ut alienum non laedas.[29] This principle can be discerned in the *Corfu Channel* case and *Lac Lenoux*, but the fundamental problem is that its meaning is not clear, even in domestic American law. "The dearth of [international] caselaw deprives the principle of sic utere of the specificity that applications to particular instances of transboundary pollution would arguably furnish it. Instead, sic utere remains an abstraction, an empty concept that commentators hope to fill with substantive content...."[30] At what level does environmental injury reach the level of "significance" or "unacceptable damage" in transboundary situations? Is *any* injury compensable, thereby bringing into international law a straightforward "polluter-pays" liability as a cost-of-doing-business rule? Or does it import some theory of fault and negligence? Must a state act to prevent normal production-based pollution, or is due diligence focused on accidental catastrophes? Does due diligence imply a strict liability standard, or a negligence, or intentional tort type standard? The closer the definitions move toward strict liability,[31] the more resistance will be raised by both industrial states and LDCs[32] that want to get in on the money of industrial production.

The ambiguities of defining customary law are further increased by some commentators' assertion that a rule can be regarded as "customary" between two party litigants based on their own prior practice, even though it is not customary between any other nation states. This makes a distinction between duties based on a framework of general custom, and the "specific custom" of the disputing states as it lends content to that framework. Further, to assert that a rule is "customary" to a state, must it be shown to be applied in its domestic law, or is it to be based on the state's customary behavior in the international arena? In either event, much definition has to be done before a rule of law ready for ICJ jurisdiction is presented.

As to the "general principles of law recognized by civilized nations" in Article 38, these focus almost exclusively on procedural rules, such as res judicata, and have never been the sole foundation of an ICJ decision.[33] As to the use of "judicial decisions and the teachings of publicists," this basis for ICJ doctrine is traditionally

29. "One should use one's own property in such a manner as not to injure that of another."

30. Developments in the Law – International Environmental Law, 104 Harv. L. Rev. 1484, 1501 (1991).

31. Some commentators hopefully assert that strict liability is already the customary standard. See Goldie, Transfrontier Pollution, 12 Syracuse J. Int'l L. and Commerce 185 (1985).

32. "Less developed country" is the current euphemism for Third World states.

33. H. Lauterpacht, Private Law Sources and Analogies of International Law 215–217 (1970).

regarded as highly subordinate, not sufficient in itself to base a decision, and merely a source of definition for Article 38's first three bases of legal responsibility.

6. State responsibility for nonaccidental pollution, before the fact as well as after the fact? Does it make a difference whether transboundary environmental damages are caused by a one-shot disaster, or by the normal course of business pollution created by industrial technologies? The focus of transboundary pollution cases has most often been on "one-shot" occurrences, which are universally identified as disasters. Arguably, however, international liability applies equally to normal pollution, analogous to American intentional tort doctrines. Under this reasoning, a "due diligence" formula addresses a state's duty to insure the environmental safety of behavior within its borders in both accidental and non-accidental settings; it would apply both before the fact, in prevention, as well as after the fact in terms of response to transboundary pollution. In the Sandoz spill, Switzerland could be accused of violating a duty to monitor, investigate, and prevent dangerous instrumentalities from injuring the environment, as well as duties arising after the fact to warn downstream states that a pollution incident had occurred, facilitating rescue and response efforts to mitigate harms. The fact that Switzerland did neither, despite the fact that there were Rhine treaties as well as arguable customary law, emphasizes the shaky standing of such international environmental principles.

7. Is international law really law? The tools of international environmental law raise a fundamental riddle, especially for American observers. Is international law really "law" if it fundamentally does not have to be obeyed? Americans with their Wild West background tend to think that law isn't law unless it is directly enforceable. Because jealous guarding of sovereignty is such a fundamental principle of international legal policy, each state hesitates to the point of stalemate in yielding authority to higher levels of international authority. Accordingly a number of environmental activists have concluded that the most powerful tools for applying international principles are consumer boycotts in developed Northern industrial societies and the media. United Nations police actions, which theoretically could be the enforcement mechanism of international law, are twice limited. First, they are extremely difficult to mobilize, requiring a resolution of the Security Council where one veto can block an initiative, even if the fundamental principle being enforced is clearly a violation of the U.N. Charter or international law. Second, police actions by the U.N. are at best crude, blunt instruments, as unwieldly as they are rare. For the most part, international environmental law will never be able to rely upon U.N. direct enforcement efforts, and will have to be based on less assertive principles.

8. Overview. Looking back at the Sandoz Spill and the transboundary pollution issues it raises, what strength do you discern in the potential legal devices for responding to transboundary pollution? After the Chernobyl disaster, two international conventions dealing with future nuclear catastrophes were quickly promulgated and ratified by many states including the Soviet Union, but like the post-Sandoz Seveso Directive they dealt primarily with notification and emergency assistance.[34] Both conventions, moreover, provide specifically that states may ratify these conventions provisionally, opt out from particular paragraphs imposing mandatory duties, or "denounce" the treaty at any point and thereby de-ratify it. No legal actions for determining liability or damages have been filed, despite the drastic radioactive pollution consequences of the Chernobyl meltdown.[35]

B. THE GLOBAL COMMONS

There have been a number of important international legal initiatives attempting to deal with problems of the global commons. The Montreal Convention on Protection of the Ozone Layer, for example, provides a fascinating example of the interplay between international concerns and domestic constraints in its moves to limit the production of chlorofluorocarbons (CFCs) that destroy stratospheric ozone.[36] Global warming, endangered species, population management, preservation of antiquities, Antarctica – all these and more could be the basis of extended international case studies.

This chapter part, however, chooses the more prosaic issue of whaling and its effects on the world's whale populations as its relatively clear and instructive example of international responses to problems of the global commons.

Section 1. WHALING, A CLASSIC RESOURCE DEPLETION DILEMMA

P. Birnie, Whaling: End of an Era (1985)

Herman Melville shipped out on the whaling vessel Acushnet early in 1841 from New Bedford, Massachusetts, bound for Cape Horn and the South Pacific. The 22-year-old was between jobs during a period of hard times. But it was a boom time for the New England whaling industry. More than 700 American ships prowled the seas in search of whales during the 1840s. New Bedford was the busiest whaling port in the world. Crewing on a whaler was difficult and dangerous, and Melville left his ship in mid-voyage after 18 months. But his adventures were the fodder for *Moby Dick*, which many believe is the quintessential American novel.

Commercial whaling changed radically just a few years after the 1851 publication of *Moby Dick*. By the late 1860s the explosive harpoon had replaced the hand-thrown weapon used in Melville's day, and steam-powered catcher boats allowed

34. Vienna Convention on Early Notification of a Nuclear Accident, 25 I.L.M. 1370 (1986), and Vienna Convention on Assistance in the Case of a Nuclear Accident or Radiological Emergency, 25 I.L.M. 1377 (1986).

35. For coverage of the Chernobyl issue generally, see Phillippe Sands, Chernobyl: Law and Communication (1988).

36. See the Vienna Convention for the Protection of the Ozone Layer, 26 I.L.M. 1516 (1987)(defining obligations of participating nations with regard to CFCs); Protocol on Chlorofluorocarbons (the "Montreal Protocol"), 26 I.L.M. 1541 (1987)(mandating reductions in CFC use pursuant to the Vienna Convention). Other important examples are the Basel Convention on the Control of Transboundary Movements of Hazardous Wastes and Their Disposal, 28 I.L.M. 657 (1989)(governing international restrictions on hazardous waste import and export); the Convention on the Regulation of Antarctic Mineral Resource Activities (the Wellington Agreement), 27 I.L.M. 859 (1988)(protecting the Antarctic environment from military and mining activity); and the Third United Nations Conference on the Law of the Sea (UNCLOS III), 21 I.L.M. 1261 (1982)(a noble thwarted attempt to govern the use and protection of the world's ocean resources).

whalers to hunt faster-swimming whales and to range farther in search of them. By the end of the 1930s whaling fleets from around the world had drastically depleted the numbers of eight of the nine largest species of whales, a group of mammals known as the great whales.

World War II interrupted nearly all commercial whaling, but in the late 1940s a handful of nations resumed operations. At the same time several nations with whaling industries took steps to ensure a continuous supply of whales, an effort that until recently was characterized more by political dissension than success. However, all but a handful of countries – notably the Soviet Union and Japan...agreed to end commercial whaling in 1986, and those two countries...indicated they will end their operations in 1988.

Some conservationists believe that may be too late for some species. Whalers were prohibited from hunting the slow-swimming right whale in 1936. But it is estimated that fewer than 4,000 right whales live today. "The population is at best stabilized, or at worst continuing to decline," said Peter Dykstra, a spokesman for Greenpeace, the environmental action group. Bowhead whales, which swim in extreme northern waters, also were decimated in the late 19th century. Although bowheads have not been hunted commercially since 1935, there are believed to be fewer than 5,000 alive today. Six other great whales – the gray, blue, fin, sei, humpback and sperm – are considered endangered due to overharvesting.

Concerned by a decline in whale stocks...during the 1930s the antarctic whaling nations entered into several voluntary agreements designed to protect whales. Some of them – including the Geneva Convention of 1931, the eight-nation London Agreement of 1937 and a British-German-Norwegian agreement signed the following year – succeeded in reducing the number of whale catchers and limiting the time periods for hunting some species. But none of those agreements stopped the whales' decline. Several whaling nations set up the International Whaling Commission (IWC) in 1946 to try to safeguard the whales and keep the industry alive.... [The IWC] was the first international body given the power to grant complete protection to endangered species and set up yearly hunting quotas for the other species. In addition, the IWC could limit whaling to specific seasons and ban the taking of nursing whales, whale calves, and adults under certain sizes. The commission also carries on regular inspections of whaling operations.... Nearly everyone agrees that the IWC has failed to achieve either goal. "It is widely known that the International Whaling Commission...presided during the first 20 years of its existence over the depletion of nearly all the world's whale populations," British biologist Sidney Holt, a longtime international fisheries expert, asserted. "And the whaling industry, instead of enjoying an orderly development, experienced a disorderly, though long drawn-out collapse."

A resurgence of whaling followed World War II, but by the early 1960s only the Soviet Union and Japan maintained extensive whaling operations. Those two nations, along with Norway, Iceland, Brazil, South Korea, Denmark, Peru, Spain and the Philippines, are the only countries with commercial whaling industries today. A drop in whale oil prices during the worldwide Depression of the 1930s accounted for some of the decline. But the more important factor by far was the decimation of virtually every species of antarctic whale. The relatively slow-swimming humpback was the first to be hunted – and the first to be overharvested. Antarctic whalers killed so many humpbacks beginning in 1904 that they all but disappeared by 1916. Then the blue whale was hunted practically to extinction. "When there were too few blue whales to hunt, the whalers turned to the next largest species, the fin whale, then to the sei [in the mid-1960s], and finally to the little minke [in the mid-1970s]," Richard Ellis noted....

The discovery in the 1960s that the blue whale, the largest creature that has ever lived on earth, was in danger of extinction sparked an international "Save the Whales" campaign. Wildlife, environmental, animal-welfare and conservation groups lobbied heavily to get nations to stop commercial whaling. The IWC first discussed a ban in 1972. But 10 years passed before the commission in 1982 voted to phase out all commercial whaling by 1986.

Under the terms of the IWC charter, nations that file formal objections to commission rulings do not have to abide by them. Japan, Norway and the Soviet Union – the nations with the largest commercial whaling operations – promptly filed the requisite formal complaints. Japan and Norway claimed that the ban was not based on scientific evidence and would wipe out profitable domestic whaling industries. The Soviet Union said that "political considerations," not scientific information, motivated the whaling ban. Japan, Norway, and the Soviet Union, however, indicated they would end their commercial ocean whaling operations by 1988.... "The handwriting is on the wall for commercial whaling," Patricia Forkan of the Humane Society of the United States commented....

It is generally conceded that, despite its unprecedented powers, the IWC did little to safeguard diminishing whale species until the 1970s. Still, unlike its predecessors, the commission continued to operate. The IWC "is really a remarkable organization in that it's managed to hold together through all these years and still has a certain amount of legitimacy. It actually seems to function," biologist Scott Krauss of the New England Aquarium in Boston said. "It may not function to my liking, but it does still function." Under increasing pressure from conservationists, the IWC in the late 1970s began cutting quotas and working toward implementing a total moratorium on commercial whaling. This led to the total ban that the commission adopted at its 1982 meeting.

The first unilateral U.S. restrictions on commercial whaling came with passage of the Endangered Species Act in 1969, which placed eight of the nine great whales on the U.S. endangered list and barred the granting of whaling licenses for those species. At the time there were only two small commercial whaling operations in this country, the Del Monte and Golden Gate Fishing companies in Richmond, California. The Marine Mammal Protection Act of 1972, which put a permanent moratorium on most killing of ocean mammals within the U.S. fishing zone and on importation of their products, "was the nail in the coffin for any commercial whaling in the United States," said Tom McIntyre, marine resources management specialist with the National Marine Fisheries Service.

CHANCES FOR SURVIVAL

Commercial whaling almost certainly will end within the next few years. But that does not mean that all other types of whaling also will cease. Article VII of the 1946 International Convention for the Regulation of Whaling gives countries the right to kill whales "for the purposes of scientific research." Thus far Iceland and South Korea have officially notified the IWC that they intend to carry out comparatively widescale whaling for scientific purposes.... Whalers in Japan and Brazil reportedly are pushing for those nations to undertake scientific whaling as well. Iceland planned to kill 80 fin whales, 80 minke whales and 40 sei whales annually from 1986 to 1989. South Korea said it would take 200 minkes a year.

Icelandic and South Korean officials maintain that the whales will be taken solely for research studies. But conservationists say those nations are actually trying to circumvent the IWC ban on commercial whaling. Conservationists point out that Iceland plans to export the meat from its whales to Japan. "Iceland has made no bones about the fact that they intend to sell [the whale meat] to Japan," Forkan said. "What we are looking at is the potential to make $30 million or so over the four years for a million and a half dollars' worth of research. We think that's commercial whaling."

The IWC allows another exception to its whaling bans, including those on catching totally protected species. IWC regulations permit the taking of whales so long as "the meat and products are to be used exclusively for local consumption by the aborigines." Aboriginal whaling has been permitted in recent years in Greenland where the Eskimos kill fin and humpback whales, in the Soviet Union where Siberian Eskimos take gray whales, and in the United States where Alaskan Eskimos kill bowheads. Conservationists have strenuously objected to these aboriginal whaling activities, alleging that the meat of the gray whales killed in Siberia is used illegally to feed animals on fur farms and that the Eskimos in Greenland and Alaska are killing too many of the rare humpbacks and bowheads.

"U.S. Eskimos are wreaking havoc on the bowhead stocks," Potter said. The problem is not so much the number of whales killed, but the much larger number of those struck and not killed, nearly 90 percent of which die. "The number of whales struck and not landed skyrocketed in the late '70s, early '80s," Potter said. "Given the very low population estimates of these bowhead whales, there is great concern that [the Eskimos] are clearly taking more animals than are being reproduced each year. If you've only got a couple of thousand, it doesn't take long to extinct the species." Some IWC scientists have pushed to end Alaskan bowhead aboriginal whaling. The U.S. government, under pressure from the Alaska Eskimo whaling commission, requested that the IWC allocate 35 bowhead strikes for 1985. The commission eventually allocated the Eskimos 26 strikes a year for 1985, 1986, and 1987.

Then there is the issue of coastal whaling. At the 1985 IWC meeting, Japan asked the commission to give "special consideration" to whaling that takes place solely within 200 miles of a nation's coastline. It would be "totally improper," the Japanese said, for the IWC to have jurisdiction over "any additional species whose utilization is confined exclusively to the 200-mile zone." This was the start, conservationists say, of a Japanese lobbying campaign to reclassify coastal whaling as subsistence whaling, which would be exempt from IWC jurisdiction. Norway and other nations are expected to join Japan in seeking unrestricted coastal subsistence whaling.

THE CONTROVERSY OVER COUNTING POPULATIONS

What continued hunting means for the various whale populations is unclear. The International Whaling Commission has been setting quotas based on whale populations for decades. Yet the process of counting whales is an inexact science at best. This has led to charges by conservation groups that the IWC, bowing to pressure from whaling nations, continually overestimates whale populations. Whaling nations and IWC officials, for their part, claim that conservation groups deliberately understate their figures. "We tend on a worldwide basis to set quotas for the numbers of whales that can be killed without any firm idea of how many there are and whether or not those numbers may be harmful," said Dykstra of Greenpeace.

"If you were to talk to a scientist who works for the Japanese government...[and] a scientist who works for a country that may tend towards conservation, you might find as much as a 5,000 percent difference in the estimate of a certain stock."

COMMENTARY AND QUESTIONS

1. Whales as a global commons. "The oceans of the world continue to suffer from the survival of the philosophy of the commons. Maritime nations still respond automatically to the shibboleth of the 'freedom of the seas.' Professing to believe in the 'inexhaustible resources of the oceans,' they bring species after species of fish and whales closer to extinction." So wrote Garret Hardin.[37] To what extent does the imperiling of the whales reflect a global commons, and to what extent is it susceptible to the legal strategies that Hardin proposed in his famous article? See page 34 *supra*.

2. Whales, extinction, the public trust doctrine and other general principles of international environmental law. It is ultimately probably in the best interests of all to prevent the extinction of whales, but because every market participant can make short-term profit by ignoring long-term resource destruction, and none trusts the others to forebear, the whales as a resource base are exploited into a downward spiral. In the case of many endangered species, moreover, the rarer the remaining individuals, the higher the unit price that is likely to be offered for them, which only accelerates the extinction.

Could this international environmental law problem find legal resolution in the absence of directly actionable legal mechanisms? Could it be litigated? There would of course be all the problems noted earlier as to transboundary pollution of finding a supra-national tribunal capable of wrestling with the actions of several independent sovereigns, especially where the actions and injuries took place on the high seas or other nonterritorial locations.

Assuming jurisdiction in some tribunal, what "general principles" or "custom" or "jurisprudence of civilized nations" would permit the tribunal to take account of extinction of such a valuable and beautiful global resource? Granted, a few nations have passed relevant endangered species protections, but these municipal laws do not rise to the level of general principles. Is the public trust doctrine capable of supplying such a general principle? Although analytically the public trust doctrine, deriving from the ancient code of Justinian, offers some customary basis for argument,[38] its subsequent development in Anglo-American jurisdictions would only coincidentally make it a global legal doctrine. For the same reason the public trust doctrine in general, and a prohibition of extinctions in particular, is hardly likely to be classed as customary in general or between the contending parties. Nor would prior caselaw and the comments of scholars be likely to create principles rising to the level of international law.

---

37. Hardin, The Tragedy of the Commons, 162 Science, 1243, 1245, Dec. 13, 1968.

38. See Nanda and Ris, The Public Trust Doctrine: A Viable Approach to International Environmental Protection, 5 Ecol. L.Q. 291 (1976).

3. International declarations, the Brundtland Commission, and "sustainable development." Over the years, the United Nations and regional and other international bodies have issued a series of declarations and resolutions which may have applicability in the international environmental law area. The 1972 United Nations' Stockholm Conference on the Human Environment and its Declaration were aspirationally very significant, but the latter's terms were resolutely general and lacked enforcement mechanisms. In 1983, the General Assembly of the United Nations established a "World Commission on Environment and Development" chaired by Gro Harlem Brundtland, then-Prime Minister of Norway. It was charged with the task of analyzing worldwide environmental problems and prescribing long-term strategies for resolving them to achieve a sustainable natural and human world for the future. The blue ribbon commission consisted of eminent delegates from two dozen nations. Its 1987 report, Our Common Future, is a startling and highly detailed analysis of global environmental challenges. Its proposals for reform include most significantly a "Summary of Proposed Legal Principles for Environmental Protection and Sustainable Development" adopted by the WCED Experts' Group on Environmental Law. Again, however, reading closely through this carefully negotiated and drafted document, it is evident that the product is aspirational, looking to further implementation by international groups, and is in no sense itself actionable "law," customary or otherwise. Nor is a series of United Nations resolutions using the concept of "common heritage of human kind" or "world natural reserves" a foundation for asserting actionable international environmental law principles in an adjudicative forum.

"Sustainable Development" – the Brundtland Commission's concept for a principle of international environmental policy – quickly became a catchword for discussions at the Rio UNCED conference, however, and the Commission's assertions of the stark necessities of comprehensive environmental acountability indicate that the rhetoric and mechanisms of international law in the environmental sphere are changing.

4. Of sovereignty and enforceability. As already discovered in the transboundary example, one of the classic problems of international environmental law is that there is no supra-national sovereign authority to play the role of Hardin's unitary owner who would incorporate and rationalize all costs and benefits of resource exploitation. The dilemma of the whales is a small example of dozens of major issues of the global environmental commons which lead many wistful observers like ex-U.N. Secretary General U Thant to urge the creation of a new "global authority...a governing body capable of establishing binding standards...and an enforcement authority with power to make conclusive determinations as to compliance."[39] The United Nations is obviously not such an entity. Despite the fact that most lawyers in developed countries presume the necessity of a superior enforcement entity, the international community flees from such proposals. The

39. Public Papers of the Secretaries-General of the United Nations, Volume 8, 350 (1977); see Chayes, International Institutions for the Environment, in Law, Institutions, and the Global Environment at 2 (1972).

wonder is that the International Whaling Commission has any mandatory powers at all. Article 1 of the International Agreement for the Regulation of Whaling provides that "the contracting Governments will take appropriate measures to ensure the application of the provisions of the present Agreement and the punishment of infractions," but it is far from clear what this means beyond providing inspectors on whaling factory ships. Article V, paragraph 3, as in many treaties, provides for a one-nation veto of IWC decisions by the filing of an "objection" to IWC quotas or regulations. In 1971 when the IWC voted 25 to 1 for a zero quota on North Pacific male sperm whales, Japan dissented, lodged an objection, and continued whaling with impunity.

Reading through any major multilateral treaty or convention collected in the International Environment Reporter, for example, one is repeatedly struck by the typical legal minuet between attempts to pin down meaningful standards, which may deter nation states from agreeing to them, and the creeping vacuity and loopholes that make a document agreeable to general concensus and ratification. The more meaningful provisions tend to be drafted and accepted after disasters occur, but even then, as in the Chernobyl example, states are hesitant to erode their hermetic sovereignty. Is protective international action therefore more likely to come from politics and media than from the evolution of law?

5. IGOs and their actions. The IWC is an example of an IGO, an inter-governmental organization. There are literally dozens of IGOs that have direct or indirect jurisdiction over international environmental problems. The United Nations is the premier IGO, and has gathered under its aegis most other IGOs through a process of coordination managed by the U.N. Economic and Social Council (ECOSOC). After the Stockholm conference, the general assembly created the United Nations Environment Programme (UNEP), now based in Nairobi. The UNEP, however, since it was created merely by an Assembly resolution and not by ratification by the states, has an uncertain legal status and no enforcement authority whatever, serving explicitly as a "coordinating body" to lead the environmental activities of other IGOs. The IWC, which predates the United Nations, coordinates with UNEP and ECOSOC, but analytically has separate legal status based on the treaty ratifications that created it.

What can IGOs do? Basically they can talk, formulate aspirational declarations, gather information in compendious detail, and enforce little or nothing. Yet through them one can understand some of the ultimate suasions of international law. In 1985, a group representing displaced indigenous plantation workers petitioned the International Labor Organization (ILO)[40] to investigate the Indian Sardar Sarovar and Narmada dam-building programs. These projects were systematically causing serious environmental destruction, and displacing tens of thousands of rural

40. See Matthew Tuchow, Tribal Land Protection: Lessons from the Sardar Sarovar Conflict (student paper, Harvard Law School, 1987), as reported (with dropped citation) in Plater, Multilateral Development Banks, Environmental Diseconomies, and International Reform Pressures on the Lending Process: the Example of Third World Dam-Building Projects, 9 Third World L.J. 169, 201–202 (1989).

workers in violation of ILO Convention Article 107. The resulting ILO investigation received immediate attention from the Indian government, even though the ILO had no enforcement powers.[41] The prospect of being censured or suspended by the ILO and made to look delinquent in the eyes of the world community – the potential "mobilization of shame" that gives impact to so much of international law's unenforceable mandates – prompted India to take the ILO's investigation extremely seriously. (The fact that subsequent pressure from India forced the ILO to suspend its investigation in spite of clear cut violations of the ILO Convention is a further realistic example of how the game of international law plays out.)

6. NGOs. An important and understated feature of many international environmental law issues like the IWC whaling story is the critical role played by intense pressure from non-governmental organizations (NGOs) in the evolution of conservation-oriented legal principles. Like many IGOs, the IWC was from the beginning susceptible to "capture" by industrial groups and the dozen whaling nations. (Indeed it was they who made up the IWC, and they held the predictable power and perspective of market participants who stand to make greater short-term revenues when conservation restrictions are minimal.) Even when IGOs are made up of broader, or even universal, state membership, they are unlikely to be rigorous in conservation measures due to constraints of inertia and diplomatic compromise. As one scholar has noted, IGOs and the development of international legal principles are often limited by the phenomonenon of the "slowest boat" as well as the "freerider" problem.[42] The slowest boat phenomenon means that agreements tend to be drafted initially to attract maximum numbers of ratifying states, and therefore tend to have the loosest possible mandatory controls. After ratification, moreover, whatever mandatory provisions that exist tend to be designed to be least burdensome on out-voted minority members, thus reflecting a further lowest common denominator "bottom line."

The history of whaling and the IWC, however, was dramatically changed in the early 1960s by NGO pressure groups, based primarily in the United States. Judy Collins recorded a bestselling record album using hydrophone recordings of humpback whale songs as accompaniment to her plaintive ballads. Greenpeace and other citizen groups began a domestic and international program of media intervention and direct action (consumer boycotts; disrupting whale harpooners with little zodiac boats; ramming whaler ships with derelict old scows) designed to show the public the cruelties and needlessness of whale slaughter. More established environmental groups, working out of Washington, San Francisco, and New York, brought pressure to bear upon the federal government to pass tough domestic legislation

---

41. Some observers see the ILO as an interesting model for improving the post-Rio Conference United Nations Environment Programme (UNEP). State delegations to the ILO contain two nongovernmental members (one labor, one employer-based) as well as two government officials. Under Article 26, *any* delegate may petition for adjudication of a matter by the ILO Committee of Experts. ILO thus offers an interesting combination of deliberative functions (its annual Council meetings) and adjudicative, both giving a significant institutionalized role to nongovernmental players.

42. Peter Sand, Lessons Learned in Global Environmental Governance, 18 Envtl Aff. L. Rev. 213, 220 et seq. (1991).

noted in the next section and to impel active U.S. participation in the IWC. Pressure upon the State Department in turn produced U.S. diplomatic pressures on a number of nonwhaling states to join the IWC, thereby outnumbering the whaling nations that previously had controlled it.

As their political force grew in the United States, Canada, and several Western European nations, NGOs became regular observer participants at IWC annual meetings, completely changing the nature of scientific debate and political compromise. NGOs hired scientists who were not in thrall to the whaling industry, hired cameramen for the production of beautiful books, calenders, and horrifying videos of whaling, and prepared press kits and educational materials for schools all over the United States and Europe, to focus aroused environmental consciousness upon the problem of whale killing.

As the success of Western NGOs became evident, citizens groups were formed in a variety of other countries, including LDCs, broadening and focusing the political pressures.

At first most official IGOs, like the IWC, took the position that "the organization will speak only with nation states." After repeated political torture at the hands of NGOs (and reminders that the IGOs had always been quite happy to talk with non-governmental industrial corporations and market organizations), the international community has now been largely pried open to the insistent and integrated participation of NGOs.[43] In this way too the lessons of environmentalism in the United States have become a matrix for the evolution of international environmental law. Without the pluralistic intervention of citizen NGOs, what level of response would have come from the international legal community to the environmental challenges of the past two decades?

C. EXTRATERRITORIAL MUNICIPAL LAW, AND OTHER EVOLVING INTERNATIONAL STRATEGIES AND PRINCIPLES

The preceding examples of transboundary pollution and the problems of regulating whales in a global commons present many fundamental issues of international environmental law. A few further specific areas serve to complete this quick survey of the field.

43. The World Bank, the International Marine Organization, and other IGOs with establishment perspectives long held such exclusionary policies. Now the picture has changed, for functional as well as political reasons. As Mooen Quereschi, Senior Vice President of the World Bank in Washington has said, "As late as ten years ago what we knew about [our own] World Bank operations in many countries depended mainly on bureaucratic lines of information and supervision.... In today's global village, NGO networks can report a problem in rural northeast Brazil...within a week. Where [our own] bureaucratic eyes are astigmatic, NGOs provide vivid images of what is really happening at the grass roots." Speech to Society for International Development (Washington, April 22, 1988).

Section 1. MUNICIPAL LEVERAGE AND EXTRATERRITORIAL LAW?

As the whaling example illustrates, the development of international law ultimately can build upon the actions of domestic law as well as the action of international organizations or treaties. Without NGO pressures applied through the U.S. and a few Western governments, efforts to apply IWC conservation restrictions would probably still be stalled. International environmental law must increasingly internalize the stalemate-breaking pressure mechanisms available through well-targeted municipal law.

Many treaties, of course, foresee local enforcement by domestic law. In this regard, the Convention on International Trade in Endangered Species (CITES) led to enforcement actions by federal agencies in the United States,[44] to federal statutes like the Endangered Species and Marine Mammal Protection Acts, and to legislation by states of the union. Trade in endangered species depends on markets in developed nations; to the extent that these markets (for furs, whale oil products, etc.) can be closed off, the incentive for killing is diminished. Local market restrictions are thus a practical avenue for enforcing the mandates of conventions without going through the burdensome process of hauling states to the ICJ, even where that is jurisdictionally possible. Similar domestic enforcement can usefully be applied in the settings of other international agreements.

INTERNATIONAL ISSUES IN DOMESTIC COURTS

Another way the courts of one nation may have international environmental impact is by extending their reach to include jurisdiction over incidents occurring abroad. When a U.S. company ships defective pharmaceuticals overseas to sell them in a Third World country, or designs its overseas chemical plants so as to invite subsequent disasters, the victims of these instrumentalities may be well advised to try to sue the defendants in a U.S. courtroom. Lawsuits filed in Bolivia, Nigeria, Indonesia, or India, for example, are less likely to draw upon the heightened tort law awareness of American common law and juries. (The doctrine of forum non conveniens, however, is often a bar to such actions, where defendants argue disingenuously that it would be more convenient for all concerned to have the case litigated in the country in which the accident occurred.) Extended application of domestic jurisdiction can be quite dramatic. In Filartiga v. Pena-Irala, 630 F.2d 876 (2d Cir. 1980), 577 F. Supp. 860 (E.D.N.Y. 1984), a human rights case arising from the torture killing of a Paraguayan by a Paraguayan official in Paraguay, a U.S. district court nevertheless allowed a civil lawsuit to be brought in the United States when the plaintiff family was able to serve a complaint on defendant when he happened to be visiting Disney World. Could a village of Indonesian forest-dwellers bring suit in the U.S. against a Japanese timber corporation doing business in the U.S. for its environmental or "genocidal" depredations in mountainous areas of Borneo?

---

44. Convention on International Trade in Endangered Species of Wild Fauna and Flora, Mar. 3, 1973, 27 UST 1087, TIAS No. 8249, 993 UNTS 243. The trade bans of the Convention have been enforced under importation restrictions of the U.S. Customs Service at ports of entry. Under Article VI §2 of the U.S. Constitution, of course, ratified treaties become part of the "Supreme Law of the Land."

DOMESTIC LEGISLATION WITH INTERNATIONAL EFFECTS

At another level, there has been an insistent argument that domestic legislation like NEPA and the endangered species act can have a beneficial effect on the world environment, by forcing American agencies that are involved with development projects abroad to comply with American environmental standards. One of the principles of the legal advisory group to the World Commission on Environment and Development was that states shall apply, as a minimum, at least the same standards for environmental conduct and impacts regarding transboundary resources and environmental interferences as are applied domestically – paraphrased officially as "Do not do to others what you would not do to your own citizens."[45] If the Federal Highway Administration is building a highway through virgin jungle in Panama, does NEPA apply? See Sierra Club v. Adams, 578 F.2d 389, 392 n.14 (D.C. Cir. 1978)(assuming that it does); and see also President Jimmy Carter's Executive Order 12, 114 (44 Fed. Reg. 1,957 (1979)), accepting the application of NEPA, though modifying some of its requirements in international projects. Does the Endangered Species Act apply when the United States Agency For International Development (AID) finances a development scheme that would destroy the jungle habitat of Sri Lankan elephants, or other such international projects? Lujan v. Defenders of Wildlife, 911 F.2d 117 (8th Cir. 1990), cert. granted 111 S. Ct. 2008 (1991) is a case the Supreme Court is deciding, as this book goes to press, whether the constraints of the Endangered Species Act apply to federal agency actions overseas. The environmental applications of extraterritorial jurisdiction are obvious, and still very much in evolution.

But is it proper for environmental law to use the legal pressure of a major state's legislation to force the adoption of international environmental conservation practices? Several examples of such "altruistic bullying" raise the issue.

In the international whaling controversy, a critical moment occurred when NGOs successfully pressured the U.S. Congress to pass the Pelly amendment to the Fishermans Protective Act.[46] Under this provision, upon certification by the Secretary of Commerce that any nation's actions "diminish the effectiveness of an international fishery conservation program," the President is empowered to bar all or a portion of the offending nation's fish products from the U.S. market. When presidential enforcement lagged, Congress in 1979 added the Packwood-Magnuson amendment to the Fisheries Conservation and Management Act, requiring *mandatory* cuts in foreign fishing quotas within the 200-mile U.S. fishery conservation zone.[47] Backed by this unilateral market blackmail, U.S. negotiators persuaded Japan and the U.S.S.R. to abide by minke whale quotas, pushed Peru, Chile, and South Korea to join the IWC, and pressured Iceland and Japan to curtail "scientific" whaling.[48] Even though the Reagan administration persuaded its Supreme Court to enlarge the role of executive enforcement discretion,[49] the threat of unilateral

45. World Commission on Environment and Development (Brundtland Commission), Our Common Future, Annexe One, Principle 13 (1987).

46. Pub.L 92-219, 22 U.S.A. §1978 (1971).

47. Pub.L. 96-61, 16 U.S.C.A. §1821(e)(2).

48. For an excellent though dispirited analysis see Wilkinson, The Use of Domestic Measures to Enforce International Whaling Agreements, 17 Denv. J. Int'l L. & Pol'y 2 (1989).

49. Japan Whaling Assoc. v. American Cetacean Society, 478 U.S. 221 (1986).

statutory sanction exerted useful pressure and established a useful precedent for application in other areas of global concern.

MARINE MAMMALS AND THE 1991 GATT PANEL DECISION

An interesting backlash against American legislative attempts to reinforce the IWC and other marine mammal conservation efforts occurred in September, 1991. Mexico (reportedly at the suggestion of the Bush administration[50]) won a provisional decision from a trade tribunal panel under the international General Agreement on Tariffs and Trade (GATT) that U.S. restrictions on tuna imports violated free trade principles. Mexican fishermen set nets around dolphins in order to capture the tuna swimming below, in a process that ends up slaughtering thousands of dolphins. Under the Pelly-Packwood legislation, these actions raise problems for seafood imports from Mexico. Under Articles 11 and 20 of GATT, the panel recommended that domestic legislation not be applied to have extraterritorial effects on production methods in other countries, unless there are domestic human or ecological effects.[51]

The future course of this confrontation between international trade policy and international conservation policy is unclear. Under GATT, a panel's decision has no effect until it is adopted, by consensus, at the GATT Council monthly meeting. Suddenly fearful that the panel decision would sour congressional support for the North American Free Trade Agreement, the U.S. administration successfully pressured Mexico to "defer indefinitely" its presentation of the panel decision to the Council. Simultaneously the GATT Working Group on Trade and Environment – which in its 20 years of existence had never held a meeting – was called to define some future basis for balancing production and trade practices in light of environmental concerns.[52]

DOMESTIC LEGISLATION AND MULTILATERAL LENDING INSTITUTIONS

In the case of the World Bank and other multi-lateral development banks (MDBs), a coalition of NGOs applied the same kind of domestic legislative pressures to force international lenders to consider the negative effects of their development projects upon environmental quality and the rights of indigenous people. MDB projects had provided textbook examples of how development planners can disastrously ignore the predictable physical, environmental, and human consequences of their projects.[53] The NGOs persuaded a powerful member of the U.S. Senate to attach a rider to annual appropriations bills for funding the World Bank, instructing the U.S. Executive Director of the Bank not to vote for any project which violated these criteria. The effect of such pressure can be extraordinarily practical in achieving environmental quality improvements internationally. The fact remains that it was

50. Divine Porpoise, World Politics & Current Affairs, The Economist, American Survey 31 (Oct. 5, 1991).

51. GATT Panel – U.S.: Restrictions on Imports of Tuna (September 3, 1991).

52. On Oct. 7, when it withdrew the matter on the day before the Council meeting, Mexico also announced its own domestic dolphin conservation program.

53. See Plater, Multi-lateral Lending Banks, Environmental Diseconomies, and the International Lending Process: The Example of Third World Dams, 9 Third World L.J. 169, 208–212 (1989)(on the problems and the legal propriety of such long-arm pressures).

produced by a unilateral decision by one country to force its will on the community of nations or upon an IGO, and what works benignly in one case may be malign in another.

What is the international legal propriety of donor nation pressure on MDBs? Even if one assumes that quite salutary environmental reforms have been so instigated, the use of direct pressure on an international compact entity raises worrisome concerns in some observers' minds. No matter how altruistic, the fact remains that certain nations are able to have this effect upon the MDBs in part because they possess financial leverage on the Bank board. For constructive reforms on the international stage to rely upon altruistic bullying is a troubling concept indeed.

The question is presented with particular clarity in the World Bank initiatives because there the Congress applied its pressure via direct statutory enactment. A spectrum of arguments may be applied to such situations. At one end of the spectrum is the opinion of those members of Congress who have attached or attempted to attach policy conditions to appropriations bills for funding international lending organizations. As one senator said, it is always the right of a sovereign people to determine how their taxpayer dollars are going to be spent; if legislators attach directive conditions to their funding bills, or threaten a cut-off of their taxpayers' contributions based on particular policy positions, that is no more than one would expect and demand as a right of a democratic people.

At the other end of the spectrum is the quite skeptical position taken by Dr. Ibrahim Shihata, Vice-President and General Counsel of the World Bank, arguing that all such unilateral threats or suasions applied by donor nations are improper and even *contra legem* under international agreements, unless the policy conditions are directly related to the economic integrity of the Bank and its loans to member states.

Somewhere in the middle between the two polar positions is the opinion of several MDB legal counselors who informally expressed a fundamental pragmatism about such donor-nation pressures on international lending. Indeed, political reality indicates that some unilateral pressure on MDBs is completely inevitable and will take place regardless of whether or not it is formal or informal, direct or indirect, linked to economic concerns or not. From this middle perspective, the application of pressure to the appointees of member states, or to the elected representatives of blocks of member states, is perhaps best regarded with a shug. In any event, the compromise position would note, the directives are typically not an attempt to *bind* the MDB organization as such.

According to the middle position, then, the only case where donor nations' political interference with lending decisions becomes *contra legem* is the case where political considerations lead to rescission in whole or part of a member state's prior commitment to contribute a specified amount of funding. In such cases a prior binding international agreement is being unilaterally abrogated. In other situations, including conditional refusals to commit further supplementary contributions, a member state is merely exercising its right to contract or to decline to do so.

Section 2. PROCEDURAL REFORMS

Faced with the difficulty of defining substantive standards for environmental protection, another interesting trend can be discerned in concerned jurists' exporation of the efficacy of procedural approaches to international environmental quality. Broad scale requirements for environmental impact statement procedures are an obvious example. More than 20 countries have adopted some form of environment assessment requirement, as well as a number of IGOs, including lending institutions, in order to implement the common sense rationality of looking broadly and carefully before you leap. The problem, of course, is that, as the NEPA experience reveals in the United States, the pressures of short-term economic profit making and political momentum tend to undercut the broad principles represented by environmental impact assessment. Nations as well as federal agencies play with the definition of what is a "significant" project affecting the environment, and with the specificity required in the statements themselves.

Other commentators have focused on a specific express or implied "duty to inform or disclose," the kind of requirement that was expressly included in the post-Chernoybl nuclear notification convention. Such a duty encounters similar problems in defining what relevant and available information must be disclosed and how quickly and how specifically it must be revealed. Because states perceive the specific obligation of prior disclosure as contrary to their interests, the duty is abstracted to such a level of generality that states may plausibly construe a wide range of conduct to satisfy the obligation.[54]

Yet another procedural approach is to add periodic official review and report procedures to international conventions. Thus in the 1987 Montreal Protocol on ozone depletion, the 1988 Sofia Protocol on long range air pollution, and the 1989 Basel Convention on the Control of Transboundary Movements of Hazardous Wastes and Their Disposal, each of the agreements was limited in the stringency of substantive requirements for which it could achieve ratification, but provided for subsequent high-level investigation and regular reporting. It is a technique that forces nation states to remain sensitive to the factual realities of an issue and to world opinion, and may thereby promote compliance with standards higher than the lowest common denominator.

Section 3. NGOs

Clearly, the legitimacy of NGOs on the world stage has evolved over the last 20 years, with major legal consequences. With the ongoing delegitimation of authoritarian states, there is the prospect that lessons of pluralism developed in the American environmental movement will be echoed by enfranchising the voices of concerned citizens in states throughout the world community. The role of NGOs continues to have special impact in the environmental area, as NGOs participate actively in the councils of IGOs and international law. If the ILO model noted above is applied to international environmental organizations like UNEP, nongovernmental voices will be straightforwardly incorporated into official international discourse.

---

54. Developments – International Environmental Law, 104 Harv. L Rev. 1484, 1518 (1991).

Pending such official incorporation of NGOs, the current confrontational adversarial/negotiation model of interaction between NGOs and IGOs is likely to continue. The role of indigenous Third World NGOs is growing, owing not only to philosophical principle but also to the fact that local NGOs are often the only accurate source of information on projects and their consequences.

Where indigenous NGOs lack the resources and sophistication to mount campaigns in international capitals, there is also a growing tendency for developed nations' NGOs to set up "partnerships" with Third World groups, to their mutual benefit.

> Until the international community creates adjudicatory mechanisms to give aggrieved members of the public in developing countries direct access to the foreign aid decision-making process, the partnership model of public policy advocacy is the best prospect for improving the environmental quality of development assistance.... Partnerships with overseas counterparts enhance the legitimacy, efficacy, and accuracy of American environmental activism on these issues. Over time, and with continued successes, such partnerships may pave the way for greater accountability in development assistance and, ultimately, international legal processes generally. Wirth, Legitimacy, Accountability, and Partnership: A Model for Advocacy on Third World Environmental Issues, 101 Yale L.J. _ (1991).

Section 4. INTERGENERATIONAL EQUITY

In ongoing discussions of international environmental policy, increasing prominence is being found for a principle that echoes the public trust doctrine in environmental law. Called variously the theory of "intergenerational equity" or the principle of "common heritage of human kind," its message is that in fundamental ethical terms no present generation has the right to consider itself the ultimate decisionmaker for global ecological changes. The doctrine is presented in the following excerpt from the work of Professor Edith Brown Weiss.

E. Brown Weiss, Our Rights and Obligations to Future Generations for the Environment

84 American Journal of International Law 198, 198–202 (1990)

We, the human species, hold the natural environment of our planet in common with all members of our species: past generations, the present generation, and future generations.[55] As members of the present generation, we hold the earth in trust for future generations. At the same time, we are beneficiaries entitled to use and benefit from it.

There are two relationships that must shape any theory of intergenerational equity in the context of our natural environment: our relationship to other generations of our own species and our relationship to the natural system of which we are a part.

The human species is integrally linked with other parts of the natural system; we both affect and are affected by what happens in the system. The natural system,

55. E. Brown Weiss, In Fairness to Future Generations: International Law, Common Patrimony and Intergenerational Equity (1989).

contrary to popular belief, is in many ways a hostile one. Deserts, glaciers, volcanoes, tsunamis can bring havoc to our species. Moreover, the natural environment can be toxic to our species, as through the natural toxicity of some plants and animals or the dramatic release of toxic clouds of carbon dioxide from Lake Nyos in the Cameroon, which killed 1,700 people. On the other hand, the natural system makes life possible for us. It gives us the resources with which to survive and to improve human welfare.

Our actions affect the natural system. We alone among all living creatures have the capacity to shape significantly our relationship to the environment. We can use it on a sustainable basis or we can degrade environmental quality and the natural resource base. As part of the natural system, we have no right to destroy its integrity; nor is it in our interest to do so. Rather, as the most sentient of living creatures, we have a special responsibility to care for the planet.

The second fundamental relationship is that between different generations of the human species. All generations are inherently linked to other generations, past and future, in using the common patrimony of earth.

To define intergenerational equity, it is useful to view the human community as a partnership among all generations. In describing a state as a partnership, Edmund Burke observed that "as the ends of such a partnership cannot be obtained in many generations, it becomes a partnership not only between those who are living but between those who are living, those who are dead, and those who are to be born."[56] The purpose of human society must be to realize and protect the welfare and well-being of every generation. This requires sustaining the life-support systems of the planet, the ecological processes and the environmental conditions necessary for a healthy and decent human environment.

In this partnership, no generation knows beforehand when it will be the living generation, how many members it will have, or even how many generations there will ultimately be. It is useful, then, to take the perspective of a generation that is placed somewhere along the spectrum of time, but does not know in advance where it will be located.[57] Such a generation would want to inherit the earth in at least as good condition as it has been in for any previous generation and to have as good access to it as previous generations. This requires each generation to pass the planet on in no worse condition than it received it in and to provide equitable access to its resources and benefits. Each generation is thus both a trustee for the planet with obligations to care for it and a beneficiary with rights to use it.

Intergenerational equity calls for equality among generations in the sense that each generation is entitled to inherit a robust planet that on balance is at least as good as that of previous generations. This means that all generations are entitled to at least the planetary health that the first generation had. In practice, some generations may improve the environment, with the result that later generations will inherit a richer and more diverse natural resource base. In this case, they would be treated better than previous generations. But this extra benefit would be consistent with intergenerational equity, because the minimum level of planetary robustness would be sustained and later generations would not be worse off than previous generations. The converse is also possible, that later generations would receive a badly degraded environment with major loss of species diversity, in which

56. E. Burke, Reflections on the Revolution in France 139-40 (1790), in 2 Works of Edmund Burke 368 (London 1854).

57. See J. Rawls, A Theory of Justice (1971).

case they would be treated worse than previous generations. This latter case would be contrary to principles of intergenerational equity. Equity among generations provides for a minimum floor for all generations and ensures that each generation has at least that level of planetary resource base as its ancestors. This concept is consistent with the implicit premises of trusteeship, stewardship and tenancy, in which the assets must be conserved, not dissipated, so that they are equally available to those who come after....

I have proposed three basic principles of intergenerational equity. First, each generation should be required to conserve the diversity of the natural and cultural resource base, so that it does not unduly restrict the options available to future generations in solving their problems and satisfying their own values, and should also be entitled to diversity comparable to that enjoyed by previous generations. This principle is called "conservation of options." Second, each generation should be required to maintain the quality of the planet so that it is passed on in no worse condition that that in which it was received, and should also be entitled to planetary quality comparable to that enjoyed by previous generations. This is the principle of "conservation of quality." Third, each generation should provide its members with equitable rights of access to the legacy of past generations and should conserve this access for future generations. This is the principle of "conservation of access."

Planetary rights and obligations coexist in each generation. In the intergenerational dimension, the generations to which the obligations are owed are future generations, while the generations with which the rights are linked are past generations. Thus, the rights of future generations are linked to the obligations of the present generation. In the intergenerational context, planetary obligations and rights exist between members of the present generation. They derive from the intergenerational relationship that each generation shares with those who have come before and those yet to come. Thus intergenerational obligations to conserve the planet flow from the present generation both to future generations as generations and to members of the present generation, who have the right to use and enjoy the planetary legacy.

Section 5. "SOFT LAW"

In a fascinating article surveying innovative approaches to practical environmental protection through international law, Peter Sand explores a variety of tacks for circumventing constraints imposed by 150 jealous national sovereignties.[58] One of his interesting inquiries focuses on "soft law" –

> States may decide to forgo treatymaking altogether and to recommend common rules of conduct by joint declarations – usually referred to as "soft law" to distinguish them from the "hard law" of formal legal agreements. Environmental diplomacy has produced a wide variety of such declaratory instruments and resolutions. Their recognized practical advantage is that since they are not subject to national ratification, they can take instant effect. Their inherent risk, however, is precisely that lack of formality that makes them attractive as a shortcut....
>
> One of the most prolific makers of soft law has been the UNEP Governing Council. Since 1978, the UNEP has addressed a whole series of "environmental law guidelines and principles" to states, drafted in typical treaty language

58. Sand, Lessons Learned in Global and Environmental Governance, 18 Envtl Aff. L. Rev. 213 (1991).

except for the copious use of "should" in the place of "shall." Once adopted by ad hoc groups of experts nominated by governments, these provisions normally are approved by the UNEP Governing Council for submission to the UN General Assembly, which either incorporates them in resolution (as in the case of the 1982 World Charter for Nature) or, less solemnly, recommends them to states for use in the formulation of international agreements or national legislation (as in the case of the 1982 Conclusions of the Study of Legal Aspects Concerning the Environment Related to Offshore Mining and Drilling Within the Limits of National Jurisdiction). In a number of cases, however, promulgation did not go beyond the level of a UNEP Governing Council decision (e.g., the 1980 Provisions for Co-operation Between States on Weather Modification).

Soft law may be "hardened" by later international practice. When the government of Uganda, under gentle World Bank pressure, had to consult other Nile Basin countries on a proposed water use project for Lake Victoria in December 1983, it did so by way of reference to, among other documents, the 1978 UNEP Principles of Conduct in the Field of the Environment for the Guidance of States in the Conservation and Harmonious Utilization of Natural Resources Shared by Two or More States. Three months later, the governments of Egypt and Sudan in their replies in turn referred to the guidelines as "jointly honored principles of cooperation," thereby quietly promoting them to the status of common regional standards. UNEP soft law instruments have also served [in the area of hazardous wastes and chemical notification compacts] as forerunners of treaty law.... Sand, Lessons Learned in Global Environmental Governance, 18 Envtl Aff. L. Rev. 213, 239-240 (1991).

Section 6. THE NORTH-SOUTH SPLIT

A fundamental fact of international environmental law is the great difference between the "North," the developed world, and the "South," the less-developed world. Developed countries are pleased to urge less developed countries to conserve their forests, mountains and wilderness, to halt destructive burning, and the like. LDCs resent any limitations on their efforts to follow industrial societies into greater economic productivity. They point the finger at developed countries for generating the vast amount of past pollution, and the majority of present carbon dioxide, CFCs that plague the global environment. The debate has led to calls for global redistribution of economic resources and a constraint on self-righteous preaching by developed countries to forbid the kind of environmental despoliation that accompanied their own economic industrial development. Mzee Jomo Kenyatta, the first president of Kenya, argued in his Arusha Principle that if the North wishes LDCs to take care of the world environment, the North should help pay for it. The Montreal ozone protocol actually put money where that message was. The protocol provided for a $240 million CFC "transition fund" to help pay for the cost of converting LDCs to less ozone-destructive chemical materials. Given the votes possessed by each state in IGOs and the United Nations, irrespective of economic strength or population, it is evident that some form of accommodation between rich and poor nations will increasingly be a part of international agreements for environmental protection. "The primary goal of the [1992 Rio "Earth Summit"] will be to lay the foundation for a global partnership between developing and more industrialized countries based on mutual need and common interests to ensure the future of the planet," declared Maurice Strong, Secretary General of the United Nations' Rio Conference.

Section 7. ONE WORLD/ONE TRIBE?[59]

The global reality of environmental law is the indivisibility of environmental causes and effects. Over the past decades many jurists have wistfully hoped for the emergence and growth of legal mechanisms of international cooperation and coordination to cope with the environmental and economic realities of global interconnectedness. Some have hoped for some form of One World government. Many have watched the development of the European Community as an extraordinarily important experiment in supra-national law. In the 1980s, the European Community began moving toward integration of legal systems and affirmation of continental environmental norms.

There is a corresponding centrifugal tendency, however, that has lately been painfully evident around the world, with corollaries in environmental law .

A fundamental stumbling block in international law noted throughout this chapter has been the jealously-held sovereignties of 159 independent nation states, states that often were created – and behave – without regard to the common setting in which they exist. In the past several years, the pressures of divisive fractionalizing have dramatically expanded rather than diminished. Hungarians and Romanians, Serbs and Croats, Uzbeks and Kirghiz, Armenians and Azerbaijanis, Russians and Chechen-Ingushis, Hmung and Vietnamese – these insular allegiances represent a powerful human tendency to seek communal identity in narrowed terms.[60]

These insularizing tendencies can be seen within the domestic legal realm as well, including environmental law. Modern politics is characterized in many theaters, including environmental protection and natural resources management, by battlelines of narrow single-issue combatants and factional allegiances.

In fact, under the pressures of modern circumstances the governing metaphor for human relationships – local, regional, national, and international – may be atavistic tribalism.

TRIBALISM

Viewing the narrowed perspectives and localized interests of contemporary natural resources decisionmaking as "tribalism" offers a useful analytical perspective on its symptoms and consequences. Tribalism, as the anthropologists describe

---

59. The text of this section is adapted from Plater, A Modern Political Tribalism in Natural Resources Management, 11 Public Land L. Rev. 1 (1990).

60. Germany's reunification marked a reinvigoration of nationalism rather than the contrary international tendency. It is not at all clear that the European Community's supra-national experiments for resolving shared problems can survive the nationalistic fervors unleashed in Eastern Europe and the resurrection of the German nation. The trend previously was clear: the European Community's environmental policies were going to act as a matrix model for the rest of the world. Now the passions of that process may be going in the opposite direction.

it, denotes the way groups of people live in a form of cohesive affiliation and narrowed community of interest, systematically including all members of that community, and deprecating or excluding all others as "outsiders."[61]

Tribalism has both positive and negative attributes. Both are periodically revealed in international and domestic legal systems,[62] and environmental conflicts often reflect the tensions of such latter-day tribalism. In an unfortunate paradox, moreover, preclusive local, national, and international tribalisms seem to increase the more that there are strains and limitations upon resource systems and the global commons, in precisely those circumstances where increased integration and cooperation would seem to be most necessary.

In some circumstances it is drastically important that narrowed, localized, "tribal" interests be represented at the heart of complex management decisions. It appears to be a completely functional instinct on the part of many of us, when faced with the complexity and stresses of modern politics and economics, to seek out a narrower affinity rather than to trust to some broader community. Even today, tribalism functions as a utilitarian phenomenon rather than a mere atavistic throwback. If we wish to be heard, and to have our interests reflected in governmental decisions, we trust more to the focused pressures of our affiliated tribe than to our marginal individual weight in governmental processes.

There is, however, a countervailing peril in tribalism. One of the fundamental tragedies of many Third-World societies is that the nature of tribalism, by definition a narrowed, non-comprehensive, preclusive affiliation, seeks to dominate and preempt all other interests. A tribalism may bring important information and policy considerations into a decision, but if it completely dominates the decision, its effects will only be rational in terms of the interests it represents. Tribal localisms have a valid place in the consideration of resource decisionmaking; the problem is to what extent a tribal localism should be accorded dominating or determinative weight in a decisional system.

Ultimately the balance comes down to a perplex of pluralistic democracy. A diversity of tribal voices is critically important to coping with the breadth and depth of complex realities we face on the planet. But tribal voices are inherently unreliable, unless they can cultivate an instinct for the integration of external views. We may aspire as a goal to rise above tribalism: a triumphal process of research, intellectual analysis, and forward-looking coordination of human activities, necessarily encompassing an overarching comprehensive rationality, is certainly one of the implicit objectives of futurists, academics, political philosophers, and our own profession. But perhaps that asks too much of human nature and the

---

61. A characteristic of tribalism that separates it from mere civic groupings within the body politic is its members' intense sense of internal identification and loyalty, one with the other, amounting to a broad and cohesive extended familyhood, with, moreover, a sense of focus that all share as a common mission the advancement of tribal interests as a top priority.

62. In the international realm, besides the diverse sovereignties, there are religious tribes, North-South tribes, haves and have-nots.... In Washington D.C. it would seem quite realistic for a political anthropologist to discern the existence of a Sun Belt tribe and a Rust Belt tribe, an Urban tribe and a Farm Country tribe, a Pork-barrel public works subsidy tribe and an Environmental tribe, a Pro-life tribe and a Pro-choice tribe, and perhaps others — a Black tribe and a White tribe and so on.

human intellect.[63] If the future of the planet is to be a long-term proposition in which humans continue to play a part, however, we should strive to play the role of shepherds, acting in a cohesive, integrated, planet-wide systematic perspective. Decisions affecting the equilibrium and natural balance of this fragile place increasingly require comprehensive thought and cooperation.

Faced with the problems posed by contentious sovereignties and a human tendency in the face of adversity to move toward tribalism, perhaps we will find international law moving toward a single tribalism, a global tribalism, as ironically predicted a generation ago by Aldous Huxley.[64] In the end it may be politics and social evolution, not law, that build the requisite foundations for international environmental protection.

63. As Shaw said, socialism doesn't work because it would take too many evenings.

64. "I don't see that it's in the least likely that we shall be able to breed a race of beings, at any rate within the next few thousand years, sufficiently intelligent to be able to form a stable non-tribal society.... In a few generations it may be that the whole planet will be covered by one vast...tribe." Chelifer and Cardan in A. Huxley, Those Barren Leaves (1925). Tribalism, if we all feel ourselves part of the same tribe, would get us to the same destination of an integrated organic planetary rationality.

Afterword:

FACING THE FUTURE

For two reasons, our generation will bear a heavier responsibility for the future of planet Earth than any generation before it has. First, we know better – having gained access to an unprecedented wealth of new scientific information and a vastly improved capacity for analysis and prediction. Second, we can do better – having accumulated enough experience, technological and institutional, to take the necessary...action.[1]

Predicting the future of environmental law – a field characterized by diverse legal approaches to scientific uncertainty – is itself a risky venture. Environmental law has evolved in response to unexpected and unsettling discoveries and events. Rachel Carson's identification of the pernicious effects of DDT on food webs led directly to major revisions of the Federal Insecticide, Fungicide, and Rodenticide Act; the Environmental Defense Fund's discovery of toxic chemicals in the lower Mississippi River, which serves as the potable water supply for New Orleans, was instrumental in the enactment of the Safe Drinking Water Act; the Kepone debacle resulted in developments in common law and criminal law, and was partially responsible for the passage of the Resource Conservation and Recovery Act; and the Exxon-Valdez disaster has already stimulated the passage of a new Oil Pollution Act (OPA '90), and is initiating innovations in other areas of law as well. Why should the future of environmental law be any more predictable than its first decades?

Nevertheless, we can discern comparatively recent but established legal trends that are likely to continue into the foreseeable future. Some of these developments have been discussed in previous chapters: the dynamic growth of toxic tort law; the application of corporate, contract, and property law concepts to environmental issues; the increasing interactions between common law and statutes; the evolution of environmental criminal law; the unfolding of the public trust doctrine; the tension and competition between federal and state governments; the wrangling over competing uses of public lands; the increasingly sophisticated implementation of market incentives for pollution control; new types of environmental land-use mechanisms; the increased use of alternative dispute resolution; and the emergence of international environmental law.

There will be further amendments, extensions, applications, administrative and judicial interpretations, and enforcement (and nonenforcement) of existing environmental statutes. Congress may enact a limited number of new federal statutes – which may appear as amendments to existing acts – covering areas ignored or

---

1. Peter Sand, Lessons Learned in Global Environmental Governance, 18 Envtl. Aff. L. Rev. 1 (1990).

inadequately addressed by prior federal legislation, like groundwater pollution, indoor air pollution, and protection of biodiversity. Even though the emphasis during the next twenty years of environmental law will probably be on the implementation, fine-tuning, and interpretation of existing federal statutes, we must always be prepared for the revelations or catastrophes that galvanize the creation of new environmental law. And if the federal government shows increasing laxity in its approach to environmental protection, then – as in the field of civil rights – the cutting edge of the law will move to state legislatures and courts, and to the international realm.

A TRIAD OF ENVIRONMENTAL CHALLENGES

Professor Arnold Rietze pointed out that global environmental degradation can be attributed to three categories of human activity – population, consumption, and pollution – and of the three only the last (which is perhaps least important) has received major attention.[2]

POPULATION

There are currently between 5 and 6 billion people on earth. Because population grows exponentially, unless we have a global nuclear war or widespread famine and disease, by 2100 the earth's population will be 10.4 billion – more than twice that in 1988. Most of this increase will take place in the impoverished Third World.

Lester R. Brown of the Worldwatch Institute describes the environmental consequences of what has been called the Population Bomb:

> Ecologists looking at biological indicators...see rising human demand, driven by population growth and rising affluence, surpassing the carrying capacity of local forests, grasslands, and soils in country after country. They see substainable yield thresholds of the economy's natural support systems being breached throughout the Third World. And as a result, they see the natural resource base diminishing even as population growth is expanding.... Continuing rapid population growth and spreading environmental degradation have trapped hundreds of millions in a downward spiral of falling incomes and growing hunger. With the number of people caught in this life-threatening cycle increasing each year, the world may soon be forced to reckon with the consequence of years of population policy neglect.[3]

But population control runs afoul of deep-seated moral and religious convictions and human instincts, and comes close to being an intractable challenge.

CONSUMPTION

Critics of our inefficient, wasteful, consumption-oriented "throwaway" society advocate modes of sustainable economic activity that maintain a long-term equilibrium between production and ecological integrity.

---

2. Reitze, Environmental Policy – It Is Time for a New Beginning, 14 Colum. J. Envtl. L. 111 (1989), at page 10 *supra*.

3. In Population: The Neglected Issue,Worldwatch Institute, State of the World 1991, 15–18.

William Ruckelshaus, a former EPA Administrator and now the Chief Executive Officer of the world's largest waste handling firm, notes the shift toward concepts of sustainability:

> Sustainability is a nascent doctrine that economic growth and development must take place, and be maintained over time, within limits set by ecology in the broadest sense – by the interrelations of human beings and their works, the biosphere, and the physical and chemical laws that govern it. The doctrine of sustainability holds too that the spread of a reasonable level of prosperity and security to the less developed nations is essential to protecting ecological balance and hence essential to the continued prosperity of the wealthy nations. It follows that environmental protection and economic development are complementary rather than antagonistic processes....[4]

For Ruckleshaus, the fundamental principles of a sustainable economy would be to recognize that:

- The human species is part of nature. Its existence depends on its ability to draw sustenance from a finite natural world; its continuance depends on its ability to abstain from destroying the natural systems that regenerate this world....
- Economic activity must account for the [full] environmental costs of production....
- The maintenance of a liveable global environmental depends on the sustainable development of the entire human family.

Globally, as the Brundtland Commission declared, the concept of Sustainable Development is not just an aesthetic; it is a necessary principle for long-term survivability. It involves not only the prevention of global threats such as global warming and ozone depletion, but also the assurance that citizens of less developed nations will receive equitable material treatment.[5]

Sustainability also means a commitment to maximizing biodiversity, both because other species may be necessary for human well-being, and also because all species are essential participants in ecological integrity. Sustainability cannot be achieved without conservation – of resources, of energy, and of a quality existence for all species on earth. Reaching a state of sustainability will certainly require the moderation of the wasteful modes of life that have become instinctive in some affluent nations.

POLLUTION

Pollution control efforts will become increasingly proactive, emphasizing pollution prevention rather than the infernal complexities of end-of-pipe command and control systems and cleanup liability.

---

4. Toward a Sustainable World, 261 Scientific American (No. 1) 166, 167–68 (Sept. 1989).

5. Adlai Stevenson, who supplied the image of Spaceship Earth with which the Introduction to this casebook began a thousand pages ago, continued by saying that –

> We cannot maintain it half fortunate, half miserable, half confident, half despairing, half slave to the ancient enemies of mankind, half free in a liberation of resources undreamed of until this day. No craft, no crew, can travel safely with such vast contradictions. On their resolution depends the survival of us all.

The Pollution Prevention Act of 1990[6] illustrates that trend. Its basic premise is that source reduction "is fundamentally different and more desirable than waste management and pollution control." It envisions source reduction as a win/win opportunity for EPA and the regulated community because of "significant opportunities for industry to reduce or prevent pollution at the source through cost-effective changes in production, operation, and raw material use." These changes, in turn, ensure "reduced raw material, pollution control, and liability costs as well as help to protect the environment and reduce risks to worker health and safety." The most forceful language in the statute is its unequivocal declaration of policy:

> The Congress hereby declares it to be the national policy of the United States that pollution should be prevented or reduced at the source whenever feasible; pollution that cannot be prevented should be recycled in an environmentally safe manner, whenever feasible; pollution that cannot be prevented or recycled should be treated in an environmentally safe manner whenever feasible; and disposal or other release into the environment should be employed only as a last resort and should be conducted in an environmentally safe manner.

Thus far, pollution prevention has been hortatory rather than mandatory, but EPA possesses the legal authority to include pollution prevention requirements in permits and enforcement settlements; agencies in other nations are already far along that trail.

EVOLVING PRINCIPLES AND PROCESSES:

INTEGRATED ENVIRONMENTAL PLANNING AND MANAGEMENT

Throughout this book we have provided examples of the traditional, incremental, medium-specific and site-specific approach to environmental protection. We can no longer afford, however – either in an economic or an environmental sense – to hold to this narrow and reactive style of environmental management. The resulting array of laws is in too many ways an uncoordinated, unruly mess that is ineffective, or, even worse, counter-productive.

A more integrated approach is inevitably necessary. An integrated overview would consider the cumulative impacts and multi-media exposures threatened by a potential polluting or resource-depleting activity or series of activities, facilitating more accurate assessments of risk, with attendant improvement in setting environmental protection priorities and issuing permits. The most salient problem with integrated environmental control is implementation. Institutions capable of making the necessary holistic assessments are not yet in existence, and the track record of governmental central management systems does not inspire confidence. The inertia and institutional investments of the present fragmented systems assure that any fundamental reorienting will meet with significant resistance. But principles of integrated overview are ultimately unavoidable, and must eventually be built into the diverse mechanisms that drive our societies.

---

6. Pub. L. 101–508, Title VI, §§6601–6610, 42 U.S.C.A. §§13101–13119.

INSTITUTIONALIZED CAUTION

Institutionalized caution – a principle enunciated in the Endangered Species Act that also serves more broadly as a general reminder of the importance of looking before we leap – implies a functional and effective planning process. The National Environmental Policy Act prescribes a basic form of that rational process, although most of the inside players still resist taking the medicine.

Meaningful environmental planning systems must be established in both the public and private sectors, and at all levels of government – local, state, interstate, national, regional, and international. The design and implementation of these innovative modes of environmental planning will constitute one of the profound and difficult challenges facing humankind during the 21st century.

CITIZEN ACTION

Citizen environmentalists over the years have all too often felt like Cassandra. The daughter of King Priam of Troy rejected the seductive blandishments of Apollo, and in retaliation the god burdened her with a terrible curse: she would accurately see the future – the impending onslaughts of storms, droughts, death lurking in the belly of the Trojan horse – but she would not be heeded.

Modern environmentalists' warnings about ecological dangers – acid rain, leukemia from hazardous wastes, the diminishing legacy of natural resources, pollution-caused health and welfare costs – have been important, as are environmentalism's systemic process warnings about narrow-minded decisionmaking, inattention to noneconomic values, erosions of civic responsibility and governmental integrity, regressions in the state of the federal courts, the low level of the national information process, and many more. Despite chronic inertia and resistance within corporate and governmental establishments, there has been a significant increase in popular dismay about systemic environmental problems. Environmental concerns can no longer be dismissively caricatured as just a whimsical aesthetic fad, and the minions of the media, though typically superficial and erratic, know that it is important to try to tell the story.

Environmental law, which was built by citizen efforts in legislatures, courts, and agencies, will continue to assure that citzens play a fundamental role in the governance of our society. Because environmental law has become such a major presence in the law books and in public awareness, environmentalism is not likely ever to go away, nor ever again to be the lonely domain of a tiny group of unheard seers.

THE COMMON HERITAGE OF HUMANKIND

Our environment is indeed a global public trust. We have inherited from predecessor generations the responsibility for managing and shepherding it for our descendants and all other life forms. The principles of intergenerational equity advanced by Edith Brown Weiss, at page 1027 *supra*, suggest that rights and responsibilities of ecological stewardship are owed across political borders and the boundaries of time, ultimately as a matter of law as well as ethics. If we are to fulfill this fiduciary responsibility successfully, we must overcome what one of the authors of this book has referred to as a modern form of divisive tribalism:

> As the problems of managing the economy and ecology of this nation become ever more complex, subtly-interrelated, pressured and demanding, our processes of legal and political governance might be expected to become more integrative and comprehensive in scope. Instead, however, there often appears to be a contrary dysfunctional tendency. The more complex and stressed an issue becomes, the more its political actors retreat into a narrow, insulated factionalism that can be viewed as a form of latter-day tribalism.[7]

In framing environmental problems, it helps to conceive of humans and all other forms of life as members of a global tribe, a comprehensive and integrated social unit that transcends the incessant territorial skirmishing of fragmented factions.

The ancient Greeks understood that the core philosophical problem is how to maintain a balance between the individual and the community, between unity and diversity. We must learn to retain the energy and richness of our disparate individual diversities, while creating the national, international, and intergenerational cooperation necessary for ten billion human beings to live in relative harmony, managing a sustainable future for the planet and its natural systems. Facing the future it seems that, fundamentally, we're all in this together.

7. See page 1031 *supra*.

REFERENCE

Acknowledgments of Permission to Reprint

The authors gratefully acknowledge the cooperation and generosity of many authors and publishers who consented to have portions of their works excerpted and reprinted in this book. The works are arranged here listed in alphabetical order by last name of first author. Photographs and charts are acknowledged where they appear in the text.

Bruce A. Ackerman and Richard B. Stewart, Comment: Reforming Environmental Law, 37 Stanford Law Review 1333. Reprinted material first appeared in 37 Stanford Law Review at page 1333. Copyright © 1985 by the Board of Trustee of Leland Stanford Junior University. Reprinted by permission of the copyright holder, the authors, and Fred B. Rothman Company.

J.P. Acton, Understanding Superfund: A Progress Report. Reprinted by the permission of the Rand Corporation, Santa Monica, Ca.

Robert K. Anderberg, Wall Street Sleaze: How the Hostile Takeover of Pacific Lumber Led to the Clear-Cutting of Coastal Redwoods, 10 Amicus Journal 8. © 1988, The Amicus Journal, a publication of the Natural Resources Defense Council, reprinted with permission.

Applegate, The Perils of Unreasonable Risk: Information, Regulatory Policy and Toxic Substance Control, 91 Colum. L. Rev. 261, 308–09, 312–13, 320 (1991). Reprinted by permission of the Columbia Law Review.

Patricia Birnie, "Whaling: End of an Era" International Whaling Regulation, 1985. Copyright 1985, Oceana Publications, reprinted with permission.

Rachel Carson, Silent Spring (1962). Copyright © 1962 by Rachel L. Carson. Reprinted by permission of Houghton Mifflin Company. All rights reserved.

Coggins, Charles, The Law of Public Rangeland Management IV: FLPMA, PRIA, and the Multiple Use Mandate, 14 Environmental Law 1 (1983). Reprinted by permission of Environmental Law.

Conservation Foundation, State of the Environment: A View Toward the Nineties (1987). Reprinted by permission of the Conservation Foundation, Washington, D.C.

Peter N. Davis, Groundwater Pollution: Case Law Theories For Relief, 39 Mo. L. Rev. 117. Reprinted by permission of the Missouri Law Review.

Ray Druley & Girard Ordway, The Toxic Substance Control Act, pages 1–4 (1977). ©1977 by the Bureau of National Affairs, Inc., Washington, D.C. 20037. Reprinted by permission.

Steven Ferrey, Hard Time Criminal Prosecution For Polluters. © 1988, The Amicus Journal, a publication of the Natural Resources Defense Council, reprinted with permission.

William Goldfarb, Health Hazards in The Environment: The Interface of Science and Law, 8 Environmental Law 645. Reprinted by permission of Environmental Law.

Robert W. Hahn and Gordon L. Hester, Marketable Permits: Lessons for Theory and Practice, 16 Ecology L.Q. 361. © 1989 by Ecology Law Quarterly. Reprinted from Ecology Law Quarterly, Vol. 16, No. 2, pp. 361–406 by permission.

G. Hardin, The Tragedy of the Commons, 162 Science 1243–48 (12–13–68). Reprinted by permission of Science magazine.

Samuel Hays, Clean Air: From The 1970 Act To The 1977 Amendments, 17 Duq. L. Rev. 33. Reprinted by permission of the Duquesne Law Review.

Peter Huber, Safety and the Second Best: The Hazards of Public Risk Management in the Courts, 85 Columbia Law Review 277. Copyright © 1985 by the Directors of the Columbia Law Review Association, Inc. All Rights Reserved. This article originally appeared at 85 Colum. L. Rev. 277 (1985) Reprinted by permission.

James Krier, The Environment, the Constitution, and the Coupling Fallacy, 32 Michigan Law Quadrangle Notes 35 (1988). Copyright 1988. Reprinted with permission of James E. Krier, Earl Warren DeLano Professor of Law, University of Michigan.

Howard Latin, Ideal Versus Real Regulatory Efficiency: Implementation of Uniform Standards and "Fine-Tuning" Regulatory Reforms, 37 Stanford Law Review 1267. Reprinted material first appeared in 37 Stanford Law Review at page 1267. Copyright © 1985 by the Board of Trustee of Leland Stanford Junior University. Reprinted by permission of the copyright holder, the author and Fred B. Rothman Company.

Aldo Leopold, A Sand County Almanac. Copyright © 1949, 1977 by Oxford University Press, Inc. Reprinted with permission.

Mann, Polluter-Financed Environmentally Beneficial Expenditures: Effective or Improper Abuse of Citizen Suits Under the Clean Water Act?, 20 Environmental Law 176, 182–85 (1990). Reprinted by permission of Environmental Law.

Meyers, Old Growth Forest, The Owl, And Yew: Environmental Ethics Versus Traditional Dispute Resolution Under The Endangered Speciaes Act And Other Public Lands And Resources Law, 18 B.C.Env.Aff.L.R. 623 (1991). Reprinted by permission of the Boston College Environmental Affairs Law Review.

Marshall Miller, "Federal Regulation of Pesticides" in Environmental Law Handbook, 10th Edition pp. 473–483 (1989) Reproduced with permission. The entire publication, Environmental Law Handbook, is available from Government Institutes, Inc., 4 Research Place, suite 200, Rockville, Maryland 20850.

Herbert L. Packer, The Limits Of The Criminal Sanction (1960). Reprinted from The Limits of the Criminal Sanction, by Herbert L. Packer with the permission of the Publishers, Stanford University Press. © 1968 by Herbert L. Packer.

Peter Passell, Rebel Economists Add Ecological Cost to Price of Progress, 27 Nov. 1990, C1. Copyright © 1978 by the New York Times Company. Reprinted by permission.

Zygmunt J. B. Plater and William Lund Norine, Through the Looking Glass of Eminent Domain: Exploring the "Arbitrary and Capricious" Test and substantive Rationality Review of Governmental Decisions, 16 B. C. Envtl. Aff. L. Rev. 661. Reprinted by permission of the Boston College Environmental Affairs Law Review.

Zygmunt J. B. Plater, Statutory Violations and Equitable Discretion, 70 Cal. L. Rev. 524. Reprinted by permission of the California Law Review.

Arnold W. Reitze,Jr., Environmental Policy-It Is Time for a New Beginning, 14 Columbia Journal of Envtl. Law 111. Reprinted by permission of the Columbia Journal of Environmental Law.

Michael Renner, Rethinking the Role of the Auto, World Watch Paper 84, June 1988. Reprinted by permission of the World Watch Institute.

David A. Rich, Personal Liability for Hazardous Waste Cleanup: An Examination of CERCLA Section 107, 13 B.C.Env.Aff.L.R. 643. Reprinted by permission of the Boston College Environmental Affairs Law Review.

William L. Rosbe and Robert L. Gulley, The Hazardous and Solid Waste Amendments of 1984: A Dramatic Overhaul of the Way America Manages Its Hazardous Wastes, 14 ELR 10458. Copyright 1984 Environmental Law Institute. Reprinted with permission from the Environmental Law Reporter.

Mike Royko, A Road. Reprinted by permission of Mike Royko.

Thomas A. Sancton, "What On Earth Are We Doing?, TIME, January 2, 1989. Copyright 1989 The Time Inc. Magazine Company. Reprinted by permission.

Frank E. A. Sander, Alternative Methods of Dispute Resolution: An Overview, 37 University of Florida L.Rev. 1. Reprinted with the permission of the Florida Law Review. Copyright 1985.

Joseph L. Sax, The Public Trust Doctrine in Natural Resource Law: Effective Judical Intervention, 68 Mich. L. Rev. 471 (1970). Reprinted by permission of the Michigan Law Review.

Joseph L. Sax, Defending the Environment: A Stategy for Ciltizen Action (1970). Reprinted with permission of Joseph L. Sax and the University of California at Berkeley.

Joseph L. Sax, Liberating the Public Trust Doctrine from Its Historical Shackles, 14 U.C.Davis L.Rev. 185. Reprinted by permission of the University of California Davis Law Review.

Joseph L. Sax, The of Private Rights in Public Waters, 19 Environmental Law 473. Reprinted by permission of Environmental Law.

Joseph L. Sax, Environmental Law in the Law Schools: What We Teach and How We Feel Abodut It, 19 ELR 10251. Copyright 1989 Environmental Law Institute. Reprinted with permission from the Environmental Law Reporter.

J. Sax, R. Abrams & B. Thompson, Legal Control of Water Resources 588–96 (2d. ed. 1991). © 1991, West Publishing Company. Reprinted with permission.

Aaron L. Schwabach, The Sandoz Spill: The Failure of International Law to Protect the Rhine from Pollution, 16 Ecology L.Q. 443. © 1989 by Ecology Law Quarterly. Reprinted from Ecology Law Quarterly, Vol. 16, No. 2, pp. 443–480 by permission.

Lawrence E. Starfield, The 1990 National Contilngency Plan—More Detail and More Structure, But Still a Balancing Act, 20 ELR 10222. Copyright 1990 Environmental Law Institute. Reprinted with permission from the Environmental Law Reporter.

Jan Stevens, Air Pollution and the Federal System: Responses to Felt Necessities, 22 Hastings Law Journal 661. Copyright 1971 Hastings College of Law, reprinted from 22 Hastings L. J. 661 by permission.

Richard B. Stewart, The Reformation of American Administrative Law, 88 Harv. L. Rev. 1669. Copyright 1975 by the Harvard Law Review Association.

Joseph E. Stiglitz, Economics of the Public Sector (1986) pp. 226– 227. Reprinted by permission of W.W. Norton & Company.

Susskind and McMahon, The Theory and Practice of Negotiated Rule Making, 3 Yale J. Reg. 133 (1985). © Copyright 1985 by Yale Journal on Regulation, Box 401A Yale Station, New Haven, CT 06520. Reprinted from Volume 3:133 by permission. All rights reserved.

A. R. Talbot, Settling Things: Six Case Studies in Environmental Mediation 6–24 (1983). Reprinted with permission of the Conservation Foundation, Washington, D.C.

Hal R. Varian, Intermediate Microeconomics: A Modern Approach. Reprinted by permission of Hal Varian.

Edith Brown Weiss, Our Rights and Obligations to the Future Generations for the Environment, 84 Am.J. Intl. Law 198. Reproduced with permission from 84 Am. J. Int'l L. 198 (1990).

Charles F. Wurster, Of Salt..., 4 March 1978. Copyright © 1978 by the New York Times Company. Reprinted by permission.

Glossary of Acronyms

Page numbers, where they appear, are references to a description of that term in the text. For further references, see the Tables of Authorities and Index.

ACO	Administrative Consent Order (CERCLA), 925
ADR	Alternative Dispute Resolution, 979
AEC	Atomic Energy Commission (now NRC)
APA	Administrative Procedure Act, 538
AQCR	Air Quality Control Regions (CAA), 810
ARARs	Applicable, Relevant, Appropriate Requirements (CERCLA), 895
BANANA	Build Absolutely Nothing Anywhere Near Anybody (see NIMBY)
BAT	Best Available Technology, 729, or, Best Available Technology Economically Achievable (CWA), 836
BCT	Best Conventional Control Technology (CWA), 836
BDAT	Best Demonstrated Available Technology (RCRA), 895
BDT	Best Available Demonstrated Control Technology (CWA), 837
BLM	Bureau of Land Management (DoI), 685
BMP	Best Management Practices, 843
BNA	Bureau of National Affairs
BOD	Biological Oxygen Demand (CWA), 834
BPT	Best Practicable Control Technology Currently Available (CWA), 836
CAA	Clean Air Act, 245
CAP	Capacity Assurance Plan (RCRA), 945
CEQ	Council on Environmental Quality (executive office of the President), 599
CERES	Coalition for Environmentally Responsible Economics, 229
CERCLA	Comprehensive Envtl Response, Compensation, and Liability Act (Superfund), 252
CERCLIS	CERCLA Information System, 886
CFCs	Chlorofluorocarbons, 1013
CFR	Code of Federal Regulations
CGL	Comprehensive General Liability insurance, 295
CITES	Convention on International Trade in Endangered Species, 1022
CMA	Calcium Magnesium Acetate (road salt substitute), or, Cooperative Management Agreement (PRIA), 699
Corps	U.S. Army Corps of Engineers
CSO	Combined Sewer Outflows (CWA), 844
CWA	Clean Water Act (FWPCA), 825
CZMA	Coastal Zone Management Act, 948
DEIS	Draft Environmental Impact Statement (NEPA)
DMR	Discharge Monitoring Report, 857
DNR	Department of Natural Resources

DOA	U.S. Department of Agriculture
DOI	U.S. Department of Interior
DOJ	U.S. Department of Justice
DOT	U.S. Department of Transportation
EA	Environmental Assessment (NEPA), 619
EBEs	Environmentally Beneficial Expenditures (CWA), 858
EC	European Community
ECJ	European Court of Justice, 1007
ECRA	Environmental Cleanup Responsibility Act (NJ), 910
EDF	Environmental Defense Fund
EIS	Environmental Impact Statement (NEPA), 599
ELR	Environmental Law Reporter (by Environmental Law Institute)
EO	Executive Order
EPA	U.S. Environmental Protection Agency
EPCRA	Emergency Planning and Community Right to Know Act, 254
EPCRTKA	EPCRA
ERC	BNA Environmental Reporter – Cases, or Environmental Reduction Credit (CAA), 871
ESA	Endangered Species Act, 656
ESD	Explanation of significant differences (CERCLA), 888
FDA	U.S. Food and Drug Administration
FDF	Fundamentally Different Factors (FDF), 840
FEIS	Final Environmental Impact Statement (NEPA)
FEPCA	Federal Environmental Pesticide Control Act, 248
FHWA	Federal Highway Administration
FIFRA	Federal Insecticide, Fungicide, Rodenticide Act, 248
FIP	Federal Implementation Plan (CAA), as in "the state's SIP got shot down and FIPped," 817
FLPMA	Federal Land Policy and Management Act, 685
FOE	Friends of the Earth
FOIA	Freedom of Information Act, 255
FONSI	Finding of No Significant Impact (NEPA), 619
FR	Federal Register
FRCP	Federal Rules of Civil Procedure
FWPCA	Federal Water Pollution Control Act (CWA), 247
FWS	Fish and Wildlife Service (DoI)
GAO	General Accounting Office (Congressional)
GATT	General Agreement on Tariffs and Trade, 1024
HRS	Hazard Ranking System (CERCLA), 882
HSWA	Hazardous and Solid Waste Amendments (of 1984), 929
ICJ	International Court of Justice (The Hague)
ICS	Individual Control Strategy
IGO	Intergovernmental organization
IJC	International Joint Commission (US-Canada)
ILM	International Legal Materials
ILO	International Labour Organisation, 1019
IPM	Integrated Pest Management, 748
ISC	Interagency Scientific Committee (ESA), 675
ITC	Interagency Test Committee (ToSCA), 755

IWC	International Whaling Commission
LAER	Lowest Achievable Emissions Rate (CAA), 815
LDCs	Less-Developed Countries
LDR	Land Disposal Restrictions (CERCLA), 895
LULU	Locally Unwanted Land Use (see NIMBY)
MACT	Maximum Available Control Technology, 792
MBTA	Migratory Bird Treaty Act
MCL	Maximum Contaminant Level (CWA), 845
MCLG	Maximum Contaminant Level Goals, 845
MDB	Multilateral Development Bank, 1024
MEPA	Michigan Environmental Protection Act, 421
MMT	Million Metric Tons
MoA	Memorandum of Agreement
MUSY	Multiple Use-Sustained Yield Act, 692
NAAQS	National Ambient Air Quality Standards, 773
NAM	National Association of Manufacturers
NASQUAN	National Ambient Stream Quality Accounting Network (CWA), 831
NCP	National Contingency Plan (Superfund), 884
NEPA	National Environmental Policy Act of 1969, 596
NESHAPs	National Emissions Standards for Hazardous Air Pollutants (CAA), 790
NFMA	National Forest Management Act, 674
NGO	Non-Governmental Organization
NIMBY	Not In *My* Back Yard! Syndrome, 67
NMFS	National Marine Fisheries Service
NOAA	National Oceanographic and Atmospheric Administration (Dept. of Commerce)
NPDES	National Pollutant Discharge Elimination System (CWA), 827
NPL	National Priority List (Superfund), 881
NPS	National Park Service
NRA	Negotiated Rulemaking Act (ADR), 995
NRC	U.S. Nuclear Regulatory Commission, or (state) Natural Resources Commission
NRDC	National Resources Defense Council
NSPS	New Source Performance Standards (Air)
NTAs	Negotiated Test Agreements (ToSCA), 755
NWF	National Wildlife Foundation
NWQS	National Water Quality Standards (CWA), 825
OCS	Outer Continental Shelf
OMB	Office of Management and Budget (executive offices of the President)
ONRW	Outstanding National Resource Waters, 853
OPA '90	Oil Pollution Act of 1990, 570, 898
ORV	Off-Road Vehicle, 707
OSHA	Occupational Safety and Health Act, Occupational Safety and Health Administration, 245
OSWER	Office of Solid Waste and Energy Response, 918
OTA	Office of Technology Assessment (congressional), 896
PLLRC	Public Land Law Review Commission, 690
PMNs	Pre-marketing Notifications (ToSCA), 756

POTW	Publicly Owned Treatment Works (CWA), 830
PRIA	Public Rangelands Improvement Act, 690
PRP	Potentially Responsible Party (Superfund), 280, 883
PSD	Prevention of Significant Deterioration, 819
RACHEL	Reauthorization Act Confirms How Everyone's Liable (SARA's unofficial alternate name), 280
RACT	Reasonably Available Control Technology (CAA), 817
RAM	Real-time Air-quality-simulator Model, 802
RAP	Refuse Act Permit, 43
RARE I, II, III	Roadless Areas Review and Evaluation (Wilderness Act)
RCRA	Resource Conservation and Recovery Act, 251
RD	Remedial Design (CERCLA), 886
RI/FS	Remedial Investing/ Feasibility Study (CERCLA), 886
ROD	Record of Decision, 676
RPAR	Rebuttable Presumption Against Registration (ToSCA), 745
RRA	Resource Recovery Act, 251
SARA	Superfund Amendment and Reauthorization Act, 252
SCLDF	Sierra Club Legal Defense Fund
SCS	U.S. Soil Conservation Service
SDWA	Safe Drinking Water Act, 254
SEIS	Supplementary Environmental Impact Statement (NEPA), 644
SIP	State Implementation Plan (CAA), 766
SIR	Supplemental Information Report (NEPA), 648
SLAPP	Strategic Lawsuits Against Public Participation, 121
SMCRA	Surface Mining Control and Reclamation Act, 236
SPCC	Spill Prevention, Control, and Countermeasure (CERCLA), 898
SRF	State Revolving Loan Funds (CWA), 843
Superfund	CERCLA
SWDA	Solid Waste Disposal Act, 251
TDRs	Transferable Development Rights, 974
TDS	Total Dissolved Solids (CWA), 832
ToSCA	Toxic Substance Control Act, 250
TRE	Toxicity Reduction Evaluation (CWA), 853
TRO	Temporary Restraining Order
TSCA	ToSCA, 250
TSD	Treatment, Storage, and Disposal (CERCLA), 884, 931
TTP	Trial Type Process (APA), 541
TVA	Tennessee Valley Authority
UCATA	Uniform Contribution Among Tortfeasors Act, 181
UCFA	Uniform Comparative Fault Act, 181
UNEP	United Nations Environment Programme
USDA	U.S. Department of Agriculture
USFS	United States Forest Service
USGAO	United States General Accounting Office
WQBELs	Water Quality Based Effluent Standards (CWA), 825, 852
WQS	Water Quality Standards (CWA), 825

Table of Cases

Table of Authorities

BOOKS

Table of Authorities

ARTICLES, MONOGRAPHS, ETC.

Table of Authorities

STATUTES, CONVENTIONS, REGULATIONS, ETC.

Federal Regulations

State Constitutions and Statutes

State Regulations

Index